STRATEGIC MARKETING MANAGEMENT CASES

THE IRWIN/MCGRAW-HILL SERIES IN MARKETING

Peter & Donnelly
A PREFACE TO MARKETING
MANAGEMENT
EIGHTH EDITION

Peter & Donnelly
MARKETING MANAGEMENT:
KNOWLEDGE AND SKILLS
SIXTH EDITION

Peter & Olson
CONSUMER BEHAVIOR AND
MARKETING STRATEGY
SIXTH EDITION

Rangan
BUSINESS MARKETING STRATEGY:
CASES, CONCEPTS &
APPLICATIONS
FIRST EDITION

Rangan, Shapiro & Moriaty
BUSINESS MARKETING STRATEGY:
CONCEPTS AND APPLICATIONS
FIRST EDITION

Rayport, Jaworski & Breakaway
Solutions
INTRODUCTION TO E-COMMERCE
FIRST EDITION

Rayport & Jaworski
E-COMMERCE
FIRST EDITION

Rayport & Jaworski
CASES IN E-COMMERCE
FIRST EDITION

Stanton & Spiro
MANAGEMENT OF A SALES FORCE
TENTH EDITION

Stock & Lambert
STRATEGIC LOGISTICS
MANAGEMENT
FOURTH EDITION

Sudman & Blair
MARKETING RESEARCH: A
PROBLEM SOLVING APPROACH
FIRST EDITION

Ulrich & Eppinger
PRODUCT DESIGN AND
DEVELOPMENT
SECOND EDITION

Walker, Boyd & Larreche
MARKETING STRATEGY: PLANNING
AND IMPLEMENTATION
THIRD EDITION

Weitz, Castleberry & Tanner
SELLING: BUILDING
PARTNERSHIPS
FOURTH EDITION

Zeithaml & Bitner
SERVICES MARKETING
SECOND EDITION

SEVENTH EDITION

STRATEGIC MARKETING MANAGEMENT CASES

David W. Cravens
Charles W. Lamb, Jr.
M. J. Neeley School of Business
Texas Christian University

Victoria L. Crittenden
The Wallace E. Carroll School of Management
Boston College

Boston   Burr Ridge, IL   Dubuque, IA   Madison, WI   New York   San Francisco   St. Louis
Bangkok   Bogotá   Caracas   Kuala Lumpur   Lisbon   London   Madrid   Mexico City
Milan   Montreal   New Delhi   Santiago   Seoul   Singapore   Sydney   Taipei   Toronto

McGraw-Hill Higher Education

A Division of The **McGraw-Hill** *Companies*

STRATEGIC MARKETING MANAGEMENT CASES
Published by McGraw-Hill, an imprint of The McGraw-Hill Companies, Inc., 1221 Avenue of the
Americas, New York, NY, 10020. Copyright © 2002, 1999, 1996, 1993, 1990, 1986, 1983 by The
McGraw-Hill Companies, Inc. All rights reserved. No part of this publication may be reproduced
or distributed in any form or by any means, or stored in a database or retrieval system, without
the prior written consent of The McGraw-Hill Companies, Inc., including, but not limited to,
in any network or other electronic storage or transmission, or broadcast for distance learning.
Some ancillaries, including electronic and print components, may not be available to customers
outside the United States.

This book is printed on acid-free paper.

domestic   1 2 3 4 5 6 7 8 9 0 QPD/QPD 0 9 8 7 6 5 4 3 2 1
international   1 2 3 4 5 6 7 8 9 0 QPD/QPD 0 9 8 7 6 5 4 3 2 1

ISBN 0-07-242946-1

Publisher: *John E. Biernat*
Executive editor: *Linda Schreiber*
Developmental editor: *Sarah Crago*
Marketing manager: *Kim Kanakes Szum*
Project manager: *Karen J. Nelson*
Production supervisor: *Carol A. Bielski*
Producer, media technology: *Todd Labak*
Coordinator freelance design: *Artemio Ortiz, Jr.*
Associate supplement producer: *Joyce J. Chappetto*
Photo researcher coordinator: *Jeremy Cheshareck*
Photo researcher: *Connie Gardner*
Cover and interior design: *Artemio Ortiz, Jr.*
Typeface: *10/12 Times Roman*
Compositor: *ElectraGraphics, Inc.*
Printer: *Quebecor World Dubuque Inc.*

Library of Congress Cataloging-in-Publication Data

Cravens, David W.
     Strategic marketing management cases / David W. Cravens, Charles W. Lamb, Victoria
L. Crittenden. — 7th ed.
       p.   cm.
     Includes index.
     ISBN 0-07-242946-1 (alk. paper)
     1. Marketing—Case studies.   I. Lamb, Charles W.   II. Crittenden, Victoria Lynn.   III.
Title.
HF5415.C6944   2002
658.8'02—dc21   2001044566

INTERNATIONAL EDITION ISBN 0-07-112325-3
Copyright © 2002. Exclusive rights by The McGraw-Hill Companies, Inc. for manufacture and export.
This book cannot be re-exported from the country to which it is sold by McGraw-Hill.
The International Edition is not available in North America.

www.mhhe.com

To Our Children:

Karen Cravens
Christine Stock and Jennifer Lamb
Carl, Drew, and John Crittenden

PREFACE

The seventh edition of *Strategic Marketing Management Cases* focuses on the major issues faced by marketing managers as businesses enter the new millennium. The decade of the 1990s witnessed critical twists and turns as managers addressed both new and traditional marketing concerns in an emerging electronic, global world.

This edition has been substantially revised and reorganized to reflect marketing management priorities in the 21st century. The part topics highlight both the traditional and the new elements faced by today's marketer:

- Market Orientation and Organizational Learning
- Marketing Program Development
- Growth Strategies
- Innovation and Strategic Brand Management
- Supply Chain Management and Partnership Alignment
- Cross-Functional Integration
- Implementing Marketing Plans and Assessing Performance

The reorganization and the new direction have allowed for the inclusion of many current issues in the rapidly changing business environment. While a market-driven, customer-oriented strategy remains the driver in strategic market planning, businesses are focusing on specific areas of concern within strategic marketing. This edition includes three of these major marketing-related topics as individual sections: innovation, the supply chain, and cross-functional integration. Woven throughout all the sections and topics is the issue of the changing environment reflected in doing business in an electronic world. Therefore, this edition includes an e-business case in each of the seven parts.

Several major features are included in the seventh edition:

- We continue to use the versatile, flexible paperback format to meet the rapid changes in curricula at both the undergraduate and graduate levels.
- Each part presents an electronic business case that has appeared in *Business Week* in 2000 and beyond.
- One-half of the cases in this edition are new or revised. Many of the cases that have been carried over from the last edition have been placed in new sections and highlight these new topics.

- The cases are all current. All but one focus on issues managers faced in the 1990s and beyond.
- Substantial emphasis continues to be placed on international marketing strategies. Cases in this edition focus on marketing decisions faced by managers in Canada, France, Hungary, India, Ireland, Japan, Mexico, the Netherlands, the Philippines, Russia, South America, and Switzerland. Additionally, cases address growth issues as companies attempt to expand into new international markets.
- Cases continue to reflect the changing role of women in business. Over 25 percent of the case scenarios feature women protagonists or women as major players in the decision-making process.
- Seven video cases accompany the book. Another video available in libraries is noted in the *Instructor's Manual*.

Many instructors prefer that students focus their case analyses on the time frame and situation described in the case. However, Web information may be useful as a follow-up to the class discussion of the case. The *Instructor's Manual* lists Web addresses for 25 of the cases.

We have also retained key features from previous editions.

- The cases illustrate marketing problems and decisions faced by large, medium-sized, and small organizations, goods and services marketers, manufacturers and channel intermediaries, business and consumer products firms, profit and nonprofit organizations, and domestic, foreign, and multinational companies.
- The selection of cases includes a balance of short, medium-length, and long cases.
- Over half of all cases include some form of quantitative data, most frequently financial information.
- Situations described in this edition do not fall neatly into individual marketing mix categories. Rather than organize the book around the four P's (product, place, price, and promotion), we have chosen section classifications that more realistically reflect the types of decisions frequently encountered by today's marketing managers.
- The *Instructor's Manual* continues to provide detailed, comprehensive analyses and supporting materials for each case. Several teaching notes include epilogues describing actions taken by the organization and/or how it has fared since the case was prepared. Suggestions for course design are also included in the *Instructor's Manual*.
- To meet the teaching/learning preference of instructors who wish to use the case analysis process described in detail in the Appendix, a substantial portion of the teaching notes follow this format. The discussion questions are not listed at the end of the cases so instructors can assign questions in advance or raise them during case discussions.

Acknowledgments

We appreciate the opportunity to include cases in this edition prepared by the following colleagues:

Lisa Robie Adam
Boston College

David Angus
Boston College

Reinhard Anglemar
INSEAD

Gary Armstrong
*University of North Carolina
at Chapel Hill*

Thierry Azalbert
INSEAD

Gyula Bosnyak
Taurus Hungarian Rubber Works

Lew G. Brown
*University of North Carolina at
Greensboro*

Christine L. Connolly
Boston College

Victoria L. Crittenden
Boston College

William F. Crittenden
Northeastern University

Mary Cronin
Boston College

Lee Dahringer
Butler University

Niraj Dawar
INSEAD

John Devoy
Boston College

Sharon M. Doherty
Northeastern University

Jennifer Fraser
Boston College

Andrew Fried
International University of Japan

John E. Gamble
University of South Alabama

Laura Gow
Boston College

Timothy J. Halloran
Washington and Lee University

Paula J. Haynes
University of Tennessee at Chattanooga

Marilyn M. Helms
University of Tennessee at Chattanooga

Charles Hoffheiser
University of Tulsa

Richard Keeley
Boston College

Raymond Keyes
Boston College

Allison Kleva
Boston College

Suresh Kotha
New York University

Philip Kotler
Northwestern University

Lawrence M. Lamont
Washington and Lee University

Frederick W. Langrehr
Valparaiso University

Thomas D. Lowell
Washington and Lee University

Ken Manning
Gonzaga University

Gordon McDougall
Wilfrid Laurier University

Richard McGowan
Boston College

Carlo Mobayed
INSEAD

Jakki Mohr
University of Montana

Donna Moore
Boston College

Wolfgang Munk
INSEAD

Michael Murphy
University College–Cork, Ireland

Patrick E. Murphy
University of Notre Dame

Lester A. Neidell
University of Tulsa

James E. Nelson
University of Colorado at Boulder

Eric Nyman
Boston College

Don O'Sullivan
University College–Cork, Ireland

Sean O'Sullivan
Boston College

Marie Pribova
Czechoslovak Management Center

Erin L. Quinn
Boston College

Piyush K. Sinha
Xavier Institute of Management

Anne Stöcker
Nijenrode University, Netherlands

Elizabeth W. Storey
Washington and Lee University

Sara Streeter
University of Montana

Tammy L. Swenson
University of Tennessee at Chattanooga

George Tesar
University of Wisconsin–Whitewater

Arthur A. Thompson, Jr.
University of Alabama

Gregory Trompeter
Boston College

Janos Vecsenyi
International Management Center, Budapest

Cathy Waters
Boston College

Joseph Wolfe
University of Tulsa

We were fortunate to have the input of the following colleagues in developing this edition and previous editions of *Strategic Marketing Management Cases:*

C. L. Abercrombie
University of Memphis

Seymour T. R. Abt
McGill University

Scott Alden
Purdue University

Robert P. Allerheiligen
Colorado State University

Robert M. Ballinger
Sienna College

Benny Barak
Hofstra University

Joseph L. Bonnici
Bryant College

Betty Bose
University of Alaska at Anchorage

E. Wayne Chandler
Eastern Illinois University

John I. Coppett
University of Houston at Clear Lake

Jack R. Dauner
Fayetteville State University

M. Wayne DeLozier
Nicholls State University

Laurence P. Feldman
University of Illinois at Chicago

Troy A. Festervand
Middle Tennessee State University

Charles W. Fojtik
Pepperdine University

Jack E. Forrest
Middle Tennessee State University

Frank J. Franzak
Virginia Commonwealth University

Betsy D. Gelb
University of Houston

Ralph W. Giacobbe
Southern Illinois University at Edwardsville

Myron Glassman
Old Dominion University

Kenneth Grant
Monash University

Michael T. Greenwood
Suffolk University

David E. Hansen
Ohio University

Ray Hehman
San Francisco State University

Mary A. Higby
University of Detroit at Mercy

Foo Nin Ho
San Francisco State University

William M. Kawashima
University of North Carolina at Greensboro

D. M. King
Avila College

Max E. Lupul
California State University at Northridge

Richard Mahan
Anna Maria College

Oswald A. Mascharenhas
University of Detroit at Mercy

Joseph McAloo
Fitchburg State College

Dennis McDermott
Virginia Commonwealth University

Rob M. Morgan
University of Alabama at Tuscaloosa

Cliff Olson
Southern College

Peter W. Olson
Hartford Graduate Center

Thomas J. Page, Jr.
Michigan State University

Charles R. Patton
University of Texas at Brownsville

Gordon L. Patzer
University of Northern Iowa

A. M. Pelham
University of Northern Iowa

Linda Rochford
University of Minnesota at Duluth

William N. Rodgers
University of San Francisco

Mary Rousseau
Delta College

Nancy Panos Schmitt
Westminster College

Gary R. Schornack
University of Colorado at Denver

Patrick L. Schul
University of Memphis

Carol A. Scott
University of California at Los Angeles

Harold S. Sekiguchi
University of Nevada

Richard J. Shenkus
Central Michigan University and Highland Park College

Kirk Smith
Boise State University

Theodore F. Smith
Old Dominion University

Ravi Sohi
University of Nebraska

Sudhir Tandon
Prairie View A&M University

Jennifer Tarbell
Davenport College

Peter K. Tat
University of Memphis

James W. Taylor
California State University at Fullerton

R. Viswanathan
University of Northern Colorado

Several of our research assistants have made essential contributions to this edition of the book, especially Enrico Lange at Texas Christian University and Christine Connolly and Allison Kleva at Boston College. Special thanks to Debra Proctor at TCU and Elizabeth Shanley at Boston College for their assistance in various aspects of the project. We appreciate the support and encouragement of our deans, Robert F. Lusch and Helen Frame Peters, and our colleagues in the marketing departments at TCU and Boston College.

Finally, we would like to acknowledge the support and suggestions we have received from adopters of the previous five editions of this book. Many features of this edition were implemented in response to advice and counsel from colleagues around the world.

David W. Cravens
Charles W. Lamb, Jr.
Victoria L. Crittenden

CONTENTS

Part 1

Market Orientation and Organizational Learning

Market orientation highlights the central importance of the customer as the focal point of business operations. "A business is market-oriented when its culture is systematically and entirely committed to the continuous creation of superior customer value."[1] The term *market orientation* often is confused with *marketing orientation* although the two are significantly different. A market orientation refers to everyone in the organization being committed to the customer and adapting in a timely way to meeting the changing needs of the customer.[2] A market*ing* orientation implies that the marketing function is the most important function within the organization and that all other functional areas are driven by the demands of the marketing department. Market orientation is an organizational rather than functional responsibility.

Today's globally competitive environment demands that companies, in order to survive, focus on meeting the value requirements of worldwide customers quickly and efficiently. Southwest Airlines is an interesting example of a company that has performed very well by adopting a market orientation. The regional, point-to-point carrier has a major advantage over many competing U.S. domestic airlines. Southwest's distinctive competencies center on performing air carrier activities more efficiently than do competing airlines. The entire Southwest work force is market-driven, being guided by a culture committed to providing superior customer value. A key advantage is the airline's high aircraft utilization, which is achieved by minimizing the time between landing and take-off. Southwest does not serve meals or provide seat reservations, and so it does not meet the needs of passengers who want those amenities. Nonetheless, the economy airline has developed a substantial customer base which consistently reports high levels of satisfaction.

Becoming market-oriented does not happen overnight. To grow more market-oriented, managers must identify rapidly changing customer needs and wants, determine the impact of those changes on customer satisfaction, increase the rate of product innovation, and develop strategies to gain a competitive advantage. We first describe the characteristics and features of a market-oriented organization and consider the importance of becoming market-oriented. Next, the issues and hurdles confronting the transition to a market-oriented organization are discussed, and we look at the role of organizational learning and its close relationship with market orientation. Finally, we consider how marketing strategy guides the organization's efforts to deliver superior customer value.

What Is Market Orientation?

Achieving a market orientation involves obtaining information about customers, competitors, and markets; examining the information from a total business perspective; determining how to deliver superior customer value; and implementing actions to provide value to customers (Exhibit 1). Market orientation blends a culture committed to customer value and a process of continuously creating superior value for buyers.[3] Market orientation requires a customer focus, competitor intelligence, and interfunctional coordination.

Customer Focus

The importance of the customer was first highlighted in the marketing concept articulated by a General Electric executive in the 1950s. In fact, there are many similarities between the marketing concept and market orientation. The *marketing concept* advocates starting with customer needs and wants, deciding which needs to meet, and involving everyone in the process of satisfying customers. The important distinction is that market orientation extends beyond the philosophy of the marketing concept, also offering a process for delivering customer value. The market-oriented organization understands customers' preferences and requirements and then combines and directs the skills and resources of the entire organization to satisfy customers.

"That model of competing, which links R&D, technology, innovation, production, and finance—integrated through marketing's drive to own a market—is the approach that all competitors will take to succeed in the 1990s," writes Regis McKenna.[4]

Achieving a customer orientation requires finding out what values buyers are looking for to help them meet their purchasing objectives. Buying decisions are guided by the attributes and features of the brand that offers the best value. The buyer's experience in using the brand is compared to expectations to determine customer satisfaction.[5]

EXHIBIT 1   Components of Market Orientation

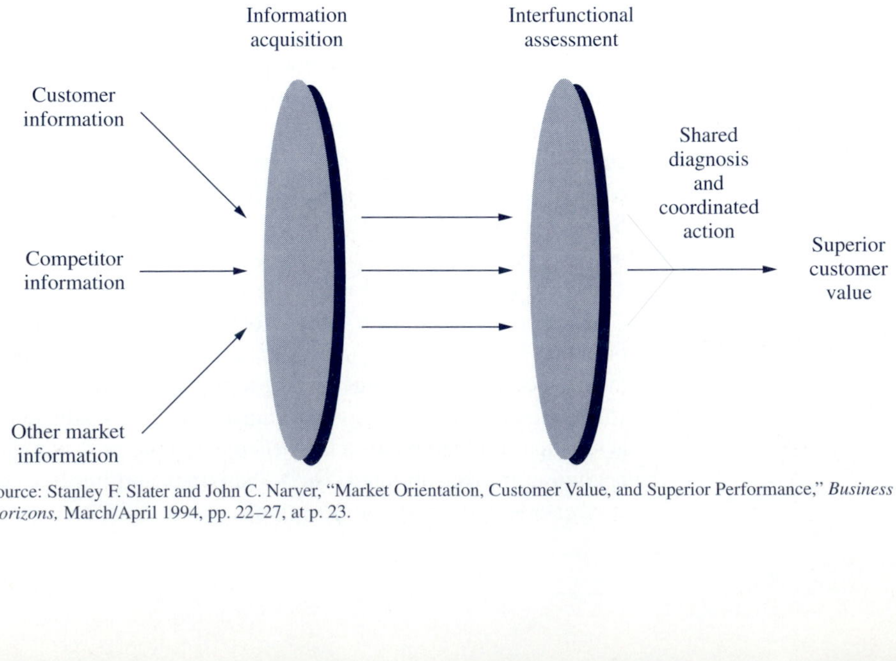

Source: Stanley F. Slater and John C. Narver, "Market Orientation, Customer Value, and Superior Performance," *Business Horizons,* March/April 1994, pp. 22–27, at p. 23.

Competitor Intelligence

Market orientation is about the competition as well as the customer.

> The key questions are which competitors, and what technologies, and whether target customers perceive them as alternate satisfiers. Superior value requires that the seller identify and understand the principal competitors' short-term strengths and weaknesses and long-term capabilities and strategies.[6]

Complacency leads to disaster in today's turbulent marketplace. For example, Western Union failed to define its competitive area as telecommunications, concentrating instead on its telegraph services, and eventually was outflanked by fax technology. If Western Union had been a market-oriented company, its management might have better understood the changes taking place, seen the competitive threat, and developed strategies to counter the threat.

In the 1980s Wal-Mart's management recognized the changes taking place in retailing. By investing heavily in information systems technology, the power retailer was able to improve inventory management, lower costs, and increase customer satisfaction. Wal-Mart's private satellite system links retail stores, distribution centers, headquarters, and suppliers. Store reorders are sent direct to the supplier and shipped to distribution centers. Often the centers are able to unload and load for delivery to stores within 24 hours.

Interfunctional Coordination

Market-oriented companies are successful in getting all business functions to work together to provide customer value. The tendency to "box" management functions so that manufacturing does not talk with research and development (R&D), R&D does not talk with marketing, marketing does not talk with manufacturing, and sales does not talk with anyone in the organization creates functions empty of responsibility and void of interaction. In contrast, interfunctional cooperation and shared decision making lead to the achievement of customer value objectives.

Becoming a Market-Oriented Organization

As shown in Exhibit 1, becoming a market-oriented company involves several interrelated requirements. These include information acquisition, interfunctional assessment, shared diagnosis, and coordinated action.

Information Acquisition

"A company can be market-oriented only if it completely understands its markets and the people who decide whether to buy its products or services."[7] For example, Wal-Mart's information system provides a wealth of information about popular store items, supplier responsiveness, and differences in customer preferences in various regions.

Interfunctional Assessment

Rubbermaid has overcome the hurdles of getting people from different functions to work together to conceive and develop new houseware products. It is important that new product planning involve all functions because they all contribute to customer satisfaction.[8] Rubbermaid's entrepreneurial teams seem to overcome problems with conflicting functional objectives and other differences.

Shared Diagnosis and Action

The remaining cornerstone of the market orientation paradigm is deciding what actions to take. This involves shared discussions and analysis of trade-offs.[9] An effective multifunctional team approach to decision making facilitates diagnosis and coordinated action. Rubbermaid's teams are empowered to make decisions and are responsible for the results.

Becoming market-oriented is challenging and quite different from an organization that does not have close and shared responsibilities across business functions. Nonetheless, mounting evidence suggests that the market-oriented organization has an important competitive advantage in providing customer value and achieving superior performance.

Ethics in Marketing

The ethical responsibilities of managers and professionals include (1) identifying ethical issues, (2) determining guidelines for ethical behavior, and (3) encouraging employees to practice ethical behavior. The typical ethical appeal is based on moral philosophy—doing good because it is right. The reality is that "Back in the real world, however, no businessman is going to sacrifice his company on the altar of such altruistic extremism."[10] The marketing manager wants (and needs) guidelines for coping with the pressures of self-interest and encouraging altruism. The challenge is to show that practicing good ethics leads to long-term favorable business performance.

The situations that are most difficult and perhaps are encountered most frequently are those described as amoral management.[11] Amoral judgments may be intentional (managers do not include ethical considerations in their decisions) or unintentional (managers do not recognize the ethical impact of their decisions). Both situations should be avoided.

Ethical guidelines that are too general provide limited direction for employees who want to practice ethical behavior. Such guidelines also give people who lack a strong commitment to ethics a basis for pursuing unethical behavior. The following checklist offers a useful basis for evaluating a situation that may require ethical decision making:[12]

- Does my decision presume that I or my company is an exception to a common practice or convention? In other words, do I think I have the authority to break a rule?
- Would I offend customers by telling them about my decision?
- Would I offend qualified job applicants by telling them about my decision?
- Have I made this decision without input from others so that important issues might be overlooked?
- Does my decision benefit one person or group but hurt or not benefit other individuals or groups?
- Will my decision create conflict between people or groups in the company?
- Will I have to pull rank and use coercion to enact my decision?
- Would I prefer to avoid the consequences of this decision?
- Did I avoid truthfully answering any of the above questions by telling myself that I could get away with it?

Pragmatic, easily understood guidelines like these should enhance the possibilities of making ethical decisions. Evaluating the ethical implications of decision situations is a continuing challenge for managers.

Corporations are placing unprecedented emphasis on the ethical behavior they expect of their personnel. One estimate indicates that over three-quarters of major U.S. companies are actively trying to encourage ethical behavior in their organizations.[13] Companies employ several methods to encourage managers to recognize the ethical content of their decisions. Such methods include workshops, drawing up corporate and industry codes of ethics, and the establishment of leadership role models.

Organizational Learning

Learning about markets requires developing a process throughout the organization for obtaining, interpreting, and acting on information from sensing activities. The learning processes of market-oriented companies follow four steps: open-minded inquiry, synergistic information distribution, mutually informed interpretations, and accessible memory usage.[14]

Open-Minded Inquiry

A danger to be avoided is not being open to exploring new views about markets and competition. This sometimes is referred to as "out-of-the-box" thinking; the idea is to not be bound to past views about markets and how they are likely to change in the future. A search for information is of little value if management already has a view on which new information will have no influence.

The members of the market-oriented organization recognize the importance of market sensing and coordinated interpretation of market intelligence to guide strategies. Not all companies see the value in continuous learning about markets. Managers who are not part of market-driven cultures may be unwilling to invest in information for decision making. Unfortunately, these companies often encounter problems because of faulty or incomplete market sensing.

Continuous learning allows firms to capture more information about their customers, suppliers, and competitors. This capability provides the potential for growth based on decisions made by open-minded managers who take into account a more complete representation of the competitive environment. Also, firms can respond much more quickly to competitors' actions and take advantage of situations in the marketplace.

Synergistic Information Distribution

This part of the learning process encourages the widespread distribution of information throughout the organization. The intent is to leverage the value of the information by cutting across business functions to share information on customers, channels of distribution, suppliers, and competitors. Traditional information processing in organizations allocates relevant information to each business function. Synergistic distribution works to remove functional hurdles and practices. Multifunctional teams help encourage the transfer of information across functions.

Mutually Informed Interpretations

The mental model of the market guides managers' interpretation of information. The intent is to reach a shared vision about the market and the impact of new information on this vision. The market-oriented culture encourages market sensing. But the process requires more than gathering and studying information. "This interpretation is facilitated by the mental models of managers, which contain decision rules for deciding how to act on the information in light of anticipated outcomes."[15] The model reflects the executives' vision of the forces influencing the market and likely future directions of change. Learning occurs as members of the organization evaluate the results of their decisions based on their vision at the time the decisions were made.

Accessible Memory Usage

This phase in the learning process emphasizes the importance of gaining access to prior learning. The objective is not to lose valuable information that can continue to be used.

Urban Outfitters, Inc., a successful specialty retailer, is guided by management's shared vision of the market. The company has an effective learning process. The retailer's products include fashion apparel, accessories, household items, and gifts. Urban Outfitters' unique strategy is the shopping environment it provides to the 18-to-30 targeted age group. To stay ahead of its unpredictable buyers' whimsical tastes, management employs over 75 fashion spies who sense what is happening fashionwise in neighborhoods in New York, California, London, and Paris.[16] Salaries and expenses of this market-sensing team total $4 million annually. Market feedback guides new product decisions and signals when buyer interest is slowing. Management is testing new retail concepts to appeal to its buyers when they move into an older age group.

Hewlett-Packard's (H-P) Inkjet product strategy illustrates market orientation and organizational learning. In the early 1980s H-P's product team developed a shared vision of how the global printer market would change. The team believed that dot matrix technology would be replaced by a better method of printing that was less expensive than laser printers. H-P developed inkjet technology as an alternative to dot matrix printers. The team's decision to target the higher-volume dot matrix market instead of positioning against laser printers is an impressive example of higher-order learning. This strategy offered H-P a value proposition for differentiating the printer and lowering cost by serving the mass market instead of a high-end niche. Following the market-orientation process, H-P's product team made a major effort to sense market needs by using information from customers, competitors, and distributors. These inputs guided design, production, and marketing decisions.

Marketing Strategy

Exhibit 2 shows the four-step process of designing and managing a marketing strategy (analysis, planning, implementation, and management) that we follow in this book.[17] First, the situation analysis considers market and competitor analysis, market segmentation, and continuous learning about markets. Second, designing a marketing strategy entails customer targeting and positioning strategies, marketing relationship strategies, and planning for new products. Third, marketing program development consists of product/service, distribution, price, and promotion strategies designed and implemented to meet the needs of targeted buyers. Fourth, strategy implementation and management look at organizational design and marketing strategy implementation and control. A brief overview of each stage in the marketing strategy process follows.

Marketing Situation Analysis

Marketing management needs the marketing situation analysis to guide the design of a new strategy or change an existing strategy. The situation analysis is conducted on a regular basis to guide strategy changes.

Exhibit 2
Designing and Managing Marketing Strategy

Analyzing Markets and Competition.   Markets need to be defined so that the buyers and competition can be analyzed. For a market to exist, there must be people with particular needs and wants and one or more products that can satisfy those needs. Also, buyers must be both willing and able to purchase a product that satisfies their needs and wants.

A product market consists of a specific product (or line of related products) that can satisfy a set of needs and wants for the people (or organizations) willing and able to purchase the product. The term product refers to either a physical good or an intangible service. Analyzing product markets and forecasting how they will change in the future will supply vital information for business and marketing planning. Decisions to enter new product markets are critical strategic marketing choices. The objective is to identify and describe the buyers, understand their preferences for products, estimate the size and rate of growth of the market, and find out which companies and products are competing in the market.

Evaluation of competitors' strategies, strengths, limitations, and plans is also a key aspect of the situation analysis. It is important to identify both existing and potential competitors. A few of the firms in an industry are often a company's key competitors. Analysis includes evaluating each competitor. The analyses highlight the competition's important strengths and weaknesses. A key issue is trying to figure out what the competition is likely to do in the future.

Market Segmentation.   Segmentation considers the nature and diversity of buyers' needs and wants in a market. It offers an opportunity for an organization to focus its business competencies on the requirements of one or more specific groups of buyers. The intent of segmentation is to consider differences in needs and wants and identify segments within the product market of interest. Each segment includes buyers with similar needs and wants for the product category of interest to management. The segments are described by using the various characteristics of people, the reasons they buy or use certain products, and their preferences for certain brands of products. Segments for business product markets may be formed according to the type of industry, the uses for the product, the frequency of product purchase, and various other factors.

Designing Marketing Strategy

The situation analysis identifies market opportunities, defines market segments, evaluates competition, and assesses the organization's strengths and weaknesses. This information plays a key role in designing marketing strategy, which includes market targeting and positioning analysis, building marketing relationships, and developing and introducing new products.

Market Targeting and Positioning Strategy.   Market targeting determines the people (or organizations) that management decides to pursue with the marketing program. The target(s) typically consist of one or more market segments. The targeting decision sets the stage for setting objectives and developing the positioning strategy.

The options range from targeting most of the segments to targeting one or a few segments in a product market. The targeting strategy may be influenced by the market's maturity, the diversity of buyers' needs and preferences, the firm's size compared to the competition, corporate resources and priorities, sales potential, and financial projections.

Positioning seeks to position the product in the eyes and mind of the buyer and distinguish the company, product, or brand from the competition. The positioning strategy is the combination of product, channel of distribution, price, and promotion strategies a firm uses to position itself against its key competitors in meeting the needs and wants of the market target. This strategy is also called the marketing mix or the marketing program.

Marketing Relationship Strategies.   Marketing relationship strategies are intended to create high levels of customer satisfaction through collaboration of the parties involved. Marketing relationship partners may include end user customers, marketing channel members, suppliers, competitor alliances, and internal teams. The intent is for a company to enhance its ability to satisfy customers and cope with a rapidly changing business environment through partnering.

Building long-term relationships with customers offers companies a way to gain competitive advantage. Similarly, forging relationships with suppliers, channel of distribution members, and sometimes competitors helps provide superior customer value.

New Product Strategies.   New products are needed to replace old products because of declining sales and profits. Strategies for developing and positioning new market entries involve all functions of the business. Closely coordinated new product planning is essential to satisfy customer requirements and produce high-quality products at competitive prices. New product decisions include finding and evaluating ideas, selecting the most promising for development, designing marketing programs, market testing the products, and introducing them to the market. New product planning includes both goods and services.

Marketing Program Development

Market targeting and positioning strategies for new and existing products set guidelines for the choice of strategies for the marketing mix components. Product, distribution, price, and promotion strategies are combined to form the positioning strategy selected for each market target.

The marketing mix decisions help implement the positioning strategy.[18] The objective is to achieve favorable positioning while allocating financial, human, and production resources to markets, customers, and products as effectively and efficiently as possible.

Product/Strategy.   Marketing management needs the following information on current and anticipated performance of the products (services) to guide product strategy decisions:

1. Consumer evaluation of the company's products, particularly their strengths and weaknesses vis-à-vis the competition (i.e., product positioning by market segment information).
2. Objective information on actual and anticipated product performance on relevant criteria such as sales, profits, and market share.[19]

Product strategy includes (1) managing existing products and (2) deciding what actions to take on problem products (e.g., improve product performance, lower cost, reposition).

Distribution Strategy.   Market target buyers may be contacted on a direct basis using the firm's sales force or, instead, through a distribution channel of marketing intermediaries (e.g., wholesalers, retailers, or dealers). Distribution channels often are used in linking producers with end user household and business markets. Decisions include (1) the type of channel organization to use and (2) the intensity of distribution appropriate for the product or service.

Price Strategy.   Price plays an important role in positioning a product or service. Customer reaction to alternative prices, the cost of the product, the prices of the competition, and various legal and ethical factors establish management flexibility in setting prices. Price strategy involves choosing the role of price in the positioning strategy, including the desired positioning of the product or brand as well as the margins necessary to satisfy and motivate distribution channel participants.

Promotion Strategy.   Advertising, sales promotion, sales force, direct marketing, and public relations help the organization communicate with its customers, cooperating organizations, the public, and other target audiences. These activities make up the promotion strategy, which performs an essential role in positioning products in the eyes and minds of buyers. Promotion informs, reminds, and persuades buyers and others who influence the purchasing process.

Implementing and Managing a Marketing Strategy

Selecting the customers to target and the positioning strategy for each target moves marketing strategy development to the final stage, implementation, shown in Exhibit 2. Here we consider the design (or modification) of the marketing organization and implementation and control of the strategy.

The Marketing Organization.   A good organization design matches people and work responsibilities in a way that is best for accomplishing the firm's marketing strategy. Deciding how to assemble people into organizational units and assigning responsibility to the various mix components that make up marketing strategy are important influences on marketing performance. Organizational structures and processes must be matched to the business and marketing strategies that are developed and implemented. Restructuring and reengineering of many organizations in the 1990s led to numerous changes in the structure of marketing units.

Implementing and Assessing Marketing Strategy.   Marketing strategy implementation and assessment consists of (1) preparing the marketing plan and budget, (2) implementing the plan, and (3) managing and assessing the strategy on an ongoing basis.

The typical marketing plan includes details concerning targeting, positioning, and marketing mix activities. The plan indicates what is going to happen during the planning period, who is responsible, how much it will cost, and the expected results (e.g., sales forecasts).

The marketing plan includes action guidelines for activities to be implemented, who does what, the dates and location of implementation, and how implementation will be accomplished. Several factors contribute to implementation effectiveness, including the skills of the people involved, organizational design, incentives, and the effectiveness of communication within the organization and externally.

Marketing strategy is an ongoing process of making decisions, implementing them, and gauging their effectiveness over time. In terms of its time requirements, evaluation is far more demanding than planning is. Evaluation and control are concerned with tracking performance and, when necessary, altering plans to keep performance on track. Evaluation also includes looking for new opportunities and potential threats in the future. It is the connecting link in the strategic marketing planning process shown in Exhibit 2.

Segmentation, Targeting, and Positioning

The interrelationships between segmentation, targeting, and positioning are shown in Exhibit 3. The process begins by defining and analyzing the product market to be segmented. Application of segmentation methods seeks to identify market segments as shown by segments A through E in Exhibit 3. Next, management must decide which (and how many) segments to target. The positioning strategy determines how management wants the buyers in a particular market target to perceive the organization's offering. For example, Nike uses symbolic positioning for its athletic shoes, featuring sports celebrities to promote Nike products. Finally, the marketing program spells out the

EXHIBIT 3
Segmentation, Targeting, and Positioning

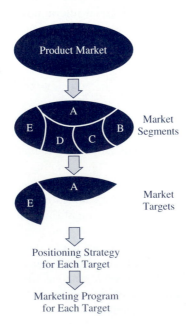

product, distribution, pricing, and promotion strategies intended to position the product with the buyers in the market target.

The market target decision sets in motion the marketing strategy, as shown in Exhibit 3. Choosing the right market targets is a most important decision affecting the enterprise. This decision is central to properly positioning a firm in the marketplace. Locating the firm's best competitive advantage may first require detailed segment analysis. Market target decisions are central to business and marketing planning. These decisions establish key guidelines for planning, and the market target decision provides the focus for the remaining marketing strategy decisions.

End Notes

1. Stanley F. Slater and John C. Narver, "Market Orientation, Customer Value, and Superior Performance," *Business Horizons,* March–April 1994, p. 22.
2. Thomas Bonoma, "A Marketer's Job Is to Self-Destruct," *Marketing News,* June 25, 1990; and Regis McKenna, "Marketing Is Everything," *Harvard Business Review,* January–February 1991.
3. Slater and Narver, "Market Orientation."
4. McKenna, "Marketing Is Everything," p. 72.
5. Philip Kotler, *Marketing Management,* 8th ed. (Englewood Cliffs, NJ: Prentice-Hall, 1994), Chapter 2.
6. Slater and Narver, "Market Orientation," p. 23.
7. Benson P. Shapiro, "What the Hell Is Market Oriented," *Harvard Business Review,* November–December 1988, p. 120.
8. Ibid., p. 121.
9. Ibid., p. 122.
10. *The Economist,* "How to Be Ethical and Still Come Out on Top," June 5, 1993, p. 71. See also Andrew Stark, "What's the Matter with Business Ethics," *Harvard Business Review,* May–June 1993, pp. 38–48.
11. Archie B. Carroll, "In Search of the Moral Manager," *Business Horizons,* March–April 1987, pp. 7–15.
12. Stark, "What's the Matter with Business Ethics," p. 38.
13. Adapted from Michael R. Hyman, Robert Shipper, and Richard Tansey, "Ethic Codes Are Not Enough," *Business Horizons,* March–April 1990, pp. 15–22.
14. The following discussion is based on George S. Day, "The Capabilities of Market-Driven Organizations," *Journal of Marketing,* October 1994, p. 43. See also Stanley F. Slater and John C. Narver, " 'Market-Oriented' Isn't Enough: Build a Learning Organization," Report no. 94-103 (Cambridge, MA: Marketing Science Institute, 1994).
15. Day, "The Capabilities of Market-Driven Organizations," p. 43.
16. Robert La Franco, "It's All about Visuals," *Forbes,* May 22, 1995, pp. 108–12.
17. This section is adapted from David W. Cravens, *Strategic Marketing,* 6th ed. (Chicago: Irwin/McGraw-Hill, 2000), Chapter 2.
18. Frederick E. Webster, Jr., "The Changing Role of Marketing in the Organization," *Journal of Marketing,* October 1992, p. 11.
19. Yoram Wind and Henry J. Claycamp, "Planning Product Line Strategy: A Matrix Approach," *Journal of Marketing,* January 1976, p. 2.

CASES FOR PART 1

The eight cases in Part I consider a broad range of marketing issues in various types of companies. Both for-profit and not-for-profit organizations are discussed in the cases. Within this mix, products and services such as rental cars, medical equipment, coffee, golf courses, and art museum gift items are covered. From a nonprofit perspective, two cases are featured; however, their services and markets are quite different. New to the casebook is the marketing of a baseball club. The focus on e-business highlights the strategic marketing initiatives of a computer powerhouse.

The video case, **Enterprise Rent-A-Car (Case 1–1),** looks at an interesting strategy for competing in a mature, highly competitive industry. Developing successful strategies in this industry is a major management challenge. Enterprise offers career opportunities for college graduates.

Medical Products, Inc.: Developing New Products for the Twenty-First Century (Case 1–2) focuses on the environment that the medical equipment industry faces in the new millennium. The company needs a long-term strategic plan that will lead it to become a dominant competitor in the industry. This plan will help the vice president make a decision concerning a new product proposal.

Case 1–3, The Boston Red Sox, offers a unique case approach to examining the world of professional sports. Presented in the format of newspaper articles, the case looks at the economics of baseball.

Case 1–4, Battered Women Fighting Back! (video), is about a nonprofit human rights organization. The executive director thinks that marketing can benefit BWFB! However, she is not quite sure where to start and what to do regarding BWFB!'s marketing challenges.

Providing Web site addresses to gather information, **Filterfresh (Case 1–5)** presents an interesting situation involving the mix of technology and marketing. A competitor's assertion of superior technology and its attempt to strike agreements with suppliers were challenging Filterfresh on its home turf.

Decreasing government support, changing tax laws regarding charitable giving, and rising expenditures are forcing the management of the **Metropolitan Museum of Art (Case 1–6)** to become more self-sufficient. Management must find creative ways to sustain financial stability by generating additional revenue. The museum's merchandising activities may be the key to generating additional internal sources of funds.

Performance is not quite up to par at the **Bear Creek Golf Range (Case 1–7).** Beginning its second year of operations, the golf range has not come close to meeting its first-year objectives. The future survival and success of the business depend on the development and implementation of a sound marketing program.

The e-business case (**Case 1–8**) in this part focuses on **Sun Microsystems** and its mission to become as dominant and reliable as Ma Bell. Utilizing its strategy, management techniques, and technology, can Sun become a dominant computer company in the Internet age?

CASE 1-1
ENTERPRISE RENT-A-CAR: SELLING THE DREAM

On a bright January 1997 morning, Dean Pittman, Enterprise Rent-A-Car's area rental manager for Durham/Chapel Hill, North Carolina, got out of his car at Enterprise's new office on Hillsborough Road in Durham. He reached back in to retrieve his cellular phone and locked the new Dodge Intrepid, his latest company car. Then, leaning against the car, he admired the line of clean cars and the new office with its green and white Enterprise sign. To Dean, it seemed that dreams really did come true.

In the Fast Lane

A little over six years earlier, Dean had graduated with a degree in industrial relations from the University of North Carolina at Chapel Hill. In the job-search process, he had scheduled an interview with Enterprise Rent-A-Car, even though he'd known little about the firm. During the first part of the interview Dean had been skeptical. He wasn't certain that he liked the idea of renting cars for a living or of working at a retail job that included doing work such as washing cars. But he'd seen the potential to advance quickly, develop strong management skills, and learn about running a business. Enterprise had hired Dean and assigned him to Durham's University Drive office. He was promoted quickly to management assistant and then to branch manager at Enterprise's new office in Rocky Mount, North Carolina. Dean performed well, and a year ago the company made him an area manager, giving him responsibility for the Durham/Chapel Hill area. He now supervised three branch offices with 22 employees, 495 cars, and annual revenues of more than $3 million. Even though he worked for a big company, he felt as though he were running his own business. Enterprise gave its managers considerable autonomy and based their pay on a percentage of their branches' profits. Dean's starting salary was in line with those of his classmates, but within three years his pay had doubled, and now it had tripled. There couldn't be many other companies, Dean thought, where a person his age could have so much responsibility, so much fun, and such high earnings. He still had to work long hours and do his share of grunt work, but the rewards were there.

Dean's good fortune mirrored that of Enterprise itself. Starting its rental operation in 1962 with a single location and 17 cars in St. Louis, Missouri, Enterprise had grown dramatically to become the nation's largest rent-a-car company in terms of fleet size and number of rental locations. By 1997, the company had more than 3,000 locations, 325,000 cars, $3.1 billion in sales, $5 billion in assets, and 30,000 employees (see Exhibit 1). In 1996, Fortune ranked Enterprise 37th on its list of the top 50 privately held U.S. firms. If it were public, Enterprise would have ranked about 390th among the Fortune 500.

The company's success resulted from its single-minded focus on one segment of the rent-a-car market. Instead of following Hertz, Avis, and other rent-a-car companies by

This case was prepared by Dr. Lew Brown, Joseph M. Bryan School of Business and Economics, University of North Carolina at Greensboro; Dr. Gary Armstrong, Kenan-Flagler Business School, University of North Carolina at Chapel Hill; and Dr. Philip Kotler, Kellogg Graduate School of Management, Northwestern University. The authors wish to thank officials at Enterprise Rent-A-Car and Auto Rental News for their support in the development of this case. The case is for classroom discussion purposes only. Copyright © 1997 Lew Brown, Gary Armstrong, Philip Kotler. All rights reserved.

EXHIBIT 1   Enterprise Rent-A-Car Growth in Units, Locations, and Employees

Number of Rental Units

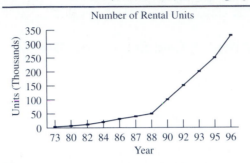

Number of Locations

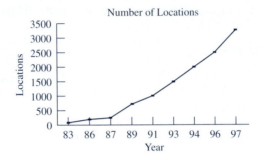

Total Employees
Full- and Part-time

setting up branches at airports to serve national travelers, Enterprise built an extensive network of neighborhood locations serving the "home-city" market—people who needed rental cars as replacements when their cars were wrecked or in the shop being repaired. Because these customers were often stranded at a body shop or repair garage and had no easy way to get to a rental office, Enterprise offered to pick them up. Enterprise's home-city strategy had been very successful—by 1997, the company had captured more than 50 percent of the replacement car segment. In recent years, Enterprise had consistently led the industry in growth and profitability.

A Surprise Guest

Out of the corner of his eye, Dean saw two men getting out of a nearby car. Dean recognized Dan Miller, Enterprise's regional vice president who was responsible for operations in eastern North and South Carolina, and Andy Taylor, Enterprise's president and

chief executive officer. Andy had attended a management meeting in Raleigh the day before, and Dan had suggested that they visit the new Durham branch this morning before Andy's plane left for St. Louis, where Enterprise still had its international headquarters.

Dan knew that Andy liked to visit branches whenever he had the chance. As the son of Enterprise's founder, Jack Taylor, Andy started working for Enterprise at the age of 16 in his father's first office. Like Enterprise's other top executives who had started as entry-level branch employees, Andy still had branch operations in his blood. He and other executives visited branches regularly to stay in touch with employees and customers, learn about new ways to grow the market, and offer support to branch personnel. In fact, most Enterprise executives boasted that on occasion they still "got their ties caught in the vacuum cleaners" while cleaning cars and performing other chores to help out while visiting busy branches.

"Good morning!" Dean hailed across the parking lot.

"Hi, Dean," Andy responded as he threw up his hand. "Good-looking new office. That's a nice suit. Is it new, too?"

"Yes. I needed some new suits to go with the office. Glad you were able to stop by, Andy. I've scheduled an interview with a prospective employee this morning. Perhaps you'd like to sit in for a few minutes."

"That sounds great. Who's the candidate?"

"Her name is Rachael Van Doren. Based on her résumé and a preliminary interview by one of our recruiters, she seems to be bright, ambitious, and not afraid of hard work. More important, she seems to be a real people person, someone who'd do well marketing to our referral sources and working with our customers. She also seems to be a team player with great management potential."

"I'd like to meet her," Andy responded. "Good people are the key to our business. As you know, we've got to hire a lot of new people this year if we are going to continue our rapid growth. In fact, recruitment may be the number one issue we face this year. We need to attract more employees with the right expectations and help them see that although it may not seem as glamorous as some other careers, working at Enterprise offers real opportunity."

As the three men entered the office, Dean spotted Rachael in the waiting area. "Good morning, Rachael, I'm Dean Pittman. I hope you didn't have trouble finding the office."

"No, your directions were very good."

"I appreciate your coming for an interview on such short notice. As it turns out, we're going to have a special guest in your interview. Rachael Van Doren, meet Andy Taylor, Enterprise's president and chief executive officer. And this is Dan Miller, our regional vice president."

"Hello, Mr. Taylor, Mr. Miller. It's a pleasure to meet you," Rachael responded as she shook hands.

"Please call us Andy and Dan—we aren't very formal at Enterprise," Andy responded. "I hope we're not overwhelming you. Whenever I have the chance, I like to visit our branch offices. Do you mind us sitting in?"

"Oh, no. That's fine," Rachael answered. "I guess I'm lucky to get to meet the president of the company."

"Well, Rachael, the branch office is the key to our company's success—it's where all the important action takes place. So it's always exciting when I get to spend time at a branch. We've grown more than 25 percent in each of the past 11 years. Needless to say, a key factor in continuing such growth is developing quality employees who want to run their own branches."

The Interview

As they walked through the office, Dean introduced the group to the other branch employees and showed off the new office. They stopped by a break room to pick up coffee, and Dean pointed out pictures on the bulletin board from the previous weekend's New Year's party. The Durham and Chapel Hill branches had held a contest in December to see which branch could grow its business the most that month. The Durham branch had won, and so the Chapel Hill group had arranged and paid for the party. "We're always competing like that," Dean noted. "It really adds excitement and challenge to our work."

The group moved to Dean's office, and he began the interview. "Rachael, we're interviewing you for a position in the Chapel Hill office. Normally, the branch manager, Sally Pinon, would be here, but she's on maternity leave now. Why don't you start by telling us a little about your background and how you came to apply at Enterprise?"

"I'm originally from Abington, Virginia," Rachael explained. "I graduated from the University of North Carolina at Greensboro last May with a degree in marketing. When I graduated, I wasn't sure what I wanted to do. I interviewed for a number of jobs but didn't find anything that really appealed to me. So for the last few months I've been working in a temporary administrative position at Duke University Medical Center while I continued looking for a permanent position.

"Last month, I went to a job fair in Raleigh and met one of your recruiters. I gave her my résumé, and she gave me some information on the company. Apparently, she sent my résumé to Hamilton Morales, your regional recruiter in Raleigh, and he called me for a preliminary interview last week."

"Did you know anything about Enterprise before you met our recruiter at the job fair, Rachael?" Andy asked.

"No, sir. I really didn't know much about the company. Once I looked at your materials, I did remember seeing some of your television ads with the wrapped car."

"After reading the brochures," Dan asked, "were you interested in the company?"

"To be honest, no," Rachael answered. "Enterprise seemed like a good company, but I had brochures from lots of companies at the job fair. I don't think I would've been interested if Hamilton hadn't called and invited me to the interview. My reaction was that a rent-a-car company didn't sound like a business that required someone with a college degree. I couldn't see myself renting cars like those uniformed people you see behind the counters at the airport."

"Did your interview with Hamilton change your opinion?" Dean asked.

"Yes. I could sense his excitement about working for Enterprise and his feeling that he had a real future with the company. I also met some of the other employees at the regional office, and I could tell they enjoyed their jobs. I learned that there's a lot more to this business than just working behind a counter."

Company Background

"I've also learned a lot about the company," Rachael continued, "but I'd be interested in your thoughts on why Enterprise has been so successful."

"Many factors have contributed, Rachael," Andy answered. "First, cars have become more important to people. People today just can't do without their cars, even for a day or two. And as more and more families have both adults working or are single-parent families, there is often no one else in the family who can pick you up when you have car problems. Tied in to this, the courts ruled in the 1970s that insurance companies have to offer coverage so that insured motorists can rent a replacement car if they lose the use of their car. As a result, those insurance companies began to offer rental replacement coverage in their policies.

"But perhaps the most important reason for our success is that we've adhered closely to my father's initial beliefs about how we should run the business. First and most important, we believe that we're here to serve the customer. That's why, from day 1, my father urged his employees to do whatever they had to do to make the customer happy. Sometimes it means waiving charges. Other times it means stopping everything and running out to pick up a stranded customer. Our employees know that they need to do whatever it takes to make customers happy.

"When my father first started this company, he also believed—and he still believes—that after customers come employees. If we're going to satisfy our customers, we need to have satisfied, challenged employees working as a team." Andy explained that all of Enterprise's branch employees, from assistant manager on up, earn a substantial portion of their pay based on branch profitability. In addition, the company has a profit-sharing plan for all employees. Enterprise hires primarily college graduates and promotes from within. Ninety-nine percent of its managers start as management trainees at the branch level. "As a result," Andy concluded, "they really know how our business works and understand our customer-centered culture."

Dean Pittman agreed. "That's really true. Jack Taylor believes that if you take care of the first two—customers and employees—profits will follow."

"A final piece of the puzzle," Andy continued, "is our conviction that Enterprise is a local-market business. We believe strongly that our branch employees know how best to respond to customer needs in their markets. We see our business not as a broad, national business but as a network of small, independent businesses—more than 3,000 of them now.

"We let our managers run their businesses, and we like to create friendly competition between branches. For example, employees at each branch see revenue and profit information for neighboring branches. As a result, all of these locally managed operations come up with many ideas about how to expand their businesses and serve their customers better. We weed out the ideas that don't work and share those that do with other Enterprise operating groups.

"Enterprise is a highly decentralized operation with a very small corporate staff," Andy explained. "The corporation provides capital to help branches fund their growth and a national marketing program. The only other centralized component of our business is our information system." As of 1997, the company had 23 IBM AS/400 computers in St. Louis, connected in real time via satellites to each branch worldwide. At peak times, the system processed some 834,000 transactions an hour. Enterprise knew the status of every car in its fleet at all times and was the only home-city rental company with that capability. The system also gathered all the information that corporate and branch managers needed to monitor each branch's performance. Another system allowed customers around the country to call just one telephone number and be connected to the nearest Enterprise office.

Marketing Strategy

"You mentioned that Enterprise began its rental business by targeting the home-city replacement market. Are you targeting other market segments?" Rachael asked.

"Yes, Rachael," Andy answered. "Although the majority of our business is in the replacement market, we're in two other markets as well. In the replacement market, of course, our end customers are the individuals who rent the cars. However, our initial customer is often the referral source—the insurance agent or auto body shop employee who recommends Enterprise to the stranded customer. Few of our customers get up in the morning thinking they'll need to rent a car—but then they're involved in a wreck. So referral sources are extremely important to us.

"The second segment of the home-city market is the 'discretionary' or 'leisure/vacation' segment. Friends or relatives may visit and need a car, or the family may decide to take a vacation and feel that the family car is not dependable. More and more people are renting for trips just to keep the extra miles off the family car. This is a rapidly growing segment for us as more people learn about Enterprise's nearby locations and low prices.

"Finally, we are seeing growth in our business from what we call the local corporate market. Many small businesses and some large ones have found that it's cheaper and easier for them to rent their fleets from Enterprise rather than trying to maintain their own fleets. For example, we do a lot of business with colleges and universities that have realized that it's cheaper to rent a 15-passenger van from us when the soccer team travels than to keep a van full-time for only occasional use."

"How big is the home-city market?" Rachael asked.

"That's a good question," Andy responded. "It's very hard to define accurately, but the trade publication *Auto Rental News* has made some estimates and sees the market growing at 10 to 15 percent per year (see Exhibit 2). The entire rent-a-car market, including airport rentals—what we call the travel segment—is about $14.6 billion."

"I also read in several news articles that Enterprise's rental rates are about 30 percent lower than those of the rent-a-car companies that operate at airports. Is that true?" Rachael asked.

"Our local rates are much lower than those you typically find at the airport," Dean answered. "We tend to locate our offices where the rent is much lower than at the airport. We also keep our cars a little longer than the typical airport-rental company. These two factors, along with our efficient operations, help us keep our rates lower." Because home-city market car rentals peak during the workweek, Enterprise experiences excess capacity during weekends. Therefore, it also offers attractive weekend promotional prices in most markets, Dean explained.

"Who is your competition?" Rachael asked.

"We have a greater share of the total home-city market than any other single competitor," Andy answered. "A handful of major regional competitors, such as Spirit and Snappy, when combined, capture an equivalent share of the market. The airport-rental companies, such as Hertz, Avis, and Alamo, get only a small portion of the home-city business. In fact, Hertz is just now starting a small operation that focuses on the home-city replacement market. Local 'mom-and-pop' firms that often have just one office and a few cars serve the remainder of the market."

"As I noted earlier," Rachael began, "I'd never really heard of Enterprise. I'm very impressed with what I have learned, but I must admit that I wonder why so few people seem to know about the company. When I told my friends I was coming for an interview, few of them recognized the company name until I mentioned your ads with the car wrapped in paper and the 'Pick Enterprise. We'll pick you up' slogan."

"That's a problem," Dan agreed. "When our recruiters go to a university's career day, they often find that students sign up for interviews without knowing who we are. I'm sure even more would sign up if we were more widely known."

"We grew up as a very quiet company," Andy joined in. "We have always depended on word of mouth and our referral sources. It wasn't until 1989 that we did our first national advertising. At that time, marketing research showed that we had low awareness. If you showed people a list of company names and asked them to identify the rent-a-car companies, only about 20 percent picked us. We then started advertising nationally but still kept our ads low-key. Since then we have more than quadrupled our annual advertising and promotion spending."

"Our research shows that Enterprise's awareness is now up substantially. Still, only about one-third of those surveyed are aware of our pickup service, and only about one-third are aware that we have branches nearby. Further, few college-age people have

EXHIBIT 2   The Replacement Car Rental Market
Competitors, Revenue Estimates, and Other Market Data

I. Competitor	*1996 U.S. Revenue*	*% Replacement*[1]	*Cars in Service (U.S.)*
1. Enterprise Rent-A-Car	$2.61 billion[2]	78%	315,000
2. Ford and Chrysler Systems	$490 million	92	82,250
3. Snappy Car Rental	$100 million	100	15,500
4. U-Save Auto Rental	$115 million	60	13,500
5. Rent-A-Wreck	$85 million	35	10,942
6. Premier Car Rental	$66 million	100	9,500
7. Advantage Rent-A-Car	$76 million	33	9,000
8. Spirit Rent-A-Car	$50 million	100	7,500
9. Super Star Rent-A-Car	$43 million	100	5,250
10. Many independent companies	$750 million	53	
11. Airport-based companies: Hertz, Avis, Budget, Dollar, National, Thrifty, Alamo[3]	$360 million	100	—

II. Industry Average Pricing

Estimated industry average price per day for replacement rentals, not including additional insurance coverages or other rentals, such as cellular phones: Industry average daily rental is $23. Industry average rental period for replacement rentals is 12 days.

Additional insurance coverages produce about 5 percent of revenue, with other rental options producing about 2 percent of revenue. Per-day rental rates are often established through national contracts with insurance companies or automobile manufacturers' or dealers' warranty reimbursement programs.

There are approximately 150 major U.S. airport rental markets. Airport-based rental rates vary widely, depending on the competition. Airport rental companies also negotiate corporate rates with individual companies.

III. Overall Rent-a-Car Market

Overall 1996 U.S. market estimated at $14.62 billion broken down as follows: business rentals, 40 percent; leisure/discretionary rentals, 33 percent, replacement rentals, 27 percent.

IV. Advertising

Advertising Age estimated that U.S. car rental companies spent $384.4 million in measured advertising in 1994, about 2.8 percent of revenue. It estimated that Enterprise spent $22 million in 1994, up from $13 million in 1993. Enterprise's 1994 spending compared with $47 million spent by Hertz, $31 million by Alamo, and $24 million by Avis (Sept. 27, 1995).

Source: *Auto Rental News*

Note: Estimates provided by *Auto Rental News.* Data are for case discussion purposes only. Use in case does not imply certification of estimates by Enterprise.

[1] Replacement market includes insurance replacement rentals, mechanical repair rentals, dealer loaner rentals, and warranty rentals.

[2] *Auto Rental News* estimate of U.S. rental revenue excluding leasing. Seven percent of revenue is from airport/traveler rentals, and 93 percent is from local market rentals. Local market includes replacement, business, and leisure rentals, with business and leisure about equal for Enterprise.

[3] Includes the portion of airport-based companies' revenue from local market operations that target the replacement market, including Hertz H.I.R.E. operations with 70 locations and Alamo with 115 locations. Hertz total fleet included 250,000 cars; Avis, 190,000; Alamo, 130,000; Budget, 126,000; National, 135,000; Dollar, 63,500; and Thrifty, 34,000.

direct experience with us even though we are one of the few companies that will rent to someone under 25 years of age. We realize that we still have a way to go in getting our name out."

The Management Trainee's Job

"I'd also like to know more about the management trainee position. Exactly what are the responsibilities of that position?" Rachael asked.

"When you come to work for Enterprise, your goal should be to learn all aspects of developing a business. First, you're assigned to a branch," Dean answered. "After initial training and orientation, we continue your on-the-job training by putting you on the front line to work alongside the other branch team members, dealing with customers who are renting or returning cars. Besides the work at the computer terminal, this involves picking up customers. Even though many of our branches have employees called 'car preps' who are assigned specifically to washing and preparing our cars for renting, all branch employees help prepare cars from time to time. They also check the repair status of customers' cars and inform insurance adjusters about how the repairs are coming along. In addition, they constantly monitor the branch's income statement and operating information to learn the logistics of running a business. This is exactly how Andy and our other senior managers started."

Dean went on to explain that aside from direct interaction with rental customers, the most important aspect of the trainee's job is managing relationships with referral sources. Each week, trainees spend time visiting the insurance agents, claims adjusters, and body shop and repair shop employees who generate much of the company's business by referring customers to Enterprise. "We visit these people every week, often taking donuts or pizzas, as a way of saying thank you for their business," Dean noted. In addition, trainees also make cold calls on referral sources and others who are not yet doing business with Enterprise. Building and maintaining these relationships is one of the most important parts of the job, he said.

"There is a lot of room for aggressiveness and creativity in this job, Rachael," Dean continued. "We need people who are willing to work hard for long hours (about 52 hours a week) while keeping a positive, friendly attitude toward customers and other employees. Our people must be dedicated to learning all aspects of branch operations, and they need to have good communication and interpersonal skills. They also need to be able to make decisions quickly, an important skill as they move up in management."

"What happens after the first few weeks?" Rachael asked.

"You spend several months learning how to run our business," Dan answered. "After six to nine months, your manager will give you what we call the Management Qualification Interview. Our employees call it 'the Grill.' The manager takes a couple of hours to ask you a full range of questions about every aspect of running a branch. If you pass this test, you get a raise and a promotion to management assistant, and you're on your way to becoming a manager." Dan explained that successful trainees move up quickly at Enterprise. Frequently within another six to nine months, they become the assistant manager of a branch. Then, within two to three years of joining the company, they are promoted to branch manager, assuming full responsibility for a branch with four to six employees and 100 to 150 cars. Within five to seven years, a successful employee could expect to become an area manager, with responsibility for two or more branches. Beyond that were positions as city managers, group rental managers, group managers, corporate vice presidents, and, of course, Andy Taylor's job as CEO.

"With advancement comes the opportunity for significant increases in income," Dan continued. "A management trainee starts at a competitive salary based on local market conditions, along with a full range of benefits and company profit sharing. Our typical branch manager is 27 years old and has doubled his or her initial salary. Managers continue to earn a percentage of the profits of the branches for which they are responsible as they move up in the organization."

"In my case," Dan noted, "I started with Enterprise 10 years ago in southern California. In about two years I became a branch manager with responsibility for satisfying customers, watching the bottom line, motivating employees, and managing more than $1 million in assets. Within seven years I was a group rental manager in Birmingham, Alabama. Two years ago I moved to Raleigh to become a regional vice president with responsibility for 30 offices and 4,000 cars, $60 million in assets, in eastern North and South Carolina. Our region grew 43 percent last year, creating lots of opportunities for advancement. One of my friends, Rob Hibbard, is now a corporate vice president after only 91/2 years, at the ripe old age of 33! In fact, you'd be amazed at how young our corporate officers are."

"That's impressive," Rachael responded, "but I'm not sure I'm very excited about starting out at a retail salary, working such long hours, and having to wash cars. As I mentioned earlier, I've been working at Duke University Medical Center in a temporary position. The center has offered me a permanent, full-time job with a higher starting salary and a more normal nine-to-five work schedule. I've also been interviewing with a large pharmaceutical firm that has outside sales positions starting at $30,000 with a company car. When I told my father that I was going to interview with you, he was a little skeptical. I'm not sure he sees working for a rent-a-car company as a good use of my college degree."

"We realize that people like you have lots of options," Dean answered. "That's why we think it's important that you understand our job and expectations so that you can decide if there's a good fit. The Duke job sounds like a good opportunity, but Enterprise employees typically prefer moving about and working with people rather than working behind a desk all day. Outside sales jobs like the one you mentioned often come with lots of travel, and some require you to relocate periodically. Perhaps more important, at Enterprise, unlike many other jobs, your pay increases significantly because it reflects your increasing value to the company. Further, although you can apply for open positions anywhere in our system, we don't force you to relocate. I guess it comes down to your deciding what is most important to you."

"Well, I've been thinking about those issues. I was a waitress while I was in college, and I know that I like being active and working with people. It's also important to me that I enjoy what I do. One thing I've noticed is that the Enterprise people I met in Raleigh and here this morning seem to be happy and to enjoy their work."

Role Playing

"It seems to me that you've been doing a better job interviewing us than we have of interviewing you," Andy joked. "Let me ask you a question like one you might get in the 'Grill' exam we mentioned. This question is based on an actual incident that Dan told me about this morning—something one of our employees faced last Friday at the Chapel Hill office. A management trainee went to pick up a young man at the university hospital's main entrance in order to bring him to the branch to get a rental car. The customer was a third-year medical student whose car had 'died' several weeks earlier. He wanted to rent one of our cars for the weekend at our special weekend rates. It was about 4:30 on a cold, rainy afternoon with lots of traffic congestion. With four employees on duty, our office was extremely busy. When our employee, who'd been on the job only about seven weeks, arrived at the hospital, the customer informed her that he'd just realized that his license had expired. Of course, we can't rent to someone with an expired license. The customer said he'd just called the Department of Motor Vehicles office, located about three miles away, and the DMV officer had indicated that if he came over, it would take only a few minutes to renew the license. The question is, If you were the employee, what would you do?"

Rachael thought for a moment. "Well, you said the office was very busy, and if I did what the customer asked, I'd be away from the office longer than expected. So I guess I'd call the office to see if it was okay to take the customer to the DMV office," Rachael answered.

"Okay," Andy replied. "Let's assume you can't locate a phone quickly. What then?"

This time Rachael didn't hesitate. "You said earlier that customer satisfaction is number one. If I don't take the customer, he'll probably be without a car for the weekend. So I'd take him to the DMV office and try to call our office from there to let them know that I'd been delayed. Hopefully, it wouldn't take the customer long to renew the license, and I'd wait and take him back to our office to complete the rental."

"Well done, Rachael! Great answer," Andy exclaimed. "That's exactly what we'd expect from an Enterprise employee."

Back to the Airport

Dan broke in. "Excuse me, Rachael, but I've got to get Andy to the airport now. We'll leave you with Dean to complete your interview. Thanks for letting us sit in."

"I enjoyed the discussion, Dan," Rachael answered. "I learned a lot about your company. It was nice to meet you, Andy. I hope you have a good trip back to St. Louis."

*****

"Rachael seemed very sharp," Andy observed as he and Dan walked to the car.

"Yes, I wish we could find more prospective employees like her. But we have awareness and image problems. In this economy, with good college grads having so many choices, we've got to deal with those issues."

"How's your recruiting coming?" Andy asked.

"Pretty well. Hamilton Morales, my regional recruiter, has been on the job for three months now. I created that job and promoted him from one of our branch offices. This gives me someone who concentrates full-time on recruiting. We're doing all the normal recruiting activities, like going to college career days and advertising in the college newspapers. But we've got to find other sources and be creative if we are going to meet our hiring goals. We've got to hire about 75 college grads to meet our growth targets and cover normal turnover. I understand we need more than 5,000 recruits companywide.

"We learned last year," Dan continued, "how important it is to keep up the supply of good employees. Our demand skyrocketed. It's easy to add 40 to 50 cars to an office to meet demand, but we can't add people that fast.

"I've asked Hamilton to put together a recruiting plan for our region that outlines the general types of activities we should carry out. I've encouraged him to do some 'out-of-the-box' thinking. We've got to find new and more effective ways to recruit college grads if we're going to meet our growth goals."

Andy nodded. "I have just gotten some results from several recruitment studies that the corporate office commissioned. I think this information will be helpful to you (see Exhibit 3). I was surprised by the results, especially the reasons candidates turned down

---

EXHIBIT 3   Enterprise Rent-A-Car Recruiting Study Results

1. Top eight messages to communicate in recruitment advertising:[1]
   a. Fun and friendly work environment.
   b. Great earning potential.
   c. Earnings and responsibility are performance-based.
   d. Great place to start.
   e. Perfect place for well-rounded people.
   f. Promote from within.
   g. Not a desk job.
   h. Run a business in two years.
2. Top six messages to communicate to prospective employees:[1]
   a. Opportunity to advance.
   b. Promotion from within.
   c. Future earnings potential.
   d. People you work with.
   e. Learn a business.
   f. Team environment.

3. Backgrounds of successful managers:[2]
   a. Active in extracurricular activities.
   b. Worked their way through school.
   c. Officers in clubs/organizations.
   d. Come from full-time job.
   e. Active in athletics.
4. Top reasons our offers are turned down:[2]
   a. Compensation.
   b. Prestige.
   c. Hours versus pay.
   d. Don't see potential.
5. Why people leave[1]
   a. Long hours.
   b. Stress.
   c. Low pay.

Source: Enterprise Rent-A-Car.

[1] Based on a written questionnaire to 103 students and 53 graduates at 10 campuses.
[2] Based on a survey of 188 current Enterprise managers and 107 recruiters.

our offers and why people chose to leave. It seems we aren't getting the word out about the future opportunities in terms of both pay and prestige."

"Andy, I think we've got to understand that recruiting is a marketing problem," Dan said. "We can use marketing techniques to attack this problem just as we use them to develop strategies to serve our customers. We're selling a dream."

"Yes," Andy replied. "And good recruiting will be essential if we want to keep growing at our current pace. We think we can double revenues again by the year 2001, but we're wrestling with a number of growth-related issues. What markets should we target? How should we position ourselves? Are there new services that we might offer? Do we need to be doing more to get the Enterprise story out to customers? How are we going to respond when Hertz and others decide to attack our home-city markets? And how can we keep up this rapid growth without losing our focus and the wonderful culture we've developed?

"All of our growth is driven not to create fame and wealth for Enterprise but to serve new customers and create opportunity for our employees. You're right, Dan. We do have a dream to sell—my father's dream. The Enterprise dream."

CASE 1–2
MEDICAL PRODUCTS INC.:
DEVELOPING NEW PRODUCTS FOR THE TWENTY-FIRST CENTURY

As Sally Roan, vice president of Medical Products Inc. (MPI), arrived at her Lexington office, her thoughts were on new product development. New products had to be developed for MPI to stay competitive and profitable in the changing medical industry, and Roan had to prove to critics that MPI could continue to operate in that industry, as well as in the non-medical industries that had helped make the company profitable over the years. She remained confident in MPI's ability to produce a variety of products that would not only take advantage of the company's reputation for producing high-quality products but also produce the type of financial returns shareholders had come to expect from MPI throughout the 1990s. (See Appendix 1 for financial information.) Roan knew that she needed to develop a long-term strategic plan to demonstrate that MPI was in fact a dominant competitor in the medical products and service industry.

MPI markets medical products and services, as well as offering medical supply products, to its customers. Roan had just received a proposal to produce a new ultrasound product that would be used primarily by cardiologists but also could be used for general medical purposes. Her initial reaction to the proposal was positive, but she needed to review the environment that the medical equipment industry would face in the future.

The Company

The entry of MPI into the medical field started with the Morley Company of Quincy, Massachusetts (USA). Matthew Morley, a civil engineering professor at Boston University, used two products to launch his firm: a water level recorder and a blood pressure outfit. In the 1940s, Morley Company came out with a series of medical products such as the metabolism tester, the pulse wave recorder, and the first table-model electrocardiograph. It was the electrocardiograph that led Morley to form many working partnerships with physicians from Massachusetts Hospital. In late 1960 Morley decided that he wanted to expand his firm's product line beyond cardiology. To acquire the funds for expansion, he would have to sell the firm. Three Massachusetts doctors—Seamus Begley, John Nylen, and Christopher Shub—bought Morley Company in April 1961. Together, they renamed the firm Medical Products Inc. and named Matthew Morley president and chief executive officer.

MPI's research orientation had three criteria: (1) An idea had to pass close examination before it was accepted, (2) it had to fill a need, and (3) it had to provide an economical solution to that need. Hence, MPI had a panel of nurse consultants state their needs and provide input to engineers during the product design phase. As a result of this "practical" orientation, MPI took a leadership role in products designed for patient safety and ease of use. MPI's patient-monitoring instruments became the standard of excellence during the 1970s.

In the mid-1970s the growth of MPI was the highest attained by any corporation. MPI built a reputation in the medical field for developing high-quality products coupled with professional field sales and customer support second to none. In June 1977 the charters of MPI were realigned. Patient monitoring remained in Quincy, where another new business operation emerged that eventually became the Hospital Supplies Division. Framingham, Massachusetts (USA), became home to the diagnostic product division. Fetal and neonatal products were the thrust of a new division established in West Germany. In 1983 the Framingham division purchased the assets of Jankey Medical Systems of Stamford, Connecticut (USA), in order to broaden the mechanical imaging technology of the ultrasound product line.

As a result of various purchases and mergers, MPI entered the 1990s as one of the world's leading suppliers of electronic measurement, communications, and information systems for hospitals, medical clinics, and other health-care facilities. From ultrasound imaging and patient-monitoring systems to the latest computer workstations, MPI was well known by medical professionals.

During the 1990s, 60 percent of MPI's customers were in the United States (whereas nearly 56 percent of total orders were international). However, the group was hoping to grow its business in Europe and Asia. MPI's medical products were sold in dozens of countries, and it maintained a business and manufacturing center in Germany. The company also had strategic alliances in key markets such as Japan and China. It hoped that its formula of the highest quality and the latest in medical technology would work outside the United States.

Throughout its 30-year history MPI's medical customers were typically medium-size to large hospitals (200 to 1000 beds). Through alliances with "cutting-edge" medical researchers, MPI's name was associated with the elite of the medical community. Its products were of the highest quality, and MPI coupled this feature with unmatched customer support. Hence, if a hospital wanted medical electronics that were state of the art, it went with MPI. But the 1990s had brought a radical transformation of the manner in which medical care in the United States was provided. With medical costs outpacing inflation by almost four to one, the pressure to control costs mounted. "Managed" care, or health maintenance organizations (HMOs), was the primary vehicle used to control these costs. This change would force MPI to rethink who its customers were and what the needs of those future customers were.

The Changing Health Care Industry

Exhibit 1 provides a dramatic illustration of the popularity of HMOs compared with the traditional indemnity option. In a traditional indemnity plan, individuals are insured by

EXHIBIT 1:   The Rise of the HMO

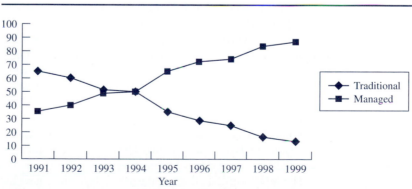

Source: KPMG survey of employer-sponsored health benefits.

EXHIBIT 2 National Health Expenditures (in billions of US$)

Year	1970	1980	1990	1992	1994	1996	1998	2000*
Hospital care	28	102.7	256.4	305.3	335.7	358.5	383.2	418.4
Physician services	13.6	45.2	146.3	175.9	190.4	202.1	221.4	253.1
Home health care	0.2	2.4	13.1	19.6	25.6	30.2	33.2	38.2
Drugs	8.8	21.6	59.9	71.2	79.5	91.4	106.1	124.5
Technology	1.6	3.8	10.5	11.9	12.5	13.3	14.3	15.8
Nursing homes	4.2	17.6	50.9	62.3	70.9	78.5	87.3	96.4
Research	5.3	11.6	24.5	27.5	30.5	31.5	33.5	36
Other†	11.5	39.4	137.6	162.9	200.6	229.6	267.8	312.8
Total expenditures	73.2	247.3	699.5	836.6	945.7	1,035.1	1,146.8	1,295.2

* Estimated.

† Includes all government health activities.

Source: Health Care Financing Administration, 1998.

one organization (a private insurance firm) and provided medical care by another (one of many private sector medical providers). HMOs, however, combine these functions; the financing and the delivery of medical care are integrated into one organization. The primary tool that an HMO uses in controlling costs is its method of reimbursement, which has as its goal to shift most of the financial risk to providers (doctors and hospitals). Shifting risk discourages overutilization of services—primarily the use of expensive technology and specialty referrals. Some HMOs negotiate a fee-for-service schedule that represents a discount from the fees that are normally charged. Hospitals or doctors who agree to these discounts are rewarded with a larger volume of the HMO's patients. Clearly, all these factors have put HMOs in a very strong position to control the rate of growth in health-care expenditures.

HMOs and Expenditures on Health Care

Exhibit 2 shows how dramatically health-care expenditures have grown over the last 30 years (by the year 2000, health-care spending was predicted to have increased by 17.6 times the amount that was spent in 1970).

Yet the rate of growth in health-care expenses in each of these decades was dramatically different. The 1970s had the greatest rate of increase in health-care expenditures, at 3.38. During the 1980s, the rate of increase had slowed to 2.83, while the 1990s had reined in this increase to 1.85 times the health-care expenditures of the previous decade.

Certainly, the rise of HMOs coincided with the 1990s slowdown in health-care costs. How did the HMOs manage to slow the rate of growth in health-care costs? Clearly, some of the sectors of the health-care industry were winners or losers. While the overall dollar amounts spent on each category increased from 1970 to 2000, there was a dramatic shift in the way in which health-care dollars were spent.

In 1970, nearly 60 percent of all health-care expenditures was spent on either hospital care or physician services. Government services, such as Medicare, accounted for approximately 16 percent of the total, while technology and research constituted nearly 7 percent of total medical spending. The remaining 18 percent of health-care expenditures was divided among drug costs, home care services, and nursing homes (Exhibit 3).

The advent of the HMO in the 1990s brought a new list of priorities to the way in which health-care expenditures were divided. By 2000, spending on hospitals and doc-

──────

EXHIBIT 3   **Percent of National Health Expenditures**

	1970	1980	1990	2000*
Hospital care	38.2	41.5	36.7	32.3
Physician services	18.6	18.3	20.9	19.5
Home health care	—	1	1.9	2.9
Drugs	12	8.7	8.6	9.6
Technology	2.2	1.5	1.5	1.2
Nursing homes	5.7	7.1	7.3	7.4
Research	7.2	4.7	3.5	2.8
Other†	15.7	15.9	19.7	24.2

* Estimated.

† Includes all government health activities.

Source: Adapted from Health Care Financing Administration, 1998.

tors' services had decreased by 8 percent (to 52 percent of all health-care expenditures). Research and technology accounted for only 4 percent of all health-care expenditures, falling 6 percent from its 1970 high of 7 percent. Government spending had increased to over 24 percent of total health-care expenditures, while home care, drugs, and nursing homes had increased their take of the pie to 20 percent.

It appeared that HMOs' efforts to hold down medical costs had relied primarily on three factors: (1) shifting services away from hospitals and doctors, (2) decreasing funding for technology and research, and (3) shifting services to outpatient centers. The great unknown in the future of the health-care industry was the role of government. Certainly, government spending on health care had increased dramatically over the last 30 years, but this rate of increase would not continue in the future. Yet there was a larger question: What side would Congress take in the battle between doctors and insurers on who gets to decide when treatment is medically necessary? If the doctors won the battle, health care spending probably would increase. If managed care (HMOs) won, the determination of what goods and services would be paid for would be quite different.

While there was growing sentiment among the American public to change the way health care was delivered and financed, no single plan had gathered enough public support to win approval in the U.S. Congress. The following three health-care plans had achieved almost equal public acceptance:

1. *All-government single-payer option:* Under this system, everyone would participate in a single health plan administered and financed by the government or a quasi-governmental agency. A basic benefits package defined to cover all medically necessary services would be available to the entire population.

2. *Expanded use of the market to encourage and enable individuals to purchase insurance:* This was considered the "market"-based alternative. The market approach to health-care reform was most commonly associated with the use of the tax code to make people more sensitive to the cost of medical care and health insurance reform to improve access among the uninsured. Tax credits and vouchers were suggested as one way to encourage low-income families to buy their own health insurance. The proposed market solution also would include measures to provide incentives to enroll in managed care plans. The market alternative was built around the core idea that individual decisions are better than collective decisions.

3. *Managed competition:* This was the central element of President Clinton's reform package of 1993. In most employer-provided plans, the employee has little choice. As members of the same group, all employees get the plan provided by the employer—fee-for-service or managed care—and rarely get to choose between the two. The Clinton plan also included universal coverage as an entitlement, uniform fee schedules, and an employer mandate to provide health insurance. Essentially, Clinton was trying to propose a compromise between the two previous alternatives. It was a proposal that was defeated.

Roan wondered how MPI was preparing to handle the new economic and political environment facing the health-care industry. Could MPI still utilize its reputation for producing high-quality and innovative medical products? What strategy would need to be developed to compete in a health-care industry whose major concern was still costs? What type of health-care plan would the federal government adopt eventually? Above all, who were the competitors in this medical equipment arena, and could MPI obtain any sort of strategic advantage over them?

Competitors in the Medical Equipment Industry

By the late 1990s MPI's competitors in the medical equipment industry could be divided into two groups: (1) "traditional" ones whose strategy evolved from their ability to introduce technological innovations and (2) large corporate competitors whose distinctive advantage was their ability to produce low-cost, high-quality medical equipment and provide outstanding servicing of that equipment.

"Traditional" Medical Equipment Makers

Acuson Corporation.   Chairman and CEO Samuel H. Maslak, Sc.D., and former Medical Products Inc. engineers Daniel Horning and Adam Wenke founded Acuson in 1979. Incorporated in 1982, the company designs, manufactures, markets, and services the Sequoia, the Aspen, and the 128XP ultrasound platforms as well as the AEGIS digital image and data management system. Acuson is a leading supplier of diagnostic ultrasound systems to the hospital radiology and cardiology markets. To date, more than 13,000 Acuson 128XPs, as well as 1,500 Sequoia and 1,500 Aspen systems, have been installed in hospitals and medical centers globally.

Acuson introduced its first product, the Acuson 128 Computed Sonography System, in 1983. Developed at a time when ultrasound was thought to have reached its peak, the 128 system garnered praise from the medical community as "the fourth generation in medical ultrasound." Acuson quickly earned a reputation for providing physicians with "gold standard" ultrasound image quality and system performance. The Aspen system was based on select technologies from the Sequoia ultrasound systems, combined with other Acuson innovations to create an entirely new high-performance platform at a lower price than Sequoia technology.

Acuson is a leading manufacturer, international marketer, and service provider of medical diagnostic ultrasound systems and image management products for hospitals, clinics, and health-care delivery systems throughout the world. Located in Mountain View, California, Acuson had sales of US$455 million in 1998. The company currently employs more than 1,800 people.

Advanced Technology Laboratories Inc. (ATL).   ATL Ultrasound, a Philips Medical Systems company, was founded in 1969. Its goal was to become a worldwide leader in the development, manufacture, distribution, and service of diagnostic medical ultrasound systems. Philips Medical Systems was a leading supplier of diagnostic imaging systems and related services worldwide that employed more than 11,000 people in more than 100 countries.

During a 1996 presentation to investors at the ninth annual Bear Stearns Health Care Conference held in New York, it was reported that ATL was on track to achieve its goal of a 15 percent return on shareholder equity by the end of 1998. Growth opportunities for ATL and the ultrasound industry were expected to increase over the next several years. ATL achieved a return on equity of 5 percent, excluding nonrecurring gains and charges, in 1995. The company expected to take a leadership position in digital, scanhead, and software ultrasound technologies.

The New Corporate Giants

Toshiba.   In 1973, Toshiba entered the medical industry in the United States when it began selling diagnostic equipment through Litton Industry's medical division. Around 1977, it developed its first ultrasound imaging product with broad potential application in America. For the next 12 years Toshiba struggled to gain a significant U.S. presence in the production of imaging equipment. Toshiba America Medical Systems Inc. did not become a major player until the purchase of the MRI Division of Diasonics Inc. in 1989 made it the nation's third largest manufacturer of magnetic resonance imaging (MRI) systems, with a 15 percent market share. This acquisition boosted Toshiba America's annual sales to about US$350 million from US$200 million and nearly doubled its work force to 1,200 employees.

Through a full line of medical imaging systems—encompassing x-ray, MRI, computed tomography (CT), nuclear medicine, and ultrasound—Toshiba has become the world's third largest manufacturer of medical imaging systems and the number one worldwide manufacturer of ultrasound equipment. While Toshiba's equipment was not the result of technological innovation, its equipment was known for high quality and reliability as well as low cost.

Siemens AG.   Werner von Siemens, who helped patent and manufacture the world's first x-ray tubes in 1895, established Siemens. This discovery sparked an exploration of medical imaging technologies and ultimately led to Siemens's early forays into medical ultrasound. Until the 1950s Siemens's use of ultrasound was primarily in mechanical engineering. The company's first ultrasound systems were used primarily to test the composition and strength of the materials used in heavy equipment. The company's introduction to medical ultrasound came in 1953, when two Swedish professors sought Siemens's help in using ultrasound as a tool to assess the composition of the human body. Dr. Carl Hellmuth Hertz and Dr. Inge Edler had developed a special motion scanner that operated with a Siemens ultrasound system to map the movement of the heart by capturing the echoes of ultrasound waves.

Major changes in the company's ultrasound systems began in the late 1970s with the advent of revolutionary linear arrays. These linear arrays not only improved image quality by replacing fixed-focus mechanical sector scanners with adjustable systems, they were significantly lighter. These lighter, more flexible systems made ultrasound a much more practical real-time diagnostic tool. At the same time, Siemens began investigating innovative ultrasound systems, many of which are only now becoming commercially viable. In 1979 Siemens created the very first 1.5 D array, a diagnostic tool that allowed clinicians to focus on a particular elevation direction within an ultrasound image. The technology became marketable only in the 1990s, after scientific advances in microelectronics. As early as the 1980s Siemens was investigating use of digital imaging in ultrasound, an advance only now becoming widely available.

Siemens Ultrasound is part of Siemens Medical Systems, Inc., of Iselin, New Jersey (USA), and Siemens Medical Engineering Group, based in Erlangen, Germany. Siemens Medical Engineering Group is one of the world's leading providers of diagnostic imaging products and advanced medical systems, with worldwide annual sales in 1996–1997 of US$4.7 billion and approximately 21,200 employees. It is headquartered near Seattle in Issaquah, Washington (USA). Siemens Ultrasound designs and manufactures a comprehensive line of ultrasound systems. Siemens's commitment to innovation in ultrasound began when the company pioneered real-time ultrasound in the 1960s. Today, nearly half of Siemens Ultrasound's employees are dedicated to the research and development of technologies that push the limits of diagnostic ultrasound. More than 48,000 Siemens ultrasound systems are in use in hospitals, clinics, and physicians' offices worldwide, making it the world's second largest supplier of ultrasound systems.

General Electric Co.   General Electric (GE) believes it is well positioned to take advantage of the upheaval in health care. Several years before President Clinton made health-care reform a household debate, GE's medical division was busy revamping operations. The division's work force had shrunk to 3,800 from 5,500 in the mid-1980s, with many of the cuts resulting from layoffs. However, productivity was up. The smaller work force churned out the same number of machines each year: several hundred in each category. John Trani, GE Medical Systems president, also cut the cost and time to build its machines. The price of the superconducting magnet in an MRI machine was cut in half in five years, and making a CT scanner took one and a half weeks, compared with seven or eight weeks in the mid-1980s. The goal was to cut that time to 24 hours. GE also had cut the cost of servicing its medical products. It had begun doing maintenance checks remotely over telephone wires on 90 percent of its CT scanners and MRI machines. The ability to service its equipment quickly had become a strong selling point for GE Medical Systems.

Since 1993, increases in the prices in the medical device industry had hovered at or below the general rate of inflation. GE's prices had actually fallen in that period. That was in contrast to price increases for health care in general and for prescription drugs in particular, where costs have climbed on average at several times the rate of inflation. Despite the downward pressure on prices and a slowdown in domestic sales, which had fallen 8 percent to 10 percent, GE Medical Systems had produced record sales of US$3.5 billion by the late 1990s, as well as record profits. By 2000, 45 percent of GE's medical device sales were outside the United States, compared with 15 percent five years earlier.

In 1996 GE Medical Systems acquired Specialty Underwriters' health-care operations in an attempt to bolster its efforts in the multivendor service business. Multivendor service offerings give health-care providers a more efficient solution for managing and servicing hundreds of pieces of clinical and biomedical equipment across their departments.

GE Medical Systems was a leading provider of diagnostic imaging systems and related services. Its products included x-ray, computed tomography, ultrasound, magnetic resonance, and nuclear medicine systems. Its services ranged from maintaining equipment to providing productivity training and asset management. It employed around 14,000 people worldwide.

Conclusion

As Roan was about to review the ultrasound proposal, she realized that the project faced a number of crucial questions before she could give her approval (or refuse it). What would the health-care industry resemble in the years to come? Would the U.S. model of providing health care through a system of HMOs be the future of health care worldwide, or would government take a more active role in providing universal coverage? While MPI had a reputation for producing high-quality, innovative medical equipment, could it use that reputation to gain an advantage in the ever-changing medical equipment market? Could MPI provide the type of service that customers seemed to demand when they purchased medical equipment? Roan knew that a better understanding of the health-care environment was needed before reading the proposal.

APPENDIX 1
MEDICAL PRODUCTS INC.

Balance Sheet Information ($US millions)

	1996	1997
Cash and investments	$13,625	$13,471
Accounts receivable	27,176	29,106
Total inventories	26,817	25,697
Other current assets	4,226	5,365
Total current assets	**71,844**	**73,639**
Property and equipment	20,557	23,799
Other noncurrent assets	15,293	17,794
Total Assets	**107,694**	**115,232**
Total current liabilities	$45,175	$39,823
Long-term debt	6,837	12,602
Other noncurrent liabilities	4,111	4,398
Shareholder's equity	51,571	58,409
Total Liabilities	**107,694**	**115,232**
Net Income	**2,433**	**2,735**

Ratio Analysis		
Current ratio	1.7	1.9
Return on assets	9.8%	10.5%
Return on equity	20.2%	21.1%
Book value per share	$12.83	$15.04

1996–1997 Orders and Revenues ($US millions)

1996	Orders	Revenues
Computer products	$31,852	$31,458
Electronic T & M	3,912	3,798
Medical electronics	1,399	1,388
Chemical analysis	895	858
Electronic components	831	918
Totals	**$38,889**	**$38,420**

1997	Orders	Revenues
Computer products	$35,444	$35,447
Electronic T & M	4,432	4,299
Medical electronics	1,318	1,265
Chemical analysis	941	909
Electronic components	964	975
Totals	**$43,099**	**$42,895**

CASE 1–3
THE BOSTON RED SOX

Mike Miller, a writer for a Boston newspaper, was given the task of writing a series of articles on the economic state of the Boston Red Sox and Major League Baseball (MLB). Mike assumed that the average baseball fan did not think about baseball economics. However, he knew that folks around Boston were wondering how baseball had gotten itself into its current economic situation and how that situation might affect the Red Sox.

In thinking about various aspects of the articles, Mike believed that salary trends should be examined because of the amazingly high contracts that had been signed during the late 1990s. Additionally, the economic conditions surrounding the proposal to build a new Fenway Park in Boston would definitely need to be looked at (at 87 years old, Fenway was one of the oldest parks in Major League Baseball).

As a reporter, Mike realized that behind the bright lights, baseball is a business—an enterprise whose existence relies on more than talented participants. While athletes will continue to draw crowds, sales and profits ultimately will determine baseball's future. Minimal research about the present state of the sport yielded the notion that MLB and its ball clubs were composed of far more than balls, bats, and player statistics. Modern-day baseball is a business whose roster far exceeds those who play the game. Lawyers, accountants, architects, financiers, investors, bankers, and marketers affect the continuance and success of Major League Baseball.

Mike's byline appeared on a series of baseball-related articles on three consecutive days.

April 2, 2000

"Baseball as Big Business," Boston, MA—With the Red Sox set to begin the new season in a couple of days, many of us will shift our focus to Major League Baseball. The anticipation for "America's pastime" is building as it has each year since the late 1800s, when the game was first played. For numerous reasons, many of us hold baseball up to a different standard than other sports. The Red Sox, one of the oldest and best-known teams, started playing in 1901. The Sox have played in the same stadium for 87 years.

Major League Baseball has been afforded the benefit of being unique in relation to other sports—it is exempt for antitrust laws. This is the result of a 1922 ruling by the U.S. Supreme Court. The question put before the Court at that time was whether "the monopoly they had established or had attempted to establish was a monopoly of any part of interstate commerce."[1] The plaintiff who brought the suit against baseball contended the "mere act of a person allowing himself to be transported from one state to another" created interstate commerce.[2] It was argued before the courts that organized baseball was in the business of "giving exhibitions of baseball, which are purely state

This case was prepared by Sean O'Sullivan, honors student, Carroll School of Management, Boston College, and Gregory Trompeter, associate professor, Boston College, as the basis for class discussion rather than to illustrate effective or ineffective handling of a managerial situation. Development of the case was funded by a grant from the General Electric Fund at Boston College.

affairs."[3] It was also argued that the games involved teams from different states but that "the transport is a mere incident, not the essential thing."[4]

The court's decision stated, "Organized Baseball is not interstate commerce and does not constitute an attempt to monopolize within the Sherman Act."[5] This exemption allowed owners to restrict the establishment of new franchises as well as the relocation of other franchises. The decision allowed baseball to flourish earlier in the century, and as a result, many Americans associate baseball with their childhood. However, this association appears to be changing as baseball becomes more like a business than a game.

Some subtle and some not so subtle changes have occurred over the last 50 years. These changes have begun to transform the game of baseball as we knew it growing up. In 1950, there were 16 major league teams. All were concentrated in the northeastern United States. Chicago, Illinois, and St. Louis, Missouri, were the westernmost outposts, and a trip to play the Senators in Washington, D.C., was described as a southern road trip. Players traveled by train or bus, and only the greatest superstars could dream of earning the astronomical sum of US$100,000 per year. At the start of the 1999–2000 season, the league had 30 teams—stretching from San Francisco, California, on the West Coast to Boston, Massachusetts, on the East Coast and as far south as Miami, Florida, and north into the Canadian cities of Montreal and Toronto.

Many of the changes over time, from expansion and internationalization to the doubleheader and Astroturf, have upset baseball fans. However, none have caused such discontent for MLB as the ongoing transformation from a Walt Whitmanesque national pastime into the multi-billion-dollar business it has become. The economics have begun to overshadow the sport—so much so that many fans are more likely to know players' salaries than to know their batting averages or home run totals.

An unstable situation regarding the commissioner of baseball has also eroded confidence in the American pastime. Until 1999, Major League Baseball had spent seven years without an official commissioner. Thus, there was no dominant authority figure to punish owners, teams, players, and/or coaches for inappropriate conduct. The position of commissioner was created in 1921 after the gambling scandal in 1919 in which eight players admitted to purposely losing World Series games.[6] The first commissioner was Judge Kenesaw Landis. After being elected by team owners, he was given absolute authority over matters involving baseball. The position was constructed so that the commissioner's decisions were final and could not be challenged in court. Landis was given the authority to rule on anything that he deemed was "not in the best interests of baseball."[7] Over the years, commissioners have on numerous occasions suspended players and owners for their actions. The commissioner also plays an integral role in labor relations. In 1990, Commissioner Faye Vincent presided over labor negotiations that delayed the start of the season by a week. However, a full 162-game season was played.

With only an acting commissioner in the position in 1994, fans were given reason to hate the big business of baseball. It was during that year that players went on strike and cut short the 162-game season as well as delaying the start of 1995 spring training. The biggest blow of all was that baseball fans were left without a World Series for the first time since 1904.[8] This, combined with the increase in popularity of the National Basketball Association (NBA) and the National Hockey League (NHL), left the future of baseball in doubt.

During the strike season many fans vowed to stay away from the game forever. Attendance figures for 1995 were down from the prestrike totals. In 1995, average per game MLB attendance was 26,202—down from 31,377 in 1993 (Exhibit 1). However, in the year after the strike, revenues immediately started to increase and by 1999 were increasing at a greater rate than they had been increasing before the strike. The average

Exhibit 1   Total and Per Game MLB Attendance

Total MLB Attendance

Year	Total ($millions)	Per Game
1940 (1)	9.82	7,949
1950 (2)	17.46	14,174
1960 (3)	19.91	16,162
1970 (4)	28.75	14,788
1980 (5)	43.01	20,425
1990 (6)	54.82	26,032
1991 (7)	56.81	26,977
1992 (8)	55.87	26,529
1993 (9)	70.26	31,377
1994 (10)	50.01	31,612
1995 (11)	50.29	26,202
1996 (12)	60.1	26,889
1997 (13)	63.02	28,288
1998 (14)	70.59	29,376

Source: David Schoenfeld, "Success, but at What Price?"

team revenue was US$63 million in 1993; by 1998 it was around US$89 million (Exhibit 2). Part of this revenue growth was attributed to the expansion MLB experienced twice during the decade. Two new teams were formed in 1992 and again in 1998. These teams resulted in franchise revenues of US$190 million in 1992 and US$270 million in 1998. Beyond these initial franchise costs, the new teams brought in additional merchandising revenue.

Another change resulting from the owners' quest for more money has been the expansion of the playoffs. The first expansion of postseason play occurred in 1969 when the league championship series was added.[9] The next and most recent expansion was met with skepticism as two more teams from each league were given a chance to play in the postseason. The first round is a best of five game series, and so there is a possibility of revenue from an additional 20 postseason games (which are typically sold out). This was perceived by some as another change to squeeze money from loyal fans. The Boston Red Sox benefited from this expansion. The team has been the "wild card" team twice in the five years in which this extended format has existed.

Although the Red Sox baseball club has benefited from the expansion, the players have benefited the most. They receive 60 percent of gate receipts from the games in each postseason series.[10] The players' shares totaled US$39.3 million in 1998.[11] Most of the remaining 40 percent and the revenue from any additional games go to Major

EXHIBIT 2 **Total Revenue Ranked by Total, 1990–1998 (in $millions)**

Rank	Team	1990	1991	1992	1993	1994	1995	1996	1997	1998	Total	Average	Average 1995–1998
1	New York Yankees	$98.0	$90.0	$94.6	$107.6	$71.5	$93.9	$133.3	$144.7	$175.5	$1,009.1	$112.1	$136.9
2	Baltimore Orioles	47.9	50.6	83.5	81.3	53.1	75.1	105.3	134.5	140.5	771.8	85.8	113.9
3	**Boston Red Sox**	**68.5**	**81.5**	**90.6**	**77.5**	**49.9**	**67.9**	**88.4**	**92.1**	**106.9**	**723.3**	**80.4**	**88.8**
4	Los Angeles Dodgers	64.4	79.3	84.2	79.7	49.5	70.9	88.6	94.3	107.9	718.8	79.9	90.4
5	New York Mets	81.1	91.1	86.9	80.8	45	61.5	68.3	80.5	99.7	694.9	77.2	77.5
6	Toronto Blue Jays	77.5	88.7	87.7	88.4	56.4	62.5	70.2	67.1	73.4	671.9	74.7	68.3
7	Atlanta Braves	35.4	40.3	50.7	79	55.8	60.7	79.1	119.6	142.7	663.3	73.7	100.5
8	Cleveland Indians	34.8	42	39.9	48.8	41	60.2	95.4	134.1	149.7	645.9	71.8	109.9
9	Texas Rangers	50.3	61.5	66.2	60.3	50.1	61.9	87.7	97.6	108.1	643.7	71.5	88.8
10	Chicago Cubs	50.3	64.5	64.9	82.8	53.8	62.9	76.6	81.5	93.1	630.4	70.0	78.5
11	Chicago White Sox	49	78	77.9	78.8	45.5	55.7	70.3	82.3	74.1	611.6	68.0	70.6
12	St. Louis Cardinals	55.8	59.1	50.9	64.8	39.3	48.8	69.8	82.9	97.8	569.2	63.2	74.8
13	Colorado Rockies				52.2	43.5	70.3	95.6	116.6	124.6	502.8	83.8	101.8
14	San Francisco Giants	50	48.9	47	69.1	43.1	46.4	51.8	69.8	73.3	499.4	55.5	60.3
15	Oakland Athletics	57.9	64.9	64.4	60.1	36.7	41.2	49.4	56.4	56.7	487.7	54.2	50.9
16	Houston Astros	40	46	43.3	60.5	34.3	44.4	62.4	68	82.5	481.4	53.5	64.3
17	Anaheim Angels	48.6	54.1	55.8	53.8	30	39	42.5	62.6	88.5	474.9	52.8	58.2
18	Philadelphia Phillies	61.9	48.2	50	48.8	41.1	45.3	50	57.1	66	468.4	52.0	54.6
19	Seattle Mariners	34	44.7	45.4	50.7	27.4	36.7	57.6	89.8	81.3	467.6	52.0	66.4
20	San Diego Padres	47.2	48.4	53.6	47.7	25	28.2	52.8	57.6	78.9	439.4	48.8	54.4
21	Kansas City Royals	53.2	53.6	52	51.7	31.9	35.8	43.1	51.2	53.5	426	47.3	45.9
22	Cincinnati Reds	48.7	49	49.6	52.9	30.6	40.4	45.3	50.2	54.4	421.1	46.8	47.6
23	Detroit Tigers	38	51.6	50.5	55.6	33	39.1	44.4	50.6	54.2	417	46.3	47.1
24	Minnesota Twins	38.6	44.1	52.8	48.9	26.2	30.2	41.1	46.8	46.8	375.5	41.7	41.2
25	Pittsburgh Pirates	41.1	45.8	50.1	43	25.6	24.9	39.9	49.3	51.7	371.4	41.3	41.5
26	Milwaukee Brewers	38.4	38.8	43.3	46.3	26	29.5	41.6	46.9	55.5	366.3	40.7	43.4
27	Montreal Expos	35.3	39.4	46.7	46.2	25.8	29.3	40.9	43.6	46.5	353.7	39.3	40.1
28	Florida Marlins				44.9	40.9	47.8	55.8	88.2	69.5	347.1	57.9	65.3
29	Arizona Diamondbacks									116.3	116.3	116.3	116.3
30	Tampa Bay Devil Rays									93.7	93.7	93.7	93.7
	Total	1,345.9	1,504.1	1,582.5	1,762.2	1,132.0	1,410.5	1,847.2	2,215.9	2,663.3	15,463.6		
	Average	$51.8	$57.9	$60.9	$62.9	$40.4	$50.4	$66.0	$79.1	$88.8	$515.5	$65.1	$73.1

Source: David Schoenfeld, "Team-by-Team Total Revenue," and Burt Badenhausen and William Sicheri, "Baseball Games."

EXHIBIT 3 Fan Cost Index

NFL Season	Average Ticket Price	Ticket % Change	FCI*	FCI % Change
1991	$25.21		$151.55	
1992	27.19	7.8	163.19	7.6
1993	28.68	5.5	173.33	6.2
1994	30.56	6.6	182.72	5.4
1995	33.52	9.7	199.09	9
1996	35.58	6.1	207.8	4.4
1997	38.09	7.1	221.17	6.4

NHL Season	Average Ticket Price	Ticket % Change	FCI*	FCI % Change
1994–95†	$32.75		$193.10	
1995–96	34.75	6.1	203.46	5.4
1996–97	38.34	10.3	220.72	8.5
1997–98	40.64	6	228.39	3.5

NBA Season	Average Ticket Price	Ticket % Change	FCI*	FCI % Change
1991–92	$23.24		$144.10	
1992–93	25.16	8.3	158.17	9.8
1993–94	27.12	7.8	168.68	6.6
1994–95	28.63	5.6	177.12	5
1995–96	31.56	10.2	191.31	8
1996–97	33.77	7	202.14	5.7
1997–98	36.32	7.6	214.28	6

MLB Season	Average Ticket Price	Ticket % Change	FCI*	FCI % Change
1991	$8.64		$77.40	
1992	9.3	7.6	86.24	11.4
1993	9.6	3.2	90.84	5.3
1994	10.45	8.9	95.8	5.5
1995	10.55	1	96.83	1.1
1996	11.19	6.1	102.58	5.9
1997	12.36	10.5	107.13	4.4
1998	13.6	10	114.82	7.2

Source: Team Marketing Report, Chicago, and "Take Me Out to the Ball Game."

* The Fan Cost Index includes the cost of four average-price tickets, four small soft drinks, two small beers, four hot dogs, parking for one car, two game programs, and two souvenir caps.

† No NHL surveys were conducted before 1994–1995.

League Baseball and the American and National leagues. Participating individual teams receive only concessions and what is left of the gate receipts.[12] They do, however, receive the benefit of being showcased on national television during the playoffs, which helps in selling team merchandise, securing advertising for the future, and negotiating broadcast rights.

Concessions represent another revenue source that has been exploited by team owners. The fan cost index (FCI), which factors in concession revenues, has risen every year in Major League Baseball. This index looks at the average amount a family of four spends at a baseball game. It considers four average-price tickets, two small beers, four small sodas, four hot dogs, parking for one car, two game programs, and two caps. The Red Sox FCI was the second highest among major league teams. The average family of four spends US$160 at Fenway Park, which is US$40 higher than the league average.[13] However, the average FCIs for the three other major professional sports (basketball, hockey, and football) were well over US$200 (Exhibit 3).

It looks like the business of baseball has started to overshadow the game of baseball.

April 3, 2000

"Making Money at the Park," Boston, MA—As evidenced by player salaries, baseball has become big business. The only way owners can afford to pay such steep salaries is by generating revenues. With the exception of player strike periods, revenues increased steadily during the 1990s. The decade began well for baseball but fell hard as the players union went on strike in August 1994. There were no games, resulting in no ticket, broadcasting, parking, concession, or advertising revenues for the end of the 1994 season. The strike took place at the worst part of the season. There could be no postseason games—a time when the league generated substantial revenue. MLB revenue dropped US$600 million from the previous season, with the strike-shortened season seeing revenue of US$1.13 billion. However, by 1998, MLB revenue was at US$2.63 billion.

The Red Sox were not strangers to the revenue boom. In 1990 Red Sox revenue was a modest US$68.5 million, but it dropped to US$49.9 when the 1994 strike occurred. However, by 1998 the Red Sox had reached an all-time revenue high of US$106.9 million (Exhibit 4). Baseball had indeed recovered from the strike. Fans who had vowed never to return to the parks had returned with open wallets.

In 1994 attendance at Fenway Park dropped to 1.78 million. By end of the 1990s, however, attendance was at 2.5 million (Exhibit 5). While the number of fans was growing, so were ticket prices. By 1999 the average price for a ticket to see the Red Sox at Fenway park was US$23.84—the highest in Major League Baseball.[14]

The Boston Red Sox receive relatively high revenues from television and radio broadcasting rights. The team averaged US$32.3 million in media revenues in the 1990s. That was third in MLB, behind the two New York teams (Exhibit 6). The New York teams benefit from playing in the largest television market in the country. The Red Sox are in the seventh largest market (Exhibit 7).

Although Major League Baseball teams have enjoyed an increase in revenues, this increase has been accompanied by an equal or greater rise in expenses. Player salary is the most significant expense for ball clubs. Since 1976, the average salary has increased in every year except 1987 and 1995 (Exhibit 8). Even more troubling is the fact that the average player's salary has more than doubled in the 1990s. In 1990 the average major league player earned US$589,438 yearly. By 1998 the average salary had skyrocketed to US$1,377,196.

The Red Sox were no strangers to this trend. In 1990 the club had the second highest payroll with US$21.8 million. By 1999 the payroll figure had jumped to US$72.3 million (Exhibit 9). This significant payroll increase has been attributed to the 1997 acquisition of star pitcher Pedro Martinez. His contract was for US$75 million for six years, with a US$17 million club option for a seventh year. That contract made Martinez the highest paid player in baseball at that time.[15] Another high-priced Red Sox

EXHIBIT 4   1998 Revenues

Rank	Team	Current Value (millions)	One-Year Change in Value (%)	Revenues (millions)	Operating Income (millions)	Debt/Value (%)
1	New York Yankees	$491	36%	$175.50	$23.00	3%
2	Cleveland Indians	359	12	149.7	19	16
3	Atlanta Braves	357	19	142.7	16.4	6
4	Baltimore Orioles	351	9	140.5	8.5	28
5	Colorado Rockies	311	3	124.6	19.5	11
6	Arizona Diamondbacks	291		116.3	22.5	47
7	Texas Rangers	281	11	108.1	0.5	71
8	Los Angeles Dodgers	270	14	107.9	−11.7	5
9	**Boston Red Sox**	**256**	**12**	**106.9**	**−7.6**	**8**
10	New York Mets	249	29	99.7	−5.2	5
11	St. Louis Cardinals	205	18	97.8	1.6	7
12	Tampa Bay Devil Rays	225		93.7	20.6	33
13	Chicago Cubs	224	10	93.1	−7.9	6
14	Anaheim Angels	195	24	88.5	−0.2	10
15	Houston Astros	239	26	82.5	−3.7	67
16	Seattle Mariners	236	−6	81.3	−8.6	35
17	San Diego Padres	205	27	78.9	−8	63
18	Chicago White Sox	178	−17	74.1	0.2	8
19	Toronto Blue Jays	162	15	73.4	−9.5	8
20	San Francisco Giants	213	13	73.3	−6.4	80
21	Florida Marlins	153	−4	69.5	8.6	0
22	Philadelphia Phillies	145	11	66	4.5	9
23	Oakland Athletics	125	6	56.7	3.3	11
24	Milwaukee Brewers	155	22	55.5	−8.8	80
25	Cincinnati Reds	163	20	54.4	0.6	18
26	Detroit Tigers	152	11	54.2	−4.5	96
27	Kansas City Royals	96	−11	53.5	−10.9	21
28	Pittsburgh Pirates	145	9	51.7	2.6	62
29	Minnesota Twins	89	−5	46.8	−7.1	93
30	Montreal Expos	84	−4	46.5	5.6	60
	League average	220	11	88.8	1.9	32

Source: Burt Badenhausen and William Sicheri, "Baseball Games."

player was Nomar Garciaparra. Garciaparra accepted a five year, US$23.25 million contract with a chance for it to extend to a seven-year deal worth US$45.25 million if the Red Sox picked up two options on him.[16] Despite these two highly paid players, the Red Sox had only the seventh highest payroll among MLB teams.

The increase in salaries began in 1976, when the average player's salary was US$52,300. The salary growth is attributed to the start of the free agency. Curt Flood opened the gates to free agency by fighting Major League Baseball for control over where he could play. Although he lost the case, his argument attracted public support, with the rule change coming only three years after Flood's case. Before free agency, ball clubs could trade players without the players having a say in the matter. Also, a player was allowed to sign with his current team only when his contract expired. Players were not able to negotiate with others teams and therefore did not have any leverage in signing new contracts. Basically, if a player did not like the contract that was being offered, he would not be playing professional baseball.

EXHIBIT 5   **Annual Attendance**

Rank	Team	1990	1991	1992	1993	1994	1995	1996	1997	1998	1999	Total	Average
1	Colorado Rockies				$4.48	$3.28	$3.39	$3.89	$3.89	$3.79	$3.48	$26.20	$3.74
2	Baltimore Orioles	2.42	2.55	3.57	3.64	2.54	3.1	3.65	3.71	3.68	3.43	32.29	3.23
3	Toronto Blue Jays	3.89	4	4.03	4.06	2.91	2.83	2.56	2.59	2.45	2.16	31.48	3.15
4	Arizona Diamondbacks										3.02	3.02	3.02
5	Los Angeles Dodgers	3	3.35	2.47	3.17	2.28	2.77	3.19	3.32	3.08	3.1	29.73	2.97
6	Atlanta Braves	0.98	2.14	3.08	3.88	2.54	2.56	2.9	3.46	3.35	3.28	28.17	2.82
7	St. Louis Cardinals	2.57	2.45	2.42	2.84	1.87	1.75	2.66	2.63	3.19	3.24	25.62	2.56
8	Texas Rangers	2.06	2.3	2.2	2.24	2.5	1.99	2.89	2.95	2.92	2.77	24.82	2.48
9	Cleveland Indians	1.23	1.05	1.22	2.18	2	2.84	3.32	3.4	3.46	3.47	24.17	2.42
10	**Boston Red Sox**	**2.53**	**2.56**	**2.47**	**2.42**	**1.78**	**2.16**	**2.32**	**2.23**	**2.31**	**2.45**	**23.23**	**2.32**
11	Chicago Cubs	2.24	2.31	2.13	2.65	1.85	1.92	2.22	2.19	2.62	2.81	22.94	2.29
12	New York Yankees	2.01	1.86	1.75	2.42	1.68	1.71	2.25	2.58	2.95	3.29	22.5	2.25
13	Seattle Mariners	1.51	2.15	1.65	2.05	1.1	1.64	2.72	3.19	2.65	2.92	21.58	2.16
14	Cincinnati Reds	2.4	2.37	2.32	2.45	1.9	1.84	1.86	1.79	1.79	2.06	20.78	2.08
15	Anaheim Angels	2.56	2.42	2.07	2.06	1.51	1.75	1.82	1.77	2.51	2.25	20.72	2.07
16	Philadelphia Phillies	1.99	2.05	1.93	3.14	2.29	2.04	1.8	1.49	1.71	1.83	20.27	2.03
17	Florida Marlins				3.06	1.94	1.7	1.75	2.36	1.72	1.37	13.9	1.99
18	Chicago White Sox	2	2.93	2.68	2.58	1.7	1.61	1.68	1.86	1.38	1.35	19.77	1.98
19	New York Mets	2.73	2.28	1.78	1.87	1.15	1.27	1.59	1.77	2.28	2.73	19.45	1.95
20	San Diego Padres	1.86	1.8	1.72	1.38	0.95	1.04	2.19	2.09	2.55	2.52	18.1	1.81
21	San Francisco Giants	1.98	1.74	1.56	2.61	1.7	1.24	1.41	1.69	1.92	2.08	17.93	1.79
22	Houston Astros	1.31	1.2	1.21	2.08	1.56	1.36	1.98	2.05	2.45	2.71	17.91	1.79
23	Oakland Athletics	2.9	2.71	2.49	2.04	1.24	1.17	1.15	1.26	1.22	1.43	17.61	1.76
24	Tampa Bay Devil Rays										1.75	1.75	1.75
25	Kansas City Royals	2.24	2.16	1.87	1.93	1.4	1.23	1.44	1.52	1.49	1.5	16.78	1.68
26	Minnesota Twins	1.75	2.29	2.48	2.05	1.4	1.06	1.44	1.41	1.1	1.2	16.18	1.62
27	Pittsburgh Pirates	2.05	2.07	1.83	1.65	1.22	0.91	1.33	1.66	1.55	1.64	15.91	1.59
28	Milwaukee Brewers	1.75	1.48	1.86	1.69	1.27	1.09	1.33	1.44	1.8	1.7	15.41	1.54
29	Detroit Tigers	1.5	1.64	1.42	1.97	1.18	1.18	1.17	1.37	1.4	2.03	14.86	1.49
30	Montreal Expos	1.37	0.93	1.67	1.64	1.28	1.31	1.62	1.5	0.91	0.77	13	1.30
	MLB average	2.23	2.39	2.32	2.77	1.99	2.10	2.49	2.59	2.65	2.68	22.44	2.47
	Total MLB attendance	$54.83	$56.79	$55.88	$70.23	$50.02	$50.46	$60.13	$63.17	$64.23	$70.34	$596.08	$65.62

Sources: David Schoenfeld, "Yearly Attendance Chart," "NL Attendance Report," and "AL Attendance Report."

EXHIBIT 6   Media Revenue Ranked by Yearly Average (in $millions)

Rank	Team	1990	1991	1992	1993	1994	1995	1996	1997	Average
1	New York Yankees	$69.4	$61.0	$61.0	$63.0	$36.4	$54.3	$69.8	$69.8	$60.6
2	New York Mets	38.3	50	50	46.1	22.2	33.6	30.9	38.3	38.7
3	**Boston Red Sox**	**34.1**	**40.5**	**40.1**	**38**	**18**	**24.2**	**30.9**	**32.2**	**32.3**
4	Los Angeles Dodgers	29.7	32.5	33	34	15.3	24.4	31.8	33.3	29.3
5	Chicago Cubs	24.2	27.5	28	36	17	21.1	29.3	32.2	26.9
6	Toronto Blue Jays	28	30	28	31.6	12.9	20.7	28.4	29.4	26.1
7	Baltimore Orioles	22.5	24.4	25	27.4	11.4	18.9	30.6	36.3	24.6
8	Atlanta Braves	20	18.9	17.3	35	16.6	22.1	30.3	33.3	24.2
9	Detroit Tigers	22.3	28.8	28.8	30.3	12.5	18.1	24.7	22.4	23.5
10	St. Louis Cardinals	27.4	25	25.5	27	10.7	19.8	25.7	23.8	23.1
11	San Francisco Giants	23.3	26.2	24.5	27.5	10.7	19.8	25.5	27.3	23.1
12	Oakland Athletics	21.2	27	25	27.4	13.2	17	25.2	27.1	22.9
13	Texas Rangers	24.6	25.5	26.8	27.5	10	16.9	24.3	24.3	22.5
14	Chicago White Sox	24.2	25.7	26.2	26.2	7.2	16.4	24.3	28.3	22.3
15	Philadelphia Phillies	35	23.2	23.7	21	10.3	15.9	21.4	26.6	22.1
16	Anaheim Angels	24	27.9	28.2	26.7	8.7	12.8	18.3	29.9	22.1
17	Houston Astros	24.2	25.2	24.1	25.2	8	15.3	22.3	25.8	21.3
18	Cleveland Indians	20	23.7	23	23.7	5.4	15.7	21.6	29.7	20.4
19	Cincinnati Reds	21.8	24.4	24.4	25	8.4	13.6	21.5	21.3	20.1
20	San Diego Padres	25.1	23.1	25.5	25	9	11.1	16.5	19.8	19.4
21	Montreal Expos	20	23.5	24	24	7.8	12.1	19.4	18.5	18.7
22	Pittsburgh Pirates	20	21.9	23.3	23.5	8.6	12.2	17.7	19.6	18.4
23	Seattle Mariners	17	22	22	21	6.3	11.6	17.2	28.5	18.2
24	Minnesota Twins	20.8	20.5	20	22.3	5.4	14.3	20.4	20.3	18.0
25	Florida Marlins				5	12.7	19	23.9	29.4	18.0
26	Milwaukee Brewers	19	19.4	19.8	21.5	6.3	9.6	15.1	24	16.8
27	Kansas City Royals	19	20.5	21	21	5.4	10.9	16.5	19.1	16.7
28	Colorado Rockies				5	6.2	14.9	22.8	32.3	16.2
	Total	675.1	718.3	718.2	766.9	322.6	516.3	706.3	802.8	653.3
	Average/team	$26.0	$27.6	$27.6	$27.4	$11.5	$18.4	$25.2	$28.7	$24.1

Source: Rodney Fort and James Quirk, *Hard Ball,* and Michael Ozanian, "Selective Accounting."

The lack of a salary cap in baseball is another significant factor in the continuing rise in salaries. Major League Baseball owners unsuccessfully attempted to install a salary cap in 1994—thus, one reason for the player strike. The owners proposed to split revenues with players 50–50. However, players viewed the owners' proposal as a means of limiting their salaries, not as profit sharing.

The NFL and NBA both have some form of a salary cap. For example, the NBA has had a cap since the mid-1980s that limits salaries to 53 percent of total league revenues divided by the number of teams.[17] In the 1981–1982 season, 18 of the 21 NBA teams reported a financial loss. The league, however, has prospered since the implementation of the salary cap.[18] The NFL instituted a salary cap in 1993.

Although it might seem outrageous to pay a baseball player US$15 million a year, some players appear to be worth the money because they draw fans to the stadium, which increases merchandise sales. Two very attractive baseball players in the late 1990s were Mark McGwire and Ken Griffey, Jr. Griffey's impact on the Cincinnati Reds was felt immediately as fans waited in long lines to buy tickets to see him play. In

EXHIBIT 7   **Teams Ranked by Winning Percentage**

Team	Winning Percentage	Payroll	Attendance	City (Market Size)	Operating Income*	Revenue†
Atlanta Braves	0.595	2	5	12	20	7
New York Yankees	0.548	1	11	1	1	1
Cleveland Indians	0.531	11	8	16	14	8
Chicago White Sox	0.526	17	17	3	13	11
Boston Red Sox	**0.523**	**4**	**9**	**7**	**5**	**3**
Houston Astros	0.523	18	21	11	16	16
Cincinnati Reds	0.520	13	13	24	28	22
Texas Rangers	0.519	7	7	9	6	9
Toronto Blue Jays	0.516	6	3	10	9	6
Los Angeles Dodgers	0.513	5	4	2	7	4
Baltimore Orioles	0.512	3	2	4	2	2
San Francisco Giants	0.508	10	20	5	24	14
Montreal Expos	0.500	28	28	15	12	27
Pittsburgh Pirates	0.498	27	25	21	21	25
Oakland Athletics	0.497	20	22	5	18	15
New York Mets	0.494	9	18	1	4	5
Seattle Mariners	0.493	16	12	14	26	19
St. Louis Cardinals	0.488	15	6	20	11	12
San Diego Padres	0.487	21	19	19	15	20
Colorado Rockies	0.478	8	1	22	3	13
Milwaukee Brewers	0.478	24	26	26	25	26
Chicago Cubs	0.476	14	10	3	8	10
Anaheim Angels	0.475	12	14	2	19	17
Philadelphia Phillies	0.471	23	15	6	17	18
Kansas City Royals	0.468	19	23	25	27	21
Minnesota Twins	0.463	26	24	17	22	24
Detroit Tigers	0.453	22	27	8	23	23
Florida Marlins	0.442	25	16	13	10	28

*Operating Income does not include 1998 and 1999.

† Revenue does not include 1999.

Source: Compiled from other charts and David Schoenfeld, "The Truth Behind the Numbers."

the 1998 season the St. Louis Cardinals set a record for attendance of 3.2 million. This was an increase from 2.63 million the year before McGwire joined the team.[19] Simultaneously, merchandise sales increased more than 100 percent and concession sales increased 50 percent.[20] McGwire was also deemed responsible for an estimated extra US$60 million in the St. Louis, Missouri, economy.[21]

Despite a revenue stream that is increasing at a rapid rate, baseball club owners claim that they are losing money. Many people have questioned whether this claim is true, since some of the owners' choices of accounting methods are debatable. One area of debate has been the way teams account for the cost of players. When owners buy a team, the initial roster cost (essentially the cost representing the players), which can account for up to 50 percent of the purchase price, is written off. The write-off is allocated over a six-year period after the team purchase.[22] For example, if a team is bought for US$300 million, up to US$150 million can be written off over the next six years. Therefore, there is an additional expense of US$25 million attributable to operations. This lowers the team's income and leads to disagreements between owners and players who want

EXHIBIT 8   Average MLB Salary Since 1976

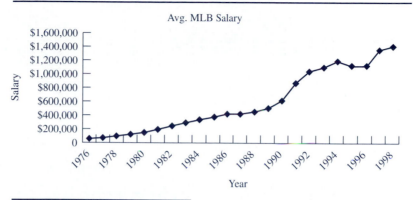

Year	Average Salary	Increase (%)
1976	$52,300	
1977	74,000	41.49
1978	97,800	32.16
1979	121,900	24.64
1980	146,500	20.18
1981	196,500	34.13
1982	245,000	24.68
1983	289,000	17.96
1984	325,900	12.77
1985	368,998	13.22
1986	410,517	11.25
1987	402,579	−1.93
1988	430,688	6.98
1989	489,539	13.66
1990	589,483	20.42
1991	845,383	43.41
1992	1,012,424	19.76
1993	1,062,780	4.97
1994	1,154,486	8.63
1995	1,094,440	−5.2
1996	1,101,455	0.64
1997	1,314,420	19.33
1998	1,377,196	4.78

Source: "Average Payrolls Since 1976."

higher salaries and between owners and local governments that frequently are asked to pay for new ball parks because the team appears to be losing money. Some people, however, think the cost should be associated with the purchase and not with operations.[23]

The selling price for baseball teams can be phenomenal. The Cleveland Indians ball club, the only major league team that is publicly traded, was sold in 1999 for US$320 million.[24] In 1998, the Texas Rangers were sold for US$250 million and the Los Angeles Dodgers sold for US$311 million. The Dodgers deal involved a considerable amount of real estate around the stadium.[25] In 1996, an offer of US$220 million was made for the Boston Red Sox.[26] The team's value in 1999 was estimated to be between

EXHIBIT 9 **Team Annual Payroll (millions)**

Rank	Team	1990	1991	1992	1993	1994	1995	1996	1997	1998	1999	Total	Average	1995–1999 Average
1	New York Yankees	$19.3	$31.4	$34.9	$46.6	$47.5	$58.2	$61.5	$73.4	$73.8	$92.0	$538.6	$53.9	$71.8
2	Arizona Diamondbacks									32.8	70	102.8	51.4	51.4
3	Atlanta Braves	10.9	21.2	35.9	47.2	44.1	47	53.4	53.1	61.7	79.3	453.8	45.4	58.9
4	Baltimore Orioles	8	14.4	24	29.3	38.7	48.7	55.1	64.6	74	75.4	432.2	43.2	63.6
5	Boston Red Sox	21.8	35.5	42.1	46.2	36.3	38.2	38.6	40.6	59.3	72.3	430.9	43.1	49.8
6	Los Angeles Dodgers	20.4	35.6	42.1	33.5	38.8	36.7	37.3	48.5	60.7	76.6	430.2	43.0	52.0
7	Toronto Blue Jays	16.3	31	49.4	51.9	42.3	42.2	28.7	49	37.3	48.8	396.9	39.7	41.2
8	Texas Rangers	12.6	22.5	26.2	36	32.4	35.9	41.1	44.6	62.1	80.8	394.2	39.4	52.9
9	Colorado Rockies				14.9	23.7	38	41	46.1	47.9	54.4	266	38.0	45.5
10	New York Mets	21.8	32.4	44	40.8	30.9	13.1	24.9	35	58.7	71.5	373.1	37.3	40.6
11	San Francisco Giants	18.8	32.1	33.2	36.3	42.3	33.7	34.6	43.1	47.9	46	368	36.8	41.1
12	Cleveland Indians	13.8	13.1	9.3	16.7	31.7	40.2	47.6	58.9	56.6	73.5	361.4	36.1	55.4
13	Anaheim Angels	21.4	32	32.6	27.4	24.5	34.7	25.1	46.7	54.2	51.3	349.9	35.0	42.4
14	Cincinnati Reds	14.9	26.2	35.4	41.6	41.5	47.7	43.7	38.2	20.7	38	347.9	34.8	37.7
15	Chicago Cubs	13.7	26.6	32.4	36	32.5	36.8	32.6	30.8	50.7	55.4	347.5	34.8	41.3
16	St. Louis Cardinals	19.2	22.3	28.7	24.2	29.6	28.7	38.6	50.2	47.6	46.3	335.4	33.5	42.3
17	Seattle Mariners	11.9	16.4	26.4	33.3	28.5	38	43.1	46.3	44.7	45.4	334	33.4	43.5
18	Chicago White Sox	9.8	16.7	30.2	42.1	40.1	40.8	44.8	41.8	37.8	24.5	328.6	32.9	37.9
19	Tampa Bay Devil Rays									27.7	37.9	65.6	32.8	32.8
20	Houston Astros	17.1	12	14.9	30.1	33.1	33.6	29.6	34.9	48.3	56.4	310	31.0	40.6
21	Kansas City Royals	22	31.1	32	40.2	40.7	31.2	20	33.9	35.6	16.6	303.3	30.3	27.5
22	Oakland Athletics	21.8	38.9	48	35.4	34.6	33.4	22.5	12.9	18.6	25.2	291.3	29.1	22.5
23	San Diego Padres	16.7	23.3	27.7	12.8	13.8	25	33.1	32.8	53	46.5	284.7	28.5	38.1
24	Detroit Tigers	18.2	24.2	28.2	38	41.1	28.7	18	21	23.3	37	277.7	27.8	25.6
25	Philadelphia Phillies	14	20.4	25.5	28.7	31.1	30.3	30.4	31.1	29.9	30.4	271.8	27.2	30.4
26	Milwaukee Brewers	18.2	23.8	30	25.6	24.8	17.4	11.7	26.6	36.9	43	258	25.8	27.1
27	Florida Marlins				21.2	19.5	23	25.3	52.3	19.1	14.7	175.1	25.0	26.9
28	Minnesota Twins	13.5	22.5	27.3	27.1	24.5	15.4	21.3	32.2	22	15.8	221.6	22.2	21.3
29	Pittsburgh Pirates	14.7	25.3	36.2	24.3	21.5	17.7	17	15.1	13.7	23.7	209.2	20.9	17.4
30	Montreal Expos	15.8	16.7	16.1	17.6	18.8	13.1	17.3	18	8.3	15	156.7	15.7	14.3
	Average	$16.4	$24.9	$31.3	$32.3	$32.5	$33.1	$33.5	$40.1	$42.2	$48.8	$313.9	$34.3	$39.8

Source: David Schoenfeld, "Team Payrolls in the '90's," and "1999–1995 Payroll Comparison."

US$200 million and US$230 million.[27] One can only assume that this value would increase with a new Fenway Park.

April 4, 2000

"A New Fenway Park," Boston, MA—Recently, there has been a boom in new baseball stadiums, with nine new stadiums built in the 1990s. New stadiums have sprung up in San Francisco (California), Houston (Texas), Detroit (Michigan), Milwaukee (Wisconsin), Pittsburgh (Pennsylvania), and Cincinnati (Ohio). The new stadiums are larger, with a significant increase in the number of luxury boxes. Luxury boxes are the latest trend and typically are purchased by businesses at a hefty price. Additionally, larger stadiums offer fans a greater variety of concessions. It is estimated that more luxury/club seating and concessions can generate US$17 million in a new ballpark.[28] However, new stadiums are often met with opposition by local neighborhoods that might be heavily affected by a larger operation.

The Boston Red Sox claim that they are losing out on significant revenue because they have to play home games in the 87-year-old Fenway Park. The stadium seats 33,871 fans, a number far less than the capacity of other stadiums. The Red Sox ball club has proposed a new stadium. Plans for a new stadium target seating of 44,130. This is in line with other new stadiums that seat around 45,000.[29] As far as luxury seating, the Red Sox would like to become more in line with other parks. For example, Camden Yards (Baltimore, Maryland) has 72 luxury suites, and Jacobs Field (Cleveland, Ohio) has 119 suites.[30] Currently, Fenway Park has only 40 luxury boxes that sell for US$100,000 per season and 610 club seats priced at US$6,000 per season.[31] The proposal for a new Red Sox stadium includes 55 additional luxury boxes priced at US$150,000 and a total of 5,000 club seats.[32]

It was estimated that annual operating income increased US$23 million from 1991 to 1992 when the Baltimore Orioles opened Camden Yards in 1992. The Chicago White Sox's operating income went from US$9 million in 1990 to US$18 million in 1992 when the new Comiskey Park opened. The Colorado Rockies opened Coors Field in 1995 and saw operating income increase to US$12 million from US$5 million in the previous year. The Seattle Mariners opened a new ball park in 1998 and expect to increase their income by US$25 million after losing US$1.7 million in 1996.[33] (See Exhibit 10 for ball clubs' operating incomes between 1990 and 1998.)

With those financial data in mind, the Boston Red Sox want to build a new park in Boston. The club has presented two main options: (1) refurbish the current Fenway Park to preserve the park and team's history and (2) build a new park close to the current Fenway. The team's preference is the construction of a new stadium. The main argument in favor of this option is that there are too many issues to address in bringing the 87-year-old structure into the twenty-first century. The new stadium plans presented by the club do, however, try to preserve history by incorporating the old stadium into a new one.

The Red Sox face a major obstacle in building a new stadium. Not surprisingly, this obstacle is funding. Many of the new stadiums built recently have been financed with public money. The current Red Sox proposal has the new stadium construction costing US$600 million. The Red Sox are expected to seek between US$200 million and $250 million in public funding.[34]

Jacobs Field in Cleveland (Ohio) cost US$173 million to build in 1994, with the public covering 88 percent of the bill.[35] The Arizona Diamondbacks spent US$338 million on Bank One Ballpark in 1998 and paid only 5 percent of the construction costs.[36] The Seattle Mariners had expected the public to pay 89 percent of the cost of their new

EXHIBIT 10 Estimated Operating Income (in $millions)

Rank	Team	1990	1991	1992	1993	1994	1995	1996	1997	1998	Average
1	New York Yankees	$24.5	$30.4	$25.0	$18.2	$8.7	$24.0	$38.3	$21.4	$23.0	$24.2
2	Baltimore Orioles	9.6	11.1	34.2	28.9	5.5	6.0	19.0	18.7	8.5	16.3
3	Colorado Rockies				12.7	4.6	11.5	23.0	38.3	19.5	13.0
4	New York Mets	15.8	20.7	5.6	4.9	(2.2)	20.8	11.0	8.1	(5.2)	10.9
5	**Boston Red Sox**	**12.3**	**10.7**	**11.7**	**7.4**	**0.2**	**15.4**	**16.3**	**7.7**	**(7.6)**	**10.6**
6	Texas Rangers	9.1	13.9	14.8	1.1	5.2	7.6	18.9	9.1	20.6	10.1
7	Los Angeles Dodgers	7.6	7.3	14.7	11.1	(4.1)	12.8	13.5	0.9	(11.7)	9.0
8	Chicago Cubs	9.2	6.5	5.1	7.4	3.7	4.8	18.3	8.1	(7.9)	7.9
9	Toronto Blue Jays	13.9	26.3	(1.3)	1.3	1.4	(1.6)	14.5	(20.5)	(9.5)	7.8
10	Florida Marlins				12.5	9.0	6.8	2.8	(5.5)	8.6	7.8
11	St. Louis Cardinals	10.5	12.7	3.3	20.0	(4.0)	0.9	3.2	2.4	1.6	6.7
12	Montreal Expos	6.4	(4.2)	11.8	12.4	(3.8)	7.1	6.2	(3.7)	5.6	5.1
13	Chicago White Sox	8.8	18.0	16.7	10.7	(5.8)	(8.0)	(5.2)	(4.2)	0.2	5.0
14	Cleveland Indians	(10.5)	(4.2)	13.6	13.3	(4.5)	1.4	15.6	15.4	19.0	3.5
15	San Diego Padres	8.5	(0.4)	(0.3)	17.5	(1.6)	(5.1)	2.5	(6.7)	(8.0)	3.0
16	Houston Astros	(13.5)	14.5	11.4	6.7	(8.4)	(4.5)	11.5	2.3	(3.7)	2.5
17	Philadelphia Phillies	11.1	4.8	(0.3)	0.5	(3.7)	3.4	(6.5)	(2.5)	4.5	1.3
18	Oakland Athletics	12.4	(1.7)	(12.8)	(0.4)	(10.6)	(4.8)	11.3	7.5	3.3	(0.9)
19	Anaheim Angels	8.7	(7.6)	(0.3)	2.6	(8.7)	(3.0)	(2.4)	(9.6)	(0.2)	(1.5)
20	Atlanta Braves	7.8	(0.5)	(9.0)	(1.4)	(5.3)	(2.9)	(0.4)	18.2	16.4	(1.7)
21	Pittsburgh Pirates	(0.7)	(4.0)	(9.9)	4.1	(6.1)	(1.7)	1.4	7.5	2.6	(2.4)
22	Minnesota Twins	(6.5)	(4.5)	0.2	1.0	(9.6)	2.5	(1.3)	(16.5)	(7.1)	(2.6)
23	Detroit Tigers	5.1	(2.8)	(3.2)	(5.4)	(15.7)	(5.3)	3.8	(0.4)	(4.5)	(3.4)
24	San Francisco Giants	9.0	(4.4)	(11.1)	(0.7)	(10.3)	(1.4)	(6.0)	0.2	(6.4)	(3.6)
25	Milwaukee Brewers	3.9	(11.4)	(12.8)	(2.2)	(12.0)	1.0	6.6	(4.8)	(8.8)	(3.8)
26	Seattle Mariners	(3.1)	2.9	(2.4)	(4.0)	(12.1)	(9.8)	(1.7)	11.4	(8.6)	(4.3)
27	Kansas City Royals	(9.8)	(7.2)	(5.1)	(6.3)	(17.4)	(6.9)	4.7	(11.8)	(10.9)	(6.9)
28	Cincinnati Reds	11.0	0.2	(11.8)	(5.0)	(16.8)	(11.8)	(14.0)	(19.9)	0.6	(6.9)
	MLB Average	$6.2	$4.9	$3.4	$6.0	($4.4)	$2.1	$7.3	$2.5	$1.2	$3.2

Source: Rodney Fort and James Quirk, *Hard Ball,* Michael Ozanian, "Selective Accounting," and Burt Badenhausen and William Sicheri, "Baseball Games."

stadium.[37] However, there were over US$100 million in cost overruns which brought the total cost of the stadium to US$517 million.[38] The public ended up paying US$372 million of the cost of construction.[39]

To secure public funding for the new park, however, the citizens of Boston must vote on whether they want their tax dollars to fund a new sports complex. Another issue that has come up is the acquisition of the 15-acre lot needed to build the stadium and parking garages. The easiest way for the Red Sox to gain access to this land is for the city to declare the buildings in the area as "blighted or substandard" so that the city can give the site to the developers.[40]

It's expected that the Red Sox proposal will meet considerable resistance among local residents and business owners. Inhabitants in the area targeted for development view the stadium as a community threat. In addition to this concern over maintaining residences and businesses, the currently overcrowded area can expect an extra 10,000 people on a regular basis. The area has narrow streets with buildings practically on top of each other. The public transportation system is very old and is barely adequate for everyday traffic. "Locals" doubt that the system could handle an extra 10,000 commuters without substantial improvements.

There are also people who simply do not agree with public funding of sports complexes. They believe it diverts money from issues such as education, welfare, and housing. Some people, such as those in the "Save Fenway Park!" group, believe that Fenway Park is a landmark and should not be torn down.

The Red Sox argue that local businesses will benefit from an increase in the number of people visiting the area. A recent study by the Greater Boston Chamber of Commerce and Visitors Bureau estimated that a new Fenway Park would generate US$16 million in additional annual spending in Boston and create 1,032 permanent jobs.[41] A study by MASSPIRG, however, discounts some of these benefits and views them as overly optimistic. The study by MASSPIRG claimed that the Boston Chamber of Commerce study exaggerated predicted attendance figures.[42] The MASSPIRG report also suggests that the Chamber of Commerce's study overestimated the number of out-of-state fans who would attend games, resulting in an overestimation of the revenue that could be generated. In relation to new jobs, MASSPIRG claims that new construction jobs would not be created. Rather, construction workers would substitute work on the stadium for other jobs. The MASSPIRG study even went so far as to say that jobs might be lost as a result of the new stadium because the project would draw funding away from important areas, such as education and housing.

While there are pros and cons to the new stadium, folks in Boston know that getting a new stadium will not be easy for the Red Sox ball club.

Mike's newspaper articles generated considerable discussion in the local community. At the local level, the articles fed the new stadium versus old stadium debate. On a larger level, however, broader issues were raised: (1) Were threats outweighing the opportunities for Major League Baseball? (2) Does Major League Baseball have a competitive advantage over other professional sports? (3) How will a salary cap affect the MLB and its players? As Major League Baseball surges into the next millennium, it is faced with a dual interest—dedicating itself to the fans (satisfying the crowds) while remaining a profitable business (the bottom line).

Mike did not have any answers or solutions. Rather, his research and his articles made him realize that baseball is big business, not unlike computer software, banking, and consumer package goods. He, too, wondered what needed to be done to satisfy all the stakeholders.

End Notes

1. *Federal Baseball Club of Baltimore, INC. v. National League of Professional Baseball Clubs, et al,* 259 U.S. 200 (42 S. Ct. 465).
2. Ibid.
3. Ibid.
4. Ibid.
5. Ibid.
6. "The Commissionership: An Historical Perspective" (February 15, 2000), http://www.majorleaguebaseball.com.
7. Ibid.
8. "History & Records" (March 2, 2000), http://www.majorleaguebaseball.com.
9. Ibid.
10. Gregg Krupa, "Pennant Games Are More Symbolic Than Lucrative for Baseball Teams," *Boston Globe,* October 16, 1999, p. G9.
11. Ibid.
12. Ibid.
13. "Exhibition Baseball," *Charleston Gazette,* April 2, 1999, p. 2b.
14. Chuck Johnson, "Baseball's Big Ticket Situation: 22 Teams Make a Hike for Payrolls," *USA Today,* February 11, 1999, p. 3C.
15. Gordon Edes, "Sox Make Big Deal of Martinez: Pitcher Is Signed to a Record Contract," *Boston Globe,* December 13, 1997, p. G1.

16. Larry Whiteside, "Garciaparra Scoops a Record Contract," *Boston Globe,* March 11, 1998, p. 2.

17. Rodney Fort and James Quirk, *Hard Ball: The Abuse of Power in Pro Team Sports* (Princeton, NJ: Princeton University Press, 1999), p. 65.

18. Ibid.

19. Jason Strait, "St. Louis a Big Winner: Mac Made $60M for City," *The Record, Northern New Jersey,* September 30, 1998, p. S07.

20. Ibid.

21. Ibid.

22. George Sorter, "Baseball: A Game of Numbers." *Houston Chronicle,* August 13, 1985, p. 15.

23. Ibid.

24. Cosmo Macero, et al., "Indians Sale Shows Why Sox Covet Public Funding for Park," *Boston Herald,* November 6, 1999, p. 10.

25. Fort and Quirk, *Hard Ball,* p. 212.

26. Macero et al., "Indians Sale," p. 10.

27. Ibid.

28. Meg Vaillancourt, "Fresh Parks Are Proving a Boon for Many Teams," *Boston Globe,* May 17, 1999, p. A1.

29. Rob Sargent, "Major League Steal: The Economic Folly of Public Subsidies for a New Red Sox Stadium." *MASSPIRG,* March 2000, p. 1.

30. Mike Dodd, "Indians' New Facility Blends Many Elements," *USA Today,* September 30, 1993, p. 6C.

31. Gregg Krupa, "Temporary Seats at Fenway Remain," *Boston Globe,* July 23, 1999, p. E7.

32. Ibid.

33. Nicholas K. Geranios, "Baseball Equation: New Stadium Equals Better Record," *Associated Press,* July 26, 1999.

34. Sargent, "Major League Steal," p. 4.

35. Fort and Quirk, *Hard Ball,* p. 219.

36. Ibid., p. 222.

37. Ibid., p. 224.

38. Hunter T. George, "The Safe Opens for Business," *Associated Press,* July 16, 1999.

39. Ibid.

40. Sargent, "Major League Steal," p. 4.

41. Ibid.

42. Ibid., p. 1.

Sources

"AL Attendance Report." http://www.fastball.com/auto/mlb/stats/alattend.html (January 10, 2000).

Anderson, Chris. "Veterans Say Show Me the Money Later: Deferred Payments Give Devil Rays Room to Maneuver in the Free Agent Market." *Sarasota-Herald Tribune,* February 21, 2000, p. 1C.

"Average Payrolls Since 1976." http://www.fastball.com/stats/archives/1998/payavg.html (March 12, 2000).

Badenhausen, Burt, and William Sicheri. "Baseball Games." http://www.forbes.com/forbes/99/0531/6311112tab1.htm (November 20, 1999).

"Cleveland Indians Annual Report, 1998." http://www.primark.com (February 10, 2000).

"The Commissionership: An Historical Perspective." http://www.majorleaguebaseball.com (February 15, 2000).

Dodd, Mike. "Fan's Top Wish: Shorten Break between Innings." *USA Today,* June 9, 1995, p. 3C.

Dodd, Mike. "Indians' New Facility Blends Many Elements." *USA Today,* September 30, 1993, p. 6C.

Edes, Gordon. "Sox Make Big Deal of Martinez: Pitcher Is Signed to a Record Contract." *Boston Globe,* December 13, 1997, p. G1.

Eckberg, John, and John Fay. "Commercial Appeal: Radio Advertisers Will Pay More: Fox Sports Net Hasn't Decided About TV Rates." *Cincinnati Enquirer,* February 11, 2000, p. C7.

"Exhibition Baseball." *Charleston Gazette,* April 2, 1999, Sports, p. 2b.

Federal Baseball Club of Baltimore, INC. v. National League of Professional Baseball Clubs, et al. 259 U.S. 200 (42 S. Ct. 465).

Fort, Rodney, and James Quirk. *Hard Ball: The Abuse of Power in Pro Team Sports.* Princeton, NJ: Princeton University Press, 1999.

George, Hunter T. "The Safe Opens for Business." *Associated Press,* July 16, 1999.

Geranios, Nicholas K. "Baseball Equation: New Stadium Equals Better Record." *Associated Press,* July 26, 1999.

"Goldman Sachs Helping Out." *American Banker-Bond Buyer,* May 31, 1999, p. 1.

"History & Records." http://www.majorleaguebaseball.com (March 2, 2000).

"Jacobs to Sell Indians for $320 Million." http://espn.go.com/mlb/news/1999/1104/150665.html (November 6, 1999).

Johnson, Chuck. "Baseball's Big Ticket Situation: 22 Teams Make a Hike for Payrolls." *USA Today,* February 11, 1999, p. 3C.

Krupa, Gregg. "Pennant Games Are More Symbolic Than Lucrative for Baseball Teams." *Boston Globe,* October 16, 1999, p. G9.

Krupa, Gregg. "'Temporary' Seats at Fenway Remain." *Boston Globe,* July 23, 1999, p. E7.

"Living Room Seat without Leaving Ballpark." *Fresno Bee,* April 4, 1996, p. E1.

Lubinger, Bill, and Zach Schiller. "Indians to Revise Stock Lineup," *Cleveland Plain Dealer,* July 31, 1998, p. 1C.

Macero, Cosmo, Jack Sullivan, and Greg Gatlin. "Indians Sale Shows Why Sox Covet Public Funding for Park." *Boston Herald,* November 6, 1999, p. 10.

Markiewicz, Mark. "Corporations Paying More to Put Brand-Names on U.S. Sports Arenas." *Fort Worth Star-Telegram,* December 18, 1997.

Morse, Steve." Summer Season a Sizzler for Concert Promoters." *Boston Globe,* September 6, 1999, p. C6.

"NL Attendance Report." http://www.fastball.com/auto/mlb/stats/nlattend.html (January 10, 2000).

"1999–1995 Payroll Comparison." http://www.slam.ca/BaseballMoney Matters (December 8, 1999).

Ozanian, Michael. "Selective Accounting." http://www.forbes.com/tool/toolbox/sports/asp/teamvaluations.asp (November 20, 1999).

Sargent, Rob. "Major League Steal: The Economic Folly of Public Subsidies for a New Red Sox Stadium." MASSPIRG, March 2000.

Schoenfeld, David. "Success, but at What Price?" http://espn.go.com/mlb/state/dayone.html (June 17, 1999).

Schoenfeld, David. "The Truth behind the Numbers." http://espn.go.com/mlb/state/daytwo.html (June 17, 1999).

Schoenfeld, David. "Win-Loss Records in the '90's." http://espn.go.com/mlb/features/01072249.html (June 17, 1999).

Schoenfeld, David. "Team Payrolls in the '90's." http://espn.go.com/mlb/features/01072323.html (June 17, 1999).

Schoenfeld, David. "Yearly Attendance Chart." http://espn.go.com/mlb/features/01076017.html (June 17, 1999).

Schoenfeld, David. "Team-by-Team Total Revenue." http://espn.go.com/mlb/features/01076707.html (June 17, 1999).

Sorter, George. "Baseball: A Game of Numbers." *Houston Chronicle,* August 13, 1985, p. 15.

Strait, Jason. "St. Louis a Big Winner: Mac Made $60M for City." *The Record, Northern New Jersey,* September 30, 1998, p. s07.

"Take Me Out to the Ball Game." http://ea.grolier.com/ea-online/wsja/text/ch10/tables/sp001.htm (March 3, 2000).

Vaillancourt, Meg. "Fresh Parks Are Proving a Boon for Many Teams." *Boston Globe,* May 17, 1999, p. A1.

Whiteside, Larry. "Garciaparra Scoops a Record Contract." *Boston Globe,* March 11, 1998, p. 2

"Why Renovation Makes Sense: The Once and Future Fenway." http://www.savefenwaypark.com/case/statement.cfm (April 19, 2000).

 *

CASE 1–4
BATTERED WOMEN FIGHT BACK!

Stacey Kabat, executive director and founder of Battered Women Fighting Back!, would always have a vivid recollection of the 1994 Academy Awards. She looked into the glaring lights and saw thousands of heads that resembled bobbing apples. As they received their Oscars for best short documentary, *Defending Our Lives,* the other two filmmakers thanked everyone. Then Stacey said, "Domestic violence is the leading cause of injury to women in the United States, more than rapes, muggings, and automobile accidents combined. Please, we need all your help to stop this."

Stacey's comment was cited the next day in the *Los Angeles Times* as one of the most memorable moments at the Academy Awards. However, Stacey could not allow herself to sit back and enjoy this rare moment of glory. Battered Women Fighting Back!, a human rights organization, had been catapulted into a unique position to nationally frame the issue of domestic violence.

First and foremost, Stacey wanted to stop domestic violence. To do that, however, Stacey and Battered Women Fighting Back! needed funding. Stacey was not a businessperson, but she knew she had a big marketing job on her hands.

Domestic Violence

There were between 2 million and 4 million victims of domestic abuse yearly in the United States.[1] Domestic violence was a crime that in most cases involved the assault of a woman by a man who was her spouse or boyfriend. A national crime survey had found that women were the victims of violent crime committed by family members at a rate three times that of men and that a woman was in nine times more danger at home than on the streets. By 1992, domestic violence occurred in one out of four American families.

Domestic violence was a leading cause of birth defects. Studies had even found that violence against women increased during pregnancy. Other statistics showed the following:

- Over 80 percent of violent offenders in prison came from homes with histories of domestic violence. (Men who saw their parents attack each other physically were three times more likely to hit their wives as than were those who had not seen such violence at home, and sons of the most violent parents beat their wives at a rate 1,000 times greater than that of the sons of nonviolent parents.)

- Sixty-three percent of boys under age 18 in prison for murder were jailed for killing their mother's abuser.

---

* The video for this case may be available at your local library.

[1] This range was cited from "Domestic Violence: Help and Resources for Battered Women." *The Boston Parents' Paper,* October 1994. The Commonwealth Fund in New York reported that 3.9 million women had admitted being beaten by a husband or male friend during a 12-month period. This translated to a woman being beaten somewhere in the United States every nine seconds.

This case was prepared by Jennifer Fraser, MBA student, and Victoria L. Crittenden, associate professor of marketing, Boston College, as the basis for class discussion rather than to illustrate either effective or ineffective handling of a managerial situation. Research assistance was provided by Stephanie Hillstrom, Boston College. Revised 1997.

- Seventy percent of men who abused their female partners also abused their children. (As violence against women became more severe and common, children experienced a 300 percent increase in physical violence and 30 percent of children from violent households became abusive parents.)
- Nationally, 50 percent of all homeless women and children were on the streets because of violence in the home.
- Sixty-three percent of abused women permanently left their partners.
- Seventy-three percent of women treated medically for abusive injuries were separated, single, or divorced, and 35 percent of hospital emergency room visits by women related to battering.
- Ninety-two percent of abused women did not tell their medical doctors.
- Businesses lost $3 billion to $5 billion yearly due to absenteeism from work because of domestic abuse. (This included women who were battered and men who battered and had to take time away from work for court appearances, etc.) Around 70 percent of battered women were employed when abused.
- Abusive men were as likely to be educated, middle-class, or employed as they were to be uneducated, poor, or unemployed.
- Fifty percent of abusive men were between 26 and 35 years of age; 26 percent were between 36 and 50 years old.
- Domestic violence against women was still considered acceptable in many countries.
- There were three times as many animal shelters in the United States as there were shelters for battered women and their children.

While the concentration of domestic violence occurred in women between the ages 15 and 35, domestic abuse crossed all monetary, geographic, and cultural categories (Exhibit 1).

Awareness.   Secretary of Health and Human Services Donna Shalala had called for a national awakening to "domestic terrorism," the "unacknowledged epidemic" in America.[2] During the 1990s, the domestic violence issue was magnified on a national and international scale by incidents such as those involving Charles Stuart in Boston, Massachusetts, and O.J. Simpson in Los Angeles, California.

The murder of Carol Stuart made international headlines in October 1989 when a white man, Charles Stuart, alleged that he and his pregnant wife had been shot by a black man after a Lamaze class at Beth Israel Hospital in Boston, Massachusetts. All evidence, however, suggested that Charles Stuart had killed his wife. Stuart committed suicide in 1990 when the evidence became overwhelming to accuse him of first-degree murder.

The murders of Nicole Brown Simpson and Ronald Goldman in 1994 created chaos, confusion, and doubt among many communities and brought new attention to the issue of domestic violence. Several allegations against O.J. Simpson by Nicole Brown Simpson detailing domestic violence for several years had been recorded. Nicole Brown Simpson's telephone calls, however, did not instigate police investigation or action because the issue of domestic violence was considered a "private matter" that involved only a "certain population." As a result of the Nicole Brown Simpson case, some negative conceptions of and assumptions about individuals and families involved in domestic violence were challenged.

---

[2] Speech delivered before the American Medical Association (AMA) National Conference on Family Violence, Washington, D.C., March 11, 1994.

EXHIBIT 1   Victim Description

Demographics	
Sex	Female
Age	15–35 years old
Income	All levels
Occupation	All types
Education	All levels
Ethnic background	All
Family life cycle	All
Household size	Any size
Psychographics	
Social class	All classes
Personality	Compulsive
Geographic	
Region	All regions
City size	All sizes

Legislation/Business Support.   As early as 1948 the Universal Declaration of Human Rights, adopted by the United Nations, assured life, liberty, and security of person as well as freedom from torture and other cruel, inhuman, or degrading treatment. In June 1993 the United Nations World Conference on Human Rights was held. Additionally, the Global Tribunal on Violations of Women's Human Rights was held in 1993. This conference was sponsored by the Center for Women's Global Leadership at Douglass College in New Jersey. The aim of the conference was to draw international attention to gender-driven crimes.

The Violence against Women Act was part of the 1994 federal government's crime bill. This act stipulated that gender-based crimes violated a woman's civil rights. This made women eligible for compensatory relief and damages. The act authorized $1.8 billion over five years to aid police, prosecutors, women's shelters, and community prevention programs. The sponsor of the act was U.S. Representative Connie Morella from Maryland, who also sought $1 million to establish a national domestic violence hotline that would be operated 24 hours a day in more than two dozen languages. The U.S. Congress had designated October as Domestic Violence Awareness Month.

A nonprofit organization, the Advertising Council, selected domestic violence as one of 28 national pro bono projects for 1994. This resulted in roughly $20 million in free ads. Corporations including DuPont, Ryka, Liz Claiborne Inc., and Polaroid had identified domestic violence as a major area of social responsibility as well.

DuPont offered workshops on spouse/child abuse, and volunteers operated 24-hour rape hotlines. Ryka, a women's athletic shoe company, established the ROSE Foundation to end violence against women. The company pledged 7 percent of pretax earnings to the foundation. Also, along with Lady Foot Locker, the Ryka ROSE Foundation made grants to rape crisis centers and prevention programs. Liz Claiborne Inc. supported the Women's Work Program, which consisted of community-based public art projects designed to heighten awareness of domestic violence. Polaroid donated

$42,000 to seven battered women's shelters in Massachusetts as well as offering self-image groups for battered employees.

Intervention Resources.   At the beginning of 1993 almost 550,000 U.S. charities were eligible to receive tax-deductible donations.[3] This was an almost 50 percent increase since 1985 and a 71 percent increase since 1980. Included in these charitable organizations were intervention resources to assist victims of domestic violence.

Intervention resources consisted of five common services. Battered women service providers could offer one or any combination of intervention resources. The five common resources were as follows:

- *Shelter.* This resource sought to provide a safe haven for a battered woman and her children. This was considered one of the most costly services provided by an intervention resource.

- *Hotline.* It was found that many battered women made their first contact or call for help via the crisis telephone line. The hotline volunteer had to make a quick judgment about whether the caller was in immediate danger and/or needed emergency medical attention. Hotlines were operated 24 hours a day, seven days a week.

- *Emergency medical assistance.* This was a referral service in which the battered woman was referred to a hospital emergency room or private physician known by the referral service to be highly qualified to administer to a battered woman.

- *Financial assistance.* This program provided financial assistance to assist the battered woman with personal and children's needs and/or to aid the woman in meeting her needs for entering the work force.

- *Support services.* This all-encompassing program could provide counseling, legal assistance, employment information, child care, and other types of services.

Exhibit 2 lists intervention resources in the greater Boston, Massachusetts, area. The services offered by these organizations varied from counseling, support groups, and shelters to education and lobbying.

Battered women and their children could call the Brookline Women's Shelter in emergency situations. While many of the women were battered, many were homeless. This shelter did not receive any outside funding. Thus, the organization sheltered women and children on a temporary basis when funds allowed. Additionally, the shelter helped the women and children find other places to go.

At Community Services for Women, one-half of the women who called were battered. The other half were substance abusers. The service counseled drug abusers and referred battered women to Battered Women Fighting Back! and/or RESPOND.

RESPOND offered counseling, support groups, and shelter for battered women. The organization was funded privately and by the Massachusetts Department of Social Services.

The Massachusetts Coalition of Battered Women's Service Groups was neither a shelter nor a counseling service. Rather, the group provided referrals to shelters and counseling. The group's primary focus was lobbying for laws for battered women's rights.

---

[3] In 1993, *Financial World* identified eight characteristics sought by grant givers when selecting charitable organizations to target their giving: (1) a focused mission, (2) results that could be evaluated, (3) inspired and dedicated leadership, (4) the organization's responding to a proven community need, (5) a board of directors that understood its role and reflected the diversity of those served, (6) money spent on programs that exceeded administration and fund-raising costs, (7) training for volunteers and efforts to develop leadership skills, and (8) innovative, creative programs.

**EXHIBIT 2   Domestic Violence Help Resources
in the Greater Boston,
Massachusetts, Area**

Alternative House
Asian Women's Project
Battered Women Fighting Back!
Battered Women's Hotline
Battered Women's Resources
Brockton Family and Community Resources
Brookline Women's Shelter
Casa Myrna Vasquez
Community Services for Women
Daybreak
Domestic Violence Program
Dove House
Elizabeth Stone House
FINEX House
Harbor Me
Help for Abused Women and Their Children
Independence House
Mary Forman House of CMV
Massachusetts Coalition of Battered Women Service Groups
My Sister's Place
Network for Battered Lesbians
New Bedford Battered Women's Project
New Hope Inc.
Our Sister's Place
Rosie's Place
Renewal House
RESPOND
Second Step Inc.
Services Against Family Violence
South Shore Women's Center
Transition House
Waltham Battered Women's Support Committee
Womansplace
Women's Center
Women's Crisis Center
Women's Protective Services
Women's Resource Center

Source: "Domestic Violence: Help and Resources for Battered Women," *The Boston Parents' Paper,* October 1994, p. 53.

Battered women and children could go to Services Against Family Violence for one-on-one counseling and support groups. The women who went there were emotionally and/or physically abused. This service had court advocacy in Woburn, Massachusetts, and Malden, Massachusetts, and an advocate in the Malden police station. A 24-hour hotline and legal referrals were offered. Shelter was not provided, but the group did refer women to shelters.

At the national level, the National Resource Center on Domestic Violence (NRC) located at the Pennsylvania Coalition against Domestic Violence in Harrisburg, Pennsylvania, was funded in 1993 through a three-year grant by the U.S. Department of Health and Human Services. The NRC's goal was to strengthen existing support systems for battered women and their children in addition to identifying and filling information and resource gaps that tended to perpetuate domestic violence in U.S. communities. Three other national resource centers included Battered Women's Justice Project in Duluth, Minnesota; Resource Center on Child Protection and Custody in Reno, Nevada; and Health Resource Center on Domestic Violence in San Francisco, California.

In addition to organized resource groups, there were local events to raise awareness and funds for battered women's programs. One example was the Jane Doe Safety Fund's 10K Walk for Women's Safety. This walk served to increase domestic violence awareness as well as raising funds for programs.

Battered Women Fighting Back!

Battered Women Fighting Back! (BWFB!) was a Boston, Massachusetts–based education and advocacy group that addressed the severity of domestic violence as a human rights violation. Its primary charge was to create and disseminate educational programs designed to eradicate domestic violence in society and promote human rights for everyone.

Begun as both a prison support group for battered women who had defended their lives and a diverse grassroots task force dedicated to raising community awareness on domestic violence, BWFB! was incorporated in Boston, Massachusetts, in November 1992. BWFB!'s official 501(c)(3) agency status[4] was the culmination of work performed for years by over 100 volunteers dedicated to freeing the "Framingham Eight."[5] The goal of the new organization was to heighten community awareness of the indisputable fact that domestic violence was a direct violation of a person's fundamental human right as stated in the Universal Declaration of Human Rights. Stacey Kabat was the visionary and driving force behind BWFB!

In 1994 BWFB! operated on what Stacey referred to as "a shoestring" budget of approximately $150,000. The agency solicited and received funding from individual donors (usually people committed to the domestic violence cause), corporations (e.g., Reebok and Aveda), foundations (e.g., the Public Welfare Foundation), and sponsorship/events. Exhibit 3 breaks down the sources of solicited funds.

The program was run by three full-time employees, three part-time staff members, and a group of volunteers. Volunteers answered the phones, did administrative work, networked, and/or assisted in writing grant proposals. Essentially, volunteers did whatever they were capable of doing at the time.

Stacey Kabat.   Stacey Kabat was the woman behind BWFB! whose spectrum of experience helped create the agency. Stacey was the daughter and granddaughter of battered women.

Stacey began her human rights work by establishing an Amnesty International Campus Network while at Bates College in Maine. She later traveled to London to work for

---

[4] Organizations with this status were charities that accepted tax-deductible donations. The organizations had to submit Form 990s to the IRS yearly to detail their finances.

[5] The Framingham Eight were eight women who had become famous for killing their batterers. The cases became landmark political and social cases. This was the first time a Massachusetts governor had proposed pardoning prisoners based on evidence that the woman was a victim of battering. Each of the eight women testified that her partner abused her to the point that she feared for her own life and in effect killed in self-defense. As of June 1994, four of the eight were freed on parole, two were granted commutations, one persuaded a judge to revise her sentence, and one remained in jail.

EXHIBIT 3   Sources of Funding

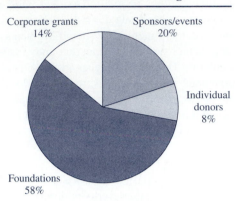

Corporate grants
14%

Sponsors/events
20%

Individual
donors
8%

Foundations
58%

the International Secretariat. She worked for an antiapartheid organization, IDAF, transcribing radio broadcasts out of southern Africa, and visited families in refugee camps in the Middle East. Upon returning to the United States, Stacey worked for two years at the Renewal House, a shelter for battered women in Roxbury, Massachusetts. Later, through her work at MCI–Framingham with battered women and substance abusers, Stacey and a group of eight women incarcerated for defending themselves from their batterers (the Framingham Eight) founded BWFB!. The organization was intended initially as a support group for women imprisoned for killing their batterers.

Local and National Recognition.   Both Stacey Kabat and the BWFB! agency had received local and national recognition. Stacey and her two film comrades from Cambridge Documentary Films had won the 1994 Academy Award for best documentary for *Defending Our Lives.* The documentary exposed the severity of domestic violence in the United States. Along with winning a prized award, Stacey had made many Hollywood connections. Her office boasted many pictures of Stacey with such celebrities as Glenn Close, Angela Bassett, Nicole Kidman, and Steven Spielberg. The Academy Award, however, was not BWFB!'s only claim to fame. Stacey Kabat had won the Reebok Human Rights Award in 1992, and BWFB! was named one of "America's Best Run Charities" in 1993 by *Financial World.* As well, BWFB!'s documentation and publication of domestic violence homicides in Massachusetts had led Massachusetts Governor William Weld and Lieutenant Governor Paul Cellucci in 1992 to declare a "state of emergency" in response to the ever-increasing cases of domestic violence.

Existing Violence Prevention Program.   The theme of BWFB!'s violence prevention program was "Peace in the World Begins at Home." The name of the program was based on the belief that everyone could help stop domestic violence if given the proper tools and information. The program was designed as a public awareness/education tool designed to both prevent and stop domestic violence by doing the following:

1. Shattering myths about domestic violence.
2. Identifying warning signs.
3. Encouraging help for those who were victims of such violence.

EXHIBIT 4   **Contents of the Booklet *Domestic Violence: The Facts***

Since receiving the 1992 Reebok Human Rights Award for my work on domestic violence I have created a grassroots public education campaign entitled 'Domestic Violence: The Facts' geared toward heightening cross-cultural awareness, providing tools for intervention and enlisting greater community involvement.

Stacey Kabat

Contained within *Domestic Violence: The Facts* you will find

1. Statistics
2. Myths and Facts
3. Controlling Behaviors Warning List
4. Violence Wheel
5. Cycle of Domestic Violence
6. Non-Violence Wheel
7. Basic Suggestions for Offering Help
8. Personalized Safety Plan
9. Excerpts from the Universal Declaration of Human Rights
10. Hotline Numbers
11. Bibliography and Resources

The materials for the "Peace in the World Begins at Home" program included the 1994 award-winning documentary *Defending Our Lives* and a booklet, *Domestic Violence: The Facts.* (Exhibit 4 shows the contents of the booklet.) These items could be disseminated to places such as high schools, universities, places of worship, physician's offices, libraries, and any number of public places.

Current Situation

In June 1994, Stacey Kabat knew that the issue of domestic violence was in the public eye. While telephone logs were not kept, Stacey felt certain that inquiries and calls had surged in the past few months. Requests for educational information and materials for awareness programs had quadrupled. Stacey had to capitalize on this level of interest. How could she most effectively obtain funding to distribute BWFB!'s materials and implement worldwide the "Peace in the World Begins at Home" program? While other resources were available for victims of domestic violence, Stacey felt that BWFB! was unique.

Stacey pondered her many marketing challenges:

- First and foremost, how could she get information to the people who needed it most?
- Could she market BWFB!'s idea and frame domestic violence as a human rights violation—not "just a women's issue"—to the public?
- Could she obtain funding for resources and education for domestic violence educational programs across the United States, if not the world?
- Where should she start with each of these challenges?
- What did she need to do?

Sources

"Domestic Violence: Help and Resources for Battered Women." *The Boston Parents' Paper,* October 1994, p. 53.

Engelken, Cort. "Fighting the Costs of Spouse Abuse." *Personnel Journal,* March 1987, pp. 31–34.

Frum, David. "Women Who Kill." *Forbes,* January 18, 1993, pp. 86–87.

Giobbe, Dorothy. "Publicizing Domestic Abuse." *Editor & Publisher,* December 18, 1993, p. 13, 45.

Gold, Jacqueline S. "Finding Gems among the Rhinestones." *Financial World,* August 3, 1993, pp. 46–58.

Kessler, Hannah. "Washington Watch." *Working Woman,* June 1993, p. 16.

Marmon, Lucretia. "Domestic Violence: The Cost to Business." *Working Woman,* April 1994, pp. 17–18.

Miller, Cyndee. "Tapping Into Women's Issues Is Potent Way to Reach Market." *Marketing News,* December 6, 1993, pp. 1, 13.

National Resource Center on Domestic Violence. Harrisburg, PA.

Nichols, Paula. "Reaching the Compassionate Consumer." *American Demographics,* November 1993, pp. 26–27.

Sabatino, Frank. "Hospitals Cope with America's New Family Value." *Hospitals,* November 5, 1992, pp. 24–30.

Shalala, Donna E. "Domestic Terrorism." *Vital Speeches of the Day,* May 15, 1994, pp. 450–53.

"Too Much of It About." *The Economist,* July 16, 1994, p. 25.

"When Did You Stop Beating Your Wife? After Seeing All Those Ads, Doubtless." *Adweek,* August 1, 1994, p. 17.

On Wednesday, November 4, 1998, Brian King read the Emerging Business section of the *Boston Globe* with keen interest. The headline read, "Brewing Competition: Wakefield Firm Elbows into Single-Cup Market with Fresh Idea." The subject of the story was Keurig, Inc., an aggressively funded entrant into the office coffee system (OCS) market. As president of Filterfresh, the pioneering firm in single-cup coffee brewing, King was quite familiar with competition.

Coffee in the United States

Coffee was a big business in the United States. In 1997, the National Coffee Association (NCA) reported 109 million daily coffee drinkers, 41 million weekly drinkers, and 14 million occasional drinkers. Coffee beverage sales from vending machines, shops, and workplaces amounted to US$55 billion in 1998. By the NCA's account, office coffee consumption totaled 17 percent of all coffee consumed each year in the United States.

Americans consume a variety of coffee and purchase coffee in many forms. Some consumers choose to brew coffee with beans, others prefer ground coffee in vacuum-packed cans, and other consumers, eager for the taste of coffee but reluctant to wait for the brewing of an entire pot, select instant coffee.

The 1980s and 1990s saw the burgeoning of the gourmet coffee culture. Following the Continental European style, coffee shops and outlets offering gourmet selections flourished, especially in sophisticated urban locales. Specialty coffees such as French or Italian roasts, cappuccinos, and lattes captured a growing share of the market. The Specialty Coffee Association of America (SCAA) noted the dramatic development of this industry. In 1969, the SCAA counted only 50 specialty coffee retailers, 20 of which roasted their own beans on the premises. The number increased to 250 with 40 roasters by 1979 and continued to rise to 1,000 coffeehouses with 385 roasters a decade later. The SCAA maintained its belief in market expansion with its projected forecast of 2,500 shops with 1,400 roasters in 1999. This was a profitable trend, with the café segment of the specialty coffee industry (includes cafés, kiosks, and carts) totaling sales of nearly US$3.2 billion in 1997.

The SCAA attributed the shift away from "regular brewed coffee" to older Americans cutting back their consumption (www.scaa.org/stories/080799/part2.html). In the 1960s, 75 percent of the population identified themselves as coffee drinkers. Per capita consumption has since declined to only 48.5 percent. The 1.4-cup-per-day consumption by the late 1990s was a drastic change from 3.12 cups per day in the 1960s.

While the baby boom generation moved away from "regular" coffee, specialty coffee simultaneously gained popularity. Between 1997 and 1998, the number of identified

This case was prepared by Richard Keeley, Boston College, as the basis for class discussion rather than to illustrate effective or ineffective handling of a managerial situation. Development of the case was funded by a grant from the General Electric Fund at Boston College.

specialty coffee drinkers rose from 80 million to 108 million Americans. A substantial part of this growth was attributed to generation X-ers.

Coffee at Work

By the year 2000, office or workplace coffee was a part of pop culture. While it signified many things for the modern-day worker—a place to gather with fellow employees, the destination for caffeine replenishment, a location for a five-minute break in the middle of the day—the coffee machine was an office temple as well as a moneymaker. The NCA found that office consumption of coffee accounted for nearly one-fifth of U.S. total coffee consumption. The small market was a surprisingly competitive arena where negotiating for the office coffee dollar was intense.

In the office coffee system (OCS) industry, Filterfresh's specialty, single cup brewing was a niche market. Most OCS providers, such as Bunn and Grindmaster, operated in multi-cup or pot brewing systems. The Bunn BCM2 Coffee Management System touted its "computer controlled automatic coffee management system, the machine's . . . self cleaning capabilities, its push button operation, and batch sizes from .25 decanter up to 2 gallons." Grindmaster prided its Grind 'n Brew Grinderbrewer for its "European style, its digital timers, and the single or double bean hoppers." Both companies competed on speed of delivery, quantity brewed, and freshness of coffee.

Filterfresh had successfully built its niche by challenging these three competencies: Its machines worked quickly, a single cup of coffee was produced within 12 seconds, and the customer was never faced with drinking "old coffee." Proud of the ability to produce fast, full cups of fresh coffee, Filterfresh marketed its distinction by emphasizing its speed advantage: "Each person, his or her own brewer, in his or her own time." (For details of the process, take a virtual tour at www.filterfresh.com.)

Although it was the largest provider of single cup coffee brewing, Filterfresh was not the only company serving the office/work coffee market. While some competitors attempted to penetrate the market, many OCS providers were not convinced of the merit of the single cup model. Many OCS vendors were loathe to introduce single-cup brew systems. There was concern that the single cup market was not only higher priced, but that it also involved a technology that required a high service component.

Apart from the internal competition, providers of office coffee systems, like Filterfresh, viewed the proliferation of specialty coffee cafes outside the workplace as a growing threat. President Brian King referred to these cafes as ". . . 'intercept' marketers. Filterfresh was focusing considerable attention on how to combat them. Unfortunately, the specialty travel mug, quite visible in office cubicles, symbolized the increasing presence of specialty coffee retailers and the diminishing OCS market." On the flip side, however, the specialty coffee industry had helped the OCS market by educating the customer's coffee palate.

Of course, other beverages challenged coffee within the workplace. Long an office mainstay, the water cooler had grown quite popular in the wake of health concerns about caffeine consumption. The identification of bottled water as a chic, new healthy alternative to caffeine was also leading many workers to abandon their office coffee dependency.

Filterfresh: History and Operation

Named after the company founder, Alan King, Filterfresh was originally known as Vend King International. A native of Canada, the largely self-taught engineer and entrepreneur created the first single-cup coffee-brewing machine in 1969. The company name was abbreviated to VKI in 1987, and later that year Filterfresh was established as a wholly owned franchising subsidiary.

Like many entrepreneurial leaders, King was involved with all aspects of his company. In response to an engineer who complained of his interference in the design process, King stressed his ownership in replying, "It's my company, and I will do what I want." Alan protected his vision for Filterfresh and secured its future by appointing his son, Brian, as its current president. Brian complemented his undergraduate studies in engineering with an MBA from Stanford University.

The company remained partially privately held until A. L. VanHoutte completed a buyout of the remaining 49 percent shares for CDN\$21 million. A. L. VanHoutte bought VKI, and in turn, Filterfresh. VanHoutte then sold Filterfresh to Selena, its coffee service subsidiary. Operating under the same parent company, VKI is a Filterfresh supplier. In a press release announcing the acquisition of the final block of stocks, Paul Andre-Guillotte, President and CEO of A. L. VanHoutte, noted that the development in the coffee service market had been the driving force of VKI's growth. It was thought that this acquisition would enable VanHoutte to accelerate its expansion into the North-American single cup niche.

Filterfresh operates with three business models. It (1) sells independent franchises, (2) operates some joint venture partnerships, and (3) owns 10 percent of some operations. With around 50 outlets in the United States and a presence in 27 states, Filterfresh became the nation's largest single-cup coffee service network by the late 1990s.

The Keurig Challenge

Although Filterfresh held the preeminent position in its market, King had reason to be concerned with Keurig, Inc. As a privately funded start-up, Keurig had an entrepreneurial flexibility that Filterfresh, as a subsidiary, could not match. Its top management appeared strong. King noted the trio of MBAs among top management, including one person who had preceded him by several years at Stanford. Keurig was rich with venture capital, though King often wondered if the company was spending at a rate that would alarm current and potential investors.

Among the most threatening challenge was Keurig's assertion of technological supremacy. The start-up claimed it had built a better, more efficient single brewing system than the market leader. The key to the Keurig system, and the source of its alleged advantage, was the introduction of the "K-Cup." The K-Cup sealed freshly roasted and ground coffee into a plastic cup impervious to oxygen, light, and moisture. One of the company's web FAQ ("frequently asked questions) argued that, "most single-serve brewers were loaded with coffee one to five pounds at a time. Then, the coffees were supposedly dumped into large hoppers that were not sealed to prevent oxygen from entering, therefore, if that coffee was not used quickly, it would go stale." By these standards, Filterfresh machines, utilizing the large hopper system, delivered inferior quality coffee to its customers.

Not only was Keurig attempting to usurp Filterfresh's dominant market share on the technological front, it also was attempting to beat the leader in potential markets. Keurig aggressively pursued markets that Filterfresh was actively seeking as well as striking agreements with shared suppliers. Filterfresh used a variety of coffees, including Green Mountain. Keurig used Green Mountain as its exclusive supplier. Filterfresh had an established program at a range of supermarkets, including the Stop and Shop chain, where coin-operated coffee dispensers often were located in the bakery area. But early in 1999, Green Mountain Coffee, utilizing Keurig machines, launched a coffee program at 172 Stop and Shop locations.

    As King finished reading the *Boston Globe* article, he wondered what, if anything, Filterfresh should do in response to Keurig. Filterfresh enjoyed a commanding position in the market, built up over many years. Could Keurig continue to expand and attract Filterfresh customers? What would be a fitting response to the Keurig challenge? Was this an issue of technology or of marketing? Or was it both?

    Brian King took a long sip of his freshly brewed coffee and settled into thought.

Sources

(http://www.bunnomatic.com)

(http://1st-line.com/machines)

(http://www.Keurig.com/faq.html)

The New York Metropolitan Museum of Art (Met) ended the 1990–1991 fiscal year with an operating deficit of $2 million. The deficit occurred in part because of decreases in auxiliary revenue, increases in operation expenditures, and decreases in admissions revenue. Even though the base museum attendance figures exceeded those of previous years, the absence of large-scale ticketed exhibitions, or "blockbusters," curtailed admissions revenue in 1990. During 1991, however, admissions revenues increased due to rising admission prices and the return of large-scale exhibitions.

The Met is dependent on external sources of revenue, including interest on endowments, gifts, governmental appropriations, and grants, as well as internal sources of revenue from merchandising operations, auditorium rental, parking garage fees, restaurants, admissions, memberships, royalties, and fees. Operating expenses include the costs of the curatorial departments, educational programs, libraries, and public information programs; costs associated with development, including marketing research; stocking merchandise inventories for auxiliary operations; and various additional administrative costs.[1] Because total expenditures are rising at a faster rate than total revenues, future deficits are predicted. Management of the museum must find creative and effective ways to sustain financial stability.

History

The state of New York established the museum on April 13, 1870, by granting a charter to a group forming a corporation in the name of the Metropolitan Museum of Art. The corporation was formed for the purpose of "establishing and maintaining in the city of New York a museum and library of art, of encouraging and developing the study of the fine arts, and the application of arts to manufacturing and practical life, of advancing the general knowledge of kindred subjects, and, to that end, of furnishing popular instruction and recreation."[2] The mission remains unchanged to date with one exception—the word *recreation* has been removed.[3]

City Support

The city of New York owns the building housing the museum, but the collections are the property of the corporation that operates the Met. The city continues to appropriate funds to the museum to be used for maintaining the building as well as providing utilities at no charge to the Metropolitan. The allocations in 1991 totaled $15,633,609, which is 9.3 percent of the total operating revenue for the year; however, the allocations are increasing at a decreasing rate due to the fiscal instability of the city of New York. A history of support from the city of New York is included in the five-year summary shown in Exhibit 1.

This case was prepared by Marilyn M. Helms, Paula J. Haynes, and Tammy L. Swenson of the University of Tennessee at Chatanooga. This case is intended for classroom discussion only, not to depict effective handling of administrative situations. All rights reserved to the authors.

EXHIBIT 1   The Metropolitan Museum of Art: Five-Year Summary

	1991	1990	1989	1988	1987
Operating Fund: Revenue and Support					
Total income from endowment, including the Cloisters	$ 14,169,461	$ 12,815,529	$ 10,838,371	$ 10,849,935	$ 9,912,411
City of New York					
Funds for guardianship and maintenance	9,645,657	10,193,481	9,892,601	9,970,936	8,339,423
Values of utilities provided	6,068,111	5,398,227	5,489,227	4,910,772	4,768,439
Memberships	11,723,453	10,809,726	10,557,710	9,732,467	9,674,124
Gifts and grants					
Education, community affairs, and special exhibitions	5,784,889	5,921,025	4,419,936	2,481,572	3,852,564
General-purpose contributions	15,864,740	14,126,525	11,492,125	9,862,288	9,596,497
Income for specified funds utilized	439,330	539,539	403,308	323,237	360,722
Admissions	8,621,001	7,304,343	10,032,361	6,588,169	8,343,996
Royalties and fees	1,814,579	1,222,951	1,438,572	878,547	838,063
Other	3,817,124	4,941,078	4,393,423	4,737,758	2,241,464
Gain on partial termination of pension plan	—	—	—	7,828,874	—
Income before auxiliary activities	77,948,345	73,272,424	68,957,634	68,164,555	57,927,703
Revenue from auxiliary activities	90,154,977	79,565,366	78,480,090	64,967,946	61,088,135
Total revenue and support	168,103,322	152,837,790	147,437,724	133,132,501	119,015,838
Expenses					
Curatorial					
Curatorial departments, conservation, and cataloging	16,617,016	15,091,929	14,921,578	13,266,536	12,724,858
Operation of the Cloisters	3,253,558	2,913,132	2,801,680	2,484,003	2,322,191
Special exhibitions	5,789,990	6,242,448	5,061,807	3,407,668	5,056,044
Education, community programs, and libraries	5,300,858	5,104,734	5,700,470	4,351,743	3,641,121
Financial, legal, and other administrative functions	6,084,069	5,542,451	5,046,463	4,646,079	4,483,464

Collections

The Met is a nonprofit, tax-exempt [501(c)(3)] organization located on the east side of Central Park. Museum collections include ancient and modern art from Egypt, Greece, Rome, the Near and Far East, pre-Columbian cultures, and the United States. Exhibit 2 shows the floor plan. The Cloisters, a branch museum, houses the European medieval art collection. Opened in 1938, this gallery is located in Fort Tryon Park on the far northern tip of Manhattan Island. The structure is constructed from parts of five European monasteries (see Exhibit 3). The land and the building were donated to the city of New York, and much of the art within was donated by John D. Rockefeller, Jr.[4]

Facilities

The museum consists of many gallery wings, a 250,000-volume library of art and reference materials used by graduate students in accordance with the museum's affiliation

EXHIBIT 1   (Concluded)

	1991	1990	1989	1988	1987
Public information, development, and membership services	5,431,390	6,649,179	5,398,638	4,809,956	5,259,375
Operations					
Guardianship	15,404,915	14,981,129	13,497,933	12,305,602	12,434,875
Maintenance	9,994,162	8,460,979	8,075,233	7,284,095	6,721,522
Operating services	5,359,190	4,870,045	4,572,179	3,870,884	3,586,939
Value of utilities provided by the city of New York	6,068,111	5,398,227	5,489,227	4,910,772	4,768,439
Nonexhibition capital construction and renovation	2,088,713	2,530,557	1,163,930	—	—
Expenses before auxiliary activities	81,391,972	77,784,810	71,729,138	61,337,338	60,998,828
Cost of sales and expenses of auxiliary activities	88,672,214	77,647,773	72,223,048	61,555,170	53,968,101
Total expenses	170,064,186	155,432,583	143,952,186	122,892,508	114,966,929
Revenue and support (under) over expenses	(1,960,864)	(2,594,793)	3,485,538	10,239,993	4,048,909
Transfer of gain on partial termination of pension plan and net pension income to endowment funds	—	—	—	9,195,557	—
Net (decrease) increase in operating fund balance	$(1,960,864)	$(2,594,793)	$ 3,485,538	$ 1,044,436	$ 4,048,909
Additional information					
Endowment funds balance	$450,890,594	$425,725,761	$396,149,106	$331,790,406	$353,836,762
Capital construction expenditures	$ 22,978,339	$ 20,434,301	$ 15,476,598	$ 30,866,842	$ 22,299,538
Acquisitions of art	$ 16,945,340	$ 18,259,644	$ 17,107,754	$ 15,845,522	$ 7,000,695
Full-time employees	1,627	1,659	1,568	1,542	1,503
Visitors to the main building and the Cloisters	4,702,078	4,558,560	4,816,388	3,978,404	4,859,522

Source: The Metropolitan Museum of Art, *Annual Reports.*

with New York University, a 708- and a 246-seat auditorium, three classrooms, a restaurant and cafeteria, a parking garage, and a museum store. Ten other museum stores are operated by the Metropolitan off-site in New York City, Connecticut, California, Ohio, and New Jersey.[5]

Activities

Activities at the museum include guided tours, lectures, gallery talks, concerts, formally organized educational programs for children, intermuseum loans, and permanent, temporary, and traveling exhibitions.[6]

Management

Currently, the Met is operated by a dual management system, as shown in Exhibit 4. The president and the director report directly to the board of trustees. The dual management system was started in 1978, when the board decided the museum was too complex and large for one person to manage.[7] Before the board's action in 1978, Thomas Hoving had been the

EXHIBIT 2   The Metropolitan Museum of Art: Floor Plan

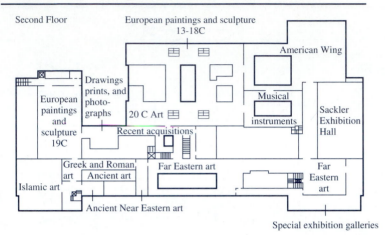

Second Floor

European paintings and sculpture 13-18C

American Wing

Drawings prints, and photographs

European paintings and sculpture 19C

20 C Art

Recent acquisitions

Musical instruments

Sackler Exhibition Hall

Islamic art

Greek and Roman art

Ancient art

Far Eastern art

Far Eastern art

Ancient Near Eastern art

Special exhibition galleries

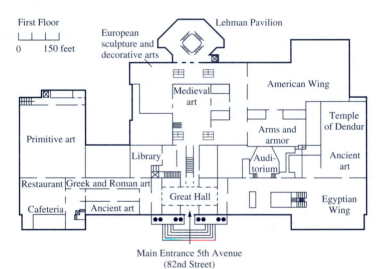

First Floor

0   150 feet

European sculpture and decorative arts

Lehman Pavilion

American Wing

Medieval art

Temple of Dendur

Primitive art

Arms and armor

Auditorium

Ancient art

Library

Restaurant

Greek and Roman art

Egyptian Wing

Cafeteria

Ancient art

Great Hall

Main Entrance 5th Avenue
(82nd Street)

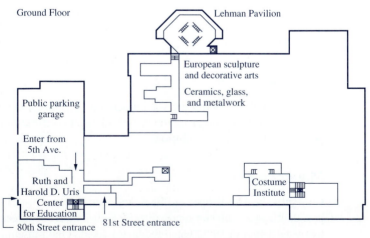

Ground Floor

Lehman Pavilion

European sculpture and decorative arts

Ceramics, glass, and metalwork

Public parking garage

Enter from 5th Ave.

Ruth and Harold D. Uris Center for Education

Costume Institute

80th Street entrance

81st Street entrance

EXHIBIT 3   The Cloisters: Floor Plan

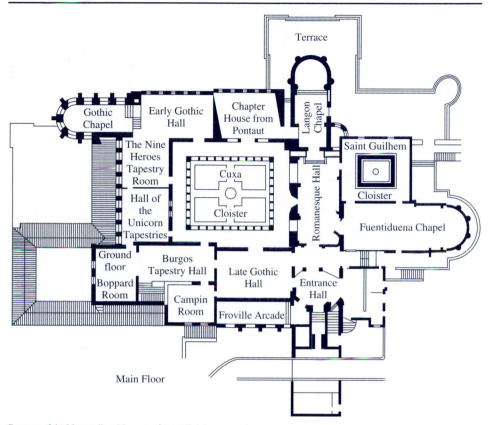

chief executive at the museum since 1967. Hoving often was disparaged as a publicity-seeking showman; by 1971 he had brought the museum to a fiscal crisis through his excessive acquisitions and expansion projects.[8] Some of these included the 1975 addition of the Lehman Wing, a glass-covered garden court; in 1978 the Sackler Wing, a climate-controlled glass-roofed room, housing the Temple of Dendur; and in 1980 the American Wing. Major renovations of the Great Hall and Costume Institute were completed in 1970 and 1971.[9]

Most of the controversy surrounding Hoving's tenure was due to his role in institutionalizing the "blockbuster" event at the Metropolitan as an answer to the financial crisis. Because the public is most attracted to temporary events, attendance figures were high at the large-scale ticketed events.[10] An example of these types of events was the "Treasures of Tutankhamen" show in 1978 and 1979, in which 1.2 million tickets were sold. Other examples of large-scale ticketed events include "The Great Age of Fresco," "Mexico: Splendors of Thirty Centuries," and the controversial "Harlem on My Mind."[11] The blockbuster issue has been intensely debated, however. Supporters of these events say the attraction of new audiences will diminish the elitist image of museums. Those against such exhibitions, such as Sherman Lee, director of the Cleveland Museum, feel that the values of the marketplace, if applied carelessly, may undermine public confidence in the museum's integrity.

Both of these views aside, the revenue earned from additional attendees has helped support all the museum's activities in the last 10 years. Since Lee's retirement from the

EXHIBIT 4   The Metropolitan Museum of Art: Organization Chart, October 1990

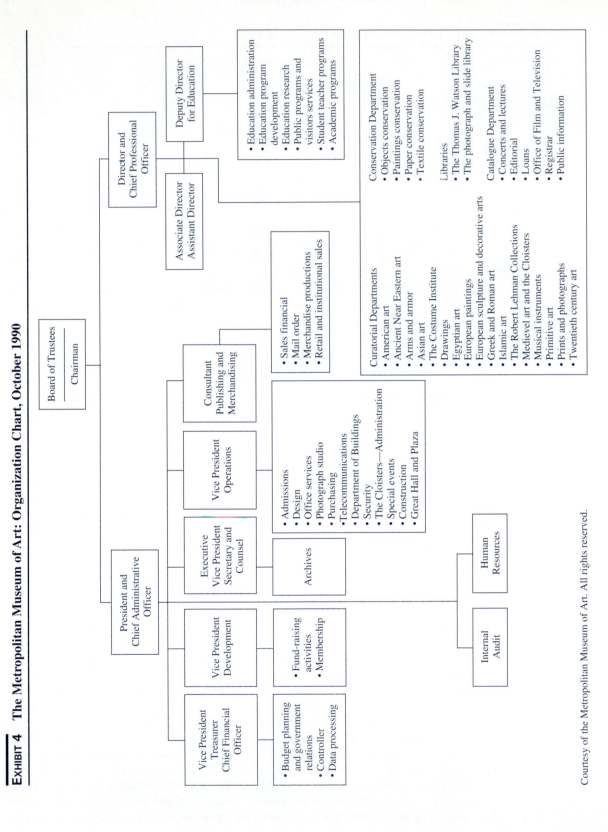

Cleveland Museum, Philippe de Montebello, the current director of the Metropolitan and Hoving's successor, has taken on the leadership of the antiblockbuster cause. Mr. de Montebello's position is to "lament the cost-effective mentality that places any museum activity that does not generate attendance or immediate income in jeopardy."[12] For the year ended June 30, 1990, there were no large-scale ticketed events at the Metropolitan, and the total revenue from admissions decreased by 27 percent.[13] However, during 1991 the museum's increased admission prices and large-scale exhibition offerings increased total admission revenues.

Currently, de Montebello and William H. Luers, the president, share the responsibility of managing the Met. Philippe de Montebello, a graduate of Harvard and New York University, is primarily responsible for all curatorial functions, conservation departments, libraries, and educational activities. William H. Luers, a former U.S. Ambassador to Czechoslovakia, is responsible for the business side of the Metropolitan. His basic responsibilities include daily operations, merchandising, development, human resources, internal auditing, and all financial matters, including budgeting. Even though the president is responsible for the development of the Metropolitan, including fund-raising, de Montebello is also involved heavily in this activity as well as in acquiring donations of works of art and money. Mr. Luers stated, "Philippe should be perceived as the man who gives esthetic and artistic vision to the museum. And I am the manager, diplomat, executive, fund-raiser, and basically a communicator."[14]

Fund-Raising

In 1982, the Met began a public campaign to raise $150 million to offset operating deficits and enhance the endowment. Even though large gifts have been solicited for specific projects on several occasions, this campaign was the first formal fund-raising drive ever conducted. These funds were supposed to help the Metropolitan Museum achieve financial stability, allow all galleries to stay open when the museum is open, and finance the existing educational programs, the work of curatorship, and the conservation library.[15] This five-year drive was completed in 1987 and was successful in meeting the $150 million goal; however, the Metropolitan experienced an operating deficit of $2.6 million for the 1989–1990 fiscal year and a $2.0 million deficit for 1990–1991 with future deficits predicted. The development staff at the Metropolitan has implemented the following fund-raising techniques in an attempt to offset deficits.

Endowed Chairs.   An effective fund-raising technique borrowed from universities and hospitals has been soliciting funds for existing curatorships in the form of endowed chairs. All major art dealers in New York as well as industry leaders are approached for endowments. These chairs would carry the name of the donor, who would add to the endowment indefinitely. This drive was the first attempt to raise the salaries of curators so that the Metropolitan could be competitive within the job market by attracting the best people and retaining the people it already had by increasing their existing salaries. Raises of this type would have not otherwise been possible due to the operating fund shortfalls.[16]

Corporate Sponsorships.   As governmental funding decreases, corporations have come under increasing pressure to take the lead in funding social and community programs. Based on a 1991 study performed by *American Demographics,* the largest share of corporate support goes to education (38 percent), with health and human services (34 percent) following. The results of this survey do not present a promising future for corporate sponsorship of the arts because most corporations practice "strategic philanthropy," focusing philanthropic efforts to maximize their returns.[17] At the Metropolitan, great effort is given to matching the 30 annual special exhibits to corporations' activities to entice them to fund the exhibits; otherwise, an exhibit might not be shown.[18] One example of matching a corporation's activities to an exhibit was a gift of $500,000 from the Hunting World Group of Companies to maintain a gallery displaying American arms.[19]

A corporate patron program is also available and requires an annual donation of $30,000. This gives companies the right to have one party a year, at their own expense, in the Temple of Dendur, the American Wing, or the Medieval Sculpture Hall. Proceeds from this program cover operating costs. Even though private use of public space is a controversial issue, it has proved to be a successful way to generate funding. Philippe de Montebello said, "There is no ministry of culture in the United States. We don't receive a check from Washington, so we have to seek ways to provide revenues."[20]

Memberships.   The museum has various levels of membership and councils. The chair's council members donate $25,000 annually and are included in the governance of the museum. Membership in this council is by invitation only. The Real Estate Council is responsible for raising money for special showings that are not fully financed. Each member is given 15 invitations to a special showing.[21] There are many memberships available to the public. Members get free admission and receive the *Bulletin,* a quarterly magazine, and the bimonthly events listing, the *Calendar.* They also receive catalogues of the museum at no cost and are given 10 percent off all merchandise. The Metropolitan Museum's membership is now over 100,000. In addition, the contribution levels required for all categories of membership were increased in 1991. See Exhibits 5 and 6 for a comparison of the number of members by category for 1987 through 1991.

Government Grants.   For the year ended June 30, 1991, the Met received funding from the local, state, and federal governments. The city of New York provides the building that houses the museum, the utilities, and appropriate funds for maintaining the building. The state of New York provides an annual allocation from the New York State Council on the Arts for general operating and program support. Special capital funds from the National Heritage Trust were received for support of the special exhibitions programs. Federal agencies such as the National Endowment for the Arts and the Institute of Museum Services provided support for specific projects and general operations. Funds provided from governmental sources amounted to $17,059,604 for the year ended June 30, 1991. Most governmental support is appropriated on an annual basis; therefore, during recessionary periods this external funding is uncertain.[22]

Gifts.   The 1986 Tax Reform Act (TRA86) curtailed donations of works of art to the Metropolitan and other museums. The change in the tax law reduced the tax deduction donors could take for appreciated art objects. This move resulted in many of these objects being sold to the highest bidder in auction houses.[23] A survey conducted by *American Demographics* found that charitable giving by corporations fell by 12 percent after the 1986 Tax Reform Act became effective.[24] In March 1991 the Metropolitan received the largest gift it had received in over 50 years, probably due to a temporary "tax window," a one-year restoration of tax deductions for the full market value of art donated in 1991. Valued at $1 billion, the paintings donated by Walter Annenberg will not become the property of the Metropolitan until Annenberg's death.[25]

Admissions.   The Met is the number one tourist attraction in New York City. For the year ended June 30, 1991, there were 4,702,078 visitors to the museum and the Clois-

EXHIBIT 5   Annual Members

Current Prices*	1991	1990	1989	1988	1987
Student ($30)	1,557	1,575	1,517	1,309	1,381
Individual ($70)	29,175	33,054	34,548	30,425	32,379
Dual ($125)	21,261	23,299†	24,485‡	22,440	23,826
Sustaining ($300)	6,539	7,329	7,729	6,486	7,047
Supporting					
Contributing ($600)	1,547	1,671	1,885	1,798	1,773
Donor ($900)	555	611	634	562	581
Sponsor ($2,000)	507	521	541	524	577
Patron ($4,000)	156	182	175	142	82
Upper patron ($6,000)	51	62	51	45	36
Nat'l asso. ($35)*	32,848	31,555	29,777	31,058	27,189
Total	94,196	99,859	101,342	94,789	94,871

Source: The Metropolitan Museum of Art, *1991 Annual Report.*

* Rates for all membership categories were increased an average of 21 percent in 1991.

† Includes life members.

‡ Nonresident membership.

EXHIBIT 6   Members of the Corporation

	1991	1990	1989	1988	1987
Honorary fellows for life	3	3	3	3	4
Fellows for life	873	901	911	936	965
Fellows in perpetuity	329	336	342	349	357
Benefactors	355	389	372	364	334
Total corporation members	1,560	1,629	1,628	1,652	1,660
Total annual members	95,756	99,859	101,342	94,789	94,871
Grand total	97,316	101,488	102,970	96,441	96,531

Source: The Metropolitan Museum of Art, *1991 Annual Report.*

ters. (Exhibit 1, for attendance figures from 1987 through 1991.) Attendance decreased in 1990 because there were no large-scale ticketed exhibitions like the two in 1989. Because of this, revenue from admissions decreased by $2,728,000 (27 percent). This decrease is 3.7 percent of the total revenue before auxiliary operations. The management of the museum has decided to veer away from ticketing exhibitions in an effort to make special exhibitions more spontaneous and more rewarding for frequent visitors.[26]

Hours of Operation

Evening hours were added on Friday and Saturday nights in place of opening on Tuesday evening in an attempt to increase attendance. Attendance on Tuesday evening averaged 2,500, while attendance on Friday and Saturday evenings is averaging between 3,500 and

EXHIBIT 7   **Museum Hours and Admission Charges**

Hours of Operation	
Sunday, Tuesday–Thursday	9:30 AM–5:15 PM
Friday, Saturday	9:30 AM–8:45 PM
Monday	Closed
Donation for Admission	
Adults	$5.00
Students and seniors	2.50
Children under 12	Free

Source: *The Official Museum Directory 1990,* National Register Publishing Company.

5,000.[27] See Exhibit 7 for the hours of operation and the suggested donations for admission to the museum.

Target Customer

Many surveys are conducted by the Metropolitan each year to determine the key demographics of its visitors. See Exhibit 8 for the demographics of the average visitor to the Met. The Met's management feels that understanding the demographics of the current average visitor is the key to marketing the museum's services effectively. Of the 1,357 visitors surveyed, 48 percent were New York City residents, 39.6 percent were residents of other areas of the United States, and 12.4 percent were foreign residents.[28]

Volunteers

Approximately 800 volunteers work at the Metropolitan Museum. Three hundred of them are docents, or volunteers, who lead tours of schoolchildren and other groups.[29] Unfortunately, the Met's traditional volunteer pool is shrinking. According to a Census Bureau study conducted in 1989, 59 percent of the women in the United States are now

EXHIBIT 8   **Customer Demographics**

Demographics	*Data*	*Percent*
Number of visits within 1 year	1–3 visits	32.8%
Time spent in museum	2 hours	36.0
Primary reason for visiting museum	Special exhibition	51.1
Median age of visitors	Age 38	
Sex of visitors	Female	57.0
Education of visitors	Baccalaureate	33.5
Occupation of visitors	Teachers/other professionals	47.5
Ethnicity of visitors	Caucasian	76.1
Museum membership	Member	15.5

Source: *The Metropolitan Museum of Art,* January 1991.

employed. As women continue to enter the work force, nonprofit organizations are finding it difficult to attract volunteers to work during the daytime hours.[30]

Auxiliary Operations

Today, at the Metropolitan, there are a growing number of business executives on the board because of the recognition that the museum has evolved into a big enterprise with an investment portfolio and business activities such as a reproduction studio and retail outlets. Because external funds can no longer be relied on, greater emphasis must be placed on the generation of internal sources of revenue.

Museum Shops.   Retail shops are operated within the museum, at the Cloisters, and in 10 off-site locations. Four of these satellite shops are in New York: Rockefeller Center, New York Public Library, the Americana at Manhasset, and Macy's. Two are in Connecticut: Stamford Town Center and Westfarms Mall. Two are in California: Century City Shopping Center in Los Angeles and Southcoast Plaza in Costa Mesa. One is in Ohio at Columbus City Center, and one is in New Jersey at the mall at Shorthills.[31] Because the Met is a tax-exempt, nonprofit organization, it does not have to pay taxes on profits realized from retail operations; therefore, some feel it has an unfair advantage over other retailers that sell similar goods.[32] The museum is required to pay income taxes only on retail items unrelated to its mission, in accordance with section 511 (imposition of tax on unrelated business income of charitable organizations) of the Internal Revenue Code.

The purpose of the unrelated business income tax is to prevent tax-exempt organizations from competing unfairly with businesses whose earnings are taxed. Unrelated business income is any income derived from any unrelated trade or business. The term *unrelated trade or business* is defined in section 511 of the Internal Revenue Code as

> the case of any organization subject to the tax imposed by section 511, any trade or business the conduct of which is not substantially related (aside from the need of such organization for income or funds or the use it makes of the profits derived) to the exercise or performance by such organization of its charitable, educational, or other purpose or function constituting the basis for its exemption under section 501.[33]

The museum's stores sell greeting cards, posters, calendars, postcards, sculptures, glass, and jewelry. Nearly all the items offered are reproductions of or adaptations from the museum's collections. These items are not available for sale at any other retail location. Items are sold in the museum shops or through mail order. The museum management contends that the sale of the items in the shops falls within the mission of the museum in that the sale of an item makes people think about the museum outside its walls and serves as an extension of their visits. Groups that represent small businesses are lobbying for changes in the tax code because some commercial ventures undertaken by nonprofit institutions compete unfairly with private companies that sell nearly the same merchandise. These groups want the tax code rewritten to detail specifically which items would be considered tax-exempt.

The Metropolitan's merchandising activities resemble those of commercial businesses in some ways but are unique in others. The resemblances include the Met's desire to introduce such technology as a point of sale (POS) computerized inventory system into its stores. The differences include the requirement that all merchandise sold in the museum must reflect the permanent collection to preclude assessment of taxes on the earnings. Therefore, the decision on the types of items to sell does not necessarily reflect customers' desires. Marketing research consists of showing pictures of items in the permanent collection to randomly selected customers in the museum shop to determine if the items should be reproduced for sale.

The museum almost never advertises except to invite people to join its catalog mailing list. Six catalogs per year are mailed out to members and other customers on the mailing list. The Christmas catalog is mailed out to 3 million people, and the others are mailed to a smaller number. Some of the merchandising policies, such as buying large quantities of an item to get it at a lower price, have led to inventory storage problems. It is not unusual for an item to remain in the inventory for up to two years. The museum manufactures the molds to make the copies of art in its own reproduction studio. The art books are printed in the United States and around the world.[34]

The museum leases space for off-site retail stores and for the warehouse that serves as the headquarters for the mail order business and as a storage facility for inventory. Lease costs for all rented spaces used solely for the retail operation amounted to $1,456,295 and $1,675,519 for the years ended June 30, 1990, and 1991, respectively.[35]

Restaurants.   The museum operates a restaurant, cafeteria, and bar. The restaurant and bar are open to accommodate the evening hours on Fridays and Saturdays. The museum has received approval to open a new restaurant to replace the current restaurant and cafeteria so that space can be used for additional galleries.[36]

Other Auxiliaries.   Other auxiliary operations at the Metropolitan are the parking garage and the auditorium. The parking garage is located adjacent to the museum for use by its patrons at the rate of $8.50 for the first hour, $1.00 for each additional hour up to the fifth, $17.50 for 5 to 10 hours, and $19.50 beyond 10 hours.[37]

Auxiliary Results of Operations.   Net income from merchandising operations was $787,852 for the year ended June 30, 1991. Though sales from mail order were up 4 percent, the total revenue was less than forecasted. A general softening of the retail industry was thought to be the reason for this shortfall. The net contribution to the museum's operations from auxiliaries totaled $1.48 million in 1991. See Exhibit 9 for the balance sheet and Exhibit 1 for the five-year summary.

Future Outlook

The future financial stability of the Met is the key concern of management. The fiscal instability of the city of New York could lessen future support. Threatened reductions in federal funding also could have an adverse effect on the museum's operations. The national recession could affect the museum in terms of attendance and retail sales.

According to the book *Megatrends 2000,* researchers predict that the arts will begin to replace sporting events as society's primary leisure activity. The authors cite a 1988 report by the National Endowment of the Arts calculating that Americans spend $28 billion on sports events compared to $3.7 billion on art events. However, more than 500 million people visited American museums last year, far more than attended professional sporting events.[38]

Growth in the future must continue to come from individual and corporate donations. Statistics from *The Economist* show that while the French government spends approximately $30 per capita on the arts and the British $9, the U.S. federal and state governments together spend only about $2. This means others, including corporate America, will be required to help reduce this differential.[39]

EXHIBIT 9   The Metropolitan Museum of Art: Balance Sheet for the Years Ended June 30, 1987–1991

	1991	1990	1989	1988	1987
Assets					
Cash	$ 606,396	$ 907,578	$ 395,529	$ 1,237,648	$ 1,915,744
Investments, at market	531,292,293	521,786,251	500,028,584	425,091,168	444,762,386
Receivables	41,046,111	33,443,105	34,426,235	26,112,389	13,697,322
Merchandise inventories	18,019,006	19,710,828	15,528,500	13,110,043	10,848,449
Fixed assets, at cost, net	18,609,096	13,413,486	9,953,319	8,580,484	8,548,091
Deferred charges, prepaid expenses, and other assets	7,042,756	5,622,154	4,092,675	4,900,913	4,510,822
Total assets	$616,615,658	$594,883,402	$564,424,842	$479,032,645	$484,282,814
Liabilities and Fund Balance					
Accounts payable	$ 21,631,963	$ 27,182,146	$ 27,075,186	$ 23,926,641	$ 16,527,236
Accrued expenses, primarily payroll, annual leave, and pension	14,112,100	14,363,817	13,080,930	9,636,881	6,003,065
Deferred income, principally memberships, gifts, and grants	11,038,712	10,700,500	9,801,820	8,716,301	7,533,288
Notes payable	15,800,000	7,750,000	8,000,000	10,400,000	8,000,000
Loan payable	46,915,000	47,655,000	48,260,000	48,260,000	44,990,000
Total liabilities	$109,497,775	$107,651,463	$106,217,936	$100,939,823	$ 83,053,589
Fund (deficit) balance	507,117,883	487,231,939	458,206,906	378,092,822	401,229,225
Total liabilities and fund balance	$616,615,658	$594,883,402	$564,424,842	$479,032,645	$484,282,814

Source: The Metropolitan Museum of Art, *Annual Reports.*

Many people believe the resurgent interest in the arts will bring success for the museum shops. Patrons want to support local culture and are spending generously on books, maps, models, posters, replicas, and other museum shop items. The Metropolitan sold more products than did any other museum in 1991 and remains the only museum that manufactures its own line of merchandise. Second in sales was the Smithsonian Institution in Washington, D.C., which sells through its nine museum shops and catalog. Other shops with a minimum of $1 million in annual sales include the Museum of Modern Art and Whitney Museum of American Art in New York, Boston's Museum of Fine Art, the San Francisco Museum of Modern Art, the Art Institute of Chicago, the Los Angeles County Museum of Art, the Philadelphia Museum of Art, and the San Diego Museum of Art.[40]

Competition for museum shops is not limited to museum locations. The Museum Company, a retailer based in East Rutherford, New Jersey, has opened stores in seven states in two years and sells merchandise from the Louvre in Paris, the British Museum, and other art institutions and pays royalties to the museums. Its first-year revenues topped $10 million.

Other Museum Competition

Because there are multiple demands for the free time of museum visitors, many activities, outings, and other forms of recreation and leisure are potential substitutes. The direct competitors—other museums—are plentiful, and many are in the New York area.

They include the American Museum of Natural History, the Museum of Modern Art, the Whitney Museum, and the Museum of the City of New York.

Other activities and forms of available recreation range from sporting events to theatrical presentations. The New York metropolitan area is the home of two National Basketball Association teams, three National Hockey League teams, two National Football League teams, two baseball teams, and two racetracks. Broadway, the most celebrated street in America, offers daily productions in 40 theaters, and there are numerous off-Broadway shows for tourists and residents in New York.

In addition, each of the five New York boroughs has many attractions to choose from including the Statue of Liberty, the Bronx Zoo, and the National Historic Landmark district on Staten Island. Central Park and the World Trade Center are easily accessible to all visitors via the New York City subway.

End Notes

1. The Metropolitan Museum of Art, *1990 Annual Report.*
2. W. Howe, *A History of the Metropolitan Museum of Art* (New York: Arno Press, 1913), p. 125.
3. *The Metropolitan Museum of Art—Charter, Constitution, and By-Laws,* p. 3.
4. *Collier's Encyclopedia,* 1981, Volume 16, p. 70f.
5. *The Official Museum Directory 1990* (National Register Publishing Company, 1990), p. 581.
6. Ibid.
7. G. Glueck, "The Metropolitan Museum's Diplomat at the Top," *The New York Times,* May 2, 1988.
8. M. Conforti, "Hoving's Legacy Reconsidered," *Art in America,* June 1986, pp. 19–23.
9. *Collier's Encyclopedia,* 1981, Volume 16, p. 70f.
10. Conforti, "Hoving's Legacy Reconsidered," pp. 19–23.
11. C. Tomkins, "The Art World," *The New Yorker,* February 28, 1983, pp. 94–97.
12. Conforti, "Hoving's Legacy Reconsidered," pp. 19–23.
13. The Metropolitan Museum of Art, *1990 Annual Report.*
14. Glueck, "The Metropolitan Museum's Diplomat at the Top."
15. J. Russell, "Met Museum Opens 5-Year Drive for $150 Million," *The New York Times,* October 26, 1982.
16. G. Glueck, "A Raise for Met's Curators," *The New York Times,* November 14, 1990; "Met Museum Seeks Endowed Chairs," *The New York Times,* March 15, 1983.
17. B. O'Hare, "Good Deeds Are Good Business," *American Demographics,* September 1991, pp. 38–42.
18. S. Salmans, "The Fine Art of Museum Fund Raising," *The New York Times,* January 14, 1985.
19. "$500,000 to Met Museum," *The New York Times,* December 20, 1990.
20. J. Taylor, "Party Palace," *New York,* January 9, 1989, pp. 20–30.
21. Salmans, "The Fine Art of Museum Fund Raising."
22. The Metropolitan Museum of Art, *Annual Report.*
23. G. Glueck, "For Two Museums, a Very Good Week," *The New York Times,* March 1, 1991.
24. B. O'Hare, "Corporate Charitable Gifts Reached 5.9B in 1990," *American Demographics,* September 1990, p. 38.
25. Glueck, "For Two Museums, a Very Good Week."
26. The Metropolitan Museum of Art, *1990 Annual Report.*
27. Smith, "Weekends at Dusk, a New Met Museum," *The New York Times,* March 30, 1990.
28. The Metropolitan Museum of Art, Survey, December 1990 and January 1991.
29. The Metropolitan Museum of Art, *1990 Annual Report.*
30. P. Mergenbagen, "A New Breed of Volunteer," *American Demographics,* June 1991, pp. 54–55.
31. The Metropolitan Museum of Art, *1990 Annual Report.*
32. W. Honan, "Deciding Which Profits Should Be Tax Exempt," *The New York Times,* May 15, 1988.
33. Internal Revenue Code, Section 511.
34. B. Feder, "Metropolitan Museum Shows Retailing Bent," *The New York Times,* May 27, 1988.
35. The Metropolitan Museum of Art, *1990 Annual Report.*
36. Ibid.
37. Ibid.
38. J. Naisbitt and P. Aburdene, *Megatrends 2000* (New York: William Morrow, 1990).
39. L. David, "Picture of Success: National Gallery of Art Celebrates 50th Anniversary," *International Washington Flyer,* 1992, V1, pp. 70–74.
40. S. Soltis, "Retailing Rodin: Museum Shops Carve a Profitable Niche," *International Washington Flyer,* 1992, V1, p. 73.

On a clear but cool day in mid-January, Dan Shay, co-owner and manager of Bear Creek Golf Range, stood looking out over his golf range, where two hearty golfers were taking their swings. Turning to his partner, George Patton, he observed,

> Well, George, at this time last year we were on top of the world with our plans for the new golf range. Here we are a year later, and things aren't nearly so rosy. We're starting our second year in the business and let's face it, we didn't come close to meeting our objectives last year. In fact, if we don't do a lot better this year, we'll probably go under, which will cost us both a lot of money. However, I'm not ready to throw in the towel. We had some significant start-up problems in our first year and didn't do the business that we expected, but we're still here and I think we have a chance to turn things around. But we sure have to figure out how to attract a lot more customers in 1994.

Background of the Golf Range

Bear Creek Golf Range, the newest range in the Dallas/Fort Worth area, opened for business the previous May. Dan Shay, the owner and manager, was a professional golfer who had recently retired from active tournament play. Dan graduated from Wake Forest University in 1973, where he was a member of the varsity golf team. Upon graduating, he decided to turn professional. He played on the tour for several years, and his career earnings were quite respectable. When a wrist injury forced him to retire in 1990, he had saved enough money to invest in his own business venture. Many retired golf professionals choose to continue as golf course pros at private courses, but Dan felt that he would have more independence and a higher income potential if he ran his own business. Reflecting on a career shortened by an injury, Dan observed, "If I can't make it as the best golf tour player, I will try to become the best golf teacher." Over the years he had been quite successful as a golf instructor and had earned recognition as one of the most knowledgeable PGA Class A professionals in America. He had been actively involved with Junior Golf in the north Texas area and had received many awards for his efforts. Not surprisingly, Dan's business interests focused on utilizing his experience and abilities in the area of golf instruction.

Dan was approached in early 1991 by a longtime friend and fellow PGA professional, George Patton, about the possibility of jointly starting their own driving range in the Dallas/Fort Worth area. Dan felt that this was an ideal opportunity to combine his interest in golf and golf instruction with a promising business undertaking. Although Dan and George were to be equal investors and partners in the business, George was to continue to compete on the tour while Dan assumed the responsibility for managing the day-to-day operations of the business. As they considered the requirements for success in this business, they felt that they had the necessary qualifications. They had excellent

This case has been prepared by Ray Keyes, associate professor of marketing, and Donna Moore, student, Boston College. The situation is based on an actual business experience.

golfing backgrounds, genuine knowledge of the game, and good contacts in the golfing community to go along with their experience as golfing instructors. Also, between them, they had adequate financial resources. They were confident that they could raise additional funds if necessary.

In discussing their ideas for the new driving range, the partners agreed that they should focus on serious golfers who were interested in improving their golfing skills through practice and instruction. The range would cater to serious golfers by providing first-class facilities (driving range and hitting areas), high-quality equipment (clubs, balls, and merchandise), and professional services (lessons, club repair, advice, and assistance). This driving range would establish an image as "the professional golfing center" run by professionals. The partners agreed that they were not interested in attracting customers who enjoyed golf as a form of entertainment. They referred to these golfers as "Yahoos." Their observations of other driving ranges led them to feel that the Yahoos were more trouble than they were worth. They tended to be loud, disruptive, very hard on equipment, and often less concerned with developing skills than with showing off. As Dan observed, "We can really do without the aggravations."

In weighing the driving range potential, the partners were aware of the growing interest in golf nationally and in the Dallas/Fort Worth area in particular. On the national level, the $40 billion golf market (golf and related products and services) had an estimated annual growth rate of 5 percent. The growth rate had been even higher in the Dallas/Fort Worth area because of the availability of golf courses and practice facilities and the warm weather found there nine months of the year. The Dallas/Fort Worth Metroplex was one of the fastest growing metropolitan areas in America. There were 86 private and municipal golf courses in the area, and several of them were new. All the courses had high memberships, and many had long waiting lists. The increase in population of Dallas/Fort Worth, the increase in beginner golfers (up 15 percent since 1980), and the warm climate led the partners to conclude that this could be a very healthy area for a golf-related business.

Dan and George decided to proceed with the driving range business. They were fortunate in identifying a 22-acre plot of land on an access road to Route 183, the connecting highway between Dallas and Fort Worth. They agreed that this would be a good location because it was midway between the two cities and very close to the Dallas/Fort Worth International Airport. The people who used the highway were primarily people living in the surrounding suburban townships of Irving, Bedford, Grapevine, Euless, Arlington, Grand Prairie, Hurst, and Coppell. Many of these people worked in either Dallas or Fort Worth and traveled regularly on Route 183. In addition, the Route 183 access road connected with the International Parkway leading to the international airport. The partners estimated that their golf range would draw people within a 10-mile radius (population 777,082). There were 15 golf courses in this market area, public and private.

The Plan

After considering several locations, the partners decided to purchase the 22-acre piece of property on Route 183 (with an option to purchase the adjacent 10-acre plot of land). They secured a mortgage on the property and set about developing their plan. First they visited a number of driving ranges in the state to get ideas. Then they identified the facilities and services that they felt would be most appropriate for the kind of professional range that they had in mind. The plan included the following facilities and services.

Facilities and Equipment

- A first-class driving area with high-quality grass for the range, several target greens, distance flags, and a system of trees and fencing around the outer rim of the range. The back tree-lined boundary would be 300 yards from the driving tees.
- Thirty-five individual hitting areas (tees) with Astroturf mats. Six of the tees would be set aside as a teaching area. The teaching area was to include a sand trap.
- Video equipment for instructional purposes.
- An awning to cover 12 of the hitting areas for golfers to use in inclement weather.
- A top-quality putting green for lessons and practice.
- Hitting areas and range to be lit for night use.
- A permanent clubhouse-style building that included

  customer service counter

  snack bar/restaurant with tables and chairs

  business office

  video game area

  bulletin boards

  sink and toilets (indoor plumbing)

  merchandise sales area (pro shop) where they would sell items (gloves, balls, spikes, golf shirts, sweatshirts, etc.) at lower prices than the typical golf course pro shop

  picture windows that looked out over the tees and the driving range

  public telephones

- A paved parking area (for approximately 30 cars).
- A lighted sign visible from Route 183 (both lanes).
- Landscaping and decorative shrubbery.

Services

- PGA instruction (individual and group lessons).
- Custom club fitting and repair.
- Advice and ordering of merchandise (clubs, bags, etc.).

Exhibit 1 provides a sketch of the facility as they planned it, and Exhibit 2 shows their financial development plan.

Competitive Situation.   The partners reviewed the competitive situation in their market area. There were two full-service golf ranges and two limited-service ranges within the 10-mile radius. The two full-service ranges were very different from each other, and each offered a significant competitive threat to the Bear Creek Range. The larger of the two, Greenbrier Golf Range, was a full-service range with 40 hitting areas, a putting green, two golf instructors, a full-service snack bar (with hot dogs, hamburgers, sandwiches, cold drinks, etc.), and a retail golf equipment and supplies shop. Although the proprietors of Greenbrier were not recognized PGA golfing pros, they were experienced and knowledgeable golf enthusiasts known to be good instructors. The driving range and buildings were well constructed, and everything about the operation was first class. It was not unusual to see long lines, especially on summer evenings and weekends, when the wait could run as long as an hour. At these busy times some golfers became impatient and went to one of the other golf ranges in the area where there were no waiting lines. Although there were no published figures on Greenbrier's profitability, it was generally believed that the business was quite profitable.

EXHIBIT 1   Bear Creek Golf Range

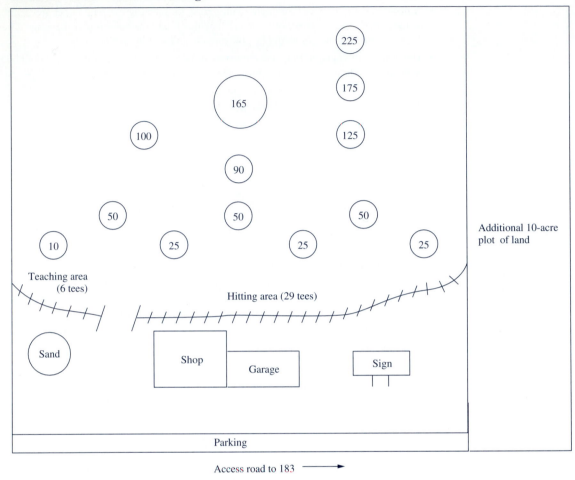

The second successful driving range, the Golfarama Golfing Center, was closer to Dallas, where it appealed to less serious golfers with its entertainment-oriented facility. The facility included a driving range with 30 hitting areas, a pitch-and-putt area, and an 18-hole miniature golf course. Golfarama also attracted good crowds on summer evenings and weekends, but waiting was not as much of a problem because of the other activities for customers to engage in while waiting for open tees. In fact, significant numbers of people came specifically to play miniature golf and the other games. Golfarama was located next to the Bowlarama Bowling Center (owned by the same company), which featured 10 bowling alleys, six pool tables, and a video game arcade. They had added an indoor/outdoor pitching machine and a batting cage. The Golfarama/Bowlarama complex also featured a restaurant and a separate sports bar that was quite popular with the younger sports crowd. As the Golfarama Center was part of the overall entertainment complex, it was difficult to determine its profitability. However, the parent company for this national chain of franchise recreation centers was regularly reporting growth in units, sales, and profits.

EXHIBIT 2

FINANCIAL DEVELOPMENT PLAN
Bear Creek Golf Range
for Year Ending December 31, 1993

	Planned	*Actual*
Sources of Net Working Capital		
Net income	$ 50,000	($ 24,942)
Depreciation	500	500
Long-term debt	240,000	240,000
Owner/manager input (Shay)	100,000	100,000
Partner input (Patton)	100,000	100,000
Total sources	$ 490,500	$ 415,558
Applications of Net Working Capital		
Procurement of land	$ 180,000	$ 180,000
Land clearing	10,000	12,000
Installation of electricity	5,000	5,790
Installation of water main, pipes	4,000	4,200
Auto parking area (paved)	18,750	5,400
Construction of building	165,000	75,000
Fairway construction (grading, etc.)	30,000	40,000
Toilet and septic tank	9,500	2,000
Lights for night play	8,000	8,450
Practice putting green	10,000	0
Equipment	20,000	22,000
Signs	12,800	4,250
Awning	3,000	0
Landscaping (trees, shrubs, fencing)	13,500	2,000
Drainage system (additional)	0	40,000
Total applications	$ 489,550	$ 401,090
Increase in net working capital	$ 950	$ 14,468

The other two driving ranges, the Hit 'Em Out Range and the Discount Driving Range, were both minimum operations. They were cleared fields with some crude hitting areas, inexpensive balls and clubs, and low prices.

At various times during the summer and fall months, Dan Shay and/or one of his employees would scout the competitors to observe their levels of business activity. On the basis of these observations, Dan was able to develop some estimates of the hitting area usage and the market shares for the five golf ranges in his market area. Exhibit 3 presents a summary of these business activity estimates and a review of the facilities and services offered by each of the driving ranges.

Pricing.   Dan noted that price elasticity in the golf range business varied with the kind of golfing customer. Serious golfers tended to be less price-sensitive and more willing to pay a higher price if the facilities and instruction were superior. The frequent golfers were more price-conscious, yet they too were influenced by the quality of the facilities. Occasional golfers were unpredictable. Some were interested primarily in hitting as many balls as possible for the lowest price. They were not particularly concerned with the quality of the range, the equipment, or the balls. Other recreational golfers were

EXHIBIT 3   **Area Golf Ranges**

	Greenbrier	Golfarama	Bear Creek	Hit 'Em Out	Discount
Total number of tees	40	30	35	24	20
Tees available for lessons	6	—	6	—	—
Price per bucket balls	$7.50/100	$6.00/100	$6.50/90	$4/100	$4/100
Individual lessons* (3/4 hr.)	$25	—	$60	—	—
Group lessons† (3–6)	$15	—	$20	—	—
Paved parking	yes	yes	gravel	dirt	gravel
Putting green	yes	—	—	—	—
Covered hitting area	yes	yes	—	—	—
Pitch and putt	—	yes	—	—	—
Miniature golf	—	yes	—	—	—
Golf equipment and supplies	yes	yes	will order	—	—
Restaurant	—	yes	—	—	—
Snack bar	yes	yes	—	—	—
Vending machines	yes	yes	yes	yes	yes
Video games	—	yes	—	—	—
Club cleaning and repair	yes	—	yes	—	—
Usage rate‡	35%	33%	20%	25%	25%

*The cost of lessons includes balls and video analysis.

†The cost of lessons includes balls.

‡Usage rate was determined by noting the number of hitting areas in use at a given time as a percentage of the total number of hitting areas in the range. Hourly counts of golfers were recorded for days, evenings, and weekends to determine patterns of play and percentage of use.

willing to pay higher prices if the surroundings provided a variety of entertainment opportunities.

Each of the driving ranges used different pricing approaches to differentiate themselves from the others and promote higher usage. They sold different sizes of buckets of balls at the following prices:

Bear Creek	$2.75 for 30	$4.50 for 60	$6.50 for 90	$10.50 for 150
Greenbrier	$4.50 for 50	$6.00 for 75	$7.50 for 100	
Golfarama	$4.00 for 50		$6.00 for 100	(2 for 1 specials)
Hit 'Em Out	$2.50 for 50		$4.00 for 100	
Discount	$2.50 for 50		$4.00 for 100	

All the ranges provided golf clubs for their customers, and the quality of the clubs varied significantly. Bear Creek provided premium irons (3, 5, and 7 irons) for both men and women. It did not provide woods (drivers) because of the cost of repairs when they were misused by inexperienced golfers. Most serious golfers brought their own clubs (irons and woods), and so this was not much of a problem for Bear Creek. Greenbrier followed a similar policy but had a limited amount of woods available. The other ranges provided irons and woods that were of an inferior grade. These ranges reasoned that their customers were not as concerned with the quality of the clubs and balls as they were with the entertainment value of driving the balls as far as possible. Both Bear Creek and Greenbrier used high-quality, durable (premium) golf balls. These balls were of higher quality and cost than those normally used on golf courses. The other ranges tended to use seconds and used balls, which were considerably less expensive.

The pricing of golfing instruction presented a different situation. Many serious golfers were inclined to shop around for an instructor whose style produced "winning golfers." The price for golfing lessons related directly to the reputation and success record of the instructor. Experienced teachers and golf course pros set their prices in line with the value of the service they provided. A few highly respected pros charged as much as $100 to $200 per 3/4-hour instruction session. With Dan's background on the tour and recognized teaching success, he felt comfortable charging $60 per 3/4 hour. This was higher than the $30 to $40 charged by most of the golf course pros in the area and more than the $25 per 3/4 of an hour charged by the two instructors at the Greenbrier Range. The other three ranges did not have instructors on site but could make arrangements to have an instructor available by appointment.

The First Year (1993)

By the end of October 1992 Dan and George had completed the arrangements to purchase the property and were ready to proceed with their building plans. Their schedule called for them to complete the land preparations (clearing, grading, seeding, fencing, etc.) during November and December. The hitting areas, fairway, greens, clubhouse facilities, and parking area were to be completed during January and February. They hoped to have their work completed by the end of the off-season and the driving range ready to operate by March 1, the beginning of the busy golfing season. This would give them 10 business months to operate. They did not believe that the abbreviated year was a negative factor as most of the golf courses and driving ranges were inactive during the off-season months of November through February. Dan and George projected reasonable profits for the first year.

Full of optimism and naivete, the two partners set out on November 1 to launch the new business. Almost immediately they ran into difficulty getting the necessary clearances from the local planning board. Complications in the application led to delays in processing the papers. However, a potential delay of two months was reduced to three weeks with a timely $500 contribution to the political campaign fund of one of the planning board's members. However, just when they thought that they were ready to proceed, the Environmental Protection Agency raised questions concerning whether putting a building on this protected floodplain area was appropriate. After several hearings and three more weeks of delay, the agency agreed that the driving range was an appropriate use of floodplain land and the clubhouse building could be built on higher ground beyond the boundaries of the floodplain area. In the middle of December, all the necessary clearances were received and work was begun. Unfortunately, the delays put them into the worst part of the winter, and weather conditions were unusually severe. As a result, land clearing was delayed and the costs of clearing and preparing the site ran almost 27 percent higher than they had originally projected. The whole project was threatened again in mid-February when it became apparent that the land preparations had disturbed an underground spring at the front of the property and water was seeping onto the access road leading to Route 183. Once again, local authorities objected and required that the owners install a culvert and drainage system to carry the water away. This unanticipated development cost them an additional $40,000.

By the targeted March 1 opening date the golf range was only partially completed. The range itself was in good shape but the building, the parking lot, and the landscaping had not been started. At this point it was painfully obvious to the owners that they were running out of money to complete their dream. They did not have adequate financial resources to complete the facility as planned. If they delayed much longer, they would be so late in opening that they would suffer significant revenue losses. Faced with the cash squeeze and the impact of further delays on their revenues, the owners decided to take some emergency steps to get the facility opened by May 1. They determined that they could not afford to build the permanent clubhouse that they had originally envisioned. However, they were fortunate in locating a portable classroom building which they were able to transport to the site and refurbish to meet their immediate needs (see Exhibit 4). This resulted in considerable savings. They also decided to go with a gravel parking area instead of the paved one, minimal exterior landscaping, and a more modest sign. The snack bar, the practice putting green, and the awning were put on hold, and they decided to have outdoor portable toilets for the immediate future. Although he was disappointed at not being able to start out with their dream facility, Dan believed that most of the necessary changes had been in areas that he considered "cosmetic." The range, the hitting areas, the equipment, and the services were all in place to meet the primary requirements of their prospective golfing customers.

On May 1, Bear Creek Driving Range finally opened for business. Dan assumed responsibility as manager and instructor. He hired an assistant inside manager and three employees to work outside on maintenance tasks (ball collecting, lawn cutting, cleanup, etc.). In June he hired a college student on a part-time basis to assist him with customer service, administrative details, and paperwork. Dan half-seriously introduced his new employee as "Martha Rawls, my new vice president of marketing."

EXHIBIT 4   Bear Creek Shop Layout

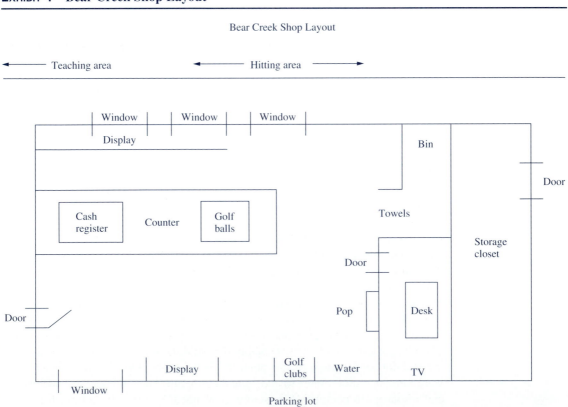

Bear Creek Shop Layout

By the first of September, Bear Creek was not doing the business that the partners had envisioned when they laid out their business plan for the year. Although a fair number of customers were finding the range, there were not enough of them to generate a positive cash flow. It was not unusual to see most of the 35 hitting areas unoccupied. According to Dan's calculations, the range needed a 33 percent usage rate during the summer months to break even for the year. This usage rate called for an average daily rate of 105 customers. (This assumes that the typical customer hits 90 balls and takes a little less than an hour to do so.) Bear Creek's actual usage rate during the year was closer to 20 percent. What was most disturbing to Dan was the apparent disparity between his usage rate and that of his two major competitors. While there were no formal data available on the usage rates of the driving ranges, Dan had developed a way of monitoring his competitors to observe their business activity. Using a system devised by his college student, Martha, the activity rates (percentage of hitting areas being used) were recorded for each of the competitors at various times during the week. On the basis of these observations, Dan could conclude that his range was capturing a significantly smaller share of the business than his competitors were. According to these calculations, Dan's in-season usage rate was 20 percent compared to 35 percent for Greenbrier, 33 percent for Golfarama, and a surprising 25 percent for each of the two discount ranges. Although the methodology was crude, the result was clear. Bear Creek Driving Range was not capturing its fair share of the business in spite of its new facilities and professional orientation.

Dan began to think more about his customers. As he had anticipated, many of them were serious golfers who came because they knew about Dan and his golfing know-how. In discussions with these customers, several of them observed that they liked the easy, informal atmosphere of the place but missed some of the amenities, such as telephones, indoor plumbing, snacks, and a lounge area. Although most of these serious golfers were members of local golf courses, they chose to come to Bear Creek because of its convenient location, first-class hitting areas and fairway, excellent instruction, and privacy. Not surprisingly, a high proportion of these customers used their own clubs. In her scouting trips, Martha noted that the golfers at the other ranges were more apt to use clubs provided by the driving range.

As the summer progressed, Dan began to question one of his earlier decisions in relation to advertising and promotion expenditures. Caught up in the financial squeeze, the partners decided that they could not afford to allocate scarce dollars for advertisements in local papers or in the *Par Fore* or *North Texas Golfer* magazines. However, they did purchase a listing in the local *Yellow Pages*. Both of their competitors advertised in local papers and in the trade journals, offering coupons and specials (two-for-one offers). Dan was not convinced that aggressive advertising and couponing was the way to attract the kind of customers they were seeking. Up until this time he had felt that word-of-mouth advertising would be sufficient for attracting serious golfers to Bear Creek. Now he wasn't so sure. He wondered if their emphasis on and preoccupation with the serious golfer segment were too limiting.

The rest of the year showed no great improvement. Bear Creek plugged along with a modest business base, but the partners were forced to seek short-term financing to get them over the hump. The usage rate averaged 20 percent for the first year instead of the desired 33 percent. No additional facilities improvements were accomplished, and this left the range without a permanent clubhouse, snack bar, pro shop, putting green, awning, or paved parking area. One bright spot had been the demand for golf lessons. Dan's excellent reputation did in fact attract customers for individual lessons and group clinics. Revenues from this source exceeded the forecasts by almost 16 percent. However, in spite of this hopeful sign, the end of the year results were discouraging, with an operating loss as of December 31 of $24,942. The loss not only placed them in a difficult financial position but also deprived them of this important source of funds which they had included in their financial development plan. As they reviewed the financial returns for the first year (Exhibits 5 and 6), the partners were anxious for ideas to improve their operations and customer usage rate.

The Market Study

Dan referred to his part-time employee, Martha Rawls, as his "marketing vice president," and he was quite serious about calling on Martha to assist him in strengthening the marketing aspects of the business. As a marketing major and a member of the women's golf team at the University of Texas, Arlington, Martha was willing to help Dan gain a better understanding of the golf range market in the Dallas/Fort Worth area. She was even able to conduct a market study as part of a project in one of her marketing courses in the fall semester. Upon reviewing Martha's study, Dan noted the following relevant facts and figures concerning the golfing industry and the local market situation:

The Industry
- The golfing industry as a whole (golf, golf equipment, instruction, club repair, soft goods merchandising, playing facilities, practice facilities, etc.) was a $42 billion business.
- There were 24.8 million golfers in the country, and the market was growing at a rate of approximately 3 percent per year.
- Women constituted the fastest-growing segment of the market and accounted for 5.4 million of the 24.8 million total. Women made up 37 percent of beginner golfers, up from 23 percent in 1983. The female golfer spent about $1,789 per year on the sport, about $100 more than her male counterpart.

The Dallas/Fort Worth Area
- The total population of the Dallas/Fort Worth area was 3,855,415. The population in the 10-mile radius that constituted the Bear Creek market area was 777,082. Seventy percent were adults (16 years old or over).
- There were eight private golf courses and seven public courses in the market area.
- The average membership at a private club was approximately 1,500, with 80 percent being family memberships with an average of four golfers per family unit.
- The number of individual golfers using each of the public golf courses (at one time or another during the year) was estimated to be 13,500.
- Because of the excellent climate and the long season, golf was a very popular form of recreation in the Dallas/Fort Worth area. It was estimated that 25 percent of the adult population played golf with varying frequencies during the year. In addition, a sizable and growing number of nongolfers enjoyed the sport of hitting balls for recreation at local driving ranges.
- There was an increasing interest on the part of young adults (age 16 to 36) in sports-related recreational activities. This included attendance at sporting events (Dallas Cowboys, etc.), participation in sports activities (team sports, video games, baseball hitting machines, golf ranges, etc.), and socializing at sports bars and clubs featuring large-screen television and other sports-centered entertainment. This sports segment was spending significant dollars on various sports-related activities. However, problems sometimes developed with this younger group when alcohol and exuberance combined to produce unruly behavior.

EXHIBIT 5

INCOME STATEMENT
Bear Creek Golf Range
December 31, 1993

	Pro Forma	Actual
Income		
Range ball revenue	$ 190,000	$ 124,900
Lessons	47,280	54,660
Merchandise	24,000	17,609
Club repair	5,000	5,400
Food and beverages	35,000	3,705
Total income	$ 301,270	$ 206,274
Expense		
Cost of Sales		
Merchandise	10,000	16,750
Repair supplies	3,250	3,530
Food and beverages	16,000	1,950
Total cost of sales	$ 29,250	$ 22,230
Payroll		
Salaries	60,000	60,000
Hourly wages	52,000	49,144
Total payroll	$ 112,000	$ 109,144
Range Expenses		
Range balls	6,000	6,200
Equipment	2,500	2,350
Fertilizer, seed, chemicals	15,000	11,490
Total range expenses	$ 23,500	$ 20,040
Operating Expenses		
Office expenses and supplies	3,000	2,520
Utilities	3,000	2,412
Telephone	4,000	3,328
Auto and truck expense	7,000	7,275
Depreciation and amortization	5,050	5,050
Insurance and liability	7,500	6,012
Irrigation	0	1,350
Legal and accounting	3,500	3,875
Postage and freight	500	630
Sales taxes, other taxes	3,000	1,360
Advertising and promotion	5,000	800
Miscellaneous	1,400	1,430
Total operating expense	$ 42,950	$ 36,042
Professional Expenses		
Dues, education, fees	3,000	3,212
Travel, entertainment, lunches	4,000	4,237
Total professional expense	$ 7,000	$ 7,449
Interest	36,000	36,311
Total expense	$ 250,700	$ 231,216
Profit/Loss (before income tax)	$ 50,570	$ (24,942)

EXHIBIT 6

BALANCE SHEET
Bear Creek Golf Range
December 31, 1993

	Pro Forma	Actual
Assets		
Current Assets		
Cash	$ 4,000	$ 3,217
Accounts receivable	3,220	6,451
Prepaid interest	0	472
Total Current Assets	$ 7,200	$ 10,140
Fixed Assets		
Land	$ 180,000	$ 180,000
Improvements	57,000	70,440
Building	174,500	77,000
Parking area	18,750	5,400
Practice green	10,000	0
Equipment	20,000	22,000
Other fixed assets	29,300	46,250
Total Fixed Assets	$ 489,550	$ 401,090
Total Assets	$ 496,770	$ 411,230
Liabilities and Net Worth		
Liabilities		
Current liabilities		
Accounts payable	$ 4,000	$ 4,472
Accrued taxes	2,000	250
Expenses payable	0	1,000
Total Current Liabilities	$ 6,000	$ 5,722
Long-term liabilities		
Bank loans	$ 240,000	$ 230,450
Total long-term liabilities	$ 240,000	$ 230,450
Total Liabilities	$ 246,000	$ 236,172
Net Worth		
Shay, capital	$ 100,000	$ 100,000
Patton, capital	100,000	100,000
Retained earnings	50,770	(24,942)
Total Net Worth	$ 250,770	$ 175,058
Total Liabilities and Equity	$ 496,770	$ 411,230

Market Segments. In her study of the golf market, Martha identified and described the major segments as follows:

1. **Serious golfers:** Serious golfers were those who played frequently (25 or more rounds per year), generally belonged to private clubs, had low handicaps, used premium equipment, and played to win. They enjoyed the game for its competitive aspects and enjoyed it more if there was money on the line ("$10 Nassau," "Skins," "Birdies," "Sandies," "Greenies," etc.). Serious golfers wanted to be the best. They practiced and took lessons if they thought it would

help them improve their games. Money was not an obstacle. Serious golfers accounted for approximately 9 percent of the total golfing population.

2. **Frequent golfers:** Frequent golfers enjoyed the game, played when possible (between 7 and 24 times per year), had respectable handicaps, might have belonged to private clubs or played at public courses, and played to win. They would play more often if business and/or personal circumstances allowed it and often combined business with golf. They enjoyed the camaraderie and worked to improve their games. They also took lessons. Frequent golfers accounted for 29 percent of the golfing population.

3. **Occasional golfers:** Occasional golfers played when invited to do so (between one and six times per year). They enjoyed the game but were not usually skilled players. They would play more often if time and economic circumstances permitted it. Typically, occasional golfers played on public courses or as guests at private courses. They would have liked to be able to play more often and more skillfully but were not likely to take lessons. They described themselves as recreational golfers rather than serious golfers. Occasional golfers made up 62 percent of the total golfing population.

Martha considered other ways to segment the market by focusing on characteristics other than "frequency of play." She considered the "Women's Golf Segment," which was the fastest growing segment, at 5.4 million players. She learned that the profile of a woman golfer was age 43, four years of college, $60,000 annual earnings, and married with no children living at home. One-third were members of a golf facility. Private clubs were changing their rules to allow equal playing opportunities for women members.

Martha identified another significant segment that she identified as the "Learners Segment." Each year a significant number of newcomers joined the golfing community. New golfers included young players, females, retired people, and midlifers who enjoyed exercising. Learners often were confronted with confidence problems as they struggled to master the game. They were good candidates for lessons in group or individual instruction sessions. Many were interested in learning the rules of the game (golfing etiquette) as well as the skills.

Finally, Martha considered a less obvious segment composed of "Wanabee Golfers" or "Entertainment Golfers." This growing segment included persons who did not have the skills or the economic status to be golfing regulars. Nevertheless, they saw and heard about golf often and enjoyed an occasional opportunity to play the game. They played for fun. For this aspirational group, driving ranges, miniature golf games, pitch-and-putt facilities, and video games offered opportunities that were both economical and enjoyable.

Martha's research indicated that the competitors were active in marketing their ranges to the various markets. Greenbrier advertised periodically in the *Par Fore* and *North Texas Golfer* publications, featuring its up-to-date facilities and excellent instructional services and equipment. Golfarama appeared regularly in the daily and weekly newspapers with its special promotions (two-for-one offerings). It aimed specifically at the recreational market, emphasizing in its ads the variety of entertainment opportunities at the center, "the place to come for Sports Entertainment." The discount ranges mainly featured their low prices in their ads.

Martha learned that the costs for advertising in the local media were not unreasonable. A quarter-page ad in the *Yellow Pages* cost $110 per month. The local golf magazines charged $150 per weekly issue, and the daily newspapers ran between $50 and $100 per insertion, depending on ad size and frequency.

Business Operations. In her review of the local golf range market, Martha noted that local weather conditions permitted outside activities for most of the year, but for all practical purposes, the driving range "season" ran from March 1 through October 31. Most area ranges closed during the four-month off-season. In this first year, however, Dan decided to remain open during the off-season to try to make up some of the business lost due to the delayed opening in the spring. Success in this business depended on making the numbers in the eight-month period. During the season, Bear Creek, like the other ranges in the area, was open 11 hours a day (10:00 am to 9:00 pm). During the week business was slow during the daytime hours and picked up after 5:00 pm. Saturdays and Sundays were the busiest for both range business and lessons. It was not unusual during June and July to have all 35 hitting areas in use on evenings and on weekends. On good days, the range had 100 to 150 customers. However, according to Dan's daily records, the range averaged closer to 75 customers per day over the six-month period and 10 per day in the off-season.

Martha was concerned about the low customer traffic during the weekday daytime hours. Although this was understandable, she pointed out the importance of building more off-hour business. She suggested various ways to attract customers to the range during these daytime hours, including off-hour pricing, introductory offers, special group rates for high school and college golf teams, discount prices for learner clinics, coupons for visitors staying at local hotels and motels in the airport area, and other promotional devices designed to introduce customers to the range. Overall, Martha's report to the partners showed that the market was healthy and growing but that Bear Creek was not exploiting the opportunities that were there.

Reconsideration of Strategy

After reviewing Martha's data and the disappointing results from their first year's business, the Bear Creek partners met to discuss possible ways to increase the number of golfing customers to accomplish their targeted 33 percent usage rate.

Dan was experiencing some misgivings concerning the practice and instructional focus of the range. Although the majority of serious golfers were members of private golf courses that had their own practice ranges and professional instructors, Dan was convinced that many of these golfers would be attracted to a practice range that offered high-quality facilities, a convenient location, and a congenial golfing milieu. He believed that his reputation as a top-flight teacher would attract people to the range for lessons and advice. He thought that would encourage these customers to use the range for their regular practice sessions. This idea was working to some extent, but it was not generating enough customers to accomplish Dan's objectives. Dan and George realized that the shortened six-month year had accounted for some of their customer shortfall. They were confident that things would improve with a full year of operation and with further easing of the recession. They also felt that business would improve as their existing customers spread the word about their practice range.

In terms of their financial constraints, they were inclined to postpone further range improvements pending the results of the second year. However, they were concerned that customers were turned off by the unfinished facilities. They were further concerned that they might be overlooking the recreational golfers, a significant, high-spending segment of the market. Keeping in mind that this segment was attracted by such additional activities as miniature golf, pitch and putt, video games, and sports bars, the partners gave some thought to expanding their operation to include some of those attractions. The opportunity was available to them because the 10-acre adjoining piece of property was offered to them on a 10-year lease/buy arrangement. The partners believed that these additional facilities would bring in more customers, but they still wondered if this was the kind of customer they wished to attract.

Time for Action. It was now January 1994, and Martha Rawls knew that Dan and his partner were looking forward to her recommendations concerning the marketing strategy for the coming year and the years ahead. As she reviewed her experience working at Bear Creek Golf Range and the information she had collected, she felt that the future survival and success of the business depended largely on the implementation of a sound marketing program. This program would identify the appropriate market segments to explore, determine the needs and behavior of the golfing customers in those markets, and weigh various alternatives (product/service offerings, pricing tactics, and promotional programs) for responding to the needs of the target markets. As she learned in her marketing courses, Martha needed to provide a sound analysis of the situation as a basis for evaluating the options and supporting her recommendations. Her resulting recommended marketing strategy should include a full description of the marketing strategy, its objectives, necessary changes, and specific action steps for carrying it out.

CASE 1–8
SUN'S BID TO RULE THE WEB

Late last June, Sun Microsystems Inc. President Edward Zander got the kind of call every tech executive dreads. After eBay Inc. suffered a 22-hour outage of its Web site and a spate of smaller crashes, CEO Margaret Whitman called to tell Zander that the problem was a bug in Sun's top-of-the-line server. Sun would learn something just as startling over the next few days of round-the-clock meetings with eBay: The Internet upstart didn't have a clue about running a $1 million-plus computer. The company hadn't provided sufficient air conditioning to keep the machine cool. And even though there had been a software problem with the machine for which Sun had issued a patch many months before, eBay had simply neglected to install it. The list went on—fueling the sentiment, as one Sun manager put it, that "selling computers to some of these dot-coms is like giving a gun to a 5-year-old."

That's when Zander realized things could get much worse. For most dot-coms, starting their business on a Sun server is almost a given. Already, more than 40% of the servers found in the computing centers that house most Web sites are Sun's, and that market is expected to boom as everyone from new Net companies to the click-and-mortar crowd set up shop online. "It suddenly hit me," says Zander. "How many future eBays are buying their first computer from us this very minute?" Adds Sun CEO Scott G. McNealy: "It was our Pentium moment," comparing the eBay incident to the lesson Intel Corp. learned in 1994 after the chip giant angered customers by initially trying to downplay a bug in its new Pentium chip. "That's when we realized it wasn't eBay's fault," says McNealy. "It was our fault."

McNealy and Zander didn't need another wake-up call. Since then, the two have been tearing apart Sun and rebuilding it in an effort to make the Net as reliable as the telephone system. Just as AT&T became Ma Bell, providing that always available dial tone, Sun is shooting for no less than Ma Web, the supplier of super-reliable Web tone. To do that, Sun is moving far beyond Web servers to providing many of the technologies required to make this possible: storage products, a vast array of e-business software, and consultants that not only supply all the gear but also hold customers' hands every step of the way (Exhibit 1).

Safe Bet

If the duo can pull it off, Sun could emerge as the King of the Net—every bit as dominant as Big Blue in its mainframe heyday or Microsoft Corp. in the PC era. Just as high-tech managers used to say, "No one gets fired for choosing IBM," Zander aims to have the same said of Sun. "I want to be the safe bet for companies that need the most innovative technology," he says.

Sun hopes to go down in the history books as that rare company with the vision to change an industry and the ability to cash in on that vision. Since it was founded in 1982, Sun has promoted the notion that "the network is the computer," a view of computing where the action isn't on desktop PCs but on big central servers where computing can be doled out in easy-to-use chunks, wherever and whenever desired. With the

EXHIBIT 1   The Net Effect

Almost from its founding in 1982, Sun has pursued a vision in which computing power resides on huge servers, whisking data and other services to PCs, handheld gadgets, and other devices. Thanks to the Web, Sun's vision is becoming reality. So Sun is honing its strategy, management techniques, and technology to become the dominant computer company in the Internet Age.

Strategy

Redefine Net Software: Today, hundreds of niche software outfits hawk a mind-numbing patchwork of applications. Sun wants to create a new category of software that combines many Net programs into one super-reliable whole that's included with its server.

As Reliable as the Phone Network: Sun is moving beyond just hardware to offer pretested configurations that include storage, Net software, and popular applications. That's how telco switchmakers like Lucent and Nortel managed to make the phone network fail-safe.

Lock Up the Service Providers: Having guessed right that software would be delivered over the Net rather than as CDs to be installed on PCs, Sun has the early lead with companies that will deliver the software—from Net newbies to huge telcos.

Management

Central Authority: On July 1, Sun created into one uber-sales operation, rather than fiercely independent server, software, chip, and services units. That way, customers can deal with one salesman. More important, engineers are working together to design resilient systems by making sure, for example, that Net software can detect chip or disk-drive failures.

No More Cowboys: Sun has been known as the freewheeling cowboy of the computer business. Now it's adding big-company processes—such as extensive audits of a customer's tech operations before taking the order.

Technology

The Grand Design: Sun is the architect of some of the sexier elements of the Web, such as its Java Net software. Now engineers are focusing on keeping the Net running all the time—like how to build backup systems to avoid failures in chips, servers, software, and networks.

Pay-as-You-Grow: Sun is working on hardware and software components that allow fast-growing customers to add what they need without ever having to scrap old equipment.

The Storage Is the Network: New VCR-sized storage devices that can be located anywhere on the Net—instead of just in central data centers—putting information closer to users.

Leadership

Forging Industry Standards: With Java a Net standard, Sun continues to push its Jini technology, which promises to let any digital device talk to any other. That way, your browser-equipped cell phone could print on any nearby Jini-ready printer.

Setting Ground Rules: Not all Net companies know how to operate around the clock. So Sun has a program to lay out best practices, from how to ensure backup to how to prevent data centers from becoming overheated. Some 300 companies have qualified for this stamp of approval of the Net Age.

---

explosion of the Internet and rapid deployment of high-bandwidth networks, Sun's vision finally is becoming a reality. "McNealy held out for the pot of gold," says Bill Raduchel, a former Sun executive who is now chief technologist at America Online Inc. "It took a decade to play out, but now the pot of gold is here."

That's why Sun has been on a tear. In the most recent quarter, revenue climbed 35%—more than any other computer company, including PC darling Dell Computer Corp., which grew 30%. Sun is growing faster than at any time since 1991, when it was one-fifth the size it is today. And with gross profit margins of 52%, it is the most profitable computer maker in all of techdom.

McNealy vows this is just the beginning. Known for having the strategic vision, slickest sales reps, and hottest new products—but not the best service—Sun has made reliability the top priority. That means pumping up the services business and overhauling the way the company designs and sells its products. In the past year, Sun has reduced the number of configurations it sells from thousands by pushing customers to choose from under 200 models. And now, managers and sales reps are compensated largely on customer satisfaction. What's more, McNealy, a sometime golfing buddy of General Electric Co. Chairman John F. Welch, has become a convert of GE's Six Sigma quality program that builds in checks to make sure customers' operations stay up and running. By far, the boldest element of McNealy's plan is software. Sun is trying to define and dominate a new category of software that combines many of today's e-business software segments, including e-mail, e-commerce portals, and programs for serving up Web pages and wireless applications. The idea: Wrap a suite of applications into one fail-safe whole available on any Sun server. On July 17, iPlanet, Sun's Net software joint venture formed with AOL last year, unveiled the new suite, along with an audacious goal: Within 18 months, the company expects to hit the $1 billion mark in e-commerce software sales, according to Margaret Breya, iPlanet's vice-president of marketing. By 2005, she says Sun could have a $5 billion to $10 billion software business. Other executives, however, say it may take a buying binge to get there.

Put it all together, and Sun is designing its own take on an old trend: vertical integration, in which it sells software, hardware, and services as one—just like telecom equipment makers Lucent Technologies or Nortel Networks Corp. do with their phone switches. "The computing model of tomorrow is the telecom model of today," says Masood Jabbar, Sun's senior vice-president of sales. How does Sun fit in? It plans to make the "big frigging Webtone switches," as McNealy calls them—the powerful servers that can whisk billions of bits around the Net, along with the software that manages Web pages, dishes up data, and executes transactions. "The world's moving in our direction at 8 gazillion miles per hour. Our biggest problem is just trying to keep up," says McNealy.

That's why he has lit a bonfire under Sun. After the eBay incident, Zander called a meeting of all managers and read them the riot act. Late last summer, his staff identified 14 key initiatives, such as new processes for conducting customer audits, with one of Zander's top vice-presidents in charge of each. And on July 1, McNealy reorganized Sun, combining fiercely independent sales operations within product units into one single sales organization. Now, customers see one sales rep for their entire business, instead of being bombarded by reps from different divisions. And McNealy has created a Customer Advocacy Organization to make sure all divisions are putting reliability and customer satisfaction first. Division president Mel Friedman, for instance, has authority to request the redesign of any Sun product for suspected glitches. Says Breya: "It's about Sun growing up."

As we all know, though, growing up is hard to do. For Sun to shake off its upstart ways, it will have to make the shift from an engineering-driven company to a full-service company. That means mastering software sales, a historic weakness, and building up consulting to help companies design their e-business around Sun gear. And it must do all this while holding off heavyweights such as IBM and Hewlett-Packard. The stalwarts may have been slow to grok the Net, but they have a legacy of ultra-dependable products that could be a major advantage. "Sun rode the wave of dot-coms, but those companies have different needs now. And taking care of those needs is IBM's and HP's forte, not Sun's," says Bruce L. Chovnick, senior vice-president at Network Solutions, a Web registry company that recently ditched a Sun high-end server for a mainframe from IBM.

McNealy will have to stare down other challengers, as well. At a time when servers based on Sun's new UltraSparc3 chip are a few months late, longtime PC industry rivals are massing for yet another assault on the server market. Using Microsoft's four-month-old Windows 2000 program or the free Linux operating system, PC makers will continue to chip away at the market for less powerful servers—especially after Intel brings out its new IA-64 chips, due by year end. "Customers are willing to pay high prices and go with the safe bet [Sun] in these early days of the Net. But ultimately, we'll be able to redefine the economics of the Internet," says Compaq Computer Corp. CEO Michael D. Capellas. Adds International Data Corp. analyst Jean S. Bozman: "Everyone is shooting at Sun, there's no question about it."

The company with the most ammunition is Microsoft. On June 22, Microsoft announced its version of Sun's Webtone scheme—an initiative dubbed .net that is designed to make the Web much easier to use. In it, unrelated Web sites, Net services, and traditional Windows software programs can be linked together to do useful things—say, to get your bank's Web site to transfer money to your e-broker, who buys a stock and then records the trade to your Microsoft Money program on your PC. Such complexity requires software expertise, snorts Microsoft CEO Steve A. Ballmer, "and Sun's not really a software company." Counters Sun chief scientist Bill Joy: "I've been writing about network-based computing for 20 years. Microsoft embraced it last week."

Sniping aside, Sun faces even more software challenges. Throw into the mix programs such as Napster that make it easy to link files directly from PC to PC, altogether bypassing huge servers, and some analysts think McNealy & Co. could face a resurgence of powerful PCs that can store and move data around the Net. That could put a squeeze on server profits. Sanford C. Bernstein & Co. analyst Toni Sacconaghi thinks profit margins for Sun's servers could fall from the mid-50s to the low-30s within three years. So it's crucial that Sun crank up sales of hugely profitable software and storage products, with gross profit margins of 80% and 60%, respectively.

Only then can Sun continue to fund its $2 billion research-and-development effort and keep spending at an industry-leading rate of 10% of revenue. If it can't, Sun may find itself boxed into a high-end corner of the computer industry, adding to the list of once proud computer companies such as Digital Equipment Corp. that have been whittled away by PC makers.

Sun has managed to outfox the doomsayers before. In the early 1990s, when profits collapsed for the technical workstations that brought in 90% of the company's revenue, McNealy bet the next big opportunity would be servers. He poured billions into developing technologies such as the Solaris operating system. Now, servers and related gear bring roughly 80% of Sun's $11.7 billion in sales. Even more remarkable is Sun's assault on the high-end server market once dominated by IBM mainframes. While the market for $1 million-plus servers shrank 17.8% last year, to $11.4 billion, Sun's revenue has rocketed 28% because of runaway sales of its e10,000 Starfire machines, according to IDC (Exhibit 2).

Unlike high-tech dynasties such as IBM or Microsoft, Sun's grand plan is not based on locking customers into its own proprietary technology. IBM and Microsoft modulated the flow of new technology in the mainframe and PC eras largely by maintaining control of technical interfaces that others would need to create compatible programs and peripherals. But Sun wants to dominate Internet-style—that is, by doing as much innovation as possible, licensing leading-edge work as the standard for others, and then racing to stay ahead.

That puts the pressure on Sun's big thinkers, like Joy (Exhibit 3). For starters, Joy and Sun's other technologists have coined the term "Net Effects" to describe the challenge of keeping up with spiraling demand as a billion people use the Net more often, from more devices, and in different ways over the next few years. To keep pace, Sun's servers will have to accelerate in power at a rate at least 100 times faster than Moore's

EXHIBIT 2

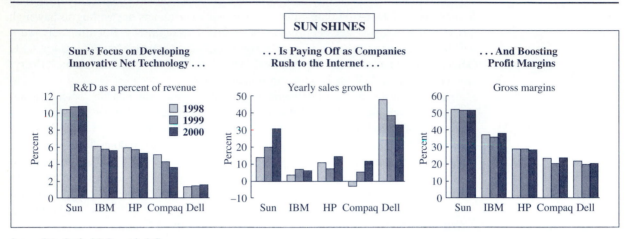

SUN SHINES

Sun's Focus on Developing Innovative Net Technology . . .

R&D as a percent of revenue

. . . Is Paying Off as Companies Rush to the Internet . . .

Yearly sales growth

. . . And Boosting Profit Margins

Gross margins

Source: Data; Sanford C. Bernstein & Co.

Law, which holds that chips double in speed every 18 months, says Sun chief technologist Greg Popadopolous. Sun is working on two tracks—massive single machines with millions of microprocessors, as well as distributed computing schemes so the computing load can be divvied up between smaller machines linked by high-speed networks.

Sun also is betting it can leapfrog the competition by giving customers the essential software they need to run their e-businesses in one neat, foolproof package. Today, companies face a blizzard of offerings—application servers to host and handle e-mail, Web servers to manage and send out Web pages, and portal programs on which to give the sites a unique look and feel. While these stand-alone software products may deliver the latest bells and whistles, it costs a fortune in consulting fees to make them work together.

Sun's approach is different. iPlanet packs snazzy programs into a suite known as the Internet Service Deployment Platform. Don't be fooled by the clunky name. Using this suite, customers can get up and running quickly because Sun has made sure the software works in sync. With the price starting at $500,000, Sun isn't looking to undercut the competition. Instead, customers will save on installation. "This could cut my development time by 30%," says Norbert Nowicki, a senior partner with Computer Sciences Corp., an El Segundo (Calif.) computer services consultancy.

Sun isn't the only company offering such a suite. Oracle, IBM, and Microsoft do, as well. But none of those companies is the dominant provider of the computers on which the software must run. "Sun isn't just dragging the software along anymore," says Goldman, Sachs & Co. analyst Laura Conigliaro. "It can be a serious driver of new business." Especially with partner AOL using the software suite internally and promoting it to its Net customers. "AOL is customer No. 1 for iPlanet," says David Gang, an AOL executive who recently became iPlanet's executive vice-president. "If we can build products that satisfy AOL, it should work for everyone else."

The irony of McNealy's software approach is that he's stealing a page from the Microsoft playbook—a twist on Microsoft's "embrace and extend" strategy of absorbing fresh technologies into its Windows software. Instead, Sun wants to either bundle or weave Net software into its Solaris operating system. The process already has begun. While competition used to be fierce in the market for arcane directory software, where companies store their databases of employees, customers, and suppliers, now Sun dominates because it has embedded directory software into the latest version of Solaris. "This could be every bit as big as Oracle's [$7.4 billion database] business," says Mark Tolliver, general manager of iPlanet.

In recent months, the company has made a push into hot new areas, such as a wireless server that will go head-to-head with IBM and others, and e-commerce and e-marketplace applications that will compete with offerings from Commerce One, Oracle, and others. And while iPlanet doesn't have a product to rival red-hot programs like Vignette's software for managing Web pages, Sun may develop offerings in this niche or buy the pieces necessary to offer it. "With our stock where it is, we'd be remiss if we didn't look at this," says Jonathan Schwartz, recently named Sun vice-president for corporate strategy.

Storage Breakthrough

One area where Sun hasn't been able to get off the ground is storage. The company has made two failed attempts to introduce new products in the last three years. "This business takes focus, but storage was an afterthought for Sun," says Raduchel. No more.

EXHIBIT 3   The Joy of Questioning

It was a bona fide mood killer. On May 15, the 100 or so chief technology officers at San Francisco's Palace Hotel were flying high. They spent the morning at a high-tech conference getting jazzed about how they could help their companies cash in on the limitless wealth-making potential of the Internet. Then Bill Joy took the stage. The Sun Microsystems Inc. chief scientist used his lunchtime keynote to lay out his view of technology: He fears that rapid high-tech advances could lead to man-made electronic and biological scourges—and the possible extinction of the human race by mid-century. For most of the speech, the audience sat in respectful silence. Then Joy gave a sense of what the future could hold by reading a long description of a horrific plague that wiped out much of medieval Greece. Nervous chuckles began to break the uncomfortable silence.

Joy is a surprising candidate to be making such dire warnings. After all, he has helped shape Sun's vision of superfast computers zipping all manner of digital transactions along the Net. And, he admits, it's computers from Sun and others that will make possible the scientific advances he fears. Still, no one at Sun is trying to talk Joy down from his high-tech bully pulpit. "The concept took me by surprise," admits Sun CEO Scott G. McNealy. "A lot of people think Bill is shooting the golden goose. But hey, I've got kids, too, and Bill's [discussing his views] in a very prudent, responsible way. He's not some lunatic. He's not a prophet of doom." Adds Melvin Schwartz, a Nobel prize winner for physics in 1988: "He's thinking about the things that should be thought about. What sounds wild today won't be in 20 to 30 years."

Indeed, Joy says he's out to shake the mindset that technology offers boundless good. Since publishing an article in *Wired* magazine last April entitled "Why the Future Doesn't Need Us," the 45-year-old Joy has been spending a third of his time on his latest concern. Discoveries in genetic engineering, robotics, and molecular-level engineering (nanotechnology) will soon make it possible for terrorists to unleash mayhem far more dangerous than the nuclear threat, he says. "These technologies are going to create a quadrillion dollars of wealth in the next century," says Joy. "But we do have to deal with the risks. The future is rushing at us at incredible speed, and people just haven't thought it through."

There have been plenty of doomsayers in the past, but few have Joy's credentials. In 1976, as a graduate student, Joy created a version of the Unix operating system that is the standard for most Web sites. In 1982, he co-founded Sun, and was a driving force behind its Java software. These days, Joy is working on new technology to make computers resistant to software bugs.

Joy is by no means turning his back on the Information Society that has made him rich. He says he's simply trying to start a debate. He suggests that companies exploring planet-threatening technologies pay high insurance premiums to discourage them from simply dabbling in such technology. Joy fears the only answer could be one that appalls scientists—including himself: put an end to the spirit of unfettered freedom of scientific inquiry. Lewis M. Branscomb, IBM's former chief scientist and a professor emeritus at Harvard University, credits Joy with raising important issues, but cautions that "once the politicians are allowed to start censoring 'dangerous knowledge,' we will lose both our democracy and our ability to understand how to manage our future." For Joy, the debate is just beginning.—*Peter Burrows*

Source: Peter Burrows, "Sun's Bid to Rule the Web," *Business Week E.Biz,* July 24, 2000, EB 31–EB 42.

Sun claims it has made a breakthrough and has created a specialized sales and support organization to push it. Never mind lining up big cabinet-size storage racks tethered to servers—the way most storage farms operate. Instead, customers put Sun's new T3 storage boxes wherever makes the most sense—without having to be within close proximity to a server. An Internet service provider, for example, could put one in a Boston office to speed Red Sox scores to the locals—regardless of whether that site uses servers from Sun or a rival. "The upside for Sun in storage is immense," says Goldman's Conigliaro, who thinks Sun's $2 billion business will grow 25% a year for the next three years. Still, in that time frame, rival EMC Corp. is expected to shoot past the $15 billion mark.

When did Sun get so serious about growing up? Rumblings began in 1998, when Sun's brain trust began to sense that customers' needs for keeping their Web sites up and running were far outstripping Sun's know-how. But for McNealy and Zander, the eBay incidents in mid-1999 underscored how fast those requirements were rising—and far behind Sun really was.

Sun sprang into action to solve eBay's problem, and within weeks, it worked out a plan with software partners Oracle and Veritas Software Corp. to stabilize eBay's server—even devising back-up systems that have kept eBay out of the news despite six or so crashes in recent months. "We were pushing Sun's products to places they'd never had to go," says eBay Chief Technology Officer Maynard Webb, who last fall nearly switched to IBM. "For Sun to still have our business is a testament to their ability to solve those issues."

Zander was worried it was more like dumb luck. He knew last-minute heroics would not be possible should eBay-like debacles become commonplace. So in early July, Zander assigned Vice-President John C. Shoemaker to come up with a set of initiatives to meet customer demand for rock-solid gear. By the end of August, after key areas for improvement were identified, Zander decided it was time to turn up the pressure inside Sun, calling for daily 8 A.M. meetings with the management team to discuss any problems at customer sites. "Scott and I decided to ruin everyone's morning," he says.

Now, all high-end systems must be pretested with the customer's software before they ship. Another team is making sure that all new products can be monitored remotely from one of Sun's data centers, finally bringing it up to speed with rivals such as EMC and IBM. Sun has also done two-day, lengthy audits of 75 top customers, sometimes issuing 100-page reports that recommend making changes such as adding a humidity sensor to ensure that atmospheric conditions are optimal for Sun equipment.

And McNealy has become a crusader for the new quality program, dubbed Sun Sigma. Now, Sun's top execs will get four days of training and will then lead teams that will get four weeks of training in Six Sigma-style practices. Any manager who doesn't lead such a team over the next 18 months, says Zander, can forget getting promoted to vice-president.

Why the hardball tactic? With 35,000 employees, Sun will have to start behaving less like a mob of high-tech freedom fighters and more like an icon of big management control. If McNealy can pull that off, then Sun might one day truly be worthy of the nickname Ma Web.

2 Marketing Program Development

Marketing strategy entails selecting target markets, setting marketing objectives, and developing, implementing, and managing marketing program positioning strategies. Marketing strategy builds competitive advantage by combining the customer-influencing strategies of the firm or business unit into an array of market-focused actions.

Part II focuses on setting objectives and designing marketing program positioning strategies. We also provide guidelines for preparing the marketing plan.

Setting Objectives

A marketing objective is a statement of what is to be accomplished through marketing activities, such as getting 150 people to test-drive a new car during the month of January 2002 or obtaining customer satisfaction ratings of at least 90 percent on the 2002 annual customer satisfaction survey. Each objective should be clear, specific, and realistic; in addition, it should indicate a desired level of performance, how it will be measured, and who will be responsible for meeting it. Each marketing objective should also be relevant to the overall results desired and should be consistent with other marketing and business objectives. Well-stated objectives also include benchmarks such as a product's current sales volume per period and the current level of product awareness or preference in the target market.

When objectives meet these criteria, they provide direction for those charged with achieving the objectives. They also can serve as standards by which both the organization and employees can gauge their performance.

The process of developing objectives also can force executives to sharpen and clarify their thinking. Written objectives enable efforts toward developing, implementing, and evaluating a marketing plan to be pointed in a consistent direction.

Among the troublesome problems encountered in setting objectives are the interrelationships among objectives and the shared responsibility for achieving them. Each objective does not fit neatly into an isolated task. Thus, considerable skill is required in determining a balanced set of objectives for different organizational levels and across different functional areas (e.g., advertising and personal selling).

Marketing objectives normally are set at the following levels:

1. The entire marketing organization within a particular company or business unit in a diversified firm.
2. Each target market served by the company or business unit.
3. The major marketing functional areas, such as product planning, distribution, pricing, and promotion.
4. Subunits within particular functional areas (for example, objectives for individual salespeople).

The extent to which various levels of objective setting are relevant in a particular firm depends on the size and complexity of the organization.

Marketing Program Positioning Strategy

Positioning involves developing a specific marketing mix to influence potential customers' overall perceptions of a brand, product line, or organization. *Position* is the place a product item, line, brand, or organization occupies in potential customers' minds relative to competing offerings. For example, Procter & Gamble markets 11 different laundry detergents, each with a unique position. Tide is positioned as a tough and powerful cleaner, Bold as a detergent with a fabric softener, Dash as a value brand, Oxydol as a bleach-enhanced detergent for whitening, and so forth.[1]

Positioning assumes that potential customers compare products on the basis of important features. Choosing the positioning concept for a product item, line, brand, or business unit is an important first step in developing a marketing program positioning strategy. Effective positioning requires assessing the positions occupied by competitors and choosing a position where the organization's marketing efforts will have the greatest impact.

Once a position is selected, product, distribution, pricing, and promotion strategies are designed to communicate and reinforce the desired position. These marketing mix elements represent a bundle of actions designed to (1) produce mutually satisfying exchanges with target markets and (2) achieve marketing objectives. Exhibit 1 illustrates the major decisions involved in marketing program positioning strategy development. An overview of these decisions follows.

Product Strategies

The heart of a marketing program positioning strategy is the firm's product portfolio. It is hard to develop a promotion program or distribution strategy or to set prices without knowing the product to be marketed. Product strategy includes the following:

- Deciding how to position a firm or business unit's product items, lines, and/or mixes.
- Setting strategic objectives for each product item and product line.
- Selecting a branding strategy.
- Developing and implementing strategies for managing products.

Product Positioning and Objectives.   Product positioning consists of deciding how to compete with a product or line of products against key competitors in the target markets selected by management. Key decisions about quality, price, and features establish guidelines for product development and improvement. Closely associated with posi-

EXHIBIT 1   **Major Decisions in Marketing Program Positioning Strategy Development**

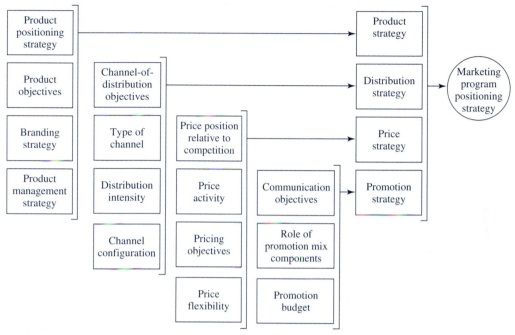

Source: Adapted from David W. Cravens, *Strategic Marketing,* 6th ed. (Burr Ridge, IL: Irwin, 2000), p. 195.

tioning decisions are the strategic objectives for the product strategy. Examples of objectives are market penetration, profit contribution, and the establishment of a reputation for quality.

Branding Strategy.   The major alternatives in the branding decision by a manufacturer are to

- Make no attempt to establish brand identity but instead offer a generic (no brand name) product.
- Produce products for private labeling by distributors—for example, True Value (hardware) or Janet Lee (Albertson's grocery stores).
- Establish brand names for lines of products, such as Sears' Craftsman tools.
- Build a strong brand identification for individual products, as in the case of Procter & Gamble (eg. Tide).
- Use a combination of these strategies.

Product Management.   Organizations with multiple products often use product managers to direct the marketing programs of one or more products within a product line or product mix. The primary responsibilities of product managers are to

- Create strategies for improving and marketing assigned product lines or brands.
- Make financial and operating plans for those products.
- Monitor the results of plans and revise tactics to meet changing conditions.

Some firms that market similar products to diverse target markets assign market managers to coordinate marketing efforts designed to reach a particular group of customers rather than guiding a particular group of products. For example, personal computers are used by households, educational institutions, small businesses, government institutions, and large businesses.

Distribution Strategies

The channel of distribution (supply chain) connects suppliers and producers with end users of goods and services. An effective, efficient distribution channel provides the member organizations with an important strategic edge over competing channels. Distribution strategies focus on getting a firm's products to its target markets. While some producers market their products directly to end users, many others utilize various types of wholesalers and retailers to perform distribution functions and activities. A good distribution strategy requires a penetrating analysis of the available alternatives to select the most appropriate channel network.

Channel Objectives.   Management may seek to achieve one or more objectives by using channel strategies. While the primary objective is gaining access to end users, other objectives—such as gaining promotional support, providing customer service, and obtaining market information—also may be important.

Type of Channel.   The major types of channels are conventional channels and vertical marketing systems (VMSs). A conventional channel of distribution is a group of loosely aligned manufacturers, wholesalers, and retailers that bargain with each other at arm's length, negotiate aggressively over the terms of sale, and otherwise behave independently.

In contrast, a VMS consists of producers and intermediaries working together to achieve operating economies and maximum market impact. Three common types of vertical marketing systems are corporate, contractual, and administered.

- A *corporate* VMS exists when one firm owns successive stages in a channel of distribution, such as Sherwin-Williams, which operates over 2,000 paint stores.
- A *contractual* VMS exists when independent firms at different channel levels coordinate their distribution activities by contractual agreement. Franchises such as McDonald's and Holiday Inn illustrate this type of VMS.
- An *administered* VMS exists when a strong organization (usually a manufacturer or retailer) assumes a leadership position. The leader of an administered system influences or controls the policies of other channel members so that the channel works as a team to achieve efficiencies and market impact. Companies such as Procter & Gamble and Wal-Mart are widely recognized as leaders of administrative channels.

Distribution Intensity.   Distribution intensity concerns how many outlets carry a product. Choosing the right distribution intensity depends on management's targeting and positioning strategies plus product and market characteristics. Low-cost convenience products typically are available in a large number of outlets in any area. *Intensive* distribution is aimed at maximum market coverage. *Selective* distribution is achieved by using only a few distributors within a geographic area. The most restrictive intensity of distribution is *exclusive* distribution, which entails one or a few distributors within a metropolitan area.

Channel Configuration.   Channel configuration refers to the number of levels and the specific kinds of intermediaries used at each level. The type (conventional versus VMS) of channel and the distribution intensity selected help in deciding how many channel levels to use and the kinds to use at each level. Other factors include where end users expect to buy the product and whether the producer wishes to control pricing, positioning, and brand image. Products that are more complex, customized, or expensive tend to be marketed through shorter, more direct channels compared with simpler, standardized, inexpensive ones. Sometimes, however, the types of intermediaries, experience, skill level, and motivation desired are not available. Some channels are difficult to break into because of existing exclusive relationships.

Price Strategies

Pricing strategies are determined largely by three interrelated decisions: (1) the decision on price position relative to the competition, (2) the decision on how active price will be in the marketing program, and (3) pricing objectives. The extent of price flexibility also influences price decisions. Price position is closely linked to several other aspects of the positioning strategy, such as product quality, distribution strategy, and advertising and personal selling programs. Price position establishes, for example, how price will be used in advertising and personal selling efforts.

Price Activity.   Exhibit 2 illustrates possible options in deciding how active price will be in the marketing program. A high–active strategy sometimes is used for prestige brands seeking an affluent image. When the buyer cannot easily evaluate the quality of a product, price may serve as a signal of value. A high–passive strategy entails marketing high-priced items by featuring nonprice factors such as product characteristics and performance. A low–active strategy often is used when price is an important factor in buyers' decisions. It is most effective for firms that have cost advantages. A low–passive strategy entails selling at a relatively low price but not featuring the low price for fear of creating or reinforcing perceptions of low quality. So-called off brands with less expensive features targeting price-sensitive market segments often feature their value or economy rather than low prices. Once decisions have been made regarding price position relative to the competition and how active price will be, guidelines can be established for price objectives.

Pricing Objectives.   To survive in today's highly competitive market environment, firms need pricing objectives that are specific, attainable, and measurable. Pricing objectives require periodic monitoring to determine the effectiveness of the firm's pricing strategies. Three general categories of pricing objectives are profit-oriented, sales-oriented, and status quo. Examples of profit-oriented objectives are profit maximization, satisfactory profits, and target return on investment. Sales-oriented pricing objectives include market share and sales maximization goals. Status quo objectives entail maintaining existing prices and meeting competitors' prices.

Price Flexibility.   Demand and cost factors determine the extent of pricing flexibility. Within these upper and lower boundaries, competition as well as legal and ethical considerations also influence pricing decisions. Management must determine where to price within the gap. In competitive markets, the feasibility range may be very narrow. New markets or emerging market segments may give a firm more flexibility in price strategy selection.

EXHIBIT 2   Pricing Options

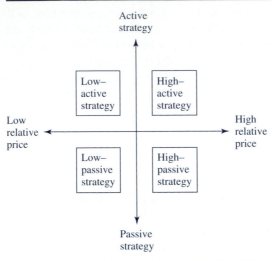

Source: David W. Cravens, *Strategic Marketing,* 6th ed. (Burr Ridge, Ill: Irwin, 2000), p. 346.

Promotion Strategies

Promotion is communication by marketers that attempts to inform, persuade, or remind present or potential customers or other selected audiences in order to influence their opinion or elicit a response. The promotion mix includes advertising, personal selling, sales promotion, direct marketing, and public relations. Target markets and product, distribution, and price decisions influence (1) the role of promotion strategies in the total marketing program and (2) the specific communications tasks of the promotion mix.

Major components of promotion strategy are (1) setting communication objectives, (2) deciding on the role of promotion mix components in the overall promotion strategy, and (3) determining the promotion budget.

Communication Objectives.   Objectives need to be selected for the entire promotional program and for each promotion component. Certain objectives, such as sales and market share targets, are shared with other marketing program components. Illustrative promotion objectives include the following:

- Creating or increasing buyers' awareness of a product item, line, or brand.
- Influencing buyers' attitudes toward a company, product item, line, or brand.
- Increasing the level of brand preference of the buyers in a targeted segment.
- Boosting sales and market share for specific customer or prospect targets.
- Generating repeat purchases of a brand.
- Encouraging customers to try a new product.
- Attracting new customers.

Deciding on the Role of Promotion Mix Components.   Promotion objectives can be linked to the specific role of each component in the promotion mix. For example, the role of the sales force may be to obtain sales or instead to inform the channel of distribution organizations about product features and applications. Advertising may play a major or minor role in the promotion strategy. Sales promotion (e.g., trade shows) may be used to achieve various objectives in the promotion mix.

Early in the development of the promotion strategy, it is useful to set some guidelines for the promotion mix components. These guidelines help determine the strategy for each promotion component. It is necessary to decide which communications objective(s) will be the responsibility of each component. For example, advertising may be responsible for creating awareness of a new product. Sales promotion (e.g., coupons, samples) may encourage trial of the new product. Personal selling may be assigned the responsibility for getting retailers to stock the new product. It is also important to decide how large each promotion component's contribution will be. Indicating the relative contribution of each component will help determine the promotion budget.

Promotion Budget.   Theoretically, the promotion budget should be set at a level that maximizes profitability. This theory is not easy to apply, however, because it requires knowledge of the actual monetary benefits resulting from the promotion effort.[2] Factors other than promotion, such as competitors' efforts, influence sales.

The most popular and most scientific approach to setting a promotion budget is the objective and task approach. First, management sets objectives. Second, it defines the communication tools required to achieve those objectives. Then a budget is built by adding up the costs of the planned promotion activities. This approach requires that management understand the effectiveness of various promotion tools. It also assumes that achieving the objectives will be worth the costs. The major advantage of the objective and task method is that it explicitly incorporates planning into the budgeting process: Objectives are defined, alternatives are analyzed, and the costs of each element in the promotion plan are determined.

Preparing the Marketing Plan

The marketing plan spells out the marketing strategy. Plans vary widely in scope and detail. Nevertheless, all plans need to be based on analyses of the product market and segments, the industry and competitive structure, and the organization's competitive advantage.

An outline for a typical marketing plan is shown in Exhibit 3. We briefly discuss the major parts of the outline, highlighting the nature and scope of the planning process. The market target serves as the planning unit.

The Situation Summary.   This part of the plan describes the market and its important characteristics, size estimates, and growth projections. Market segmentation analysis indicates the segments to be targeted and their relative importance. The competitor analysis indicates the key competitors (actual and potential), their strengths and weaknesses, probable future actions, and the organization's competitive advantage(s) in each segment of interest. The situation summary should be brief. Supporting information for the summary can be placed in an appendix or separate analysis.

Description of the Market Target.   A description of each market target—including size, growth rate, end users' characteristics, positioning strategy guidelines, and other available information useful in planning and implementation—is an essential part of the plan. When two or more targets are involved, it is important to assign priorities to aid in resource allocation.

EXHIBIT 3   Outline for Preparing an Annual Marketing Plan

Strategic Situation Summary
A summary of the strategic situation for the planning unit (business unit, market segment, product line, etc.).

Market Target(s) Description
Define and describe each market target, including customer profiles, customer preferences and buying habits, size and growth estimates, distribution channels, analysis of key competitors, and guidelines for positioning strategy.

Objectives for the Market Target(s)
Set objectives for the market target (such as market position, sales, and profits). Also state objectives for each component of the marketing program. Indicate how each objective will be measured.

Marketing Program Positioning Strategy
State how management wants the firm to be positioned relative to the competition in the eyes and mind of the buyer.
A. *Product Strategy*
   Set strategy for new products, product improvements, and product deletions.
B. *Distribution Strategy*
   Indicate the strategy to be used for each distribution channel, including the role of middlemen, the assistance and support provided, and the specific activities planned.
C. *Price Strategy*
   Specify the role of price in the marketing strategy and the planned actions regarding price.
D. *Promotion Strategy*
   Indicate the planned strategy and actions for advertising, publicity, personal selling, and sales promotion.
E. *Marketing Research*
   Identify information needs and planned projects, objectives, estimated costs, and timetable.
F. *Coordination with Other Business Functions*
   Specify the responsibilities and activities of other departments that have an important influence on the planned marketing strategy.

Forecasts and Budgets
Forecast sales and profit for the marketing plan and set the budget for accomplishing the forecast.

Objectives for the Market Target(s).   In this part of the plan we discuss what the marketing strategy is expected to accomplish during the planning period. Objectives are needed for each market target, and they may be financial, market position, and customer satisfaction targets. Objectives also are usually included for each marketing mix component.

Marketing Program Positioning Strategy.   The positioning statement indicates how management wants the targeted customers and prospects to perceive the brand. Specific strategies for product, distribution, price, and promotion are explained in this part of the plan. Actions to be taken, responsibilities, time schedules, and other implementation information are indicated.

Planning and implementation responsibilities often involve more than one person or department. A planning team may be assigned the responsibility for each market target and each marketing mix component. The planning process should encourage participation from all the areas responsible for implementing the plan.

EXHIBIT 4   Sonesta Hotels: Marketing Plan Outline

Note: Please keep the plan concise—maximum of 20 pages plus summary pages. Include title page and table of contents. Number all pages.

  I. *Introduction.* Set the stage for the plan. Specifically identify marketing objectives such as "increase average rate," "more group business," "greater occupancy," and "penetrate new markets." Identify particular problems.

 II. *Marketing Position.* Begin with a single statement that presents a consumer benefit in a way that distinguishes us from the competition.

III. *The Product.* Identify all facility and service changes that occurred this year and are planned for next year.

 IV. *Marketplace Overview.* Briefly describe what is occurring in your marketplace that might have an impact on your business or marketing strategy, such as the economy or the competitive situation.

  V. *The Competition.* Briefly identify your primary competition (three or fewer), specifying number of rooms, what is new in their facilities, and marketing and pricing strategies.

 VI. *Marketing Data*
   A. Identify top five geographic areas for transient business, with percentages of total room nights compared to the previous year.
   B. Briefly describe the guests at your hotel, considering age, sex, occupation, what they want, why they come, etc.
   C. Identify market segments with percentage of business achieved in each segment in current year (actual and projected) and projected for next year.

VII. *Strategy by Market Segment*
   A. Group
    1. *Objectives:* Identify what you specifically wish to achieve in this segment (for example, more high-rated business, more weekend business, larger groups).
    2. *Strategy:* Identify how sales, advertising, and public relations will work together to reach the objectives.
    3. *Sales Activities:* Divide by specific market segments:
      a. Corporate
      b. Association
      c. Incentives
      d. Travel agent
      e. Tours
      f. Other

      Under each category include a narrative description of specific sales activities geared toward each market segment, including geographically targeted areas, travel plans, group site inspections, correspondence, telephone solicitation, and trade shows. Be specific on action plans and designate responsibility and target months.
    4. *Sales Materials:* Identify all items so that they will be budgeted.
    5. *Direct Mail:* Briefly describe the direct mail program planned, including objectives, message, and content. Identify whether we will use existing material or create a new piece.
    6. *Research:* Indicate any research projects you plan to conduct, identifying what you wish to learn.
   B. Transient (The format here should be the same as it was under "Group" throughout.)
    1. *Objectives*
    2. *Strategy*

Contingency plans may be included in the plan. These plans consider possible actions if the anticipated planning environment is different from what actually occurs. The contingency plan considers how the marketing strategy will be changed if the future is different from what was anticipated.

EXHIBIT 4   (concluded)

---

      3. *Sales Activities:* Divide by specific market segments:
        a. Consumer (rack rate)
        b. Corporate (prime and other)
        c. Travel agent: business, leisure, consortia
        d. Wholesale/airline/tour (foreign and domestic)
        e. Packages (specify names of packages)
        f. Government/military/education
        g. Special interest/other
     4. *Sales Materials*
     5. *Direct Mail*
     6. *Research*
  C. Other Sonesta Hotels
  D. Local/Food and Beverage
     1. *Objectives*
     2. *Strategy*
     3. *Sales Activities:* Divide by specific market segments:
        a. Restaurant and lounge, external promotion
        b. Restaurant and lounge, internal promotion
        c. Catering
        d. Community relation/other
     4. *Sales Materials* (e.g., banquet menus, signage)
     5. *Direct Mail*
     6. *Research*
VIII. *Advertising*
  A. Subdivide advertising by market segment and campaign, paralleling the sales activities (group, transient, F&B).
  B. Describe objectives of each advertising campaign, identifying whether it should be promotional (immediate bookings) or image (longer-term awareness).
  C. Briefly describe contents of advertising, identifying key benefit to promote.
  D. Identify target media by location and type (newspaper, magazine, radio, etc.).
  E. Indicate percentage of the advertising budget to be allocated to each market segment.
IX. *Public Relations*
  A. Describe objectives of public relations as it supports the sales and marketing priorities.
  B. Write a brief statement on overall goals by market segment paralleling the sales activities. Identify what proportion of your effort will be spent on each segment.
X. *Summary:* Close the plan with general statement concerning the major challenges you will face in the upcoming year and how you will overcome these challenges.

Source: Adapted from Howard Sutton, *The Marketing Plan in the 1990s* (New York: The Conference Board, Inc., 1990), pp. 34–35.

Forecasting and Budgeting.   Financial planning includes (1) forecasting revenues and profits and (2) estimating the costs necessary to carry out the marketing plan. The people responsible for market target, product, geographic area, or other units may prepare the forecast. Comparative data on sales, profits, and expenses for prior years are useful to link the plan to previous results.

    Exhibit 4 shows the marketing plan outline for Sonesta Hotels. The activities include making the situation assessment, setting objectives, developing targeting and positioning strategies, deciding on action programs for the marketing mix components, and preparing supporting financial statements (budgets and profit-and-loss projections).

End Notes

1. Jennifer Lawrence, "Don't Look for P&G to Pare Detergents," *Advertising Age,* May 3, 1993, p. 2.
2. Peter J. Danaher and Roland T. Rust, "Determining the Optimal Level of Media Spending," *Journal of Advertising Research,* January–February 1994, pp. 28–34.

CASES FOR PART 2

The seven cases in this part focus on the development of market-oriented marketing programs in various types of organizations. Not only are the companies diverse in their locations (the Netherlands, France, United States), they also are diverse in their product offerings (bagels, medical equipment, hockey). The e-business case looks at how Oracle Corp. is attempting to assemble an e-business powerhouse in various markets.

In the video case, **Dunkin' Donuts (Case 2–1),** we see an attempt to transform a firm's image from quality donut seller to bagel expert. The bagel introduction was Dunkin' Donuts' largest initiative ever, and a host of problems erupted, mostly in supply and distribution. With two weeks left before the largest advertising campaign the bagel industry had ever experienced, the supply chain dried up. The purchasing director responsible for coordinating supply had to make an immediate recommendation about the continued rollout of the new product line.

Medical Products Inc: The "Wolverine" Project (Case 2–2) picks up on Case 1–2, which examined the medical equipment industry. The company approved the proposal for a new state-of-the art ultrasound imaging system. The interfunctional development team at MPI was waiting for the marketing staff to deliver on its marketing plan.

L'Oréal Nederland B.V. (Case 2–3) is the Netherlands subsidiary of the L'Oréal Group. Headquartered in Paris, L'Oréal was the largest cosmetics manufacturer in the world. The subsidiary had to decide whether to introduce a facial skin care line, a hair colorant, or both. If a decision was made to market one or both of the product lines, appropriate marketing programs had to be developed.

The New York Islanders Hockey Club, Inc. (Case 2–4), is looking for a marketing plan that will restore fan interest and increase ticket and merchandise sales. But how will a marketing plan help provide a winning team—the thing fans seem to want most?

The senior marketing manager in **Pfizer, Inc., Animal Health Products (A), Case 2–5,** is wondering if his team's approach to the marketplace is becoming outdated. While the company has positioned its products on a combination of superior science and high-quality production/control techniques, the marketing manager is not sure his group is using comparable quality in its segmentation approaches when developing its marketing strategies in a changing marketplace.

Case 2–6, Apache Power, Inc., focuses on the introduction of a new gasoline engine. The introduction takes API into a new market of large engines, and the company has invested a substantial amount of money in the development of the engine. The product manager needs a marketing program.

Case 2–7, the e-business case in this part, examines **Oracle Corp.**'s aggressive strategy to provide the first-ever "e-business suite" of products. Competition in this market is tough, but the company appears to be assembling an e-business powerhouse.

CASE 2–1
DUNKIN' DONUTS

It was a hot Massachusetts day in late August 1996, and Chris Booras, the Dunkin' Donuts purchasing director responsible for coordinating supply, was feeling the heat. It was a trying time for Dunkin' Donuts as it tried to transform its image from quality donut seller to bagel expert. The bagel introduction was the largest initiative ever for Dunkin' Donuts, and a host of problems had erupted, mostly in supply and distribution. With two weeks left before the largest advertising campaign the bagel industry had ever experienced, the supply chain had dried up.

Chris Booras stared forlornly out the window. A lot was at stake here. The pressure was definitely on. Jack Shafer, the COO overseeing Dunkin' Donuts, had recently commented,

> The combination of the new Dunkin' Donuts freshly baked bagels and our legendary coffee is the key to our future growth. We have invested a year and a half developing the perfect bagel. When paired with the magic of the Dunkin' Donuts name, the equity in our coffee business, our advertising strength and our far reaching network of shops, we become uniquely positioned to lead the bagel category.[1]

Dunkin' always moved fast to stay ahead. Chris hoped he could get the supplier problems straightened out and keep pace with the expectations of the company's top management.

The Background

> Dunkin' Donuts will strive to be the dominant retailer of high quality donuts, bakery products and beverages in each metropolitan market in which we choose to compete.

> > company mission statement

In 1948 Bill Rosenberg had a dream. He envisioned a morning destination shop centered on quality donuts and the freshest coffee. He opened his first donut shop, the Open Kettle, on the Southern Artery in Quincy, Massachusetts. The popularity of this shop convinced Rosenberg of his concept's potential, and for the next five years he opened one shop per year. In 1950, with a six-store operation, Rosenberg opened the first Dunkin' Donuts.

Rosenberg quickly realized that to maximize his organization's growth potential, he would have to franchise. In 1955 he signed the company's first franchise agreement, and he went to work aligning himself with business partners willing to take on the risks of the franchise system. Those risks included paying Rosenberg a percentage of sales, paying a fee for the franchise name, and paying large up-front costs for land and con-

---

[1] Editor. *Milling and Baking News* (June 25, 1996): 1.

This case was prepared by Eric Nyman, Boston College, under the supervision of Victoria L. Crittenden, associate professor of marketing, Boston College, as the basis for class discussion rather than to illustrate either effective or ineffective handling of a managerial situation.

struction. This strategy allowed Rosenberg to grow Dunkin' Donuts to a 24-shop chain in New England with annual sales of US$3 million by 1960.[2]

Astronomical growth continued into the next decade. In 1963, the 100th shop opened and the company attained revenues of US$10 million. In 1968, with Rosenberg at the helm as president and CEO, Dunkin' Donuts went public. Operating with the pledge to make donuts fresh every four hours and to brew fresh coffee every 14 minutes, Dunkin' Donuts reached US$44 million in sales by 1969.

The 1970s was a big decade for the company. During this period, the company expanded internationally and developed new products. In 1974 the Dunkin' Munchkin was released and became one of the food service industry's most successful product spin-offs ever. The Munchkin, a donut hole, was offered in a variety of flavors and was considered to "truly be a bite-sized treat." Sales were strong, with the Munchkin remaining a mainstream product into the 1990s.

As the chain entered the 1980s, sales reached US$300 million in 1,000 shops. Plans were formulated to accelerate expansion. The strategy for growth and profits centered on distribution, advertising, new products, remodeling, and standards improvement. To implement the strategy, Dunkin' Donuts developed what would become known as the gold standard in franchise distribution when it created the first of six regional distribution centers. These regional distribution centers allowed for quick delivery to individual stores along with good pricing for all outlets in a given region. This period also marked the national advertising debut of "Fred the Baker." Fred was a hero to working-class America as he rose at all hours of the night as a franchise owner to ensure that his customers were always given fresh products and a smile. Fred popularized the saying "It's time to make the donuts." Dunkin' began to remodel stores during this period as well. Brightly lit, colorful nonsmoking stores were created to replace the dimly lit, smoky coffee shops consumers had been accustomed to. Standards were improved to ensure freshness across all product lines.

In 1990 Dunkin' Donuts, with a firm balance sheet and strong brand equity in the morning food retail business, became an attractive takeover target. After trying unsuccessfully to ward off a hostile takeover, Dunkin' Donuts was acquired under friendly terms by Allied Domecq, a world leader in spirits and retailing. Its international spirits brands included Ballantines, Beefeater, and Kahlua. Allied was the world's leading brandy company and the second largest distributor of Scotch whiskey, tequila, and liqueurs. The company had over 13,800 retail outlets that included 4,100 pubs and 8,200 franchised stores, including the popular California-based Baskin-Robbins ice cream chain. After the takeover, Dunkin' Donuts, acting as a wholly owned subsidiary of Allied Domecq, operated over 3,200 shops with total sales in excess of US$1 billion.[3]

By the mid-1990s, Dunkin' Donuts franchise stores were seeing sales between US$20,000 and US$50,000 a month. Dunkin' Donuts reported sales of US$1.4 billion around the globe in 1995. Entering the mid-1990s, however, Dunkin' Donuts was experiencing organizational turbulence. Both of Allied Domecq's American concerns, Baskin-Robbins (based in California) and Dunkin' Donuts (headquartered in Massachusetts), were attempting to merge cultures, which was causing some discomfort on both sides. Baskin-Robbins had been experiencing flat growth for several years, and it was

---

[2] The New England states include Connecticut, Maine, Massachusetts, New Hampshire, Rhode Island, and Vermont.

[3] Twenty-seven hundred of these shops were owned by Dunkin' Donuts; the rest were acquired when Dunkin' bought Mister Donuts.

thought that the merger with Dunkin' Donuts would instill some life into the brand. Initial problems included simple logistics, resentment from the Baskin-Robbins organization over placement of Dunkin' Donuts people in high-level Baskin positions, and general fear among all parties about whether their jobs would continue to exist. To further complicate matters, Dunkin' Donuts was restructuring along the lines of category management. That meant that individuals in a given department (e.g., marketing, purchasing, quality assurance) would be given a product category to manage. These categories included bakery, beverages, and the product expected to redefine Dunkin' donuts—bagels.

The Bagel Market

Once an ethnic specialty food, bagels had gained acceptance as an American breakfast and lunch item. Bagels were a low-fat, boiled bread product. A study of national eating trends conducted by the NPD Group Inc., a Chicago-area research firm, found that per capita bagel consumption soared 65 percent between 1990 and 1995. Market reports revealed that the bagel business was a US$2.5 billion industry by the mid-1990s.[4]

By 1995, there were over 700 bagel retail outlets and wholesale bakeries in the United States, with annual sales of over US$1 billion. The market's growth rate was estimated at over 30 percent.[5] Analysts projected that growth would remain steady throughout the decade. The major players in this primarily breakfast food segment were Bruegger's, Manhattan Bagel, and Einstein Brothers. The rest of the market was dominated by small chains and mom-and-pop operations. No dominant national market presence by any single company had been established.

Most retailers agreed that the popularity of bagels was a long-term trend. However, food retail analysts expected a shakeout as the marketplace became increasingly crowded. Nancy Krause, vice-president of Technomic, Inc., thought that success in this industry was related to the rate of increase of bagel shops and the extent to which they cluster in the same markets.[6]

The bagel marketplace was divided among various types of outlets. Approximately 44 percent of all bagels were sold in retail shops and bakeries, 26 percent at in-store bakeries, 20 percent by food services, and 10 percent frozen by wholesale bakeries. At the beginning of 1995 only 15 percent of these sales were by multiunit chains. Furthermore, 70 percent of the bagel stores were concentrated in New York, New Jersey, Florida, and California. This alluded to a positive growth situation as bagel stores spread across America.[7]

The chains competed on quality of product, physical appearance of their facilities, flavor variety of both bagels and cream cheese, and the bagel "experience" (a hard-to-quantify atmosphere that bespoke freshness and a homemade feel). These bagel shops were beginning to grab market share from the dominant player in the breakfast food category, Dunkin' Donuts, as more and more health-minded Americans jumped on the bagel bandwagon. The product fit the perfect nutrition profile, as a plain 2.5-ounce bagel had approximately one gram of fat. As a spokesperson from Lender's Bagels said, "Bagels are the food of the nineties."[8]

---

[4] Brown, Jennifer. *Bagel Boom* (July 1996): 62.

[5] Malovany, Dan. *Bakery Production and Marketing* (May 24, 1995): 12.

[6] Brown, Jennifer. "Bagel Boom," *Baking & Snack,* Kansas City, MO: Sosland Publishing Company, July 1996.

[7] Ibid.

[8] Malovany, Dan. "Don't Change that Dial; Wholesale Bakery Industry Trends," *Bakery Production and Marketing.* Chicago: Delta Communications, May 24, 1995.

The outlook for the bagel chains' future appeared to include rapid expansion through franchising and acquisition. Consolidation was predicted, and so speed to market was essential. Already, Einstein Bros. had acquired Noah's Bagel, and Manhattan Bagel had joined forces with Specialty Bakeries, a franchiser of the Bagel Builders chain. The top two or three dominant players in this industry were expected to be the last ones standing. As stated by Krause, "Only those who really have established their brand image and dominance within their trade areas will survive."[9]

Dunkin' Donuts' Market Entry

In 1995 it was becoming quite clear to Dunkin' Donuts President Will Kussell and many members of senior management that the bagel industry, while hurting Dunkin' sales at that point, held a great deal of potential for the company. The Dunkin' Donuts sales mix at that time was as follows:

Coffee	65%
Donuts	25
Muffins and cookies	10

Kussell envisioned the company's sales mix changing dramatically and foresaw Dunkin' Donuts becoming the biggest and most dominant player in the bagel industry. Simple math revealed that if Dunkin' Donuts jumped into the bagel business with its 2,700 North American outlets, it would more than triple the entire retail industry's 700 outlets. Furthermore, the sales opportunity that bagels could inspire in this growing billion-dollar U.S. retail market was staggering. After some initial research of the industry and a search for a high-quality supplier, Dunkin' Donuts made the decision to compete in the bagel business.

The company's goal was to have the best product in the market and to be the largest bagel retailer in the United States. Several research and development tests were conducted to discover the attributes that customers found most appealing in a bagel. The results of those tests showed that consumers desired a large bagel in a variety of flavors and insisted on the complementary product of cream cheese. Dunkin' Donuts then designed a bagel around these considerations and created a new cream cheese line to go with it.

The Search for Supply.   Dunkin' Donuts felt that it had developed the perfect bagel. Consistent with its outsourcing strategies for muffins and cookies, it needed someone to produce the bagel in large enough quantities to supply its geographically dispersed retail outlets.

Many suppliers wanted to get into the bagel business with Dunkin' Donuts. Manufacturing giants such as Harold's Bakery Products,[10] Sara Lee, and Brooklyn Bagel Boys bid on the business. Criteria for supplier selection included a proven track record, a sizable cash flow to enter into a new business, and, most important, the speed to act quickly in building new lines for bagel production. No company had the existing capacity for a project of this scope. Therefore, when Harold's promised a nine-month delivery time on new bagel production lines with the ability to sign copacker relationships in the interim, a deal was consummated. Harold's was chosen as the vendor that would supply Dunkin' Donuts with its fresh bagels.

---

[9] Brown, *Bagel Boom:* 62.

[10] A pseudonym is used to protect the Dunkin' Donuts supplier relationship.

Harold's gave Dunkin' Donuts a standard volume guarantee, including a nine-month construction promise for new lines. The $8 million cost of the new lines would be paid for by Harold's. However, the costs were to be amortized on those lines—meaning that the finished cost to Dunkin' Donuts for the bagels would be lower over the long term. Dunkin' provided Harold's with a volume guarantee along with the promise that outside vendors would not be looked at unless Harold's violated the supply guarantee. The supply guarantee centered on production numbers at Harold's and at copackers' plants. (Copackers were short-term outside vendors that would assist Harold's in supplying the Dunkin' system with bagels while the Harold's lines were being built.)

Dunkin' Donuts' Planned Rollout

Using Harold's theoretical capacity numbers on lines that had not yet been built, along with the projected capacity of copackers, the Dunkin' Donuts marketing team went to work. A national rollout plan was developed that called for 2,700 stores to be supplied with bagels in one year. Some objections were raised by both purchasing and quality assurance, as both departments pointed out the risks of creating such an aggressive schedule. However, these concerns were overshadowed by senior management's drive to get fiscal year 1997 (which started in September 1996) off to a great start. The new budget was built around the expectation that the bagel program would be a rousing success, with franchisees targeted to achieve a 10 percent growth in sales with the $0.55 bagel, up from an average of 2 to 4 percent.[11] Cream cheese would sell for US$1.29 to US$1.99. Expected bagel-related sales per store were projected at over US$1,000 a week for many stores.

There were several steps to follow for a Dunkin' franchisee to get into the bagel program. The cost of construction (to the franchisee) was expected to be around $25,000, as all enrolling shops were required to remodel with new signs, bagel cases, and cream cheese merchandisers to give the look and feel of a bagel enterprise. The marketing department expected that 80 percent of all shops in a given market would enroll and used that number as a goal for franchisee sell-in. Importantly, all shops did not have to sign up as bagel carriers. However, a franchisee that did not sign up initially would go to end of the line on the rollout schedule. This could mean that a shop in Boston that did not sign up on the first rollout opportunity could have to wait up to nine months while the rest of the country's 2,700 stores were remodeled before being allowed to sell bagels. Furthermore, all participating shops had to agree to carry all of Dunkin' Donuts' proprietary bagel products (including all flavor varieties of bagels and all cream cheese types created by the company).

Before attempting to sell the product to franchisees, Dunkin' Donuts selected 20 of the best stores (termed fast-track stores—traditionally high performers) in various markets to serve as model stores. Dunkin' Donuts then used the fast-track stores' impressive sales results with the new bagels to entice other franchisees to join the bagel program. The average fast-track store had a sales boost of 15 percent with the new bagel program.

The U.S. rollout was to start in the New England states, the company's strongest sales region. From there, the rollout would go on to the Mid-Atlantic (which included New York, Baltimore, and Washington D.C.), continue to the Midwest (where markets such as South Bend, Indiana, existed), and finish off in the Southeast (which included

---

[11] This would mean greater profits for Dunkin' Donuts, which received a percentage of sales from the franchisees both for marketing support and for the brand equity the Dunkin' Donuts name provided.

Atlanta, Georgia, and Orlando, Florida). Once this phase of the rollout was complete, Dunkin' Donuts planned to head westward, where its presence was much smaller, and then into Canada. The plan was to supply 65 stores a week with bagels starting the second week of May 1996 and continue until all interested Dunkin' Donuts stores were selling bagels.

Sales Projections.   Taking an aggressive approach, the bagel marketing team used past and present data to determine how many bagels the average shop would use. A case contained 96 bagels. The highest-performing fast-track store (in South Weymouth, Massachusetts) had sold 60 cases a week of the new bagels—amazingly, without any advertising support!

Bagel usage projections therefore built in this preadvertising sales jump. The marketing department projected that the average store would sell 18 cases of the new bagels each week before advertising. Once advertising began, historical Dunkin' figures showed that a 100 percent sales jump usually occurred. With this prediction, a US$25 million advertising campaign was planned.

The Crisis

Dunkin' Donuts' bagel team projected that with advertising, it would be selling almost 40 cases of bagels a week per store. Through the month of July 1996, with no advertising, the current system supply of 14,500 cases per week was being used up on a weekly basis. This presented both short- and long-term problems.

In the short term, volume promises from the supplier were not being met, and that was hurting the rollout plan. The rollout already had been delayed for three weeks in July, as demand had exceeded capacity. It was costly to delay the rollout, as lost sales could never be recaptured.

Supplying the system in the long term presented challenges as well. Harold's was already experiencing several problems with regard to constructing the new lines. Harold's was having difficulty locating the proper equipment and suffering product-related problems with one of its copackers.

The Decision

At a supplier meeting, Kussell had stated,

> Bagels are a tremendous opportunity for our company. It is once in a lifetime that an opportunity comes along in the food service industry with this kind of growth. The speed at which the bagel market is growing is the kind of growth that high technology companies in the Internet are seeing. We cannot afford not to be in this game. Another point, however, is a business decision. I want to be out ahead of the competition. I don't want to send the message that we are pulling back, only that we are plowing ahead.

Chris Booras had several decisions to make. Should the rollout be slowed? Could the shops delayed in July be added back into the rollout schedule? Should advertising be pushed back and, if so, to what date? Should the contract with Harold's be reevaluated? Should Dunkin' Donuts begin looking for a new supplier?

These decisions were the basis for three options under consideration by Booras and the Dunkin' Donuts bagel team:

1. They could continue the rollout at the current pace with a partial product line.

2. They could slow the rollout by limiting advertising or limiting the pace of store expansion.
3. They could stop the rollout until there was some certainty of supply.

If the Dunkin' team decided to stop the rollout until supply was guaranteed, it would have to do one of two things: (1) work with Harold's to find more copackers in the short term or (2) terminate the contract with Harold's, since Harold's had been unable to keep its short-term supply commitments, and begin the process of finding a new supplier. Before dissolving the contract with Harold's, however, the Dunkin' team had to keep in mind the rumor that all U.S. production facilities capable of making bagels were signing long-term supplier contracts with different firms, leaving very few opportunities for additional capacity to be obtained.

Chris Booras knew that his and his team's reputations were on the line with Allied Domecq and the franchise community. And a recommendation had to be made immediately!

Case 2–2
Medical Products Inc.:
The "Wolverine" Project

In late 1994 management at Medical Products Inc. (MPI) assigned a cross-functional team to determine the feasibility of introducing new products into the worldwide ultrasound imaging marketplace. Code-named Wolverine, the project successfully proceeded through various stages of development.

By early 1997 Wolverine had developed into a state-of-the art ultrasound imaging system. A full-scale model of Wolverine had been built, a mock-up of the Wolverine display formats and their control structure had been developed, customer input had been solicited, and both the user interface and the model had been evaluated by typical users in Japan and South America. The interfunctional development team was ready for deliverables from various functional areas.

With considerable information from research and development, manufacturing, and legal, as well as both internal and external marketing information, the Wolverine marketing team had promised to deliver a detailed draft of its marketing plan by fall 1997. The marketing staff leading the development of the marketing plan included Elizabeth Sweeney (marketing plan owner), Tim Green (technical marketing contributor), Caitlin Murphy (marketing development contributor), James Harris (marketing communications contributor), and Claudia Zaborsky (learning products contributor).

MPI

Located in Lexington, Massachusetts (USA), Medical Products Inc. marketed more than 400 medical products and services (e.g., patient monitors, defibrillators, electrocardiographs, and ultrasound imaging systems) and offered over 1,000 medical supply products (e.g., cables and leads, electrodes, paper, stethoscopes, and temperature probes). These health-care products and services were designed and marketed to medical professionals in cardiology, acute care, surgery, obstetrics, neonatology, and radiology and to medical clinics, physicians' offices, and emergency services. MPI employed around 5,000 people and generated annual revenues of around US$1 billion from its medical electronics market segment.

Traditionally, Medical Products Inc.'s health-care customers were medium-size to large hospitals (200 to 1,000 beds). However, the company had also begun to service specialty centers and group physician offices. Recognizing that the health-care industry was moving away from extended hospital stays and supplanting them with more outpatient/preventive care solutions, MPI saw home health care as a growth opportunity that would take the company into the next millennium. The home health-care market would require low-cost, high-performance clinical measurement solutions.

Sixty percent of MPI's customers were in the United States. However, MPI's products were sold in dozens of countries, with Europe, Latin America, and the Asia/Pacific region representing major growth opportunities. MPI maintained a business and manufacturing

This case was prepared by Victoria L. Crittenden, Boston College, as the basis for class discussion rather than to illustrate effective or ineffective handling of a managerial situation. Development of the case was funded by a grant from the General Electric Fund at Boston College. Research assistance was provided by Christine Connolly, Allison Kleva, and Jennifer Moisan. Quantitative data have been disguised, and pseudonyms are used throughout.

center in Boeblingen, Germany, and strategic alliances in Japan (Yokagama MPI) and China (MPI Medical Products Qingdao) in addition to the Massachusetts center.

Ultrasound Imaging

Ultrasound diagnosis is a noninvasive, safe way to perform medical imaging. The technique involves waves of sound that are sent to or through a person's body. The waves are reflected by the part of the body being imaged. A machine collects the reflections, producing a mirror image of the object on a video monitor.

By the mid-1990s, Medical Products Inc. was the worldwide leader in cardiovascular ultrasound imaging and was number one in the United States in cardiac ultrasound imaging. To accomplish this market position, MPI marketed the IMAG line of cardiovascular ultrasound imaging systems. This system allowed real-time visualization of the beating heart and the associated vasculature, which assisted cardiologists and vascular specialists in the treatment of adult and pediatric cardiovascular disorders. Imaging equipment was prevalent not only in hospitals but also in outpatient and ambulatory settings.

To further its position in one of its flagship businesses, ultrasound imaging, MPI had approved the development of the company's first general radiology imaging system. This multispecialty, high-performance ultrasound system was code-named for internal purposes as Wolverine.

Wolverine

The development of Wolverine began in November 1994. At that time a nine-person team was formed to investigate technology alternatives for developing a low-cost product based on the IMAG platform. The team decided that a new MPI product—Wolverine—would leverage MPI's technology in order to tap into new markets.

Medical Products Inc.'s traditional imaging market—cardiovascular departments—was serviced by the IMAG line of products. The primary users of the IMAG products were cardiologists. Current market data, however, suggested that a new product should incorporate not only cardiovascular but also mixed-application imaging system capability (e.g., abdominal, transrectal, and transvaginal). Radiologists would be the primary users of a mixed-application imaging system.

Sufficient data existed to define the cardiovascular market's requirements for the Wolverine product adequately as well as justify it financially within the cardiovascular market segment. A cardiology product must have sensitive spectral and color Doppler, crisp valve definition, clear endocardial borders, transesophageal capabilities, and an integrated stress solution. However, the mixed-application market needs were significantly different. The market data available to the Wolverine project team gave a reasonably clear picture of those market requirements. Radiologists required completely different image quality to discern differences in tissue, a wide array of transducers to provide total body imaging, controls arranged for easy image acquisition, hard-copy devices (film), power angiography, and a discrete screen format to display crucial system settings.

While the members of the project team thought that their ability to define the market adequately was still suspect, they felt that the time necessary to gain complete knowledge of the market would result in a significant loss of R&D productivity. Therefore, the Wolverine project team opted to accept the currently available market data for the worldwide cardiovascular and mixed-application market requirements and proceed with the development of the business plan for the Wolverine product.

The development process for Wolverine followed the traditional phase reporting process at Medical Products Inc. That is, the process started at Phase 1. When the goals and objectives of that phase were thought to be met, the product concept was evaluated and a determination was made whether to proceed with the development process. Upon the successful completion of a phase, the product moved into the next phase. Each successive development phase brought the product closer to marketplace introduction.

The Wolverine project had proceeded through three development phases by early 1997.

Phase 1 *(November 1994–October 1995).* At the end of this one-year phase of analysis, the Wolverine interfunctional management triad [consisting of the release coordinator (R&D), product marketing, and manufacturing] and the interfunctional definition team (consisting of release coordinator, R&D, regulatory, marketing, manufacturing, and finance) determined that Wolverine was a viable project that would allow Medical Products Inc. to make significant inroads into the worldwide market for cardiovascular and mixed-application imaging. Exhibit 1 shows the proforma data sheet for the Wolverine product concept that resulted from initial analysis over a one-year period.

The team developed the following prioritized program objectives to help guide the decision-making process over the life of the Wolverine project:

EXHIBIT 1   **Pro Forma Data Sheet**
Medical Products Inc.

Wolverine
(Preliminary)

Product Description

Wolverine evolves the IMAG 100 platform into a very low cost ultrasound system adaptable to a broad spectrum of worldwide diagnostic imaging requirements in

- Cardiovascular
- Vascular
- Abdominal
- Fetal
- Gynecological
- Pediatric and neonatal
- Small parts
- Operating room

Contribution

- A complete MPI cardiovascular imaging system with Doppler and color flow for $104.5K
- A complete MPI mixed-application (MAP) system option which combines cardiovascular capabilities with general mixed applications needs for $134K
- Best value in price class
- Easiest to use in its class

Cost Goals

- Total factory cost of standard system < $30K
- Total factory cost of MAP system < $37K

Schedule Goals

- Phase 3—May 1996
- Phase 5—Q1 FY98

1. Meet market segment cost goals.
2. Superior competitive performance.
3. Meet minimum applications.
4. Ease of use/productivity.
5. Uptime/support.
6. Time to market.
7. Competitive feature set.
8. Upgradability.

Having determined that Wolverine was a viable project, the team was authorized to move forward with the development process. The early phases of the process focused on the technical and operational viability of this type of ultrasound imaging system as well as the determination of a marketplace need.

Phase 2 *(November 1995–May 1996).*   Exhibit 2 shows the pro forma data sheet developed during Phase 2 of the Wolverine project. Changes from Phase 1 to Phase 2 were mostly in the area of the schedule and R&D resources. These changes were the result of a better understanding of the mixed-application market. At this design stage, the primary goal of Wolverine was to provide a very low cost, high-performance system for

**EXHIBIT 2   Revised Pro Forma Data Sheet
Medical Products Inc.**

Wolverine

Product Description

Wolverine evolves the IMAG 100 platform into a very low cost ultrasound system adaptable to a broad spectrum of worldwide diagnostic imaging requirements in

- Cardiovascular
- Vascular
- Abdominal
- Fetal
- Gynecological
- Pediatric and neonatal
- Small parts
- Operating room

Contribution

- A complete MPI cardiovascular imaging system with Doppler and color flow for $104.5K
- A complete MPI mixed-application (MAP) system option which combines cardiovascular capabilities with general mixed applications needs for $112K
- Best value in price class
- Easiest to use in its class

Cost Goals

- Total factory cost of standard system < $30K
- Total factory cost of MAP system < $37K

Schedule Goals

- Phase 3—October 1996
- Phase 5—Q3 FY98

the price-sensitive/price-performance worldwide imaging market. The project utilized the company's core product, IMAG, for the product platform.

The completion of this phase of the product development process meant that the company was certain that there was a market for a new ultrasound imaging system and could produce such a product.

Phase 3 *(May 1996–January 1997).* During this phase the Wolverine project team further developed the product and began moving toward the development of final functional-level plans that would take the product to market. At this time the decision priority list changed. Time to market increased in priority from number six to number four and became more important than ease of use and uptime. The company had generated marketplace interest in the product concept by means of its inclusion of customers in the product's development process. Now it was becoming increasingly important to deliver the product to the marketplace.

Also at this time, the project team set performance/reliability/costs/delivery (PRCD) goals. Performance goals were set by using historical knowledge and competitive information. The risks associated with Wolverine's performance goals were considered minimal. Reliability goals were set by using established projection techniques for similar types of circuitry as well as historical data on failure rates. Again, the risks associated with meeting the reliability goals were considered minimal. The cost goals were set by using a bottom-up technique. In Wolverine's case, the electronics hardware design had consistently been ahead of the mechanical hardware design (due to the staffing history of the project). Thus, significant portions of the electrical design were complete and costing was accomplished by using established parts lists. The costs associated with the mechanical components of the design were traditionally more difficult to estimate accurately. Therefore, the following process was used to generate accurate mechanical costing estimates:

1. A full-scale model of Wolverine was designed that reflected not only the external "look" of the product but also first-pass design elements.

2. The model was used to generate assembly breakdowns that were broken down further into mechanical component lists.

3. Each component was assigned a price estimate. Each estimate was generated by using as accurate a technique as possible.

4. All high-risk components with projected high costs were quoted by at least one external vendor. This included components such as the keyboard and cart sheet metal.

5. All these estimates were totaled to generate a "standard" mechanical cost estimate that was used to generate the overall Wolverine cost goal.

6. Each component price estimate was assigned a risk factor determined by the price estimation technique. For example, a component that was currently being purchased by MPI would have a low risk factor. Conversely, a component that was not similar to an existing component would have a high risk factor.

7. A second "high" component price estimate was determined by increasing the original component price estimate by an amount proportional to the degree of risk associated with the part.

This process resulted in both a "high" and a "standard" cost estimate. The high mechanical cost estimate was US$971 more than the standard estimate. This suggested that the mechanical costs needed to be managed aggressively in order to meet the overall goals. The final Phase 3 factory cost goal was US$51,300 for the mixed-application model.

Wolverine's delivery goal was established by using a bottom-up scheduling approach. The project team utilized historical scheduling issues from similar platform projects to incorporate estimates that accounted for foreseeable problems. Those possible problems included digital scanner debugging and software development issues. This resulted in the schedule presented in Exhibit 3, with an estimated delivery date of first quarter 1999.

The Phase 3 retrospective shown in Exhibit 4 is a list of the top three issues that did and did not go well in the processes to complete Phase 3. Included in the list is the best guess at the root cause for each issue as well as a recommendation on how to enhance what went well and eliminate what went poorly.

EXHIBIT 3   Wolverine Schedule

Task Name	Completion
Wolverine Tentative Checkpoint Schedule	11/06/97
Phase 3: Specifications	01/27/97
Phase 3B: Design	07/25/97
Phase 4A: Implementation	05/03/98
Phase 4B: Process	07/09/98
Phase 5: Validation	11/06/98
Phase 6: Manufacturing release	11/06/98
First image	07/05/97
First lab prototype	10/25/97
Software quality started	11/15/97
Cardiac lab prototype clinical completed	02/15/98
Lab prototype error tests completed	04/16/98
Abdominal lab prototype clinical completed	04/16/98
First production prototype built	07/17/98
Production prototype error tests completed	10/02/98
Software quality completed	10/15/98
30–50 production prototypes	11/01/98

	1997				**1998**			
Q1	*Q2*	*Q3*	*Q4*	*Q1*	*Q2*	*Q3*	*Q4*	*Q1*

```
V_____V
+
              _____
                      _____
                                        _____
                                                 ____
                                                 V___V
          + July 6
                  + October 25
                + November 15
                      + February 15
                          + April 16
                          + April 16
                                  + July 17
                                      + October 2
                                      + October 15
                                          + November

Task  _____        Summary  v_____v     Milestone     +
```

EXHIBIT 4   Phase 3 Positive/Negative Retrospective

Wolverine Phase 2A Positive Retrospective		
Positive Effect	*Root Cause*	*Recommendation*
An extremely complete and customer-focused product definition and specification at 2A that will be the foundation for a stable and efficient product development effort	"Define and specify before you build" product development focus. Construction of model and its use in worldwide customer surveys. Extensive use of clinical forum input.	Continue to force product development to follow the established phase review process when the project is large in scope or the market is new to MPI. Institutionalize use of clinical forum and models when appropriate.
Maintenance of aggressive factory cost goals and establishment of additional aggressive low-cost service goals with plans to achieve them	Divisionwide commitment to low-cost products and sustained emphasis on Wolverine's highest-priority goal. Team enthusiasm (R&D, marketing, and manufacturing) that cost is truly important.	Continue high-level management focus on cost. Proper selection of project priorities.
Maintenance of reasonable project scope	Early expectation of limited project resource availability that kept product features lean. Emphasize that the product doesn't have to be perfect but focus on high-priority customer and safety needs. This allows extensive leverage of common hardware and software.	Continued emphasis on efficiency and the attitude that it isn't always necessary to be perfect at any cost.

Wolverine Phase 3 Negative Retrospective		
Negative Effect	*Root Cause*	*Recommendation*
Field selling cost still not well understood	Difficulty in accessing field selling cost data to establish baseline.	Work with international groups to strip out data.
Overall product cost not as low as it could be	Lack of resources to staff low-cost transducer project.	Continue to invest in low-cost transducer development as resources become available.
Inefficient product development	Late availability of mechanical resources caused hardware and mechanical design to be out of phase. Late management focus on platform leverage caused a redesign to accommodate common hardware.	More balanced product staffing plans. Clear goals before designing starts.

The material developed in Phase 3 of the project provided significant information for the marketing program that would have to be developed for Wolverine. While the information was still general in nature, the marketing group was ready to move forward on developing a marketing plan.

Marketing Plan Information

Phase 3 of the project began to address functional-level plans more clearly. The next phase of the development process, Phase 4, entailed bringing these functional-level plans together to make sure all functions were in tune with each other.

From a marketing perspective, the goal of the Wolverine project was to provide a product that would satisfy imaging customers with needs ranging from cardiovascular applications to general-purpose abdominal applications. With this in mind, every attempt was made to gather data to ensure that appropriate features and benefits, pricing, physical appearance, keyboard layout, and total cost of ownership would satisfy the needs of the marketplace. Reduced cost was the number one project goal, not only in product design but also in all aspects of the total product. This included reduced cost in technical support, training, learning products, distribution, and marketing communications. To this end, "low cost" guided the development of new marketing programs. The objective was to bring the Wolverine product to market as a cost-effective solution for the price-performance/price sensitive worldwide customer base.

U.S. Market Analysis.   Exhibit 5 shows a 1998 snapshot projection of market segmentation, market size, installations, competitors, and target market share for Medical Products Inc. in the U.S. marketplace. The goal of this projection was to understand how the price/performance market was segmented in the United States and the market share Medical Products Inc. could expect in year 2 (FY98) after Wolverine's introduction (which was expected in the first quarter of FY97).

International/Distribution.   During Phase 3, a total of 22 customers in the Asia/Pacific region (Kobe, Japan) and Europe (Boeblinger, Germany, and Bergamo, Italy) were visited by a marketing/engineering team and interviewed regarding many aspects of the Wolverine project. Competitive systems were evaluated during this process, and no new competitors had entered either the cardiac or the general-purpose marketplace. The competitive picture was found to be relatively the same in all geographic areas. The major competitors would be Toshiba, Aloka, Hitachi, Interspec, and General Electric.

Nori Kunje, product marketing manager of the Asia/Pacific region, reported that dealers/distributors were positioned geographically for coverage, especially in China. Unlike the United States and Europe, where growth would come from new application areas, China would use dealers to expand sales coverage to realize market share growth. In Japan, dealers could handle the general-purpose customers and distributors could manage the cardiology business.

The need for a low-cost cardiology product in Europe was apparent. Wolverine would serve as a complementary product to the current product offerings of the IMAG line and could be distributed by the European direct sales force. The expected area for growth, however, was the internal medicine general-purpose market. Unfortunately, there was uncertainty about how best to approach that market. There was a distinction between dealers and distributors in the European market. Distributors were responsible for all products, including warranty, installation, and training. The distributor's compensation was embedded in the final selling price to the customer. European distributors were located in areas where MPI did not have a legal entity. The dealer network in Europe was well established. Dealers signed a contract for dollar volume. Warranty was covered by the company, with installation and training paid for by the dealer. Exhibit 6 shows MPI's cost data for the European marketplace.

Pricing.   A goal of the Wolverine project was to develop a product that would maintain acceptable profitability over a five-year product life. The pricing challenge therefore was to predict what could be done to offer value to customers over the years in order to command sustainable pricing in light of competitive pricing pressures.

EXHIBIT 5 U.S. Ultrasound Market Analysis (Wolverine Opportunity)

Market Segment	Customer Profile	Systems Installed in 1995		Purchases per Year in 1998		Competitors	MPI Target in 1998
		Total	Wolverine Equivalent	Total	Wolverine Equivalent		
Cardiovascular–Hospital							
Echo Lab	100+–bed hospitals 200+–bed hospitals	9,500	1,000	1,000	200	Acuson, Toshiba, Vingmed, GE, ATL/Interspec	60% Share 120 units
Open Heart	Open Heart ORs 980 with 2.1 rooms Target = CV surgeons	220	30	100	75	Acuson, ATL/Interspec	70% share 50 units
General OR	Hospitals with OH programs 980 with 10 rooms Target = anesthesiologists	50	10	50	50	Acuson, ATL/Interspec	50% share 25 units
Vascular Surgery	Not Addressable—missing intraoperative probes						
Cardiovascular–Office							
Cardiovascular–Office	Single physician, 2–4 physicians, 5+ physicians	8,000	4,000	750	400	Acuson, Biosound, ATL/Interspec, GE	60% share 240 units
General Purpose–Hospital							
Community Hospital	Less than 200 beds with ultrasound department	3,500	1,000	550	250	Acuson, ATL, Toshiba, Diasonics	10% share 25 units
Emergency Room	More than 200 beds with ER	Negligible	Negligible	150	100	Acuson, ATL/Interspec	25% share 25 units
Radiology Department	200+–bed hospitals needing price/performance and portable machine	11,700	2,000	1,300	300	Acuson, ATL, Toshiba, Diasonics	15% share 45 units
Labor and Delivery	Hospitals with L&D units	4,500	1,000	300	100	ATL, Aloka, Acuson, GE	20% share 20 units
General Purpose–Office							
OB/GYN Group Practice	Single physician, 2–5 physicians, more than 5 physicians	11,500	2,000	1,770	300	ATL, Aloka, Acuson, GE	15% share 45 units
Mobile Services							
General Imaging	Independently owned Hospital-owned	1,000	500	200	150	ATL/Interspec, Acuson, Toshiba	40% share 60 units

EXHIBIT 6   **Direct and Indirect Selling Expenses for Europe**

	Direct Expenses	*Indirect Expenses*
Gross orders	$108,790	$42,952
Discounts	32,637	17,568
Field selling costs	18,129	3,411
Net contribution	58,024	21,973

Customer Support.   Three areas of marketing (technical marketing, learning products, and clinical marketing) dealt with the customer support deliverables. Those three areas submitted a "customer support plan" that included the line of business costs associated with the cost of ownership (see Exhibit 7 for plans for year 1 and years 2 through 5).

In keeping with the low-cost theme for Wolverine, the product support strategy had to do everything possible to reduce expenses to both MPI and the customer—without a reduction in the quality of support. The proposed scenario would be that a customer with a product failure would call the local response center. The response center would remotely interrogate the system and determine the location of the failure. If the failure was in one of the customer replaceable units, the response center would make arrangements for the replacement parts to be sent to the customer. If it was not a replaceable unit, an MPI designate would be sent to the site.

The supportability improvements to be included with the Wolverine were customer-installable media (a 3½-inch floppy disk for installation purposes), remote diagnostics (ability to remotely access the system via modem), improved scanner fault isolation, and customer-replaceable modules (making it easy for the customer to replace such items as the keyboard, VCR, and peripherals).

The learning products aspect of the plan included worldwide customer training through product training materials a week before product arrival, MPI instructor training at the time of installation, and response center calls as follow-up assurance of use. Sending training materials before installation meant that those materials would have to be very customer-friendly.

Marketing Communications.   Wolverine was designed as a low-cost, mixed-application ultrasound imaging system targeted for the price-sensitive/price-performance worldwide market. All marketing communications activities would have the following objectives:

- Communicate a consistent MPI message and image.
- Build recognition for MPI in the general-purpose ultrasound imaging market.
- Build recognition for Wolverine as the best value and the easiest to use mixed application.
- Enhance the effectiveness of the sales process.
- Generate inquiries and leads for sales activities.
- Help achieve product revenue goals.

Financial Analysis.   The nature of the Wolverine project and the targeted segment at the low end of the price/performance market placed many pressures on the cost structure. The interfunctional team recognized that it needed a creative way to examine

EXHIBIT 7   **Support Line of Business Costs**

	Year 1		
	Cost*		
Type	*U.S.†*	*Europe†*	*Asia/Pacific†*
Installation	$ 502	$ 627	$ 430
Basic training	167	201	143
Clinical training	5,104	5,104	4,895
Training materials	373	373	373
Warranty	2,013	2,252	1,877
Preventative maintenance	669	836	573
Preventative assistance	335	418	287
Total	9,163	9,811	8,578

* At FY96 internal labor rates: U.S. $167 per hour
Europe $209 per hour
Asia/Pacific $143 per hour

†U.S. dollars.

	Years 2–5		
	Cost*		
Type	*U.S.†*	*Europe†*	*Asia/Pacific†*
Parts/labor	$2,415	$2,655	$2,268
Preventative maintenance	669	836	573
Preventative assistance	329	418	287
Field overhead and profit	1,465	1,681	1,341
Total	4,878	5,590	4,469

*At FY96 internal labor rates: U.S. $167 per hour
Europe $209 per hour
Asia/Pacific $143 per hour

†U.S. dollars.

profitability—something that would include business costs over time as well as different geographic cost structures. However, until a new approach was developed, Wolverine would have to be analyzed by using the traditional historical approach to financial analysis. Exhibit 8 provides an estimate of product profitability using this historical approach.

Spring 1997

The marketing group was in the middle of the next stage of the Wolverine project. The project was moving full steam ahead, with marketing scheduled to have marketing ideas in place by the fall.

The official worldwide launch of Wolverine was scheduled to take place at the Radiological Society of North America conference to be held on December 1–5, 1998. While a year might seem like a long time, the marketing group knew that it was a long way from the final product. A tentative marketing plan would have to be approved at the end of this fourth phase of evaluation. Once approval was obtained, which would have to be in conjunction with all other functional plans, the marketing group knew it would have little time to get its prerelease material into the marketplace.

EXHIBIT 8   Product Profitability

	*$/Unit**
Gross revenue	$143,159
Trade discount	38,233
Net revenue	104,936
Factory costs	40,691
Trading expense	2,204
Warranty	3,673
Direct expense/allocated overhead	24,765
Field selling cost	19,098
Operating profit	14,505
Net profit	$ 8,413

*U.S. dollars.

CASE 2–3
L'ORÉAL NEDERLAND B.V.

Yolanda van der Zande, director of the Netherlands L'Oréal subsidiary, faced two tough decisions and was discussing them with Mike Rourke, her market manager for cosmetics and toiletries. "We have to decide whether to introduce the Synergie skin care line and Belle Couleur permanent hair colorants," she told him. Synergie had recently been introduced successfully in France, the home country for L'Oréal. Belle Couleur had been marketed successfully in France for two decades. Mr. Rourke responded:

> Yes, and if we decide to go ahead with an introduction, we'll also need to develop marketing programs for the product lines. Fortunately, we only need to think about marketing, since the products will still be manufactured in France.

Ms. van der Zande replied:

> Right, but remember that the marketing decisions on these lines are critical. Both of these lines are part of the Garnier family brand name. Currently Ambre Solaire (a sun screen) is the only product we distribute with the Garnier name in the Netherlands. But headquarters would like us to introduce more Garnier product lines into our market over the next few years, and it's critical that our first product launches in this line be successful.

Mr. Rourke interjected, "But we already sell other brands of L'Oréal products in our market. If we introduce Garnier, what will happen to them?" After some more discussion, Ms. van der Zande suggested:

> Why don't you review what we know about the Dutch market. We've already done extensive marketing research on consumer reactions to Synergie and Belle Couleur. Why don't you look at it and get back to me with your recommendations in two weeks.

Background

In 1992 the L'Oréal Group was the largest cosmetics manufacturer in the world. Headquartered in Paris, it had subsidiaries in over 100 countries. In 1992, its sales were $6.8 billion (a 12 percent increase over 1991) and net profits were $417 million (a 14 percent increase). France contributed 24 percent of total worldwide sales, Europe (both western and eastern countries, excluding France) provided 42 percent, and the United States and Canada together accounted for 20 percent; the rest of the world accounted for the remaining 14 percent. L'Oréal's European subsidiaries were in one of two groups: (1) major countries (England, France, Germany, and Italy) or (2) minor countries (the Netherlands and nine others).

The company believed that innovation was its critical success factor. It thus invested

Copyright © 1994 by the *Case Research Journal* and the authors.

This case was prepared by Frederick W. Langrehr, Valparaiso University; Lee Dahringer, Butler University; and Anne Stöcker. This case was written with the cooperation of management solely for the purpose of stimulating student discussion. All events and individuals are real, but names have been disguised. We appreciate the help of J. B. Wilkinson and V. B. Langrehr on earlier drafts of this case.

heavily in research and development and recovered its investment through global introductions of its new products. All research was centered in France. As finished products were developed, they were offered to subsidiaries around the world. Because brand life cycles for cosmetics could be very short, L'Oréal tried to introduce one or two new products per year in each of its worldwide markets. International subsidiaries could make go/no go decisions on products, but they generally did not have direct input into the R&D process. In established markets such as the Netherlands, any new product line introduction had to be financed by the current operations in that country.

L'Oréal marketed products under its own name as well as under a number of other individual and family brand names. For example, it marketed Anaïs Anaïs perfume, the high-end Lancôme line of cosmetics, and L'Oréal brand hair care products. In the 1970s it acquired Laboratoires Garnier, and this group was one of L'Oréal's largest divisions. In France, with a population of about 60 million people, Garnier was a completely separate division, and its sales force competed against the L'Oréal division. In the Netherlands, however, the market was much smaller (about 15 million people), and Garnier and L'Oréal products would be marketed by the same sales force.

Dutch consumers had little, if any, awareness or knowledge of Garnier and had not formed a brand image. The Garnier sunscreen was a new product, and few Dutch women knew about the brand. It was therefore very important that any new Garnier products launched in the Netherlands have a strong concept and high market potential. To accomplish this, the products needed to offer unique, desired, and identifiable differential advantages to Dutch consumers. Products without such an edge were at a competitive disadvantage and would be likely not only to fail but to create a negative association with the Garnier name, causing potential problems for future Garnier product introductions.

The Dutch Market

In the late 1980s, 40 percent of the Dutch population (about the same percentage as in France) was under 25 years old. Consumers in this age group were the heaviest users of cosmetics and toiletries. But as in the rest of Europe, the Dutch population was aging and the fastest-growing population segments were the 25-or-older groups.

Other demographic trends included the increasing number of Dutch women working outside the home. The labor force participation rate of women in the Netherlands was 29 percent. That was much lower than the 50 percent or above in the United Kingdom or the United States, but the number of women working outside the home was increasing faster in the Netherlands than it was in those countries. Dutch women were also delaying childbirth. As a result of these trends, women in the Netherlands were exhibiting greater self-confidence and independence; women had more disposable income, and more of them were using it to buy cosmetics for use on a daily basis.

Despite their rising incomes, Dutch women still shopped for value, especially in cosmetics and toiletries. In the European Union (EU), the Netherlands ranked fourth in per capita income, but it was only sixth in per capita spending on cosmetics and toiletries. Thus, Dutch per capita spending on personal care products was only 60 percent of the amount spent per capita in France or Germany. As a result of both a small population (15 million Dutch to 350 million EU residents) and lower per capita consumption, the Dutch market accounted for only 4 percent of total EU sales of cosmetics and toiletries.

Synergie

Synergie was a line of facial skin care products that consisted of moisturizing cream, antiaging day cream, antiwrinkle cream, cleansing milk, mask, and cleansing gel. It was made with natural ingredients, and its advertising slogan in France was "The alliance of science and nature to prolong the youth of your skin."

Skin Care Market.   The skin care market was the second largest sector of the Dutch cosmetics and toiletries market. For the past five quarters unit volume had been growing at an annual rate of 12 percent, and dollar sales at a rate of 16 percent. This category consisted of hand creams, body lotions, all-purpose creams, and facial products. Products in this category were classified by price and product type. Skin care products produced by institutes such as Shisedo and Estée Lauder were targeted at the high end of the market. These lines were expensive and were sold through personal service perfumeries that specialized in custom sales of cosmetics and toiletries. At the other end of the price scale were mass-market products such as Ponds, which were sold in drugstores and supermarkets. In the last couple of years a number of companies, including L'Oréal, had begun to offer products in the midprice range. For example its Plénitude line was promoted as a high-quality, higher-priced—but still mass-market—product.

Skin care products also could be divided into care and cleansing products. Care products consisted of day and night creams; cleansing products were milks and tonics. The current trend in the industry was to stretch the lines by adding specific products targeted at skin types, such as sensitive, greasy, or dry. An especially fast-growing category consisted of antiaging and antiwrinkling creams. Complementing this trend was the emphasis on scientific development and natural ingredients.

Almost 50 percent of the 5 million Dutch women between the ages of 15 and 65 used traditional skin care products. The newer specialized products had a much lower penetration, as shown in Exhibit 1.

The sales breakdown by type of retailer for the middle- and lower-priced brands is shown in Exhibits 2 and 3.

EXHIBIT 1   **Usage of Skin Care Products by Dutch Women**

Product	Percentage of Women Using
Day cream	46%
Cleansers	40
Mask	30
Tonic	26
Antiaging cream	3

EXHIBIT 2   **Sales Breakdown for Skin Care Products in Supermarkets and Drugstores**

Type of Store	Unit Sales (%)	Dollar Sales (%)
Supermarkets	18%	11%
Drugstores	82	89
	100	100

EXHIBIT 3   Sales Breakdown for Skin Care Products by Type of Drugstore

Type of Drugstore	Unit Sales (%)	Dollar Sales (%)
Chains	57%	37%
Large independent	31	39
Small independent	12	24
	100	100

EXHIBIT 4   Competitive Product Lines of Cosmetics

	Price Range (Guilders)*	Positioning
Lower End		
Nivea Visage†	9.50–11.50	Mild, modest price, complete line
Ponds	5.95–12.95	Antiwrinkle
Middle		
Dr. vd Hoog	10–11.95	Sober, nonglamorous, no illusions, but real help, natural, efficient, relatively inexpensive
Oil of Olaz (Procter & Gamble)	12 (day cream only)	Moisturizing, antiaging
Plénitude (L'Oréal)	10.95–19.95	Delay the signs of aging
Synergie	11.95–21.95	The alliance of science and nature to prolong the youth of your skin
Upper End		
Yvs Rocher	10–26.95	Different products for different skins, natural ingredients
Ellen Betrix (Estée Lauder)	12.95–43.50	Institute line with reasonable prices, luxury products at nonluxury prices

* One dollar = 1.8 guilders; one British pound = 2.8 guilders; 1 deutschmark = 1.1 guilders.

† Although Nivea Visage had a similar price range to Dr. vd Hoog, consumers perceived Nivea as a lower-end product.

Competition.   There were numerous competitors. Some product lines, such as Oil of Olaz (Oil of Olay in the United States) by Procter & Gamble and Plénitude by L'Oréal, were offered by large multinational companies; other brands, for example, Dr. vd Hoog and Rocher, were offered by regional companies. Some companies offered a complete line, while others, such as Oil of Olaz, offered one or two products. Exhibit 4 lists a few of the available lines along with the price ranges and positioning statements.

The Dutch market was especially competitive for new brands such as Oil of Olaz and Plénitude. The rule of thumb in the industry was that share of voice for a brand (the percentage of total industry advertising spent by the company) should be about the same as its market share. Thus, a company with a 10 percent market share should have had advertising expenditures around 10 percent of total industry advertising expenditures. But there were deviations from this rule. Ponds, an established and well-known company with loyal customers, had about 9 percent share of the market (units) but accounted for only about 2.5 percent of total industry ad expenditures. Alternatively, new brands such as Oil of Olaz (10 percent market share, 26 percent share of voice) and Plénitude (5 percent market share, 13 percent share of voice) spent much more. The higher ad spending for these brands was necessary to develop brand awareness and, ideally, brand preference.

Any innovative products or new product variations in a line could be quickly copied. Retailers could develop and introduce their own private labels in four months; manufacturers could develop a competing product and advertising campaign in six months. Manufacturers looked for new product ideas in other countries and then transferred the product concept or positioning strategy across national borders. They also monitored competitors' test markets. Since a test market typically lasted nine months, a competitor could introduce a product before a test market was completed.

Consumer Behavior.   Consumers tended to be loyal to their current brands. This loyalty resulted from the possible allergic reaction to a new product. Also, facial care products were heavily advertised and sold on the basis of brand image. Thus, users linked self-concept with a brand image, and this increased the resistance to switching. While all consumers had some loyalty, the strength of this attachment to a brand increased with the age of the user. Finally, establishing a new brand was especially difficult since Dutch women typically purchased facial creams only once or twice a year. Dutch women were showing an increasing interest in products with "natural" ingredients, but they were not as familiar as the French were with technical product descriptions and terms.

Market Research Information.   Earlier, Mike Rourke had directed his internal research department to conduct some concept and use tests for the Synergie products. The researchers had sampled 200 women between the ages of 18 and 55 who used skin care products three or more times per week. They sampled 55 Plénitude users, 65 Dr. vd Hoog users, and 80 users of other brands.

The participants reacted positively to Synergie concept boards containing the positioning statement and the terminology associated with the total product line. On a seven-

---

EXHIBIT 5   Buying Intentions for Synergie Products

	All Participants	Plénitude Users	Dr. vd Hoog Users	Other Brand Users
Price Not Known				
Antiaging daycream				
After trial	5.37*	5.63	5.00	5.42
After use	5.26	5.55	5.08	5.17
Moisturizing cream				
After trial	5.34	5.60	5.38	5.11
After use	5.51	5.74	5.56	5.22
Price Known				
Antiaging daycream				
After trial	3.75	4.13	3.82	3.44
After use	3.60	3.76	3.54	3.54
Certainly buy†	24%	21%	23%	27%
Moisturizing cream				
After trial	4.08	4.36	4.17	3.77
After use	4.06	4.26	4.13	3.78
Certainly buy	39%	52%	38%	30%

* Seven-point scale with 7 being most likely to buy.

† Response to a separate question asking about certainty of buying with "certainly buy" as the highest choice.

point scale with 7 being the most positive, the mean score for the Synergie line for all the women in the sample was 4.94. The evaluations of the women who used the competing brands, Plénitude and Dr. vd Hoog, were similar at 4.97 and 4.88, respectively.

The researchers then conducted an in-depth analysis of two major products in the line: antiaging day cream and moisturizing cream. Participants reported their buying intentions after they tried the Synergie product once and again after they used it for a week. Some participants were told the price, and others did not know the price. The results of this analysis are shown in Exhibit 5 on page 139.

Belle Couleur

Belle Couleur was a line of permanent hair coloring products. It had been sold in France for about two decades and was the market leader. In France the line had 22 shades that were mostly natural shades and a few strong red or very bright light shades. It was positioned as reliably providing natural colors with the advertising line "natural colors, covers all gray."

Hair Coloring Market.   There were two types of hair coloring: semipermanent and permanent. Semipermanent colors washed out after five or six shampooings. Permanent colors disappeared only as the hair grew out from the roots. Nearly three-quarters (73 percent) of Dutch women who colored their hair used a permanent colorant. Over the past four years, however, the trend had been toward semipermanent colorants, with an increase from 12 percent to 27 percent of the market. Growth in unit volume during those years for both types of colorant had been about 15 percent per annum. The majority of unit sales in the category were in chain drugstores (57 percent), with 40 percent equally split between large and small independent drugstores. Food retailers accounted for the remaining 3 percent.

Competition.   In the Netherlands 4 of 10 total brands accounted for 80 percent of the sales of permanent hair colorants, compared to 2 brands in France. Exhibit 6 gives the market share of the leading permanent color brands in the period 1987–1989. Interestingly, none of them had a clear advertising positioning statement describing customer benefits. By default, then, Belle Couleur could be positioned as "covering gray with natural colors."

EXHIBIT 6   Major Brands of Hair Colorant

Market Shares of	*1987*	*1988*	*1989*
Upper end (14.95 guilders)			
Recital (L'Oréal brand)	35%	34%	33%
Guhl	9	12	14
Belle Couleur (12.95 guilders)	—	—	—
Lower-priced (9.95 guilders)			
Andrelon	12	14	17
Poly Couleur	24	23	21
Others	20	17	15
Total	100	100	100

Hair salons were indirect competitors in the hair coloring market. The percentage of women who had a hairstylist color their hair was not known, nor were the trends in the usage of this method known. It was projected that as more women worked outside the home, home coloring probably would increase because it was more convenient.

L'Oréal's current market entry (Recital) was the leading seller, although its share was declining. Guhl's and Andrelon's increases in shares between 1986 and 1989 reflected the general trend toward using warmer shades, and these two brands were perceived as giving quality red tones. In the late 1980s Guhl had changed its distribution strategy and started selling the brand through drug chains. In 1987 less than 1 percent of sales were through drug outlets; in the first quarter of 1990 drug-outlet sales had reached nearly 12 percent. Guhl also had become more aggressive in its marketing through large independents, with its share in those outlets climbing from 16 to 24 percent over the same period. Both the increasing shares of the smaller brands and the decreasing shares of the leaders sparked a 60 percent increase in advertising in 1989 for all brands of hair coloring.

Consumer Behavior.   Consumers perceived permanent hair color as a technical product and believed its use was very risky. As a result, users had strong brand loyalty and avoided impulse purchasing. When considering a new brand, both first-time users and current users carefully read package information and asked store personnel for advice.

Traditionally, hair colorants had been used primarily to cover gray hair. Recently, however, coloring hair had become more of a fashion statement. This partially accounted for the increased popularity of semipermanent hair coloring. In one study the most frequently cited reason (33 percent) for coloring hair was to achieve warm/red tones; another 17 percent reported wanting to lighten their hair color, and covering gray was cited by 29 percent. It was likely that the trend toward using colorants more for fashion and less for covering gray reflected the increase in hair coloring by consumers less than 35 years old. In 1989, 46 percent of Dutch women (up from 27 percent in 1986) colored their hair with either semipermanent or permanent hair colorants. Exhibit 7 contains a breakdown of usage by age of user.

Hair coloring was purchased almost exclusively in drugstores; only 3 percent of sales were through supermarkets. The percentage of sales for drug outlets was chains, 58 percent; large independents, 22 percent; and small independents, 20 percent.

Market Research.   As with Synergie, Mr. Rourke had the L'Oréal market researchers contact consumers about their reactions to Belle Couleur. Four hundred twelve Dutch women between the ages of 25 and 64 who had used hair colorant in the last four months were part of a concept test, and 265 of those women participated in a use test. A little over 25 percent of the participants colored their hair every six weeks or

---

EXHIBIT 7   Hair Coloring by Age (%)

	1986	1989
Less than 25 years	35%	50%
25–34	24	54
35–49	32	55
50–64	24	33
65 and over	15	19

EXHIBIT 8   Buying Intentions

	Price-Unaware	*Price-Aware*	*After Use*
Certainly buy (5)	18%	26%	29%
Probably buy (4)	60	57	30
Don't know (3)	12	5	9
Probably not (2)	7	7	11
Certainly not (1)	3	6	21
Total	100%	100%	100%
Mean score	3.85	3.92	3.35

more often, while another 47 percent did it every two to three months. (The average French user colored her hair every three weeks.) Nearly 60 percent used hair color to cover gray, while the remainder did it for other reasons.

After being introduced to the concept and being shown some sample ads, participants were asked their buying intentions. The question was asked three times—before and after the price was given and after Belle Couleur was used. The results are shown in Exhibit 8.

In most product concept tests (as with the Synergie line) buying intentions declined once the price was revealed. For Belle Couleur, buying intentions increased after the price was given but decreased after actual use. As the exhibit shows, the percentage of participants who would probably or certainly not buy the product after using it increased from 13 to 32 percent. In Exhibit 9 only participants who gave negative after-use evaluations of Belle Couleur are included, and they are grouped according to the brands they were using at the time.

To try to determine why some users didn't like the product, the dissatisfied women were asked to state why they disliked Belle Couleur. The results are shown in Exhibit 10.

Many of the women thought that their hair was too dark after using Belle Couleur and said it "didn't cover gray." Those who thought Belle Couleur was different from expected were primarily using the blond and chestnut brown shades of colorant. This was expected, since in France Belle Couleur was formulated to give a classical, conservative dark blond color without extra reflections or lightening effects and the product had not been modified for the Dutch test. The competing Dutch-manufactured hair colorant competitors, by contrast, were formulated to give stronger lightening effects. Thus, some of the negative evaluations of Belle Couleur were due to the fact that Dutch women tended toward naturally lighter hair colors, and the French toward darker shades.

Role of Distributors

Distributors' acceptance of the two product lines was critical for L'Oréal's successful launch of both Synergie and Belle Couleur. At one time, manufacturers had more control in the channel of distribution than did retailers. Retailers, however, had been gaining power as a result of the increasing size of retailers, the development of chains with their central buying offices, and the proliferation of new brands with little differentiation from brands currently on the market. Retailers had also increasingly been offering their own private-label products, since they earned a higher-percentage profit margin on their own brands.

EXHIBIT 9   Purchase Intentions and Evaluation of Belle Couleur by Brand Currently Used

	Brand Currently Used				
	Total Sample	*Andrelon*	*Poly Couleur*	*Guhl*	*Recital (L'Oréal)*
After-Use Purchase Intentions of Belle Couleur					
Probably not (2)	11%	12%	12%	14%	5%
Certainly not (1)	21	24	29	20	5
	32%	36%	41%	34%	10%
Overall mean score	3.35	3.4	3.1	3.4	3.95
Evaluation of Final Color of Belle Couleur					
Very good (1)	25%	24%	31%	22%	35%
Good (2)	43	40	31	44	49
Neither good or bad (3)	10	10	14	6	8
Bad (4)	12	14	5	18	8
Very bad (5)	9	12	19	10	. . .
Mean	2.37	2.5	2.5	2.5	1.89
Comparison to Expectations					
Much better (1)	11%	12%	14%	14%	14%
Better (2)	26	12	21	24	38
The same (3)	29	38	26	28	32
Worse (4)	19	24	19	18	11
Much worse (5)	15	14	19	16	5
Mean	3.0	3.17	3.07	2.98	2.57
Compared with Own Brand					
Much better (1)		17%	17%	24%	14%
Better (2)		21	19	24	32
The same (3)		21	31	14	30
Worse (4)		21	12	16	16
Much worse (5)		19	21	22	8
Mean		3.05	3.02	2.88	2.73

Following are the criteria, listed in order of importance (3 being "most important"), that retailers used to evaluate new products:

1. Evidence of consumer acceptance   2.5
2. Manufacturer advertising and promotion   2.2
3. Introductory monetary allowances   2.0
4. Rationale for product development   1.9
5. Merchandising recommendations   1.8

L'Oréal's goal for developing new products was to introduce only products that had a differential advantage with evidence of consumer acceptance. It did not want to gain distribution with excessive reliance on trade deals or higher than normal retail gross margins. L'Oréal also wanted to have its Garnier product lines extensively distributed in as many different types of retailers and outlets as possible. This approach to new product introduction had been effective for L'Oréal, and it currently had a positive image with Dutch retailers. L'Oréal was perceived as offering high-quality, innovative products supported with good in-store merchandising.

EXHIBIT 10   **Reasons for Negative Evaluations of Belle Couleur by Brand Currently Used**

	Brand Currently Used				
	Total Sample	*Andrelon*	*Poly Couleur*	*Guhl*	*Recital (L'Oréal)*
Hair got dark/darker instead of lighter	13%	14%	17%	14%	5%
Irritates skin	8	10	7	2	11
Ammonia smell	5	7	—	2	—
Didn't cover gray	5	12	2	4	3
Color not beautiful	5	7	5	6	3
Color different from expected	5	5	10	4	3

Note: Some of the cell sizes are very small, and caution should be used when comparing entries of less than 10 percent.

For L'Oréal's current products, 35 percent of sales came from independent drugstores, 40 percent from drug chains, and 25 percent from food stores. For all manufacturers, drug chains and supermarkets were increasing in importance. These stores required a brand with high customer awareness and some brand preference. The brands needed to be presold since, unlike independent drugstores, there was no sales assistance.

Introducing a line of products rather than just a product or two resulted in a greater need for retail shelf space. Although the number of new products and brands competing for retail shelf space frequently appeared unlimited, the space itself was a limited resource. With Belle Couleur, L'Oréal had already addressed this issue by reducing the number of Belle Couleur colorants it planned to offer in the Netherlands. Although 22 shades were available in France, L'Oréal had reduced the line to 15 variations for the Netherlands. As a result, 1.5 meters (about five linear feet) of retail shelf space was needed to display the 15 shades of Belle Couleur. Synergie required about half this shelf space.

Decision Time

After reviewing the information on the market research on the two product lines, Ms. van der Zande summarized the situation. L'Oréal Netherlands could leverage its advertising of the Garnier name by promoting two lines at once. Consumers would hear and see the Garnier name twice, not just once. As a result, Dutch consumers might see Garnier as a major supplier of cosmetics and toiletries. But she was concerned about the selling effort that would be needed to sell the L'Oréal brands that were already in the Dutch market and at the same time introduce not just one but two new brand name product *lines*. The Dutch L'Oréal sales force would have to handle both family brands, since the much lower market potential of the Netherlands market could not support a separate Garnier sales force, as in France. She was also concerned about retailer reaction to a sales pitch for two product lines.

Ms. van der Zande reflected that she was facing three decision areas. First, she had to decide if she should introduce one or both product lines, and she had to make this decision knowing that L'Oréal would not reformulate the products just for the Dutch market. Second, if she decided to introduce either one or both of the product lines, she needed to develop a marketing program. This meant she had to make decisions on the promotion of the product line(s) to both retailers and consumers as well as the pricing and distribution of the line(s). Third, given that the Garnier product introductions might negatively affect the sales of her current product lines, she needed tactical marketing plans for those products.

THE NEW YORK ISLANDERS HOCKEY CLUB, INC.

The National Hockey League (NHL) has become one of the most popular sports leagues in the United States. With the latest surge in its popularity, marketing strategies are becoming necessary for teams throughout the league to succeed.

As hockey gets more popular, it is ironic that teams are having financial problems. In June 1999 the NHL commissioner, Gary Bettman, said that "some of the financial problems affecting about three-quarters of the league's 27 teams are their own fault."[1] The New York Islanders team is struggling to draw fans, pay its players, and free the team from a binding lease.

In October 1999 the Islanders played at home versus the Atlanta Thrashers. Fans bought only 5,219 tickets (approximately 11,000 tickets shy of capacity), and the turnstiles accounted for only 3,062 attending fans. The rest of the season continued in the same fashion, with low attendance and merchandise sales. Something had to be done before the Islanders were forced to fold or relocate to another city.

Professional Sports Industry

The professional sports industry has been and will continue to be an industry characterized by profit, competition, and growth. Professional U.S. baseball, basketball, football, and hockey teams together generate sales of about $8 billion per year. Revenues broken down among the four major sports in the industry are shown in Exhibit 1. Baseball, basketball, and football have always been considered American sports even though they may have roots in other nations. Each sport showed growth in revenue from 1997 to 1998 and will continue to grow as each league has shown interest in expansion.

Some professional sports teams are owned by major corporations. For example, the News Corporation owns the Los Angeles Dodgers baseball team and the Molson Companies owns the Montreal Canadiens hockey team. Some teams are owned by individuals. For example, George Steinbrenner owns the New York Yankees baseball team and Jerry Reinsdorf owns the Chicago Bulls basketball team.[2] Corporations are not allowed to own teams in the National Football League; NFL football teams are owned by individuals or groups of individuals.

Revenues from professional sports include ticket profits, media revenues, licensing fees for names and logos, merchandising revenues, endorsements, parking fees, luxury sky boxes, and concessions. Professional athletes, through endorsements of products or

---

[1] Dave Fay, "Bettman Assails Clubs' Spending, Caps' Lagging Ticket Sales," *Washington Times,* June 10, 1999, p. B3

[2] Hoover's Online-Professional Sports Industry Snapshot, April 9, 2000, http://www.hoovers.com/industry/snapshot/0,2204,33,00.htm.

This case was written by Christine Lynn Connolly under the supervision of Victoria L. Crittenden, associate professor of marketing at Boston College, as a basis for class discussion rather than to illustrate either effective or ineffective handling of an administrative situation. The material was taken from secondary sources.

Exhibit 1   Major League Team Revenues[1]

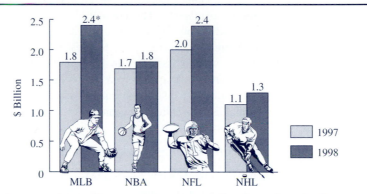

[1] Includes gate receipts, media revenues, venue revenues, licensing, and merchandise revenues.
*Estimate.

Source: Hoover's and Forbes, www.hoovers.com.

services, also add to the revenues of these sports. Michael Jordan, one of the most famous basketball players and athletes of all time, earned a whopping US$45 million for endorsements in 1998, while Tiger Woods, a professional golfer, earned US$28 million. Attending a professional sporting event can be very expensive. After tickets and souvenirs have been bought, parking has been paid for, and the concession stand has been visited, the spectator has contributed greatly to the revenue of the team as well as to that of the league to which the team belongs. While baseball, basketball, and football have all been popular since the inception of U.S. professional sports, hockey has taken a longer time to catch on among spectators and fans. Hockey has, however, moved into the spotlight with famous players such as Wayne Gretzky and Bobby Orr and will continue to shine as advertising, youth participation, fan interest, and league size grow.

Hockey, the Beginning

Ice hockey is a game of skill, power, balance, and agility. The sport is played on an ice surface. There are six players on the ice for each team, consisting of three offensive players, two defensive players, and a goalie who guards the team's goal. There are fewer players on the ice if a team incurs a penalty; the player who commits the penalty has to serve a designated amount of time in the penalty box. The players usually are equipped with helmets, gloves, ice skates, elbow guards, shin guards, padded pants, shoulder pads, and sometimes mouth and neck guards. Each player carries a hockey stick in order to handle and shoot the puck, which is a very small piece of rubber, into the opposing team's goal.

Hockey has a history of which many people are unsure. The sport cannot be accredited to a specific inventor, nor can anyone find an exact date for the birth of this winter pastime. "Once a relatively obscure recreation for people who lived in the north country, hockey is now played all over the world and has become one of the most popular winter sports."[3]

---

[3] http://www.nhl.com/history/evolution.htm.

Many people believe that hockey began somewhere in Europe and then migrated to North America. Games were first played in Canada, and soon some organization to the competitions developed. "The continent's first hockey league was said to have been launched in Kingston, Ontario, in 1885, and it included four teams."[4] As more organized competitions occurred, Lord Stanley of Preston, the English governor general of Canada, "was so impressed that in 1892 he bought a silver bowl with an interior gold finish and decreed that it be given each year to the best amateur team in Canada."[5] Today the team that wins the National Hockey League finals is honored with the same trophy, which is now called the Stanley Cup.

The National Hockey League Then

Before the National Hockey League was born, several smaller leagues existed. The International Pro Hockey league began in 1904 but ended in 1907. The National Hockey Association followed, and after that the Pacific Coast League began. World War I caused the uprooting of those leagues. After the war ended, a new organization was started, and this one was here to stay. The National Hockey League held its first game on December 19, 1917. The five original teams were the Montreal Canadiens, the Montreal Wanderers, the Ottawa Senators, the Quebec Bulldogs, and the Toronto Arenas. The Pacific Coast League still existed, but it was short-lived. In 1926 the NHL formed two divisions and had 10 teams. Those teams would play for the Stanley Cup. Slowly the NHL expanded, and hockey players and equipment improved. Teams started showing up throughout Canada and in the United States.

The National Hockey League Now

The NHL currently has 28 teams divided into two conferences, the Eastern and Western conferences, which are further divided into six divisions: the Atlantic Division, the Northeast Division, the Southeast Division, the Central Division, the Northwest Division, and the Pacific Division (Exhibit 2). Two more expansion teams, the Columbus Blue Jackets and the Minnesota Wild, are expected to begin play in the 2000–2001 season. The reward for winning the playoffs is still the famous Stanley Cup, which the members of the winning team hold above their heads as they lap the rink after the final victory. The Stanley Cup is one of the most prestigious athletic awards in the world.

The NHL commissioner, Gary Bettman, stated that in the 1998–1999 season attendance was up 41 percent from seven years earlier even though there had been attendance slumps with some teams, including the New York Islanders.[6] See Exhibit 3 for a comparison of team attendance in the 1998–1999 and 1999–2000 seasons. Even with the general league increase in attendance at NHL games, many teams are still losing money. The salaries of the players are increasing faster than revenues are.[7] In 1991, an average player's salary was around $270,000; it increased to approximately $1.2 million in 1998.[8]

Despite the teams' losses in profits and even though hockey trails other American sports, some people say that investment in the NHL and its teams could prove to be ben-

---

[4] Ibid.

[5] Ibid.

[6] Fay, "Bettman Assails Clubs' Spending."

[7] Ibid.

[8] Ibid.

EXHIBIT 2   **The National Hockey League**

Eastern Conference		
Atlantic Division	*Northeast Division*	*Southeast Division*
New Jersey Devils	Boston Bruins	Carolina Hurricanes
New York Islanders	Buffalo Sabres	Atlanta Thrashers
New York Rangers	Montreal Canadiens	Florida Panthers
Philadelphia Flyers	Ottawa Senators	Tampa Bay Lightning
Pittsburgh Penguins	Toronto Maple Leafs	Washington Capitals
Western Conference		
Central Division	*Northwest Division*	*Pacific Division*
Chicago Blackhawks	Calgary Flames	Mighty Ducks of Anaheim
Detroit Red Wings	Colorado Avalanche	Dallas Stars
Nashville Predators	Edmonton Oilers	Los Angeles Kings
St. Louis Blues	Vancouver Canucks	Phoenix Coyotes
San Jose Sharks		
Expansion Teams		
Columbus Blue Jackets		
Minnesota Wild		

eficial due to the room in the league for improvement and growth. From 1994 to 2000, the league experienced an NHL-licensed merchandise sales increase of approximately 20 percent, while NBA merchandise sales went down 36 percent.[9] Paul Much of Houlihan Lokey Howard and Zukin, a Chicago investment banking firm, states, "Hockey is the growth stock of professional sports. The best value plays are teams that have been poorly marketed, or in situations where the arena economics can be improved."[10]

The marketing solutions for teams in the National Hockey League have varied by team. "Teams are trying discounts, frequent-buyer rewards and snappy advertising campaigns to lure fans, with mixed results."[11] A marketing strategy that almost every team has tried is the building or renovation of a hockey arena. "In the last five years alone, eleven state-of-the-art arenas for NHL teams have opened their doors. Four more will debut this year and three in the 2000–2001 season."[12] The three teams still playing in older, less sophisticated arenas are the New York Islanders, the New Jersey Devils, and the Detroit Red Wings. Some teams, however, are still seeing a slump in sales, even with newer arenas.

Some people blame a team's slump in sales on not having a winning record. After the wonderful sales and popularity of an expansion team's first few years in the league,

---

[9] David Olive, "Interest in Hockey Heats Up as Owners Launch Vigorous Marketing Campaign," *National Post,* January 1, 2000, Financial Post section, p. D05.

[10] Ibid.

[11] Helene Elliott, "The NHL: Fan-Friendly Moves Get Mixed Results," *Los Angeles Times,* November 2, 1999, p. D3

[12] Steve Zipay, "State of The Islanders/Arena of Dreams/Isles May Study Many Blue Prints," *Newsday,* July 4, 1999, Sports, p. C06.

EXHIBIT 3   TEAM-BY-TEAM COMPARISON OF ATTENDANCE

Team	Games	1998–1999	1999–2000
Boston Bruins	18	288,500	287,904
Buffalo Sabres	19	331,050	327,708
Calgary Flames	16	247,055	235,172
Carolina Hurricanes	17	126,599	215,999
Chicago Black Hawks	17	284,700	281,796
Colorado Avalanche	12	192,732	216,194
Dallas Stars	16	269,425	272,016
Detroit Red Wings	19	379,677	379,677
Edmonton Oilers	17	272,214	258,737
Florida Panthers	17	311,195	263,340
Los Angeles Kings	16	199,570	255,106
Mighty Ducks of Anaheim	20	313,460	280,244
Montreal Canadiens	17	349,389	336,127
Nashville Predators	18	281,644	299,212
New Jersey Devils	19	315,861	269,197
New York Islanders	17	191,679	164,850
New York Rangers	19	345,800	345,800
Ottawa Senators	17	272,826	291,410
Philadelphia Flyers	20	391,333	390,464
Phoenix Coyotes	17	266,409	249,126
Pittsburgh Penguins	16	225,677	230,484
San Jose Sharks	20	327,729	342,468
St. Louis Blues	20	374,858	347,829
Tampa Bay Lightning	16	167,415	230,524
Toronto Maple Leafs	23	361,608	438,596
Vancouver Canucks	19	301,259	265,496
Washington Capitals	15	267,903	186,234

Source: National Hockey League, Mighty Ducks of Anaheim, and Chris Foster, "Ducks' Act No Longer Good Enough to Pack House: Hockey: High Ticket Prices, Mushrooming Player Salaries and Flawed Marketing Strategy Blamed for Attendance Decline," *Los Angeles Times,* December 31, 1999, p. D15.

fans lose interest if a team does not win. Others claim that the slump in ticket sales for some teams may be due to the league's ticket prices. The average ticket price last season was $45.70, and a four-person family can expect to spend an average of $254.48 after paying for tickets, concession visits, and parking, according to the Team Marketing Report in Chicago.[13] This ticket price is the highest among the four professional sports leagues in North America.[14] In the 1998–1999 season, only six teams—Tampa Bay, Pittsburgh, Washington, Phoenix, Buffalo, and the New York Islanders—lowered the average ticket cost, while the majority of teams increased ticket prices.[15]

Ticket sales are important for hockey teams. They are more essential than is the case for football, baseball, and basketball because hockey receives less money from televi-

---

[13] Chris Foster, "Ducks' Act No Longer Good Enough to Pack House: Hockey: High Ticket Prices, Mushrooming Player Salaries and Flawed Marketing Strategy Blamed for Attendance Decline," *Los Angeles Times,* December 31, 1999, p. D15.

[14] David Holzman, "Second Thoughts: Islanders' Arena Sees Attendance Sink Steeply," *Arkansas Democrat-Gazette,* October 19, 1999, p. C2.

[15] "NHL Ticket Price Average Is Up," *Tampa Tribune,* October 15, 1999, Sports, p. 5.

sion stations than do the other three sports. "While NFL teams each receive $71 million from television, NHL teams each get $4.5 million."[16] With less seating than there is in other sports arenas, hockey teams must strive to fill to capacity and keep tickets at a price at which people will buy them.

The New York Islanders

On November 8, 1971, Long Island was assigned an expansion team of the National Hockey League. The team's home was and remains the Nassau Veteran's Memorial Coliseum. The Islanders began play on October 7, 1972, losing that game to the Atlanta Flames. However, this would not prove to be a team that went down easily. In the following years the Islanders remained competitive with the other teams in the league. Their dominating years were yet to come.

The early 1980s are known as the Islander dynasty to any true National Hockey League fan. March 10, 1980, was the day the Islanders acquired one of their best remembered players, Butch Goring. Goring joined the team in time to create memories that will live forever in the hearts of Islander fans everywhere. In the same year, on May 24, the Islanders won their first Stanley Cup by defeating the Philadelphia Flyers in overtime. The following year, the team won the cup again, this time leaving the Minnesota North Stars in second place. The streak would not stop there, as the Islanders would go on to be the NHL champions in 1982 and 1983. Throughout this dynasty period the Islanders accrued many adoring fans. Long Island was hopping with blue and white jerseys decorated with favorite players' numbers and autographs. The Islanders became the dominant team of the first part of the decade. After their win in the 1983 finals, the team went to the White House, where goalie Bill Smith gave President Ronald Reagan a goalie stick inscribed with "The Puck Stops Here."[17]

Smith spoke too soon. In the Stanley Cup finals in 1984, the Islanders were defeated by the Edmonton Oilers, four games to one. The Islanders have yet to see another title round game since that time.

As the team entered the slump it would find difficult to recover from, fan attendance began to decrease. In 1992, the Islanders tried a direct mail campaign to market the home opener versus the New York Rangers. The campaign was said to "metaphorically label the team as 'new and improved!' " and called that season "the new ice age."[18] During the 1991–1992 season, the Islanders' average attendance, lowest in the league at that time, was 10,099 per game, a staggeringly low figure considering that the Coliseum holds approximately 16,297 fans.[19] The Islanders knew that they had to get their irritated and disappointed fans back into the Coliseum. The campaign targeted those consumers by asking for another chance to live up to fans' standards and bring home another Stanley Cup. This advertising did not work. Performance was what the fans wanted.

In 1995 the Islanders participated in yet another marketing strategy. "At least seven teams—more than a quarter of the league—[had] petitioned the NHL for the right to change uniforms, logos, colors and/or mascots."[20] The Islanders, along with the other

---

[16] Foster, "Ducks' Act No Longer Good Enough."

[17] Editors: Chris Botta, Kerry Gwydir, Jason Lagnese, "In Islanders History," *New York Islanders 1999–2000 Media Guide,* pp. 138–43.

[18] Stuart Elliot, "The Media Business: Advertising: Marketing a Hockey Team as a New, Improved Product," *New York Times,* August 18, 1992, p. D1

[19] Elliot, "The Media Business."

[20] Mike Patterson, "NHL Teams Focus on Marketing," *Omaha World Herald,* March 5, 1995, p. C13.

NHL teams, believed that that idea would raise merchandise sales and fan interest. And it did raise fan interest, but not in the way the teams desired. Fans organized themselves into Save the Islanders Coalition, abbreviated as STICK. This group believed that changing the uniform detracted from their memories of Stanley Cup wins and claimed that the owners during that time, Howard and Edward Milstein and Steven Gluckstern, were "bleeding the team dry," especially as they reaped the benefits of expensive Coliseum parking.[21] The fans convinced Islander management to discard the new logo and revert back to the traditional logo.

STICK is still a voice in the Islander community. During an Islander home game in the Coliseum, you can hear the chanting from a section where Islanders fans sit. They chant, "SMG, set us free!" SMG manages the Coliseum and has a lease with the Islanders until the year 2015. The fans want SMG to allow the Islanders to break the lease or develop a more favorable lease. The present lease is making it even more difficult to get a new arena. The Coliseum is in desperate need of renovation. The Islanders are in need of an upgrade or a new arena.

On April 30, 1999, ex-Islander player and Stanley Cup winner Butch Goring was introduced as the team's ninth coach. The organization was feeling the pressure of poor attendance, declining ticket and merchandise sales, and the need to invigorate the team and fans. With an extremely small payroll, management did all that was possible. The strategy was to focus on nurturing a product that would sell. Management recognized that the product demanded by the customers was a winning team. It also realized that the development of this product would not come instantly. Instead of trying to squeeze the payroll account to afford one expensive superstar, they invested in talented youth such as Mariusz Czerkawski, Tim Connolly, and Roberto Luongo. The plan was to keep the young players together to form a solid foundation. The Islanders began to build from the bottom up and work toward their goal of managing a winning team.

Some fans are showing some support of the new strategy. They are excited to have Butch Goring as head coach. Attendance, however, has not improved. In the 1999–2000 season, attendance was down again (see Exhibit 3). The young team had only won 24 games, the same as the previous season. Player trades occurred throughout the year, and the Islanders traded their highest paid player, goalie Felix Potvin. Although the number of wins did not improve, General Manager Mike Milbury gave a postseason address, stating, "It's safe to say that there are a lot of good things ahead for this team."

Milbury did not know at that time how right he was. On April 26, 2000, Howard and Edward Milstein and Steven Gluckstern announced the sale of the New York Islanders. The team was bought by Charles Wang, Computer Associates founder and CEO, and Computer Associates' president and chief operating officer, Sanjay Kumar.[22]

The team, management, and new owners all show excitement at the possibility of having a larger payroll and more money to work with. With fans on their last legs, the owners will have to restore fan interest, increase ticket and merchandise sales, and, most difficult, provide a winning team. Will Wang and Sanjay be able to develop a strategy to pull the team out of its miserable slump with the help of management and the players? Or will the task prove to be too much and cause a loss because of the extremely low fan attendance and difficulty in breaking a lease with SMG in order to renovate the arena or build a new one?

---

[21] Ibid.

[22] http://www.newyorkislanders.com/news/islessale.htm, accessed May 4, 2000.

CASE 2–5
PFIZER, INC., ANIMAL HEALTH PRODUCTS (A):
MARKET SEGMENTATION AND INDUSTRY CHANGES

Kipp Kreutzberg was putting the finishing touches on his marketing plan for the coming year. As the senior marketing manager of Pfizer's Cow/Calf Division, he was responsible for a full range of animal health products that Pfizer marketed to cattle ranchers, including vaccines for newborn calves and their mothers, medications (dewormers, antidiarrheals, etc.), and antibiotics (for pneumonia and other diseases). Pfizer positioned its products on the combination of superior science (resulting from its significant R&D efforts) and high-quality production/quality control techniques. Pfizer's pride in its sophisticated research and development was based on its new and useful products for the market. The company invests more in research and development than any other animal health company does.

Pfizer historically had segmented ranchers in the cow/calf business on the basis of herd size, as shown in Exhibit 1. "Hobbyists" are so called because in many cases these ranchers run their cattle as a sideline to another job. For example, a schoolteacher may keep a herd of cattle simply because he grew up on a ranch and couldn't imagine not doing so. In many cases hobbyists' ranch income accounts for a minor percentage of their overall income. The average age of hobbyists is 50 years, and 15 percent have a college degree. They have been in the cattle business for an average of 26 years and spend 51 percent of their time with their cattle businesses.

The main livelihood of "traditionalists" is their cattle operation. The average age of traditionalists is 51 years, and 26 percent have a college degree. They have been in the cattle business for 30 years and spend 70 percent of their time with their cattle operations.

The "business" segment operations are headed by ranchers who average 53 years of age, 22 percent of whom have a college degree, and who average 33 years in the business. They spend 80 percent of their time with their cattle. These large ranch businesses are owned either by a family or by a corporation.

Pfizer had an extensive network of field sales representatives who visited ranchers to inform them of products, offer seminars on herd health, and sponsor industry activities such as stock shows and 4-H. Time spent with accounts typically is allocated on the basis of volume of product purchased. Ranchers then buy the animal health products they need from either a veterinarian or a distributor/dealer (typically, animal feed stores and similar establishments). The field sales reps also call on the vets and distributors/dealers to help them manage inventory and inform them of new products and merchandising programs.

Some of the information in this case has been modified to protect the proprietary nature of firms' marketing strategies. The case is intended to be used as a basis for class discussion rather than to illustrate either effective or ineffective marketing strategies.

This case was written by Jakki Mohr and Sara Streeter, University of Montana. © Copyright by Jakki J. Mohr, 1999. All rights reserved. Support from the Institute for the Study of Business Markets, Pennsylvania State University, is greatly appreciated.

Exhibit 1   Pfizer Market Segmentation, 1998

Segment	No. Cattle	No. Operations	Percent of National Cattle Inventory
Hobbyist	<100	808,000	50%
Traditionalist	100–499	69,000	36
Business	500+	5,900	14

The Problem: Industry Challenges and Change and a Need to Evaluate Segmentation Practice

As the leader of the marketing team, Kipp recognized that his customers were facing some daunting challenges that would result in significant changes in the industry, changes that probably would affect Pfizer's animal health business. For example, the market share of beef products had declined from 44 percent in 1970 to 32 percent in 1997, while pork and poultry had gained share. The decline in beef consumption was due in part to well-known concerns about cholesterol and fat. In addition, preparation issues affected the demand for beef, as they did for poultry and pork demand as well. For example, two-thirds of all dinner decisions are made by a consumer on the same day. In these same-day decisions, three-fourths of the consumers still don't know what they are going to make as late as 4:30 PM. Obviously, many beef products require cooking and preparation time, and this limits consumer selection.

Of course, other types of meat products also require cooking and preparation time. A key difference, however, is that consumers were being bombarded with new products from the poultry and pork industries. For example, in 1997 Tyson Foods introduced stuffed chicken entrees, roasted chicken dinners, Southwest-style blackened fajitas, and a host of other creative products. The names Tyson and Purdue are well recognized by the public, unlike the names of most beef products.

Some of the changes that had occurred in the poultry and pork industries were expected to diffuse into the cattle industry. Industry analysts believed that the beef industry would need to develop products that could be more easily prepared and develop branded products that consumers could recognize and rely on for quality and convenience.

In addition, industry analysts believed that the beef industry would have to improve the quality of its products in terms of more consistent taste and tenderness. Beef quality is assessed on the basis of U.S. production targets for tenderness, juiciness, flavoring, and marbling (fat) of cuts of beef. The targets are based on two dimensions. The first dimension is based on taste quality (tenderness and juiciness) and specifies that 70 percent of beef production should be rated high quality (choice or prime). The second dimension is based on yield and specifies that 70 percent of beef cattle should be rated grade 1 or grade 2 (implying a good amount of beef for the carcass size), with 0 percent poor yield (meaning that the carcass did not yield much meat). Currently, only 25 percent of beef cattle meet these criteria.

One way to improve the percentage of cattle meeting these criteria is participation in the Beef Quality Assurance program run through the federal government. This is a voluntary quality control program that is based on the education, awareness, and training of cattle producers to influence the safety, quality, and wholesomeness of beef products. It specifies injection sites (neck versus rump) for shots, a seven-step quality check for cows, a method and location for branding, and so forth. Forty percent of ranchers say they have participated in this program in the last two years, among whom 67 percent have changed the way they manage their cattle.

In summary, consumer demand for beef products had declined over the years, resulting in a situation of overcapacity, which depressed prices. A flood of imports resulting from NAFTA regulations further worsened the situation, as did high prices for feed. Most industry analysts were predicting a period of consolidation and alliances. Furthermore, many industry experts expected that beef would have to improve in quality and be better marketed and packaged to fit consumers' changing lifestyles.

Kipp wondered how the ranchers, who were the lifeblood of his division's sales, would handle the changes. From reports from the sales representatives in the field, he knew that the situation was dire for many ranchers. He wondered whether Pfizer's approach to marketing took account of the complicated situation. In particular, the Cow/Calf Division had been segmenting the market of ranchers on the basis of herd size for at least 15 years. In light of the significant challenges posed by industry changes, Kipp wondered whether his team's approach to the marketplace was still a useful one. Perhaps a different approach to segmenting the market might allow his division to develop more effective marketing strategies in light of the changes looming on the horizon.

Research Method

To provide some insight into the continued viability of segmenting the market on the basis of herd size, Kipp asked Joan Kuzmack, the manager of marketing research for the Livestock Division, to conduct a series of depth interviews with cattle ranchers in the Rocky Mountain/Midwest region. These interviews offer qualitative insights into behavioral and attitudinal differences among cow/calf ranchers. More specifically, the objectives of the research were to do the following:

- Identify the inputs driving ranchers' success as cow/calf producers.
- Identify whether ranchers' values and beliefs about herd management differed by herd size.
- Determine what motivates cow/calf producers in selecting products.
- Examine ranchers' views about the future.

A stratified random sample was used to select ranchers for interviews. Rocky Mountain and Upper Midwest ranchers in each of the three groups (hobbyist, traditionalist, and business) were identified and randomly selected from within those strata. Exhibit 2 provides descriptive statistics on the types and numbers of ranchers interviewed.

Ranchers were asked a variety of questions, using a semistructured questionnaire. The questionnaire focused on their herd management activities; attitudes, values, and beliefs about herd management; and views of the future trends in their industry.

Research Findings

Inputs Driving Ranchers' Success as Cow/Calf Producers.   The results from the interviews suggested that commercial producers across all three herd-size categories look for maximum output (weight gain, number of calves) with the minimum inputs. They attempt to improve the quality of their calves through *health and nutrition programs, genetics, and herd culling.* Activities used to manage the herd include vaccinations, nutrition, and breeding programs. Ranchers also strive for uniformity in the calves, typically on the basis of size. These goals in managing the herd are traded off against the cost of achieving them. As one respondent stated:

EXHIBIT 2   Summary of Types of Ranchers Interviewed

	Hobbyist	*Traditionalist*	*Business*
Number of Interviews	3	6	3
Size of Herd			
<100	3		
100–250		2	
251–500		4	
501–1000			2
>1,000			1
Percent of Time Spent with Cattle			
<80%	2		1
81–90%			
91–99%		1	
100%	1	5	2
Percent of Income from Cattle			
<80%	3	2	1
81–90%		2	1
91–99%		1	1
100%		1	
Type of Operation*			
Seed stock	2	2	
Commercial	1	4	3

* *Seed-stock operators* focus on breeding high-quality bulls for use by commercial producers. The bulls are measured by the quality of their offspring. Desirable characteristics include low birth weight, rapid growth, high carcass yield, and grading of choice or better-quality meat. *Commercial producers* raise calves to sell to feedlots. The feedlots fatten the calves, are sold to packing houses, and move on to the retail distribution channel for consumers. In some cases, commercial producers retain ownership of their calves, in which case the rancher pays the feedlot to feed out the calves but the rancher still owns them. Then the rancher sells the calves to the packing houses.

> We strive for the largest amount of production with the least amount of input going in. That's really the only thing we can control at this point with the economy the way it is. We can't control the price that we get for our product, so the only way we can make ends meet is to control the input cost.—Traditionalist

Some ranchers also focused on range management of their grasslands as another objective in managing their operations:

> Basically I think of us as ranchers; we're in the business of grass managers. We grow grass, and if we don't manage our lands to grow a lot of grass, the right kind of grass, we can't run the cows properly. All the genetics in the world won't be of use without the right grass. —Traditionalist

The degree to which ranchers felt that *health management* was critical to their herds' success varied greatly. Some valued herd health as one of the most important concerns:

> You start off with the best breeding that you think you can do through bull selection. From there, it goes on with nutrition and herd health. You're expecting more from the cows. You have to put more into them with nutrition and herd health. You can't cut corners on either one of those. Some feeds will be cheaper some years than others, but we stay with the same drugs.—Traditionalist

Others tended to put in the bare minimum into herd health, sometimes because they were uncertain what results the health management programs yielded:

> We only do the bare minimum on health care. We do more of a preventative maintenance than anything else. We don't do any more than we have to because you can vaccinate for so many things. Our philosophy has been, if you don't need it, don't do it. You can get an awful lot of money in your cows giving them shots of stuff I don't know if you need.—Traditionalist

> I try to keep them healthy with shots and nutrition. I don't want to skimp on the health of a cow, but if I can save some money by supplementing different things in the ration or with vaccinations. . . .—Hobbyist

Seed-stock producers were seeking "best genetics," a loosely defined goal that commonly focused on breeding bulls that would maximize weight gain in commercial calves. Seed-stock producers consistently used artificial insemination in their cows and kept computer records to track information on their herds. They used software programs provided through the breed association to record animal registry and performance information.

Use of Information in Herd Management.   To aid in herd management, most of the ranchers in the hobbyist and traditionalist categories collected information on their cows and calves. The information collected on calves included birth date, birth weight, sex, and weaning weight. The information collected on the cows included calving history, mothering ability (temperament and/or milk production), calving ease, and which cows birthed the replacement heifers. This information typically was handwritten in a book of some type. The ranchers maintained an intimate familiarity with their cattle and saw them as individuals.

> We knew everything there was to know about our cattle. . . . We knew more about our cattle than we did about our family. We could tell you every calf a cow had, pretty much the exact minute she had it every year. I've got little books here that I wrote everything down exactly.—Traditionalist

In the business category, ranchers collected some information on their cows and calves. That information might be collected on an exception basis because of the number of head with which the ranchers were working. The ranchers were familiar with their cattle, but not to the degree demonstrated by the owners of smaller herds.

Some ranchers used a very sophisticated approach to gathering information in order to refine their herd management practices. For example, one purebred operation sent some of its calves to a test station where all the calves from various ranches were fed and cared for similarly. This allowed the rancher to show how well his bulls stacked up to bulls from other ranches in a controlled experiment. Another rancher stated:

> We've performed quite a few experiments of our own over the years, and still do. I have a fair sense of what a true experiment is with controls and so forth. We get a lot of cooperation from the pharmaceutical industry. We've tested new products such as ear tags. We get a lot of things free as long as we're willing to put in some controls and report on the results. I enjoy that sort of thing. We've had some experiments going for a couple of years on range management. The opportunities are out there if you're cooperative. I think I probably have an advantage because I know how to conduct an experiment. We can get information first-hand from experiments we conduct ourselves. . . . We've changed our method of supplementing cattle in the winter. We're using more expensive supplements that don't rely on salt. We seem to distribute cattle better. I think it worked. It's cheaper in the long run because you have more grass.—Business

The changes made on the basis of the information ranchers collected varied in their sophistication. Some made changes that were based primarily on judgment and intuition.

> It's done by eye and is not as scientific as it could be.—Business

> A lot of times you know in the back of your mind what you want to do with a cow. It's sure nice to have the records, because you go back and refer to it.—Hobbyist

Many of the ranchers attempted to get information back from the feedlot on their calves in order to assess how well they did after leaving the ranch. In some cases they also received carcass data, which allowed them to assess weight gain, quality of the meat, and other types of information.

There were isolated but notable exceptions to gathering and using information about the herd. One rancher kept no information on his herd, did not attempt to get new information on herd management practices, and relied strictly on the information "in his head" based on his cumulative years of experience. Another said:

> It was just a matter of whatever the good Lord gives them when they come out; that's what they are. I can't change that very much.—Hobbyist

The information ranchers gathered was used primarily as a tool in culling the herd. Culling of open (not pregnant) cows or those that were "unsatisfactory producers" usually occurred in the fall. In general, it seemed that changes in herd management were highly judgment-based. Cause-and-effect links for possible problems were hard to establish. For the larger herds, information was not collected on a detailed enough level to analyze and draw specific conclusions.

> Where I've got a thousand head, and we've got one full-time employee, we don't track detailed information on a cow-by-cow basis. I've always got a book with me, so when we're working them, I put things down in the book. That information will be put on the computer. After a while you kind of know your cows. It's visual, when you see things you don't like.—Business

Motivations in Selecting Products.   Ranchers as a whole were interested in getting additional information about how to manage their operations better. They read industry trade publications, attended seminars, and talked to neighbors. They were most likely to view information as credible if it came from a local source that was familiar with specific local conditions. As a whole, it was clear that the person the ranchers trusted most was the veterinarian. The ranchers also found the animal health product firm reps to be a good source of information, but not as credible as the veterinarian.

> On a drug situation, I wouldn't necessarily trust one person over another, but I would certainly pay attention to my veterinarian. He knows my area and my situation better than the drug rep from the company does. Even though I know the drug rep from that company is going to represent the drugs he sells, I don't necessarily not trust what he says. I just like to have more information about what works in my environment.—Traditionalist

Ranchers bought their animal health products from both veterinarians and supply houses. Price was an important consideration but not an overwhelming concern.

Ranchers' Views about the Future.   The ranchers all expressed concern about the future. The number one concern among the commercial hobbyists and traditionalists was the low prices for their calves. While business producers also were concerned about price for their "outputs" (cattle), they were concerned about the input side of the equation (expenses) as well. All the ranchers noted that with the low prices they were getting for their calves, they couldn't afford to maintain and replace the old, dilapidated equipment they were using.

> It takes a lot of calves to buy a new pickup, when they want about $30K or something. —Hobbyist

> [My number one concern is] pricing, and not just the price of the product but the price of what it costs to produce that product. Compare the price of beef with the price of machinery. Calves are bringing what they brought in the 60s, but a tractor costs three times as much.—Traditionalist

In addition, they noted the high price of land. One rancher stated, "The land around here grows houses better than cattle."

Ranchers spoke vehemently against NAFTA and the influx of cheaper imports.

> Well, the biggest issue we have right now is NAFTA. NAFTA is probably the worst thing they've come up with. It has lowered our cattle market so bad, it's put a lot of people out of business, driving the prices down so low. It is not fair trade from the standpoint of shipping Australian cattle into Mexico; they become Mexican cattle and come right into the U.S. They can get our top dollar (whatever we're getting here—say, 60 cents) but were brought in through Mexico at 30 cents. They flooded the market. They didn't have to make as much; they don't have as much in their cattle. With this R-Calf thing, they're investigating Canada. Let's face it: They're overrunning our market. It takes away the supply and demand. It's not just affecting us, it's affecting everybody—for example, the beef business, the car business, the timber industry.—Traditionalist

Tightening environmental regulations (the Endangered Species Act, pesticides, water quality, etc.) also had an impact on the economics of ranching operations.

The increasing market strength of the packers was viewed with fear and trepidation and also with a sense of increasing helplessness. Ranchers sold their calves to the feedlots, which in turn sold them to the meatpackers. Packer concentration (four packers controlled 80 percent of the market) and the packers' perceived ability to set prices (the implication is "collusively") for the industry was a recurring theme. Moreover, fears of vertical integration by the packers, or packers that own their own cattle and feedlots, further worried the ranchers.

> We have no market for our agriculture products. To back that up, when you've got packers controlling 80 percent of the cattle and they'll buy cattle for a half hour in the middle of the week, you either take the offer or you leave it. If you turn them down, pretty soon they won't come back and look at your cattle or price your cattle. This is where we're going to have to have more players in our market or we're going to have to become one of the major players against the packer in supplying food to the consumer. We cannot compete with packers that own their own cattle and slaughter their own cattle instead of paying the market value for cattle they don't own. So that's why I say we have no market. The grain is the same way, because basically, the same companies that control the grain control the cattle: Cargill, Con-Agra, ADM. You just look through the hall of mergers. One of these days, if things don't change, we will know the true value of our food when the corporations get it and we're all working for those people. The consumer will find out what the value of it is.—Business

In general, the view among the commercial producers was one of extreme pessimism. They saw a lot of other ranchers going broke (but usually not themselves).

> I think it's all offset by the good things, but sometimes you wonder. You have to wonder about your mentality. You work and you work and you work and you work and you work and then you sell your cows at a loss, and you think, "Why am I doing this?" Either I'm really stupid or really stubborn.—Traditionalist

> I think the day that the old rancher who gets on his horse at daybreak and gets off his horse at sunset and never sees another human being, and everybody is knocking on his door to buy his calves—those days are through. I hate to admit it, but everywhere you turn, somebody is trying to put you out of business. If it isn't the Bambi-huggers, then it's the prices, and if it isn't that, then somebody's coming along with those brainy ideas. The small producer is really going to have to work at it to stay in business.—Traditionalist

Solutions: Value-Added Marketing, Branded Beef, and Quality.   Ranchers were asked about possible solutions to the depressed prices they were facing. The solutions discussed in industry publications included value-added marketing, or marketing strategies designed to increase the value and quality customers receive from beef purchases, and a branded beef model. The development of branded beef would require a tracking system from "birth to beef" in the supply chain. Such tracking would allow standardized health, quality, and management protocols as well as improved feedback through the entire production model.

Branded beef production would move the industry from a cost-based (production) model to a value-added model. This change also would require the producers to be more closely linked to the feedlots to improve the quality of the beef. Better coordination along the supply chain would ensure an increased flow of information from the consumer to the producer. Alliances between the cow/calf producers and the feedlots would allow ranchers to better track the success of their calves (based on health and weight gain). Those data could allow the ranchers to further improve the genetics of their herds by tracking which cow-bull combinations had delivered the higher-yield calves. As part of these trends, some degree of integration or vertical coordination would occur in the beef industry. Ranchers would have to participate to ensure market access for their product. Ranchers would have to think beyond the boundaries of their own ranches.

Most ranchers were familiar with the concepts of value-added marketing and a branded beef model. However, most were dubious about their viability and impact on ranchers' independence.

> I don't know if any kind of marketing at this point is going to get us where we need to be without a change in the price structure of cattle.—Traditionalist

> If there is a demand for high-quality beef, then the market should show it, and the packers will start bidding more for a piece of that quality. There may be some niches somewhere that people can fall into, but it's not going to be the salvation of many ranches. What we need is a mass market. Whatever niche there is, is going to be saturated very quickly, and the price will come down. I think the solution is cutting costs. People are eating a tremendous amount of beef, but the production is enormous as well. Numbers are down, but tons are up. The amount of beef being eaten is still quite high. I just think that some people have got to quit producing beef.—Business

> We are concerned about the vertical marketing approach big companies are introducing into the system. Ranchers are very independent-minded people. We are fearful about the control that companies will be able to exert on us.—Traditionalist

Skepticism about value-added marketing is also derived from history: Other programs used in the past to provide a more consistent product to the feedlots, with supporting documentation, did not result in noticeable price differences. Of all the information ranchers collected on their herds, only vaccination records seemed to be valued by cattle buyers. Ranchers with complete histories of their cattle were selling their calves at the same price as ranchers without that information. Hence, the information was not viewed as a way to command a premium for the calves.

> For many years, it seemed like having good health records on the calves didn't matter. One herd would keep excellent records and be real progressive, and the next-door neighbor was the exact opposite, and it was the exact same price for both. The local cattle buyers didn't give a premium to keep the records, give the vaccines. . . . There were green tag programs in the 1980s (we followed one) where the vet certified you used them [preconditioning records]. But the cattle buyers didn't pay a premium for them. They as much as said, "We don't care." Today, 10 years later, cattle buyers are starting to ask, Will you precondition your calves? Will they be "bunkbroke" (so when they get to the feedlot, the calves will be trained to go to a feedbunk to eat)? Will they be weaned? There's a stress period associated with weaning. So there's more of a focus on those questions now than there has been. But there's still no rule; it's not a given. It's still ambiguous when it comes to marketing the cattle whether the information matters or not [results in a better price for the cattle]. —Traditionalist

The feeling was that price premiums, if any, would accrue to others in the supply chain (the packers, retailers, and others). Despite that, some with more progressive views noted the need to have more of a consumer focus in their efforts:

> We need better beef quality if we're going to increase consumption. A lot of the breed associations are concentrating on carcass quality right now. There's measurement; there's selection for marbling and yield on cattle. I think as long as there is a possibility there might be some added value, a person should start working on it a little bit, along with the other production traits. I think it's something to pay attention to.—Traditionalist

> I think in the future, all ranchers are going to have to retain ownership of their cattle more and follow them closer to the consumer. I think that's part of our problem right now with our packer concentration. The producer's going to have to be a meat producer and not just sell calves. I think some of our long-range goals are going to have to be to get closer to the consumer with our product and know what he wants instead of listening to the packer tell us what he wants.—Business

> The money in agriculture is not in producing it. It's in processing it. This is where more ranchers and farmers have to realize that you can't produce the raw product anymore; you've got to follow it on through.—Business

Ranchers also noted that the idea of consistent quality beef was important.

> I'm expecting to see a change to where quality is more important. I think, down the road, that it's going to be mandatory that you know exactly what your cattle are doing. Those that aren't producing well at the kill floors are going to come back to haunt you.—Business

Interestingly, each of the respondents who was interviewed felt that the quality of his or her beef was above average. However, there was some doubt about whether consistent quality could be achieved easily with range cattle.

> That's going to be pretty tough with cattle. With chickens and hogs, you can throw up a confinement building. One person can control x amount of hogs and turkeys and chickens. But how do you do that with cattle? You can only have so many cattle in one spot because they're bigger and they need more feed. You're going to have to have pasture. It's going to be pretty tough to get everything uniform. There are a lot of small producers with just a few cows around.—Hobbyist

> I'm not convinced that branded products are going to magically save the beef industry. I think we're in competition on a world scale, and we're going to have to cut our costs of production. I think we could get our costs down to about 45 cents per pound of critter sold if we had to. Our total production would go down, but I think our costs would go down more.—Business

Because of the doubts about the viability of moving to a branded beef model, ranchers tended to focus more on controlling the cost of inputs and weathering the current downturn in the production cycle. One respondent cited earlier summed this up as "striving for the largest amount of production with the least amount of input."

Rancher's Concluding Thoughts. Despite these hardships and concerns, the ranchers were passionate about their love for their lifestyle, feeling that the benefits of living a life on the land outweighed the drawbacks.

> You get up in the morning and go out there, and everything's bright and fresh. We're fortunate in this part of the world that we don't have a lot of noise from cars and trains. It's gratifying to see what happens when spring turns around, new things start to grow, new animals come into the world. It's pretty special, something that you can't explain to a lot of people because they don't understand what you're talking about. . . . It isn't the highest-paying job in the world, but it's got a lot of happiness that money can't buy.—Traditionalist

They expressed pride in their work and a sense of ownership for feeding the country's people.

Back to the Segmentation Decision

As Joan perused the findings from the qualitative interviews, she wondered what she would report to Kipp about possible changes in their approach to market segmentation. Joan wondered whether their historical approach to segmenting the market on the basis of herd size was consistent with the changes in the industry and the changing needs of ranchers.

Despite the insights gathered, there was a lack of understanding of the various segments of beef consumers and their needs, how brand marketing could affect consumer demand, and how alliances within the supply chain could affect the ranchers' situation. Unfortunately, the fragmented nature of the cow/calf producers, combined with their focus on production rather than marketing, meant that the beef industry was not very consumer-focused.

As she pondered how all these pieces fit together, Joan began to brainstorm new ways to look at the market. She wanted to work with Kipp in developing a plan to maintain Pfizer's market position in light of the changes in the industry.

CASE 2–6
APACHE POWER, INC.

It was February 2000. Kristy Furnas, product manager for gasoline engines at Apache Power, Inc. (API), was contemplating how to introduce and price a new gasoline engine, the FE21, for large outdoor power equipment. The FE21 was the first engine API had produced for use in large outdoor power equipment.

Background

API was principally a manufacturer of gasoline engines used in small outdoor power equipment (OPE), such as lawn mowers, rotary tillers, and snow throwers. API did not manufacture the completed piece of outdoor power equipment. Rather, it focused on designing and manufacturing engines and then selling them to outdoor power equipment manufacturers. In 1999, API's sales of small engines accounted for about 85 percent of total sales. The other 15 percent came from parts and services. Exhibit 1 presents operating figures for the last five years. Exhibit 2 provides balance sheet information for three years. Apache manufactured exclusively in the United States, and virtually all sales were domestic.

API had an excellent reputation for the quality and dependability of its products in the small engine market. It was known for providing fast and reliable service. The company had been in business for over 90 years and had developed an established customer base. Its customers included Deere & Co., Toro, and Snapper. Additionally, it sold engines for use in private label brands, such as the Sears Craftsman line. Some of API's current customers also manufactured large outdoor power equipment. API's "newest" customer began buying from the company 25 years before.

API used its own sales force to sell engines to small outdoor power equipment manufacturers. It employed 22 salespeople responsible for selling engines and parts. The salespeople were paid a base salary plus a commission on sales. The salespeople were technically knowledgeable about the engines and spoke with the manufacturer and understood what was wanted or needed from API. Unfortunately, it had become difficult finding qualified people to sell the engines in recent years.

The FE21 was a larger engine than API had ever produced. With the addition of the FE21, API was hoping to successfully expand into the large outdoor power equipment market. In 1998 and 1999, API experienced successive sales declines from previous years. However, this decline was experienced by the U.S. market overall. The economic downturn and unusually dry weather were generally considered as causes for the decline in the demand for OPE, and with slight regional variations this was expected to continue throughout 2000. API was hoping its new engine and a turnaround in the economy would boost sales for 2001. Exhibit 3 provides actual and projected unit sales of small and large outdoor power equipment in the United States.

This case was prepared by Associate Professor William F. Crittenden and MBA candidate Sharon M. Doherty of Northeastern University as the basis for class discussion. The case situation is hypothetical and is not intended as an accurate portrayal of the outdoor power equipment engine industry or of any of the participating companies. Pietro Berardi, MBA candidate at Boston College, updated the case in 2000.

EXHIBIT 1   Income Statement—Apache Power, Inc.
(in thousands of dollars)

	1999	1998	1997	1996	1995
Gross sales	$25,112	$25,968	$26,190	$26,032	$25,876
Sales discounts	2,498	2,544	2,620	2,604	2,588
Net sales	$22,614	$23,424	$23,570	$23,428	$23,288
Cost of goods sold					
Raw materials	9,724	10,072	10,088	10,028	9,968
Direct labor	4,512	4,662	4,668	4,592	4,564
Variable overhead	1,356	1,358	1,368	1,382	1,350
Shipping	384	398	398	396	396
Gross margin	6,638	6,934	7,048	7,030	7,010
Selling costs	0	0	0	0	0
Advertising	18	18	18	18	18
Salaries	1,108	1,078	1,060	1,030	1,002
Commissions	452	468	472	468	466
Promotional materials	452	468	448	448	490
Other costs	0	0	0	0	0
Administrative	696	684	664	660	652
Depreciation	194	188	184	182	174
Research and development	3,166	3,046	2,180	702	698
Supplies	226	210	200	188	164
Insurance	374	368	360	358	350
Interest	334	332	330	328	326
Operating income	−$382	$74	$1,132	$2,648	$2,670
Taxes	−160	30	476	1,112	1,122
Income after taxes	−$222	$44	$656	$1,536	$1,548

Industry and Economic Information

Over the last 10 years, fluctuations in the U.S. dollar had given API and most other U.S. manufacturers products a higher price compared to international competition. Although competition came from around the globe, small engine manufacturers from the Far East had especially taken advantage of this trend and gained significant market share. Japanese manufacturers in particular provided technologically advanced products. Their products generally were viewed as more reliable and fuel-efficient than the American manufacturers' engines. OEMs continued to seek improvements from their engine suppliers in fuel efficiency, noise and air pollution abatement, and safety.

There had also been a trend in the buying behavior of the end user, the consumer. Over the past few years consumers had been buying more powerful OPE that could do a variety of tasks, such as garden tractors, instead of buying a few smaller OPE for individual tasks.

Small OPE Engines.   The average market price to an original equipment manufacturer (OEM) for a small outdoor power equipment gasoline engine was $55 in 1998. The typical range was from $45 to $110. After adjusting for trade/sales discounts, the industry had seen no price increase the last two years. Total market in sales to OEMs of small engines was estimated at $252,400,000 in 1999. Finished small OPE products typically listed at retail from $150 to $500, although discounters might have offered specials up to 25 percent off in highly competitive markets.

**EXHIBIT 2   Balance Sheet—Apache Power, Inc.
(in thousands of dollars)**

	1999	1998	1997
Current assets			
Cash	$ 1,256	$ 1,708	$ 1,850
Accounts receivable	12,910	11,780	12,206
Inventory	6,658	6,292	7,438
Prepaid expenses	2,680	2,348	2,046
Total current assets	$ 23,504	$ 22,128	$ 23,540
Fixed assets			
Land	5,000	5,000	5,000
Building, net	32,696	32,340	32,400
Machinery, net	74,836	65,430	62,004
Total fixed assets	$112,532	$102,770	$ 99,404
Total assets	$136,036	$124,898	$122,944
Current liabilities			
Accounts payable	$ 4,976	$ 4,244	$ 4,994
Notes payable	3,268	3,974	6,114
Accrued liabilities	7,102	6,908	7,744
Total current liabilities	$ 15,346	$ 15,126	$ 18,852
Long-term liabilities			
Notes payable	$ 29,268	$ 18,098	$ 12,430
Total liabilities	$ 44,614	$ 33,224	$ 31,282
Equity			
Common stock	18,000	18,000	18,000
Retained earnings	73,422	73,674	73,662
Total equity	$ 91,422	$ 91,674	$ 91,662
Total liabilities and equity	$136,036	$124,898	$122,944

**EXHIBIT 3   Actual and Forecasted Unit Sales
of Outdoor Power Equipment
(in thousands of units)**

Year	OPE Using Small Engines	OPE Using Large Engines
1997	5,646	1,471
1998	5,754	1,554
1999	5,610	1,510
2000	5,410	1,520
2001	5,600	1,580
2002	5,800	1,630

API's main competitor in the small engine market was Brighams, a U.S. manufacturer of engines for OPE. Although not a finished goods manufacturer, Brighams had exceptionally strong name recognition among males 35 years and older. It had been in the business for a long time and had an established customer base. No longer considered the industry's technological leader, Brighams still maintained an excellent reputation for the dependability of its products, and its parts and service network was second to none. Brighams currently was the small engine market leader with a 30 percent market share.

Hachi, a Japanese manufacturer of engines that manufactured its own OPE, was also a formidable, yet indirect, competitor. Vertically integrated, with 98 percent captive sales, Hachi was second in small engine sales with approximately 13 percent of the market.

Brighams and Hachi were the only small engine manufacturers perceived as national in sales and distribution. The rest of the U.S. small engine market was fragmented on a regional basis among 25 U.S. and international manufacturers, including API. Three U.S. manufacturers had recently left the industry, citing decreasing margins and increased capitalization needs. Increased competition in the small engine market and changing consumer behaviors prompted API to expand its product line into larger engines.

Large OPE Engines. Principal competitors in the large engine market were Brighams, Hachi, two other U.S. manufacturers, and a few companies that manufactured engines for their own large outdoor power equipment. Hachi's strengths in the market were its exceptional performance record, superior technology, and lower price. Hachi had been written up as the best engine in many trade journals. Its weaknesses included its distribution network for large finished OPE and the availability of parts since all parts were manufactured in Japan.

Brighams virtually created the large engine market, working closely with an OEM that recognized the need for outdoor power equipment products that were smaller and lower-priced than those needed on a farm but larger than those available for the consumer market. With its established name recognition, reputation, and parts and service network, Brighams was the natural source for those OEMs not seeking vertical integration. In the large engine market, Brighams was again the leader with a 42 percent market share. Exhibit 4 provides estimated costs for the Brighams Large Engine Division.

Captive manufacturing accounted for approximately 33 percent of the large engine market. Based on retail sales, Hachi appeared to have an 8 percent market share, all of it captive. Two other U.S. manufacturers held 6 percent and 7 percent, respectively, of the market. These firms sold exclusively to the OEM market. Remaining market share for large engine sales was fragmented among a few smaller U.S. and international manufacturers, all supplying the small engine market as well. The market price to an OEM averaged $450, with a typical range of $400 to $600. Exhibit 5 shows financial ratios for the gasoline engine market.

New Product Information

API had invested a lot of time and money designing its large engine. The increased investment appeared to be paying off. API had developed a large gasoline engine for garden tractors that was even more fuel-efficient, emitted lower noise levels, and included more safety features than any other large engine on the market. For example, API's new large gasoline engine, the FE21, was 7 percent more fuel-efficient than any other engine in its class currently on the market. In addition, the noise level was much softer and the cutting blade would stop within one second of when the tractor had been turned off (or turned over).

To design this new engine, API invested $6 million toward engineering costs, and an additional $12 million was spent modifying and buying new equipment in order to manufacture the engine. It was estimated that an additional $3 million in expenses would be needed for the engine to be completely ready for release to the market by midyear, when OEMs finalized product decisions for the upcoming model year. API's total pro-

EXHIBIT 4

FINANCIAL DATA—BRIGHAMS:
Large Engine Division*
(in thousands of dollars)

Net sales	$285,390
Cost of goods sold	198,348
Raw materials	$115,298
Direct labor	63,643
Variable overhead	15,983
Shipping	3,424
Gross margin	$ 87,042
General, sales & administration expenses	$ 75,546
Advertising	$ 3,139
Commissions	12,842
Promotional materials	6,422
Depreciation	5,708
Interest	7,136
R&D	10,703
Supplies	1,913
Insurance	4,281
Salaries	23,402
Operating income	$ 11.496

*Note: These approximations were made using Brighams' consolidated financial statements and suggestions made by industry experts.

EXHIBIT 5   **Select Financial Ratios for U.S. Publicly Held Gasoline Engine Manufacturers, 1999**

Current	1.63
Quick	1.02
Net profit margin	7.07%
Gross profit margin	20.33%
Return on investment	24.52%
Inventory turnover	9.35
Collection period	98 days
Payables period	52 days
Days of inventory	178 days
Debt to asset	16.66%
Debt to equity	40.03%
Long-term debt to equity	30.97%
Times interest earned	1.17

Note: All gasoline engine manufacturers do not supply the outdoor power equipment industry, although the majority do. Furthermore, these ratios do not include data from captive manufacturers or those divisions and subsidiaries where information is reported only in consolidated statements.

duction capacity was 700,000 engines. The plant and equipment modifications allowed API to produce 75,000 large engines a year.

Product Introduction Alternatives

In the past API had not spent much on promotion of its engines. Usually API just put together sales materials that included product brochures, gave moderate trade discounts, and had a few ads in trade journals. Since it had held a solid market position for so long and had many of the same customers year after year, it had seen no reason to push its name and products aggressively. With the development of the large engine, API was contemplating increasing its promotional activity in order to compete in the market.

Furnas was investigating various promotion program alternatives. One alternative was to increase the number of ads in trade journals. It was estimated that Brighams spent about $4 million a year on trade journal advertising. Another alternative was to give more generous trade discounts. API's current trade discount was 10 percent, about the industry average. Furnas wondered if increasing the trade discount would increase sales. The final alternative being considered was using TV advertising to increase customer awareness. It was thought that if end consumers knew more about API, they would buy OPE made with API's engines. Hachi currently spent $12 million on TV advertising, while Brighams spent about $5 million.

Furnas had to decide what marketing program or combination of marketing programs would be most beneficial to the sale of API's new engine and overall sales while considering what the company could afford to do and the price of the new engine.

For the past decade, Lawrence J. Ellison has been Silicon Valley's Bad Boy. The chairman of No. 2 software maker Oracle Corp. watched with unbridled envy as the PC industry became the most powerful force in the Information Age—and William H. Gates III and his Microsoft Corp. along with it. But Oracle, after its initial success as a flashy Silicon Valley startup, seemed stuck in Dullsville. The company's database software, with its ability to organize reams of information, was a crucial but oh-so-boring adjunct to grey-flannel-suit corporate computing.

So Ellison squawked for attention. He tried to buy a Russian MiG for $20 million—but ran afoul of U.S. Customs. He riled authorities in San Jose by repeatedly landing his executive jet after the 11 P.M. curfew. He was nearly killed winning the Sydney-to-Hobart race in his 78-foot yacht, Sayonara. And he cooked up one Oracle announcement after another that seemed to be aimed at upstaging Gates. Interactive TV would merge Hollywood with Silicon Valley to create Siliwood. Oracle would build a stripped-down "network computer" that would make PCs obsolete. Neither happened. The headlines were entertaining, but few took Ellison seriously.

Database Fever

Now, as the Information Age gives way to the Internet Age, Silicon Valley's Bad Boy is having his revenge. Suddenly, databases are all the rage, as troves of information—from product catalogs on Amazon.com to the global order stats of GE Medical Systems—are being made instantly available to customers and employees over the Internet. Two-and-a-half years ago, when the Web was still in short pants, Oracle's database sales inched along at 3% and 5% growth per quarter. Last quarter, they surged 32%, to $778 million.

And that could be just a warmup. Envisioning a day when companies would shift their internal operations to the Net, Ellison began creating software programs that hooked into his database to do a host of other big corporate jobs over the Web, such as purchasing and managing inventory (Exhibit 1). Now that daunting engineering effort looks to be paying off. Since November, Oracle has landed big-name customers such as Ford Motor, Chevron, and Sears. They've signed on for technology that allows them to operate virtual marketplaces on the Web in which anybody who wants to sell them supplies or services places a bid. "I always saw Oracle as a database company," says David J. O'Reilly, CEO of Chevron. "But they've come a long way to transform themselves into an Internet software company."

And Oracle's stock shows it. After puttering along for more than five years, Oracle's shares have joined the superheated elite. Since November, the company's stock has nearly quadrupled, to about 72 a share, giving the world's No. 2 software maker a market cap of $205 billion—surpassing mighty IBM. Though the tech correction brought Oracle's price down from an all-time high of 90, it has weathered the storm far better than the Nasdaq composite, which has dropped 28% from its peak and is down 10% year-to-date. Oracle is up 29% for the year, bolstered most recently by a rave report

EXHIBIT 1   **Squeezing Savings Out of an E-Business**

Tom Scott and Tom First started off in business on Nantucket in 1989 by delivering supplies to visiting yachts. When they added fresh juice to their repertoire, Nantucket Nectars was born. Now, the company is installing Oracle software to help it keep growing at 40% a year.

1 Suppliers

In the past, Nantucket Nectars communicated with its 900 suppliers the old-fashioned way—by phone and fax. Besides being slow and costly, the system didn't keep track of inventories or demand well. Oracle software allows them to create more accurate forecasts and will enable them to forge close links with the likes of Ocean Spray.

2 Bottlers

Nantucket Nectar's six bottlers are also its warehouses. With better forecasting and Web links, the company can alert bottlers to rev up production lines. It enables bottlers to better plan so their plants aren't idle. Nantucket Nectars also can size up inventories at the warehouses and ship juices from one if stocks are low at another.

3 Headquarters

Anybody in sales, marketing, or operations can tap into the computer system via a Web browser and check on the status of orders, inventory levels, and changes in demand. Executives like the two Toms and sales managers can dice sales data by region, distributor, and salesperson. If somebody is asleep at the switch, they'll know it instantly.

4 Sales Force

Each morning, Nantucket Nectars' 85 field salespeople can log on to the Internet from their homes and tap into NectarNet, the company's business Web site. If they see that Orange Mango has to be substituted for Pineapple Orange Guava in a shipment, they'll be able to warn the customer. Plus, they can track promotions at sports events.

5 Distributors

The 150 distributors can log into NectarNet to place and check orders. If a drink is out of stock, they can avoid an unwanted substitution by specifying what they'd like instead. Nantucket's marketers can check promotional budgets to see if distributors have kept up their commitments to pass out coolers to retailers.

6 Retailers

The company uses sales-analysis software to help retailers figure out how to stock the right juices. Marketers at headquarters can review sales records for various distributors in a given region and rate which combination of drinks does best. The company alerts distributors, who pass the info on to mom-and-pop shops.

7 Web Site

Nantucket Nectars sells T-shirts, hats, and frisbees decorated with its logo on its Web site www.Juiceguys.com. It's planning a major overhaul that will turn the Web site into a real store and is sizing up Oracle's iStore software to power the site. Possible merchandise: Juice blenders, herbs, nutrition items, and health aids.

from Lehman Bros. And Microsoft? Its stock price was hammered down 15.6% on Apr. 24 by the double-whammy of a disappointing third-quarter report and word that the Justice Department might call for a breakup of the company. The capper: To Ellison's delight, on Apr. 25 his stake in Oracle actually surpassed Gate's Microsoft holdings, by $52.1 billion to $51.5 billion.

Ellison revels in Oracle's good fortune. "We're cool again," he says. And aiming to stay that way. With his database business on cruise control. Ellison is about to launch Phase Two of his Net assault. In May, Oracle plans to unveil its most important product update in years. It's a suite of business applications that work seamlessly with one another to handle everything from customer service on one end to relationships with suppliers on the other. And it's all rejiggered to run on the Web.

Ellison's vision for what he calls the first-ever "e-business suite" is to create something as popular as Microsoft's Office desktop suite. Now, Ellison figures, everyone from giant corporations to tiny dot-coms can buy a single package from Oracle to run their e-businesses, rather than buying software from a host of competitors and trying to stitch it all together.

It it works, Ellison's dream of knocking Gates down a peg might actually come to pass. As computing moves from desktop PCs to huge Internet servers that run everything from Web sites to complex corporate networks, Oracle's skills and technologies are taking center stage. Ellison gloats that Microsoft's tangle with Netscape Communications Corp. over Web browsers, which landed it in hot water with the Justice Department, didn't get it ahead in the Net-server realm. "They robbed the wrong bank," Ellison says. Now, if Microsoft is actually broken up, the ensuing confusion would help Oracle, though long term, it might make Microsoft's database program a stronger competitor if it is adapted to run on other operating systems besides Microsoft's Windows. For now, Oracle has a shot at becoming the biggest supplier of crucial software that extends beyond the PC, out onto the Web, and into the heart of a company. "We have a chance to pass Microsoft and become the No. 1 software company," Ellison says. "If I said that two years ago, I would have been sedated and locked up. But now we're the Internet and they're not."

Such braggadocio frosts Oracle's competitors. They would all love to burst what they see as its stock-price bubble. They erupt at the mere mention of Ellison's name. When it comes to electronic marketplace software, "Oracle has nothing to offer. They have no position," says Steven A. Ballmer, Microsoft's CEO. Steven A. Mills, general manager of software strategy at IBM, charges that Oracle's hyperaggressive sales force will promise anything to make a deal. "They take the P.T. Barnum approach to business: There's a sucker born every minute," he says. And Thomas Siebel, chairman of customer-management software leader Siebel Systems Inc., calls Oracle's e-business suite "vacuous." Claims Siebel: "After all their chest-beating, they're basically failing in applications."

Behind Schedule

Clearly, the long knives are out. With Oracle's stock runup and early successes with e-business, it's a target for some of the most powerful companies in software. Oracle faces Microsoft and its allies such as corporate software kingpin SAP on one side and IBM and its cronies such as Siebel Systems on the other. IBM, for instance, has agreed that its 163,000-person consulting and sales team will hawk Siebel's customer-management software—a daunting prospect for Oracle, given the size of its 30,000-person consulting and sales force.

And it's no cinch that Oracle's e-business suite will be a runaway hit. The broad package of programs will go head to head with products by the biggies and by dozens of smaller companies that have a one- or two-year lead and are focused on doing one thing really well. Already, Oracle's e-business suite is a year late. David Yockelson, director of e-business strategies at Meta Group Inc., believes there's no way Oracle can build all of this technology itself and match the capabilities of its rivals. "Oracle has a not-invented-here philosophy," he says. "And building it all themselves is going to be too slow." Even after the suite ships, consultants such as Gartner Group Inc. warn corporate customers that it probably won't be stable enough to handle the most crucial jobs until the end of the year.

If Ellison is worried, he isn't showing it. Sitting in his four-story Pacific Heights home in front of a breathtaking panorama of the Golden Gate Bridge, he concedes that development of the e-business suite has been devilish. "It's a huge job," he says. "But it's the right strategy for Oracle." Indeed, he insists that the suite, called Oracle Release

11i, is on track for a May launch and will catapult the company to dizzying heights. It offers customers a simpler approach: one software product from one company—no more lavish consulting fees for making disparate products work together. "You ain't seen nothin' yet," he vows. "If this e-business-suite plan works, we're going to be an extraordinary company."

Not that Oracle is a slouch now. The company's core business looks rock-solid (Exhibit 2). It leads in the fastest-growing piece of the database market with a 40% market share to IBM's 18%, according to International Data Corp. And with its critical application-suite upgrade on the way, Oracle seems poised for a new burst of growth. Oracle's third-quarter revenues for the period ended Feb. 29 grew 18%, to $2.4 billion. And profits? They shot up 80%, to $498 million. Oracle's application-software business also saw a healthy rise—35% growth, to $199 million. Next fiscal year looks like another winner, with applications revenue forecasted to grow 35%, according to Goldman, Sachs & Co. "They've gone from out of the game to the front of the pack," says analyst Robert Austrian of Banc of America Securities.

Samurai Warrior

Product sales don't deserve all the glory. Surprisingly, Ellison has turned Oracle into a tightly run company. Gone are the days when a "let's-make-a-deal" negotiating philosophy ruled the sales force and feudal country managers ran their businesses as they saw fit. A year ago, Ellison kicked off a massive belt-tightening blitz that has curbed the company's free-spending ways. The workforce has been pared by 2,000 in the past two quarters. Routine sales are being shifted to the Web and away from high-paid reps. And hundreds of computing systems are being consolidated into a handful.

The result: Oracle has trimmed $500 million from expenses and boosted operating margins from 19.4% to 31.4% over the past nine months. Ellison promises he can wipe out another $1.5 billion in costs and push the margin to 40% or more in the next year, which would make Oracle one of the most efficient software outfits on the planet—though still less so than Microsoft with its 50%-plus margin.

Ellison, a penny-pinching model of efficiency? Hard to believe, but true. This is the guy, after all, who spent $3 million for Sayonara, his carbon-hull sailing yacht—the fastest craft under sail in its class. He owns a Japanese-style home in tony Atherton, Calif., where his graceful gardens and *koi* ponds are overshadowed only by the suits of samurai armor on display inside. Along with his glass, steel, and stone home overlooking the Golden Gate Bridge, construction is under way on a $40 million estate in the Santa Cruz foothills that's modeled on a medieval Japanese palace and will be built around a man-made lake. But all this has come from his personal fortune.

When it's Oracle's money, Ellison is downright parsimonious. But he's not tight-fisted just for the sake of goosing margins. The millions that Oracle has saved so far serves as a bold advertisement for what Oracle's technologies can do for its customers. Ellison had watched other companies such as Dell Computer Corp. harness the Web to make themselves more efficient, which attracted new customers. "Why not us?" he recalls asking. So Ellison, who had long kept to product development and marketing, grabbed hold of operations with a vengeance. "Larry has got Buddhas all over his house, but he's not a Buddha. He's a samurai warrior. He's the destroyer, the transformer. It's what he does best," says Marc Benioff, a former Oracle executive who is now chairman of Web startup Salesforce.com, in which Ellison has invested $2 million.

Everywhere that Ellison looked, he saw something that needed fixing. Each of Oracle's 70 country operations had its own computing systems and ways of tracking sales,

EXHIBIT 2   **Assembling an E-Business Powerhouse**

Oracle Corp.'s software is the foundation for Web sites, e-commerce, and corporate networks. Here are its most crucial markets:

Data Storehouses	*Business Applications*	*E-Marketplaces*
Database software for storing and analyzing corporate data, inventories, and customer info.	For running everything from accounting to customer management to Web sales.	Web-site and internal software for transactions between companies, including auctions.
Market Size $10.5 billion in 1999 for software and maintenance; heading for $16.6 billion in 2003.	**Market Size** $26 billion in 1999; heading for $33 billion this year.	**Market Size** $3.9 billion in 1999; heading for $18.6 billion in 2003.
Oracle's Third-Quarter Sales Software-license sales grew 32%, to $778 million.	**Oracle's Third-Quarter Sales** Up 35%, to $199 million.	**Oracle's Third-Quarter Sales** $26 million for supply-chain and procurement software.
Market Share 40%, compared with 18% for IBM, 5.7% for Informix, and 5.1% for Microsoft.	**Market Position** Oracle is a distant second behind SAP in the market for core corporate applications. Siebel Systems leads in customer-management software.	**Market Position** The procurement market is expanding into e-exchanges, and Oracle is an early leader along with Commerce One, Ariba, and i2.
Prospects Oracle dominates the database-software realm on both Unix and Windows NT operating systems. Analysts predict it will hold off the competition indefinitely, thanks to its strong technology and new cachet with dot-coms.	**Prospects** In May, Oracle plans to release the most comprehensive package of business applications available. It has a good chance to gain market share because its applications are integrated, while others offer pieces that have to be stitched together.	**Prospects** Oracle has deals to power exchanges for Ford, Sears, and Chevron and is expected to have staying power, thanks to its army of 7,000 software programmers.

Source: International Data Corp., AMR Research, Companies.

revenues, and profits. Not for long. By the end of this year, the company will eliminate 2,000 server computers scattered around the world and consolidate on 158 machines at its Redwood Shores (Calif.) headquarters. All the company's data will be stored on one central database accessible via the Web. That makes it easy for executives to get a comprehensive view of operations and spot trouble before it gets out of hand. "Larry has the people in this company screwed down tight," says Chief Financial Officer Jeffrey O. Henley.

The Oracle boss has been just as aggressive about establishing new business practices. Ellison personally rewrote sales contracts and established standard pricing to cut down on dickering by field salespeople. He changed the compensation system to prevent more than one salesperson from getting a full commission on a sale. And he compensated country managers for meeting ambitious profit-margin targets—not meeting sales goals at any cost.

It's all about centralized control—with Ellison in charge. The way he sees it, he's creating a management style for the Internet Age. "When you're an e-business, everything is mediated by computers," says Ellison. "All the individuality is bled out of the system and replaced by standards. People don't run their own show anymore."

That has been tough on some of Ellison's sidekicks. Oracle President Raymond J. Lane remembers getting the phone call from Ellison in December, 1998, when the boss decided to insert himself into every corner of the company's business, including Lane's sales and consulting operations. "My mouth just hit the table," he recalls. Since then, everything has changed. "All of sudden, Larry is in your mess kit drilling down for four hours. Some days, I'll walk out of a meeting saying, 'I don't need this.' But then you look at the stock price. What Larry's doing is working. There's not a hotter company around."

To get staffers to bend to his will, Ellison uses the carrot first—and then the stick. When European country managers were slow to give up their computing systems, he offered them an option: If they kept control of their computers, they had to pay the cost out of their own budgets. Otherwise, they got their computing for free. That ended the holdout. Canada was another story. The subsidiary dragged its feet even after Ellison dispatched Gary Roberts, senior vice-president of global information technology, to Canada last August to deliver an ultimatum. "We had to send a Navy SEAL team to blow up our Canadian data center," quips Ellison. What really happened was just as effective: He shuffled management responsibilities and the problem melted away.

One of the cornerstone's of Ellison's e-engineering is the Oracle Business Online Web site. Launched last October, it targets small and midsize businesses, selling them programs for accounting and planning. What's unusual about it is that Oracle then runs the software for them as a service, charging a monthly fee. This saves small fry the cost of buying their own computers. For Pointclick.com Inc., a company in American Fork, Utah, that offers product purchase-incentive programs on the Web, Oracle Business Online provided an accounting system for $5,000 a month. And Pointclick got going in just two weeks.

Calling All Newbies

In the past, dot-coms simply couldn't afford Oracle software. They often bought Microsoft's then-less-expensive database and made do with accounting software designed for small businesses. But Oracle has made a concerted effort to turn itself into an easy choice for newbies (Exhibit 3). For starters, it gives away versions of its database software for free on its Web site to software developers. Later, when they are ready to go into business, they pay their license fees. But Oracle makes that affordable, too. Last October, it began selling a starter kit of all the basic software a "garage" startup needs to establish a Web site for just $6,750. In the first month, 150 companies signed on. And, Oracle knocked about 40% off its standard database prices in December, making them competitive with Microsoft's.

The strategy is to win over dot-coms when they're in the cradle and keep them when they grow up to be adult businesses. It's already starting to work. Pointclick.com now plans on buying several million dollars' worth of Oracle database and accounting software. "We're going to be spending so much money with Oracle, it's not even funny," says Craig Brown, the company's chief technology officer. Partly to stimulate the dot-com business, Oracle has set aside $500 million in an Oracle Venture Fund to invest in promising startups. One condition: They've got to buy Oracle software.

Thanks to these ventures—and the fact that high-flying dot-coms like eBay Inc. use its stuff—Oracle has become a favorite for Net companies. These startups often buy high-octane technology right on the starting line, figuring they won't have to switch later when they're in fast-growth mode. "You talk about the four horsemen of the Internet—it's Sun Microsystems, Cisco, EMC, and Oracle," says James Schanzenbach, chief technology officer for Drug Emporium Inc., a Columbus (Ohio) company that launched an online drugstore in September using Oracle software.

To reinforce that image, Oracle has forged tight partnerships with other horsemen. For example, Oracle and EMC Corp., the leading maker of data storage computers, tune their technologies to run together well and avoid downtime—which is death to

EXHIBIT 3   Putting His Money Where His Passion Is

When it comes to his personal investments, Larry Ellison the visionary often gets the better of Lawrence J. Ellison the businessman. The chairman of Oracle Corp. has spent more than $500 million of his own money on 30 or so investments in e-commerce, network appliances, and biotechnology. But few of his personal investments have turned into barn-burners—not yet, anyway. Ellison doesn't seem to mind, though. His 24% stake in Oracle is where he makes his money. Beyond that, he indulges himself.

Ellison is playing a game that's only for the rich. He can afford to bet early and wait for years for a company to blossom. For others, his advice is simple: "Stick to companies with profits." His own investments are about doggedly pursued ideas, not sure-fire returns.

Good Fight. Case in point: so-called network computers. Five years ago, Ellison proposed a low-cost device for accessing the Net, which he predicted would turn PCs into dinosaurs. Despite a flood of publicity, the devices never took off. Ellison thinks it was just an idea ahead of its time. Now he's putting $10 million into something called New Internet Computer Co., which will make non-PC devices. "I only invest in things I know something about—biotech and the Internet are two of them. Education is the third," he says.

It's all about fighting the good fight for something he believes in. Ellison backs cancer research through biotech companies such as SuperGen Inc. of San Ramon, Calif. He bets on technologies that take full advantage of the Internet, such as Salesforce.com of San Francisco, which lets sales reps manage their accounts on the Net. Often, he backs companies whose founders he knows and trusts, like accounting software maker NetLedger.com Inc. in San Mateo, Calif., which is run by a former Oracle engineer, Evan Goldberg.

Ellison Dabbles in Startups

Here's a sample of Oracle Chairman Lawrence Ellison's personal investments:

Investment	Amount	Why
Salesforce.com Web-based services	$2 million	Replaces desktop software for salespeople
New Internet Computer Co. Net access devices	$10 million	Ellison hopes the devices will supplant the PC as the preferred way to get on the Internet
SuperGen Inc. Biotech research	$23 million	Working on treatments for cancer, which his mother died from

Data: Ellison and companies

While he's not overly worried about making quick returns, he's careful with his money. In 1997, Joseph Rubinfeld, president and chairman of SuperGen, needed Ellison's help to acquire the rights to a drug designed to treat pancreatic cancer. Before investing $23 million, Ellison had two chemists and a dozen lawyers scrutinize the young company, says Rubinfeld. It was a smart bet: Ellison has made seven times his initial investment since an IPO in February.

Ellison is a patient investor. In 1988, he bought nCUBE, which builds machines to speed multimedia technologies such as videoconferencing over the Web. For years, it looked like a bust. Today, however, thanks to the growing use of high-speed Net connections, nCUBE has more than 100 customers and is on track for an IPO within a year.

Net Currency. Perhaps the most adventurous Ellison investment is London-based beenz.com, which has created a faux currency for Internet shoppers. Ellison believes this kind of electronic currency can be used more easily and more safely than credit cards. But skeptics abound. "I'm of the opinion that this is like Disney Dollars," says Gene Alvarez, program director for electronic business strategies at market researcher Meta Group Inc. "They're great in the park. But what do you do after you leave?" Beenz.com executives insist they are quite different from a handful of Net scrip companies that have come and gone. "Larry wouldn't have gotten involved, if it was just a vanilla investment," says CEO Philip Letts.

Most importantly, perhaps, the beenz.com Web site is built on an Oracle database. For Ellison, there's nothing plain-vanilla about that.

By Jim Kerstetter in San Mateo, Calif.

e-commerce Web sites. "Oracle has been right on track riding the dot-com wave," says EMC CEO Michael C. Ruettgers.

That partnership is a far cry from the gut-it-out-alone approach Oracle used when it nabbed e-marketplace customers like Ford, Chevron, and Sears. Late last year, e-marketplaces—which connect buyers and sellers of products in specific industries such as chemicals or cars—were starting to explode on the Web. Stocks of B2B companies have declined of late, but the long-term software market opportunity seems strong: On-line business-to-business transactions are pegged to climb to $1.4 trillion by 2004.

B2B Edge

Oracle wanted a piece of the action. Oracle's Lane learned that both Ford Motor Co. and General Motors Corp. wanted to tap the Internet to overhaul the way they buy $160 billion a year in parts and supplies and were looking for a software partner to help out. Lane hoped he could pull off a coup by making deals with each of them. So he ping-ponged between meetings in Detroit. But on Oct. 28, talks with GM broke down because Oracle wouldn't surrender a chunk of its stock to GM as part of the deal, say sources close to the discussions.

Lane was more determined than ever to win over Ford. He raced across town with a proposal to set up an independent company co-owned by Ford and Oracle that would let Ford get bids from suppliers via a Web site. Lane had no time to waste. He knew GM was negotiating a similar agreement with Oracle rival Commerce One Inc., and he didn't want to leave empty-handed. Even though Lane had to fly to a wedding in Los Angeles that Saturday, he kept up the pressure through the weekend—clinching the deal by promising to spend whatever it took to get the e-marketplace up and running quickly. He nailed down the final agreement in face-to-face talks with Ford CEO Jacques A. Nasser in Las Vegas on the following Monday, Nov. 1. A day later, both GM and Ford announced their exchanges, and Oracle's stock took off. "These were the first major exchange announcements ever," says Lane. "We had to be in the game." The two e-marketplaces later merged.

Now Ellison is hoping he can build on these early e-marketplace successes with his e-business suite. And customers are starting to buy in. Take GE Medical Systems, a $7.4 billion operation that sells in more than 100 countries and has dozens of factories in places like China, Hungary, France, and the U.S. In December, the GE subsidiary agreed to buy Oracle's entire 11i suite and install it worldwide. The plan is to operate one database accessible to both customers and employees—rather than scattering information across a handful of computing systems. "We're creating a global e-business," says Joseph F. Eckroth, the subsidiary's CIO. "With Oracle, it's integrated. I don't have to make connections between a lot of different pieces of software." Eckroth, who has dealt with Oracle for more than seven years, says the company has become much easier to work with. Because of Oracle's new sales and pricing policies, it took only two days to negotiate a deal. In the past, it might have taken weeks.

Other large organizations will be a tougher sell. Many companies choose the software that they feel is best for each task—whether it's running a Web site, managing a field sales force, or coordinating relationships with suppliers. Siebel Systems, for instance, specializes in sales-force software. Broadvision Inc. focuses on personalizing Web sites. And i2 Technologies is the leader in supply-chain software. Each is considered the best in its category. Even some major Oracle database customers, such as BellSouth Corp., prefer to mix and match so-called best-of-breed programs. BellSouth is considering other suppliers in addition to Oracle for its customer-management software. "Yes, it's important for applications to be integrated, but we can pick what we think is best and do some of the integration ourselves," says Francis A. Dramis, chief information and e-commerce officer for BellSouth.

There's another negative to selling a soup-to-nuts suite. By trying to do so much itself, Oracle misses out on benefits it could get from partnerships with other software makers (Exhibit 4). While it's going it alone in the exchange business, i2, procurement-software maker Ariba, and IBM announced late last month that they will pool their resources to create e-marketplaces. Former Oracle executive Barry M. Ariko, now CEO of supply-chain specialist Extricity Software Inc., believes Ellison is making a serious mistake. "The notion that you can do everything flies in the face of what the Net is all about," he says. "A lot of the new technology comes from the smallest companies. You can work with them—or you can try to do everything yourself and be 18 months behind."

Ellison admits he's playing catch-up. But he's betting that his 7,000 software programmers can deliver a package whose pieces are in some cases every bit as good as software from the specialists. He has 800 programmers focusing on customer-management software alone. Oracle still has more to do to make its e-marketplace software robust enough for the most demanding jobs. Even Oracle Business Online has run into glitches.

EXHIBIT 4   How Long Will Microsoft Play Second Fiddle?

Microsoft Corp. CEO Steven A. Ballmer could barely contain himself after announcing a deal on Mar. 13 with Andersen Consulting. Andersen would train 25,000 consultants to put together high-end computer systems using the software giant's technology. Ballmer called it a "pinch me" moment. Now Microsoft would have the consulting firepower to bid on huge contracts, especially in the lucrative market for business-to-business Internet software.

It may take more than a nip-on-the-arm moment for Microsoft to beat back archrival Oracle Corp., especially if it faces a possible breakup. When it comes to PC software, Microsoft only sees Oracle through its rearview mirror. But in the world of database and e-commerce software for building robust Web sites, Microsoft is sucking Oracle's exhaust. "Microsoft has not been a factor in the B2B market. They're not driving any business momentum—and that's the big growth area," says Morgan Stanley Dean Witter analyst Charles E. Phillips.

Beefing Up. Microsoft denies it's an also-ran. "What's so good about their performance?" Ballmer says of Oracle. "Maybe they'll pull it off. But I wouldn't trade spots with them." He's confident because Microsoft is in the midst of a massive effort to leapfrog ahead in the e-business sphere. The software giant's new Windows 2000 software is the company's first product that has enough muscle to power the biggest computer network. Combine that with SQL Server 2000, its new database that will be released later this year, and Microsoft says it will be able to handle the busiest Web sites. Moreover, the company is beefing up its software for Web-site sales and is creating technology that helps companies trade products with one another via the Web.

Still, all of Ballmer's bravado could be for naught. The federal government may push to split Microsoft's operating-system business from its software-applications operations to remedy the software giant's monopolistic abuses. If it succeeds, Windows 2000 may end up in a different company than the database program and the two products would have to compete with Oracle independently. That could make the gap between Microsoft and Oracle Grand Canyon-esque.

Even then, don't count Microsoft out. It has gained a smidgen of ground in the database business. According to Dataquest Inc. analyst Norma Schroder, Microsoft's SQL Server 7.0, launched in November, 1998, helped the company line up dot-com business and crack the corporate computer market. She hasn't completed her analysis of 1999, but preliminary data suggest that Microsoft's share of the database market may grow a couple of percentage points from the 10.2% she gave it in 1998.

Still Oracle's lead in selling databases for both the Windows 2000 and Unix operating systems will put it well ahead of Microsoft in 1999—with a market share in the high 20s. Analyst Carl Olofson of International Data Corp., who measures the database market differently, gave Microsoft just a 5.1% market share in 1998 and believes leaders Oracle and IBM will hold their own against Microsoft when the results are in for 1999.

Just the notion that Oracle is leading in e-business software gets under Microsoft's skin. Microsoft isn't used to playing second fiddle, particularly to a company run by Larry Ellison, who has made a sport of mocking it. "That will keep Microsoft alive and running like hell," says Usama Fayyad, a former senior Microsoft researcher who helped develop the soon-to-be-released SQL Server 2000 and recently left Microsoft to start his own Internet startup, digiMine.com.

With the intense Ballmer leading its charge, it's a safe bet that Microsoft won't let up until it's a serious player in e-business software.

By Jay Greene in Seattle

"It was harder to get going than we expected," admits Oracle Executive Vice-President Gary L. Bloom. The service's first 50 customers had to put up with frequent service interruptions. Now, Oracle is forging alliances with telecoms to obtain more trustworthy network connections.

Oracle had better get this right. Ellison believes that over the next few years, the company will stop being a traditional software company and deliver most of its technology to customers the way its Oracle Business Online operation does—as an online service for a monthly fee. Already, about 70% of the software in the new e-business suite is designed to be dished up that way.

That means Ellison's troops are in for several more years of roiling change. "Life is like a shark," he says. "You have to continue to move forward and do things better every day, or you die." And Ellison is enjoying being cool too much to slow down now.

Source: Steve Hamm, "Oracle: Why It's Cool Again," *Business Week,* May 8, 2000, 115–126.

3 Growth Stategies

In this part we examine growth strategies from two perspectives. First, we explore alternative directions of growth that may be taken from a company's core (initial) business. Second, we examine strategic challenges and opportunities in growth markets.

Company Growth Strategies

A business can achieve growth by marketing current or new products in existing or new markets. Management must be aware of any marketing opportunities, strategic windows, or potential differential advantages. A useful tool to help identify alternatives is the strategic opportunity matrix shown in Exhibit 1. The matrix organizes opportunities into four categories based on product and market considerations.

Market Penetration. A firm pursuing a market penetration strategy tries to increase market share in the existing market. If Kraft Foods started a major promotional campaign for Maxwell House coffee, with aggressive advertising and cents-off coupons to existing coffee users, it would be following a penetration strategy.

Market Development. Market development entails attracting new customers to existing products. Ideally, new uses for old products stimulate additional sales to existing customers while also bringing in new buyers. McDonald's, for example, has opened restaurants in Russia, China, and Italy and is eagerly expanding into Eastern Europe. In the nonprofit area, the growing emphasis on continuing education and executive development by colleges and universities is a market development strategy.

Product Development. A product development strategy entails the creation of new products for present markets. The "eating healthy" trend of the early 1990s led ConAgra—the maker of Banquet, Morton, Patio, and Chun King frozen dinners—to develop Healthy Choice frozen dinners, which are low in fat, cholesterol, and sodium. Responding to the same trend, Kraft Foods introduced no-cholesterol mayonnaise and General Mills and Kellogg brought out high-fiber, low-fat, and low-sodium cereals. Managers who follow this strategy can rely on their extensive knowledge of the target

EXHIBIT 1   Strategic Opportunity Matrix

Present Products	*New Products*
Market penetration	Product development
Market development	Diversification

audience. They usually have a good feel for what customers like and dislike about current products and which existing needs are not being met. In addition, managers can rely on established distribution channels.

Diversification.   Diversification is a strategy of increasing sales by introducing new products into new markets. For example, Sony practiced a diversification strategy when it acquired Columbia Pictures; although motion pictures are not a new product in the marketplace, they were a new product for Sony. Coca-Cola manufactures and markets water-treatment and water-conditioning equipment—a challenging task for the traditional soft-drink company. A diversification strategy can be quite risky when a firm is entering unfamiliar markets. However, it can be very profitable when a firm is entering markets with little or no competition.

Movement beyond the core business is not unusual as businesses grow and mature. Several factors may influence the rate and direction of company growth strategies, including available resources, management's preferences, pending opportunities and threats, and the desire to reduce dependence on the core business. For example, when growth in the apparel market began slowing in the late 1980s, Benetton grew by acquiring sporting goods firms. Nordica Spa (ski equipment), Prince (tennis rackets), and Rollerblade (inline skates) now account for about one-fifth of Benetton's worldwide sales.

Sometimes a company relies on its own expertise to grow. At other times it uses the expertise of others. Three primary ways of accomplishing a growth strategy are leveraging a core competency, engaging in mergers and acquisitions, and establishing a joint venture or strategic alliance.

- *Leveraging a core competency.* A company may use its own expertise in a particular field to grow. For example, Honda's diverse line of products—including cars, garden tillers, motorcycles, lawn mowers, snowblowers, snowmobiles, power generators, and outboard motors—seems to be a growth strategy of diversification into unrelated markets. However, Honda has simply exploited its core competency in small-engine technology and manufacturing and its brand recognition to leverage growth into diverse power equipment markets.

- *Mergers and acquisitions.* In the past decade these initiatives have been a leading growth strategy of companies in a variety of industries. Toymaker Mattel acquired Fisher-Price to gain entry into the preschool and infant markets. Disney acquired Capital Cities/ABC to expand movie and television producers' ability to distribute their products. Ernst & Young, the Big Six accounting firm, acquired Kenneth Leventhal & Company, a smaller accountancy firm specializing in real estate, to grow in that industry.

- *Establishing a joint venture or strategic alliance.* Companies often form partnerships with other corporations to develop products. An example is the partnership between Apple, IBM, and Motorola to develop the PowerPC microchip. Another reason to form an alliance is to vertically align with specific suppliers or customer groups. An example is Boeing Corporation developing long-term relationships with a core group of suppliers and involving its customers in designing products.

Marketing Strategy in Growth Markets[1]

Growth markets typically are characterized by escalating industry sales, new competitors entering the market, large companies acquiring pioneering firms, and healthy industry profits. The strategic focus shifts from stimulating generic or primary demand to aggressive selective or brand demand stimulation. Large firms are likely to enter markets at the growth stage, utilizing superior skills and resource advantages to overcome some of the timing advantages of market pioneers. Large firms also have the advantage of evaluating the attractiveness of product markets during initial development. The uncertainties about the size and scope of the emerging market may encourage a wait-and-see position on the part of large potential competitors.

Procter & Gamble (P&G), for example, sometimes enters growth markets dominated by well-entrenched competitors. Instead of launching me-too or single-segment products, P&G introduces a succession of products aimed at different segments. Each entry creates a loyal following and takes some business away from the competitor. Soon the competitor is surrounded, its revenue is weakened, and it is too late to launch new brands at outlying segments. This presents an opportunity for P&G to introduce a brand to compete head-on in the major market segment dominated by the competitor. This approach has been labeled an "encirclement" strategy.[2]

Growth markets present interesting strategic challenges and opportunities. Key issues that marketing managers must consider include market segmentation, targeting, and positioning.

Market Segmentation. If not already defined in the emerging market, segments should be defined, described, and analyzed in the growth stage. Identifying customer groups with similar needs improves targeting, and "experience with the product, process, and materials technologies leads to greater efficiency and increased standardization."[3] The market environment moves from highly uncertain to moderately uncertain during the growth stage. Further change is likely, but information is available about the forces that influence the size and composition of the product market. Analysis of existing buyers' characteristics and preferences yields useful guidelines for estimating market potential. Anticipating the directions of change is important in developing or maintaining a competitive advantage. The potential for segment growth, profitability, and stability must be evaluated by management.

Targeting. The major influences on targeting decisions in growth markets are (1) the capabilities and resources of the organization, (2) the competitive environment, (3) the extent to which the product market can be segmented, (4) the future potential of the market, and (5) the market entry barriers confronting potential competitors.

A concentrated or niche targeting strategy may be appropriate when buyers' needs are differentiated or when product differentiation occurs. A new market entrant may identify segments that are not served by large competitors. These segments provide an opportunity for the small firm to gain competitive advantage. The market leader(s) may not find small segments attractive enough to allocate the skills and resources necessary to gain a position in them.

A company that seeks to appeal to multiple market segments by using a differentiated targeting strategy must determine how much variation exists in buyers' needs and wants. During the growth stage of the business market for personal computers, the three major segments were small, medium-size, and large companies. Microsegmentation (many segments) in a growth market is typically not necessary. A small number of segments can be identified by one or a few general characteristics (e.g., size of business). When no segments are apparent, undifferentiated targeting is guided by a general profile of buyers. This average-buyer profile becomes the target.

Positioning Strategy.   As product markets shift from emerging to growth, positioning strategies typically change. Exhibit 2 illustrates positioning strategies found in emerging, growth, and mature product markets. These strategies are illustrative because many factors influence the choice of a strategy.

As product markets shift from emerging to growth, the strategic focus shifts from stimulating generic or primary demand to aggressive selective brand stimulation. The expanded number of models and competitors contributes to this shift. Another reason for this shift in strategies is that most potential customers and distributors are aware of generic product features, advantages, and benefits. The promotion emphasis changes from education, product awareness, and primary demand stimulation to developing brand loyalty.

Distribution becomes a major key to success in growth markets. Manufacturers scramble to sign up dealers and distributors and to begin building long-term relationships. Without adequate distribution, it is impossible to establish a strong market position.

Toward the end of the growth phase, profits normally begin falling from the peak level. Price reductions result from increasing economies of scale and rising competition. Also, most firms have recovered their development costs by this time, and their priority is to increase or retain market share and enhance profits.

Intuit Corporation found success in the growth stage of what otherwise might have become a commodity market:

EXHIBIT 2   Illustrative Positioning Strategies in Emerging, Growth, and Mature Markets

Positioning Strategy Component	Emerging Markets	Growth Markets	Mature Markets
Product strategy	Limited number of models; frequent product modification	Expanded number of models; frequent product modifications	Large number of models
Distribution strategy	Distribution usually limited, depending on product; intensive efforts and high margins often needed to attract distributors	Expanded number of distributors; margins declining; intensive efforts to retain distributors and shelf space	Extensive number of dealers; margins declining; intensive efforts to retain distributors and shelf space
Promotion strategy	Develop product awareness; stimulate primary demand; use extensive personal selling to distributors; use sampling and coupons to consumers	Stimulate selective demand; advertise brand aggressively; promote heavily to retain dealers and customers	Stimulate selective demand; advertise brand aggressively; promote heavily to retain dealers and customers
Pricing strategy	Prices are usually high to recover development costs	Prices begin to fall toward end of growth stage as a result of competitive pressure	Prices continue to fall

Intuit makes microcomputer software. Its flagship product is Quicken, a program that allows consumers and small businesses to write checks and keep track of their finances on a personal computer. Quicken is probably the most successful personal finance program ever written, holding a market share estimated at 60 percent.[4]

Intuit's secret formula? A faster, cheaper, hassle-free, and, above all, easy-to-use program supported by extensive and continuous product development, testing, customer research, and technical support representatives who share management's obsession with customer satisfaction. Intuit's success frequently is linked to its corporate philosophy of doing whatever it takes to satisfy a customer.

End Notes

1. Much of the material in this section is from David W. Cravens, *Strategic Marketing,* 6th ed. (Burr Ridge, IL: Irwin/McGraw-Hill, 2000), pp. 184–185.

2. Philip Kotler, *Marketing Management,* 8th ed. (Englewood Cliffs, NJ: Prentice-Hall, 1994), p. 376.

3. Mary Lambkin and George S. Day, "Evolutionary Processes in Competitive Markets: Beyond the Product Life Cycle," *Journal of Marketing,* July 1989, p. 14.

4. John Case, "Consumer Service: The Last Word," *INC.,* April 1991, p. 89.

CASES FOR PART 3

Growth occurs in various forms of product development and market development. The seven cases in this part portray growth strategies in small entrepreneurial organizations as well as growth options in large international corporations. The product offerings examined in these cases range from karate lessons to computer software.

The video case, **Rollerblade, Inc.: Doing Business in a Mature Market (Case 3–1),** examines the company's challenges in an industry that is trying to rebound from an enduring maturation phase. Rollerblade, Inc., is looking to expand the scope of in-line skating by creating new ways and reasons to skate. The bottom line is that the company needs to revitalize its growth.

The Indian market for home water filtration and purification is difficult to understand. In **Blair Water Purifiers India (Case 3–2),** Blair Company has to determine the optimal mode of market entry into this new market. Can the company consolidate the market and stimulate growth?

SystemSoft Corporation (Case 3–3), a provider of system-level software, has been very successful with its core product lines. The company has to decide whether it should push into new product categories and segments by entering the call avoidance software business. The rewards for pioneering a new product category could be tremendous. Yet pursuing this opportunity could stretch SystemSoft's resources at a time when the company has to begin to understand and manage growth.

In **Transvit of Novgorod, Russia (Case 3–4),** a consortium of radio and television electronic component manufacturers needs to grow in the international marketplace since the Japanese have infiltrated the domestic market. The group intends to capture more value-added manufacturing processes while increasing its international and domestic customer base.

Case 3–5, Shorin-Ryu Karate Academy, examines the challenges and opportunities of managing a small business. The owner has collected market research data and must decide whether growth entails opening new facilities and/or expanding its current facility.

Taurus Hungarian Rubber Works (Case 3–6) has decided that it needs to diversify away from its traditional dependence on truck and farm tires. The company's strategy is to seek cooperative strategic alliances to accelerate growth. Taurus must determine the appropriate grouping of its current product lines. These changes will help define the company's attractiveness in terms of future relations with other companies.

Case 3–7, the e-business case, looks at whether **Vignette Corp.,** the leading maker of software to manage Web content, can morph into an all-in-one e-business software shop. The content management market is characterized by fast growth. Will Vignette be able to match, and capture, this growth?

CASE 3–1
ROLLERBLADE, INC.
DOING BUSINESS IN A MATURE MARKET

For Rollerblade, Inc., to remain the market leader in the competitive in-line skating industry, the company must continually innovate its product offerings in response to changing consumer desires. In an industry trying to rebound from an enduring maturation phase, Rollerblade continues to lead in-line skating into the next millennium.

Over the last 20 years Rollerblade has made technical, aesthetic, and practical improvements in its products as well as introducing extensive new product lines that have developed into dependable moneymakers. In attempting to maintain consumer interest in an industry which is experiencing declining sales, Rollerblade looks to expand the scope of in-line skating by creating new ways and reasons to skate. As the company looks ahead and considers the long-range in-line skating market conditions, it faces a challenging question: In what directions should Rollerblade go, and what strategies should it pursue to maintain its market share and revitalize its growth?

The Company

As a 19-year-old goaltender for a minor league hockey team, Scott Olson divined a simple idea that soon led him to multimillionaire status. The simple idea was ice skates that could work without ice.

In 1979 Olson came across a pair of roller skates in which the wheels were arranged in a single row rather than two by two. This "in-line" skate originated in the Netherlands in the 1700s and was said to be the first roller skate.[1] Although slow and clumsy, the skate provided the feel of skating on ice. As a hockey player, Olson knew the outstanding potential of a skate targeted toward hockey players that could simulate the feel of ice skating but allow a hockey player to perform off the ice and during the off-season.

After locating the manufacturer of the in-line skate and buying up back stock (the manufacturer had quit making the skate by then), Olson proceeded to refine the skates (through good skate boots and better wheels for a faster, smoother ride) and began building them in his basement. In 1983 Olson's company, Rollerblade, Inc., based in Minnesota, became the only manufacturer of in-line skates. Olson soon sold most of his holdings in Rollerblade, Inc., to Robert O. Naegele, Jr., and in 1985 Olson left Rollerblade after a business dispute.[2]

The success of the company continued through the late 1980s and into the 1990s, with Rollerblade, Inc., maintaining its number one position in a growing market expe-

---

[1] In-line skating was a fad in the 1860s.

[2] Olson introduced Switch-It skates in 1985. Those skates had interchangeable ice and in-line blades. Fifty percent of the business was sold in 1990, and Olson went on to start two more businesses. Nuskate Inc. focused on a product that married in-line skates to a cross-country ski track exerciser. O.S. Designs sold other Olson sporting good designs, such as a lightweight golf bag with wheels and a built-in pull handle.

This case was prepared by Allison E. Kleva under the supervision of Victoria L. Crittenden, associate professor of marketing at Boston College, as the basis for class discussion rather than to illustrate either effective or ineffective handling of a managerial situation. All information was derived from secondary sources. January 2001.

riencing increased competitive activity. In 1991 Rollerblade, Inc., embarked on a partnership with Nordica Sportsystem (Italy). Nordica, a division of Edizione Holding (controlled by the Benetton family) and the world's number one ski boot maker, purchased 50 percent of Rollerblade, Inc., for an undisclosed sum.[3] Edizione Holding's product lines, under the Benetton Sportsytem umbrella, also included Prince tennis rackets, Asolo mountain boots, and Kastle Skates. In November 1997 Rollerblade, Inc.'s, Minnesota headquarters closed, and the company was relocated to Bordentown, New Jersey. There all facets of the manufacturing, sales, marketing, and distribution of Benetton's Sports brands were consolidated in one place.

In-Line Skating

In the 1990s in-line skating permeated the recreation, fitness, and athletics industry at a startling pace. According to the Sporting Goods Manufacturers Association (SGMA), U.S. in-line participation had grown 858 percent in the last 10 years. An estimated 32 million Americans were in-line skaters, a striking contrast to the reported 3.6 million participants in 1994. At 22 percent, up 7 percent from 1995, household penetration of in-line skating was on the rise. A recent SGMA study noted in-line skating as the fastest-growing sport of 1999. While the number of new participants continued to increase and the sport maintained its evolution, the industry faces a decline in sales resulting from the onset of maturation.

The in-line craze of the early 1990s led to the presence of almost 30 manufacturers in the industry by 1995. Large sporting goods companies entered the market. Nike and Fila capitalized on their footwear popularity and entered the market in 1996. Ski boot manufacturers Rossignol, Salomon, and K2 joined as well, building their in-line businesses on their quality ski equipment images. The abundance of product offered to customers by these competitors as well as numerous other independent manufacturers contributed to the industry's continuous sales decline in the late 1990s.

Maturation for in-line skating began as it approached its 20-year presence in the sporting goods industry. After soaring sales and consistent years of double-digit growth rates, numerous companies entered the market, hoping to take advantage of the popularity of in-line skating. The competitive saturation produced inevitable overinventoried, overstored tanking across the industry. The continual lowering of skate prices, resulting from competitive pricing and the presence of so many skate manufacturers in the market, resulted in a steady decline in dollar sales in the late 1990s. Sales in 1999 were $305 million, down 35 percent from the previous year. In 1998, sales were $322.4 million, while 1997 posted $374 million and 1996 reported $418 million in sales. Future sales performance was expected to follow this trend. While in-line skating remained popular, preseason orders project sales in 2000 to continue to decrease 15 to 25 percent.

Major competitor brands exited the in-line market in the second half of the decade. In 1999 Nike, Fila, and Rossignol, strong brands looking to capitalize on their brand equity and the in-line craze, recognized their efforts as unprofitable and decided to end distribution of their respective skate products. Both their presence and their absence

---

[3] Nordica ski boots and Rollerblade in-line skates were made from the same basic plastic composite material. Machines at the Nordica production plant in Italy could switch easily between components for the ski boot and those for the Rollerblade skate shell. Plans were for up to 50 percent of Rollerblade production to take place at Nordica plants. In the United States, Rollerblade operated out of its Minnesota facility and Nordica operated out of its Vermont facility.

were felt by other manufacturers and retailers. The entrance and exit of manufacturers in the industry had created an excess inventory problem. This "problem" evolved into inventory pileups, product dumping, and inventory rollovers. With the consumer's hunt for the cheapest pair of skates and the absence of upgrade purchases, the industry faced a discouraging decline.

The slow and steady recovery of the in-line skating market began in the new millennium as "inventory pipe-lines are finally getting cleared out and the closeouts haunting the business begin to subside."[4] New products and skating opportunities were being developed, and with fewer major players in the market, industry leaders were better able to maintain and grow their market share. The four major players in the industry (Rollerblade, 36 percent; K2, 34 percent; Salomon, 5.8 percent; and Bladerunner, 2.6 percent) continued to lead the market in the year 2000, presenting consumers with new and innovative products.

Product Line

Over the years, changing consumer patterns and industry trends led to a redefinition of the original market segments. The company had introduced new products in those segments based on customer usage. By listening to the consumers and devoting itself to extensive research and development, Rollerblade sustained market dominance by developing skates that addressed buyers' needs and desires. Since the industry slowdown in the mid-1990s, Rollerblade had worked hard to create new markets, which in turn generated new product lines for the company.

In 1998 the in-line industry had plateaued. Skates were used for fitness, recreation, transport, and playing hockey. While in-line users continued to skate, nothing "new" was introduced to motivate or excite the market. Rollerblade capitalized on this monotony by creating a new category of skating. Innovation had, since the origin of the sport, been the lifeblood of in-line. Concept and design innovation stimulated media hype and consumer attention. With the launch of Rollerblade's Coyote skate in 1998, all-terrain, off-road skating was born.

The introduction of all-terrain skating resulted in the evolution of new sports in the industry; aggressive skaters, lured by the exciting terrain made accessible by product attributes, brought skating to an entirely new level with grass skating, downhill slalom, bump competition, and rough-terrain racing. Rollerblade marketed the Coyote as a downhill-specific,[5] off-road, all-terrain skate and introduced Blade Cross at the 1998 Summer X Games. Competitors, apprehensive about consumer response, waited until aggressive skating became mainstream before manufacturing off-road skates. This trepidation allowed Rollerblade, Inc., to dominate the aggressive market. According to Rollerblade, Inc.'s, vice president of sales and marketing, Mike Klein, the development of the Coyote was essential because aggressive skating was the direction in which in-line skating was headed in the future.

Rollerblade, Inc., continued to innovate its products to satisfy consumer needs in the late 1990s. Its original transportation skate, the Metroblade, had served the desired function but lacked any distinct beneficial feature. In late 1998 Rollerblade introduced a specialty transport skate, the Nature. The product functioned as a high-end skate with

---

[4] Carpenter, Kristen. "The Buzz," *Sporting Goods Business,* June 22, 1998, p. 38.

[5] Blade Cross is a downhill all-terrain skating event. Five or six off-road skaters navigate a downhill course which is designed to showcase excitement and be spectator-friendly.

a removable frame so that the boot could be worn separately. The skate, created with the student and local commuter in mind, featured a boot designed by Benetton Sportsystem partner Asolo. The success of the Nature skate among consumers led to the development of three new models launched in January 2000: Derby, Derby-Grey, and Drop skates (boot designs differed among the three).

Joining the product launches of 1998 was Rollerblade, Inc.'s, first footwear offering. The Grind shoe, introduced to the consumer market simultaneously with the Coyote and the Nature skate, was designed for grinding on curbs and rails, sliding, and jumping. This everyday shoe, featuring Rollerblade's patented Twin Bar Roller System, capitalized on the company's brand equity to introduce a new product line and skating concept to the consumer market. Yet again Rollerblade succeeded in expanding its product offering to uncharted territory while maintaining quality image consistency.

By the start of the new millennium Rollerblade offered consumers many products in five major product lines: fitness/performance, transportation, aggressive/specialty, recreation, in-line hockey, and kids.

Focus on the Future

While in-line skating had entered a stage of maturity and sales had decreased significantly, it was possible for Rollerblade to recover and increase its business. To grow in the new millennium, Rollerblade must focus on developing a marketing strategy that will drive future sales in a stagnant market. As Rollerblade must continue to present the market with new and innovative products, it also has to respond to consumer trends. As aggressive market sales slow, children's and high-performance fitness skates are becoming the focus.

Children's in-line skating participation was steadily rising, causing Rollerblade to acknowledge that market as an important growth segment and regard it as a legitimate investment. RB Kids introduced the Xtenblade in 1996, and improvements and design modifications were made continually. The skate's technology accommodated children's growing feet by creating an adjustable frame that extended four full sizes with the turn of a screw. Included in the 2000 skate line for children was the SAX, a new softboot offering an ABT brake designed to accommodate users' short legs and limited braking leverage.

Another segment in which Rollerblade hoped to generate sales was high-performance fitness. A study outlining the fitness benefits of in-line skating resulted in Rollerblade focusing its energies on a fitness campaign. Much of the 2000 line would reflect design changes to Rollerblade's high-end fitness skates. Unveiled in late 1999, the 2000 skate line aimed not only to provide the consumer with upgraded, high-performance fitness skates but also to re-enter the market segment at higher prices than it had had in the recent past (due to the presence of competitors who were forcing prices down). The stylish new line featured a variety of softboot skates with advances in braking, comfort, and performance.

The 2000 skate line reflected technical and innovative improvements on existing products. The previously mentioned transportation skate models, accompanied by improvements to the aggressive skates as well as the debut of two new grind shoes, would join Rollerblade's 2000 line.

Long-range in-line market conditions and opportunities had to be considered before Rollerblade could implement its future marketing strategy. The company needed alternative marketing strategies to combat the sales slump it was experiencing. Additionally, Rollerblade had to evaluate the market's current state, consumer desires, and industry trends before executing a strategy aimed at increasing sales. As Rollerblade faced growth in a declining market, it was challenged with the task of recognizing future opportunities in a changing consumer market as well as focusing on marketing efforts that would capitalize on those opportunities.

Rollerblade segmented its market in multiple ways. Therefore, considering marketing strategies, it was imperative to recognize the age and benefit segments to which Rollerblade catered with its product offerings. Rollerblade's marketing efforts were not based on gender segmentation due to the presence of an almost equal male-female in-line representation (male, approximately 57 percent; female, approximately 43 percent). The previously mentioned product lines correspond with certain markets:

Fitness/performance: men and women ages 20 to 50, core group between 25 and 40, professional and highly educated

Aggressive/specialty: 18- to 24-year-olds

Kids: under 18 years old

Recreation: 18 to 55 years old

In-line hockey: children, adolescents, and younger adults

Transportation: local commuters and students

To develop an effective marketing strategy, Rollerblade must identify which market(s), if not the general in-line skating market (men and women age 18 to 55), it will focus on. The company must then direct its promotional efforts toward the chosen market.

Rollerblade, Inc., must examine the following four potential growth areas:

1. Market Penetration
   - Rollerblade could engage in grassroots marketing efforts which would involve marketing directly to its customers through promotional activities and events. In providing interactive workshops, seminars, festivals, shows, and other various events, Rollerblade would reintroduce its consumers to its products.

2. Product Development
   - Rollerblade had consistently delivered new and improved products to the market over the last 20 years. The development of innovative products had been the key to its success as well as its market domination.
   - The introduction of aggressive skating products to the consumer market in 1998 aimed to boost sales in the existing in-line market. The new aggressive line, along with the introduction of all-terrain skating as a sport, led the market to change to a more challenging skate. Perhaps introducing another skate product category to the existing market would spur sales.
   - Recent studies suggested that in-line skating was linked to being fit. The focus on in-line skating as a top cardiovascular, balance, and muscular endurance fitness activity could be beneficial to Rollerblade's future. If the company capitalized on the increase in contemporary health/fitness consciousness and took advantage of the rising interest in alternative methods of exercise, Rollerblade could develop its existing fitness market into a top moneymaker. In developing new and innovative products for this growing market, Rollerblade could simultaneously increase profits and gain a larger customer base.

3. Market Development
   - Rollerblade could continue to grow internationally. While it had expanded in Europe (Finland, Greece, Italy, Netherlands, Turkey, the United Kingdom), the Middle East (Saudi Arabia, the United Arab Emirates, Israel), Asia (Korea, Japan, Hong Kong, Malyasia, Philippines, Singapore), Central and South America (Argentina, Brazil, Chile, Columbia, Mexico, Panama, Venezuela), the Caribbean (Dominican Republic,

St. Maarten, and Trinidad), and Australia and New Zealand, Rollerblade could seek to permeate new, more obscure markets.

- Recent research had noted that in-line skating was tremendously helpful for children in mastering motor skills. In-line skating was credited with aiding developmentally delayed children in their mental and physical progress. Perhaps making some efforts toward the creation of an educational/developmental children's market focusing on the psychological and physical benefits of in-line skating would prove beneficial to company sales.

4. Diversification.

- Rollerblade took the first step in this direction with the development of the Grind shoe in 1998. The product expanded Rollerblade's market penetration to encompass footwear.
- An option for growth could lie in the development of product lines outside the in-line industry. Perhaps, in keeping with its image as an alternative sporting goods manufacturer, Rollerblade could extend its product lines to include other extreme sports, such as skateboarding and snowboarding. Rollerblade could possibly capitalize on the recent scooter craze and introduce its own line to the consumer market. Two-wheeled, lightweight portable scooters had become popular among short-range commuters, students, adults, and children. Investment in this current trend could prove profitable for the company.

Given the four options, which one(s) would prove to be most lucrative in the long term? What should Rollerblade, Inc., do to be successful in the selected growth area(s)?

Sources

Carpenter, Kristen. "Wheels: Meet the More Mature Inline Market," *Sporting Goods Business,* June 21, 1999, pp. 26–28.

Carpenter, Kristen. "The Dirt," *Sporting Goods Business,* June 22, 1998, p. 40.

Carpenter, Kristen. "The Buzz," *Sporting Goods Business,* June 22, 1998, pp. 38–39.

McIntyre, Jason. "Your Game: On the Inline Fast Track," *Provincial Journal,* May 20, 2000, p. 7D.

Riddle, John D. "In-Line Skating Rolls Out Initiatives to Counter Market Woes," *2000 State of the Industry Report,* February 9, 2000.

www.rollerblade.com.

www.skating.com. "Rollerblade Aims High," September 10, 1999.

CASE 3–2
BLAIR WATER PURIFIERS INDIA

"A pity I couldn't have stayed for Diwali," thought Rahul Chatterjee. "But anyway, it was great to be back home in Calcutta." The Diwali holiday and its festivities would begin in early November 1996, some two weeks after Chatterjee had returned to the United States. Chatterjee worked as an international market liaison for Blair Company, Inc. This was his eighth year with Blair Company and easily his favorite. "Your challenge will be in moving us from just dabbling in less developed countries [LDCs] to our thriving in them," his boss had said when Chatterjee was promoted to the job last January. Chatterjee had agreed and was thrilled when he was asked to visit Bombay and New Delhi in April. His purpose on that trip was to gather background data on the possibility of Blair Company entering the Indian market for home water purification devices. The initial results had been encouraging and had prompted the second trip.

Chatterjee had used his second trip primarily to study Indian consumers in Calcutta and Bangalore and to gather information on possible competitors. The two cities represented quite different metropolitan areas in terms of location, size, language, and infrastructure, yet both cities faced similar problems in terms of the water supplied to their residents. Those problems could be found in many LDCs and were favorable to home water purification.

Information gathered on both visits would be used to make a recommendation on market entry and on the elements of an entry strategy. Executives at Blair Company would compare Chatterjee's recommendation to those from two other Blair Company liaisons who were focusing their efforts on Argentina, Brazil, and Indonesia.

Indian Market for Home Water Filtration and Purification

Like many things in India, the market for home water filtration and purification took a good deal of effort to understand. Yet despite expending this effort, Chatterjee realized that much remained either unknown or in conflict. For example, the market seemed clearly a mature one, with four or five established Indian competitors fighting for market share. Or was it? Another view portrayed the market as a fragmented one, with no large competitor having a national presence and perhaps 100 small regional manufacturers, each competing in just one or two of India's 25 states. Indeed, the market could be in its early growth stages, as reflected by the large number of product designs, materials, and performances. Perhaps with a next-generation product and a world-class marketing effort, Blair Company could consolidate the market and stimulate tremendous growth—much like the situation in the Indian market for automobiles.

Such uncertainty made it difficult to estimate market potential. However, Chatterjee had collected unit sales estimates for a 10-year period for three similar product cate-

This case was written by Professor James E. Nelson, University of Colorado at Boulder. He thanks students in the class of 1996 (batch 31), Indian Institute of Management, Calcutta, for their invaluable help in collecting all the data needed to write this case. He also thanks Professor Roger Kerin, Southern Methodist University, for his helpful comments. The case is intended for educational purposes rather than to illustrate either effective or ineffective decision making. Some data as well as the identity of the company are disguised. ©1997 by James E. Nelson. Used with permission.

gories: vacuum cleaners, sewing machines, and color televisions. In addition, a Delhi-based research firm had provided him with estimates of unit sales for Aquaguard, the best-selling water purifier in several Indian states. Chatterjee had used the data in two forecasting models available at Blair Company along with three subjective scenarios—realistic, optimistic, and pessimistic—to arrive at the estimates and forecasts for water purifiers shown in Exhibit 1. "If anything," Chatterjee had explained to his boss, "my forecasts are conservative because they describe only first-time sales, not any replacement sales over the 10-year forecast horizon." He also pointed out that his forecasts applied only to industry sales in larger urban areas, which was the present industry focus.

One thing that seemed certain was that many Indians felt the need for improved water quality. Folklore, newspapers, consumer activists, and government officials regularly reinforced this need by describing the poor quality of Indian water. Quality suffered particularly during monsoons because highly polluted water entered treatment plants and because of numerous leaks and unauthorized withdrawals from water systems. Such leaks and withdrawals often polluted clean water after it had left the plants. Politicians running for national, state, and local government offices also reinforced the need for improved water quality through election campaign promises. Governments at these levels set standards for water quality, took measurements at thousands of locations throughout the nation, and advised consumers when water became unsafe.

During periods of poor water quality many Indian consumers had little choice but to consume the water as they found it. However, better-educated, wealthier, and more health-conscious consumers took steps to safeguard their families' health and often continued these steps all year. A good estimate of the number of such households, Chatterjee thought, would be around 40 million. These consumers were similar in many respects to consumers in middle- and upper-middle-class households in the United States

---

EXHIBIT 1 **Industry Sales Estimates and Forecasts for Water Purifiers in India, 1990–2005 (thousands of units)**

Year	Unit Sales Estimates	Unit Sales Forecast Under		
		Realistic Scenario	Optimistic Scenario	Pessimistic Scenario
1990	60			
1991	90			
1992	150			
1993	200			
1994	220			
1995	240			
1996		250	250	250
1997		320	370	300
1998		430	540	400
1999		570	800	550
2000		800	1,200	750
2001		1,000	1,500	850
2002		1,300	1,900	900
2003		1,500	2,100	750
2004		1,600	2,100	580
2005		1,500	1,900	420

and the European Union. They valued comfort and product choice. They saw consumption of material goods as a means to a higher quality of life. They liked foreign brands and would pay a higher price for such brands as long as those products outperformed competing Indian products. Chatterjee had identified as his target market these 40 million households plus another 4 million households whose members had similar values and lifestyles but made little effort to improve water quality in their homes.

Traditional Method for Home Water Purification.   The traditional method of water purification in the target market relied not on a commercially supplied product but on boiling. Each day or several times a day, a cook, maid, or family member would boil two to five liters of water for 10 minutes, allow it to cool, and then transfer it to containers for storage (often in a refrigerator). Chatterjee estimated that about 50 percent of the target market used this procedure. Boiling was seen by consumers as inexpensive, effective in terms of eliminating dangerous bacteria, and entrenched in a traditional sense. Many consumers who used this method considered it more effective than any product on the market. However, boiling affected the palatability of water, leaving the purified product somewhat "flat" tasting. Boiling also was cumbersome, time-consuming, and ineffective in removing physical impurities and unpleasant odors. Consequently, about 10 percent of the target market took a second step by filtering their boiled water through "candle filters" before storage. Many consumers took this action despite knowing that water could become recontaminated during handling and storage.

Mechanical Methods for Home Water Filtration and Purification.   About 40 percent of the target market used a mechanical device to improve their water quality. Half of this group used candle filters, primarily because of their low price and ease of use. The typical candle filter contained two containers, one resting on top of the other. The upper container held one or more porous ceramic cylinders (candles) which strained the water as gravity drew it into the lower container. Containers were made of plastic, porcelain, or stainless steel and typically stored between 15 and 25 liters of filtered water. Purchase costs depended on materials and capacities, ranging from Rs.350 for a small plastic model to Rs.1,100 for a large stainless-steel model (35 Indian rupees was equivalent to US$1.00 in 1996). Candle filters were slow, producing 15 liters (one candle) to 45 liters (three candles) of filtered water in 24 hours. To maintain this productivity, candles regularly had to be removed, cleaned, and boiled for 20 minutes. Most manufacturers recommended that consumers replace candles (Rs.40 each) either once a year or more frequently, depending on sediment levels.

The other half of this group used "water purifiers," devices that were considerably more sophisticated than candle filters. Water purifiers typically employed three water-processing stages. The first removed sediments, the second objectionable odors and colors, and the third harmful bacteria and viruses. Engineers at Blair Company were skeptical that most purifiers claiming the latter benefit could deliver on their promise. However, all purifiers did a better job here than candle filters. Candle filters were totally ineffective in eliminating bacteria and viruses (and might even increase this type of contamination) despite advertising claims to the contrary. Water purifiers generally used stainless-steel containers and sold at prices ranging from Rs.2,000 to Rs.7,000, depending on the manufacturer, features, and capacities. Common flow rates were one to two liters of purified water per minute. Simple service activities could be performed on water purifiers by consumers as needed. However, more complicated service required that units be taken to a nearby dealer or necessitated an in-home visit from a skilled technician.

The remaining 10 percent of the target market owned neither a filter nor a purifier and seldom boiled their water. Many consumers in this group were unaware of water problems and thought their water quality was acceptable. However, a few consumers in this group refused to pay for products that they believed were mostly ineffective. Overall, Chatterjee believed that only a few consumers in this group could be induced to change their habits and become customers. The most attractive segments consisted of the 90 percent of households in the target market that boiled, boiled and filtered, only filtered, or purified their water.

All the segments in the target market showed a good deal of similarity in terms of what they thought important in the purchase of a water purifier. According to Chatterjee's research, the most important factor was product performance in terms of sediment removal, bacteria and virus removal, capacity (in the form of storage or flow rate), safety, and "footprint" space. Purchase price also was an important concern among consumers who boiled, boiled and filtered, or only filtered their water. The next most important factor was ease of installation and service, with style and appearance rated almost as important. The least important factor was warranty and the availability of financing for purchase. Finally, all segments expected a water purifier to be warranted against defective operation for 18 to 24 months and to perform trouble-free for 5 to 10 years.

Foreign Investment in India

India appeared attractive to many foreign investors because of government actions begun in the 1980s during the administration of Prime Minister Rajiv Gandhi. The broad label applied to these actions was *liberalization*. Liberalization had opened the Indian economy to foreign investors, stemming from a recognition that protectionist policies had not worked very well and that Western economies and technologies—seen against the collapse of the Soviet Union—did. Liberalization had meant major changes in approval requirements for new commercial projects, investment policies, taxation procedures, and, most important, the attitudes of government officials. These changes had stayed in place through the two national governments that followed Gandhi's assassination in 1991.

If Blair Company entered the Indian market, it would do so in one of three ways: (1) joint working arrangement, (2) joint venture company, or (3) acquisition. In a joint working arrangement Blair Company would supply key purifier components to an Indian company, which would manufacture and market the assembled product. License fees would be remitted to Blair Company on a per-unit basis over the term of the agreement (typically five years, with an option to renew for three more). A joint venture agreement would have Blair Company partnering with an existing Indian company expressly for the purpose of manufacturing and marketing water purifiers. Profits from the joint venture operation would be split between the two parties per the agreement, which usually contained a clause describing buy/sell procedures available to the two parties after a minimum time period. An acquisition entry would have Blair Company purchasing an existing Indian company whose operations then would be expanded to include the water purifier. Profits from the acquisition would belong to Blair Company.

Beyond understanding these basic entry possibilities, Chatterjee acknowledged that he was no expert in the legal aspects of the project. However, two days spent with a Calcutta consulting firm had produced the following information. Blair Company had to apply for market entry to the Foreign Investment Promotion Board, Secretariat for Industrial Approvals, Ministry of Industries. The proposal would go before the board for an assessment of the relevant technology and India's need for the technology. If approved by the board, the proposal then would go to the Reserve Bank of India, Ministry of Finance, for approvals of any royalties and fees, remittances of dividends and interest (if any), repatriation of profits and invested capital, and repayment of foreign loans. While the process sounded cumbersome and time-consuming, the consultant assured Chatterjee that the government usually completed its deliberations in less than six months and that his consulting firm could "virtually guarantee" final approval.

Trademarks and patents were protected by law in India. Trademarks were protected for seven years and could be renewed on the payment of a prescribed fee. Patents lasted for 14 years. On balance, Chatterjee had told his boss that Blair Company would have "no more problem protecting its intellectual property rights in India than in the United States—as long as we stay out of court." Chatterjee went on to explain that litigation in India was expensive and protracted. Litigation problems were compounded by an appeal process that could extend a case for a generation. Consequently, many foreign companies preferred arbitration, as India was a party to the Geneva Convention covering foreign arbitral awards.

Foreign companies were taxed on income arising from Indian operations. They also paid taxes on any interest, dividends, and royalties received and on any capital gains received from a sale of assets. The government offered a wide range of tax concessions to foreign investors, including liberal depreciation allowances and generous deductions. The government offered even more favorable tax treatment if foreign investors would locate in one of India's six Free Trade Zones. Overall, Chatterjee thought that corporate tax rates in India probably were somewhat higher than those in the United States. However, so were profits; the average return on assets for all Indian corporations in recent years was almost 18 percent, compared to about 11 percent for U.S. corporations.

Approval by the Reserve Bank of India was needed for the repatriation of ordinary profits. However, approval could be obtained easily if Blair Company could show that repatriated profits were being paid out of export earnings of hard currencies. Chatterjee thought that export earnings would not be difficult to realize because of India's extremely low wage rates and its central location in regard to wealthier South Asian countries. "Profit repatriation is really not much of an issue, anyway," he thought. Three years might pass before profits of any magnitude could be realized; at least five years would pass before substantial profits would be available for repatriation. Approval of repatriation by the Reserve Bank might not be required at that time, given liberalization trends. Finally, if repatriation remained difficult, Blair Company could undertake cross-trading or other actions to unblock profits.

Overall, investment and trade regulations in India in 1996 meant that business could be conducted much more easily than ever before. Hundreds of companies from the European Union, Japan, Korea, and the United States were entering India in all sectors of the country's economy. In the home appliance market, Chatterjee could identify 11 such firms: Carrier, Electrolux, General Electric, Goldstar, Matsushita, Singer, Samsung, Sanyo, Sharp, Toshiba, and Whirlpool. Many of those firms had yet to realize substantial profits, but all saw the promise of a huge market developing over the next few years.

Blair Company, Inc.

Blair Company was founded in 1975 by Eugene Blair after he left his position in research and development at Culligan International Company. Blair Company's first product was a desalinator used by mobile home parks in Florida to remove salt from the brackish well water supplied to residents. The product was a huge success, and markets quickly expanded to include nearby municipalities, smaller businesses, hospitals, and bottlers of water for sale to consumers. Geographic markets also expanded, first to other coastal regions near the company's headquarters in Tampa, Florida, and then to desert areas in the southwestern United States. New products were added rapidly as well, and by 1996 the product line included desalinators, particle filters, ozonators, ion exchange resins, and purifiers. Industry experts generally regarded the product line as superior in terms of performance and quality, with prices higher than those of many competitors.

Blair Company sales revenues for 1996 would be almost $400 million, with an expected profit close to $50 million. Annual growth in sales revenues had averaged 12 percent for the last five years. Blair Company employed over 4,000 people, with 380 having technical backgrounds and responsibilities.

Export sales of desalinators and related products began at Blair Company in 1980. Units were sold first to resorts in Mexico and Belize and later to water bottlers in Germany. Export sales grew rapidly, and Blair Company found it necessary to organize its international division in 1985. Sales in that division also grew rapidly and would reach almost $140 million in 1996. About $70 million would come from countries in Central America and South America, $30 million from Europe (including shipments to Africa), and $40 million from South Asia and Australia. The international division had sales offices, small assembly areas, and distribution facilities in Frankfurt, Germany; Tokyo, Japan; and Singapore.

The Frankfurt office had provided the impetus in 1990 for the development and marketing of Blair Company's first product targeted exclusively at consumer households— a home water filter. Sales engineers at the Frankfurt office began receiving consumer and distributor requests for a home water filter soon after the fall of the Berlin Wall in 1989. By late 1991 two models had been designed in the United States and introduced in Germany (particularly to the eastern regions), Poland, Hungary, Romania, the Czech Republic, and Slovakia.

Blair Company executives watched the success of the two water filters with great interest. The market for clean water in LDCs was huge, profitable, and attractive in a socially responsible sense. However, the quality of water in many LDCs was such that a water filter usually would not be satisfactory. Consequently, in late 1994 executives had called for the development of a water purifier that could be added to the product line. Engineers had given the final design in the project the brand name Delight. For the time being Chatterjee and the other market analysts had accepted the name, not knowing if it might infringe on an existing brand in India or in the other countries under study.

The Delight Purifier

The Delight purifier used a combination of technologies to remove four types of contaminants from potable water: sediments, organic and inorganic chemicals, microbials or cysts, and objectionable tastes and odors. The technologies were effective as long as the contaminants in the water were present at "reasonable" levels. Engineers at Blair Company had interpreted this to mean the levels described in several World Health Organization (WHO) reports on potable water and had combined the technologies to purify water to a level above WHO standards. Engineers had repeatedly assured Chatterjee that Delight's design in terms of technologies should not be a concern. Ten units operating in the company's testing laboratory showed no signs of failure or performance deterioration after some 5,000 hours of continuous use. "Still," Chatterjee thought, "we will undertake a good bit of field testing in India before entering. The risks of failure are too large to ignore. And besides, the results of our testing would be useful in persuading consumers and retailers to buy."

Chatterjee and the other market analysts still faced major design issues in configuring technologies into physical products. For example, a "point of entry" design would place the product immediately after water entry to the home, treating all water before it

---

EXHIBIT 2   Wall-Mount and Countertop Designs

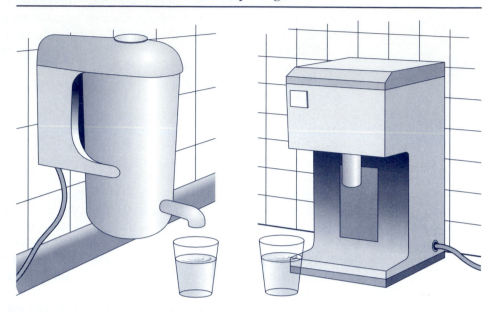

flowed to all water outlets. In contrast, a "point of use" design would place the product on a countertop, on a wall, or at the end of a faucet and treat only water arriving at that location. Based on cost estimates, designs of competing products, and his understanding of Indian consumers, Chatterjee would direct the engineers to proceed only with point of use designs for that market.

Other technical details had not yet been worked out. For example, Chatterjee had to provide engineers with suggestions for filter flow rates, storage capacities (if any), unit layout, and overall dimensions, plus a number of special features. One such feature was the possibility of a small battery to operate the filter for several hours in case of a power failure (a common occurrence in India and many other LDCs). Another might be one or two "bells or whistles" to tell cooks, maids, and family members that the unit indeed was working properly. Yet another might be an "additive" feature that would permit users to add fluoride, vitamins, or even flavorings to their water.

Chatterjee knew that the Indian market eventually would require a number of models. However, at the outset of market entry, he probably could get by with just two—one with a larger capacity for houses and bungalows and the other a smaller-capacity model for flats. He thought that model styling and specific appearances should reflect a Western, high-technology design to distinguish the Delight purifier from competitors' products. To that end, he had instructed a graphics artist to develop two ideas that he had used to gauge consumer reactions on his last visit (see Exhibit 2). Consumers liked both models but preferred the countertop design to the wall-mount design.

Competitors

Upward of 100 companies competed in the Indian market for home water filters and purifiers. While information on most of those companies was difficult to obtain, Chatterjee and the Indian research agencies were able to develop descriptions of three major competitors and brief profiles of several others.

Eureka Forbes.   The best established competitor in the water purifier market was Eureka Forbes, a joint venture company established in 1982 between Electrolux (Sweden) and Forbes Campbell (India). The company marketed a broad line of "modern, lifestyle products," including water purifiers, vacuum cleaners, and mixers/grinders. The brand name used for its water purifiers was Aquaguard, a name so well established that many consumers used it to refer to other water purifiers or to the entire product category. Aquaguard, with its 10-year market history, was clearly the market leader and came close to being India's only national brand. However, Eureka Forbes had recently introduced a second brand of water purifier called PureSip. The PureSip model was similar to Aquaguard except in its third-stage process, which used a polyiodide resin instead of ultraviolet rays to kill bacteria and viruses. This meant that water from a PureSip purifier could be stored safely for later use. Also in contrast to Aquaguard, the PureSip model needed no electricity for its operation.

However, the biggest difference between the two products was how they were sold. Aquaguard was sold exclusively by a 2,500-person sales force that called directly on households. In contrast, PureSip was sold by independent dealers of smaller home appliances. Unit prices to consumers for Aquaguard and PureSip in 1996 were approximately Rs.5,500 and Rs.2,000, respectively. Chatterjee believed that unit sales of PureSip were much lower than unit sales for Aquaguard but were growing at a much faster rate.

An Aquaguard unit typically was mounted on a kitchen wall, with plumbing required to bring water to the purifier's inlet. A two-meter-long power cord was connected to a 230-volt AC electrical outlet—the Indian standard. If the power supply dropped to 190 volts or lower, the unit would stop functioning. Other limits of the product included a smallish amount of activated carbon, which could eliminate only weak organic odors. It could not remove strong odors or inorganic solutes such as nitrates and iron compounds. The unit had no storage capacity, and its flow rate of one liter per minute seemed slow to some consumers. Removing water for storage or connecting the unit to a reservoir tank could affect water quality adversely.

Aquaguard's promotion strategy emphasized personal selling. Each salesperson was assigned to a specific neighborhood and was monitored by a group leader, who in turn was monitored by a supervisor. Each salesperson was expected to canvass his or her neighborhood, select prospective households (those with annual incomes exceeding Rs.70,000), demonstrate the product, and make an intensive effort to sell the product. Repeated sales calls helped educate consumers about their water quality and reassure them that Aquaguard service was readily available. Television commercials and advertisements in magazines and newspapers (see Exhibit 3) supported the personal selling efforts. Chatterjee estimated that Eureka Forbes would spend about Rs.120 million on all sales activities in 1996, or roughly 11 percent of its sales revenues. He estimated that about Rs.100 million of that Rs.120 million would be spent in the form of sales commissions. Chatterjee thought the company's total advertising expenditures for the year would be only about Rs.1 million.

Eureka Forbes was a formidable competitor. The sales force was huge, highly motivated, and well managed. Moreover, Aquaguard was the first product to enter the water purifier market, and the name had tremendous brand equity. The product itself was probably the weakest strategic component, but it would take a lot to convince consumers of this. And while the sales force provided a huge competitive advantage, it represented an enormous fixed cost and essentially limited sales efforts to large urban areas. More than 80 percent of India's population lived in rural areas, where water quality was even lower.

EXHIBIT 3   **Aquaguard Newspaper Advertisement**

DON'T JUST GUARD YOUR FAMILY THIS MONSOON.

AQUAGUARD IT.

The monsoons bring a welcome relief from the long hot summer. But they also bring along some of the most dangerous water-borne diseases. Like cholera, dysentry, gastro-enteritis and jaundice. Which is why you need an Aquaguard Water Purifier, to safeguard your family.

Today, Aquaguard is synonymous with clean, pure and safe drinking water.

Aquaguard is a 3 stage water purification system using the latest Ultra Violet technology, which destroys disease causing bacteria and virus in the water. It also has a unique

Electronic Monitoring System which stops water flow automatically if the purification level falls below pre-determined standards.

In addition, with Aquaguard you have the Eureka Forbes guarantee of After-Sales-Service at your doorstep.

So install an Aquaguard today. And help your family enjoy the monsoons better.

For a free demonstration at your home call the friendly man from Eureka Forbes or write to us at the addresses given below

Aquaguard
EUREKA FORBES LTD.

Calcutta: Mani Tower, Block Uttara, 1st Flr., 31/41 Vinoba Bhave Rd., Calcutta - 700 036. Tel: 4786645/5444. * 27 A, Lal Mohan Bhattacharjee Rd., 2nd Flr., Calcutta - 700 014. Tel: 2451548/2325. * 12 D, Chakraberia Rd. (North), Calcutta - 700 020. Tel: 746411/5326. * 177, Raja Dinendra Street, Opp. Desbandhu Park, Shyam Bazar, Calcutta - 700 004. Tel: 5545729/7248. * 21 G, Deodar Street, Calcutta - 700 019. * Guwahati: G.N.B.Rd., Silpukhuri, Above Jungle Travels, Near Goswami Service Station, Guwahati - 781 003. Tel: 31574. * Howrah: 105/106 A Panchsheel Apt., 1st Flr., 493, B.G.T. Road (South), Howrah - 711 102. Tel: 6606042. * Siliguri: 521 Swamiji Sarani, 1st Flr., Hakimpara P.O. Siliguri, Dist. Darjeeling. Tel: 29332.

Ion Exchange.   Ion Exchange was the premier water treatment company in India, specializing in the treatment of water, processed liquids, and wastewater in industrial markets. The company began operations in 1964 as a wholly owned subsidiary of British Permutit. Permutit divested its holdings in 1985, and Ion Exchange became a wholly owned Indian company. The company currently served customers in a diverse group of industries, including nuclear and thermal power stations, fertilizers, petro-chemical refineries, textiles, automobiles, and home water purifiers. Its home water pu-rifiers carried the family brand name ZERO-B (Zero-Bacteria).

ZERO-B purifiers used a halogenated resin technology as part of a three-stage pu-rification process. The first stage removed suspended impurities with filter pads, the second eliminated bad odors and taste with activated carbon, and the third killed bacte-ria by using trace quantities of polyiodide (iodine). The last feature was attractive be-cause it helped prevent iodine deficiency diseases and permitted purified water to be stored up to eight hours without fear of recontamination.

The basic purifier product for the home carried the name Puristore. A Puristore unit typically sat on a kitchen counter near the tap, with no electricity or plumbing hookup needed for its operation. The unit stored 20 liters of purified water. It sold to consumers for Rs.2,000. Each year the user had to replace the halogenated resin at a cost of Rs.200.

Chatterjee estimated that ZERO-B captured about 7 percent of the Indian water pu-rifier market. Probably the biggest reason for the small share was a lack of consumer awareness. ZERO-B purifiers had been on the market for less than three years. They were not advertised heavily and did not enjoy the sales effort intensity of Aquaguard. Distribution also was limited. During Chatterjee's visit, he could find only five dealers in Calcutta carrying ZERO-B products and none in Bangalore. The dealers he contacted were of the opinion that ZERO-B's marketing efforts soon would intensify; two had heard rumors that a door-to-door sales force was planned and that consumer advertis-ing was about to begin.

Chatterjee confirmed the latter point with a visit to a Calcutta advertising agency. A modest number of 10-second television commercials soon would be aired on the Zee TV and DD metro channels. The advertisements would focus on educating consumers with the position "It is not a filter." Instead, ZERO-B was a water purifier and was much more effective than a candle filter in preventing health problems. Apart from this ad-vertising effort, the only form of promotion used was a point of sale brochure that deal-ers could give to prospective customers (see Exhibit 4).

On balance, Chatterjee thought that Ion Exchange could be a major player in the market. The company had over 30 years' experience in the field of water purification and devoted upward of Rs.10 million each year to corporate research and development. "In fact," he thought, "all Ion Exchange really needs to do is recognize the market's po-tential and make it a priority within the company." However, that might be difficult to do because of the company's emphasis on industrial markets. Chatterjee estimated that ZERO-B products would account for less than 2 percent of Ion Exchange's 1996 total sales, estimated at Rs. 1 billion. He thought the total marketing expenditures for ZERO-B would be around Rs.3 million.

Singer.   The newest competitor to enter the Indian water purifier market was Singer India Ltd. Originally, Singer India was a subsidiary of the Singer Company, located in the United States, but a minority share (49 percent) was sold to Indian investors in 1982. The change in ownership led to the construction of manufacturing facilities in India for sewing machines in 1983. The facilities were expanded in 1991 to produce a broad line of home appliances. Sales revenues in 1996 for the entire product line—sewing ma-chines, food processors, irons, mixers, toasters, water heaters, ceiling fans, cooking ranges, and color televisions—would be about Rs.900 million.

During Chatterjee's time in Calcutta he had visited a Singer Company showroom on Park Street. Initially he had hoped that Singer might be a suitable partner to manufac-ture and distribute the Delight purifier. However, much to his surprise, he was told that

EXHIBIT 4   Zero-B Sales Brochure

Singer now had its own brand on the market, Aquarius. The product was not yet available in Calcutta but was being sold in Bombay and Delhi.

A marketing research agency in Delhi was able to gather some information on the Singer purifier. The product contained nine stages (!) and sold to consumers for Rs.4,000. It removed sediments, heavy metals, bad tastes, odors, and colors. It also killed bacteria and viruses, fungi, and nematodes. The purifier required water pressure (8 psi minimum) to operate but needed no electricity. It came in a single countertop model that could be moved from one room to another. The life of the device at a flow rate of 3.8 liters per minute was listed as 40,000 liters—about four to six years of use in the typical Indian household. The product's life could be extended to 70,000 liters at a somewhat slower flow rate. However, at 70,000 liters, the product had to be discarded. The agency reported a heavy advertising blitz accompanying the introduction in Delhi, emphasizing television and newspaper advertising, plus outdoor and transit advertising as support. All 10 Singer showrooms in Delhi offered vivid demonstrations of the product's operation.

Chatterjee had to admit that the photos of the Aquarius purifier shown in the Calcutta showroom looked appealing. And a trade article he found had described the product as "state of the art" in comparison to the "primitive" products now on the market. Chatterjee and Blair Company engineers tended to agree—the disinfecting resin used in Aquarius had been developed by the U.S. government's National Aeronautics and Space Administration (NASA) and had been proved to be 100 percent effective against bacteria and viruses. "If only I could have brought a unit back with me," he thought. "We could have some test results and see just how good it is." The trade article also mentioned that Singer hoped to sell 40,000 units over the next two years.

Chatterjee knew that Singer was a well-known and respected brand name in India. Further, Singer's distribution channels were superior to those of any competitor in the market, including those of Eureka Forbes. The most prominent of Singer's three distribution channels were the 210 company-owned showrooms in major urban areas around the country. Each sold and serviced the entire line of Singer products. Each was very well kept and was staffed by knowledgeable personnel. Singer products also were sold throughout India by over 3,000 independent dealers, who received inventory from an estimated 70 Singer-appointed distributors. According to the marketing research agency in Delhi, distributors earned margins of 12 percent of the retail price for Aquarius, while dealers earned margins of 5 percent. Finally, Singer employed over 400 salespersons who sold sewing machines and food processors door to door. As with Eureka Forbes, the direct sales force sold products primarily in large urban markets.

Other Competitors.   Chatterjee was aware of several other water purifiers on the Indian market. The Delta brand from S & S Industries in Madras seemed to be a carbon copy of Aquaguard except for a more eye-pleasing countertop design. According to the promotional literature, Delta offered a line of water-related products: purifiers, water softeners, iron removers, desalinators, and ozonators. Another competitor was Alfa Water Purifiers, Bombay. That company offered four purifier models at prices from Rs.4,300 to Rs.6,500, depending on capacity. Symphony's Spectrum brand sold well around Bombay at Rs.4,000 each but removed only suspended sediments, not heavy metals or bacteria. The Sam Group in Coimbatore recently had launched its Water Doctor purifier at Rs.5,200. The device used a third-stage ozonator to kill bacteria and viruses and came in two attractive countertop models with 6- and 12-liter storage, respectively. Batliboi was mentioned by the Delhi research agency as yet another competitor, although Chatterjee knew nothing else about the brand. Taken together, unit sales of all purifiers at these companies plus ZERO-B and Singer probably would account for around 60,000 units in 1996. The remaining 190,000 units would be Aquaguards and PureSips.

At least 100 Indian companies made and marketed candle filters. The largest probably was Bajaj Electrical Division, whose product line also included water heaters, irons, electric light bulbs, toasters, mixers, and grillers. Bajaj's candle filters were sold by a large number of dealers who carried the entire product line. Candle filters produced by other manufacturers were sold mostly through dealers who specialized in small household appliances and general hardware. Probably no single manufacturer of candle filters had more than 5 percent of any regional market in the country. No manufacturer attempted to satisfy a national market. Still, the candle filters market deserved serious consideration; perhaps Delight's entry strategy would attempt to "trade up" users of candle filters to a better, safer product.

Finally, Chatterjee knew that the sales of almost all purifiers in 1996 in India were in large urban areas. No manufacturer targeted rural or smaller urban areas, and at best, Chatterjee had calculated, existing manufacturers were reaching only 10 to 15 percent of the entire Indian population. An explosion in sales would come if the right product could be sold outside metropolitan areas.

Recommendations

Chatterjee decided that an Indian market entry for Blair Company was subject to three "givens," as he called them. First, he thought that a strategic focus on rural or smaller urban areas would not be wise, at least at the start. The lack of adequate distribution and communication infrastructure in rural India meant that any market entry would begin with larger cities, most likely on the west coast.

Second, market entry would require manufacturing the units in India. Because the cost of skilled labor in India was around Rs.20 to Rs.25 per hour (compared to $20 to $25 per hour in the United States), importing complete units was out of the question. However, importing a few key components would be necessary at the start of the operation.

Third, Blair Company should find an Indian partner. Chatterjee's visits had produced a number of promising partners: Polar Industries, Calcutta; Milton Plastics, Bombay; Videocon Appliances, Aurangabad; BPL Sanyo Utilities and Appliances, Bangalore; Onida Savak, Delhi; Hawkins India, Bombay; and Voltas, Bombay. All those companies manufactured and marketed a line of high-quality household appliances, had one or more strong brand names, and had established dealer networks (a minimum of 10,000 dealers). All were involved to greater or lesser degrees with international partners. All were medium-size firms—not so large that a partnership with Blair Company would be one-sided and not so small that they would lack managerial talent and other resources. Finally, all were profitable (15 to 27 percent return on assets in 1995) and looking to grow. However, Chatterjee had no idea if any company would find the Delight purifier and Blair Company attractive or might be persuaded to sell part or all of their operations as an acquisition.

Field Testing and Product Recommendations.   The most immediate decision Chatterjee faced was whether to recommend a field test. The test would cost about $25,000, placing 20 units in Indian homes in three cities and monitoring their performance for three to six months. The decision to test really was more than it seemed; Chatterjee's boss had explained that a decision to test was really a decision to enter. It made no sense to spend this kind of time and money if India was not an attractive opportunity. The testing period also would give Blair Company representatives time to identify a suitable Indian company as a licensee, joint venture partner, or acquisition.

Fundamental to market entry was product design. Engineers at Blair Company had taken the position that the purification technologies planned for Delight could be "packaged in almost any fashion as long as we have electricity." Electricity was needed to operate the product's ozonator as well as to indicate to users that the unit was functioning properly (or improperly, as the case might be). Beyond this requirement, anything was possible.

Chatterjee thought that a modular approach would be best. The basic module would be a countertop unit much like the one shown in Exhibit 2. The module would outperform anything on the market in terms of flow rate, palatability, durability, and reliability and would store two liters of purified water. Two additional modules would remove iron, calcium, or other metallic contaminants that were specific to particular regions. For example, Calcutta and much of the surrounding area suffered from iron contamination, which no filter or purifier on the Indian market could remove to a satisfactory level. Water supplies in other areas in the country were known to contain objectionable concentrations of calcium, salt, arsenic, lead, or sulfur. Most Indian consumers would need neither of the additional modules, some would need one or the other, but very few would need both.

Market Entry and Marketing Planning Recommendations.   Assuming that Chatterjee recommended proceeding with the field test, he would need to make a recommendation concerning the mode of market entry. In addition, his recommendation should include an outline of a marketing plan.

Licensee Considerations.   If market entry was in the form of a joint working arrangement with a licensee, Blair Company's financial investment would be minimal. Chatterjee thought that Blair Company might risk as little as $30,000 in capital for production facilities and equipment, plus another $5,000 for office facilities and equipment. Those investments would be completely offset by the licensee's payment to Blair Company for technology transfer and personnel training. Annual fixed costs to Blair Company should not exceed $40,000 at the outset and would decrease to $15,000 as soon as an Indian national could be hired, trained, and left in charge. The duties of this individual would be to work with Blair Company personnel in the United States and with management at the licensee to see that units were produced per Blair Company's specifications. Apart from this activity, Blair Company would have no control over the licensee's operations. Chatterjee expected that the licensee would pay royalties to Blair Company of about Rs.280 for each unit sold in the domestic market and Rs.450 for each unit that was exported. The average royalty probably would be around Rs.300.

Joint Venture/Acquisition Considerations.   If entry was in the form of either a joint venture or an acquisition, financial investment and annual fixed costs would be much higher and would depend largely on the scope of operations. Chatterjee had roughed out some estimates for a joint venture entry, based on three levels of scope (see Exhibit 5). His estimates reflected what he thought were reasonable assumptions for all needed investments plus annual fixed expenses for sales activities, general administrative overhead, research and development, insurance, and depreciation. His estimates allowed for the Delight purifier to be sold either through dealers or through a direct, door-to-door sales force. Chatterjee thought that estimates of annual fixed expenses for market entry through acquisition would be identical to those for a joint venture. However, estimates for the investment (purchase) might be considerably higher, the same, or lower. It depended on what was purchased.

Chatterjee's estimates of Delight's unit contribution margins reflected a number of assumptions: expected economies of scale, experience-curve effects, the costs of Indian labor and raw materials, and competitors' pricing strategies. However, the most important assumption was Delight's pricing strategy. If a skimming strategy was used and the product was sold through a dealer channel, the basic module would be priced to dealers at Rs.5,500 and to consumers at Rs.5,900. "This would give us about a Rs.650 unit contribution once we got production flowing smoothly," he thought. In contrast, if a penetration strategy was used and the product was sold through a dealer channel, the basic module would be priced to dealers at Rs.4,100 and to consumers at Rs.4,400 and would yield a unit contribution of Rs.300. For simplicity's sake, Chatterjee assumed that the two additional modules would be priced to dealers at Rs.800 and to consumers at Rs.1,000 and would yield a unit contribution of Rs.100. Finally, he assumed that all

EXHIBIT 5   Investments and Fixed Costs for a Joint Venture Market Entry

	Operational Scope		
	Two Regions	*Four Regions*	*National Market*
1998 market potential (units)	55,000	110,000	430,000
Initial investment (Rs. thousands)	4,000	8,000	30,000
Annual fixed overhead expenses (Rs.thousands)			
Using dealer channels	4,000	7,000	40,000
Using direct sales force	7,200	14,000	88,000

products sold to dealers would go directly from Blair Company to the dealers (no distributors would be used).

If a direct sales force was employed instead of dealers, Chatterjee thought that the prices charged to consumers would not change from those listed above. However, sales commissions would have to be paid in addition to the fixed costs necessary to maintain and manage the sales force. Under a skimming price strategy, the sales commission would be Rs.550 per unit and the unit contribution would be Rs.500. Under a penetration price strategy, the sales commission would be Rs.400 per unit and the unit contribution would be Rs.200. These financial estimates, he would explain in his report, would apply to 1998 or 1999, the expected first year of operation.

Skimming versus penetration was more than just a pricing strategy. Product design for the skimming strategy would be noticeably superior, with higher performance and quality, a longer warranty period, more features, and a more attractive appearance compared with the design for the penetration strategy. Positioning also most likely would be different. Chatterjee recognized several positioning possibilities: performance and taste, value for the money/low price, safety, health, convenience, attractive styling, avoidance of diseases and health-related bills, and superior American technology. The only position he considered "taken" in the market was that occupied by Aquaguard—protect family health and service at your doorstep. While other competitors had claimed certain positions for their products, none had devoted financial resources to a degree that prevented Delight from dislodging them. Chatterjee believed that considerable advertising and promotion expenditures would be necessary to communicate Delight's positioning. He would need estimates of those expenditures in his recommendation.

"If we go ahead with Delight, we'll have to move quickly," Chatterjee thought. "The window of opportunity is open, but if Singer's product is as good as they claim, we'll be in for a fight. Still, Aquarius seems vulnerable on the water pressure requirement and on price. We'll need a product category 'killer' to win."

Case 3–3
SystemSoft Corporation

William O'Connell, senior vice president of strategic accounts and business development at SystemSoft Corporation, sat in his office and contemplated his company's future direction. SystemSoft had experienced tremendous growth since its founding in 1991 and was now the world's leading supplier of PC card software.[1] SystemSoft had gone public in August 1994, and now, just one year later, O'Connell faced a difficult decision regarding the company's growth strategy.

SystemSoft developed system-level software that allowed the operating system of a PC to interface with the hardware. The company had been highly successful in its core product lines of BIOS (basic input/output system), PC card, and power management software. SystemSoft operated in a highly competitive environment in which technological innovation was a key driver of success. O'Connell had to decide whether to proceed in developing a new "call avoidance" product category.[2] Call avoidance software had a significant market potential, and there was no comprehensive problem resolution software on the market.

O'Connell knew that SystemSoft had to continue to innovate and push into new categories and segments, but he was concerned that the call avoidance software was too different from the company's core product mix. While the rewards for pioneering a new product category could be tremendous, pursuing this opportunity could stretch SystemSoft's resources too far at a time when the company had to begin to understand and manage its growth. Pursuing growth through a strategy of product development would have far-reaching effects within SystemSoft. For example, O'Connell would have to decide whether the salespeople should be organized by product line or should be generalists, representing all of SystemSoft's products to an account. Some questioned whether SystemSoft should delve into this new category, given that it differed from its core product lines in many ways. O'Connell wondered, Was market penetration a safer route?

Company Overview

SystemSoft was cofounded in 1991 by four people from Phoenix Technologies as a developer of system-level software. SystemSoft's mission was to become the leading provider of connectivity and other system-level software for microprocessor-based devices. Its strategy was focused on technological leadership, strategic alliances, key customer relationships, further expansion into the desktop market, and finding additional

---

[1] Formerly termed PCMCIA (Personal Computer Memory Card International Association). This is the industry standard for expansion slots on portable computers. PCMCIA slots accept a variety of PCMCIA cards from a variety of manufacturers. They can be used to add things such as memory, a modem, a fax, or LAN cards.

[2] Call avoidance software is intended to solve user problems on a PC, reducing the number of technical support calls to manufacturers.

This case was prepared by Lisa Robie Adam, graduate assistant, Boston College, under the supervision of Victoria L. Crittenden, associate professor of marketing, Boston College. This case was written to facilitate classroom discussion rather than to illustrate effective or ineffective corporate decision making.

EXHIBIT 1

SystemSoft Corporation
Consolidated Balance Sheet, January 31

	1995	1994	1993
Assets			
Current assets:			
Cash and cash equivalents	$ 7,716,687	$ 2,758,318	$ 696,249
Restricted cash	—	—	125,000
Marketable securities	4,885,069	—	—
Accounts receivable, net of doubtful accounts	4,572,757	2,423,612	1,439,477
Receivable from related party	73,500	89,950	43,082
Prepaid and other current assets	481,626	298,142	62,761
Deferred income taxes	1,218,812	—	—
Total current assets	18,948,451	5,570,022	2,366,569
Property and equipment, net	1,060,048	521,437	447,595
Purchased software, net	—	—	575,293
Software development costs, net	1,088,926	1,302,990	429,148
Total assets	$ 21,097,425	$ 7,394,449	$ 3,818,605
Liabilities and Stockholders' Equity (Deficit)			
Current liabilities:			
Accounts payable	$ 614,501	$ 354,259	$ 1,032,226
Accrued expenses	302,392	284,229	208,927
Income taxes payable	391,143	7,000	—
Accrued commissions	734,715	339,752	318,846
Accrued compensation and benefits	622,470	563,502	205,797
Accrued royalties	237,707	122,263	318,591
Deferred revenue from related party	260,000	540,000	—
Notes payable, current portion	—	359,123	189,901
Total current liabilities	$ 3,162,928	$ 2,570,128	$ 2,274,288
Notes payable, net of current portion	—	60,045	183,943
Deferred income taxes	276,600	—	—
Commitments			
Redeemable convertible preferred stock	—	12,080,511	8,656,702
Warrant	—	500,000	—
Stockholders' equity (deficit)			
Common stock	98,611	29,393	28,997
Paid-in capital	22,453,812	—	—
Less treasury stock	(128,696)	(128,696)	(105,596)
Accumulated deficit	(4,765,830)	(7,716,932)	(7,219,729)
Total stockholders' equity (deficit)	17,657,897	(7,816,235)	(7,296,328)
Total liabilities and owners' equity	$ 21,097,425	$ 7,394,449	$ 3,818,605

markets for PC card software and power management technology. Exhibits 1 and 2 show SystemSoft's balance sheet and income statement for the past several years.

System-level software provides a layer of connectivity and ease of use for personal computers by allowing the operating system to recognize, configure, and communicate with the system hardware, including the peripherals. Exhibit 3 describes system-level software. The end user typically is not familiar with system-level software because it operates between the computer chips and the operating system. In 1995, SystemSoft

EXHIBIT 2

SystemSoft Corporation
Consolidated Statement of Operations, January 31

	1995	1994	1993	1992
Revenues				
Software license fees	$10,223,294	$6,281,190	$4,425,216	$2,188,881
Engineering services	2,532,588	1,279,630	1,153,129	481,575
Related party	2,419,298	1,077,408	711,488	260,251
Other	46,077	515,364	—	—
Total revenues	15,221,257	9,153,592	6,289,833	2,930,707
Cost of Revenues				
Software license fees	1,303,769	850,006	960,202	808,084
Engineering services	951,023	1,046,140	1,028,102	837,465
Related party	1,817,343	616,093	513,776	276,517
Other	40,181	455,977	—	—
Total cost of revenues	4,112,316	2,968,216	2,502,080	1,922,066
Gross profit	11,108,941	6,185,376	3,787,753	1,008,641
Operating Expenses				
R&D	2,252,491	1,506,891	1,076,379	709,301
Sales and marketing	5,073,194	2,685,619	2,250,633	1,750,793
General and administrative	1,900,779	1,579,877	1,782,670	1,593,646
Litigation settlement	—	—	1,019,225	—
Total operating expenses	9,226,464	5,772,387	6,128,907	4,053,740
Income (loss) from operations	1,882,477	412,989	(2,341,154)	(3,045,099)
Interest income	298,726	15,857	28,480	41,417
Interest expense	(10,005)	(38,164)	(37,092)	(12,432)
Income (loss) before income taxes	2,171,198	390,682	(2,349,766)	(3,016,114)
Provisions for income tax	125,798	160,340	242,495	157,185
Net income (loss)	2,045,400	230,342	(2,592,261)	(3,173,299)
Accretion of preferred stock	(412,640)	(759,378)	(497,986)	(144,246)
Net income (loss) available to comm. shareholders	$1,632,760	($529,036)	($3,090,247)	($3,317,545)
Net income (loss) per share	$ 0.22	($0.15)	($0.87)	($0.93)
Weighted average number of shares outstanding	7,342,619	3,559,074	3,554,381	3,568,687

offered three categories of software products: PC card, power management, and BIOS. The company dominated the mobile computer market, but its share of the desktop computer market remained negligible.

Products and Competition

The advent of mobile computers had dramatically changed the way people worked and communicated by the mid-1990s. The rapid development of mobile devices created a need for additional technologies that addressed the limitations of mobile computers. For example, PC cards provided expanded memory and increased flexibility/functionality, while power management lengthened life between battery charges. Power management had also become more important on desktop PCs due to rising energy costs and the

---

EXHIBIT 3   System-Level Software

SystemSoft is a supplier of PCMCIA and other system-level software to the rapidly growing market for mobile computers, which consist of laptops, notebooks, subnotebooks, and personal computing devices. PCMCIA is a published industry standard which enables PCs and electronic devices to automatically recognize, install, and configure peripherals (including, for example, modems, flash memory, and network cards) incorporated in credit card–size PCMCIA cards. System-level software provides both a connectivity layer, which facilitates the addition, configuration, and use of peripheral devices, and a hardware adaptation layer, which includes the communication link between a PC's operating system software and hardware. Each new version of hardware or operating system software generally requires new system-level software. PC manufacturers are able to offer enhanced functionality, flexibility, and ease of use by using the company's software in their products.

System-level software is one of the four basic technologies in the architecture of a PC: application software, operating system software, system-level software, and hardware.

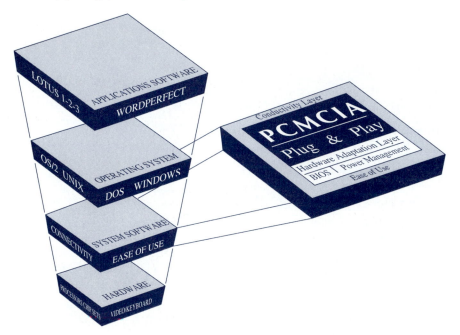

Application software is designed to perform end user tasks such as word processing and data analysis. WordPerfect and Lotus 1-2-3 are examples of widely used application programs. Operating system software allows PC hardware to control the sequencing and processing of applications and respond to a PC user's commands, such as storing data, displaying data, and running an application program. Microsoft's DOS and Windows are the dominant operating systems in the IBM-compatible PC market. System-level software is a necessary component in every PC, enabling the computer's operating system to recognize, configure, and communicate with the hardware, including peripherals. PC hardware consists of microprocessors, also known as central processing units (CPUs), CPU-support chipsets, memory, input–output devices (such as monitors and keyboards), and various other peripheral devices (such as printers, modems, and CD-ROM drives). Intel's x86 and Pentium chips are the leading CPUs in the PC market.

Environmental Protection Agency's (EPA's) Energy Star Program.[3] The following list is a brief description of the functionality of SystemSoft's core product lines:

---

[3] Energy Star is a voluntary program between the U.S. EPA and computer, monitor, and printer manufacturers that was developed in 1992 to conserve energy. To qualify for Energy Star, a computer must have a "sleep" feature that powers down the computer when it is not in use. This feature can cut power usage by up to 75 percent.

EXHIBIT 4 Market Share by Product Category, 1995

Product	Market Share
BIOS and power management	
Notebook market	20% of available market,* 10% of overall market
Desktop market	Negligible
PC Card	64%

* The available market refers to personal computers that shipped with third-party BIOS and power management software. All OEMs used third-party manufacturers for PC card software.

- *BIOS (basic input/output system)* software enables PC hardware components to accept commands from and deliver commands to the operating system software.
- *PC card* software gives users immediate access to the features contained in add-on peripheral cards. Users insert credit card–size cards into sockets built into PCs in a manner similar to the insertion of a floppy disk. PC card software enables a computer to identify the inserted card and reconfigure and allocate system resources without manual intervention by the user (such as setting jumper switches or configuring operating system software). PC cards incorporate a standard published by the Personal Computer Memory Card International Association.
- *Power management* software reduces the power consumption of PCs by slowing or stopping the operation of specific system components when a computer is not in use.

SystemSoft had different competitors in each type of software it developed. Phoenix Technologies was the only competitor that had developed software in all of System-Soft's product categories. American Megatrends (AMI) was a leading competitor in the BIOS segment. Award competed with SystemSoft in the PC card segment.

SystemSoft's greatest success was its dominance of the PC card market. The company had approximately a 64 percent market share in 1995 and supplied 14 of the top 15 notebook vendors. Its BIOS and power management software were also highly successful, with approximately a 20 percent share of the available notebook market in 1995[4] (see Exhibit 4). Phoenix was the leader in the notebook BIOS and power management market; AMI was second. SystemSoft's share of the desktop BIOS and power management market was small, but the company was looking to expand it.

Companies in the mobile computer industry operated in a highly competitive, rapidly changing technological environment. Innovation and the ability to change rapidly drive success. In addition to the leading direct competitors, there was always the competitive threat that operating system vendors would enter the market or incorporate enough features to decrease SystemSoft's revenues from original equipment manufacturers (OEMs).

Sales and Marketing

SystemSoft's sales and marketing efforts were focused on personal selling and attending trade shows. The company distributed data sheets on its products but did little advertising and promotion. Exhibit 5 shows a sample data sheet. SystemSoft's sales were driven by a direct sales force complemented by independent manufacturers' representatives for international sales. SystemSoft had a national sales office in California and international offices in Taiwan and Japan (the international headquarters). The software

---

[4] The available market refers to notebooks that ship with a third-party BIOS. The available market is approximately 50 percent of 10 million units.

EXHIBIT 5   Sample Data Sheet

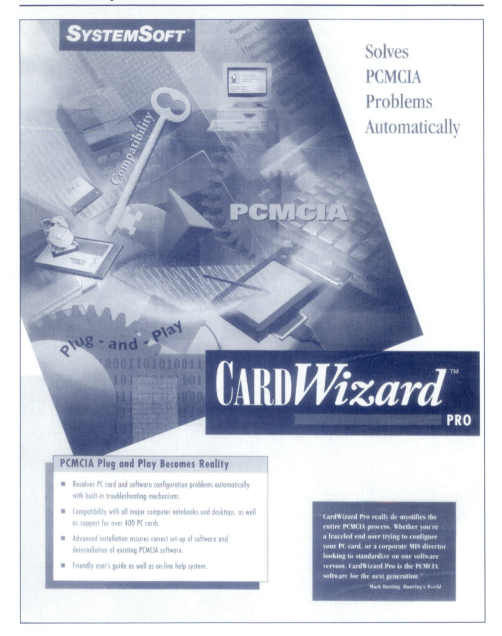

was licensed to OEMs, and SystemSoft received royalties on the systems shipped. There was no initial charge for the software unless SystemSoft customized or made adjustments to it for the customer.

Revenues from BIOS software ranged from US$0.10 to US$1.00 for every unit shipped. Power management software typically was sold along with BIOS software and added about 20 to 50 percent to the BIOS revenue. PC card software generated approximately US$1 to US$3 for each unit shipped, and the proposed call avoidance product was expected to generate US$3 to US$7 per unit.

EXHIBIT 5   **(Continued)**

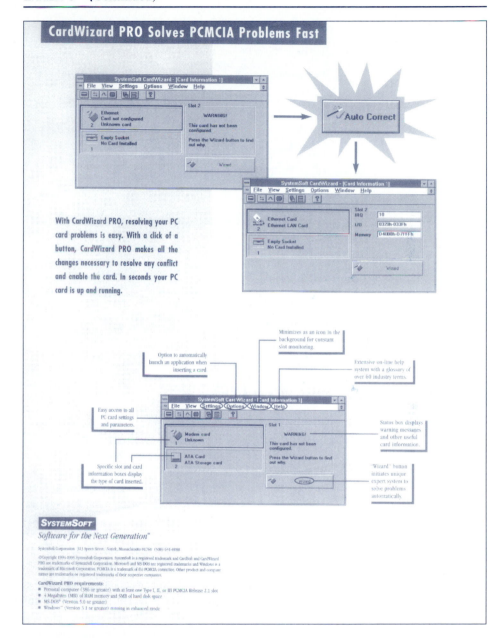

Customer Base

SystemSoft licensed its products to OEMs, including PC manufacturers, hardware component manufacturers, PC card manufacturers, and operating system software companies. The company had licensed its software to more than 100 PC manufacturers and more than 45 PC card manufacturers. Exhibit 6 lists a number of SystemSoft clients in various segments.

Much of SystemSoft's success was attributed to a number of key customer relationships and strategic alliances that it had developed over a few short years. In 1993, SystemSoft

EXHIBIT 6   Sample Customer List by Segment

Hardware Component Manufacturers
Intel
Advanced Micro Devices (AMD)

PC Manufacturers

Acer	Hewlett-Packard	NCR/AT&T
AST Research	Hitachi	NEC
Citizen	Hyundai	Seiko Epson
Clevo	IBM	Sotec
Compaq	ICL	Twinhead
Dell	Inventec	Wacom
Digital Equipment	LiteOn	
Gateway 2000	Mitsui	

Operating System Software Companies
Microsoft
Geoworks

PC Card Manufacturers

Adaptec	Megahertz
Advanced Micro Devices	Motorola
AMP	National Semiconductor
Epson America	New Media
Hayes	Qlogic
Integral Peripherals	Standard Microsystems
Kingston Technology	US Robotics

entered into a development and license agreement with Intel by which Intel licensed certain technologies to SystemSoft. SystemSoft in turn developed those technologies into products marketed under the SystemSoft name. The Intel agreement stipulated that the two companies would meet quarterly to identify new product opportunities. In addition to this agreement, Intel had around 10 percent equity ownership in SystemSoft. The agreement with Intel was the most comprehensive agreement for SystemSoft. However, the company also worked with other companies, such as Microsoft, to codevelop software.

The Call Avoidance Marketplace

When an end user has trouble with her personal computer, she frequently calls the manufacturer's technical support line. This call involves an "interview" stage in which the technical support representative asks a series of questions to diagnose the problem. Many of these calls are for routine problems, yet the sheer volume of calls is quite costly to the manufacturer. SystemSoft's goal was to develop an expert system to diagnose and solve common PC problems. The proposed product was expected to solve many problems, including scanning for and repairing viruses as well as remedying general protection faults, resource conflict, and configuration problems. Automating this process would decrease the number of calls to technical support centers significantly, reducing both the cost to manufacturers and the number of unanswered technical support calls.

The idea for the new product was a result of SystemSoft's huge success with CardWizard, a product launched in early 1995 to solve problems with PC cards. CardWizard enabled mobile computer users to change PC cards without having to stop what they were doing, an ability called hotswapping. Before the release of CardWizard, users often had to restart Windows or even reboot the computer with a different configuration to change cards. CardWizard simplified changing PC cards because it automatically solved configuration problems, allowing PC cards to be recognized upon insertion. SystemSoft assumed that if it could develop a successful product to solve problems on a specific part of the PC, it could expand the concept of CardWizard to the PC as a whole.

The market research firm Dataquest estimated that more than 200 million calls would be received at technical support centers nationwide in 1996, more than a 67 percent increase from 1992. Dataquest attributed this rise to the dramatic increase in the complexity of new hardware, operating system, and application software products. With the average cost per call exceeding $20, the PC industry would spend nearly $4 billion on "help desk" support in 1996. SystemSoft's proposed call avoidance software would help the PC industry handle its increasingly large number of customer support calls, significantly decreasing the enormous expense of technical support to PC manufacturers.

CyberMedia was the largest competitor in the call avoidance product category. CyberMedia had a call avoidance software package, First Aid 95, in the retail channel, but the company did not have an OEM presence. First Aid 95 automatically caught problems with PCs and offered a variety of diagnostic programs that let the user pinpoint the cause of other problems, such as the wrong drivers for a sound card. While CyberMedia's product detected common problems, SystemSoft's new product entry would detect and remedy such problems on the spot. No company had developed such complete problem resolution software.

Issues with the New Product

The proposed new product raised both engineering and sales issues for SystemSoft. For the proposed call avoidance software to be successful, SystemSoft would have to enlist the help of many players in the PC industry. The company would need knowledge from software vendors, hardware vendors, and OEMs regarding what should be built into the software. While SystemSoft had established relationships and experience with OEMs, the company did not have experience with either hardware or software vendors. SystemSoft therefore approached Intel and Digital Equipment Corporation (DEC) to solicit feedback on the new product idea and request development assistance. Intel was excited about the possibilities of call avoidance software and provided SystemSoft with access to relevant patent portfolios to develop the product. DEC also was excited about the possibilities that call avoidance software offered. DEC's service arm, Multivendor Service Customer Support, expressed interest in helping SystemSoft determine product requirements and develop the product.

It was also clear that SystemSoft would need to hire additional engineers and create a separate engineering group for the new product. The company had two engineering groups: one dedicated to BIOS software and the other dedicated to PC card software. The two groups required similar skill sets and experience, and engineers could be transferred easily from one group to the other. However, the proposed product would run off servers and builders; therefore, it would require different engineering skills than did SystemSoft's line of system-level software.[5] SystemSoft would have to hire engineers

---

[5] Servers are the hardware and software to which all machines on the network are connected. They run the network and store shared information. Builder software is a developmental tool for engineers that allows them to program new information into the knowledge base. It is used to enter information on new problems to keep the problem resolution software updated.

with the appropriate skill sets and create a separate engineering group to maintain and enhance the call avoidance product.

If O'Connell decided to pursue the new product, he had to recommend whether SystemSoft should market it to OEMs as it did its current products or launch it to the retail trade to compete directly against CyberMedia. While CyberMedia's call avoidance software was distributed through the retail channel, SystemSoft lacked a retail presence.[6] The retail channel was different from the OEM channel, particularly with regards to co-op funding and advertising. SystemSoft was an engineering-driven company, and large dollar outlays for such expenses did not fit with its core competencies or corporate strategy.

Selling the call avoidance product through the OEM channel required a very different sales process from that used for SystemSoft's other products. Basically, every PC needs BIOS software and all notebooks need PC card software. As a result, the decision for OEMs is simply a make-or-buy decision—they either purchase the software from another company or develop it themselves. Almost all OEMs purchase BIOS and PC card software as opposed to developing it on their own. Engineering departments typically decide which software to put into the PC; therefore, SystemSoft's sales force had experience in selling solutions directly to engineers.

Call avoidance software, by contrast, was not a necessary product. Thus, the sales force would have to convince companies of the benefits of this new product rather than simply persuading them to purchase SystemSoft software. Furthermore, the product was more complex than system-level software and the decision-making power did not rest with engineers. The technical support center would need a server with special software to run the call avoidance system, and the software would have to be included on each individual PC.

The complexity of the call avoidance system required that the product be sold to several people. SystemSoft's sales force would first have to convince the OEM call center that this product could significantly reduce the amount of calls it received and demonstrate the cost savings that would result from the product.[7] Second, the product manager for the PC line had profit-and-loss responsibility. Therefore, SystemSoft had to persuade the product manager to invest in the product to include it in the PCs. In effect, SystemSoft would have to sell both the call center and the product manager, a time-consuming process since the call center and headquarters of many OEMs are located in different areas of the country.

If O'Connell recommended pursuing the call avoidance market through the OEM channel, how should the sales force be structured? Selling the call avoidance product was more complex and required a different skills set than did selling system-level software. O'Connell could take the most successful salespeople from the PC card and BIOS software and have them sell the new product, but he was unsure how that would affect the current business. Furthermore, it would result in two SystemSoft salespeople calling on each account, which could confuse the customer.

The Decision

The call avoidance market represented a tremendous opportunity for SystemSoft to further its reputation as a technology leader. A successful new product could propel the company into new segments and help stimulate growth in the coming years. However,

---

[6] SystemSoft launched its CardWizard PC card product into the retail channel in mid-1995, and while it received strong product reviews, retail was not a successful distribution channel for the company.

[7] An OEM call center is the facility at which technical support calls from customers are received.

the risks were numerous. In addition to organizational issues surrounding engineering and sales, another factor complicated O'Connell's decision. The stockholders were pressuring SystemSoft to lower its rising software capitalization costs. Software companies are permitted to capitalize R&D expenses once a product reaches technological feasibility. O'Connell knew that pursuing this new product would boost the software capitalization even higher for up to two years. The capitalized costs threaten future earnings because they eventually have to be expensed through amortization. Would the stockholders accept that, or would many begin to sell shares, causing a decline in the valuation of the company?

Should O'Connell pursue this opportunity, or should he recommend that SystemSoft focus on pushing its core products into emerging technologies and further developing SystemSoft's presence in the desktop PC market?

CASE 3–4
TRANSVIT OF NOVGOROD, RUSSIA

Alexander Kolesjonkov, an assistant director and the head of Transvit's newly created marketing department, is currently facing a number of problems associated with the restructuring of Russia's economy. With the simultaneous fall of communism and the Berlin Wall and the disintegration of the Soviet Union as a relatively homogeneous economic bloc, rapid inflation has ensued, demand for certain domestically produced products has fallen markedly, and superior foreign and nervous domestic producers are entering once-protected markets. The foreign competitors are in search of new profits and first-mover advantages, while the domestic producers are trying to survive. Transvit is in the process of restructuring, although its near-term goals are to protect its current market share, which consists primarily of Russian manufacturers of home electronic equipment; increase its sales in Western markets; and capture a greater amount of value added from its manufacturing operations by obtaining International Electronics Component IEC-65 Standards for its products.

The Transvit Company

The Transvit Company was founded in Novgorod, Russia, in 1961 by the Soviet Ministry of Radio and Electronics. That city is the largest metropolis in Russia's northwestern Novgorod Region, with a population of about 240,000. It sits astride the Volchov River and lies approximately 120 miles south of St. Petersburg on a route leading to Moscow. Novgorod is one of the country's oldest cities, dating back at least to 859, before the creation of Russia. For many years it was a city of major economic, military, and political importance. But after Russia gained an entrance to the Baltic Sea and founded St. Petersburg to the north as an ocean port city, Novgorod lost much of its commercial and economic importance by the 1700s.

During World War II the city was completely destroyed by the German occupation, which began on August 19, 1941. Over the next 2½ years the Soviet Army's defense line resided on the banks of the Maly Volkhovets River, a tributary of the Volchov River just south of the city. After the war the government scheduled the city for immediate recovery, and within eight years the city was essentially rebuilt. In the process many of its architecturally significant cathedrals, churches, and monasteries were resurrected, drawing thousands of tourists every year.

The city of Novgorod was a logical choice for establishing an electronic-components manufacturing firm, as a radio electronics research institute had been established there a number of years earlier. Transvit began its operations in an old brick factory and was part of a consortium of electronic equipment manufacturers. Other regional consortium

This case was prepared by Joseph Wolfe, College of Business Administration, University of Tulsa, Tulsa, Oklahoma. Funding for this case research project was provided by Portland State University's Free Market Business Development Institute in conjunction with its Russian-American School of Business Administration. The case was created to highlight the various issues involved and encourage intelligent discussion of managerial actions which might be taken and should not be considered a judgment of the subject company's management skills or of the wisdom of past actions or decisions. The case writer wishes to express his deepest appreciation to Yuri Kirpichenko and Eric Romanov for their help during this study's field research.

EXHIBIT 1   **Sales Proportions by General Product Line**

Product Line	Percent of Total
Power transformers	67.5%
Throttles	22.5
Reeled magnetic cores	2.5
Printed circuit boards	2.5
Electronic units	2.5
Consumer goods	2.5

Source: Company estimates.

members were the Kometa, Ellipse, Horizont, and Elbor companies as well as the radio electronics institute. Ellipse, Horizont, and Elbor specialized in making transformer electromagnetic parts, while Kometa specialized in making tools and equipment for Elbor, Horizont, and Ellipse and ultimately for Transvit. Close relationships were formed quickly between Transvit and the consortium, aided by the fact that the same person, Anatolii Nesterov, headed the consortium and the research institute as well as serving as Transvit's general manager. In the late 1980s Nesterov was suceeded by Igor Susanin, the company's present head.

Transvit specializes in making some of the electronic parts found in such consumer durables as television sets, radios, record players, and audio and videocassette recorders (VCRs). Its main products are power transformers in the 1.5- to 350-volt range with outputs up to 300 watts, throttles, and reeled magnetic cores for radio electronic utility and indusrial equipment. Exhibit 1 shows the firm's typical product mix for the last few years; there is an annual variation in the four smaller product lines based on specific contracts obtained within the year. Exhibit 2 is an example of a specification sheet for the typical transformer sold by Transvit.

The Small Electrical Transformer Industry

The transformer was invented in 1831 by Michael Faraday. In the typical home entertainment product it "steps down" domestic power supply voltages of 110/120 volts in the United States (220 volts in Europe) to voltages typically in the 4- to 12-volt range. Because transformers of this type are a known and mature technology and have almost become products within the electronics industry, manufacturers have limited alternatives at their disposal. Some have created highly automated manufacturing processes and mass-produce these units in large numbers. To ensure quality control standards and obtain as much profit per unit as possible, companies sometimes set up vertical integration or supplier joint ventures. May & Christe GmbH, a German producer of transformers as well as lighting ballasts and other electrical equipment, integrated its operations in early 1992 with MagneTeck, an electrical equipment manufacturer. Some transformer manufacturers have become almost captive in-house suppliers to their customers. Other manufacturers have attempted to create in-use value added by employing unique proprietary raw materials or materials that are highly reliable or overspecified. These materials make their products highly dependable or functional under extremely severe or divergent operating conditions. Armco and the Canadian steel-maker Dofasco finish specialty steels

EXHIBIT 2   Specification and Product Description Sheet for a Typical Transvit Transformer

173001, г. Новгород.
ул. Б. Санкт-Петербургская, 51.
Факс: 7-32-37.
Телекс: 237123 WEBER

Russia, 173001, Novgorod.
B. Sanct-Peterburgskaja, 51
Fax: 7-32-37
Telex: 237123 WEBER

ТРАНСФОРМАТОР ПИТАНИЯ ТП-20
POWER TRANSFORMER TYPE ТП-20

Трансформатор соответствует
стандарту IEC 65.
Трансформатор питания для
печатного монтажа.
Класс трудногорючести по UL 94
V-0 или V-1.
Класс изоляции T 60/E.
Электрическая прочность изоляции:
первичная-вторичная 3000 В эфф — 1 сек.
первичная-сердечник 3000 В эфф — 1 сек.
Допустимое отклонение вторичных
напряжений ±3%.
Напряжение питания 220 В,
частота 50 Гц.
Масса не более 0,37 кг

The transformer are in conformity
with IEC 65 STANDART.
Power transformers for the
PC mounting.
Flameability class — UL 94
V-0 or V-1.
Insulation class T 60/E.
Electric insulation strength:
primary-secondary 3000 Veff — 1 sec.
primary-core 3000 Veff — 1 sec.
Tolerances of secondary voltages
deviation ±3%.
Nominal voltage 220 V, 50 Hz.
Weight less than 0.37 kg.

ГАБАРИТНЫЕ РАЗМЕРЫ
DIMENSIONS

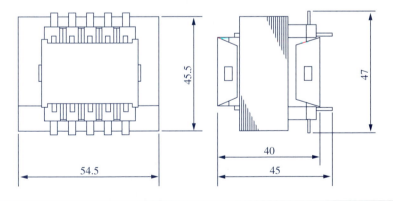

that are particularly appropriate for transformer applications, while Japan's NKK Corporation has created a new, less brittle 6.5 percent silicon electromagnetic steel designed for the special transformers found only in audiovisual equipment.

Another profit source comes from capitalizing on new electrical products that require modest modifications in transformer technology. The coming of the personal computer, as well as the highly automated business office with both its freestanding workstations and local area networks (LANs), has provided new growth areas for the transformer. Today's office requires more electrical outlets and connections, and all of its electrical components, such as power, lighting and heating, and ventilating and air-conditioning, must be designed as a total integrated system. The office's computers need an uninterrupted and nonvariable power supply. Surge-suppression devices such as voltage regulators and line conditioners use transformers to provide constant output voltage over a wide range of input voltages.

Through various fresh designs, transformers also have found new applications within both standing systems and new electrical devices. Through the use of a highly efficient transformer that interfaces balanced and unbalanced signal lines, Tut Systems has created an Ethernet implementation that employs ordinary and less expensive flat telephone wire or twisted-pair in-wall telephone wire. The need for high-volume portable disk drives that support graphical software programs and PC-based presentations has increased the need for the transformers found in these units. Diablo Engineering's state-of-the-art lightbulb uses a high-frequency electric transformer to light a phosphor-coated glass bulb. The bulb emits little or no heat, is dimmable, reduces energy use by 70 to 75 percent, and lasts over 20,000 hours in normal use.

Although certain developments have maintained or even increased the demand for the small transformer as a piece of technology, other developments may reduce its overall importance or eliminate it completely in certain applications. Sonic System's microScsi Ethernet adapter is small and lightweight and does not need an AC transformer. Some fluorescent-fixture manufacturers have switched to electronic ballasts. These ballasts provide quick starts for the tubes, increasing their life and completely eliminating the core-and-coil transformer and its annoying humming sound.

Transvit's Markets

For many years Transvit sold its products only to Russian manufacturers. Exhibit 3 shows the various consumer home entertainment products which used Transvit's products. Based on company estimates, the firm has a 30 percent market share of the audio tape recorder market, an 11 percent share of the radio set market, a 100 percent share of Russian VCR (Electronika BM-12) production, and an 8 percent share of the television set market. Kolesjonkov noted, however, that Transvit's transformers were used only in the television sets' remote-control circuits, missing out on many of that product's other transformer applications.

Although it was once a supplier to only Russian firms, Transvit's export sales had increased in the past few years. Exhibit 4 shows the company's domestic and export sales in millions of units since 1981. Foreign sales were now being made in Germany and Italy. Until recently Transvit had supplied the Thompson Company of France with parts. That relationship was discontinued, however, when Thompson phased out its

---

EXHIBIT 3   Russian-Made Home-Entertainment Equipment

Videocassette recorders: Electronika BM-12, BM-18, BM-20, BM-32
Television sets: Rubin, Temp, Sadko, Raduga, Record, Gorezont, Foton, Shiljalis, Slavutich, Electron
Radios: VEF, Okean, Selga, Tourist, Sonata, Alpinist, Leningrad, Vega
Audio tape players: Dnepr, Nota, Sonata, Vega, Mayak, Orel
Record players: Berdsk, Amphiton, Rigonda, Electronika, Vega, Aria

EXHIBIT 4   Unit Sales by General Market Area (in millions of units)

Year	Domestic	Export	Total
1981	6.56		6.56
1982	6.78		6.78
1983	6.79		6.79
1984	7.06		7.06
1985	6.67		6.67
1986	6.04	0.05	6.09
1987	4.26	0.16	4.42
1988	4.35	0.20	4.55
1989	4.23	0.20	4.43
1990	3.69	0.24	3.93
1991	3.13	0.43	3.56
1992	1.45	0.96	2.41
1993	1.09	1.87	2.96

Note: No distinction has been made between West European sales and sales to former Soviet republics.

Source: Company records.

EXHIBIT 5   Target Market Profit and Growth

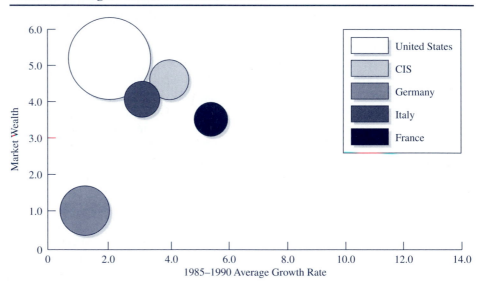

Source: "BI Market Indexes, 1980, 1985, 1990," *Business International,* July 6, 1992, p. 216.

television sets that used Transvit's TP-60-8 transformer. Kolesjonkov noted that a buyer's market existed in Western Europe, although his firm had been price-competitive over the years. Exhibit 5 shows the 1985–1990 profit and market growth rates in various countries that Transvit competed in or was targeting for future sales growth. Exhibit 6 shows data on the near-past and expected near-future growth rates and per capita wealth for these targeted countries.

EXHIBIT 6   Growth Rates and Per-Capita Wealth of Target Markets

Country	Year 1993	Year 1994	Wealth
France	–0.9	1.3	$22,995
Germany	–1.3	0.7	25,793
Italy	–0.2	1.4	20,675
Russia	–14.0	–9.8	7,050
United States	2.8	3.1	23,438

Sources: Blue Chip Economic Indicators and "Emerging-Market Indicators," *The Economist,* May 7, 1994, p. 118 for market growth rates; Vienna Institute for Comparative Economic Studies for Russian GDP data; and OECD Economic Surveys for GDP data on remaining countries.

Domestic Demand and the Marketing of Electronic Components

Within the last two years major inroads into Russia's consumer electronics market had been made by such Pacific Rim companies as Sony, Panasonic, Sharp, Technics, Samsung, Shivaki, Funai, and Aiwa. Only minor penetrations, however, had been made by Western Europe's manufacturers, such as Phillips and Grundig, as the Pacific Rim's products featured more attractive designs and offered more value. The extent of Japan's penetration into the Russian market could be sensed by examining the number of distributors in Exhibit 7 operating in mid-1994 in Moscow, Russia's largest wholesale electronics center.

Kolesjonkov blamed these falling sales on the low actual or perceived quality of his country's home entertainment devices. As Japan's products entered the Russian market, the demand for Russia's domestically produced equipment fell drastically. This was also the case in the United States and to a lesser degree in Western Europe. Japan's products were more fully featured, were well made, and presented good value, although they were high-priced by Russian standards. For example, when the Russian-made Electronika BM-27 VCR was in production, it sold for $100 (300,000 rubles), while a comparably featured Sony unit sold for $320 (640,000 rubles). The major difference between the two products, however, resided in the Sony unit's superior quality and reliability. For Kolesjonkov's company to do well, he believed that Russia's manufacturers would have to improve the quality of their products, but he did not believe this would happen very soon. In the meantime, he recognized that he had to deal with the products being manufactured closer to home. New competition had come from the Vega Radio Equipment Factory of Berdsk in Siberia and, within the Commonwealth of Independent States, from the newly formed 50th Jubilee of Lenin Comsomol Factory of Nikovaev in Ukraine. Some of Transvit's major customers in western Siberia also began to produce transformers in-house to eliminate the transportation costs associated with working with Transvit. Closer to home in the Novgorod region, Kometa had begun making electronic components, and Transvit had lost about 10 percent of its sales to Kometa. The electronics research institute, although in the process of being privatized and seeking new profit-making opportunities, did not possess enough production capacity to pose a competitive threat to Transvit. Moreover, Transvit had begun to design its own products rather than relying on the product development skills of the research institute.

EXHIBIT 7   Wholesale Distributors in the Moscow Home Entertainment Center Market

Company/Brand	Distributors
Television sets	
Panasonic 14L3R	56
Funai 2000MK7	144
Sony 2100	133
Sony 1400	94
Sony 2185	64
Sony 2530	55
Sony 1485	54
Sony 14DK1	38
JVC 21Z	41
JVC 14Z	41
Videocassette recorders	
Panasonic SD-25AM	69
Panasonic SD-11AM	57
Funai V8008CM	45
Sony X57	69
Sony X37	48
Sony 426	42
Sony 226	34
JVC 1200	29
AIWA 925	36
SUPRA 21	25
Videocassette players	
Panasonic P04	71
Funai 5000 HC	86
Funai 5000 LR	39
Sony P51	38
Sony X130	37
JVC P28	69
Akai 120	143
Samsung 31R	32
Orion 688	30
Orion 388	30

Source: Appendix, *Komsomol Pravda,* April 22, 1994, p. 12.

The Production and Product Development Cycle

During the Soviet Union's planned-economy days Transvit faced few problems in estimating production and sales. Little seasonal demand existed, although a large amount of production-related "storming" occurred at the end of each quarter and year as the company struggled to meet its production goals and quotas. Three shifts plus Saturday and Sunday overtime were normal during those periods until the early 1990s. Since that time, owing to falling demand and the need to lower labor costs, Transvit had been a two-shift, straight-time operation. Overall employment had fluctuated around the level of 3,000 since 1971. Through the combined effects of falling demand and automation, the company projected an employment level of 2,500 in the near future.

EXHIBIT 8   **Transvit Company Income Statements
(in thousands of rubles)**

	1992	1993
Sales	1,368,767	6,832,142
Cost of goods sold	750,122	5,118,754
Gross profit	618,645	1,713,388
Expenses		
Depreciation	58,462	83,083
Personnel	56,039	388,439
Telephone and utilities	52,706	427,509
Freight	31,011	175,636
Advertising and auditing	18,952	1,119,868
Interest	9,288	424,918
Services	3,623	23,322
Travel and entertainment	1,126	9,593
Miscellaneous	18,142	149,725
Profit before tax	369,296	(1,088,705)
Value-added tax	180,917	1,092,630
Profit after tax	188,379	(2,181,335)

Source: Constructed by the case writer from unaudited internal company records.

Although Kolesjonkov had a mandate to preserve domestic market share and increase sales in Western Europe, much of the company's business had been obtained through contacts and personal relationships rather than through direct marketing campaigns. An electronic equipment manufacturer typically designs a new product and then contacts past suppliers to make specially engineered components for the new final product. Depending on the uniqueness of the component, the prospective supplier may work closely with the final user in designing the component, often making suggestions regarding changes in the component's configuration or specifications. If the component manufacturer becomes an authorized supplier, a sales contract is created and sales will ensue for the component, depending on the ultimate demand for the end product. Repeat business has been the rule for Transvit, as it has a good reputation within the industry, and it has never lost a customer due to quality control or delivery conditions under its direct control.

A period of one to six months may elapse between the component-solicitation stage and the initial manufacturing run. The length of the development cycle depends on the new product's compatibility and the know-how associated with previously developed products. Kolesjonkov has found that a high degree of knowledge transfer prevailed in the past and that the rate of technological advance has slowed over the years in the electronic-parts industry. Moreover, Transvit has learned how to develop new products faster by using existing parts for successor products more intelligently and unifying the firm's design and development stages.

Once the product has been launched, certain cost-saving experience-curve effects take hold and are built into the product's quoted selling price. The length of the component's production run may be from one to five or more years, based on the end product's commercial life or the component's transferability to successor end user products. Break-even profits typically occur when production levels amount to 10,000 units per month, with manufacturing markups of 20 to 28 percent typically employed.

EXHIBIT 9   Transvit Company Balance Sheets (in thousands of rubles)

	1990	1991	1992	1993
Assets				
Current assets				
Cash	1	1	1,172	74,581
Deposits and other cash	541	93	48,806	251,167
Accounts receivable	6,446	13,862	315,442	1,303,766
Raw materials	14,732	34,065	290,499	1,009,872
Parts and supplies	2,400	3,868	25,820	18,190
Goods in progress	3,511	7,838	35,814	148,289
Finished goods	3,160	4,575	54,962	400,061
Budget payments	0	0	68,294	144,843
Total current assets	30,791	64,302	840,809	3,350,769
Fixed plant and equipment				
Current plant and equipment	55,316	55,084	1,083,106	1,133,815
Less depreciation	−26,374	−23,123	−584,337	−644,480
Net current plant and equipment	28,374	31,961	498,769	489,335
New equipment purchased	0	1,473	10	11,443
Capital in progress	0	3,704	32,985	62,094
New plant fund	0	1,000	6,227	631,389
Total plant and equipment	28,942	38,138	537,991	1,194,261
Total assets	59,733	102,440	1,378,800	4,545,030
Liabilities				
Current liabilities				
Short-term loan	12,501	26,380	112,384	287,901
Employee bank credit	45	44	22	1
Accounts payable				
Salaries and wages	2,331	5,610	147,696	858,744
Social security	772	2,544	21,206	312,206
Insurance	30	938	7,961	73,029
Budget	0	19	161	4,604
Other creditors	68	3,205	76,103	268,975
Total accounts payable	3,201	12,316	253,127	1,517,558
Total current liabilities	15,747	38,740	365,533	1,805,460
Long-term loan	0	2,000	1,927	1,877
Total debt	15,747	40,740	367,460	1,807,337
Special-purpose funds	1,674	10,594	655,744	767,005
Ministry support	0	0	42,150	46,100
Advance payments	97	513	136,756	884,975
Earnings of future periods	0	0	0	567,913
Anticipated expenses and payments	697	264	19,338	42,306
Bad-debt allowance	0	0	523	435
Owner's equity				
Paid-in capital	41,475	50,329	50,329	115,559
Retained earnings	43	0	106,500	313,400
Total equity	41,518	50,329	156,829	428,959
Total liabilities	59,733	102,400	1,378,800	4,545,030

Unfortunately, Kolesjonkov noted that high inflation rates, which affect raw material costs, combined with lagging customer payments, resulted in zero or negligible unit profits. Transvit's financial results in the form of balance sheets and income statements can be found in Exhibits 8 and 9.

Exhibit 10   Transvit's Cost of Goods Sold
Components (in thousands
of rubles)

	1992	1993
Labor	145,260	1,004,081
Raw materials and components	4,761	46,710
Purchased components and sub-assemblies	563,735	3,885,647
Subcontracting	36,366	182,316
Cost of goods sold	750,122	5,118,754

Value-Added Recovery

Owing to a lack of international certification, Transvit often sold its products to others, such as the Neotype Company, as semifinished goods. Those companies altered the products slightly by installing plugs or connectors, subjecting the finished component to a certification test that certain customers required, and embossing the revised product with their logo. They then added a markup of 5 to 10 percent over Transvit's price. To obtain this markup for itself, Transvit completed phase 1 of the IEC-65 Standards certification process, and a decision on product certification was to be made in May 1994 in Geneva, Switzerland. If this certification was obtained, Transvit would be able to offer its own products. Although the additional markup percentage was a welcome feature of this activity, Kolesjonkov observed that certification also would increase the company's target customer base by 20 percent. Exhibit 10 provides a breakdown of the company's most recent cost of goods sold components.

Organization Structure

For over 20 years Transvit had operated with the organization structure shown in Exhibit 11. Although not completely formalized at the time of writing, the structure shown in Exhibit 12, necessitated primarily by the fact that Transvit has become a joint stock corporation, was to be implemented within the year. In addition to fulfilling the governance requirements for a joint stock company, Kolesjonkov believed that this structure's virtues lay in its emphasis on his company's need for a serious marketing effort.

As an advantage for his company's new marketing emphasis, Kolesjonkov brought to his job a number of years of engineering experience. He had graduated from the Novgorod Technical Institute as a tests and measurements engineer and had served as another local company's main statistical engineer for seven years. For eight succeeding years he functioned as Transvit's metrology department chief before heading its new marketing department. Kolesjonkov studied marketing concepts and theories at the Portland State University's Russian-American School of Business Administration (RASBA) program in Novgorod and keeps a Russian version of the most popular U.S. marketing textbook. As a result of this formal education in marketing, he says, "My present knowledge is deficient both professionally and personally, and the only training I've received in marketing is what I've learned at RASBA. But I think I know the preliminaries, and that's good enough for now."

EXHIBIT 11   Transvit's Current Organization Structure

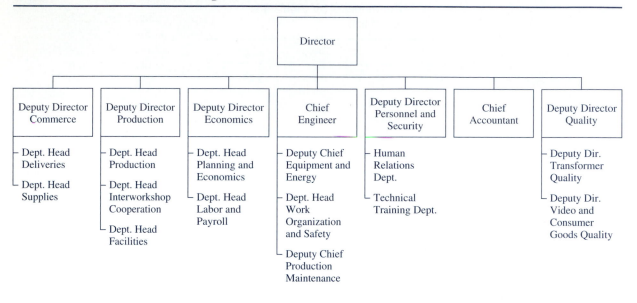

EXHIBIT 12   Transvit's Proposed Organization Structure

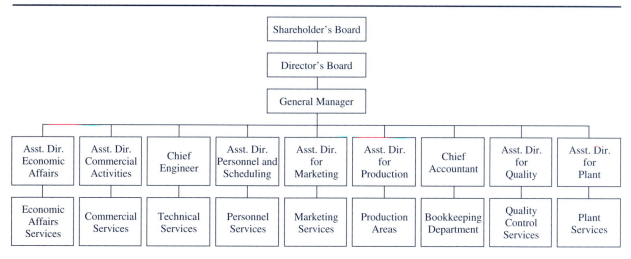

Future Marketing Efforts

In looking for new applications for Transvit's transformer manufacturing capabilities, the company was thinking about selling transformers to computer printer manufacturers in the United States as well as components in halogen lighting installations in the Commonwealth of Independent States (CIS). Transvit did not have reliable information on the demand for halogen installations. They were being made throughout the country, although most products came from the West. If CIS companies entered this market, Kolesjonkov believed his main competitors would be Elecon of Kasan, Promelectro of Moscow, and Lisma of Saransk. Transvit was also doing product development research for applications in automobile service centers as well as automobile recharging devices. Given Russia's fleet of aging automobiles and the fact the nearby Novgorod State University has an automobile service center education program, Transvit was optimistic about the success of these endeavors. Production was scheduled to begin in September 1994.

CASE 3–5
SHORIN-RYU KARATE ACADEMY

Classes were over for the day at the Shorin-Ryu Karate Academy in Waltham, Massachusetts, and Sensei[1] James True (the owner) had just received a call from one of the MBA students who had been working with him for the past four months. Eric had called excitedly to tell Jim that he and his MBA consulting team had just won the finals of the consulting project presentation competition. The team of MBA students had contacted Jim in January 1996 to see if they could work with him as partial fulfillment of their degree program requirements. Jim had jumped at the chance to have a team of outsiders take a look at his business and the issues he was just starting to address.

Sensei Jim had started the academy in 1980 in the garage of his home. The academy was now located in a state-of-the-art training facility in Waltham and had a customer base of 324 active students. Jim had reached a point in both his business and karate careers in which he felt the need to grow. Jim had identified five areas that the student consulting team had focused on in its project. One, could he develop a better sense of managing the karate business? Two, could he increase the number of students at the academy? Three, were his students (and their parents) becoming dissatisfied with his use of student instructors? Four, was his advertising effective? Five, was he at the point where he could and/or should open a second location?

Jim was excited for the student consulting team. He thought they had worked hard over the past few months, and they were a nice group of people. (One of the consulting team members had even started karate classes during the consulting project.) The team had provided Jim with some interesting information and recommendations. It was up to Jim, however, to ensure the steady growth of his business.

The Martial Arts Industry

While the origins of karate date back to around the seventeenth century, martial arts were not popularized in the United States until the late 1940s. By the middle 1990s, the U.S. commercialized martial arts instruction market was estimated to be a $1.5 billion business (the first karate school in the United States opened in 1956) and was second only to computer networking services in its 1994 growth rate.[2] While interest in the martial arts had grown substantially in the United States, Japan had experienced an equally substantial decrease in demand. Apparently, Japanese youth regarded karate as a sport for the poor, with foreign sports such as football and basketball taking precedence.

The martial arts arena consisted of many disciplines, each representing various styles, forms, and techniques:[3]

---

[1] *Sensei* means "teacher" or "instructor."

[2] Ferguson, Tim W. "Let's Talk to the Master." *Forbes* (October 23, 1995): 138–42.

[3] Much of this information was taken from Bob Condor, "Spirited Workout," *Chicago Tribune* (March 7, 1996), sec. 5, p. 4.

This case was prepared by Victoria L. Crittenden, associate professor of marketing at Boston College, and William F. Crittenden, associate professor of management at Northeastern University. Research assistance was provided by David Angus, Boston College/Andersen Consulting Fund. The case is designed as the basis for class discussion.

- *Karate,* developed in Okinawa in the seventeenth century, was an ancient Japanese tradition that consisted largely of punching and kicking in a linear fashion.
- *Aikido* ("aye-key-doe") was also a Japanese practice and incorporated a Zen philosophy in its doctrine. The practice was based on the use of the opponent's energy to defeat the opponent.
- *Judo,* also stemming from the Japanese culture and developed in 1882, consisted of grappling or wrestling with the opponent.
- *Taekwondo* (the form used in the Olympic Games) was a Korean discipline. While similar to karate, taekwondo involved more spinning and back kicks. While potentially the most deadly of the arts, taekwondo was thought to be the most popular of the martial arts in the United States.
- *Hapkido* was also a Korean discipline. Considered the least "spiritual" of the art forms, this form emphasized the fighting aspect.
- *Tai chi* had its origins in China. Considered more meditative than most martial arts, it was gaining favor in the United States due to its gentle orientation (although in China the form could be very violent).[4]
- *Kung fu* was very intense and involved many blocks and retaliation techniques in its fighting. Kung fu was popularized in the United States via Hollywood (e.g., the "Kung Fu" television series in the 1970s with David Carradine).

Self-defense and concerns about children's safety fueled interest in the martial arts. Classes were dedicated to safety tips and demonstrations of physical tactics children and adults could use to thwart an assault or abduction. Also, the media had done a good job of plugging martial arts with movies and television series such as *Karate Kid, Mortal Kombat, Teenage Mutant Ninja Turtles,* and "Mighty Morphin Power Rangers." Some estimates suggested that in the early stages of market development, close to 99 percent of all students enrolled in martial arts classes to learn to protect themselves.

However, personal discipline had become a driving force in martial arts instruction by the mid-1990s. In particular, karate combined the mastery of combat skills with the mastery of self-protection and the development of character and virtue. Martial arts training could help build a person's confidence and self-esteem, which could also aid in resisting the forces of violence. The physical fitness boom in American society also had fueled interest in the martial arts. Martial arts enhanced hand–eye coordination and flexibility and conditioned the body for other sporting activities.

There were thousands of martial arts businesses throughout the United States. While the typical academy had 75 to 100 students, some operations boasted several hundred students and multiple locations. Such large chains included Y.H. Park with seven locations in the New York area and around 3,500 students, Master Glazier's Karate International based in New Jersey and similar in size to Y.H. Park, and East West Karate with 1,200 students. Additionally, there were several professional associations. The National Association of Professional Martial Artists (NAPMA) was headquartered in Florida, and the World Traditional Taekwondo Union was based in Arkansas.

Many companies were able to capitalize on the fragmented martial arts industry. Both Education Funding Co. (Chevy Chase, Maryland) and United Professionals, Inc. (Coral Springs, Florida), were in the billing business. United Professionals was reported to have collected around $18 million in 1994 by handling the billing for almost 500 schools. The largest martial arts uniform and equipment manufacturer in the United

---

[4] While tai chi was practiced by more people worldwide than any other martial art, it was not as popular among Americans as karate and judo.

States was the Century Martial Art Supply of Oklahoma with yearly sales around $40 million. The second largest supplier was Macho Products of Florida.

The Marketplace.   Before the middle to late 1980s, about 90 percent of martial arts enrollees were between ages 16 and 25. By the middle 1990s, however, students spanned all ages. The American Taekwondo Association offered "Tiny Tigers" classes for students age 3 to 5 all the way to "Silver VIPs" for those age 50 to 75 (and sometimes older). However, there were no national statistics on the number of children or adults taking martial arts lessons.

The lack of national statistics made it difficult to segment the market by age. However, estimates were that preteens accounted for about 40 percent of martial arts students in the United States. Parents were enrolling their children in martial arts classes for discipline training, self-defense, and physical fitness. As was mentioned earlier, the influence of television and movies had spurred children's interest in the martial arts. Martial arts programs were found in affluent suburbs and in the inner city. (Many inner-city programs were the result of larger antiviolence programs.) Martial arts training was thought to be of special value to children with physical or mental disabilities, with these students seeing improvement in physical coordination (particularly relating to their motor skills) and self-confidence. Additionally, there appeared to be growing interest in parent/child martial arts classes.

Regarding older Americans, the Dallas area's Steel Magnolias was a karate demonstration group of four women over age 62. The group performed at nursing homes, store openings, ceremonial events, and karate tournaments. The women in the group credited karate with multiple benefits, such as improved balance, stronger bodies, and increased self-confidence.

While considered a traditionally male preserve, the martial arts were increasingly focused on by women. Female membership in various martial arts associations was increasing steadily. For example, the U.S.A. Karate Federation of New Jersey tripled its female membership from 1988 to 1993, and the United States Tae Kwon Do Union had seen steady growth in female membership. Factors contributing to this increase were the physical fitness boom, crumbling cultural barriers, self-defense, and perceived psychological benefits related to careers. Women reported that the martial arts changed their personalities, making them more assertive in all areas of their lives (e.g., home, workplace). The major stumbling block for women in the early stages of their martial arts training was fighting (called kumite). Initially, women were reluctant to fight, but they typically lost this inhibition as training continued.

The martial arts also had entered the American workplace. Business organizations such as the Trump Taj Mahal Casino Resort, Cigna, and Peco Energy Company sponsored in-house martial arts lessons. Workplace benefits were thought to include improved physical fitness, relief from stress, enhanced teamwork skills, better personal relations skills, and humility.

In response to the growing adult interest in the martial arts, classes were being offered such as "cardio-karate," which combined karate movement with aerobic exercise. Cardio-karate focused on strengthening the heart muscle, making the class particularly valuable for people with heart conditions. Classes such as this did not follow the same regimen as typical karate classes in that the students did not wear the martial arts uniform and no self-defense training was involved.

Leisure Time.   Leisure was one of the biggest growth industries in the 1990s. It was estimated that the average household spent anywhere from $1,500 to $3,500 a year on entertainment.[5] Middle-aged Americans were the largest group when it came to spending money on leisure time. In the 1990s this group consisted of the baby boomers, and so leisure time was devoted toward family-oriented activities. However, this group was experiencing a decline in the amount of leisure time.

The Americans' Use of Time Project grouped leisure activities into 13 categories: adult education, religious services, other organizational (club) activities, going to entertainment places, visiting, conversing, sport and outdoor activities, hobby/craft/game activities, watching TV, reading, listening to the radio/recordings, thinking/relaxing, and travel to/from leisure activities.[6] Of these categories, adult education was one of the fastest-growing areas. Additionally, time spent on sports and outdoor activities had more than doubled in a 20-year period, with TV watching and family conversations also showing increases. These gains appeared to come at the expense of newspaper reading and visiting.

From a gender perspective, the time project found that men spent more time than did women on sports and outdoor activities and adult education. However, the two sexes spent almost an equal amount of time on activities in the other 11 categories.

Concerns about children's health had begun creeping into the leisure time of both children and their parents. In the early 1990s the President's Council on Physical Fitness reported that 40 percent of children between the ages of five and eight were overweight, had high blood pressure, or had high cholesterol levels. This led to a huge increase in the number of health clubs offering children's fitness programs. Also, child care and sports programs began addressing the health and fitness concerns of children in their programs.

Instruction.   Students of the martial arts generally attributed their selection of techniques not to the technique but to the instructor. Reinforcing this selection process, taekwondo instructor Charlie Lee said that it did not matter what form of martial arts a student took since the basic principles of martial arts were the same (discipline, respect, confidence, self-defense).[7] He said that what was important was the instructor.

Basically, the "right" martial arts school used positive reinforcement, emphasized education, and focused on self-control (not confrontation). Suggested selection criteria when looking at martial arts programs included parental access to lessons, free or cheap introductory lessons, willingness of the head instructor to discuss teaching methods before a student's enrollment, whether the head instructor actually taught classes, willingness of the head instructor to allow the potential student access to current students and their opinions, proof of liability insurance, and language skills (strong English-speaking skills).[8]

A typical martial arts class was attended twice a week and consisted of stretching, arm and leg movements,[9] *katas* (choreographed movements designed for offensive/

---

[5] Cutler, Blayne. "Where Does the Free Time Go?" *American Demographics* (November 1990): 36–38; Robinson, John P. "As We Like It." *American Demographics* (February 1993): 44–48; "That's Entertainment!" *American Demographics* (July 1993): 16. Exact numbers were difficult to calculate for the entertainment/leisure industry since estimates could include everything from clothes to cable television.

[6] Robinson, John P. "The Leisure Pie." *American Demographics* (November 1990): 39.

[7] McManus, Kevin. "Karate Chops for Children." *Washington Post* (August 21, 1992), sec. NJ, p. 1, col. 3.

[8] Ibid.

[9] These exercises were typically done to the count of 10 in Japanese. *"Ichi! Ni! San! Shi! Go! Roku! Shi-chi! Ha-chi! Ku! Ju!"* After saying *"go"* and *"ju,"* students yell *"Kiai!"* The *kiai* was the expelling of breath from the inner soul and was thought to provide the martial arts student with greater strength.

defensive postures), and sparring (fighting). Respect was a dominant theme in any karate class. The teacher was always addressed as "Sensei," and students and instructor bowed as a show of mutual respect at the beginning and end of every class as well as at the beginning and end of a sparring match. This respect extended beyond the dojo (training room) to both school and home. Many instructors expressed interest in school events and in grades.[10] At home, parents might suggest asking Sensei to help resolve a disagreement.

Participant ranking in a martial arts class was denoted by belt color. A beginning student was awarded a white belt after a few weeks of instruction. A black belt was the highest belt ranking that could be achieved. Colors in between were typically orange, gold, purple, green, blue, and brown. (There were several degrees of both brown and black belts.) In class, students gathered according to rank—highest belts in the class lined up first, then in descending order to white or no belt.

From the school owner's perspective there were some standards or benchmarks regarding the number of students at the school. A rough barometer was 100 to 150 students per 1,000 square feet of space. The number of "active students" was an important measure. Basically, active students could be broken down into three components: active paying students, active nonpaying students, and nonactive paying students. The active paying student measure was the number of students paying monthly tuition (and attending classes). The gauge was that this would be about 80 percent of the active students. Active nonpaying students were those who had paid in full or had bartered services for tuition remission (e.g., helped around the academy through assisting with class teaching or office/maintenance activities). Nonactive paying students were students on the monthly payment plan who were not attending classes. The owner could not depend on these students as long-term revenue generators unless the owner did something to get them to attend classes again.

American Shorin-Ryu Karate Association

The American Shorin-Ryu Karate Association (ASKA) was a nonprofit 501(c)3 organization under the guidance of Papa Paul Keller, Papa Christopher Clarke, Papa Joe Hays, Shihan Dai Jules Pomier, and Dai Sempei James True. The association studied the Matsubayashi style of Shorin-Ryu karate. The Matsubayashi Shorin-Ryu Family Tree is shown in Exhibit 1.

The ASKA was a nationally prominent karate association that sponsored clinics and camps for all levels of students. The president of the ASKA was Paul Keller. Papa Keller, a former U.S. weapons champion, was a leader in the field of VIP protection. The head instructor of the ASKA was Christopher Clarke. Papa Chris, who worked for the U.S. Department of State, was regarded as an expert on martial arts history. He spoke and read Chinese. There were three ASKA Massachusetts schools: the Shorin-Ryu Karate Academy in Waltham, the Northeast Shorin-Ryu Karate Academy in Andover, and the Academy of Traditional Karate in Wilmington.

The Shorin-Ryu Karate Academy in Waltham was led by Sensei James True. Sensei Jim was the head instructor and had achieved the rank of fifth-degree black belt as well as fourth-degree black belt in Kobudo (Okinawan weapons). Sensei Jim was assisted by

---

[10] The American Taekwondo Association offered the "Karate for Kids" program, which awarded victory patches to children who displayed growth in three areas: (1) making the honor roll or making grade improvements in school, (2) participating in extracurricular activities, and (3) good conduct at home and work in the community.

EXHIBIT 1   **Matsubayashi Shorin-Ryu Family Tree**

Sensei Michael Pepe, fourth-degree black belt. The school offered a wide variety of classes for ages four years and up.

The Northeast Shorin-Ryu Karate Academy in Andover was led by Sensei Dick Wolnik, who was a third-degree black belt and had assistant instructor certification. The school was run through the Andover Department of Community Service and met twice a week at a local elementary school. Youth classes started at eight years of age, and adult classes were held for students 12 years and older. Sensei Wolnik was assisted by Sensei Thomas Wirtanen, fourth-degree black belt.

The Academy of Traditional Karate in Wilmington was led by Sensei Todd Keane, who was a full instructor and held the rank of third-degree black belt. The Wilmington school offered a wide variety of classes for all ages.

Students in the association participated at the following ranks (designated by belt color): no belt, white, orange, gold, purple, purple with green stripe, green, blue, brown, and black.[11]

The Shorin-Ryu Karate Academy

The mission statement of the Academy was

> to develop and build an individual's confidence, discipline, respect, and achievement, while offering an opportunity to enrich a person's inner and outer life by the short-term accumulation of physical stamina and coordination and the long lasting benefit of inner strength and peace.

---

[11] According to the rules of Shorin-Ryu, students could not attain the status of black belt until the age of 16.

Sensei Jim was a 1980 graduate of Bentley College in Waltham. He held a bachelor of arts in education and the social sciences. Jim began his karate training in 1975 and completed his black belt training in 1979. It was during this four-year training process that Jim decided that he wanted to own a karate academy.

In addition to owning, managing, and instructing at the academy, Jim was active in taking karate into the Waltham community. Jim held classes for the Waltham YMCA (for all ages), the Greater Waltham Association of Retarded Citizens, and the Waltham High School Adult Evening Division.

Location.   After an initial start-up in Jim's garage, the academy moved to a 2,500-square-foot, custom-designed facility in Waltham. The facility included three dojos (training rooms), male and female locker rooms, a small retail counter, an observation area (where visitors could observe classes), and Jim's office.[12]

Waltham, Massachusetts, was located in the middle of several affluent Boston-area suburbs. Seventy-seven percent of the academy's customer base resided in Waltham (56 percent), Watertown (12 percent), and Newton (9 percent). Newton was the largest and wealthiest of the three suburban communities, with a 1990 population of 82,585 and 58.9 percent of its annual household incomes over US$50,000. Waltham's 1990 population was 57,878, with 43.9 percent of its annual household incomes over US$50,000. The smallest of the three communities was Watertown. Its 1990 population was 33,284, and 24.7 percent of its households had annual incomes over US$50,000.

Students.   Youth members of the academy fell into four major groups: (1) Pee Wee Beginners were called *Little Dragons* (ages 4 to 6), (2) Junior Youth Beginners were called *Junior Ninjas* (ages 7 to 9), (3) Youth Beginners were called *Samurais* (ages 10 to 14), and (4) Youth Intermediate to Advanced were called *Daimyos* or *Shoguns* (ages 8 to 14, with the group depending on belt color). Also, there was a fifth group, *Teen Class,* for ages 13 to 17. The youth market accounted for 65 percent of the academy's membership base.

Adults attended class in the evenings with the appropriate level of student. For example, a beginning adult could attend class 7 to 8 PM on Tuesday or Thursday or 6 to 7 PM on Wednesday. Adult membership ranged in age from 21 to 50, with the majority of students in their twenties and thirties.

Jim used a software package, Black Belt Management, to maintain information (e.g., enrollment, advancement) on each of his students. Black Belt Management was designed specifically for karate institutions.

To gather additional information about youth students, the MBA consulting group had administered a survey to the parents and guardians of students attending the youth classes. The survey was based on a convenience sample. The survey was administered to adults watching youth classes at various times during a one-week period. Exhibit 2 shows the quantitative and qualitative results of the survey from parents of 66 of the youths.

Programs and Pricing.   Most karate students attended two classes a week at the academy. However, the school did allow students to attend one class a week, and members of one of the black belt clubs attended classes three times per week. The academy was open

---

[12] Retail sales accounted for around 4 percent of 1995 revenue. In addition to purchasing all the necessary equipment (e.g., protective fighting gear), students could buy sweatshirts, T-shirts, jackets, duffel bags, and patches from the academy.

EXHIBIT 2   MBA Consulting Team's Youth Survey Results

1. How did you hear about Shorin-Ryu?

Child's friend	33%
Other parent	14
Advertising	21
YMCA program	32

2. If you looked at other schools, why did you choose Shorin-Ryu?

Jim/instruction	32%
Recommendation/reputation	14
Other	12
Didn't look at other schools	42

3. Why does your child take karate?

Likes it	13%
Self-esteem/confidence	43
Discipline	27
Fun/new skills	07
Other	10

4. What is your town of residence?

Waltham	56%
Newton	09
Watertown	12
Belmont	06
Other	17

5. What is your annual income?

Less than $20,000	06%
$21,000–30,000	13
$31,000–40,000	05
$41,000–50,000	18
Greater than $50,000	58

6. Do you have dual income in your household?

Yes	53%
No	47

7. Would you like to see the range of classes expanded?

Yes	39%
No	50
Undecided	11

8. Would you like to see the range of hours expanded?

Yes	27%
No	62
Undecided	11

9. How do you feel about the current size of classes?

Too small	00%
Too large	45
Just right	55

10. How does karate compare to other activities costwise?

Much less	34%
Less	21
Same	12
More	15
Much more	08
Undecided	10

11. How does karate compare to other activities timewise?

Much less	06%
Less	21
Same	42
More	26
Much more	01
Undecided	04

12. Does your child participate in other sports?

Yes	89%
No	11

13. Did you consider any other school(s) before joining Shorin-Ryu?

Yes	29%
No	71

14. Was Shorin-Ryu (as a style) important in your decision to join?

Yes	11%
No	89

15. Whose decision was it to join karate?

Parent	36%
Child	32
Both	32

16. Has either parent ever taken karate lessons?

Yes	15%
No	85

Qualitative Comments

"Jim is wonderful . . . he is inspirational, but he is the school. When he is not here, the level of instruction is not the same."

"I like the idea that the school is like a community with the kids getting involved in the parties, movies, and car washes and participating in walk-a-thons and bike-a-thons. It's great that the kids don't just go to and from classes and that's [the extent of their involvement]."

"Jim is wonderful!"

"I worry that my child will get bored with being a brown belt for so long."

from 3 to 10 PM weekdays and 9 AM to 1 PM Saturdays. Children's classes were taught in the afternoons and Saturday mornings; adult classes were taught in the evenings.

Regular programs included introductory special, 3- and 6-month trials, 12-month martial arts, black belt and junior black belt clubs, spring/summer vacation camps, women awareness, and private lessons. Monthly payment schedules were possible for

**Exhibit 3   Student Enrollment per Program,
January–April, 1996**

Program	*Number of Students*
Introductory special	0
3-month	10
6-month (1 class/week)	62
6-month (2 classes/week)	20
6-month family (1 class/week)	32
6-month family (2 classes/week)	2
12-month (1 class/week)	49
12-month (2 classes/week)	32
12-month family (1 class/week)	16
12-month family (2 classes/week)	17
Junior black belt (18 months)	16
Adult black belt (18 months)	13
24-month black belt	13
36-month black belt	3
Black belt, 18-month family	39

Source: Consulting report.

all but the introductory offering. However, to encourage payment in full, a 10 percent discount was offered if full tuition was paid at the start of the program. Additionally, upon request, Sensei Jim offered various demonstrations and martial arts talks to particular interest groups.[13] Birthday parties (including a martial arts demonstration) could be held at the academy. Exhibit 3 provides an overview of the number of students enrolled in various programs in the first half of 1996.

Introductory Special.   The $19.95 introductory special included a karate gi (uniform), a 30-minute private lesson, and a beginner's group lesson (with an appropriate age group). This introductory offer was designed to provide the prospective student with a sense of karate. Participation also allowed Sensei Jim to gauge the student's level of interest and maturity, which was particularly important with very young students.

Three- and Six-Month Trials.   These programs were available to the student who (or whose family) did not feel comfortable making a long-term commitment to learning karate. The three-month program was priced at $120, and the six-month program cost $390 for two lessons a week and $240 for one lesson a week. To encourage family member participation at the academy, the second family member received a 20 percent discount from the regular price, with each additional member receiving a 50 percent discount.

Twelve-Month Martial Arts Program.   This 12-month program was offered for the student who knew that she wanted to learn karate and advance through the various levels. The program was priced at $720 for two lessons per week and $420 for one lesson per week. Family memberships were $1,020 for two lessons per family member a week and $750 for one lesson per family member per week.

Black Belt Clubs.   The black belt clubs consisted of junior and adult academy members. Students in these clubs were required to attend three classes per week. Club members were eligible to join the SWAT (*S*tudents *W*orking *A*s *T*eachers) and demon-

---

[13] For example, Sensei Jim provided a martial arts demonstration to one student's Cub Scout troop. In addition to demonstrating various katas and weapons, Jim talked to the group about how to defend themselves against bullies. This demonstration resulted in one of the Cub Scouts becoming an active student at the academy.

stration teams and could participate in extra fighting and weapons classes.[14] Membership fees were $1,260 for 18 months, $1,560 for 24 months, and $1,980 for 36 months. An 18-month family black belt program was priced at $1,800.

Spring/Summer Vacation Camps.   The academy offered weeklong spring and summer vacation camps (9 AM to 2 PM) for students age six and above. Daily programs were designed to be both entertaining and a learning experience. A typical day included kata, kumite, karate kick ball, and karate stories. The price of the camp was $75 for one child per family, $135 for two children per family, and $185 for three children per family.

Women Aware.   This was a four-week program focusing on physical and psychological techniques designed to stop an attacker. The course was offered twice a year (October and May) at a price of $75.

Private Lessons.   Students could sign up for private lessons, which Sensei would give at a mutually convenient time. A 30-minute private lesson was $20, with a one-hour lesson priced at $35.

Extracurricular Activities.   Jim felt that even non-karate-practicing parents would want to participate in activities at the academy. The academy had a parent organization that planned and coordinated monthly events for the youth members. Examples of such activities included movie nights, holiday parties, pool parties, picnics, and field trips for the older youth.

Marketing Communications.   A major promotional event held at the academy was the "Bring a Friend" Week. During this week each student was asked to bring a friend to class.[15] The friend participated in all class activities and at the end of the session was recognized by Sensei Jim and provided with a packet of information about the academy. (The packet also included a karate belt key chain.) Historically, there had been 20 to 25 friends attending the academy during the promotional week. However, no follow-up or tracking of the program was conducted.

Consistent with most martial arts programs, Shorin-Ryu ran promotional events such as a free introductory lesson, half-price tuition for additional family members, and a free uniform with enrollment.

In 1995 the Shorin-Ryu Karate Academy spent $11,910 advertising in local newspapers, in the Yellow Pages, on cable TV, on shopping carts, and through direct mail. Exhibit 4 breaks down the expenditures for each medium.

The MBA consulting group working with Sensei Jim had utilized the information stored in Jim's student database to obtain an overall idea of student responsiveness to the academy's marketing communications effort. Exhibit 5 provides this overview. Additionally, the consulting team had tracked the communication media in relation to the geographic density of the academy's student base. Exhibit 6 relates this spending to customer attraction in Waltham, Newton, and Watertown.

Internal Operations.   Three major operating areas of the academy were staffing, financial management, and the membership renewal process.

In regard to staffing, Sensei Michael Pepe assisted Jim with classes whenever possible.[16] Other than Sensei Mike's help, Jim relied on students to help him with classes. As in all martial arts training programs, students worked as nonpaid instructors as part of their advanced training. Because of this volunteer nature, however, there was a lack of consistency in both the availability and the quality of help.

---

[14] Kobudo, the study of weapons, is considered karate's sister art.

[15] The friend (or parent) had to fill out and sign a disclaimer of liability (which included address and other demographic information) before participating in the class.

[16] Mike was a firefighter; karate was his avocation.

**EXHIBIT 4   Advertising Expenditures
by Medium, 1995**

Shopping cart	$ 1,310
Cable TV	1,667
Newspaper	3,811
Direct mail	2,501
Yellow pages	2,263
Other	358
Total	$11,910

Source: Consulting report.

**EXHIBIT 5   Student Responsiveness to Marketing
Communications**

Medium	Percentage of Student Base Response
Referral	45%
Newspaper	19
Yellow pages	15
YMCA program	11
Direct mail	05
Bring-a-Friend Week	03
Other	02

Source: Consulting report.

**EXHIBIT 6   Student Responsiveness to Marketing
Communications by Town**

Medium	Waltham	Newton	Watertown
Referral	48%	46%	38%
Newspaper	21	23	28
Yellow pages	2	—	7
YMCA program	24	23	10
Direct mail	2	8	7
Bring-a-Friend Week	1	—	4
Other	2	—	6

Source: Consulting report.

The academy utilized a cash basis of accounting. Under this method, revenues were recognized when cash was received and expenses were recognized when cash was expended. Company finances were maintained with the use of the QuickBooks software package. (See Exhibits 7 and 8 for the company's 1994 and 1995 financial statements and 1994–1996 balance sheet.)

Membership renewal was an important component of the academy's operational process. In the middle of each month, Jim used his student database to sort and develop a list of students whose memberships expired at the end of that month. Jim would print

EXHIBIT 7   Profit and Loss Statement, 1994–First Quarter 1996

	1994	*1995*	*1st Quarter 1996*
Income			
After school	$ 3,420.00	$ 3,595.00	$ 7,420.34
Camps	—	—	—
Vacation camp	—	$ 1,015.00	$ 510.00
Other	—	$ 2,220.00	—
Total camps	$ 1,485.00	—	—
Deposit 95	$ 10.00	$ 21,946.12	—
Reirrb Exp	($299.00)	—	—
Sales	$ 7,320.59	$ 6,653.56	$ 1,187.37
Seminars	$ 4,028.39	$ 3,645.00	—
Services	$ 296.16	$ 463.08	$ 63.00
Special rates	—	$ 792.00	—
Testing	$ 5,575.93	$ 3,645.00	$ 1,410.00
Tournaments	$ 7,445.49	$ 4,672.68	—
Tuition	—	—	—
ASKA Fee	—	$ 360.00	$ 150.00
Intro. lesson	$ 892.50	$ 439.05	$ 179.60
Down payments	$ 21,295.50	$ 21,666.00	$ 7,215.00
Monthly dues	—	$ 142.45	$ 13,307.35
Other	$ 99,598.44	$ 74,929.25	$ 7,407.00
Woman Aware	—	$ 375.00	$ 300.00
Total Income	$ 151,069.00	$ 146,559.19	$ 39,149.66
Expenses	—	$ 126.00	—
Accounting services			
Advertising	—	—	—
Newspaper ad	—	—	$ 939.78
Shopping cart sign	—	—	$ 177.50
Sign fee	—	$ 18.00	$ 9.00
Yellow Pages	—	—	$ 788.00
Other	—	$ 11,891.95	$ 200.00
Total advertising	$ 14,318.85	—	—
Auto	—	—	—
Auto gas	—	$ 919.79	$ 221.07
Jeep expense	—	$ 445.77	—
Registry renewal	—	—	$ 30.00
Other	—	$ 6,248.13	$ 1,474.25
Total auto	$ 17,474.12	—	—
Charges	—	—	—
Bank	$ 110.50	—	—
Other	$ 0.50	—	—
Total charges	—	—	—
Business expense	$ 1,517.44	$ 4,692.46	$ 1,352.52
Cleaning	$ 644.81	$ 616.05	$ 106.52
Contributions (donations)	$ 532.98	$ 382.29	—
Customer satisfaction	$ 195.00	—	—
Deposit correction	$ 14.55	($3.00)	—
Donation	$ 460.00	$ 321.48	$ 25.10
Dues	$ 2,302.73	$ 1,980.00	$ 500.00
Equipment rent	$ 334.00	$ 634.60	—
Giveaway	$ 1,527.42	$ 3,954.42	$ 498.22
Home insurance	$ 495.00	—	—

EXHIBIT 7   **Profit and Loss Statement, 1994–First Quarter 1996 (Continued)**

	1994	*1995*	*1st Quarter 1996*
Insurance	—	—	—
Insurance—building con't.	—	$ 318.00	—
Life insurance	—	—	$ 156.60
Other	—	$ 1,808.96	$ 316.74
Total insurance	$ 2,781.89	—	
Interest expense	—	—	—
Loan	($ 11,369.26)	($246.50)	—
Total interest expense	—	—	
Magazine subscription	—	$ 28.94	
Miscellaneous expense	—	$ 109.42	$ 10.35
New car	$ 1,615.00	$ 751.16	—
New home	$ 14,809.73	$ 7,178.85	
Office supplies	$ 2,138.20	$ 4,780.58	$ 374.75
Payout fees (travel)	—	$ 1,245.67	
Personal	$ 3,909.72	$ 13,399.72	$ 6,400.00
Printing	$ 148.03	$ 801.15	$ 221.88
Professional fees	$ 1,823.00	$ 907.76	$ 50.00
Refund	$ 45.00	$ 1,025.00	$ 95.00
Rent	$ 19,349.98	$ 25,899.96	$ 6,474.99
Repairs	—	—	
Building	—	$ 122.97	—
Other	—	$ 666.51	—
Total repairs	$ 3,719.76	—	—
Returned check	$ 928.95	$ 366.47	$ 50.00
School equipment	$ 8,316.37	$ 6,452.42	$ 267.88
Shipping and handling	$ 89.70	$ 463.82	$ 127.09
Special	$ 23,433.70	$ 4,509.00	$ 600.00
Supplies	$ 509.52	$ 6,619.13	$ 1,728.73
Travel and entertainment	—	—	
Meals	$ 84.58	$ 620.13	—
Travel	$ 357.00	$ 1,026.87	$ 1,597.50
Other	$ 511.50	$ 1,006.60	—
Total travel and entertainment	—	—	—
Taxes	—	—	—
Federal	$ 6,000.00	—	—
Local	$ 50.55	—	$ 73.81
Property	—	$ 21.31	
State	$ 1,910.00	$ 2,960.00	$ 1,452.00
Other	$ 28,044.27	$ 32,187.87	$ 184.21
Total taxes	—	—	—
Telephone	—	—	—
Car phone	—	$ 708.02	$ 137.05
Local	—	—	$ 109.27
Long distance	—	—	$ 47.18
Other	—	$ 1,585.79	$ 45.39
Total telephone	$ 3,335.30	—	—
Uncategorized	$ 6,634.48	—	—
Utilities	—	—	—
Electric	$ 1,979.24	$ 2,856.54	$ 733.03
Total Utilities	—	—	—
Wages	—	$ 5,800.00	$ 1,100.00
Total expenses	$ 161,084.11	$ 158,210.06	$ 28,675.41
Net income	($10,015.11)	($11,650.87)	$ 10,474.25

a hard copy of the renewal list. A renewal letter (Exhibit 9) and a listing of current karate programs were then handed to each of these students when they attended their next class. (Jim would highlight the program that he felt best suited the needs of the individual student.) Once a renewal letter was distributed, Jim would highlight (on his hard copy), in yellow, the name of the student who had received the letter.

Memberships were renewed at the student's own pace. Basically, students could renew their membership, could fail to renew and tell Sensei Jim that they would not be continuing in the program, or could fail to respond. Students who renewed membership or told Jim that they were not renewing were crossed off the renewal list. Students

---

EXHIBIT 8   Balance Sheet, December 31, 1994, 1995, 1996

	1994	*1995*	*1996*
Assets			
Current assets			
Checking/savings Shorin-Ryu	$ 24,575.50	$ 14,918.99	$ 27,235.47
Accounts Receivable	$ 1,626.00	($214.90)	($2,258.00)
Total current assets	$ 26,201.50	$ 14,704.09	$ 24,977.47
Total assets	$ 26,201.50	$ 14,704.09	$ 24,977.47
Liabilities & equity			
Liabilities			
Current liabilities			
Sales tax	$ 110.50	$ 238.71	$ 268.64
Total current liabilities	$ 110.50	$ 238.71	$ 268.64
Total liabilities	$ 110.50	$ 238.71	$ 268.64
Equity			
Earnings	—	($10,015.11)	($21,895.98)
Net income	($10,015.11)	($11,650.87)	$ 10,474.25
Open bal. equity	$ 36,106.11	$ 36,131.36	$ 36,130.56
Total equity	$ 26,091.00	$ 14,465.38	$ 24,708.83
Total liabilities & equity	$ 26,201.50	$ 14,704.09	$ 24,977.47

EXHIBIT 9   Renewal Letter

Dear Parents of _____ ,

I am writing to you as a reminder to let you know that your current karate program will be completed on the 30th of this month, 1996.

DON'T DELAY, take time NOW to decide on your next KARATE PROGRAM to further your KARATE EDUCATION!!!

I have enclosed a copy of our current karate programs and have highlighted the one that I feel would best help you maintain and achieve your short and long term goals of becoming a BLACK BELT.

If you have any questions, please feel free to call and discuss them with me. Thanks for your help and support in making the students and instructors of the SHORIN-RYU KARATE ACADEMY the BEST THAT THEY CAN BE!!!

YOURS IN KARATE-DO

SENSEI JAMES A. TRUE

EXHIBIT 10   Local Competition

School	Martial Arts	Monthly Price	Promotions	Student Enrollment
Waltham				
Bushido-Zen Martial Arts	Karate	$ 60	Free introductory lessons	15+
Chung Do Kwan-Tae Kwan Do	Tae kwon do	65	None	65
Integrated Martial Arts Development Center	Mixture	70	Free introductory lessons	<100
Masters Self Defense Center	Karate, tai chi, judo	50	2 weeks free & 1/2 off for 2ᵈ family member	200
Savoy School of Self Defense	Mixture	70	None	150
Villar's Self Defense Center	Mixture	35	2 weeks free & 1/2 off for 2ᵈ family member	65
Newton				
Chos Olympic Tae Kwon Do	Tae kwon do	90	1 month free introductory lessons	200
Chung Moo Doe	Chinese American	90	2 free lessons & free uniform for 3-month introductory lessons	100
Esposito's Academy of Self Defense	Karate	50	None	120
Masters of Karate	Karate	57	Free introductory lessons	150
Ye-Sheu Way of the Fist	Mixture	30	None	100
Watertown				
American Karate Academy	Karate	120	None	150
DiRico's Rocky School of Kempo Karate	Karate	60	2 half-hour private lessons for beginners	55
Tokyo Joe's Studio of Self Defense	Mixture	60	2 free introductory lessons & 1/2 off for 2ᵈ family member	65
Wah Lum Kung Fu Academy	Kung fu	50	Free introductory lessons	160

Source: Consulting report.

whose names were not crossed off the list eventually were transferred to the inactive student file. Jim estimated that about one-half of his students renewed their membership through this process.

Competition.   The MBA consulting group had identified 15 direct martial arts competitors in the three communities from which Shorin-Ryu derived a majority of its customers. Exhibit 10 identifies each of these competitors along with the type of martial arts instruction received, the monthly price, regular promotions offered, and the reported student enrollment.

The Academy's Future

Jim felt that with the help of the MBA consulting group, he had obtained a lot of valuable information. Additionally, the consulting group had made some recommendations based on its survey and secondary research.

A major recommendation was that to achieve Jim's objective of increasing enrollment by 175 students by the year 2000, Jim should target the youth segment (ages 5 through 17). The student team had gone so far as to provide information for this age group for Waltham, Newton, and Watertown. Basically, there were 6,119 individuals in Waltham, 10,887 in Newton, and 3,124 in Watertown in this age category. Among the youths in these towns, 0.25 percent (Newton), 2.30 percent (Waltham), and 0.93 percent (Watertown) were active students at Shorin-Ryu.

Jim wondered, however, if he could further penetrate this youth market. If so, what was the best approach? Also, should he focus on growing this market base and just try to maintain his adult market, or should he do something in the adult market as well?

A related issue was what (if anything) Jim needed to be doing to better manage his current (and future) business. Also, should he begin looking into that second location he had started dreaming about? If so, what communities would make sense?

The consulting team's information would go far in helping Jim look at the marketplace and issues that he needed to address. Sensei Jim was happy for the team and glad it had won the presentation competition. He had watched them in the preliminary round of the competition. The quality of their presentation had made him proud of them and also very proud of his business.

Sources

American Taekwondo Association. "Taking Martial Arts into the 21st Century to Set the Standard for Others to Follow." *Arkansas Business* (July 31, 1995): S18(1).

Cimons, Marlene. "A Mesmerized Mom Jumps into the Act." *Los Angeles Times* (September 26, 1995), sec. E, p. 1, col. 4.

Cimons, Marlene. "Kick Backs." *Los Angeles Times* (September 26, 1995), sec. E, p. 1, col. 4.

Condor, Bob. "Spirited Workout." *Chicago Tribune* (March 7, 1996), sec. 5, p. 4, col. 1.

Cutler, Blayne. "Where Does the Free Time Go?" *American Demographics* (November 1990): 36–39.

Dickey, Linda. "My Son, the Black Belt." *New York Times* (January 2, 1994), sec. CY, p. 11, col. 2.

Dolan, Carrie. "Health: Concern about Kids' Safety Spurs Rise in Karate and Other Fitness Programs." *The Wall Street Journal* (April 12, 1993), sec. B, p. 1, col. 3.

Ferguson, Tim W. "Let's Talk to the Master." *Forbes* (October 23, 1995): 138–42.

Fields, Suzanne. "Karate for Hansel and Gretel." *Washington Times* (April 19, 1993), sec. E, p. 1, col. 3.

Goodrich, Robert. "Heart Patients Take to Karate." *St. Louis Post Dispatch* (November 14, 1994), sec. I, p. 1, col. 5.

Graden, John. *Black Belt Management: Learn to Run a Highly Profitable School.* St. Petersburg, FL, National Association, Professional Martial Artists, January 1997.

Kadaba, Lini S. "New Corporate Kicks." *Chicago Tribune* (July 10, 1995), "Evening" sec., p. 7, col. 3.

Kata Consulting Group. "Shorin-Ryu Karate Academy" (May 1996), n.p. (used with permission of Sensei James True).

"Kicking the Habit." *The Economist* (November 20, 1993): 37.

Linke, Denise. "Families That Kick Together Stick Together." *Chicago Tribune* (February 26, 1993), sec. 2D, p. 1, col. 2.

McManus, Kevin. "Karate Chops for Children." *Washington Post* (August 21, 1992), sec. WW, p. 52, col. 1.

Mitchell, Kent. "Martial Art Tai Chi 'Meditation in Motion.'" *Atlanta Constitution* (August 30, 1991), sec. H, p. 4, col. 3.

Musante, Fred. "Where Discipline and Confidence Meet." *New York Times* (April 4, 1993), sec. CN, p. 12, col. 3.

Robinson, John P. "As We Like It." *American Demographics* (February 1993): 44–48.

Shaheen, Jacqueline. "Whether for Exercise or Self-Defense, More Women Take Up the Martial Arts." *New York Times* (November 7, 1993), sec. NJ, p. 1, col. 3.

"That's Entertainment." *American Demographics* (July 1993): 16.

Wexler, Natalie. "Karate Kids." *Washington Post* (July 7, 1996), sec. WMAG, p. 5, col. 1.

Case 3–6
Taurus Hungarian Rubber Works

Although Taurus had adjourned the three-day top management planning session conducted at its Lake Balaton retreat less than two years earlier, many major company decisions had been made since that time. Still, the basic implementation of the company's diversification strategy had not been accomplished. As director of the company's Corporate Development Strategic Planning Department, Gyula Bosnyak recognized both the timing and the importance of the events and issues involved. In early 1988 the Hungarian government had passed its Corporation Law, which put all state-owned firms on notice to reprivatize and recapitalize themselves. Not only did the firm have to deal with the mechanics of going public, it had to obtain the ideal mix of debt and equity capital to ensure solid growth for a company that was operating in a stagnant economy and a low-growth industry. Top management was also concerned about the route it should follow in its attempts to invigorate the company. It was an accepted fact that Taurus had to maintain or even improve its international competitiveness and that it had to diversify away from its traditional dependence on the manufacturing of truck and farm tires.

Rather than viewing this situation as a bothersome threat, Gyula had seen this as an opportunity for Taurus to deal with its working capital problem as well as to begin serious diversification efforts away from its basically noncompetitive and highly threatened commercial tire manufacturing operation. Now, in spring 1990, he was beginning to sort out his company's options before making his recommendations to both Laszlo Geza, vice president of Taurus's Technical Rubber Products Division, and Laszlo Palotas, the company's newly elected president.

Rubber and Rubber Production

Christopher Columbus was probably the first European to handle rubber. Haitian natives had used it for centuries to make a football-size sphere that they threw into a hole in the wall of a playing field. These balls were derived from a dried milky liquid obtained by cutting the bark of a "weeping wood," or cauchuc, tree. While the Haitians also used this substance to make shoes, bottles, and waterproof cloth, the Western world's commercial use of the product was limited until two discoveries greatly expanded rubber's usefulness and properties. In 1819 Thomas Hancock discovered that latex rubber could be masticated, which allowed it to be converted into products of different shapes by the use of pressure and the addition of other materials. Unfortunately, mastication deprived rubber of its elastic qualities.

The discovery of vulcanization by Charles Goodyear in 1839 solved this problem and also kept rubber products from becoming tacky. Goodyear found that the addition

This case was prepared by Joseph Wolfe, University of Tulsa; Gyala Bosnyak, Taurus Hungarian Rubber Works; and Janos Vecsenyi, International Management Center, Budapest. © 1990 University of Tulsa, Tulsa, Oklahoma, USA. Distributed by the European Case Clearing House Ltd, Cranfield Institute of Technology, Cranfield, Bedford MK43 OAL, England. This publication may not be reproduced, stored, transmitted or altered in any way without the written consent of the copyright owner, except as permitted under the Copyright, Designs and Patents Act 1988.

This case is intended for classroom discussion only, not to depict effective or ineffective handling of administrative situations. All rights reserved to the authors.

of sulfur to crude rubber at a temperature above its melting point improved rubber's mechanical properties and resistance to temperature changes. After these twin discoveries, the commercial uses of rubber multiplied greatly, with the greatest impetus coming from J. B. Dunlop's rediscovery of the pneumatic tire, which he applied to his son's bicycle in 1888. Shortly thereafter, the rise of the automobile industry at the century's turn resulted in a tremendous increase in the demand for rubber and its principal application in the manufacture of automobile and truck tires. The world's long ton consumption of rubber before World War II in approximate 30-year periods was as follows:

1840–1872	150,000
1873–1905	1,000,000
1906–1940	18,850,000

The production of natural rubber entails collecting the juice of the 60- to 80-foot-high *Hevea brasiliensis* tree, which is now plantation-grown in such tropical countries as Brazil, Malaysia, and Indonesia. The trees are tapped by cutting through the bark, which contains latex tubes. A flow of liquid amounting to about five pounds per year can be obtained from each tree. The milky substance is dehydrated for shipment by spraying and drying; by acidification, coagulation, washing, and rolling; or by drying it with smoke. Natural rubber usually is transformed into sheet or crepe. Sheet rubber is smoke-dried and turns a dark brown color, while crepe is air-dried, is much lighter in color, and is passed through heavy rollers at the beginning of the drying process.

As shown in Exhibit 1, a wide range of rubber applications can be obtained through the addition of various ingredients to latex rubber during its masticating or compounding manufacturing stages. Carbon black is added for high abrasion resistance, oils to make the material more workable, and paraffin for better light resistance. Other ingredients, such as antioxidants, activators, and various organic and inorganic coloring substances, are also employed, and various accelerators are used to (1) hasten the vulcanization process, (2) allow it to occur at room temperature, and (3) improve the product's ultimate quality.

Because of the tremendous increase in the need for natural rubber in the early 1920s and the realization of its strategic importance by both Germany and Russia from their World War I experiences, vigorous research into the creation of a synthetic rubber was conducted in the 1930s. The first butadiene-styrene copolymer from an emulsion system (Buna S) was prepared at the research laboratories of I.G. Farbenindustrie, followed shortly thereafter by the analogous butadiene-acrylonitrile copolymer (Buna N). By 1936, Germany was able to produce 100 to 200 tons of synthetic rubber a month; by 1939, the factories at Schkopau and Hüls could produce 50,000 tons per year.

EXHIBIT 1   Major Non-tire Rubber Uses

Mechanical goods	Hard rubber products
Latex foam products	Flooring
Shoe products	Cements
Athletic goods	Drug sundries
Toys	Pulley belts
Sponge rubber	Waterproof insulation
Insulated wire and cable	Conveyor belts
Footwear	Shock absorbers and vibration dampeners
Waterproofed fabrics	

EXHIBIT 2   **Predicted Demand for Synthetic Rubbers in 1992 (nonsocialist countries, in thousands of metric tons)**

Synthetic Rubber	Forecast
Styrene-butadiene*	2,819
Carboxylated styrene-butadiene	1,015
Polybutadiene	1,142
Ethylene-propylene diene	556
Polychloroprene	268
Nitrile	238
All others†	1,025
Total	7,063

Source: Adapted from International Institute of Synthetic Rubber Producers; Bruce F. Greek, "Modest Growth Ahead for Rubber," *Chemical & Engineering News* 66, no. 12 (March 21, 1988), p. 26.

*In both liquid and solid forms.

†Includes polyisoprene and butyl.

The "Buna" rubbers are produced by polymerizing butadiene, with sodium (natrium) acting as a catalyst. This process originally was conducted at a temperature of about 50° centigrade, but the copolymerization of butadiene and styrenes is now usually done in aqueous phase.[1] In an emulsion copolymerization process carried out at 50° centigrade, so-called *cold rubber,* the hydrocarbons to be polymerized are in emulsion and contain a constituent of the activator system dissolved in them. The second part of the activator system is present in the watery medium of the emulsion. The combined activator system initiates the process of polymerization, and the molecule size of the polymer is regulated by adding various substances. The entire process is stopped after about 60 percent of these substances have reacted. The resulting product is very much like latex rubber and from this phase on can be treated like the natural substance. A large variety of other synthetic rubbers can be produced in addition to the Buna rubbers. Exhibit 2 presents a forecast of the demand for these rubbers for the year 1992.

Combining both natural and synthetic rubbers, it has been estimated that world consumption of these substances will be about 15.9 million metric tons in 1992. According to William E. Tessmer, managing director of the International Institute of Synthetic Rubber Producers, this is an 11 percent increase from the 14.4 million tons estimated for 1987. As shown in Exhibit 3, about 70 percent of the world's rubber consumption is in the form of synthetic rubber. Exhibits 4 and 5 show the predicted geographic distribution of rubber demand for the year 1992.

Worldwide Rubber Company Competition

Rubber firms now compete on the international level because of a number of driving forces. Automobiles and trucks, which are the major users of tire and rubber products,

---

[1] *Polymerization* is a reaction involving the successive addition of a large number of relatively small molecules (monomers) to form a final compound or polymer. A *polymer* is a giant molecule formed when thousands of molecules have been linked together end to end. A *copolymer* is a giant molecule formed when two or more unlike monomers are polymerized together.

EXHIBIT 3   Predicted World Consumption of Rubber (in millions of metric tons)

Type	1986	1987	1988	1989	1990	1991	1992
Synthetic	9.5	9.8	9.8	9.9	9.9	10.0	10.0
Natural	4.5	4.6	4.9	5.1	5.4	5.7	5.9
Total	14.0	14.4	14.7	15.0	15.3	15.7	15.9

Source: Based on Bruce F. Greek, "Modest Growth Ahead for Rubber," *Chemical & Engineering News* 66, no. 12 (March 21, 1988), pp. 25–26.

Note: One metric ton equals 2,204.6 pounds.

EXHIBIT 4   Predicted Changes in Rubber Demand by Geographic Area (in thousands of metric tons)

Geographic Area	1987	1992	Change
North America	3,395	3,432	1.09%
Latin America	788	944	19.80
Western Europe	2,460	2,953	20.04
Africa & Middle East	259	324	25.10
Asia & Oceania	3,060	3,541	15.72
Socialist countries	4,057	4,706	16.00
Total	14,019	15,900	13.42%

Source: Based on Bruce F. Greek, "Modest Growth Ahead for Rubber," *Chemical & Engineering News* 66, no. 12 (March 21, 1988), p. 26.

EXHIBIT 5   Predicted Demand for Rubber in Socialist Countries (in millions of metric tons)

Socialist Group	1987	1992
Eastern European		
Synthetic	2.90	3.30
Natural	0.40	0.37
Total	3.30	3.67
Asian Socialist		
Synthetic	0.30	0.43
Natural	0.47	0.61
Total	0.76	1.04

Source: Based on Bruce F. Greek, "Modest Growth Ahead for Rubber," *Chemical & Engineering News* 66, no. 12 (March 21, 1988), pp. 25-26.

are ubiquitous; the high operating scales required for efficient plant operations compel manufacturers to find markets that can support them, and growth opportunities no longer exist in many of the manufacturers' home countries. As has been the case in its domestic automobile industry, the United States has been invaded by a number of very competitive and efficient foreign tire and rubber manufacturers. Those foreign competitors in turn have acquired firms or have entered into joint ventures on a global scale, increasing their penetration into a number of countries. Exhibit 6 displays the financial

EXHIBIT 6   **Selected Company Sales and Profits (in U.S. dollars)**

Company	1984		1988	
	Sales (billion)	*Profits (million)*	*Sales (billion)*	*Profits (million)*
B.F. Goodrich (U.S.)	$ 3.40	$ 60.6	NA*	NA
Bridgestone (Japan)	3.38	65.1	$ 9.30	$ 310.2
Cooper (U.S.)	0.56	23.9	0.73	35.0
Firestone (U.S.)	4.16	102.0	NA†	NA
GenCorp (U.S.)	2.73	7.2	0.50	NA‡
Goodyear (U.S.)	10.24	391.7	10.90	330.0
Michelin (France)	5.08	(256.5)	8.70	397.4
Pirelli (Italy)	3.50	72.0	7.01	172.1
Taurus (Hungary)	0.26	11.5	0.38	9.0
Uniroyal (U.S.)	2.10	77.1	2.19	11.8

Sources: *Akron Beacon Journal,* January 13, 1986, p. B8; "Powerful Profits around the World," *Fortune* 120, no. 3 (July 31, 1989), pp. 292, 294; Gary Levin, "Tire Makers Take Opposite Routes," *Advertising Age* 60, no. 6 (February 6, 1989), p. 34.
*Merged with Uniroyal in 1987.
†Acquired by Bridgestone in 1988.
‡Acquired by Continental in 1987.

results that have been obtained by the major world rubber manufacturers in 1984 and 1988; Exhibit 7 reviews the alternative strategies and recent actions of the industry's principal actors. As best as can be determined, Exhibit 8 demonstrates that Michelin has recently become the world's largest tire manufacturing firm, with a worldwide market share of 21.3 percent, with Goodyear and Bridgestone basically tied for second place in world sales.

Taurus Hungarian Rubber Works

Today's Taurus Hungarian Rubber Works has an ancestry dating back more than a century. From its earliest days with the founding of the factory by Erno Schottola, it has been Hungary's most important rubber producer. In growing to its current size, Taurus has both grown internally and acquired several smaller manufacturers.

The first Hungarian rubber factory was established in 1882, and in 1890 it became a public company under the name Magyar Ruggyantaarugyar Rt. Because Hungary lacked a domestic producer of automobiles at the turn of the century, the company supported the creation of an automobile plant, which was ultimately located in Arad, and the formation of the Autotaxi company in Budapest. During the period before World War I, Magyar Ruggyantaarugyar grew rapidly and was soon exporting between 30 percent and 35 percent of its products outside Hungary. Its rubber balls, toys, asbestos-rubber seals, and Palma heels gained a worldwide reputation for quality.

During the interwar period, the Hungarian rubber sector declined dramatically, with its export sales dropping to 15 to 18 percent of total production. Its factory equipment deteriorated, and only its lines of rubber yarns and latex products could remain internationally competitive. Pre–World War I global market shares of 0.6 percent fell to 0.3 percent, and its annual sales growth rates dropped to 1.5 to 2.0 percent per year.

After the nationalization of all rubber firms after World War II, the Hungarian government pursued a policy of extensive growth for a number of years. From 1950 to 1970

EXHIBIT 7   Recent Activities of Various Tire and Rubber Companies

Bridgestone Corporation: Bridgestone's acquisition of the Firestone Tire & Rubber Company in 1988 for $2.6 billion vaulted it into a virtual tie with Goodyear as the world's second largest tire company. The acquisition has been a troublesome one for Bridgestone, with Firestone losing about $100 million in 1989, causing the parent company's 1989 profits to fall to about $250 million on sales of $10.7 billion. Bridgestone has already invested $1.5 billion in upgrading Firestone's deteriorated plants, and an additional $2.5 billion will be needed to bring all operations up to Bridgestone's quality standards. Last year's North American sales were $3.5 billion, and the firm plans to quadruple the output of its La Vergne, Tennessee, plant. Currently, Bridgestone is attempting to increase its share of the American tire market while slowly increasing its share of the European market as Japanese cars increase their sales in that area. In mid-1989, nine top executives were forced to resign or accept reassignment because of disputes about the wisdom of the company's aggressive growth goals. Bridgestone is a major factor in Asia, the Pacific, and South America, where Japanese cars and trucks are heavily marketed.

Continental Gummi–Werke AG: Continental is West Germany's largest tire manufacturer and is number two in European sales. It purchased General Tire from Gencorp in June 1987 for $625 million and is basically known as a premium-quality tire manufacturer. Continental entered a $200 million joint radial tire venture in December 1987 with the Toyo Tire & Rubber Company and Yokohama Rubber Company for the manufacture of tires installed on Japanese cars being shipped to the American market. Another part of the venture entails manufacturing radial truck and bus tires in the United States.

Cooper Tire and Rubber Company: This relatively small American firm has been very successful by specializing in the replacement tire market. This segment accounts for about 80 percent of its sales, and nearly half of its output is sold as private-labeled merchandise. Cooper has recently expanded its capacity by 12 percent, with about 10 percent more capacity scheduled for completion in late 1990. About 60 percent of its sales are for passenger tires, while the remainder are for buses and heavy trucks. The company is currently attempting to acquire a medium truck tire plant in Natchez, Mississippi, to enable it to cover the tire spectrum more completely.

Goodyear Tire and Rubber Co.: The last of two major rubber companies left in the United States, Goodyear has diversified itself into chemicals and plastics, a California-to-Texas oil pipeline, and the aerospace industry. Automotive products, which include tires, account for 86 percent of sales and 76 percent of operating profits. Its recent sales growth has come from African and Latin American tire sales, where the company has a dominant market share. Additional plant expansions have been started in Canada and South Korea (12,000 tires daily per plant) and will be available in 1991 although they should not produce significant revenues until 1992. Goodyear is attempting to sell off its All America pipeline for about $1.4 billion to reduce its interest charges of $275 million per year on $3.5 billion worth of debt.

Michelin et Cie: Although it lost $1.5 billion between 1980 and 1984, Michelin has become profitable again. In late 1988, the company acquired Uniroyal/Goodrich for $690.0 million, which made it the world's largest tire company. Uniroyal had merged in August 1986 with the B.F. Goodrich Co., creating a company in which 29 percent of its output was in private brands. Passenger and light truck tires were sold in both the United States and overseas, and sales grew 44.5 percent although profits fell 11.1 percent. Michelin has entered a joint venture with Okamoto of Japan to double that company's capacity to 24,000 tires a day. While a large company, Michelin is much stronger in the truck tire segment than it is in the passenger tire segment.

Pirelli: After having been frustrated in its attempts to acquire Firestone, Pirelli purchased the Armstrong Tire Company for $190 million in 1988 to gain a foothold in the North American market. Armstrong, under the guise of Armtek Corporation, was attempting to diversify out of the tire industry by selling off its industrial tire plant in March 1987. Pirelli, which is strong in the premium tire market, obtained a company whose sales are equally divided between the original equipment and replacement markets and that has over 500 retail dealers. In the acquisition process Pirelli obtained a headquarters building in Connecticut, three tire plants, one tire textile plant, and one truck-tire factory. Armstrong's 1988 sales were $500 million.

EXHIBIT 8   Top Market Shares in World Tire Market

Company	1985	1990
Goodyear	20.0%	17.2%
Michelin	13.0	21.3
Bridgestone	8.0	17.2

Source: Adapted from Stuart J. Benway, "Tire & Rubber Industry," *The Value Line Investment Survey* (December 22, 1989), p. 127.

annual production increases of 12.5 percent a year were common, while the rubber sector's employment and gross fixed asset value increased an average of approximately 6.2 percent and 15.7 percent per year, respectively. Although growth was rapid, great inefficiencies were incurred. Plant utilization rates were low, and productivity ratios lagged by about 1.5 to 3.0 times those obtained by comparable socialist and advanced capitalist countries. Little attention was paid to rationalizing either production or the product line as sales to the Hungarian and Eastern bloc countries appeared to support the sector's activities. At various times, the nationalized firm produced condoms, bicycle and automobile tires, rubber toys, boots, and raincoats.

During this period the government also restructured its rubber industry. In 1963, Budapest's five rubber manufacturers—PALMA, Heureka, Tauril, Emerge, and Cordatic—were merged into one company called the National Rubber Company, and new locations in Vac, Nyiregyhaza, and Szeged were created. Purchasing, cash management, and investment were centralized, and a central trade and research and development apparatus was created. Contrary to the normal way of conducting its affairs, however, the company pioneered the use of strategic planning when the classic type of centralized planning was still the country's ruling mechanism.

In 1973, the company changed its name to the Taurus Hungarian Rubber Works, and it currently operates rubber processing plants in Budapest, Nyiregyhaza, Szeged, Vac, and Mugi as well as a machine and mold factory in Budapest.

As shown in Exhibits 9 through 12, Taurus operates four separate divisions while engaging in a number of joint ventures. Sales have increased annually to the 20.7 billion forint mark with an increasing emphasis on international business.

Tire Division.   The tire division manufactures tires for commercial, nonpassenger vehicles after having phased out its production of automobile tires in the mid-1970s. Truck tires, as either bias-ply or all-steel radials, account for about 34 percent of the division's sales. Farm tires are its other major product category as either textile radials or bias-ply tires. Farm tires accounted for about 20 percent of the division's sales in 1988. A smaller product category includes tire retreading, inner tubes, and forklift truck tires. About 58 percent of the division's volume consists of export sales, of which the following countries have accounted for the greatest amounts (in millions of forints):

United States	351.7
Algeria	298.2
Czechoslovakia	187.3
West Germany	183.5
Yugoslavia	172.0

The division recently finished a World Bank–financed capacity expansion in the all-steel radial truck tire operation. This project began in December 1986. Eleven new tires within the Taurus Top Tire brand have been scheduled for the market, of which two were completed in 1988 and another three in early 1990. The division is also developing a new supersingle tire under a licensing agreement with an American tire manufacturer.

Technical Rubber Division.   This division manufactures and markets an assortment of rubber hoses, air springs for trucks and buses, conveyor belts, waterproof sheeting, and the PALMA line of camping gear. The PALMA camping gear line has a 15 percent world market share, while the company's rotary hose business is a world leader with 40 percent of all international sales. The demand for high-pressure and large-bore

EXHIBIT 9   Taurus Hungarian Rubber Works Organization Structure

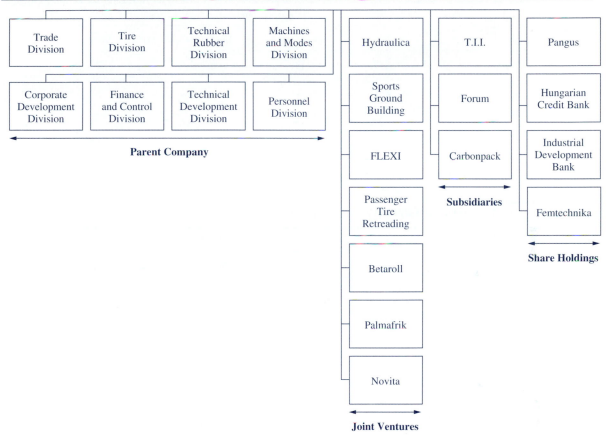

Source: *1988 Annual Report,* p. 17.

EXHIBIT 10   Total Company Sales (selected years; in millions of forints)

Market	1981	1983	1985	1986	1987	1988	1989	1990
Export	2,560	2,588	3,704	4,055	4,517	5,349	6,843	7,950
Domestic	7,890	9,024	9,381	9,979	11,174	12,255	12,056	12,716
Total	10,450	11,612	13,085	14,034	15,691	17,604	18,899	20,666

Source: *1988 Annual Report* and internal company data.

hoses is closely related to offshore drilling activity, while the sale of air springs for commercial vehicles is expected to increase as this technology gains increasing acceptance with vehicle manufacturers. The former Soviet Union is this division's largest customer, with 1989 sales of 380 thousand forints. In recent years, sales within the division have been distributed in the following fashion:

EXHIBIT 11   Selected 1988 Division Performance Information (in millions of forints)

	Division			
Item	*Tires*	*Technical Rubber*	*Machines and Molds*	*Trade*
Revenues	6,591	6,484	212	5,612
Assets				
Gross fixed assets	5,201	2,756	268	—
Net fixed assets	2,934	1,199	123	—
Inventories	1,024	601	100	—
Employees	3,987	3,912	557	208

Note: Machine and mold sales include output used in-house.

EXHIBIT 12   Selected 1989 Division Performance Information (in millions of forints)

	Division			
Item	*Tires*	*Technical Rubber*	*Machines and Molds*	*Trade*
Revenues	8,547	7,183	242	4,694
Assets				
Gross fixed assets	5,519	2,787	292	—
Net fixed assets	3,016	1,120	135	—
Inventories	1,126	545	104	—
Employees	4,021	3,851	552	198

Note: Machine and mold sales include output used in-house.

Large-bore high-pressure hoses	6.7%
Rotary hoses	27.1
Hydraulic hoses	14.7
Camping goods	18.0
Waterproof sheeting	13.9
Air springs	5.3
Conveyor belts	14.3

Machine and Molds Division.   This division manufactures products that are used in-house as part of Taurus's manufacturing process as well as products used by others. About 70 percent of its sales are for export, and its overall sales were distributed as follows in 1988:

Technical rubber molds	24%
Polyurethane molds	17
Machines and components	25
Tire-curing molds	34

Trade Division.   The Trade Division conducts Eastern European purchases and sales for Taurus as well as performing autonomous distribution functions for other firms. Its activities serve both Taurus's other divisions and those outside the company. It is expected that this division will continue to function as Taurus's purchasing agent while increasing its outside trading activities; its status with regard to trading in the former Eastern bloc is in a state of flux.

Implementing Taurus's Strategy of Strategic Alliances

Immediately after returning from his company's top management conference, Gyula began collecting materials to confirm the tentative decisions that had been made at Lake Balaton. By examining the secondary data collected and assembled into Exhibits 13 and 14, he could see that the general rubber industry had fallen from a better than average industry growth performance in the 1960–1970 period to one that was far inferior to the industrial average during the 1980–1990 period. He also saw that other industries, such as data processing, aircraft, medical equipment, and telecommunication equipment, had obtained sizable growth rates from 1977 to 1988. Moreover, he was extremely aware of the increasing concentration occurring in the tire industry through the formation of joint ventures, mergers, cooperative arrangements, and acquisitions. It was obvious that at least the rubber industry's tire segment had passed into its mature stage. In response to

EXHIBIT 13   **Comparative Average Annual Growth Rates**

Period	Rubber Sector	All Industry
1960–1970	8.3%	6.8%
1970–1980	4.0	4.1
1980–1990	1.7	4.3
Average	4.7%	5.1%

Source: Internal company report.

EXHIBIT 14   **Ten-Year Growth Rates for Selected Industries (1977 to 1988)**

Sector	Annual Growth Rate
Data processing equipment	21.0%
Transistors	17.0
Aircraft	16.0
Medical equipment	15.0
Measuring and control equipment	13.5
Electronic games	13.2
Telecommunication equipment	12.9
Metal processing equipment	10.4
Synthetic fibers	7.8
Steel	7.4
Building materials	7.3
Fertilizers	7.0
Agricultural equipment	4.5
Coal	3.2
Passenger cars	2.5
Crude oil	0.5

Source: Internal report.

this situation, most major rubber companies had diversified away from the heavy competition within the industry as well as attempting to find growth markets for their rubber production capacity. For the year 1988 alone, Gyula listed the various strategic alliances shown in Exhibit 15, while Exhibit 16 reviews the diversification activities of Taurus's major tire competitors in 1990.

Within the domestic market, various other Hungarian rubber manufacturers had surpassed Taurus in their growth rates as they jettisoned their low-profit lines and adopted newer ones with higher growth rates. Taurus's market share of the Hungarian rubber goods industry had slowly eroded since 1970, and this erosion increased greatly in the decade of the 1980s due to the creation of a number of smaller start-up rubber companies encouraged by Hungary's new private laws. While the company's market share stood at about 68 percent in 1986, Gyula estimated that Taurus's market share would

---

EXHIBIT 15   Strategic Alliances in 1988

Goodrich (USA) and Uniroyal (Great Britain) operate as a joint venture.

Pirelli (Italy) acquired Armstrong (USA).

Firestone (USA) acquired by Bridgestone (Japan), which has another type of alliance with Trells Nord (Sweden).

General Tire (USA) acquired by Continental Tire (West Germany), which in turn operates in cooperation with Yokohama Tire (Japan). Continental also owns Uniroyal Englebert Tire.

Toyo (Japan) operates in cooperation with Continental Tire (West Germany) while also operating a joint venture in Nippon Tire (Japan) with Goodyear (USA).

Michelin (France) operates in cooperation with Michelin Okamoto (Japan).

Sumitoma (Japan) operates in cooperation with Nokia (Finland), Trells Nord (Sweden), and BTR Dunlop (Great Britain).

Source: Corporate annual reports.

EXHIBIT 16   Rubber Company Diversification

Rubber Company	Nontire Sales (%)	Major Diversification Efforts
Goodyear	27%	Packing materials
		Chemicals
Firestone	30	Vehicle service
Cooper	20	Laser technology
Armstrong	NA	Heat transmission equipment
General Tire	68	Electronics
		Sporting goods
Carlisle	88	Computer technology
		Roofing materials
Bridgestone	30	Chemicals
		Sporting goods
Yokohama	26	Sporting goods
		Aluminum products
Trelleborg	97	Mining
		Ore processing
Aritmos	NA	Food processing
Nokia	98	Electronics
		Inorganic chemicals

Note: Major diversifications as of 1990.

fall another 3 percent by 1992. Exhibit 17 displays the figures and estimates he created for his analysis.

With the aid of a major consulting firm, Taurus had recently conducted the in-depth analysis of its business portfolio shown in Exhibit 18. It was concluded that the company operated in a number of highly attractive markets but that the firm's competitive position needed to be improved for most product lines. Accordingly, the firm's emphasis was to be placed on improving the competitiveness of the company's current product lines and businesses. In 1991 Taurus was to implement two types of projects: software projects dealing with quality assurance programs, management development, staff training efforts, and the implementation of a management information system and hardware projects dealing with upgrading the agricultural tire compounding process as well as upgrades in the infrastructures of various plants.

EXHIBIT 17   Distribution of Rubber Goods Production between Taurus and All Other Hungarian Rubber Manufacturers

	Percent of Market			
Manufacturer	*1970*	*1980*	*1986*	*1992*
Taurus	95%	80%	68%	65%
All others	5	20	32	35

Source: Internal company data for years 1970 to 1986 and personal estimate for 1992.

EXHIBIT 18   The Taurus Portfolio

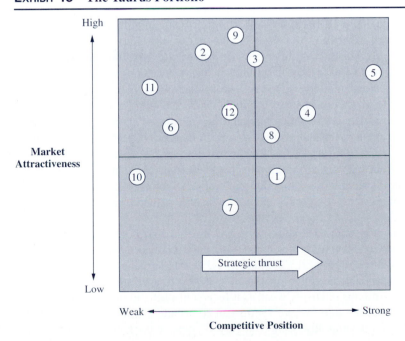

1. Bias tires
2. Steel radial truck tires
3. Agricultural tires
4. Rotary hoses
5. Special hoses
6. Conveyor belts
7. Camping mattresses
8. Rubber sheets
9. Air springs
10. V-belts
11. Precision technical rubber
12. Machines and molds

Source: Company documents and consulting group's final report.

EXHIBIT 19   Taurus's Strategy for the 90s

The decade of the 1990s is predicted to be a busy stage of the rubber sector worldwide.

There are strong factors of concentration in traditional manufacturing business(es), particularly in tire operations. The role of substitute products is growing in several areas. On the other hand, the fast end-of-century growth of industrial sectors is expected to stimulate the development of sophisticated special rubber products. In the face of these challenges, Taurus bases its competitive strategy on the following:

A continuous structural development program has been started aimed at *increasing the company's competitive advantage,* with the scope to cover a range from manufacturing processes, through quality assurance, to the reinforcement of strengths and elimination of weaknesses.

Efficiency is a prerequisite of any business activity. The company portfolio must be kept in good balance.

Associated with profitability, the company keeps developing its sphere of operations, determining the direction of diversification according to the criteria of potential growth and returns.

Our pursuit of competitive advantages and diversification must be supported by a powerfully expanding *system of strategic alliance and cooperation.*

Source: Taurus's *Annual Report.*

Fundamental to Taurus's desire to be more growth-oriented was the newly enunciated strategy shown in Exhibit 19. As formally stated, the company was seeking strategic alliances for certain business lines rather than growth through internal development, which had been its previous growth strategy. While it was felt that internal development possessed lower risks, as it basically extended the company's current areas of expertise, benefited the various product lines already in existence, and better served the present customer base while simultaneously using the company's store of management knowledge and wisdom, internal development presented a number of impediments to Taurus's current desires for accelerated growth. Paramount was its belief that management was too preoccupied with its current activities to pay attention to new areas outside its specific areas of expertise.

Now ranked at thirtieth in size in the rubber industry, Taurus found it was facing newly formed international combinations with enormous financial strength, strong market positions, and diverse managerial assets. Given the high degrees of concentration manifesting themselves in the rubber industry and the fact that even the largest firms have had to establish international cooperative relationships, Taurus determined that it too should seek cooperative, strategic alliances. In seeking those affiliations, the company would be very open and responsive to any type of reasonable alternative or combination that might be offered. These alliances could include participating with companies currently in operation or creating new, jointly held companies, whether related or unrelated to the rubber industry. The only real criteria for accepting an alliance would be its profitability and growth potential.

In pursuing strategic alliances, Gyula notes that Taurus's bargaining position differs greatly between the various business lines in its portfolio. As an aid to understanding its bargaining strategy with potential allies, Taurus's businesses are placed into one of the three categories shown in Exhibit 20. Category I types are those where Taurus's bargaining position is relatively weak as it feels it has little to offer a potential suitor. Category II types are those where Taurus can contribute a sizable "dowry" and has much to offer the potential ally, while category III types are businesses with mixed or balanced strengths and weaknesses.

EXHIBIT 20 Cooperation Potentials by Product Line

Product Lines	Cooperation Category		
	I	II	III
Truck tires	•		
Farm tires			•
Rotary hoses		•	
Specialty hoses			•
Hydraulic hoses	•		
Waterproofing sheets		•	
Belting	•		
Camping goods			•
Air springs			•
Machines and molds		•	
Precision goods			•

Source: Internal company report.

The problem now becomes the restructuring of the company's current divisions to make them into rational and identifiable business units to outside investors as well as serving Taurus's need for internal logic and market focus. Which product lines should be grouped together, and what should be the basis for their grouping? Gyula saw several different ways to do this. Products can be grouped on the basis of a common production process or technology. The groupings can be based on their capital requirements, markets served, or trade relations that have already been established by Taurus. Depending on how he defines the company's new strategic business units (SBUs), he knows he will be making some major decisions about the attractiveness of the company's assets as well as defining the number and the nature of Taurus's potential strategic alliances. As he explained,

> If I create an SBU that manufactures hoses, a good joint venture partner might be someone who manufactures couplings for hoses—this would be a match that would be good for both of us, and it would be a relatively safe investment. If, on the other hand, I create a business that can use the same hoses in the offshore mining and drilling business, and this is a business that is really risky but one that could really develop in the future, what do I look for in partners? I need to find an engineering company that's creating large mining exploration projects. For every type of combination like this I can create, I have to ask myself each time, "What are the driving questions?"

In reviewing the company's portfolio, he immediately saw three new SBUs he could propose to Laszlo Geza, vice president of the Technical Rubber Division. One SBU will serve the automobile industry through the manufacture of rubber profiles (rubber seals and grommets) that provide watertight fits for car windows; V-belts for engines and engine components such as air-conditioning, power steering, and electrical units; and special engine seals. Another unit would serve the truck and bus industry by manufacturing the bellows for articulated buses and air springs for buses, heavy-duty trucks, and long-haul trailers. The last newly created SBU will target the firm's adhesives and rubber sheeting at the construction and building industry, where the products can be used to waterproof flatroofs as well as serve as chemicalproof and watertight liners in irrigation projects and hazardous waste landfill sites.

Although top management knows that "the house is not on fire" and that a careful and deliberate pace can be taken regarding the company's restructuring, Gyula wants to make sure the proposals he is about to make are sound and reasonable. Moreover the success or failure of this restructuring will set the tone for Taurus's future diversification efforts.

Sources

Benway, S.J. "Tire & Rubber Industry." *The Value Line Investment Survey* (December 22, 1989), p. 127.

Garvey, B.S., Jr. "History and Summary of Rubber Technology." In *Introduction to Rubber Technology,* ed. M. Morton. New York: Reinhold, 1959, pp. 1–43.

Greek, B.F. "Modest Growth Ahead for Rubber." *Chemical & Engineering News* 66, no. 12 (March 21, 1988), pp. 25–29.

Thompson, A.A., Jr. "Competition in the World Tire Industry." In *Strategic Management: Concepts and Cases,* A.A. Thompson, Jr., and A.J. Strickland. Homewood, Ill.: Richard D. Irwin, 1990, pp. 518–48.

APPENDIX 1
FINANCIALS

Taurus Hungarian Rubber Works Income Statements for 1988–1990 (in millions of forints; year ended December 31)

	1988*	1989	1990
Basic activities	10,637.7	12,193.4	14,918.6
Nonbasic activities	6,270.0	6,705.5	5,747.0
Total revenues	16,907.7	18,898.9	20,665.6
Direct costs	12,022.1	13,095.0	13,819.6
Indirect costs	4,235.6	4,963.3	5,714.8
Production and operating costs	16,257.7	18,058.3	19,534.4
Before-tax profit	650.0	840.6	1,131.2
Taxes	290.0	386.0	491.4
After-tax profit	360.0	454.6	639.8

*1988 data adjusted for better comparability to reflect the effects of tax changes initiated in 1989.

Taurus Hungarian Rubber Works Balance Sheets for 1988–1990 (in millions of forints; year ended December 31)

	1988*	1989	1990
Assets			
Cash, bank deposits, and receivables	2,491.1	3,157.0	3,763.2
Inventories	2,749.6	2,803.8	2,888.3
Other current assets and capital investments	577.4	739.7	938.6
Current assets	5,818.1	6,700.5	7,590.1
Property	2,480.7	2,772.0	3,008.6
Machines and equipment	4,718.2	6,202.6	6,357.9
Fleet	46.3	46.4	48.6
Other	27.9	25.9	25.6
Fixed asset value	7,273.1	9,046.9	9,440.7
Accumulated depreciation	3,977.0	4,303.8	4,687.7
Unaccomplished projects	541.4	272.2	541.6
Total fixed assets	3,837.5	5,015.3	5,294.6
Total assets	9,655.6	11,715.8	12,884.7
Liabilities			
Short-term loans	1,531.7	1,684.3	1,444.0
Accounts payable	922.7	1,378.5	2,072.8
Accrued expenses	95.8	141.4	151.6
Provisions for taxes	(274.1)	195.0	34.7
1989 long-term debt service	267.0	129.9	314.3
Other liabilities due within 12 months	58.0	5.4	242.1
Total current liabilities	2,601.1	3,534.5	4,259.5
Provisions and noncurrent liabilities	61.4	335.1	.4
Long-term loans	725.4	1,453.1	1,815.7
Equities and funds reserves	5,907.7	5,938.5	6,169.2
Current year after-tax profit	360.0	454.6	639.8
Total equity and funds	6,267.7	6,393.1	6,809.0
Total liabilities	9,655.6	11,715.8	12,884.6

*1988 data adjusted for better comparability to reflect the effects of tax changes initiated in 1989.

It's a beautiful warm spring evening in downtown Austin, Tex., and the patrons are flitting around Serranos bar and restaurant, eyeing name tags and ordering $5 frozen margaritas. More than 1,000 people are here for Austin's High-Tech Happy Hour, a monthly schmooze fest. Most work for the local dot-coms springing up all over, but nearly everyone wishes they worked for Vignette Corp. "Vignette is the dot-com that made it," says Harry Pape, 32, a freelance marketing consultant and longtime Austin resident who cofounded the happy hour. "They're the example that everyone looks up to."

Granted, Vignette may not be a household name like Yahoo! or eBay. But when it comes to the Web, Vignette's software plays a crucial behind-the-screens role. Vignette makes software that helps companies publish and manage content on the Internet and elsewhere. Sounds simple, but consider this: Today there are nearly 1 billion Web pages, and 3 million new ones are being unleashed every day. If this material were not carefully indexed and delivered by software from companies like Vignette, the Web would look like a giant Jackson Pollock painting.

Tending to all that Web content has placed Vignette at the vanguard of the New Economy. Since going public in February, 1999, the five-year-old company's stock has spiked more than 1,500%, from $19 to a split-adjusted $300, giving Vignette a market capitalization of nearly $9 billion—even after Wall Street's recent oscillations. Its market cap is bigger than any other Web software company except BroadVision Inc., whose valuation nears $11 billion. And its 700-customer base is more than double its closest rival. In the quarter ended Mar. 31, Vignette reported $55.2 million in revenues, up 505% from the year-ago quarter, and an operating loss of $5.3 million. Analysts expect the company to turn profitable by the fourth quarter.

Soup to Nuts

But Vignette CEO Gregory A. Peters has his eye on bigger pastures. The 40-year-old former All-American high-school quarterback from Little Rock says he wants Vignette to "become the fastest software company in the world to reach $1 billion in revenue." The record, held by security-software maker Network Associates Inc., is nine years. Peters figures he can do it in seven or eight. To get there, he must transform Vignette into a soup-to-nuts e-business software supplier, offering clients the ability to run their entire business online, from sales to customer service to marketing. Throughout this year, Peters will roll out software to handle online billing and payments, as well as ways for merchants to track thousands of orders (Exhibit 1).

The prize for pulling off this transformation is huge. E-business software is predicted to mushroom into an $18 billion market by 2003, up 300% from $6 billion this year, according to Banc of America Securities. With so many greenbacks up for grabs, the market is fiercely competitive, and growing more so every day. Vignette faces tough rivals such as BroadVision, which specializes in building online stores; Art Technology

Source: *Business Week* e.biz/June 5, 2000

EXHIBIT 1   **Handicapping Vignette**

Vignette is the leading maker of software to manage Web content. Now it wants to morph into an all-in-one e-business software shop. Through its own development and partnerships, the company plans this year to add applications to run every aspect of an online business. As Vignette expands, here are its prospects:

Content Management Software
These programs are essential if companies are going to organize and manage thousands of pages and dozens of Web sites.
Market Size: $917 million this year, growing to $2.5 billion by 2003.
The Competition: Vignette is the leader. But BroadVision is getting into this business through its Interleaf acquisition. And Interwoven's software is gaining popularity. Still, Vignette's momentum will make it hard for rivals to gain much traction.

E-commerce
Web companies need software to help build product catalogs for online stores, collect payments, and track deliveries.
Market Size: By yearend, this business will hit $2 billion and skyrocket to $4.4 billion by 2003.
The Competition: A definite weakness for Vignette. BroadVision is No. 1 here. To gain ground, Vignette is partnering with IBM for e-commerce and database software. Art Technology Group's software has a strong following, too.

Online Marketing
This software helps marketeers segment customers by profitability, time spent on the site, or pages visited.
Market Size: Expected to reach $564 million this year. It will more than triple, to $1.9 billion, by 2003.
The Competition: E.piphany is the Big Kahuna here, but Vignette has a chance to catch up by releasing its own relationship marketing software based on technology it gained through the January acquisition of DataSage.

Customer Service
These programs automate customer-service tasks such as responding to e-mail queries about billing, deliveries, or products.
Market Size: By yearend, this will be a $433 million market, ballooning to $1.8 billion by 2003.
The Competition: Kana Communications' software is tops. Vignette will release its software later this year. Unless it's a quantum improvement over Kana's, it's not apt to gain much ground.

Source: Banc of America Securities, *Business Week.*

Group, which sells e-commerce software to build Web pages; and fellow content manager Interwoven. And it's only a matter of time before it butts heads with giants such as Oracle Corp. and SAP as they create new software to run online businesses. "There will only be two or three [software] companies that survive the e-business wars," predicts BroadVision Executive Vice-President Rani Merritt.

Peters is unfazed. Colleagues say he's the Gary Cooper of Web software—the strong but silent type. "Greg is very self-effacing," says Laurie Frick, Vignette's senior vice-president for marketing. And he's not one to duck a challenge. In 1996, three weeks after becoming the chief financial officer of Logic Works Inc., a database-software company, it failed to meet Wall Street's earnings expectations, and its stock nosedived. "I was like, 'I can't believe I moved my whole family to Princeton, N.J., for a catastrophe,'" recalls Peters, who today likes to kick back on his 24-foot boat with his wife and two kids. He got the company back on its feet before selling it to Platinum Technology International, Inc. for $175 million in March, 1998.

Peters has a different ending in mind for Vignette. From his first days there, he has built a strong service organization to hold customers' hands. Now, he's shoring up Vignette's product gaps by crafting a series of technology and marketing partnerships. In a ringing endorsement of its products and strategy, Andersen Consulting agreed on Apr. 10 to train 500 consultants to install and maintain Vignette's software, and, *Business Week* has learned, if the deal is successful, Andersen will take a minority stake in the company. Last September, Vignette teamed up with IBM to integrate Big Blue's e-commerce software with Vignette's programs. This will offer Vignette's customers software for online billing, electronic catalogs, and a simplified way to track thousands of orders at once.

Chaos

The strategy seems to be working. On May 10, Vignette landed its largest deal ever, a $10 million order from Telefónica's Terra Networks to manage the content for the Spanish Internet service provider. At the same time, current customers such as First Union Corp. are eager for the new software. "We've been very pleased," says Parrish Arturi, a vice-president of First Union Corp. "But we're more excited" about the new applications.

Vignette's path wasn't always so clear. The startup was founded in late 1995 by Ross Garber and Neil Webber, friends who had worked together at Austin printer-management software outfit Dazel Corp. (Exhibit 2). With little idea of what they wanted to do, the duo cold-called 300 businesses trying to identify big problems that needed to be solved. The message: Help us bring order to the chaos of Web publishing.

Garber called CNET Networks Inc., because he knew the tech-news and retail site had developed its own sophisticated online publishing system. The two companies struck a deal: In exchange for $500,000 and a 35% equity stake in Vignette, CNET sold Vignette the patent, source code, and all future development rights to its Web publishing system. That investment is worth some $150 million today. "Besides CNET and Snap [CNET's Web portal], Vignette is one of the three things I'm most proud of," says CNET Chairman Halsey Minor.

EXHIBIT 2   Meet Vignette Corp.

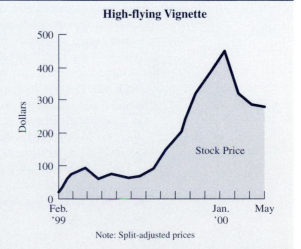

Founded: 1995

What It Does: Vignette makes software that helps companies manage and publish content on the Net and elsewhere. The software also enables Web sites to craft personalized pages on the fly, realizing the Net's promise of one-to-one marketing.

Financial Performance: In 1999, Vignette lost $42.5 million on sales of $82.9 million. But analysts expect the company to turn profitable by this year's fourth quarter, earning $6 million on annual revenues of $280 million, a 335% year-over-year revenue growth rate. Thanks to the Nasdaq plunge, Vignette's current stock price, in the $50 range, is well off its 52-week high of $100. Still, the company's market capitalization of around $9 billion is the highest of any Web software firm except BroadVision, whose market cap nears $11 billion.

Financial Prospects: Vignette dominates the content-management market. A $1 billion market this year, analysts expect it to reach $2.5 billion in 2003. But the company wants to reach $1 billion in sales in two or three years, making it the fastest software company ever to do so. To get there, Vignette aims to become an all-in-one supplier of e-commerce software, with applications for sales, customer service, and marketing. And it just might succeed. Thirteen of the 16 analysts covering Vignette rate it a strong buy—with three recommending buy ratings.

High-flying Vignette

Note: Split-adjusted prices

Source: Commodity Systems Inc.

"Hot Sites"

The deal gave Vignette the launchpad it needed. Within three months, the company was shipping product. By mid-1998, realizing the company had become too complex for them to run, the two founders stepped down from day-to-day management, and in came Peters.

Since coming on board as employee No. 115 in June, 1998, Peters has sharpened the company's focus on customer service. Today, Vignette is a 1,300-person organization, with nearly 40% of its employees in service-oriented jobs. At the weekly senior-management meeting, the first item of business Peters discusses is "hot sites"—customers that are having trouble with the company's products. Peters also designed a way to make the sales staff sensitive to customer needs: As much as a quarter of a sales-person's salary is tied to customer satisfaction. And rather than booking revenue after shipping its software or during the period when customers are installing its programs—as most software companies do—Vignette records a sale when the software is up and running. This keeps Vignette employees focused on ensuring buyers' satisfaction. "We'll bend over backward, and then bend over some more, to make the customer successful," says Vignette's Senior Vice-President for Development Bill Daniel.

That doesn't mean every deal goes smoothly. "They're making all the right moves now, but it was initially painful," notes Jan Hier-King, a senior vice-president for Charles Schwab Corp., one of Vignette's first big customers. The launch date of Smart Investor, Schwab's new personal finance Web site, has been pushed back six months, says Hier-King, partly because Vignette wasn't familiar with the product-development procedures, security systems, and legal and regulatory requirements of a big firm like Schwab. It is now.

Nor does Peters want Vignette to get caught flat-footed when it comes to technology. His engineers have developed a pack of applications that includes a search engine and a bookmark tool that lets customers quickly access the content they want. And, until Vignette can offer more home-grown software, it's partnering with other companies to fill out its offerings. An alliance with Inktomi, for example, will help e-commerce companies distribute content faster. And its partnerships with E.piphany and NetGenesis give Vignette customers a way to help marketers gauge the success of online sales pitches, as well as segment customers by profitability or pages visited. Analysts applaud these deals as smart short-term moves but warn that Vignette could get burned if it fails to cook up its own applications.

One encouraging sign: Vignette's move to non-PC devices. Sprint Corp.'s service, which provides wireless access to the Web, is using Vignette technology. This allows Sprint's content partners to write "10-second applications" that would enable a bank, say, to notify a client of the arrival of a money wire—all via cell phone. In many countries, "the Net-enabled phone will be the primary way people access the Internet," says Richard Schwartz, Vignette's senior vice-president for technology.

The question is: Can Vignette leverage its content-management strength to become a $1 billion supplier of e-commerce software? If not, Austin's best and brightest will dream of working elsewhere.

4 Innovation and Strategic Brand Management

The importance of innovation for competing in today's complex and rapidly changing marketplace is acknowledged by many executives. However, executives may rank customer satisfaction and the use of technology ahead of innovation. Importantly, a major research initiative sponsored by *Forbes ASAP* and Ernst and Young placed innovation at the top of eight potential value drivers, whereas the use of technology (number 7) and customer satisfaction (number 8) were not statistically significant drivers of market values.[1] The researchers analyzed the primary nonfinancial factors which create market value (above that explained by traditional accounting metrics) for a corporation.

Broad-based innovation is an important requirement for survival in the global marketplace.[2] Innovation includes new goods and services, ideas, processes, and business practices. While the importance of innovation is recognized, what is less clear is which strategies will be successful in pursuing innovation opportunities. Organizations must foster a culture of innovation and develop effective new product planning processes to achieve their innovation objectives.

Both incremental improvements to existing products and new-to-the-world innovations may be essential to sustaining a competitive advantage. Accumulating evidence indicates that innovation pays off. For example, the top 20 percent of companies in *Fortune* magazine's annual innovation survey have generated double the shareholder returns of their peers since 1985. Often successful innovations are identified, developed, and brought to market by large, well-established companies.[3] The more successful of these companies employ small entrepreneurial units to stimulate innovation.

Many companies identify their new products through brand names. A company may link all of its products to an umbrella brand such as Nike or instead manage a portfolio of brands, as Procter & Gamble (P&G) does. Developing and managing brand strategies are important corporate initiatives.

Procter & Gamble is an interesting example of a company that is trying to create a culture that stimulates innovation while also managing a large portfolio of brands. P&G spends over $1 billion on research and development each year,[4] yet it has not introduced a breakthrough new product since the 1960s. The Olestra fat substitute was supposed to be the company's next big success but has not been a big winner. There have been some new products, but the results have been mixed. The Dryel home dry-cleaning product has not performed well, whereas P&G's Swiffer floor-cleaning mop has been very successful although not a breakthrough product. P&G faces an array of complex innovation and brand strategy challenges, including dealing with competition between new products and existing brands for marketing support, coping with the increasing power of giant retail claims, determining Internet strategies, and achieving better focus in new product planning activities.

In this part we first consider new product planning; that is followed by a discussion of strategic brand management.

New Product Planning

Deciding on the best new product strategy is challenging. Incremental improvement strategies for existing products seem to work well for many companies. Nonetheless, rapid changes in markets and technologies are creating threats and uncertainties for a wide range of old economy companies, forcing them to examine the feasibility of value migration innovations. Consider, for example, the pervasive impact of digital technology and Internet development in nearly every industry. Companies such as AT&T, Polaroid, IBM, and Xerox, among many others, recognize that continuing to improve existing products incrementally may not be sufficient for gaining a competitive edge in the future.

Defining the Scope of New Ideas for Consideration

Companies normally concentrate their new product planning in certain product categories (e.g., personal computers) and markets (e.g., PCs for business and other organizations). Product scope may be broad as in the case of Procter & Gamble's packaged goods or narrow as in the case Rolex in watches. Importantly, the firm's idea scope should be defined to help guide idea generation activities.

It is useful for management to develop a written statement indicating the technology focus of the firm, product type(s) or category, and customer segment(s) of interest to the firm. This statement spells out the organization's new product strategy. It can be used to evaluate the strategic fit of new product ideas. Ideas that fall outside the scope statement are not excluded from consideration. However, management is alerted to the extent to which those ideas depart from the firm's new product scope statement.

The objective of the new product strategy is to identify the most promising opportunities for a company to pursue. This strategy should take into account the organization's distinctive capabilities and market opportunities that provide a good customer value match with those capabilities. For example, some observers question Amazon.com Inc.'s brand extension from books and CDs into several unrelated product categories. Will Amazon's success in marketing books transfer to tools and hardware, electronics, and housewares? How does the Amazon brand name relate to these product categories? Amazon's e-retailing strategy requires warehouse and distribution centers, large inventories, brand name leveraging, and extensive promotional efforts.

A major benchmarking study of 161 business units from a broad range of industries in the United States, Germany, Denmark, and Canada indicates that a carefully formulated and articulated new product strategy is a cornerstone of superior new product performance. A successful new product strategy includes the following:[5]

1. Setting specific written new product objectives (sales, profit, contribution, market share, etc.).

2. Communicating across the organization the role of new products in contributing to the objectives of the business.

3. Defining the areas of strategic focus for the business in terms of product scope, markets, and technologies.

4. Including longer-term projects involving new technology in the portfolio along with incremental projects.

New Product Planning Process

Both executives and researchers agree that the new product development process should follow an interrelated sequence of stages. These stages include searching for ideas, screening and evaluating product concepts, moving promising concepts into the development/design stage, use testing, marketing strategy development, market testing, and full-scale market introduction (Exhibit 1). A brief overview of these stages follows.

Searching for and Screening Ideas.   The objective of this stage is to generate new ideas and screen them against criteria such as strategic fit, market potential, financial requirements, and competition.

Evaluating Product Concepts.   Ideas that pass through initial screening require comprehensive evaluation and business analysis. Up to this point in the process the product is a concept that is under consideration for possible development into a new product.

EXHIBIT 1   New Product Planning Process

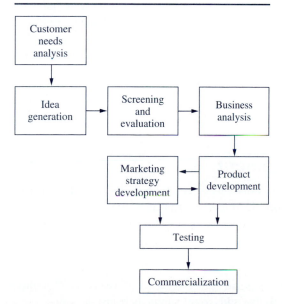

Source: David W. Cravens, *Strategic Marketing,* 6th ed. (Chicago: Irwin/McGraw-Hill, 2000), p. 238.

Product Development.   At this stage the new product concept moves into design. Product development may include designing a physical product or service.

Marketing Strategy Development.   In this stage the market targeting and positioning strategies are determined. Marketing strategy guidelines usually are developed during the concept stage and refined during product development.

Testing.   This stage may include use testing of the product and market testing. Neither is a requirement. Use testing is part of the design process, whereas market testing requires that the product design be complete and sufficient quantities be produced for market testing.

Commercialization.   This is the final stage in the process. The product may be introduced regionally, nationally, or internationally. Typically, international introduction follows national introduction of the market.

Comprehensive analysis at the concept stage is essential before resources are committed to actual product development. Cooper emphasizes the essential role of market and technical assessments of new product concepts before beginning the development of the product.[6] This "up-front" effort should create a clearly defined concept and its market target, value offering, and intended positioning. Cooper also stresses the need for demanding evaluation throughout the entire process, quality of execution, and flexibility in moving through each stage of the process.

The Intelligent Quisine (IQ) line of functional foods offering therapeutic benefits that was developed by the Campbell Soup Company in 1997 apparently did not receive sufficient up-front evaluation at the concept stage. Over 70 million Americans have diabetes or cardio-vascular disease. However, determining how many people might be attracted to the IQ concept is the issue that is important to Campbell.[7] Market tests in Ohio were halted after 18 months, and the IQ line was withdrawn from the market. The clinical (use) tests for IQ were extensive, and the results were impressive. However, during the market tests, sufficient numbers of buyers were not attracted, apparently because of relatively high prices, limited variety, and a lengthy use period. Some authorities propose that IQ could have been withdrawn too soon from the market. Another option for Campbell might have been to partner with a company with marketing and technical capabilities for health foods like IQ. In any event, the evidence suggests that Campbell would have benefited from more extensive concept tests concerning IQ's proposed therapeutic benefits, its prices, people's willingness to commit to long-term meal plans, and users' variety requirements before moving the concept into the product development stage.

Strategic Brand Management

New products that are successful become part of the organization's product portfolio. We now consider important aspects of strategic brand management, including brand equity, brand portfolio management, and brand leveraging.

Brand Equity

Aaker defines brand equity as "a set of assets (and liabilities linked to a brand's name and symbol) that adds to (or subtracts from) the value provided by a good or service to a firm and/or that firm's customers."[8] Managing brands such as BMW to enhance their value (equity) is an important management responsibility. The brand's value is a strategic asset and represents a major source of competitive advantage.

Measuring brand equity across products and markets is useful because it allows firms to compare themselves (benchmark) with strong firms. Brand equity provides guidelines for brand building, and the concept and measures provide the tools to manage the brand portfolio.

Methods of measuring brand equity incorporate the various assets that constitute equity. For example, Aaker proposes a combination of 10 measures representing five equity categories: loyalty, perceived quality/leadership, associations/differentiation, awareness, and market behavior.[9] The consulting firm Interbrand uses seven factors (leadership, stability, market, internationality, trend, support, and protection) to evaluate brand strength. Young & Rubicam, a global advertising agency based in New York, measures brand equity by using the following four sets of measures: differentiation, relevance, esteem, and knowledge of the brand. The intent of the brand equity measure is that it can be used across different products and markets. Equity measurement gives executives a method to quantify intangible assets.

Equity measures also may signal critical weaknesses.[10] For example, in the process of implementing its international growth strategy, Skoda Cars (the Czechoslovakian car manufacturer which once had the status now enjoyed by BMW) actually displayed a "negative brand equity." Consumers' perceptions of the value of Skoda cars and their likelihood of purchase were higher in certain overseas markets when the Skoda brand identity was removed from the vehicles. This pointed to the need for a major brand-building initiative. Skoda's management has succeeded in turning the brand around, and Skoda now holds a favorable position in the European J. D. Powers rankings.

Brand Portfolio Management[11]

Companies often have several brands that need to be managed as an interrelated system.[12] Strategic brand measurement looks at the different roles brands play in the product portfolio and the relationships among the brands. Portfolio management seeks to achieve synergy from the brand system while avoiding inconsistencies in how the brands are positioned. A central consideration is to link brand management efforts across the brands rather than managing each brand on an independent basis.

Colgate-Palmolive's management has been very successful in managing the Colgate brand toothpaste portfolio. By using targeting and positioning initiatives for the various brands to offer different bundles of value to buyers, Colgate achieved over a 26 percent market share by the end of 1997. Colgate gained a 1 percent lead over the market leader, Procter & Gamble's Crest toothpaste. Colgate Total toothpaste was introduced in the United States in early 1998 with a planned $100 million promotion expenditure during the first year. Total was positioned to help prevent cavities, gingivitis, and plaque while fighting tartar and offering long-lasting fresh breath. Interestingly, Total could have focused on preventing gingivitis since it had the approval of the American Dental Association. Instead, by using the more extensive appeal, Total gained a strong market position in 1999. Total previously had been introduced in over 100 countries.

Proactive efforts are necessary to strengthen brands, and sometimes actions may be necessary to revitalize brands. Brands that are no longer making a positive contribution to the portfolio need to be eliminated. Brand retirement is often difficult after extensive brand-building efforts. For example, Anheuser-Busch worked for 16 years to gain a profitable market position with the Eagle chips brand before management decided to leave the market.

Brand Leveraging[13]

A brand that has a strong market position can facilitate the introduction of new products using the brand name, either within the product line or in other categories. This initiative in leveraging the brand name offers several advantages over introducing new products under new brand names. Leveraging strategies benefit from the established market position of the core brand.

Types of Brand Leveraging.   The major ways of leveraging are line extensions and brand extensions. Line extensions involve adding one or more products to an existing product line. This strategy may include additional flavors, added features, and other extensions within the same product line. Brand extension leverages the brand name into another product category (e.g., Swiss Army knives to watches).

Line and brand extensions account for a major percentage of new product introductions every year. The advantages include instant name recognition, reduced brand promotion, and the use of common distribution channels. Leveraging also may enhance brand equity. Nonetheless, extensions present possible risks if the extended brand is not successful and damages brand equity. Line extension may cannibalize sales from the core brand(s). Too many line extensions may confuse buyers. Brand extensions into unrelated product categories may not offer logical leveraging avenues.

An example of successful brand leveraging is the Healthy Choice portfolio of foods. The brand initially was launched as a line of frozen meals and positioned to appeal to both men and women seeking the benefits of healthy foods that taste good. ConAgra Inc. extended the Healthy Choice brand to deli meats, cheeses, and soups.

Cobranding involves a combination of two brand names. The intent in cobranding is to gain the advantages of two powerful brands from different product categories. Examples include airline and credit card joint promotions, the Healthy Choice line of Kellogg cereals, and Coca-Cola and McDonald's partnering projects.

Brand Equity Considerations.   Brand leveraging has both positive and possible negative impacts on brand equity. For example, we know that the brand extension strategy used by Healthy Choice has had a positive impact on brand equity. However, Gap's trial entry into a lower-priced apparel retail concept using the Gap name did not perform well and, if continued, could have damaged Gap's brand equity. Management aborted the strategy and adopted the Old Navy retail concept, which has been very successful.

Concluding Note

Many companies develop strategies around pivotal products. Companies such as Coca-Cola and Intel position their business strategies around key products in their portfolios. Several important trends have emerged in the marketplace, such as the blurring of market boundaries, escalating customer diversity, demanding customer requirements, and increasing global competitive challenges. These pressures create urgency for executives to develop and adopt market-driven product strategies. At the center of these strategies are new product planning and strategic brand management initiatives.

End Notes

1. Geoff Baum, Chris Ittner, David Larcker, Jonathan Low, Tony Siesfeld, and Michael S. Malone, "Introducing the New Value Creation Index," *Forbes ASAP*, April 3, 2000, pp. 140–43.

2. Rajesh K. Chandy and Gerald J. Tellis, "Organizing for Radical Product Innovation," MSI Report No. 98–102, 1998.

3. "Innovation in Industry," *The Economist,* December 20, 1999, p. 15.

4. Charles L. Decker, "P&G Will Crest Again," *The Wall Street Journal,* March 10, 2000, p. A14.

5. Robert Cooper, "Benchmarking New Product Performance: Results of the Best Practices Study," *European Management Journal,* February 1998, pp. 1–17.

6. Ibid.

7. Vanessa O'Connell, "Food for Thought: How Campbell Soup Saw a Breakthrough Menu Turn into Leftovers," *The Wall Street Journal,* October 6, 1998, pp. A1, A12.

8. David A. Aaker, *Building Strong Brands* (New York: Free Press, 1996), pp. 7–8.

9. Ibid.

10. This example is drawn from David W. Cravens, Nigel F. Piercy, and Ashley Prentice, "Developing Market-Driven Product Strategies," *Journal of Product & Brand Management,* Vol. 9, No. 6, 2000, pp. 369–388.

11. This section is drawn from Cravens, Piercy, and Prentice, "Developing Market-Driven Product Strategies."

12. Aaker, *Building Strong Brands.*

13. This section is drawn from Cravens, Piercy, and Prentice, "Developing Market-Driven Product Strategies."

CASES FOR PART 4

Innovation and strategic brand management are critical to long-term success. Included in this part are cases involving well-known international companies that must continue to innovate and manage their company brands. A "classic" in this part is the Coca-Cola (Japan) case. This case has proved popular in the classroom, with users rating it as one of the most successful cases in the book. The company's focus on both innovation and strategic brand management makes the case a great fit for this new section in the book. In addition to traditional product innovation and brand issues, however, this part takes a hard look at the new economy that involves new ways of doing business and the resulting brand management that has occurred.

As a video case, **Coca-Cola (Japan) Company (Case 4–1)** focuses on the decision whether to enter the Japanese canned tea market. Tea is a "drink of tradition" in Japan, and there is concern about the long-term acceptance of canned tea. The stakes are high not just for Coca-Cola (Japan) Company but for the brand manager making the go/no-go recommendation.

Under the American Express corporate umbrella, **the American Express Corporate Purchasing Card (Case 4–2)** did not have a strong organizational identity. The employee charge card was an innovative concept in the business-to-business marketplace, but how could the company convince prospective customers that card use would result in measurable cost reduction?

Case 4–3, The Quaker Oats Company, Gatorade, and Snapple Beverage, examines the brand portfolio of Quaker Oats' worldwide production and sales operations. The company was committed to real earnings growth. To make this happen, Quaker was restructuring its food products brands.

Case 4–4, Cruisers, examines brand name strength in the motorcycle marketplace. In a market with plenty of growth opportunity, the question becomes one of which motorcycle company has the brand recognition to offer the longest ride.

Cima Mountaineering, Inc. (Case 4–5), a manufacturer of mountaineering and hiking boots, is trying to determine the best strategy for future growth. Margaret Simon, the company's president, favors one approach, while her brother, Anthony, the executive vice president, favors another.

Murphy Brewery Ireland, Limited (Case 4–6), is a brewery faced with developing a global strategy in a very competitive environment. Murphy has become a recognized international brand while maintaining a unique identity in Ireland.

Brand credibility is critical in **Slendertone (A): Creating a World-Class Brand (Case 4–7).** The company, BioMedical Research, has gone from being product-oriented to being market-oriented. The future, however, is highly dependent on Slendertone's brand recognition.

The e-business case examines the merger of two well-known companies. **AOL Time Warner (Case 4–8)** exemplifies the new Net economy of the twenty-first century. As the new company combines its resources, new brands could emerge and, linked with older companies' brands, could lead to new and exciting customer relationships.

CASE 4–1
COCA-COLA (JAPAN) COMPANY

It was October 1987. Arthur Grotz, brand manager, was pacing the floor in his Tokyo office. He was pondering whether to recommend that Coca-Cola launch a ready-to-drink tea in Japan. Since 1981, four notable Japanese companies had entered the tea market. The decision had to be made quickly and was critical to Grotz's career. For him it was "sink or swim." A success for Coca-Cola would mean career advancement; a failure could result in dire consequences.

Grotz's research and final suggestion would pass through many hands within the Coca-Cola Company. Approval would have to come first from the president of Coca-Cola (Japan). Ultimate approval would come from corporate headquarters in Atlanta, Georgia. Thus, the final decision would rest with Roberto C. Goizeuta, chairman and chief executive officer of the Coca-Cola Company. Grotz mused, Should Coca-Cola enter the tea market in Japan?

The Coca-Cola Company

The Coca-Cola empire was founded in 1886, when John C. Pemberton, an Atlanta, Georgia, pharmacist, developed Coca-Cola, a carbonated soft drink. Following a strategy of international and national expansion, the company, by the late 1980s, was the world's largest producer and distributor of soft drink syrups and concentrates. The company's products were sold through bottlers and fountain wholesalers and distributors in more than 155 countries. Soft drinks generated approximately 81 percent of operating revenues and 96 percent of operating income in 1987. (Exhibit 1 provides summary revenue and income information from 1984 through 1987.)

Coca-Cola operated two business sectors: the North American Business Sector and the International Business Sector. The North American Business Sector consisted of Coca-Cola USA, Coca-Cola Ltd. (Canadian operations), and Coca-Cola Foods (juice drinks). The International Business Sector had four geographic-oriented groups: Greater Europe, Latin America, Middle and Far East, and Africa.

Japan

Japan, located in the Pacific Ocean, consists of four main islands—Honshu (mainland), Hokkaido, Kyushu, and Shikoku—covering 145,856 square miles. The population in the late 1980s was around 123 million, of whom 75 percent were urban dwellers.

The Japanese economy had improved considerably in the 1980s. Consequently, a growing number of Japanese people enjoyed a rising standard of living with an annual income of US$25,000. This led to a boom in consumer spending for both durable and nondurable goods. The yen had been appreciating in value from 1985 to 1987. (See

This case was prepared by Laura Gow, MBA student, under the supervision of Victoria L. Crittenden, associate professor of marketing, Boston College, as the basis for class discussion rather than to illustrate either effective or ineffective handling of a managerial situation. Information was derived from secondary sources. Pseudonyms were used. Revised 1997.

EXHIBIT 1

**Operating Revenues and Income
Soft Drink Products**

	Revenues	*Income*
1984	67%	86%
1985	67	86
1986	81	89
1987	81	96

**International Operating Revenues and Income
for Soft Drink Products**

	Revenues	*Income*
1984	42	51
1985	42	50
1986	53	75
1987	55	74

Source: Coca-Cola Company annual reports.

EXHIBIT 2   **Average Exchange Rates, Japanese
Yen/U.S. Dollar, 1970–87**

Year	*Rate*
1970	360
1975	297
1977	269
1980	227
1981	221
1982	249
1983	238
1984	238
1985	239
1986	169
1987	145

Exhibit 2 for exchange rates.) Economists were positive about the future, but consumers were guarding their purse strings carefully.

The 1980s Japanese consumer was more concerned with health issues than ever before. This was due in part to an aging population interested in longevity and feeling well. Additionally, it was aided by a desire to be fit and trim. This health trend appeared to be continuing and possibly gaining in popularity into the late 1980s. Along with this consumer interest came a proliferation of nutritious food and beverage products.

Japanese Beverage Market.   The Japanese beverage industry was worth US$18 billion by 1987. The market consisted of the following segments:

Colas	10%
Other carbonated drinks	9
Juices	26
Teas	9
Coffees	21
Waters	16
Sports drinks	9

Japanese Tea Market. Originating in the fifteenth and sixteenth centuries, when leaders in China began to boil tea leaves in water, tea preparation traditionally had been considered an almost ceremonial event. In the mid-1970s the founder of Ito En Ltd., a packager and wholesaler of dried tea, decided that the future for his company and its current product was limited. Therefore, Mr. Masanori Honjo decided to follow the trend toward more convenience-oriented products by developing an unsweetened tea packaged in a can. The product was introduced in Japan in 1981. By that time a canned oolong tea was already available in China.

The ready-to-drink tea segment consisted of three basic categories of tea: oolong (57 percent of the market), black (31 percent of the market), and green (12 percent of the market). From 1985 to 1987, oolong tea growth had averaged 42 percent annually and black tea growth had averaged 60 percent annually. Rapid growth was expected to continue in the canned black tea market. Western-style tea (tea with milk and/or sugar) also was experiencing strong growth of about 60 percent annually. Tea sold in cans (250 milliliters) for around 100 yen and also in larger PET containers (1,500 milliliters).

Tea, along with other beverages, was sold in grocery stores, convenience stores, restaurants, and vending machines. Grocery stores had experienced an annual average growth rate of 5.1 percent by the middle 1980s (1985 grocery store sales of 4.8 million yen). Convenience stores had an annual average growth rate during that period of 15.8 percent (1985 convenience store sales of 3.4 million yen). Vending machine sales, which accounted for approximately 50 percent of beverage sales, continued to grow. In fact, a well-placed machine was expected to sell about 10,000 cans of beverage per year, similar to a convenience store. Japan had about 5 million vending machines, with 2 million selling canned drinks. The average drink machine had 20 spots in 250-milliliter or 350-milliliter sizes.

In crowded urban areas a consumer usually had a choice among many machines and alternative products. Aside from canned drinks, vending machines offered everything from flowers to comic books to lingerie. Companies competed not only in vending machine accessibility but also in machine appearance and interactive capabilities—a talking or singing machine was not uncommon. A downside to vending machine distribution, however, was vandalism.

The Coca-Cola (Japan) Company

The Coca-Cola (Japan) Company Limited (CCJC) was established in Tokyo in 1957. Since trade regulations prohibited Coca-Cola from expanding to other Japanese locations, company executives focused on making local connections, assessing the competitive environment, and gaining a solid understanding of Japanese culture. This information and knowledge provided a strong foundation for future growth. In 1961, when the Japanese government enacted trade deregulation policies, CCJC was ready to pursue expansion and unrestricted advertising.

A major part of CCJC's strategy was to form strategic alliances with powerful Japanese corporations. The three most notable partners were Mitsui, Mitsubishi, and Kikkoman. By forming strong relationships with these local bottlers, CCJC was able to reap immediate economies of scale and scope as well as gain Japanese consumer confidence and buy-in.

In the 1960s Coca-Cola's sales in Japan soared, with revenues doubling every year, making Coca-Cola the best-selling soft drink in Japan by 1965. Important to CCJC's revenue figures was the return the company saw in concentrate prices. CCJC made four to five times as much on a gallon of syrup as did its U.S. counterparts. By 1985 CCJC had solidified its dominance in the market, becoming the industry leader in improving quality standards and introducing new products. To establish itself as an integral part of the Japanese lifestyle, CCJC actively promoted cultural, educational, and athletic activities.

CCJC Success.   Two factors were thought to have contributed to CCJC's leadership position: (1) the company's direct marketing approach and (2) the company's distribution system of independent local franchisees. In addition to supplying bottlers with syrups and concentrates, the company provided support in distribution and the entire marketing effort—"from the TV set to the store shelf."

The Japanese market was divided into 17 regions serviced by 17 individual bottlers. (See Exhibit 3 for a geographic view of the market and the company's bottlers.) The direct sales concept (which was pioneered by Coca-Cola in its start-up operations in the United States) had encountered stiff resistance in Japan initially. Traditional Japanese business practices involved several wholesalers. However, the enthusiasm of the bottlers and strong sales of Coca-Cola eventually convinced local retailers of the benefits of the new system. A key element of the distribution system was that it generated activity in the local economy because CCJC's system established partnerships with local businesses. In principle, bottlers acted as independent corporations, sourcing their raw materials locally and completing all aspects of production on-site. The CCJC unified this assembly of disparate players through a carefully crafted strategy of aggressively monitoring all regional operations, creating all marketing strategies, and initiating new product development. By the end of the 1980s, however, CCJC had become worried about the diversification efforts of the bottlers. Non–Coca-Cola brands were accounting for 20 to 40 percent of total annual sales at some of the bottlers.

Although CCJC offered a variety of products (Exhibit 4), three products were Japan's favorites:

- *HI-C.* The HI-C line of products with 50 percent fruit content was introduced in 1973. The product line opened the way for a new fruit juice drink market and, in the process, helped avert a crisis for Japanese citrus farmers. An overproduction of *mikan,* Japanese tangerines, had caused a serious problem for individual growers and agricultural cooperatives. Coca-Cola had stepped in and bought the bumper crop to produce its HI-C products. This led to a lasting relationship between CCJC and the growers.
- *Georgia.* In 1975 CCJC launched a ready-to-drink coffee, Georgia.[1] Although Japan was projected to become one of the largest canned coffee markets in the world, CCJC had taken several years to introduce a canned coffee product into the Japanese market. The lack of a canned coffee product had been the source of mild controversy between CCJC and its local Japanese bottlers. Once introduced, the Georgia brand quickly became the leading brand in this very competitive market segment, with 34 percent of the market by

---

[1] The name Georgia came from the home state of Coca-Cola's headquarters in the United States.

EXHIBIT 3   Individual Bottler Regions in Japan

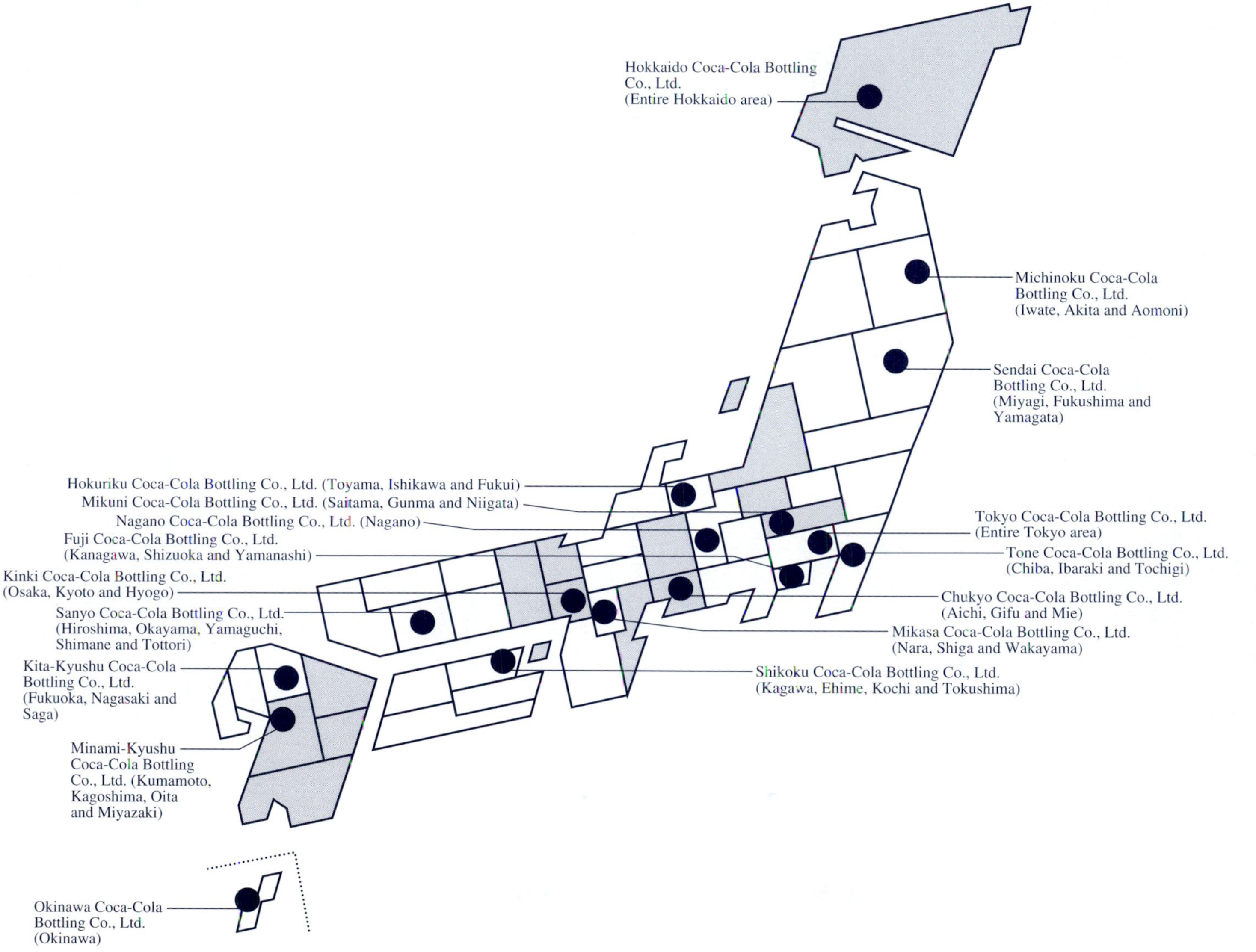

Hokkaido Coca-Cola Bottling Co., Ltd. (Entire Hokkaido area)

Michinoku Coca-Cola Bottling Co., Ltd. (Iwate, Akita and Aomori)

Sendai Coca-Cola Bottling Co., Ltd. (Miyagi, Fukushima and Yamagata)

Tokyo Coca-Cola Bottling Co., Ltd. (Entire Tokyo area)

Tone Coca-Cola Bottling Co., Ltd. (Chiba, Ibaraki and Tochigi)

Chukyo Coca-Cola Bottling Co., Ltd. (Aichi, Gifu and Mie)

Mikasa Coca-Cola Bottling Co., Ltd. (Nara, Shiga and Wakayama)

Shikoku Coca-Cola Bottling Co., Ltd. (Kagawa, Ehime, Kochi and Tokushima)

Hokuriku Coca-Cola Bottling Co., Ltd. (Toyama, Ishikawa and Fukui)

Mikuni Coca-Cola Bottling Co., Ltd. (Saitama, Gunma and Niigata)

Nagano Coca-Cola Bottling Co., Ltd. (Nagano)

Fuji Coca-Cola Bottling Co., Ltd. (Kanagawa, Shizuoka and Yamanashi)

Kinki Coca-Cola Bottling Co., Ltd. (Osaka, Kyoto and Hyogo)

Sanyo Coca-Cola Bottling Co., Ltd. (Hiroshima, Okayama, Yamaguchi, Shimane and Tottori)

Kita-Kyushu Coca-Cola Bottling Co., Ltd. (Fukuoka, Nagasaki and Saga)

Minami-Kyushu Coca-Cola Bottling Co., Ltd. (Kumamoto, Kagoshima, Oita and Miyazaki)

Okinawa Coca-Cola Bottling Co., Ltd. (Okinawa)

Source: Coca-Cola (Japan) Company.

EXHIBIT 4   CCJC Product Line

Coca-Cola
Coca-Cola Light
Fanta
Sprite
HI-C
Aquarious
Ambasa Water
Georgia Coffee
Real Gold
Mello Yello

1987. The young Japanese businessman was the primary target for the Georgia brand. The sweet, milky flavor deterred the female consumer, who preferred unsweetened, lower-calorie drinks.

- *Aquarious.* Soon after the 1983 introduction, the Aquarius line of isotonic drinks became as popular as Georgia and HI-C. Touted as a health drink, it was ideal for replenishing fluid and electrolytes lost through perspiration.

CCJC commanded 90 percent of the cola market, slightly less than 60 percent of the noncola carbonated market, and approximately 10 percent of the remaining drink market. Coca-Cola beverage sales in Japan accounted for 21.5 percent of Coca-Cola's worldwide profits, compared with 18 percent for the United States, with profit per gallon four times higher than it was in the United States. CCJC owned and operated around 750,000 vending machines (accounting for almost 65 percent of canned beverage sales) and distributed to approximately 1 million retail stores and food service outlets. CCJC invested in around 100,000 new vending machines annually at a cost of US$4,000 per machine. Routine replacement was due to technology change, not machine life, which was around 10 years. (Exhibits 5 and 6 provide select financial information.)

Competition

The soft drink industry was highly competitive, with up to 1,000 new product introductions each year and around 8,000 products in the marketplace. Competitors included producers of other nationally and internationally advertised brands as well as regional producers and private-label suppliers. Other beverages competed with soft drinks. Advertising and sales promotional programs, the introduction of new packaging and new products, and brand and trademark development protection were important competitive factors. Ito En Ltd., Suntory Ltd., Kirin, Hitachi Zosen Corp., and Asahi Breweries Ltd. were the leading competitors in the tea market.

Ito En Ltd. was the leading Japanese canned tea marketer. The company initiated the canned tea boom in 1981 by marketing the first unsweetened tea in a can. In 1985 it introduced the first can of Japanese green tea, Ryokucha. Ito En spent months perfecting systems to manufacture and produce a canned tea that was free from oxidation and did not change color, taste, or aroma even when subjected to drastic temperature changes. While the company's focus was tea, there were rumors that the company had plans to enter the canned tea market.

EXHIBIT 5   CCJC Financial Data: Summary of Operations, 1986–87
(in U.S.$ millions)

	1987	1986
Net operating revenues	$7,658	$6,977
Cost of goods sold	3,633	3,454
Gross profit	4,025	3,523
S,G,&A	2,665	2,446
Provisions for restructured operations and divestment	36	180
Operating income	1,324	897
Interest income	232	154
Equity income	297	208
Other income (deductions)—net	113	152
Gain on sale of stock by former subsidiaries	—	35
Income from continuing operations before income taxes	40	375
Income taxes	1,412	1,405
Income from continuing operations	496	471
	916	934

Source: Coca-Cola Company annual reports.

**EXHIBIT 6   Coca-Cola Company Net Operating Revenues and
Operating Income, 1986–87** *(in U.S.$ millions)*

	1987	1986
United States		
Net operating revenues	$3,459.1	$3,277.9
Operating income	384.5	273.8
Latin America		
Net operating revenues	558.0	555.5
Operating income	153.2	140.8
Europe and Africa		
Net operating revenues	1,709.5	1,628.9
Operating income	508.1	354.6
Pacific and Canada		
Net operating revenues	1,917.0	1,502.4
Operating income	453.3	352.4

Source: Coca-Cola Company annual reports.

Suntory Ltd. was Japan's largest distiller. The company also was gaining ground in its nonalcoholic divisions. In 1981 Suntory introduced a canned oolong tea called Tess. By 1987 Suntory held nearly 50 percent of the oolong tea market. Additionally, the company produced colas, green tea, and health tonics. The company planned to enter the canned coffee market by the end of the 1980s.

Kirin was the first to produce a canned black tea, called Afternoon Tea, in 1986. The fifth largest Japanese brewery, Kirin had 50 percent of the Japanese beer market. The company also was one of Japan's leading soft drink producers and marketers, with canned soft drink sales of around US$1 billion. Kirin also produced fruit drinks, vitamin-enriched drinks, and sports drinks as well as posting brisk sales in its canned coffee.

Hitachi Zosen Corp. was a "Big Five" shipbuilder in Japan that diversified into biotechnology and developed a new tea from the Chinese tochu tree. In 1987 it introduced this "healthy" unsweetened tea in cans and bottles. For centuries the Chinese had used the bark of the tochu tree in herbal medicine to treat high blood pressure as well as liver and kidney ailments. The bark was also rich in calcium, iron, and magnesium.

Asahi Breweries Ltd. was the first producer to market a Western-style canned tea with milk and/or sugar. Asahi was also a major player in the canned coffee market.

The Tea Decision

In the early 1970s a Japanese company began marketing a canned ready-to-drink beverage that contained coffee, milk, sugar, and water. Served cold, it was considered a soft drink under Japanese food laws. For approximately 50 years Coca-Cola had been looking into coffee-flavored technologies that would enable the canned coffee to be served hot or cold, depending on the season, from a vending machine. Despite the fact that the technology was available and a sales opportunity existed, it took CCJC five years to arrive at the decision to enter the coffee market. It then took several years to capture a portion of the growing canned coffee market.

Would ready-to-drink tea, like coffee, be a success in the long term, or was it a passing fad? Would the Japanese truly embrace a canned version of their traditional beverage? Arthur Grotz knew this could make or break his career at Coca-Cola (Japan) Company. Should he recommend that Coca-Cola enter the ready-to-drink tea market? What were the pros and cons of this strategic move? Grotz knew that other soft-drink issues were simmering in Japan. For example, how would generic colas affect the Japanese cola market? Was the trend moving toward fruit-flavored drinks? These issues weighed heavily on his thinking. Should his attention be on products other than tea?

Whatever the decision, Grotz needed to present his recommendation to the vice president of marketing the next week. What should he do?

Sources

Benjamin, Todd. "Ready-to-Drink Tea Catches On in Japan." Cable News Network, Inc., October 13, 1992.

Beverage World. *Coke's First 100 Years.* Kentucky: Keller International Publishing, 1986.

Casteel, Britt. "Japan's Taste for Canned Tea Growing." *The Daily Yomiuri,* January 6, 1991.

Coca-Cola Company. *Annual Reports.*

Coca-Cola Company. *The Chronicle of Coca-Cola since 1886.*

Coca-Cola Company. Web site information.

Coca-Cola (Japan) Company, Limited. *The Coca-Cola Business in Japan.*

"Consumption of Upmarket Goods Booms in Japan." *Business Asia,* October 22, 1990.

"Drink Makers Read Tea Leaves, Discover Canned Teas Are Trend." *Nikkei Weekly,* August 29, 1994.

Eisenstodt, Gale. "Japan's New Business Heroes." *Forbes,* July 4, 1994.

Fukui, Makiko. "At Your Convenience; 24-Hour Services Take Root in Urban Areas." *The Daily Yomiuri,* September 9, 1993.

Hideko, Taguchi. "Tea Reading." *Asia Inc.,* May 1994.

Hoover's Handbook of World Business. *Kirin Brewery Company, Ltd.* 1993.

Japan Economic Newswire. "Breweries Beefing Up Soft Drinks Divisions." March 8, 1991.

Karassawa, Kazuo. "Canned Coffee Sales Regain Two-Digit Growth; Japanese Coffee Sales." *Tea & Coffee Trade Journal,* March 1991.

Kilburn, David. "Pepsi's Challenge: Double Japan Share." *Advertising Age,* December 10, 1990.

Kilburn, David. "Suntory Splashes in Softer Drinks." *Advertising Age,* March 25, 1991.

Killen, Patrick. "Business Talk; Coca-Cola Light Bubbles to No. 2 in Cola Market." *The Daily Yomiuri,* February 20, 1990.

Killen, Patrick. "Coke Chief Sees Japan." *The Daily Yomiuri,* December 21, 1993.

Lin, Diane. "Canned Tea New Battleground in Japanese Food War." *The Reuter Library Report,* July 30, 1992.

Market Reports. "Japan—Health Foods." *1993 National Trade Data Bank,* October 15, 1993.

Mitari, Shin. "The Japanese Beverage Market." *Prepared Foods New Products Annual,* 1991.

Miyatake, Hisa. "Shipbuilder Berths in Tea Market and Sales Soar." *Japan Economic Newswire,* March 12, 1994.

Morris, Kathleen. "The Fizz Is Gone." *Financial World,* February 1, 1994.

Nakayama, Atsushi. "Canada Dry Rights Buy-Up Rattles Bottlers." *Japan Economic Journal,* September 8, 1990.

Nomiyama, Chizu. "Fickle Public Makes Japan Soft Drinks Tough Market to Tap." *The Reuter Library Report,* January 29, 1991.

Pepper, Thomas, Merit Janow, and Jimmy Wheeler. *The Competition Dealing with Japan.* New York: Praeger, 1985.

Reuter Textline. "Japan: Canned Tea New Battleground in Japanese Food War." *Reuter News Service,* August 10, 1992.

Reuter Textline. "Japan: Canned Tea Sales Look Set to Rise Further." *Nikkei Weekly,* October 13, 1990.

Reuter Textline. "Japan: Green Tea Making Comeback in Cans." *Nikkei Weekly,* May 24, 1993.

Reuter Textline. "Japan: Marketing Weekly Spotlight on Marketing and Media Information." *Marketing Week,* April 11, 1991.

Reuter Textline. "Japan: Producers Banking on Strong Sales of Canned Coffee." *Nikkei Weekly,* September 21, 1992.

Reuter Textline. "Japan: Soft-Drink Makers Focus on Blended Tea in Push for Share." *Nikkei Weekly,* February 21, 1994.

Reuter Textline. "Japan: Sugar-Free Tea Enjoys Revival." *Marketing Week,* September 20, 1991.

Stinchecum, Amanda. "The Where and Ware of Hagi." *The New York Times,* July 3, 1988.

The Nikkei Marketing Journal. "Rivals Thirst to Reduce Coca-Cola's Lead; Some Cautious, Other Bold—But All Challengers Are Still Far Behind." *The Japan Economic Journal,* April 27, 1991.

Thomson, Robert. "Setting Out to Get the Coffee Market in the Can." *Financial Times,* December 10, 1990.

Tsukiji, Tatsuro. "Tea Brings in Wave of Beverage Market Profit." *The Japan Economic Journal,* January 19, 1991.

"Unsweetened Soft Drinks Soar on Health Fad." Report from Japan, Inc., 1990.

Watters, Pat. *Coca-Cola.* New York: Doubleday, 1978.

Coca-Cola Company References

Mr. Jean-Michel Bock
Vice President
Coca-Cola International
Pacific Group
PO Drawer 1734
Atlanta, GA 30301

Mr. John Elwood
Assistant to President
Coca-Cola (Japan) Company, Limited
Shibuya PO Box 10
Tokyo 150
Japan

Introduction

The small interior conference room where Thayer Stewart, vice president of marketing and new business development for the Corporate Purchasing Card (CPC) group of American Express Corporate Services, usually met with his management team did not offer many amenities. Its basic, all-business style was a good match for the territory that this American Express program had staked out in the corporate purchasing arena. The CPC group was about to wrap up its fourth year of existence with over $46 million in revenues on an estimated charge volume of $2 billion by over 200 corporate customers, netting $3 million in profits. That was a track record that would have been considered very successful for a stand-alone start-up company. But within the $16 billion context of the American Express corporate umbrella, the CPC program still looked like a tiny upstart without a strong organizational identity. As Stewart prepared for a critical planning meeting in December 1997, he reflected that jump-starting the CPC growth rate was just one of the challenges his management team faced in the coming year.

After four years of slow, steady growth, the CPC business goals for 1998 included a significant increase in revenues based on a higher volume of charge activity and more aggressive targets for new customer acquisition. Top AMEX executives wanted to see the CPC capture a greater share of the business-to-business purchasing market and were prepared to invest the marketing and sales dollars required for a major new campaign to overtake the competition. That was the good news, and one of the agenda items for today's meeting was a review of the 1998 marketing plan and proposals for an expanded advertising campaign in the second quarter.

Stewart knew, however, that it would take more than a bigger advertising budget to overtake the direct and indirect competition that loomed in the corporate purchasing realm. He had spearheaded the launch of the CPC in 1994, convincing key managers within the Corporate Services Division of AMEX that the high-volume, low-cost purchases that made up the bulk of purchasing transactions at large corporations was a huge untapped business opportunity waiting for a purchasing card solution. Back in those days most large organizations were wedded to cumbersome homegrown or proprietary vendor purchasing systems that required multiple approvals and mountains of paperwork. Managing those transactions with a simple employee charge card was an innovative concept with a special appeal to organizations looking for measurable cost reductions from their business process reengineering efforts. The marketing challenge was to convince prospective customers that the CPC could offer the same level of control and functionality provided by traditional purchasing systems at a lower cost.

Purchasing directors who were initially uneasy about cutting back on internal forms and record keeping could be reassured by sales demonstrations of the detailed records that the American Express network was gathering behind the scenes to reconcile every

This case was prepared by Mary Cronin, Boston College, as the basis for class discussion rather than to illustrate effective or ineffective handling of a managerial situation. Development of the case was funded by a grant from the General Electric Fund at Boston College.

purchase order handled through the CPC. The back end of the CPC system—a powerful network that handled customer authorization, purchase orders, fulfillment and payment transactions, and daily reports to customer accounting systems—was integrated with the proprietary American Express network based in Phoenix. The rest of the CPC group, including marketing, sales, and customer support, operated as a separate program within Corporate Services with its management team based in one of AMEX's satellite office locations near Wall Street. This separation allowed the CPC group to market its product directly to purchasing directors at target organizations, underscoring the message that the new American Express purchasing program was committed to meeting the specialized requirements of high-volume business-to-business transactions.

Since those early days, the CPC management had been through more than one period of reorganization and strategic redirection. However, the core product description had remained the same: a business-to-business charge card that allowed companies to streamline the way employees bought supplies and made other repetitive purchases. Now, however, as Stewart considered the shifting terrain of corporate purchasing practices, he wondered if the time had come for a redefinition of the CPC itself. On the one hand, direct alternatives to the CPC were providing tougher competition: Visa and MasterCard were making inroads into the CPC customer base with their own versions of the all-in-one corporate card. On the other hand, solutions that did not involve charge cards at all also were proliferating. At the higher end, SAP and enterprisewide software programs were taking on purchasing processes as part of their solutions for financial and accounting systems. More and more companies seemed to be ready to adopt the Internet as a platform for business-to-business transactions that could be carried out on secure Extranets or even the public Web.

In terms of the total market opportunity, only a small percentage of overall corporate and large organizational purchase transactions used any of these alternatives. As Stewart knew all too well, most of the multi-billion-dollar market was still wedded to traditional purchasing practices. Total corporate purchasing activity in the United States amounts to more than $5,800 billion annually, and only a tiny percentage of that amount was currently processed through any type of purchasing card. It wasn't enough to beat out the direct competition. Real growth would require persuading a lot more organizations to change their approach to purchasing. To break through resistance to adoption, the CPC group needed a compelling value proposition for its program and possibly a different mix of products and services that could address the issues of a changing marketplace.

There will be a lot to discuss at this afternoon's meeting, thought Stewart, as he looked over his notes. It might be a good idea to start with a review of the major developments in the CPC program to date and some background on the competition and the opportunities in a changing marketplace. With so much at stake, he wanted to make sure that everyone in the group had the information needed to contribute to the discussion.

Launching the Corporate Purchasing Card: Round One

American Express entered the corporate purchasing card market in 1994, when the concept of using a charge card to manage purchasing more effectively was still a novelty to many companies. The original positioning of the CPC card was based on an analysis of overall U.S. corporate purchasing activity. Because most large companies have different channels and internal processes to purchase different kinds of goods and services, it was important to get a handle on how to target a particular market segment. The AMEX analysis started with a division of the purchasing universe into four distinct quadrants according to the dollar size and strategic impact of purchases in relation to

---

EXHIBIT 1   The Four Areas of Purchasing

High

IV Specialty High-dollar, low-frequency company expenditures such as capital equipment, taxes, utilities, and high-level services; typically contracts that are negotiated on a one-off basis	**III Strategic** Mission-critical purchases which go into the company's end products (raw materials or component parts for autos, computers, etc.)
I Sundry Low-cost assorted supplies and services where the individual purchaser can select from a variety of suppliers	**II Staples** Low-cost, high-frequency purchases that typically are provided by a designated group of corporate suppliers

Dollar Volume (vertical axis label)

Low ———————————— *Frequency of Purchase* ———————————— *High*

EXHIBIT 2   Estimate of Overall U.S. Volume of Specialty, Strategic, Staples, and Sundry Spending in the Corporate and Public Sectors in 1995

Spending Quadrant	Percentage of Total Transactions	Total Purchasing ($billions)	Percent $ Manufactoring Sector Purchasing	Percent $ Services Sector Purchasing
IV Specialty	0.7%	$1,994	29%	57%
III Strategic	11.3	1,872	49	15
II Staples	**78**	**1,136**	**18**	**23**
I Sundry	10	261	4	5

Source: Center for Advanced Purchasing Studies.

the number and frequency of transactions. The four major areas of purchasing that emerged from this analysis are shown in Exhibit 1.

A feature of a purchasing card program is the ability to streamline the process for making routine, repetitive purchases. Quadrants III and IV, where the typical cost of each purchase is high and the process often requires individual contracts, did not seem like good matches for the charge card approach. Both sundries and staples, as defined by AMEX, were suitable target markets. Adding data on the annual volume of dollars spent and transactions completed in each quadrant, as summarized in Exhibit 2, helped highlight the appeal of Quadrant II.

Even though the absolute dollar amounts spent on lower-cost supplies (Quadrant II) and the relative percentage of purchasing budgets devoted to this quadrant were lower than the totals for specialty and strategic goods, Quadrant II represented the overwhelming majority of purchasing transactions in large corporations. This concentration of transactions made it a perfect match for a charge card that would help reduce the red tape and indirect costs associated with routine, repetitive purchases. While the CPC could potentially handle the even lower-cost purchases that characterized Quadrant I, this was a less attractive target for the program launch for three reasons. First, the total purchasing volume, while considerable, was significantly less than that of the other three quadrants. Second, sundries typically represented less than 10 percent of overall purchasing transactions for large organizations.

Third, even corporations that had complex authorization and vendor selection systems for higher-ticket purchases often allowed individuals to manage their own low-cost sundry purchases on a reimbursement basis. This meant that the record-keeping and tracking capabilities of the CPC program might not be perceived as useful for a Quadrant I purchase.

EXHIBIT 3   Curb Rising Processing Costs and Increase Efficiency

"Our strategy included using The Card for high transaction volume vendors. We found that the bankcard in our pilot program had limitations. We turned to American Express® because of the enhanced data capture capabilities at the point-of-sale, as well as technical support."

> David Smith,
> Division Manager,
> Accounts Payable, Bethlehem Steel.

- An inefficient purchasing process requires too many steps, too much paperwork and too much of your people's time.
- The average cost to process a purchase order is $100–$150.
- 80% of a company's transactions account for 20% of dollars.
- American Express Corporate Purchasing System lowers purchasing and accounts payable processing costs by providing customized, automated solutions that provide you with greater control.
- Now, you can confidently empower key employees as Cardmembers so that your time is free to focus on strategic issues.

A New Way of Purchasing That's Made to Order

With the large volume of transactions your company makes, it's more important than ever to lower processing costs. The American Express Corporate Purchasing System will help you do so. Here's how it works:

- Cardmember orders directly from supplier.
- Supplier processes order.
- American Express authorizes transaction based on predetermined controls.
- Supplier ships product and bills American Express.
- American Express pays supplier.
- American Express sends a monthly consolidated bill to Company.
- Company receives MIS reporting and data file.
- Transactions are automatically distributed to company's general ledger or accounts payable system.
- Cardmember gets monthly report of spending for reconciliation.
- Company sends one payment to American Express.

Consistent, Comprehensive Data Capture Capabilities

Bankcards have multiple issuers and merchants, each with their own third party processors, preventing them from controlling data content and integrity. American Express One Network System has the ability to consolidate static information directly from the Cardmember and the supplier, with dynamic information at the point-of-sale. This means you receive comprehensive detail consistently throughout your preferred supplier network. As a result the American Express Corporate Purchasing System offers comprehensive, consistent data capture. Monthly Data Capture Reports ensure data integrity by measuring and identifying exceptions and errors in the sales tax, ship-to-zip code and Cardmember reference fields. Here's how the Corporate Purchasing System can help your Company:

Purchasing

- Eliminates purchase orders and requisition forms.
- Improves commodity management reporting, which leads to improved supplier negotiations.
- Saves processing time.
- Delivers goods and services more quickly and accurately.
- Provides flexible spending controls.
- Monthly reports track spending that can consolidate multiple levels.
- Standard MIS reports include sales/use tax, 1099 information, minority business, industry spending.
- Improves policy control with activity and exception reporting.
- Eliminates maintenance and set-up of new suppliers in vendor master database.
- Decreases cycle times.

EXHIBIT 3   (Continued)

Accounts Payable

- One invoice for all low dollar purchases.
- Elimination of the cost associated with inputting and processing multiple invoices and issuing multiple checks.
- Automates general ledger distribution.
- Increases control of general ledger and other accounts.
- Reduces suspense costs and invoice reconciliation.
- Identifies exceptions prior to posting.
- Consolidated reporting provides a comprehensive view of all transactions.

Tax and Audit

- Monthly sales and use tax reporting.
- Monthly spending by Taxpayer ID Report.
- A number of states have issued favorable rulings on the Corporate Purchasing Card Sales Tax Reports.
- Report features facilitate tax planning and monitoring.
- Saves time and money spent in manual reporting.
- Streamlines record retention.

Receiving

- Eliminates goods receipt against purchase order.
- Package routes directly to Cardmember.

An essential step in converting the multi-billion-dollar market in Quadrant II into a profit center for American Express was persuading target customers (large corporations and government agencies) that it was worth changing their existing purchasing processes. That meant defining the value of the CPC program in terms that middle management purchasing directors, who were seen as the most likely decision makers for card adoption, would find convincing. The marketing material that the CPC group adopted to highlight the value of the card to prospective customers is presented in Exhibit 3.

However, it was not enough to win over just the buying organization. American Express also had to persuade a critical mass of popular vendors and suppliers to adjust their order and billing systems to accept the CPC. Widespread supplier acceptance was especially important because deducting a percentage of the total charge from the money paid to suppliers was expected to be the primary source of CPC revenues. To make a profit, the CPC program had to persuade customers to use the card to buy a significant percentage of their staple items and ensure that large volume suppliers could handle these charges efficiently. One strategy that CPC managers adopted to help persuade suppliers to participate in the program was asking each corporation that signed on as a CPC customer to provide a list of the major suppliers it wanted to have accept its CPC American Express charges. The prospect of having a large customer using the card was seen as a good leverage point to persuade suppliers to make the necessary adjustments in their systems and to be willing to pay a percentage of their revenue collection to the CPC. The percentage discount rate adopted by the CPC group was 2.5 percent. This was set to be slightly higher than the sundry card programs that were emerging from Visa and MasterCard, with the differential justified by the greater record-keeping and accounting functionality provided by American Express.

Behind the scenes, one of the American Express purchasing card's strongest differentiators was its One Network Advantage, which creates a direct data channel linking

---

EXHIBIT 4   Build Your Business with the American Express® Corporate Purchasing Card

---

The '90s: A New Era of Expense Management

These days, bringing spending under control is first and foremost on the minds of your corporate customers. They're revamping their traditional, centralized purchasing process for day-to-day expenses. The reason for this is clear: processing a purchase order for a box of staples can cost them as much as processing a purchase order for a mainframe computer system. Your customers can no longer afford to devote the same valuable time and money to both types of purchases. They are looking for you to partner with them to help decrease transaction costs.

The corporations that are looking ahead to the future are prepared to make changes. They're delegating purchasing to a wider range of authorized employees. And by using the American Express Corporate Purchasing Card, they're successfully maintaining control over their spending.

Take Advantage of This New Purchasing Process

As a supplier, you can benefit from your customers' new way of managing expenses. In fact, by welcoming the American Express Corporate Purchasing Card, you can both increase your sales by appealing to a greater number of potential customers and get paid faster. Most importantly, you can offer your customers enhanced services and a more streamlined way to process their transactions.

Receive Faster Payment—in as Few as Three Days

Welcoming the Corporate Purchasing Card can improve your cash flow, putting profits to work for you sooner. Instead of the traditional 45- to 60-day payment cycle you experience with purchase orders and invoices, you can receive payment in as few as three days. Furthermore, payment is guaranteed because Corporate Purchasing Card transactions are paid to you directly by American Express.

Reduce Billing and Collection Costs

Because you'll receive payment directly from American Express, you'll have both fewer invoices to mail and unpaid invoices to follow up on. Therefore, postage costs, data processing time, and printing costs for forms can be significantly reduced.

Boost Sales and Improve Customer Service

At a Glance: The Advantages of welcoming the American Express Corporate Purchasing Card:

- Faster payment.
- Reduced billing and collections costs.
- Orders direct from end-users, resulting in:
  - increased sales
  - reduced paperwork and errors in ordering
  - reduced order turn-around time
- Complimentary listing in the American Express Corporate Purchasing Card Supplier Directory; used by our corporate clients to help in their supplier selection.
- Exposure to all Corporate Purchasing Cardmembers and an additional 6.5 million American Express® Corporate Cardmembers.
- Improved customer service.

Since your corporate customers are authorizing numerous employees to purchase your goods and services directly with the Corporate Purchasing Card, you can increase sales by expanding your customer relationships beyond the purchasing department. By selling directly to the end-users, there will be fewer errors in ordering and you have the ability to substitute out-of-stock items and offer promotions.

---

the client and the supplier through American Express. This allows AMEX to control data capture of transactions at the point of sale and create another benefit: the ability to get line item information such as sales tax and use tax, 1099 information, minority status, product description, and spending by SIC code. Clients can use this information to gain greater control over tax planning and monitoring, corporate buying policies, product pricing, and supplier management. Bank cards, by contrast, have multiple issuers and merchants, with each one having its own third-party processor, which prevents bank card issuers from controlling point of sale data capture.

The description of CPC benefits that was designed to persuade suppliers to participate in the program is presented in Exhibit 4.

EXHIBIT 4   **(Continued)**

Attract New Customers

To help you open your doors to new business from Corporate Purchasing Cardmembers across the country, we'll feature your
company in the Corporate Purchasing Card Supplier Directory. This database is provided free to all Corporate Purchasing customers,
to help them locate their preferred suppliers—the businesses that welcome the Corporate Purchasing Card and provide the required
transaction information.

Process Transactions in Four Easy Steps

While accepting the Corporate Purchasing Card may require some small changes in the way you manage a transaction, each purchase
can be completed with these simple steps:

The Order
Your customer places an order in person, by phone, or by fax.

Authorization
You obtain direct authorization for the total amount of the transaction from American Express by using one of three convenient
electronic payment processing systems.

Fulfillment & Submission
You fill and ship the order and then electronically submit the charge to American Express for quick and easy payment.

Payment
American Express's electronic payment system sends payment directly to your bank account in as few as three days.

Enjoy Unparalleled Customer Service

When you welcome the Corporate Purchasing Card, you can depend on the exemplary customer service American Express has always
provided. Customer Service representatives are available during all business hours to provide assistance.

Choose the Payment Processing System That's Right for You

Corporate Purchasing Card transactions can be quickly and efficiently integrated into your business operations. Several payment
processing options are available.

To find out more about the American Express Corporate Purchasing Card, contact your American Express Sales Representative or call
1-888-TAKE CPC.*

---

*If the telephone system in your area is not equipped to reach the 888 exchange, please call 1-800-686-5493.

From Customer Acquisition to Program Implementation

Once the target market was established and the CPC program was defined in terms of
its value to both buying organizations and suppliers, the focus shifted to an aggressive
strategy for acquiring new customers. The CPC direct sales force met with a positive
corporate response to the presentation of the purchasing card as a way to streamline
routine processes while retaining control of accounting and expenditures. At this stage
there seemed to be relatively few barriers to sales. Prospective customers did need to
make a number of organizational commitments to get the program up and running. In
addition to installing basic CPC software, most companies had to adjust their internal
purchasing procedures to take advantage of the card's features and ensure that their suppliers also were ready to accept card payment. But the corporate customers did not have
to make a significant advance payment to contract for the CPC program, and the sales
presentations promised clients that AMEX resources would help with card implementation and signing on their choice of suppliers.

In 1994 the CPC program was very successful at signing large corporate customers; by
the end of the year AMEX had 259 new CPC clients, exceeding its targets for the first year

of customer acquisition. During 1995, however, it became clear that customer acquisition success did not guarantee that the CPC program would meet its revenue targets. By the middle of 1995, even though more customers were being signed monthly, only 107 of all the CPC clients were actively using the American Express card for purchasing transactions. A midyear customer survey by AMEX managers found that only 45 percent of all clients had even installed the core program "Payment Link" software, which automates charge card transactions and captures data to authorize payment and settle shipments. Without this step, they were not in a position to use the system at all. Even the customers that had the program up and running were not charging at the volume rate projected in the original revenue forecasts for the CPC. Many companies had implemented the purchasing card with a small pilot group or department and were waiting to evaluate the results or sign on more suppliers before rolling it out to the majority of employees.

To find out more about the barriers to implementation, AMEX hired a market research firm to review selected CPC clients and AMEX corporate purchasing field employees. Participants in this study included newly signed accounts, strong accounts that had implemented the program successfully, and early clients that had low or no card purchases. Twenty-one American Express CPC staff members also were interviewed to gain their perspective on the customer support and implementation challenges they had encountered.

Clients that were lagging behind in CPC implementation had one thing in common—the lack of a clear focus on the internal value of supply chain management. Often purchasing managers had underestimated the time and effort required to transform their established purchasing processes to take advantage of the card or had run into unexpected departmental resistance to changing end user procedures. Some complained that they simply could not get the attention of their own IT departments to retool the existing purchasing system or install the CPC software. Not infrequently, the CPC project was on a list of IT projects that were delayed because more urgent priorities kept emerging. These companies were interested in having more CPC support for training and system implementation. They also expected the CPC staff to take more of the initiative in signing on the suppliers with which they were used to doing business.

The CPC field support staff personnel were strongly committed to providing as much hands-on support as possible to facilitate customer implementation. They were, however, frustrated to find that many of the factors influencing the pace of implementation seemed to be beyond the control of their primary customer contact inside the company. They wanted faster turnaround time from AMEX's own IT division in rolling out new charge card features and system enhancements for the advanced customers and at the same time requested more CPC resources on basic card value and "best purchasing practices" to meet the needs of clients at the early stages of implementation.

The study also underscored the differences between active clients and early-stage clients in signing on suppliers. The companies that were less active in using the card actually suggested that many more supplier leads be added to the CPC system because they had not taken any internal steps to consolidate their vendor relationships. As a result, the AMEX support group was dedicating more than 50 percent of its resources to pursuing suppliers recommended by clients that generated only 12 percent of the overall charge volume.

This study helped CPC managers recognize that their initial client targeting had been too broad and that many of the customers who had nominally adopted the CPC program might still be years away from generating significant revenues. Even worse, the least profitable customers tended to require a disproportionate amount of field support resources.

On the basis of these insights, management developed a new CPC strategy for 1996. Sales efforts were limited to mining a targeted list of about 75 high-charge-volume prospects, with the expectation of signing 20 to 25 new accounts. Support for companies that had signed up for the program but did not seem to have realistic plans for high-volume charge activity was transferred to a centralized AMEX support facility based in Phoenix. Reallocated staff resources were dedicated to increasing the volume of charge activity at the top 60 companies that already had implemented the program.

To deal with supplier sign-up more effectively, managers enhanced supplier communications and took responsibility for supplier training and activation. A supplier sign-up program was developed to standardize implementation, and a national supplier database was created to leverage suppliers across multiple clients.

By the end of 1996, the majority of companies that had been designated as targeted CPC clients were active program participants and the volume of charge activity had increased significantly. For the first time the CPC was operating in the black.

Time for Another Look: Competitive and Market Shifts

In 1997, the CPC program was continuing to add card features and charge volume was expanding at a steady rate, but a disturbing trend had emerged. Signing up new clients was slower than AMEX managers had projected and the CPC program was losing some customers to competitors. This was partly due to the refocused strategy that deemphasized broad marketing and sales campaigns and restricted new customer acquisition to

---

EXHIBIT 5   Marketplace Solutions

A variety of solutions have emerged to meet the reengineering requirements in each spending quadrant. Given the size and importance of Quadrants III and IV, most efforts have focused on implementing high-end solutions to cut costs. Only recently have companies started looking at Quadrants I and II as a potential source of savings.

Quadrant Characteristics	Current Solutions	
	Ordering	*Payment*
IV: Speciality High-value contracts which are negotiated on a one-off basis.	• Orders are executed (manually, fax, or EDI) from an electronic requisitioning system	• Financial EDI (electronic invoice; EDI payment) • Check requests
III: Strategic Mission-critical strategic purchases which go into the end product. Contracts are highly leveraged and very price-sensitive.	• Orders executed via EDI from a just-in-time materials requirements planning system	• Financial EDI • Electronic summary billing • Evaluated receipts settlement
II: Staples High-volume contracts which are negotiated up front under "blanket" agreements. Requesters are authorized to go "directly" to the supplier.	• Desktop catalog systems • Internet-based catalog systems • Integrated supply (vendor is responsible for replenishing, buying, and managing item inventories)	• Financial EDI • Purchasing cards • Electronic summary billing
I: Sundry Typically no contract in place. End user can choose from a variety of suppliers.	• None	• Purchasing cards • Petty cash • Check requests

prospects with the highest charge volume. Many of these attractive prospects, however, were looking for low-dollar, low-volume Quadrant I solutions, which they found lacking in the AMEX program.

Options for implementing corporate purchasing card programs and the supply management goals of many large companies had undergone some important changes since the introduction of the CPC in 1994. Competition for card customers was much stronger in 1997, and AMEX has not fared well in gaining the attention of the marketplace. Of those companies actively using or planning to implement corporate purchasing cards, only 19 percent were aware of AMEX's product, while 28 percent knew about Visa purchasing cards and 35 percent were aware of or already using MasterCard.

EXHIBIT 5   Quadrant I Challenges (Continued)

The banks are the primary solution providers for Quadrant I. The number of banks in the market has dramatically increased, and they share a consistent market position. The banks offer a quick, easy-to-use charge card for low-dollar purchasing.

# of Bankcard Competitors	1	2	3	4	6	7	9	–	60–75
Year	89	90	91	92	93	94	95	96	97YTD

First Bank Systems (V)
Corestates (V)
Nations Bank (V)
First Chicago (MC)
GE Capital (MC)
Citibank (V/MC)
American Express
Chase (V/MC)
Bank of America (MC)
Firstar (V)
Wells Fargo (MC)
First USA (V)
Harris (V)
PNC (V)
Sun Trust (V)

Source: PSI, 1996

Positioning

Visa (Quadrant I)	Stresses program simplicity and ease of implementation; leverages widespread supplier acceptance for convenience and utility; extends coverage superiority (versus AmEx) into commercial market.
MasterCard (Quadrants I/II)	Stresses ease of implementation and the ability to meet supplier coverage needs; tactically responsive to client needs (e.g., high ROC pricing/enhanced data capture initiatives).
American Express (Quadrant II)	Promotes enhanced procurement solution; attempts to support strategic procurement initiatives such as supplier consolidation with enhanced data capture and reporting; promises transactional and unit cost reduction.

EXHIBIT 5   Quadrant III/IV Challenges: Impact on Quadrant II (Continued)

The proliferation of the enterprise system not only drives low P-card awareness but also fuels the perception of P-card value. Enterprise systems facilitate the use of alternative procurement methods (e.g., EDI). As the use of these systems grows, so does the use of alternatives. For the purchasing card to displace the alternatives, clients and client influencers must widely accept the purchasing card as the most valuable method of procurement for Quadrant II.

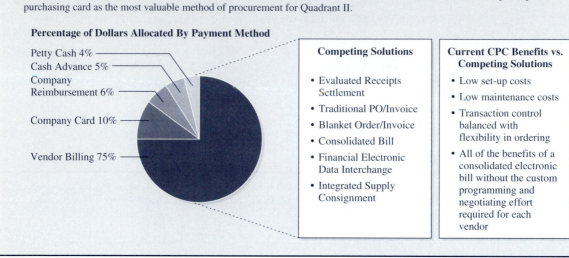

Percentage of Dollars Allocated By Payment Method

Petty Cash 4%
Cash Advance 5%
Company Reimbursement 6%
Company Card 10%
Vendor Billing 75%

Competing Solutions

• Evaluated Receipts Settlement
• Traditional PO/Invoice
• Blanket Order/Invoice
• Consolidated Bill
• Financial Electronic Data Interchange
• Integrated Supply Consignment

Current CPC Benefits vs. Competing Solutions

• Low set-up costs
• Low maintenance costs
• Transaction control balanced with flexibility in ordering
• All of the benefits of a consolidated electronic bill without the custom programming and negotiating effort required for each vendor

Source: 1996 PSI Commercial Card Research Program: *Capitalizing on Purchasing Cards; Purchasing,* August 1997.

To see where it stood competitively against bank card providers that capture low-dollar, low-transaction spending and enterprise solutions providers that capture strategic and specialty high-dollar transactions, the CPC management initiated another purchasing solutions market review. The results of this study are summarized in Exhibit 5.

This study served as a wake-up call for AMEX. Behind the reassuring increase in overall charge volume, CPC managers saw serious competitive threats to their program. At the lower level they could be squeezed by less fully featured bank cards that had succeeded in positioning themselves as a faster, easier-to-implement corporate purchasing solution, a message that had special appeal to companies that were not ready to undertake a purchasing reengineering project. At the high end, it seemed that expensive integrated enterprise solution vendors such as SAP were adding procurement software to their product mix. Companies that had already invested millions in implementing SAP across their organizations seemed likely to want a purchasing solution that was fully integrated with their financial and accounting systems. The finding that more companies were at least considering using the Web for purchasing activity could be either a threat or an opportunity for the CPC program. Electronic commerce on the Internet offered a standards-based, low-cost approach to business-to-business transactions and opened the purchasing services market to even more competitors. But if the CPC could integrate a Web interface successfully into its own program, that could accelerate the pace of implementation for many clients and broaden the appeal of the purchasing card to a larger group of buyers and suppliers.

The 1998 CPC strategic plan, which Stewart's management team already had reviewed at earlier meetings, was designed to respond to both the threats and the opportunities that had emerged from the latest procurement marketplace analysis. Key elements of the plan included the following:

EXHIBIT 5   Quadrant III/IV Challenges (Continued)

We also face challenges from Quadrant III and IV providers. SAP, PeopleSoft, Baan, and the like, offer comprehensive integrated procurement systems. These providers are partnering with market influencers (Andersen, Price Waterhouse), and together they have captured the attention and funding of client senior management, based on their ability to meet Quadrants III and IV requirements as well as those of Quadrant II.

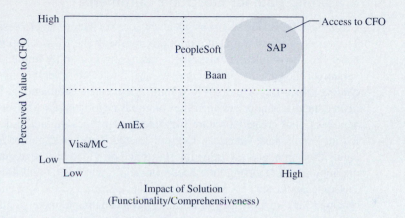

Enterprise System Stakeholders and Position

Systems Provider Position
- Comprehensive system with built in hooks to EDI, General Ledger, Inventory Management
- Used for a variety of expenditure types
- "One-stop purchasing solution"

Consultant Position
- Revenue enhanced by long implementation time frame
- Attempt to find technology solution to fit all purchasing processes

Client Impact
- Push purchases through the system to justify heavy investment in system
- Long implementation cycle takes attention away from other initiatives

1. Moving from a primary focus on Quadrant II commodity and MRO purchases to a more comprehensive coverage of all types of purchasing within the organization.
   - Expand card coverage to present a low-end sundry purchase solution.
   - Partner with high-end solution providers to integrate the card with organizationwide systems.
   - Enhance sales and service capabilities in this area.
2. Expanding card functionality to establish dominance in the commodity purchase arena.
   - Add capabilities such as line item detail that customers have been requesting.
   - Further expand supplier participation.
3. Providing Web-based purchasing card options.
   - Implement Web purchasing transactions using the Open Buying on the Internet (OBI) standard.

- Develop an Internet purchasing module (OrderLink) that simplifies Web purchasing implementation for both customers and suppliers.
- Implement a full-featured, information-rich CPC Web site for buyers and suppliers; encourage program administrators to use this for on-line card administration.

A Starring Role for Electronic Commerce?

Using the CPC on the Web was not a new idea for American Express managers. In 1994 Thayer Stewart had initiated a pilot program with the Massachusetts Institute of Technology to streamline the university's purchasing system by implementing a Web-based version of the CPC for MIT employees. MIT selected several of its major suppliers, including Office Depot and VWR Scientific, to create customized on-line catalogs that reflected the discount prices and range of goods negotiated for MIT departments. The university IT staff created a secure Web interface for locating and ordering supplies called E-Cat. For its part, American Express created Web-based authorization, payment, account allocation, and reporting interfaces and provided back-end automated budget reconciliation and reporting interfaces with MIT's purchasing and finance departments.

Based on the success of the E-Cat project, several of the key university participants obtained MIT support to split off and start a separate company called SupplyWorks in 1996. The new company continued to work with Stewart and the CPC program to expand the Web purchasing opportunity and determine the demand for Web solutions among large buying organizations. American Express awarded a market research contract to SupplyWorks to conduct an in-depth market research study on how purchasing directors regarded Internet-based purchasing solutions and the potential for the adoption of Web-based procurement systems. This research revealed that large corporations were attracted to the Web's promise of interoperability and freedom from proprietary vendor software to support their purchasing systems but a general sense that the Internet was not ready to handle large-volume secure transactions. In particular, both buying organizations and large suppliers expressed concern about the lack of explicit Internet purchasing standards that could guide the development of truly interoperable systems.

This issue presented a barrier to immediate adoption of Web-based purchasing programs, but it also seemed to offer a golden opportunity to help shape the longer-term direction of Internet purchasing activity. Taking the lead in setting standards had become a successful strategy for many companies committed to growing business on-line. This line of reasoning led Stewart to advocate for American Express sponsorship of the Internet Purchasing Roundtable in 1996. This group brought together purchasing representatives from Fortune 500 corporations with major selling organizations to discuss the need for standards creation. By the middle of 1997, the Internet Purchasing Roundtable had reached a consensus on the need for a vendor-neutral Internet purchasing standard for business, and had developed a prototype standard called Open Buying on the Internet (OBI). An interview with Stewart in summer 1997 highlights his personal support for OBI (Exhibit 6).

The OBI standard is for high-volume, low-dollar transactions, which account for about 80 percent of most organizations' purchasing. Version 1.0 of the OBI standard included a comprehensive technical specification, information about secure transport, OBI objects, and the OBI EDI specification. The standard is free for any organization to use to develop solutions, products, and services. It is intended for use by buying and selling organizations, technology companies, financial institutions, service providers, and other organizations interested in business-to-business Internet commerce. By the end of 1997

EXHIBIT 6   Setting Standards for Corporate Purchasing on the Internet

American Express aimed to foster online systems that would boost the use of its services to buy business supplies. It may wind up abetting Web-based competition.

Mary J. Cronin

Three years ago, Thayer Stewart began pondering the billions of dollars companies spend each year on paper clips, pens, and all the other consumables in their supply closets. As vice president of American Express's corporate services division, he dreamed of channeling such purchases through Amex. The costs of ordering and processing payments for keeping a myriad of business supplies in stock often exceed outlays for the goods themselves. That suggested a gambit: Help companies cut costs by offering them an efficient online purchasing system with Amex inside.

But when Stewart convened a buyer-seller focus group to define the features of a killer purchasing system, the list of demands was sobering. The system would have to be open to all vendors, be easy to implement on the buyer's end, and use existing hardware and software—pricey proprietary software was definitely out. It also would need a single simple interface for ordering, approval, and secure online payment. When Stewart showed the list to his colleagues at *American Express,* the reaction was: "This isn't a set of specifications; it's the Holy Grail." But when he ran it by Peter Roden, who was developing an online purchasing system at Massachusetts Institute of Technology with Amex and supplies vendors, his response was simply: "Sounds like the Web."

Roden had found it relatively easy to sell the idea of Web-based purchasing at MIT, where the culture was imbued with the Internet and cutting costs was a high priority. Roden's team developed an online catalogue, and American Express provided payment services, including invoicing and back-end accounting. The project's success stirred corporate interest, convincing Stewart and Roden that selling Web purchasing systems would work as a business. Funded by Amex, Roden and several colleagues left MIT in April 1996 to start SupplyWorks.

The company quickly encountered a daunting reality: Many companies are wedded to proprietary computer systems for business-to-business purchasing. Offering purchasing software on the Web wouldn't induce them to abandon investments in such systems, especially in the absence of a widely accepted standard that could ensure compatibility among buyers and sellers. Going back to the drawing board, Stewart and Roden sketched out Plan B: Develop standards for buying supplies on the Internet, hastening the day when the Web would be the preferred medium for such transactions.

Last fall, SupplyWorks, with additional funding from Amex, organized an Internet purchasing roundtable to pursue that goal. A score of Fortune 500 companies with big buying budgets accepted the invitation to join. Like Stewart's original focus group, their primary goals were to help different buying systems interact seamlessly and put vendors on an equal footing. The group's first draft, issued in May, is called Open Buying on the Internet, or OBI. Recently the roundtable was reorganized as a nonprofit consortium open to all interested organizations. SupplyWorks handles administrative functions.

As a general framework for business-to-business transactions, OBI offers multiple payoffs. It will discourage software vendors from populating the Web with proprietary systems that can't interact. It will encourage innovative vendors to jump in, since customers needn't buy from a dominant vendor to ensure their software can interact with others' systems. A critical mass of companies already has endorsed the standards, including sellers of purchasing software; big buyers and sellers of corporate supplies, such as Ford and Office Depot; and major Web-commerce players, such as Microsoft, General Electric, and Oracle.

But will Amex reap extra benefits from having spearheaded the standards? Officially, it is just another member of the standards group. Amex is betting that OBI will foster ever more transactions on the Web, and that many will be authorized, invoiced, and paid through its purchasing-card programs. If the standards consortium does its job well, however, this lucrative new niche will be open to competitors, even companies from entirely different industries. Amex could lose corporate-card customers to suppliers of Web interface software that branch out to offer payment services. Providers of Internet communications links might also make a play for the business.

Stewart says that risk is intrinsic to Internet commerce: "Trying to hold on to a proprietary advantage on the Internet is like putting up a dam after the river has run dry. If the market adopts Web purchasing in a big way, we'll definitely be competing with alternative card and vendor programs. But at least the flow of business will keep growing." Amex can count on at least one reward from its efforts, though: It will be perfectly positioned to stock up on paper clips.

Mary J. Cronin is a professor of management at Boston College and strategic adviser to Mainspring Communications. An expanded version of her column is available online at www.mainspring.com. Cronin can be reached at cronin@mainspring.com. http://www.pathfinder.com/fortune/digitalwatch/0908dig4.html.

the Roundtable had won widespread recognition and support for OBI and had formed a nonprofit consortium to promote its adoption.

Taking a leadership role in Internet standards development was a strong statement of CPC interest in electronic commerce, but it had not led to any immediate changes in the CPC product definition during 1997. In fact, the value of devoting more resources and marketing attention to Web-based purchasing solutions during 1998 was a topic of heated management debate within Stewart's group. Advocates for more emphasis on the Web argued that the CPC should capitalize on its leadership in establishing the OBI standard to position itself as the premier provider of electronic commerce purchasing solutions. In particular, they saw an electronic commerce strategy as a vital component in reviving the rate of new customer acquisition. Skeptics maintained that it was still too soon for most large corporations to move their purchasing activities to the Internet and that focusing on Web-based services would distract the CPC group from addressing the enhancements to the current program that had been requested by high-volume customers.

Setting the Agenda

Stewart looked at his watch. It was time to finalize the afternoon's agenda. The last item in the stack of materials that he had reviewed in preparation was a recent survey of corporate purchasing directors conducted by *Purchasing* magazine. Like many of the other materials, this article seemed to offer both opportunities and threats. It reported that even though the majority of corporate buyers were not actively using the Internet in 1997, 80 percent indicated plans to use the Net for business purposes in 1998 and 97 percent expected it to be an important tool in purchasing activity within five years. Would those corporate buyers use the Internet as an alternative to the CPC, or could they be won over by a more aggressive AMEX electronic commerce strategy? Stewart was not sure whether it was a good idea to introduce these new data into the discussion. He wanted to end the meeting with a consensus on the short-term priorities for 1998 and the longer-term changes needed to propel the CPC program to the forefront of the purchasing solutions market. It was going to be a long afternoon.

CASE 4–3
THE QUAKER OATS COMPANY, GATORADE, AND SNAPPLE BEVERAGE

In November 1994 Quaker Oats Co. negotiated a deal to acquire the iced tea and fruit drink marketer Snapple Beverage Corp. for $1.7 billion in cash, a move that took Quaker off the list of rumored takeover targets and greatly strengthened its position as a producer-marketer of beverage substitutes for soft drinks. Quaker's Gatorade brand commanded 85 percent of the sports drink segment in the United States, generated worldwide sales of almost $1.2 billion, and was Quaker's fastest-growing, most lucrative product. Snapple had 1993 sales of $516 million, up from $95 million in 1991, and was the clear-cut market leader in New Age or alternative beverages, with a national distribution capability and growing brand awareness among consumers. Quaker's acquisition of Snapple elevated it into a nonalcoholic beverage powerhouse with nearly $2 billion in sales, trailing only Coca-Cola and PepsiCo.

Quaker agreed to pay Snapple shareholders $14 a share for the 121,620,000 shares outstanding, a price roughly equal to the $13.75 to $14.25 trading range of Snapple stock in the few days before the agreement was announced. Shares of Snapple, which had traded in range of the $28 to $32 in late 1993 and early 1994, had fallen in recent months when sales growth during the first three quarters of 1994 slowed significantly, and ready-to-drink tea products carrying the Lipton and Nestea brands began to capture almost 50 percent of sales in supermarkets. The Lipton line was jointly produced and marketed by PepsiCo and Unilever's Thomas J. Lipton subsidiary; the Nestea line was the product of an alliance between Coca-Cola and Nestlé (Nestlé was the world's largest food products company and the producer of Nestea-brand teas).

Hours before the Quaker–Snapple agreement was announced, Snapple reported a third-quarter earnings drop of 74 percent, which analysts attributed to oversized inventories and intensifying competition. In NYSE trading on the following day, Quaker's stock fell nearly 10 percent, from $74.50 to $67.125. The drop in price was said to be a combination of Snapple's poor earnings report, the reduced likelihood that Quaker would be a takeover target, and the high acquisition price Quaker was paying for Snapple. Wall Street analysts regarded the outlook for Snapple's future sales and earnings as very uncertain. Whereas Snapple's management indicated in May 1994 that it was comfortable with a 1994 earnings per share projection of 86 cents a share, the confidential business plan Snapple gave Quaker during their negotiations contained a projection of only 55 cents a share; in a filing with the Securities and Exchange Commission in the week after the acquisition announcement, Snapple indicated that 1994 earnings of 40 cents a share appeared more reasonable.[1] The $14 acquisition price represented a multiple of 35 times Snapple's latest earnings projection of 40 cents per share and a multiple of nearly 20 times Snapple's estimated 1994 operating earnings (the latter multiple was well above the multiples of 10 and 11 that other recently acquired beverage companies had commanded).[2]

This case prepared by Arthur A. Thompson, Jr., the University of Alabama, and John E. Gamble, Auburn University of Montgomery. Copyright © 1995 by Arthur A. Thompson, Jr.

[1] Reported in *The Wall Street Journal,* November 7, 1994, p. A4.
[2] *The Wall Street Journal,* November 3, 1994, pp. A3, A4.

To finance the Snapple acquisition, Quaker borrowed $2.4 billion from Nations-Bank. Quaker planned to use the loan proceeds to (1) make cash payments of $1.7 billion to Snapple's shareholders for the outstanding 121,620,000 shares, (2) pay off $100 million in Snapple debt, (3) refinance $350 million in Quaker's debt, and (4) retain $250 million for working capital. Quaker management reportedly was seeking buyers for its European pet foods business and Mexican chocolate subsidiary (combined sales of $900 million) as part of an ongoing restructuring of its food products lineup and presumably to raise cash to pay down debt associated with the Snapple acquisition.

The Quaker Oats Company

In 1994 Quaker Oats was the twelfth largest food and beverage company in the United States, with worldwide sales of $6 billion (see Exhibit 1). The company operated 54 manufacturing plants in 16 states and 13 foreign countries and had distribution centers and sales offices in 21 states and 18 foreign countries. Nearly one-third of corporate revenues came from sales outside the United States. Quaker's worldwide grocery prod-

EXHIBIT 1 **The 25 Largest Food and Beverage Companies in the United States**
(ranked by 1993 food and beverage sales, in millions of dollars)

Company	1992	1993
1. Philip Morris	$33,024	$34,526
2. ConAgra Inc.	16,201	16,499
3. PepsiCo	13,738	15,665
4. Coca-Cola	13,039	13,937
5. IBP Inc.	11,128	11,671
6. Anheuser-Busch	10,741	10,792
7. Sara Lee	6,622	7,206
8. H. J. Heinz	6,582	7,103
9. RJR Nabisco	6,707	7,025
10. Campbell Soup	6,263	6,586
11. Kellogg	6,191	6,295
12. Quaker Oats	5,576	5,731
13. CPC International	5,502	5,636
14. General Mills	5,234	5,397
15. Seagram Company	5,214	5,227
16. Tyson Foods	4,169	4,707
17. Ralston Purina	4,558	4,526
18. Borden Inc.	4,056	3,674
19. Hershey Foods	3,220	3,488
20. Procter & Gamble	3,709	3,271
21. Dole Foods	3,120	3,108
22. Hormel Foods	2,814	2,854
23. Chiquita Brands	2,723	2,522
24. Dean Foods	2,220	2,243
25. International Multifoods	2,281	2,224

Source: The Food Institute.

uct portfolio included such well-known brands as Quaker Oats, Cap'n Crunch, Rice-A-Roni, Gatorade, Aunt Jemima, Ken-L Ration pet foods, and Van Camp's bean products; 81 percent of the company's sales came from brands holding the number one or number two position in their respective categories. Moreover, 82 percent of Quaker's worldwide sales came from brands positioned in categories where sales volumes were growing. Hot cereals were Quaker's oldest, best-known, and most profitable products. Of the top 25 cereal brands, Quaker had 4: Instant Quaker Oatmeal, Cap'n Crunch, Old Fashioned and Quick Quaker Oats, and Life Cereal.

Quaker's top management was committed to achieving real earnings growth of 7 percent and providing total shareholder returns (dividends plus share price appreciation) that exceeded the S&P 500 stock index over time. Management also believed it could enhance shareholder value by prudently using leverage. Before the Snapple acquisition, Quaker issued $200 million in medium-term notes, increasing total debt to $1 billion. In fiscal 1994 Quaker used its debt proceeds and cash flow from operations to repurchase 3 million shares of common stock, make four small acquisitions, extend the company's record of consecutive dividend increases to 27 years, and make $175 million in capital investments to support growth and efficiency improvements. Exhibit 2 provides a 10-year financial summary of Quaker's corporate performance.

Quaker's Corporate Organization and Brand Portfolio. Quaker Oats' worldwide production and sales operations were structured around two broad geographic groups: U.S. and Canadian Grocery Products and International Grocery Products. The U.S. and Canadian Grocery group was subdivided into four product divisions: Breakfast Foods, Gatorade Worldwide, Diversified Grocery Products (pet foods and grain products), and Convenience Foods. The International Grocery Products group had three geographic operating divisions: Europe, Latin America, and Pacific. Exhibit 3 shows the financial performance of the two major product groups. Exhibit 4 shows the brands and sales of the divisional units.

The Gatorade Worldwide Division. Gatorade was developed in 1965 for the University of Florida Gators; it was sold to Stokely-Van Camp in 1967. Quaker acquired the Gatorade brand in 1983 when it bought Stokely-Van Camp. At that time Gatorade sales were about $100 million. Since the acquisition, sales of Gatorade had grown at an average annual compound rate of 22 percent, spurred by the addition of flavor and package-size variety as well as wider geographic distribution. Worldwide sales were just over $1.1 billion in 1994, up 21 percent over fiscal 1993. U.S. and Canadian volume increased 19 percent; international volume was up 31 percent. According to Quaker estimates, Gatorade held a 77 percent share of the $1.3 billion U.S. sports beverage category as of mid-1994 (down from 90 percent–plus in 1990–1991) and more than 40 percent of the global sports drink market. Quaker management believed that Gatorade's science-based rehydration ability to replace salts and fluids lost during exercise, strong identification with sports, and leading position domestically and globally made it an exceptionally profitable growth opportunity worldwide. Gatorade was Quaker's number one growth priority, and the stated mission of the Gatorade Worldwide division was "to quench hot and thirsty consumers in every corner of the world."

Gatorade's Market Scope. In 1994, Gatorade was marketed in 26 countries on five continents and had the leading market position in most of those locations. The brand's biggest markets in 1994 were the United States, Mexico, South Korea, Canada, Venezuela, Italy, Germany, and Taiwan. In 1994 sales of Gatorade totaled nearly $900 million in the United States and approximately $220 million in the other 25 countries

EXHIBIT 2 Financial Summary for Quaker Oats Company, 1984–1994 (dollars in millions, except per-share data)

Year Ended June 30	5-Year CAGR[1]	10-Year CAGR[1]	1994	1993	1992	1991	1990	1989	1988	1987	1986	1985	1984
Operating Results[2,3]													
Net sales	4.1%	7.7%	$5,955.0	$5,730.6	$5,576.4	$5,491.2	$5,030.6	$4,879.4	$4,508.0	$3,823.9	$2,968.6	$2,925.6	$2,830.9
Gross profit	6.3%	10.8%	3,028.8	2,860.6	2,745.3	2,652.7	2,350.3	2,229.0	2,114.6	1,750.7	1,298.7	1,174.7	1,085.7
Income from continuing operations before income taxes and cumulative effect of accounting changes	9.6%	6.0%	378.7	467.6	421.5	411.5	382.4	239.1	314.6	295.9	255.8	238.8	211.3
Provision for income taxes	10.3%	4.0%	147.2	180.8	173.9	175.7	153.5	90.2	118.1	141.3	113.4	110.3	99.0
Income from continuing operations before cumulative effect of account changes	9.2%	7.5%	231.5	286.8	247.6	235.8	228.9	148.9	196.5	154.6	142.4	128.5	112.3
Income (loss) from discontinued operations, net of tax			—	—	—	(30.0)	(59.9)	54.1	59.2	33.5	37.2	28.1	26.4
Income from the disposal of discontinued operations, net of tax			—	—	—	—	—	—	—	55.8	—	—	—
Cumulative effect of accounting changes, net of tax			—	(115.5)	—	—	—	—	—	—	—	—	—
Net income	2.7%	5.3%	$ 231.5	$ 171.3	$ 247.6	$ 205.8	$ 169.0	$ 203.0	$ 255.7	$ 243.9	$ 179.6	$ 156.6	$ 138.7
Per common share:													
Income from continuing operations for cumulative effect of accounting changes	12.3%	9.5%	$ 3.36	$ 3.93	$ 3.25	$ 3.05	$ 2.93	$ 1.88	$ 2.46	$ 1.96	$ 1.77	$ 1.53	$ 1.35
Income (loss) from discontinued operations			—	—	—	(0.40)	(0.78)	0.68	0.74	0.43	0.47	0.35	0.32
Income from the disposal of discontinued operations			—	—	—	—	—	—	—	0.71	—	—	—
Cumulative effect of accounting changes			—	(1.59)	—	—	—	—	—	—	—	—	—
Net income	5.6%	7.2%	$ 3.36	$ 2.34	$ 3.25	$ 2.65	$ 2.15	$ 2.56	$ 3.20	$ 3.10	$ 2.24	$ 1.88	$ 1.67
Dividends declared:													
Common stock	8.1%	12.2%	$ 140.6	$ 136.1	$ 128.6	$ 118.7	$ 106.9	$ 95.2	$ 79.9	$ 63.2	$ 55.3	$ 50.5	$ 44.4
Per common share	12.1%	14.4%	$ 2.12	$ 1.92	$ 1.72	$ 1.56	$ 1.40	$ 1.20	$ 1.00	$ 0.80	$ 0.70	$ 0.62	$ 0.55
Convertible preferred and redeemable preference stock			$ 4.0	$ 4.2	$ 4.2	$ 4.3	3.6	—	—	—	$ 2.3	$ 3.6	$ 3.9
Average number of common shares outstanding (in thousands)			67,618	71,974	74,881	75,904	76,537	79,307	79,835	78,812	79,060	81,492	80,412
Financial Statistics[4,5]													
Current ratio			1.0	1.0	1.2	1.3	1.3	1.8	1.4	1.4	1.4	1.7	1.6
Working capital			$ (5.5)	$ (37.5)	$ 168.7	$ 317.8	$ 342.8	$ 695.8	$ 417.5	$ 507.9	$ 296.8	$ 400.7	$ 316.8
Property, plant, and equipment, net			$1,214.2	$1,228.2	$2,173.3	$1,232.7	$1,154.1	$ 959.6	$ 922.5	$ 898.6	$ 691.0	$ 616.5	$ 650.1
Depreciation expense			$ 133.3	$ 129.9	$ 129.7	$ 125.2	$ 103.5	$ 94.2	$ 88.3	$ 81.6	$ 59.1	$ 56.3	$ 57.4
Total assets			$3,043.3	$2,815.9	$3,039.9	$3,060.5	$3,377.4	$3,125.9	$2,886.1	$3,136.5	$1,944.5	$1,760.3	$1,726.5
Long-term debt			$ 759.5	$ 632.6	$ 688.7	$ 701.2	$ 740.3	$ 766.8	$ 299.1	$ 527.7	$ 160.9	$ 168.2	$ 200.1

EXHIBIT 2 **(Concluded)**

Year Ended June 30	*5-Year CAGR*[1]	*10-Year CAGR*[1]	*1994*	*1993*	*1992*	*1991*	*1990*	*1989*	*1988*	*1987*	*1986*	*1985*	*1984*
Financial Statistics[4,5] **(Continued)**													
Preferred stock (net of deferred compensation) and redeemable preference stock			$ 15.3	$ 11.4	$ 7.9	$ 4.8	$ 1.8	—	—	—	—	$ 37.9	$ 38.5
Common shareholders' equity			$ 445.8	$ 551.1	$ 842.1	$ 901.0	$1,017.5	$1,137.1	$1,251.1	$1,087.5	$ 831.7	$ 786.9	$ 720.1
Net cash provided by operating activities			$ 450.8	$ 558.2	$ 581.3	$ 543.2	$ 460.0	$ 408.3	$ 320.8	$ 375.1	$ 266.9	$ 295.5	$ 263.6
Operating return on assets[6]			19.9%	21.1%	18.9%	18.8%	20.4%	14.4%	18.3%	22.1%	25.8%	24.5%	24.4%
Gross profit as a percentage of sales			50.9%	49.9%	49.2%	48.3%	46.7%	45.7%	46.9%	45.8%	43.7%	40.2%	38.4%
Advertising and merchandising as a percentage of sales			26.6%	25.7%	26.0%	25.6%	23.8%	23.4%	24.9%	22.9%	21.7%	19.4%	18.4%
Income from continuing operations before cumulative effect of accounting changes as a percentage of sales			3.9%	5.0%	4.4%	4.3%	4.6%	3.1%	4.4%	4.0%	4.8%	4.4%	4.0%
Total debt–total capitalization ratio[7]			68.8%	59.0%	48.7%	47.4%	52.3%	44.2%	33.8%	50.2%	35.7%	28.9%	35.4%
Common dividends as a percentage of income available for common shares (excluding cumulative effect of accounting changes)			63.1%	48.9%	52.9%	58.9%	65.1%	46.9%	31.3%	25.9%	31.2%	33.0%	32.9%
Number of common shareholders			28,197	33,154	33,580	33,603	33,859	34,347	34,231	32,358	27,068	26,670	26,785
Number of employees worldwide			20,000	20,200	21,100	20,900	28,200	31,700	31,300	30,800	29,500	28,700	28,400
Market price range of common stock—High			$ 82	$ 77	$ 75¼	$ 64⅞	$ 68⅛	$ 66¼	$ 57⅛	$ 57⅝	$ 39¼	$ 26⅛	$ 16⅛
—Low			$ 61⅞	$ 56⅛	$ 50¼	$ 41¾	$ 45⅛	$ 42⅝	$ 31	$ 32⅝	$ 23½	$ 14¼	$ 10¾

[1] CAGR = compound average growth rate.

[2] Fiscal 1994 results include a pretax restructuring charge of $118.4 million, or $1.09 per share, for work force reductions, plant consolidations, and product discontinuations and a pretax gain of $9.8 million, or $0.13 per share, for the sale of a business in Venezuela.

[3] Fiscal 1989 results include a pretax restructuring charge of $124.3 million, or $1.00 per share, for plant consolidations and overhead reductions and a pretax charge of $25.6 million, or $0.20 per share, for a change to the LIFO method of accounting for the majority of U.S. Grocery Products inventories.

[4] Income-related statistics exclude the results of businesses reported as discontinued operations. Balance sheet amounts and related statistics have not been restated for discontinued operations, other than Fisher-Price, due to materiality.

[5] Effective fiscal 1991, common shareholders' equity and number of employees worldwide were reduced as a result of the Fisher-Price spin-off.

[6] Operating income divided by average identifiable assets of U.S. and Canadian and International Grocery Products.

[7] Total debt divided by total debt plus total shareholders' equity including preferred stock (net of deferred compensation) and redeemable preference stock.

Source: 1994 Annual Report.

EXHIBIT 3   **Financial Performance of Quaker's Two Major Grocery Products Groups, 1989–1994**
(dollars in millions)

Product Group	Fiscal Year Ended June 30					
	1989	*1990*	*1991*	*1992*	*1993*	*1994*
U.S. and Canadian Grocery Products						
Net sales	$3,630	$3,610	$3,860	$3,842	$3,930	$4,253
Operating income	256	373	429	435	447	431
Identifiable assets	2,055	2,150	2,229	1,998	1,877	1,999
Return on net sales	7.1%	10.3%	11.1%	11.3%	11.4%	10.1%
Return on assets	13.1%	17.7%	19.6%	20.6%	23.1%	22.2%
International Grocery Products						
Net sales	$1,250	$1,421	$1,631	$1,734	$1,800	$1,702
Operating income	93	172	104	105	128	106
Identifiable assets	482	638	656	842	745	786
Return on net sales	7.5%	12.1%	6.4%	6.1%	7.1%	6.2%
Return on assets	20.0%	30.7%	16.1%	14.0%	16.2%	13.9%

Source: 1994 Annual Report.

where it was marketed. Management's objective was to increase sales in Latin America, Europe, and the Pacific to $1 billion by the year 2000.

In Latin America, Gatorade's sports drink share was in the range of 90 percent in all the countries where it was available. Mexico was Gatorade's second largest market after the United States. In 1994 sales in Brazil increased fourfold as Gatorade was relaunched successfully in the São Paulo region. Sales volumes continued to rise in Venezuela and the Caribbean, and Gatorade was introduced into Chile. To deal with the growing sales volume in Latin America, Quaker was investing in additional production facilities.

Competition in the sports beverage market in Europe was fierce because in a number of important countries the market was already developed. When Gatorade was introduced in those country markets, it had to win sales and market share away from established brands. Quaker had pulled Gatorade out of the competitive British and French markets. Given the varying competitive intensity from country to country, Quaker's Gatorade division was focusing its marketing resources on the most promising European country markets. Sales were currently biggest in Germany and Italy. In 1994 Gatorade was introduced in Holland and Austria. Quaker management anticipated that Gatorade sales in Europe would evolve more slowly than they would in other global locations. In 1994 volume grew 9 percent in Europe, but sales revenue was lower because of weaker European currencies against the U.S. dollar.

Throughout most of the Pacific, Gatorade was sold primarily through licensing agreements. Quaker's most successful licensing agreement was with Cheil Foods in South Korea, where Gatorade was a strong second in the sports beverage segment. Gatorade volume in South Korea ranked third, behind the United States and Mexico. In fiscal 1994 Gatorade was introduced in Australia (where the brand was sold through an arrangement with Pepsi-Cola bottlers in Australia), Singapore, and Hong Kong. Although Gatorade was not the first sports drink marketed in Australia, the brand captured the leading share by mid-1994, less than 12 months after it was introduced.

The expense of underwriting Gatorade's entry into new country markets had pinched Gatorade's international profit margins. Quaker's profits from international sales of

EXHIBIT 4   Quaker Brands and Sales by Division, 1989–1994 (dollars in millions)

Division/Category	Brands/Products	1989	1990	1991	1992	1993	1994
		— Sales in Fiscal Year Ending June 30					
Breakfast foods	Quaker Oatmeal, Cap'n Crunch, Life, Quaker rice cakes, Quaker Chewy granola bars, Quaker grits, Aunt Jemima cornmeal	$1,292	$1,280	$1,322	$1,313	$1,425	$1,573
Pet foods	Ken-L Ration, Gaines, Kibbles 'n Bits, Puss 'n Boots, Cycle	608	518	531	531	529	539
Golden Grain	Rice-A-Roni, Noodle Roni, Near East Golden Grain, Mission	283	275	297	309	269	305
Convenience foods	Aunt Jemima breakfast products, Celeste frozen pizza, Van Camp's canned beans, Wolf chili, Burry cookies, Maryland Club coffee, Proof & Bake frozen products, Petrofsky's bakery products	857	901	978	953	949	924
Gatorade (U.S. and Canada)	Gatorade	584	630	724	727	750	906
Europe	Quaker cereals, Gatorade, Felix cat food, Bonzo dog food, Cuore corn oil	969	1,085	1,326	1,355	1,336	1,164
Latin America and Pacific	Quaker cereals, Gatorade	281	336	305	380	465	538

Source: 1994 Annual Report.

Gatorade were expected to remain subpar as the company pushed for expanded penetration of international markets. Quaker management believed that increased consumer interest in healthy foods and beverages, growing sports participation, expanded sports competition in the world arena, increasing acceptance of international brands, and a growing population in warm-climate countries and youthful age segments—especially in Latin America and the Asian Pacific region—all boded well for Gatorade's continued sales growth in international markets.

The U.S. Market Situation.   The Gatorade brand was coming under increased competitive pressure in the U.S. market as a number of companies introduced their own sports beverage brands:

Brand	Marketer
Powerade	Coca-Cola Co.
All Sport	Pepsi-Cola Co.
10-K	Suntory (Japan)
Everlast	A&W Brands
Nautilus Plus	Dr Pepper/Seven Up
Snap-Up (renamed Snapple Sport in April 1994)	Snapple Beverage Co.

Soft-drink companies were looking for new market segments because the $47 billion retail soft-drink market had grown less than 3 percent annually since 1980. Both Coca-Cola and Pepsi were moving to market their brands directly against Gatorade's well-developed connections to sports teams, coaches, trainers, and celebrity athletes (Michael Jordan was Gatorade's athlete spokesman). Coca-Cola had maneuvered successfully to get Powerade named the official sports drink of the 1996 Olympic Games in Atlanta and was running Powerade ads to sponsor World Cup Soccer. Coca-Cola's Powerade ads on local television and radio carried the tag line "More power to ya." Coca-Cola had signed pro baseball–football star Deion Sanders to appear in Powerade ads. Pepsi-Cola's commercials for All Sport touted the theme "Fuel the fire" and showed gritty scenes of youths playing fast-action sports such as blacktop basketball. Pepsi also had enlisted pro basketball's Shaquille O'Neal to appear in its ads and was sponsoring telecasts of NCAA basketball games. Snapple's ads for Snap-Up/Snapple Sport featured tennis celebrities Ivan Lendl and Jennifer Capriati. Suntory was seeking to attract preteens to its 10-K brand with ads featuring a 12-year-old boy who played five sports. Gatorade rivals were expected to spend $30 million to $40 million advertising their brands in 1994. Pepsi's All Sport and Coca-Cola's Powerade were considered particularly formidable brands because they were backed by nationwide networks of local soft-drink bottlers that delivered daily to major supermarkets (and at least weekly to other soft-drink retailers and vending machine outlets) and typically stocked the shelves of retailers and set up in-store aisle displays. With such distribution muscle both Powerade and All Sport could gain market exposure everywhere soft drinks were available.

To counter rivals' efforts to horn in on Gatorade's market share, Quaker doubled its 1994 ad budget to nearly $50 million and created ads that reduced Michael Jordan's role in favor of product-benefit claims. Quaker also expanded Gatorade's line to eight flavors, compared to four for Powerade and All Sport. Still, Gatorade's estimated market share was five percentage points lower in fall 1994 than it had been a year earlier.

In an attempt to develop a new beverage category, the Gatorade division was test-marketing a new product named SunBolt Energy Drink, designed for morning consumption or any time consumers wanted a "pick-me-up." SunBolt contained three carbohydrate sources, caffeine, and vitamin C equivalent to a whole orange; it was offered in four flavors. SunBolt was positioned in the juice aisles of grocery stores, where Gatorade was shelved.

Despite the entry of other sports beverages, Quaker management regarded water as Gatorade's biggest competitor as a "thirst quencher." Moreover, in many supermarkets Gatorade was located alongside fruit juices, whereas Powerade and All Sport often were located in the soft-drink section, something Gatorade executives believed was an advantage. Gatorade executives also believed that the entry of competing sports drink brands would help grow the category enough so that Gatorade sales would increase despite a declining market share. According to Quaker President Phil Marineau:[3]

> When you have a 90 percent share of a category and competitors like Coke and Pepsi moving in, you're not foolish enough to think you won't lose some market share. But we're going to keep our position as the dominant force among sports drinks. Greater availability is the key to the U.S. success of Gatorade.

Gatorade's Marketing and Distribution Strategies.   Quaker executives concluded in early 1994 that U.S. sales of Gatorade were approaching the limits of its traditional grocery channel delivery system—Gatorade was shipped from plants to retailer warehouses, and stores ordered what they needed to keep shelves stocked. Sustaining Gatorade's sales growth in the United States meant stretching the distribution strategy for Gatorade to include other channels. Donald R. Uzzi, a Pepsi executive, was hired in March 1994 as president of Gatorade's U.S. and Canada geographic unit. Uzzi's top strategic priority was to develop additional sales outlets for Gatorade; the options in-

---

[3] As quoted in "Gatorade Growth Seen Outside U.S.," *Advertising Age,* November 15, 1993, p. 46.

cluded fountain service for restaurants and fast-food outlets, vending machines, direct deliveries to nongrocery retail outlets, and point of sweat locations such as sports gyms and golf courses. The customary way of accessing such outlets was by building a network of independent distributors who would market to and service such accounts. In 1994, Gatorade's strongest markets were in the South and the Southwest. In foreign markets, Gatorade relied on several strategies to establish its market presence:

- Shipping the product in, handling the marketing and advertising in-house, and partnering with a local distributor to sell retail accounts, gain shelf space, and make deliveries. This approach was being utilized in Greece with a food distribution company.
- Handling the marketing and advertising in-house and having a local partner take care of manufacturing, sales, and distribution. This approach was being used in Australia.
- Contracting with a soft-drink bottler to handle production, packaging, and distribution, with Gatorade taking care of marketing functions and supervising the contractor. This strategy was used in Spain, where the contractor was a Pepsi-owned bottler.
- Handling all functions in-house: manufacturing, marketing, sales, and distribution. Such was the case in Venezuela, where Quaker had built facilities to produce Gatorade.

Snapple Beverage Corp.

Snapple Beverage Corp. originated as a subchapter S corporation in 1972. The company, operating as Mr. Natural, Inc., was the brainchild of three streetwise entrepreneurs: Leonard Marsh, Arnold Greenberg, and Hyman Golden. Marsh and Greenberg were lifelong friends, having gone to grade school and high school together; Golden was Marsh's brother-in-law. Mr. Natural, headquartered in Brooklyn, marketed and distributed a line of specialty beverages for the New York City area; the company's products were supplied by contract manufacturers and bottlers. The company's sales and operating scope grew gradually. Its all-natural products sold well in health food stores; later, delicatessens and convenience stores began to carry the line. By 1988, the company had become a regional distributor and headquarters operations were moved to East Meadow on Long Island, New York. Exhibit 5 summarizes key events in the company's history.

Capitalizing on consumers' growing interest in natural and healthy beverage products, the three entrepreneurs launched an all-natural beverage line under the Snapple name in 1980. Over the years, more flavors and varieties were added; Snapple iced teas were introduced in 1987. The introduction of the iced tea line was supported with a creative and catchy advertising campaign stressing the message, "Try this, you'll love the taste, and it's good for you." Snapple's recipe for making a good-tasting iced tea involved making it hot and then bottling it; artificial preservatives and colors were avoided. Snapple's strategy was simple: make all-natural beverages that taste great and keep introducing new and exciting flavors. As sales grew (principally because devoted health-conscious consumers spread the word among friends and acquaintances), company principals Marsh, Greenberg, and Golden plowed their profits back into the Snapple brand. Wider geographic distribution was attained by signing new distributors and granting them exclusive rights to distribute the Snapple line across a defined territory.

By 1991 sales had reached $95 million. Revenues jumped to $205.5 million in 1992 and to $516.0 million in 1993 as distribution widened and more consumers tried the line. Snapple's sales in 1993 ranked it number 35 on the top 50 beverage companies list. Exhibits 6 and 7 present Snapple's financial statements. The company went public in December 1992 as Snapple Beverage Corp., with the three founders retaining 23.1 percent of the stock (7.7 percent each). After the initial public offering at a split-adjusted

EXHIBIT 5   **Summary of Key Events in Snapple Beverage Corporation's History**

1972

Marsh, Golden, and Greenberg form a company in association with a California juice manufacturer to distribute 100% natural fruit juices in New York City, primarily through health food distributors.

1979

A production plant is purchased in upstate New York to produce a line of pure, natural fruit juices.

1980

The name *Snapple* makes its first appearance when Snapple Beverage Corporation became the first company to manufacture a complete line of all-natural beverages.

1982

Snapple introduces Natural Sodas and pioneers the natural soft drink category.

1986

All Natural Fruit Drinks join the Snapple family, including Lemonade, Orangeade, Grapeade, and more.

1987

Snapple launches its All Natural Real Brewed Ice Tea and revolutionizes the beverage industry with the first tea to be brewed hot instead of mixed from cold concentrate. Snapple's signature wide-mouth bottle also makes its first appearance.

1990

Snapple introduces Snapple Sport, the first isotonic sports drink with the great taste of Snapple.

1991

Snapple recruits its first international distributor in Norway.

1992

The Thomas H. Lee Investment Company buys Snapple and leads an effort to take the company public. The stock triples in the first three months and is listed among the hottest stocks in the country. The three cofounders retain 23.1% of Snapple's common stock, and Thomas H. Lee ends up owning 47.5% of Snapple's common shares.

1992–1993

Fruit Drink line expands to include such exotic flavors as Kiwi-Strawberry Cocktail, Mango Madness Cocktail, and Melonberry Cocktail.

1993

Snapple goes international, signing on distributors in the United Kingdom, Canada, Mexico, the Caribbean, Hong Kong, and elsewhere.

1994

Snapple introduces seven new products, including Guava Mania Cocktail, Mango Tea, Amazin Grape Soda, Kiwi Strawberry Soda, and Mango Madness Soda as well as new diet versions of some best-sellers—Diet Kiwi Strawberry Cocktail, Diet Mango Madness Cocktail, and Diet Pink Lemonade.

Source: Company promotional materials.

EXHIBIT 6   **Snapple's Income Statement, 1992 and 1993**

	1992	*1993*
Net sales	$205,465,595	$516,005,327
Cost of goods sold	127,098,086	298,724,646
Gross profit	78,367,509	217,280,681
Selling, general, and administrative expenses	45,455,818	105,693,741
Nonoperating expenses	10,626,742	9,116,664
Interest expense	19,086,213	2,459,297
Income before tax	3,198,736	100,010,070
Provisions for income taxes	1,262,919	32,387,498
Net income before extraordinary items	1,935,817	67,623,481
Extraordinary item	(2,632,904)	0
Net income	$ (697,087)	$ 67,623,481

Source: Company annual report.

EXHIBIT 7 **Snapple Beverage Corporation Balance Sheet, 1992 and 1993**

	1992	1993
Assets		
Cash	$ 97,486,632	$ 13,396,949
Receivables	17,428,379	53,010,325
Inventories	16,166,183	40,922,888
Other current assets	6,788,585	4,192,759
Total current assets	137,869,779	111,522,921
Net property, plant, and equipment	1,053,399	10,751,597
Deferred charges	3,705,001	18,552,625
Intangibles	82,770,827	97,819,997
Other assets	1,338,166	304,745
Total assets	$ 226,737,172	$ 238,951,885
Liabilities and Shareholders' Equity		
Accounts payable	$ 6,100,345	$ 7,326,411
Current long-term debt	150,469	8,949,665
Accrued expenses	16,999,258	17,573,454
Income taxes	446,892	6,034,860
Other current liabilities	90,000,000	3,860,844
Total current liabilities	113,696,964	43,745,234
Long-term debt	18,226,138	26,218,911
Other long-term liabilities	4,000,000	5,011,000
Total liabilities	135,923,102	74,975,145
Minority interest	0	1,499,717
Common stock net	1,213,766	1,216,096
Capital surplus	90,297,391	94,334,533
Retained earnings	(697,087)	66,926,394
Total shareholders' equity	90,814,070	162,477,023
Total liabilities and shareholders' equity	$ 226,737,172	$ 238,951,885

Source: Company annual report.

price of $5, the stock traded as high as $32.25 in late 1993 before trading as low as $11.50 in mid-1994. Responding to the concerns of investors and Wall Street analysts about whether the company's rapid growth was sustainable, Marsh said:

> For those of you who might have heard mumblings that we've grown too far, too fast, I suggest you consider Snapple in the proper context. The average American drank 500 soft drinks last year (1993) . . . and the average American drank only five Snapples last year. That's a 1 percent share of a $64 billion pie.[4]

During the summer months of 1994 Snapple marketed 75 varieties and flavors in five categories (ready-to-drink iced teas, fruit drinks, natural sodas and seltzers, fruit juices, and sports drinks) and had distributors in all 50 states. Despite sales of more than $500 million, Snapple had fewer than 200 employees; production, bottling, packaging, and distribution were handled by contractors and independent distributors. Company activities focused on marketing, new product development (the company had expertise in flavor technology), and overall management of contractors and distributors. In May 1994, however, management

---

[4] As quoted in Beverage World's *Periscope,* February 28, 1994, p. 21.

EXHIBIT 8   **Per Capita Consumption of Liquid Beverages in the United States, 1983–1994** (in gallons)

	1983	1984	1985	1986	1987	1988	1989	1990	1991	1992	1993E	1994P
Soft drinks	37.0	38.8	41.0	42.3	44.3	46.2	46.7	47.6	47.8	48.0	48.9	49.6
Coffee*	26.1	26.3	26.8	27.1	27.1	26.5	26.4	26.4	26.5	26.1	25.9	26.0
Beer	24.3	23.9	23.9	24.2	24.0	23.8	23.6	24.0	23.3	23.0	22.8	22.5
Milk	19.7	19.8	20.0	19.9	19.8	19.4	19.6	19.4	19.4	19.1	18.9	19.1
Tea*	7.2	7.2	7.3	7.3	7.3	7.4	7.2	7.0	6.7	6.8	6.9	7.0
Bottled water	3.4	4.0	5.2	5.8	6.4	7.3	8.1	9.2	9.6	9.9	10.5	11.2
Juices	8.2	7.0	7.9	7.8	8.3	7.7	8.0	7.1	7.6	7.1	7.0	7.0
Powdered drinks	6.5	6.4	6.3	5.2	4.9	5.3	5.4	5.7	5.9	6.1	6.0	5.9
Wine†	2.2	2.3	2.4	2.4	2.4	2.3	2.1	2.0	1.9	2.0	1.7	1.6
Distilled spirits	1.9	1.9	1.8	1.8	1.6	1.5	1.5	1.5	1.4	1.3	1.3	1.3
Subtotal	136.5	137.6	142.6	142.6	146.1	147.4	148.6	149.9	150.1	149.4	149.9	151.2
Imputed water consumption‡	46.0	44.9	39.9	39.9	36.4	35.1	33.9	32.6	32.4	33.1	32.6	31.3
Total	182.5	182.5	182.5	182.5	182.5	182.5	182.5	182.5	182.5	182.5	182.5	182.5

* Coffee and tea data are based on a three-year moving average to counterbalance inventory swings, thereby portraying consumption more realistically.
† Includes wine coolers beginning in 1984.
‡ Includes all others.
E = estimated; P = projected.

Source: John C. Maxwell, "Annual Soft Drink Report," *Beverage Industry Supplement,* March 1994, p. 6.

initiated construction of the company's first production facility—a $25 million plant in Arizona, scheduled to begin operations in 1995 and to employ 100 people.

Snapple was widely credited with catalyzing a more pronounced consumer trend toward New Age beverages, spurring added sales growth in bottled waters, sports drinks, and juices as well as its own line of flavored teas and fruit drinks. In 1993, New Age or "alternative" beverages constituted a $3 billion product category. Exhibit 8 shows trends in the per capita consumption of liquid beverages in the United States during the 1983–1994 period.

Snapple's Marketing and Distribution Strategies.   In Snapple's early days the product wasn't selling well; market research revealed that consumers thought the bottles were ugly and difficult to store. A packaging redesign followed, resulting in the use of clear wide-mouth 16-ounce glass bottles—a container that management said was "perfectly suited to the hot-brewed process we use to make Snapple beverages." The new bottles were affixed with redesigned labels. Sales perked up quickly, buoyed by an offbeat and catchy media campaign.

The company sparked demand for Snapple products with offbeat, witty ads and catchy themes. Snapple had gotten the greatest mileage out of an ad featuring a stereotypical receptionist, "Wendy the Snapple Lady" (who was actually employed in the company's marketing department), responding to customer inquiries. Snapple ads sometimes poked fun at things. Print ads compared Snapple sales to "hot cakes" and "greased lightning" with "more flavors than you can shake a stick at." Ivan Lendl and Rush Limbaugh appeared in Snapple television ads as celebrity endorsers. Most of Snapple's distributors were local soft-drink bottlers/distributors that had third-place or fourth-place market shares (usually behind Coca-Cola and Pepsi) and were eager to take on product lines where competition was less intense and profit margins were bigger. The average price per case for New Age beverages was around $9 to $11 versus $5 to $6 per case for soft drinks. On average, soft drinks offered bottlers and distributors a $1 margin per case compared with about $3 per case for New Age products. These distributors delivered Snapple directly to supermarkets, convenience stores, delicatessen outlets, and up-and-down-the-street retailers on trucks carrying an assortment of branded beverages (low-volume soft-drink brands, bottled waters, club soda, tonic water, ginger ale, and perhaps canned Gatorade). Snapple's distributors were responsible for everything—selling retail accounts, keeping shelves stocked, handling point of sale displays, and setting prices. Retail prices for a 16-ounce bottle were typically around 75 cents. Snapple's surging sales in 1992 and 1993—a boom that reportedly began in convenience stores and delicatessens, where trend-setting consumers bought Snapple from the cooler and drank it straight from the bottle—helped it recruit distributors willing to commit time and resources to the Snapple line. Snapple established a nationwide network of distributors in a matter of months, something few alternative beverage brands had been able to do. The attractive profit margins distributors earned on Snapple sales were a key factor in the company's ability to recruit distributors willing to invest time and resources in building the Snapple brand. Snapple's market research showed that half the U.S. population had tried Snapple by the end of October 1993. Snapple's sales were strongest in California and the Northeast; sales were weakest in the South and Southwest. By mid-1994 Snapple had begun introducing its brands in Europe. Launches in Britain, Ireland, and Norway came first, followed by Sweden and Denmark. Test marketing was under way in France and Spain. As of November 1994 only 1 percent of Snapple's sales were derived from overseas markets.

In April 1994 Snapple announced it had developed an exclusive glass-front vending machine capable of offering 54 different flavors simultaneously; the machine held 18 cases of the company's 16-ounce wide-mouth bottles. The company expected to place 10,000 units in service by year end to broaden its distribution beyond supermarkets, convenience stores, and delicatessens.

Competition in the Iced Tea/New Age Segment.   Snapple's success in developing consumer interest in ready-to-drink iced teas and teas spiked with fruit juices attracted other competitors quickly. In 1993 Coca-Cola, Pepsi-Cola, Dr Pepper/Seven-Up, and Cadbury Schweppes/A&W Beverages all launched New Age offerings. Several regional products, most notably Arizona Iced Tea (packaged in distinctive tall cans with a Southwestern motif), also entered the market. As of 1994, the major players in the ready-to-drink iced tea segment were the following:

Brand	Marketer
Snapple	Snapple Beverage Corp.
Lipton	Pepsi-Cola and the Thomas J. Lipton division of Unilever
Nestea	Coca-Cola Nestlé Refreshments (a joint venture of the Coca-Cola Company and Nestlé)
Tetley	A&W Brands and Tetley Tea Co. partnership
Luzianne	Barq's Inc. and Wm. B. Reily partnership
All Seasons	Cadbury Beverages and Omni Industries
Celestial Seasonings	Perrier Group of America and Celestial Seasonings
Arizona	Ferolito, Vultaggio and Sons

Besides the major players, there were 5 to 10 niche brands of bottled teas. In addition, Pepsi-Cola had teamed with Ocean Spray Cranberries, Inc., to introduce a line of juices and lemonade. Minute Maid had announced a new line of juices, Very Fine and Tradewinds were planning lemonade entries, and Gatorade introduced its eighth flavor, Gatorade Iced Tea Cooler. An Information Resources survey of supermarket sales of canned and bottled iced teas during the 12 weeks ended April 17, 1994, showed the following:[5]

Brand	Case Volume (in millions)	Dollar Volume (in millions)
Snapple	2.5	$22.3
Lipton	2.3	14.9
Nestea	1.0	7.8
Arizona	0.5	5.0

Snapple's market share (based on dollars) was 17 percentage points lower in this survey than in the comparable year-earlier period. The Arizona brand was gaining share and had edged out Snapple as the market leader in several markets in the West. However, Snapple's market share of convenience store sales was estimated to be in the range of 75 percent. Exhibit 9 presents estimated case sales of alternative beverage companies.

Industry analysts estimated that wholesale volume for iced tea flavors grew from $500 million in 1992 to more than $1 billion in 1993. Alternative beverage sales were breaking out into 40 percent take-home purchases and 60 percent single-service and on-premise consumption. Ready-to-drink teas and juice-based drinks were the fastest-growing products in the New Age category, while sales of "clear" products dropped to the range of 8 to 9 percent (down from 44 percent growth in 1992). Analysts were divided in their assessments about how long the booming growth in ready-to-drink teas and fruit beverages would last. Some analysts believed that teas and fruit drinks would experience continued growth because of their healthy, "all-natural" image with consumers and because the proliferation of brands and varieties would help develop greater buyer interest. Others were skeptical, observing that trendy products had comparatively short life cycles and that three or four growth years were all many product categories ever experienced. While some cola bottlers had derisively referred to Snapple as a member of the "brand of the day" club, unconvinced of its power to sustain broad consumer interest, market research indicated that younger consumers (who had fueled the growth in New Age beverages) had gravitated to Snapple, Arizona, and unusual niche brands with distinctive packaging and a certain mystique. In fall 1994 industry observers saw bottled tea as becoming increasingly complex to market successfully because the market was overcrowded, the costs to support a brand were rising, shelf space was harder to obtain, and image was such a dominant factor in a brand's success or failure.

In late August 1994 Coca-Cola and Nestlé unexpectedly announced the dissolution of their iced tea alliance; Nestea sales had been disappointing, falling well behind supermarket sales of both Snapple and Lipton. It was not clear whether Nestlé would continue to market Nestea bottled teas on its own. Meanwhile, Pepsi-Lipton had begun running a series of radio ads attacking Snapple as being "mixed up from a tea powder." The announcer said, "Snapple. Isn't that a cute name. Kinda snappy. I bet they call it Snapple 'cause it's iced tea made in a snap." The spot went on to boast that Lipton Original varieties were "real brewed," a trait that Pepsi-Lipton believed was its best weapon against rivals.[6] Pepsi had also run Super Bowl ads for Lipton Original and promoted Lipton Original heavily in supermarkets, including a 99-cent value pack containing one bottle each of Lipton Original, All Sport, and Ocean Spray Lemonade.

---

[5] As reported in *The Wall Street Journal,* June 9, 1994, p. B6.
[6] As quoted in *The Wall Street Journal,* June 9, 1994, p. B6.

EXHIBIT 9   **Estimated Case Sales of Alternative Beverage Companies, 1992–1993**

Company/Brand	Case Sales (in millions)	
	1992	1993
Snapple Beverage Company		
Snapple Iced Tea	28.33	52.63
Snapple drinks	19.73	45.41
Snapple sodas	1.52	3.10
Snapple Snap-Up/Sport	0.51	1.03
Snapple juices	0.51	1.03
Total	50.60	103.20
Coca-Cola Company		
Nestea	14.00	33.00
Powerade	1.20	10.00
Minute Maid Juices-to-Go	5.00	15.00
Total	20.20	58.00
PepsiCo		
Ocean Spray	6.50	16.00
Lipton	—	33.00
All Sport	2.00	3.00
H2 Oh!	0.50	0.63
Total	9.00	52.63
Perrier Group		
15-Brand totals	30.40	36.70
Cadbury beverages/A&W brands		
Tetley	2.90	4.30
Everlast	—	—
Others	17.30	17.30
Total	20.20	21.60
Ferolito, Vultaggio and Sons		
Arizona	—	2.00
All others	169.60	175.37
Segment totals	300.00	449.50

Source: Compiled from "Annual Soft Drink Report," *Beverage Industry Supplement,* March 1994, pp. 22–23.

Snapple management indicated its iced teas were made from "the finest tea leaves in India" but wouldn't specify how it was produced. Arnold Greenberg said:

> Pepsi would die to make tea taste so great. People don't care how it's made. They just care that it tastes good.[7]

Snapple management also pointed out that the less expensive Lipton Brisk varieties, sold in cans and 64-ounce bottles, were not "real brewed." Analysts estimated that during the first five months of 1994, about 60 percent of Pepsi's prepared iced teas were Lipton Brisk varieties. To counter the increased competition from rival teas, Snapple more than doubled its 1994 advertising budget and launched a new $65 million media campaign in April 1994.

---

[7] Ibid

CASE 4–4
CRUISERS

Beecy Eagle sighed in exasperation as he read the promotional material on the Indian Motorcycle Company Web site. Rey Sotelo, the president of the company, was quoted saying on June 16, 1999: "With the Indian Chief on the road, we've successfully revived one of America's greatest icons." Sotelo was speaking about the debut of the Limited Edition 1999 Indian Chief cruiser motorcycle, a motorcycle sometimes referred to as "legendary" and last built in 1953. The Indian Motorcycle Company had been formed in November 1998 through a $30 million merger involving Indian Motorcycle Company Inc., American Indian Motorcycle Company, and California Motorcycle Company and its six related companies to create the second largest producer of heavy cruisers in North America. The largest producer was Harley-Davidson, with 1998 revenues of $2,064 million and income of $214 million (Exhibit 1).

The Indian Motorcycle Company had been as legendary as Harley-Davidson back in the early 1900s, and among motorcycle buffs the brand was revered. However, between 1953 and 1997 the Indian trademark had been in contention, resulting in multiple attempts to capitalize on the brand. The Indian Motorcycle Company Web site alluded to the years of trademark confusion: "Even the Indian brand has been resurrected by so many people, you'd need a program to tell them apart. We've been on the ride of our lives to give you the ride of yours." The promotional material continued, "Real Legends never Die."

Beecy could understand the strategy behind Indian's product positioning, since he had just accepted a marketing position with the Excelsior-Henderson Motorcycle Manufacturing Company. In the 1930s, Excelsior-Henderson, Indian, and Harley-Davidson were the "big three" manufacturers of cruiser motorcycles. Excelsior-Henderson had gone defunct in the middle of the Depression of the 1930s. Indian had lasted through World War II by becoming a supplier of motorbikes for the U.S. armed forces. Harley-Davidson had persisted and, after some struggles with Japanese competition in the early 1980s, had roared into the 1990s bolstered by market share and heritage.

In 1998 Harley commanded 48 percent of the North American cruiser motorcycle market. The company, based in Milwaukee and known by the faithful as The Motor Company, evoked a nostalgic reaction in motorcycle fans that was based on its enduring heritage. Harley's motorcycles were intended for sport, not transportation, as were some of the lighter-weight Japanese-manufactured bikes.

"King of the Road" summed up the Harley image of a burly, leather-dressed biker comfortably ensconced on his large, loud, chrome-bedecked cruiser. "You buy a Harley to be a part of a family," said Buzz Kanter, publisher of *American Iron* motorcycle magazine.[1] The brotherhood of the Harley Owners Group, also known as H.O.G., held annual rallies in Sturgis, North Dakota, and Daytona, Florida. The rallies did not welcome non-Harley bikers. Harley customers were explained as buying "emotion, attitude, and the American flag."

This case was written by Cathy Leach Waters, adjunct instructor of marketing, Boston College Carroll School of Management, as the basis for class discussion rather than to illustrate effective or ineffective marketing. All material was from secondary sources. All rights reserved to the author. December 2000.

---

[1] Machan, Dyan, "Is the Hog Going Soft?" *Forbes,* March 10, 1997, p. 114.

EXHIBIT 1 Harley-Davidson Revenues and Income (in $millions)

	1998	1997	1996
Sales	$2,064	$1,750	$1,500
Income	$ 214	$ 174	$ 160

EXHIBIT 2 Total Motorcycle Industry Sales (units)

	1997	1998
Dirt bike	94,544	118,469
Dual-purpose bike	12,698	12,647
Street (cruisers, touring, sport bikes, racers)	235,395	276,132
ATV	366,742	439,696
Scooter	11,045	12,986
Total	720,424	859,930

EXHIBIT 3 Share of Total Motorcycle Market by Segment (units)

	1990	1997
Sport bikes	29.5%	22.6%
Standard	11.2	4.7
Dual-purpose	10	6.3
Cruisers	37	53.1

Cruiser Motorcycles

Cruiser motorcycles are heavyweight machines with large, slow-revving engines, large saddles for upright riding, and lots of chrome. They are low-slung and comfortable, better for highway cruising than for racing around winding roads. In contrast, lighter performance "sport" bikes are ridden hunched forward and achieve higher top speeds than cruisers do.

Other segments in the motorcycle market are standard bikes (used for transportation), touring bikes (for longer distances), and dual-purpose bikes. The "two-wheeled motorcycle market" was divided into the following categories: dual-purpose, street (including standards, touring bikes, sport bikes, and cruisers), and dirt bikes. Dirt bikes were used for off-road riding and frequently were purchased for youths by their parents. Roughly 118,000 dirt bikes were sold in 1998. Also included in industry sales were scooters and ATVs (all-terrain vehicles).[2] Exhibit 2 summarizes the percentage that each segment contributes to the entire category. Exhibit 3 depicts the change in each

[2] ATVs are used for off-road riding and have three or four wheels.

segment's share of the motorcycle market ("dual-purpose and street motorcycles," not including dirt bikes, scooters, and ATVs) from 1990 to 1997.

Cruiser Market

Cruisers accounted for 53 percent of the American motorcycle market in 1997. By 2000, the cruiser segment was expected to increase to 60 percent of the motorcycle category. Cruiser sales are summarized in Exhibit 4. Motorcycle sales in 1998 were $2.9 billion, up from $1.5 billion in 1992. According to the Motorcycle Industry Council in Irvine, California, motorcycle sales nationally in 1999 were increasing 20 percent per quarter. Industry experts expected cruiser sales to grow 12 to 15 percent a year for several years. The average price of a cruiser was $11,000.

In Massachusetts, where Beecy Eagle had just graduated from college, there were 98,729 registered motorcycles in 1999, compared with 65,807 in 1989. The growth trend regionally and nationally explained the proliferation of new and newly resurrected motorcycle companies. Among the newly resurrected was Beecy's future employer, Excelsior-Henderson.

Excelsior-Henderson

Excelsior-Henderson had a heritage too. From 1917 through 1931, the Excelsior Supply and Henderson Companies had produced four-cylinder luxury motorcycles and V-twin sport bikes. "V-twin" engines, with two big pistons in a V-for-victory configuration, were prominent on cruisers. In 1912 the Excelsior was the first motorcycle to exceed 100 miles per hour.

In 1993 founders and brothers Dave and Dan Hanlon and Dave's wife, Jennie, acquired all rights to the names and trademarks of the old Excelsior-Henderson Company. Dave had been a truck leasing company manager for Rollins Leasing. Dan, with an MBA from the University of St. Thomas in St. Paul, had worked for Honeywell. Dan had founded and sold a company that made biodegradable packing peanuts.

The Hanlons used their business acumen to raise the financing to build a factory, hire an experienced staff, and then design a motorcycle. They raised $60 million from over 300 private investors, $30 million from an initial public offering in July 1997, and $7 million in Minnesota state loans. They used roughly $100 million to hire experienced people to build the manufacturing, engineering, design, sales, and marketing operations. Traded on NASDAQ (stock symbol BIGX), Excelsior-Henderson had a stock-market value of $41 million in late 1999. The firm employed 210 workers in its new $50 million headquarters and factory, a 160,000-square-foot brick building in the Hanlons' home town of Belle Plaine, 45 miles from Minneapolis.

EXHIBIT 4   **Total Cruiser Sales (units): Selected Years**

Year	Units
1993	86,000
1994	94,000
1996	123,205
1997	131,829
1998	153,000

EXHIBIT 5   The Super X

The average employee was about 30 years old. Nine of every 10 workers were licensed bikers, as were the founding Hanlons. The Hanlon brothers owned five Harley-Davidsons. As longtime riders, the Hanlons rode their Harleys to the annual Sturgis rally, the world's biggest event for bikers, in South Dakota in the early 1990s. With over 350,000 bikes at the rally, the market for cruisers was evident.

The Super X.   Excelsior-Henderson's entry in the cruiser market, the Super X, was supposed to be ready in late 1998. Bolstered by feature articles in *USA Today* and *Inc.* magazine and by an appearance at the Sturgis rally, Excelsior-Henderson had orders for 5,500 Super X's before any had been produced. The first Super X, priced at $18,000, had rolled off the production line in February 1999. The bike was declared by *American Iron* as "the best cruiser motorcycle for the money in the world today."[3]

The Super X was praised for its handling and power. Visually, it made a strong statement with its high-tech, retro look and unique front-fork-through-the-fender design (Exhibit 5). The frame had classic styling and curved around a 1,386-cc engine which had double overhead camshafts, four-valve cylinder heads, and fuel injection. In a recent article, the publisher of *American Iron* magazine had predicted that people would "get over the 'unusual' looking front end of the Excelsior and discover what a terrific machine it really is (even if they don't advertise in *American Iron* Magazine)."[4]

On July 26, 1999, Excelsior-Henderson shipped the thousandth Super X motorcycle. The firm's plant had the capacity to manufacture 20,000 motorcycles a year. The plan was

[3] *American Iron,* www.americaniron.com, July 1999.
[4] Ibid.

to make 4,000 bikes in 1999 and increase production to the maximum capacity by 2003. The Super X's steel frame was welded in the factory. Most of the other parts were manufactured elsewhere and shipped to the Belle Plaine plant for paint and final assembly.

The Super X was sold through 100 dealers nationwide; two-thirds of them were Harley dealers who carried the Super X as a second line. The Super X had been declared the official motorcycle of the Minnesota Vikings team in the National Football League. A specially painted cycle was going to lead the team onto the field at home games.

At the August 9, 1999, Sturgis rally, Excelsior-Henderson introduced its new 2000 Super X lineup. The new model was called the Deadwood Special. It featured blacked-out components, chrome front forks, a single-piece seat, new "flame" logos, drag bars, and white letter tires in an "outlaw tribute to Deadwood, South Dakota."

Super X Positioning.   The Super X was positioned as a choice for bikers who wanted an "American bike with a great heritage and authenticity." The Hanlon brothers viewed Excelsior-Henderson as a "brand with soul" and on the same par as Harley. The Super X was positioned head to head with Harley's Softail and Fat Boy models and similarly priced at $18,000 to $20,000. Regarding Japanese bikes that could be purchased for less, Dan Hanlon had asked, "You ever see a biker with a Honda tattoo?" About Polaris, another competitor, Dave Hanlon had said, "Our bike has an authenticity. Theirs doesn't."[5]

Polaris

Polaris Industries Inc. also was based in Minnesota, in the Minneapolis suburb of Plymouth. This had complicated Beecy's search for employment when he had returned to his home state after graduating from college with a degree in marketing. In contrast to the excitement of the newly minted Excelsior-Henderson, Polaris had been in business since 1954. The snowmobile market leader was ranked among the top three firms in market share for all-terrain vehicles and personal watercraft.[6] Polaris had converted an assembly line in one of its factories to produce motorcycles.

With sales of $1.2 billion, Polaris had leveraged its existing manufacturing infrastructure and had spent only $20 million to develop its Victory motorcycle. Polaris, headed by a Harvard MBA, W. Hall Wendel, Jr., had introduced the Victory, a retro V-twin cruiser, in 1997 and began full production in the spring of 1998. The firm planned to produce 2,000 to 3,000 motorcycles in 1998 and double that number in 1999. It then hoped to sell 40,000 to 50,000 bikes per year.

To develop the Victory, the motorcycle-development team had accumulated cruisers from Harley, the top four Japanese makers, BMW, and Ducati and had taken them apart and picked what it liked best. Polaris made a discrete decision to develop its own engine and hired designer Mark Bader to design an engine described by one reporter as one that "pulls with authority while leaving one's dental fillings in place." The motors were assembled at a Polaris plant in Wisconsin, where steel tubing for the bikes' frames was bent.

The company believed it was important to make the frames in-house. Like Excelsior-Henderson, Polaris assembled its bikes mostly from outsourced parts. Engines and other parts were put together on a slow-moving assembly line staffed by nine two-person teams that moved from station to station, each building an entire motorcycle. Polaris planned to move more operations in-house if the bike met company objectives.

---

[5] Strauss, Gary, "Minnesota Motorcycles Take on Harley," *USA Today,* November 5, 1997, p. 1B.

[6] Personal watercraft are designed for one or two riders and propel the rider across the water.

The firm planned to develop a series of models and had its sights set on 10 percent of the global market in less than 10 years. The first Victory, the V-92, was priced at $13,000, in line with Japanese rivals' prices. Initially the Victory was sold through about 200 of Polaris's over 2,000 dealers. Matt Parks, the general manager of Polaris's Victory Motorcycle Division, had commented, "We're not a Harley clone, and our price will be significantly lower."[7]

Polaris had considered entering the lower end of the motorcycle market (dirt bikes for off-road riding), but thin margins and the rapidly changing technology of the segment dissuaded it. The growth in the cruisers segment offered the best opportunity, and the firm intended to be a global force in motorcycles. Thirty percent of Polaris's existing customers were already cyclists.

Polaris already was competing successfully with the Japanese companies that manufacture motorcycles: Honda, Kawasaki, Suzuki, and Yamaha. Polaris planned to stay out of Harley's way and compete with the Japanese on price, quality, and technology. A billboard outside Polaris headquarters showed a pair of Victorys in dramatic Monument Valley, Arizona, with the slogan, "It's a free country. Act like it."

Japanese Competition

Japanese firms Honda, Yamaha, Kawasaki, and Suzuki collectively owned 48.5 percent of the cruiser market in 1998. Since 1995, the four firms had each introduced a Harley clone: the Yamaha Virago, the Honda American Classic, the Kawasaki Vulcan, and the Suzuki Marauder. The clones all featured Harley look-alike styling and the loud "potato-potato-potato" growl characteristic of the Harley engine. While a top-of-the-line Honda motorcycle can cost as much as $20,000, the Honda American Classic sold for $9,599.

The Japanese companies were acknowledged leaders in producing sport bikes, lightweight racers that owners frequently traded in for more technologically advanced models. New technology that produced higher speeds and better handling tended to drive demand in the sport bike segment. Sport bike sales for 1998 had increased 16 percent over the previous year.

While sport bikes were oriented toward the future, cruisers focused on the past and connoted heritage and icons; the chief icon was Harley-Davidson. According to some industry observers, the Japanese made the best cruisers, and at a better price than their American competition. Honda, the world's largest motorcycle company, had an extensive network of 1,200 stores and competed in almost every segment of the power sports industry (motorcycles, dirt bikes, all-terrain vehicles). Honda's aim was to dominate the market in the category segments in which it competed. Honda, with a 42.5 percent share of the dirt bike market in 1997, was the market leader. Kawasaki had a network of 1,500 dealers for its motorcycles, all-terrain vehicles, and watercraft. Yamaha was strongest in the dirt bike market. Exhibit 6 lists cruiser unit sales by manufacturer. Exhibit 7 shows motorcycle unit sales by manufacturer.

Other International Competition

BMW had entered the market in 1999 with the R 1200 C, a $14,500 cruiser that combined fluid lines, a smooth ride, and BMW's well-known German engineering. BMW had taken its time entering the market because with 15 percent of the world market in each of the

---

[7] Stevens, Karen, "That Vroom! You Hear May Not Be a Harley," *Business Week,* October 20, 1997, p. 159.

EXHIBIT 6 Cruiser Sales (units) by Manufacturer: Selected Statistics

	1997	1998
Harley-Davidson	68,103	74,970
Honda	29,845	30,970
Suzuki	13,680	
Kawasaki	12,582	
Yamaha	12,687	

EXHIBIT 7 Unit Sales by Manufacturer: Dual-Purpose and Street Bikes

	1996	1997	1998
Harley-Davidson	82,396	91,160	109,240
Honda	51,821	53,806	61,213
Suzuki	30,741	36,010	37,619
Kawasaki	35,033	31,349	36,351
Yamaha	20,181	20,979	24,718
BMW	4,921	5,700	7,313
Ducati	2,112	2,853	3,609
Triumph	1,758	2,933	3,422
Buell	1,626	1,646	2,553
Moto Guzzi	303	400	660
KTM	230	401	428
Victory	0	0	130
Total	231,122	247,237	287,126

segments in which the firm competed, it wanted to make sure the cruiser market was viable. Cruisers were known more for appearance than for BMW's competencies of performance and technology. The R 1200 C was the first cruiser to have antilock brakes and fuel injection. BMW hoped to set the technological standard in the segment.

BMW aimed for customers who liked to remove limits in their lives. Demographically, the BMW cruiser customer earned an average of $75,000, with 27 percent of the target market earning $100,000 or more.

Norton Motorcycle Company, originally in Shenstone, England, had been established in 1898. On April 16, 1999, Norton Motorcycles, Inc., acquired all Norton assets and relocated to Eden Prairie, Minnesota. The new Norton company was going to reintroduce and produce motorcycles under the famous British brand. According to the promotional literature, the company had new corporate offices, new designers, brand-new and newly designed motorcycles, and "much more to come."

Norton had announced an agreement with the British firm Vepro, Ltd., to prepare the company's motorcycles for production in the areas of vehicle engineering and homologation. Vepro had recently worked with both Triumph and Excelsior-Henderson in a similar capacity. Norton had just appointed the former Purchasing Manager at Excelsior-Henderson as its new supply chain manager.

Indian

The 1999 Indian Chief had been introduced only five months after the Indian Motorcycle Company had secured the rights to the Indian Motorcycle trademark. The bike was produced at the company's new 150,000-square-foot plant, which had a production capacity of 3,000 units a year. The firm planned to expand capacity to 25,000 units by the year 2000. The Indian Motorcycle Company, in northern California, was headed by the former founder of the California Motorcycle Company. The California Motorcycle Company had produced 10 different models of a hand-built cruiser that closely resembled a Harley-Davidson. Prices had ranged from $15,000 up to $30,000 for a customized bike.

Custom Bikes

Customizing bikes with accessories was a big business. Bikers would spend thousands of dollars adding nameplates, windshields, mirrors, cylinder heads, carburetors, and other accessories to customize and outperform the original bike. Andrew's cams, S&S SuperE carburetors, and Rich Thunderheader exhausts were some of the brands produced by aftermarket companies to replace Harley-Davidson original parts. In addition to these parts, the aftermarket companies made bigger, faster copies of Harley's Big Twin 1,340-cc engine. Some customers would spend as much as $3,000 to widen a bike's front end or get a custom paint job. One customer opined that the mechanically minded were attracted to motorcycling: "You can individualize your bike by adding equipment or taking off things. That's why it's said, for example, that no two Harleys are the same."[8]

Many companies built "non-Harley Harleys" with their own parts. One firm, Big Dog, was started by Sheldon Coleman, grandson of the founder of Coleman's camping and sporting goods. Coleman built his first bike in 1993 and began manufacturing a year later. Big Dog bikes sold for $22,000 or more versus about $16,000 for a Harley. One die-hard Harley rider said about Big Dog: "Everything I wanted a Harley to be without spending time and money to customize it myself."[9]

A Colorado Springs firm, Castle KR-SuperSportt, introduced the KR-SuperSportt in 1993. Castle motorcycles looked and sounded like a Harley, but the handmade cycles had twice the power and were priced at $27,695. In 1996 Castle produced 15 motorcycles. The company hoped to make 300 to 500 motorcycles in 1997.

Buell Motorcycle Company

In the late 1980s an ex-Harley engineer and road racer named Erik Buell began building high-performance sports bikes that used a modified Harley engine and formed the Buell Motorcycle Company. In 1993 Harley-Davidson bought a 49 percent stake in Buell and began selling Buells through its dealer network. In 1998 Harley acquired another 49 percent of the company, and Buell became a Harley subsidiary. Company literature maintained that Buell manufactured a complete line of American sport bikes that appealed to a young, diverse group of riders who demanded the ultimate in performance and handling. Like Harley's loyal owners group, H.O.G., Buell had its own affinity group, B.R.A.G. (Buell Riders Adventure Group).

---

[8] Bushnell, Davis, "Motorcycles Ride New Wave of Popularity," *Boston Sunday Globe*, June 27, 1999, p. 8NW.

[9] Stevens, "That Vroom! You Hear May Not Be a Harley."

American Quantum Cycles

American Quantum Cycles manufactured high-performance, custom-made cruisers and touring-style motorcycles with state-of-the-art engines utilizing a patented four-valve head for greater power and lower pollutant emissions. Using a PC-based kiosk Intranet/Extranet system installed in dealer showrooms, customers could select a precise motorcycle design with options tailored to their requirements.

For the quarter ended July 1999, American Quantum had sales of $343,000, up 105 percent over the same quarter the previous year. Quarterly expenses were $581,000 versus $1,232,000 a year earlier. CEO Rich Hagen announced that this improvement had come one and one-half months before the closing of a secondary stock offering of $8.5 million.

American Quantum had attracted attention with a memorable advertisement created for the firm by Della Femina/Jeary and Partners. The print ad was remembered more for its tag line than for its photograph of the motorcycle it featured. The tag line stated: "For the 65 million men who don't need Viagra." Viagra, manufactured by Pfizer, was a drug used to treat male impotence. The ad ran just once on the back page of *The Wall Street Journal*.

Harley-Davidson

There had been complaints about Harley-Davidson from the firm's loyal macho riders. Some felt that success had made the company too corporate, too mainstream, and overly focused on merchandising and image building. For example, one Harley dealership had been transformed from a grimy place that prominently featured parts and service to a sleek, neon-lit showcase for Harley-Davidson clothing and collectibles. When a sweaty California biker wheeled his oil-dripping bike in for repairs, a salesman asked him to take it off the lot because the "bike was pretty dirty."[10]

Harley had 600 franchised dealers in the United States and 1,200 dealers worldwide. The dealers had been required to remodel their stores at their own cost to showcase Harley's Motorclothes and other souvenirs along with the motorcycles. In 1996 Motorclothes accounted for $90 million of Harley's revenues.

While the required remodeling was an imposition, most Harley dealers did not have to work very hard to sell the motorcycles. Harley had a strategy of keeping supply lower than demand, which resulted in dealer waiting lists, dealers charging premiums for bikes they did not have in stock, and waits of up to two years for some models. "Because of the Harley name, many dealers today are just order takers," an industry observer had said.[11] One dealer interviewed in June disclosed that business was so good that he would not have another bike to sell until August. Another dealer stopped maintaining a waiting list of orders and sold Harleys only on a first-come, first-served basis. With Harley dealers frequently out of stock, the competition took the leftovers.

Harley Demand and Supply. Harley's 57 percent share of the cruiser market in 1994 had eroded. In 1997 Harley President Richard Teerlink said that the company was losing market share because it could not keep up with demand. Harley had increased production, from 118,000 bikes in 1996 to 131,000 in 1997. The firm had spent $800 million between 1994 and 1999 to open two new factories and intended to raise its annual production capacity to 200,000 by 2003, Harley's hundredth anniversary. Harley machined most of the parts for its V-twins. Harley had developed a new motor, the Twin

---

[10] Machan, "Is the Hog Going Soft?"
[11] Bushnell, "Motorcycles Ride New Wave of Popularity."

Cam 88, the first totally new Harley engine since 1936, which was designed to win back some of the sales the company had lost to aftermarket companies. The Twin Cam 88, at 1,450 cc, had about 10 percent more horsepower than Harley's Big Twin. The first Twin Cams were produced in June 1998.

Cruiser Buyers

Beecy Eagle could understand the excitement around the cruiser market. He had opted to take a position with Excelsior-Henderson because of the huge potential for growth. While motorcyclists in the 1970s were often called "easy riders" and stereotyped as a tough crowd, today the label "Rolex riders" fit better. Cruiser buyers were more affluent, better educated, and certainly not just Hell's Angels anymore.

A survey of male motorcyclists found that they were five times as likely to cry during a romantic movie than were men who did not ride motorcycles. The top movie that motorcyclists reported made them cry was Walt Disney's animated film *The Lion King*. As the general manager of the largest insurer of motorcycles in the country reported, "We always knew that they [male motorcyclists] were passionate about their bikes, but what we are finding is that they are as passionate about many other things."[12]

The cruiser target market consisted of 35- to 55-year-old males with household incomes of $60,000 and over. They were baby boomers who wanted "toys that they did not have when they were much younger." According to the Motorcycle Industry Council, the median income of motorcyclists in 1998 was $44,300. Fifty-nine percent of motorcyclists were white-collar workers or retirees.

Harley had recently reported that women made up 9 percent of its customers, up from 2 percent in 1985. In fact, according to J.D. Power and Associates, women now accounted for almost 25 percent of first-time new motorcycle owners. About 5 percent of Polaris's Victory motorcycle customers were women. The newest Victory offering, the Victory SportCruiser, was a hybrid between a sport bike and a cruiser and had a lower seat height, making it easier for women to straddle. Kawasaki had lowered some seat heights on its bikes and added colors to appeal to women.

Motorcycle riding had become more mainstream and less rebellious and was even a family activity, with so many dirt bikes being bought for children by their parents. There were over 5,000 motorcycle clubs in the United States, compared with 200 in the late 1980s. The Department of Commerce had reported that Americans were spending $573 billion a year on recreation, tripling the proportional rate of economic output from two generations earlier.

The motorcycle market appeared to be full of opportunity. All the same, Beecy wondered whether he had chosen the right company when he had moved back home. It was exciting to be living in an area where so many motorcycle firms were based, and he hoped to make the trip to Sturgis on his own bike the next summer. The question was, Which company offered the best long ride?

---

[12] Bailey, Ruby L., "More Women Are Grabbing the Handlebars in Motorcycle Market," *Knight-Ridder/Tribune Business News,* Oct. 6, 1999.

Sources

Alper, Mila. "Playing Around." *Forbes,* August 9, 1999, p. 148.

"American Quantum Cycles," *Business Wire,* October 6, 1999.

Bailey, Ruby L. "More Women Are Grabbing the Handlebars in Motorcycle Market." *Knight-Ridder/Tribune Business News,* October 6, 1999.

Ballon, Marc. "Born to Be Wild." *Inc.,* November 1, 1997, p. 42.

Brown, Don J. "An Industry in Perpetual Motion?" *Dealernews,* January 1999, vol. 35, p. 28.

Brown, Don J. "A Real Head of Steam." *Dealernews,* July 1999, vol. 35 (7), p. 80.

Brown, Don J. "Retail Sales Finish 1997 at 720,422 Units." *Dealernews,* March 1998, vol. 34, n3, p. 78.

Brown, Don J. "Teetering on the Brink of 1 Million Units." *Dealernews,* February 1998, vol. 34, n2, p. 36.

Brown, Don J. "There's Nothing Like Unbridled Enthusiasm, but Is the Motorcycle Industry Looking at Too Much of a Good Thing?" *Dealernews,* February 1999, vol. 35, n2, p. 38.

Brown, Stuart F. "Gearing Up for the Cruiser Wars." *Fortune,* August 3, 1998, p. 128B.

Bushnell, Davis. "Motorcycles Ride New Wave of Popularity." *Boston Sunday Globe,* June 27, 1999, p. 8.

Doyle, Rob. "Battle of the Muscle Bikes." *Business Week,* October 11, 1999, p. 10.

Hammond, Mark. "Kawasaki Covers New Sales Data Terrain." *PC Week,* September 6, 1999, p. 79.

Hartfiel, Robin. "Lightning Does Strike Twice: Behind the Scenes with Buell." *Dealernews,* October 1996, vol. 32, n10, p. 66.

"The Honda Way for 2000: Engineering, Performance, Leadership." *PR Newswire,* September 9, 1999.

Hopkins, H. Donald. "Using History for Strategic Problem-Solving: The Harley-Davidson Effect." *Business Horizons,* March–April 1999, vol. 42, i2, p. 52.

Kiley, David. "E-Z Rider." *Brandweek,* August 18, 1997, vol. 38, n31, p. 24.

Koss-Feder, Laura. "Be Reborn to Be Wild on Today's Powerful Retro Motorcycles." *Money,* April 1997, vol. 26, n4, p 174.

Machan, Dyan. "Is the Hog Going Soft?" *Forbes,* March 10, 1997, p. 114.

McCraw, Jim. "Three Biker-Entrepreneurs Take on Mighty Harley." *The New York Times,* August 20, 1999, p. P1.

McMains, Andrew. "Print Ad Proves Potent." *ADWEEK Eastern Edition,* May 18, 1998, vol. 39, n20, p. 10.

Miller, Karen Lowry. "On Beyond Born to Raise Hell." *Business Week,* June 7, 1999, p. 96.

"1997 Honda Valkyrie: Is Bigger Better?" *Dealernews,* March 1996, vol. 32, n3, p. 52.

Osterholm-Cox, Nancy. "California-Made Motorcycles Challenge Harley-Davidson in Colorado." *Knight-Ridder/Tribune Business News,* April 17, 1997, p. 417B1313.

Stevens, Karen. "That Vroom! You Hear May Not Be a Harley." *Business Week,* October 20, 1997, p. 159.

Strauss, Gary. "Minnesota Motorcycles Take on Harley." *USA Today,* November 5, 1997, p. 1B.

Web Sites

www.americaniron.com *(American Iron)*

www.americanmotor.com (American Motorcycle Network)

www.buell.com (Buell Motorcycle Company)

www.excelsior-henderson.com (Excelsior-Henderson Motorcycle Manufacturing Co.)

www.harley-davidson.com (Harley-Davidson Motor Company)

www.indianmotorcycle.com (Indian Motorcycle Company)

www.nortonmotorcycles.com (Norton Motorcycle Company)

www.quantumcycles.com (American Quantum Motorcycles)

CASE 4–5
CIMA MOUNTAINEERING, INC.

"What a great hike," exclaimed Anthony Simon as he tossed his Summit HX 350 hiking boots into his car. He had just finished hiking the challenging Cascade Canyon Trail in the Tetons north of Jackson, Wyoming. Anthony hiked often because it was a great way to test the hiking boots made by Cima Mountaineering, Inc., the business he inherited from his parents and owned with his sister, Margaret. As he drove back to Jackson, he began thinking about next week's meeting with Margaret, the president of Cima. During the past month they had been discussing marketing strategies for increasing the sales and profits of the company. No decisions had been made, but the preferences of each owner were becoming clear.

As illustrated in Exhibit 1, sales and profits had grown steadily for Cima, and by most measures the company was successful. However, growth was beginning to slow as a result of foreign competition and a changing market. Margaret observed that the market had shifted to a more casual, stylish hiking boot that appealed to hikers interested in a boot for a variety of uses. She favored a strategy of diversifying the company by marketing a new line of boots for the less experienced weekend hiker. Anthony also recognized that the market had changed, but he supported expanding the existing lines of boots for mountaineers and hikers. The company had been successful with those boots, and Anthony had some ideas about how to extend the lines and expand distribution. "This is a better way to grow," he thought. "I'm concerned about the risk in Margaret's recommendation. If we move to a more casual boot, then we have to resolve a new set of marketing and competitive issues and finance a new line. I'm not sure we can do it."

When he returned to Jackson that evening, Anthony stopped by his office to check his messages. The financial statements shown in Exhibits 2 and 3 were on his desk, along with a marketing study from a Denver consulting firm. Harris Fleming, vice president of marketing, had commissioned a study of the hiking boot market several months earlier to help the company plan for the future. As Anthony paged through the report,

EXHIBIT 1 Cima Mountaineering, Inc., Revenues and Net Income, 1990–95

Year	Revenues	Net Income	Profit Margin (%)
1995	$20,091,450	$ 857,134	4.27%
1994	18,738,529	809,505	4.32
1993	17,281,683	838,162	4.85
1992	15,614,803	776,056	4.97
1991	14,221,132	602,976	4.24
1990	13,034,562	522,606	4.01

Lawrence M. Lamont is professor of management at Washington and Lee University and Eva Cid and Wade Drew Hammond are seniors in the class of 1995 at Washington and Lee, majoring in management and accounting, respectively. Case material was prepared as a basis for class discussion and not designed to present illustrations of either effective or ineffective handling of administrative problems. Some names, locations, and financial information have been disguised. Copyright © 1995, Washington and Lee University.

EXHIBIT 2   **Cima Mountaineering, Inc., Income Statement, Years Ended December 31, 1995, and December 31, 1994**

	1995	1994
Net sales	$20,091,450	$ 18,738,529
Cost of goods sold	14,381,460	13,426,156
Gross margin	5,709,990	5,312,373
Selling and admin. expenses	4,285,730	3,973,419
Operating income	1,424,260	1,338,954
Other income (expenses)		
Interest expense	(160,733)	(131,170)
Interest income	35,161	18,739
Total other income (net)	(125,572)	(112,431)
Earnings before income taxes	1,298,688	1,226,523
Income taxes	441,554	417,018
Net income	$ 857,134	$ 809,505

two figures caught his eye. One was a segmentation of the hiking boot market (see Exhibit 4), and the other was a summary of market competition (see Exhibit 5). "This is interesting," he mused. "I hope Margaret reads it before our meeting."

History of Cima Mountaineering

As children, Anthony and Margaret Simon had watched their parents make western boots at the Hoback Boot Company, a small business they owned in Jackson, Wyoming. They learned the craft as they grew up and joined the company after college.

In the late 1960s the demand for western boots began to decline, and the Hoback Boot Company struggled to survive. By 1975 the parents were close to retirement and seemed content to close the business, but Margaret and Anthony decided to try to salvage the company. Margaret, the older sibling, became the president, and Anthony became the executive vice president. By the end of 1976, sales had declined to $1.5 million and the company earned profits of only $45,000. It became clear that to survive, the business would have to refocus on products with a more promising future.

Refocusing the Business.   As a college student, Anthony attended a mountaineering school north of Jackson in Teton National Park. As he learned to climb and hike, he became aware of the growing popularity of the sport and the boots being used. Because of his experience with western boots, he also noticed their limitations. Although the boots had good traction, they were heavy and uncomfortable and had little resistance to the snow and water always present in the mountains. He convinced Margaret that Hoback should explore the possibility of developing boots for mountaineering and hiking.

In 1977 Anthony and Margaret began 12 months of marketing research. They investigated the market, the competition, and the extent to which Hoback's existing equipment could be used to produce the new boots. By the summer of 1978 Hoback had developed a mountaineering boot and a hiking boot that were ready for testing. Several instructors from the mountaineering school tested the boots and gave them excellent reviews.

EXHIBIT 3   **Cima Mountaineering, Inc., Balance Sheet, Years Ending December 31, 1995, and December 31, 1994**

	1995	1994
Assets		
Current assets		
Cash and equivalents	$ 1,571,441	$ 1,228,296
Accounts receivable	4,696,260	3,976,608
Inventory	6,195,450	5,327,733
Other	270,938	276,367
Total	12,734,089	10,809,004
Fixed assets		
Property, plant, and equipment	3,899,568	2,961,667
Less: accumulated depreciation	(1,117,937)	(858,210)
Total fixed assets (net)	2,781,631	2,103,457
Other assets		
Intangibles	379,313	568,087
Other long-term assets	2,167,504	1,873,151
Total fixed assets (net)	$ 18,062,537	$ 15,353,699
Liabilities and shareholder equity		
Current liabilities		
Accounts payable	$ 4,280,821	$ 4,097,595
Notes payable	1,083,752	951,929
Current maturities of long-term debt	496,720	303,236
Accrued liabilities		
Expenses	2,754,537	2,360,631
Salaries and wages	1,408,878	1,259,003
Other	1,137,940	991,235
Total current liabilities	11,162,648	9,963,629
Long-term liabilities		
Long-term debt	3,070,631	2,303,055
Lease obligations	90,313	31,629
Total long-term liabilities	3,702,820	2,334,684
Other liabilities		
Deferred taxes	36,125	92,122
Other noncurrent liabilities	312,326	429,904
Total liabilities	14,672,043	12,820,339
Owner's equity		
Retained earnings	3,390,494	2,533,360
Total liabilities and owner's equity	$ 18,062,537	$ 15,353,699

The Transition.   By 1981 Hoback was ready to enter the market with two styles of boots: one for the mountaineer who wanted a boot for all-weather climbing and the other for men and women who were advanced hikers. Both styles had water-repellent leather uppers and cleated soles for superior traction. Distribution was secured through mountaineering shops in Wyoming and Colorado.

Hoback continued to manufacture western boots for its loyal customers, but Margaret planned to phase them out as the hiking boot business developed. However, because they did not completely understand the needs of the market, they hired Harris Fleming, a mountaineering instructor, to help them with product design and marketing.

EXHIBIT 4 **Segmentation of the Hiking Boot Market**

	Mountaineers	Serious Hikers	Weekenders	Practical Users	Children	Fashion Seekers
Benefits	Durability/ruggedness Stability/support Dryness/warmth Grip/traction	Stability Durability Traction Comfort/protection	Lightweight Comfort Durability Versatility	Lightweight Durability Good value Versatility	Durability Protection Lightweight Traction	Fashion/style Appearance Lightweight Inexpensive
Demographics	Young Primarily male Shops in specialty stores and specialized catalogs	Young, middle-aged Male and female Shops in specialty stores and outdoor catalogs	Young, middle-aged Male and female Shops in shoe retailers, sporting goods stores, and mail order catalogs	Young, middle-aged Primarily male Shops in shoe retailers and department stores	Young marrieds Male and female Shops in department stores and outdoor catalogs	Young Male and female Shops in shoe retailers, department stores, and catalogs
Lifestyle	Adventuresome Independent Risk taker Enjoys challenges	Nature lover Outdoorsman Sportsman Backpacker	Recreational hiker Social, spends time with family and friends Enjoys the outdoors	Practical Sociable Outdoors for work and recreation	Enjoys family activities Enjoys outdoors and hiking Children are active and play outdoors Parents are value-conscious	Materialistic Trendy Socially conscious Nonhikers Brand name shoppers Price-conscious
Examples of brands	Asolo Cliff Raichle Mt. Blanc Salomon Adventure 9	Raichle Explorer Vasque Clarion Tecnica Pegasus Dry Hi-Tec Piramide	Reebok R-Evolution Timberland Topozoic Merrell Acadia Nike Air Mada, Zion Vasque Alpha	Merrell Eagle Nike Air Khyber Tecnica Volcano	Vasque Kids Klimber Nike Merrell Caribou	Nike Espirit Reebok Telos Hi-Tec Magnum
Estimated market share	5% Slow growth	17% Moderate growth	25% High growth	20% Stable growth	5% Slow growth	28% At peak of rapid growth cycle
Price range	$210–$450	$120–$215	$70–$125	$40–$80	Up to $40	$65–$100

EXHIBIT 5 **Summary of Competitors**

Company	Location	Mountaineering (Styles)	Hiking (Styles)	Men's	Women's	Children's	Price Range
Raichle	Switzerland	Yes (7)	Yes (16)	Yes	Yes	Yes	High
Salomon	France	Yes (1)	Yes (9)	Yes	Yes	No	Mid
Asolo	Italy	Yes (4)	Yes (26)	Yes	Yes	No	High
Tecnica	Italy	Yes (3)	Yes (9)	Yes	Yes	No	Mid/high
Hi-Tec	United Kingdom	Yes (2)	Yes (29)	Yes	Yes	Yes	Mid/low
Vasque	Minnesota	Yes (4)	Yes (18)	Yes	Yes	Yes	Mid/high
Merrell	Vermont	Yes (5)	Yes (31)	Yes	Yes	Yes	Mid
Timberland	New Hampshire	No	Yes (4)	Yes	No	No	Mid
Nike	Oregon	No	Yes (5)	Yes	Yes	Yes	Low
Reebok	Massachusetts	No	Yes (3)	Yes	Yes	Yes	Low
Cima	Wyoming	Yes (3)	Yes (5)	Yes	Yes	No	High

Source: Published literature and company product brochures, 1995.

A New Company. During the 1980s Hoback prospered as the market expanded along with the popularity of outdoor recreation. The company slowly increased its product line and achieved success by focusing on classic boots that were relatively insensitive to fashion trends. By 1986 sales of Hoback Boots had reached $3.5 million.

Over the next several years distribution was steadily expanded. In 1987 Hoback employed independent sales representatives to handle the sales and service. Before long, Hoback boots were sold throughout Wyoming, Colorado, and Montana by retailers specializing in mountaineering and hiking equipment. Margaret decided to discontinue western boots to make room for the growing hiking boot business. To reflect the new direction of the company, the name was changed to Cima Mountaineering, Inc.

Cima Boots Take Off. The late 1980s was a period of exceptional growth. Demand for Cima boots grew quickly as consumers caught the trend toward healthy, active lifestyles. The company expanded its line for advanced hikers and improved the performance of its boots. By 1990, sales had reached $13 million and the company earned profits of $522,606. Margaret was satisfied with the growth but was concerned about low profitability as a result of foreign competition. She challenged the company to find new ways to design and manufacture boots at a lower cost.

Growth and Innovation. The next five years were marked by growth, innovation, and increasing foreign and domestic competition. Market growth continued as hiking boots became popular for casual wear in addition to hiking in mountains and on trails. Cima and its competitors began to make boots with molded footbeds and utilize materials that reduced weight.[1] Fashion also became a factor, and companies such as Nike and Reebok marketed lightweight boots in a variety of materials and colors to meet the

---

[1] Two processes are used to attach the uppers to the soles of boots. In classic welt construction, the uppers and soles are stitched. In the more contemporary method, a molded polyurethane footbed (including a one-piece heel and sole) is cemented to the upper with a waterproof adhesive. Many mountaineering boots use classic welt construction because it provides outstanding stability, while the contemporary method often is used with hiking boots to achieve lightweight construction. Cima used the classic method of construction for mountaineering boots and the contemporary method for hiking boots.

demand for styling in addition to performance. Cima implemented a computer-aided design (CAD) system in 1993 to shorten product development and devote more attention to design. Late in 1994, Cima restructured its facilities and implemented a modular approach to manufacturing. The company switched from a production line to a system in which a work team applied multiple processes to each pair of boots. Significant cost savings were achieved as the new approach improved the profit and quality of the company's boots.

The Situation in 1995.   As the company ended 1995, sales had grown to $20.0 million, up 7.2 percent from the previous year. Employment was at 425, and the facility was operating at 85 percent of capacity, producing several styles of mountaineering and hiking boots. Time-saving innovations and cost reduction also had worked, and profits reached an all-time high. Margaret, now 57, was still president, and Anthony remained executive vice president.

Cima Marketing Strategy

According to estimates, 1994 was a record year for sales of hiking and mountaineering boots in the United States. Retail sales exceeded $600 million, and about 15 million pairs of boots were sold. Consumers wore the boots for activities ranging from mountaineering to casual social events. In recent years, changes were beginning to occur in the market. Inexpensive, lightweight hiking boots were becoming increasingly popular for day hikes and trail walking, and a new category of comfortable, light "trekking" shoes was being marketed by manufacturers of athletic shoes.

Only a part of the market was targeted by Cima. Most of its customers were serious outdoor enthusiasts. They included mountaineers who climbed in rugged terrain and advanced hikers who used the boots on challenging trails and extended backpacking trips. The demand for Cima boots was seasonal, and most of the purchases were made during the summer months, when the mountains and trails were most accessible.

Positioning.   Cima boots were positioned as the best available for their intended purpose. Consumers saw them as durable and comfortable with exceptional performance. Retailers viewed the company as quick to adopt innovative construction techniques but conservative in styling. Cima intentionally used traditional styling to avoid fashion obsolescence and the need for frequent design changes. Some of the most popular styles had been in the market for several years without any significant modifications. The Glacier MX 350 shown in Exhibit 6 and the Summit HX 350 boot shown in Exhibit 7 are good examples. The MX 350, priced at $219.00, was positioned as a classic boot for men and had a unique tread design for beginning mountaineers. The Summit HX 350 was priced at $159.00 and was a boot for men and women hiking rough trails. Exhibit 8 describes the items in the mountaineering and hiking boot lines, and Exhibit 9 provides a sales history for Cima boots.

Product Lines.   Corporate branding was used, and "Cima" was embossed on the leather on the side of the boot to enhance consumer recognition. Product lines were also branded, and alphabetic letters and numbers were used to differentiate items in the line. Each line had different styles and features to cover many of the important uses in the market. However, all the boots had features that the company believed were essential to positioning. Standard features included water-repellent leather uppers and high-traction soles and heels. The hardware for the boots was plated steel, and the laces were made of tough, durable nylon. Quality was emphasized throughout the product lines.

EXHIBIT 6   **The Glacier MX 350 Mountaineering Boot**

EXHIBIT 7   **The Summit HX 350 Hiking Boot**

Glacier Boots for Mountaineering.   The Glacier line featured three boots for men. The MX 550 was designed for expert all-weather climbers looking for the ultimate in traction, protection, and warmth. The MX 450 was for experienced climbers taking extended excursions, while the MX 350 met the needs of less-skilled individuals beginning climbing in moderate terrain and climates.

EXHIBIT 8   Cima Mountaineering, Inc., Mountaineering and Hiking Boot Lines

Product Line	Description
Glacier	
MX 550	For expert mountaineers climbing challenging mountains. Made for use on rocks, ice, and snow. Features welt construction, superior stability and support, reinforced heel and toe, padded ankle and tongue, step-in crampon insert, thermal insulation, and waterproof inner liner. Retails for $299.
MX 450	For proficient mountaineers engaging in rigorous, high-altitude hiking. Offers long-term comfort and stability on rough terrain. Features welt construction, deep cleated soles and heels, reinforced heel and toe, padded ankle and tongue, step-in crampon insert, and waterproof inner liner. Retails for $249.
MX 350	For beginning mountaineers climbing in moderate terrain and temperate climates. Features welt construction, unique tread design for traction, padded ankle and tongue, good stability and support, and a quick-dry lining. Retails for $219.
Summit	
HX 550	For experienced hikers who require uncompromising performance. Features nylon shank for stability and rigidity, waterproof inner liner, cushioned midsole, high-traction outsole, and padded ankle and tongue. Retails for $197.
HX 450	For backpackers who carry heavy loads on extended trips. Features thermal insulation, cushioned midsole, waterproof inner liner, excellent foot protection, and high-traction outsole. Retails for $179.
HX 350	For hikers who travel rough trails and a variety of backcountry terrain. Features extra cushioning, good stability and support, waterproof inner liner, and high-traction outsole for good grip in muddy and sloping surfaces. Retails for $159.
HX 250	For hikers who hike developed trails. Made with only the necessary technical features, including cushioning, foot and ankle support, waterproof inner liner, and high-traction outsole. Retails for $139.
HX 150	For individuals taking more than day and weekend hikes. Versatile boot for all kinds of excursions. Features cushioning, good support, waterproof inner liner, and high-traction outsoles for use on a variety of surfaces. Retails for $129.

EXHIBIT 9   Cima Mountaineering, Inc., Product Line Sales

	Unit Sales (%)		Sales Revenue	
Year	Mountaineering	Hiking	Mountaineering	Hiking
1995	15.00%	85.00%	21.74%	78.26%
1994	15.90	84.10	22.93	77.07
1993	17.20	82.80	24.64	75.36
1992	18.00	82.00	25.68	74.32
1991	18.80	81.20	26.71	73.29
1990	19.70	80.30	27.86	72.14

Summit Boots for Hiking.   The Summit line featured five styles for men and women. The HX 550 was preferred by experienced hikers who demanded the best possible performance. The boot featured water-repellent leather uppers, a waterproof inner liner, a cushioned midsole, a nylon shank for rigidity, and a sole designed for high traction. It was available in gray and brown with different types of leather.[2] The Summit HX 150 was the least expensive boot in the line, designed for individuals who were beginning to take more than the occasional "weekend hike." It was a versatile boot for all kinds of excursions and featured a water-repellent leather upper, a cushioned midsole, and excellent traction. The HX 150 was popular as an entry-level boot for outdoor enthusiasts.

Distribution. Cima boots were distributed in Arizona, California, Colorado, Idaho, Montana, Nevada, New Mexico, Oregon, Washington, Wyoming, and western Canada through specialty retailers selling mountaineering, backpacking, and hiking equipment. Occasionally, Cima was approached by mail order catalog companies and chain sporting goods stores offering to sell its boots. The company considered the proposals but had not used those channels.

Promotion. The Cima sales and marketing office was located in Jackson. It was managed by Harris Fleming and staffed with several marketing personnel. Promotion was an important aspect of the marketing strategy, and advertising, personal selling, and sales promotion were used to gain exposure for Cima branded boots. Promotion was directed toward consumers and to retailers that stocked Cima mountaineering and hiking boots.

Personal Selling. Cima used 10 independent sales representatives to sell its boots in the Western states and Canada. Representatives did not sell competing boots, but they sold complementary products such as outdoor apparel and equipment for mountaineering, hiking, and backpacking. They were paid a commission and handled customer service in addition to sales. Management also was involved in personal selling. Harris Fleming trained the independent sales representatives and often accompanied them on sales calls.

Advertising and Sales Promotion. Advertising and sales promotion also were important promotional methods. Print advertising was used to increase brand awareness and assist retailers with promotion. Advertising was placed in leading magazines such as *Summit, Outside,* and *Backpacker* to reach mountaineers and hikers with the message that Cima boots were functional and durable and had classic styling. In addition, cooperative advertising was offered to encourage retailers to advertise Cima boots and identify their locations.

Sales promotion was an important part of the promotion program. Along with the focus on brand name recognition, Cima provided product literature and point of sale display materials to assist retailers in promoting the boots. In addition, the company regularly exhibited at industry trade shows. The exhibits, staffed by marketing personnel and the company's independent sales representatives, were effective for maintaining relationships with retailers and presenting the company's products.

---

[2] Different types of leather are used to make hiking boots. *Full grain:* High-quality, durable, upper layer of the hide. It has a natural finish and is strong and breathable. *Split grain:* Underside of the hide after the full-grain leather has been removed from the top. Light weight and comfort are the primary characteristics. *Suede:* A very fine split-grain leather. *Nubuk:* Brushed full-grain leather. *Waxed:* A process in which leather is coated with wax to help shed water. Most Cima boots were available in two or more types of leather.

Mountaineering and hiking boots are made water-repellent by treating the uppers with wax or chemical coatings. To make the boots waterproof, a fabric inner liner is built into the boot to provide waterproof protection and breathability. All Cima boots were water-repellent, but only styles with an inner liner were waterproof.

Pricing.   Cima selling prices to retailers ranged from $64.50 to $149.50 a pair, depending on the style. Mountaineering boots were more expensive because of their construction and features, while hiking boots were priced lower. Retailers were encouraged to take a 50 percent margin on the retail selling price, and so the retail prices shown in Exhibit 8 should be divided by two to get the Cima selling price. Cima priced its boots higher than competitors did, supporting the positioning of the boots as the top-quality product at each price point. Payment terms were net 30 days (similar to competitors), and boots were shipped to retailers from a warehouse in Jackson, Wyoming.

Segmentation of the Hiking Boot Market

As Anthony reviewed the marketing study commissioned by Harris Fleming, his attention focused on the market segmentation shown in Exhibit 4. It was interesting, because management had never seriously thought about the segmentation in the market. Of course, Anthony was aware that not everyone was a potential customer for Cima boots, but he was surprised to see how well the product lines met the needs of mountaineers and serious hikers. As he reviewed the market segmentation, he read the descriptions for mountaineers, serious hikers, and weekenders carefully because Cima was trying to decide which of these segments to target for expansion.

Mountaineers.   Mountain climbers and high-altitude hikers are in this segment. They are serious about climbing and enjoy risk and adventure. Because mountaineers' safety may depend on their boots, they need maximum stability and support, traction for a variety of climbing conditions, and protection from wet and cold weather.

Serious Hikers.   Outdoorsmen, who love nature and have a strong interest in health and fitness, are the serious hikers. They hike rough trails and take extended backpacking or hiking excursions. Serious hikers are brand-conscious and look for durable, high-performance boots with good support, a comfortable fit, and good traction.

Weekenders.   Consumers in this segment are recreational hikers who enjoy casual weekend and day hikes with family and friends. They are interested in light, comfortable boots that provide a good fit, protection, and traction on a variety of surfaces. Weekenders prefer versatile boots that can be worn for a variety of activities.

Foreign and Domestic Competition

The second part of the marketing study that caught Anthony's attention was the analysis of competition. Although Anthony and Margaret were aware that competition had increased, they had overlooked the extent to which foreign bootmakers had entered the market. Apparently, foreign competitors had noticed the market growth and were exporting their boots aggressively into the United States. They had established sales offices and independent sales agents to compete for the customers served by Cima. The leading foreign brands, such as Asolo, Hi-Tec, Salomon, and Raichle, were marketed on performance and reputation, usually to the mountaineering, serious hiker, and weekender segments of the market.

The study also summarized the most important domestic competitors. Vasque and Merrell marketed boots that competed with Cima, but others were offering products for segments of the market where the prospects for growth were better. As Anthony examined Exhibit 5, he realized that the entry of Reebok and Nike into the hiking boot market was quite logical. They had entered the market as consumer preference shifted from wearing athletic shoes for casual outdoor activities to wearing a more rugged shoe. Each was marketing footwear that combined the appearance and durability of hiking boots with the lightness and fit of athletic shoes. The result was a line of fashionable hiking boots that appealed to brand- and style-conscious teens and young adults. Both firms were expanding their product lines and moving into segments of the market that demanded lower levels of performance.

Margaret and Anthony Discuss Marketing Strategy

A few days after hiking in Cascade Canyon, Anthony met with Margaret and Harris Fleming to discuss marketing strategy. Each had read the consultant's report and studied the market segmentation and competitive summary. As the meeting opened, the conversation went as follows:

Margaret: It looks like we will have another record year. The economy is growing, and consumers seem confident and eager to buy. Yet I'm concerned about the future. The foreign bootmakers are providing some stiff competition. Their boots have outstanding performance and attractive prices. The improvements we made in manufacturing helped control costs and maintain margins, but it looks like the competition and slow growth in our markets will make it difficult to improve profits. We need to be thinking about new opportunities.

Harris: I agree, Margaret. Just this past week we lost Rocky Mountain Sports in Boulder, Colorado. John Kline, the sales manager, decided to drop us and pick up Asolo. We were doing $70,000 a year with them, and they carried our entire line. We also lost Great Western Outfitters in Colorado Springs. They replaced us with Merrell. The sales manager said that the college students there had been asking for the lower-priced Merrell boots. They bought $60,000 last year.

Anthony: Rocky Mountain and Great Western were good customers. I guess I'm not surprised, though. Our Glacier line needs another boot, and the Summit line is just not deep enough to cover the price points. We need to have some styles at lower prices to compete with Merrell and Asolo. I'm in favor of extending our existing lines to broaden their market appeal. It seems to me that the best way to compete is to stick with what we do best, making boots for mountaineers and serious hikers.

Margaret: Not so fast, Anthony. The problem is that our markets are small and not growing fast enough to support the foreign competitors that have entered with excellent products. We can probably hold our own, but I doubt if we can do much better. I think the future of this company is to move with the market. Consumers are demanding more style, lower prices, and a lightweight hiking boot that can be worn for a variety of uses. Look at the segmentation again. The "Weekender" segment is large and growing. That's where we need to go with some stylish new boots that depart from our classic leather lines.

Anthony: Maybe so, but we don't have much experience working with the leather and nylon combinations that are being used in these lighter boots. Besides, I'm not sure we can finance the product development and marketing for a new market that already has plenty of competition. And I'm concerned about the brand image that we have worked so hard to establish over the past 20 years. A line of inexpensive, casual boots just doesn't seem to fit with the perception consumers have of our products.

Harris: I can see advantages to each strategy. I do know that we don't have the time and resources to do both, so we had better make a thoughtful choice. Also, I think we should reconsider selling to the mail order catalog companies that specialize in mountaineering and hiking equipment. Last week I received another call from REI requesting us to sell them some of the boots in our Summit line for the 1997 season. This might be a good source of revenue and a way to expand our geographic market.

Margaret: You're right, Harris. We need to rethink our position on the mail order companies. Most of them have good market penetration in the East, where we don't have distribution. I noticed that Gander Mountain is carrying some of the Timberland line and that L.L. Bean is carrying some Vasque styles along with its own line of branded boots.

Anthony: I agree. Why don't we each put together a proposal that summarizes our recommendations, and then we can get back together to continue the discussion.

Harris: Good idea. Eventually we will need a sales forecast and some cost data. Send me your proposals, and I'll call the consulting firm and have them prepare some forecasts. I think we already have some cost information. Give me a few days, and then we can get together again.

The Meeting to Review the Proposals

The following week, the discussion continued. Margaret presented her proposal, which is summarized in Exhibit 10. She proposed moving Cima into the "Weekender" segment by marketing two new hiking boots. Anthony countered with the proposal summarized in Exhibit 11. He favored extending the existing lines by adding a new mountaineering boot and two new Summit hiking boots at lower price points. Harris presented sales forecasts for each proposal, and after some discussion and modification, they were finalized as shown in Exhibit 12. Cost information was gathered by Harris from the vice president of manufacturing and is presented in Exhibit 13. After a lengthy discussion in which Margaret and Anthony were unable to agree on a course of action, Harris Fleming suggested that each proposal be explored further by conducting marketing research. He proposed the formation of teams from the Cima marketing staff to research each proposal and present it to Margaret and Anthony at a later date. Harris presented his directions to the teams in the memorandum shown in Exhibit 14. The discussion between Margaret and Anthony continued as follows:

> *Margaret:* Once the marketing research is completed and we can read the reports and listen to the presentations, we should have a better idea of which strategy makes the best sense. Hopefully, a clear direction will emerge and we can move ahead with one of the proposals. In either case, I'm still intrigued with the possibility of moving into the mail order catalogs, since we really haven't developed these companies as customers. I just wish we knew how much business we could expect from them.
>
> *Anthony:* We should seriously consider them, Margaret. Companies like L.L. Bean, Gander Mountain, and REI have been carrying a selection of hiking boots for several years. However, there may be a problem for us. Eventually the catalog companies expect their boot suppliers to make them a private brand. I'm not sure this is something we want to do, since we built the company on a strategy of marketing our own brands that are made in the U.S.A. Also, I'm concerned about the reaction of our retailers when they discover we are selling to the catalog companies. It could create some problems.
>
> *Harris:* That is a strategy issue we will have to address. However, I'm not even sure what percentage of sales the typical footwear company makes through the mail order catalogs. If we were to solicit the catalog business, we would need an answer to this question to avoid exceeding our capacity. In the proposals I asked each of the teams to provide an estimate for us. I have to catch an early flight to Denver in the morning. It's 6:30; why don't we call it a day.

The meeting was adjourned at 6:35 PM. Soon thereafter, the marketing teams were formed, with a leader assigned to each team.

EXHIBIT 10   Margaret's Marketing Proposal

MEMORANDUM

TO: Anthony Simon, Executive Vice President
           Harris Fleming, Vice President of Marketing
FROM: Margaret Simon, President
RE: Marketing Proposal

I believe we have an excellent opportunity to expand the sales and profits of Cima by entering the "Weekender" segment of the hiking boot market. The segment's estimated share of the market is 25 percent, and according to the consultant's report, it is growing quite rapidly. I propose that we begin immediately to develop two new products and prepare a marketing strategy as discussed below.

Target Market and Positioning

Male and female recreational hikers looking for a comfortable, lightweight boot that is attractively priced and acceptable for short hikes and casual wear. Weekenders enjoy the outdoors and a day or weekend hike with family and friends.

The new boots would be positioned with magazine advertising as hiking boots that deliver performance and style for the demands of light hiking and casual outdoor wear.

Product

Two boots in men's and women's sizes. The boots would be constructed of leather and nylon uppers with a molded rubber outsole. A new branded line would be created to meet the needs of the market segment. The boots (designated WX 550 and WX 450) would have the following features:

	WX 550	WX 450
Leather and nylon uppers	X	X
Molded rubber outsole	X	X
Cushioned midsole	X	X
Padded collar and tongue	X	X
Durable hardware and laces	X	X
Waterproof inner liner	X	

Uppers: To be designed. Options include brown full-grain, split-grain, or suede leather combined with durable nylon in two of the following colors: beige, black, blue, gray, green, and slate.
Boot design and brand name: To be decided.

Retail Outlets

Specialty shoe retailers carrying hiking boots and casual shoes and sporting goods stores. Eventually mail order catalogs carrying outdoor apparel and hiking, backpacking, and camping equipment.

Promotion

Independent sales representatives	Point of sale display materials
Magazine advertising	Product brochures
Co-op advertising	Trade shows

Suggested Retail Pricing

WX 550: $89.00
WX 450: $69.00

Competitors

Timberland, Hi-Tec, Vasque, Merrell, Asolo, Nike, and Reebok.

Product Development and Required Investment

We should allow about one year for the necessary product development and testing. I estimate these costs to be $350,000. Additionally, we will need to make a capital expenditure of $150,000 for new equipment.

EXHIBIT 11   Anthony's Marketing Proposal

MEMORANDUM

TO: Margaret Simon, President
         Harris Fleming, Vice President of Marketing
FROM: Anthony Simon, Executive Vice President
RE: Marketing Proposal

We have been successful with boots for mountaineers and serious hikers for years, and this is where our strengths seem to be. I recommend extending our Glacier and Summit lines instead of venturing into a new, unfamiliar market. My recommendations are summarized below:

Product Development

Introduce two new boots in the Summit line (designated HX 100 and HX 50) and market the Glacier MX 350 in a style for women with the same features as the boot for men. The new women's Glacier boot would have a suggested retail price of $219.99, while the suggested retail prices for the HX 100 and the HX 50 would be $119.00 and $89.00, respectively, to provide price points at the low end of the line. The new Summit boots for men and women would be the first in the line to have leather and nylon uppers as well as the following features:

	HX 100	HX 50
Leather and nylon uppers	X	X
Molded rubber outsole	X	X
Cushioned midsole	X	X
Padded collar and tongue	X	X
Quick-dry lining	X	X
Waterproof inner liner	X	

The leather used in the uppers will have to be determined. We should consider full-grain, suede, and nubuck since they are all popular with users in this segment. We need to select one for the initial introduction. The nylon fabric for the uppers should be available in two colors, selected from among the following: beige, brown, green, slate, maroon, and navy blue. Additional colors can be offered as sales develop and we gain a better understanding of consumer preferences.

Product Development and Required Investment

Product design and development costs of $400,000 for the MX 350, HX 100, and HX 50 styles and a capital investment of $150,000 to acquire equipment to cut and stitch the nylon/leather uppers. One year will be needed for product development and testing.

Positioning

The additions to the Summit line will be positioned as boots for serious hikers who want a quality hiking boot at a reasonable price. The boots will also be attractive to casual hikers who are looking to move up to a better boot as they gain experience in hiking and outdoor activity.

Retail Outlets

We can use our existing retail outlets. Additionally, the lower price points on the new styles will make these boots attractive to catalog shoppers. I recommend that we consider making the Summit boots available to consumers through mail order catalog companies.

Promotion

We will need to revise our product brochures and develop new advertising for the additions to the Summit line. The balance of the promotion program should remain as it is since it is working quite well. I believe the sales representatives and retailers selling our lines will welcome the new boots since they broaden the consumer appeal of our lines.

Suggested Retail Pricing

MX 350 for women:	$219.00
HX 100:	$119.00
HX 50:	$89.00

Competitors

Asolo, Hi-Tec, Merrell, Raichle, Salomon, Tecnica, and Vasque.

EXHIBIT 12   Cima Mountaineering, Inc., Sales Forecasts for Proposed New Products (Pairs of Boots)

	Project 1		Project 2		
Year	*WX 550*	*WX 450*	*MX 350*	*HX 100*	*HX 50*
2001–02	16,420	24,590	2,249	15,420	12,897
2000–01	14,104	21,115	1,778	13,285	11,733
1999–2000	8,420	12,605	897	10,078	9,169
1998–99	5,590	8,430	538	5,470	5,049
1997–98	4,050	6,160	414	4,049	3,813

Note: Sales forecasts are expected values derived from minimum and maximum estimates.

Some cannibalization of existing boots will occur when the new styles are introduced. The sales forecasts provided above have taken into account the impact of sales losses on existing boots. No additional adjustments need to be made.

Forecasts for WX 550, WX 450, HX 100, and HX 50 include sales of both men's and women's boots.

EXHIBIT 13   Cima Mountaineering, Inc., Cost Information for Mountaineering and Hiking Boots

	Inner Liner	*No Inner Liner*
Retail margin	50%	50%
Marketing and Manufacturing Costs		
Sales commissions	10	10
Advertising and sales promotion	5	5
Materials	42	35
Labor, overhead, and transportation	28	35

Cost information for 1997–98 only. Sales commissions, advertising and sales promotion, materials, labor, overhead, and transportation costs are based on Cima selling prices. After 1997–98, annual increases of 3.0 percent apply to marketing and manufacturing costs and increases of 4.0 percent apply to Cima selling prices.

EXHIBIT 14   Harris Fleming's Memorandum to the Marketing Staff

MEMORANDUM

TO: Marketing Staff
CC: Margaret Simon, President
             Anthony Simon, Executive Vice President
FROM: Harris Fleming, Vice President of Marketing
SUBJECT: Marketing Research Projects

Attached to this memorandum are two marketing proposals (see case Exhibits 10 and 11) under consideration by our company. Each proposal is a guide for additional marketing research. You have been selected to serve on a project team to investigate one of the proposals and report your conclusions and recommendations to management. At your earliest convenience, please complete the following.

Project Team 1: Proposal to enter the "Weekender" segment of the hiking boot market.

Review the market segmentation and summary of competition in Exhibits 4 and 5. Identify consumers who would match the profile described in the market segment and conduct field research using a focus group, a survey, or both. You may also visit retailers carrying hiking boots to examine displays and product brochures. Using the information in the proposal, supplemented with your research, prepare the following:

EXHIBIT 14   (concluded)

1. A design for the hiking boots (WX 550 and WX 450). Please prepare a sketch that shows the styling for the uppers. We propose to use the same design for each boot, the only difference being the waterproof inner liner on the WX 550 boot. On your design, list the features that your proposed boot would have, considering additions or deletions to those listed in the proposal.

2. Recommend a type of leather (from among those proposed) and two colors for the nylon to be used in the panels of the uppers. We plan to make two styles, one in each color for each boot.

3. Recommend a brand name for the product line. Include a rationale for your choice.

4. Verify the acceptability of the suggested retail pricing.

5. Prepare a magazine advertisement for the hiking boot. Provide a rationale for the advertisement in the report.

6. Convert the suggested retail prices *in the proposal* to the Cima selling price and use the sales forecasts and costs (shown in Exhibits 12 and 13) to prepare an estimate of before-tax profits for the new product line, covering a five-year period starting in 1997–98. Assume annual cost increases of 3.0 percent and price increases of 4.0 percent beginning in 1998–99. Discount the future profits to present value, using a cost of capital of 15.0 percent. Use 1996–97 as the base year for all discounting.

7. Determine the payback period for the proposal. Assume product development and investment occur in 1996–97.

8. Provide your conclusions on the attractiveness of these styles to mail order catalog companies and their customers. You may wish to review current mail order catalogs to observe the hiking boots featured. Assuming that Cima is successful selling to mail order catalog companies, estimate the percentage of our sales that could be expected from these customers.

9. Prepare a report that summarizes the recommendations of your project team, including the advantages and disadvantages of the proposal. Be prepared to present your product design, branding, pro forma projections, payback period, and recommendations to management shortly after completion of this assignment.

10. Summarize your research and list the sources of information used to prepare the report.

Project Team 2: Proposal to extend the existing lines of boots for mountaineers and hikers.

Review the market segmentation and summary of competition in Exhibits 4 and 5. Identify consumers who match the profile described in the market segment and conduct field research using a focus group, a survey, or both. You also may visit retailers carrying hiking boots to examine displays and product brochures. Using the information in the proposal, supplemented with your research, prepare the following.

1. Designs for the hiking boots (HX 100 and HX 50). Please prepare sketches showing the styling for the uppers. We propose to use a different design for each boot, so you should provide a sketch for each. On each sketch, list the features that your proposed boots would have, considering additions or deletions to those listed in the proposal. No sketch is necessary for the mountaineering boot, MX 350, since we will use the same design as the men's boot and build it on a women's last.

2. Recommend one type of leather (from among those proposed) and two colors for the nylon to be used in the panels of the uppers. We plan to make two styles, one in each color for each boot.

3. Verify the market acceptability of the suggested retail pricing.

4. Prepare a magazine advertisement for your hiking boots. Include a rationale for the advertisement in the report.

5. Using the suggested retail prices *in the proposal,* convert them to the Cima selling prices and use the sales forecasts and costs (shown in Exhibits 12 and 13) to prepare an estimate of before-tax profits for the new products covering a five-year period starting in 1997–98. Assume annual cost increases of 3.0 percent and price increases of 4.0 percent beginning in 1998–99. Discount the profits to present value using a cost of capital of 15.0 percent. Use 1996–97 as the base year for all discounting.

6. Determine the payback period for the proposal. Assume product development and investment occur in 1996–97.

7. Provide your conclusions on the attractiveness of these styles to mail order catalog companies and their customers. You may wish to review current mail order catalogs to observe the hiking boots featured. Assuming that Cima is successful selling to mail order catalog companies, estimate the percentage of our sales that could be expected from these customers.

8. Prepare a report that summarizes the recommendations of your project team, including the advantages and disadvantages of the proposal. Be prepared to present your product design, pro forma projections, payback period, and recommendations to management shortly after completion of this assignment.

9. Summarize your research and list the sources of information used to prepare the report.

CASE 4–6
MURPHY BREWERY IRELAND, LIMITED

Patrick Conway, marketing director for Murphy's, picked up his issue of *The Financial Times* and read the following headline on May 13: "Grand Met, Guinness to Merge." He pondered the impact on his firm. Guinness was Murphy's most formidable competitor not only in Ireland but worldwide. Since a staff meeting was already scheduled for later Tuesday morning, he decided to examine the article closely and discuss it with his team. As he read on, the £22.3 billion merger between two of the four largest distillers (Seagram's headquartered in Canada and Allied Domecq, another British company, were the other two) appeared to have much synergy. The article pointed out that the geographic and brand fits were good between the two companies. The new firm, which will be called GMG, will be approximately equal in size to such major multinationals as Unilever, Procter & Gamble, and Philip Morris.[1]

During the 11 AM staff meeting, Patrick brought the merger to the attention of his colleagues. His company was in the middle of preparing its 1998 global marketing plan, and this news brought some urgency to the task ahead. Patrick stated that he felt a major assessment of Murphy's status in the worldwide market was needed. He called on David Ford, his export manager, to examine Murphy's position in the British and European markets. He said he would phone Michael Foley of Heineken USA (distributor of Murphy's in the states) to report on Murphy's progress there and asked Dan Leahy to look into Murphy's status in Ireland. He asked each man to report back to him within a week.

As part of his personal preparation, Patrick decided to dig into the files and reacquaint himself with the company history, since he had joined the firm only a few years previously. He also wanted to find out more about the merger. He rang the communications department to clip and route all articles from business publications on this topic to him. Patrick considered the impact these developments would have on Murphy's brands.

In 1997 Murphy's had become a truly international brand that maintained a unique identity in Ireland. The name Murphy, the most common surname in the entire country, is recognized internationally for its Irish heritage. Exhibit 1 shows that about 85 percent of Murphy's sales came from export business in 1996 and that the company now employs 385 people. He located a report from several years earlier that provided a historical perspective on the company.

Historical Background

James J. Murphy and Company Limited was founded in 1856 in Cork City, Ireland, by the four Murphy brothers—James, William, Jerome, and Francis. In 1890 they were described as follows: "These gentlemen applied themselves with energy and enterprise to

This case was prepared by Patrick E. Murphy, professor of marketing, University of Notre Dame, Indiana, and former visiting professor of marketing, University College Cork in Ireland, and Don O'Sullivan, lecturer in marketing, Department of Management and Marketing, University College Cork. The case was distributed by the European Case Clearinghouse.

This case is intended to serve as a basis for a class discussion rather than to illustrate either effective or ineffective handling of a business situation. The authors would like to thank Patrick Conway, David Ford, and Dan Leahy of Murphy Brewery Ireland and Michael Foley of Heineken USA for their assistance in writing this case.

EXHIBIT 1 **Export Sales versus Total Company Volumes**

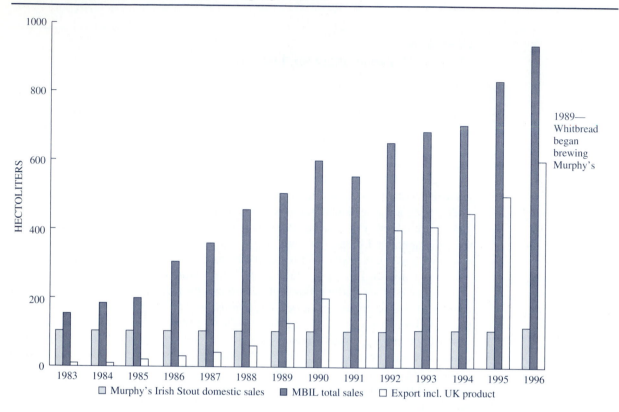

1989—
Whitbread
began
brewing
Murphy's

□ Murphy's Irish Stout domestic sales   ■ MBIL total sales   □ Export incl. UK product

the manufacture of an article, the reputation of which now extends far beyond the South of Ireland where the firm's stout and porter have been long and favorably known and where they command a very exclusive sale."[2]

James J. Murphy inherited the family business skills. His grandfather, also called James, had founded, with his brothers, the distillery James Murphy and Company in Midleton, County Cork (15 miles to the east of Cork City), in 1825. These Murphy brothers prospered as ship owners and tea importers and had been paid quite a large sum of money before founding their distillery. This company experienced significant growth and in 1867 amalgamated with four Cork distilleries to create Cork Distilleries Company Ltd. That firm enjoyed great success over the next century and in 1966 joined with the Dublin distillery John Jameson and Son and John Power and Son to create Irish Distillers Limited.

The Murphy Brewery is located at Lady's Well in Cork, whose name derives from a celebrated well on the hill opposite of the premises. It was dedicated to Our Lady and believed to possess miraculous properties. To the present day, pilgrimages take place to the shrine every year in the month of May. During the nineteenth century Lady's Well was one of Cork's largest breweries and was mentioned in the 1890 publication *Noted Breweries of Great Britain and Ireland,* which indicated that Murphy's Stout had become a formidable rival to Guinness in the south of Ireland.[3]

Initially, Murphy's brewed porter, but it switched exclusively to stout (the name *stout* denotes strong beers—see Exhibit 2 for a description of the product), and this remained

---

EXHIBIT 2   **What Is Stout, and How Was It Promoted?**

Stout is a black beer with a thick white head. The black color is due mainly to the fact that it contains malted barley which is roasted in a similar way to coffee beans. The creamy white head is created from the "initiation" and "surging" of bubbles of nitrogen and carbon dioxide gas as the beer is poured. The gas enters the keg and forces the beer out. It is actually the nitrogen which causes the tight, creamy head.

The word *stout* has long been used to describe strong beers; it also meant stout, as in stout ale. The strength may have been in terms of taste or alcohol or both. Standard stout ranges in alcohol content from 4 percent to 5 percent. The word *stout* gradually made the transition from adjective to noun. The basic constituent of stout is barley, which consists mainly of starch. The barley becomes a malt and during this process is converted to sugar, which is fermentable. When the malt is roasted beyond the normal limits, this gives the stout its unusual dark hue. The highly roasted dark malt is 500 times darker than a pale malt and adds its distinctive color as well as flavor.

The resulting sugary liquid, called wort, is eventually formed. At this stage hops are added and boiled with wort to produce the liquid. When boiled for an hour or two, the hops release oils and resins which produce the characteristic bitterness and aroma. A comparison of the bitterness level among the leading brands of stout conducted by the European Brewery Convention found that Guinness rates 45 to 48 European units of bitterness, Beamish 40, and Murphy's 36 to 38.

Stout is synonymous with Ireland, and nowhere else is stout as popular or as intrinsically part of everyday life. The criterion by which a pub often is judged is likely to be whether it sells a good pint of stout. In the pub, pouring pints of stout is an activity full of tradition and custom. The pouring of the product is seen as having a major impact on product quality. Stout is poured in two stages. First the glass is filled to 75 percent capacity and allowed to "settle" so that the creamy head will separate from the dark body. To top off the pint, the tap is pushed forward slightly until the head rises just below the rim. This activity takes a minute or two and results in stout taking longer to pour. Interestingly, the product is poured in one go/pull outside Ireland.

Stout has its roots in colder climates in Ireland and Scandinavia, and traditionally it has been a winter brew. Comments such as "typically consumed in the dark winter months" and "a seasonal beer brewed only in the winter" are used regularly by stout breweries worldwide. Stout is thought to be a drink suited to quiet, reflective sipping. Both in Ireland and worldwide, it is now a year-round drink.

To return to the definition, stout is often considered a strong drink. Therefore, both Murphy's and Guinness have extensively used strength in their marketing and advertising. Murphy's utilized a circus strongman who was shown lifting a horse off the ground with the label "Murphy's Stout gives strength" for many years in the late 1800s and 1900s. Guinness has utilized posters throughout Ireland depicting superhuman strength achieved by drinking Guinness with the slogan "Guinness for strength."

Source: Partially adapted from Brendan O'Brien, The Stout Book (Dublin: Anna Livia Press, 1990).

its sole beer product until 1965. Over the years the brewery acquired a number of licensed products and developed a wholesale spirits and soft drinks bottling business.

Although Murphy's opened up trade in London, Manchester, South Wales, and other parts of England early in the twentieth century, the company began experiencing financial problems in the 1960s. There was considerable anxiety among the staff of 200 in Murphy's Brewery Cork concerning the continuity of their employment in the early 1970s. At that time they had an English partner (Watney and Mann), which wanted to dissolve the partnership. Colonel John J. Murphy, chairman of Murphy's, stated that "we are confident that we can satisfy" certain financial conditions to meet the demands of the creditors. The company at this time was well over 100 years old and had overcome difficult periods in the past.

In February 1975 Murphy's approached Heineken N.B. (the Amsterdam-based brewery which had been founded by Garard Adriann Heineken the same year the Murphy brothers opened their brewery in Ireland) with a proposal to begin a licensing operation for Heineken in Ireland. Heineken examined the possibilities of the Irish market and found them favorable, and a license agreement was signed. A marketing company, Heineken Ireland Limited, was set up as a fully owned subsidiary of Heineken N.B. Heineken was well known for its lager beer, which complemented the Murphy's Irish Stout offering.

Murphy's new policy of expanding as a broad-based competitor to the leading brands (e.g., Guinness and Beamish and Crawford) worked well at first. However, the company was hit by recessionary problems, and J.J. Murphy and Company Limited went into receivership in 1982. At that time the company employed 235 people. On July 14, 1982, the *Cork Examiner* confirmed a commitment from the Dutch brewing company Heineken to invest 1.6 million pounds in the brewery.

In 1983 Heineken International purchased the assets of James J. Murphy and Company Limited, which was then in receivership. Murphy Brewery Ireland Limited became a wholly owned subsidiary of Heineken International, a move which gave a new lease on life to Murphy's Brewery. This development preserved the long and respected tradition of brewing in the Cork area and the well-known brand name. Since then Murphy Brewery Ireland Limited has continued its brewing and marketing of Murphy's Irish Stout and Heineken. The adoption of Murphy's Irish Stout by Heineken International as one of its corporate brands meant that the brand became available to drinkers worldwide.

The Heineken Era

Heineken International is the world's second largest brewer (see Exhibit 3) and a private company. Its flagship Heineken lager, the world's most exported beer, and the Amstel brand are also brewed under license by third parties. They are produced in over 100 plants and sold in 170 countries on all continents. The Heineken brand is sold in the same green bottle and promoted with the same brand imagery in the same price tier in China, Spain, the United States, and elsewhere. Heineken was the first beer to be imported into the United States after Prohibition was lifted in 1933. The United States is now its largest market.

Murphy's management during the Heineken years has been led by four managing directors. Currently, Marien Kakabeeke, a native of Holland, serves in that position. He

---

EXHIBIT 3   **World's Largest Brewers, 1994**

Company	HQ	Prod./Vol.[1]	World Share	% of Sales in Exports
Anheuser-Busch	United States	105.1	9%	6%
Heineken	Netherlands	59.6	4.8	89
Miller	United States	50.1	3.9	5
Kirin	Japan	35.1	2.7	5
Foster's	Australia	34.7	2.7	73
Carlsberg	Denmark	30.4	2.3	82
Danone Group	France	27.7	2.4	65
Guinness	United Kingdom	24.2	2.1	84

Source: Havis Dawson, "Brand Brewing." *Beverage World,* October 1995, p. 52.
1994 is the latest year available.

[1] Production/volume is measured in hectoliters: 1 hectoliter = 26.4 gallons or .85 barrel.

assumed the post in August 1993. Heineken has demonstrated its commitment to Murphy's by opening a new office complex in the old Malthouse at the brewery. Murphy's became accredited in 1992 with the ISO 9002 mark for all aspects of operations—the first brewery in Europe to achieve that distinction.

Murphy's Brands and Packaging

Internationally, Murphy's Irish Stout (MIS) is now available in 63 countries worldwide, up from only 20 in 1992. Export sales of the brand grew by almost 200 percent during 1996. Growth markets include the United States, where MIS sales increased 163 percent, and Germany, France, Spain, Italy, and the Netherlands, where sales volumes grew 82 percent. MIS's output has grown by 700 percent in the last decade. Most of this increase was fueled by international consumption, with sales in Ireland increasing only 10 percent over that time (see Exhibit 1).

This growth is reflected in an increased turnover for MBI from Ir £125 million to Ir £140 million. The total company volume now stands at almost 950,000 hectoliters.

For most of its first 135 years Murphy's Irish Stout was available only in draft form in pubs throughout Ireland. A packaging innovation (draughtflow cans) was launched in October 1992. A plastic device (called a widget) is fitted into the bottom of the can which nitrates the liquid after the can is opened, creating the famous creamy head and giving the product a publike taste. Consumer acceptance of the can is reflected in the distribution growth of the product, which makes it available in off-licenses/liquor stores. Within Europe a 330-milliliter cream-colored can is sold, while in the United States a 14.9-ounce can is marketed. One distinguishing feature of the can in Europe is the message "Chill for at least two hours. Pour contents into glass in one smooth action. Best before end—see base," which is reprinted in four languages on the cans.

Another packaging innovation for MIS was developed in 1995. A draughtflow bottle is now available in both the U.S. and European markets. The 500-milliliter (16.9-oz.) bottle has a long neck and is dark brown in color. It is used as a powerful unique differentiating point for the brand. The back labels acclaim the benefits of the draughtflow technology. Warning labels concerning alcoholic beverages are shown on the U.S. labels.

Murphy's Irish Amber, a traditional Irish ale, was launched in 1995 as Murphy's Irish Red Beer in Germany and France. It is brewed in Cork but is not available domestically in Ireland. In the United States Murphy's Irish Amber was introduced in both draft and a 12-ounce bottle in September 1996. The bottles are amber in color. The label's dark blue and red colors accented by gold signal a high-quality product. Compelled by the need for a stronger Murphy's portfolio due to increased interest in genuine red beers, the company believed this product would be successful. Thus far, Murphy's Irish Amber's success has far exceeded expectations.

Murphy's also offers Heineken's low-alcohol beer called Buckler. It contains 1/2 of 1 percent alcohol and about half the calorie content of normal beer. It sells in 330-milliliter bottles in bars, off-licenses, and supermarkets in the served markets.

The Competition

After returning from a business trip to the Continent a week later, Patrick Conway found on his desk a stack of articles sent to him from the communications department discussing the Guinness–Grand Met merger. Before turning his attention to them, he reflected on what he knew regarding the Guinness brand both in Ireland and elsewhere. Guinness Stout was the pioneer in this category and an even older firm than Murphy's.

It was founded in 1759 by Arthur Guinness in Dublin. It was now the eighth largest brewer in the world in terms of volume, with over a 2 percent market share. Murphy's parent, Heineken, is in second place worldwide (see Exhibit 3).

Guinness is brewed in almost 50 countries and sold in over 130.[4] In the stout category, it is the proverbial "500-pound gorilla" in that it commands a 70 to 90 percent share in almost all markets. When it moves, Murphy's and other competitors invariably pay close attention. The Guinness name defines the stout market in most countries and is the "gold standard" against which all other competing brands are measured. The company's marketing prowess is well known in that Guinness Stout is positioned as "hip in the United Kingdom," "traditional in Ireland," and a source of "virility" in Africa; a special microbrew is aimed at "creating a new generation of beer snobs" in the United States. Guinness plans to continue targeting continental Europe, the United States, and Asia in a bid to expand its markets and grow its business.

Guinness has been very successful in building its stout brand around the world. The company is identified with its quirky advertising campaigns in Ireland and its high profile regarding other marketing and promotional endeavors. One significant effort involved the Irish national soccer team, which endorsed Guinness as its official beer for the 1994 World Cup. Sales of Guinness Stout rose dramatically in the United States during the World Cup finals. Another U.S.-based promotion program designed to appeal to the over 40 million Americans of Irish descent was the "Win Your Own Pub in Ireland" contest. This competition has been going on for several years and is featured in Guinness's Web page currently. Third, the huge development of the Irish pub concept around the world helped Guinness brands abroad and contributed to an increase in export sales of 10 percent in 1996. The company launched the Guinness pub concept in 1992, and there are now 1,250 "Guinness" Irish pubs in 36 countries. Four hundred more are expected to open in 1997.[5]

Patrick turned his attention to several articles about the Guinness and Grand Met merger. A rationale for the merger was that these firms could acquire new brands more easily than they may be able to find new consumers in the U.S. and European marketplace, where alcohol consumption is falling, the population is aging, and concerns about health are rising. The new firm will be a formidable force in the race to open up new markets in liquor and beer. The companies have complementary product lines and will be divided into four major divisions (see Exhibit 4). The Guinness Brewery worldwide divison will feature its signature stout, Harp (a lager), Kilkenny (a red ale), Cruzcampo (a Spanish beer), and Red Stripe.

The Economist noted that even though GMG will be the seventh largest company in the world, it faces major obstacles. One is that even though its brands are very well known, the combined company will lack focus. Grand Met has a long history of trying its hand at different businesses but has done so with mixed success. Guinness, however, has an even longer history of not doing much besides brewing beer, and its spirits business has been a struggle for the firm. *The Economist*'s conclusion gave Mr. Conway encouragement and reflected his own impression when the magazine stated: "Unless GMG manages to show very rapidly that they can mix these ingredients into something fairly tasty, then pressure will grow on it to simplify itself."[6]

Patrick recalled that Guinness is not the only competitor of Murphy's. Beamish & Crawford, also located in Cork, was founded in 1792 and currently employs about 200 people. In 1987 the company joined the Foster's Brewing Group. The primary brands offered by the company are Beamish (stout), Foster's (lager), and Carling Black Label (lager).

Beamish stout is available in most pubs throughout the southern part of Ireland. The brand is positioned on its Irishness, the heritage of Beamish Stout, and the fact that it is

EXHIBIT 4 GMG Brands

Division	Turnover (millions)	Pretax Profit (millions)
Guinness Brewing Worldwide:	£2,262	£283
Guinness Stout, Harp, Cruzcampo (Spanish), Red Stripe		
United Distillers & Vintners (Guinness Brands)	£2,468	£791
Dewar's, Gordon's Gin, Bell's, Moet Hennessey, Johnnie Walker, Black and White, Asbach		
(Grand Met Brands)	£3,558	£502
Smirnoff, Stolichnaya, J&B (whisky), Gilbey's Gin, Jose Cuervo, Grand Marnier, Bailey's, Malibu, Absolut		
Pillsbury	£3,770	£447
Pillsbury, Green Giant, Old El Paso, Häagen-Dazs		
Burger King	£859	£167

Source: "GMG Brands: What the Two Sides Will Contribute," *Financial Times,* May 13, 1997, p. 27.

Note: Turnover and pretax profit numbers denote millions of pounds sterling.

the only Irish stout exclusively brewed in Ireland. In the last three years Beamish has been marketed in Europe (Italy and Spain mostly) and North America (Canada and the United States). It is distributed through the Foster's Brewing Group in those markets.

The Irish Market

Dan Leahy sent Patrick the following report on the market for Murphy's in Ireland. His memo discussed both the importance of pub life in the country and the competitive situation. Patrick read with interest Dan's assessment of the Irish market:

> With a population of less than 4 million people, the Irish market is small in international terms. However, it is the market in which stout holds the largest share at nearly 50 percent of all beer sales. With one of the youngest populations in the developed world and one of the fastest-growing economies, it is an important and dynamic market for all stout producers. This is added to by the fact that the three competitors—Murphy's, Guinness, and Beamish—all use their Irishness as a key attribute in product positioning. A presence in the Irish market is viewed as being central to the authenticity of the Irishness claim.
>
> Pubs have long been a central part of Irish life, particularly in rural areas, where pubs are semi-social centers. Irish pubs are regularly run by owner-operators who buy products from different breweries. This is quite different from most international markets, where pubs tend to be run by or for the breweries. For example, in the Dutch market Heineken has 52 percent of the outlets. Partly as a result of this, Irish consumers are highly brand-loyal. Also, in the Irish market, breweries engage in higher levels of promotion.
>
> Irish pubs are perceived very positively in many parts of the world. They are seen as places which are accessible to all the family. Irish pubs are intimately linked with musical sessions and viewed as being open, friendly places to visit. This positive perception has resulted in a proliferation of Irish-themed pubs, particularly in the last decade. This development has been used extensively by Guinness and lately by Murphy's as a means of increasing distribution.
>
> Guinness dominates the Irish stout market with an 89 percent market share. Murphy's and Beamish have roughly equal shares of the rest of the market. Guinness's dominance of the market is reflected in the fact that the term *Guinness* is synonymous with stout. In many

parts of the country it is ordered without reference to its name simply by asking for "a pint." Similarly, in Britain 1 million pints of Guinness are sold every day, with 10 million glasses a day sold worldwide.

Guinness Ireland turned in a strong performance in 1996 with sales up 8 percent to 764 million pints.[7] The company began a 12-million-pound advertising campaign last year called "The Big Pint" and engaged in extensive billboard advertising emphasizing the size and strength of the brand.

In Ireland, Beamish Stout is positioned as a value for money, Irish stout selling at 20 pence (10 percent) lower than the competitors. It is slightly ahead of Murphy's currently in the race for second place in Ireland. As with Murphy's, Beamish's traditional base has been in the Cork-area market. Today, 1 in every 4 pints of stout consumed in Cork is Beamish and 1 in every 14 pints in Ireland is Beamish.

Within the lager market in Ireland, Heineken dominates with nearly 40 percent of the market, while Budweiser and Carlsberg (both distributed by Guinness) each have just over a 20 percent market share. Harp, which once held an overwhelming 80 percent share, now accounts for only 8 percent.

Murphy's is priced on a par with Guinness in all markets in the country. The average price of a pint of stout in the market is Ir £2.00.

In parts of the market where demand for the brand is low, Murphy's has begun selling the product in an innovative 3/5-keg (a keg is a barrel containing 50 liters) size. This ensures that the product reaches the customer at the desired level of quality.

Murphy's has pursued market growth through the development of export markets and development of the take-home market. The development of these markets is driven by the fact that the domestic draught market is mature with static sales over the last number of years. In 1995 pub sales fell by almost 2.5 percent, while off-license sales grew by 37 percent. The growth in the off-license business is due in part to the impact of the new stronger drunk-driving legislation and in-home summer consumption.[8]

Both of these markets rely heavily on canned and bottled packaging for the product. Traditionally this has posed a difficulty for stout products as there is a perceived deterioration in quality compared to the draught version. Murphy's is selling its product in bottles and dedicating some advertising to the superior bottled taste and using it as a differentiating feature for all of Murphy's products and using the draught bottle as a brand icon for the firm.

Conway thought about the report on the Irish market and how difficult it was to compete against Guinness and the extreme brand loyalty of the Irish consumer to it. He thought about the new three-year 5-million-pound advertising campaign launched in 1996 and hoped that the unique approach would win new customers. One memorable TV ad featured a group of Japanese samurai warriors who arrive in a line at a bar, knock back bottles of Murphy's, and leave while a Guinness drinker drums his fingers on the counter waiting for his pint to settle. Conway believed that brand awareness was growing. One successful promotional endeavor is the company's sponsorship of the Murphy's Irish Open, which was part of the PGA European Golf Tour.

He knew that strides were being made in the distribution network outside its traditional stronghold of Cork City and County. One of the inducements the company was using was a lower trade price to the pubs so that they made more on each pint sold. The company followed this philosophy internationally as well in the effort to compete with Guinness.

He also recalled two *Irish Times* articles that gave his and Kakabeeke's views on the importance of the Irish market to the company. He asked his secretary to retrieve them from the files and routed them to the marketing group. Conway was quoted as saying, "Murphy's believes it has to have an advertising spend comparable to Guinness if it is ever to achieve a critical mass in Ireland. We have to differentiate ourselves, and there's no use doing it with a whisper. A better market share in Ireland would also provide Murphy's Irish Stout with a backbone from which to grow exports."⁹ Mr. Kakebeeke said that "the brewery is not happy with the 5 percent position in the Irish market and with the level of domestic growth being achieved by Murphy's Irish Stout. I feel that sales can be improved in Ireland."¹⁰

The UK and Continental European Markets

The United Kingdom (England, Scotland, Wales, and Northern Ireland), Ireland's closest neighbor, represents the world's largest stout market in terms of consumption at 60 million hectoliters. The total population of the UK is approximately 60 million consumers. Murphy's market share stands at 15 percent, while Guinness (78 percent) and Beamish (6 percent) are the other two major competitors. MIS was launched in the UK in 1985 and has enjoyed continued growth in that market since then. Murphy's success in the UK may be attributed to several factors.

First, Heineken and Murphy's are distributed in the UK through the Whitbread Beer Company in Luton. Whitbread has an association with over 27,000 pubs in the country, which translates to an automatic distribution network for Murphy's products. Recently Whitbread has opened a series of themed bars under the banner "J. J. Murphy and Company" throughout the country. These outlets reflect the desired image for Murphy's and help raise the profile of the brand in the UK. As a point of comparison, Beamish is distributed in 10,000 outlets in Britain.

Second, Murphy's has also been successful with its advertising in the UK. Its continuing advertising theme "Like the Murphy's, I'm not bitter" campaign is a tongue-in-cheek poke at Guinness's taste. The campaign has received several awards and has resulted in a unique identity developed for the brand (see Exhibit 2 on stout). The firm has also sponsored the Murphy's English Open Golf Championship for five years.

Third, the brand has gained momentum since it was voted product of the year by the UK Vintners in 1990. Murphy's has a strong position in the minds of the British who prefer darker ales. The brand represents a viable option to those who do not like the taste of Guinness and/or seek an alternative to their favorite UK-based brands such as Thomas Hardy, Newcastle, Samuel Smith, Watney's, and Young's.

MIS is available in all Western European markets. It has excellent distribution in the Netherlands, where Heineken is headquartered. Guinness's recent Irish pub expansion program has also helped raise awareness for all entries in the Irish stout category. Murphy's experienced dramatic growth in volume and market share across Europe in 1996.

In Germany, the establishment of Murphy's Trading GmbH, a wholly owned subsidiary of Murphy Brewery Ireland, allows for greater focus and control of the Murphy's brands within this critical market. The year 1996 also saw Murphy's gain the exclusive beer rights to Paddy Murphy's, the largest chain of Irish theme pubs throughout Germany. Also, in Denmark MIS is distributed in the Paddy Go Easy chain in several Danish cities.

In 1996 new markets were developed in Eastern Europe, including Hungary and the Czech Republic. The potential of the emerging Russian market is also anticipated. With the introduction of the brand in Finland, Murphy's is now available in all the Nordic countries.

The American Market

As he reached for the phone to ring Michael Foley, current CEO of Heineken USA (Van Munching & Co. is the importer's name) and former managing director of Murphy Brewery Ireland from 1989 to 1993, Patrick thought about the United States. He knew that the United States, with its 270 million consumers and general high standard of living, represents the most lucrative beer market in the world. The $40 billion beer market in the United States is dominated by the "giants" Anheuser-Busch (10 brands and 45 percent market share), Miller (9/23 percent), and Coors (7/11 percent).[11]

Michael gave Patrick a status report on the Murphy's brand in the United States as of June 1997. Michael reiterated that the U.S. strategy is to "build slowly" and gain acceptance of Murphy's products by endorsement by customers rather than attempting to buy market share with mass advertising. The plan is to "keep off TV because it is too expensive." Murphy's is seeking a premium brand positioning aimed at the specialty imported niche rather than the mass market.

Foley indicated that he was very optimistic about the Murphy growth possibilities in the United States. "Our 1996 sales were up 180 percent, and our target is 1 million cases by mid-1998," he said. Both Murphy's Irish Stout and Irish Amber are meeting the expectations set for them by Heineken USA.

Murphy's Irish Stout has been available in the United States since 1992 and has experienced steady growth since then. MIS has been on a gradual progression, from 100,000 gallons in 1992 to 400,000 gallons in 1994 and 600,000 gallons in 1995. It is now on tap at over 5,000 bars and pubs throughout the country. The distribution tends to be concentrated in the eastern corridor running from Boston through New York City (the largest market) to Washington, D.C. Another area of intense distribution is in south Florida. The "gold coast" area running from Miami to Fort Lauderdale is a stronghold for Murphy's, partially due to its attraction to British tourists who are already familiar with the brand. Other areas of focus for MIS are the major metropolitan areas of Chicago, Los Angeles, and San Francisco.

For the off-premises/carryout market, MIS has been available in cans since 1993. Their size is 14.9 ounces, and they are cream colored (like the "head" of the drink) and are priced relative to domestic U.S. beers at a premium level—$1.76 versus $1.99 for Guinness in the same size can. Foley stated that cans generally signify a "down market product" and the company would like to present more of a prestige image. Therefore, in September 1996 Murphy's introduced the draughtflow bottle in the United States. While Foley believes the glass package is "more premium," the company has experienced a problem with it in the United States. The serving size of 16.9 ounces is not correct for the market since most beer glasses hold only 12 ounces. The usual price is $1.99 per bottle. The size is not that important for in-home consumption, but in bars where MIS is sold by packages rather than on draft, this is a significant issue for the company. Another issue that has arisen is that the thick brown bottle takes substantially longer to cool than does a can.

Murphy's Irish Amber was introduced into the American market in late 1996. Its on-premise penetration has exceeded company expectations, and according to Foley, "the product is doing very, very well. It is the 'real deal' and replacing nonauthentic Irish products such as Killian's in many areas." The product is available in six-packs for off-site consumption. The rich-looking green and red package makes it attractive. The company has positioned it against Bass Ale and other premium-quality ales. Its price is in the $7.50 range, which is substantially higher than many of the specialty imports, which cost $4.00 to $6.00 per six-pack. Killian's sometimes is sale priced as low as $3.99, but its regular price is in the $5.50 to $6.00 range, and Sam Adams Red and Pete's Wicked Ale are priced at $5.49 and $5.99, respectively. Bass Ale, however, carries an even higher price ($7.79) than Murphy's.

Conway thanked Foley for his update on the status of the Murphy's brands in the United States and asked if Michael could spend a few minutes discussing trends in the beer market within the country. "I know import sales are increasing about 7 percent a year in the United States and that Heineken is the leading import brand," said Conway, "But where does Guinness fall?" Foley responded that they were in tenth place, while Bass Ale held down the eighth spot and beer imports from Ireland held the sixth position among all countries (see Exhibits 5 and 6). Foley said that he recalled reading that the top 20 brands (out of a total of 400 import brands) account for 90 percent of U.S. import sales.

Patrick asked about trends in the U.S. beer market. "It has been flat the last several years," said Foley. "The most significant recent trend domestically is the growth in microbreweries." Michael said he remembered seeing on a Web site that microbreweries, brewpubs, and regional specialty breweries totaled almost 1,300 in early 1997.[12] The microbrewery category has grown tenfold to 500 in 10 years. However, it still accounted for only a paltry 2 percent of the U.S. market in 1995.

Conway said good-bye and was just about to hang up when Foley said, "I almost forgot, but someone passed an article from *The Wall Street Journal* by me a few weeks ago that talked about Guinness and the microbrewery boom. I will send it to you with the other material" (see Exhibit 7).

Murphy's World Market Positioning and Marketing

Dan Leahy stopped by Patrick Conway's office and handed him the information requested on Murphy's status in the world market. Patrick glanced at the statistics assembled by Dan and noticed that the specialty category (into which MIS and MIA both

EXHIBIT 5   Leading Imported Beer Brands in the United States (thousands of 2.25-gallon cases)

Brand	Importer	Origin	1992[1]	1993	1994[2]	% Change 1993–1994
Heineken	Van Munching & Co.	Netherlands	26,700	29,200	31,200	6.8%
Corona Extra	Barton/Gambrinus	Mexico	13,000	14,000	16,000	14.3
Molson Ice	Molson USA	Canada	—	3,000	10,000	—
Beck's	Dribeck Importers	Germany	9,650	9,700	9,720	0.2
Molson Golden	Molson USA	Canada	8,500	8,600	8,700	1.2
Amstel Light	Van Munching & Co.	Netherlands	5,500	6,000	7,500	25.0
Labatt's Blue	Labatt's USA	Canada	5,900	6,200	6,500	4.8
Bass Ale	Guinness Import Co.	United Kingdom	2,850	3,390	4,160	22.7
Tecate	Labatt's USA	Mexico	2,900	3,400	4,000	17.6
Guinness Stout	Guinness Import Co.	Ireland	3,100	3,650	3,970	8.8
Foster's Lager[3]	Molson USA	Canada	3,500	3,700	3,800	2.7
Moosehead	Guinness Import Co.	Canada	3,400	3,350	3,340	−0.3
Molson Light	Molson USA	Canada	1,900	2,000	2,200	10.0
Dos Equis	Guinness Import Co.	Mexico	1,900	2,060	2,120	2.9
St. Pauli Girl	Barton Brands	Germany	2,200	2,000	2,000	0.0
Labatt's Ice	Labatt's USA	Canada	—	845	1,910	—
Molson Canadian	Molson USA	Canada	1,640	1,690	1,710	1.2
Labatt's Light	Labatt's USA	Canada	1,100	1,020	1,100	7.8
Corona Light	Barton/Gambrinus	Mexico	1,100	1,000	1,000	0.0

[1] Revised.
[2] Estimated.
[3] The gradual production switch from Australia to Canada began in April 1992.

EXHIBIT 6   Imported Beer Market
Market Share by Supplier, 1994 (Estimated)

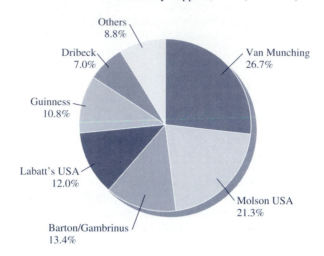

fell) had grown over the last few years (see Exhibit 8). He was concerned that it was the second smallest of the five categories.

Dan left a revision of the Murphy's Positioning Statement on which Patrick and his colleagues had been working for several months. It read:

> Murphy's is a symbol of everything authentically "Irish." Its warm history takes time to discover but its taste is easy to appreciate.

Supporting this positioning was the image of Ireland that Murphy's planned to convey in its marketing strategy (see Exhibit 9). While the words in the exhibit are a bit stereotypical, they describe the perception of both the country and its people. It is in this context that Irish products are viewed by consumers in other counties. The elements of the marketing mix were summarized by Dan in several accompanying pages.

The product consists of the two brands—Murphy's Irish Stout and Murphy's Irish Amber/Red Beer (MIA/RB). It is sourced in Ireland except for the UK and New Zealand markets. Ongoing new product development continues in line with positioning, umbrella branding, and premium packaging.

The distribution objective is one of controlled distribution growth. The focus is on quality Irish bars/pubs and specialty beer outlets. Package variants are available in low-volume outlets. Dual stocking of MIS and MIA/RB will occur wherever possible. Exclusivity is a goal but not a prerequisite for stocking. The existing Heineken distribution network will continue to be used wherever possible.

The pricing strategy is one of price parity with major specialty competitors. A reasonable margin is being offered to the trade. In fact, the company prices its products slightly below the competition to the trade as an enticement to carry the products.

The promotion and communications strategy is multipronged. The brands' Irish heritage and origin continue to be reinforced. The company engages in tactical advertising and promotion rather than larger-scale strategic campaigns. For example, St. Patrick's Day and Irish music nights are exploited. The communication focus is on both brands in most markets. The company plans to use still rather than electronic media to convey the authentic Irish image of the brands.

EXHIBIT 7   Buoyed by Boom in Microbrews, Guinness Pours Its Cash into TV

Guinness Import Co. poured about 33 percent more of its signature dark draft stout in the United States last year as the microbrew boom helped lift import sales by creating a new generation of beer snobs. Now Guinness hopes to keep the beer taps flowing with its first large-scale U.S. TV ad campaign for the Irish-brewed brand, breaking today.

At a time when sales of all beer in the United States rose just 1 percent last year, several of Guinness Import's major brands, including Harp lager and Bass ale, posted double-digit gains. Overall, sales of Guinness Import's brands (including Moosehead, whose distribution rights Guinness is shedding, effective at the end of March) grew 20 percent to about 17 million cases last year, according to Guinness.

The company's success is one of the factors that contributed to an estimated 10 percent rise in the sale of beers last year, according to Frank Walters, senior vice president of research at M. Shanken Communications, publisher of *Impact,* which tracks beer sales. Final numbers on sales of domestic beers are expected to be flat, although it's estimated that the tiny microbrewery and specialty segment jumped more than 20 percent. "It's a good economy, and people are indulging themselves more," says Mr. Walters of the sales of more-expensive imports.

Guinness stout's fast sales pace in bars and stores lifted it to the number 6 or 7 ranking among imports, up from ninth place in 1995, according to Mr. Walter's estimates. Guinness Import, a unit of Guinness PLC of London, attributes its success to changing consumer tastes in the wake of the microbrew explosion and a more intense distribution and marketing effort. "People are getting more into beers with taste," said Sheri Roder, marketing development director for Guinness Import, "and at the same time, we've gotten behind our brands more."

There have been eye-catching promotions, such as the annual "Win Your Own Pub in Ireland" contest, now in its fourth year. A "Great Guinness Toast," on February 28, hopes to get into the *Guinness Book of World Records* for the largest number of people making a toast. And the number of outlets selling the brand jumped by 20 percent in 1996.

Even more unusual, Guinness has been sending out a force of "draft specialists" armed with thermometers and training brochures to visit bars and make sure they're serving Guinness under the best possible conditions. Brewers can't own bars, so they can't control whether tavern owners serve the product in sparkling clean glasses or how often they flush out built-up yeast in the lines that carry the beer from the keg to the tap.

With distribution and the quality program in place, Guinness decided the time was right to launch the TV campaign. "There's no point in advertising a lot when people can't find you," says Ms. Roder. "There's a likelihood now that people will be able to find a pint of Guinness, poured well to our exacting standards. You don't want to get people too excited about something they can't find."

The TV ad campaign, with the tag line "Why Man Was Given Five Senses," will air through St. Patrick's Day, March 17, in 18 major markets, including New York, Los Angeles, and Atlanta. Guinness won't say what it is spending on the ad campaign, which will run in late prime-time and sports programs, but calls it a significant media buy. Chicago viewers of the Super Bowl saw the ad run twice; Guinness also has spots in NBC's high-rated Thursday prime-time lineup.

The quirky ad, which goes through the ritual of ordering a pint of Guinness, from the nod to the bartender to the long wait for the beer to settle, was created by Weiss, Stagliano of New York City. It got a five-week tryout in Chicago and Boston last fall with convincing results: Sales of Guinness in Boston were up 24 percent in December over a year earlier, compared with just an 11 percent gain for the rest of the Guinness portfolio, while in Chicago, sales are up 35 percent from a year ago, with distribution up 22 percent.

Source: Elizabeth Jensen, *The Wall Street Journal,* February 10, 1997, p. B2.

Murphy's Future Direction

Patrick Conway assembled the reports on the Irish, UK, European, and American markets as well as the world positioning and strategy. He circulated them to the members of his group with a memo calling a meeting in early June 1997. Conway indicated that he wanted to develop a long-term strategy for the Murphy's brand to take to

EXHIBIT 8   World Beer Market

Category	1994	1995	1996	Volume (Hectoliters)
Specialty	6.5%	7.4%	8.2%	103,000,000
Sophistication	11.9	12.4	12.9	162,000,000
Standard savings	63.3	62.7	61.2	763,000,000
Stay fit	15.9	15.5	15.8	189,000,000
Stay clear	2.1	2.0	2.1	24,000,000
Total	100	100	100	1,250,000,000

EXHIBIT 9   Image of Ireland

Perception of Country	Personality of People
Green	Relaxed
Environmentally friendly	Sociable
Natural	Friendly
Unspoiled	Different
Lost Arcadia	Humorous/witty
Underdeveloped	Pub atmosphere

Heineken management rather than develop a knee-jerk reaction to the Guinness–Grand Met merger.

He believed that Murphy's reputation was improving both in Ireland and throughout the world. He did not want to jeopardize the gains made in the last several years. However, he was concerned with the stagnant nature of the beer industry in Europe and North America. He called a meeting for June 10, 1997, to discuss the marketing strategy for Murphy's.

Before he met with the marketing department members, he stopped by Marien Kakebeeke's office. The managing director reminded him of the corporate goal for Murphy's, which is 20 percent of the world's stout market by the year 2000. "I know that is ambitious, Patrick, but I am confident you and your staff can achieve it."

"Do you realize that the Cork Brewery is almost at capacity now?" asked Patrick. "Even if we stimulate demand, how will we be able to meet it with production limits? Also, recall that we expanded the brewery in 1995."[13]

When Patrick, D. Ford, and Dan Leahy sat down that morning to discuss the future of Murphy's, they considered several questions:

How important is a strong showing in the Irish domestic market to Murphy's? Must it make a strong showing there to be successful worldwide?

Should Murphy's employ a global rather than local marketing strategy worldwide? The "I'm not bitter" campaign has been successful in the United Kingdom, so should several possible strategies be used, especially in the large markets of the United States and continental Europe?

Is Murphy's destined to be a "niche" product forever? Will these brands ever reach a place where they command a substantial market share?

Should the company continue to make the two brands only at the Cork brewery for the lucrative U.S. market, or should it consider making the product in that country? It worked for automobiles; why not beer?

Will Murphy's ever be able to achieve the status of other products that are famous for their Irish heritage, such as Guinness, Bailey's Irish Cream, Jameson Irish Whiskey, Waterford Crystal, and Belleek China?

End Notes

1. John Willman and Ross Tieman, "Grand Met, Guinness to Merge," *Financial Times,* Tuesday, May 13, 1997, p. 1.
2. *Murphy Brewery Limited: A Profile,* undated.
3. Company sources.
4. Company fact sheet.
5. Barry O'Keeffe, "'Black Stuff' Underpins Profit Raise at Guinness," *The Irish Times,* March 21, 1997.
6. "Master of the Bar," *The Economist,* May 17, 1997, p. 73.
7. O'Keeffe, "'Black Stuff' Underpins Profit Raise at Guinness."
8. Paul O'Kane, "Murphy Boosts Exports," *The Irish Times,* March 7, 1996.
9. Paul O'Kane, "Murphy's Aims to Double Its Sales in Three Years," *The Irish Times,* June 14, 1996.
10. O'Kane, "Murphy Boosts Exports."
11. "Domestic Beer Shipments Drop 2.1% in '95 While Volume Dips 1.7%," *Beverage Industry,* January 1996, pp. 24–32.
12. "Craft-Brewing Industry Fact Sheet—February 1997," http://www.Beertown.org/craftbrew.html.
13. Paul O'Kane, "Murphy's Plans Major Expansion," *The Irish Times,* August 16, 1995.

Local auctioneer Eamonn McBride still remembers clearly the day in 1990 when Kevin McDonnell arrived in the truck in Bunbeg: "Kevin had asked me to organize accommodations for some employees of a new business he was setting up. I went to look for him on the industrial estate. I found him outside the factory in a big truck. He pointed to the equipment in the back of the truck and said, 'That's it there,' referring to his new business. I was totally stunned." McDonnell wanted to buy the remaining assets of a company called BMR, which had gone into liquidation. The deal included ownership of the company's brand names, NeuroTech and Slendertone. McDonnell had decided, against the advice of many, to reestablish the business in an old factory on the industrial estate outside Bunbeg. Bunbeg is a remote, windswept coastal village in the Gaeltacht (Irish-speaking) region of northwest Donegal. Within a few weeks McDonnell and five employees had begun production.

McDonnell says that he knew little about the business he was getting into when he loaded the truck in Shannon and drove north to Donegal. An accountant by training, he thought that on paper it seemed like a viable business. He now employs over 150 people in Ireland and another 70 in international subsidiaries of his company, BioMedical Research Ltd. Company revenue in 1998 was £22 million, £17 million of which was from sales of Slendertone, up nearly 60 percent from the previous year. The company has received a number of design, export, and enterprise awards, and McDonnell was voted Donegal Businessman of the Year in 1995. But McDonnell has little time or desire to reflect on his substantial achievements to date—not while he has still to attain one of his greatest goals: to develop Slendertone into a world-class brand.

McDonnell believes that Slendertone can be a £100 million a year business by the year 2002. He likes to relate how Slendertone now outsells popular brands such as Impulse and Diet Pepsi in the United Kingdom; or how Slendertone is now available in Selfridges, the prestigious department store in London. McDonnell is under no illusions about the arduous challenge that lies ahead. However, he believes he has the strategy to achieve his goal. He is confident that the recent marketing strategy devised by Brian O'Donohoe will enable Slendertone to achieve sales of over £100 million in two years and become a world-class brand. O'Donohoe, now managing director of Slendertone, joined the company as marketing director for Slendertone in April 1997.

According to O'Donohoe, "BioMedical Research has gone from being a product-oriented company to a market-led one." In the process O'Donohoe has had to identify and deal with a number of critical issues. He believes that the foremost issue facing the Slendertone brand is credibility. He stresses the need to get away from the "gadget" image associated with Slendertone. O'Donohoe is confident that his strategy to reposition the brand will resolve this issue successfully. Product credibility is one of a num-

This case was written by Michael J. Murphy, University College Cork. It is intended to be used as the basis for class discussion rather than to illustrate either effective or ineffective handling of a management situation. The case was made possible by the cooperation of BioMedical Research Ltd. Copyright 1999 by M. J. Murphy, University College, Cork. Some of the figures, names, and other information in this case have been altered to protect company and customer confidentiality. However, all the data are representative of the actual position.

ber of important issues that have arisen since Slendertone's creation over 30 years ago. O'Donohoe knows that the future of Slendertone as a world-class brand depends on how well his strategy deals with these and other issues which have arisen more recently as a result of the company's dramatic growth.

Slendertone: The Early Years

Slendertone originally was developed by a company called BMR Ltd. in 1966. The company moved from England to the tax-free zone in Shannon in 1968. BMR manufactured a range of electronic muscle stimulation (EMS) devices under the Slendertone[1] and NeuroTech brands, serving the cosmetic and medical markets, respectively. By the end of the 1980s BMR's total annual sales were £1.5 million. Around 40 percent of revenue came from the sale of NeuroTech products, which were used by medical practitioners and physiotherapists to treat conditions such as muscle atrophy. The balance came from sales of Slendertone, which was used mostly for cosmetic purposes. Ninety-five percent of Slendertone sales were to the professional (beauty salon) market, with the remaining 5 percent coming from a limited range of home use products. The home use units were very basic and had few features. They retailed for between £250 and £400. Margins on all products were high. BMR claimed that Slendertone was available in over 40 countries by the late 1980s. All international sales were being handled by small local distributors or companies with diverse product interests (including an oil importer and a garden furniture dealer).

Kevin McDonnell was a creditor of BMR at the time of its liquidation; he had been supplying the company with printed circuit boards for four years. In that time he had learned something about the company's operations. When he heard BMR was going into liquidation, he immediately saw an opportunity. In an interview with *The Financial Times* in 1995 he stated: "I thought it was a bit odd that the company could go out of business, and yet, according to its business plan, it was capable of a 20 percent return on turnover." Few shared McDonnell's belief in the future of the Slendertone business. The managing director of BMR's German office felt that Slendertone was a fad which had little future.

McDonnell was not deterred. By the end of 1990 he had notched sales of £1.4 million, producing and selling much of the original BMR product range. With his focus initially on production, McDonnell continued to sell most of his products through distributors, many of which had previously worked with BMR. Over the next two years revenue grew gradually through increasing sales to distributors of the existing product range. McDonnell reinvested all his earnings in the business. Research into biomedical technology, with a view to developing new products, consumed much of his limited investment resources. The production facilities also were being upgraded: The company acquired a new and much larger factory in the Bunbeg industrial estate. McDonnell always believed that new product development was the key to future growth. By using distributors to develop export markets, he could focus his limited resources on developing better products.

The Gymbody 8.   In late 1993 the Gymbody 8 was launched, the first "new" product produced by BioMedical Research Ltd. Designed primarily to meet the demands of

---

[1] This case study focuses on the Slendertone division. Readers who are not familiar with EMS or Slendertone are advised to read the appendix before proceeding with the case.

a distributor in France, this "eight-pad stomach and bottom styler" was soon to outsell all the company's other products combined. Although it was much more stylish than anything else on the market at that time, initial sales of the Gymbody 8 were disappointing. Sales in general for home use products were very limited. Most sales of home use EMS-based consumer products were through mail order catalogs, small advertisements in the print media, and a very limited number of retail outlets, mainly pharmacies. After a few months of lackluster sales performance, the French distributor tried using an American-style direct response "infomercial" on the national home shopping channel, M6. This 30-minute "chat show," featuring interviews with a mixture of "ordinary" and celebrity users of the Gymbody 8, produced immediate results. Between interviews and demonstrations showing how the product worked, viewers were encouraged to order a Gymbody 8 by phone. By the end of 1994 Gymbody 8 sales (ex-factory) to the French distributor totaled £3.4 million. The French promotional strategy also involved the wide use of direct response (DR) advertisements in magazines and other print media. Over time retail distribution was extended to some pharmacies and a few sports stores. The soaring sales in France indicated a large untapped market for home use EMS products, a market larger than anyone in the company had anticipated.

Other Slendertone markets were slower to grow even after the introduction of the Gymbody 8. Those markets included mainland Europe, South America, Japan, and Australia. Sales in Ireland for the Gymbody 8 began to rise but were small relative to the sales in France. The Gymbody 8 was listed in a few English mail order catalogs, but sales were low. A distributor in Colombia was the only other customer of any significance for the Gymbody 8.

Distribution

With the exception of the home market, all sales of Slendertone were through distributors. By using distributors, the company believed it could develop new markets for Slendertone (or redevelop previous markets) more cost-effectively and quickly. The company's marketing resources were very limited because of the investments being made in research and production. Some of the distributors had handled Slendertone products previously for BMR, while others were newly recruited. Most of the distributors tended to be small operators, sometimes working from their homes. Most did not have the resources to invest in large-scale market development. Efforts to attract larger distributors already in the beauty market were proving unsuccessful in spite of the potential returns indicated by the ever-growing French market. Yet management was of the view that small distributors could also generate sales quickly by using direct marketing. Without the need to secure retail distribution and with an immediate return on all promotional spending, going direct would not require the levels of investment usually associated with introducing a new product to the market. The growing sales of Slendertone in Ireland from a range of direct marketing activities was proof of this.

Along with poorly resourced and inexperienced distributors, sluggish growth in most markets was blamed on legal restrictions on DR activity and cultural factors. In Germany, DR television was not allowed.[2] Combined with a very low use of credit cards, this did not augur well for a DR-oriented strategy in Germany. Other countries also had restrictions on DR activities. With regard to cultural factors, a number of BioMedical Research personnel felt that the Germans were less likely to be interested in a product

---

[2] Restrictions on DR activity in Germany, including TV broadcasts, have since been relaxed.

like Slendertone than were the Spanish, the French, and the South Americans. It was believed that the latter countries had a stronger "body culture" and that their people were not as conservative as those in Germany and Switzerland. Yet, it was argued, this couldn't explain the rapidly growing sales of Slendertone in Ireland, a relatively conservative country.

Direct Response Television.   In the summer of 1995 a small cable television company in Ireland agreed to broadcast a locally produced infomercial. The infomercial featured local celebrities and studio guests and adopted the French "chat show" format. Broadcast periodically throughout the summer to a potential audience of fewer than 200,000 viewers, the infomercial resulted in direct sales of almost 1,000 Gymbody 8's. Sales of Gymbody 8's also increased in a handful of retail outlets within the cable company's broadcast area. There also appeared to be an increase in demand for Slendertone beauty salon treatments in this area. The success of the Irish infomercial campaign, along with the French campaign, convinced management that DR television was the best way to sell Slendertone. It was believed that if infomercials worked well in both France and Ireland, it was likely that they would work in most other countries. The focus of the sales strategy switched from developing local distributors to securing more DR television opportunities. Intensive research was undertaken to identify infomerical opportunities around the globe, from South America to the Far East. A number of opportunities were identified, but the initial costs of producing infomericals for separate far-flung markets were a constraint. It was then decided to target "home shopping" companies. These companies buy TV time in many countries and then broadcast a range of direct response programming.

By the end of 1995 a deal had been signed with Direct Shop Ltd., which was broadcasting home shopping programming in over 30 countries at that time. The advantages of using Direct Shop were that it had access to TV space across a number of markets, would handle all negotiations with the TV companies, would buy product up-front, and could handle large numbers of multilingual sales calls. BioMedical Research produced a new Slendertone infomercial exclusively for Direct Shop, using the successful chat show format. Direct Shop ran the infomercial on satellite channels such as Eurosport and Superchannel, usually late at night or early in the morning, when broadcasting time was available. The Slendertone infomericals often were broadcast alongside presentations for car care products, kitchen gadgets, fitness products and "exercisers," and various other products. Direct Shop, like all TV home shopping companies, operated on high margins. This meant that BioMedical Research would get less than 25 percent of the £120 retail price for the Gymbody 8. The company was selling this product to other distributors for around £40. Direct Shop also had a liberal customer returns policy. This resulted in return rates of product from customers as high as 35 percent. Very often the outer packaging hadn't even been opened by the purchasers. Direct Shop also returned much unsold product when TV sales were lower than expected for some countries.

Sales to Direct Shop were not as high initially as management had expected. After a few months sales began to increase, reaching monthly sales of around 3,000 Gymbody 8's. The majority of these sales were to television viewers in England.

The Direct Model.   Total sales of Slendertone continued to grow rapidly. Sales (from the factory) to the French distributor totaled £5.6 million in 1995. By early 1996 it appeared that annual sales to France for that year would be considerably higher than the budgeted £7.2 million. Irish sales for 1995 were £0.4 million and were well ahead of budget in early 1996. Sales to Direct Shop were on the increase, though not by as much as management had budgeted. Sales on the order of £0.75 million were being made annually to the Colombian distributor. In early 1996 those four markets were accounting for over 90 percent of total Slendertone sales. Management continued to refine the direct model because of its success in those diverse markets.

One of the critical success factors of the direct approach was believed to be the way it allowed company representatives (either on the telephone directly to customers or through extended TV appearances) to explain clearly how the product worked. Management felt it would not be as easy to sell this product through regular retail channels. Retail sales, it was thought, required too much explanation by the sales staff, which might not be very knowledgeable about the products. Retail usually was limited to pharmacies and some sports stores. There was no definite strategy for developing retail channels. It was thought that there were some people who did not want to buy direct but who got their initial information from the infomercials, the company's telemarketing personnel, or other customers.

Going direct also allowed more targeted marketing efforts. While the target market for Slendertone was defined as "women between the ages of 25 and 55," a few niche segments also were targeted, including "prenuptials," "postnatals," and men. Postnatals were defined as women who had given birth recently and were now eager to regain their prepregnancy shape. Customer feedback had indicated that EMS was particularly effective in retoning the stomach muscles, which normally are "stretched" during pregnancy. This segment was reached by means of direct response advertisements in magazines aimed at new mothers and the "bounty bags" which are distributed in maternity wards. Bounty bags consist of free samples from manufacturers of baby-related products. The company would include a money-off voucher along with a specially designed brochure explaining how EMS can quickly and easily retone the stomach muscles. Prenuptials, those about to get married, were reached through wedding fairs and bridal magazines. EMS would allow the bride to be to quickly and easily tone up for the big day. It also was reported that increasing numbers of men were using the home use products. As an optional accessory the company supplied nonstick rubber pads which are attached to the body with a strap. These pads are suitable for men, for whom body hair can make adhesive pads uncomfortable.

Direct response enabled the company to gauge the effectiveness of all advertising and promotions directly. Advertisements were placed in a range of media, using different copy, graphics, and selling points to identify the most effective advertising methods. Direct response also meant that every advertisement produced immediate revenue or could be pulled quickly if it wasn't generating enough sales. This approach did not require the level of investment in brand development normally associated with introducing a new product to the market. In effect, all advertising became immediately self-financing.

Another important element of the direct strategy was to allow the company to develop an extensive customer database that could be used to market other products that the company would develop in the future. It had not yet been decided what those products would be other than that they would be sold under the Slendertone brand. The database also could be used to sell other products of interest to Slendertone customers and could be traded with other companies. The personal data from customers also proved useful for research purposes, helping the company identify its market.

Finally, for some customers, buying direct provided privacy when purchasing what some considered a personal product. One Irish pharmacist with a number of retail outlets reported that some customers would buy a Slendertone product at a pharmacy far from where they lived, presumably to avoid recognition by the staff or other customers. Some users of Slendertone products were reluctant to tell others they were using the company's products even when complimented on how well they were looking. The reasons given included, "No one says they are using these gimmicks" and "Because people would say to you, 'You don't need that.'" Some customers were reluctant to tell even a spouse that they had bought or were using Slendertone.

Customer Feedback

Attitudes regarding the sensitive nature of the purchase were revealed in a focus group of Irish customers conducted in 1995. A number of favorable comments about the Gymbody 8 were recorded, such as, "It's fabulous; I lost inches around the waist, and my sister got it and she looks fantastic." Some of the comments reflected an initial doubt about the efficacy of the product but subsequent satisfaction: "It's fabulous, I'm delighted, it's wonderful—it does actually work." One user was not so satisfied: "It's not very effective. I didn't see a visible difference; no one else did—no one commented."

The majority of the participants thought it was a very good value at £99. In determining "value" they tended to compare it to the cost of EMS treatment in a salon, joining a gym, taking fitness classes, or buying exercise equipment. The research also revealed generally low long-term use of the product. One issue raised related to uncertainty about using the unit, particularly how to place the pads on the body correctly. Another issue that arose was that using the products involved a certain amount of "hassle": attaching the pads to the unit, placing the pads on the body, and actually using the product for 40 minutes and then putting it all away again. All the focus group participants had bought their unit "off the TV," having seen the Irish infomercial. Most thought that the infomerical was very effective in explaining the product and that "it looked like a good product." Some found the TV presentation interesting and even entertaining (with some people watching it a number of times), while others thought it was "a bit over the top" or "false-looking."

The findings of this research supported anecdotal evidence and customer service feedback received by company personnel: initial doubt about the product's efficacy, a certain degree of surprise that it actually worked, mixed satisfaction (though mostly very high) with the results attained, and low long-term use. The low usage levels were confirmed by the low levels of replacement sales of the adhesive pads (which are used with the home use units to apply the current to the body and need to be replaced after 35 to 40 uses).

The Competition

Slendertone was the only product of its kind being marketed on television in 1995. A number of new EMS products entered the market during the mid-1990s, using a similar direct response approach in magazines, mail order catalogs, and other media. Other products had been available for many years, sold mostly through the mail order channel. With the exception of Ultratone, an English product, the competitor products in almost all markets tended to be of much poorer quality than Slendertone (though they were not necessarily much cheaper to buy). In this very fragmented market there were no international leaders. For instance, in Italy there were at least eight products on the market, none of which was sold outside the country. Other than the occasional mail order product, there did not appear to be any EMS units for sale in Germany. Ultratone was one of the biggest players in England but did not sell in France, which then was estimated to be the largest market for EMS products. In Spain a low-quality product called the Gymshape 8 was launched; it was priced lower than the Gymbody 8.

Management saw Slendertone as being at the "top end" of the market, based on its superior quality. Although the company had by then lost most of its mail order business to lower-priced (and lower-quality) competitors, management's attitude was that the biggest and most lucrative markets lay untapped. It was felt that the company had the products and the know-how to exploit those markets, as evidenced in France and Ireland. However, the increasing competition continued to put pressure on prices; most of the cost savings being achieved through more efficient production were being passed on to the distributors. From 1993 to the beginning of 1996 the retail price of the Gymbody 8 had fallen over £40 in France. To satisfy the French distributors' demand for cheaper products for certain channels, a "low-price" range under the Minibody and Intone brands was launched by BioMedical Research. Those products did not feature the Slendertone logo anywhere.

Given the fragmented nature of the market and a complete lack of secondary data for the EMS product class, it was hard to determine what market share different companies had. Lack of data also made it difficult to determine the size of the existing market for EMS products in each country. For planning purposes the company focused on the potential market for EMS, based on the belief that most countries had a large latent demand for EMS-based cosmetic products. Potential demand for each country was calculated on the basis of the size of the target market and the niche segments in that country. As revealed in the market research findings, the competition also had to be viewed in terms of the other means to improve body shape: the gym, fitness classes, exercise equipment, diets, diet foods, and the like.

The Professional Market

The salon business in Ireland experienced a big revival in the mid-1990s. The extensive marketing for the home use products helped create new or renewed awareness among salon users of EMS treatments and the Slendertone brand. Intensive media campaigns in Ireland were run to promote the salon products. In conjunction with salons, the company placed full-page "feature" advertisements in papers such as the *Sunday Independent*. A certain amount of tension arose between the company and the salon owners because the company was simultaneously marketing salon and home use units. For the price of 15 salon treatments one could buy a Gymbody 8.

The redevelopment of the salon market in the mid-1990s attracted a number of competitors to Ireland, including Ultratone, Eurowave, CACI, and Arysis. The increased competition led to greater promotional activity, which increased the demand for salon EMS treatments. Even though Slendertone had become a generic term for salon EMS treatment in Ireland, research in early 1996 indicated that some customers thought it represented "old" technology. Ultratone had positioned itself as the product with "newer" technology, one that was more effective and more comfortable and offered faster results in spite of using very similar, if not more basic, technology. In 1996 BioMedical Research promoted the fact that Slendertone had been in existence for 30 years. A special thirtieth-anniversary logo was featured on the promotional literature for the professional market. This was done to give buyers the assurance of long-term company marketing support and technical backup in the face of many new entrants into the market. Little effort was being made by the international distributors to develop the professional market in other countries in spite of very high margins on the larger professional units, which retailed at over £4,000. The French distributor was showing no interest in the professional market in France. It believed the size of the home use market offered much greater potential, and it did not require a sales team.

Product Development

After the success of the Gymbody 8, a number of other home use EMS products were developed by BioMedical Research before 1996, primarily to meet the requirements of the French distributor. Along with the low-cost Minibody and InTone brands, products developed under the Slendertone brand included the Bustyler (for lifting the breasts), the Face Up (a facial antiaging unit), and the Celluforme (to combat cellulite). Little market research was undertaken by the company while developing these products (the research that was done mostly consisted of prototype testing on a number of volunteers recruited locally in Galway, Ireland). The products would be developed, mostly in-house, according to criteria determined by the French distributor. The distributor also indicated the cost at which units would have to be supplied so that it could achieve certain retail price points in the targeted channels.

Rapid Growth

In March 1996 it appeared that annual Slendertone sales (from the factory) could break the £10 million barrier by year end. Sales for the Gymbody 8 represented over 70 percent of all Slendertone sales (including professional units). Over 75 percent of Gymbody 8 units being produced were for the French distributor. New employees were being recruited in a number of areas, including a large number of temporary workers in production. Many other workers chose to work overtime. There was a real sense of excitement throughout the company as orders continued to increase. The potential for Slendertone was enormous. If other countries achieved even a quarter of the per capita sales levels being attained in France or Ireland, the company would soon be a major Irish exporter. Plans were being drawn up to extend the factory and build a new headquarters in Galway. In spite of the impressive growth and the exciting potential, the board of the company was concerned about the growing dependence on one distributor.

The French distributor was becoming more demanding with regard to margins, product development, and pricing strategies. It continued to develop its own promotional material for the Slendertone range. The products were being sold as a form of "effortless exercise": "the equivalent of 240 sit-ups in just 40 minutes, while watching TV!" Some advertising featured topless models alongside sensational claims for the products' effectiveness: "the body you've always wanted in just three weeks." The distributor in France had arranged in 1996 for a well-known blond television celebrity to endorse the product. In the words of one of the Irish marketing staff, the distributor's approach was "very tacky" (see Exhibit 1). Still, few could argue with the ever-increasing sales. The distributor appeared to have found a large market that responded favorably to this type of promotion. Analysis of the French sales database, which was not computerized, indicated that sales were mostly to younger females; however, the distributor was very reluctant to share sales data with the company.

Developing the UK Market.   A number of marketing meetings were held in April 1996 to develop a plan to reduce the company's growing dependence on this single customer. It was decided to develop the UK market directly, without any distributor involvement. This decision was made on the basis of a number of factors: the failure to attract good distributors in the past, the success of the company's direct campaign in Ireland, the reasonably successful sales to UK viewers by Direct Shop, and finally, geographic and cultural proximity to Ireland.

EXHIBIT 1   Direct Response Advertisement Used in France

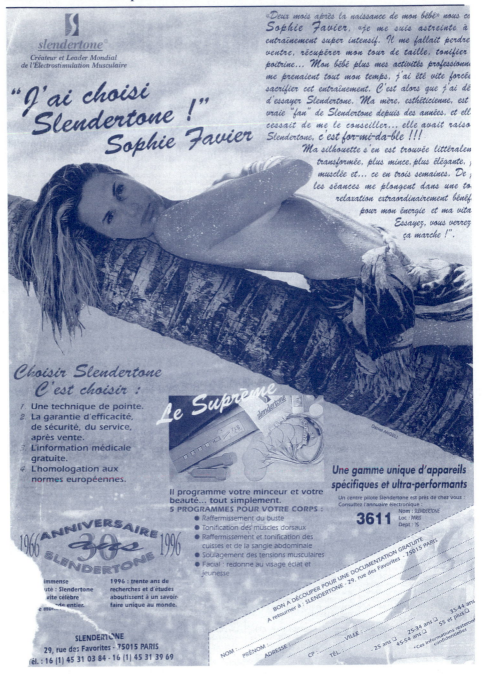

In May 1996 the board supported management's decision to develop the British market directly. This was going to require a substantial investment in terms of both money and management time. By the end of July an office had been established in London, with a general manager and two staff members. Direct response advertisements were soon being placed in a number of different print media, from *The Sunday Times Maga-*

zine to the *News of the World*'s color supplement. Responses and sales were monitored closely to gauge the more likely market for the products. Sales were slow to grow; by the end of the first quarter the UK subsidiary was behind budget. The cost of maintaining an office in London also was affecting profitability. However, the Slendertone staff in both Ireland and England was optimistic about the longer-term prospects.

APPENDIX
WHAT IS SLENDERTONE?

Beauty salons buy electronic muscle stimulation (EMS) units such as Slendertone so that they can provide their customers with a toning/body-shaping treatment. EMS devices work by delivering a series of electrical charges to the muscle through pads placed on the skin over the muscle area. Each tiny charge "fires" the motor points in the muscle. These charges are similar to the natural charges sent by the brain, through the nervous system, to activate particular muscles and thus cause movement. EMS therefore has the effect of exercising the muscle, but without the need to move the rest of the body. Customers use the EMS treatment over a period of weeks to help tone a particular area, primarily with the aim of improving body shape. This treatment also can improve circulation and the texture of the skin. EMS gives users improved body shape through improved muscle tone rather than through weight loss. Customers typically book a series of 10 or 15 one-hour treatments that are administered once or twice weekly. A qualified beautician who is trained in the use of EMS as part of the standard professional training for beauticians administers the treatment in the salon. A series of 10 salon treatments in Ireland costs in the range of £70. An alternative salon treatment to tone muscles is a manual "toning table," which works the muscles by moving different parts of the body attached to the table. Home use EMS units allow users to treat themselves in the comfort, privacy, and convenience of their own homes. A home use unit such as the Slendertone Body currently retails for £100 in Ireland. In terms of treatment, the home use unit should offer the user similar results to a salon treatment if used correctly and consistently.

Some customers prefer to go to a salon for EMS treatment, possibly enjoying the professional attention they get in a salon environment and the break it offers from everyday life. Booking and paying for a series of treatments in a salon also encourage customers to complete the treatment. Others prefer the convenience, privacy, and economy offered by the home use units. However, the home treatment requires a certain discipline to use the unit regularly. Home users sometimes report that they are uncertain if they are using the unit correctly; this mostly involves proper pad placement. EMS has been available in salons for over 30 years, but the home use market began to develop significantly only in the last 10 years.

Is EMS/Slendertone Safe?

EMS originally was developed for medical use. A common application of EMS is the rehabilitation of a muscle after an accident or a stroke. EMS frequently is used by physiotherapists for muscle rehabilitation after sports injuries and other injuries. Slendertone was developed to enable healthy users to "exercise" muscles without having to do any exercise. By remaining seated, lying down, or even doing minor chores, users could get the benefit of a vigorous workout. The effect of EMS is similar to that of regular exercise of a muscle. For many years the company compared the effect of using EMS (as applied to the abdominal muscles) to the effect gained from doing sit-ups. With the exception of well-stated contraindications (EMS should not be used by pregnant women, on or near open wounds, on or near ulcers, by diabetics, and on or near the throat area), EMS has proved to be perfectly safe for a variety of uses. Some people wonder what might happen when one stops using EMS. Again, the effect is like regular exercise: If one stops exercising, one may regain the shape one had before starting to exercise.

The U.S. Food and Drug Administration (FDA) has classified this type of EMS-based product as a Class II device. Class II devices must be prescribed by a "licensed practitioner" and only for very specified medical purposes. The FDA regulations governing the sale and use of EMS devices are based on proven efficacy and safety. According to the FDA, there is insufficient clinical evidence to support claims such as "body shaping," "weight loss," and "cellulite removal" for EMS treatments. The FDA's decision to impose stringent controls on the use of EMS was made after a number of home use EMS users suffered minor injuries. Users of a direct-current, home use EMS unit available in the United States in the 1970s suffered skin "burns" around the pad placement area. All Slendertone products, like the other cosmetic EMS products on the market today, only use alternating current, which will not cause burns.

CASE 4–8
AOL TIME WARNER

On the surface, it looked like just another awesome megadeal. There were the top executives up on stage, palling around like local-TV anchors—and assuring everyone that this would be a merger of equals, a careful blending of two companies, two cultures, But make no mistake: America Online is the acquirer. The trading symbol for the new company, tellingly, is AOL.

Given the realities of the New Economy, it could hardly be otherwise. By now, the pattern is clear: The digital will prevail over the analog, new media will grow faster than old, and the leaders of the Net economy will become the 21st century Establishment. If the ascendance of the Net economy were not clear already, the Jan. 10 announcement of America Online Inc.'s $183 billion deal to purchase Time Warner—the biggest deal ever—should be taken as proof positive. AOL has just one-fifth the revenue and 15% of the workforce of Time Warner, itself the combination of publishing and entertainment empires that have been fixtures in America culture since the 1920s. But with a New Economy stock that investors valued at nearly twice that of the Old Economy icon, AOL had the resources to be the buyer, not the bought. "The deal shows the torch has passed," says Bruce Leichtman, director of media and entertainment strategies at research firm Yankee Group.

Now, New Economy titans Stephen M. Case and Robert W. Pittman will team up with Old Economy strategist Gerald M. Levin—CEO until 2003—to assemble a new kind of conglomerate whose very existence will likely change the contours of information and entertainment media—digital and otherwise. Case, who will be chairman of AOL Time Warner, is making a huge bet that by melding the Time Warner colossus with his Internet empire, he will create a hybrid with unmatched advantages as the long-anticipated convergence of entertainment, information, communications, and online services comes about in the next few years (see Exhibit 1).

It is a bid to define the future. By assembling more assets and audiences and advertisers for the new digital marketplace than anyone has previously even thought of, Case and AOL President Pittman see a chance to move so far ahead that others won't catch up for years—the way Alfred P. Sloan audaciously engineered the creation of General Motors Corp. in the 1920s—producing the corporation that dominated the U.S. in the Auto Age. "This should provide encouragement for other combinations that wouldn't have been thought possible," Time Warner Chairman Levin told *Business Week* on Jan. 11.

Costly Bet

But deal handicappers are scratching their heads, trying to figure out how to come close to this combo. "There just isn't another AOL out there," says Robert "Dob" Bennett, president of Liberty Media Corp., which owns a 9 percent nonvoting stake in Time Warner. "This was a landmark deal, and I don't know if it can be duplicated."

Source: "Welcome to the 21st Century," *Business Week,* January 24, 2000, 37–47.

EXHIBIT 1   How the Giant Fits Together

The AOL Time Warner conglomerate will bring together a unique blend of media assets and methods to put them before the public

	Content	*Distribution*
Print	**Music**	**Cable**
Time	Warner Music	Time Warner Cable
People		
Sports Illustrated	**Television**	**Internet Service**
Entertainment Weekly	CNN	America Online
Money	TNT	Roadrunner
Fortune	TBS	CompuServe
And 27 other titles	HBO	
Book Publishing	The WB Network	**Telephone**
		Deals with regional
	Digital Content	Bells for DSL
Film	AOL Sites	service
Warner Bros.	CNNi	
Studios	Magazine Web sites	**Satellite**
New Line Cinema	MapQuest	AOL owns a stake
Turner Classic Movies	Moviefone	in DirecTV

It is also an immensely costly move: To secure this strategic stronghold, AOL proposed to pay a 71 percent premium over what Time Warner was valued at in the market. In the following days, however, AOL's high-flying stock was quickly devalued as investors focused on how tying up with Time Warner may produce a company with rates of return usually associated with the Old Economy (Exhibit 2). Pittman, who will start out as co-chief operating officer with Time Warner President Richard D. Parsons, says the market is wrong in thinking that AOL will come to resemble Time Warner rather than vice versa. Time Warner has "traditional businesses with big brands, long consumer relationships, strong cash flow," he argues. "All you need to do is put a catalyst to it, and in a short period, you can alter the growth rate. The growth rate will be like an Internet company, but built on businesses that have already built their brands."

Still, there is a fundamental risk to AOL that goes beyond stock valuation. Although the acquirer, it could become the captive of the sprawling Time Warner empire, which has 82,000 employees and a distinctly Old Economy management culture that could rob 15-year-old AOL of the flexibility, speed, and entrepreneurial drive that are crucial in the New Economy (Exhibit 3).

That's the big picture. For now, however, you can think of the combination in simpler terms: pipes and content. With its cable systems serving 20% of the country, Time Warner gives AOL a clearer path into broadband than it had with its previous plans to rely solely on upgrades in local telephone lines and satellite TV. The speedy new links—available across Time Warner systems by next year—not only will make existing Web fare far more appealing but will also make practical all sorts of new things, including AOL TV, a service to deliver the Web to TV sets that the company is rolling out this June. "We're now at the cusp of a fundamental new Internet experience, enabled by broadband access," says Case. "It's [about] a whole range of experiences, including a more engaging multimedia experience on a whole range of devices, of which TV is increasingly prominent."

EXHIBIT 2   Running the Numbers on the Deal

Ted Turner may think that the joining of Time Warner and America Online is as good as making love for the first time, but average investors took a more dispassionate view. By Jan. 12, two days after the Merger of the Millennium was announced, the combined market value of AOL and Time Warner was actually lower than before the announcement—$260 billion, vs. $270 billion pre-deal. In the eyes of Wall Street, the much lauded deal actually destroyed value.

That could well change in the days ahead, of course. Shares of AOL are notoriously volatile, and investors may learn to love the combination. But what the early sell-off showed is the difficulty of merging not just two companies but two sets of shareholders with different views of the world. AOL shareholders bought their shares as an Internet play. Time Warner shareholders acquired what they thought was a media company. Now, both groups will become owners of a hybrid that wasn't what either exactly bargained for.

Missing Billions. Time Warner shareholders, to be sure, have nothing to complain about. Their company's market value was still up $22 billion as of Jan. 12, thanks to the generous ratio of shares they are slated to receive in the new AOL Time Warner Inc. The big losers were shareholders of AOL, whose market value fell 19%, or $32 billion, in the days immediately following the announcement of the deal. Out of that $32 billion, about $22 billion was effectively transferred to Time Warner shareholders and about $10 billion simply vanished in the stock's fall—in effect, the market was concluding

that the companies were worth less together than apart.

The deal calls for America Online shareholders to receive one share in the new company for each of their current shares, and for Time Warner shareholders to receive 1.5 shares for each of theirs. That represents a 70 percent premium for Time Warner shareholders, based on the

pre-deal prices of the stocks and the numbers of shares outstanding. It gives AOL shareholders 55 percent and Time Warner shareholders 45 percent of the new company.

In an interview with *Business Week,* AOL Chairman and Chief Executive Stephen M. Case said he thought last fall that the deal should be a "merger of equals." Ordinarily, that would mean giving each set of shareholders 50 percent of the new company. When AOL shares started running up, he decided to ask for better terms. "We were prepared to pay a premium, but there are practical limits," he says.

Based solely on pre-deal market capitalization, Case says, AOL shareholders should have gotten 65 percent of the new company. On the other hand, basing the ratio on the

companies' revenues or cash flow would have given AOL shareholders just 20 percent of the company, he notes. Says Case: "They recognized the leap of faith that Internet valuations are real. We took a similar leap of faith that media assets are valuable and underappreciated. And we arrived at some place in the middle."

Earnings Hit. So how much is AOL really worth, given its deal to acquire Time Warner? The method that Case favors—and that Wall Street analysts often use—is to project the combined companies' per-share earnings before interest, taxes, depreciation, and amortization (EBITDA)—roughly speaking, operating cash flow. That measure ignores the giant hit to net earnings that AOL will take by writing off about $15 billion of goodwill annually for 10 years. (Goodwill is the gap between the purchase price for Time Warner and the book value of the company's net assets.)

Pre-deal, Time Warner shares traded at a multiple of 14 times EBITDA, while AOL's shares traded at an EBITDA multiple of 55 because of its higher growth rate. The multiple for the blended company will depend on whether investors see the hybrid as more like AOL or more like Time Warner. Merrill Lynch & Co. analyst Henry Blodget expects the multiple to range between 25 and 40, implying a price for AOL stock between $55 and $90 (see the table). In a Jan. 11 report, he advised that, if the merger goes well, the price could be $90 to $100 in a year. If so, AOL is a great buy at $60. If not, AOL shareholders may get a new message: "You've got losses."

By Peter Coy in New York, with Catherine Yang in Washington

One Stab at Valuing the Stock

Merrill Lynch & Co. analyst Henry Blodget projects the combined companies' earnings before interest, taxes, depreciation, and amortization (EBITDA) in 2001. Different assumptions about the multiple the market will pay for EBITDA produce a target stock price of $55 to $90 a share.

Total Shares in New AOL Time Warner	4.8 billion
Stand-Alone AOL EBITDA	$3.5 billion
Stand-Alone Time Warner EBITDA	$6.5 billion
Gains from Synergy	$1 billion
Total EBITDA	$11 billion or $2.30 per share
Conservative Projection of Combined Companies' EBITDA Multiple	25
EBITDA × Multiple	About $55 a share
Aggressive Projection of Combined Companies' EBITDA Multiple	40
EBITDA × Multiple	About $90 a share

Source: Merrill Lynch & Co.

King Content

And when all that bandwidth and all those gizmos are hooked up, AOL Time Warner will have the world's greatest trove of content with which to attract the largest audience, the most subscribers, and the most ads and e-commerce. From *In Style* magazine to Turner Classics' movie vault to CNN to the latest Kid Rock CD, Time Warner has something for everybody. Nobody knows that better than Levin, who has spent hundreds of millions in efforts to leverage those assets in cyberspace—and had budgeted as much as $500 million for 2000. But many projects, such as the *Pathfinder* Web portal, went nowhere. And Time Warner's Old Economy balance sheet and shareholders would not permit the years of losses required to fund a massive online effort—the way pure Internet companies such as AOL can.

EXHIBIT 3   Is This Baby Built for Cyberspace?*

"I feel betrayed. I bought a company that was going to change the world. I didn't buy a big, fat, stupid conglomerate. And now I've got one."
—Alan Towers

Does Towers, a New York consultant and AOL shareholder, know something that the architects of the world's biggest merger don't?

America Online founder Steve Case has shown a keen ability for seizing on a world-changing vision and sticking with it. The boyish entrepreneur has defied the odds and the calamitous predictions to create the largest and most profitable company in cyberspace. And his audacious plan to take over Time Warner is the grandest manifestation of that vision yet—a behemoth that can place more digital content in front of more consumers than anyone on the horizon. In short, a General Motors for the New Economy.

Dated Strategy. Case's remarkably bold stroke is in fact reminiscent of the architecture designed by Alfred P. Sloan at GM in the 1920s. Through monumental acquisition and vertical integration, Sloan created a giant that outdistanced its rivals on every measure and dominated the world auto industry for nearly half a century. Sloan's strategy was simple but powerful: GM built a car "for every purpose and purse" and sewed up more of the market than anyone else.

Seven decades later, Case is pursuing a similar strategy of vertical integration and conglomeration to rule cyberspace. There is, however, an inherent problem in the analogy: Case is using Old Economy tools in a New Economy that he has helped to define.

Leaders in this economy have generally understood that, unlike in the world of iron foundries and stamping plants, the attributes of size—access to greater resources, economies of scale, and stability—are not nearly as crucial as flexibility, speed, and agility. They know that partnerships, without the fixed costs, inventories, and management headaches of pure ownership are the antithesis of vertical integration. And they've learned that melding a sleek, fast-growing organization with a big established enterprise is the quickest way to slow growth and smother creativity.

Indeed, few people have mastered that lesson better than Case himself. The giants of old media, including Time Inc., were the first to enter the online services business with ill-fated experiments. Then came Prodigy, the joint venture of IBM and Sears Roebuck. But AOL was the one that triumphed—thanks to Case's focus on brand building and a strategy of turning cyberspace into a friendly place for everybody.

Obsolete Pipe. The Time Warner deal smacks of an endgame maneuver—in a single strategic stroke putting miles between AOL and the competition. But who's to say that there won't be a new Steve Case who will use the tools of the New Economy—alliances, technological knowhow, and an inspired workforce—to leap over this giant combination? Alternate broadband technologies over copper, satellite dish, or wireless phone lines could render the AOL Time Warner cable "pipe" into the home obsolete. Smart new entrepreneurs could align with other content providers to create similarly large audiences. Timothy Koogle of Yahoo!, for one, says he "sees no necessity" to own content when you can partner for it.

After the front-page hype and hoopla, after the i-bankers collect their fat fees, the dealmakers face the daunting challenge of making a sprawling and bureaucratic empire work. Just as Sloan did in his day. It's something that Tower and other shareholders ought to worry about.

*By John A. Byrne

In the end, that helped convince Levin and his eclectic management team—including Vice-Chairman Ted Turner—that it was worth giving up corporate control to secure their company's berth in the New Economy. "It's damn hard," says Parsons. "We could work for a decade and maybe still not get up to a level that would be competitive."

AOL also gains things that it needed but could not get on its own: access to broadband distribution and more compelling content. The company, which dialed back its own efforts to develop new content in recent years, now realizes that it can't thrive long-term as mainly a glorified Internet-access provider. "AOL woke up one day and understood that their core competency wasn't pipes, but content," says Edward J. Zander, president and chief operating officer of Sun Microsystems Inc. "It's like when the train companies figured out they're not train companies, but transportation companies."

How will AOL get the most from Time Warner's distribution and content—and Time Warner gain from its links to the world's biggest online community? (Exhibit 4) Even before the deal closes later this year, the companies are making plans to work more closely together. Entertaindom, the first of several miniportals Time Warner is starting, will be featured on AOL's entertainment channel. And Warner Brothers stores will have prominent displays of AOL sign-up disks.

But that's just cross-promotion. The key to the deal is developing new types of Web sites and services using Time Warner's rich content and getting them up quickly using AOL's vast Web infrastructure. Another plus: The companies will combine sales forces and back-end functions such as sales and customer support call centers. In all, the two companies promise to generate $1 billion in extra cash flow from "synergies" in their first full year together. That includes eliminating some of the $800 million AOL spends on advertising by using house ads across Time Warner media.

Tuneful

The first big stab at synergy may come in online music. Look for artists from Warner Music Group to be featured on AOL's music channel, where consumers can sample music and order CDs online—from CDNow Inc., which Time Warner partly owns. There is also potential for selling downloads on AOL. "We can help reinvent the business," says Case. "In the long run, we have the opportunity to create a personal jukebox

---

EXHIBIT 4   A Little Help from the Feds

How can a Net company that has never covered a war or made a movie swallow a premiere news and entertainment conglomerate? In part, America Online Inc. can thank government policy for helping it get a stock valuation that lets it absorb Time Warner Inc.

How so? Web traffic, like long-distance calls, must use the local phone network to reach customers—a service for which long-distance providers until recently paid local carriers as much as $30 billion per year. But back in 1983, the Federal Communications Commission exempted data carriers—then, an "infant industry"—from those fees. That meant annual savings of $5 billion to $7 billion, according to Legg Mason Precursor Group.

Although the infant has grown up, the exemption still stands, letting AOL and other Internet service providers offer unlimited surfing for roughly $20 a month. "The day [AOL] started offering flat-rate service, demand went through the roof," recalls online consultant George Sacerdote. The fees "would have bankrupted them," he says.

Another boost has come from the federal moratorium on Net taxation. These breaks mean more customers, more ads, and a market capitalization that allows an upstart to buy a giant.

that you carry with you—so you can listen to it on a pay-for-play, subscription, or pay-once-and-play-for-life basis."

Perhaps the greatest strength of the two companies going into the merger is the subscriber relationships they have with more than 100 million consumers. AOL has 22 million subscribers, and Time Warner's biggest sources of revenue are 28 million subscriptions to its magazines, 13 million cable subscribers, and 35 million paying viewers at its cable-movie service HBO. Plus, it draws fees from the 75 million households that take the TBS and TNT channels, and from TV services around the world that carry CNN. In addition, the new companies have a huge presence on the Web. Along with the AOL properties, including the Netscape portal, Time Warner has hundreds of sites including CNN.com.

Slice and Dice

That's a promising venue for advertisers, notes Renatta McCann, managing director for Starcom North America, a media buyer with $8.5 billion in annual billings. "The combined company will have a fantastic database," says McCann. "They will have a phenomenal way of slicing and dicing their consumer database to deliver the specific target audiences that I want."

That's the theory. How well it works in practice depends largely on how well the management of the two companies mesh. Ironically, the AOL deal was announced 10 years to the day after Time Inc. agreed to merge with Warner Communications. That deal, too, was supposed to deliver quick synergies but got off to a rocky start as execs from both sides jockeyed for position. "In any big transaction, probably the most significant risk is really people risk," says Levin. The 61-year-old Time Warner chairman plans to stay on as CEO of the new company until at least 2003. And he can't be removed unless three-quarters of the new company's board—which will be composed of eight directors from each company—agree. Even now, however, the media industry is betting that Pittman, 46, a former Warner exec who helped start MTV, will be the successor to Levin.

By most accounts, there is good chemistry between the scholarly Levin and the preppy Case. Their friendship blossomed last September on the 50th anniversary of the founding of the People's Republic of China. While attending a conference in Beijing, Case and Levin took in the festivities. "We stood together watching the tanks, the planes, and fireworks roll by," recalls Case. The next month, it was Case who called Levin to propose the idea of buying Time Warner—and keeping Levin as CEO. "If he had said no, I would have persevered," says Case. "Luckily, he's a smart guy and recognized . . . that it would be complicated to pull off but worth taking a shot."

Strong Pipes

If AOL Time Warner does get sidetracked by internal politics, there are dozens of rivals looking for an opening (Exhibit 5). Players across the digital landscape—from Web rivals such as Microsoft and Yahoo! to the telecom giants to media companies like Walt Disney and Viacom—may have to recalibrate their strategies in the wake of the deal. AT&T, for example, plowed $110 billion into cable. But it has shied away from content and focused instead on creating broadband and local-phone links to homes—and a deal with Time Warner has been long delayed. Now, Levin says, he'll have broadband pipes, content, and the potential to add Internet telephony. Moreover, Case told *Business Week* in an interview that he has been talking with both AT&T and MCI Worldcom—on whose board he sits—about phone ventures.

EXHIBIT 5 So Who's Next?

MICROSOFT

UPSIDE Microsoft hopes AOL's alignment with Time Warner pushes other entertainment and news organizations into its arms—either as partners or customers for its "enabling" technology for Web-site operators. It has even gone so far as to spin off content properties such as Expedia to avoid clashing with potential customers.

DOWNSIDE The greatest threat to Microsoft is the heightened competition for its MSN and WebTV Internet services. AOL now has a rich array of content and a cable-delivery system the software giant can't match. With only about 3 million Net access subscribers for MSN and WebTV combined, Microsoft lags far behind AOL's 22 million customers. And so far, it has forged close relationships only with smaller Web content players like WebMD, a health-care site.

PROGNOSIS Microsoft swears it isn't seeking a major merger or exclusive partnership, but analysts envision all sorts of couplings. "Could AT&T, Disney, and Microsoft get together in a huge *keiretsu?* It's very intriguing," says Michael Kwatinetz, an analyst at Credit Suisse First Boston.

AT&T

UPSIDE When it completes the acquisition of MediaOne Group, AT&T will become the largest cable operator in the U.S., with connections to more than 25 percent of the country's cable customers. The birth of AOL Time Warner could encourage other content companies to seek access to this system, which is being upgraded to carry data at broadband speeds.

DOWNSIDE On the Internet, AT&T holds a weak hand. Its WorldNet Internet service is only a fraction of the size of AOL. Meanwhile, Time Warner has pledged "open access" for its high-speed cable-modem service—putting pressure on AT&T to do the same and stop favoring Excite@Home, of which it is a partial owner. AT&T's biggest hole now: no content.

PROGNOSIS The AOL-Time Warner deal means AT&T and other carriers must take another look at alliances and deals in the media world. "Most traditional telecom companies have shied away from content," says Yankee Group Research telecom analyst Brian Adamik. "The content-distribution model is very powerful. It will cause telecom companies to wonder if owning a pipe alone is enough."

YAHOO

UPSIDE Yahoo! is sitting in the e-catbird seat. The largest portal on the Web, Yahoo attracts 120 million unique visitors a month worldwide; 65 percent of U.S. Web users visit the site. And as one of the few profitable Web media outlets, Yahoo boasts a $94 billion-plus market cap that gives it tremendous buying power. Yahoo says that it has no plans to buy content companies—though some speculate it could make a play for Disney—but, "We have strong relationships with a pretty broad range of content providers. We're going to continue on that path," says Chairman Tim Koogle.

DOWNSIDE Yahoo has little guaranteed distribution to make sure its site remains widely available. If broadband operators refuse to open their networks to all content providers, Yahoo might be left out in the cold. And since it doesn't offer Net access services, Yahoo's hold on users is more tenuous than AOL's.

PROGNOSIS Since Yahoo continues to rapidly increase its registered users, it seems likely to remain one of the Web's leaders. But if media players continue to consolidate, Yahoo may be forced to make some dramatic acquisitions.

DISNEY

UPSIDE AOL is coming around to agree with what CEO Michael D. Eisner has long believed: Content is king. He says that Walt Disney Co.'s brands and its ability to churn out world-class content are its strongest bets in the New Media world. It owns a winning collection of household names including Disney, ESPN, and ABC. And it has decades of experience at cross-selling—leveraging its worldwide theme parks, cable-TV holdings, and a TV network to promote its films.

DOWNSIDE Disney identified the Web as a new opportunity early, but properties such as the Go portal could be dwarfed by the combination of AOL and Time Warner Inc. And it has been unable to conjure up a broadband strategy.

PROGNOSIS With its stock on the floor due to problems at its company stores and home-video units, the company could face a takeover. One possible suitor: AT&T.
"One of the first things I thought about after hearing about the AOL-Time Warner deal was that Disney is next," says Lee Masters, president of Liberty Digital, John C. Malone's Internet acquisition vehicle.

VIACOM

UPSIDE The AOL-Time Warner deal bolsters Viacom Chairman Sumner M. Redstone's view that content and brands matter on the Internet. And he owns plenty of both, from the Paramount studio to cable networks MTV and Nickelodeon. When his $80 billion merger with CBS closes, the company will add the most popular broadcast TV network and the No. 1 radio network in the U.S.

DOWNSIDE Viacom and CBS have both been building up online businesses lately, but they were slow off the mark and still have to figure out how to integrate the online businesses of the two parents. Morever, Viacom's lucrative cable music channels MTV and VH-1 face heavy online competition from AOL Time Warner, which will have a big presence in digital downloading and online music sales.

PROGNOSIS With CBS dealmaker Mel Karmazin as Viacom's CEO for the next three years, little can be ruled out. If he thinks the best move for Viacom stock is to partner with or be acquired by an Internet company, Karmazin will make it happen. Says Redstone: "If there's a deal out there, we'll look at it, but we're going to look at it very carefully."

NEWS CORP.

UPSIDE News Corp., owner of the Old Media icon Fox film studios, has impressive worldwide distribution assets with satellites in Asia, Europe, and Latin America and the Fox TV network in the U.S. The Fox brand has been extended to sports, news, and children's networks on cable. The company also owns newspapers in Britain, Australia, and the U.S. and book publisher HarperCollins. It has spent lavishly to acquire top-notch sports teams to provide programming for its broadcast and cable outlets.

DOWNSIDE Bruised relationships with cable operators slowed efforts to place cable channels on U.S. systems. Not yet a presence on the Net, it has earmarked $300 million for New Media investments. It has few assets in the music industry.

PROGNOSIS The family-run empire isn't likely to cede control in any deal. More likely are content-sharing joint ventures with Net companies. "We're comfortable with our position," says James Murdoch, Rupert's son and an executive vice-president of News Corp. "But clearly the whole sector will start to undergo a lot of activity as people start to get worried."

Another complication for AT&T is the AOL Time Warner pledge to provide open access on its broadband networks. AT&T, which owns 26 percent of cable-modem service Excite@Home, has resisted open access, which would require it to let all online services use its cable pipes on the same terms as Excite@Home. "It's probably the nail in the coffin of the whole open-access debate," says Excite@Home CEO Thomas Jermoluk.

To compete more broadly with the New New Media giant, some analysts predict closer links between AT&T and Microsoft, possibly with ties to content companies such as Disney or Viacom. "This merger will make it easier for us to find partners among the other media companies," says Yusuf Mehdi, Microsoft Network's marketing director. "Will they want to partner with AOL now?"

Indeed, in the tangled media business, the AOL deal with Time Warner already produces complications: What happens with AOL's joint venture with Germany's Bertelsmann to roll out AOL in Europe? Bertelsmann competes heavily with Time Warner and its chairman has quit the AOL board.

Those are issues that Case, Pittman, and Levin will have to address—if the deal closes as expected later this year. Despite the falloff in AOL's stock and the retreat in Time Warner shares after an initial 50 percent surge, the merger is not in danger of immediate collapse because there is no "collar" on the deal that dictates the limits of share prices on either side. That was a concession that Time Warner made to get the 71% premium. At one critical board meeting, AOL director James Barksdale, the former CEO of Netscape Communications Corp., told fellow AOL directors: "Well, that's the price of eggs."

Twists

Another twist in the deal is the use of purchase accounting rather than a pooling of interests, which companies with hot stocks usually use. That, say people close to the deal, means the company will have to write off some $150 billion in goodwill. Bottom line: Charges of at least $15 billion a year against earnings for the next decade. But, insiders point out, it also gives the combined company the chance to pursue further acquisitions, joint ventures, or asset sales. Under a pooling of interests deal, AOL Time Warner would not be able to transfer more than 10 percent of its assets for two years. "We did not want to be hamstrung by the rules of pooling accounting," says Michael Kelly, AOL's CFO.

That means a long-rumored alliance between Time Warner and General Electric Co.'s NBC is still not out of the question. Nor are deals to bolster the slumping Warner Music Group, perhaps by joining up with British music group EMI PLC. And the company could buy up more cable systems to expand its broadband reach. "We have a lot," says Case. "I wouldn't say we have everything we need forever." So the deal of the century may not be the last for the AOL Time Warner team.

Supply Chain Management and Partnership Alignment

The supply chain extends from suppliers to consumer and organizational end users. The organizations that participate in the supply chain include manufacturers, agents, distributors, wholesalers, dealers, and retailers. Also frequently involved in supply chain activities are transportation firms, financial service providers, and other facilitating organizations. In the past, the supply chain referred to supplier and manufacturer links whereas the channel of distribution referred to links from the manufacturer to end users. Increasingly, the term *supply chain* (also termed the *value-added chain*) is used to identify the group of organizations aligned together in moving goods and services from sources of supply to end users.

Thus, the supply chain consists of the network of business processes and organizations that move raw materials through producers and distribution organizations to consumer and organizational end users. Supply chain management seeks to achieve high levels of effectiveness and efficiency. Effectiveness involves the supply chains that provide the most effective combination of organizations. Efficiency involves operating the supply chain at the highest feasible level of efficiency.

Determining which supply chain(s) to use and effectively integrating multiple chains are important strategic initiatives. These decisions may be made by producers and other supply chain participants. Conflicts may occur between different supply chains, but revenue opportunities may be lost if multiple strategies are not pursued. The explosive growth of the Internet has introduced a new dimension into supply chain management by providing direct access to end users and supply chain members.

First, we discuss the major decisions involved in developing supply chain strategies. Next, several aspects and challenges of managing the supply chain are examined. Finally, we consider what is involved in partnership alignment.

Supply Chain Strategy

The core issue in developing the supply chain strategy is deciding how to access the end user of goods and services. We examine the major decisions involved in supply chain strategy, highlighting important considerations in building the supply chain network.

Direct versus Use of Intermediaries

An important initial step in formulating the supply chain strategy is deciding whether to go directly to end users or instead to access them through partnering organizations. Typically, this decision is made by the producer of goods or services. However, the decision also may be made by an Internet-based organization such as Amazon.com. Dell Computer is an example of a producer that utilizes direct distribution to business customers by using salespeople, telecommunications, and the Internet.

Several factors that may point to the use of direct distribution are shown in Exhibit 1. Not all of these factors necessarily apply in a particular direct distribution decision. However, unless one or more factors apply in a particular decision situation, the use of intermediaries may be indicated. These factors fall into three major categories: buyer considerations, product characteristics, and financial and control considerations.

The Internet offers an important direct distribution capability, particularly for producers of products for business firms and other organizations. Many producers have developed Internet access to their end users as a part of their multichain strategies. For example, AMP Inc. supplies electronics components to organizational customers. It has an on-line catalog, and the site has 130,000 contacts every day from 132,000 registered users in 144 countries around the world.[1]

E-Business Strategy

It is important for all companies to examine the relevance of e-business. E-business strategies are a form of direct marketing and have been adopted by many companies to achieve various customer access objectives. E-business differs from e-commerce in that it does not necessarily involve Web transactions. Management needs to first decide what the e-business strategy should include, such as on-line lead identification, Web-based surveys, e-mail-based customer support, and on-line profile management.[2]

After deciding on the role e-business will play in the organization, management needs to formulate and implement the following initiatives:[3]

EXHIBIT 1   Factors Favoring Distribution by the Manufacturer

Source: David W. Cravens, *Strategic Marketing,* 6th ed. (Chicago: Irwin/McGraw-Hill, 2000), p. 307.

- Develop the marketing strategy to be pursued.
- Articulate the strategy with a marketing plan.
- Communicate the strategy to all the participants.
- Achieve close coordination between sales, marketing, and information technology participants.
- Integrate the e-business strategy with other supply chain channels that may be affected.

E-business is a reality in many industries and markets. While many of the specific strategy initiatives represent key marketing strategy decisions (market targeting, strategic and tactical positioning, and marketing mix strategies), linking e-business technology with marketing strategy requires close coordination and teamwork between sales, marketing, operations, and information technology personnel.

Types of Supply Chains

There are three major types of supply chains: conventional, managed, and collaborative.

Conventional Chain.   A conventional supply chain consists of a group of organizations that are aligned together for the purpose of moving goods and services from suppliers to end users. Each organization operates on an independent basis rather than as a participant in an integrated and coordinated supply chain system. No specific firm in the channel has sufficient power and influence to manage the entire supply chain.

Managed Chain.   Leadership by one of the firms in the supply chain occurs in a managed supply chain. The term *vertical marketing system* (VMS) may be used to describe a managed supply chain, although a VMS typically considers the manufacturer–end user portion of the chain. The firm that manages the supply chain seeks to achieve close coordination among the participants and efficiencies in moving goods and services through the system.

Collaborative Chain.   No single firm has control over the entire supply chain in a collaborative chain. However, unlike the conventional chain, members cooperate and build relationships. This type of chain is more likely to occur when the members want to integrate supply chain activities but are unwilling to commit to having one firm manage the entire chain.

Conventional supply chains can be found in several product categories, such as small food retailers, dry cleaning, construction companies, and automobile services. McDonald's and other fast-food franchisers are examples of managed supply chains. Kimberly-Clark's exclusive relationship with Costco in supplying the giant discount retailer with diapers is an example of a collaborative supply chain. The producer is responsible for keeping Costco stores stocked, and the retailer makes detailed sales information available to Kimberly-Clark.

Supply Chain Configurations[4]

As shown in Exhibit 2, there are five possible levels in the supply chain, beginning with suppliers to manufacturers/producers. Several possible configurations may be used, depending on the supply chain under consideration. The decision criteria that are often relevant in selecting a particular configuration include the following:

EXHIBIT 2
Alternative Supply
Chain Configurations

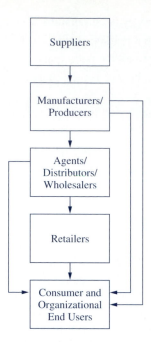

- Market coverage of each supply chain configuration under consideration.
- Functions needed at each level in the supply chain.
- Revenue and cost analyses.
- Product characteristics.
- Legal constraints.
- Management control considerations.
- Availability of qualified organizations.

The company that is concerned with selecting (or changing) the supply chain configuration is usually the producer or retailer. However, a powerful essential supplier such as Intel Corp. may play a key role in decisions involving channel configuration. There are also examples of distributors and wholesalers that have significant influence on the formation of supply chains.

Managing the Supply Chain[5]

Several issues may be important to the firm(s) managing the supply chain. We briefly overview each one, highlighting relevant issues.

Leadership.   There is substantial evidence indicating that some form of leadership for the supply chain will enhance the performance of the entire chain. Informal leadership may emerge in the conventional chain as a result of the size and influence of one of the members. In a managed supply chain, one firm performs the leadership role. Examples include The Limited and Gap in apparel, Frito Lay in snacks, and Tiffany in jewelry. Examples of key partners in a collaborative chain are Boeing and the major airlines.

The supply chain leader is not always viewed in a positive context. Conflicts may occur, since what is best for the entire supply chain may have undesirable consequences for individual members. For example, Compaq Computer's e-business strategy and partnership with Radio Shack may draw sales away from distributors and other retailers.

Building Relationships.   Relationship strategies may be developed between companies and end user customers, suppliers and manufacturers, distribution channel members, companies at the same level in the value chain, and different business functions within the organization. The purposes underlying these strategic relationships include gaining access to new markets, reducing the risks characteristic of the rapidly changing business environment, obtaining needed skills and resources, and reducing the time necessary to develop and implement business and marketing strategies.

The rapid growth of Tommy Hilfiger illustrates the benefits of partnering with suppliers, channel members, and industry members. That apparel company has about 2600 employees and should generate nearly $2 billion in sales in 2001, nearly three times the level of its 1996 sales. Hilfiger's profits have chalked up similar growth records. The company manages a network of relationships with other organizations. Hilfiger's competencies include very successful product designs and effective strategic partnering. The company has leveraged its powerful brand image by licensing its name to companies in related product categories, such as Estée Lauder, which produces Tommy fragrances.

Conflict Resolution.   The multiorganizational structure of the supply chain is certain to create conflicts between the members. These problems should be anticipated when the chain is formed, and processes should be set up to handle conflicts when they occur. Effective communications are important in anticipating possible conflicts and attempting to reduce the impact of conflicts.

Conflict often occurs when the supply chain leader adds one or more additional supply chains. Avon Products' opening of boutiques in Penney's retail stores in 2001 is likely to steal sales away from Avon's direct sales representatives. In an effort to avoid this problem the cosmetics in the boutiques were introduced under a different brand label.

Supply Chain Performance

Two supply chain performance issues need to be considered. First, each firm is concerned with its individual revenue and expense performance. Second, the supply chain manager is interested in the overall performance of the supply chain. While both types of performance are related, the effects are not necessarily the same in that high supply chain performance does not necessarily result in high performance for all the participants.

Rapid changes in markets and competitive situations require monitoring of supply chain performance on a continuing basis. Business applications software used in accounting, customer management, and Web sales offers impressive monitoring capabilities. For example, in the year 2000 Oracle Corp. released a comprehensive and integrated software package of business applications.

Partnership Alignment

Various types of strategic relationships may be formed between the members of the supply chain. The previously mentioned partnership of Kimberly-Clark and Costco is illustrative.

Customer Relationships

Relationship marketing starts with the customer—understanding needs and wants and how to satisfy customers' requirements and preferences:

> Customers think about products and companies in relation to other products and companies. What really matters is how existing and potential customers think about a company in relation to its competitors. Customers set up a hierarchy of values, wants, and needs based on empirical data, opinions, word of mouth references, and previous experiences with products and services. They use that information to make purchasing decisions.[6]

Understanding customers' needs and wants encourages the development of long-term collaborative relationships. Driving the necessity of staying in close contact with buyers is the reality that customers often have several suppliers of the products they wish to purchase. Customer diversity compounds the competitive challenge. Developing a customer-oriented organization includes the following:

- Instilling customer-oriented values and beliefs supported by top management.
- Integrating market and customer focus into the strategic planning process.
- Developing strong marketing managers and programs.
- Creating market-based measures of performance.
- Developing customer commitment throughout the organization.[7]

Supplier-Manufacturer Relationships

The relationships between suppliers and customers range from transactional to collaborative partnerships.[8] Collaboration may include product and process design, applications assistance, long-term supply contracts, and just-in-time inventory programs. While supplier-producer collaboration is employed by companies in various industries, the logic of these relationships needs to take into account the following factors.[9]

1. *Philosophy of doing business.* The partners' approach to business should be compatible. For example, if one firm has adopted a total quality management (TQM) philosophy and the other partner does not place a high priority on TQM, conflicts are likely to develop in the working relationship.

2. *Relative dependence of the partners.* Collaborative relations are more likely to be successful if the dependence is important and equivalent between the two organizations.

3. *Technological edge contributions.* The buyer may represent an opportunity for a supplier to improve its product or process because of the customer's leading-edge application of the supplier's product or service. For example, collaborative codesign of industrial equipment can increase the supplier's competitive advantage.

Collaborative relationships require trust and commitment by both partners, since a considerable amount of proprietary information is shared. Evaluating the extent to which a supplier or manufacturer should enter into a collaborative relationship is an important concern for both partners. Several companies have drastically reduced the number of suppliers from which they purchase and are working more closely with each supplier. For example, by the early 1990s, Xerox had reduced its suppliers by 90 percent, from 5,000 to 500.[10]

Distribution Channel Relationships

Distribution channel relationships may involve transactional ties between producers, wholesalers, retailers, and consumer and industrial end users. Alternatively, more collaborative relationships may be developed through ownership, contractual commitments, or power and influence exercised by one of the channel organizations. For example, Wal-Mart has established strong relationships with the producers of the products it sells in retail stores.

Coordinating relationships with distribution channel members is an important responsibility for each of the organizations involved. The role of a channel member may be to direct and coordinate the activities of the entire channel or instead to be managed by the firm that has gained control of the entire channel. Channel relationships vary from situations where one organization manages the channel to those where no channel member manages the channel.

Developing Effective Relationships

Executives from marketing and other business functions may be responsible for managing relationships with customers, suppliers, producers, internal functions, and partner organizations. The success of these relationships is enhanced by spelling out the objective(s) of the relationship and developing relationship management guidelines.

Relationship Objectives

Objectives have to be developed for each of the major types of relationships. Included in these guidelines is establishing how much collaboration will be involved. In some situations, close collaboration may not be of interest to either party in the relationship. For example, if the partners differ concerning the type of relationship they seek, this issue must be resolved. Unless both partners develop trust in and a commitment to the relationship, it will not be successful. The partners must have compatible objectives.

Relationship Management Guidelines

Guidelines are available for managing relationships between buyers and sellers, channel members, and internal departments. Perhaps the most challenging relationship management situation is the strategic alliance. Collaboration among competitive firms is contrary to the traditional view of competition. The starting point is making a good choice of a partner. These relationships require careful planning, trust, willingness to share information, conflict resolution processes, leadership structure, recognition of interdependence and cultural differences among the partners, decisions about how to transfer technology, and means of learning from partners' strengths.[11]

Successful strategic alliances offer powerful advantages to the participants, but many alliances are not successful. Different cultures, lack of trust and commitment, and poor matching of shared competencies create problems between partners. Northwest Airlines and KLM Royal Dutch Airlines formed a successful alliance in the early 1990s that generated substantial profits for both partners. Nonetheless, by 1997 lack of trust and conflicting objectives threatened the future of the alliance.

After each partner yielded to the concerns of the other partner, Northwest and KLM agreed in 1997 to extend the alliance for 10 years. KLM sold its Northwest Airlines stock to Northwest, more than doubling the investment. The initial alliance allowed either partner to exit after giving 12 months' notice.

End Notes

1. Melanie Berger, "It's Your Move," *Sales & Marketing Management,* March 1998, pp. 45–46.
2. Erin Strout, "Launching an E-Business: A Survival Guide," *Sales & Marketing Management,* July 2000, pp. 89–96.
3. Ibid.
4. The following discussion is based on David W. Cravens, *Strategic Marketing,* 6th ed., Chapter 10 (Burr Ridge, IL: McGraw-Hill, 2000).
5. Ibid.
6. Regis McKenna, *Relationship Marketing* (Reading, MA: Addison-Wesley, 1991), p. 43.
7. Frederick E. Webster, Jr., "The Rediscovery of the Marketing Concept," *Business Horizons,* May–June 1988, p. 37.
8. James C. Anderson and James A. Narus, "Partnering as a Focused Market Strategy," *California Management Review,* Spring 1991, pp. 96–97.
9. Ibid., pp. 100–03.
10. John R. Emshuiler, "Suppliers Struggle to Improve Quality as Big Firms Slash Their Vendor Roles," *The Wall Street Journal,* August 16, 1991, p. B1.
11. Timothy M. Collings and Thomas L. Dooley, *Teaming Up for the 90s* (Homewood, IL: Business One Irwin, 1991), pp. 101–02.

CASES FOR PART 5

The network of business processes and organizations that allow the movement of materials from producers and distributors to consumers and organizational end users is vast in today's business world. The seven cases in this part examine this network in a wide variety of companies.

Case 5–1, Alligator Records, a video case, describes the distribution decision faced by that company. Could an independent blues recording label survive with regional distribution? Or should the company jump on the bandwagon of national Web distribution?

In **Case 5–2, Electro-Products Limited** (EPL) is a manufacturer of small home appliances. Located in a semirural area of the Czech Republic, the company exports a large proportion of its production under an exclusive agreement with a large European-based international electronics manufacturing and marketing firm. EPL would like a closer working relationship with this European firm; however, the export company is not interested.

Case 5–3, Konark Television India, considers the distribution strategy for a medium-size manufacturer of television sets in India. A slowing market growth rate is complicated by dealer activities thought to be damaging to Konark. Immediate actions need to be taken with respect to dealer relations. However, selecting the appropriate action is difficult without a long-term distribution strategy.

Several foreign companies are courting the Magnolia Group in **San Miguel Corporation: The Magnolia Group (Case 5–4).** The companies want to license Magnolia to produce and distribute ice cream products in the Philippines. Magnolia has to decide whether it needs a foreign partner. If it does, it can select from three companies expressing interest in a partnership or can pursue relations with other companies.

Entering the European market in 2001 appeared feasible for **Camar Automotive Hoist (Case 5–5).** There were three investment options for expanding into that market: (1) licensing, (2) a joint venture, and (3) direct investment. The key is determining which option will keep the company on the fast growth track.

Wentworth Industrial Cleaning Supplies (Case 5–6) in Lincoln, Nebraska, is experiencing a slowdown in growth. Sales of its products are below the projected volume. Total sales for the industry have increased, but Wentworth's competitors have been the benefactors. The vice president of marketing has been directed to identify the factors that are stunting growth and institute a program that will facilitate expansion.

The e-business case (**Case 5–7**) focuses on **Avon Products Inc.** and its new model of supply chain management and representative partnership. CEO Andrea Jung is helping to reconcile the door-to-door selling pioneer with the explosive growth of the Internet.

CASE 5–1
ALLIGATOR RECORDS

The National Association of Recording Merchandisers Independents Conference held in the fall of 1996 reflected changing times in the independent music community. Attendance at the conference was down. In the words of Chris Morris, writer for *Billboard,* "The consolidation of indie[1] distribution and the rise of exclusive national representation, which resulted in an erosion of the labels' presence in 1995, were again felt in declining numbers this year."[2]

With independent labels jumping on the consolidated distribution system train, Alligator Records, an independent blues recording label, was left with a distribution decision to make.

The Music Industry

The music industry provides a variety of products for its selective consumers. In the United States in 1998, 33 percent of music sales were in the rock genre, while country, rhythm and blues, pop, and rap accounted for 15 percent, 10 percent, 10 percent, and 10 percent, respectively. Other music categories were pooled to result in 22 percent of sales in 1998 (Exhibit 1). CDs had become the most prominent form of recording sales as a result of technological advances, convenience, and sound quality superior to that of cassettes and records.

The six nationally recognized companies in the music industry were Warner, PolyGram, Sony, BMG, MCA, and EMI. See Exhibits 2 and 3 for those companies' percentages of the US$11 billion music industry and overall recording sales. The independent companies tend to be "specialty" companies that concentrate on a specific genre of music. While the larger companies tend to sign popular groups without concern about which form of music an artist performs, the independent recording companies are inclined to focus on a specific genre. Alligator Records, an independent company, is dedicated solely to the blues.

What Are the Blues, and Who Got the Blues First?

As defined in the *Encyclopedia Britannica,* blues are the "secular folk music of American blacks" with "obscure origins among Southern blacks in the early 20th century." Blues music contains certain pitch inflections along with a call and response pattern. Instruments such as the guitar and harmonica often accompany a blues artist, although the

---

[1] *Indie* is an abbreviation typically used for the word *independent;* in this case it is used to describe independent distributors.

[2] Morris, Chris, "Declaration of Independents: Gloomy Atmosphere Pervades Narm Indies Conference," *Billboard,* October 26, 1996, online.

This case was written by Christine Lynn Connolly under the supervision of Victoria L. Crittenden, associate professor of marketing, Boston College, as a basis for class discussion rather than to illustrate either effective or ineffective handling of an administrative situation. The material was taken from secondary sources.

EXHIBIT 1   Music Market by Genre, 1996

Rock	33%
Country	15
Rhythm and blues	10
Pop	10
Rap	10
Other	22

Source: 1998 Gale Research, Inc., *Market Share Reporter.*

EXHIBIT 2   The $11 Billion Music Industry, 1995

Warner (Time Warner)	22.65%
PolyGram (Philips)	14.37
Sony (Sony)	13.19
BMG (Bertelsmann)	12.12
MCA (Seagrams)	10.42
EMI (Thorn-EMI)	8.61
Independents	18.64

Source: 1997 Gale Research, Inc., *Market Share Reporter.*

EXHIBIT 3   Company Shares Based on Album Sales, January–mid-May 1997

Warner Music	17.30%
Universal Music	14.91
EMI Music	13.50
BMG	13.21
PolyGram	11.82
Sony Music	11.61
Other	17.65

Source: 1997 Gale Research, Inc., *Market Share Reporter.*

lyrics and the singing are dominant. Blues singers use their voices to express their emotions and employ techniques such as "bending guitar strings on the neck of the guitar to create a whining sound."[3]

With its origins consisting of field hollers and work songs, the blues' hazy beginnings lay in the southern part of the United States after the Civil War. At first, the blues were sung mostly by southern black men, many of whom had been slaves on agricultural plantations. Other influences on the blues included church music, ragtime, and the folk and popular music of whites during that period. The first published composition came from W. C. Handy, titled "Memphis Blues," in 1912. After that, many songs claimed to fall in the blues genre. Georgia, the Carolinas, Texas, and Mississippi are the home of the rural blues. While each territory had a unique blues style, the Mississippi Delta blues were the most intense and influential. Although the blues were most notable

---

[3] "Blues," *Encyclopedia Britannica Online,* http://www.eb.com:180/bol/topic?eu=15992&sctn=1 (August 3, 1999).

among southern black men, some of the first recordings were made in the 1920s by black women who usually sang with a jazz band behind them. Mamie Smith, Ma Rainey, and Bessie Smith were among the women whose style became known as the classic blues.

Blues began to spread as black Americans left the South to migrate to cities in the North during the Great Depression and the two world wars. The northern urban areas created a new environment for the blues. With the addition of percussion and electric guitars, the blues form was altered again. Blues took root in northern cities such as St. Louis (Missouri), Detroit (Michigan), and Chicago (Illinois), where Alligator Records was later born.

Who's Got the Blues Now?

Those who are not fans may consider blues music to be on the way to extinction. However, ask a blues fan about this genre of music and he or she will tell you that the blues is experiencing healthy growth and is now more popular than ever. "Veteran observers say that the popularity of the music today is virtually unprecedented."[4] The vice president of catalog development at MCA, Andy McKaie, states, "The audience for the blues is the largest that the blues has had, period. This revival is not going away at any time."[5] Interest in the blues genre has become evident at the cash registers as well. Bruce Iglauer, owner of Chicago's top independent blues label, Alligator Records, says, "I'm looking at our best year for us, and without a blockbuster release. . . . It looks to me like we're going to end up billing $500,000 to $750,000 more than last year."[6]

Not only are the independent specialty companies prospering from the popularity explosion of the blues, the major labels are tapping the source as well. RCA Records recently released *Damn Right, I've Got The Blues,* an album by the Chicago blues guitarist Buddy Guy. That release resulted in sales of close to 250,000 copies. There is a demand for blues, and the supply is plentiful. With both independent and major blues labels thriving in the music industry, there has been change in the distribution system.

How Do We Get the Blues?

Two types of distribution systems exist in the music industry: national webs and regional systems. Major labels, such as Sony and BMG, generally use national webs of distribution. That is, large distributors have gained access to retailers across the nation and have managed to develop an intricate system of distributing music products nationwide. Major labels use these webs to disperse their wide variety of different artists' music to the large, diverse fan population.

However, the independents have taken issue with national distribution. Bruce Iglauer of Alligator Records stated, "How much of the business is dominated by five or 10 buyers in the country? You've got 10 people making decisions for the majority of the stores in the U.S."[7] This statement mirrored the problems with national distribution systems. There were fewer choices for the recording companies in terms of distribution options.

---

[4] Morris, Chris, "Current Boom Dwarfs 1960's: New And Vintage Music Shakes Its Moneymaker on Stage, Disc, Radio," *Billboard,* May 14, 1994.

[5] Ibid.

[6] Ibid.

[7] Morris, Chris, "Indies Consolidate, Re-evaluate Their Relationship with the Majors—and Undergo Some Major Changes," *Billboard,* May 15, 1993, p. 57.

Smaller, independent companies can either join the major labels in using the national webs of distribution or stand by the regional distribution system. Regional distribution systems allow distributors to maintain a well-managed, efficient distribution web in one area of the country. Within the blues market, the target market and the consumers' blues artist preferences vary in different areas of the country. The South has proved to be a hot-selling area for the blues genre. Nonchain retail outlets have helped black-oriented albums post large sales numbers. "Peggy Scott-Adams' Miss Butch/Mardi Gras Records album, 'Help Yourself,' developed out of the regional popularity of the song 'Bill.' "[8]

With distribution systems changing, some regional distributors had left the business while others had been purchased by larger distribution companies. "Many observers tie the radical realignment of the indie picture to the concurrent consolidation of national music retailing, which has seen a shift in recent years from a preponderance of regional chains to a focus on centralized ownership of a greatly reduced number of national webs."[9] Regional distribution systems, however, were not lost. "The kind of regionals we saw in the past will continue to exist, but they will do more niche marketing. There will always be a product that can't be handled in the mass market"[10]

Clay Pasternack of Cleveland's Action Music Sales said it most clearly when he described the changing and competitive world of music distribution: "All it does is give people more options. It's a matter of what's right for people. But I still tend to think that one of the advantages of regional distribution is that you're right there in the market and better able to react to what's going on."[11]

Alligator Records

Alligator Records, founded by CEO Bruce Iglauer, is a dominant independent label in the blues music industry. The name was given to Iglauer by a girlfriend who called the record company entrepreneur an alligator because Iglauer had a habit of clicking his teeth when he listened to music. The company started when Iglauer decided to use a US$2,500 inheritance to support his love for the blues by opening a blues recording company in Chicago. He did this so that he could produce an album for his favorite band, Hound Dog Taylor and the House Rockers. Iglauer produced 1,000 copies of the album. The distribution system consisted of Iglauer and his car. Iglauer drove from Chicago to New York, stopping on the way many times to promote his first production. He got airtime on radio stations and sold albums at some of the progressive colleges on the way. Eventually, the album got enough airtime and Bruce could head to nearby distributors and say, "I got two or three radio stations in your area to play this album. Would you sell it to the stores for me?"[12] Alligator Records was born.

Slowly the company grew. Alligator Records became popular with recordings by artists such as Koko Taylor and Albert Collins. In 1975 Alligator hired its first employee and moved out of Bruce's apartment and into a three-bedroom house on the north side of Chicago. After several more years and a few Grammy-winning artists under its belt, Alligator once again was growing too big for its home. In 1985 Alligator relocated to a nearby building. At that time, the company had seven full-time employees and was

---

[8] Morris, Chris, "Blues Sees Major Shift in Marketplace," *Billboard,* March 1, 1997, p. 1.

[9] Morris, "Indies Consolidate, Re-evaluate Their Relationship with the Majors."

[10] Ibid.

[11] Ibid.

[12] http://www.alligator.com.

making some serious promotional efforts. The label maintained its own promotion, publicity, and marketing departments. Alligator also grew internationally by expanding into Australia, Argentina, and Europe. The production of albums increased sevenfold.

By 1996 the Alligator staff had grown and gained strength in the blues community. As Iglaver explained, the focus had not changed: "I just want to keep bringing the blues to new fans and getting them as excited about it as I am."[13] Alligator had become the largest independent contemporary blues label in the world. The company had a catalog of over 150 titles and had won many prestigious blues artist awards, including Grammys and the W. C. Handy awards. Knowing that times were changing, Iglauer began to evaluate the company's position. With many independent companies falling through the cracks, Iglauer had reason to be concerned. Should he stick with the regional distribution even though many of the smaller distributors were being bought or banding together, or should he jump on the wagon and use national webs to distribute his pride and joy, blues music?

----

[13] Ibid.

Sources

"Blues." *Encyclopedia Britannica Online,* http://www.eb.com:180/bol/topic?eu=15992&sctn=1 (August 3, 1999).

Morris, Chris. "Indies Consolidate, Re-evaluate Their Relationship with the Majors—and Undergo Some Major Changes." *Billboard,* May 15, 1993, p. 57.

Stack, Peter. "Record Label Has a Right to Sing the Blues, Alligator's Koko Taylor, Lonnie Brooks, Katie Webster." *San Francisco Chronicle,* Daily Datebook, February 10, 1993, p. E2.

Mr. Josef Novak,[1] recently appointed manager of marketing and marketing analysis at Electro-Products Limited (EPL), is faced with a dilemma. A number of marketing issues important to his firm have surfaced suddenly. Some of these issues relate directly to the role marketing needs to play in the future operations of the firm; others relate to the strategic question of survival. The issue that is most troublesome is EPL's relationship with a large European client.

EPL, located in a semirural area of Czechoslovakia, is a manufacturer of small home appliances. Currently, a significant portion of EPL's production is being exported under an exclusive agreement with a large European-based international electronics manufacturing and marketing firm (LIEM). Under this agreement, EPL is responsible for manufacturing hand-held vacuum cleaners for LIEM. LIEM markets those products under its own brand name in Western markets. EPL has exclusive rights to market the products domestically under its own brand name, ZETA.

The Czechoslovak economy is going through a major transition. A competitive domestic market is emerging. Domestic and foreign competitors are entering the market. Both EPL and LIEM have realized that the Czechoslovak market needs to be reexamined systematically in light of all the changes taking place. Not only is EPL looking for market opportunities in its own domestic market, it also is concerned with survival in a rapidly changing economy—dealing with privatization, foreign ownership, and new consumer demand among other strategic uncertainties.

Before the changes in Czechoslovakia that began in late 1989, LIEM had no interest in its internal market. Since the changes, however, LIEM is actively looking for market opportunities in EPL's domestic market. EPL's small marketing group is faced with several issues that potentially could evolve into major confrontations with LIEM.

EPL realizes that its agreement with LIEM helps EPL understand product development efforts in the context of a large firm. It also helps EPL engineers comprehend the quality control requirements of Western markets. And to a certain degree, the agreement assures EPL of future revenue. However, LIEM is a large international firm that views EPL as a captive supplier of a product whose attributes are set by LIEM's marketing personnel.

Mr. Novak would like to develop a cooperative relationship with LIEM. He is interested in working closely with LIEM's marketing personnel so that he and his staff can learn more about marketing practices in Western Europe. Mr. Novak is particularly curious about the entire product development process used by LIEM. He would like to know more about it. LIEM's management is not interested and is ignoring any such overtures from EPL.

---

[1] All names of individuals and firms, domestic or foreign, have been changed.

This case was prepared by George Tesar, visiting professor, Umeå Business School, Umeå University, Umeå, Sweden, and Marie Pribova, Czechoslovak Management Center, Celakovice, Czechoslovakia. At the time this case was written, Professor Tesar was on sabbatical leave from the University of Wisconsin, Whitewater.

EPL organized a small marketing group over two years ago. Until recently this group did not play a significant role in EPL's strategic management. Under the current leadership of Mr. Novak, marketing concepts are slowly being recognized and accepted in the strategic development and growth of the firm. The marketing group is being asked to generate new opportunities for the entire firm. Plans and strategies are being developed as part of this new marketing effort.

The latest plans developed by the marketing group have three important objectives: (1) developing an effective and efficient domestic distribution and sales network for its products, (2) broadening its cooperation with foreign firms in the areas of product development and cross-marketing arrangements, and (3) improving the overall image of its ZETA brand name in Western European markets.

According to Mr. Novak, these are realistic and strategically implementable objectives under normally operating market conditions. However, given the nature of the transitional economy in Czechoslovakia today, these objectives present a complex combination of challenges not only to the small marketing group but also to the entire firm.

Background Information

EPL has been manufacturing and exporting small home appliances since 1943. After the general nationalization in the late 1940s it became the sole producer of small home appliances in Czechoslovakia, and since late 1989 it has been trying to become an important competitor in the international small home appliance industry.[2]

In the past EPL produced a wide range of small home appliances and heating elements. Its current catalog lists the range of products available for domestic and export sales (Exhibit 1). However, before late 1989, approximately 43 percent of its total production consisted of vacuum cleaners and 13 percent consisted of steam and dry irons. These two product lines accounted for a total of 56 percent of EPL's production.

EPL exported about one-quarter of its products to Eastern and Western European markets. Western European markets demanded higher quality and better-designed products from EPL. Quality was not an issue in Eastern Europe due to general shortages of consumer products in those markets. Vacuum cleaners accounted for 68 percent of exports, and dry irons for 24 percent; all remaining products produced by EPL accounted for only 8 percent (Exhibit 2).

The primary activity of EPL has been manufacturing vacuum cleaners. According to the marketing group, hand-held vacuum cleaners represent the most lucrative and most advanced product in EPL's product line. They believe that these products exemplify the level of quality found in most Western European products intended for the demanding Western consumer.

From the overall perspective of EPL's management, the contract with LIEM enabled the technical and administrative staff of EPL to understand the dynamics of Western markets. It enabled EPL to raise its manufacturing standards to world-class production, and consequently, EPL is in a better position to market its own products in world markets.

The marketing group, now under the leadership of Mr. Novak, was formed at the end of 1990. It is positioned too low in the organization to make significant impact on top

---

[2] EPL has a relatively long history among manufacturers in Czechoslovakia. Over the past 50 or more years its ownership has been in question. Between the late 1940s and November 1989 it held a monopoly on the manufacture of small home appliances and a variety of home and industrial electrical heating elements. EPL still makes most of these products, but their overall contribution to its operations and profits is not known.

EXHIBIT 1   Small Appliances Currently Produced by EPL

Blenders
Coffee grinders
Coffeemakers
Dry flatirons
Electric countertop units
Electric frying pans
Electric pans
Food mixers
Food processors
Hand-held food mixers
Heating elements (domestic use)
Heating elements (industrial use)
Plastic welding units
Portable electric plates
Portable grills
Portable space heaters
Roasting ovens
Steam irons
Vacuum cleaners
Warm air ventilators

EXHIBIT 2   Production of Small Home Appliances and Domestic and Foreign Sales before 1989

Product Line	Production	Sales		
		Domestic	Foreign	Total
Vacuum cleaners	43%	32%	68%	100%
Steam and dry irons	13	76	24	100
Other	44	92	8	100
Total	100%			

Note: These percentages are estimates only. Actual production figures are not available.

management's decision-making performance. Mr. Novak came to the group from engineering; he was in charge of product design and development. Currently he and his group are developing promotional, retailing, and distribution strategies for EPL products in the domestic market.

Working with a Trading Company

In the past EPL was represented exclusively by Alfa, a state-owned export trading company in Prague. Alfa was responsible for all of EPL's exporting activities, including initiation of contacts, negotiations of sales agreements, and delivery of finished products. EPL's marketing personnel, or in the past the individuals responsible for product development and sales, had little or no direct contact with customers. Alfa also was responsible for all communications between EPL and its customers abroad.

This was not unusual before late 1989. State-owned export trading companies represented all Czechoslovak manufacturing firms and state-owned enterprises abroad. Management of many firms and enterprises had no direct contact with foreign customers or consumers. It was only in early 1990 that Czechoslovak firms and enterprises became free to conduct business abroad without the state-owned export trading companies. But even after these changes were made, the state-owned export trading companies retained important information about foreign contacts, clients, customers, and consumers. In other words, they withheld the export technology from the firms they had represented.

In some cases, the client firms were completely dependent on individuals within the export trading companies and could not operate without them. This dependency resulted from the structural inability to communicate with the outside world, the lack of foreign language competency, and even the inability to travel to foreign markets.[3]

Consequently, EPL's top management and the entire engineering, manufacturing, and purchasing staffs had little or no direct contact with clients such as LIEM. They did not understand LIEM's consumers. Alfa served as a filter for all marketing and competitive information.

The Agreement with LIEM

An agreement between EPL and LIEM to produce a new hand-held vacuum cleaner was negotiated by Alfa in 1987. Before the November 1989 political changes in Czechoslovakia, LIEM had insisted that the agreement be kept secret. The agreement clearly defines the roles and responsibilities of each party. LIEM is responsible for the development of product specifications based on marketing information. The overall product specifications can be classified into several categories, as shown in Exhibit 3.

These product specifications not only represent engineering specifications, they also provide clear cost and expense guidelines. In other words, under this contract EPL became a captive fabricator and supplier of hand-held vacuum cleaners to LIEM.

It also was agreed that during the engineering process, testing would be conducted by both parties separately. This included testing, verification, and documentation of each step in the engineering process. Any tooling, dies, and fixtures were subject to inspection and testing. The prototypes and products produced during pilot production runs would be subject to testing by both parties.

EPL was able to calculate the cost of engineering and manufacturing at the end of the pilot production of all models specified under the contract. It became apparent that EPL could not deliver any of the three models at the price specified by LIEM. After a series of negotiations, LIEM agreed to a price increase of 18 percent. At the same time the projected mix of models based on the original set of specifications was also changed, as indicated in Exhibit 4.

An important factor in the arrangement between the two firms was the way in which the representatives of the two firms met to discuss important points during the engineering of the hand-held vacuum cleaner. All meetings were scheduled by Alfa, and five were held during the product engineering process, as shown in Exhibit 5. Notes were taken during each meeting; the main points on which both sides agreed were recorded; new deadlines were set; and managers responsible for specific tasks were appointed.

---

[3] Many of these situations were created by government policies. Individual manufacturing firms had no input into the creation or implementation of those policies.

EXHIBIT 3   Product Specifications for a Hand-Held Vacuum Cleaner

Dimensions and technical parameters
Physical design and color specifications
Number and type of models (economy, standard, and deluxe)
Purchase price of each model
Annual purchase schedule of each model for the next four years

EXHIBIT 4   The Original Purchase Schedule by LIEM Compared to the Final Purchase Schedule for 1991

	Model		
Purchase Schedule	*Economy*	*Standard*	*DeLuxe*
Original	25%	55%	20%
Final	35	45	20

EXHIBIT 5   Hand-Held Vacuum Cleaner: List of Individual Steps from the Time of Negotiations to Product Completion

Beginning of 1987	Negotiations between EPL and LIEM begin.
January 21, 1988	Product developed by LIEM.
March 15, 1988 Meeting	Product designed and engineering specifications completed by LIEM.
May 1, 1988 Meeting	Mutual agreement between EPL and LIEM on the final product design, engineering specifications, and cost structure.
August 1, 1988	Production of the first functional prototype by EPL.
November 1, 1988	Production of the final prototype by EPL.
December 1, 1988 Meeting	Testing and verification of the final prototype by LIEM.
February 1, 1989 Meeting	Product changes and modifications by EPL resulting from final prototype testing by LIEM.
February 1, 1990	Technical development and manufacturing engineering for mass production of the final product by EPL.
March 1, 1990	Delivery of manufactured products by EPL to LIEM for final testing and verifications. End of pilot production run for EPL.
May 1, 1990 Meeting	Testing completed by LIEM. Calculation of final costs by EPL completed.
July 1, 1990	Final product modifications completed by EPL.
October 1, 1990	LIEM's purchasing process begins.
December 1, 1990	Mass production by EPL begins.
January 15, 1991	First shipment leaves EPL's production facility.

EPL's representatives included the chief design engineer, the engineer directly responsible for the product, and the manager responsible for the pricing and delivery of the product. From the LIEM side the meetings were attended by the product manager, product designer, technical specialist, quality control specialist, and sales manager. Top management of EPL did not meet routinely with the product manager from LIEM but held only informal discussions during trade fairs or industrial exhibitions.

Once the product engineering process had been completed for the hand-held vacuum cleaner, all the decisions regarding the production machinery, sourcing of raw material and components, and sourcing of packaging material were the responsibility of EPL. Product modifications during manufacturing were not allowed under the agreement. Only minor production changes or changes that did not alter the cosmetic or functional characteristics of the product could be made without LIEM's approval.

Additional factors such as cosmetic modifications, including color changes, were incorporated into the engineering process as necessary. Color specifications were changed four times during the engineering process. Final performance and quality testing before commercialization was completed by LIEM. The final product was shown at two major exhibitions. Two months after the presentation of the product, the product was available for sale in retail outlets.

From the perspective of Mr. Novak, the agreement between EPL and LIEM has several problems:

1. EPL is not part of the marketing process managed by LIEM.
2. LIEM ignores requests by EPL for one or more of its managers to visit LIEM's operations.
3. EPL cannot communicate directly with LIEM due to the lack of language capabilities.

The language barrier presents the most important problem for EPL. Representatives from Alfa sit in on all meetings, including meetings that are strictly technical in nature, and serve as translators and interpreters. Recently, LIEM offered to work directly with EPL without involving Alfa, but EPL does not have marketing personnel with the language capabilities needed to conduct negotiations.

EPL's Marketing Perspective

The situation at EPL has been changing rapidly since late 1989. The marketing department wants to play a larger role in the strategic management of the firm. According to Mr. Novak, EPL as a manufacturer has learned a great deal from cooperation with LIEM. EPL has learned how to enter highly competitive foreign markets at the same time that its domestic market is going through a major transition.

Cooperation with a large international firm that is consistently concerned about product quality in highly competitive markets offers an opportunity for EPL to learn what these markets demand so that in the future EPL can enter them on its own. From a marketing perspective, this cooperation enables EPL, to a degree, to develop a fundamental understanding of the role marketing plays in the development and engineering of consumer products and at the same time realize how important quality standards are in competitive markets abroad.

EPL's management offered to cooperate with LIEM as part of the new marketing perspective. LIEM appears uninterested. The relationship with Alfa changed significantly after late 1989. Alfa's management established a new unit concerned only with exporting EPL's products. Mr. Novak sees a strong potential for cooperation with this unit. EPL, with Alfa's assistance, also exports some of its vacuum cleaners to Western Europe under brand names owned by various retail store chains.

LIEM is interested in entering the Czechoslovak market with its own brand name, even with products manufactured by EPL. The same products manufactured under

LIEM's label and under EPL's label would compete side by side. EPL offered to represent LIEM in the Czechoslovak market, but LIEM declined the offer and opened offices for all its products in Prague and Bratislava. Recently, LIEM's unit dealing with small home appliances offered EPL the possibility of negotiating representation in the future.

As part of the new marketing effort at EPL, some of the marketing specialists suggest that perhaps EPL should improve the image of its ZETA brand name and concentrate on sales and distribution of its own products in Western Europe.

EPL is at a crossroads for its manufacturing and marketing operations. It wants to become better known in its own domestic market. It also realizes that it needs to enter foreign markets to generate foreign capital for its operations. The agreement with LIEM is bothersome for EPL's marketing group. And most significantly, EPL's business climate and the domestic market are progressing through rapid changes.

CASE 5–3
KONARK TELEVISION INDIA

On December 1, 1990, Mr. Ashok Bhalla began to prepare for a meeting scheduled for the next week with his boss, Mr. Atul Singh. The meeting would focus on distribution strategy for Konark Television Ltd., a medium-size manufacturer of television sets in India. At issue was the nature of immediate actions to be taken as well as long-range planning. Mr. Bhalla was the managing director of Konark, responsible for a variety of activities, including marketing. Mr. Singh was the president.

The Television Industry in India

The television industry in India started in late 1959 with the Indian government using a UNESCO grant to build a small transmitter in New Delhi. The station soon began to broadcast short programs promoting education, health, and family planning. Daily transmissions were limited to 20 minutes. In 1965 the station began broadcasting variety and entertainment programs and expanded its programming to one hour per day. Programming increased to three hours per day in 1970 and to four hours by 1976, when commercials were first permitted. The number of transmission centers in the country grew slowly but steadily during this period.

In July 1982 the Indian government announced a special expansion plan, providing 680 million rupees (Rs) to extend its television network to cover about 70 percent of India's population. By early 1988 the 245 TV transmitters in operation were estimated to have met this goal. The government then authorized the construction of 417 new transmitters, which would raise network coverage to over 80 percent of India's population. By late 1990 daily programming averaged almost 11 hours per day, making television the most popular medium of information, entertainment, and education in India. The network itself consisted of one channel except in large metropolitan areas, where a second channel was available. Both television channels were owned and operated by the government.

Despite the huge increase in network coverage, many in the TV industry still would describe the Indian government's attitude toward television as conservative. In fact, some would say that it was only the pressure of TV broadcasts from neighboring Sri Lanka and Pakistan that forced India's rapid expansion. Current policy was to view the industry as a luxury industry capable of bearing heavy taxes. Thus, the government charged Indian manufacturers high import duties on the foreign manufactured components that they purchased plus heavy excise duties on sets they assembled; in addition, state governments charged consumers sales taxes that ranged from 1 to 17 percent. The result was that duties and taxes accounted for almost one-half of the retail price of a color TV set and about one-third of the retail price of a black and white set. Retail prices of TV sets in India were estimated at almost double the prevalent world prices.

This case was written by Fulbright Lecturer and Associate Professor James E. Nelson, University of Colorado at Boulder, and Dr. Piyush K. Sinha, associate professor, Xavier Institute of Management, Bhubaneswar, India. The authors thank Professor Roger A. Kerin, Southern Methodist University, for his helpful comments on this case. The case is intended for educational purposes rather than to illustrate either effective or ineffective decision making. Some data in the case are disguised. © 1991 by James E. Nelson.

EXHIBIT 1   **Production of TV Sets in India
(00,000 omitted)**

	Black and White			
Year	*36 cm**	*51 cm**	*Color*	*Total*
1980	—	3.1	—	3.1
1981	—	3.7	—	3.7
1982	—	4.4	—	4.4
1983	—	5.7	0.7	6.4
1984	1.8	6.6	2.8	11.2
1985	4.4	13.6	6.9	24.9
1986	8.2	13.3	9.0	30.5
1987	17.0	14.0	12.0	43.0
1988	28.0	16.0	13.0	57.0
1989	32.0†	18.0†	13.0†	63.0†

* Diagonal screen measurement.

† Estimated.

Such high prices limited demand. The number of sets in use in 1990 was estimated at about 25 million. This number provided coverage to about 15 percent of the country's population, assuming five viewers per set. To increase coverage to 80 percent of the population would require over 100 million additional TV sets, again assuming five viewers per set. This figure represented a huge latent demand, almost 16 years of production at 1989 levels (see Exhibit 1). Many in the industry expected that the production and sales of TV sets would grow rapidly if prices were reduced.

Indian Consumers

The population of India was estimated at approximately 850 million people. The majority lived in rural areas and small villages. The gross domestic product per capita was estimated at $450 for 1990.

In sharp contrast to the masses, however, the television market concentrated on the affluent middle and upper social classes, variously estimated at some 12 percent to 25 percent of the total population. Members of this segment exhibited a distinctly urban lifestyle. They owned videocassette recorders, portable radiocassette players, motor scooters, and compact cars. They earned MBA degrees, exercised in health spas, and traveled abroad. They lived in dual-income households, sent their children to private schools, and practiced family planning. In short, members of this segment exhibited tastes and purchase behaviors much like those of their middle-class, professional counterparts in the United States and Europe.

While there was no formal marketing research available, Mr. Bhalla thought he knew the consumer fairly well: "The typical purchase probably represents a joint decision by the husband and wife to buy. After all, they will be spending over one month's salary for our most popular color model." That model was now priced at retail at Rs 11,300, slightly less than the retail prices of many national brands. However, a majority in the target segment probably did not perceive a price advantage for Konark. Indeed, the segment seemed somewhat insensitive to differentials in the range of Rs 10,000 to Rs 14,000, considering their TV sets to be valued possessions that added to the furnishing of their drawing rooms. Rather than price, most consumers seemed more influenced by promotion and dealer activities.

TV Manufacturers in India

Approximately 140 different companies manufactured TV sets in India in 1989. However, many produced fewer than 1,000 sets per year and could not be considered major competitors. Further, Mr. Bhalla expected that many would not survive 1990; the trend definitely was toward a competition between 20 or 30 large firms. Most manufacturers sold in India only, although a few had begun to export sets (mostly black and white) to nearby countries.

Most competitors were private companies whose actions ultimately were evaluated by a board of directors and shareholders. Typical of this group was Videocon. The company was formed in 1983, yet it was thought to be India's largest producer of color sets. A recent trade journal article had attributed Videocon's success to a strategy that combined higher dealer margins (2 percent higher than industry norms), attractive dealer incentives (Singapore trips, etc.), a reasonably good dealer network (about 200 dealers in 18 of India's 25 states), an excellent price range (from Rs 7,000 to Rs 18,000), and an advertising campaign that featured Indian film star Sridevi dressed in a Japanese kimono. Onida, the other leader in color, took a different approach. Its margins were slightly below industry standards, its prices were higher (Rs 13,000 to Rs 15,000), and its advertising strategy was the most aggressive in the industry. Many consumers seemed sold on Onida before they ever visited a retailer.

The major competitors in the black and white market were considered by Mr. Bhalla to be Crown, Salora, Bush, and Dyanora. Those four companies distributed black and white sets to most major markets in the country. (Crown and Bush manufactured color sets as well.) The strengths of these competitors were considered to be high brand recognition and strong dealer networks. In addition, several Indian states had one or two brands, such as Konark and Uptron, whose local success depended greatly on tax shelters provided by state governments.

All TV sets produced by the different manufacturers could be classified into two basic sizes: 51 centimeters and 36 centimeters. The larger size was a console model, while the smaller was designed as a portable. Black and white sets differed little in styling. Differences in picture quality and chassis reliability were present; however, these differences tended to be difficult for most consumers to distinguish and evaluate. In contrast, differences in product features were more noticeable. Black and white sets came with and without handles, built-in voltage regulators, built-in antennas, electronic tuners, audio and video tape sockets, and on-screen displays. Warranties differed in terms of coverage and time periods. Retail prices for black and white sets across India ranged from about Rs 2,000 to Rs 3,500, with the average thought by Mr. Bhalla to be around Rs 2,600.

Differences between competing color sets seemed more pronounced. Styling was more distinctive, with manufacturers supplying a variety of cabinet designs, cabinet finishes, and control arrangements. Konark and a few other manufacturers recently had introduced a portable color set in hopes of stimulating demand. Quality and performance variations were again difficult for most consumers to recognize. Differences in features were substantial. Some color sets featured automatic contrast and brightness controls, on-screen displays of channel tuning and time, sockets for video recorders and external computers, remote control devices, high-fidelity speakers, cable TV capabilities, and flat-screen picture tubes. Retail prices were estimated to range from about Rs 7,000 (for a small-screen portable) to Rs 19,000 (large-screen console), with an average around Rs 12,000.

Advertising practices varied considerably among manufacturers. Many smaller manufacturers used only newspaper advertisements that tended to be small. Larger manufacturers, including Konark, also advertised in newspapers but used quarter-page or larger advertisements. Larger manufacturers also spent substantial amounts on magazine, outdoor, and television advertising. Videocon, for example, was thought to have spent about Rs 25 million, or about 4 percent of its sales revenue, on advertising in 1989. Onida's percentage might be as much as twice that amount. Most advertisements for TV sets tended to stress product features and product quality, although a few were based primarily on whimsy and fantasy. Most ads would not mention price. Perhaps 10 percent of newspaper advertising appeared in the form of cooperative advertising, featuring the product prominently in the ad and listing local dealers. Manufacturers would design and place cooperative ads and pay upward of 80 percent of media costs.

Konark Television Ltd.

Konark Television Ltd. began operations in 1973 with the objective of manufacturing and marketing small black and white TV sets to the Orissa state market. Orissa is on the east coast of India, directly below the state of West Bengal and Calcutta. The early years of operation found production leveling at about 5,000 sets per year. However, in 1982 the company adopted a more aggressive strategy when it became clear that the national market for TV sets was going to grow rapidly. At the same time, the state government invested Rs 1.5 million in Konark in order to produce color sets. Konark also began expanding its dealer network to nearby Indian states and to more distant large metropolitan areas. Sales revenues in 1982 were approximately Rs 80 million.

The number of Konark models produced grew rapidly to 10, evenly divided between color and black and white sets. (Exhibit 2 shows a sales brochure describing Konark's top-of-the-line color model.) Sales revenues increased as well, to Rs 640 million for 1989, based on sales of 290,000 units. For 1990, sales revenues and unit volume were expected to increase by 25 percent and 15 percent, respectively, while gross margin was expected to remain at 20 percent of revenues. In early 1990 the state government added another Rs 2.5 million to strengthen Konark's equity base despite an expectation that the company would barely break even for 1990. Employment in late 1990 was almost 700 people. Company headquarters remained in Bhubaneswar, the state capital.

Manufacturing facilities also were in Bhubaneswar except for some assembly performed by three independent distributors. Assembly activity was done to save state sales taxes and lower the prices paid by consumers; that is, many Indian states charged two levels of sales taxes depending on whether the set was produced within the state. The state of Maharashtra (containing Bombay), for example, charged a sales tax of 4 percent for TV sets produced within the state and 16.5 percent for sets produced outside the state. Sales taxes for West Bengal (Calcutta) were 6 percent and 16.5 percent, while rates for Uttar Pradesh (New Delhi) were 0 percent and 12.5 percent. State governments were indifferent to whether assembly was performed by an independent distributor or by Konark as long as the activity took place inside the state borders. Current manufacturing capacity at Konark was around 400,000 units per year. Capacity easily could be expanded by 80 percent with the addition of a second shift.

The Konark line of TV sets was designed by engineers at Grundig, Gmbh., a German manufacturer known for quality electronic products. This technical collaboration saved Konark a great deal of effort each year in designing and developing new products. And the resulting product line was considered by many in the industry to be of higher quality than the lines of many competitors. Circuitry was well designed, and production engineers at the factory paid close attention to quality control. In addition, each

EXHIBIT 2 Konark Sales Brochure

Presenting the amazing new colour TV 'Galaxy Plus'

EXHIBIT 2 (continued)

The New Colour TV from Konark. 'Galaxy Plus'.
Incorporating all the sophisticated features likely to be introduced in the next few years.

Superior German technology. That's what sets the new 'Galaxy Plus' apart from all other colour TVS.

One of the latest models of GRUNDIG (W. Germany), world leaders in entertainment electronics. Brought to you by Konark Television Limited.

A symbol of German perfection

The Galaxy Plus combines the best of everything: World-famous German circuitry and components. The latest international TV technology. And the most demanding standards of picture and sound quality.

All of which make it more sophisticated. More dependable.

Features that are a connoisseur's delight.

The Galaxy Plus has several advanced features which offer you an extraordinary audio-visual experience, the like of which you will probably not feel with any other make.

What the Galaxy Plus offers you that other TVs don't

Never-before picture quality

 Through the world's latest Colour Transient Improvement (CTI) technology. Which reduces picture distortion. And improves colour sharpness. Giving you a crystal-clear picture and more natural colours.

Programmes from all over the world

The Galaxy Plus is capable of bringing you the best of international TV networks. Thanks to satellite dish antenna, a unique 7-system versatility, and 99 channels with memory.

These features of the Galaxy Plus also help it play all types of Video Cassettes. Without any picture or sound distortion.

Simultaneous connection with external devices

 An exclusive 20 pin Euro AV socket helps you connect the Galaxy Plus simultaneously with all external audio/video devices: Computers, VCRs, Video games. And cable TV.

While its automatic colour and brightness tuning save you the bother of frequent knob-fiddling.

Catch all your favourite programmes. Always.

You can preset the Galaxy Plus to switch itself on and off for your favourite programmes. Or, for worry-free operation by your children, in your absence.

Your own musical alarm clock

An on-screen time display reminds you of an important programme or appointment. While a built-in chimer wakes you up every day. Pleasantly.

Automatic pre-selection and operation

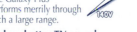 Select specific stations or external functions, code them in the 39+AV programme memory of the Galaxy Plus. And then, get them at the touch of a button. On the full-function Remote Control.

Handles wide voltage fluctuation

From a heart-stopping low of 140V. To a shocking high of 260V. The Galaxy Plus performs merrily through such a large range.

Richer, better TV sound

A higher audio output (8W) brings you all the beauty and power of full-bodied sound and clarity.

Saves power and money

Unlike other TVs, the Galaxy Plus uses only 60W. Besides, it also switches to the stand-by-mode automatically, when there is no TV signal for over 10 minutes.

Both features help you save precious electricity and money.

From Konark Television Limited

The futuristic Galaxy Plus is brought to you by Konark Television Limited. Through its nationwide network of over 500 sales outlets. Each of which also provide you prompt after-sales service. Should you ever need it.

The revolutionary new Galaxy Plus. See it in action at your nearest dealer. Compare it with every other make available in the local market.

And see how, feature by advanced feature, the Galaxy Plus is truly years ahead of its time. And the competition.

A marvel of German Technology

Konark Television Limited
(A Government of Orissa Enterprise)
Electronic Bhawan, Bhubaneswar 751 010. Phone: 53441 Telex: 0675-271

Konark set was operated for 24 hours as a test of reliability before being shipped. The entire line reflected Konark's strategy of attempting to provide the market with a quality product at prices below those of the competition. In retail stores in Orissa, the lowest-priced black and white model marketed by Konark sold to consumers for about Rs 2,200, while its most expensive color set sold for about Rs 15,000. Sales of the latter model had been disappointing to date. The premium market for color sets was quite small and seemed to be dominated by three national manufacturers.

Konark had a well-established network of more than 500 dealers located in 12 Indian states. In eight states Konark sold its products directly to dealers through branch offices (Exhibit 3) operated by a Konark area manager. Each branch office also contained two or three salesmen who were assigned specific sales territories. Together, branch offices were expected to account for about 30 percent of Konark's sales revenues and cost Konark about Rs 10 million in fixed and variable expenses for 1990. In three states Konark used instead the services of independent distributors to sell to dealers. The three distributors carried only Konark TV sets and earned a margin of 3 percent (based on cost) for all their activities, including assembly. All dealers and distributors were authorized to service Konark sets. The branch offices monitored all service activities.

In the state of Orissa, Konark used a large branch office to sell to approximately 250 dealers. In addition, Konark used company-owned showrooms as a second channel of distribution. Konark would lease space for showrooms at one or two locations in larger cities and display the complete line. The total cost of operating a showroom was estimated at about Rs 100,000 per year. Prospective customers often preferred to visit a showroom because they could easily compare different models and talk directly to a Konark employee. However, they seldom purchased—only about 5 percent of Orissa's unit sales came from the 10 showrooms in the state. Buyers preferred instead to purchase from dealers because dealers were known to bargain and sell at a discount from the list price. In contrast, Konark showrooms were under strict orders to sell all units at list price. About half of Konark's 1990 revenues would come from Orissa.

The appointment of dealers either by Konark or by its distributors was made under certain conditions (Exhibit 4). Essential among them was the dealer's possession of a suitable showroom for the display and sale of TV sets. Dealers also were expected to sell Konark TV sets to the best of their ability, at fixed prices, and in specified market areas. Dealers were not permitted to sell sets made by other manufacturers. Dealers earned a margin ranging from Rs 100 (small black and white model) to Rs 900 (large color model) for every TV set they sold. Mr. Bhalla estimated that the average margin for 1990 would be about Rs 320 per set.

The Crisis

The year 1990 seemed to represent a turning point in the Indian TV industry. Unit demand for TV sets was expected to grow only 10 percent, compared to almost 40 percent for 1989 and 1988. Industry experts attributed the slowing growth rate to a substantial hike in consumer prices. The blame was laid almost entirely on increases in import duties, excise taxes, and sales taxes, plus devaluation of the rupee—despite election year promises by government officials to offer TV sets at affordable prices! In addition, Konark was about to be affected by the Orissa government's decision to revoke the company's sales tax exemption beginning on January 1, 1991. "Right now we are the clear choice, as Konark is the cheapest brand with a superior quality. But with the withdrawal of the exemption, we will be in the same price range as the 'big boys,' and it will be a real run for the money to sell our brand," remarked Mr. Bhalla.

EXHIBIT 3   Branch Offices and Distributors for Konark Television India

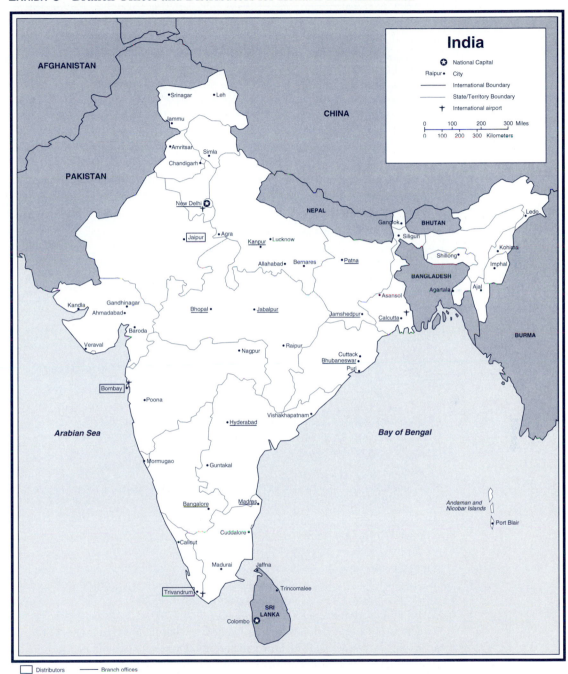

Distributors   Branch offices

EXHIBIT 4 **Terms and Conditions for Dealers of Konark TV Products**

1. The Dealer shall canvass for, secure orders, and affect sales of Konark Televison sets to the best of his ability and experience and will guarantee sale of minimum of sets during a calendar month.

2. The Company shall arrange for proper advertisement in the said area and shall give publicity of their product through newspapers, magazines, cinema slides, or by any other media and shall indicate, wherever feasible, the Dealer's name as their Selling Agents. The cost of such advertisements may be shared by the Company and the Dealer as may be mutually agreed to.

3. The appointment shall be confirmed after 3 months and initially be in force for a period of one year and can be renewed every year by mutual consent.

4. The Company reserves the right to evaluate the performance of a Dealer.

5. This appointment may be terminated with a notice of one month on either side.

6. The Company shall deliver the Konark Television sets to the Dealer at the price agreed upon cash payment at the factory at Bhubaneswar. On such delivery, the title to the goods would pass on to the Dealer and it will be the responsibility of the Dealer for the transportation of the sets to their place at their cost and expenses.

7. The Company may, however, at their discretion allow a credit of 30 (thirty) days subject to furnishing a Bank Guarantee or letter of credit or security deposits toward the price of Konark Television sets to be lifted by the Dealer at any time.

8. The Company shall not be responsible for any damage or defect occurring to the sets after delivery of the same to the Dealer or during transit.

9. The Dealer shall undertake to sell the sets to customers at prices fixed by the Company for different models. Dealer margins will be added to wholesale prices while fixing the customer's price of the television sets.

10. The Dealer will not act and deal with similar products of any other company so long as his appointment with Konark Television continues.

11. The Dealer shall not encroach into areas allotted to any other Dealer.

12. Any dispute or difference arising from or related to the appointment of the Dealership shall be settled mutually and, failing amicable settlement, shall be settled by an Arbitrator to be appointed by the Chairman of the Company whose decision shall be final and binding upon the parties. The place of arbitration shall be within the State of Orissa and the Court in Bhubaneswar (Orissa) only shall have jurisdiction to entertain any application, suit, or claim arising out of the appointment. All disputes shall be deemed to have arisen within the jurisdiction of the Court of Bhubaneswar.

13. Essential requirements to be fulfilled before getting Dealership:
    a. The Dealer must have a good showroom for display and sale of Television sets.
    b. The Dealer should have sufficient experience in dealing with Electronics Products (Consumer Goods).

Mr. Bhalla also was concerned about some dealer activities that he thought were damaging to Konark. He knew that many dealers would play with the assigned margin and offer the same Konark product at differing prices to different customers. Or, equally damaging, different dealers might quote different prices for the same product to a single customer. Some dealers recently had gone so far as to buy large quantities of TV sets from Konark and sell them to unauthorized dealers in Bhubaneswar or in neighboring districts. This problem was particularly vexing because the offending dealers—while few in number—often were quite large and important to Konark's overall performance. Perhaps as much as 40 percent of Konark's sales revenues came from "problem" dealers.

Early in 1990 Mr. Bhalla thought that an increase in the margins that Konark allowed its dealers was all that was needed to solve the problem. However, a modest change in dealer compensation had resulted in several national competitors raising their dealer margins even higher—without an increase in their retail prices. The result was that prices of Konark's models became even closer to those of national competitors, and Konark's decline in market share had actually steepened. By late 1990 Konark's unit share of the Orissa market had fallen from 80 percent to just over 60 percent. "Unless something is done soon," Mr. Bhalla thought, "we'll soon be below 50 percent."

The Decision

Some immediate actions were needed to improve dealer relations and stimulate greater sales activity. An example was Konark's quarterly "Incentive Scheme," which had begun in April 1989. The program was a rebate arrangement based on points earned for a dealer's purchases of Konark TV sets. Reaction was lukewarm when the program was first announced. However, a revision in August 1989 greatly increased participation. Other actions yet to be formulated could be announced at a dealers' conference Mr. Bhalla had scheduled for next month.

All such actions would have to be consistent with Konark's long-term distribution strategy. The problem was that this strategy had not yet been formulated. Mr. Bhalla saw this void as his most pressing responsibility as well as a topic of great interest to Mr. Singh. Mr. Bhalla hoped to have major aspects of a distribution strategy ready for discussion at the next week's meeting. Elements of the strategy would include recommendations on channel structure—branch offices or independent distributors, company showrooms or independent dealers—in existing markets as well as in markets identified for expansion. The latter markets included Bombay, Jaipur, and Trivandrum, areas that contained some 2 million consumers in the target segment. Most important, the strategy would have to address actions to combat the loss of the sales tax exemption in Orissa.

CASE 5–4
SAN MIGUEL CORPORATION: THE MAGNOLIA GROUP

"I've done some initial analysis/data gathering. The easy part is putting together the information on 'what' is going on in the frozen desserts and snacks marketplace in the Philippines. My problem is not so much with the 'what' but with 'how' to maintain our market dominance," said Andrea Bratten, senior assistant vice president and operations director of the frozen desserts and snack business of the Magnolia Division of the San Miguel Corporation. She was facing an unfamiliar competitive situation in the ice cream marketplace. Magnolia was the Philippines' first and only name in ice cream and frozen confections. Even with prices slightly higher generally than competitors' prices, Magnolia's market share in 1991 was around 77 percent. Suppliers of major raw materials for ice cream (e.g., Universal Flavors, Inc.) and manufacturers of dairy equipment (e.g., Alfa-Laval and APV) advertised Magnolia in the same league as Häagen-Dazs and Baskin-Robbins as "world-class" users of their products. However, the Philippines' continuing import liberalization program was broadening the competitive arena. Non–ice cream food items from foreign brands had high acceptance in the country, and consumers appeared to be willing to pay a premium for imported products. Magnolia's domestic competitors expressed interest in having some sort of "tie-ups" with foreign brands.

Foreign companies were courting Magnolia with the notion of licensing Magnolia to produce and distribute their products in the Philippines. But if Magnolia was already "among the world's best," did it need a foreign brand segment? Would Magnolia lose its place in the premium segment to its own foreign brand segment? In short, should Andrea and Magnolia management in general consider and possibly accept any offers from foreign investors?

San Miguel Corporation

Founded in 1890 and incorporated in 1913, San Miguel Corporation manufactured, distributed, and sold food products, beverages, packaging products, and animal feed throughout the Philippines. San Miguel Corporation was the Philippines' largest publicly held food and beverage company. It generated about 4 percent of the country's gross national product and contributed about 7 percent of the government's tax revenues. In 1993, San Miguel was rated number 27 in the top 100 emerging market companies. Exhibit 1 shows San Miguel's fundamental and historical philosophy, and major milestones of the San Miguel Corporation are included in Exhibit 2.

The San Miguel Corporation did business in four major market segments: (1) beverages, (2) food and agribusiness, (3) packaging, and (4) property development. The beverage segment consisted of five companies, with a contribution to sales of 69 percent and a contribution to operating income of 70 percent. The food and agribusiness segment

This case was prepared by Victoria L. Crittenden, associate professor of marketing, and Erin L. Quinn of Boston College and William F. Crittenden, associate professor of management, Northeastern University, as the basis for class discussion rather than to illustrate either effective or ineffective handling of a managerial situation. Revised 2001.

EXHIBIT 1   Fundamental and Historical Philosophy

Profit with Honor

The following objectives are indivisible and together represent the broad aims of the Corporation and should be interpreted in the light of this philosophy.

Objectives

To be constantly aware of the aspirations of the people and of the nation and to ensure that San Miguel continues to make a major contribution toward the achievement of these aspirations.

To manufacture, distribute, and sell throughout the Philippines food products, beverage, packaging products, and animal feeds, being ready at all times to add, modify, or discontinue products in accordance with changes in the market.

To diversify into fields that will ensure optimum utilization of management resources and a substantial contribution to corporate profits.

To seek and develop export markets for new products as well as for those already being produced by the Corporation.

To generate a return on funds employed sufficient to ensure an adequate rate of growth for the Corporation and to provide satisfactory returns to stockholders.

To provide an environment that is conducive to the development of the individual and that encourages employees to realize their full capabilities.

To maintain the highest ethical standards in the conduct of our business.

To adopt a flexible and objective attitude toward change and to pursue an active policy of innovation.

EXHIBIT 2   Milestones in San Miguel's History

1890	San Miguel Brewery is founded.
1895	San Miguel Beer wins its first well-deserved recognition when it is named the "product of the highest quality" in the Exposicion Regional de Filipinas.
1913	The enterprise becomes a corporation.
1925	The Magnolia Ice Cream Plant is founded.
1927	San Miguel Brewery secures exclusive rights for bottling and distributing Coca-Cola in the Philippines.
1938	The pilot glass plant starts operations, manufacturing beer bottles at first and later bottles for other San Miguel products.
1942–45	Operations of the corporation are interrupted by the Japanese occupation of Manila and the seizure as enemy property of San Miguel Brewery including all its plants, equipment, and inventories.
1954	San Miguel enters poultry and livestock feeds processing.
1963	San Miguel Brewery changes its name to San Miguel Corporation.
1973	Sales exceed P1 billion and net profits are over P100 million for the first time.
1977	The company celebrates the fiftieth anniversary of the Coca-Cola bottling franchise in the Philippines.
1978	Construction of the new Magnolia chicken-processing plant begins at Cabuyao, Laguna.
1981	San Miguel Beer firms up its worldwide reputation for excellence when it wins four of the top awards in the prestigious Monde Selection held in Brussels. Pale Pilsen Regular, Pale Pilsen Export, and Dark Beer won gold medals, and Lagerlite won a silver medal.
1982	The company's highly automated and efficient brewery at San Fernando, Pampanga, commences operations in July.
1991	The Magnolia Division spins off as a separate corporation.

EXHIBIT 3   **Magnolia Financial Overview**

	1991	*1990*	*1989*	*1988*
For the Year[1]				
Net sales	53,332	43,815	36,714	30,866
Income from operations	5,556	4,303	3,860	3,611
Net income before nonrecurring items	2,519	1,880	1,858	1,895
Earnings per share before nonrecurring items[2]	1.77	1.32	1.31	1.35
Net income after nonrecurring items	2,812	1,796	2,431	2,052
Earnings per share after nonrecurring items[2]	1.97	1.26	1.72	1.46
Cash dividends	432	432	417	374
At Year-End[1]				
Working capital	7,247	5,411	3,569	2,962
Total assets	42,338	35,684	29,554	23,893
Property, plant, and equipment, net	17,880	15,514	12,287	8,766
Stockholders' equity	14,916	12,633	10,866	8,401

Source: Annual report.

[1] Pesos in millions (except per share).

[2] Based on the average number of shares outstanding during each year with retroactive adjustments for the stock split/stock dividends.

consisted of eight companies with a sales contribution of 21 percent and operating income contribution of 16 percent. Packaging included five companies with a sales contribution of 10 percent and operating income contribution of 14 percent. The property development segment began operation in 1991 and was managed by one company.

San Miguel believed that strategic alliances were important because of the increasingly competitive global environment. Examples of such partnerships included relations with Conservera Campofrio S.A. of Spain, Yamamura Glass Co., Ltd., of Japan, and Guangzhou Brewery of China. It was believed that substantial benefits could be attained from synergies and the sharing of the cost of research and development.

Exhibit 3 provides a financial overview of the firm.

The Philippines

An island country of Southeast Asia, the Philippines lies on the western edge (about 600 miles, or 960 km) from mainland Asia. Its 1992 population was around 62 million. The capital and largest city was Manila, with around 8 million inhabitants in metro Manila.[1] There were two major airports in the Philippines: one in Manila and one in Cebu (population around 1 million). Exhibit 4 provides a geographic look at the country. Major storms approached the Philippines from the southeast. Most products were distributed by sea from Manila.

The Philippine economy contracted in 1991. The effects of the Gulf War, restrained government spending, the full implementation of an ad valorem tax on beer, the imposition of additional indirect taxes such as the import levy, high interest rates and inflation, and the damage caused by the eruption of Mount Pinatubo and other natural

---

[1] The latest published census report was dated 1991 with population data for 1980; however, a country spokesperson provided estimates for 1992 population data. This was almost a 30 percent increase in population from 1980 to 1992.

EXHIBIT 4
The Philippines

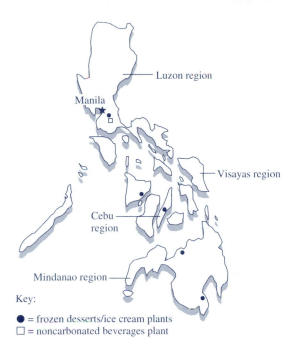

Manila

Luzon region

Visayas region

Cebu
region

Mindanao region

Key:

● = frozen desserts/ice cream plants
□ = noncarbonated beverages plant

calamities weakened consumer demand and set back employment opportunities as well as investment and industrial activity. Additional factors that were expected to affect economic conditions included the government's continued implementation of fiscal and monetary measures aimed at economic stabilization, the ramifications of a severe drought in Mindanao, the critical water supply situation, and increased power rates that would add to industrial costs. Additionally, there were no antitrust laws in the Philippines.

As a result of increased travel, improved communications, and the homogenization of consumer tastes, a universal lifestyle appeared to be emerging in the Philippines. Foreign food and beverage companies, technology, and financial resources were expanding and globalizing their operations. With the easing of trade and investment barriers, the availability of more foreign products was expected. Foreign companies—alone or in partnership with local firms—were taking advantage of business opportunities in the Philippines.

Magnolia

In 1925 San Miguel Corporation bought the trademark "Magnolia" when it purchased a small ice cream plant on Aviles Street in Manila. In 1969, the Magnolia Dairy Products Plant was established on Aurora Boulevard in Quezon City just north of Manila. In 1981, a joint venture with the New Zealand Dairy Board formed the Philippine Dairy Products Corporation (PDPC). The PDPC, managed by Magnolia, was 70 percent owned by San Miguel. PDPC's businesses were butter, margarine, and cheese. The Magnolia Division was transformed into a wholly owned subsidiary of San Miguel Corporation in 1991. Exhibit 5 provides an overview of the organizational structure of Magnolia.

414

EXHIBIT 5 Organization Structure

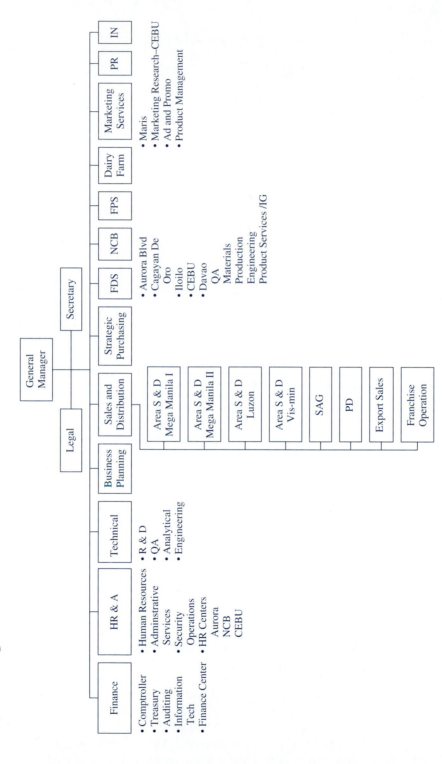

EXHIBIT 6
Business Portfolio

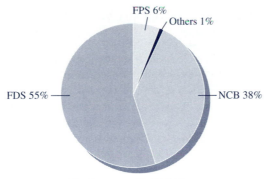

Total revenue: P2.830 billion

Magnolia was the only dairy manufacturer in the Philippines with its own dairy farm. The Magnolia Dairy Farm in the hills of Alfonso, Cavite (just south of Manila), was at the forefront of a major effort to develop, through computerized breeding, a dairy herd suitable to the tropics. Besides being the biggest in Southeast Asia, the farm was one of the most modern and advanced in all Asia.

Magnolia's businesses included frozen desserts and snacks (FDS), noncarbonated beverages (NCB), and food preparation and supplements (FPS), with a 1991 total revenue of P2.83 billion.[2] Fifty-five percent of Magnolia's revenue came from its frozen desserts and snacks, 38 percent from noncarbonated beverages, and 6 percent from food preparation and supplements (Exhibit 6).

The frozen desserts and snacks product line consisted of three major line offerings (Bulk Ice Cream, Single-Serves, and Soft-Serve Ice Cream/Others), with wide variety in each one. Exhibit 7 lists the offerings within each line. Magnolia launched new products and flavors consistently in the frozen desserts and snacks category. Sixteen new products were at some stage of development and were expected to be introduced between 1993 and 1997. Between January and July 1992, the company introduced five new flavors of Gold Label and All Time Favorites (Swisse mocha, mangoes n' cream, double cheese supreme) and two Sorbetes flavors (sesame karoy espesyal, tsohalle real) as well as a new Sorbet in five flavors. In the Single-Serves category, Magnolia introduced a fruit bar in four flavors (nangha, ube, sweet corn, orange). Additionally, Magnolia Ice Cream Special in two flavors and five new single-serves were proposed for introduction between August and December 1992.

Exhibit 8 shows the product offerings in the noncarbonated beverages line. Exhibit 9 lists the food preparation and supplements offerings.

Magnolia had six manufacturing plants. A major capacity expansion to be completed by the beginning of 1993 was expected to almost double the current capacity. The Aurora Plant in Quezon City produced items for the frozen desserts and snacks and food preparation and supplements lines, with the Mandaluyong plant producing noncarbonated beverages. Four ice cream plants had opened since the early 1980s. The Ceba Ice Cream Plant opened in 1983, the Davao Ice Cream Plant in 1989, the Cagayan Ice Cream Plant in 1990, and the Iloilo Ice Cream Plant in 1991. Eighteen sales offices were located in Luzon, eight in Visayas, and nine in Mindanao. (Exhibit 4 shows the

---

[2] P = peso.

EXHIBIT 7   Frozen Desserts and Snacks Product Lines

Bulk Ice Cream
Magnolia Gold Label (Premium and Super Premium)
Magnolia Flavor-of-the-Month
Magnolia All Time Favorites
Magnolia Sorbetes
Magnolia Lite n' Creamy (sugar-free ice cream)
Magnolia Ice Cream Cakes and Moulds

Single-Serves
Magnolia Chocolate Pinipig Crunch (stick bar)
Magnolia Twin Popsies (stick bar)
Magnolia Ice Drop (stick bar)
Magnolia Drumstick
Magnolia Crunchies (ice cream bar)
Magnolia Ice Cream Sundae (cup)
Magnolia Ice Cream Cups
Magnolia Chocolait Bar

Soft-Serve Ice Cream and Others
Magnolia Curly Creams Soft-Serve Ice Cream
Magnolia Soft-Serve Ice Cream Mixes (powdered and liquid)
Magnolia Ice Cream Cones
Magnolia Soda Fountain Syrups
Magnolia Frozen Yogurt (customized)

plants' locations.) With its extensive geographic spread, Magnolia was able to ship from various locations throughout the Philippines, unlike its competitors, which distributed from Manila only. Thus, inclement weather did not pose a threat to maintaining a steady flow of products to consumers.

Competitors.   Major Filipino industry players in each of Magnolia's product categories were the following:

Company	Brand
Frozen Desserts and Snacks	
RFM	Selecta
Purefoods	Sorbetero
	Coney Island
CPC	Presto
	Tivoli
Ready-to-Drink Juice, Milk, and Chocolate	
SEMEXCO	Zest-O
	Sun-Glo
General Milling	Granny Goose
	Alaska
Nestlé	Bear Brand
Cream	
Nestlé	

EXHIBIT 8   Noncarbonated Beverages Product Lines

Magnolia Fresh Cow's Milk (pasteurized)
Magnolia Low-Fat Milk (pasteurized)
Magnolia Flavored Milk (pasteurized)
   Chocolait
   Melon Milk
Magnolia Fruit Juice (pasteurized)
   Orange
   Mango
Magnolia Fresh n' Lite (pasteurized, sugar-free)
   Orange
   Mango
Magnolia Fresh Milk (UHT)*
Magnolia Full Cream (UHT)
Magnolia Flavored Milk (UHT)
   Chocolait
   Strawberry
Magnolia Sweet Dairy Milk (UHT sweetened full cream)
Magnolia Fruit Drinks (UHT)
   Orange
   Mango
   Guyabano (soursap)
   Calamansi (Philippine lemon)
   Buco (young coconut water)
   Hi-C Fruit Drinks (UHT)
   Nestee
   Milo
Magnolia Fruit Juice Concentrate

* UHT refers to ultra high temperature and is a form of cooking juice to preserve the taste, flavor, and odor during processing.

EXHIBIT 9   Food Preparation and Supplements Product Lines

Creams
Magnolia Dip n' Dressing
Magnolia All Purpose Cream (UHT)
Magnolia Whipping Cream (pasteurized)
Magnolia Fresh Whipping Cream
Magnolia Sour Cream

Fermented Products
Magnolia Cottage Cheese
   Plain
   Fruited
Magnolia Bulgarian Yogurt
   Plain
   Flavored
   Fruited
Magnolia Lite n' Rite (sugar-free yogurt)
   Flavored
   Fruited

Frozen Desserts and Snacks

Industry volume in the frozen desserts and snacks category was expected to double by 1998, with the future belonging to single-serves and the targeting of provincial areas.[3] In the first half of 1992 Magnolia's market share in the ice cream marketplace was about 75 percent, compared to 77.3 percent in 1991. The division's objective was to strengthen its market dominance and translate it into higher profits for the corporation. The strategies for achieving this objective were (1) a focus on the consumers' driving force (impulse buying), (2) expansion of capacity to meet market demand, and (3) attaining international quality standards.

Consumer Buying Behavior.   Magnolia's market research found that 86 percent of Filipino consumers bought ice cream on impulse. The major reasons for eating ice cream were specific occasion/purpose, taste/flavor, fondness, and refreshment. Ninety-eight percent of consumers ate ice cream at home, with 73 percent eating it as an afternoon snack.

The research also suggested that while consumers bought on impulse, brand and flavor were determined before purchase. This implied to Magnolia that product availability, visibility, and desirability (key success factors in the industry) needed to be ensured and that there was a need to strengthen top-of-mind awareness and brand image. Distribution was such that about 60 percent of Magnolia's frozen dessert and snack products were sold through retail stores (e.g., supermarkets, convenience stores), and about 30 percent through prepared food outlets (e.g., bakeshops, restaurants, ice cream shops). Communication activities included trade promotions (e.g., raffles with prizes such as generators), consumer promotions (e.g., "buy one, get one free," free gift items with minimum purchase), and advertising (e.g., media and free signage).

Since taste and quality were major motivations for eating ice cream (i.e., desirability), Magnolia managers felt that the division needed to work on improving product quality and product formulation continually. As the market leader in the industry, Magnolia felt that it must dictate the tempo of development in the areas of new product introduction, flavors, and packaging to create excitement in the marketplace.

Competition.   Philippine consumption of ice cream was well behind that of other nations. The United States was the leader in 1989, with per capita consumption of 5.95 gallons. New Zealand was next with 5.05 gallons, followed by Australia (4.70), Canada (3.83), Japan (2.00), and South Korea (1.14). Per capita consumption in 1989 in the Philippines was 0.24 gallon, which was expected to be the same in 1992.

Including Magnolia, four major competitors existed in 1992 to capture this untapped marketplace in the Philippines.

Selecta.   With a market share in the ice cream industry of 15 percent for the first half of 1992 (7.3 percent in 1991), Selecta's overall strategy seemed to be a frontal attack on Magnolia. The elements of this strategy appeared to be a parity of product offerings along with parity pricing and premium positioning of its products. Selecta was focusing on major retail outlets in key provincial urban centers.

Recent developments within Selecta included (1) a doubling of capacity (an increase from 4,000 to 8,000 gallons per day, equivalent to 2.1 million gallons per year), (2) the purchase of a new single-serve machine capable of producing 3,000 gallons per day (equivalent to 0.8 million gallons per year), and (3) the purchase of 22 new refrigerated

---

[3] A province is a geographic region in the Philippines.

route trucks. Along with these internal operational developments, Selecta had started negotiations with Cadburry IC Bar for its single-serves.

Coney Island/Sorbetero.   Purefoods was also posing a frontal attack on Magnolia through a multibrand strategy. Coney Island (2.4 percent market share in 1991) was using an "All American" positioning in the premium segment; Sorbetero (3.1 percent market share in 1991) was using its Filipino ice cream to attack Magnolia's Flavor of the Month, Special, Regular, and Sorbetes directly.

Purefoods' attack against Magnolia included (1) taking a census of Magnolia carrito vendors[4] to attract them to carry Purefoods' products instead of Magnolia's and (2) parity pricing with Magnolia as of February 1992. Additionally, Purefoods had acquired an APV Glacier brand machine to produce single-serves, expanded distribution using Smokey's/Scoops n' Steaks outlets, launched three new flavors for Sorbetero Ice Sarap, and started offering a 10 percent rebate to selective retail outlets.

Presto.   Presto's overall strategy was to focus on single-serve novelty items and lower pricing. Market share in the total ice cream marketplace in 1991 for Presto was 10 percent. However, Presto's 1991 market share for single-serve ice cream was almost 30 percent (compared to Magnolia's 69 percent). In bulk ice cream, Presto was averaging only around a 5 percent share.

Presto followed the launch of Magnolia Sundae with Tivoli Sundae and Funwich. Presto's new entries in the candy bar segment in 1992 had been the Big Bang and Cloud Nine. Additionally, Presto planned to introduce two new variants of the Tivoli Bar (Ube-Nangka and Strawberry).

Exhibits 10 through 12 provide capacity information for all three of Magnolia's major competitors in the frozen desserts and snacks category.

Foreign Investors

Corporate management knew of three foreign companies with interests similar to Magnolia: Nestlé, Häagen-Dazs, and Mars.

Nestlé.   Nestlé S.A. (Switzerland) was a holding company in the food processing industry. Its principal products were drinks (coffees, chocolate drinks, tea, mineral water, fruit juices), dairy products (milk, cream, cheese, butter, breakfast cereals), infant and dietetic products (formula, baby foods), culinary products (soups, condiments, sauces), frozen foods and ice cream (entrees, pizza, Lean Cuisine), refrigerated products (yogurt, cold meat products, fresh pasta), chocolate and confectionery (Kit Kat, Nestlé Crunch), pet foods (cat and dog foods), restaurants and hotels (through Stouffer Corporation), pharmaceutical products, and cosmetics. Nestlé S.A. had 423 factories spread across 61 countries. Exhibit 13 analyzes Nestlé's sales by product groups.

Acquisitions and joint ventures had been important to Nestlé's growth since its incorporation in 1866. For example, Nestlé had acquired (and in some cases later sold off) such companies as Stouffer Corporation (which operated a chain of restaurants and a frozen food division) in 1973, Alcon Laboratories (ophthalmic products) in 1977, Beech-Nut Corporation (baby foods and dietetic specialty products) in 1979, and Hills Brothers Coffee in 1985. Coca-Cola and Nestlé S.A. had formed a joint venture to manufacture and market concentrates and beverage bases for the production of ready-to-drink coffee and tea beverages under the Nescafé and Nestea brand names.

---

[4] A carrito vendor is a vendor who sells items from a pushcart.

Exhibit 10
Selecta Capacity

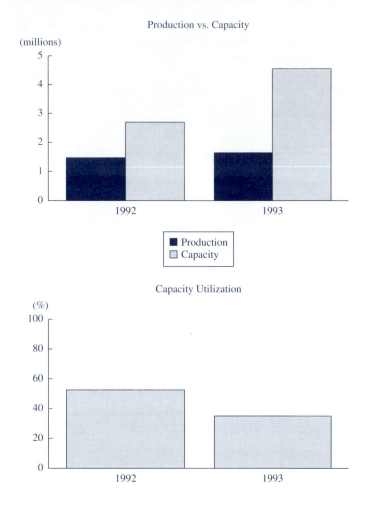

Nestlé Philippines, Inc., was an affiliate company of the San Miguel Corporation (51 percent of Nestlé Philippines being owned by San Miguel and 49 percent by Nestlé). The affiliate produced and marketed instant drinks, full cream and filled milk, soya-based products, infant foods, and culinary products in the food and agribusiness market segment. There were four manufacturing plants.

Häagen-Dazs. Häagen-Dazs, a private subsidiary of Grand Metropolitan PLC (incorporated in England), made superpremium ice cream and frozen yogurt products. The company operated in the United States, Japan, Canada, and Europe. Headquartered in Teaneck, New Jersey, the company had 1,100 employees, with an estimated annual revenue of $340 million. Häagen-Dazs was committed to building its business worldwide and invested heavily in advertising, consumer promotions, manufacturing facilities, and research and development.

Häagen-Dazs accounted for approximately 60 percent of the superpremium ice cream (butterfat content between 14 and 18 percent) market in the United States. Its major U.S. competitors were Ben and Jerry's, Mars, and Breyers. Major European competitors included Carte d'Or, Movenpick, and Loseley. In Japan, competitors included Meiji, AYA, and Lady Borden. Häagen-Dazs expected a significant portion of its

**EXHIBIT 11
Coney Island/Sorbetero
Capacity**

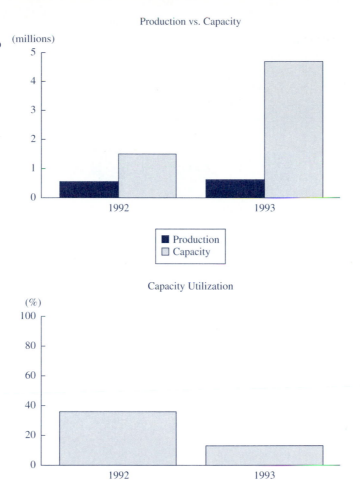

Production vs. Capacity

Capacity Utilization

growth to come from Europe (the largest frozen dessert market outside North America). The company was making major inroads into the Far East through joint ventures in Japan and Korea.

Grand Metropolitan PLC conducted operations through three groups: Food (35 percent of turnover and 28 percent of trading profit in fiscal 1991), Drinks (28 percent of turnover and 42 percent of trading profit in fiscal 1991), and Retailing (23 percent of turnover and 22 percent of trading profit in fiscal 1991). Discontinued operations accounted for 14 percent of turnover and 8 percent of trading profit in 1990.[5]

The food group consisted of several well-known companies: Pillsbury Company for bakery, pizza, vegetable, dough, frozen, and canned products (brands included Pillsbury, Green Giant, Totino's, Jeno's, and Hungry Jack); Häagen-Dazs; Alpo Petfoods with its cat and puppy food and dog treats (Alpo brand name); Grand Metropolitan Foodservice USA, which made and supplied bakery and frozen foods at the food service, bakery, and deli level (Green Giant and Pillsbury brands); Express Foods Group, which produced cheese, butter, and milk-based products in the United Kingdom and Ireland; and

---

[5] Standard & Poor's, *Standard Corporate Descriptions* (New York: McGraw-Hill, 1992).

EXHIBIT 12
Presto Capacity

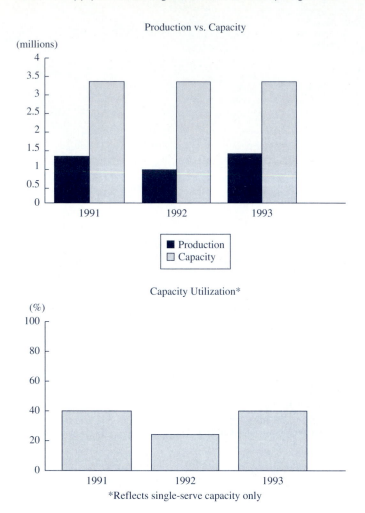

Production vs. Capacity

(millions)

■ Production
□ Capacity

Capacity Utilization*

(%)

*Reflects single-serve capacity only

EXHIBIT 13   Nestlé S.A. Sales by Product Groups

	1990	1989	1988
Drinks	23.6%	24.7%	27.4%
Cereals, milks, and dietetic	20.1	20.0	20.3
Chocolate and confectionery	16.0	15.3	12.4
Culinary products	12.7	12.4	12.2
Frozen foods and ice cream	10.1	10.8	10.5
Refrigerated products	8.9	8.5	8.7
Pet foods	4.5	4.4	4.2
Pharmaceuticals and cosmetics	3.0	2.8	2.2
Other products and activities	1.1	1.1	2.1
	100.0	100.0	100.0

Source: *Moody's International Manual,* 1991, Vol. 2 (New York: Moody's Investors Service), pp. 3705–9.

EXHIBIT 14   **Wholly Owned Principal Subsidiaries of Grand Metropolitan PLC**

Pillsbury Co.
Burger King Corp.
Pillsbury Danada Ltd.
Pillsbury GmbH
Häagen-Dazs Co. Inc.
Pilstral SA
S&E&A Metaxa Distilleries SA
Paddington Corp.
Belin Surgeles SA
Conservas Chistu, SA
Express Foods Group (International) Ltd.
Express Foods Group Ireland Ltd.
Alpo Petfoods Inc.
International Distillers and Vintners Ltd.
R&A Bailey & Co. Ltd.
Carillon Importers Ltd.
Gilbey Canada Inc.
International Distillers and Vintners (UK) Ltd.
Justerini & Brooks Ltd.
Heublein Inc.
Driehock Beheer, BV
AED SA
Croft & Ca Lda
Croft Jerez SA
Pearle Inc.
Chef & Brewer Group Ltd.
Grand Metropolitan Estates Ltd.
Grand Metropolitan Finance PLC
Wyvern International Ltd.
(Cinzano International SA is an affiliate of Grand
   Metropolitan PLC, with the corporation having 25 percent
   ownership.)

Source: Standard & Poor's, *Standard Corporate Descriptions* (New York: McGraw-Hill, 1992), p. 5279.

European Baked Goods and Prepared Foods (brands included Brossard, Erasco, and Peter's). Exhibit 14 lists the principal wholly owned subsidiaries of the corporation.

Mars.   A privately held company headquartered in McLean, Virginia, M&M/Mars Inc. was number two to Hershey Foods Corporation in the $8.7 billion (wholesale) U.S. confectionery business. As of May 1991, Mars had a 38 percent share of chocolate product sales through wholesalers, a 2.5 share point gain over the same period a year earlier.[6] Four major divisions constituted Mars Incorporated: M&M/Mars (candy bars), Kal Kan Foods (pet foods), Uncle Ben's Inc. (rices and sauces), and Dove International (ice cream bars and snacks). Total worldwide sales in 1989 and 1990 were $8 billion. Advertising spending for the corporation totaled $272.4 million for the 1990–1991 fiscal year.

_____
[6] "P&G Spends $2.28 Billion, Surges to Head of Top 100," *Advertising Age,* September 25, 1991, pp. 47-48.

As of 1992 Dove International had introduced three ice cream bars: Snickers, Three Musketeers, and Milky Way. According to Nielsen Marketing Research, the Snickers bar had become a top 10 seller in the frozen novelties market. Other products produced by this division included Dove ice cream bars and Rondos bite-size ice cream snacks.

The Strategic Issue

The entry of foreign brands was expected to generate greater competitive activities in the global ice cream industry. More innovative new products, flavors, and packages were expected. Thus, the industry probably would see an intense battle for shelf space, with heavy advertising and promotion activities and a greater deployment of trade assets. All in all, the industry expected to see the production of world-class and state-of-the-art products.

The strategic question facing Magnolia was how best to maintain its competitive dominance in this rapidly changing industry where barriers to entry included strong brand loyalty; large capital requirements in manufacturing, selling, and distribution; and strong economies of scale. What should Bratten recommend to San Miguel corporate? Was some kind of foreign partnership the way—maybe even the only way—to proceed as number one?

CASE 5–5
CAMAR AUTOMOTIVE HOIST

In September 2000 Mark Camar, president of Camar Automotive Hoist (CAH), had just finished reading a feasibility report on entering the European market in 2001. CAH manufactured surface automotive hoists, a product used by garages, service stations, and repair shops to lift cars for servicing (Exhibit 1). The report, which had been prepared by CAH's marketing manager, Pierre Gagnon, outlined the opportunities in the European Union and the available entry options.

Mr. Camar was not sure if CAH was ready for this move. While the company had been successful in expanding sales into the U.S. market, he wondered if this success could be repeated in Europe. He thought that with more effort, sales could be increased in the United States. However, there were some positive aspects to the European idea. He began reviewing the information in preparation for the meeting the following day with Mr. Gagnon.

Camar Automotive Hoist

Mr. Camar, a design engineer, had worked for eight years for the Canadian subsidiary of a U.S. automotive hoist manufacturer. During those years he had spent considerable time designing an aboveground, or surface, automotive hoist. Although Mr. Camar was very enthusiastic about the unique aspects of the hoist, including a scissor lift and wheel alignment pads, senior management expressed no interest in the idea. In 1990, Mr. Camar left the company to start his own business with the express purpose of designing and manufacturing the hoist. He left with the good wishes of his previous employer, who had no objections to his plans to start a new business.

Over the next three years Mr. Camar obtained financing from a venture capital firm; opened a plant in Lachine, Quebec; and began manufacturing and marketing the hoist, which was called the Camar Lift (see Exhibit 1).

From the beginning Mr. Camar had taken considerable pride in the development and marketing of the Camar Lift. The original design included a scissor lift and a safety locking mechanism which allowed the hoist to be raised to any level and locked in place. Also, the scissor lift offered easy access for the mechanic to work on the raised vehicle. Because the hoist was fully hydraulic and had no chains or pulleys, it required little maintenance. Another key feature was the alignment turn plates that were an integral part of the lift. The turn plates would allow mechanics to perform wheel alignment jobs accurately and easily. Because it was a surface lift, it could be installed in a garage in less than a day.

Mr. Camar continually made improvements to the product, including adding more safety features. In fact, the Camar Lift was considered a leader in automotive lift safety. Safety was an important factor in the automotive hoist market. Although hoists seldom malfunctioned, when they did, it often resulted in a serious accident.

This case was prepared by Gordon McDougall, Wilfrid Laurier University, as the basis for class discussion rather than to illustrate either effective or ineffective handling of an administrative situation. © Gordon McDougall 2001.

EXHIBIT 1   Examples of Automotive Hoists

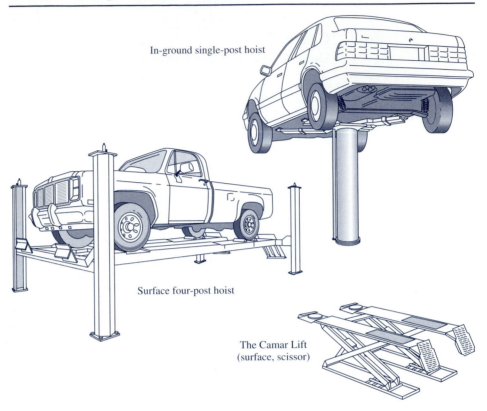

In-ground single-post hoist

Surface four-post hoist

The Camar Lift
(surface, scissor)

The Camar Lift developed a reputation in the industry as the "Cadillac" of hoists; the unit was judged by many as superior to competitive offerings because of its design, the quality of the workmanship, the safety features, the ease of installation, and the five-year warranty. Mr. Camar held four patents on the Camar Lift, including the lifting mechanism on the scissor design and a safety locking mechanism. A number of versions of the product were designed that made the lift suitable (depending on the model) for a variety of tasks, including rustproofing, muffler repairs, and general mechanical repairs.

In 1991 CAH sold 23 hoists and had sales of $172,500. During the early years the majority of sales were to independent service stations and garages specializing in wheel alignment in the Quebec and Ontario market. Most of the units were sold by Mr. Gagnon, who was hired in 1992 to handle the marketing side of the operation. In 1994 Mr. Gagnon began using distributors to sell the hoist to a wider geographic market in Canada. In 1996 he signed an agreement with a large automotive wholesaler to represent CAH in the U.S. market. By 1999 the company had sold 1,054 hoists and had sales of $9,708,000 (Exhibit 2). In 1999 about 60 percent of sales were to the United States, with the remaining 40 percent going to the Canadian market.

Industry

Approximately 49,000 hoists were sold each year in North America. Hoists typically were purchased by any automotive outlet that serviced or repaired cars, including new car dealers, used car dealers, specialty shops (for example, mufflers, transmission,

EXHIBIT 2   Camar Automotive Hoist, Selected Financial Statistics (1997–1999)

	1997	1998	1999
Sales	$6,218,000	$7,454,000	$9,708,000
Cost of sales	4,540,000	5,541,000	6,990,000
Contribution	1,678,000	1,913,000	2,718,000
Marketing expenses*	507,000	510,000	530,000
Administrative expenses	810,000	820,000	840,000
Earnings before tax	361,000	583,000	1,348,000
Units sold	723	847	1,054

Source: Company records.

* Marketing expenses in 1999 included advertising ($70,000), four salespeople ($240,000), the marketing manager, and three sales support personnel ($220,000).

wheel alignment), chains (for example, Firestone, Goodyear, Canadian Tire), and independent garages. It was estimated that new car dealers purchased 30 percent of all the units sold in a given year. In general, the specialty shops focused on one type of repair, such as mufflers or rustproofing, while "nonspecialty" outlets handled a variety of repairs. While there was some crossover, in general CAH competed in the specialty shop segment and, in particular, shops that dealt with wheel alignment. This included chains such as Firestone and Canadian Tire as well as new car dealers (for example, Ford) which devoted a certain percentage of their lifts to the wheel alignment business and independent garages that specialized in wheel alignment.

The purpose of a hoist was to lift an automobile into a position where a mechanic or serviceperson could easily work on the car. Because different repairs required different positions, a wide variety of hoists had been developed to meet specific needs. For example, a muffler repair shop required a hoist where the mechanic could gain easy access to the underside of the car. Similarly, a wheel alignment job required a hoist that offered a level platform where the wheels could be adjusted and there was easy access for the mechanic. Mr. Gagnon estimated that 85 percent of CAH's sales were to the wheel alignment market to service centers such as Firestone, Goodyear, and Canadian Tire and to independent garages that specialized in wheel alignment. About 15 percent of sales were made to customers who used the hoist for general mechanical repairs.

Firms that purchased hoists were part of an industry called the automobile aftermarket. This industry was involved in supplying parts and service for new and used cars and was worth over $54 billion at retail in 1999 while servicing the approximately 14 million cars on the road in Canada. The industry was large and diverse; there were over 4,000 new car dealers in Canada, over 400 Canadian Tire stores, over 100 stores in each of the Firestone and Goodyear chains, and over 220 stores in the Rust Check chain.

The purchase of an automotive hoist was often an important decision for a service station owner or dealer. Because the price of hoists ranged from $3,000 to $15,000, this was a capital expense for most businesses.

For the owner-operator of a new service center or car dealership the decision involved determining what type of hoist was required and what brand would best suit the company. Most new service centers and car dealerships had multiple bays for servicing cars. In these cases the decision would involve what types of hoists were required (for example, in-ground, surface). Often more than one type of hoist was purchased, depending on the service center/dealership needs.

Experienced garage owners seeking a replacement hoist (the typical hoist had a useful life of 10 to 13 years) usually would determine what products were available and then make a decision. If the garage owners were also mechanics, they probably would be aware of two or three types of hoists but would not be very knowledgeable about the brands or products currently available. Garage owners and dealers who were not mechanics probably knew very little about hoists. The owners of car or service dealerships often bought the product that was recommended and/or approved by the parent company.

Competition

Sixteen companies competed in the automotive lift market in North America: 4 Canadian and 12 U.S. firms. With the advent of the North American Free Trade Agreement in 1989, the duties on hoists between the two countries were phased out over a 10-year period, and in 1999 exports and imports of hoists were duty-free. For Mr. Camar, the import duties had never played a part in any decisions; the fluctuating exchange rates between the two countries had a far greater impact on selling prices. In the last three years the Canadian dollar had fluctuated between $0.65 and $0.70 versus the U.S. dollar ($1.00 CDN bought $0.65 U.S.) and forecasted rates were expected to stay within that range.

A wide variety of hoists were manufactured in the industry. The two basic types of hoists were in-ground and surface. As the name implies, in-ground hoists required a pit to be dug "in-ground" where the piston that raised the hoist was installed. In-ground hoists were either single-post or multiple-post, were permanent, and obviously could not be moved. In-ground lifts constituted approximately 21 percent of total lift sales in 1999 (Exhibit 3). Surface lifts were installed on a flat surface, usually concrete. Surface lifts came in two basic types: post lift hoists and scissor hoists. Compared to in-ground lifts, surface lifts were easy to install and could be moved if necessary. Surface lifts constituted 79 percent of total lift sales in 1999. Within each type of hoist (for example, post lift surface hoists) there were numerous variations in terms of size, shape, and lifting capacity.

The industry was dominated by two large U.S. firms, AHV Lifts and Berne Manufacturing, that together held approximately 60 percent of the market. AHV Lifts, the largest firm, with approximately 40 percent of the market and annual sales of about $60

EXHIBIT 3   **North American Automotive Lift Unit Sales by Type, 1997–1999**

	1997	*1998*	*1999*
In-ground			
Single-post	5,885	5,772	5,518
Multiple-post	4,812	6,625	5,075
Surface			
Two-post	27,019	28,757	28,923
Four-post	3,862	3,162	3,745
Scissor	2,170	2,258	2,316
Other	4,486	3,613	3,695
Total	48,234	50,187	49,272

Source: Company records.

million, offered a complete line of hoists (in-ground and surface) but focused primarily on the in-ground market and the two-post surface market. AHV Lifts was the only company that had its own direct sales force; all the other companies used only wholesalers or a combination of wholesalers and a company sales force. AHV Lifts offered standard hoists with few extra features and competed primarily on price. Berne Manufacturing, with a market share of approximately 20 percent, also competed in the in-ground and two-post surface markets. It used a combination of wholesalers and company salespeople and, like AHV Lifts, competed primarily on price.

Most of the remaining firms in the industry were companies that operated in a regional market (for example, California, British Columbia) and/or offered a limited product line (for example, four-post surface hoist).

Camar had two competitors that manufactured scissor lifts. AHV Lift marketed a scissor hoist that had a different lifting mechanism and did not include the safety locking features of the Camar Lift. On average, the AHV scissor lift was sold for about 20 percent less than the Camar Lift. The second competitor, Mete Lift, was a small regional company with sales in California and Oregon. It had a design that was very similar to that of the Camar Lift but lacked some of its safety features. The Mete Lift, which was regarded as a well-manufactured product, sold for about 5 percent less than the Camar Lift.

Marketing Strategy

As of early 2000, CAH had developed a reputation for a quality product backed by good service in the hoist lift market, primarily in the wheel alignment segment.

The distribution system employed by CAH reflected the need to engage in extensive personal selling. Three types of distributors were used: a company sales force, Canadian distributors, and a U.S. automotive wholesaler. The company sales force consisted of four salespeople and Mr. Gagnon. Their main task was to service large "direct" accounts. The initial step was to get the Camar Lift approved by large chains and manufacturers and then, having received the approval, sell to individual dealers or operators. For example, if General Motors approved the hoist, CAH could sell it to individual General Motors dealers. CAH sold directly to the individual dealers of a number of large accounts, including General Motors, Ford, Chrysler, Petro-Canada, Firestone, and Goodyear. CAH had been successful in obtaining manufacturer approval from the big three automobile manufacturers in both Canada and the United States. Also, CAH had received approval from service companies such as Canadian Tire and Goodyear. To date, CAH had not been rejected by any major account, but in some cases the approval process had taken over four years.

In total, the company sales force generated about 25 percent of the unit sales each year. Sales to the large "direct" accounts in the United States went through CAH's U.S. wholesaler.

The Canadian distributors sold, installed, and serviced units across Canada. Those distributors handled the Camar Lift and carried a line of noncompetitive automotive equipment products (for example, engine diagnostic equipment, wheel-balancing equipment) and noncompetitive lifts. They focused on the smaller chains and the independent service stations and garages.

The U.S. wholesaler sold a complete product line to service stations as well as manufacturing some equipment. The Camar Lift was one of five different types of lifts that the wholesaler sold. Although the wholesaler provided CAH with extensive distribution in the United States, the Camar Lift was a minor product within the wholesaler's total line. While Mr. Gagnon did not have actual figures, he thought that the Camar Lift probably accounted for less than 20 percent of the total lift sales of the U.S. wholesaler.

Both Mr. Camar and Mr. Gagnon felt that the U.S. market had unrealized potential. With a population of 264 million people and over 146 million registered vehicles, that market was almost 10 times the size of the Canadian market (population of over 30 million and approximately 14 million vehicles). Mr. Gagnon noted that the six New England states (population of over 13 million), the three largest mid-Atlantic states (population of over 38 million), and the three largest Mideastern states (population of over 32 million) were all within a day's drive of the factory in Lachine. Mr. Camar and Mr. Gagnon had considered setting up a sales office in New York to service those states, but they were concerned that the U.S. wholesaler would not be willing to relinquish any of its territory. They also had considered working more closely with the wholesaler to encourage it to "push" the Camar Lift. It appeared that the wholesaler's major objective was to sell a hoist, not necessarily the Camar Lift.

CAH distributed a catalog-type package with products, uses, prices, and other required information for both distributors and users. In addition, CAH advertised in trade publications (for example, *AutoInc.*), and Mr. Gagnon traveled to trade shows in Canada and the United States to promote the Camar Lift.

In 1999, Camar Lifts sold for an average retail price of $10,990 and CAH received on average $9,210 for each unit sold. This average reflected the mix of sales through the three distribution channels: (1) direct (where CAH received 100 percent of the selling price), (2) Canadian distributors (where CAH received 80 percent of the selling price) and (3) the U.S. wholesaler (where CAH received 78 percent of the selling price).

Both Mr. Camar and Mr. Gagnon felt that the company's success to date had been based on a strategy of offering a superior product that was targeted primarily at the needs of specific customers. The strategy stressed continual product improvements, quality workmanship, and service. Personal selling was a key aspect of the strategy; salespeople could show customers the advantages of the Camar Lift over competing products.

The European Market

Against this background, Mr. Camar had been thinking of ways to maintain the rapid growth of the company. One possibility that kept coming up was the promise and potential of the European market. The fact that Europe had become a single market in 1993 suggested that it was an opportunity that should at least be explored. With this in mind, Mr. Camar asked Mr. Gagnon to prepare a report on the possibility of CAH entering the European market. The highlights of Mr. Gagnon's report follow.

History of the European Union.   The European Union (EU) had its basis in the 1957 Treaty of Rome, in which five countries decided it would be in their best interest to form an internal market. Those countries were France, Spain, Italy, West Germany, and Luxembourg. By 1990 the EU consisted of 15 countries (the additional 10 were Austria, Belgium, Denmark, Finland, Greece, Ireland, the Netherlands, Portugal, Sweden, and the United Kingdom) with a population of over 376 million people. Virtually all barriers (physical, technical, and fiscal) in the EU were scheduled to be removed for companies within the EU. This allowed the free movement of goods, persons, services, and capital.

In the last 15 years many North American and Japanese firms had established themselves in the EU. The reasoning for this was twofold. First, those companies regarded the community as an opportunity to increase global market share and profits. The market was attractive because of its size and lack of internal barriers. Second, there was continuing concern that companies not established within the EU would have difficulty exporting to the EU due to changing standards and tariffs. To date, this concern had not materialized.

Market Potential.   The key indicator of the potential market for the Camar Lift hoist was the number of passenger cars and commercial vehicles in use in a particular country. Four countries in Europe had more than 20 million vehicles in use, with Germany having the largest domestic fleet, 44 million vehicles, followed in order by Italy, France, and the United Kingdom (Exhibit 4). The number of vehicles was an important indicator since the more vehicles there were in use, the greater the number of service and repair facilities which needed vehicle hoists and potentially the Camar Lift.

An indicator of the future vehicle repair and service market was the number of new vehicle registrations. The registration of new vehicles was important, as it maintained the number of vehicles in use by replacing cars that had been retired. Again, Germany had the most new cars registered in 1997 and was followed in order by France, the United Kingdom, and Italy.

Based primarily on the fact that a large domestic market was important for initial growth, the selection of a European country should be limited to the "Big Four" industrialized nations: Germany, France, the United Kingdom, and Italy. In an international survey companies from North America and Europe ranked European countries on a scale of 1 to 100 on market potential and investment site potential. The results showed that Germany was favored for both market potential and investment site opportunities, while France, the United Kingdom, and Spain placed second, third, and fourth, respectively. Italy did not place in the top four in either market or investment site potential. However, Italy had a large number of vehicles in use, had the fourth largest population in Europe, and was an acknowledged leader in car technology and production.

Little information was available on the competition within Europe. There was no dominant manufacturer as there was in North America. At that time there was one firm in Germany that manufactured a scissor-type lift. That firm sold most of its units within the German market. The only other available information was that 22 firms in Italy manufactured vehicle lifts.

Investment Options

Mr. Gagnon felt that CAH had three options for expansion into the European market: licensing, a joint venture, or direct investment. The licensing option was a real possibility, as a French firm had expressed an interest in manufacturing the Camar Lift.

EXHIBIT 4   Number of Vehicles (1997) and Population (2000 estimate)

Country	Vehicles in Use (thousands)		New Vehicle Registrations (thousands)	Population (thousands)
	Passenger	*Small Commercial*		
Germany	41,400	2,800	3,500	82,100
France	28,000	4,900	2,200	59,000
Italy	33,200	2,700	1,800	56,700
United Kingdom	23,500	4,000	2,200	59,100
Spain	15,300	2,800	1,000	39,200

In June 2000, Mr. Gagnon had attended a trade show in Detroit to promote the Camar Lift. At the show he met Phillipe Beaupre, the marketing manager for Bar Maisse, a French manufacturer of wheel alignment equipment. The firm, located in Chelles, France, sold a range of wheel alignment equipment throughout Europe. The best-selling product was an electronic modular aligner which enabled a mechanic to utilize a sophisticated computer system to align the wheels of a car. Mr. Beaupre was seeking a North American distributor for the modular aligner and other products manufactured by Bar Maisse.

At the show Mr. Gagnon and Mr. Beaupre had a casual conversation in which both explained what their respective companies manufactured, exchanged company brochures and business cards, and went on to other exhibits. The next day Mr. Beaupre sought out Mr. Gagnon and asked if he might be interested in having Bar Maisse manufacture and market the Camar Lift in Europe. Mr. Beaupre felt that the lift would complement Bar Maisse's product line and the licensing would be beneficial to both parties. They agreed to pursue the idea. Upon his return to Lachine, Mr. Gagnon told Mr. Camar about those discussions, and they agreed to explore the possibility.

Mr. Gagnon called a number of colleagues in the industry and asked them what they knew about Bar Maisse. About half had not heard of the company, but those who had commented favorably on the quality of its products. One colleague with European experience knew the company well and said that Bar Maisse's management had integrity and the firm would make a good partner. In July Mr. Gagnon sent a letter to Mr. Beaupre stating that CAH was interested in further discussions and enclosing various company brochures, including price lists and technical information on the Camar Lift. In late August Mr. Beaupre responded, stating that Bar Maisse would like to enter a three-year licensing agreement with CAH to manufacture the Camar Lift in Europe. In exchange for the manufacturing rights, Bar Maisse was prepared to pay a royalty rate of 5 percent of gross sales. Mr. Gagnon had not yet responded to this proposal.

A second possibility was a joint venture. Mr. Gagnon had wondered if it might not be better for CAH to offer a counterproposal to Bar Maisse for a joint venture. He had not worked out any details, but he felt that CAH would learn more about the European market and probably make more money if it was an active partner in Europe. Mr. Gagnon's idea was a 50-50 proposal in which the two parties shared the investment and the profits. He envisaged a situation where Bar Maisse would manufacture the Camar Lift in its plant with technical assistance from CAH. Mr. Gagnon also thought that CAH could get involved in the marketing of the lift through the Bar Maisse distribution system. Further, he thought that the Camar Lift, with proper marketing, could gain a reasonable share of the European market. If that happened, Mr. Gagnon felt that CAH was likely to earn greater returns with a joint venture.

The third option was direct investment, in which CAH would establish a manufacturing facility and set up a management group to market the lift. Mr. Gagnon had contacted a business acquaintance who recently had been involved in manufacturing fabricated steel sheds in Germany. On the basis of discussions with his acquaintance, Mr. Gagnon estimated the costs involved in setting up a plant in Europe at (1) $250,000 for capital equipment (welding machines, cranes, other equipment), (2) $200,000 in incremental costs to set up the plant, and (3) carrying costs to cover $1 million in inventory and accounts receivable. While the actual costs of renting a building for the factory would depend on the site location, he estimated that annual building rent, including heat, light, and insurance, would be about $80,000. Mr. Gagnon recognized that these estimates were guidelines but felt that the estimates were probably within 20 percent of the actual costs.

The Decision

As Mr. Camar considered the contents of the report, a number of thoughts crossed his mind. He began making notes concerning the European possibility and the future of the company:

- If CAH decided to enter Europe, Mr. Gagnon would be the obvious choice to head up the direct investment option or the joint venture option. Mr. Camar felt that Mr. Gagnon had been instrumental in the success of the company to date.
- While CAH had the financial resources to go ahead with the direct investment option, the joint venture would spread the risk (and the returns) over the two companies.
- CAH had built its reputation on designing and manufacturing a quality product. Regardless of the option, Mr. Camar wanted the firm's reputation to be maintained.
- Either the licensing agreement or the joint venture appeared to build on the two companies' strengths: Bar Maisse had knowledge of the market, and CAH had the product. What troubled Mr. Camar was whether this apparent synergy would work or whether Bar Maisse would seek to control the operation.
- It was difficult to estimate sales under any of the options. With the first two (licensing and a joint venture), it would depend on the effort and expertise of Bar Maisse; with the third, it would depend on Mr. Gagnon.
- CAH's sales in the U.S. market could be increased if the U.S. wholesaler would "push" the Camar Lift. Alternatively, the establishment of a sales office in New York to cover the Eastern states also could increase sales.

As Mr. Camar reflected on the situation, he knew he probably should get additional information, but it wasn't obvious exactly what information would help him make a yes or no decision. He knew one thing for sure: He was going to keep this company on a "fast growth" track, and at tomorrow's meeting he and Mr. Gagnon would decide how to do it.

CASE 5–6
WENTWORTH INDUSTRIAL CLEANING SUPPLIES

Wentworth Industrial Cleaning Supplies (WICS), located in Lincoln, Nebraska, is experiencing a slowdown in growth; sales of all WICS products have leveled off far below the volume expected by management. Although total sales volume has increased for the industry, WICS's share of this growth has not kept pace. J. Randall Griffith, vice president of marketing, has been directed to determine the factors that are stunting growth and institute a program that will facilitate further expansion.

Company and Industry Background

WICS is a division of Wentworth International, competing in the janitorial maintenance chemical market. According to trade association estimates, the total market is roughly $2.5 billion in 1992. Exhibit 1 shows the nature of this market. Four segments make up the institutional maintenance chemical market, which consists of approximately 2,000 manufacturers that provide both national and private labels.

EXHIBIT 1   **Institutional Maintenance Chemical Market**

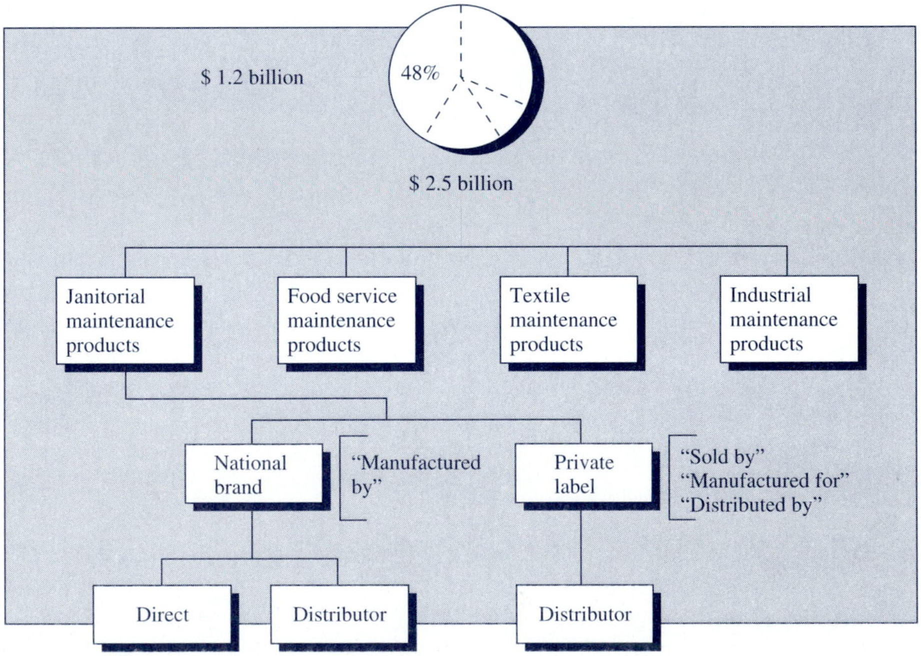

Reprinted by permission from Gilbert A. Churchill, Jr., Neil M. Ford, and Orville C. Walker, Jr., Sales Force Management, 4th ed. (Burr Ridge, IL: Richard D. Irwin, Inc., 1993), pp. 861–77.

EXHIBIT 2   WICS "Served" Portion of the Janitorial Maintenance Chemical Market

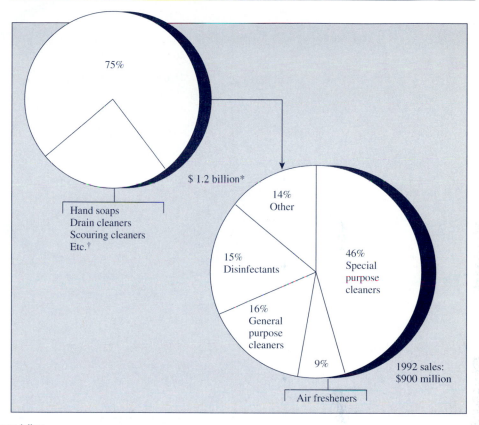

*End user dollars.

†Includes some general-purpose cleaners and air fresheners that WICS does not manufacture.

Total industry sales volume in dollars of janitorial supplies is approximately $1.3 billion. Exhibit 2 shows the breakdown by product type for the janitorial market. WICS addresses 75 percent of the market's product needs with a line of high-quality products. The composition of WICS's product line is as follows:

Special-purpose cleaners	46%
Air fresheners	9
General-purpose cleaners	16
Disinfectants	15
Other	14

The janitorial maintenance chemical market is highly fragmented; no single firm, including WICS, has more than 10 percent market share. Agate and Marshfield Chemical sell directly to the end user, while Lynx, Lexington Labs, and WICS utilize a distributor network. Most of WICS's competitors utilize only one channel of distribution; only Organic Labs and Swanson sell both ways. Most private-label products move through

EXHIBIT 3   **Janitorial Maintenance Chemical Market (End User Dollars)**

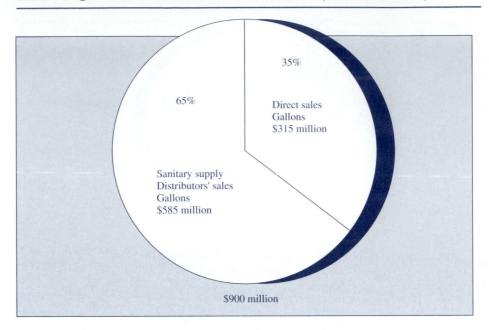

distributors. Sanitary supply distributors (SSDs) deliver 65 percent of end user dollars, while direct-to-end-user dollar sales account for 35 percent (Exhibit 3).[1] The following list shows the sales breakdown by target market, by type of distribution:

Distributor Sales	
Retail	20%
Industrial	18
Health care	18
Schools	11
Building supply contractors	10
Restaurants	3
Hotels	3
Other	17

Direct Sales	
Retail	47%
Building supply contractors	35
Health care	15
Hotels	2
Restaurants	1

Trade association data plus information from other sources estimate the number of SSDs to be between 5,000 and 6,000. The following list shows the sales volume breakdown for the SSDs based on an average 5,500:

---

[1] Includes paper supply distributors that carry janitorial supplies.

Size in Sales Volume	
Less than $100,000	1,210
$100,000–$500,000	2,475
$500,000–$1,000,000	1,375
More than $1,000,000	440
Total	5,500

According to a recent analysis of end users, WICS provides cleaning supplies for approximately 20,000 customers. WICS's sales force is expected to call on these accounts as well as prospect for new business. These 20,000 end users receive product from the SSDs that supply cleaning supplies manufactured by WICS and others as well. About one-third of the average SSD's total sales is accounted for by WICS's products. An exception is the paper supply distributor, where WICS's products account for an average of 10 percent of sales.

The typical SSD carries other related items. In fact, according to a survey conducted by an independent firm, SSDs almost always carry a private-label line of cleaning supplies plus one to two additional branded products besides the WICS line. This survey revealed that 60 percent of the SSDs carry a private-label line along with WICS and one other national brand. Forty percent carry two national labels and WICS and a private label. The private label may be a regional label or the SSD's own label.

WICS places almost total reliance on selling through the SSDs, although a small amount of sales (less than 10 percent) are made direct. WICS sells its janitorial maintenance products through roughly 400 distributors, who in turn "see" 65 percent of the end user dollar market. Thus, 65 percent of sales in the total janitorial maintenance market are made through SSDs (35 percent are direct sales), and the 400 SSDs used by WICS provided 65 percent coverage. The market seen by each distributor, referred to as his or her *window* on the market, is a function of

Product lines carried (paper versus chemical).

Customer base (type and size).

Nature of business (specialization by market versus specialization by sales function).

The combination of these factors produces end user market coverage of 42 percent (65 percent distributor sales × 65 percent coverage). WICS has very limited direct sales.

To reach its market, WICS uses a sales force of 135 area managers, 21 territory managers, and 4 regional managers (Exhibit 4). Regional managers are located in San Francisco, Denver, Chicago, and Boston. Although WICS is viewed as a giant in the industry, it does not produce a complete line of janitorial chemicals. Janitorial chemicals are rated based on their performance. WICS produces products that have average to premium performance ratings: WICS has no products in the economy class. Moreover, due to various factors, WICS's coverage in the average and premium classes is not complete. The emphasis on premium and average products results in providing only 75 percent of the market's product needs.

To provide high distributor margins and extensive sales support, WICS charges premium prices. Recent estimates reveal that only 40 percent of the served market is willing to pay these premium prices. The impact of WICS's limited product line coupled with its premium price is evident in Exhibit 5.

An overall description of WICS's marketing program shows that it has focused on market development. Distributors receive high margins (30 to 40 percent), and sales costs are high (10 to 15 percent) due to the emphasis on selling technical benefits,

EXHIBIT 4   WICS's Access to the Market

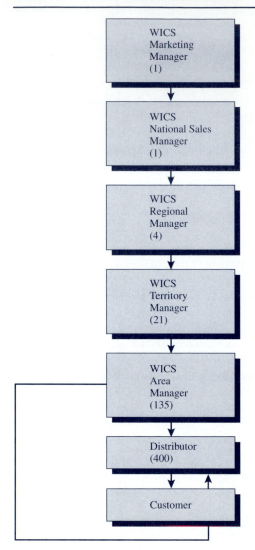

demonstrations, and cold calls. Area managers call on prospective end users to develop the market for the SSD. By comparison, WICS's competitors offer SSDs low margins (15 to 20 percent) and incur low sales costs (5 to 8 percent).

Griffith recently received a memo from Steve Shenken, WICS's national sales manager, reporting on a study of the effectiveness of SSDs. Territory managers evaluated each SSD in their respective regions on a basis of reach (advertising and promotional programs) and frequency of sales calls. The composite report indicated that distributors as a whole were doing an excellent job servicing present accounts. In other words, 400 SSDs provide WICS with a sizable share of the market.

Area managers (AMs) represent WICS in distributor relations. The AMs' prime focus is to sell and service existing key end user accounts and selected new target

EXHIBIT 5   End User Product Coverage

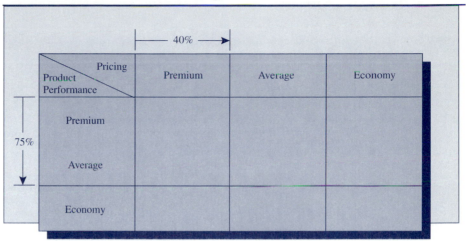

accounts in their assigned territories. According to a recent study, maintenance of current accounts represents approximately 80 percent of the AMs' time (Exhibit 6). In addition to handling old accounts, the AM makes cold calls on prospective distributors as directed by the territory manager. However, the number of cold calls made monthly has decreased substantially in the past year since the major SSDs now carry WICS products. A study of AM and SSD attitudes, conducted by MGH Associates, management consultants, is presented in Appendixes A and B. Some of the sales management staff question the use of AM time; however, there has been no indication that formal changes will be made in the future regarding sales force organization and directives. The AM job description has seen few revisions, if any, during the firm's last 10 years of rapid growth (Exhibit 7).

Area managers are compensated with a straight salary, enhanced periodically by various incentive programs and performance bonuses. Incentive programs generally require that AMs attain a certain sales level by a specified date. For example, the "Christmas Program" necessitated that AMs achieve fourth-quarter quotas by November 15; on completion of this objective, the AM received a gift of his or her choice, such as a color television. To date, management considers the Zone Glory Cup the most effective incentive program. The Glory Cup is an annual competition among areas within territories which entails meeting or exceeding sales objectives by a specified date. An all-expenses-paid vacation at a plush resort for area, territory, and regional managers and their "legal" spouses is the prize for the winning team. However, management at WICS believes that prestige is the prime motivator in this competition and the underlying reason for the program's success.

In a recent meeting, Terry Luther, executive vice president of the WICS division of Wentworth International, expressed his concern to Griffith about WICS's mediocre performance. Luther indicated that corporate cash flow expectations from WICS were not being met and that a plan was needed from Griffith concerning how WICS could improve its overall operating performance. Griffith was quite aware that Wentworth International would make personnel changes to meet corporate objectives and that selling off

EXHIBIT 6   Allocation of Area Manager Duties*

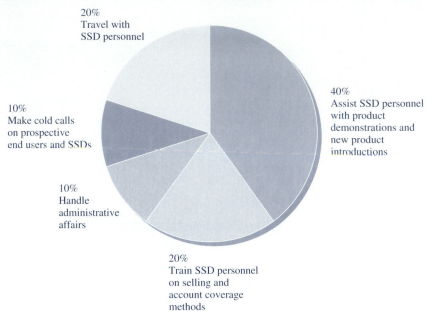

20%
Travel with
SSD personnel

40%
Assist SSD personnel
with product
demonstrations and
new product
introductions

10%
Make cold calls
on prospective
end users and SSDs

10%
Handle
administrative
affairs

20%
Train SSD personnel
on selling and
account coverage
methods

*Based on an analysis of call reports.

divisions not able to meet corporate expectations was not unlikely. Griffith informed Luther that an action plan would be developed and be on his desk within 30 days.

Griffith's first step was to approve an earlier request made by Mike Toner, sales and distributor relations manager, for a study of sales force and distributor attitudes and opinions (Appendixes A and B). Next, the following memo was sent, discussing Griffith's assignment from Luther:

Intra-Office Memorandum

To: Steve Shenken, National Sales Manager
      Caitlin Smith, Manager—Sales Analysis
      Ryan Michaels, Manager—Sales Training
      Calla Hart, Manager—Special Sales Program
      Charlotte Webber, Senior Product Manager
      Mike Toner, Sales and Distributor Relations Manager

From: Randall Griffith, Vice President—Marketing

Subject: WICS Performance Review

As you all know, our performance has not met corporate expectations. To rectify this situation, before we all lose our jobs, we need to meet to discuss ways for improving our market performance.

At our next meeting, I want each of you to develop proposals for your areas of responsibility. These proposals need not be detailed at this time. For the moment, I am seeking ideas, not final solutions.

Staff reaction to Griffith's memo was one of frustration and anger. Several managers thought they had already complied with Griffith's request. One person

EXHIBIT 7 **Wentworth Industrial Cleaning Supplies Position Description**

Date: January 1, 1983	Position:	Area Manager, Maint. Prods.
Approved by: (1) _____	Incumbent:	135 Positions Nationally
(2) _____		
(3) _____	Division:	Janitorial Maintenance Products Division
		Reports to: Territory Manager, Janitorial Maintenance Products Division

POSITION PURPOSE:

To sell and service user accounts and authorized distributors in an assigned territory to assure that territory sales objectives are attained or exceeded.

DIMENSIONS:

Annual sales:	$300 M	(average)
Number of distributors:	4	(average)
Number of distributor salesmen:	12	(average)
Annual expense budget:	$4.2 M	(average)
Company assets controlled or affected:	$8 M	(average)

NATURE AND SCOPE

This position reports to a territory manager, janitorial maintenance products. Each district is subdivided into sales territories that are either assigned to an individual member of the district or to a team effort, based on market and/or manpower requirements.

The janitorial maintenance products division is responsible for developing and marketing a broad line of chemical products for building maintenance purposes.

The incumbent's prime focus is to sell and service existing key user accounts and selected new target accounts in his assigned territory. He multiplies his personal sales results by spending a major portion of his time working with distributor sales personnel, selling WICS maintenance products and systems to key accounts such as commercial, industrial, institutional, and governmental accounts, and contract cleaners. When working alone, he sells key user accounts through an authorized distributor as specified by the user customer.

The incumbent plans, schedules, and manages his selling time for maximum sales productivity. He interviews decision makers and/or people who influence the buying decision. He identifies and evaluates customer needs through careful observation, listening and questioning techniques to assure proper recommendations. He plans sales strategy to include long-term/quick-sell objectives and develops personalized user presentations to meet individual sales situations, utilizing product literature, manuals, spot demonstrations, and sales aids to reinforce presentations. This position sells systems of maintenance to major volume user accounts through the use of surveys and proposals, test programs, and other advanced sales techniques. He develops effective closing techniques for maximum sales effectiveness. This position trains custodial personnel in product usage techniques through the use of product demonstrations and/or audiovisual training to assure customer satisfaction. He follows up through the use of product demonstrations and/or audiovisual training to assure customer satisfaction. He follows up promptly on customer leads and inquiries. He services customer

commented, "I've told Randy numerous times what we need to do to turn the division around, and all he does is nod his head. Why go through this 'wheel-spinning' exercise again?" Another said, "The only time old J. R. listens to us is when the top brass leans on him for results." Despite staff reaction, the meeting would be held, and everybody would have suggestions for consideration.

To provide adequate time, Griffith scheduled an all-day meeting to be held at Wentworth's nearby lodge, located on Lake Woebegone. Griffith started the meeting by reviewing past performance. Next, he asked each manager to outline his or her proposal. First to speak was Steve Shenken, who indicated that Mike Toner would present a proposal combining both of their ideas. Shenken also said he would listen to all sales force proposals and try to combine the best parts into an overall plan.

EXHIBIT 7   (concluded)

and distributor complaints or problems and provides technical support as required. On a predetermined frequency basis, he surveys and sells assigned local accounts currently being sold on national contract. He represents the division in local custodial clinics and trade shows as required. He maintains an adequate current supply of literature, forms, and samples and maintains assigned equipment and sales tools in a businesslike condition.

The incumbent is responsible for training, developing, and motivating distributor sales personnel. This is accomplished by frequent on-the-job training in areas of product knowledge, selling skills, and demonstration techniques. He sells distributor management and assists distributors to maintain an adequate and balanced inventory of the full product line. He introduces marketing plans and sells new products and sales promotions to distributor management. He participates in distributor sales meetings to launch new products or sales promotions, or for training and motivational purposes. He keeps abreast of pertinent competitive activities, product performance, new maintenance techniques, and other problems and opportunities in the territory. Periodically, he communicates Wentworth growth objectives versus distributor progress to distributor management (i.e., sales coverage, volume and product sales, etc.). He assists the distributor to maintain a current and adequate supply of product literature, price lists, and sales aids.

The incumbent prepares daily sales reports, weekly reports, travel schedules, weekly expense reports, and the like, and maintains territory and customer records. He maintains close communication with his immediate supervisor concerning products, sales, distributor and shipping problems.

He controls travel and business expenses with economy and sound judgment. He handles and maintains assigned company equipment and territory records in a businesslike manner.

Major challenges to this position include maintaining established major users, selling prospective new target accounts, and strengthening distribution and sales coverage to attain or exceed sales objectives.

The incumbent operates within divisional policies, procedures, and objectives. He consults with his immediate supervisor for recommendations and/or approval concerning distributor additions or terminations, exceptions to approved selling procedures, and selling the headquarter's level of national or regional accounts.

Internally, he consults with the editing office concerning distributor shipments, credit, and so forth. Externally, he works closely with distributor personnel to increase sales and sales coverage and with user accounts to sell new or additional products.

The effectiveness of this position is measured by the ability of the incumbent to attain or exceed territory sales objectives.

This position requires an incumbent with an in-depth and professional knowledge of user account selling techniques, product line, and janitorial maintenance products distributors, and a minimum of supervision.

PRINCIPAL ACCOUNTABILITIES

1. Sell and service key user accounts to assure attainment of territory sales objectives.
2. Sell, train, develop, and motivate assigned distributors to assure attainment of product sales, distribution, and sales coverage objectives.
3. Plan, schedule, and manage personal selling efforts to assure maximum sales productivity.
4. Plan and develop professional sales techniques to assure maximum effectiveness.
5. Train custodial personnel in the use of Wentworth products and systems to assure customer satisfaction.
6. Maintain a close awareness of territory and market activities to keep the immediate supervisor abreast of problems and opportunities.
7. Perform administrative responsibilities to conduct an efficient territory operation.
8. Control travel and selling expenses to contribute toward profitable territory operation.

Mike Toner's Proposal

Toner's proposal was rather basic. If improving market performance was WICS's objective, more SSDs were needed in all territories. According to Toner,

> Each area manager serves, on the average, four SSDs. Since we can only get so much business out of an SSD, then to increase sales we need more SSDs. I suggest that each area manager add two more distributors. Of course, this move will require that either we add more area managers or we hire and train a special group to call on new end users and new distributors. It's difficult to attract new SSDs unless we show them a group of prospective end users who are ready to buy WICS's products. Now, I have not made any estimates of how many more people are needed, but we do know that present AMs do not have enough time to adequately seek new business.

After Toner presented this proposal, Griffith asked if the existing AMs could not be motivated to apply more effort toward securing new business. Calla Hart thought the AMs could do more and that her proposal, if adopted, would alleviate the need for expansion of the AMs and SSDs.

Calla Hart's Proposal

As expected, Hart's proposal revolved around her extensive experience with WICS's incentive programs. This satisfactory experience led Calla to suggest the following:

> If I thought that the AMs and the SSDs were working at full capacity, I would not propose more incentive programs. But they are not! We can motivate the AMs to secure more new business, and we can get more new business from our distributors. We all know that the SSDs are content to sit back and wait for the AMs to hand them new business. Well, let's make it worthwhile to the SSDs by including them in our incentive programs. For the AMs I suggest that we provide quarterly incentives much like our Christmas Program. AMs who achieve their quotas by the 15th of the second month of the quarter would receive a gift.
>
> In addition, we need to develop a program for recognizing new end user sales. Paying bonuses for obtaining new end user accounts would be one approach. For example, let's reward the AM from each territory who secures the highest percentage increase in new end user accounts. At the same time, we need to reward the distributor from each territory who achieves the highest percentage increase in new end user sales dollars. And let's recognize these top producers each quarter and at year end as well. Our incentive programs work. We know that, so let's expand their application to new sales.
>
> Finally, on a different note, I support establishing quotas for our distributors. We have quotas for our sales force, and we enforce them. AMs who do not make quotas do not stay around very long. Why not the same procedures for some of our SSDs? We all know that there are some distributors who need to be replaced. Likewise, I have not made any cost estimates but feel that we are just searching for new ideas.

Griffith thanked Hart for her comments. He wondered whether applying more pressure to the distributors was the most suitable approach. He agreed with Hart that WICS's incentive programs seemed to be very popular but questioned if other techniques might not work. Griffith then asked Ryan Michaels for his comments.

Ryan Michaels's Proposal

During his short time with WICS Michaels has gained respect as being very thorough and analytical. He is not willing to accept as evidence such comments as "We know it works" as a reason for doing something. Determining the value of sales training, Michaels's area of assignment, has caused him considerable concern. He knows it is useful, but how useful is the question he is trying to answer. According to Michaels, WICS needs to examine the basic selling duties of the area managers:

> Before we recruit more AMs and SSDs or try to motivate them to obtain more new business with incentive programs, we need to examine their job activities. I favor doing a job analysis of the area manager. Some evidence that I have seen indicates that job descriptions are outmoded. AMs do not perform the activities detailed in the job descriptions. For example, most AMs spend very little time calling on prospective end users. Accompanying distributor sales reps on daily calls does not lead to new end user business. Possibly the AMs could better spend their time doing new account development work. But before we make any decisions concerning time allocation, we need to conduct a job analysis. And, while we are collecting data, let's ask the AMs what rewards are important to them. How do they value

promotions, pay increases, recognition, and so forth? Maybe the AMs do not want more contests.

Griffith agreed that the job descriptions were out of date. He also contended that this is typical and nothing to be concerned about in the short run. The idea of finding out what rewards AMs value intrigued Griffith. Next, Griffith asked Charlotte Webber for her reactions to WICS's market share problem.

Charlotte Webber's Proposal

Webber's proposal was more strategic in nature than the previous suggestions. Her experience as a product manager led her to consider product-oriented solutions and to suggest the following:

> I think we can increase market share and sales volume through the expansion of current lines and the addition of a full line of economy-based products. We can expand our present premium and average lines to cover 100 percent of the product class by adding air fresheners and general-purpose cleaners. In addition we must introduce the economy-based products to counter competition.
>
> The proposed plan would not be costly because we could use our existing distributor network. If additional SSDs are necessary, we can select those in the $500,000 to $1,000,000 sales volume range. I feel that through these extensions and an increased number of SSDs we can address 75 percent of the SSD end user dollars.

Griffith agreed that line extensions were a viable means of achieving some corporate goals. He expressed concern over entry into the low-quality segment of the market due to WICS's present customer perceptions of the company as a high-quality producer. Griffith turned to Caitlin Smith for additional suggestions on how to increase market share.

Caitlin Smith's Proposal

Smith's proposal came as no surprise to those attending the meeting. Her position in sales analysis made her critically aware of WICS's high cost of sales. It was only recently, however, that she had developed a plan incorporating market share and cost of sales. Her views were accurate but often were given little weight due to her inexperience. According to Smith,

> Our cost of sales are currently running at 10 to 15 percent, while our competitors' costs average 5 to 8 percent. As many of you know, I am in favor of changing the job description of the area manager and the sales presentation. These changes are necessary due to our products' stage in the life cycle and customer service level preferences. Recently I have become convinced that there is another means of reducing sales costs. By reducing prices we could increase sales volume and reduce the cost of sales. This strategy would also increase penetration and market share.

Griffith conceded that price reductions were a possibility but expressed concern over the possibility of weakening consumer perceptions of WICS as a high-quality manufacturer. He also questioned Smith's assumption that the industrial cleaning supplies industry was presently in the mature stage of the product life cycle.

Following these comments, Griffith thanked the participants for their input and adjourned the meeting. On retiring to his room, he reflected on the suggestions presented during the meeting and his own beliefs. He knew he must begin to formulate an action plan immediately since the 30-day deadline was drawing near.

APPENDIX A
CONCLUSIONS OF STUDY OF AREA MANAGER ATTITUDES

MGH Associates, management consultants, was retained by WICS to investigate attitudes and opinions of field personnel and sanitary supply distributors. Initially, MGH conducted lengthy interviews with selected individuals, followed by the administration of a comprehensive questionnaire. The results below identify role expectations and attitudes toward their reasonableness.

Territory Manager's Role Expectations

MGH Associates' interviews included territory managers because the territory manager is really the only management level contact the distributor has.

The territory manager interprets his or her role to be that of an overseer, to assure that WICS objectives are achieved and that quotas are met.

The territory manager interprets his or her role to include

- Training the area managers to
    Sell WICS products.
    Train and motivate the distributor sales force.
- Coordinating area manager activities with headquarters in Lincoln.
- Hiring and firing area managers.
- Striving for new product commitments from the distributors.
- Acting as "referee" for competition between distributors.
- "Building the book" for the adding or deleting of distributors.
- Submitting the "study" to the regional manager, who writes a proposal based on the territory manager's "study." It is submitted to corporate management, where the final decision is made.

Area Manager's Role Expectations

The following is the area manager's view of the role he or she believes WICS management expects to be performed:

- Multiply sales effort through distributor's sales force (listed first because it was consistently mentioned first).
- Teach and motivate the distributor's sales force to sell WICS products.
- Introduce new products to the market through
    Direct calls on end users.
    Distributors.
- Keep margins high to keep distributors happy. If they are happy, they will push WICS.
- Follow through on direct sales responsibilities.
- Collect information for management.

445

- Fulfill responsibilities relating to incentives.

    New gallon sales.

    Repeat gallon sales.

    Demonstrations.

    30, 35, 40? calls/week.

    Major account calls.

    Cold calls—"to develop business the distributor is reluctant to go after."

Area Manager's Role Problems

The area manager's perception of what management expects does not imply that the area manager feels that management's approach is working. In general, the sales force appears frustrated by a sales role they see as ineffective:

- A sales role that stresses

    New gallon sales.

    Cold calls on end users.

    Product demonstrations.

    New product introduction.

- "Checking the boxes" rather than being "creatively productive."

    15 demos.

    10 cold calls.

    5 distributor training sessions.

- Incentives stress selling techniques that may not be the most productive ways to sell.

    Emphasis is on new gallon sales over repeat gallon sales. Incentives weigh new gallons over repeat gallons (two to one).

    Emphasis to "demonstrate as often as possible" for the points. Demonstrate to show you are a "regular guy" who gets his or her hands dirty, not necessarily to show product benefits.

- Bonus incentives appear to be a "carrot" only for those who don't regularly make bonus; that is, "hit 106 for maximum bonus and minimum quota increase."

- The sales role gives the area manager little ability to affect his or her own success to

    Change distribution.

    Move distributor outside his or her window.

- The area manager describes his or her role as

    A "lackey."

    A "chauffeur."

    A "caretaker of old business."

Area Manager's Role: Making Cold Calls

One of the causes of area manager frustration is the general ineffectiveness of their cold calls sales role:

- The area manager makes cold calls on end users not currently sold by the WICS distributor, with the difficult objective of moving these accounts to the WICS distributor.

- If the area manager succeeds in moving this account over to WICS products, chances are small that the distributor will keep the business. Without a major portion of the account's total purchases, the distributor cannot afford to continue to call on the account.

    Distributor sales rep is on commission.

    After five calls, will stop calling if purchases have not begun to increase.

- The distributor that lost the account will try extremely hard to get back the business. This may mean giving the product away to keep control of the account—maintain majority of the account's purchases. Past experience indicates it is very difficult to move distributors outside their "window."

APPENDIX B
CONCLUSIONS OF STUDY OF WICS SANITARY SUPPLY DISTRIBUTOR ATTITUDES

WICS Distributor's Role Expectations

The following is the WICS distributor's role as outlined by WICS management and sales force.

- Act as an extension of the WICS sales force.
- Push and promote WICS product line in a *specified area.*

  Sell WICS over other brands.

  Always sell the premium benefits of WICS products to the end user instead of distributor's private label.

  Be aware that the WICS line could be lost if private-label sales grow too large.
- Actively market new WICS products.

Distributor's Role Problems.   Distributors have been angered by WICS's attempt to run their businesses ("WICS is trying to tell me what to do").

- WICS makes demands—"uses pressure tactics."

  Distributors say they are told "our way or no way."

  Distributors feel they are forced to carry products they don't want.

  High minimum buy-ins.

  "Won't see area manager if we don't carry the new product."

  Distributors say WICS management doesn't "realize we make our living selling all our products—not just WICS."
- Communication is poor with WICS management.

  One way—"Our opinions never reach Lincoln."
- "WICS uses the distributor as a testing ground for new products."

  Distributor is not told what to expect.

  After 14-week blitz, "You never hear about the product again."

  The distributor sales force is not trained to sell to, and cannot afford to call on, certain segments of the market.
- Growth takes the distributor into new geographic market areas, and WICS may elect not to go/grow with the distributor.

  New branch in different city.

  Growth may take distributor sales personnel out of area manager's district.

  Receives no support from WICS.

  Worst case—distributor sales rep's territory is completely outside district.

  No WICS representative at any accounts.

  Prefer to sell other than WICS.

- WICS does not realize that a distributor's total business extends beyond "its own backyard" in many markets.

Distributor's Role Selling Costs.   Distributors have shown concern over the high cost of selling WICS products. Sales costs are approximately 45 percent of the total operating costs.

- "WICS products are basically no better than anyone else's."
- Yet WICS asks distributors to switch competitor's accounts over to WICS products.

    Price advantage is very rare.

    A problem must exist.

    A demonstration is required.
- All these make the "problem-solving" sale time-consuming and costly.
- Result: When WICS product is sold, it is easy for competitive WICS distributors to cut price to try to get the business.

    They have very low sales costs.
- Required action: Original distributor must cut margin to keep the business.

    This frustrates distributor salespeople.

    Causes them to sell private label.

CASE 5–7
AVON: THE NEW CALLING

It's 8:30 on a Sunday evening in summer. Outside the Thomas & Mack Center in Las Vegas, where temperatures have hovered around 110°F all weekend, the desert heat is still oppressive. Inside is another matter. The air-conditioning has made for a chilly stage as Andrea Jung waits in the wings to address the biggest crowd she has ever faced. And Jung herself couldn't be more cool and composed. In her red floor-length ball gown with spaghetti straps and white shoes with sharp-pointed toes, Jung, at 41, looks more like a movie star than the CEO of a $5.3 billion company. As she strides onto the stage, she is met by an explosion of applause from some 13,000 mostly forty- and fifty-something Avon women reps who have traveled to Las Vegas from all across the U.S. to see Avon's new product lines, listen to Engelbert Humperdinck, applaud Suzanne Somers' keynote speech, and do aerobics with Richard Simmons to songs like *Breaking Up Is Hard to Do.* The contrast is striking: the svelte, fashionable, Ivy League–educated, New York fast-tracker preaching to the mostly Middle American moms and grandmas whose fashion tastes lean toward slacks for dressy occasions and sweat suits and sneakers for the rest of the convention.

Still, with a mike in her hand giant TV screens in the background projecting her image, Jung has no problem firing up the crowd. "Avon is first and foremost about you," she proclaims. "I stand here before you and promise you that that will never change." She vows that Avon Products Inc. can be as big in the women's beauty business as Walt Disney Co. is in entertainment. She confides her proudest moment: Jung, the daughter of Chinese immigrants, traveled to China last year for the first time in her life to meet and speak to women in a Chinese factory. "We will change the future of women around the world!" she exclaims. And as the audience rises to a standing ovation, Jung wraps up with the most amazing declaration of all: "I love you all!"

To the uninitiated, it all sounds like a lot of hooey. But for Jung the stakes are huge: She desperately needs the support of the company's million sales reps worldwide to answer Avon's new calling: getting today's women to buy a brand that hit its peak when their mothers were first trying on lipstick. The pioneer of door-to-door selling, founded in 1886, Avon is at a critical turning point in its history (Exhibit 1). At the dawn of the Internet Age, when three-quarters of American women work, Avon's direct-sales model, dated for a generation, now seems positively antiquated. As direct selling gets redefined by such Web players as Dell Computer Corp. and Amazon.com Inc., Avon ladies seem in danger of going the way of the horse and buggy. If it weren't for Avon's success in such markets as Latin America and Asia, the company would surely have faded long ago. Indeed, according to industry trackers Kline & Co., direct selling represented only 6.8% of the $27 billion of cosmetics and toiletries sold in the U.S. in 1999, down from 8% in 1995. Avon itself has seen sales growth—up only 5% a year over the past decade—slow even further, to a 1.5% increase in 1999. And though the company reversed a two-year decline in operating profits last year to post a 16% increase to $549 million, over the past 10 years profits are up only an anemic 4% a year.

Source: Nanette Bynes, "Avon: The New Calling," *Business Week,* September 18, 2000, 136–148.

EXHIBIT 1   From Ding-Dong to Dot.Com: 114 Years of Avon Ladies

Started in the 19th century, Avon has seen it all, from failed acquisitions and hostile takeover attempts to moves into retail and the Internet

1886 California Perfume Company founded in New York by salesman David Hall McConnell. Its first product: the Little Dot Perfume Set. First Avon lady, Mrs. P.F.E. Albee, launches direct-selling in Winchester, N.H.

1914 With nearly $1 million in sales, Avon opens its first international office in Montreal.

1928 First products sold under the "Avon" name, which founder McConnell adopted after visiting Shakespeare's birthplace in Stratford-upon-Avon.

1954 "Ding-Dong, Avon Calling" TV commercial debuts. Company begins selling in Latin America.

1960s Heavy advertising in magazines and television helps make the Avon Lady an American icon.

1970s Stock, which first traded publicly in 1946, is named to the "Nifty Fifty" by Morgan Guaranty Trust.

1979 Launches disastrous diversification binge, buying upscale jeweler Tiffany & Co. Later adds a chemical maker and a health-product company.

1988 Takes the second of two write-offs totaling $520 million for dismantling its health-care investment. Debt reaches $1.2 billion, and Avon stock hits a low of $5 per share after splits.

1989 Avon becomes target of the first of a series of hostile bids, including one from Amway Corp. with Minneapolis-based corporate raider Irwin L. Jacobs and another from Texas billionaire Robert M. Bass. Company successfully fends them off.

1997 Avon.com Web site launched, selling directly to customers for the first time and creating tension with many of Avon's 500,000 U.S. sales reps. Results have been uninspiring.

1998 Sets up mall kiosks around the country, its first U.S. retail stores, marking a major strategic shift.

1999 Andrea Jung named Avon's first female CEO.

2000 Relaunching Web site with emphasis on making Avon reps available online. Separately negotiating with big retailers for a new product line to be sold only in stores.

Avon profits are rebounding . . .

Millions of dollars — Annual net income
'96 '97 '98 '99 '00

. . . but sales have barely climbed . . .

Billions of dollars — Annual sales
'96 '97 '98 '99 '00

making investors wary

Dollars — Monthly stock close
July '95   Sept. 5 '00

*Estimates, Bank of America Securities
Data: Bloomberg Financial Markets

"We're in one of the greatest economies of all times, and Avon's still finding it hard to increase sales," says Allan Mottus, a consultant to beauty and retail companies.

The huge task of fixing Avon falls squarely on Jung's shoulders. Jung landed the top job last November in the wake of a fourth-quarter sales and earnings shock that sent Avon shares down 50%. Soon afterward, Jung's predecessor, Charles R. Perrin, resigned. Jung, with very little operating experience under her belt, was suddenly running a company with millions of independent sales reps and operations in 137 countries.

Now, with the need to reconcile the intersection of the Internet's explosive growth with the company's Old Economy direct-sales business model, Jung is faced with what is shaping up to be one of Corporate America's toughest consumer-products turnarounds.

For a marketer who cut her teeth in high-end fashion at ritzy retailers like I. Magnin and Neiman Marcus, reinventing a dowdy megabrand like Avon would seem an unlikely career high. Precocious from the start, Jung was second-in-command at I. Magnin & Co. before she was 30 years old. At 32 she was in charge of all women's apparel for Neiman Marcus and regularly jetted to Europe for the runway shows. Two years later, in 1993, Jung married Bloomingdale's CEO, Michael Gould, 15 years her senior, left her job at Neiman Marcus in Dallas, and moved to Manhattan. Gould, whose previous job had been running the Giorgio Beverly Hills perfume business that Avon then owned, was already in the upper echelons of the New York retailing *glitterati*. In 1994, Jung joined Avon, making her mark by unifying Avon's many regional brands into one powerful global label.

Now, with her mission at Avon, Jung joins one of Corporate America's most elite groups: women, like Carly Fiorina of Hewlett-Packard Co., who are leading complex and problem-ridden corporations. "She's a young woman with a very big job," says executive headhunter Herbert Mines. "She has an opportunity to really demonstrate her abilities, and if she does well, others will undoubtedly reach for her." But if she fails, the business world will witness the collapse of one of the most-watched careers in American business. Another Jill Barad? It's possible. Even her supporters acknowledge that Jung has no easy task ahead. "Anytime you expand your business beyond your existing universe of operations, you have risk," says Larry D. Coats, portfolio manager at Oak Value Capital Management, which holds 1.7 million shares of Avon stock. "The key is in the execution—the careful, thoughtful, and deliberate execution."

Jung's vision for a new Avon is what she grandiosely calls the "ultimate relationship marketer of products and services for women." Her idea is to rebuild the organization from the ground up into a company that does much more than sell lipstick door-to-door. The Avon that Jung envisions will one day be the source for anything and everything a woman wants to buy. More than that, she wants to give busy women a choice in how they do their buying: through an Avon rep, in a store, or online. "Do you have an Avon rep? I don't," offers Avon board member Brenda C. Barnes. "People like us should be able to get the product."

The new Avon would be a radical departure from decades-old ways of doing business. For one thing, Jung is pushing into traditional retail, which Avon had always avoided for fear of competing against its reps. A trial run of 50 kiosks based in shopping malls is luring younger customers who had never before bought an Avon product. To squash any possible rep opposition, the kiosks are now being franchised to them. And this fall, in its boldest move yet, Avon will announce a deal to create a separate line of products for sale at a store-within-a-store at a major mass retailer such as Wal-Mart Stores Inc. or Kmart Corp.

It's the Web, however, that is Avon's best hope for the future, Jung says (see Exhibit 2). Her biggest dilemma is figuring out just where all those Avon ladies fit in. One thing she's sure of: they will play a key role in Avon's reinvention. Jung knows independent sales reps have been the backbone of the company ever since one Mrs. Albee of Winchester, N.H., sold her neighbor a package of assorted perfumes in 1886. Today, reps still produce 98% of the company's revenue, though the top 20% of producers account for about 80% of sales. "If we don't include them in everything we do, then we're just another retail brand, just another Internet site, and I don't see the world needing more of those," says Jung.

EXHIBIT 2 **'I've Gone Through a Learning Curve That's Staggering'**

Len Edwards likes to think of himself as an entrepreneur. Since coming to Avon Products Inc., he has launched a bunch of new businesses. The most successful is a line of children's books and how-to videos for all ages that boasts more than $200 million in sales a year.

All that, however, might be small change compared to what Edwards is trying to pull off now. He is the man behind the Avon ladies' new Web site, which Avon says will have its official launch in late September. But even the most successful corporate entrepreneur has to learn a new set of rules when it comes to the Net. And Edwards is about to come face to face with just how tough it can be to attract online customers. He's facing a rash of new and fast-growing competitors with plenty of entrepreneurial energy of their own. "I've gone through a learning curve that is staggering," says Edwards, 52, who has worked at Avon for 17 years and, Net or no Net, still isn't averse to wearing a well-cut blue suit.

Looking for Action. That alone makes him a sharp contrast to the founders of the No. 1 beauty site, Eve.com. Eve's co-founders, Mariam Naficy, 29, and Varsha Rao, 30, are former roommates who have had more than their share of bumps along the way—such as having to buy the domain name Eve.com from a precocious 7-year-old in Virginia. With financial backing from Pasadena (Calif.)-based idealab! and a new management team from posh retailer Barneys New York, they're moving past just beauty products and into jewelry and accessories as well. "The chances of any venture succeeding are really slim," says Rao. "We wanted to do something where even if it wasn't a success, we'd have learned a lot and had a good time."

These days, everyone seems to want in on the good times. With online sales of health and beauty products at $756 million in the first six months of this year, it's no wonder major real-world beauty names like Avon, LVMH's Sephora stores, and Estée Lauder are all looking for a piece of the action. But as Avon and the rest of the pack come online, they have to face the fact that much of what they know about cosmetics in the real world just doesn't apply. For one thing, online customers are more affluent and better educated than the general population. Their purchasing behavior is different, too. Generally, makeup and skin care are thought of as "replacement" businesses—70% of what sells is someone's next tube of her favorite cream. But at Eve.com, Rao and Naficy have found that replenishment is only 40% of the Eve.com buying. The biggest share of sales are impulse buys, something a customer has never tried before. And the pair have also found that make-up brands with very little presence in the real world—like BeneFit and Nars—are among their most popular. "The Web is not similar to a physical store," says Naficy. "The shopping behavior is completely different."

Still, a real-world presence can have its advantages. Jim Kenny, chief executive officer of Sephora.com, says that by knowing what the hot products are in the stores, he can better stock his site. Avon's Edwards sees another plus: He says the $100 million Avon is spending on advertising this year has helped direct more motivated buyers to his site. The result is that 4% to 6% of people visiting his site actually buy something—compared with 1% to 2% for most sites.

Sites like Eve and Sephora offer a lot of choice, but's an eclectic mix and doesn't include some of the biggest names such as Estée Lauder and Clinique. Those brands are teaming up with Chanel and Clarins to relaunch their gloss.com Web site next year. That powerful team may force a shakeout among the online beauty sites, says Forrester Research Inc. analyst Evie Black Dykema. Whatever happens, rest assured that by then, all the rules will have changed again.

Late Start

Can Jung really move Avon forward into an e-tailing future while keeping her reps happy? It's a long shot, but she has an ambitious plan. Jung is promising to offer them more business on the Net and ways for them to better manage the new reps that they recruit. She's earmarked $60 million to build a Web site focused around the reps and the Avon catalog. For $15 a month, any rep can become what Avon calls an "eRepresentative" who can sell online and earn commissions ranging from 20% to 25% for orders shipped direct or 30% to 50% for ones they do deliver. That's good money for very little work. And it's also good business for Avon. Today, most reps still fill out 40-page paper order forms in No. 2 pencil and send them in by mail or fax. The cost of processing that order is 90¢. On the Web, it's 30¢. Says Chief Operating Officer Susan Kropf: "Anything we can get off of paper has a significant cost advantage to us."

Unfortunately for Jung, Avon is getting a late start. Back in 1997, the company put up an early but basic Web site that offered only a small fraction of its products for sale.

Management consciously downplayed the Net's role to avoid a backlash from reps. But as the importance of the Web became more obvious, it was clear that tack wouldn't work for long. But what would? The internal struggle over Net strategy dragged out over three long years and cost Avon its early online lead. Now, small upstarts like Eve.com are running away with the lion's share of the nearly $1 billion online beauty-products business.

While executives dawdled, reps, meanwhile, reacted with outrage last year when the company took the mild step of printing its Web address on catalogs. Many simply covered it with their own stickers and forced the company to quickly remove it. They also lambasted Avon for selling online while prohibiting reps from setting up their own sites. "It was like Avon was directly competing with the representatives that they claim to serve," says Jennifer Cobb, an Avon rep who quit nine months ago, in part out of frustration with Avon's Web policy.

Jung's response has been swift. To ensure the reps' concerns are considered, Avon has been polling them about the site, asking them what kind of technology could help them. Focus groups include both the Web-savvy and the technologically illiterate to create a site that everyone can use. The result: a Web-site design that gives customers an option to shop with Avon directly but first asks them if they'd like an eRepresentative in their Zip Code. "I don't believe [that] in the future, sitting alone in front of the Internet is how people are going to conduct their lives," says Jung. "What we do is about relationships, affiliations, being with other people. That is never going to go out." Already, 11,800 Avon reps have signed up to sell online. That's a small fraction of the total 500,000 U.S. reps, but Jung wants to get the 54% of them who aren't already online there by offering them Gateway Inc. PCs plus Internet hookups for $19.95 a month. At the Las Vegas conference, where Avon hyped the site heavily, "no one," says Len Edwards, head of Avon.com, "came up to me once and said, 'You're stealing my business.' "

If Jung's Web strategy prevails, she, for one, won't be surprised. Achievement has always been a given. Born in Canada, she grew up in Wellesley, Mass., the daughter of middle-class immigrant parents. There, she and her younger brother were raised in the demanding environment of a family determined to succeed. Her father, born in Hong Kong, received his master's degree in architecture from Massachusetts Institute of Technology. Her mother, born in Shanghai, was a chemical engineer before becoming an accomplished pianist. Jung excelled in school and studied Chinese and piano, which she still plays.

After graduating from Princeton University in 1979 with a *magna cum laude* degree in English literature, Jung surprised her family by entering the executive training program at Bloomingdale's. As she rose through the ranks there, and later at I. Magnin and Neiman Marcus, she forged friendships with such successful fashion tastemakers as designer Donna Karan and Anne Sutherland Fuchs, then publisher of *Vogue*. Karan, on whose board of directors Jung once sat, today calls her a mentor. Later in New York, Jung and her husband were regulars on the party circuit, where her Armani gowns and good looks were chronicled on the society pages.

Making the Connection

Earlier in her career, some co-workers say they found Jung "aloof" and detached. But at Avon, she has lost some of that reserve, and that has helped her connect with Avon reps. "Four years ago, I saw an extremely private, incredibly brilliant person," says Brian C. Connolly, Avon's senior vice-president for U.S. sales and operations. "Now I see a leader who's willing to tell the story of her heritage, her grandmother, her daughter. She's more comfortable in herself."

From her start at Avon, Jung seemed to look at the company differently than management old-timers. Brought in to study whether it should be moving into retail, she came back with a quick "no," arguing that neither the products nor the sales reps were ready. Her no-nonsense views impressed then-CEO James E. Preston, who offered her a job as head of marketing. Once Jung was on board, Preston became her mentor and ally. He promoted her career, asking her to speak at board meetings. That put her on a par with executives who had been at Avon for decades. "We looked at the market through one set of glasses," says Preston, one of the old guard. "She had a fresh take on what Avon could be."

More than anything, Jung proved she was decisive. She would approve a detailed, million-dollar ad campaign in as little as 15 minutes. Early on, she sacked Avon's ad agency and ordered a complete packaging redesign. She killed Avon's hodgepodge of regional brands and replaced them with global brands like Avon Color, a line of cosmetics. That cut out 35% to 40% of Avon catalog items. "You don't sell anything to Andrea. She buys it or she doesn't," says Mary Lou Quinlan, the former CEO of N. W. Ayer & Partners, the agency that Jung brought in when she ran Avon's marketing.

Still, in 1997, when the board began a search for Preston's successor, Jung had two strikes against her: She had no operating experience and she had never worked overseas, where Avon now gets two-thirds of its revenue. In the end, the board picked outsider Perrin, a former chief of Duracell. Jung became chief operating officer and heir apparent.

Though passed over for CEO, Jung's promotion leapfrogged a number of candidates with far more time at Avon, including her then-boss Christina A. Gold, who soon left the company. Preston remembers a senior manager, with 25 years at Avon, who came to him in protest after Jung was promoted. "I think this is a mistake," he recalls the executive saying. "She's unknown, unproven. She won't be accepted outside the U.S." But six weeks later, Preston says, after Jung had made a two-day visit to Latin America, the executive had changed his tune. "He said, 'You were right. I was wrong. People loved her down here.' I thought, 'Bingo!'" Preston says.

Jung will need to deploy all her charisma as she begins to move Avon beyond cosmetics, jewelry, and clothing into an array of new products and services. Next year, Avon reps around the world will begin selling nutritional supplements and vitamins manufactured by pharmaceuticals manufacturer Roche Holding Ltd., a line that Avon says could reach $300 million in sales within 5 years. She's pushing Avon hard into multilevel marketing, where reps get a percentage of the sales of those they recruit. And she has just launched Beauty Advisor, which trains Avon reps as personal advisers to their customers on what products look and work best for them. It's an area where smaller competitors such as Addison (Tex.)-based Mary Kay Inc. have long dominated. But Jung is betting that she can marshal Avon's enormous sales force to capture plenty of it. The company's offerings could eventually expand to include in-store spa facials and massages. Down the road, Avon might even offer expert financial services and legal advice targeted toward women.

Too Much at Once?

It's a lot to do. But Jung insists that moving fast on several fronts is key. Until about five years ago, for example, sales in Taiwan were growing less than 5% a year. Then Avon's management in Taiwan introduced multilevel marketing and opened showrooms to sell Avon products directly to consumers. The payoff: Avon is now growing 20% a year in Taiwan.

Still, some wonder whether Jung isn't pushing too hard. In the late 1970s and 1980s, Avon went on an expansion tear, purchasing jewelry retailer Tiffany & Co., perfumer Giorgio Beverly Hills, and even a health-care company. Almost all lost the company money, and the result was $1.2 billion in debt and three hostile takeover bids in the early 1990s. "Their efforts at distribution and diversification," says Kline & Co. consultant Susan M. Babinsky, "don't have a real good track record." And though Avon cites a de-valued Brazilian real and some weak holiday sales for its disastrous fourth quarter last year, others say the company was again trying to do too much at once: everything from exploiting technology to striving for double-digit increases in the beauty business, all while overhauling the Avon catalog in the U.S. To avoid a repeat of that kind of debacle, Jung is emphasizing open communication, including setting up a CEO advisory council of 10 top performers from every level of the company and from all around the globe.

That Jung, with her expensive designer suits and elegant jewelry, has found a way to bond with the average Avon rep may be her most surprising feat. As she walked the halls of the convention in the days leading up to her speech, Jung couldn't go more than a few steps without crowds asking her to pose for a group photo or sign an autograph. "I'm going to take a photo and have it blown up and put it on my wall for motivation," said Julie A. Mann, a 24-year-old rep from San Diego, who waited in line for 15 minutes.

Jung doesn't shrink from the idea that she's a role model, even though it's put her private life sharply in the public light. Ten years ago, she wouldn't have brought her daughter in to work. If she had a pediatrician's appointment, she would say she had an outside meeting. Today, she wants to set a different example, and her daughter, now 11, regularly visits the Avon offices and, for an occasional treat, Avon's Fifth Avenue spa. Not that Jung doesn't have her share of challenges at home. She's now separated from Gould, though they are both raising her daughter from a previous marriage and a 3-year-old adopted son. "She's the kind of woman that most women aspire to be," says Donna Karan. "But you're always asking, 'Oh my God. How does she do it all?'"

Just being home can be a challenge. Jung, who traveled to 20 countries last year and has plenty of long workdays in New York, admits to occasional doubts and guilt. Does her 11-year-old know that Jung is the boss? "Not really. But she did ask me one time what it means to be CEO," says Jung. "I try to make her feel like she's no different from anyone else's daughter."

With so many eyes on her, Jung is under intense pressure to perform. So far, few are betting against her. Since her first day as CEO, Avon's stock is up 23%, compared to an 11% gain for the Standard & Poor's 500-stock index. Excluding a special charge last year, sales and earnings for the first half of 2000 are up 9% and 40% respectively. "She bit off a lot. The challenges are great," says investor Robert Hagstrom, senior vice-president of Legg Mason Fund Manager and director of Legg Mason's Focus Capital. But "at this point, it would be very hard to give her anything less than A's."

That's good for starters. Now Jung has to bring the same magic that she showed off in Las Vegas to the bottom line. Maybe then, Jung can turn Avon back into an "A" company.

Cross-Functional Integration

Traditionally, each functional area performs specialized portions of the organization's tasks. Dating back to the late 1700s, this division of labor is the basis for much departmentalization because of the commonsense appeal of having functions that are performed by experts in specific fields. For example, marketing resolves questions concerning which markets to target, the breadth of the product offering, and the appropriate marketing mix elements. These vertical activities are tackled more easily, since they require expertise in only one functional area. Horizontal activities, however, cut across functional lines and require substantially more coordination among functions. An organization's success with its marketing strategy in a specific product market depends on the effective coordination of strategies and activities across functions.

Companies such as General Electric, Hewlett-Packard, Ford Motor Company, Deere & Company, and Motorola have all recognized that success is dependent on managing across functional boundaries. Success in marketing strategy formulation and implementation requires the input and cooperation of all the players in the organization. The tendency to "box" management functions—so that manufacturing does not talk with research and development, research and development does not talk with marketing, marketing does not talk with manufacturing, and salespeople do not talk with anyone in the organization—creates functions that are empty of responsibility and devoid of interaction.

As one of the broadest areas in management, encompassing dimensions from all major business functions, marketing is in a strong boundary-spanning position in the company. Drivers behind the need for the marketing department to partner with major functions of the organization, as well as potential conflicts between functions, are discussed in this part. The marketing department's lead role in the successful implementation of a market-oriented corporate strategy becomes evident as key relationships and interactions are identified.

Drivers of Cross-Functional Integration

As marketing has developed and adapted strategies to meet customers' expectations, several issues have arisen that necessitate greater internal partnering between marketing and other business functions. These issues include

- Speeding products to market.
- Mass customization.
- Quality and the internal marketing link.

Speeding Products to Market

The 1990s witnessed a shift in the way businesses attempt to gain competitive advantage. Recognizing that product life cycles were becoming shorter and shorter—and that the penalties for being late to market were becoming higher and higher—several companies turned to speed as a way to compete. Often referred to as time-based competition or quick response, speed as a marketing strategy encompasses both new products and product modifications. Speed involves moving products from concept to market in less time than can be done with traditional methods, ultimately reducing time throughout the company's value chain.

The key in speeding products to market is a multidisciplinary approach to marketing. In this approach business functions work simultaneously on the new or modified product. In this simultaneous development process, the traditional relay-race approach to bringing products to market—passing the baton from design to manufacturing to marketing—is replaced with a new and more exciting rugby match in which design, manufacturing, and marketing rush a new product downfield together.[1]

Regardless of whether speed is established as a strategic paradigm, the long-term effects of time-based competition will continue to reside in the multidisciplinary framework that has resulted from such competition; that in and of itself will be a sustainable competitive advantage.

Mass Customization

While speed as a marketing strategy is gaining a foothold in businesses worldwide, another new marketing paradigm has emerged—mass customization—which has some of the same underpinnings. Mass customization encompasses the low-cost production of high-variety, individually customized products and services to almost all customers.[2] There are four basic innovations that come together to achieve mass customization:

- Just-in-time production and delivery.
- Reduction of setup and changeover times.
- Compression of cycle times.
- Production upon receipt of order (instead of producing to forecasts).

Mass customization is linked closely with time-based competition. Speeding products to market allows a firm to increase variety, which in turn allows the firm to satisfy a wider range of customer desires. Successful implementation of mass customization touches all aspects of the business: operational, organizational, and cultural. This overarching companywide impact has made mass customization a key driver in the need for a better understanding of cross-functional interactions in the formulation and implementation of marketing strategies. Mass customization is also inextricably linked to the role of technology in both marketing and corporate strategies.

Quality and the Internal Marketing Link

Schonberger[3] suggests that business functions such as research and development (R&D), manufacturing, accounting, and marketing form a continuous chain of customers that extends to the end user (buyer) of the product. If anyone in the chain messes up, the final product or service is put in jeopardy. In essence, everyone in the firm has a customer. The customer may be one of the following:

- Someone in purchasing who has to order the parts to complete the product's assembly.
- Someone in marketing who develops the creative component of the ad campaign.
- Someone in customer service who responds to a customer's complaint that the product is not fitting together as the instruction booklet says it should.

Attaining marketing's goal of having loyal, repeat customers is made possible by having a high-quality product that the customer wants and needs, having a high-quality product at a reasonably competitive price, and having a high-quality product at the right time. Marketing's goal is easily attainable when everyone in the company is concerned with his or her respective internal customers and with the final customer.

Achieving the internal mind-set in which the next person or group is considered a customer reinforces the need for functions to work together in an amicable manner. Also, the extension of a traditional marketing term, *customer*, into the language of all functions highlights marketing's boundary-spanning position in the firm.

Marketing's Cross-Functional Partners

The traditional functional areas of business are marketing, research and development, manufacturing/operations, accounting/finance, and human resources. Marketing is portrayed as the functional area closest to the customer, with the other functions having more of an internal focus.

The two functions that have a direct effect on marketing are R&D and manufacturing/operations. The impact of these two functions is felt particularly in the areas of product development and product management. The effect of the accounting/finance functional area generally is reflected in the company's pricing process. The human resources function is in a cross-functional facilitating position as a result of its interactions with the marketing department. This is true except in the *services industry,* where the service provider is intimately involved in the production and marketing of the service.

Marketing and Research and Development

Consider the following quote and think about what it means: "Great devices are invented in the laboratory. Great products are invented in the marketing department."[4] What is the difference between a device and a product? Most marketers probably would say that from a utility perspective, a device and a product are the same thing. However, it is the extras that turn a device into a product that is desirable to the consumer. A product, then, is an augmented device.

It is not surprising that one of the most significant causes of new product failure is a lack of integration between R&D and marketing in the early stages of product conceptualization and development. This lack of integration has been driven by what many refer to as supply-side versus demand-side marketing.[5]

Supply-side proponents argue that marketing should stay out of the research and development of new products since marketers do not produce truly new products. From this perspective, marketers are viewed as involved largely with me-too products. R&D becomes the key player, leaving marketing to make money for the company by delivering products on the basis of what Shanklin and Ryans refer to as "presumptive need." R&D

develops a product based on cutting-edge technology, and then marketing creates the market for that product.

Demand-side marketing is based on a market-pull perspective. With this market-driven approach, R&D's job becomes one of responding to marketplace needs—needs that typically are identified by marketing research. In this scenario, marketing conducts end user research to identify current and future wants and needs. Those wants and needs then are handed over to the R&D department to translate into a device. Marketing then adds value to the device and turns it into a desirable product offering.

Both sides have legitimate concerns. Supply-siders blame marketers for

- Speeding products to market (resulting in what they say is a lack of innovation and too many me-too products).
- Ignoring quality.
- Using soft data (imprecise consumer attitudinal data).
- Killing innovation.

Demand-siders blame R&D for

- Failure to identify products that satisfy consumers' wants and needs.
- Overly sophisticated products that consumers are not ready for.
- A lack of responsiveness to the marketplace.
- Inflexibility in terms of consumers' wants.
- Designing technologically successful products that are commercial failures.

Some observers suggest that the nature of the industry determines whether marketing should be supply-side- or demand-side-driven. Complexity and the industry life cycles are the determining factors here. For example, a complex industry such as high technology at first is supply-side-driven. As the industry moves toward maturity, marketing becomes more demand-side-oriented. Less complex products such as consumer packaged goods would need to be demand-side-oriented.

Marketing and Manufacturing/Operations

Manufacturing experts Hayes and Wheelwright contend, "The marketing/manufacturing interface is the focal point of much more frequent and heated disagreement than occurs between other pairs of functions."[6] These two functions are the ones involved in ultimately getting a product off the shop floor and to the customer. If a product is delayed in assembly or shipping, marketing is responsible for letting the customer know that the product will not be available. The delay may cause unhappiness or anger on the part of the customer, and the customer may vent this anger on someone in marketing. Unfortunately, the marketing person's hands are tied, and marketing probably does not feel responsible for the delay on the shop floor.

Three major categories of conflict exist between marketing and manufacturing: (1) managing diversity, (2) managing conformity, and (3) managing dependability.[7] In regard to diversity, producing a variety of items is often a requirement for meeting customer demands. Products vary in shape, size, flavor, and other dimensions. The company makes decisions pertaining to the number of items in a line, the number of different lines to offer, building to customer specifications, modifying existing products, and eliminating and adding products. Hayes and Clark[8] refer to the managerial actions related to these decisions as confusion-engendering activities. The confusion is caused, for example, by varying production rates, expediting orders, or changing production specifications.

Managing conformity takes place while marketing stimulates demand for a product and manufacturing makes certain the product is available. In the short run, manufacturing manages the transformation process through its production schedule. Over the long run, manufacturing manages the process by making decisions about capacity and facility planning.

Managing dependability requires actions by both marketing and manufacturing. Specifically, tension often occurs that relates to delivery and quality control. Marketing wants rapid delivery and high standards. However, rapid delivery may mean that manufacturing has to maintain a large inventory. Furthermore, producing high-quality products quickly is not always possible.

Marketplace demands for both wide variety and reduced delivery lead times present what McCutcheon, Raturi, and Meredith refer to as the customization-responsiveness squeeze.[9] This trend is characterized by the need to deliver highly differentiated products in less time than it takes to make them. It is unlikely that companies can manage this squeeze without some changes in the interactions and methods of both marketing and manufacturing.

Marketing and Accounting/Finance

Historically, the marketing function has tended to operate with minimal input from the financial unit. Additionally, it has eluded many of the financial constraints imposed on the company as a whole. A frequently heard complaint is that marketers do not understand the financial consequences of their marketing strategies and programs. However, Foster and Gupta report that marketing costs have received very little attention from accountants.[10]

The lack of attention given to one function by the other may be attributed to the substantial difference in functional focus: Marketing emphasizes sales volume and sales revenue, while accounting/finance emphasizes the cost of goods sold. Accountants tend to follow a production-oriented approach to business. Accordingly, accountants and financial managers have a difficult time using manufacturing cost techniques to analyze marketing costs. Marketing data cannot be imported directly into these techniques.

Foster and Gupta attribute such marketing and manufacturing costs differences to four major factors:[11]

1. Marketing costs are not inventoriable under general accounting principles or taxation laws.

2. A higher percent of marketing costs is discretionary; thus, a less clear cause-and-effect relationship exists between input and output.

3. The time span between cost commitment and cost incurrence is much shorter for marketing.

4. Marketing costs (e.g., advertising) generally are not allowed as cost items under U.S. government contracts.

However, activity-based costing (ABC) has emerged as an accounting technique that seems appropriate for interaction with the marketing function. The general idea behind ABC is to associate a particular marketing function with the activities involved in that function.

Causes of Cross-Functional Conflict

As we have seen in the preceding paragraphs, the need for coordination between marketing and other business functions is obvious. However, marketing's interface with other functional areas is frequently problematic. For example, Souder reported an element of disharmony between marketing and R&D in almost 60 percent of 289 new product projects examined in his study.[12] Additionally, anecdotal evidence is abundant describing cross-functional problems within particular companies.

Reasons for conflict between marketing and other business functions include

- Physical separation.
- Reward systems.
- Personality.
- Data differences.

In many organizations, marketing is physically separated from the manufacturing/operations functional area. Marketing may be located strategically close to customer groups, while manufacturing/operations locates in low-wage areas or close to suppliers. This physical separation generally results in a lack of communication and understanding between the two groups and may be exacerbated by language differences and cultural differences if the groups locate in different countries.

Marketing and the other business functions respond to different reward systems. Generally, marketing has a goal of, and is rewarded for, increased sales. Increasing sales often requires timely delivery, product customization, and variety in the product offering. At the same time, accounting/finance and manufacturing/operations in particular are trying to keep costs down (and are rewarded for such measures). Reducing costs means tight inventory and economies due to long production runs and few machine changeovers. Accounting/finance often feels that marketing is too extravagant in its expense accounts and willingness to extend credit terms.

Lucas and Bush report that marketing and R&D managers have different personalities and that these differences are related to perceived satisfaction of the marketing–R&D interface.[13] Typically, the salesperson stays in marketing because of his or her customer orientation, the production operator or engineer stays in manufacturing or R&D because of his or her technical orientation, and the accountant pursues the chief financial officer's position.

One only has to look at the type of data marketing deals with compared to the other business functions to see that data differences can be a major cause of conflict. The type of data collected and used in each area is different due in part to the traditional concerns with demand and supply regulations. Marketing's interests rest with concerns about what are perceived to be the customer's wants and needs, unit sales, and competitive offerings. By contrast, manufacturing/operations strictly maintains production output, cost, and cycle data and R&D has specifications regarding tensile strength, electrical usage, and battery power. Accounting/financial data are tightly controlled by general accounting procedures and well-established econometric models. Marketing data often are seen as "soft" compared to the "hard" data of other functional areas.

Whatever the root cause, the conflict generally manifests itself initially as a communication problem between marketing and the other function. The communication problem quickly escalates into distrust, which can inadvertently sabotage current as well as future interactions.

Facilitating Cross-Functional Interactions

While conflict is a normal part of any workplace environment, the conflict between marketing and other business functions has tended to be destructive to corporate, business unit, and functional planning and implementation. The central challenge is to reduce conflict in cross-functional interactions. Exhortations and predictive frameworks suggest four major facilitating mechanisms for improving interfunctional coordination:

- Organizational design.
- Evaluation systems.
- Improved communications.
- Information technology.

Many business managers and researchers support the need for an organizational design conducive to nurturing integrative activities and possibly the demise of older, functionally specialized structures.[14] Lorsch and Lawrence's seminal piece on differentiation/integration suggested that organization's first divide the total task into specialized pieces and then provide a means by which individual units coordinate their activities to achieve a unified effort.[15]

Cross-functional teams have been a major outgrowth of this focus on organizational design as a facilitating mechanism. As stated by Parker:[16]

- Individualism is out—teamwork is in.
- Specialization is out—a new-style generalism is in.
- Rigid organizational lines are out—fluid collaboration is in.
- Power is out—empowerment is in.
- Hierarchical organizations are out—network, adaptive, informal, horizontal organizations are in.

Early research on evaluation systems found that the use of a joint reward system influenced significantly the effectiveness of cross-functional integration.[17] Because it is tied closely to the firm's evaluation system, the reward system strongly affects the way employees do their jobs. In regard to interactions between marketing and R&D, Carroad and Carroad suggested different types of reward systems for cross-functional success: (1) percentage of profits that arise from products not produced five years ago, (2) percentage of initially screened ideas that reach commercialization, and (3) rewarding an employee for individual work (e.g., sales) as well as effort within a group that produces a product innovation.[18]

More recently, the "balanced scorecard" has been developed by Kaplan and Norton as a way of combining financial measures of performance with the firm's operational measures of performance.[19] The scorecard links four major business perspectives:

1. Financial perspective: How do we look to shareholders?
2. Internal business perspective: What must we excel at?
3. Innovation and learning perspective: Can we continue to improve and create value?
4. Customer perspective: How do customers see us?

A breakdown in communication may be the first sign of conflict between marketing and another business function. Thus, several authorities espouse the need for improved communications as a prerequisite for interfunctional effectiveness. One method of communication that should enhance integrative attempts is adaptive interfacing. The idea behind this method is that people should alter their form of communication to match the style of those with whom they want to interact. For example, Lucas and Bush[20] suggest that marketers temper their assertiveness and refrain from being overly enthusiastic about projects when they interact with R&D personnel since R&D managers tend to be more emotional and timid in their business dealings. A formal communication program that encourages frequent, structured communication between marketing and other business functions could facilitate this adaptive interfacing.

Not surprisingly, information technology is now at the forefront in linking marketing with its functional partners. Navistar uses a customer database linked with manufacturing/operations, with the result being market segments that provide Navistar with the opportunity to engage in micromarketing. Advances in information technology will allow marketing to understand and work within the interdependent components of the organization. Shop floor information no longer will belong only to manufacturing. Marketing will have immediate access to availability of production, allowing us to make better estimates of availability. R&D will have immediate access to market research data, allowing it to utilize customer information in the design of products.

Advances in technology are reflected in the company's bottom line. For example, scanners can automatically track inventory and create shipping bills, orders can be received and reconciled immediately with customer credit history, and orders can be received and sent simultaneously to manufacturing, with all of this eliminating redundancy and delays in company operations.

The Human Resources Partner

Whatever the facilitating mechanism(s) ultimately selected for use, successful cross-functional integration will be driven by the human resources partner. People are the heart of interactions between marketing and other business functions. Today's human resource managers will be in charge of many of the facilitating tools that we have identified. For example, a human resources manager will lead the workshops for improved communication, work with payroll to implement a joint reward system, and work closely in the management of cross-functional teams.

Hathcock[21] best sums up this human resource imperative: "The 21st century human resource imperative is to raise the company's human capital to sophisticated levels which produce competitive advantages for the enterprise."

Summary

A decade ago Regis McKenna suggested, "Marketing today is not a function, it is a way of doing business."[22] While there will always be a need for experts in particular aspects of developing a marketing program—experts housed in the traditional marketing function—this part opener has identified the critical functional interactions that must take place in the development of a successful marketing program. McKenna successfully predicted the orientation that firms would move toward in the twenty-first century and the critical nature of marketing in this orientation.

The important role of marketing and its cross-functional interactions is summed up by Schonberger, a world-renowned authority on production and manufacturing: "The marketing message doesn't belong just to the marketing people; we all must assume part of the job of presenting our products, services, talents, and capacity to the customer."[23]

End Notes

1. Hirotaka Takeuchi and Ikujiro Nonaka, "The 'New' New Product Development Game," *Harvard Business Review,* January–February 1986, pp. 137–46.
2. B. Joseph Pine II, *Mass Customization: The New Frontier in Business Competition* (Boston: Harvard Business School Press, 1993).
3. Richard J. Schonberger, *Building a Chain of Customers: Linking Business Functions to Create the World-Class Company* (New York: Free Press, 1990).
4. William H. Davidson, *Marketing High Technology* (New York: Free Press, 1986), p. 25.
5. For additional information on supply- versus demand-side marketing, see William L. Shanklin and John K. Ryans, Jr. "Organizing for High-Tech Marketing,"

Harvard Business Review, November–December 1984, pp. 164–71, and George H. Lucas, Jr., and Alan J. Bush, "The Marketing-R&D Interface: Do Personality Factors Have an Impact?" *Journal of Product Innovation Management,* December 1988, pp. 257–68.

6. Robert M. Hayes and Steven C. Wheelwright, *Restoring Our Competitive Edge: Competing through Manufacturing* (New York: Wiley, 1984), p. 199.

7. Victoria L. Crittenden, Lorraine R. Gardiner, and Antonie Stam, "Reducing Conflict between Marketing and Manufacturing," *Industrial Marketing Management,* vol. 22, 1993.

8. Robert H. Hayes and Kim B. Clark, "Exploring the Sources of Productivity Differences at the Factory Level," in *The Uneasy Alliance,* edited by Kim B. Clark, Robert H. Hayes, and Christopher Lorenz (Boston: Harvard Business School Press, 1985).

9. David M. McCutcheon, Amitabh S. Raturi, and Jack R. Meredith, "The Customization-Responsiveness Squeeze," *Sloan Management Review,* Winter 1994, pp. 89–99.

10. George Foster and Mahendra Gupta, "Marketing, Cost Management and Management Accounting," *Journal of Management Accounting Research,* Fall 1994, pp. 43–77.

11. Ibid.

12. W. E. Souder, "Managing Relations between R&D and Marketing in New Product Development Projects," *Journal of Product Innovation Management,* vol. 5, 1998, pp. 6–19.

13. Lucas and Bush, "The Marketing-R&D Interface."

14. Joe D. Goldhar and Mariann Jelinek, "Plan for Economies of Scope," *Harvard Business Review,* November–December 1983, pp. 141–48.

15. Jay W. Lorsch and Paul R. Lawrence, "Organizing for Product Innovation," *Harvard Business Review,* January–February 1965, pp. 109–20.

16. Glenn M. Parker, *Cross-Functional Teams: Working with Allies, Enemies, and Other Strangers* (San Francisco: Jossey-Bass, 1994), p. 3.

17. William E. Souder and Alok K. Chakrabarti, "The R&D/Marketing Interface: Results from an Empirical Study of Innovation Projects," *IEEE Transactions on Engineering Management,* November 1978, pp. 88–93.

18. Paul A. Carroad and Connie A. Carroad, "Strategic Interfacing of R&D and Marketing," *Research Management,* January 1982, pp. 28–33.

19. Robert S. Kaplan and David P. Norton, "The Balanced Scorecard—Measures That Drive Performance," *Harvard Business Review,* January–February 1992, pp. 71–79.

20. Lucas and Bush, "The Marketing–R&D Interface."

21. Bonnie C. Hathcock, "The New Breed Approach to 21st Century Human Resources," *Human Resource Management,* Summer 1996, p. 244.

22. Regis McKenna, "Marketing Is Everything," *Harvard Business Review,* January–February 1991, p. 69.

23. Schonberger, *Building a Chain of Customers: Linking Business Functions to Create the World-Class Company,* p. 16.

CASES FOR PART 6

The marketing function does not operate in a vacuum. The eight cases in this part focus on the cross-functional integration needed to implement marketing strategies. This integration is examined in small local companies as well as larger companies with functions located in different countries.

The video case, **Navistar International Transportation Corporation (Case 6–1),** centers on how a large corporation should implement a customer orientation program. The company must develop customer-focused programs while simultaneously cutting costs.

Floral Farms (Case 6–2) is a producer and distributor of fresh-cut flowers. The flowers are grown in South America and then marketed and distributed in the United States. The annual planning meeting has not gone well. While the marketing arm of the business (located in the United States) projects increased demand for most of the company's major products, the production arm (located in South America) seems either unable or unwilling to alter its production plans. The company's owner has told the two groups to work toward developing a mutually agreeable forecast.

Senior management at the **National Bicycle Industrial Company (Case 6–3)** is considering changes in the firm's mass-customization strategy. There are mixed feelings about whether the firm should modify its strategy in order to increase its customer base.

A privately held company, **Powrtron Corporation (Case 6–4),** was grappling with an unprecedented problem of constrained capacity. Top management had to immediately resolve capacity, delivery, and customer problems. Exacerbating these problems was the tension between the sales and marketing manager and the manufacturing manager. Manufacturing felt that sales and marketing was making unreasonable delivery commitments, while sales and marketing blamed manufacturing for customer dissatisfaction problems.

Case 6–5, Chemical Additives Corporation: Specialty Products Group, focuses on the company's strategy of moving away from large-volume commodity markets and toward niche markets. Critical to this move's success is the positioning and pricing of three corrosion inhibitors used during the transport and storage of liquid fertilizer.

A modular home construction/sales company, **Southern Home Developers (Case 6–6),** has been in business for less than a year. Potential for the company's modular homes was strong, as was nationwide demand. However, the company was beginning to experience conflict between customers' expectations and the operational side of the business.

Quality Plastics International S.A. de C.V. (Case 6–7) is a Mexico-based plastics manufacturer. It is believed that the company is successful because it gives customers what they want at a good price. However, the owner is puzzled by comments from the plant manager and the accountant. The owner's enthusiasm about the company's growth opportunities apparently is not shared by the entire management team.

The e-business case **(Case 6–8)** describes efforts at **Intel** to foster internal collaboration. Such collaborative efforts are expected to lead the company into new markets and new businesses.

CASE 6–1
NAVISTAR INTERNATIONAL TRANSPORTATION CORPORATION

> A truck is a capital good. It's purchased to do a job. It's not purchased for esoteric reasons, it's only purchased to create value for the user. The buyer is a very professional person or company. They are looking for something that's going to create a return for them. [Our job] is understanding the needs of each one of those customers.
>
> Gary E. Dewel

Gary E. Dewel, senior vice president of sales and marketing at Navistar, reflected on the strategic intent that had been a major factor in the Fortune 500 company's turnaround. A descendant of International Harvester Corporation, Navistar was on the brink of bankruptcy in 1982. Heavy debt, rising interest rates, and a struggling agricultural business resulted in the loss of $3.4 billion between 1980 and 1985. New management, facing the task of transforming the stifling bureaucracy into a flexible organization with the ability to compete in an increasingly competitive trucking industry, had chosen to focus on reducing costs and increasing customer service. Management felt that a greater familiarity with the customer would result in a competitive advantage that had been lacking in Navistar's history. Management knew, however, that a customer orientation would have to go hand in hand with new avenues for cutting costs. At the same time, Navistar had to keep abreast of market changes as a result of the North American Free Trade Agreement (NAFTA).

The Company

History.   In 1831 Cyrus H. McCormick pioneered the first mechanical grain reaper, providing the foundation for International Harvester, a company specializing in the production of farm machinery. Trucks became part of Harvester's core business in the 1920s as soldiers returning from World War I continued the industrialization of the United States. Perhaps beginning Harvester's troubles, Fowler McCormick, grandson of the late Cyrus, led the company into an era of haphazard expansion in the late 1940s, culminating in a devastating battle to dethrone Caterpillar's leadership of the construction machinery industry.

In the 20 years that followed Fowler's 1951 ousting, Harvester was hindered by an unmanageable variety of truck models. In attempting to provide such a wide product offering, Harvester ignored both production capabilities and marketing difficulties. At the same time, a lack of customer awareness resulting in a gross underestimation of tractor demand severely limited Harvester's main business. Costs soared, and profit margins disappeared.

The agricultural boom of the 1960s and 1970s provided cover for Harvester's rigid structure and rising cost base. The series of strikes and concessions to the United Auto

This case was prepared by Victoria L. Crittenden, associate professor of marketing, Boston College, and John DeVoy, MBA student, Boston College, as the basis for class discussion rather than to illustrate effective or ineffective handling of a managerial situation. Research assistance was provided by David Angus, undergraduate research assistant, Boston College/Andersen Consulting Fund. All information was derived from secondary sources. Revised 1997.

Workers (UAW) through the early 1980s resulted in operating inefficiencies throughout the corporation. Capital spending aimed at the modernization of aging factories was increased modestly but barely offset administrative inefficiencies. The most agonizing union battle came at the start of the 1980 recession, resulting in a six-month strike. Lost sales, rising interest rates, and a growing debt left the company struggling for survival. Trying to keep the company afloat, Archie McCardell, who succeeded McCormick in 1978, sold the company's profitable Solar Turbines unit to Caterpillar in 1981 and disposed of several smaller businesses, including the company's unprofitable steel mill.

New management was brought in by early 1982. Donald Lennox (on the verge of retirement from International Harvester) began presiding over the company. Unfortunately, his tenure began at the start of four of the worst years in the company's history. Saddled with tremendous debt and outdated product lines, Lennox was forced to do everything possible to keep the company from hemorrhaging cash.

With the sale of its losing agricultural business to Tenneco in 1985—along with the rights to the Harvester name—the company adopted the name Navistar and began to focus exclusively on manufacturing trucks.

Navistar International Corporation.   Navistar International Corporation, with its world headquarters in Chicago, Illinois, was a holding company. The corporation was the leading producer of heavy and medium trucks and school buses in North America. The corporation's principal operating subsidiary was Navistar International Transportation. The products were sold to distributors in certain export markets. The company had financial services subsidiaries which provided wholesale, retail, and lease financing as well as commercial physical damage and liability insurance. Dealers and retail customers constituted the majority of the financial services customers.

In 1986, led by James C. Cotting as CFO, the company posted its first full-year profit since 1979, earning $2 million on sales of $3.4 billion. Cotting maneuvered the company through a vast restructuring during the mid-1980s and became chief executive officer in 1987.

Cotting's long-range plan was for half of Navistar's revenue to come from new businesses by 1997. Those new businesses were to come from acquisitions related to Navistar's core truck business. While simultaneously seeking acquisitions, Cotting began cutting costs internally. For example, the plan was to trim 450 white-collar jobs and add more medical copayments on employee insurance by 1990.

Navistar International Transportation Corporation.   The transportation subsidiary of Navistar operated in one principal industry segment: the manufacture and marketing of medium and heavy trucks. This included school bus chassis, midrange diesel engines, and service parts.

Led by Neil A. Springer and based in Chicago, Illinois, the company had introduced 22 new models by 1989. Those models replaced S-Series units, which were introduced in 1977 and 1978. Additionally, the company began partnering with its customers and suppliers.

In late 1987, when U-Haul International wanted to revamp its medium-size rental truck, it could not initially find a supplier that would agree to make the requested design changes. No one was interested because U-Haul was requesting some nontraditional ideas. However, Navistar began working with U-Haul, and the result was that Navistar won an order for 5,400 trucks. U-Haul received a prototype five months after an agreement was reached with Navistar. Dana Corporation, Navistar's frame supplier and partner, brought the truckmaker and U-Haul together.

Started in 1986, the Navistar/Dana Corporation vertical partnership was one of the oldest and most fully developed partnerships between two companies.[1] Both companies felt that combining Dana Corporation's component design expertise and manufacturing capability with Navistar's ability to put the total system together and manage distribution would be an advantage for each firm. The success of the partnership led to partnering between Navistar and Goodyear and between Navistar and Caterpillar. When Navistar introduced two dozen new models in late 1988, the product display included drivetrains composed of Caterpillar engines, transmissions, clutches, drivelines, and axles plus Goodyear tires.

In 1987, top management supported a major cost-cutting proposal: electronic data interchange (EDI). In its simplest form, EDI involved the electronic exchange of business documents over a standard telephone line using computer information systems. Before EDI, Navistar's monthly needs were mailed to suppliers and daily production requirements were phoned in. With EDI in place, Navistar was able to instantaneously transmit and receive documents that previously had taken up to a week of processing time. As a result, inventories were reduced from 33 days' supply to an average of 6 days', and as little as four hours' inventory in some instances. Navistar was able to cut its inventory by $167 million (33 percent) in the first 18 months of EDI implementation.[2]

The U.S. Truck Marketplace

The beginning of the 1990s was not an easy time for truck manufacturers. The trucking industry was reeling from a business recession (which began for truckers around the middle of 1989) that meant both rising fleet expenses and sluggish freight traffic. The economy had posted a 1 percent decline from the third quarter of 1990 through the second quarter of 1991. Predictions were that the economy would begin working itself out of that decline, but the outlook was not good, with growth rates maybe around 2 percent. This translated into expected sluggishness in the trucking marketplace.

Truck Class. Several classes of trucks existed in the truck marketplace. Classes 1 and 2 were considered light-duty trucks. A rise in sales for Class 1 (under–6,000-lbs. GVW[3]) trucks was predicted at the beginning of 1990. Class 2 (6,001-to-10,000–lbs. GVW) sales were thought to have peaked in 1990, and declines were projected for the early 1990s. Vehicles sold for straight commercial fleet applications were expected to account for slightly over 10 percent of combined Classes 1 and 2 sales.

The emerging segment of the commercial market was Classes 3 and 4. Class 3 (10,001-to-14,000–lbs. GVW) was the only vehicle class to show growth in the early 1990s. Class 4 (14,001-to-16,000–lbs. GVW) showed signs of growth, and the outlook was positive. The smallest commercial market class in annual sales, Class 5 (16,001-to-19,500–lbs. GVW), had peaked in sales in 1985, when over 8,000 units were sold.

The medium-duty trucks encompassed Classes 6 and 7. Class 6 (19,501-to-26,000–lbs. GVW) and Class 7 (26,001-to-33,000–lbs. GVW) showed signs of growth. Medium-duty truck sales were predicated on wholesale and retail traffic. Other factors had begun affecting sales in this category as well. First, there was a large number of

---

[1] Interestingly, the partnership did not include a written contract between Navistar and Dana. The deal was consummated on a handshake and a lot of trust.

[2] Before EDI, a one-day reduction in inventory was the largest the company had been able to achieve.

[3] GVW refers to gross vehicle weight.

late-model used trucks in this range. Second, fleets had begun stretching replacement cycles due to increases in warranty mileage coverage.

Heavy trucks made up the Class 8 (over-33,000–lbs. GVW) market. The market for Class 8 trucks had been declining. Projections were that this market would not see an increase until 1992. There was concern that 1991 would be the worst year since the 1982–1983 recession. The industry's replacement-demand pattern was being reshaped due to more productive trucks and an increase in warranty mileage. The trend in the heavy-truck market was toward trucks designed specifically for a single vocation.[4]

The outlook for the mid-1990s was better than that for the beginning of the 1990s. The expected economic recovery would be further along, and carriers would begin replacing older trucks with newer-technology vehicles. Vocational or job-specific trucks[5] increasingly were being considered by buyers and sellers in Classes 3 through 8. Another trend was toward automatic transmissions. By the early 1990s around 70 percent of Class 3 trucks sold were automatics.

Buying Behavior.   Fleet managers were bombarded daily with trade magazines[6] and factory mailings regarding product offerings. Additionally, OEMs and suppliers would often bring their product directly to the offices of larger fleets. The annual International Trucking Show, however, was the premier show for truck manufacturers and truck users to interact. The show offered a hands-on introduction to the newest in trucks and refinements to existing trucks. Another show in which suppliers of trucking equipment and OEMs exhibited was the beverage industry's premier show, the InterBev.

Order specifications from a fleet owner were so detailed they could fill several pages and include as many as 200 line items. Exhibit 1 provides an example of the types of specifications requested by a fleet owner. A large percentage of items might require a specific manufacturer's part. Additionally, there was some concern that many standard parts had not been tested sufficiently before becoming standard. In 1989, estimates were that 60 percent of fleets operating fewer than 10 trucks had Class 8 trucks built to order. The number increased steadily by fleet size, with 94 percent of fleets operating over 100 Class 8 trucks requesting built-to-order trucks. This was a 35 percent increase in built-to-order compared to 1985 figures.

Many truck manufacturers had begun focusing on ways in which they could help the transportation industry address some of its most pressing concerns. A major industry concern was the turnover rate of drivers. It was not uncommon to hear of 80, 100, 110, and 200 percent annual turnover rates among U.S. private fleet owners. This problem was compounded by an increasing driver shortage attributed primarily to low pay, long hours away from home, and uncomfortable equipment.[7] Another major industry concern was holding down costs for the fleet owner.

To address the driver shortage/turnover rate problem, truck makers were concentrating on improving the driver "environment." Manufacturers were providing high-tech

[4] Some industry experts doubted that there would ever be a time when a *standard* model Class 8 truck would be popular.

[5] These were trucks tailored as much as possible to the job requirements of specific vocational applications in given market segments.

[6] Examples include *Fleet Equipment, Fleet Owner, Distribution,* and *Equipment Management.*

[7] The driver shortage problem was expected to be made worse in the short term by the Commercial Driver's License (CDL), which was to be phased in nationwide by 1991. The CDL would provide one national license instead of several state licenses for truck drivers. The short-term impact was expected to be a decrease in the number of drivers (both good and bad). The longer-term impact was expected to be an improved quality of truck driver.

EXHIBIT 1   Example of Fleet Owner Specifications

Category	Percentage of Total Items Ordered
Standard to manufacturer	27%
Improved maintenance	35
Operational requirements	11
Improved safety	8
Increased driver comfort	7
Improved appearance	7
Fuel economy	5

Source: "Spec'ed or Standard," *Fleet Equipment,* June 1989, pp. 38–42

features for comfort, maneuverability, safety, fuel economy, vehicle operation, and maintenance. Manufacturers of Classes 7 and 8 trucks were paying increased attention to drivability, ergonomics, and creature comforts.[8] Both truck manufacturers and fleet owners felt that a driver would treat the truck better if he or she was treated well.

To help fleet owners keep costs down, manufacturers were offering tremendous engineering advances with introductions of new aerodynamic and fuel-efficient designs. Also, durability had improved, with proper maintenance and repowering delaying capital expenditures for equipment replacement. There was even talk of the 1,000,000-mile truck.[9]

Industry Competitors

In the medium and heavy truck categories (principally Classes 7 and 8) there were seven leading manufacturers: Ford, Freightliner, Mack, Volvo, Peterbilt, Kenworth, and Navistar.

Ford.   Ford was the manufacturer of a complete line of light-duty through Class 8 trucks. It produced both diesel and gasoline-powered vehicles. Ford traditionally had been the industry leader in Class 7 trucks. Its major truck plant in Kentucky was dedicated to medium and heavy trucks. This facility operated a rapid scheduling system for special orders. An $18 million computer system allowed Ford to save weeks of special engineering by comparing current and historical orders as a way to utilize existing designs to speed vehicle delivery time. The company operated 28 field locations in the United States. In 1990 Ford planned to spend three times as much money on its heavy-duty truck line as it had in the previous five years. The plans were to upgrade every piece of equipment by 1995.

Ford offered a long line of Classes 7 and 8 trucks. The LTLS-9000 was designed for the heaviest applications. The most appropriate Ford truck for long-haul cargo

[8] Ergonomics is the scientific study of human factors in relation to working environments and equipment design. Examples include dashboard layout, support and seating adjustments, and outside visibility. An example of a creature comfort is an oversized sleeper cab.

[9] The 1,000,000-mile truck would go 1 million miles with good routine maintenance and without rebuilding major components.

applications was the LTL-9000. Ford's L-Series included a broad range of other heavy-duty trucks. In 1991 Ford was to offer its new AeroMax series. This aerodynamic series focused on fuel efficiency. Additionally, Ford planned to offer 24-hour emergency road service for the AeroMax.

Ford had conducted driver surveys at truck stops across North America. Those surveys focused on driver comfort issues. As a result of the information gathered, Ford had plans to offer convenience items such as a dash-mounted cup holder, lumbar support in the driver's seat, an innerspring mattress, and a television package.

Freightliner.   Among the seven leading heavy-truck manufacturers, Freightliner offered the broadest range of Class 8 equipment. In 1990 Freightliner began offering five new glider kits to complement its line of trucks. The glider kits provided an economical means for fleet owners to upgrade existing vehicles. The kits included the frame, finished cab, front axle with wheels, fuel tanks, steering systems, and electrical, cooling, and exhaust components. Basically, the kits enabled owners to turn an older truck into a new, customized truck with the high-tech features of Freightliner's new trucks.

Freightliner planned to introduce a new design focusing on interior comfort. The features to be included were an interior allowing occupants to stand anywhere in the forward compartment, a wide-open sleeper, and multiple shelves and storage units/closets in the sleeper. This new offering would provide an improved ride inside a lighter-weight, aerodynamically designed truck.

The company's production was 17,000 units in 1986 and remained relatively stable at 23,000 to 24,000 units from 1987 through 1991.

Mack.   "Built like a Mack truck" was a popular American saying. Trying to continue this tradition, Mack promoted its durability and technological innovation, particularly in its Class 8 CH600 series. The CH600 series, launched in 1990, was Mack's premier truck. The series introduced Mack's V-MAC electronics system.

V-MAC, an acronym for Vehicle Management and Control, was a fully integrated, all-vehicle electronic control system that was intended to optimize vehicle performance and driver efficiency. Mack believed that its V-MAC was the start of total vehicle management which would provide consistent vehicle performance through precise electronic control of fuel delivery and engine timing. The V-MAC offered several programmable options that would enable owners to adapt a truck to their particular needs and applications. The programmable options included cruise control, engine shutdown, idle shutdown, and a variable engine speed limit. Mack felt that the V-MAC addressed the current and future needs of the industry.

Regarding creature comforts, Mack boasted that its Class 8 CH600 had the most comfortable ride of Class 8 trucks in the industry. This was attributed to its unique air-suspended cab/sleeper combination. The CH600 was also the roomiest and quietest model Mack had ever produced. Standard in the truck were a tilt-telescoping steering wheel and a two-piece wraparound windshield. Options included power windows and door locks and a high-rise sleeper-cab configuration.

Mack's production had increased steadily from 1986 to 1988 (from 17,000 units in 1986 to 23,000 units in 1988). However, production had tapered off to 15,000 units in 1990 and 10,000 units in 1991. The company expected production to increase for 1992.

Volvo GM.   During the late 1980s Volvo and General Motors (GM) formed a new company, Volvo GM, to develop Class 8 trucks. Volvo owned 76 percent and GM owned 24 percent of the new company. Volvo GM accounted for 34 percent of Volvo

Truck Corporation's 1990 worldwide sales. Volvo's two product lines introduced in 1986, the FE Series Class 7 and Class 8 trucks, remained its two major lines at the beginning of the 1990s.

Both the Class 7 and Class 8 trucks featured dashboards, seating, and steering wheels designed to improve driver comfort and performance. The Class 8 models were designed to provide a high degree of fuel efficiency through advanced aerodynamics.

To better meet customer demands of flexibility and appeal to a wider base of customers, Volvo began assembling its FE Series Class 7 trucks in its Ohio plant in 1991. The trucks had been assembled in its Belgium plant. In another move to push the company closer to the customer, Karl-Erling Trogen, the president of Volvo GM, had plans to improve parts availability, increase training, enhance literature offerings, improve computer systems, and improve communications (via satellite) between headquarters and the company's 200 dealers. Trogen's goal was to increase the penetration of Volvo components in American trucks.

Peterbilt.   Peterbilt, a division of Paccar, offered a wide range of models in its Classes 7 and 8. Safety and driver concerns were major factors in the design of Peterbilt's newer models. To provide smoother ride quality, Peterbilt introduced its first front air suspension in 1990. To address safety concerns, the company provided a Bendix BPR-1 bobtail proportioning system as an option on its trucks. The Bendix BPR-1 was designed to prevent rear axle lockup. This reduced stopping distances and decreased uneven wear on the truck's rear tires.

Peterbilt's Class 7 line of trucks shared the same name with its sister company, Kenworth. This Mid-Ranger series was designed for ease of maintenance, better visibility and maneuverability, and a tighter curb-to-curb turning circle than a conventional Class 7 truck.

Kenworth.   The Paccar division selling Class 7 and 8 trucks along with Peterbilt, Kenworth offered several models in its Class 8 line. The models offered improved aerodynamics, which boosted fuel economy. Kenworth attempted to target its Class 8 truck models to particular market segments. For example, its T400A was marketed to fleets transporting consumer and business-to-business products such as general freight, petroleum, food, and lumber. Its K100E was targeted toward moving companies, truckload carriers, and private fleets. The company's Class 7, Mid-Ranger series mirrored Peterbilt's.

Navistar.   With production averaging around 75,000 units a year from 1986 through 1991, Navistar was the nation's largest truck manufacturer.[10] The focus of the company's truck design at the beginning of the 1990s was ergonomics. The manufacturer planned to increase driver comfort through a new axle designed to improve driver maneuverability, increase aerodynamics and driver visibility, and offer new interiors and more electronic controls (e.g., cruise control). The plan was to update 65 percent of the company's product line by the end of 1992.

Customer support also was the center of attention at Navistar. As part of the company's greatly expanded parts program, a new service maintenance kit for truck air-conditioning systems was introduced in 1990. The kit contained all the parts needed for the annual preventive maintenance of all makes of its International trucks. The kit was made available through Navistar's network of 900 North American dealers.

---

[10] Production peaked in 1988 at 85,000 units, with a low of 63,000 units in 1991.

Many of Navistar's trucks carried the International name. However, the company also offered its 8000 (Class 7) and 9000 (Class 8) series. Like Freightliner, Navistar was strong on glider kits in 1990, with the kits available for its 8000 and 9000 series models. By the beginning of the 1990s, the company had introduced 22 new truck models which replaced models brought to the market in the late 1970s. There were plans to introduce a limited-edition model focusing on the very best in driver comfort.[11]

The International Truck Marketplace

Mexico and South America were potentially large markets for truck manufacturers. With the passing of NAFTA in 1993, U.S.-based companies were presented with new challenges as well as new opportunities. In its purest form, NAFTA allowed products and services to cross borders as easily as they moved within a nation. While NAFTA was drawing immediate attention, implementation of its components was expected to take as long as 15 years. Highlights of NAFTA included

- Greater access to the Mexican marketplace for U.S. and Canadian manufacturers.
- Tariff cuts on vehicles with substantial North American parts and labor.
- Equal treatment for international and domestic companies doing business in Mexico.
- Phasing out of barriers to investment in the Mexican trucking industry.
- Continuation of individual-country environmental, health, and safety standards.

Mexico's population was estimated to be 95 million in 1995. With its accelerated population increase and significant growth in its industrial sectors, Mexico, by the beginning of the 1990s, had a larger industrial base than did Belgium, Spain, or Sweden. Mexico's government appeared adamant in expanding Mexico's infrastructure to continue to support the country's ongoing industrialization.

As part of the continued investment in infrastructure, the country's National Investment Program called for the construction of several major highways to connect industrial centers such as Kermosillo and Nogales, Monterrey and Tampico, Guadalajara, and the port of Manzanillo. One new major Mexican highway was complete by early 1993. This 163-mile toll route between Cuernavaca and Acapulco, however, cost around US$150 to travel round-trip. (There was concern that truckers would not use expensive toll roads but instead would stick to the older roads, especially since time was not considered to be worth as much as money.) In addition to new roads, Mexico had a young, cheap work force. A Mexican worker earned just US$10 to US$20 a day. Capital costs could be cut by using more of these workers and fewer robots and by using less expensive machinery.

The American Society of Transportation and Logistics estimated that 1.7 million truckloads of goods accounted for 85 percent of all freight moving between the United States and Mexico. This generated US$75 billion in annual revenue. The American Trucking Association estimated that 6 million truckloads of goods would travel between the two countries by the year 2000. Approximately 85 percent of total freight tonnage in Mexico was transported by truck. Achieving reforms instigated by NAFTA would enable private industry to their operations, allowing expanded operations in the trucking industry.

---

[11] Only 250 units would be produced. The cabs would feature air-suspended high-back leather seats with dual armrests, an easy-to-read instrument panel accented by genuine rosewood trim, and an upgraded stereo system.

This industrialization and rapid GDP growth in Mexico had led to a sharp increase in sales of medium and heavy trucks (Classes 6 through 8). Annual truck sales in 1990 were around 6,000 units but had doubled by 1991. Expectations were that unit sales would hold near the 1991 total for three to five years. The Mexican truck fleet was very large, with an estimated 550,000 trucks in operation at the beginning of the 1990s. The trucks had an estimated average age of 12 years, nearly twice the average for the U.S. truck fleet. Mathematically, industry sales would have to exceed 45,800 trucks a year to prevent further aging of Mexico's fleet.[12]

A Mexican company, Grupo Dina, dominated the Mexican truck market, with close to 50 percent of the medium- and heavy-truck market. Kenmex, the Mexican division of Paccar, assembled Kenworth and Peterbilt trucks at a plant in Mexicali. While dominating the Mexican heavy-truck market for three decades, Kenmex had begun to face intense competition. Other truck manufacturers in Mexico in the early 1990s included Daimler Benz and Chrysler.

Projections were that the South American commercial vehicle market would be around 6,500 new trucks (4,000 heavy-duty trucks and 2,500 medium trucks) by the early to middle 1990s. In 1991 around 31 percent of Classes 6, 7, and 8 trucks shipped out of North America by U.S. producers were sold in South America. The relatively sound economy in Chile offered truck exporters a solid base from which to spread into nearby countries.[13] Additionally, Chile had no vehicle import restrictions, and there was no Chilean truck manufacturing industry.

U.S. companies that had entered Chile by the early 1990s were Ford, General Motors, Navistar, Kenworth, Mack, and Freightliner. There were also manufacturers from Europe and Asia. Russia's Kamaz truck had become the best-selling truck (medium-duty). The Kamaz had edged out Mercedes-Benz, which had truck assembly operations in Argentina and Brazil.

In addition to Chile, South American countries such as Venezuela, Colombia, Brazil, and Argentina were becoming more industrialized. Although several of these countries were battling high inflation—2,937.8 percent in Brazil and 2,311.3 percent in Argentina in 1990—there were still South American countries with relatively stable economies. Chile's annual rate of inflation was 26 percent, Venezuela's was 40 percent, and Colombia's fell between the two.

A few of these countries were already producing commercial vehicles. Brazil, for instance, produced 251,600 units in 1990. However, many other South American countries were producing fewer. For example, Chile produced only 8,000 commercial vehicles in 1990. Colombia and Venezuela produced 17,700 and 21,600 units, respectively, in 1990.

As South American nations became more industrialized, they would need more commercial trucks. Usage of these trucks could be quite large considering that in 1990 South America's total population was approximately 297.01 million people (over 20 million more people than in the United States and Canada).

A Customer Orientation

Navistar was the largest truck manufacturer in the United States. But could it remain in that position long, given its competitors' customer-oriented actions? Dewel knew a customer focus was necessary to survive in the highly competitive truck marketplace. But

---

[12] Douglas Laughlin, "Automotive–Heavy Trucks: A Sunshine Industry in Mexico," *Institutional Investor,* June 1993, p. SS8.

[13] Peru was seen as the country to enter after getting established in Chile.

how could he implement this customer focus when he also had a mandate to cut costs? Weren't the two goals contradictory? Also, what about the international marketplace?

Sources

Baker, Stephen. "Detroit South—Mexico's Auto Boom: Who Wins, Who Loses." *Business Week,* March 16, 1992, n.3256 (Industrial/Technology Edition), pp. 98–103.

Birkland, Carol. "Gasoline Engine Update." *Fleet Equipment,* April 1992, pp. 14–17.

Burr, Barry B. "Navistar Joins Electronic Pay Age." *Pensions & Investment Age,* April 6, 1987, pp. 37–38.

Byrne, Harlan S. "They Almost Bought the Farm, but Navistar and Varity Are on the Road to Recovery." *Barron's,* May 2, 1988, pp. 6–7, 32–34.

Cullen, David. "Building Working Assets." *Fleet Owner,* August 1991, pp. 55–58.

Cullen, David. "The Long Pull Ahead." *Fleet Owner,* January 1992, pp. 30–36.

Darlin, Damon. "Maquiladora-ville." *Forbes,* May 6, 1996, pp. 111–12.

Deierlein, Bob. "The Next Best Thing." *Beverage World,* September 1992, pp. 92–96.

Deierlein, Bob, and Tom Gelinas. "Spec'ed or Standard." *Fleet Equipment,* June 1989, pp. 38–42.

Deveny, Kathleen. "Can the Man Who Saved Navistar Run It, Too?" *Business Week,* March 9, 1987, p. 88.

Dumaine, Brian. "How Managers Can Succeed through Speed." *Fortune,* February 13, 1989, pp. 54–59.

Duncan, Thomas W. "Adding Muscle to Light-Duty Trucks." *Fleet Owner,* August 1988, pp. 77–82.

Duncan, Thomas W. "Chile Emerging as Export Prize." *Fleet Owner,* December 1992, p. 12.

Gage, Theodore Justin. "Cash Makes a Comeback in Navistar Financing." *Cash Flow,* December 1987, pp. 53, 58.

Gonze, Josh. "EDI Users Anticipate X.12 Boost." *Network World,* November 30, 1987, pp. 2, 45.

Green, Larry. "Building the Best Business Partnership." *Equipment Management,* April 1991, pp. 18–23.

Green, Larry. "Staying Power." *Equipment Management,* June 1991, pp. 25–30.

Heinze, Bernd G. "Big Wheels Keep on Turning." *Business Mexico,* November 1995, pp. 42–43.

"Highway Tractors: Accent on the Creature Comforts!" *Traffic Management,* November 1992, pp. 49–52.

Kraul, Chris. "Hauling Down to Mexico." *Los Angeles Times,* April 11, 1996, section D, p. 1.

Laughlin, Douglas K. "Automotive—Heavy Trucks: A Sunshine Industry in Mexico." *Institutional Investor,* June 1993, p. SS8.

Martin, James D. "Attention Returns to Heavy-Duty Trucks." *Distribution,* November 1990, pp. 54–62.

Mele, Jim. "The 1,000,000 Mile Truck." *Fleet Owner,* April 1994, pp. 77–83.

Milbrandt, Ben. "EDI: A More Efficient Way to Operate." *Corporate Cashflow,* August 1990, pp. 34–35.

Milbrandt, Ben. "Making EDI Pay Off." *Corporate Cashflow,* December 1988, pp. 24–28.

Moore, Thomas L. "Forging Partnerships." *Fleet Owner,* May 1992, p. 4.

Moore, Thomas L. "New Volvo GM Head Pushes Customer Focus." *Fleet Owner,* February 1, 1992, p. 96.

Najlepszy, Frank. "Turnaround in Truck Design." *Machine Design,* April 7, 1988, pp. 40–48.

Navistar 1993 Annual Report.

"Navistar's New Lines of Medium-, Heavy-Duty Conventionals Replace S-Series Models." *Fleet Owner,* January 1989, pp. 58–61.

Palmeri, Christopher. "Bridge Financing." *Forbes,* November 8, 1993, pp. 43–44.

Stavro, Barry. "A Surfeit of Equity." *Forbes,* December 29, 1986, pp. 62, 64.

"Supplier Partnerships . . . Who Benefits?" *Fleet Equipment,* July 1989, pp. 43–45.

Teresko, John. "Speeding the Product Development Cycle." *Industry Week,* July 18, 1988, pp. 40–42.

"The Construction Market in Mexico." *Construction Review,* July–August 1991, pp. ix–xiv.

"Truck Makers Feature Safety, Driver Comfort." *Traffic Management,* October 1991, pp. 73–77.

Case 6–2
Floral Farms

Flowers are a perfect replica of human life: planting, growth, bloom and withering. I guess flowers say it best from birth to death.

Jim Moretz[1]

It was very late on an unusually warm, humid evening on January 29, 1998. Marketing executives at Floral Farms, a producer and distributor of fresh-cut flowers, were brooding over the day's planning meeting. Leslie Stair, marketing manager, and John August, vice president/sales manager, were sitting in Leslie's office discussing the exchange between the Miami-based marketing group and the Colombian-based growers.

Leslie and John had gone into the yearly planning meeting feeling better than ever! The 1998–1999 marketplace looked good, resulting in an expected sales increase for all their products. Leslie and John had presented their sales projections (with reasons why) for all 11 of Floral Farms' major flower products. The euphoric feeling had lasted all day; while questions had been asked about how projections were derived, the meeting had appeared to be going smoothly.

However, after Leslie and John had completed their presentation, Carlos Diaz, vice president of production (headquartered in Colombia), commented, "You made a very nice presentation. It's too bad that we can't increase output by the amounts you projected for the June 1998–May 1999 time period. We can't change production for any of the products for the next 11 months. What is planted is planted. I will send you an overview of product availability for the upcoming fiscal period." After asking that marketing and production work toward an agreeable projection, Manuel Ortiz, the company's owner, adjourned the meeting.

The Fresh-Cut Flower Industry

Globally, annual retail sales of fresh-cut flowers were estimated at US$25 billion. While Europeans were the largest spenders when it came to fresh flowers, the decade of the 1990s opened with Americans increasing their spending for what once had been considered a luxury item. Americans had begun buying fresh-cut flowers like Europeans— for any occasion or no occasion. While changing consumer taste was one driver for the increased purchasing behavior, availability was thought to be a major driver. Americans no longer had to purchase fresh-cut flowers from a florist, as they were available in a variety of locations. For example, supermarkets, discount stores, department stores, corner pushcarts, electronic kiosks,[2] and catalogs had become popular points of purchase,

---

[1] As quoted in Anne Keegan, "Flower Power," *Chicago Tribune Magazine,* February 16, 1991, sec. 10, p. 15.

[2] Electronic kiosks could be placed in shopping malls, airports, offices, and so on. Orders are placed with the press of a few buttons.

This case was prepared by Victoria L. Crittenden, associate professor of marketing, Boston College, and William F. Crittenden, associate professor of management, Northeastern University, as the basis for class discussion rather than to illustrate either effective or ineffective handling of a managerial situation. Research assistance was provided by David Angus, Boston College/Andersen Consulting Fund.

accounting for almost 50 percent of floral industry sales by the mid-1990s.[3] Also, American consumers could bypass FTD[4] (and the accompanying fee) by calling the toll-free telephone numbers of many large florist shops. The U.S. wholesale flower market was valued at around US$600 million.

Changes in distribution were not the only modifications taking place in the floral industry. Flower growers had begun extending the lives of fresh-cut flowers by precooling them to 36 degrees Fahrenheit before shipment. With some flower varieties, this meant a 15-day life cycle after being cut. Six states (California, Florida, Michigan, Ohio, Pennsylvania, and Texas) were considered the top floriculture producers. While many flowers were grown in U.S. greenhouses, fresh-cut flowers were imported daily. These imports were said to be making fresh-cut flowers much cheaper.

Imports. Fresh flower imports accounted for around 75 percent of the cut flowers sold in the United States. Carnations, pompons, and roses accounted for around 60 percent of imports.

In the late 1980s American growers claimed that imports from 10 countries were injurious to the domestic fresh-cut flower market. Those 10 countries were Canada, Chile, Colombia, Costa Rica, Ecuador, Israel, Kenya, Mexico, the Netherlands, and Peru. Additionally, American growers identified the five types of imported flowers causing the most harm: carnations, chrysanthemums, alstroemeria (a type of lily), gypsophila (often called baby's breath), and gerberas (a daisy). Although the International Trade Commission did rule that imports might be causing harm to domestic products, feelings were mixed among members of national floral councils. Some industry spokespeople were unclear if it was imports or the change in farm size (e.g., major producers instead of small mom-and-pop producers) driving some companies out of business. While imported flowers were not produced much more cheaply than flowers grown in the United States, they were easier to obtain year-round. Also, imported flowers arrived just as quickly as U.S. shipments did.

The Dutch held a 20 to 25 percent share of the U.S. wholesale cut flower import market and were responsible for around 65 percent of world cut flower exports. The flower industry—one of the leading industries in the Dutch economy—consisted of around 11,000 growers and 5,000 buyers. Buyers participated daily in the Dutch flower auctions. While there were seven flower auctions in the Netherlands, the Verenigde Bloemenveilingen Aalsmeer (VBA) was the largest auction of its kind worldwide, with a 43 percent share of the market. Around 14 million flowers were sold daily via the VBA. Mexico and Colombia were the top exporters to the VBA. Largely due to strict laws regarding insects and soil particles, less than 5 percent of the VBA's business was shipped into the United States.

Most flowers sold in the United States were grown in Colombia (accounting for about 70 percent of U.S. flower imports). About 80 percent of carnations and 40 percent of roses sold in the States were from Colombia. Colombia's cut flower exports amounted to US$315 million by the mid-1990s. Accounting for 10 per-

---

[3] Additionally, with gross margins of 40 to 50 percent, floral products were some of the highest-margin items at these locations.

[4] Florists' Transworld Delivery Association (FTD), a member-owned group, linked approximately 23,000 independent flower shops in North America. This allowed a customer in Boston to easily send flowers to a friend in San Francisco. The FTD florist in Boston would receive approximately 20 percent of the price, the San Francisco FTD florist received approximately 73 percent, and the FTD association received 7 percent.

cent of the world's flower exports, the floral industry was Colombia's second largest employer.

Thailand was the leading orchid grower. Thailand's fresh flower exports, of which orchids accounted for about 75 percent, equaled around US$80 million. The Japanese were the largest importers of Thai flowers (about 50 percent), with Europe importing around 25 percent of the country's flowers and the United States about 20 percent. Thai exports constituted about 1.5 percent of the total U.S. flower import market.

Floral Farms

Floral Farms grew and marketed fresh-cut flowers. The company's mission statement was as follows:

> We are in the business of growing floral products. We will grow high-quality products, of a wide variety, and distribute these products worldwide. We will have the reputation as a high-quality producer. As well, we will seek to optimize investments, maximize long-term profits, and develop human resources.

Exhibit 1 diagrams the company's organization. The company owned its own farms in Colombia. The marketing organization for Floral Farms was located in Miami, Florida.

Floral Farms had been in Manuel Ortiz's family for decades. Although Floral Farms was only a small portion of the Ortiz family wealth, Manuel maintained a strong interest in Floral Farms' success. However, he had turned active, daily responsibility and control over to Carla Williams. Manuel and Carla had met at an executive MBA program in the United States. Their mutual interest in imports–exports and their South American heritage had made it easy for a friendship to develop. Their two families had grown close. Manuel's and Carla's daughters attended the same college in California.

Customers.   Floral Farms' customers included (1) local wholesalers in different cities (which accounted for 95 percent of Floral Farms' sales), (2) supermarket retail chains, and (3) the end consumer (via the company's retail operation in New York). U.S. and Canadian sales combined represented 95 percent of the company's total sales. The remaining 5 percent of sales was to selected importers in Europe, the Caribbean, and South America.

Marketing.   The Miami-based marketing group was responsible for all U.S. and Canadian sales. Vice president/sales manager John August had been with the company for 10 years. He had 13 salespeople, with a goal of having at least 20 by the end of 1999. Leslie Stair, marketing manager, had been with Floral Farms for two years. Before that, she had worked as a buyer at a large retail chain in Florida.

EXHIBIT 1   Corporate Structure

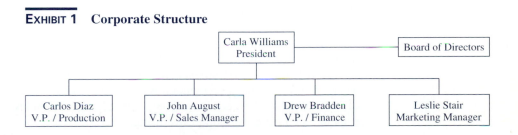

Products.   The company had 11 major flower products:

1. Alstromeria
2. Carnations
3. Miniature carnations
4. Freesia
5. Gerbera
6. Gypsophila
7. Lilies
8. Pompons
9. Roses
10. Spider mums
11. Statice

The quality of Floral Farms products was considered very high. Some lines had received various floral awards for consecutive years. Workers at Floral Farms took great pride in the care, handling, and sales of their products.

Distribution.   All Floral Farms flowers were air-shipped from Colombia into Miami. The products would clear customs at the Miami airport and then were reshipped via airfreight or trucking companies to their next destination of wholesaler, supermarket, or the New York retail outlet. (While the company had operated five retail locations at one time, the differences in marketing products to distributors and end consumers had proved too large for the company to manage effectively. Thus, four locations had been closed, leaving only one operation, New York City's, to sell flowers directly to the public.)

Fresh-cut flowers were packed in cardboard boxes of 100 to 1,000 units, depending on the variety and packing size.

Prices.   Fresh-cut flower prices followed a seasonal pattern. Moreover, in reality, prices fluctuated by the minute. The company's salespeople contacted customers by telephone from a large salesroom in the Miami office. The going rate for all fresh-cut flowers was posted constantly on the room's dry-erase board. A salesperson always had to be aware of the correct price for the products he or she was selling. For example, the salesperson could be talking to one customer in New York and quote a particular price for x number of stems of roses. Five minutes later the salesperson might be talking to another customer in New York and quote a different price for that number of stems of roses.

However, historical pricing patterns did exhibit some yearly consistency. Rose prices were higher around February 14, carnation prices were highest around February 14, pompon prices were lowest during summer months (May–July), and there was an inverse relationship between industry/Floral Farms supply and prices for all products.

Marketing Communications.   Buyers (wholesalers and supermarkets) seemed pleased with Floral Farms products. While the company did use Floral Farms as a brand name, there was no name recognition among end consumers. Basically, final purchasers of fresh-cut flowers did not know if they were buying a Floral Farms product. The company did no trade or consumer advertising.

Production.   Floral Farms owned three farms in Colombia. Each had a general manager who reported to Carlos Diaz, vice president/production. While Carlos reported to Carla Williams, Carla's Miami-based location often meant that Carlos contacted Manuel Ortiz directly when something came up and/or he needed information or guidance.

Colombian farms were in Las Palmas and Jardines de Colombia. While Floral Farms was one of around 200 floral growers in that country, it was one of the largest and most respected operations, with approximately 175 hectares available for flower production. By the late 1980s, the Colombian government had stopped its low-cost financing for carnations, roses, and pompons.

Floral Farms was considering the purchase of farm land in both Ecuador and Peru. Diaz was looking at 100 hectares in Ecuador and 144 hectares in Peru.

Ecuador was considered the second-best production country behind Colombia. Environmental elements such as better light and less temperature fluctuation were thought to be important variables to consider in future production expansion possibilities. Additionally, import laws were fairly open and labor was cheaper than in Colombia. However, transportation was complicated due to altitude limitations in Ecuador's capital, Quito. Products would have to be shipped from the coast, a seven-hour drive from the company's farm.

There were three farms available in Peru, for a total of 144 hectares. Flowers slated to be grown in Peru, should the farms be purchased, were gypsophila, statice, minicarnations, and pompons. Additionally, Diaz thought Floral Farms could utilize the climate in Peru to experiment with some new types of roses and carnations.

Exhibit 2 provides the production cycle for the 11 major products grown by Floral Farms. Due to year-round demand for floral products and the company's reputation as a full-line supplier, production for any of the products could never be zero.

The January Planning Meeting

The January planning meeting was the first of its kind at Floral Farms. A consultant hired by the company owner had recommended that the production people travel to Miami once a year for a planning session. Additionally, the marketing group had made its first trip to visit the Colombian farm sites in November 1997. It was decided to make

EXHIBIT 2   Production Cycle of Major Crops

Flower Crop	Vegetative Period (weeks)	Production Period (weeks)	Number of Plants per Square Meter	Production per Square Meter by Production Cycle
Alstroemeria	24	156	2.84	590 stems
Carnations	21	83	22.82	380 flowers
Minicarnations	21	83	21.64	42 bunches
Freesia	19	6	53.3	5.26 bunches
Gerbera	16	88	5.1	255 flowers
Gypsophila	13	10	3.42	9 bunches
Lilies	14	2	65	61 flowers
Pompons	12	1	68.9	9 bunches
Roses	18	520	5.58	900 flowers
Spider mums	12	2	58	5.6 bunches
Statice	16	36	4.62	24 bunches

the trip an annual project. The idea behind annual on-site visits, according to the consultant, was that such cross-functional interaction was necessary for the company to become market-oriented.

As part of the attempt to implement a companywide market orientation, the consultant had expressed a desire that top management participate in the cross-functional interactions. The Colombian owners, members of the board of directors, and the president of the Miami-based operations had participated actively in the November visit and were present at the January planning meeting.

Stair and August thought that they were well prepared for the meetings. They felt that their visit to the Colombian farms had added greatly to their product knowledge. It had been exciting for them to see and experience hectare after hectare of floral products. As businesspeople, they sensed they would be better able to speak the language of the production people and also be in a better position to talk to their customers.

The marketing group had worked extremely hard in preparing for the January planning meeting. Stair and August had planned to use the meeting for two major purposes: (1) to orient the production people to the marketing side of the business and (2) to share with production and top management the vast potential in the marketplace.

All meeting participants had been provided with a notebook of information detailing the analysis the marketing group had gone through to reach its recommendations. The information included three years of historical company data regarding (for each product) hectares in production, Floral Farms' unit sales, Floral Farms' percentage of the U.S. market, Floral Farms' percentage of Colombian exports to the United States, total amount sold to the United States, production costs (growing, freight, duty), average selling price, and return per square meter. Tables and graphs showed fiscal year 1997–1998 monthly product quantity and monthly average price. (Exhibit 3 shows sales projections, production costs, and average selling price for each of the 11 products, as provided to meeting participants.)

Evening of January 29, 1998.   Leslie looked at the clock. It was 10:53 PM, and she was exhausted! After going to dinner and having a couple of drinks, she and John had come back to the office. They had rehashed the meeting: Who had said and done what?

EXHIBIT 3   Marketing/Production Projections

Flower Crop	1998–99 Sales Projection	Increase over Previous Season	Production Cost (U.S.$)[1]	Average Selling Price (U.S.$)
Alstroemeria	2,080,375	115%	$0.17	$2.71
Carnations	100,022,562	25	0.08	0.14
Minicarnations	2,367,000	21	1.02	1.79
Freesia	226,500	27	0.13	1.69
Gerbera	6,076,500	45	0.19	0.22
Gypsophila	454,290	97	1.41	2.76
Lilies	1,184,000	2	0.40	0.52
Pompons	6,453,750	14	0.72	1.26
Roses	26,235,775	46	0.17	0.32
Spider mums	1,465,350	20	1.25	2.50
Statice	555,750	166	0.95	1.62

Note: Sales projections are in units, as are costs and average prices.

[1] Production cost includes growing cost, freight, and duty.

Leslie looked at John and asked, "What happens now? Should we call Carlos and plan to go to Colombia in the next couple of weeks? I don't know what it would accomplish. We really can't prepare any more marketing data. Should we wait for Carlos to call us? Manuel did say that production and marketing were supposed to work this out. So that's him the same as us. I wonder if he is worrying tonight like we are. It really ticked me off that Manuel adjourned the meeting so quickly after Carlos's statement. It was almost as though he let Carlos close the meeting. In looking back over the last few minutes of the day, the way things were handled makes me very uncomfortable."

John agreed with Leslie. He reminded her that the consultant had told all of them that they had to begin communicating more (and better). That was one of the notions behind the cross-functional site visits. However, John thought that Carlos had been very uncommunicative that day, letting them go through the entire sales forecast and then making the comment that he did.

Leslie and John decided to revisit the issue the next day. Maybe they could both think better after a good night's rest. As they were leaving the office, John said, "What can we do to make Carlos see the importance of fulfilling our sales projections? Our recommendations take Floral Farms from 1998 fiscal year sales of slightly over US$50 million to almost US$70 million for the 1999 fiscal year. What's wrong with that? The market is out there. Floral Farms production only has to provide us with the correct amount of the right products at the right time!"

Sources

Bennett, Stephen. "Flower Power." *Progressive Grocer,* November 1994, pp. 105–10.

Caughey, Terry. "Dutch Treat; Away from Amsterdam, Holland Offers a Variety of Quaint, Scenic Charms." *The Patriot Ledger,* January 11, 1997, p. 36.

"Colombian Business, Fallow Ground." *The Economist,* October 23, 1993, p. 86.

Deveny, Kathleen. "Now the Flower Business Is Blooming All Year." *Business Week,* December 23, 1995, p. 59.

Driessen, Christoph. "Dutch Market's Flower Power Growing Daily." *Chicago Tribune,* May 10, 1993, p. 8.

Faber, Harold. "A Big Drop in Flower Sales May Prompt an Industry Recount." *The New York Times Metro,* May 22, 1994, sec. 1, p. 40, col. 1.

Gillis, Chris. "The Netherlands' 'Other Airline,' Martinair Holland." *American Shipper,* July 1996, p. 73.

Grier, Peter. "A Rose Is . . . Likely to Be from South America." *The Christian Science Monitor,* February 14, 1992, p. 1, col. 2.

"Halloween Boo-quets, Anyone?" *Forbes,* October 26, 1992, pp. 206–08.

Handley, Paul. "In the Pink." *Far Eastern Economic Review,* February 27, 1992, pp. 58–59.

Hill, Helen. "Flower Power: Budding Logistics for a Worldwide Market." *Air Cargo World,* October 1996, p. 34.

"Innovating to Be Competitive: The Dutch Flower Industry." *Harvard Business Review,* September–October 1995, pp. 130–31.

Juilland, Marie-Jeanne. "Melridge Is Bustin' Out All Over." *Venture,* June 1987, pp. 33–34.

Keegan, Anne. "Flower Power." *Chicago Tribune Magazine,* February 10, 1991, sec. 10, p. 10, col. 2.

Levy, Robert. "Flower Power in the Supermarket." *Business Month,* March 1997, pp. 62–63.

"Md.'s Flower Industry Continues to Blossom." *Washington Post,* August 26, 1991, sec. WBIZ, p. 43, col. 5.

Steinmetz, Greg. "FTD to Look at Bids to Make It Bloom Again." *The Wall Street Journal,* November 2, 1994, sec. B, p. 1, col. 6.

Woodward, Richard B. "Business Is Booming." *The New York Times Magazine,* May 9, 1993, pp. 33–36.

A group of senior managers, including the managing director of National Bicycle Industrial Co. (NBIC), a subsidiary of the Japanese industrial giant Matsushita, were reflecting on the success of their firm over the last few years. NBIC is a leading manufacturer of bicycles. In 1987 the firm introduced the most innovative and revolutionary production system the Japanese bicycle industry had ever seen. The system, named the *Panasonic Order System* (POS), employed state-of-the-art techniques in bicycle production to manufacture "custom-made" bicycles. Using robots, computers, and skilled workers, the system blends human skills and advanced manufacturing automation to allow potential customers to custom-order bicycles. When ordering a custom-made bicycle, a customer can choose from about 8 million possible variations based on model type, color, frame sizes, and other features. Using this system, the firm delivers a high-quality "crafted" bicycle within two weeks of the customer's order.

With the introduction of POS the firm gained national and international attention and became the envy of the industry. In 1992 General Motors Corporation, the world's largest manufacturing firm, sent a team of executives to study the firm's "mass-customization" strategy and its implementation through the POS.[1]

Despite the firm's growing recognition, the senior management group was considering changes in the mass-customization strategy. To explore what changes were required by senior management and the questions they might raise, this case looks at the Japanese bicycle industry, NBIC's strategy and position within that industry, and the nature of issues facing the company during mid-1993.

The Japanese Bicycle Industry

The Japanese bicycle industry's history dates from the Meiji restoration period, which began around 1868. It was during that period that European-style bicycles were introduced into Japan. During the Meiji restoration, Japan's governing body and government began modeling the Japanese political system after Western governments. To end its isolation from the rest of the world, the state encouraged foreigners to visit Japan.

As foreigners arrived in the country, they brought with them their bicycles. When the bicycles needed repairs, they sought the assistance of hunting gun repair shops established during the earlier Tokugawa period. Those small shops in and around cities such as Tokyo and Osaka began to fix bicycles. Skills acquired with pipes and screws to produce guns during the Tokugawa period enabled shop owners to apply their talents to servicing and repairing bicycles. Over time those small repair shops began to produce bicycles modeled after European bicycles. The first domestic bicycle frame was manu-

---

[1] The term *mass customization* was coined by Stanley M. Davis in *Future Perfect* (Reading, MA: Addison-Wesley, 1987).

This case was prepared by Assistant Professor Suresh Kotha of the Stern School of Business, NYU, while visiting at IUJ, and research assistant Andrew Fried of IUJ as the basis for class discussion rather to illustrate either effective or ineffective handling of an administrative situation. Copyright © 1993 International University of Japan. Published with permission.

EXHIBIT 1   **Bicycle Demand in Japan, 1982–1992 (thousands of units)**

Year	Production	Shipment (1)	Export (2)	Import (3)	Total Demand (1 − 2 + 3)
1982	6,532	6,624	674	13	5,963
1983	7,039	6,996	864	6	6,138
1984	6,810	6,839	856	28	6,011
1985	6,785	6,808	888	40	5,960
1986	6,583	6,638	682	158	6,114
1987	7,379	7,742	416	580	7,636
1988	7,509	7,624	325	900	8,119
1989	7,792	7,881	200	857	8,538
1990	7,969	8,033	226	667	8,474
1991	7,448	7,416	203	940	8,153

Source: Japan Bicycle Manufacturer's Association.

factured in 1889, exactly 29 years after the invention of the bicycle by Pierre Michaux in France. Slowly, this gave rise to the Japanese bicycle industry.[2]

Bicycle demand in Japan grew rapidly in the early 1970s due to robust growth in the economy and the resulting strong consumer demand. Several environmental changes, including the growth of suburban residential areas and the building of large shopping areas in the periphery of cities, contributed to an increase in demand. The bicycles were used mainly for commuting to railway stations and shopping areas and back. Additionally, the introduction of the small bicycle, or "miniwheel," that coincided with the popularity of the "miniskirt trend" vastly improved the appeal of bicycles to women.[3] Women became an important market segment, and the industry introduced a greater variety of colors and models to appeal to that segment. The growing demand resulted in bicycle standardization and the adoption of mass production systems by Japanese manufacturers.

The 1973 "oil shock" had a chilling effect on Japan, and bicycle production dropped over 18 percent to 7.6 million. The industry hoped that demand for bicycles would develop (in lieu of automobile purchases) under a 1973 energy-saving plan, but this trend did not develop and bicycle demand plateaued at around 7 million units. Exhibit 1 shows the level of production, shipment, exports, and imports of bicycles in Japan for a 10-year period starting from 1982. The domestic production and shipment of bicycles have remained somewhat stable throughout the late 1980s and early 1990s. Exports of Japanese bicycles have declined gradually as the Japanese yen has increased in strength and imports into Japan from neighboring Taiwan and China have grown steadily during this period. Exhibit 2 shows bicycle production for the different segments in Japan.

Manufacturers and Assemblers.   Bicycle producers in Japan are subdivided by the industry into two groups: manufacturers and assemblers. The distinction between these two types lies mainly in (1) the degree of backward vertical integration achieved

---

[2] "Your Market in Japan—High-Grade Bicycle and Wear," Japan External Trade Organization report, 1990.

[3] In the past, Japanese bicycle manufacturers had produced bicycles originally designed around European models. The lower average height of Japanese women made it difficult for them to use such bicycles. The miniwheel's small wheel diameter, lower saddle mount, and U-type frames made it very appealing to women.

EXHIBIT 2   **Bicycle Production by Type (thousands of units)**

	1984	1985	1986	1987	1988	1989	1990	1991
Roadsters	57	42	37	38	35	38	35	27
Light cycles	916	1,017	1,339	2,296	2,893	3,486	3,694	3,511
Sports cycles	1,465	1,304	999	883	761	562	501	405
Juvenile cycles	756	795	726	770	772	770	788	747
Children*	566	565	542	546	555	520	527	477
Minicycles	2,871	2,753	2,687	2,570	2,192	2,065	1,822	1,426
Others†	181	308	254	275	301	350	602	855
Total	6,810	6,785	6,583	7,379	7,509	7,792	7,969	7,448

Source: Japan Bicycle Promotion Institute.

*Geared toward preschool children, with 12- to 16-inch wheels. The standard-size bicycle had wheels which were 26 or 27 inches.

†Includes adults tricycles, motorcross bikes, mountain bikes, high-risers, heavyweight load-carrying bicycles, track racing bikes, bicycles for acrobatics, and so on.

by the firms that belong to each group and (2) the level of final product assembly carried out before shipment by firms in each group. For example, the manufacturers produce their own bicycle frames and forks, the two critical structural components of the bicycle, and purchase the remaining components from parts suppliers. Also, the bicycles produced by this group were appropriately 70 percent assembled at the time of shipment to wholesalers. The assemblers purchase all their components from outside parts suppliers and only assemble the bicycles, as their name denotes. Historically, manufacturers accounted for most of the bicycles produced. Starting in the 1980s, the shipment of bicycles between the manufacturers and the assemblers was evenly split, with each accounting for approximately 50 percent of the industry.

In 1992 the Japanese bicycle industry consisted of over 80 bicycle manufacturers and hundreds of parts suppliers. The top five manufacturing firms were Bridgestone, National, Miyata, Maruishi, and Nichibei Fuji. Bridgestone Cycle Co. was the industry leader, with 18 percent of the domestic market. Bridgestone was followed by NBIC and Miyata, with 9 percent and 8 percent of the market, respectively. The top five assemblers were Yokota, Deki, Hodaka, Saimoto, and Wani. Yokota lead the group of assemblers with 9 percent of the market. Deki and Hodaka were next with 8 percent and 7 percent, respectively. Together the top five members of each group accounted for over 75 percent of the bicycles produced in Japan (see Exhibit 3).

Part Suppliers.   In 1992 there were approximately 327 firms that produced individual parts and related items. Compared to bicycle producers, parts supplier firms were in the business of producing standardized parts in large volume and were more automated than were complete bicycle producers.

In 1992 Shimano was the largest supplier of bicycle parts, commanding a dominant market share. The other major parts suppliers were Araya, Sakae, and Cat Eye. Unlike the Japanese automobile industry, where exclusive suppliers are the norm, bicycle parts suppliers sold components to multiple firms. The growing supply of bicycle parts from Southeast Asian countries made it very difficult for Japanese suppliers to compete in labor-intensive segments of the industry such as bicycle chains, pedals, and wheels. To remain competitive some suppliers began moving their production facilities to Southeast Asian countries, where labor costs were lower. Others entered into joint ventures with parts suppliers from Taiwan and China.

EXHIBIT 3   Market Shares of Major Bicycle Producers

Companies	1992 Production (thousands of units)	Market Share	1993 Production (Est.)
Top Five Manufacturers			
Bridgestone	1,400	18%	1,450
National	700	9	700
Miyata	640	8	610
Maruishi	310	4	310
Nichibei Fuji	200	3	200
	3,250	43%	3,270
Top Five Assemblers			
Yokota	710	9%	750
Deki	630	8	700
Hodaka	530	7	570
Saimoto	400	5	400
Wani	290	4	290
	2,560	34%	2,710

Source: *Cycle Press,* no. 76, February 1993.

Distribution.   Bicycles in Japan were distributed through wholesalers, retailers, supermarkets, and department stores.[4] There were approximately 1,600 wholesalers and about 38,000 retailers in 1990. While many wholesalers were subsidiaries of the large manufacturers such as Bridgestone and NBIC, among others, retail outlets for the most part were small "mom-and-pop stores." Approximately 60 percent of the bicycles sold were transferred from wholesalers to retailers, and the remainder were distributed through supermarkets and department stores throughout Japan. In the past large company-owned wholesalers dominated the distribution of bicycles. Recently, large supermarket chains and household superstores or "home centers" have started to sell bicycles. According to industry experts, the growing number of such outlets was an important reason for the steady rise in imported bicycles (see Exhibit 4).

Company Background

NBIC was Japan's second largest manufacturer of bicycles in 1992, with sales reaching about ¥20 billion. The firm marketed bicycles under three different brand names: Panasonic, National, and Hikari. NBIC targeted each brand at a unique market segment, and together the three brands covered the wide spectrum of bicycles sold in Japan. They ranged from high-quality, high-price sports and fashion bicycles (Panasonic) to bicycles that were used primarily for transportation from home to the nearest train station or supermarket and back (Hikari). National and Hikari brands together constituted the bulk of NBIC's production and sales. Panasonic, the company's more expensive line, accounted for a little less than 20 percent of total production in 1992.

NBIC began to manufacture and sell bicycles in 1952. At first growth in sales was slow, but it picked up rapidly within a few years after the firm's inception. Between

---

[4] According to industry reports, labeling firms as either wholesalers or retailers was problematic because a majority of those firms operated jointly as wholesale and retail ventures.

EXHIBIT 4   **The Japanese Bicycle Distribution System, 1992**

Bicycle Manufacturers	Wholesalers	Retailers

```
Bicycle
Manufacturers          Wholesalers              Retailers

┌────────────────┐     ┌────────────┐
│ Industrial type│     │    Own     │
│ (50% approx.)  │     │  company   │           ┌──────────────┐
└────────────────┘     │distributors│           │ Bicycle shops│
                       └────────────┘           │   (59%)      │
                       ┌────────────┐           └──────────────┘
                       │Local whole-│
                       │sale dealers│           ┌──────────────┐
                       │    and     │           │   Large      │
                       │distributors│           │ supermarkets │
┌────────────────┐     └────────────┘           │   (17%)      │           End
│Commercial type │     ┌────────────┐           └──────────────┘        Consumers
│ (50% approx.)  │     │   Large    │           ┌──────────────┐
└────────────────┘     │ wholesale  │           │  Department  │
                       │  dealers   │           │   stores     │
                       └────────────┘           │   (1%)       │
                                                └──────────────┘
                                                ┌──────────────┐
┌────────────────┐                              │ Home centers │
│Imports (super- │                              │   (19%)      │
│markets and     │                              └──────────────┘
│trading         │                              ┌──────────────┐
│companies)      │                              │   Others     │
└────────────────┘                              │   (4%)       │
                                                └──────────────┘
```

1952 and 1965 the firm produced almost a million bicycles. In 1965, due to ever-increasing demand, the firm completed the construction of a new factory in Kashihara on the outskirts of Osaka and moved its operations to that factory. At Kashihara the firm had two factories located next to each other. NBIC's management called them the mass production factory and the custom factory. The custom factory, initially conceptualized as a pilot plant, was built in 1987.

In 1992, according to published estimates, the firm produced a combined total of 700,000 bicycles in those two factories. Over 90 percent were produced in the mass production factory and shipped to Matsushita's sales subsidiaries. High-end Panasonic bicycles were produced in the custom factory and shipped to dealers to be delivered to individual customers. While most line workers worked at the mass production factory, a few of NBIC's best workers produced bicycles at the custom factory. Operating on a single-shift basis throughout the year, they produced a small fraction of the firm's production at that factory.

In early 1993 the firm employed 470 people, with a little over 66 percent classified as direct or line workers and the rest classified as indirect workers. A little over 50 percent of the indirect workers were in the production engineering and design departments of the firm. The line workers belonged to the company union and actively participated in "quality circle" programs. Workers met once a month, as part of these programs, to discuss quality and safety issues. Additionally, management periodically tested line workers and ranked them according to their skill level. The highest-skill workers were given the opportunity to work at the custom factory, where wages were higher.

NBIC "sold" its bicycles to 10 sales companies. Those sales companies distributed bicycles to approximately 9,000 retailers throughout Japan that were part of the Matsushita group. Regular monthly meetings were held between management at NBIC and the sales companies to discuss sales trends and manufacturing concerns.

Mass-Customization Strategy

The Genesis. The original idea for making custom-made bicycles came from the firm's president. The firm's managing director, who headed the team that implemented the idea, recalled:

> It all started when our president visited a famous department store in Osaka. He noticed that women could custom order dresses that were then delivered by the store in two weeks. He wondered if it was possible for National to produce bicycles in this way. When we were on a trip to the United States, he mentioned this idea. At that time we were used to making a few specially designed bicycles for some customers, such as Olympic racers, but offering a custom-made bicycle to everyone was a different matter altogether.

Within a few days after their return the managing director began giving serious thought to the idea mentioned by the firm's president. The bicycle industry was in the doldrums, demand was sluggish, and the average unit price the customer was willing to pay for a "standard" bicycle was dropping (see Exhibit 5). According to a report in *Far East Economic Review:*

> Although some Japanese component makers are riding high on the mountain bike boom, the rest of the Japanese bicycle industry is in the doldrums. The stronger yen has hurt exports of Japanese-made bicycles because of their higher cost overseas. Today, bicycle assembly for the U.S. and European markets is centered in Taiwan, dominated by such aggressive new makers as Giant, Merida, and Fairy.[5]

Although the average price of a sporting bicycle was increasing, this segment was not growing as anticipated by many large producers. It was under these conditions that the managing director, with other senior managers at NBIC, decided to change the firm's strategy by trying something bold. According to one senior manager:

> We were manufacturing bicycles in lot sizes greater than 50 in our factory. Now we were challenged by our president to produce bicycles in lot sizes of one. More important, the orders received were to be completed and delivered within two weeks. We not only had to convince ourselves that this was possible, we had to convince our design people, our manufacturing people, and the line workers that this was a *good* and *feasible* idea.

Initially, not everyone at NBIC was unanimous in supporting this revolutionary idea. Some senior members at NBIC felt that it would require a large investment and entailed a tremendous risk for the firm. They asked: What if NBIC failed in this attempt? Some also argued that the market for sports bicycles in Japan was shrinking, though admittedly at a slower pace compared to other segments (see Exhibit 2). Further, some industry analysts outside the firm said that such a strategy would be impossible to develop and implement. As one senior manager, speaking for his colleagues, recollected:

> We also had our own doubts during those early days, though we never mentioned this to our president or workers because we were committed to at least trying to see if this project would work. However, in our mind we gave it a 50 percent chance of success.

According to the managing director, the firm had only a few broad objectives when it started on the road to customization. First, the firm wanted to double the amount of

---

[5] Report published in the *Far East Economic Review,* December 7, 1989.

EXHIBIT 5   **Change in Average Production Value per Complete Bicycle Unit (yen)**

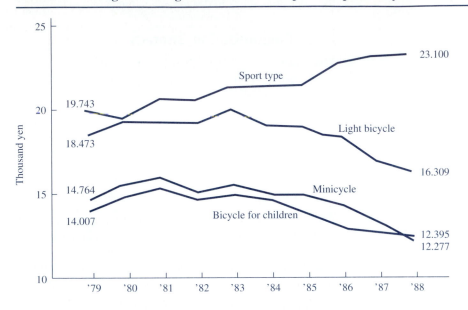

high-value-added products it sold by accommodating the *individual* needs of the customer. Second, NBIC wanted to devise a "system" of production and delivery that clearly differentiated its high-end Panasonic brand from competitors' products and also meet the growing need for variety in the marketplace. During the late 1980s, as the demand for bicycles plateaued, there was increasing competition among the manufacturers. To gain market share, firms introduced many new model types. For example, NBIC offered over 250 different model types during 1987, and within each model type customers had a choice of color and other options. Management changed about 80 percent of the models yearly. Similarly, not to be outdone, the industry's largest producer offered over 300 models during that period.

Within a few weeks of inception, the managing director assembled a project team that consisted of senior members of his management team, a designer, a few process engineers, and some highly skilled, experienced line workers. Discussing the implementation of the project, he fondly recalls:

> We worked long hours. We proposed and debated many new ideas for days. We started with a few people, but as the project began to progress, more people were added. Within a few weeks we established a pilot plant in a large empty warehouse next to the factory. Still, numerous issues had to be addressed and solved, but as time went on, we were convinced that the project was doable. We knew we had the capability, because many of us had spent most of our professional lives making bicycles.

Motivated by the relentless effort of their leader, the team successfully tackled one concern after another and completed the project in a mere four months. By July 1987 the team had converted the pilot plant to one that was fully operational and running. It was seven months since the firm's president had visited the department store in Osaka.

In June 1987 the firm unveiled its strategy to Japan's bicycle industry to the dismay and surprise of its major competitors. The new system they had devised was aptly named the *Panasonic Ordering System.*

The Panasonic Ordering System

The Order Process.   A customer ready to order a high-end bicycle walked into a Panasonic bicycle dealer equipped for POS, and the dealer, using a unique measuring and gauging machine, noted the exact physical needs of the customer, including the size of the frame, the length of the seat post, the position of the handlebar, and the extension of the handlebar stem. The customer was allowed to select the model type, the color scheme, and other features of the bicycle. Details on the number of models, colors, and options that were available are provided in Exhibit 6. When this process was completed, the dealer immediately sent this information to the control room of the custom-made factory by facsimile transmission.

Once the facsimile order form was received in the master control room of the custom factory, the receiving attendant immediately entered the information into the firm's host computer to register and control the customer's order specifications. The host computer then assigned each order a unique bar-code label. This label, which traveled with the evolving bicycle, specified and controlled each stage of manufacturing operation. At various stages in the process line workers accessed the customer's unique requirements by using the bar-code label and a scanner. This information, displayed on a CRT terminal at each station, was fed directly to the computer-controlled machines that were part of a local area computer network. Using such information, workers at each station, assisted by machines, performed the required sequence of operations. Exhibit 7 provides an overview of the entire manufacturing process used by NBIC, and Exhibit 8 illustrates the POS factory layout.

The Manufacturing Process.   At the heart of the POS lay the design and manufacturing capabilities of NBIC. Almost all the machines used in the manufacturing process were developed and built exclusively for use in the custom factory. A significant portion of this development work was carried out by the firm's own design and process engineers with assistance from the parent company's engineering staff. While the computer hardware used in POS was purchased from outside vendors, much of the software employed to control and monitor the system was developed and written internally by NBIC's software engineers.

EXHIBIT 6   **POS System: Selection of Models Available (Japan)**

	Type	*Number of Models*
Bicycles		
	Road	10
	Triathlon	5
	Time trial	3
	ATB	2
	Track	1
Frame		
	Road and triathlon	4
	Time trial	–
	ATB	–
	Track	1

Source: NBIC company records.

EXHIBIT 7   The Production Process at the Custom Factory

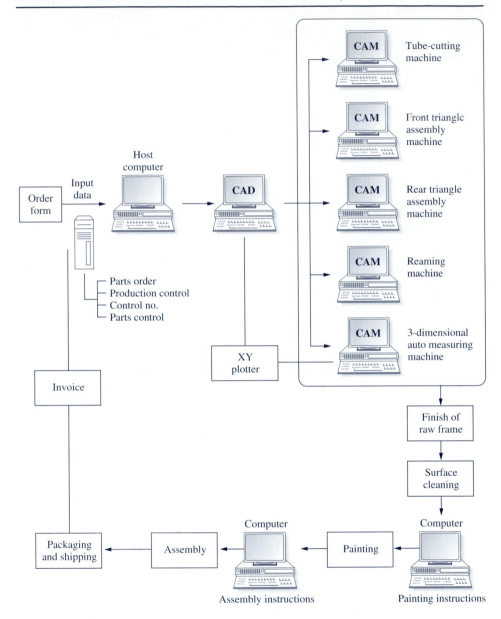

The production process began when the computer-aided design (CAD) system in the control room scanned the bar-code label to access information on the customer's order. A "blueprint" of the bicycle's frame and other structural details was produced in about three minutes.[6] Information from the CAD system was sent automatically to the raw material supplies area next to the control room. Here small lights, placed in front of the

----

[6] According to the factory manager, before the introduction of the CAD system, this process took the company draftsmen about 180 minutes.

EXHIBIT 8   **Layout of the POS/PICS Factory**

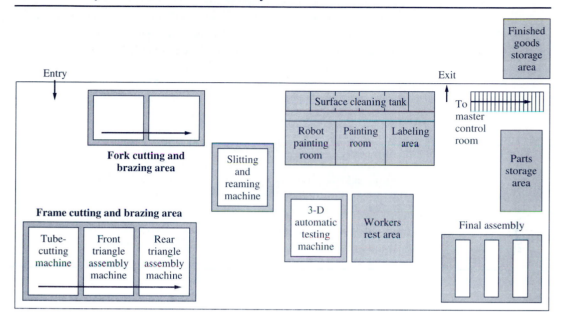

raw material bins, were automatically lit, based on the customer's specifications. The materials from the bins that were lit were picked up by a worker and sent to the factory.

Frame and Front Fork Production.   The first step on the factory floor involved the cutting of the tubes that formed the frame of the bicycle. Customer specifications were transferred to the computer-assisted "tube-cutting" machine. That machine then automatically sized and held the tubes in place while a worker cut them, using a rotary saw. The surfaces where two tubes were to be welded together were then "arch" cut, using a special machine. According to the factory manager, this process improved the rigidity of the frame and the precision of the joints during the brazing process. Small parts, such as brake guides, were carefully brazed to the frame by a skilled worker.

The tubes were carried to the "front triangle assembly" machine. This machine, using special jigs and other features, automatically aligned and held the tubes together while they were tack welded to form the front triangle of the frame. The joints of the frame were brazed by automatic brazing machines. Following this process, a worker, using the "rear fork assembly machine," tack welded the chain stay hanger section, the seat stay, and the seat lug section. These parts were brazed to the frame. These processes brought together the front and rear triangle sections to complete the bicycle frame. According to NBIC's process engineers, the automated machines used in the brazing process incorporated optical sensors capable of detecting temperature differences of + 1 percent. Such precision was required to ensure metal integrity and prevent the warping of the tubes during the process.

The final step involved the use of a "slitting and reaming" machine. In this process the seat lug, which had been attached earlier, was slit and the inside of the seat tube was reamed. This process ensured that the seat pillar could be adjusted smoothly and fixed firmly. The time taken to cut, braze, and assemble the frame was about 25 minutes.

The tubes that formed the front fork of the bicycle were cut and assembled, using processes similar to those used for the frame.

Quality Check.   The completed frame and fork were placed on a three-dimensional automatic measuring machine designed by the firm's parent company engineers. This machine checked the actual measurements of the assembled frame and fork against the customer's original specification stored in the host computer's memory banks. Small variations, if any, were detected and displayed on a CRT terminal or plotted by using the attached plotter. The process was completed in less than 60 seconds.

Painting.   Both the completed frame and the front fork were moved by overhead conveyors to the surface cleaning area and immersed in special solutions. This process prevented early rusting of the frame and improved the ability of the subsequent paint to adhere uniformly to the surfaces. The cleaning process took about 10 to 15 minutes. The bicycle frame and front fork were transferred to a "preliminary" painting room to be automatically painted by a robot. Again, the robot received its instructions from the factor's host computer via the bar-code label. According to the factory manager, NBIC was the first bicycle manufacturer to introduce a robot into the painting process for bicycles.

Two skilled workers then completed the "final" by painting the "hard-to-reach" areas, using electrostatic spray guns. Finishing touches and the customer's "special" painting instructions were completed by the workers.

Labeling and Engraving Process.   This process involved printing or engraving the customer's name on the bicycle frame or handlebar stem. A skilled worker, using a silk-screen process, printed the customer's name and transferred it onto the frame. Alternatively, a name-engraving machine engraved the name of the customer on the handle stem. With the completion of this process, the frame was ready for the final assembly process.

Final Assembly and Shipping.   The final assembly involved the mating of the completed frame and fork with the appropriate wheels, chain, gears, brakes, tires, and other components that constitute a complete bicycle. During this process the "derailleur" adjustment and the "rotation" adjustment of the bearing section were completed. Also, the seat pillar and seat lug section were checked and adjusted according to customer specifications. Each bicycle was fully assembled and tested by a single skilled craftsman. The assembly process was performed in any one of the three main assembly stations and took about 30 minutes. The completed bicycle was then boxed and sent to a holding area outside the factory to be picked up for delivery. Bicycles generally were shipped the same day.

The entire manufacturing and assembly time required to complete a single customer order was approximately 150 minutes. In 1989 the factory, employing 18 workers (15 workers were employed in 1987), had the ability to make about 60 custom-order bicycles daily. It received orders for approximately 12,000 bicycles, an increase of 20 percent over the previous two years. A significant portion of those orders were from customers in Japan.

A year after the introduction of the POS, the company unveiled a new system named the Panasonic Individual Customer System (PICS). The purpose of PICS was to offer custom-made bicycles to customers in overseas markets, especially in countries such as Australia, the United States, and Germany. PICS used the same customized manufacturing technology as the POS but offered the choice of much larger frame sizes more suitable to Western customers. The time from order to delivery was increased from two weeks to three weeks under PICS.

Marketing and Distribution.   According to the general manager of sales at NBIC, customer service, "appropriate" pricing, and extensive communication were all integral to NBIC's mass-customization strategy. Domestic customers were guaranteed a delivery time of two weeks, not a day more but also not a day less. He pointed out: "We could have made the time shorter, but we want people to feel excited about waiting for something special." According to a manager at the factory, custom-made Panasonic bicycles were priced only about 20 to 30 percent higher (depending on the particular model and features selected) than a "comparable" bicycle produced at the mass production factory.

Under the POS, the factory was given the responsibility of communicating directly with customers. Shortly after the factory received the customer's order, a personalized computer-generated drawing of the bicycle was mailed with a note thanking the customer for choosing the POS. This was followed up with a second personal note, three months later, inquiring about the customer's satisfaction with his or her bicycle. Finally, a "bicycle birthday card" was sent to commemorate the first anniversary of the bicycle.

According to the general manager in charge of sales, dealership selection played an important role in pursuing this strategy. In early 1993 only about 15 percent of 9,000 domestic dealerships were part of the POS (see Exhibit 9). The company explained the reasons for this:

> We cannot afford to make mistakes. Mistakes can be very costly. It is important that customers don't lose confidence in our system. We have to be very careful in selecting knowledgeable and committed dealers so that they send us the correct information. We can't tolerate mistakes at any stage.

Response to POS

Competitors Imitate NBIC. NBIC's strategy of offering a truly custom-made bicycle surprised all of its major competitors. Within months the two other leading manufacturers of bicycles were scrambling to develop and implement their versions of mass customization. In a year both offered their own "unique" versions of mass customization. But they were unable to duplicate all the aspects of NBIC's strategy, as was noted by a senior manager at Bridgestone in early 1993:

> The trouble with this segment is that it is too small, perhaps 10,000 or more. It costs a lot of money to advertise for such a small segment. Since NBIC was the first firm to introduce this idea, they have established a strong image in the customer's mind. When you mention

EXHIBIT 9   NBIC's Distribution System

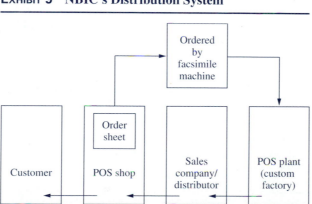

customization, the consumer thinks only of Panasonic. Also, National's parent company, Matsushita, is famous for its marketing savvy, and it is difficult for us to match them. We as a company have not paid much attention to this segment. I expect we will in the future, because we too want to be known for innovativeness.

According to a knowledgeable source in the industry, NBIC was the only company to have successfully mastered the art of mass customization, and competitors were unable to offer the same degree of variety NBIC offered. Unlike NBIC, leading competitors simply increased the inventory of frame types and model sizes they carried to accommodate the variety demand by their customers. According to the managing director:

> One of our competitive advantages is that we are located in Osaka, close to all the major parts suppliers. Frequency and reliability of parts delivery from our suppliers have helped us "truly" custom build bicycles. There is little need to hold large inventories of finished frames and other parts, unlike others outside the Kansai region.

Extensive Media Coverage.   Soon after the announcement of the POS, journalists who followed the industry began expounding on its revolutionary nature. These Japanese stories were soon picked by foreign journalists who wrote about Japanese manufacturing practices. Within a span of two years NBIC was featured in *Fortune, The New York Times,* and the *Washington Post.* One leading American television network, ABC, featured the firm in its regular prime-time "World News Tonight" program hosted by its chief anchorperson, Peter Jennings. The German Public Television network produced a documentary for European audiences. Additionally, NBIC received many requests from other manufacturing firms for information about its new system. Within a few years of the introduction of POS, *Fortune* magazine noted:

> The concept has so intrigued executives and engineers that they have been flocking from as far away as Italy to this factory in Kokubu, in western Japan, to study it. Big Japanese manufacturers of consumer goods are also taking note, hoping to improve their own production system. . . . [NBIC] built these one-of-a kind models by replacing mass production with flexible manufacturing. The method is being employed all over Japan to shrink small-lot production jobs to lots of one.[7]

While NBIC's customized bicycles manufactured under the POS system accounted for only 2 percent of total production, the effect of worldwide attention had a dramatic effect on the company's high-end segment.

Company's Sales Increase.   Before the introduction of POS, NBIC's market share was languishing behind that of its two major competitors in the high-end segment. Within a few years of the introduction of POS and PICS, the firm's total high-end (Panasonic) market share position improved dramatically. For the first time in its history NBIC became the industry's second largest manufacturer of high-end bicycles (see Exhibits 10 and 11).

Reflecting on the events of the last few years, members of the senior management at NBIC glowed with pride about the achievements of their firm. Despite the repeated attempts by other competitors to offer customized bicycles, the Panasonic name was increasingly viewed as the only "truly" mass-customized bicycle in Japan. The firm was now viewed as the leader and chief innovator in the industry. Still, this was not the time to rest on past laurels; there were some major concerns facing NBIC and the industry in 1993.

---

[7] Susan Moffat, "Japan's Personalized Production," *Fortune,* October 22, 1990, p. 132.

EXHIBIT 10 **Production by the Top Four Manufacturers (thousands of units)**

Companies	1987	1992	1992 (Estimate)
Bridgestone	1,330	1,400	1,450
National	754	700	700
Miyata	620	640	610
Maruishi	379	310	310

Source: Estimates published by *Cycle Press*, 1993.

EXHIBIT 11 **NBIC Panasonic Brand Growth, 1986–1992**

	1986	1987	1992	Future Target
Units (percent of total production)	4%	7%	18%	
Revenues (percent of total sales)	10%	13%	27%	50%

Outlook for the Future

Total company sales in 1992 grew marginally by 1.2 percent, but exports of NBIC's Panasonic bicycles were down by over 50 percent. This significant decrease in exports was the result of many factors, including the aggressive export strategies of firms in Taiwan, China, and other neighboring countries; the continued strengthening of the Japanese yen against the U.S. dollar; the softening of the demand for bicycles in Europe and the United States; and the increased competition in overseas markets. The news on the domestic front was not very encouraging either. The sales of domestic bicycles had been stagnant for some time. Forecasts for 1993 indicated only modest overall growth. According to an industry source, the Japanese industry was steadily undergoing structural change. The assemblers were beginning to exploit the growing supply of less expensive bicycle parts from overseas, to the dismay of major manufacturers. According to early industry predictions for 1993, Yokota's share of the market was expected to grow even larger in 1993, and Deki, the second largest assembler, was expected to match NBIC in the production of bicycles (see Exhibit 3).

Role of Customization at NBIC.   In early 1993, given the domestic and international situation, senior managers were pondering the future role of mass customization at NBIC. The lessons and the manufacturing skills the firm had acquired in the custom factory were readily transferable to the mass production factory. Skilled workers from the custom factory were regularly used for training line workers in the larger mass production factory. Over the last few years the mass production factory had been undergoing slow but significant changes. Lot sizes employed in production were steadily decreasing. Over the last few years lot sizes were reduced from 50 to a mere 20 in 1993.

Senior managers were examining the feasibility of turning the mass production factory into a custom shop. The goal was to increase the revenues contributed by the high-end segment to 50 percent of total sales within the next five years. More important, the likely impact on the firm's overall strategy was unclear. Some managers had the view that this custom segment should not be nurtured to grow beyond the current size. The firm should keep it as a small high-value niche market to maintain customer interest and high prices. Others argued for a strategy to increase the size of this segment.

In mid-January 1998 senior management at Powrtron Corporation was grappling with an unprecedented problem of constrained capacity. Allyson Shelton (chief operating officer), Bryce Thomason (sales and marketing manager), and Jason Stewart (manufacturing manager) were meeting to discuss the capacity situation and its snowball effect on late deliveries and customer dissatisfaction.

Tension was high at the start of the meeting, and Shelton feared that the air would only become thicker when she delivered the message from Bradley Keith, the company's principal owner and CEO. Senior management had expected Keith to announce that the company would move to a larger location within the next year. However, on the previous day Keith had informed Shelton that such a move would definitely not take place within the next 12 months. Recognizing that some type of prioritizing would have to take place, he had advised Shelton to work out the capacity, delivery, and customer problems at her meeting with Thomason and Stewart the next day.

A bottom-line person, Shelton knew that Powrtron management quickly had to devise a way to determine the appropriate mix of product development, existing product management, customer prioritization, and customer service.

The Company

Located in Newton, Massachusetts, Powrtron was a private, predominantly family-held company with sales of around $8.4 million. Founded in 1965 by three brothers, the company still operated out of its original building (with some modest additions) on land owned by the founding families.[1] From its inception and into the late 1970s the company exclusively manufactured products in the analog integrated circuit business, using designs principally developed by the youngest of the brothers (then chief engineer), Bradley Keith.[2] Most Powrtron products were designed into customers' new applications. In the late 1970s Bradley Keith developed a unique, slim design for power converters which soon became a major part of the company's business. By the beginning of 1998 Powrtron was engaged in the manufacture and sale of electronic analog circuit modules, isolation amplifiers, and power converters.

---

[1] Increased real estate prices for industrial property in Newton (an immediate suburb of Boston) made the land worth many times its original cost. Estimated value exceeded $9 million.

[2] Unlike his older brothers, who were trained as financial economists at local Ivy League colleges, Bradley Keith received two math degrees from Boston College (BC). Then, over a seven-year span, while working on various defense-related projects at a local multinational electronics firm, Keith earned an engineering degree from Northeastern University (NU) in Boston. He had received four patents. He also had a number of other process and product inventions that probably were patentable if he took the time and effort to apply. Over the years Keith also completed various graduate business courses at BC and NU, but he had not completed a business degree program.

This case was prepared by Victoria L. Crittenden of Boston College and William F. Crittenden of Northeastern University as the basis for class discussion rather than to illustrate effective or ineffective handling of a managerial situation. Powrtron is a pseudonym, and some data have been disguised. All relevant relationships remain constant.

EXHIBIT 1
Organization Structure

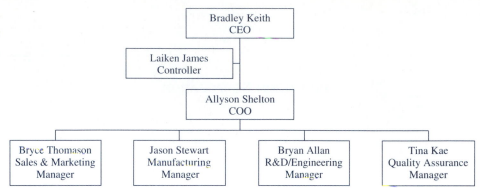

Exhibit 1 shows the firm's organizational structure. Three of the functional managers, including the heads of manufacturing and sales and marketing, had been with the firm less than two and a half years. Top management viewed manufacturing as the strongest functional area, with marketing seen as the weakest. The company's manufacturing capacity was physically constrained by the current location and a tight local labor market which made it difficult to find qualified new people at wages that would keep Powrtron's labor costs competitive. Exhibits 2 and 3 provide recent financial information.

Powrtron produced seven major products in-house. Its perceived competitive strength was providing customized, advanced-technology products to quality-conscious customers. Quality was designed into the product, and a rigorous quality assurance program kept returns at a level well below industry averages. A key accounts policy was viewed as the most effective way to take advantage of Powrtron's strengths, with a standard line of products being the means to generate accounts initially. Management believed that the key to implementing this strategy was to provide a balance of standard and custom products to its customers.

EXHIBIT 2   Income Statement

	1997	1996	1995
Sales	$8,415,393	$7,781,933	$7,548,474
Cost of sales	5,380,077	4,702,145	4,462,281
Gross margin	3,035,316	3,079,788	3,086,193
Operating costs			
Research and development	668,136	529,180	515,973
Sales and marketing	659,393	786,827	761,452
General and administration	1,067,474	1,062,321	1,028,858
OC subtotal	2,395,003	2,378,328	2,306,283
Operating income	640,313	701,460	779,910
Other income	0	0	38,900
Interest expenses			
Shareholders	264,000	264,000	264,000
Bank	118,397	121,878	128,843
Other expenses	218,837	274,584	298,821
Income before taxes	$39,079	$40,998	$127,146

EXHIBIT 3   **Balance Sheet**

	Dec 31, 1997	Dec 31, 1996	Dec 31, 1995
Current assets			
Cash	$123,812	$98,634	$93,523
Accounts receivables	803,732	784,991	787,524
Less: Allowance for bad debts	(31,000)	(31,000)	(31,000)
Inventory	318,453	321,964	326,047
Less: Allowance for obsolescence	(50,000)	(50,000)	(50,000)
Prepaid expenses	16,026	9,877	7,794
Total current assets	1,181,023	1,134,466	1,133,888
Fixed assets			
Machinery and equipment	1,457,023	1,457,023	1,457,023
Furniture and fixtures	253,685	253,685	253,685
Leasehold improvements	0	0	0
Automobile	38,979	38,979	38,979
Less: Accumulated depreciation	(1,529,223)	(1,502,623)	(1,476,023)
Net fixed assets	220,464	247,064	273,664
Total assets	1,401,487	1,381,530	1,407,552
Current liabilities			
Demand note payable	1,392,902	1,392,902	1,392,902
Current maturities of lease	0	0	0
Accounts payable	266,538	253,048	274,736
Payroll taxes payable	34,923	33,876	$35,023
Accrued payroll	235,039	243,024	293,024
Accrued interest	280,000	300,085	323,054
Other	103,726	111,234	109,067
Total current liabilities	2,313,128	2,334,169	2,427,806
Long-term liabilities			
Notes payable to shareholders	1,750,000	1,750,000	1,750,000
Shareholders' equity			
Common stock	920,000	920,000	920,000
Retained earnings	(3,581,641)	(3,622,639)	(3,690,254)
Total liabilities and equity	$1,401,487	$1,381,530	$1,407,552

Products.   Two analog business products—the pincushion integrated circuit module (PIN) and the isolation amplifier/analog multiplier (IAAM)—generally provided Powrtron with its best gross margins. The pincushion correction device corrected for geometric or focus distortion for CRT displays. Typical applications included airborne displays, air traffic control systems, medical monitors, and CAD displays. Two distinct lines of the PIN product existed. Powrtron manufactured PIN100s, with PIN300s being a buy/resale product. Isolation amplifiers could be used in a variety of situations, including industrial process control, instrumentation (data acquisition), and medical (ECG, EEG, ENG, and other types of medical monitoring). Worldwide sales of analog circuit devices were estimated at around US$12 billion, with the consumer market (video and portable phones) accounting for approximately 40 percent of demand.

With the increased use of sophisticated analog and digital devices in many types of electronic systems, DC/DC power converters were necessary products for design engineers. The converter provided the electronic system with the regulated voltage required through local transformation of power supply voltages. Applications included telecommunications, robotics, remote systems, battery-operated systems, uninterruptable power systems, test instrumentation, and ground support equipment. Five products constituted Powrtron's major lines of DC/DC converters: DCD, DCT, DCJ, DCX, and DCZ. The depths of these product lines varied and depended on such issues as power range, input voltage, output voltage, and whether output was regulated. Problems had occurred in the DC/DC converter business, however, in that Powrtron had not been able to produce large quantities of low-cost standardized products successfully.

The worldwide power converter market was estimated at around US$10 billion. These sales experienced less volatility than did the sales of the more complex integrated circuits. However, there were industrywide concerns that this market had reached maturity, leading to long-term concern about the overall health of the marketplace. At the same time, there was surprise that the market had proved to be as resilient as it was to market encroachment by analog devices.

Stewart and Thomason provided numerous personal insights and concerns about each of Powrtron's seven products. The PIN and DCT offerings were thought to be good, stable products with continued market potential. Although the IAAM was an important contributor to company margins, each manager independently expressed some concern about whether Powrtron could compete in the long term with this product. Stewart had determined that the DCD market was not growing and had plans to phase out the line. However, Powrtron had experienced recent interest in the product. Thomason was attempting to determine if this was just a short-term blip on the screen or if the market was beginning to recover. The DCJ was a small-volume business and had extremely volatile margins. However, the firm continued to make the product and had seen sales increase in 1996 and again in 1997. Stewart viewed the DCX product line as the big loser in the firm. Thomason acknowledged that the DCX was in a decline but did not agree that it was a big loser. Both Stewart and Thomason agreed that the DCZ line of products was the future of power converters at Powrtron. However, although demand had jumped 600 percent, current sales were not meeting expectations and the company was having trouble perfecting the product for the marketplace.

Additionally, Powrtron made variations of the seven products ("specials") that did not fit solely within any of the product lines. Powrtron also would purchase products for resale if its customers needed products not available from Powrtron and did not want to shop around for the product themselves.

Customers.   Powrtron had three tiers of accounts. The first tier consisted of three major customers for which Powrtron made unique, specialized products. Close business relationships existed between Powrtron and those three accounts. CEO Bradley Keith had himself made the original contact and sale with those long-time customers. Allyson Shelton, COO, now personally oversaw individual account sales of around $850,000 annually to each of those accounts. Powrtron management considered the first tier of accounts as a "separate business." The margins on business from those accounts approximated Powrtron's average, and those customers kept their promises and paid in a timely fashion.

Second-tier accounts consisted of 10 major customers and 7 minor customers, with total sales of around $4,000,000 annually. The 10 major second-tier accounts were labeled HF, TI, RO, GE, AT, GN, NA, AC, SA, and WC. Seven of the major accounts provided between $400,000 and $580,000 each in yearly sales. Thomason indicated that the remaining three major accounts had strong potential for growth. Nine of the 10 major accounts purchased Powrtron-manufactured products. Purchases from the tenth account (WC) consisted of the company's buy/resale product offering only. Shelton, Thomason, and Stewart agreed that the seven minor accounts were important to Powrtron because of their market potential or the combination of products purchased.

Exhibit 4   Product/Account Purchases

	Products							
Accounts	PIN	IAAM	DCD	DCT	DCJ	DCX	DCZ	Specials
HF				x		x		x
TI			x	x	x	x		
RO	x	x	x	x		x		x
GE	x	x						x
AT				x	x	x		x
GN	x						x	
NA			x				x	
AC								x
SA							x	

Powrtron attempted to develop second-tier accounts into key accounts (tier 1 accounts) through individual service provided by sales and marketing. However, actual purchases were made through the local sales representative and not directly to Powrtron. Sales representatives' commissions were 7 percent for sales made to three of the accounts (TI, NA, AC) and 6 percent for sales made to the remaining accounts. Exhibit 4 provides an overview of Powrtron-manufactured products purchased by the nine major accounts. Exhibit 5 shows total 1993–1997 second-tier account sales for each of the seven products manufactured by Powrtron.

The third tier of accounts consisted of around $1,900,000 in sales of Powrtron-manufactured standard products to many different customers. Individual sales to each of those customers did not amount to a large enough dollar total to warrant separate consideration of each account. These customers did not receive special sales attention from a Powrtron manager and made purchases exclusively through the local manufacturer's representative organization. The rep organization's role was simply that of order taker.

Competition

Japanese manufacturers held the leading share (35 percent) in the $12 billion analog circuit business. This was followed by the United States (25 percent), Europe (20 percent), and then the rest of the world. Leading worldwide competitors and their estimated market shares included National Semiconductor (7 percent), Texas Instruments (6 percent), Philips/Signetics (5.7 percent), Toshiba (5.6 percent), Sanyo (5.5 percent), Matsushita (5.1 percent), SGS/Thomson (4.7 percent), Motorola Inc. (4.4 percent), NEC Corp. (4.3 percent), Hitachi (4.1 percent), and Mitsubishi (4.1 percent). These large firms had significant scale advantages throughout the value chain and tended to exclusively produce highly standardized products. The battle for market share among these firms was fiercely competitive, as even a fraction of a percentage point meant millions of dollars in sales. Midsize firms (those with less than 2 percent market share) tended to come under close competitive scrutiny whenever they appeared to encroach on the high-volume, standardized portion of this business. The most profitable midsize firms tended to be subsidiaries of much larger, vertically integrated firms. Smaller firms tended to be highly focused around a single core technology that was used as the basis for quickly producing a highly customized product.

EXHIBIT 5   **Product Sales and Average Price**
for Second-Tier Accounts

	Unit Volume	Total Sales	Average Price
PIN			
1993	309	$117,487	$380
1994	310	123,054	397
1995	341	141,731	416
1996	1,890	718,281	380
1997	2,701	1,059,091	392
IAAM			
1993	17	1,683	99
1994	158	13,866	88
1995	1,558	133,987	86
1996	5,039	428,355	85
1997	5,543	509,956	92
DCD			
1993	0	0	0
1994	66	10,248	155
1995	199	32,452	163
1996	66	11,838	179
1997	398	66,466	167
DCT			
1993	627	206,910	330
1994	1,739	554,741	319
1995	1,927	447,064	232
1996	1,884	465,348	247
1997	1,841	489,706	266
DCJ			
1993	1,254	109,098	87
1994	1,326	125,970	95
1995	838	71,896	86
1996	818	80,981	99
1997	917	80,696	88
DCX			
1993	1,686	153,246	91
1994	2,806	238,510	85
1995	123	14,637	119
1996	345	36,915	107
1997	80	9,280	116
DCZ			
1993	0	0	0
1994	0	0	0
1995	0	0	0
1996	2,085	223,095	107
1997	13,694	1,410,482	103

Competition in the $10 billion power converter business was enormous, with thousands of worldwide competitors. The most successful competitors appeared to be able to blend high-margin customized production with high-volume, good-margin standardized manufacturing. There were successful small firms that focused exclusively on customized production. However, those firms often incurred substantial problems in an economic downturn. Companies operating in this industry included Vicor Corp., Theta-J, Unitech P.L.C., Rifa, Astec, and Lambda Electronics. Competitors seemed keenly aware whenever Powrtron captured significant business beyond its first-tier accounts. Thus, bids for repeat business, which would allow Powrtron to obtain some learning-curve advantages, were always highly competitive.

Operations at Powrtron

The manufacturing facility was located in the same building as management offices in Newton, Massachusetts. The manufacturing area totaled 14,500 square feet, the engineering area was 5,000 square feet, and the quality control area was 1,500 square feet. The engineering group (not including CEO Keith) had over 40 years of experience in the power design field. A computer-aided design (CAD) system was used for schematic design, layout, and documentation processes utilized by the engineering group. The CAD system had a direct parts-list link to the materials requirements planning (MRP II) system utilized by the manufacturing group. The MRP II system continuously monitored order status, inventory, and customer inquiries.

Although much of the manufacturing equipment was of an older vintage, every piece of equipment was kept in perfect operating condition. In addition, the shop floor was kept well organized and immaculate, and the equipment layout maximized the use of available space.

Powrtron employed 60 direct labor personnel and 10 indirect labor personnel in the manufacturing process. The manufacturing work force was unionized. Yet CEO Keith had a strong affinity with his production people, and labor issues were few and infrequent. Over 70 percent of the production work force had been with Powrtron for at least 20 years, and a number of workers had been with the company since its beginning. The company's location was near many long-time employees' homes and was convenient for those using mass transit systems. Keith knew all his employees and a fair amount about their families as well. During the recession of the late 1980s–early 1990s no one was ever laid off. Instead, workers were asked to take one day a month of unpaid time off.

Now that the economy was again strong and the firm was showing profitability, Stewart had suggested that a new office location/production facility be acquired to enhance the firm's capacity and production capabilities. With an order backlog of around 20 percent for tier 2 and tier 3 accounts (tier 1 account orders were prioritized and moved near the top of the queue) and sales projecting a 10 percent increase for 1998, Stewart looked toward moving to a larger facility with modern equipment and increased hiring to relieve capacity pressures.

While CEO Keith had established connections for offshore manufacturing capabilities in the Caribbean and the Far East, the company had never augmented its production volume through any of those sources. Engineering head Bryan Allan and quality assurance manager Tina Kae each expressed concerns regarding the sharing of proprietary information with firms in less developed countries (LDCs).

Every Powrtron product was subjected to a six-step quality inspection process as well as two electrical/functional tests. CEO Keith was proud that quality was designed into each of Powrtron's products and that the quality assurance program, although time-

EXHIBIT 6   Expected Allocation of Available Production Hours (Quarterly)

Product	Hours
PIN	1,300
IAAM	1,300
DCD	350
DCT	1,000
DCJ	400
DCX	350
DCZ	5,800

consuming, ensured that Powrtron maintained a lower failure rate than did most of its direct competitors.

Stewart allocated around 10,500 hours each quarter to producing the seven products for second- and third-tier accounts (approximately one-third of production time was allotted to servicing tier 1 accounts, and the remaining time was used for setup, maintenance and repair, and producing "specials" for second- and third-tier accounts). Overtime was very expensive, and most of the current work force preferred to not work extra hours. Stewart's expected allocated hourly product capacity utilization during 1998 for each product is shown in Exhibit 6. However, since the major factor was total production hour availability, Stewart used this only as a general guide to allocation. Exhibits 7 and 8 provide cost information (variable and setup) and production time for each of the major product lines.

Although Powrtron's manufacturing group had not previously dealt with constrained capacity, Stewart and the production people were not at a loss for ideas on how to approach the problem. Some people believed they should fill orders relative to the desired amount. (Some thought this meant the largest orders should be filled first, while others believed it meant the accounts with smaller orders should be filled first.) Others thought the marketing group should be forced to rank orders by account priority. Some felt they should focus on producing the most standardized requests (those requiring the least customization of the core product), while others believed they should fill a certain mini-

EXHIBIT 7   Variable Cost per Unit and Setup Cost per Run

Product	Variable Cost/Unit	Setup Cost/Run
PIN	$75.00	$5.20
IAAM	35.00	4.15
DCD	65.00	4.15
DCT	75.00	7.25
DCJ	65.00	4.15
DCX	45.00	6.25
DCZ	55.00	6.25

EXHIBIT 8   **Production Time per Unit and Setup Time per Run**

Product	Production Time/ Unit (hours)	Setup Time/ Run (hours)
PIN	1.00	0.25
IAAM	0.60	0.20
DCD	1.00	0.20
DCT	1.50	0.35
DCJ	1.00	0.20
DCX	1.05	0.30
DCZ	1.33	0.30

mum amount for each account. Other ideas generated throughout the organization included fill best prices first, fill orders by account profitability, and fill orders based on product profitability.

Current Problem

Basically, Shelton, Thomason, and Stewart were meeting to discuss how Powrtron could better balance supply and demand. But Shelton knew that the issue involved more than economics. Thomason and Stewart had literally been at each other's necks over the past couple of months. Not only did the company have irate customers due to slow or late deliveries, Powrtron's senior managers were barely speaking to each other.

Not wasting any time on social interaction at the start of the meeting, Bryce Thomason told Shelton that Stewart's group was responsible for the problems he was having with his second-tier accounts. Thomason said that Powrtron's competitors were promising (and delivering) in a maximum of six weeks from the sale. Therefore, he felt that he had to make the same commitment if Powrtron's second-tier accounts were to continue doing business with the company. Unfortunately, while Thomason indicated that Powrtron's competition was satisfying its delivery commitments, Shelton knew Powrtron had not delivered on time in the last four months. Thomason thought that Stewart was not dedicated to the firm's key account strategy. He felt that without this commitment, Powrtron might as well provide standard, off-the-shelf products and forget the key account focus.

Angrily, Jason Stewart told Thomason that sales and marketing was making unreasonable promises by pushing ahead its delivery date commitments. Stewart said that Thomason and his sales staff were being unrealistic by ignoring the firm's capacity limits, particularly with respect to backlog, run cycles, and downtime. With the current capacity situation, Stewart felt that the delivery cycle should be twice the time Thomason was telling customers. Stewart said that the only relief in sight was the upcoming move to a larger production facility. He said, "Powrtron will be able to expand its production capabilities once we are able to add equipment and laborers. Until then the company will not be able to make and deliver products any faster."

Things were heating up much more quickly than Shelton had anticipated. The meeting had not gotten off to a good start. Unfortunately, Shelton knew that her announcement about the delay in company relocation was going to make an already bad situation worse.

CASE 6–5
CHEMICAL ADDITIVES CORPORATION: SPECIALTY PRODUCTS GROUP

Nick Williamson, general manager of Specialty Products Group (SPG), gazed out his window and sighed. It was August 1990, and the atmosphere inside his office was as unpleasant as the 100-degree weather of the Fort Smith, Arkansas, headquarters of SPG. He swiveled back to face his management team and said, "Okay, I've heard your arguments about positioning and pricing 'R&D 601, 602, and 603.' I wish there were some way to get a consensus from you guys. I'll consider our options over the weekend."

The decisions facing Williamson would have a substantial impact on the future of SPG. A strategy of moving away from large-volume commodity wax markets toward becoming a premier supplier of specialty chemical additives to niche markets was not going as smoothly as anticipated. Three newly developed products might well be the catalyst to hasten that shift. These new products, known by their experimental designations R&D 601, 602, and 603, were corrosion inhibitors used during the transport and storage of liquid urea ammonium nitrate (UAN) fertilizer.

Liquid Fertilizers

Liquid fertilizers had numerous advantages over the traditional solid fertilizers principally used in U.S. agriculture: (1) excellent performance under a variety of weather conditions, (2) reduced toxicity, (3) ability to be easily blended with other nutrients, insecticides, and herbicides, and (4) milder environmental impact (but not benign; a spill or leak of undiluted UAN could still kill wildlife and vegetation).

Unfortunately, UAN liquids corroded the steel tanks, pipelines, railcars, and barges used for storage and transport, resulting in repair costs that could exceed $1 million per incident for the typical UAN producer. The industry had tried a variety of corrosion inhibitors (chemicals that were added in small doses to UAN after production) to reduce the rate at which the UAN ate away a metal surface. Inhibitors did not prevent corrosion; they slowed the chemical reaction of metal dissolving into UAN. An excellent inhibitor might increase the average life of a typical $20 million storage system from as little as 3 years to longer than 20 years.

Leaks and spills also created liabilities for EPA fines. If a tank failure resulted in massive environmental damage, federal lawsuits potentially could bankrupt a producer. Corrosion inhibitor suppliers also might be liable for leaks and environmental damage.

Manufacturers produced UAN fertilizer in continuous-process facilities with typical minimum capacities of 10,000 tons a year. They then added corrosion inhibitors and stored the inhibited UAN in tanks to await shipment. Producers shipped UAN through a distributor/dealer network that delivered the product to the right farmer, at the right time, and with appropriate other agricultural chemicals added as necessary. Some larger

This case was prepared by Charles Hoffheiser and Lester A. Neidell, University of Tulsa. Permission to reprint granted by the authors and the North American Case Research Association.

dealers provided custom-application services to apply UAN blends to fields and crops. The same distribution system also handled the solid fertilizers UAN was slowly replacing.

SPG designed these experimental products to replace its earlier entries into this market as well as to regain business previously lost to a widely used, foreign-sourced material, Corblok 105-B. The sales and marketing managers each strongly argued contrary marketing tactics. The vice president of sales, Ron White, reasoned that despite any performance advantages of the new SPG products, market conditions in the U.S. fertilizer industry required that SPG price the new products as low as possible, using only the mandatory minimum corporate markup over standard cost. White had always operated with the objective of keeping company plants operating close to capacity to minimize standard costs. Price leadership and volume were, in his eyes, the key to SPG's success.

Jim Walker, newly hired as director of marketing (a new position at SPG), vehemently favored a value-based pricing approach, recognizing both product performance and competitive conditions. The technical director regularly reminded these two managers that the three products performed differently in different producers' UANs and added, "You guys better start selling some of this stuff soon to pay off our investment of over four years of technical effort!"

Chemical Additives Corporation

SPG was one of four divisions of the Chemical Additives Corporation (CAC), a multinational company that provided solutions to production problems in oil fields, refineries, chemical plants, and other industrial applications. The corporate mission was

> to produce and market specialty chemical products and the technical service and equipment necessary to utilize CAC's products effectively.

CAC pursued a strategy of developing customized equipment and chemical treatment programs to add value to customers' operations through optimization of operating efficiency or increased reliability. CAC's strengths included expertise in organic phosphate ester chemistry (the key to advanced-technology corrosion inhibitors) and in the mixing of incompatible fluids (e.g., oil and water). It considered itself to be the worldwide leader in oil industry corrosion control and had developed and patented much of the technology historically used in these applications. However, over the last 10 years, competitors had found it increasingly easy to design products outside patent coverages, particularly as R&D departments began to use advanced computer modeling techniques. Computer modeling made it much easier to design new families of chemical products.

CAC organized its operations into four operating groups: Oil Field Chemicals, Refinery Chemicals, Instrument Group, and Specialty Products. Each group maintained its own sales, marketing, and product development functions. A central research department conducted long-range, basic chemical research for all the divisions.

The Oil Field Chemicals Group was the world's largest supplier of oil field production chemicals, including corrosion inhibitors and drilling aids. Since its products went "down the hole," appearance, odor, and handling characteristics, such as foaming, were often not of concern to customers. The sales force's requests for customer-specific products drove product development. This division had over 4,000 products in its line. The group justified this product line breadth in two ways: (1) No two oil deposits were identical in chemical makeup, and (2) as wells aged, increasing amounts of exotic chemicals were needed to enhance oil production.

Refinery Chemicals marketed process efficiency aids for the production side of refineries. It also sold fuel additives such as fuel-injector cleaners to refiners and to wholesalers of gasoline and truck diesel fuel.

The Instrument Group designed and marketed filtration and purification systems that solved a variety of water- and oil-related process problems in refineries. Customers often used this equipment in conjunction with CAC's chemical treatment programs. This group also sold a complete line of premium-quality corrosion monitoring instruments.

Specialty Products Group had two major product groups: (1) about 100 types of commodity petroleum waxes (similar but not identical to the types used in candles) that were separated from crude oil and (2) synthetic polymers based on a chemical called propylene. Common examples of polymers are plastic food wrap and vinyl siding for houses. SPG's synthetics, however, were not the type used in plastic film, cups, and containers. Customers often called them synthetic waxes because they had properties similar to those of commodity petroleum waxes. Nick Williamson tried to alter this perception through extensive trade advertising and by instructing division personnel to refer to all division products as "specialty polymers." SPG's products had hundreds of applications, ranging from shoe polish to chewing gum to cardboard box–sealing adhesives. Various SPG products also had found modest use as antidust and anticaking additives for solid fertilizers, and as a result, SPG conducted all of CAC's business in the worldwide fertilizer industry.

Exhibit 1 shows selected CAC and divisional financial data; Exhibit 2 shows the distribution of SPG revenue and profit by end use market and the allocation of salespeople.

SPG's Competitors

Each division had its own set of specialized competitors as well as competition from various divisions of large chemical companies such as DuPont, Dow, Witco, and Shell. The 1980s ushered in a new era in the chemical industry—worldwide competition. (Corblok, principal competitor to SPG's UAN anticorrosion additives, was an example of this.) Foreign suppliers also directly affected other SPG markets. They included Mitsui, BASF, Hoechst, and Dead Sea Works, an Israeli government–owned coal gasification plant that produced waxes as by-products of gasoline production. Except for Dead Sea, all the competitors were much larger than SPG (and CAC) and were reputed to be among the most efficient chemical companies in the world.

SPG found itself with a key disadvantage versus major chemical firms because its synthetic process required liquid polypropylene, a product form supplied by only one company. The majors often had captive suppliers and used much larger volumes of less expensive gaseous polypropylene, which was available from many suppliers.

SPG's Marketing.   Before 1980 SPG sold its products only through distributors. Galaxy Wax and Schmidt Associates, both of which maintained regional warehouses, served the U.S. market for SPG. The Leveque Group, headquartered in Brussels, Belgium, was responsible for sales to Europe, Africa, and the Middle East. Leveque also served as the principal distributor of wax products manufactured by BASF and Hoechst, both headquartered in West Germany. A joint venture between CAC and Nissan Trading Company (Japan) sold in the Far East.

In 1979, in an attempt to capture the distributor margin for SPG, Williamson hired Ron White to establish a direct sales force. By 1990 SPG had two regional managers and nine salespeople in the United States (see Exhibit 2). After 11 years of direct selling, there were still situations in which SPG lost business to wax distributors on price, delivery, and, in some cases, technical service.

EXHIBIT 1 **Chemical Additives Corporation Financial Data, 1985–1989**
(in thousands of dollars)

	1985	1986	1987	1988	1989
Income Statement Data					
Net sales	$253,841	$297,208	$302,567	$287,931	$294,068
COGS	160,268	189,498	181,531	174,919	171,769
Gross profit	93,573	107,710	121,036	113,012	122,299
Selling expense	33,623	41,532	49,746	53,235	56,292
R&D expense	6,370	7,520	9,487	11,537	12,065
G&A expense	10,860	12,470	14,107	14,614	15,455
Operating profit	42,720	46,188	47,696	33,626	38,487
Investment income	774	2,500	2,139	2,533	3,722
Interest expense	(2,089)	(1,893)	(1,552)	(1,384)	(1,191)
Other net	623	1,136	203	585	1,782
EBIT	42,028	47,931	48,486	35,360	42,800
Income tax	17,143	20,174	19,190	13,310	17,000
Net earnings	$ 24,885	$ 27,757	$ 29,296	$ 22,050	$ 25,800
Balance Sheet Data					
Cash	$ 16,581	$ 12,478	$ 3,018	$ 37,201	$ 43,461
Accounts receivable	45,127	61,981	55,836	51,055	56,896
Inventory	39,639	43,751	39,785	38,976	41,296
Other current assets	64,466	77,768	77,711	91,869	104,175
Total current assets	175,544	197,782	200,318	209,105	221,514
Current liabilities	44,468	48,579	39,957	39,808	45,675
Long-term debt	12,500	11,250	10,000	8,750	7,500
Stockholders' equity	112,999	132,989	145,159	153,042	164,148
Other Financial Information					
Shares (thousands)	5,972	11,864	11,864	11,865	11,715
Dividends per share	$1.20	$0.76	$0.95	$1.00	$1.03
CAC Revenue by Division					
Oil Field Chemicals	$158,048	$181,614	$201,378	$199,498	$211,804
Refinery Chemicals	33,069	32,524	32,117	30,342	32,499
Specialty Products	41,554	46,410	41,483	36,969	40,041
Instruments	21,170	36,660	27,589	21,122	9,724

Annual salary and benefit costs for each sales representative were about $80,000, while the two regional managers were paid about 20 percent more. These figures included a company car but not travel and other sales expenses, which averaged an additional 10 percent of sales revenue. These numbers did not include a profit bonus plan, which typically added 2 percent of sales revenue to selling costs. An annual "salesperson of the year" award, usually based on exceeding forecast poundage figures, provided a further bonus of 5 percent of the $50,000 base to one salesperson. Salespeople developed an annual territorial sales forecast to help plan production runs and order raw materials. The sales force devoted little time to prospecting because White kept a "sales efficiency" log for each representative that did not adjust for this sales task. Sales efficiency was calculated by dividing sales calls that yielded an order by total sales calls.

EXHIBIT 2 SPG End Use Segments in 1989

End Use Market	Percent of Total SPG Sales in Dollars	Percent of Total Pretax Profits	Product Life Cycle
Plastics	5%	12%	Late growth, maturity
Coatings	10	18	Late growth, maturity
Sealants	25	25	Mature
Food additives	5	3	Mature
Laminating wax	25	15	Decline
Others	30	27	Mostly mature

Philadelphia	East regional sales office, 1 sales representative
Atlanta	1 sales representative
Boston	1 sales representative
Cleveland	1 sales representative
Chicago	2 sales representatives
Fort Smith	1 sales representative
Houston	1 sales representative
Los Angeles	West regional sales office, 1 sales representative

The UAN Corrosion Inhibitor Opportunity

In February 1985 the general manager of the Refinery Chemicals Group (RCG) sent Nick Williamson a memo suggesting that certain CAC products might be useful in solving corrosion problems encountered by the Jackson Pipeline Company (JPL) of Fort Smith, Arkansas. One of the refinery group's (and CAC's) largest customers, JPL was a major U.S. pipeline company active in the transport of crude oil, gasoline, diesel and jet fuels, chemicals, and natural gas. The memo noted that as a result of the oil bust of 1980–1983, JPL had attempted to build its transportation volume of other products and had begun shipping UAN produced by JPL's wholly owned fertilizer company, Fertex Chemicals (also with its main plant in Fort Smith). Additional UAN shipments were procured from Farm Products (Kansas City, Missouri) and Agriproducts (Sioux Falls, South Dakota). JPL's pipeline system extended to Texas, Arkansas, Oklahoma, Missouri, Kansas, Iowa, the Dakotas, Illinois, and Indiana.

Historically, UAN was shipped by (in order of increasing cost) barge, rail tank cars, and tank trucks. To use JPL's pipeline system, UAN producers were required to incorporate a corrosion inhibitor approved by JPL. However, unexpected corrosion problems with UAN severely hurt the profitability of JPL's fertilizer-shipping business.

The RCG memo was timely; SPG too had suffered from the petrochemical industry recession of 1981–1983. Also, Williamson was being pushed by CAC's executive committee to move away from commodity wax products into chemical specialties that could provide protection against the price wars affecting chemical commodity markets.

Initial Entry into the UAN Corrosion Control Market. In late 1986 SPG introduced Stealth 3660, an oil field corrosion inhibitor, for use in transporting liquid UAN. SPG's choice of Stealth 3660 was based on its proven success in the oil field and the assumption that corrosion control was a similar phenomenon regardless of the end use environment. After testing, JPL recommended 3660 to its Fertex subsidiary and to its two other customers: Farm Products and Agriproducts. SPG priced 3660 at its standard markup, 100 percent above its standard cost. At that price, 3660 cost fertilizer producers 50 percent less than the previously approved Corblok 105-B inhibitor. All three UAN manufacturers soon switched to 3660.

However, Fertex detected toxic fumes exceeding Occupational Safety and Health Administration (OSHA)–defined lethal concentrations at the top hatch of the trucks used to deliver the product from CAC's Chicago plant. In 1987, Fertex reverted to using Corblok.

Unwilling to lose this market, Williamson instructed R&D to select another product from the oil field corrosion inhibitor line. In mid-1987 SPG introduced Stealth 3662 to JPL and its three customers. The toxicity problem appeared to be solved, while the usage cost was the same as that of 3660. By late 1987 all three fertilizer companies were buying 3662 in tank-truck quantities. As mid-1988 approached, word of mouth in the fertilizer industry persuaded firms such as Iowa Fertilizer, Ferticon, Nitrogen Industries, and Marathon Chemical, among others, to use 3662.

Like Stealth 3660, SPG priced 3662 at a 100 percent markup over standard cost. Tank-truck (40,000 pounds) quantities sold for $0.80 per pound, and 55-gallon drums for $0.83 per pound, with costs of $0.40 per pound and $0.415 per pound, respectively. According to CAC policy, if a product was not priced at least 100 percent above cost, it was not defined as a "specialty chemical" and did not qualify for recognition as supporting the corporate mission of becoming a specialty chemical firm. SPG's goal was to derive at least 30 percent of its gross sales revenue from specialties by 1990.

In late 1988 Fertex reported to SPG that its UAN was causing severe foaming problems when mixed with fertilizer components such as pesticides and herbicides, a practice that was typical at the fertilizer dealer level. By spring 1989 Fertex switched back to Corblok. As a result of the foaming incidents, SPG became aware that UAN passed through a dealer/distributor network before farmers applied it to fields and crops. SPG salespeople typically had called on fertilizer producers, not on other channel members.

Worried about SPG's ability to compete effectively in the UAN corrosion control market, Williamson directed Ron White to hire a sales engineer or product manager to get the UAN corrosion inhibitor program on track. In August 1989 Bob Brown joined SPG in that capacity. Williamson also hired a director of marketing, Jim Walker, in October 1989 and charged him with changing the culture of SPG from a sales/manufacturing/technology-driven business to a market-driven business.

SPG's 1989 organizational chart is shown in Exhibit 3; Exhibit 4 contains background information on SPG's key personnel.

Corrosion Inhibitor Technology.   Corrosion results from a complex chemical reaction that changes steel to useless iron oxide. UAN producers used two basic types of corrosion inhibitors: passivators and film formers. Passivators formed a protective coating by chemically reacting with the steel surfaces they were supposed to protect. Although some people believed them to be effective, researchers found that corrosive materials could penetrate the coating, resulting in the rapid formation of deep pits. The typical repair cost for a storage tank exceeded $1 million, and customers had even reported one or two complete tank failures.

Film formers left a microscopic layer of inhibitor on the steel surface by incompletely dissolving in the corrosive liquid UAN. This new technology was considered by the National Association of Corrosion Engineers (NACE) to be a sound alternative to designing tanks and piping using expensive, exotic steel alloys or plastics.

EXHIBIT 3   **SPG's Organization Chart**

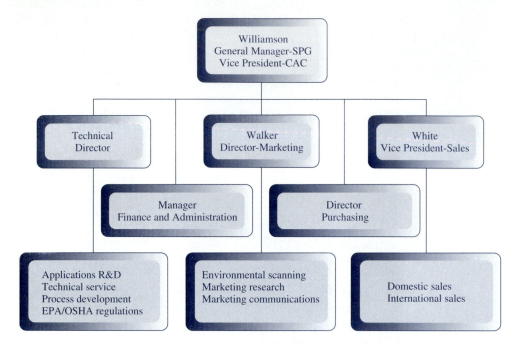

All of SPG's UAN products were of the film-forming variety. This technology and the related one of solubility control were basic and very strong technologies for CAC and were the source of numerous patents.

Corrosion Inhibitor Use in the U.S. Market.   The 1980s was traumatic for U.S. farmers and the industries that supplied them. By 1988 the fertilizer industry (including UAN producers) had experienced a shakeout that reduced industry capacity by 20 percent. One UAN plant with book assets of over $40 million netted just $3.5 million at auction. Although U.S. farmers detected improved prospects by the end of 1988, fertilizer producers faced stiff, low-cost foreign competition on their largest-volume solid products, sometimes losing money on every ton sold. The cost of liquid UAN ocean shipment kept imports from attacking the North American market, but domestic producers, in a competitive frenzy, cut UAN prices to an extent where they sometimes made only $1 per ton pretax. The shakeout led many to believe the situation would soon return to a more "normal" $30 per ton.

Corrosion control was necessary once UAN entered the distribution system. A number of different products were used over the years to reduce corrosion. Some UAN producers tried unsuccessfully to differentiate their product on the basis of the presence of a corrosion inhibitor. Dealers and farmers were more concerned with the cost per acre of fertilized land and on-time, fast delivery, especially during the hectic spring planting and fall harvest. Processing problems, such as incompatibility with other agricultural chemicals and foaming, were not tolerated. There was little dealer loyalty among farmers when they needed to plant or harvest.

Manufacturers produced UAN liquids as 28 percent and 32 percent blends in water. Dealers diluted UAN with additional water before it was suitable for crop application.

EXHIBIT 4   Key SPG Personnel

Nick Williamson—Executive Vice President and General Manager

With a degree in chemical engineering, Williamson joined SPG in 1966 as a process engineer and worked his way through the production and process engineering ranks to his current position in 1982. He had no sales, marketing, or finance experience. Along the way he completed his master's degree in chemical engineering and developed a process to make synthetic wax. He persuaded corporate management to invest $10 million in 1975 to build a plant for these products, and it came on stream in 1976. The first commercial sale of any significance occurred in 1979 to a hot melt adhesive manufacturer, a mature industry at the time. His management philosophy was to be involved in every detail of the SPG operation.

Ron White—Vice President of Sales

A personal friend of Williamson's, he was hired in 1980. A former Air Force KC-135 tanker pilot, he had for years been a member of the leading country club in Fort Smith and was a three-handicap golfer. Before his employment at SPG, he was the sole U.S. distributor of potassium permanganate, a commodity reagent widely used as a catalyst and in research laboratories. His college degree was in chemistry.

Jim Walker—Director of Marketing

With a chemical engineering degree, he joined American Cyanamid in 1970 as a process engineer. He moved to sales and marketing in 1974, responsible for contract sales of sulfuric acid and alum, and became marketing manager for specialty urethane catalysts at Dow in 1978. By that time he had earned his MBA in chemical marketing from Fairleigh Dickinson. He was appointed director of marketing for Corn Products Corp. in 1984.

Bob Brown—Sales Engineer

Brown graduated from Carnegie Mellon University with a chemistry degree in 1978 and was first employed by Firestone's chemical division, concentrating on specialty urethane adhesives sales. Three years later he became a water management chemicals and services specialist at Western Corporation. He was a highly successful salesman with specific training in consultative needs satisfaction selling and technical service.

As a rule, the more dilute the UAN was, the more corrosive it was to steel. Once a fertilizer manufacturer added a corrosion inhibitor such as Corblok 105-B or Stealth 3662 at the proper dose at the plant, corrosion control was effective through the entire distribution network.

Competitive Products.   The following inhibitors were in use in January 1989 as SPG began its program to develop a replacement for Stealth 3662. Except for borax, all were liquid materials (also see Exhibit 5).

Ammonia.   A toxic gas used as a fertilizer, ammonia was the cheapest source of nitrogen, the same nutrient provided by UAN. Some producers believed corrosion could be eliminated simply by neutralizing acids from the production process by adding ammonia. It was one of the raw materials in the manufacture of UAN. Instances of rapid pitting corrosion in 1970 led many producers to try other inhibitors. The principal advantage was that it was virtually free.

Borax.   Classified as "acceptable" by the Tennessee Valley Authority (TVA), borax was used by only one manufacturer. Several other UAN manufacturers had found it unacceptable.

EXHIBIT 5   Competitive Inhibitors, 1990

Product	Supplier	Type*	Price ($/lb.)	Treat Cost ($/ton)†
Ammonia	Many	P	0	0
Borax	Many	P	0.14–0.17	0.28–0.35
Chromate	Many	F	0.47	0.28
Corblok	IWC	F	1.87	0.47
DAP	Many	P	0.082	0.20–0.25
Stealth 3662	SPG	F	0.80	0.24
RG 2064	Western	F	1.90	0.19–0.38
OA-5	Tennessee	F	0.375	0.30

* P = passivating; F = film former.

† Treatment cost is per ton of UAN.

Sodium Chromate.   The fact that a material considered by the Environmental Protection Agency (EPA) to be a primary pollutant was allowed in fertilizer points out the strange regulatory environment typically faced by the chemical industry. This product was an excellent corrosion inhibitor but was also toxic to fish and wildlife. Only one plant used it. It was a film former.

Corblok.   This phosphate ester film former was produced in Germany by Servo, a well-respected chemical firm; supplied to North American markets by IWC, a Dutch company; and sold through M. Joseph & Co. of Philadelphia. Corblok was shipped to Houston via ocean freight. Storage facilities were leased at the port of Houston. This product did not foam and was difficult to dissolve in UAN but provided excellent corrosion protection. Technical service was the responsibility of a corrosion engineer based in Holland. The Leveque Group confirmed claims of many European customers regarding the effectiveness of this product.

DAP.   Also a fertilizer (only at 100 percent strength), DAP was made by several UAN producers and tested "effective" by the TVA. Jackson Pipeline had tried it, finding that it left deposits that interfered with pipeline pumps and that there was pitting corrosion beneath the deposits. Still, DAP had a 30 percent market share and was sold by direct sales reps or distributors, depending on location. The nutrient content that it imparted to UAN was negligible, but it had the psychological benefit of "providing crop nutrients."

Stealth 3662.   Similar in chemistry to Corblok but easily soluble in UAN, Stealth 3662 was an excellent inhibitor but, as noted previously, created foaming problems. It was produced in Chicago and Galveston, Texas, using the same process equipment used for many other CAC products.

OA-5.   Tennessee Chemical produced this material in Knoxville. SPG's own tests proved it to be effective. But it was extremely difficult to dissolve in UAN, sometimes merely floating to the surface of the UAN storage tank, even after plant operators were sure they had mixed it properly. Several plants also reported foaming problems when attempting to mix OA-5 with their UAN. This foaming was of a different type than that reported for Stealth 3662. Sold by a direct sales force, this film former was different in composition from Corblok or Stealth 3662.

RG-2064 and Equivalents.   Although neither Consolidated nor Western had promoted any products specifically for UAN transport and storage, both were strong in organic phosphate ester chemistry; however, they had applied it to water treatment applications, a market much larger than that for UAN. Both companies employed many more sales reps than did SPG and CAC and were already selling water treatment chemicals to UAN plants for boiler, cooling, and wastewater treatment applications. These operations were run by the same people who ran the UAN process equipment. These companies also were attacking CAC's oil field business and achieving significant success even though their products were more expensive to use than CAC's. Consolidated's revenue was equal to CAC's, but its profit rate was 20 percent higher than CAC's. Western had sales and profits double those of CAC.

Exhibit 6 shows the 1989 capacities of all North American UAN producers and indicates the brand(s) of inhibitor used in mid-1988 and mid-1989.

Product Development.   In 1988, after the foaming problems with Stealth 3662, SPG initiated an R&D program to develop a product specifically designed for UAN corrosion control. SPG's technical director estimated that four labor years of technical effort over two years was required. The typical cost per labor year was $100,000, including salary and benefits, the use of all group and corporate laboratory facilities, and the cost to build corrosion test apparatus. Jim Walker believed a one-labor-year marketing effort at $80,000 per year was needed to understand market needs adequately and develop literature and marketing communications programs. Hosting a hospitality suite at the Ammonium Nitrate Producers Study Group (ANPSG) meeting held each fall would increase annual marketing expenses by $5,000.

White felt confident that his department could sell any product, given a good price; the technical director was confident in the success of the development effort. Two sales efforts were possible: (1) 100 percent of Brown's time at $80,000 per year (salary, benefits, car) plus 2 percent of revenue for travel and entertainment costs (T&E) or (2) 5 percent of the entire sales force's time (including regional managers) plus the same T&E.

Williamson considered these costs and alternative sales efforts and reviewed the following data:

- Tax rate, 33 percent.
- Corporate cost of capital, 8 percent.
- Corporate mandate for 30 percent present value after-tax ROI.
- SPG requirement that new businesses generate $2 million in sales and/or $800,000 gross profit within three years of market entry.

He then instructed his technical director to develop a direct replacement for Corblok.

Early in 1989 Brown arranged a trip with a Fertex sales representative to several fertilizer dealers. His objective was to obtain extensive information about how UAN was used at the dealer level—other nutrients added, mixing techniques, blending with pesticides and herbicides, and so on. Of particular interest to Brown was the extent to which dealers were affected by the foaming problem that had precipitated SPG's new R&D efforts. He was surprised when dealers responded negatively to his questions about foaming. Despite using Fertex UAN containing Stealth 3662, they had not experienced this condition. Brown began to wonder if only certain blends and ingredients foamed and if those blends were used only in certain regions of the country.

He also learned that a considerable amount of UAN "trading" occurred in the industry. For example, if Fertex had a customer in North Dakota, it would receive the sales revenue, but Agriproducts' Sioux Falls plant would actually supply the UAN.

EXHIBIT 6   **UAN Corrosion Inhibitor Market, 1989 Capacities (0.25 lb./ton dose)**

Company*	City*	Capacity (thousands of tons)	Potential SPG Volume (thousands of lbs.)	Mid-1988 Inhibitors	Mid-1989 Inhibitors	Needs Easy Mix Product	SPG Advantage
Farm Products	Kansas City, Kan.	250	63	3662	3662	No	—
Nitron, Inc.	St. Petersburg, Fla.	10	3	3662	3662	Yes	—
Can-Am Corp.	Edmonton, Alberta	15	4	3662	3662	Yes	—
Can-Am Corp.	Lincoln, Neb.	80	20	3662	3662	Yes	—
Agriproducts	Sioux Falls, S.D.	238	60	3662	3662	No	—
Iowa Fertilizer	Dubuque, Iowa	230	58	3662	Corblok	No	Service/cost
Marathon	Toledo, Ohio	180	45	3662	Corblok	No	Service/cost
Ferticon	New Orleans	510	128	3662	Corblok	No	Service/cost
Iowa Fertilizer	Santa Fe	10	3	3662	Corblok	Yes	—
Fertex	Fort Smith, Ark.	1,400	350	3662	Corblok	No	Service/cost
Nitrogen Inds.	Spokane, Wash.	160	40	3662	Corblok	No	Service/cost
Iowa Fertilizer	Miami	51	13	3662	RG-2064	Yes	?
Nitro Products	Pensacola, Fla.	65	16	Ammonia	Ammonia	No	Performance
RJS Inc.	Idaho Falls, Idaho	230	58	Ammonia	Ammonia	No	Performance
Georgia Chemical	Savannah, Ga.	680	170	Ammonia	Ammonia	No	Performance
Jackson Chemical	Jackson, Miss.	500	125	Ammonia	Ammonia	No	Performance
Illini Fertilizer	Marietta, Ga.	329	82	Ammonia	Ammonia	No	Performance
NC Fertilizer	Jacksonville, N.C.	230	58	Borax	Borax	No	Service/pits
RJS Inc.	Fresno, Calif.	129	32	Chromate	Chromate	No	Cost/safe
Novatec	Windsor, Ontario	175	44	Corblok	Corblok	No	Service/cost
Eagle Industries	Bettendorf, Ia.	175	44	Corblok	Corblok	No	Service/cost
RJS Inc.	Winnipeg, Manitoba	210	53	Corblok	Corblok	No	Service/cost
Edsel Chemical	Sacramento	90	23	Corblok	Corblok	No	Service/cost
Edsel Chemical	Portland, Ore.	55	14	Corblok	Corblok	Yes	Service/cost
Edsel Chemical	Spokane, Wash.	200	50	Corblok	Corblok	No	Service/cost
Comanche Powder	Tucson, Ariz.	20	5	Corblok	Corblok	No	Service/cost
Illini Fertilizer	Cincinnati	150	38	DAP	DAP	No	Service/pits
Nutricorp	Council Bluffs, Iowa	500	125	DAP	DAP	No	Service/pits
Ferticon	Evansville, Ind.	80	20	DAP	DAP	No	Service/pits
US Industries	Cherokee, Ala.	65	16	DAP	DAP	No	Service/pits
Illini Fertilizer	Dalton, Ga.	100	25	DAP	DAP	Yes	Service/pits
Illini Fertilizer	La Salle, Ill.	300	75	DAP	DAP	No	Service/pits
Farm Products	Hays, Kan.	250	63	DAP	DAP	No	Service/pits
Nitrotech	Kingston, Ontario	25	6	DAP	DAP	Yes	Service/pits
Cherokee Nitrogen	Enid, Okla.	270	68	DAP	DAP	No	Service/pits
Nutricorp	Baton Rouge, La.	1,000	250	DAP	DAP	No	Service/pits
Nitrogen Inds.	Lincoln, Neb.	158	40	DAP	DAP	Yes	Service/pits
Canadian Nitrogen	Niagara Falls, Ontario	120	30	OA-5	OA-5	No	Service/foam
Fertilex	Stockton, Calif.	200	50	OA-5	OA-5	No	Service/foam
Fertilex	Compton, Calif.	100	25	OA-5	OA-5	No	Service/foam
Edsel Chemical	Burlington, Iowa	200	50	OA-5	OA-5	No	Service/foam
Total		9,740	2,435				

* Names and locations changed to protect confidentiality.

Fertex would return the favor if Agriproducts had a customer in Arkansas. Computerized accounting systems kept track of the trades, and the companies settled accounts quarterly.

In addition to these market factors, the technical director's staff, after running hundreds of corrosion and foaming tests with several producers' UANs, discovered three factors that influenced the interaction between UAN and steel surfaces: (1) higher temperature, (2) higher UAN velocity, especially in a pipeline environment, and (3) presence of impurities. The technical department also found that different producers' UANs, though identical in nutrient content, required different doses of any corrosion inhibitor for effective corrosion control. Other inhibitor suppliers (including IWC/Corblok) recommended the same dose throughout the industry. SPG's technical director suggested using an industrywide inhibitor dosage rate of 1.5 to 2.0 pounds per ton of UAN so that even the most drastic conditions would not cause corrosion problems.

While the three newly developed products were similar, each had slightly different performance characteristics. 601 worked well in Fertex UAN but would not function in several others; 601 was easier to disperse than 602, while 602 was effective in all UAN brands. Most UAN plants used high-speed pumps to move the UAN through their systems. For this reason, it was believed there would be few problems dispersing SPG's R&D 601 and 602 products into the UAN. Once dispersed, no separation occurred; 603 was the easiest to disperse (though not quite as easy as the existing 3662 product), but it exhibited a slight foaming tendency (which was not believed to be as severe as that of 3662). Also, 603 was effective in all UANs.

All three products were deliverable in tank-truck (40,000-pound) quantities. Also, in response to increased state and local regulations on the disposal of empty drums, SPG planned to offer all three products in 300-gallon returnable and reusable tote tanks, each costing $1,200. Between 30 and 40 round trips were obtainable before the tanks had to be refurbished at a cost of $300 each. Exhibit 7 shows the cost structure of SPG's products.

Sales (White) and marketing (Walker) continually debated the UAN corrosion inhibitor marketing program as fall 1990 approached. The planned October 1990 rollout would give SPG a strategic window of approximately three months as UAN producers went to high production rates to prepare for spring fertilizer consumption. Failure to obtain business by February would effectively close the window until July, when another production push would occur for fall fertilizer consumption.

EXHIBIT 7   SPG Inhibitor Costs per Pound, Tank-Car Lots (October 1989)

Product	Fixed	Variable[4]	Total
Stealth 3662	$0.100	$0.300	$0.400
R&D 601[1]	0.160	0.480	0.640
R&D 602[2]	0.160	0.480	0.640
R&D 603[3]	0.160	0.480	0.640

Note: Billing terms net 30, freight collect, FOB CAC plant.

[1] R&D 601 for "easy-to-treat" UAN such as Fertex.
[2] R&D 602 for "hard-to-treat" UAN such as Agriproducts.
[3] R&D 603 for easy dispersion, all UANs, but very slight foam.
[4] Add $0.015 to variable costs for 55-gallon drums, net weight 473 lbs. (215 kg). Add $0.06 to variable costs for 300-gallon returnable tote tanks, net weight 2,580 lbs. (1173 kg).

Market Segmentation Possibilities.   Jim Walker and Bob Brown debated the possibility that different customers had different needs. It might be advantageous to offer multiple products, each with a distinct communication and pricing program. Superior performance characteristics, such as foaming control and ease of dispersion, could command a premium price from certain customers. Other customers and potential customers were less concerned with performance (as their use of low-corrosion performance inhibitors indicated) than with price.

Walker and Brown identified three possible performance segments: (1) premium, requiring extensive corrosion control, (2) average, requiring moderate corrosion control, and (3) low, requiring minimal corrosion control. In addition, corrosion-oriented segments might be further stratified by dispersion needs and/or price. Segmentation strategies were among the issues raised at an earlier management meeting.

Decisions, Decisions, Decisions

As Nick Williamson shuffled the papers on his desk, he listed the decisions he had to make. The discussion earlier in the afternoon had focused on the pricing of the new products, but he realized that pricing was only one of the factors that had to be resolved.

CASE 6–6
SOUTHERN HOME DEVELOPERS

Initial sales inquiries had been high during the opening days of Southern Home Developers, a module home construction/sales company. Prospects were interested and excited at the possibility of having a new home in a matter of weeks at only a fraction of the cost of a site-built home. However, Bill Thompson, owner of Southern Home Developers, was concerned about the negative comments he had been receiving from his small construction crew. Additionally, Bill had begun to see an increase in construction costs (which ultimately increased the house price to the consumer) and construction time. Bill knew that his competitive advantages were low price and short cycle times. Loss of either one held dire consequences for a small company that had been in business less than a year.

The Housing Market

Richard Gentry, president of the National Association of Housing and Redevelopment Officials (NAHRO), reported in 1996 that the housing industry was in the beginning stages of a "lean cycle where spending limits and money-saving program changes will dominate."[1] The housing industry consisted of existing homes and new home starts. In the late 1980s and into the 1990s, national sales for both existing and new homes were low. However, the United States experienced a turnaround in home sales by the mid-1990s. "From the ashes of the late 1980s and early 1990s, the nation's residential real estate market is rising again . . . sales of both new and existing houses hit all-time highs nationally and in most regions in 1996."[2] (See Exhibit 1 for a historical look at existing home and new home starts in the United States.)

The demand for existing and new homes was thought to be influenced by several factors: (1) personal disposable income, (2) economic events, (3) demographic trends, (4) social attitudes toward home ownership, (5) affordability, and (6) work-related events.

The unemployment rate in the United States was holding nationally at around 5½ percent during the mid-1990s. Exhibit 2 shows unemployment rates by state for 1995 and 1996. The U.S. Bureau of Labor Statistics predicted that the labor force would increase from 131 million to 147 million in the 1994–2005 period. Compositionally, the 55-years-and-older segment of the labor force was expected to grow faster than would younger segments, reflecting the aging of the baby boomers. The segment 25 to 34 years old was expected to decrease by 4 million in this 10-year period. Also, professional and managerial occupations were expected to show the fastest growth, with

---

[1] "Richard C. Gentry: New NAHRO President." *Journal of Housing and Community Development* (November/December 1995): 43.

[2] Nick Ravo, "Housing Sales Show New Life with Good Year." *The New York Times* (December 25, 1996): sec. D, p. 1, col. 5.

This case was prepared by Victoria L. Crittenden, associate professor of marketing, Boston College, and William F. Crittenden, associate professor of management, Northeastern University. Research assistance was provided by David Angus, Boston College/Andersen Consulting Fund. The case is designed as a basis for class discussion and is not intended to portray correct or incorrect administrative styles or processes.

EXHIBIT 1   Existing Home Sales and New Home Starts in the United States

Year	Units
Existing Home Sales	
1990	3,211,000
1991	3,220,000
1992	3,520,000
1993	3,802,000
1994	3,946,000
1995	3,802,000
Housing Starts	
1987	1,620,000
1988	1,488,000
1989	1,376,000
1990	1,193,000
1991	1,014,000
1992	1,200,000
1993	1,288,000
1994	1,457,000
1995	1,354,000

Source: *Real Estate Outlook: Market Trends & Insights* (Washington, DC: National Association of Realtors); U.S. Bureau of the Census, *Current Construction Reports,* 1996.

around 5 million new workers entering this sector. These labor force statistics were combined with relatively low inflation rates.

The Dow Jones was up nearly 40 percent during late 1995 and early 1996, adding around $1 trillion to American's net worth. This gain, however, had not affected the home building market. During that period there was no significant increase in the number of housing units sold. The home building industry had a 2.8 percent net after-tax profit during 1995, which was 50 percent below the average for all industries in the United States.[3] This came at the same time that interest rates fluctuated around 7 to 9 percent (compared to double-digit rates in the late 1980s). "Bullish" builders at the beginning of 1996 had started scaling back their expectations early in that year (this was particularly evident in single-family detached homes) as foot traffic declined throughout the year.

There were around 100 million households in the United States. The number of one-person households was increasing at a faster rate than was the number of households in general. Work-related events such as working at home and four-day workweeks were expected to affect the number of purchased homes. However, household incomes were not keeping pace with housing prices. Housing costs were around one-fifth of personal consumption expenditures. Furthermore, the U.S. population was expected to grow at a decreasing rate. Throughout the 1950–1980 time period, average population growth was around 2.5 million per year. This number was expected to drop to around 1.6 million by the year 2000. However, the 1990s experienced the largest wave of immigration in U.S.

---

[3] *The Corporate Growth Weekly Report* (August 26, 1996).

EXHIBIT 2   State Unemployment Rates, June 1995
and June 1996

State	June 1995	June 1996
East North Central		
Illinois	4.5%	5.5%
Indiana	4.9	5.1
Michigan	6.3	4.9
Ohio	4.6	5.0
Wisconsin	3.7	3.7
East South Central		
Alabama	5.1	3.5
Kentucky	5.0	5.3
Mississippi	7.5	7.1
Tennessee	5.5	5.3
Middle Atlantic		
New Jersey	6.7	6.2
New York	6.0	6.1
Pennsylvania	6.0	5.2
Mountain		
Arizona	5.5	5.7
Colorado	4.4	4.5
Idaho	4.2	4.6
Montana	5.4	5.2
Nevada	6.3	5.3
New Mexico	6.8	8.0
Utah	3.8	3.7
Wyoming	4.1	3.8
New England		
Connecticut	5.5	5.0
Maine	5.8	5.1
Massachusetts	5.6	4.9
New Hampshire	3.5	4.0
Rhode Island	6.2	4.3
Vermont	3.9	3.9
Pacific		
Alaska	6.5	7.2
California	7.7	7.2
Hawaii	5.6	6.8
Oregon	5.2	5.2
Washington	5.8	5.7
South Atlantic		
Delaware	4.2	4.7
District of Columbia	9.8	9.1
Florida	5.8	5.3
Georgia	5.5	5.0
Maryland	5.5	5.1
North Carolina	4.7	4.5
South Carolina	4.9	6.2
Virginia	4.8	4.8
West Virginia	7.5	7.2

Exhibit 2 (Continued)

State	June 1995	June 1996
West North Central		
Iowa	3.3	3.1
Kansas	4.8	4.2
Minnesota	4.2	3.9
Missouri	5.0	4.4
Nebraska	2.7	3.2
North Dakota	3.4	3.3
South Dakota	2.6	2.8
West South Central		
Arkansas	4.4	5.1
Louisiana	8.0	7.6
Oklahoma	4.7	4.2
Texas	6.8	6.6

Source: Dean Crist, "Housing Activity." *Housing Economics* (August 1996): 14–23.

Note: Data are not seasonally adjusted.

history. While a large majority of immigrants lived in rental housing, home ownership increased rapidly with length of time in the United States. In 1990, 23 percent of the 1.8 million households headed by immigrants owned their homes.

Based on results from the annual Project Outlook survey,[4] forecasts were for a very different housing market in the future. Pivotal to the industry was the forecast that houses manufactured off-site (prefabricated housing sections) would be used extensively and that the number of on-site construction hours would be reduced by at least 50 percent.

Manufactured Housing

Constructed in a factory, there were two main types of manufactured houses: mobile homes and modular homes.[5] There were 188,000 manufactured homes shipped in 1990. However, by 1995 the number of manufactured homes had increased to 340,000 (12 percent more than in 1994), with 1997 expected shipments of around 375,000. Approximately one in three single-family homes sold in America in 1996 was factory-built (compared to one in four in 1990).

Mobile Homes. Section 603 of the Manufactured Home Construction and Safety Standards Act of 1974 defined a mobile home as

> a structure, transportable in one or more sections, which is eight body feet or more in width and is thirty-two body feet or more in length, and which is built on a permanent chassis and designed to be used as a dwelling unit with or without a permanent foundation when con-

---

[4] The annual Project Outlook survey brought together corporate planners, consultants, and futurists to forecast events over a 20-year period.

[5] A third type of manufactured housing exists: prefab. With prefab, components of the house (such as walls, floors, stairs, and ceilings) are manufactured in the factory. The components are then assembled at the construction site. However, prefab houses are not making as large inroads into the housing industry as are modular and mobile homes.

nected to the required utilities, and includes the plumbing, heating, air-conditioning, and electric systems contained within.

However by 1980 the U.S. Congress had recognized that calling a mobile home "mobile" was really a misnomer. In reality, few mobile homes ever left the initial home site once placed there. Thus, legislation began referring to mobile homes as manufactured homes in all federal law publications. Mobile homes were constructed to comply with the American National Standards Institute's A119.1 Standards for Mobile Homes.

In 1993 *American Demographics* profiled the mobile home consumer as

- More likely than average[6] to be a two-member household.
- Less likely than average to have a college education.
- Having a household median income of $20,026.
- More likely than average to be headed by a young adult (18 to 34 years old).
- Believing affordability was the dominant reason for purchase.

Mobile home residency increased from 4.6 million in 1980 to 13 million in the early 1990s. Exhibit 3 provides an overview of the number of mobile homes by state, based on the 1990 U.S. census.

Production of mobile homes declined from 240,000 units in 1981 to 170,000 units in 1991. The industry average for daily production was 10 home sections a day, with the top 25 manufacturers accounting for around 75 percent of the production output. Mobile home prices ranged from $10,000 to $20,000 for a single-wide unit (approximately 14 feet by 70), with prices of double-wide unit as high as $50,000. Manufacturers' operating margins ranged from around 5 to 7 percent.

Modular Homes. The similarity between mobile homes and modular homes stopped with the fact that both were built in a factory. Whereas mobile homes had wheels and essentially rolled to their destination (and other destinations thereafter), a modular home arrived at its destination in complete sections. The sections were assembled on the construction site. Once assembled, the home did not move again. Additionally, modular homes were built to the same building codes as conventional site-built homes (these codes were governed by the state in which the construction/ manufacturing took place), while mobile homes met the national HUD (U.S. Department of Housing and Urban Development) code, which might not be the same as the local state building code. Ultimately, this did not lead to visible differences in the appearance of modular and site-built homes. As with the construction of any home, a modular home had to meet zoning codes. City zoning codes generally specified a 1,800- to 2,000-square-foot minimum area in the house.

By 1996 modular homes had a 2 percent share of the nationwide housing market and 50 percent of the manufactured housing market. This market share was expected to double by the year 2001. Such growth would turn modular housing into a $2.5 billion industry. The major markets were New England (6 percent of the overall market), Mid-Atlantic (7 percent), and East North Central (4 percent). With service to the final buyer becoming foremost in the mind of large modular home builders, growth was expected in the Midwestern and Southern states.

Modular home builders were able to build, deliver, and install a single-family dwelling for about half the cost of a site-constructed house. In 1994, the typical retail price of a modular home was $50,000. (The price range was reported to be from $45,000 to

---

[6] Average is the comparison to householders in other types of home structures.

EXHIBIT 3   **Number of Mobile Homes per State, 1990 Census**
States Ranked by Percentage of Housing
Units That Are Mobile Homes

Rank	State	Percent	Number
1	South Carolina	16.9%	240,525
2	Wyoming	16.5	33,474
3	New Mexico	16.3	102,948
4	North Carolina	15.3	430,440
5	West Virginia	15.2	118,733
6	Arizona	15.1	250,597
7	Montana	15.0	54,021
8	Idaho	13.7	56,529
9	Mississippi	13.6	136,948
10	Alabama	13.4	224,307
11	Nevada	13.4	69,655
12	Arkansas	13.1	131,542
13	Florida	12.5	762,855
14	Kentucky	12.3	185,336
15	Delaware	12.1	34,944
16	Georgia	11.6	305,055
17	Louisiana	11.4	196,236
18	Oregon	11.3	134,325
19	South Dakota	10.7	31,357
20	North Dakota	9.8	27,055
21	Tennessee	9.3	188,517
22	Maine	9.3	54,532
23	Oklahoma	9.2	129,850
24	Washington	9.2	187,533
25	Alaska	8.7	20,280
26	Vermont	8.4	22,702
27	Texas	7.8	547,911
28	Missouri	7.5	164,021
29	New Hampshire	7.0	35,334
30	Indiana	7.0	156,821
31	Kansas	6.8	71,195
32	Michigan	6.4	246,365
33	Virginia	6.4	159,352
34	Colorado	6.0	88,683
35	Utah	5.8	34,986
36	Nebraska	5.6	37,046
37	Pennsylvania	5.2	254,920
38	Iowa	5.0	56,857
39	California	5.0	555,307
40	Wisconsin	4.9	101,149
41	Minnesota	4.9	90,864
42	Ohio	4.7	205,595
43	Illinois	3.3	150,733
44	New York	2.7	194,934
45	Maryland	2.3	42,729
46	Rhode Island	1.1	4,689
47	New Jersey	1.1	33,551
48	Massachusetts	1.0	23,928
49	Connecticut	0.9	12,118
50	Hawaii	0.1	389

Source: William O'Hare and Barbara Clark O'Hare. "Upward Mobility." *American Demographics* (January 1993): 26–32.

$350,000, with at least one builder selling land plus home at $550,000.) The average cost per square foot for a multisection house was $27.41, compared to an average cost of $54.65 per square foot for a site-built house.[7] Since modular homes were delivered 85 to 95 percent finished, completion of the house once it was at the site could take as little as four days but typically took three to four weeks. (Modules arrived at the site with bathroom fixtures, cabinetry, and flooring in place.) There were three major members in the channel for modular homes: the manufacturer of the modular home, the dealer (if different from the manufacturer), and the local builder. The local builder was estimated to save 10 to 20 percent in construction costs compared to site-built homes of the same quality.

There were about 500 modular housing factories in the United States. Most of these companies employed fewer than 100 employees. The target region for each of these companies was limited, generally, to a 350-mile radius of the manufacturing facility due to shipping-related costs in moving a home's sections to the construction site. (Shipping accounted for 2 to 5 percent of the total cost.) There were, however, larger players in the market: All American Homes (based in Elkhart, Indiana), Cardinal Industries (Columbus, Ohio), Chadwick International Inc. (Fairfax, Virginia), Ryland Group Inc. (Columbia, Maryland), and Westchester Modular Homes, Inc. (Wingdale, New York). Chadwick was able to capitalize on the housing shortage in various countries by manufacturing modular homes for shipment to the Ivory Coast, Benin, and Algeria.

Manufacturing Process. The modules (sections) of a modular home were designed and constructed inside the factory. By the mid-1990s, most modular manufacturers utilized state-of-the-art CAD systems in the design process. The number of modules per house ranged all the way from 2 to 22, depending on the home's style and size. Workstations in the assembly line production process generally included framing, drywall, electrical, plumbing, cabinetry, molding, and window installation. Other workstations were dependent on the level of customization provided by the manufacturer (e.g., fireplaces, dormers). Modulars contained 25 to 30 percent more lumber than did site-built homes in order to withstand the transportation process of up to 350 miles. Upon completion of the modules (which had to pass stringent inspections by local building officials), they were trucked to the construction site. Each module had a shipping weight of around 18,000 pounds.

While there was no legal restriction on the number of modules contained in a home, highway regulations governed the size of each module. To adhere to these regulations, modules generally could be no more than 16 by 60 feet. However, most builders produced 12- or 14-foot-wide modules. Upon arrival at the home site, the modules were set on the foundation with a crane and then bolted together. Builders could expect to have an airtight house on the same day.

After setting, the local builder took over the final stages of the construction process. This included utility connections, adding porches or decks, and landscaping. These final stages could take anywhere from one to four weeks, depending on the level of custom amenities desired by the prospective homeowner.

Southern Home Developers

Located in a rural town in central Arkansas, Southern Home Developers opened in spring 1997. Bill Thompson served as owner, salesperson, and plant manager. Bill's career in manufactured housing started in the late 1960s when he and a friend opened a small mobile home factory and sales office, Urbane Homes, in Missouri. Within a five-

---

[7] A. Gary Shilling, "Home Sweet Factory-Built Home." *Forbes* (February 12, 1996): 181.

year period Urbane Homes had opened factory/sales offices in Arkansas and Texas. Fifteen years after opening the first facility Bill and his partner sold the business for $10 million. Before starting Southern Home Developers, Bill had dabbled in oil and gas wells in Oklahoma and coal mines in Kentucky. Finally, Bill had returned to his first love, manufactured home production. After the receipt of a small business grant from the state government, Bill opened Southern Home Developers.

Southern Home Developers operated out of an 80- by 200-foot corrugated metal production facility. A crew of five men built the modules in the facility. Once the modules were built, the same crew located the house at the site and finished the on-site construction process. Bill's wife, Liz, did all on-site interior finishing (e.g., wallpapering, cleaning). The entire crew could take a house from module construction to move-in capability in four weeks.

Initially Bill had purchased land on which to set his modular houses. Then the houses were listed with a local real estate firm and sold through that channel for around $27,500. Until sold, these houses also served as model homes. The typical design was a house built in three modules (module 1: two bedrooms and bath, module 2: family room, module 3: kitchen, master bedroom, and bath). The three modules, when combined, resulted in a house with about 1,500 to 1,700 square feet. Exhibits 4 and 5 show the two basic floor plans built by Southern Home Developers.

Current Situation

Recently, Bill had begun taking orders for customized homes. Bill's initial idea regarding customization options was to allow the buyer to have some flexibility with the two standard designs. While highway regulations limited the size of the modules to about 16 by 60 feet, there were no restrictions on the number of modules that made up a house. Therefore, an easy route to customization was to increase the size of the house.

Randall Nyman worked for Southern Home Developers and was de facto in charge of the on-site setting and completion of a home. Randall was not too pleased with Bill's customization commitments. The first "customized" house Randall and the rest of the crew set up was basically an add-on module allowing the customer to have five bedrooms instead of three. While the setup was uncomplicated, Randall and Bill had exchanged a few words over the setup time. Basically, Bill thought that it had taken too long to set the house. Randall's response was that he was adding on almost half a house and that Bill should expect it to take 50 percent longer to set. Additionally, Randall reminded Bill that since the crew of five did both construction and setup, setup was delayed by the need to build an additional module before moving to the site.

Just the previous day, Bill had overheard one of his crew, Wayne, commenting on Bill's apparent lack of understanding of manufacturing. Bill was shocked at the comment since he had always prided himself on the building of manufactured homes. Bill's shock quickly moved to outrage, and Bill confronted Wayne about the comment. While Wayne clearly had not expected Bill to overhear him, he wasted no time letting Bill know about what he thought were unreasonable construction expectations. Basically, Wayne told Bill that if he wanted to stay in business for a while, he should stick to standardized homes. Wayne felt that there was a market for low-priced, standardized homes and predicted that customization would put Southern Home Developers out of business in less than a year.

Bill had found sleep to be somewhat elusive last night and arrived at work very early this morning. Before others arrived at the plant, Bill had already gone over the cost overruns and longer setup times for the last two houses. He was just starting to look over the specifications for a new modular home he had committed to earlier in the week when he heard Randall and Wayne arrive at the office. The house would involve more

EXHIBIT 4
Ranch Design

EXHIBIT 5
Split Design

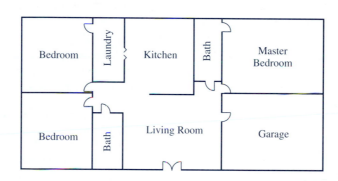

EXHIBIT 6
Side View of Cape Cod Roof

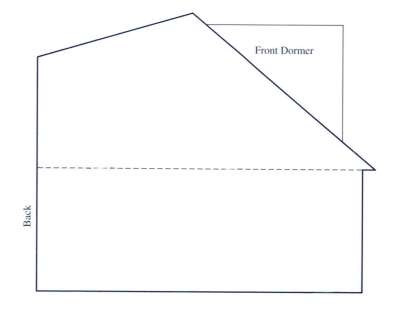

than just adding another module for enlargement purposes. This design had some new innovations, which included a second floor on half of the house. The second floor would have front dormers and a rear Dutch dormer. The dormers would give the house a Cape Cod look but would also cause a new pitch to the roof. While the Cape Cod was an unusual style for the South, it was what the customer had wanted. (Exhibit 6 diagrams the roof.) The modules and dormers would be finished when delivered but would require a significant amount of on-site detail due to the addition of the second level and the roof pitch. Now Bill was concerned that Southern Home Developers would not meet the completion deadline he had agreed on with the customer (or would not be able to make the house in a profitable fashion).

Bill wondered if his crew's inability to deliver on time and within budget was really due to unreasonable expectations on his part or if possibly the crew did not have the manufacturing expertise to mass customize his houses. What if Wayne was right? Bill's intuition told him that Wayne was wrong, but what market factors should guide Bill's decision? If Bill decided that Wayne was wrong, how could Bill convince his crew that mass customization was the way to build the business?

Bill could foresee a major conflict brewing between customer expectations and the operational side of his business. He wondered how best to address the issue.

Sources

"And Now for the Homeburger." *Economist* (August 10, 1996): 19–20.

Bady, Susan. "Builders Grow Business the Modular Way." *Professional Builder* (August 1996): 62.

The Corporate Growth Annual Report (August 26, 1996).

Crist, Dean. "Housing Activity." *Housing Economics* (August 1996): 14–23.

DiGeronimo, Richard J. "A Solution to Affordable Housing: Manufactured Homes." *The Real Estate Appraiser & Analyst* (Winter 1989): 18–25.

Enzer, Selwyn. "Project Outlook, Housing in America: Long-Term Trends." *New Management* (Winter 1987): 60–62.

Epstein, Joseph. "Home Cheap Home." *Financial World* (February 26, 1996): 48–50.

Gordon, Mitchell. "The Right Turf: Manufactured Homes Expand Hold in the Southeast." *Barron's/Investment News & Views* (June 9, 1986): 54–55.

"High Returns on Low-Income Housing." *Success* (November 1996): 30.

Kennedy, Kim. "Economic Trends Boost Manufactured Housing." *Professional Builder* (September 1996): 154.

Kroll, Luisa. "We Aim to Please." *Forbes* (November 4, 1996): 169–70.

Lahey, Karen. "Manufactured Housing: An Alternative to Site-Built Homes." *The Real Estate Appraiser & Analyst* (Winter 1989): 26–36.

Maddock, David T. "Meeting the Market with Manufactured Housing." *The Journal of Real Estate Development* (Summer 1989): 34–37.

McIntyre, Maureen. "Make Room for Modular." *Builder* (January 1996): 368.

Nolan, William T. "Modular Housing Can Help Alleviate the Nation's Housing Crunch." *The Real Estate Finance Journal* (Summer 1988): 87–89.

O'Hare, William, and Barbara Clark O'Hare. "Upward Mobility." *American Demographics* (January 1993): 26–32.

Ravo, Nick. "Housing Sales Show New Life with Good Year.'" *New York Times* (December 25, 1996): sec. D, p. 1, col. 5.

Real Estate Outlook: Market Trends & Insights. Washington, DC: National Association of Realtors.

"Richard C. Gentry: New NAHRO President." *Journal of Housing and Community Development* (November–December 1995): 43.

Rohan, Thomas M. "Affordable Homes from a Factory." *Industry Week* (January 16, 1989): 36–38.

Shilling, A. Gary. "Home Sweet Factory-Built Home." *Forbes* (February 12, 1996): 181.

Statistical Abstract of the United States, 1996.

U.S. Bureau of the Census, *Current Construction Reports.*

Wilson, Rand, and Mark Sommer. "Better Homes for Less." *Technology Review* (May–June 1990): 16–17.

CASE 6–7
QUALITY PLASTICS INTERNATIONAL S.A. DE C.V.

Sergio Trevino de Elizondo was enthusiastic regarding the potential of his plastic manufacturing business, Quality Plastics International S.A. de C.V. (QPI). Company sales and profits had increased yearly (see Exhibit 1). Exports to Canada and the United States had grown to 45 percent of revenues. Numerous new customers were added each year, and a number of North American firms were seeking quotes from QPI.

However, Trevino was puzzled by recent comments from two of his managers. Yesterday, plant manager Federico Gonzales Ojeda had grumbled about the demands being placed on manufacturing. Yet QPI had recently purchased another injection molding machine, and Gonzales had quickly and successfully brought it on line. And this morning, QPI's accountant, Rosa Maria Maldonado, had voiced concerns with the record keeping and financing involved with having so many customers.

Background

Trevino founded the plastic molding concern in 1987 to fill the tubing needs of his former employer, a local refrigerator manufacturer. Acting when another supplier failed to provide needed components in a timely fashion, Trevino recognized that many firms in Nuevo Leon, Mexico, could use a local, reliable, low-cost alternative to suppliers from the United States, Europe, or the Far East. Outsourcing trends made QPI's strategy look good. An increasing number of firms were purchasing components and parts from outside suppliers in order to concentrate on product development, assembly, and other basic strengths.

Marco Aldana de Luna, director of business development and sales, believed success resulted from two key factors:

> We give the customers what they want, and we do it at a good price.

EXHIBIT 1   QPI Operating Results
(Mexican new peso, figures in thousands)

	Sales	Net Profit
1993	8,304	298
1992	6,475	246
1991	4,385	193
1990	3,426	154
1989	2,741	110
1988	1,570	58
1987	821	<15>

Current (1993) exchange rate, 3.21 pesos per US$.

This case was prepared by Associate Professor William F. Crittenden of Northeastern University as the basis for class discussion rather than to illustrate either effective or ineffective handling of an administration situation. Names and figures have been disguised. Key relationships have been preserved. Copyright July 1994.

533

Exhibit 2 QPI's Operating Policies

We will sell quality products to satisfy the needs of various consumer and industrial segments while offering efficient and accommodating service. Our customers always deserve a good price.
We are proud of our Mexican heritage, and we want to remain an independent company.

We do not wish to be controlled by suppliers and wish to remain free to buy materials when and where we want to buy.

Single customers may not purchase more than 20 percent of our production capacity.

Excellent labor–management relations are our goal at all times. We deal with our workers each day so that all problems may be solved in an atmosphere of mutual understanding and respect.
We believe in the importance of personal and corporate integrity.

Although QPI had started as a component manufacturer, it also had been successful in cracking the market for finished products. Toy manufacturing was an especially successful segment. QPI also was involved with a promising insulated mug manufacturing venture; it would be marketing and distributing in Mexico and Central and South America.

Trevino believed that his workers were instrumental in the growth of his firm.

> We pay a good wage to attract workers, and we have a young productive work force. Our employees do not have a union, and this has given us great flexibility.

With industrial wages and benefits averaging 7.3 new pesos per hour, Mexican workers earned less than did many Asian workers (e.g., Hong Kong, 12.1 new pesos; Singapore, 14.8).

Since its inception, QPI's management had developed a management philosophy that, accompanied by certain basic guidelines, governed the operations of the business and that Trevino believed had much to do with the steady progress of the firm. The guidelines are described in Exhibit 2. Key financial data for QPI are provided in Exhibits 3 and 4. Although Trevino owned most of the company (65 percent), his top managers shared 15 percent; a Texas investment firm held the remaining 20 percent.

Exhibit 3 QPI's Income Statement Information
(constant Mexican new pesos, figures in thousands)

	1993	1992	1991	1990
Net sales	8,304	6,475	4,385	3,426
Cost of goods sold	6,228	4,662	2,937	2,261
Gross profit	2,076	1,813	1,448	1,165
Selling expenses	1,254	965	548	428
Administrative expenses	392	383	242	232
Operating income	430	465	658	505
Foreign exchange gain (loss)	28	–87	–361	–268
Income after foreign exchange	458	378	297	237
Taxes	160	132	104	83
Net profit	298	246	193	154

Source: Quality Plastics International S.A. de C.V. annual report.

EXHIBIT 4   QPI's Balance Sheets as of December 31
(constant Mexican new pesos, figures in thousands)

	1993	1992	1991	1990
Assets				
Cash and liquid securities	261	385	734	684
Accounts receivable	887	508	403	342
Inventory				
Raw materials	383	376	388	392
Work in process	269	247	186	174
Finished goods	423	412	317	298
Total current assets	2,223	1,928	2,028	1,890
Machinery and equipment	1,160	1,083	971	971
Furniture and fixtures	52	45	33	33
Vehicles	48	48	48	48
Less depreciation	181	158	108	108
Total long-term assets	1,079	1,018	944	944
Total Assets	3,302	2,946	2,972	2,834
Liabilities and Equity				
Current liabilities	915	837	688	613
Long-term liabilities	1,378	1,309	1,668	1,749
Total liabilities	2,293	2,146	2,356	2,362
Common stock	165	165	165	165
Retained earnings	844	635	451	307
Total equity	1,009	800	616	472
Total Liabilities and Equity	3,302	2,946	2,972	2,834

Note: Mexican Generally Accepted Accounting Principles (GAAP) require property, plant, and equipment depreciation, and materials and supplies are to be stated at net replacement cost.

Source: Quality Plastics International S.A. de C.V. annual report.

Quality Plastics International is located in Escobedo, Nuevo Leon, Mexico. Nuevo Leon, in northern Mexico, is known for its dynamic industrial activity. The industrial concentration, principally in the metropolitan area of Monterrey (Escobedo is part of the Monterrey metro area), has created a high level of diversification. Many of Mexico's most important industrial groups are located in this area, notably Alfa, a producer of steel, synthetic fibers, paper, and foodstuffs; Visa, specializing in beer and processed foods; Vitro, a manufacturer of glass and glass-related goods; and CYDSA, which concentrates on chemical products, petrochemicals, and synthetic fibers. A skilled work force, solid infrastructure, and close proximity to the United States contributes to Nuevo Leon's strong exports. The population is approximately 3.2 million. Approximately 30 percent of the employed work force is female. Organized labor accounts for 35 percent of the work force.

Mexico and NAFTA

Mexico is a federal democratic republic with 31 states and the Federal District (the capital). With 1,972,550 square kilometers, Mexico is the thirteenth largest country in the world and the third largest in Latin America. The economy is mixed. The government, its agencies, and government-owned/controlled companies dominate in the areas of utilities, petroleum, and certain types of basic manufacturing. Private enterprise is the principal factor in manufacturing, mining, commerce, entertainment, and the service industry. Foreign investment is found most frequently in manufacturing and mining.

The United States is Mexico's largest trade partner, accounting for 70 percent of total exports. Conversely, Mexico is the United States' third largest trading partner, accounting for approximately $75 billion in total trade. Since the mid-1980s, imports from the United States have grown from $12 billion to over $40 billion a year. Canada, members of the European Community, and members of the Latin American Integration Association also do substantial international trade with Mexico.

Industrial production accounted for about 25 percent of Mexico's GDP and had an estimated growth rate of 4.5 percent. Principal manufacturing industries included automobile and auto parts producers, steel manufacturers, the textile industry, food processing, breweries, glass, chemicals and petrochemicals, and cement and other materials for the construction industry. The Mexican plastics production industry represented 0.5 percent of Mexico's total GDP and was expected to grow 7 to 9 percent annually.

The North American Free Trade Agreement (NAFTA) presented Mexican companies with many new opportunities and challenges. Mexican firms faced expansion options in Canada and the United States while facing increased competition in home markets from Canadian and American firms. Ultimately, most goods and services will cross borders as easily as they move within each nation.

Plastic Products

Plastic was cheap, light, corrosion-resistant, and easy to fabricate. The production process for most plastic shapes was well defined. Primary inputs (monomers and polymers) were reacted with chemical reagents to impart desired characteristics and then processed by using one or more methods, such as coating, extrusion, molding, or laminating.

Consumption of plastic products was highest in the electronics, health care, construction, transportation and automotive, and food packaging industries. Material substitution (e.g., plastic for metal, wood, or glass) was not expected to contribute to growth, reflecting an already high level of substitution. However, new applications were emerging that would place greater demands on convenience and safety features. Demand for recycled and biodegradable materials was expected to continue and drive the development of more economical recycling technologies.

Plastic waste constituted a minor component of total North American solid waste collected; however, plastic waste was generally very visible, and the percentage of total plastic recycled was low compared with total production. Efforts to develop environmentally safer products in response to public pressure were an industry priority.

Although the global economy appeared to be coming out of a prolonged slump, many economists suggested that very low growth would be the norm. In addition, long-term interest rates appeared to be headed upward. Spokespersons for the North American plastics manufacturing industry indicated concerns with worldwide excess capacity.

Customers

Most customers used several criteria to determine from whom to purchase, yet Trevino believed the most important was price. Equipment capabilities and reputation for reliable delivery were other factors. Customers also considered continuity of relationships with sales representatives, although most multisourced.

EXHIBIT 5   **QPI's Major Accounts in Canada and the United States, 1993**
(U.S.$, figures in thousands)

Bombardier	$102
Carrier Air Systems	253
Fisher-Price	71
Ideal Toy	525
Little Tykes	26
Sears	32

QPI's customers were principally located in Mexico (especially Coahuila, Chihuahua, and Nuevo Leon), although the company had significant sales in Canada (Ontario and Quebec) and the United States (Texas, Illinois, and New Jersey). Exhibit 5 lists QPI's major international accounts.

According to international sales manager Juan Luis Padilla Sanchez,

> Through our own five-person sales organization, our products are sold throughout Mexico. Outside Mexico, we use brokers, who have several noncompeting clients for whom they sell. We would like to have our own direct sales force in select North American markets.

Some customers ordered one time only; others demanded a guaranteed price for a period of time. For example, a customer might plan to purchase a specific number of units every month for a year and would seek a guaranteed price for the year. However, the customer was under no obligation to actually make this purchase each month. In fact, actual purchases tended to be quite seasonal. This placed varying demands on manufacturing and on different types of equipment. For example, demand for toy manufacturing was strongest in early to late autumn, while demand for air-conditioning tubing was strongest in late spring to early summer.

Padilla believed QPI had many advantages in the North American market:

> We are a very customer-oriented company. We are very flexible and will customize products based on market demands. Our manufacturing people do not always like it, but we have to give the customers what they want.

Except for repeat business, pricing was always unique to the needs of the customer. Quotes had to be approved by a regional sales manager. Quotes generally included product specifications, lot size, price, and date(s) of delivery. Often there were immense pressures to submit a quote by a specific time.

QPI operated in the highly competitive plastic injection molding and extrusion businesses. Worldwide, some 40,000 plastic injection molding companies are in operation. Hong Kong was estimated to have at least 5,000 such firms.

QPI performed little in-house R&D. The customer delivered product specifications and often developed and owned the individual molds required to produce the product.

Competition

QPI faced four types of competitors:

1. Firms that competed exclusively in injection molding. These firms tended to be very focused on a few well-defined customer segments.

2. Firms that competed exclusively in plastic extrusion. These firms were often "captive" or had strong strategic alliances with a few large customers.
3. Multiprocessing firms with molding, extrusion, and sometimes additional capabilities. These firms often had their own R&D capabilities and could work with customers to design molds, product graphics, packaging, and so on.
4. Large, vertically integrated manufacturers. These firms required large volumes of product and could support their own plastic processing operations. Competition resulted during slack periods when these large firms would "rent" unused capacity to other firms. This added capacity to the industry and depressed prices. These firms were principally in extrusion.

Raw material manufacturers seldom vertically integrated into the plastic processing business due to the need for very different capital investment and skills. Overall, injection molding was an approximately 203-billion-peso business worldwide, with 40,000 competitors. The United States was estimated to have some 2,800 molders, while Canada had fewer than 300. Hong Kong claimed 5,000. Extrusion constituted a 165-billion-peso global business and had some 15,000 competitors.

Suppliers

Raw Materials.   Between 1987 and 1993 Mexico's consumption of plastic resins increased at an average annual rate of 6 percent, reaching 1.5 million tons. Imports were estimated to represent 35 percent of total consumption in terms of value and 24.8 percent in volume. For 1994 supply imports were estimated to exceed 2.1 billion new pesos, a 9 percent increase over 1993.

Raw material supplies from the United States dominated the Mexican import market with a 90 percent share. Mexican buyers were receptive to U.S. suppliers for several reasons: geographic proximity, familiarity with American resins and materials, perceived quality, reliability, and price competitiveness. In addition, many Mexican plastic processors were subsidiaries of U.S. companies and purchased from or through their U.S.-based counterparts.

German suppliers had approximately 4.6 percent of the market, and Japanese firms less than 1.5 percent. However, for Japanese firms this was an increase from less than 0.25 percent in 1989.

Chronic worldwide overcapacity, particularly in Europe and Japan, depressed long-term prospects and led to price declines. Plant closures and capacity cutbacks were expected to continue.

Equipment.   Plastics manufacturing was very capital-intensive. However, fierce competition between Asian, European, and North American plastic molding machine builders had depressed some equipment prices. Japanese makers had not raised prices in three years, yet they continued to add features. A recently formed group calling itself the Coalition of North American Machinery Manufacturers gave notice that it was concerned with dumping. It was alleged that machines were discounted below cost to gain market share or to sell off excess production that the market could not absorb at normal prices. However, Trevino saw this as a boon to his business, as he could purchase additional new machinery and pursue new business with much less investment than was the case when he began QPI.

QPI plant manager Federico Gonzalez Ojeda worried about the machine purchases that were being made.

Exhibit 6   QPI Machinery

Date Purchased	Manufacturer	Function	Purchase Price[1]
1987	Engel	Injection	$ 37,500 (used)
1988	Battenfelds	Extrusion	48,000 (used)
1989	Demag[2]	Injection	109,000
1990	HPM	Injection	46,000
1990	Battenfelds	Extrusion	52,000
1992	Toshiba	Injection	33,700
1993	Jinwa	Injection	24,250

[1] International purchases by Mexican firms generally are made in U.S. dollars.

[2] The Demag injection press was a multipurpose machine with broad product flexibility. Each extruder also could produce a fairly wide range of products.

> Worker training and maintenance with many different machines could become a problem. Machine changeover, service delays, and an unreliable supply of spare parts could hurt our productivity.

QPI owned two extruders and five injection molding machines. The two extruders were made by the same manufacturer. Exhibit 6 identifies the major machinery owned by QPI.

Physical Distribution

Transportation: QPI owned two trucks that were used to make deliveries in Nuevo Leon, pick up locally produced raw materials, or transport goods between two manufacturing sites and a warehouse. Outside carriers handled deliveries to other Mexican states, the United States, and Canada. If an order could not be completely filled by the deadline, partial shipments were made and the remainder was sent as a back order. This generally increased shipping costs about 20 percent more than if the total order had been shipped on time. Border-crossing delays often had been experienced in the past, chiefly due to inspections by U.S. immigration officials. Further, some local carriers were known for uneven or slow delivery but had prices 30 percent below those of their competitors.

Inventory: Each manufacturing plant had a modest storage area for raw materials and finished goods. The warehouse supported the bulk of raw material and finished goods storage, and all customer orders were shipped from the warehouse.

Conclusion

QPI had experienced tremendous growth in its seven-year history. An aggressive sales team had consistently added new customers. New equipment allowed diversification substantially beyond refrigeration tubing. More recently, NAFTA had created increased visibility for Mexican suppliers. While changes in trade barriers were important to all of Mexico, QPI's record of customer satisfaction as a supplier to Canada and the United States created excellent opportunities to gain new customers on the North American continent. Trevino was excited about gaining new customers and showing the world what QPI could do for a customer. He wished he could extend his enthusiasm to his entire management team.

CASE 6–8
THE NEW INTEL

Intel Chief Executive Craig R. Barrett sounds nearly poetic when he describes why it has been so darn hard getting the giant chipmaker to charge into new businesses—and into the Internet Age, where the old rules of computerdom no longer hold. Not surprisingly, Barrett conjures up a Western metaphor. He does, after all, live in Arizona, commuting most weeks to Intel Corp.'s Silicon Valley headquarters. Barrett compares Intel's microprocessor business to the creosote bush, a tall desert plant that drips poisonous oil, killing off all vegetation that tries to grow anywhere near it. Microprocessors so dominated the company's strategy, he says, that other businesses could not sprout around it. Chips, he says, "are a dream business, with wonderful margins and a wonderful market position. How could anything else compete here for resources and profitability?"

How, indeed, unless you have a CEO who is kicking up a sandstorm to find a way. Nearly two years after Barrett took the reins at Intel, the chip giant is in the midst of a historic overhaul that is transforming its business and its culture—for a second time. The first, back in 1985, Intel fled the memory chip business and bet the farm on microprocessors, turning itself from a diversified maker of chips into one focused solely on producing the electronic brains of personal computers. It was a brilliant move that set up the company for a golden period of growth under legendary CEO Andrew S. Grove. But now, the days of Intel concentrating virtually all its energy and investment on PC chips are gone.

The Grove era is over. Instead, Barrett is reshaping Intel into a supplier of all sorts of semiconductors for networking gear, information appliances, and, of course, PCs. More startling, he's taking Intel into radically different terrain, such as e-commerce, consumer electronics, Internet servers, and wireless phones. "We're putting a new image on top of the big powerful chip monster that eats the world," Barrett says (Exhibit 1).

And how. Last September, Intel unveiled a new family of chips for the networking and communications gear that zips data traffic through the arteries of the Internet. That's a $7 billion opportunity—and it's growing 30% faster than PC processors. In the same month, Barrett launched an even wilder scheme: Internet services, a $3 billion business worldwide that is nearly doubling each year. Intel opened the first of a dozen gigantic computer centers that it's building around the world to run Web and e-commerce sites for other companies. Over the next two years, the chipmaker will spend $1 billion on this elaborate network of Internet data facilities.

Web War

Barrett's handiwork didn't stop there. In October, he paid $1.6 billion to buy DSP Communications Inc., a leading maker of digital wireless phone technology. Then, in January, Intel rolled out an ambitious plan to sell branded information appliances—screen phones, e-mail stations, TV set-top boxes—through phone companies and Internet

Source: Andy Reinhardt, "The New Intel," *Business Week*, March 13, 2000, 110–124.

EXHIBIT 1   Intel's Path Beyond the PC

How the advent of the Internet and cheap PCs made Intel reboot

February 1997
Compaq unveils a $999 PC using a cheap Pentium clone chip. Intel execs downplay sub-$1,000 PCs as a fad, but the machines catch on, and Intel's share of the low end drops to 30%.

April 1997
Barrett wants the troops to break their old habits and diversify. He compares Intel's microprocessor business to a creosote bush, a plant that kills off nearby vegetation.

July 1997
Barrett is named president in May and, fearing the impact of low-cost chips, kicks off the first of eight seminars for Intel's top brass. The classes are aimed at getting them to dream up new businesses.

October 1997
Intel buys DEC's chip unit for $700 million. The deal contains a gem: Rights to the zippy StrongARM processor, which Intel adopts for some mobile and networking products.

December 1997
Intel ends the year with record sales of $25 billion and a blowout $6.9 billion in profits. But analysts worry about the potential financial impact of cheap PCs.

January 1998
Intel surveys 2,000 Internet service providers and discovers they want simple servers that do jobs such as encryption. So Intel develops server appliances that debut two years later.

February 1998
To kick-start a networking business, Intel hosts a press event in San Francisco and unveils dozens of products, including routers and switches.

March 1998
Barrett is named CEO. But lower chip prices in part prompt a warning of lower first-quarter results. To reclaim lost share, Intel launches the cheap Celeron chip. But it's poorly received.

July 1998
Barrett O.K.'s the launch of a new-business group to fund internal startups and asks manufacturing veteran Gerry Parker to head the new unit.

August 1998
The company forms a home-products group to develop Web appliances and Internet-enabled TVs and set-top boxes.

September 1998
Five managers, led by Renee James, study the Web-hosting business—but it's a risky leap from making chips. The board gives it the O.K. six weeks later.

November 1998
Intel completes a crash, 12-month program to set up Web-based order taking for its customers. In 1999, online revenues soar quickly to $1 billion per month.

February 1999
Intel unveils plans to codevelop a digital signal processor with Analog Devices. This could help it gain ground in markets such as cell phones and consumer electronics.

March 1999
Intel makes its largest acquisition, buying networking chipmaker Level One for $2.2 billion in stock. The company specializes in chips that connect network cards to wiring.

April 1999
Intel announces a home networking kit, the first product it will sell directly to consumers over the Web. The product sends data over phone wiring in homes.

June 1999
Straying far from its roots, Intel buys Dialogic, a maker of PC-based phone systems, for $780 million. Dialogic gives Intel technology for the convergence of voice and data networks.

September 1999
Intel unveils networking chips and opens its first Web-hosting center in Santa Clara. With a capacity for 10,000 servers, it could serve hundreds of e-commerce companies.

October 1999
Intel acquires DSP Communications, a leader in wireless phone technology, and IPivot, a maker of gear for speeding up secure e-commerce transactions.

January 2000
Barrett spells out a plan to sell into appliances through phone companies and ISPs later this year. The devices use Linux software—not Windows CE from its long-time partner Microsoft.

February 2000
Intel launches a line of seven server appliances, called the NetStructure family, that speed up and manage Web traffic. This puts Intel in competition with Cisco Systems and others.

service providers. And in February, the company barged into yet another new business, announcing a family of special-purpose network servers that manage Web traffic. The boxes will go head-to-head against gear from networking powerhouse Cisco Systems Inc. and a host of smaller rivals. "Craig stepped on the gas much more aggressively than I would have," concedes Grove, now Intel's chairman.

Each of these new schemes is ambitious in its own right. Taken together, they're a watershed. Within five years, Barrett intends all of Intel's new thrusts to be $1 billion-plus businesses and No. 1 or No. 2 in their markets. He's betting they will help Intel grow 15% to 20% a year, up from its paltry 8% compound growth over the past two years. So far, Wall Street is buying Barrett's vision, driving Intel shares up 40% since Jan. 1—easily the best growth among the 20 most widely held stocks in the U.S. By 2001, figures Merrill Lynch & Co. analyst Joseph A. Osha, products other than processors will make up a quarter of Intel's $38 billion in revenues and contribute nearly a third of its revenue growth. "Barrett is undertaking nothing less than a reinvention of Intel," says analyst Drew Peck of SG Cowen Securities Corp.

But no one is sure what he'll wind up with when he's done. Intel already is late to the Internet party. And the company is trying to break into new markets that already have scores of entrenched competitors. The result: Two years into Barrett's makeover, much of the payoff for Intel remains in the future. PC components are still the heart of its business, generating 90% of revenues and 100% of profits (Exhibit 2). "No organization its size can turn on a dime," says Peck. "This will be a slow, ponderous process, and meanwhile, expectations are very high."

Make that sky-high. Investors already are treating Barrett's plan as if success were a sure thing. That doesn't leave much margin for error. Barrett has to ensure that Intel's cash cow microprocessor business keeps throwing off beaucoup bucks to pay for the new gambits. In early March, for example, Intel will unveil the fastest PC chip ever sold, a Pentium III that runs at one gigahertz, or one billion cycles per second. But Intel's track record in its core business last year wasn't so good. The company had a rash of blunders in 1999—microprocessors and chipsets delivered months late, embarrassing design bugs, and supply shortages. Even loyal customers like Dell Computer Corp. and Gateway Inc. have taken the highly unusual step of publicly blaming the chip

---

EXHIBIT 2   Computer Processors

Still the heart of Intel's business, processors and companion chips for PCs and servers contributed 90% of revenues and 100% of profits in 1999. Analysts figure Intel's microprocessor business will account for less than 80% of total revenues in a couple of years.

THE BOSS Paul Otellini, 49, essentially No. 3 in the company, runs Intel's worldwide processor group. He's seen as a possible successor to Barrett.

PRODUCTS Pentium III and Celeron processors for desktop and mobile PCs; Xeon processors for servers and workstations. In the second half of this year, Intel will deliver its first 64-bit processor, called Itanium, which will help it grab more of the market for big corporate data systems. And it's about to introduce a gigabit chip, the fastest ever.

HOW INTEL STACKS UP Intel still has 84% market share in PC processors. But rival Advanced Micro Devices has hit big with its Athlon chip and Taiwan's Via also is coming on strong since buying the Cyrix processor from National Semiconductor.

ACQUISITION HELP Intel has made a few small acquisitions for its core business, such as graphics chipmaker Chips & Technologies and multiprocessing expert Corollary.

MARKET GROWTH The microprocessor sector just isn't the rocket ship it used to be.

Source: Robertson Stephens, Semiconductor Industry Assn.

giant's gaffes for their recent earnings problems. Gateway was so incensed over supply problems that it's giving some orders to archrival Advanced Micro Devices Inc., which has caught up to Intel in chip performance.

That's prompting analysts to wonder if top management is prepared to handle the swirl of new initiatives. For starters, Intel is heading into territory unfamiliar to its executives—all of them veterans deeply rooted in chips. Analysts worry that the company's pell-mell rush into new businesses lacks focus. "They're throwing spaghetti against the wall to see what sticks," complains analyst Jonathan J. Joseph of Salomon Smith Barney. And rivals snort that Intel lacks key expertise in networking and data services—though they admit that its rich profits give it the means to buy into new markets. Barrett himself concedes that in its new endeavors, Intel will have to "compete, scratch, and claw for market share"—a bracing change from Intel's near-monopoly in PC processors (Exhibits 3–6).

PC Pothole

Barrett had little choice. After 10 years of 30%-plus compound annual growth, Intel hit a milewide pothole in 1998. Earlier attempts to expand into new businesses such as modems and video conferencing had gone nowhere. Then falling PC prices, computer industry consolidation, and increased competition piled on top of one another, causing Intel's revenue growth to slow to 5%, while earnings declined for the first time in a decade. The bad news drove Intel's stock down 30% and kept it off its peak for most of 1998.

The biggest culprit in Intel's slowdown was a changing PC landscape. For the first time since the IBM Personal Computer exploded onto the market in 1981, PCs were

EXHIBIT 3   Networking Chips

Intel is "deadly serious" about being a player in the fast-growing networking industry, says CEO Barrett. In the past, networking was a sideline to sell more PCs. Now, Barrett is pouring billions into acquisitions, hiring, and marketing.

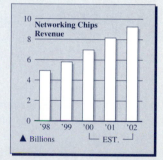

THE BOSS Mark Christensen, 40, is a rising star at Intel. With the company 18 years, he helped drive networking sales from zero to about $1 billion in the 1990s. Now he leads a 2,500-person group and reports directly to Barrett.

PRODUCTS The Network Communications Group sells chips used in modems, network interface cards, switches, and routers. Customers include Lucent, Nortel, Ericsson, and Nokia. A new family of 13 chips rolled out last September features a so-called network processor, a programmable chip that speeds and simplifies the design of new networking gear.

HOW INTEL STACKS UP Lucent Technologies Microelectronics Group is No. 1. Stalwarts like Motorola and Texas Instruments also play major roles, while newcomers Broadcom and Conexant Systems are favorites with investors. Intel is barely a blip on the radar screen in the market as a whole, but it's strong in some segments such as chips for broadband.

ACQUISITIONS Intel has spent big to get into this business. In 1999, it bought Level One Communications (for $2.2 billion), Softcom Microsystems ($149 million), NetBoost ($215 million), and the telecom chips group of Stanford Telecommunications (price not disclosed).

MARKET GROWTH Such chips are among the fastest-growing of all categories.

Source: Merrill Lynch & Co., company reports.

EXHIBIT 4   Communication Products

Nine years after launching its first networking gear, Intel has only a single-digit share of a $20 billion market. Now it's aiming for fast-growth segments: Home networking, broadband modems, PC-based telephony, and server appliances.

THE BOSS John Miner, 45, used to run the company's servers and workstations effort. Barrett tapped him last July to head a new 3,000-person Communications Products Group. Miner is gung ho: "Barrett says he'd rather come running after me and pull me back than have to push me out to the edge."

PRODUCTS Intel's lineup includes Ethernet hubs, small networking switches, and routers. It recently rolled out a line of specialized servers that manage Web traffic and speed up e-commerce. And it sells PC-based phone systems.

HOW INTEL STACKS UP Intel is up against 3Com, Nortel, and Cisco in home and small-business networking. As it pushes into broadband modems, it crosses Alcatel, Motorola, and others. And in specialty markets such as Web appliances and PC phones, it bumps into Alteon, Natural Microsystems, and others.

ACQUISITIONS Intel's most active area. In 1997, it bought Case Technology (for $72 million), a maker of low-end networking boxes. Since then, it has gobbled up the likes of iPivot ($500 million), which makes secure e-commerce servers; and Dialogic ($732 million), a leader in PC-based phone systems.

MARKET GROWTH Network gear is big business, but growth is slowing.

Communication Product Revenues (Billions), EST.: '98, '99, '00, '01, '02

Source: Cahners In-Stat, company reports.

losing some of their luster. Instead of clamoring for more power to run fatter software programs, many customers just wanted cheap PCs to get online. Low-cost PCs meant low-cost chips, something rivals realized faster. Peering into the future, says Frank Gill, Intel's former top networking exec who retired in 1998, "Intel could see that the next 10 years wouldn't be as lucrative in processors." Adds Barrett: "It used to be that the PC was the center of the action, but now it's clearly the Internet."

There's no question that Intel is now a believer. Just look at the company's semiannual developers' conference on Feb. 15. As 3,200 digit heads crammed into a ballroom at the Palm Springs (Calif.) convention center, giant video screens flashed to life and the unmistakable riff of Steppenwolf's *Born To Be Wild* blared into the hall—only it had new lyrics: "Get your modem running, head out on the I-way. Looking for e-ventures, and whatever comes our way. Born to be wired." It was the warmup for a speech by Grove, the legendary chip warrior who barely sounded as though he were still in the semiconductor business, as he went on about e-commerce, gigabit networks, and facilities filled with servers. "For the first time in 15 years, we have found it necessary to change our corporate mission statement," said Grove. Now, instead of being just the leading purveyor of PC technology, Grove says, Intel aims to make the building blocks for the entire Net Economy.

To do that means undoing much of what Grove put in place. Within weeks of taking over in May, 1998, Barrett began dismantling Grove's rigidly centralized management structure, eventually breaking Intel into five groups whose managers report directly to him (Exhibits 2–6). He loosened Intel's conservative financial management to let more of its $12 billion cash hoard flow to acquisitions, equity investments, and internal start-ups. "We had to change the culture and the way we run our business," he says. Most of

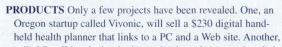

EXHIBIT 5   New Businesses

Intel's New Business Group has pumped more than $50 million into 25 small projects. They vary from a secure medical ID system for doctors on the Net to terminals installed in the backs of seats at Madison Square Garden.

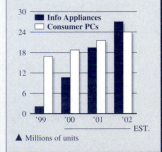

THE BOSS Gerry Parker, 56, is a widely respected 31-year Intel veteran who previously ran the company's manufacturing. Why an operations guy in business development? Because he makes things happen. "We're looking for as many ideas as possible," Parker says.

PRODUCTS Only a few projects have been revealed. One, an Oregon startup called Vivonic, will sell a $230 digital hand-held health planner that links to a PC and a Web site. Another, called PassEdge, is developing technology for protecting digital content. And the first of a dozen Web-hosting centers is now open in Santa Clara, Calif.

HOW INTEL STACKS UP It's too early to say how Intel's startups will do. But Intel is not the first to spy the opportunity for Web hosting. The top players, including Exodus and IBM, have 30% of the market—with Intel nowhere in sight. Intel thinks it can break in by offering soup-to-nuts e-commerce services.

ACQUISITIONS In 1998, Intel bought Seattle-based iCat, a maker of easy-to-use e-commerce programs aimed at small to midsize businesses.

MARKET GROWTH Web hosting is one of the fastest-growing segments of the information technology business.

Source: International Data Corp., company reports.

EXHIBIT 6   Information Appliances

A few years ago, Intel was convinced that PCs were the ultimate information appliance. But the possibility that something simpler or cheaper could attract millions of non-PC households became too attractive to ignore.

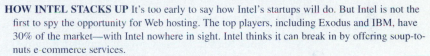

THE BOSS Claude Leglise, 44, who used to manage outside software developers, got a new mandate in August, 1998, "to move Intel into the home, somehow," he says. Just 18 months later, Intel rolled out services and prototype products that should appeal to consumers and Internet service providers.

PRODUCTS As yet undelivered, they'll use Celeron chips and Linux—not Microsoft Windows CE—software, and will be sold through phone companies and ISPs. Possible models include screen phones, e-mail terminals, and TV set-top boxes.

HOW INTEL STACKS UP There are zillions of rivals—from startups such as Network Appliance to giants like Motorola/General Instrument. Intel is behind since it hasn't shipped any products yet. Another promising avenue: Intel is moving aggressively into chips for wireless phones.

ACQUISITIONS DSP Communications ($1.6 billion).

MARKET GROWTH PC unit sales in the U.S. are expected to be eclipsed in 2002 by combined sales of e-mail terminals, Web pads, screen phones, Internet-enabled TVs, and other such high-tech gizmos.

Source: International Data Corp., company reports.

all, Barrett had to wean Intel from the defining strategy of the Grove era, when growth lay in stimulating demand for ever-more powerful PCs.

To flesh out his vision, Barrett has been on a spending spree. He's buying companies to beef up Intel's product line and help shed its notorious "not-invented-here" syndrome. In 1999 alone, the company spent $6 billion snapping up 12 companies—more, for the first time ever, than it spent on capital equipment, and nearly as much as the research-and-development and capital budgets combined. In a bid to mine fresh ideas within the company, the 60-year-old CEO has poured some $50 million into 25 homegrown start-ups that could someday become new product lines or be spun off as subsidiaries. And hundreds of other ideas are in the pipeline. Gerhard H. Parker, the Intel veteran who heads the company's New Business Group, says people are so excited about the opportunity that an employee recently chased him into the bathroom clutching a business plan. "It's wonderful to see that kind of enthusiasm," (Exhibit 5). Parker says. "It wouldn't have happened a few years ago."

Batting Average

Not without Barrett. While Grove is known for his fiery temper, Barrett is cool as ice. In his years before becoming CEO, he was known occasionally to bring a baseball bat to meetings to ensure—humorously—quick capitulation from intransigent colleagues. A native of the Bay Area, he studied metallurgy at Stanford University and went on to become an associate professor in the school's engineering department. After a sabbatical year working for Intel in 1973, he returned to Stanford for one day, then chucked it all and went back to Intel for good, rising through the ranks on the strength of his operational skills. He's credited with turning the company from an 80-pound weakling into an 800-pound gorilla in manufacturing, largely through inventing a technique called "Copy Exactly" in which every Intel plant is identical, down to the colors of paint. That made it easy for Intel to roll out new production techniques to all its factories—and dramatically boost quality and productivity.

So how did Mr. Manufacturing get Intel's troops jazzed about something besides their beloved microprocessor? He didn't need a baseball bat. When Compaq Computer Corp.'s $999 PC hit the market in February, 1997, carrying a chip from rival Cyrix Corp., Intel executives began to worry that cheap PCs could choke off its growth engine. Soon, inexpensive machines were flooding the market, and by mid-summer, Intel competitors AMD and Cyrix had grabbed 20% of the U.S. retail PC market, their highest share in half a decade.

That's when Barrett and then chief Grove decided to split Intel's Pentium line into distinct price and performance bands to target different markets. They devised the Celeron line for inexpensive PCs and the Xeon family for high-powered servers and workstations, while keeping the flagship Pentium III aimed at the middle tier of the market. Despite a cool reception at first, the Celeron has helped Intel climb back to 62% market share in sub-$1,000 PCs, up from 30% a year ago. And analysts now expect revenues from server-class chips to top $6.7 billion by 2001, up from $3.4 billion last year. The segmentation strategy has helped Intel maintain its juicy 60% gross margins by balancing high- and low-end sales.

But Barrett understood that segmentation alone wouldn't put Intel back on the growth curve investors had come to expect. Given Intel's size, growing at 20% per year required coming up with $5 billion or more in new revenues every year. And that meant Barrett had to think big. "He was looking to build Intel's next $25 billion business and knew he would have to significantly expand its charter," says David B. Yoffie, a professor at Harvard business school and a member of Intel's board.

Thinking Green

The CEO-to-be knew the first place to start was inside Intel. In July, 1997, he arranged for three corporate strategy gurus to conduct a seminar series for Intel's top 400 managers. In eight groups of 50, executives retreated for a week to hotels near Intel's offices in Santa Clara, Calif., Phoenix, and Portland, Ore. "We had to figure out how to grow new businesses in the shadow of the creosote bush," Barrett says.

The first day was led by Robert A. Burgelman, a Stanford Business School professor who has studied Intel for years and co-teaches a course at the school with Grove. Burgelman specializes in helping companies develop and nurture an entrepreneurial spirit. He urged seminar attendees to divide Intel's businesses into "blue" products, its old bread-and-butter chips businesses, and "green" products—everything new. The goal was to get managers to jump faster on green ideas and escape the gravitational pull of the blue status quo. Executives at Intel now routinely use the blue vs. green descriptions when discussing strategies. "There's been a freeing up of thinking," says Paul S. Otellini, the head of Intel's processor unit.

On the second day, managers learned about the threat posed by so-called disruptive technologies. Clayton M. Christensen, a Harvard B-school professor and author of *The Innovator's Dilemma,* explained how makers of cheap steel reinforcing bars, known as rebar, once dismissed as insignificant by industry giants, had nibbled their way into the market for higher-value steel. The PC had done the same thing to mainframe computers, he said.

"Digital Rebar"

The third day of the seminar focused on business ecosystems. Led by James F. Moore, president of consultancy GeoPartners Research Inc. and author of *The Death of Competition,* the session taught Intel execs that to move beyond the familiar PC world, they would have to construct new webs of relationships and help seed emerging business ecologies. In the first few months of the seminar series, when Intel still believed that cheap PCs would be a short-lived craze, "there was a lot of denial of the message," Moore says. Then, with AMD's market share soaring, the mood turned to despair.

The big breakthrough came in September, 1997. At a dinner with Grove and other top execs following a seminar, the famously paranoid Grove latched on to the rebar story as an analogy for cheap PCs. "If we lose the low end today, we could lose the high end tomorrow," he exclaimed. From then on, Grove referred to cheap PCs as "digital rebar," and Intel became more aggressive in promoting the Celeron, even at the risk of cannibalizing sales of pricier chips.

Intel's execs also began to accept the idea of widening the company's mission. Their vehicle of choice was an investment fund Intel launched in 1991 to dribble money into PC industry startups whose products or technologies gobbled up PC power and, in the words of Grove, created "waves of excitement" among potential PC buyers. Now renamed Intel Capital, the fund has vastly expanded its outlays, from about $300 million in 1997 to $1.2 billion last year, and has stakes in more than 350 software and Internet companies.

Intel Capital has scored some notable hits, including eToys, Red Hat, and Inktomi. Its holdings are now valued at more than $8.2 billion, and it kicked $327 million in pre-tax income into Intel's fourth-quarter results—half of the company's 6¢ upside earnings surprise. But Intel Capital wasn't conceived primarily as a moneymaker. The investment in eToys, for example, was seen simply as a way to boost the growth of e-tailing—and the purchase of PCs. "My goal is to expose the company to every facet of the Internet economy," says Leslie L. Vadasz, manager of the fund. "It has already led to an opening of minds." The model worked so well that in 1999 Intel set up a separate $250 million fund to encourage software development for its new 64-bit Itanium processor and a similar $200 million fund to spur adoption of its new networking chips.

After the seminar series ended in 1998, the minds of Intel's managers were opened a bit more than the company could handle. At each session, attendees had broken into groups to dream up new business ideas. But "Barrett had gotten all these people excited with nowhere to go," says D. Craig Kinnie, director of Intel Architecture Labs, a research group in Oregon. The new CEO soon realized he needed more than just a cultural awakening: He had to change Intel's inflexible structure to allow new ideas to thrive.

Wad of Cash

That July, Barrett came up with a solution. He and chief financial officer Andy D. Bryant threw out Intel's rulebook for funding new programs and established the New Business Group. Rather than setting tight budgets and subjecting internal startups to rigorous reviews, they were treated like venture-capital-financed companies and given a wad of cash to spend until it ran out. Under this scheme, Parker's unit has launched about 20 seed projects, each with three or four employees and a budget of several hundred thousand dollars. Seven larger projects have received $5 million to $10 million in funding. The ideas range from a scheme to equip doctors with secure IDs to encourage online medicine, to installing 3,000 information terminals on the backs of seats at Madison Square Garden for hockey fans to look up information on their favorite players. Two potential spin-offs: An Intel business called Vivonic, based in Oregon, will sell handheld computers that help users monitor their diet and fitness starting this spring. Another Portland-based venture, called PassEdge, is set to be launched this April with technology for protecting online content, such as digital music and movies, against illegal copying.

By far, Intel's biggest gamble is its nascent Web-hosting business. The idea of running Net data centers had been floated in 1996 but was shot down because top execs didn't grasp the coming rise of Web services. Two years later, in September, 1998, Barrett directed Renee James, Grove's chief technical aide, to explore the idea again. She pulled in a team of five people and spent six weeks cobbling together a plan. "We pored over reams of data, but in the end we took a flyer," James says. Intel's board quickly approved the plan in November, and by January, 1999, it was launched. Just nine months later, Intel opened its first data center in Santa Clara. With a capacity for 10,000 servers, the center is now barely occupied. So far, only about a dozen companies—including Citigroup, an Excite@Home shopping service, and several customers from Intel's Pandesic joint venture with SAP Corp.—are using the service.

Web services couldn't be further from the chip industry. But Intel execs argue that being in the business will give the company insight into e-commerce trends. Plus, it's an insurance policy in case computing moves to a pay-for-service model and PCs are eclipsed by devices connected to Web servers. Besides, Intel executives point out, the company already does $1 billion in online business every month. "We run Intel.com 24 hours a day, 365 days a year," Barrett says. "We went from selling nothing online to more than $1 billion a month over our own infrastructure. We have expertise in this space."

Wireless Way

Still, analysts remain ambivalent about the likely success of the program. "I just don't get it," says Manoj Nadkarni, president of consultancy ChipInvestor.com, an investment research house based in Federal Way, Wash., that specializes in chip companies. Noting that the leading independent Web-hosting outfits, Exodus Communications Inc. and Verio Inc., are still losing money, Nadkarni and other analysts wonder what kinds of margins Intel can get from the business. Barrett won't comment on profits. Competitors, naturally, can't resist. "This is a mistake," says William L. Shrader, CEO of Internet service provider PSInet Inc., pointing out that Intel is going into business against its customers. "Intel looks like a joke. They'll retreat in less than two years as gracefully as possible." Adds Ellen Hancock, CEO of Web-service rival Exodus Communications: "It's a stretch for them to say they have some expertise here. We've taken years to set up our operations."

Barrett rejects such notions but admits that Intel Online Services isn't the centerpiece of his strategy (Exhibit 7). By comparison, networking and communications arc "an order of magnitude" more important, he says, because the communications industry is larger than computing, yet Intel "doesn't play nearly as significant a role there." Intel, however, does stand a good chance of becoming a major supplier of wireless chip technology. The purchase of DSP Communications, combined with a joint venture with Analog Devices

---

EXHIBIT 7   The Thrill of "Clawing for Market Share" Is Back

Craig R. Barrett, CEO of Intel Corp. since May, 1998, is as cool as his predecessor Andrew S. Grove was hot. But don't let Barrett's placid mien fool you: He's as tough as they come, with a biting wit. Trained as a metallurgist, Barrett quit his job as a Stanford University engineering professor to join Intel in 1974. He rose to the top on his operations talent—Barrett is credited with turning Intel into a nonpareil manufacturer—but in the past two years, he has been moving into the role of visionary-in-chief. Barrett spoke with BUSINESS WEEK correspondent Andy Reinhardt in the CEO's unadorned conference room.

Q: *How is Intel changing?*
A: We still are driving our core [microprocessor] business as hard as ever, and [it's] still doing pretty well. But we've supplemented it with new growth initiatives, which are very exciting and very different for us. We are acquiring companies, acquiring people, and putting a new image on top of the big, powerful chip monster that eats the world.

   Whether it's networking or cellular communications, server appliances, or server farms, there's a lot more buzz and energy, which is causing the company to change the way it behaves. It's not just the big machine continuing to roll on. [We have] a bunch of smaller businesses starting up, which are forced to compete, scratch, and claw for market share.

Q: *You've started other businesses before. What's different this time?*
A: A lot of the initiatives we had in the past were not so much new business thrusts as something designed to augment and support the existing Job 1 business. But when you look at server farms [facilities with rows of computers] or cellular communications, these are pretty well removed from microprocessors. They're quite different, not just a pimple on our core business.

Q: *Why are you undertaking such a massive overhaul of your business?*
A: The PC was at the center of computing during the '90s, but if you look at the next decade, the Internet is clearly it. The PC is still very important in the Internet era. But if you want to be involved in this new era, you have to look for the new growth opportunities. That's exactly what we're trying to do.

Q: *Why are you doing so many acquisitions?*
A: We recognized one of the changes we had to make to continue to grow was to pump up the acquisitions. We really can't develop all this technology internally, so we had to go outside. This is generally accepted now as one of the ways people grow. . . . Let's stop being squeamish; let's just go out and do it.

Q: *Your plan to host the Web operations of others baffles some people because it's so different from manufacturing chips. What expertise does Intel have to offer?*
A: If the argument were that we run big silicon factories so we can run big server farms, I would question it, too. But you have to look at it from the standpoint that we run Intel.com 24 hours a day, 365 days a year. We went from selling nothing online to more than $1 billion a month over our own infrastructure. We have expertise in this space. Forget about silicon factories.

Q: *What about your plan to sell information appliances? Couldn't they undermine sales of PCs?*
A: The Internet is too big, too powerful, too multifaceted not to have multiple points of entry. But the real question is, if you're going to send e-mail with photo attachments, how are you going to do that? I would argue that you're going to do that on a standard, fairly rich PC, not on a handheld device. As long as it works that way, the PC is still at the center of the action.

to develop a new digital signal processor chip, could give Intel a bigger piece of the explosive mobile-phone business. It's already the No. 1 supplier of memory chips used in cell phones. By packaging DSPC's software with Intel's energy-efficient StrongARM processor, Barrett figures he can parlay that position into selling the more profitable brains of wireless Internet-ready phones. It's a huge opportunity: Researcher International Data Corp. figures such devices could surge to 536 million units in 2003, up from 85 million in 2000. "Wireless access is the second coming of the Internet," says IDC researcher Iain Gillott.

But rivals aren't rolling over. The $7 billion communications chip sector is on fire, with projected 20% growth this year. Established players are beefing up their portfolios. Motorola, Conexant, and Lucent Technologies, for instance, all recently bought network processor startups, and IBM has a chip of its own. Competitors pooh-pooh Intel's prospects, arguing it lacks expertise in custom chips and analog circuits—both crucial for networking. "Intel doesn't understand the communications market," snaps John T. Dickson, president of Lucent Microelectronics Group, the No. 1 supplier of communications chips. What's more, says Charles Boucher of Bear, Stearns & Co., after seeing how Intel sucked the profits out of the PC makers, networking companies "are suspicious of their intentions."

Adding talent through acquisitions could help, but Intel's track record in promoting outsiders is poor: Only three CEOs from the 20 companies Intel has bought in the last three years are now among its top 92 executives. Most others have stayed, but they toil deeper in the ranks. By contrast, Cisco's top tier is populated with former heads of acquired companies. Intel acknowledges, too, that while its overall turnover remains an enviable 4% per year, it has had trouble holding on to younger, midlevel managers who are defecting to dot-coms. Says one former Intel exec: "There aren't any whiz kids there."

Barrett is undaunted. He's driving Intel at a pace it has never known before, even during the heyday of "only-the-paranoid-survive" Grove. The new chief executive is bent on leaving a legacy every bit as large as Grove's, but he's managing a far more complex enterprise facing much greater challenges. If anything, the need to prove that Intel's success wasn't just a fluke has its managers fired up. "We felt like we had succeeded before the Net," says Sean Maloney, Intel's worldwide sales and marketing manager. "Now, we have to prove it all over again." And show the world that Intel is no creosote bush.

7 Implementing Marketing Plans and Assessing Performance

The final decade of the 20th century was an unprecedented period of organizational change. Companies realigned their organizations to establish closer contact with customers, improve customer service, reduce layers of management, decrease the time between decisions and results, and improve organizational effectiveness in other ways. Organizational changes include the use of information systems to reduce organization layers and response time, the use of multifunctional teams to design and produce new products, and the creation of flexible organization units to compete in turbulent business environments.

We first examine organization design because a sound organizational scheme must correspond to the marketing strategy. The remaining sections in this part opener examine marketing strategy implementation and performance assessment. The marketing plan guides implementation and performance assessment, indicating marketing objectives and strategies as well as tactics for accomplishing the objectives.

Organizing for the 21st Century

Organizations today have fewer levels than traditional organizations did and are beginning to be organized around processes such as order processing, new product planning, and customer services. One estimate is that the typical large business in 2010 will have fewer than half the levels of management and no more than one-third the managers of its counterpart in the late 1980s.[1] These flat organizations will be information-based. Information storage, processing, and decision-support technology will move information swiftly up and down and across the organization. Levels of management can be eliminated since people at those levels function primarily as information relays rather than as decision makers and leaders.

A major motivation for reorganizing is improving relationships with customers in the field. Many companies have restructured their sales and marketing organizations to move closer to their customers. For example, an electrical products manufacturer, previously organized on a functional basis, has set up four separate operating divisions, each with its own sales and engineering units. A packaging company, after the successful revamping of its sales force along industry lines, is now reorganizing its warehouse and customer service activities on a geographic basis to ensure more familiarity with customers by area.[2]

These actions indicate marketing executives' continuing concern about organizational effectiveness. Organizational change will occur more frequently in the future as businesses respond to market turbulence and competitive pressures.

Cisco Systems Inc. may typify the emerging model of the 21st-century corporation. For this leader in sales of networking products, 2001 sales should exceed $26 billion. Nearly 80 percent of the company's sales are over the Internet.[3] Cisco designs and markets its equipment, outsourcing manufacturing to supply chain partners that ship direct to Cisco's customers. It employs an aggressive acquisition strategy to obtain needed technologies.

Selecting an Organization Design

The design of the marketing organization is influenced by market and environmental factors, the characteristics of the organization, and the marketing strategy followed by the firm. The organization should be structured so that responsibility for results corresponds to each manager's influence on results. While this objective is often difficult to fully achieve, it is an important consideration in designing the marketing organization.

The design of an organization also affects its ability (and willingness) to respond quickly. The advantage of doing things faster than the competition is clearly important. For example, The Limited's skill in moving women's apparel from design to the store in weeks instead of months enables the retailer to market new designs ahead of its competition. Organizations that can do things faster are more competitive.

Finally, a real danger in a highly structured and complex organization is the loss of flexibility. The organization should be adaptable to changing conditions.

Implementing Marketing Plans

Marketing plans are often ineffective unless they include detailed implementation plans. An implementation plan should specify what activities are to be implemented, who will be responsible for implementation, and the time and location of implementation.

Managers are important facilitators in the implementation process, and some are more effective than others. To be effective implementers, managers need

- The ability to understand how others feel.
- Good bargaining skills.
- The strength to be tough and fair in putting people and resources where they will be most effective.
- Effectiveness in focusing on the critical aspects of performance in managing marketing activities.
- The ability to create a necessary informal organization or network to match each problem that arises.[4]

The implementation of marketing strategy may depend partially on external organizations such as marketing research firms, marketing consultants, advertising and public relations firms, channel members, and other organizations participating in the marketing effort. These outside organizations present a major coordination challenge when they actively participate in marketing activities. Their efforts should be programmed into the marketing plan, and their roles and responsibilities should be clearly established and communicated. There is a potential danger in not informing outside groups of planned actions, deadlines, and other implementation requirements. For example, the advertising agency account executive and other agency staff members should be familiar with all aspects of the promotion strategy as well as the major dimensions of the marketing strategy. Restricting information from participating firms can adversely affect their contributions to strategy planning and implementation.

Implementation/Execution Problems

Marketing managers frequently encounter problems when plans reach the implementation/execution stage. A four-year study of top marketing and general managers' key marketing concerns identified five specific problems: management by assumption, global mediocrity, empty-promises marketing, program ambiguity, and ritualization, politicization, and unavailability.[5]

Management by Assumption.   Management assumes that someone somewhere in the organization will do the analysis necessary for making knowledgeable pricing, sales promotion, or distribution decisions. Unfortunately, the function in question is often ignored until a crisis occurs.

Global Mediocrity.   Management tries to excel at all of its marketing activities rather than picking one or a few for special concentration. The firm does many things adequately but is not outstanding at anything. Ultimately, it finds itself without a competitive advantage.

Empty-Promises Marketing.   Management creates programs it does not have the subfunctional capability to execute. Declaring that a program exists and appointing a competent individual to manage it are usually not enough for subfunctional success. The existence of too many programs generally means that none is pursued with a vengeance.

Program Ambiguity.   A lack of clear identity and direction results in a multitude of programs and no unifying theme. Clever programs fail because of an absence of shared understanding about identity (i.e., theme) and strong leadership.

Ritualization, Politicization, and Unavailability.   Errors of ritual arise when the firm's systems mandate a particular course of action because "things have always been done that way." Even if good judgment dictates a different course, habitual pathways may be chosen.

Management intelligence often is undermined by the politicization of data and information. Often, daily records are not prepared until the end of the month (when much may already be forgotten) or not turned in until inflammatory data are removed.

Systems installed to make managers' lives easier may quickly become unsuitable for current environmental conditions or place the data in the hands of those completely removed from its significance. Many marketing managers do not have the data necessary to analyze profitability by segment, product, account, or order. These problems indicate that it is not enough to have a science of making plans. It is also necessary to understand how the plans are translated into actions and marketplace results.

Performance Assessment

Performance assessment consumes a high proportion of marketing executives' time and energy. Management must establish performance criteria and measures so that information can be obtained for use in tracking performance. The purpose of evaluation may be to (1) find new opportunities or avoid threats, (2) keep performance in line with management's expectations, and/or (3) solve specific problems.

The starting point in performance assessment is a *strategic marketing audit*. The audit is a comprehensive review and assessment of marketing operations. It includes a careful examination of

1. Corporate mission and objectives.
2. Business composition and strategy.
3. Buyer analysis.
4. Competitor analysis.
5. Market target strategy and objectives.
6. Marketing program positioning strategy.
7. Marketing program activities.
8. Marketing planning.
9. Implementation and management.

There are other reasons for conducting a strategic marketing audit besides its use in guiding the installation of a formal strategic marketing planning and performance assessment program:

1. Organizational changes may bring about a complete review of marketing operations.
2. Major shifts in business involvement such as entry into new product and market areas, acquisitions, and other alterations in the composition of the business may require strategic audits.

Although there is no norm for how often a strategic audit should be conducted, the nature of the audit and the costs involved suggest that the time span between audits should be at least three years and perhaps more, depending on the market and company situation.

Selecting Performance Criteria and Measures.   As marketing plans are developed, performance criteria need to be selected to monitor performance. Specifying the information needed for marketing decision making is important and requires management's concentrated attention. In the past, marketing executives could develop and manage successful marketing strategies by relying on intuition, judgment, and experience. Successful executives now combine judgment and experience with information and decision-support systems. These systems are becoming increasingly important in gaining strategic advantages.

Illustrative criteria for total performance include sales, market share, profit, expense, and customer satisfaction targets. Brand positioning analyses may also be useful in tracking position relative to key competitors. These measures can be used to gauge overall performance and for specific target markets. Performance criteria also are needed for the marketing mix components. For example, new-customer and lost-customer tracking often is included in sales force performance monitoring. Pricing performance monitoring may include comparisons of actual to list prices, extent of discounting, and profit contribution. Many possible performance criteria can be selected. Management must identify the key measures that will show how the firm's marketing strategy is performing in its competitive environment and where changes are needed.

Acquiring, Processing, and Analyzing Information.   The costs of acquiring, processing, and analyzing information are high, and so the potential benefits of needed information must be compared to the costs. Normally, information falls into two categories: (1) information regularly supplied to marketing management from internal and external sources and (2) information obtained as needed for a particular problem or situation. Examples of the former are sales and cost analyses, market share measurements, and customer satisfaction surveys. Information from the latter category includes new product concept tests, brand-preference studies, and studies of advertising effectiveness.

Deciding What Actions to Take.   Many actions are possible, depending on the situation. Management's actions may include exiting from a product market, changing the target market strategy, revising objectives, adjusting marketing strategy components, improving efficiency, and extending the existing plan into the future. Keeping track of current performance and anticipating change are the essence of performance assessment.

End Notes

1. Peter F. Drucker, "The Coming of the New Organization," *Harvard Business Review,* January–February 1988, pp. 45–53.
2. Earl L. Bailey, *Getting Closer to the Customer,* Research Bulletin no. 229 (New York: The Conference Board, Inc., 1989), p. 5.
3. "Meet Mr. Internet," *Business Week,* September 13, 1999, pp. 128–40.
4. Thomas V. Bonoma, "Making Your Marketing Strategy Work," *Harvard Business Review,* March–April 1984, p. 75.
5. Thomas V. Bonoma and Victoria L. Crittenden, "Managing Marketing Implementation," *Sloan Management Review,* Winter 1988, pp. 7–14.

CASES FOR PART 7

The eight cases in this part address various concerns related to organization, implementation, and performance assessment issues. The cases involve both consumer and business-to-business products and services.

Case 7–1, CUTCO International, a video case, describes the only U.S. cutlery manufacturer that focuses exclusively on worldwide direct selling. While the company's international sales are growing, international operations have yet to be profitable. The company has offices in Korea, the United Kingdom, Australia, Germany, and Costa Rica. Top management must develop a sequence of countries for international marketing entry.

The Bacova Guild, Ltd. (Case 7–2), is an innovative, fast-growing U.S. company. The firm has expanded operations to accommodate sales growth and now must develop and market a steady stream of new products to cover overhead and maintain profitability.

In **Case 7–3, Pfizer, Inc., Animal Health Products (B),** NAFTA's effect has been less than positive. With ranchers in Montana and Idaho seeking ways to cut costs in order to remain competitive (and viable), Pfizer is faced with the possibility of long-term customer relationships being severed due to a switch to lower-cost alternatives to vaccines and antibiotics. However, lowering the price of such products would only serve as a Band-Aid solution to a much bigger problem facing the ranchers.

Calloway Golf Company (Case 7–4) was the leader in the golf equipment industry. The company was known for its technologically advanced golf clubs that compensated for the poor swing of most amateur golfers. The company's move into golf balls is being watched closely by industry observers.

Case 7–5, Wind Technology, presents a situation requiring evaluation and marketing planning for a possible new industrial product. The company needs to generate revenues because of the cash flow problems created by its wind-profiling project.

In **Case 7–6, Slendertone (B)** is faced with an unexpected decrease in orders from its French distributor. Employees are wondering if the company can survive; the company quickly went from having a healthy cash surplus to being cash-constrained (truly overdrawn at the bank). A restructuring is in the works that involves a greater marketing effort.

Longevity Healthcare Systems, Inc. (Case 7–7), was beginning to experience increased competition and the uncertainty of health-care reform. The president is concerned that the company has neither developed a formal plan for future growth nor prepared a written marketing strategy.

The e-business situation of **Amazon.com Inc. (Case 7–8)** has raised concern over this e-tailer's apparent inability to make money. As one of the most prominent e-tailers, Amazon still plans to be more profitable than conventional retailers.

CASE 7–1
CUTCO INTERNATIONAL

It was CUTCO Cutlery's 1997 midyear companywide meeting in Olean, New York. Record sales and profits had been achieved for the first six months. CUTCO had seen record weekly shipments in June. Over 27,000 packages had gone out just the week before. Unlike some recent years, needed inventory was in place to meet seasonal demand. Further, record sales and profits were projected for the entire year. CUTCO employees could look forward to significant year-end profit-sharing bonuses.

The management team was proud of these achievements. However, Erick Laine (CEO/president, ALCAS Corporation), Fran Weinaug (president/CEO, CUTCO International), Bob Haig (president/COO, Vector Marketing Corporation), Mike Lancellot (president, Vector East), Don Muelrath (president, Vector West), and Jim Stitt (president/CEO, CUTCO Cutlery Corporation) were not satisfied. Growth was at record levels but not at plan.

According to Erick Laine, "Sales are up 11 percent over 1996, not the 20 to 25 percent we looked for. International sales in particular have been way off projections (15 percent growth versus the expected 75 percent). Although we've made some important adjustments, the second half of the year is unlikely to compensate."

He continued: "Other direct sales firms have had enormous success in the international arena. International markets are attractive to direct sellers. Direct selling allows market entry without fighting the battles of brand identity and entrenched distribution systems. With limited brick and mortar requirements, direct selling allows one to grow rapidly. We know it's [the market] there to be gotten."

CUTCO's corporate vision statement (see Exhibit 1) to be the world's "largest, most respected and widely recognized" cutlery firm required substantial growth. Although product development and company acquisitions might be part of the strategic mix, management clearly viewed the international market as a critical element to growth. Yet decisions regarding which markets to enter, which approach to use, and the sequencing and timing of entry still needed to be made.

The ALCAS Corporation (the Parent)

In 1949 Alcoa and CASE Cutlery formed a joint venture, ALCAS Cutlery Corporation, to produce kitchen cutlery known as CUTCO. The product was exclusively marketed via in-home demonstrations by WearEver, Inc. (However, CUTCO and WearEver products were treated as separate entities and were not sold together.) In 1972, Alcoa bought out CASE and ALCAS became wholly owned by Alcoa. In 1982, the local management of ALCAS, headed by Erick Laine, a longtime Alcoa employee, purchased the company from Alcoa. Management converted ALCAS into a privately held corporation with headquarters in Olean, New York. Ownership remains closely held by five of the top

This case was prepared by William F. Crittenden at Northeastern University and Victoria L. Crittenden at Boston College as the basis for class discussion rather than to illustrate effective or ineffective handling of a managerial situation. The Direct Selling Education Foundation provided partial funding for the development of this case. Revised 2001.

EXHIBIT 1

CORPORATE VISION

To become the largest, most respected and widely recognized cutlery company in the world while maintaining an equal commitment to these core values:

- Honesty, integrity and ethics in all aspects of business – founded on our respect for people.

- Recognizing and rewarding our people for dedication and high levels of achievement.

- Product pre-eminence, quality and reputation.

- First-class customer service and customer satisfaction.

- Strong consolidated corporate profitability and the strength and financial success of our field sales organization.

- Creating opportunities for our people to grow and share in the success of the enterprise.

managers. In 1996, the company acquired KA-BAR Knives, an established sporting knife company. Exhibit 2 outlines the corporate structure. Worldwide revenues from direct marketing and direct sales operations exceeded $100 million in 1996. (Sales just exceeded $20 million in 1987.) All corporations within ALCAS operate as profit centers.

CUTCO Cutlery covers a broad range of food preparation knives as well as scissors and hunting, fishing, and utility knives. (Exhibits 3 through 10 show examples of CUTCO products.) The product line is identified as "CUTCO—*The World's Finest Cutlery.*" Product pricing is consistent with this positioning at the high end of the spectrum. The product is sold as individual open stock, in wood block sets, or in a variety of gift boxed sets. According to Mark George (now international sales director and a former CUTCO sales representative), numerous features make CUTCO the world's finest cutlery: "the ergonomically designed handle, the thermo-resin handle material, the full tang triple rivet construction, the high-carbon, stain-resistant steel, and the exclusive Double-D® edge. All products are backed by the CUTCO 'Forever Guarantee.'"

Recognizing the importance of satisfied customers, CUTCO devoted considerable space in its Olean headquarters to its service department. The company has a goal of two to three days' turnaround on knives returned for free sharpening or guarantee issues.

(continued on page 564)

EXHIBIT 2

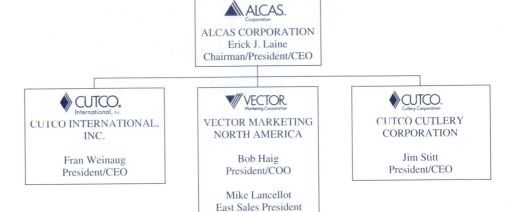

ALCAS CORPORATION
Erick J. Laine
Chairman/President/CEO

CUTCO INTERNATIONAL, INC.

Fran Weinaug
President/CEO

VECTOR MARKETING NORTH AMERICA

Bob Haig
President/COO

Mike Lancellot
East Sales President

Don Muelrath
West Sales President

CUTCO CUTLERY CORPORATION

Jim Stitt
President/CEO

EXHIBIT 3

EXHIBIT 4

EXHIBIT 5

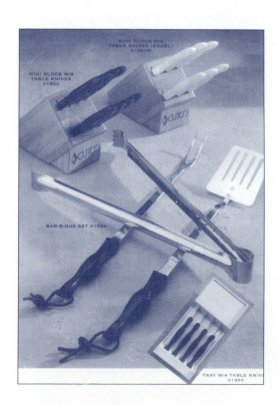

EXHIBIT 6

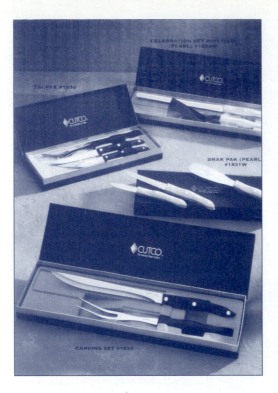

EXHIBIT 7

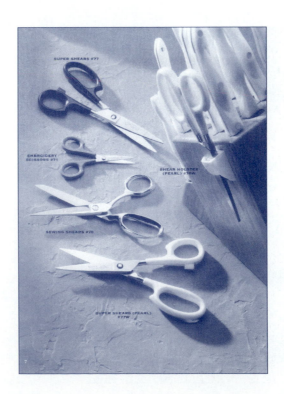

EXHIBIT 8

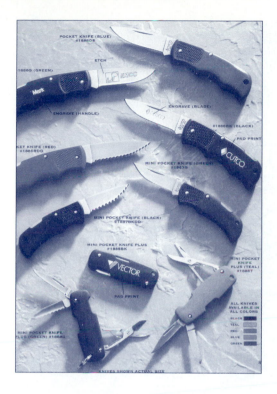

EXHIBIT 9

EXHIBIT 10
Fisherman's Solution

A total fillet knife system. Designed for lake, coastal or stream fishing.

The high-carbon, stain-resistant steel blade adjusts and locks from 6" to 9" to fillet any size fish. A patented Cam-Lock secures the blade tightly at any length. The Zytel® inner track system assures the blade's smooth adjustment. The sheath pivots open to become a gripper to help clean, skin and fillet or remove a hook. Notched line cutter and a built-in sharpening stone with a groove for fish hooks complete the sheath.

CUTCO cutlery is marketed in North America by Vector Marketing Corporation. During peak selling periods, Vector Marketing operates around 400 offices in Canada and the United States. CUTCO is sold primarily by college students who are recruited to work during vacations as sales representatives. (Exhibit 11 shows the typical seasonal percentage of sales for CUTCO products.) Some students continue to sell during the school year. Recruiting, training, and ongoing management of the sales force are done utilizing over 200 district offices. Over 200 temporary branch offices are opened during the summer months and are staffed by college students with prior selling and management experience. All sales representatives are independent contractors. Sales training is completed over a three-day period. Vector has experimented with some catalog sales and has special policies in place that demonstrate sensitivity to its sales representatives. The typical CUTCO customer has household income of approximately $60,000, is well educated (with most holding a bachelor's degree and some with postgraduate degrees), is married with older children, holds a professional or managerial position, is approximately 40 to 54 years old, is a homeowner, and enjoys cooking, gardening, reading, and traveling.

CUTCO Cutlery Corporation manufactures CUTCO products in Olean, New York, and sells at wholesale to Vector and CUTCO International. Unlike many manufacturers, CUTCO has reduced outsourcing in recent years and has backward integrated into plastic molding (e.g., knife handles and cutting boards) and wood blocks. Jim Stitt, CUTCO Cutlery Corporation president and CEO, attributed the company's ability to stay competitive to its skilled work force and considerable investment in high-technology

EXHIBIT 11   Seasonal Sales

January–April	17%
May–August	67
September–December	16

equipment. Additionally, the company processes its product very differently from competitors to provide a high level of product distinction (e.g., its unique recessed edge grind, freezing the blades, applying a mirror polish finish to the blades).

Cutlery

Cutlery is a term applied collectively to all types of cutting instruments. More specifically, in the United States it refers to knives employed in the preparation of food and for sporting and utility use. The first U.S. cutlery factory was established in Worchester, Massachusetts, in 1829. As American steel improved in quality and decreased in price, the industry developed steadily, particularly in the Northeastern states. (Exhibit 12 provides industry cutlery sales by retail outlet for 1996.)

Cutting instruments are clearly of worldwide importance—numerous international manufacturing sites have gained some renown. Sheffield in the United Kingdom and Soligen in Germany are especially well known for cutlery. However, substantial innovation at the high end and inexpensive imports at the other have hurt some of the sectors that are long known for expertise and quality. For example, the cutlery industry in Sheffield has been reduced from over 300 firms to around 12 in the past 35 years. Several cutlery manufacturers recently have expanded into other product lines, including kitchen tools, pantryware, and garden implements.

While the number of successful cutlery firms was declining, cutlery sales increased throughout the 1990s. Sales were especially strong in specialty product segments (e.g., multitool, pizza cutters, potato peelers, nonstick cheese slicers, under-the-counter knife blocks), with new product innovations initially targeting upscale channels. In 1995 and 1996, U.S. consumers demonstrated renewed interest in known brands of cutlery rather than private-label goods and were buying more expensive brands.

EXHIBIT 12   Cutlery Sales by Retail Outlet, 1996

Mass merchants	33%
Department stores	20
Specialty stores	15
Warehouse clubs	13
Catalog showrooms	5
Other[1]	14

Note: Mass merchants, specialty stores, and warehouse clubs have gained in the past 10 years, with the "Other" category seeing the greatest decline as a percentage of the total.

[1] Includes hardware stores, home centers, supermarkets, drug stores, and direct mail.

In addition to specialty product segments, many cutlery vendors had begun focusing on niche markets such as bridal registries and Internet shopping. Regarding registries, Howard Ammerman, vice president of sales for J.A. Henckels (USA), stated, "Catching consumers early helps to avoid the looming issue of affordability. [Bridal] Registries are our opportunity to gain the next generation of Henckels' cutlery customers. They need to know why they're spending the money for high-end cutlery, and that it's a lifetime investment."[1]

By 1996, some knife manufacturers and retailers also were testing the Internet as a medium for promoting and selling cutlery products. According to Brice Hereford, national sales manager at Lamson & Goodnow, "We were most intrigued by the demographics. The demographics of an Internet browser—typically a college-educated person with above-average income—fits well with the profile of most consumers of high-end cutlery. This type of person is much more likely to buy an $80 chef's knife."[2]

Direct Selling

Direct selling is a method of marketing and retailing consumer goods directly to the consumer without reliance on direct mail, product advertising, or fixed retail outlets. Most direct selling employs independent salespeople to call on consumers, mainly in their homes, to show and demonstrate products and obtain orders. The goods are then supplied by the company either directly to the consumer or through the salesperson who obtained the order. The direct sales industry exceeds US$80 billion in annual worldwide sales. The United States represents less than 25 percent of total sales. Leading international direct sales firms include Avon, Tupperware, Shaklee, Stanhome, Amway, and Mary Kay Cosmetics. The Direct Selling Association, a worldwide trade association, represents most leading direct sales firms.

Generically, direct selling is a push marketing strategy. Direct selling is an especially effective strategy for products and services with a high personal selling elasticity, where procrastination in purchasing is easy, and when the product is a household item that benefits from demonstration in that environment. Push marketing strategies have been effectively realized by direct selling firms entering newly emerging economies where distribution systems, supporting infrastructure, and capital access are limited. Further, direct selling jobs are often attractive to citizens in such economies. Direct selling often is seen as the ultimate in equal-income-earning opportunity, with no artificial barriers based on age, race, sex, or education. Independent contractors have flexible hours and can pursue earnings full-time or while pursuing an education, raising a family, or holding down another job.

Two general forms of direct selling exist: party plan and one-on-one. With the party plan method, a salesperson presents and sells products to a group of customers attending a party in one of the customer's homes. The intention is to demonstrate the quality and value of a product to a group of people, many of whom then will purchase the product. The party, however, is more than just a sales presentation and often is viewed as a socializing opportunity for busy people. The party host/hostess is principally responsible for identifying, qualifying, and inviting attendees. Tupperware and Mary Kay Cosmetics principally utilize the party plan approach. The one-on-one approach is more personalized and requires the salesperson to focus on the needs and economic demand of each potential customer. This approach is especially useful when customers may require detailed instruction regarding product quality differences or appropriate use of the product.

CUTCO's Major Competitors

Henckels.   J.A. Henckels Zwillingswerk Inc., a 266-year-old German manufacturer, is a dominant player in the upscale cutlery market and has a global presence in over 100 countries, with long-established subsidiaries in Canada, China, Denmark, Japan, the Netherlands, Spain, Switzerland, and the United States. Significant growth in sales over recent years has been attributable to increased accounts, the expansion of existing accounts, and a broadening of the company's customer base through the development of non-German sources for the production of moderately priced products for multiple channels under the Henckels International logo. Through non-German sources, Henckels has been able to offer additional price points: EverEdge, a never-needs-sharpening, Japanese-made brand has a suggested retail price of $29.99 for a seven-piece set; the Brazilian-made Classic and Traditional forged lines are considered a cost-efficient alternative at $149.99 to the German-made brands. The company offers over 10 brands in fine-edge and never-needs-sharpening cutlery, and its products are available in virtually every high-profile retail account worldwide.

Further stimulating demand for Henckels Cutlery has been the development of specialty gift sets, providing a prestigious presentation of commonly grouped individual items. Henckels also has taken a strong stance on advertising to build brand awareness, substantially increasing its television, co-op, and bridal advertising budget in recent years. Henckels also has attempted to be innovative through new packaging (e.g., clam sets) and in working with retailers to develop appropriate displays. (A clam set is one or more products in thermoformed packaging that allows a full view of product, shelf appeal, potential customer opportunity to grasp the handle, and blade protection. Clam sets can be pegged or self-supported on a shelf.) Numerous retailers and catalog firms have begun to advertise and sell their Henckels offerings through Internet Web sites. Henckels recently added new handles with an ergonomic "open-flow" design to comfortably accommodate each individual hand while maintaining safety.

In 1995, Henckels acquired German-based Wilkens tableware, moving the firm into the silverplate and stainless-steel flatware business. In 1996, the U.S. subsidiary doubled its available warehouse space to improve delivery performance. Recent estimates suggest that Henckels USA will have $70 million in 1997 trade sales. Karl Pfitzenreiter, president of J.A. Henckels, USA, explained, "We want to double our growth every five years, which we have so far been able to do by maintaining a 15 percent average annual growth rate in the U.S."[3]

Fiskars.   Fiskars, founded in 1649, is the oldest industrial company in Finland and one of the oldest in the Western world. Over the years the company has solidified a reputation as a premier steel and ironworks company manufacturing a widening range of architectural, industrial, agricultural, and houseware-related products. Main market areas include North America and Europe, with 1997 estimated sales of US$550 million (of which over 90 percent was generated outside Finland). Headquartered in Helsinki, Fiskars has subsidiaries and/or manufacturing in Canada, the Czech Republic, Denmark, France, Germany, Hungary, India, Italy, Mexico, Norway, Poland, Russia, Sweden, the United Kingdom, and the United States. Markets targeted for further development or new expansion include Eastern Europe, Southeast Asia, Australia, and Latin America. The company is considered to be very strong financially and a major innovator in its many diverse product lines.

The Montana adjustable bread knife and the Raadvad cutter for bread, cabbage, and lettuce were examples of recent innovations. Fiskars cutlery features a full tang with synthetic handles, ergonomically designed and weighted and balanced to correspond to the blade length. Gift sets are housed in handcrafted solid walnut boxes lined with velveteen fabric and intended as heirlooms. Individual units may be purchased in clam shell packaging. Fiskars's worldwide sales of cutlery products are estimated to be US$70 million. Products in its homeware lines include scissors, knives, kitchen gadgets, and sharpeners. Trademarks include Alexander, Fiskars, Gerber, Montana, Raadvad, Knivman, Kitchen Devils, DuraSharp, and CutRite. The upscale Alexander line features such gift sets as a four-piece steak knife set retailing for US$197 and a two-piece carving set at US$260. Fiskars products are carried primarily in upscale channels, but the company continues to target mass merchants with select lines within its wide array of products. The Consumer Products Group generated 59 percent of its 1997 net sales in the United States. A 35 percent jump in U.S. sales was at least partly attributable to a strengthening U.S. dollar.

In late 1994, as part of its overall expansion strategy, Fiskars acquired Rolcut & Raadvad, a supplier of kitchen cutlery and garden tools. In July 1997 a greenfield start-up, A/O Baltic Tool, began production of garden tools. In August 1997 Fiskars agreed to acquire the Italian knife manufacturer Kaimano S.p.A.

According to Stig Stendahl, the company president, "Our goal is to generate one-fourth of sales from new products which have been in the market for less than three years. Fiskars has gained a lot of positive publicity thanks to innovative product development and design."[4]

CUTCO International

In 1990, Vector Canada was established as the company's first international marketing entity. Patterned after the U.S. sales model of utilizing college students as salespeople, the international entry is considered to be quite successful. (Sales should approximate US$7.5 million in 1997.) Fueled by the rather immediate success in Canada, the company entered into the Korean marketplace in 1992 as Vector Korea.

CUTCO Korea.   CUTCO entered into the Korean marketplace with the student salesperson model that had been successful in the United States and Canada. CUTCO's strategy for entering Korea was to utilize U.S.-trained, Korean-born managers to oversee administrative operations. CUTCO Korea operated in the student salesperson mode from May 1992 until early 1995. Sales were nowhere near company expectations during this 2½-year period. With the student program faltering, CUTCO Korea began entertaining, in early 1995, the group selling (party plan) approach to selling.

Tae S. Kim, former Korean manager in charge of administration and finance and current national administration manager for CUTCO Australia, identified two major reasons for the lack of success of CUTCO's original college program approach in Korea:

1. *Cultural.* Korean college students do not value earning income during their college days in the same manner as college students in the Western part of the world do. Money is not a motivating factor for Korean students since their parents continue to provide total financial support. Mr. Kim described Korean students as less aggressive and uncertain about going into sales.

2. *Distribution.* Korean students generally do not own automobiles. The vast majority utilize public transportation (subway or bus), which does not make it easy to make sales calls.

Once CUTCO Korea understood and accepted the fact that the student model could not work in Korea, a group selling approach, with a revised commission structure, was quickly implemented. This model started in March 1995 with five female-managed offices. At that point, Korean sales exploded. The typical Korean sales representative is now a married, middle-class female age 20 to 50. The student program was abolished completely by the end of 1995. There were 21 female-managed offices by February 1996, and 1996 sales hit US$8.2 million. Unfortunately, due to the loss of sales offices, the temporary relocation of a key employee to head up a Philippine pilot office, and a very weak Korean economy, 1997 sales were likely to fall significantly below 1996 levels.

CUTCO United Kingdom.   In 1992, the company conducted a "college program" trial in the United Kingdom. An English-speaking country with a well-educated population exceeding 60 million, the United Kingdom seemed a promising market, with approximately US$1.4 billion in direct sales. Although sales were reasonably successful, high expenses (e.g., office and warehousing rent, recruiting ads) led the company to delay entry. Instead, in 1995, the company made a trial entry using a group sales (party plan) approach. This approach was not successful, and CUTCO's intention remains to re-enter with the college program in 1999.

Distributorships.   The company has utilized one independent distributor in Mauritius. Sales there are small but growing. CUTCO has tried out two other distributorships, but neither succeeded. In the distributor agreement, CUTCO sells to the distributor on wholesale terms and the distributor organizes, develops, and manages its own sales force. Chris Panus (CUTCO international finance manager) indicated that the company spent a lot of time selecting, training, and developing these distributors and wondered if the effort—versus opening up its own operation—was worth it.

CUTCO Australia.   In 1996, CUTCO entered Australia. The entry was modeled after Vector Marketing in the United States and Canada. Unlike the Korean entry, CUTCO Australia began with experienced CUTCO sales and administration people. Stephen McCarthy, national sales manager for CUTCO Australia, has been with CUTCO since 1986. Steve had a reputation as a top CUTCO sales manager. Tae Kim was transferred from Korea and appointed national administration manager for CUTCO Australia. In addition to Steve and Tae, CUTCO moved five American managers to Australia. Each of these five had been with CUTCO between 7 and 13 years, and each manages his own sales office in Australia. (Three offices are in Sydney, and two are in Melbourne.) Plans were to have a total of 21 sales offices by the end of 1998.

Australia appeared to offer a significant opportunity. According to Mark George, "Australia is a territory with 19 million English-speaking, qualified-income people and a university school break starting in November and ending in February. The culture is similar to that in the U.S."

With annual sales expected to be A$3.0 million by the end of 1997, CUTCO Australia had definitely beat the odds of the typical international startup. CUTCO products were virtually unheard of in Australia in 1996. McCarthy reported, "The Australians thought our method of marketing knives was crazy. Our solicitors, our accountants, our consultants . . . all said, 'Students? You have got to be crazy!' They could not have been more wrong! Australian students like being entrepreneurial and goal-oriented. The student model is working wonderfully in Australia."

McCarthy's goal is to make Australia the CUTCO hub for the Asia–Pacific region. He envisions an all-Asian office to manage Singapore, Thailand, and Hong Kong as well as a proposed entry into New Zealand by 1999. As with Canada and other countries entered, he says that the long-term plan is to turn management of CUTCO Australia over to the Australians.

CUTCO Germany.   In 1996 CUTCO began sales in Germany. Direct sales are extremely popular in Germany (almost US$5 billion), and other U.S. direct sales firms had experienced great success there. However, Germany appeared to be another country where recruiting college students would be difficult. Therefore, based on its Korean experience, CUTCO pursued a party plan format in Germany. The profile of sales representatives was similar to that in Korea. Unfortunately, a sales director heading up the German expansion left the company and sales had not achieved the hoped-for level of success, with 1997 sales around US$400,000 (approximately two-thirds of goal).

CUTCO Costa Rica.   A launch in Costa Rica was made in June 1997. Two managers, from inside CUTCO, were available for transfer. One manager, a Spanish speaker with a Hispanic background, was from New York; the other was from Puerto Rico.

According to Mark George, "We picked Costa Rica because it was a small market with a nice middle- and upper-class structure. It is a safe place to do business, and although it's a small country, we believe we can develop Spanish-speaking managers who can help establish markets for CUTCO in the rest of Latin America. People are well educated, and the literacy rate is around 97 percent. We utilize the university student model, which helps us qualify the recruit to be able to get into the market that can afford our product."

International Market Expansion.   CUTCO International was established in 1994 as a wholly owned subsidiary of ALCAS Corporation to manage the marketing and distribution of CUTCO products on an international basis. According to Fran Weinaug: "International operations are currently in the developmental stage." The management team had initially set a goal of wanting to open two countries each year for the foreseeable future.

Weinaug, George, and Panus all understood that a multitude of diverse issues could spring up in international markets. They had already experienced currency fluctuations, nontariff barriers, import duties, and language and gender considerations in recruiting sales representatives, plus variability in country laws for direct selling. Further, opening a market required a major outlay of capital. There are considerable cost-of-living considerations for expats (e.g., housing, cars, start-up funds). To facilitate market entry in places where language is a barrier, management has used an in-country sales manager and in-country financial officer. Selling a high-end set of cutlery isn't the same as selling plasticware or cosmetics, and using in-country managers requires a lengthy training process.

To ensure timely international delivery, CUTCO ships and warehouses product at each international site. Freight, warehousing, and insurance add approximately 10 percent to total costs. On a country-by-country basis, the company goal was to be at breakeven, covering annual costs, by its third year.

By mid-1997 international operations had yet to be profitable. Noting this lack of international profitability, Erick Laine commented, "Developing international markets is a very costly process, but we're convinced it's worth it for the long term—and we're grateful we have the financial resources to wait it out."

For the near term (in addition to a 1997 pilot test in the Philippines), Laine, Weinaug, and their management team are deciding among such diverse countries as Argentina, Austria, Brazil, Ireland, Italy, Japan, Mexico, Poland, Taiwan, and the United Kingdom. Longer-term markets under consideration include China, Hong Kong, India, and South Africa. (Exhibit 13 provides worldwide direct sales data.)

EXHIBIT 13   Worldwide Direct Sales Data

	Year	*Retail Sales (U.S.$)*	*Number of Salespeople*
Argentina	1996	1.004 billion	410,000
Australia	1996	2.02 billion	615,000
Austria	1996	340 million	40,000
Belgium	1996	111 million	13,500
Brazil	1996	3.5 billion	887,000
Canada	1996	1.825 billion	875,000
Chile	1996	180 million	160,000
Colombia	1996	400 million	200,000
Czech Republic	1996	75 million	70,000
Denmark	1996	50 million	5,000
Finland	1995	120 million	20,000
France	1995	2.1 billion	300,000
Germany	1995	4.67 billion	191,000
Greece	1996	41 million	25,000
Hong Kong	1995	78 million	98,000
Hungary	1996	53 million	110,000
India	1995	70 million	12,000
Indonesia	1995	192 million	750,000
Ireland	1995	19 million	5,000
Israel	1996	80 million	14,000
Italy	1996	2.12 billion	375,000
Japan	1996	30.2 billion	2,500,000
Korea	1995	1.68 billion	475,988
Malaysia	1995	640 million	1,000,000
Mexico	1996	1.3 billion	1,060,000
Netherlands	1993	130 million	33,750
New Zealand	1996	126.5 million	76,000
Norway	1996	90 million	9,000
Peru	1996	295 million	177,000
Philippines	1996	320 million	630,000
Poland	1996	155 million	220,000
Portugal	1995	60 million	23,000
Russia	1995	300 million	250,000
Singapore	1996	96 million	34,500
Slovenia	1994	58 million	15,500
South Africa	1994	330 million	100,000
Spain	1995	652 million	123,656
Sweden	1996	90 million	50,000
Switzerland	1996	245 million	5,700
Taiwan	1995	1.92 billion	2,000,000
Thailand	1996	800 million	500,000
Turkey	1996	98 million	212,000
United Kingdom	1996	1.396 billion	400,000
United States	1995	19.50 billion	7,200,000
Uruguay	1995	42 million	19,500
Total		79.5715 billion	22,291,094

Source: World Federation of Direct Selling Associations.

Weinaug, George, and Panus know that CUTCO management expects to move quickly into several of these new markets. During strategy meetings they have been fielding a laundry list of questions from the rest of the CUTCO management team. In developing a recommended sequence of countries for market entry (along with an overall entry timetable), the management team needs immediate answers to the following questions:

1. What criteria should CUTCO use to select countries for market entry?
2. Which countries offer the best market opportunities for CUTCO products?
3. What should be the composition of the new country's management team?
4. Should CUTCO continue to develop countries using both the party plan/hostess program approach and the college program approach?

End Notes

1. *The Weekly Newspaper for the Home Furnishing Network,* April 14, 1997.
2. *The Weekly Newspaper for the Home Furnishing Network,* February 26, 1996.
3. *The Weekly Newspaper for the Home Furnishing Network,* October 7, 1996.
4. President's Message on Fiskars Web page, 1997.

CASE 7–2
THE BACOVA GUILD, LTD.

As the director of marketing for the hardware division of the Bacova Guild, Ltd., John Walters was facing some decisions on new products that were not meeting sales expectations. The disappointing sales were of concern to senior management because the firm's growth was driven by the successful development and marketing of new products. The Bacova Guild was an innovative company, winning two *Inc.* awards in the 1980s as one of the 500 fastest-growing small companies in the United States. The firm had expanded operations to accommodate the sales growth, and it now faced a situation of having to successfully develop and market a steady stream of new products to cover a higher level of overhead and maintain profitability.

John Walters knew he faced a challenge. Product life cycles were getting shorter as competitors copied Bacova products. In addition, the product categories Bacova had entered with new products were proving to be susceptible to changing consumer tastes and economic conditions.

The hardware division, which had been very successful marketing decorative mailboxes, was also experiencing some problems with maturing markets. Division sales had fallen from $5.3 million in 1989 to $3.6 million in 1990. In response to the declining sales, the hardware division marketing group was beginning to market two new products designed to extend an existing line of outdoor decorative products for homeowners.

Postmaster, marketed in late 1989, was a complete mailbox system that could be purchased in one location to simplify the task of installing a rural mailbox. SignMaster, the newest product and the subject of this case study, is shown in Exhibit 1. It was a decorative house sign that could be used to identify a residence. Constructed of plastic in different shapes and decorative designs, it was sold with SignMaster house numbers made of peel-and-stick outdoor vinyl that the customer purchased separately and installed on the sign. Introduced during the National Hardware Show in August 1990, the product had received favorable reviews from the trade. Later in 1990, it was market-tested by a mass merchandiser and a home center store. The consumer sales had proved to be disappointing.

Bacova management believed that it was necessary to review SignMaster and its marketing strategy. Certainly changes would be made, but what was needed was not clear. Some Bacova employees believed that SignMaster had been priced improperly, while others felt that the packaging for the product did not have strong enough appeal for a self-service environment. Walters reflected that SignMaster had been introduced without trade or consumer promotion. With the end of 1991 approaching, Bacova management

This case was written by Lawrence W. Lamont, Timothy J. Halloran, and Thomas D. Lowell, all of Washington and Lee University.

Property of the Department of Management, Washington and Lee University. Case material is prepared as a basis for class discussion and is not designed to present illustrations of either effective or ineffective handling of administrative problems. Copyright © 1992 by Washington and Lee University.

The authors gratefully acknowledge the cooperation and assistance of Mr. Ben Johns and Mr. Patrick Haynes, senior management of The Bacova Guild; Mr. John Walters, director of marketing for the Hardware Division; and the employees of The Bacova Guild, Ltd.

Postmaster™, SignMaster™, and Accentbox™ are registered trademarks of The Bacova Guild, Ltd., Bacova, Virginia.

EXHIBIT **1**   **The SignMaster™ Decorative House Sign**

Shown: (top left to right) Ivy, Cardinal Chickadee, and Decoy; (bottom left to right) Floral, Classic Border, and Country House.

knew that decisions had to be made to finalize the marketing strategy and determine the role of SignMaster in the company's future.

History of The Bacova Guild, Ltd.

The Bacova Guild, Ltd., traces its origins back to 1963, when Grace Gilmore and her husband, William, began a small company known as Gilmore Designs, in New Bern, North Carolina. Grace was an artist, and the business centered on silk-screening her wildlife drawings onto paper which was laminated between fiberglass surfaces to form a flexible decorative panel. The panels were then used for television trays, card tables, and other gift items.

In 1957, Malcolm Hirsh, a retired businessman from New Jersey, purchased a "company town" in the Allegheny Mountains of Virginia. The town was named Bacova, an acronym for Bath County, Virginia. Later, in 1964, Hirsh purchased Gilmore Designs, relocated the business to Bacova, and renamed it The Bacova Guild, Ltd.

Hirsh transformed Gilmore Designs from a mom-and-pop operation into a small company that found its niche selling to retail gift shops and mail order companies. In the late 1960s he recognized that the fiberglass panels, originally used for indoor products, would also withstand the outdoor environment. This discovery led to the development of the Classic Bacova Mailbox, a product that eventually would become the cornerstone of the business. The Bacova Guild mailboxes were constructed with fiberglass covers attached to standard rural mailboxes. They utilized the original Gilmore wildlife designs and could be personalized with the name and address of the purchaser. Exhibit 2 shows the Classic Bacova Mailbox.

EXHIBIT 2   The Classic Bacova Mailbox

Source: The Bacova Guild, Ltd.

Financial difficulties led Hirsh to put The Bacova Guild up for sale in 1980. The Guild was sold in 1981 to Patrick R. Haynes, Jr., and Benjamin I. Johns, Jr., two former tennis professionals looking for a business opportunity. At the time of the purchase, there were 25 employees, a small building, and 900 customers.

The business was unprofitable in 1980, losing $40,000 on sales of $550,000. To become profitable, the partners aggressively pursued market penetration and product and market development. Bacova marketed ice buckets, waste baskets, utility barrels, and outdoor window thermometers that used the wildlife designs and the fiberglass lamination process that worked with the mailboxes. Haynes and Johns also developed additional customers through increased participation in gift trade shows and dealer recruitment. The firm achieved profitability in 1982, and by 1983 sales had grown to $1.7 million, while earnings reached $98,016.

In 1984, Bacova diversified into the textile industry. The firm developed inks and a printing process that enabled it to print the same traditional wildlife designs on indoor/outdoor doormats. The mats were an instant success with gift shops and mail order businesses that sold them with the decorative mailboxes.

The success with wildlife designs printed on doormats led Bacova to develop a line of products for mass merchandisers. The new line, branded Accentmats, used similar wildlife designs, but the mats were smaller and were priced for a market of lower-income

EXHIBIT 3	Sales and Profit History, 1981–90	
Year	*Sales*	*Net Income*
1990	$ 13,371,093	$ 39,539
1989	14,380,456	(301,914)
1988	15,766,699	866,314
1987	19,090,441	1,821,085
1986	9,599,765	807,943
1985	3,808,209	242,569
1984	2,420,683	150,197
1983	1,681,189	98,016
1982	1,116,058	64,637
1981	776,282	(10,840)

Source: The Bacova Guild, Ltd.

consumers. Within a short time, the sales of Accentmats made it the leading product line. A similar strategy was followed with mailboxes. In 1986, Bacova was successful in developing an inexpensive decorative mailbox that could be sold through the same retail outlets at prices considerably lower than the price of the original Bacova Classic Mailbox. The new mailbox line was branded with the name Accentbox. Like the doormats, the product was very successful and Bacova discovered the enormous sales and profit potential of distribution channels that reached the majority of American consumers.

Sales and profits grew rapidly, and employment and production capacity was expanded to meet the growing demand for Bacova products. The original Bacova facility was doubled in size, a new manufacturing facility was constructed across the street, additional production capacity was leased in a nearby village, and a small carpet plant was opened in Dalton, Georgia. At the end of 1987, sales reached $19 million, profits stood at $1.8 million, and about 200 people were employed at Bacova.

Bacova's success drew the attention of competitors, and they quickly copied its designs and products. During 1989 through 1990, sales declined as Bacova faced a slowing economy, maturing markets, and aggressive price competition in both hardware and textile products. The firm responded with new product development and added a product line of printed cotton throw rugs, molded plastic mailboxes, decorative mailbox cover kits that could be applied to existing mailboxes, Postmaster post kits and accessories, and SignMaster house signs. The new products helped, but as the sales and profit history in Exhibit 3 indicates, the problems persisted. For the 1990 business year, Bacova's sales had fallen to $13.4 million and the firm reported a profit of $39,539. Exhibits 4 and 5 contain the financial statements for the year ending December 31, 1990.

Bacova Marketing and Product Lines

The textile and hardware divisions of The Bacova Guild market the product lines which account for a majority of company sales. Additionally, Bacova has a gift line that includes some hardware and textile products marketed to retail gift shops and mail order companies at higher prices. However, management responsibility for the gift line falls within either the textile division or the hardware division, depending on the product.

The textile product lines include floor mats and rugs for indoor and outdoor use, while the emphasis of the hardware line is on outdoor products such as mailboxes. In

EXHIBIT 4   Income Statement, Year Ending December 31, 1990

Net sales	$13,371,093
Cost of sales	9,537,692
Gross profit	$ 3,833,401
Selling, general, and administrative	3,486,321
Operating income	347,080
Other income (expense)	
Interest expense	(338,585)
Interest income	13,556
Other, net	17,488
Net income	$ 39,539

Source: The Bacova Guild, Ltd.

EXHIBIT 5   Balance Sheet, Year Ending December 31, 1990

Assets	
Cash	$ 1,131,840
Accounts receivable	2,173,248
Inventories	1,437,035
Prepaid expenses	64,886
Total current assets	$ 4,807,009
Net fixed assets	2,518,282
Total assets	7,325,291
Liabilities and Equity	
Current installments	315,546
Accounts payable	590,413
Accrued expenses	139,221
Current liabilities	1,045,180
Long-term liabilities	2,151,792
Total liabilities	3,196,972
Stock	12,000
Paid-in capital	396,049
Retained earnings	3,720,270
Total equity	4,128,319
Total liabilities and equity	7,325,291

Source: The Bacova Guild, Ltd.

1990, the textile division accounted for 55.3 percent of Bacova sales, while the hardware division's sales were 28.1 percent. Sales of hardware and textile products to the gift and mail-order trade were 16.6 percent of total sales. Exhibit 6 provides a percentage breakdown of textile, hardware, and gift sales by product line.

Product development is conducted in Bacova, Virginia, where the firm maintains a design facility and support staff. When appropriate, Bacova also contracts with other firms for assistance with market research, product design, packaging, and the preparation of promotional materials.

EXHIBIT 6   1990 Sales by Product Line

Hardware Product Lines	*Percentage of Sales*
Accentbox	4.2%
Postmaster	15.3
Hearth Mat	6.6
Auto Mat	0.9
SignMaster	0.1
Other	1.0
Total	28.1%
Textile Product Lines	
Accentmat	33.2%
All American Rug	19.5
Braided Rug	1.2
Other	1.4
Total	55.3%
Gift and Mail Order	
Classic Mail Box	5.0%
Bacova Guild Mat	7.3
Other	4.3
Total	16.6%

Source: The Bacova Guild, Ltd.

Approximately 31 manufacturer's representative firms with a total of 75 salespeople sell Bacova products to mass merchandisers, home center stores, hardware stores, do-it-yourself lumberyards, department stores, retail gift shops, and mail order firms. Manufacturer's representatives earn sales commissions averaging 5.0 percent on sales of Bacova products. They are managed out of Bacova's New York sales office and showroom by a vice president of marketing and sales with assistance from three sales managers in the Eastern, Midwestern, and Western regions of the United States. Bacova also directs promotional literature, catalogs, and sales promotion to middlemen and is regularly represented at the major trade shows attended by its customers. Historically, Bacova has used trade shows to introduce new products such as SignMaster.

Textile Products.   The textile division markets decorative indoor/outdoor mats and cotton, braided, and berber rugs. The products usually are printed with attractive wildlife and contemporary designs and purchased as decorator items. The textile business is quite seasonal, and the majority of sales occur in the last quarter of the year. Popular designs are quickly imitated by competitors, and aggressive pricing is important to success. Bacova believes that its success in the textile market also depends on its design capability, printing technology, and ability to respond quickly to changes in consumer tastes. These unique strengths have enabled Bacova to market superior products at competitive prices.

Product Lines.   Accentmats, the best-selling product line in the company, are decorative doormats featuring the original Bacova designs printed on the mat. They are targeted at lower- and middle-income consumers looking for attractive prices. Distribution is through mass merchandisers, home center stores, and retail hardware stores.

The "All American" cotton rug is a line of indoor rugs printed with a variety of original Bacova designs. Available in four popular sizes, the rugs are made of 100 percent cotton with a nonskid backing so that they can be used in a kitchen, bathroom, or hall-way. The cotton rugs have been on the market since 1989 and are distributed through department stores and gift shops.

Two other product lines are the braided rugs and berber rugs. Braided rugs are made of 100 percent cotton, oval-shaped, and available printed with Bacova designs or un-printed. The berber rug is a new line made of synthetic fibers. It is also available with Bacova designs and a nonskid backing.

Hardware Products.   The hardware division markets mailboxes and accessories, specialty mats for automobiles and fireplace hearths, and house signs. With the excep-tion of the mats, most of the products are used as outdoor accents for residences. The specialty mats are marketed by the hardware division because the buyers for these prod-ucts purchase primarily hardware items.

Mailboxes and accessories are the hardware division products that account for the majority of sales. Bacova competes with three competitors whose products have low prices, comparable designs, and widespread retail distribution. Bacova believes it re-tains a competitive advantage because of the quality of its mailboxes, but the competi-tion has been successful in penetrating the market for decorative mailboxes. Bacova is moving to strengthen its position by marketing a full line of mailboxes and accessories.

Product Lines.   Accentbox is a line of metal mailboxes with a decorative plastic panel permanently attached to the cover. Fifteen decorative designs are available for the Accentbox, and personalization is available by special order. The Accentbox line is dis-tributed through gift shops and specialty stores to consumers who prefer an inexpensive decorative mailbox.

Postmaster is the newest line of mailboxes in the hardware division. The line in-cludes plastic mailboxes with and without decorative covers, snap-on mailbox cover kits to enable the purchaser to select and change the design on the mailbox, mounting plates, plastic posts, and an easy-mount stake that eliminates the need to dig a posthole. Postmaster is designed to be merchandised as a complete modular system and is dis-tributed through mass merchandisers, home center stores, and hardware stores.

Hearth and automobile mats complete the product lines of the hardware division. Hearthmats are used to protect surfaces in front of fireplaces and doorways. Automats are sold in sets of two and are designed to fit most automobile floorboards. The prod-ucts are constructed of synthetic fibers and are available in sporting, wildlife, and de-signer motifs.

Retail Gift Store and Mail-Order Products.   Historically, sales to retail gift shops and mail order companies were the foundation of the Bacova customer franchise. As new products were developed and distribution channels were expanded, the gift mar-ket became a smaller part of the firm's business. However, Bacova continues to market mailboxes and indoor/outdoor doormats to consumers interested in purchasing higher-quality, more expensive products through retail gift shops and mail order catalogs. The business is attractive because of the higher profit margins available through these dis-tribution channels.

Product Lines.   The Classic Bacova Mailbox and the Bacova Guild Mat line are the most important product lines marketed as gifts. The Classic Bacova Mailbox has a handcrafted decorative fiberglass cover permanently applied to a sturdy steel mailbox. About 35 different decorative designs featuring animals, wildlife scenes, birds, flowers, and sports motifs are available to consumers. The Bacova Guild Decorative Doormats are large rugged indoor/outdoor carpets with a nonskid rubber backing. The mats are available in different colors with a variety of attractive designs. If desired, the mailboxes and doormats can be personalized with the purchaser's name, address, or other message and drop shipped from the Bacova facility in Virginia to the consumer after the retailer has made the sale.

The mailboxes and doormats have strong appeal as gifts when consumers are looking for top quality and price is not a major consideration. Both products are distributed through retail gift shops and mail order firms.

SignMaster—a New Bacova Product

The most recent addition to the hardware division is SignMaster, a home identification product that enables consumers to identify residences with house numbers mounted on a decorative sign. SignMaster house signs are available in rectangular, oval, and tavern shapes with three Bacova designs for each shape. Three-inch house sign numbers made of weather-resistant peel-and-stick vinyl are displayed with the signs and selected at the time of purchase. Enclosed in the package is an alignment guide and directions to assist in applying the numbers to the sign. The house sign is 1/8-inch thick and is attached to the residence by using the double-sided adhesive mounting tape included in the package. Exhibit 7 illustrates a SignMaster Classic Border installed at a residence.

The development of SignMaster began in the spring of 1990, when management was looking for new products to extend the hardware division's line of outdoor accents. After a three-month period involving a collaborative effort between the hardware division marketing group and a firm contracted to provide product development assistance, SignMaster was ready for marketing in August 1990.

SignMaster offered a new approach to identifying a residence. Decorative house signs were generally not available to consumers except through a few mail order catalogs. The closest competitive products were the plastic, wood, aluminum, and brass numbers which consumers attached individually to their residences. The inexpensive plastic numbers were available individually or in packages of 25 or more, while the wood, aluminum, and brass numbers generally could be purchased individually from a point of purchase display. A consumer using the conventional method of numbering a residence with three numbers could expect to invest between $1.20 and $18 in house numbers, depending on the size and type of product selected.

Pricing and promotion of SignMaster house sign and numbers were important decisions. Bacova management reasoned that if the price of SignMaster to retailers was lower than it needed to be, Bacova would receive a low profit margin and fail to maximize the profits on the product. However, if a high price was established, there was a risk that it would not be acceptable to consumers and the product would not sell. Complicating the decision was the retail markup that the retailers in the distribution channels would apply to the product. Previous experience indicated that hardware chains, home center stores, and mass merchandisers usually used markups of about 40 percent.

Consumer behavior also would influence the pricing decision. Consumers purchasing the product at retail were required to make two purchasing decisions. The consumer had to select the preferred shape and decorative design and then one to four numbers, depending on the residence address. Thus, the cost to the consumer for the house sign and numbers was the total of the two purchase decisions. A second consideration centered on the fact that comparable products did not exist in the channels being considered for SignMaster. It was not clear whether consumers would simply compare the cost of installing SignMaster with the conventional approaches to numbering a residence or whether the product would be perceived as an entirely new and better solution

Exhibit 7   SignMaster Installed at a Consumer Residence

Shown in Rectangular—Classic Border.

to the problem. If the product was viewed as new, it was likely that consumer promotion would be necessary to develop an understanding of what SignMaster was before it would sell.

Costs would also be a factor in arriving at Bacova's selling price. Based on minimum production runs, the total cost for the house sign was $3.15, consisting of $2.60 variable costs and $0.55 fixed overhead. The house numbers had a cost of $.109 each, including variable costs of $.096 and fixed overhead of $.013. Management believed that these costs would remain unchanged over the next few years unless substantial changes were made in product design or packaging.

SignMaster was introduced without consumer or trade promotion in August 1990 at the National Hardware Show in Chicago. Bacova priced the house sign at $8.50 and the numbers at $0.50 each. Initial distribution was achieved in 10 Target stores, a discount department store chain owned by Dayton-Hudson, and one Lowe's store, a specialty retailer pursuing the home-center do-it-yourself business. Sales for the period September–December 1990 were $14,000. Consumers purchased an average of three numbers with each house sign.

Retail pricing was believed to be partly responsible for the disappointing sales. Pricing for SignMaster at the Target Stores was approximately $15.95, while Lowe's priced the product at $13.47. The house numbers were priced at $0.79. Late in 1990 both retailers reduced the price of the house sign to $9.95 in an attempt to stimulate sales.

Review of SignMaster Marketing Strategy

In January 1991 management decided to review SignMaster and its marketing strategy. After reflecting that consumer research had not been conducted before market introduction, management decided to retain an independent marketing research organization to survey consumers and determine their reaction to the new product. At the same time, management moved to address the pricing issue by using the research organization to assist the hardware division marketing group in the design and implementation of a test market. SignMaster was placed in retail hardware stores in six Virginia cities where three prices could be tested for consumer acceptance. The consumer survey research was completed by March. The sales results from the test market became available in November of 1991.

Research Methodology for Consumer Research.   A sample of 79 homeowners consisting of married couples and singles representing 46 different homes in 13 states was surveyed using personal interviews. The average age of survey respondents was 46, and the median market value of the homes was $140,000. After respondents had examined the house sign and numbers, they were asked a series of open-ended questions.

Survey Results.   The research confirmed that most consumers viewed SignMaster as a new product. Only 23 percent of the sample had ever seen a similar product. Most respondents believed that SignMaster would be purchased primarily by a female, although, as indicated in Exhibit 8, it was also cited as a product that might be purchased by a male or jointly or given as a gift. When asked to name the retail stores where they would expect to find SignMaster, respondents mentioned hardware stores, home-center stores, and mass merchandisers most often, as indicated in Exhibit 9. After examining the house sign in its package and the house numbers, respondents were asked what re-

EXHIBIT 8   **Expected Purchaser of SignMaster**

Purchaser	*Number*	*Percent*
Female	44	60.3%
Male	15	20.5
Joint	10	13.7
For others as gift	4	5.5
Total	73	100.0

Source: Independent market research.

EXHIBIT 9   Expected Retail Outlets for SignMaster

Retail Outlet	Number	Percent
Hardware store	42	31.3%
Home-center store	30	22.4
Mass merchandiser	27	20.1
Gift shop	13	9.7
Department store	6	4.5
Mail order catalog	5	3.7
Craft store	3	2.2
Lumberyard	3	2.2
Other	6	4.5
Total	134	100.0

Multiple response: Totals may not equal 100% due to rounding.

Source: Independent market research.

tail prices they would expect for each item. Exhibit 10 summarizes the responses for the survey sample. The significant difference in the expected price between male and female respondents was quite remarkable.

Preferred sign shapes and decorative designs were also examined in the survey research. Consumers were asked to express a preference for the shapes and decorative designs available for each shape. The most popular items were oval-Decoy, oval-Floral, tavern-Country House, and the rectangle-Classic Border. Less preference was expressed for the other combinations, although some had sold well during the market introduction in 1990.

In an effort to identify promotion opportunities, consumers were asked where they would expect to find advertising for SignMaster. Magazines were cited most frequently by both female and male respondents, although direct-mail and newspaper advertising was also mentioned. The responses are shown in Exhibit 11.

At the end of the interview, survey respondents were asked to remove the house sign from its package and carefully examine the product and instructions. Once again, consumers were asked to provide an expected retail price for a SignMaster house sign. The median price changed, with males now reporting $7.95 and females $10. In short, the perceived value of the product declined after the product was removed from the package and carefully inspected. Upon further questioning, respondents expressed concern about the strength of the adhesive mounting tape used to attach the sign to the residence,

EXHIBIT 10   Expected Retail Price (Median) of SignMaster House Sign and Numbers

	Respondents		
Product	Male	Female	Combined
House sign	$7.99	$10.99	$10.00
House numbers	0.59	0.79	0.69

Source: Independent market research.

EXHIBIT 11   **Advertising Media Mentioned for SignMaster House Sign and Numbers**

	Respondents		
Advertising Media	*Male*	*Female*	*Total*
Magazines	39.1%	38.7%	38.9%
Mail order catalog	13.0	16.1	14.8
Direct-mail flier	15.2	11.3	13.0
Newspaper supplement	10.9	8.0	9.3
Newspaper print	6.5	9.7	8.3
Television	6.5	9.7	8.3
Point of purchase	8.7	6.5	7.4
Total	100.0%	100.0%	100.0%
Number of responses	46	62	108

Multiple response: Totals may not equal 100% due to rounding.

Source: Independent market research.

the complicated instructions and multiple-step procedure for attaching the numbers, the durability of the product, and the time and patience required for installation. Respondents even suggested that the house numbers be included in the house-sign package to simplify the purchasing process. Management acknowledged that this would be possible, but to do so would require the inclusion of many more numbers than would be needed to identify a residence.

Some survey respondents also reacted negatively to the packaging used for the house sign. They asserted that it concealed the product and restricted the ability of a purchaser to determine the material used in construction and its thickness. Others felt that the light gray color of the package did not enhance the image of the product and would not be visually appealing at the point of sale.

The research was successful in identifying target markets for SignMaster. Although the findings are preliminary, three possibilities emerged when consumers were asked who they believed would purchase the product. First, young low-income couples who were owners or renters of inexpensive residences in suburban locations were mentioned as attractive prospects. Second, older retired middle-income couples living in traditional country homes in rural areas and small communities were mentioned as likely to be interested in SignMaster. Finally, the product was viewed as a decorative accent for second residences such as cottages, chalets, beach houses, townhouses, and condominiums in vacation and recreational areas.

The SignMaster Test Market.   In March 1991 John Walters decided to incorporate some of the consumer research findings into the design of an attractive display that would hold up to 12 house signs and allow consumers to visually inspect SignMaster before purchase. The point of purchase display (Exhibit 12) was designed to display a house sign with the numbers installed and feature three popular shapes and decorative designs. It was loaded with 12 SignMaster house signs and 100 house numbers and market tested in six hardware stores in small and medium-size cities in the state of Virginia. The test was designed to determine the sales response to three different Sign-

EXHIBIT 12   SignMaster Point of Purchase Display

Source: The Bacova Guild, Ltd.

Master retail prices and the acceptability of the display as a point of purchase merchandiser in hardware stores. Exhibit 13 summarizes the demographic characteristics of the test market cities, and Exhibit 14 describes the experimental design used to test retail prices of $8.95, $9.95, and $10.95 for the house sign and $0.69 for the numbers. The market test began in May 1991 and lasted six months. Each SignMaster price was tested in each store for a two-month period, and the sales made at each retail price were recorded.

Test Market Results.   The test market for the SignMaster conducted in retail hardware stores was reasonably successful. The new product sold best during the July–August test period, when consumers were likely to be making exterior home improvements.

EXHIBIT **13**   **Population Characteristics of Test Market Cities**

	Covington	Waynesboro	Harrisonburg	Buena Vista	Staunton	Lexington
Population (in thousands)	7.6	18.1	29.5	6.5	22.7	6.8
Median age	38.2	36.6	27.8	34.1	37.6	24.6
Age distribution (%)			30.2	10.2	10.9	39.0
18–24 years	9.7	9.3				
25–34 years	14.8	15.3	14.5	16.0	15.6	10.2
35–49 years	18.4	21.8	15.6	22.4	21.3	13.4
50 and over	35.7	30.7	23.9	26.1	32.5	24.2
Median household income	$20,113	$26,028	$20,047	$23,493	$24,726	$24,053
Income distr. (%)						
$10,000–19,999	28.7	22.5	28.0	24.6	22.9	22.4
20,000–34,999	29.8	30.5	24.6	35.4	28.6	24.2
35,000–49,999	13.9	17.4	13.9	17.2	17.7	13.3
50,000 and over	6.6	15.9	11.8	7.6	14.4	21.5

Source: *Sales and Marketing Management,* 1989 Survey of Buying Power, August 13, 1990.

EXHIBIT **14**   **Retail Pricing of SignMaster in Test Market Cities**

Test Period	Covington	Waynesboro	Harrisonburg	Buena Vista	Staunton	Lexington
May–June	$10.95	$10.95	$ 9.95	$ 9.95	$ 8.95	$ 8.95
July–August	8.95	8.95	10.95	10.95	9.95	9.95
September–October	9.95	9.95	8.95	8.95	10.95	10.95

House numbers priced at $0.69 each during entire test market.

Exhibit 15 summarizes the results for each two-month period of the test. The Country House was the most popular sign in the display, and a $9.95 retail price resulted in the most sales. Seventy-seven percent of the consumer purchases were made in the communities of Buena Vista, Covington, and Waynesboro, cities in which the economic base was primarily manufacturing and blue-collar employment.

Looking Ahead—1991 and Beyond

As John Walters and the hardware division marketing group pondered the future of SignMaster, they reflected on the brief history of the new Bacova product. In many ways, substantial progress had been made. SignMaster had achieved retail distribution, and even though the 1990 sales had proved disappointing, the trade had reacted favorably to the product. The consumer research, although conducted after the product had been introduced to the market, had been useful in developing a display that responded to some of the consumer questions at the point of purchase. The market test, conducted during the middle of 1991, seemed to indicate that the product would sell in a retail hardware store if it was properly priced and displayed. Yet to be considered was the desirability of offering retailers advertising allowances to build consumer awareness of SignMaster before the retail shopping experience. If management decided to add this promotional enhancement to the marketing strategy for SignMaster, the costs would re-

EXHIBIT 15   **SignMaster Sales in Test Market Cities**

	Unit Sales in Test Period			
Retail Price	*May–June*	*July–August*	*September–October*	*Sales (Units)*
$ 8.95	0	5	2	7
9.95	3	3	5	11
10.95	5	3	0	8
	8	11	7	26

Source: Independent market research.

sult in a lower before-tax profit margin on sales for the product. The display (excluding house signs and numbers) cost Bacova $7.52, while advertising allowances of $1.15 per sign probably would be necessary to motivate retailers to advertise the product.

Most of the information had now been collected, and it was time to reconsider the marketing strategy for the balance of 1991 and beyond. John Walters reflected that the market research would be helpful in improving the marketing strategy. It was obvious that some changes were needed because the 1991 SignMaster sales forecast of $250,000 (30,000 signs) would be difficult to achieve. Through the first nine months of 1991, sales were approximately $100,000 (11,338 signs).

Pricing was an important decision that needed to be finalized. The marketing group had to decide on an acceptable trade price for the house sign and numbers that would result in an attractive retail price for consumers. Promotion was another area of special concern. Research indicated that a point of purchase display was helpful, but it also seemed that some consumer promotion before the shopping experience would be desirable. Advertising allowances for retailers were one possibility, and if necessary, they could be combined with the point of purchase display that had proved successful in the market test. Whatever pricing and promotion methods were used, they had to be considered carefully because management was concerned that the house sign and numbers provide a profit margin on sales of at least 30 percent.

Packaging for the house sign was also a troubling issue. The consumer survey research seemed to indicate that improvements could be made to enhance the visual appeal of the product and simplify the application of the numbers. On the other hand, the market test results indicated that the product would sell at retail if it was properly priced and displayed.

Regardless of the marketing decisions on SignMaster, the hardware division marketing group knew that new products would be needed to meet the division's goals for sales and profitability. Experience with SignMaster seemed to indicate that a different approach to product development might be appropriate to assure success in the future.

Case 7–3
Pfizer, Inc., Animal Health Products (B):
Industry Downturns and Marketing Strategy

Gail Oss, territory manager of the Pfizer, Inc., Animal Health Group in western Montana and southeastern Idaho, was driving back to her home office after a day of visiting cattle ranchers in her territory. The combination of the spring sunshine warming the air and the snowcapped peaks of the Bitterroot Mountains provided a stunningly beautiful backdrop for her drive, but the majestic beauty provided little relief for her troubled thoughts.

The North American Free Trade Agreement with Canada and Mexico had hit the local ranchers particularly hard. The influx of beef cattle into the U.S. market from those countries, as well as beef from other countries (e.g., Australia) that entered the United States as a result of more lenient import restrictions in Mexico, had wreaked havoc over the last year. Prices of beef had declined precipitously from the prior year. Ranchers in the past had retained sufficient reserves to come back from a bad year, but this year things were particularly bad. The prices being offered for the calves by the feedlot operators were in many cases lower than the costs of raising those calves. Ranchers' objectives had changed from making a modest income from their cattle operations to minimizing their losses.

In this environment, ranchers were actively seeking ways to cut costs. Gail sold high-quality animal health products, often at a premium price. One way in which ranchers could cut costs was to scrimp on animal health-care products such as vaccines and antibiotics or switch to a lower-cost alternative. The current environment posed a particularly severe threat not only to Gail's company but also to her livelihood. Gail had spent a substantial amount of time and effort cultivating long-term relationships with these ranchers, many of whom she had had to convince of her credibility, given her gender. Because of the time and effort she had spent cultivating these relationships, as well as the camaraderie she felt with her customers, she did not want to see the ranchers in her territory go under. Ranching was an important part of the history of Montana; many ranchers had ties to the land going back generations. They took pride in producing the food for many tables in the United States and other areas of the world. Gail felt that Pfizer could use its fairly significant resources to help these ranchers. Merely lowering the price of her products (if that was possible) would be merely a Band-Aid solution to the problem.

As part of Gail's weekly responsibilities, she communicated via an automated computer system to her sales manager, Tom Brooks (also in Montana), and to the marketing managers at headquarters (in Exton, Pennsylvania). She knew she needed to report the severity of the situation, but more important, she wanted to encourage headquarters to take the bull by the horns, so to speak. She was pondering the message she would write that evening from her kitchen table.

Some of the information in this case has been modified to protect the proprietary nature of firms' marketing strategies. The case is intended to be used as a basis for class discussion rather than to illustrate either effective or ineffective marketing strategies. Support from The Institute for the Study of Business Markets, Pennsylvania State University, is greatly appreciated. This case was prepared by Jakki Mohr and Sara Streeter, University of Montana.

EXHIBIT 1 **Supply Chain for Beef**

| Cow/Calf Producers | → | Feedlot | → | Meatpacker | → | Customers (food service, retail, etc.) |

Industry Background

The supply chain (Exhibit 1) for beef begins with the cow/calf producer (the commercial rancher). Commercial ranchers are in the business of breeding and raising cattle for the purpose of selling them to feedlots. Ranchers keep a herd of cows that are bred yearly. The calves generally are born in the early spring, weaned in October, and shipped to feedlots in late October and early November. The ranchers' objectives are to minimize death loss in the herd and breed cows that give birth to low-birth-weight calves (for calving ease), produce beef that will grade low choice by having a good amount of marbling, and produce calves that gain weight quickly. Success measures include the conception rate of cows exposed to bulls, live birth rates, birth weights, weaning weights, loss from death, and profitability. By the time a rancher sells the calves to the feedlot, the name of the game is pounds. The rancher generally wants the biggest calves possible by that time.

Within a commodity market, basic laws of supply and demand are influenced by those in a position to control access to the markets. Four meatpackers controlled roughly 80 percent of the industry. Meatpackers have acted as an intermediary between the meat consumer and the meat producer. This situation has not facilitated a free flow of information throughout the supply chain, and therefore, the industry has not been strongly consumer-focused.

Exhibit 2 traces the market share for beef, pork, and poultry from 1970 through 1997 and projects changes in the market through 2003. The market share for beef has fallen from 44 percent in 1970 to 32 percent in 1997, a 27 percent drop.

Some of the reasons for the decline were

- Changes in consumer lifestyles (less time spent preparing home-cooked meals). An interesting statistic is that two-thirds of all dinner decisions are made on the same day; among those people, three-fourths don't know what they're going to make at 4:30 P.M.)

EXHIBIT 2
Per Capita Meat Consumption, Percent Market Share (Retail Weight)

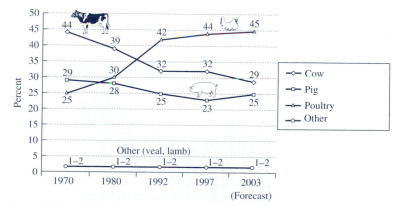

Source: USDA and NCBA.

- Health/nutritional issues (dietary considerations involving cholesterol, fat content, food-borne diseases, etc.).
- Switching to alternative meat products.

In addition, the pork and poultry industries had done a better job of marketing their products. During 1997, the number of new poultry products (for example, stuffed chicken entrees, and gourmet home meal replacements) introduced to the market increased 13 percent from the prior year, compared to an increase of only 3.5 percent for new beef products. And retail pricing for beef remained stubbornly high (although this high price did not translate into higher prices for the calves on a per weight basis to the ranchers, as discussed below).

Based on the historical data shown in Exhibit 3, the beef production cycle spans a 12-year period in which production levels expand and contract. As the exhibit shows, the amount of beef produced (bars in the chart, millions of pounds on the left-hand scale) increased through the mid-1990s despite the declining beef consumption in the United States shown in Exhibit 2. This relationship between production and consumption is consistent with other commodity markets, where there is an inverse relationship between supply and demand.

Some of the reasons for increased beef production in the mid-1990s were

- Herd liquidation: Low cattle prices coupled with the high cost of feed drove some producers out of business.
- Improved genetics and animal health/nutrition increased production yields; indeed, although cow numbers had decreased by 10 percent since 1985 (as noted in Exhibit 4, below), productivity per cow increased by 29 percent.
- Exports of beef increased sevenfold since 1985 (to 2 billion pounds); key markets include Japan (54 percent of export volume), Canada (16 percent), Korea (11 percent), and Mexico (9 percent).

Exhibit 3 also shows that the price the ranchers received for their beef cattle varied inversely with production (right-hand scale). Although calf prices were expected to rise slightly through the late 1990s and early 2000s, the prices paid were still far below the relatively high prices consumers paid at retail. One of the reasons given for the relatively low prices paid to ranchers on a per pound basis for their calves was the high degree of concentration at the meatpacker level of the supply chain. As was noted previously, four packing houses controlled access to the market. Some ranchers believed that this gave the packing houses near-monopoly power in setting prices both for what they

**EXHIBIT 3
Beef Production
and Price**

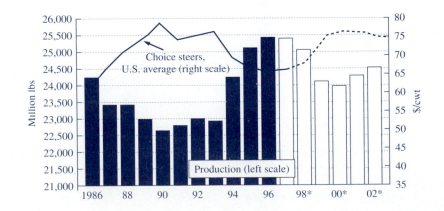

EXHIBIT 4
Total U.S. Inventory

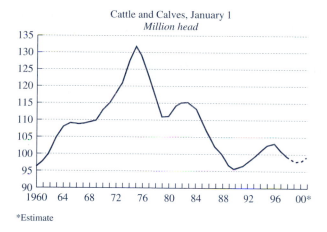

Cattle and Calves, January 1
Million head

*Estimate

would pay feedlot operators for the calves and for the prices charged to their down-stream customers (the grocery store chains). Although the U.S. government had investigated the possibility of collusion among packers, the evidence was not sufficient to draw any firm conclusions.

To further complicate matters, NAFTA, passed in 1989, had given open access to the U.S. markets to Mexican and Canadian ranchers. The lowering of trade barriers, coupled with weakness in the Canadian dollar and the Mexican peso, made imported livestock cheap compared to U.S.-grown animals. As a result, thousands of head of cattle came streaming across the borders. The flow was heaviest from Canada.

During the summer of 1998, ranchers had been quite vocal in drawing attention to the influx of cattle from Canada. Local governments were somewhat responsive to their concerns. Indeed, trucks carrying Canadian cattle had been turned back at the border for minor infractions, such as licensing. In addition, the trucks often were pulled over for inspections. A private coalition of ranchers calling itself the Ranchers-Cattlemen Action Legal Foundation (R-CALF) filed three separate petitions with the U.S. International Trade Commission (ITC) on October 1, 1998, two against Canada and one against Mexico, asking for U.S. government trade investigations. The group requested that antidumping duties be levied on meat or livestock imports from those two countries. The Montana Stockgrowers Association had been an early and steadfast supporter of R-CALF.

The ITC determined that there was evidence to support the charge that the Canadian cattle imports were causing material injury to U.S. domestic cattle producers. The Department of Commerce began to collect information on Canadian subsidies and the prices at which Canadian cattle were sold in Canada and in the United States. In the case against Mexico, the ITC determined that there was no indication that imports of live cattle from Mexico were causing "material injury" to the domestic industry in the United States. Dissatisfied with the response, R-CALF decided to appeal the case to the Court of International Trade.

Ranchers were doing whatever they could to minimize the impact of NAFTA on their livelihoods; however, some could not sustain their operations in light of the lower cattle prices. The number of cattle operations was declining. In many cases, smaller ranchers were selling out to their larger neighbors. This reality was reflected in the cattle inventory statistics shown in Exhibit 4.

The number of cattle kept by U.S. ranchers had declined from a high of approximately 132 million head in 1975 to just under 100 million head in 1998. As was noted previously, improvements in genetics and animal health and nutrition allowed ranchers to increase production yields even with fewer head.

Additional Industry Changes

Some of the changes that had occurred in the poultry and pork industries, including more ready-to-eat products and branded products, were expected to import into the cattle industry. Industry analysts believed that the beef industry would need to develop products that could be more easily prepared and develop branded products that consumers could recognize and rely on for quality and convenience. In addition, industry analysts believed that the beef industry would have to improve the quality of its products (in terms of more consistent taste and tenderness), as currently only 25 percent of the beef produced met quality targets.

The development of branded beef would require a tracking system from "birth to beef" in the supply chain. Such tracking would allow standardized health, quality, and management protocols as well as improved feedback through the entire production model. This change would also necessitate that the producers be more closely linked to the feedlots to improve the quality of the beef. Branded beef production would move the industry from a cost-based (production) model to a value-added model. Better co-ordination along the supply chain would ensure an increased flow of information from the consumer to the producer. Alliances between the cow/calf producer and the feedlots would allow ranchers to better track the success of their calves (based on health and weight gain). Such data could allow the ranchers to further improve the genetics of their herds by tracking which cow/bull combinations had delivered the higher-yield calves. As part of these trends, some degree of integration or vertical coordination will occur in the beef industry. Ranchers will have to participate to ensure market access for their product. Ranchers will have to think beyond the boundaries of their own ranches.

Pfizer Animal Health Group

Pfizer, Inc., is a research-based, diversified health-care company with global operations. Pfizer Animal Health is one of the corporation's three major business groups (the other two being the Consumer Health Care Group and U.S. Pharmaceuticals). The Animal Health Products Group accounted for roughly 12 percent of the company's revenues in 1998.

Pfizer Animal Health products are sold to veterinarians and animal health distributors in more than 140 countries around the world for use by livestock producers and horse and pet owners; the products are used in more than 30 animal species. Pfizer Animal Health is committed to providing high-quality, research-based health products for livestock and companion animals. The company continues to invest significant funds for research and development. As a result, Pfizer has many new animal health products in its research pipeline, a number of which have already been introduced in some international markets and will become available in the United States in the next several years.

As Exhibit 5 shows, the Animal Health Group is divided into a North American Region with a U.S. Livestock Division, a U.S. Companion Animal Division (cats, dogs, etc.), and Canada. The Cow/Calf division falls under the Cattle Business Unit within the Livestock Division. That division is organized further by product type.

The marketing managers for each cattle market segment work closely with product managers and sales managers to ensure that timely, accurate information is received from the field. Territory managers responsible for all sales activities report to an area sales manager, who in turn reports to the national sales and marketing manager. Territory

EXHIBIT 5
Pfizer Animal Health Organization

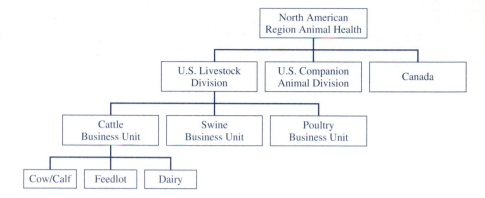

managers typically are compensated on a roughly 80 percent salary/20 percent commission basis. This percentage varies by salesperson by year: In a good year the commission might be a much higher percentage of overall earnings, while in a bad year the salary component might be a greater percentage of the salesperson's overall earnings.

Marketing Strategy

Pfizer's Cow/Calf Division offers a full range of products to cattle ranchers, including vaccines for both newborn calves and their mothers, medications (dewormers, antidiarrheals), and antibiotics (for pneumonia and other diseases). Pfizer's sophisticated research and development system has resulted in a number of new and useful products for the market. For example, Pfizer developed a long-lasting dewormer that was poured along the cow's back. This technology was a significant time-saver for the rancher, eliminating the need to administer an oral medication or an injection. Moreover, Pfizer had been the first company to come up with a modified live and killed virus vaccine, a significant technological breakthrough which provided safety in pregnant animals and the efficacy of a modified live virus.

Pfizer offered a diverse product line to cow/calf ranchers. Some of Pfizer's key product lines are compared to those of competitors in Exhibit 6.

Pfizer segmented ranchers in the cow/calf business on the basis of herd size, as shown in Exhibit 7.

Hobbyists in many cases are ranchers who run their cattle businesses as a sideline to another job. Traditionalists' main livelihood comes from their cattle operations. Business segment operations are large ranches owned by either a family or a corporation.

Pfizer's extensive network of field sales representatives visits the ranchers to inform them about new and existing products. Time spent with accounts typically was allocated on the basis of volume of product purchased.

Pfizer positioned its products on the combination of superior science (resulting from its significant R&D efforts) and high-quality production/quality control techniques. For example, although other companies in the market (particularly producers of generics) used similar formulations in their products, on occasion they did not have good quality control in the production line, resulting in batches of ineffective vaccines and recalls. Pfizer backed its products completely, using its Technical Services Department. If ranchers had any kind of health or nutritional problem with their herds, they could call on a team of Pfizer technical specialists who would work with the local veterinarian, utilizing blood and other diagnostics to identify the problem and suggest a solution.

EXHIBIT 6   **Comparison of Product Lines**

Company	Pfizer	American Home Products (Fort Dodge)	Bayer
Sales and profitability	10-year average annual sales growth increase of 3.8%; average for global veterinary market is 6.9%. Profit rate in 1997 was 8.4%; market share in 1997 was 15.3%.	10-year average annual sales growth increase of 7.8%; average for global veterinary market is 6.9%. Profit rate in 1997 was 11.0%; market share was 9.0%.	10-year average annual sales growth increase of 10.2%; average for global veterinary market is 6.9%. Profit rate in 1997 was 16.8%; market share was 10.9%.
Bovine diseases covered by product range	IBR; P1-3; BVD; BRSV; leptospira; rotavirus; coronavirus; campylobacter; clostridia; *E. coli;* pasteurellosis; *Haemophilus*	Pasteurellosis; enterotoxaemia; chlamydia; salmonella; IBR; P1-3; brucellosis; rabies; *E. coli;* anaplasmosis; tetanus; BVD; BRSV; leptospirosis; trichomonas; campylobacter; papilloma; *Haemophilus*	IBR; FMD; IPV; P1-3; balanoposthitis; clostridia; *Haemophilus;* BRSV; BVD; leptospira; *E. coli;* rhinotracheitis; campylobacter
Significant products for cattle	Comprehensive product line; anti-infectives have formed basis of product line for many years; vaccine businesses also very important; also sells a performance enhancer, virginiamycin; parasiticides, led by Dectomax, starting to make significant impact on sales; Valbazen anthelmintic; broad range of general pharmaceuticals.	Predominantly a vaccine company; antibiotics centered on antimastitis products; anti-infectives based on penicillins, tetracyclines, sulphonamides, and quinolones; parasiticides led by Cydectin; main products in general pharmaceuticals are anabolic implants for muscle growth.	Product range biased toward parasiticides, particularly ectoparasiticides, and antibiotics; overall product range is diverse; some mastitis antimicrobials; wide range of pharmaceuticals, but sales value of each product is limited; focus is more on companion animal market.
Strengths	Strong manufacturing capabilities based on fermentation expertise and capacity; global marketing coverage supported by strategic local manufacture; strong range of new products in early commercialization; broad product range with strength in companion animals	Leading global vaccine business; good international exposure; comprehensive vaccine product range; potential for growth through Cydectin	Growing market in expanding companion animal sector; solid in-house manufacturing supported by global distribution capability; business focused on key market areas
Weaknesses	North America still dominates turnover; high proportion of sales due to off-patent products; heavily dependent on performance of livestock markets.	Business with disparate parts requiring strong central focus; except for vaccines, product range is dominated by commodity products; R&D likely to be reduced.	Underweight in United States; lack of critical mass in biologicals; no blockbuster product in North American market; narrow anti-infectives product portfolio; current R&D emphasis away from new product discovery.
Percent of R&D to sales*	5	3	3
Position on quality versus price†	5	3.5	3
Price support of distribution channel‡	2	4	3

Source: Wood MacKenzie Animal Health Market Review and Veterinary Company Profiles, both done on a worldwide basis.

* Specific ratios are considered proprietary. Hence, a general rating scale is used where 5 means a higher percentage of R&D/sales and 1 is a lower percentage.

† 5 = focus on quality only; 1 = focus on low price only.

‡ 5 = strong emphasis on SPIFs (Special Promotional Incentive Funds) and price-related trade promotions; 1 = low emphasis.

EXHIBIT 7   Pfizer Market Segments, 1998

Segment	Number of Cattle	Number of Operations	Percent of National Cattle Inventory
Hobbyist	<100	808,000	50%
Traditionalist	100–499	69,000	36
Business	500+	5,900	14

Pfizer also was very deeply involved in the cattle industry. Each territory manager was given an annual budget that included discretionary funds to be spent in his or her territory to sponsor industry activities such as seminars on herd health, stock shows, and 4-H. Gail Oss, for example, chose to spend a significant portion of her discretionary funds to sponsor meetings and conferences for the Montana Stockgrower's Association which might include a veterinarian or a professor from the extension office of a state university speaking on issues pertinent to ranchers.

The majority of Pfizer's trade advertising was focused on specific products and appeared in cattle industry publications such as *Beef Magazine* and *Bovine Veterinarian.* One ad read, "More veterinarians are satisfied with [Pfizer's] Dectomax Pour-On" and went on to describe veterinarians' greater satisfaction with and likelihood of recommending Dectomax compared to a key competitor, Ivomec:

> Eighty-four percent of veterinarians who recommended Dectomax Pour-On said they were satisfied or very satisfied with its performance—compared to only 51% who were satisfied or very satisfied with Ivomec Eprinex Pour-On. . . . If choosing only between Dectomax and Ivomec, over three out of four veterinarians would choose to recommend Dectomax Pour-On.

Another ad read, "Calf Health Program Boosts Prices by Up to $21 More per Head." The data in the copy-intensive ad highlighted the fact that "cow-calf producers enrolled in value-added programs like Pfizer Select Vaccine programs are being rewarded for their efforts with top-of-the-market prices." Such programs are based on a consistent program of vaccinating animals with specific products and provide optimal disease protection. The programs result in cattle that perform more consistently and predictably in terms of weight gain and beef quality, resulting in higher prices at sale time.

Although the territory managers called on the ranchers (as well as the veterinarians, distributors, and dealers) in their territories, they sold no products directly to the ranchers. Ranchers could buy their animal health products from a local veterinarian or a distributor or dealer (such as a feed and seed store). The percentage of product flowing through vets or distributors and dealers varied significantly by region. In areas where feedlots (as opposed to cow/calf ranchers) were the predominant customers, 95 percent of the product might flow through distributors. In areas where ranchers were the predominant customers, vets might sell 50 percent of the product, depending on customer preferences.

Vets were particularly important in light of the fact that the overwhelming majority of ranchers said that the person they trusted the most when it came to managing the health of the herd was the veterinarian. Pfizer capitalizes on this trust in the vet in its marketing program. When the vet recommends a Pfizer product to a rancher, the vet gives the rancher a coded coupon which can be redeemed at either a vet clinic or a supply house. When the coupon is sent back to Pfizer for reimbursement, the vet is credited for servicing that product regardless of where the product is purchased.

Pfizer offers some trade promotions to vets and distributors, including volume rebate programs and price promotions on certain products during busy seasonal periods. However, Pfizer's competitors often gave much more significant discounts and SPIFs to distributors. As a result, when a rancher went to a distributor to buy a product the vet had recommended, the distributor might switch the rancher to a similar product on which the distributor was making more of a profit. If it was a Pfizer product the vet had recommended, the distributor might switch the rancher to a competitor's product. Pfizer historically had avoided competing on the basis of such promotional tactics, feeling instead that redirecting such funds back into R&D resulted in better long-term benefits for its customers.

As Gail pondered these various facets of the company's market position and strategies, she decided to take a strong stance in her weekly memo. It was time to cut the bull.

CASE 7–4
CALLAWAY GOLF COMPANY

As Ely Callaway walked through the sea of drivers, irons, putters, golf apparel, golf bags, and training devices displayed at the 2000 PGA Merchandise Show in Orlando, Florida, and toward Callaway Golf Company's booth, he noted that the eyes cast toward him seemed to express a greater sense of anticipation and curiosity than usual. As one of the most recognizable figures in the golf equipment industry, he had grown accustomed to his celebrity status in the golfing world and was aware that rivals and retailers alike anxiously awaited the new products his company typically launched at the industry's premier annual trade show. However, the drama and suspense surrounding Callaway's new products at the February 2000 show were very different from usual. Callaway had gone ahead and introduced its innovative Big Bertha X-14 irons and Big Bertha Steelhead Plus metal woods in January. The PGA Merchandise Show had been saved for the introduction of the highly touted and much anticipated Callaway golf ball.

Callaway Golf Company had become the leader in the golf equipment industry by developing technologically advanced golf clubs that compensated for the poor swing characteristics of most amateur golfers. During a golf swing, the clubhead travels in an arc around the golfer's body, making contact with the ball for 300 to 500 milliseconds. During this very brief period of contact, inertia is transferred from the clubhead to the ball, and the ball is propelled forward at a speed of up to 150 miles per hour. There are an infinite number of variations in a golfer's swing that can alter the swing path, causing the clubhead to strike the ball not squarely but somewhat off center, at an angle. The more a golfer's swing path deviates from square contact with the ball, the greater the loss of accuracy and distance is. A golfer loses approximately 12.5 yards of distance for every millimeter that the ball is struck off the clubhead's center.

Ely Callaway, the founder of Callaway Golf Company, understood the importance of the physics of golf, so much so that he made the phrase "You can't argue with physics" an early company slogan. Callaway Golf revolutionized the golf industry in 1990 by introducing an oversized clubhead called the Big Bertha that was more forgiving of golfers' swing imperfections. A Callaway executive stated in a 1995 *Fortune* interview that the company's objective was to design a club that would allow golfers to "miss [the center of the clubhead] by an inch" and still achieve distance and accuracy.

The company's high-tech golf clubs became so popular with golfers in the 1990s that Callaway Golf's revenues and profits grew by 1,239 percent and 1,907 percent, respectively, between 1991 and year end 1996. With the company's competitive position securely rooted and a line of innovative new clubs ready for a 1997 launch, Ely Callaway retired as CEO in mid-1996 and turned to Callaway Golf Company president Donald Dye to become the new CEO. Soon after Ely Callaway's retirement, Callaway Golf Company's fortunes reversed due to a variety of factors, including the Asian financial crisis, poor global weather conditions, strategic miscues on the part of Callaway's executives, and the introduction of innovative clubs by rivals. The reversal led to nearly an 18 percent sales decline in 1998. Callaway Golf also broke its string of 24 consecutive

This case was prepared by John E. Gamble, University of South Alabama.

quarters of growth in net income in early 1998 and went on to record a net loss of $26.5 million for the entire 1998 fiscal year.

Ely Callaway returned as CEO in November 1998 to launch a vast turnaround effort that included the development of new models of golf clubs and a $54.2 million restructuring program, which brought a number of operational improvements and cost-reduction initiatives. Callaway Golf Company returned to profitability and recaptured a great deal of its lost market share in 1999, but on February 4, 2000, the entire golf industry watched intently as Ely Callaway launched the company's new Rule 35 golf ball. Callaway's entry into the golf ball market had been vigilantly anticipated since mid-1996, when Ely Callaway announced the formation of the Callaway Golf Ball Company, and was considered by many industry participants to be the biggest event in the golf equipment industry since the debut of the Big Bertha. Callaway's managers and investors expected the entry to become a catalyst for the company's future growth. Exhibit 1 presents a summary of Callaway Golf Company's financial performance between 1989 and 1999.

Company History

When Ely (rhymes with *feely*) Reeves Callaway, Jr., graduated from Emory University in Atlanta, his father said, "Don't go to work for the family."[1] Ely Callaway, Sr., and almost everyone else in La Grange, Georgia, worked for the younger Callaway's uncle, Fuller Callaway. Fuller Callaway owned a number of farms, 23 cotton mills, the local bank, and the local department store. Heeding his father's advice, Ely Callaway, Jr., decided to join the army just before World War II. By the age of 24 he had achieved the rank of major and had become one of the army's top five procurement officers responsible for purchasing cotton clothing for the U.S. armed forces. At the peak of World War II Callaway's apparel procurement division of the U.S. Army purchased 70 percent of all cotton clothing manufactured by the U.S. apparel industry.

After the war Callaway was hired as a sales representative with textile manufacturer Deering, Millikin & Company. He rose quickly through the company's ranks by selling textiles to the manufacturers from which he had purchased apparel while in the Army. Callaway was later hired away from Deering, Millikin by Textron, which subsequently sold its textile business to Burlington Industries, at that time the largest textile manufacturer in the world. Ely Callaway was promoted to president and director of Burlington Industries, but he left the company in 1973 after losing a bid to become its chief executive officer.

Callaway had long believed that Burlington Industries' success was a result of its ability to provide customers with unique, superior-quality products. When Callaway left Burlington and the textile industry, he decided to launch his own business founded on the same philosophy. In 1974 he established Callaway Vineyard and Winery outside of San Diego. The well-known northern California vineyards scoffed at Callaway's entry into the industry and predicted a rapid failure of the venture. Not only did Callaway have no experience running a winery, no vineyard had ever been successful in the San Diego area. Ely Callaway understood the risks involved and was much better prepared to run a start-up vineyard than skeptics believed. He began by transplanting the very best vines from Italy to California and hired wine-making experts to manage the day-to-day operations of the vineyard. Callaway's strategy was to focus on a narrow

---

[1] *Inc.,* December 1994, p. 62.

EXHIBIT 1 Callaway Golf Company, Financial Summary, 1989–1996 (In thousands, except per share amounts)

	1999	1998	1997	1996	1995	1994	1993	1992	1991	1990	1989
Net sales	$714,471	$697,621	$842,927	$678,512	$553,287	$448,729	$254,645	$132,058	$54,753	$21,518	$10,380
Pretax income	$85,497	($38,899)	$213,765	$195,595	$158,401	$129,405	$69,600	$33,175	$10,771	$2,185	$329
Estimated ranking within industry —sales	1st	1st	1st	1st	1st	1st	1st	2nd	6th	14th	23rd
Pretax income as a percent of sales	12%	–6%	25%	29%	29%	29%	27%	25%	20%	10%	3%
Net income	$55,322	($25,564)	$132,704	$122,337	$97,736	$78,022	$42,862[a]	$19,280	$6,416	$1,842	$329
Net income as a percent of sales	8%	–4%	16%	18%	18%	17%	17%[a]	15%	12%	9%	3%
Fully diluted earnings per share[c]	$0.78	($0.38)	$1.85	$1.73	$1.40	$1.07	$0.62	$0.32	$0.11	$0.04	$0.01
Shareholders' equity	$499,934	$453,096	$481,425	$362,267	$224,934	$186,414	$116,577	$49,750	$15,227	$8,718	$6,424
Market capitalization at Dec. 31	$1,349,595	$769,725	$2,120,813	$2,094,588	$1,604,741	$1,127,823	$901,910	$245,254	—[b]	—[b]	—[b]

[a] Includes cumulative effect of an accounting change of $1,658,000.
[b] The company's stock was not publicly traded until February 1992.
[c] Adjusted for all stock splits through February 10, 1995, not adjusted for February 10, 1995, stock split.
Source: Callaway Golf Company annual reports.

segment of the wine market where competition with the established wineries was not as strong and barriers to entry were relatively low. Callaway Vineyard and Winery limited distribution of its products to exclusive restaurants that chose to stock only the highest-quality wines. The company made no attempt to distribute its high-quality wines through traditional retail channels. In 1981 Ely Callaway sold the company to Hiram Walker & Sons, Inc., for a $14 million profit.

In late 1982 Ely Callaway decided to enter the golf club industry and once again apply his concept of "providing a product that is demonstrably superior to what's available in significant ways and, most importantly, pleasingly different."[2] Callaway purchased Hickory Stick USA, a manufacturer and marketer of replicas of old-fashioned hickory-shafted clubs, for $400,000. From the outset, Callaway grasped the limitations of the company's hickory-shafted product line and realized that the company would have to extend its offerings beyond replicas of antique golf clubs to provide an acceptable return on his investment.

Callaway noticed that most golf equipment had changed very little since the 1920s and believed that many golfers would purchase technologically advanced golf equipment if it would improve their game. Ely Callaway and Richard C. Helmstetter —Callaway Golf's senior executive vice president and chief club designer—put together a team of five aerospace and metallurgical engineers to develop the S2H2 (short, straight, hollow hosel) line of irons. The S2H2 line was introduced in 1988 and was well received by golfers. The following year the company introduced S2H2 traditional-sized metal woods, and in 1990 it introduced the Big Bertha driver, named after the World War I German long-distance cannon. The Big Bertha was revolutionary in that it was much larger than conventional woods and lacked a hosel so that the weight could be better distributed throughout the clubhead. This innovative design gave the clubhead a larger sweet spot, which allowed a player to mishit or strike the golf ball off center of the clubhead and not suffer much loss of distance or accuracy. By 1992 Big Bertha drivers were number one on the Senior PGA, the LPGA, and Hogan tours. Callaway Golf Company became a public company on February 28, 1992. By year end 1992, its annual revenues had doubled to $132 million, and by 1996 Callaway Golf had become the world's largest manufacturer and marketer of golf clubs, with annual sales of more than $678 million.

Ely Callaway's 1996 Retirement and the Formation of the Callaway Golf Ball Company.   Callaway Golf continued to lead the golf equipment industry through the mid-1990s with innovative new lines of clubs. The company also introduced a line of golf apparel in 1996 that was available to golfers through an exclusive licensing agreement with Nordstrom. In May 1996, Ely Callaway announced that even though he would remain involved in the promotion of the Callaway Golf products, he was transferring his position as chief executive officer to the company's president, Donald Dye. Dye had been a business associate of Ely Callaway since 1974, when Callaway was in the wine business. Ely Callaway simultaneously announced that he and Charles Yash, Taylor Made Golf Company's CEO and president, would launch Callaway Golf Ball Company as a subsidiary of Callaway Golf. "We believe that there is a good and reasonable opportunity for Callaway Golf Ball Company, in due time, to create, produce and merchandise a golf ball that will be demonstrably superior to, and pleasingly different from, any other golf ball we know of," said Cal-

---

[2] *Business Week,* September 16, 1991, p. 71.

laway.[3] Yash, who had been the general manager of Spalding's golf ball business and who turned around Taylor Made with the introduction of the Burner Bubble driver, resigned his post at Taylor Made to become president and CEO of the new venture. Upon announcing his decision to work with Callaway, Yash commented, "This is an exciting and most unusual opportunity to develop a new and important golf ball franchise with Ely Callaway for Callaway Golf Company. As a competitor, I have been in awe of Callaway's accomplishments. As his partner, I look forward to the exciting opportunities and challenges Ely and I are sure to find in this new venture."[4]

Callaway Golf Company's 1998 Performance and the Return of Ely Callaway as CEO.   A variety of events occurred shortly after Ely Callaway's retirement that resulted in Callaway Golf's loss of market share in fairway woods and poor financial and market performance in 1998. The U.S. and international markets for golf clubs moved from rapid growth to maturity during 1997 and 1998 after a large percentage of avid golfers purchased titanium drivers and saw little reason to upgrade again until dramatic innovations were available. Global market maturity was compounded by the Asian financial crisis that began in late 1997 and made the exportation of U.S.-made products, especially expensive luxury goods such as Callaway golf clubs, unaffordable for many Asians. Also, heavy global rainfall caused by El Niño contributed to an overall decline in the number of rounds played around the world in 1998. In addition, many club manufacturers believed that the United States Golf Association's (USGA) discussions during 1998 to limit innovations in golf club design caused many golfers to postpone club purchases. The USGA had considered a number of limitations on club design but ultimately decided to bar only a "spring-like effect" in golf clubs. The USGA advised Callaway Golf that none of its products violated the new regulation.

The emergence of shallow-faced fairway woods had as much to do with Callaway's downturn as any other single event. Callaway had dominated the market for fairway woods since the early 1990s, when the Big Bertha line gained in popularity. By 1996 no other manufacturer came close to Callaway in building a loyal following among fairway woods customers. Even when Callaway users experimented with a rival's new driver, they frequently stayed with Callaway for their fairway woods. However, Callaway's dominance in fairway woods was severely challenged in 1997 when relatively unknown golf manufacturers Adams Golf and Orlimar Golf each heavily promoted a line of shallow-faced fairway woods that they claimed made it easier for golfers to hit a ball off the fairway or from a poor lie. The two challengers each ran a series of highly successful infomercials that demonstrated the clubs' performance and led to phenomenal sales growth for both companies. Adams's and Orlimar's success came more or less directly at the expense of Callaway. No other golf club manufacturer sold large volumes of fairway woods, and so when golfers purchased the new clubs offered by Adams and Orlimar, it was typically Callaway that lost sales and market share.

Callaway CEO Donald Dye took much of the blame for Callaway's failure to predict the popularity of shallow-faced woods and was also ultimately responsible for initiatives that took management's focus off of golf clubs. Under Dye, Callaway Golf

---

[3] "Donald H. Dye Given CEO Duties at Callaway Golf Company." *Two-Ten Communications, Ltd.,* 1996. www.twoten.press.net:80/stories/96/05/13/headlines/appointments_callaway.html, February 6, 1997.

[4] "Keeping His Eye On the Ball," *ParValu Stock Update,* 1996. www.golfweb.com:80/gi/parvalu/updates/03.html, February 6, 1997.

began new ventures in golf course and driving range management, opened interactive golf sites, created a new player development project, and launched a golf publishing business with Nicholas Callaway, the youngest son of Ely Callaway and a successful publisher of tabletop books. After a record year in 1997, the company's financial and market performance suffered immensely during 1998. In October 1998, Donald Dye resigned as Callaway's CEO and Ely Callaway returned to rebuild the company.

Ely Callaway's first efforts on his return to active management at Callaway Golf were to "direct [the company's] resources—talent, energy, and money—in an ever-increasing degree toward the creation, design, production, sale and service of new and better products."[5] As part of his turnaround strategy, Ely Callaway also initiated a $54.2 million restructuring program that involved a number of cost-reduction actions and operational improvements. During 1997 and 1998 the company had built up a large inventory of older-model clubs that were not sold before the latest clubs were shipped to retailers. Callaway management liquidated the inventory of older-generation clubs to generate cash flow and improve the company's financial position. In addition, the company divested its interest in noncore businesses begun under Dye and combined the administrative and manufacturing functions of Odyssey Golf and Callaway Golf. Callaway's business restructuring eliminated a variety of job responsibilities and thus resulted in the loss of 750 positions from all functional areas of the company. Callaway Golf Company's income statements for 1993 through 1999 are presented in Exhibit 2. Exhibit 3 presents the company's balance sheets for 1993–1999. The company's market performance is graphed in Exhibit 4.

The Golf Equipment Industry

In 1999, more than 26 million Americans played golf, among whom 5.4 million were considered avid golfers, playing more than 25 rounds of golf annually. The number of U.S. golfers was expected to grow 1 to 2 percent annually through 2010 as the baby boom generation age and had more free time and disposable income. In 1999 the typical golfer was a 39-year-old male with a household income of $66,000 who played golf about twice a month. Many women, juniors, and senior citizens also enjoyed the sport. In 1999 there were 5.7 million women and 2.1 million junior golfers aged 12 to 17 in the United States. Seniors accounted for 25 percent of all U.S. golfers in 1999. The average golf score was 97 for men and 114 for women. Only 6 percent of men and 1 percent of women golfers regularly broke a score of 80. Exhibit 5 provides the number of U.S. golfers during various years between 1986 and 1999.

Golf was popular in developed countries worldwide, especially in Asia, where there were over 3,500 courses and 16 million golfers. Most of Europe's 2 million-plus golfers resided in England, France, Germany, Scotland, Ireland, and Sweden. The sport was becoming popular in former Soviet bloc countries such as Croatia, Slovenia, the Czech Republic, Poland, and Russia but was not expected to grow dramatically until the economies of those countries stabilized. Russia's first country club opened in Moscow in 1993; by 2000 it had 550 members who had each paid a $28,000 membership fee for the privilege of playing the Robert Trent Jones–designed course. However, only 70 of the club's members were Russian. Some teaching professionals working in Russia projected that there could be 100,000 golfers in Russia by 2025, but in 2000 fewer than 500 Russians could be called avid golfers.

---

[5] Callaway Golf Company 1998 annual report.

EXHIBIT 2   **Callaway Golf Company, Income Statements, 1993–1999 ($000, except per share amounts)**

	1999	1998	1997	1996	1995	1994	1993
Net sales	$714,471	$697,621	$842,927	$678,512	$553,287	$448,729	$254,645
Cost of goods sold	376,405	401,607	400,127	317,353	270,125	208,906	115,458
Gross profit	338,086	296,014	442,800	361,159	283,162	239,823	139,187
Selling, general, and administrative expenses	224,336	245,070	191,313	155,177	120,201	106,913	—
Research and development costs	34,002	36,848	30,298	16,154	8,577	6,380	3,653
Restructuring and transition costs	(181)	54,235	—	—	—	—	—
Litigation settlement	—	—	12,000	—	—	—	—
Income (loss) from operations	79,909	(40,139)	209,189	189,828	154,384	126,530	68,416
Interest and other income, net	9,182	3,911	4,586	5,804	4,038	2,879	1,184
Interest expense	(3,594)	(2,671)	(10)	(37)	(21)	(4)	—
Income before income taxes and cumulative effect of accounting change	85,497	(38,899)	213,765	195,595	158,401	129,405	69,600
Provision for income taxes (benefit)	30,175	(12,335)	81,061	73,258	60,665	51,383	28,396
Cumulative effect of accounting change	n/a	n/a	n/a	n/a	n/a	n/a	(1,658)
Net income	$55,322	($26,564)	$132,704	$122,337	$97,736	$78,022	$42,862
Primary earnings per share	$0.79	($0.38)	$1.94	$1.83	$1.47	$1.14	$0.62
Fully diluted earnings per share	$0.78	($0.38)	$1.85	$1.73	$1.40	$1.07	$0.60
Common equivalent shares	71,214	69,463	71,698	70,661	69,855	73,104	68,964

Source: Callaway Golf Company annual reports.

The wholesale value of golf equipment sales in the United States had increased from $740 million in 1986 to over $2.7 billion in 1999. In 1999 the U.S. market for golf balls accounted for about 25 percent of the industry's wholesale sales. The wholesale value of the international golf ball market was estimated at $1.5 billion. Exhibit 6 provides wholesale sporting goods equipment sales for selected years during the 1986–1999 period. The growth in golf equipment sales during the early 1990s was attributable not so much to an increase in the number of golfers as to the introduction of technologically advanced equipment offered by Callaway Golf and other manufacturers, such as Ping and Taylor Made. Many of these technological advances made the game much easier for beginners to learn than was possible with older equipment. Additionally, experienced players frequently looked for equipment that could help them improve their game. However, it was expected that in the early 2000s sales of golf equipment would grow only modestly since most avid golfers had already upgraded their equipment and were unlikely to do so again unless major new innovations came about.

EXHIBIT 3   Callaway Golf Company, Balance Sheets, 1993–1999 ($000)

	1999	1998	1997	1996	1995	1994	1993
Assets							
Current assets							
Cash and cash equivalents	$112,602	$45,618	$26,204	$108,457	$59,157	$54,356	$48,996
Accounts receivable, net	54,525	73,466	124,470	74,477	73,906	30,052	17,546
Inventories, net	97,938	149,192	97,094	98,333	51,584	74,151	29,029
Deferred taxes	32,558	51,029	23,810	25,948	22,688	25,596	13,859
Other current assets	13,122	4,310	10,208	4,298	2,370	3,235	2,036
Total current assets	310,472	323,606	281,786	311,513	209,705	187,390	111,466
Property, plant, and equipment, net	142,214	172,794	142,503	91,346	69,034	50,619	30,661
Other assets	120,143	127,779	112,141	25,569	11,236	5,613	2,233
Total assets	$616,783	$665,827	$561,714	$428,428	$289,975	$243,622	$144,360
Liabilities and shareholders' equity							
Current liabilities							
Accounts payable and accrued expenses	$46,664	$35,928	$30,063	$14,996	$26,894	$17,678	$11,949
Accrued employee compensation and benefits	21,126	11,083	14,262	16,195	10,680	9,364	6,104
Accrued warranty expense	36,105	35,815	28,059	27,303	23,769	18,182	9,730
Accrued restructuring cost	1,379	7,389	—	—	—	—	—
Income taxes payable	—	9,903	—	2,558	1,491	11,374	n/a
Total current liabilities	105,274	184,008	72,384	61,052	62,834	56,598	27,783
Long-term liabilities	11,575	18,823	7,905	5,109	2,207	610	n/a
Shareholders' equity							
Common stock	763	751	743	729	709	680	676
Paid-in capital	307,329	258,015	337,403	278,669	214,846	75,022	60,398
Unearned compensation	(2,784)	(5,653)	(3,575)	(3,105)	(2,420)	(3,670)	(2,591)
Retained earnings	288,090	252,528	298,728	238,349	131,712	114,402	58,094
Less grantor stock trust*	(93,744)	(54,325)	(151,315)	(152,375)	(119,913)	—	—
Total shareholders' equity	499,934	453,096	481,425	362,267	224,934	186,414	116,577
Total liabilities and shareholders' equity	$616,783	$655,827	$561,714	$428,428	$289,975	$243,622	$144,360

*The sale of 5,300,000 shares to the grantor stock trust had no net impact on shareholders' equity. The shares in the GST may be used to fund the company's obligations with respect to one or more of the company's nonqualified employee benefit plans.

Source: Callaway Golf Company annual reports.

Key Technological Innovations.   The golfing industry had come up with four major innovations that made it easier for golfers to hit better shots and improve their scores: (1) perimeter weighting in the late 1960s, (2) metal woods in the early 1980s, (3) graphite shafts in the late 1980s, and (4) oversized clubheads in the early 1990s. Perimeter weighting came about due to the poor putting of Karsten Solheim, a General Electric mechanical engineer who took up golf at the age of 47 in 1954. Solheim designed a putter for himself that he found provided more "feel" when he struck the ball. Solheim moved much of the clubhead weight to the heel and toe, leaving a

EXHIBIT 4 **Monthly Performance of Callaway Golf Company's Stock Price, 1992–March 2000**

(a) Trend in Callaway Golf Company's Stock Price

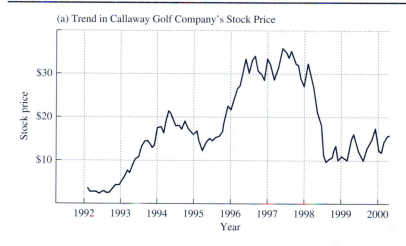

(b) Performance of Callaway Golf Company's Stock Price versus the S&P 500 Index

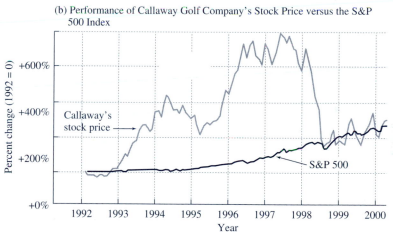

cavity at the rear and center of the club. Perimeter-weighted or cavity-back clubs had a larger "sweet spot" because of a higher moment of inertia, or resistance to twisting. The resistance to twisting reduced the gear effect of the clubhead and resulted in straighter, longer shots with irons. In addition to perimeter weighting, Karsten Solheim developed the investment-casting manufacturing process. This process allowed clubheads to be formed from molds rather than forged from steel, the traditional manufacturing process.

Solheim made his putters by hand from 1959 until 1967, when he left GE and founded Karsten Manufacturing. By the 1970s Karsten was manufacturing a full line of perimeter-weighted putters and irons that carried the Ping brand name. Solheim chose this name because of the sound the cavity-back clubhead made when it struck the ball. Karsten Manufacturing's line of Ping putters and irons was thought to be among the most technologically advanced throughout the 1980s and reigned as the market leader. Karsten Manufacturing was renamed Ping, Inc., in 1999. In 2000 over 95 percent of all irons and putters sold worldwide were perimeter-weighted.

EXHIBIT 5   Number of U.S. Golfers, 1986, 1991, 1993,
1995, 1997, 1999

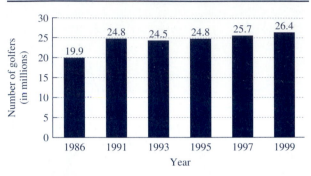

Source: National Golf Foundation.

EXHIBIT 6   Wholesale Sales of Sporting Goods Equipment, 1986, 1993–1999 (in millions of dollars)

Type of Equipment	1999*	1998	1997	1996	1995	1994	1993	1986
Exercise	$ 3,635	$ 3,400	$ 3,180	$ 2,890	$ 2,510	$ 1,825	$ 1,755	$ 680
Golf	2,770	2,800	2,749	2,463	2,130	1,793	1,490	740
Camping	1,700	1,620	1,590	1,500	1,508	1,275	1,225	580
Baseball/softball	340	340	338	350	349	348	328	240
Soccer	230	220	208	200	185	175	155	90
Tennis	220	215	235	240	235	259	380	255
Total sports equipment	$17,805	$17,350	$17,064	$16,395	$15,379	$13,877	$12,433	$8,250

*Estimated
Source: Sporting Goods Manufacturers Association, *1997–1999 State of the Industry Reports.*

Ping's investment-casting manufacturing process also made the manufacture of perimeter-weighted "metal woods" possible. Taylor Made designed the first metal wood, which, like the perimeter-weighted irons, had the advantage of a larger sweet spot than traditional clubs. Although they actually had no wood components, metal woods were so named because it had been traditional to use wooden clubs for driving from the tee and for long fairway shots. The hollow metal head made it possible to move the weight to the heel and toe of the clubhead, as was done with perimeter-weighted irons. Conventional wood heads were made of solid persimmon and had a uniform weight distribution.

The characteristics of the golf club shaft affected a club's performance almost as much as the clubhead did. Distance and accuracy were largely a function of shaft characteristics. Weak or overly flexible shafts could torque as a result of the swinging action and the weight of the clubhead. The torquing of the shaft created a gear effect that resulted in a mishit golf ball. Additionally, the flex of the shaft had the ability to increase clubhead speed and improve accuracy. Shafts with greater flex at the tip or clubhead end were advantageous to high handicappers because they helped produce greater clubhead speed at the point of contact with the golf ball, caused the ball to have a higher trajectory, and promoted greater distance. Professional and low-handicap golfers preferred shafts that flexed a few inches higher or nearer the grip because a higher flex point produced added control of the shot.

Graphite shafts were introduced in 1969 by Shakespeare but were not accepted by golfers because they flexed too much and overly dampened the feel of the club striking the ball. By the early 1990s technological advances in graphite materials, shaft design, and production had eliminated the previous torsion problems, and graphite shafts quickly gained acceptance by both amateur and professional golfers. Shaft manufacturers were using aerospace technology to improve graphite shafts that had as many as 14 to 16 layers of composite materials (carbon fibers, Kevlar, boron, glass-fiber-reinforced epoxy resins, and synthetic fibers). In 1998 graphite shafts were used in 86 percent of drivers, 77 percent of fairway woods, and 46 percent of irons. Because of the higher prices commanded by graphite, the dollar volume of graphite shaft sales exceeded that of steel alloy shafts by a margin greater than the unit volume differential.

Callaway Golf was the first golf club manufacturer to actually increase the size of the hollow metal wood and make the sweet spot bigger. The larger the clubhead, the bigger the sweet spot, but weight was the primary constraint in increasing clubhead size. If oversized clubheads were too heavy, golfers could not achieve as much speed as they could with lighter clubheads. Slower clubhead speeds resulted in shorter flight distances. The vice president of research and development for a golf club manufacturer described the challenge of trying to increase the size of metal wood clubheads as follows:

> The problem with a big driver is that you have to keep the total weight about the same as a normal-sized driver in order to give the same feel to the golfer. You can't build an overweight club or one that you can't swing at the same speed. A slightly bigger head pulls a little more drag through the air, but it's negligible. Making a bigger head is like blowing bubble gum. You have the same amount of gum but you've got to make a bigger bubble, so the metal walls will be thinner.[6]

Companies experimented with a number of materials, including stainless steel, titanium, silicon aluminum carbide, and thermoplastics, to find a way to increase clubhead size without adding weight to the clubhead or diminishing its structural integrity. By 1992, most manufacturers had discovered that titanium was the best material for oversized drivers because it was 20 percent lighter and 40 percent stronger than stainless steel. By using titanium, club manufacturers were able to increase the size of oversized drivers by about 30 percent. A golf club design engineer explained why material selection was vital to the structural integrity of the clubhead:

> Keeping weight to a minimum is the single biggest aggravation. Once you have a shape you're comfortable with, the challenge is to design a driver that will meet your weight standards. Everybody wants to go bigger, bigger, and bigger in drivers, but as you go bigger, your wall gets thinner. You could make a driver three times the normal size, but it would be like tinfoil. It would fold up and crush on impact.[7]

During the late 1990s, innovators such as Callaway Golf and Taylor Made began to use combinations of metals in the design of oversized metal woods and irons. In 1997 Callaway introduced a line of irons that were 85 percent titanium and 15 percent tungsten. A tungsten insert was placed directly at the center of the enlarged sweet spot of the titanium clubface to add weight to the portion of the clubhead that should actually strike the ball. The addition of tungsten to the clubhead concentrated 40 percent of the clubhead weight directly at the sweet spot and made it possible to create an oversized clubhead with a weight concentration designed to maximize the energy transfer from

---

[6] *Machine Design,* April 23, 1992, p. 32.
[7] Ibid.

the clubhead to the ball. Taylor Made introduced tungsten-titanium oversized clubs shortly after Callaway's introduction of its tungsten-titanium Great Big Bertha irons. In 1998, Callaway and Taylor Made introduced tungsten-titanium woods and Orlimar made clubheads that were manufactured from three different metals. Cleveland Golf introduced a four-metal oversized clubhead design in 1999. In 2000 each major golf club manufacturer had at least one oversized exotic metal driver with a graphite shaft in its product line.

Competitive Rivalry in the Golf Equipment Industry.   For decades, the golf equipment industry had been dominated by Wilson Sporting Goods, MacGregor Golf, Inc., and Spalding Sporting Goods. All three companies were very conservative in their approach to new product development, sticking to lines of the standard steel-shafted, forged-steel clubs that had been popular since the 1920s. They were caught completely off guard by the success of companies such as Ping, Taylor Made, and Callaway Golf. Amateur golfers readily accepted the technological advances offered by the new golf companies, and the market shares of the established brands of the three traditional industry leaders quickly eroded. An executive for one of the new manufacturers stated that Wilson's inability to introduce innovative products of its own had resulted in the company's market share diminishing to a "rounding error."[8]

In the late 1980s as many as 20 manufacturers accounted for about 80 percent of all golf equipment sales, but by 1997 the industry had already consolidated to the point where 6 companies commanded over 80 percent of the market for golf equipment. It was estimated that of the more than 350 manufacturers in existence, only those 6 were profitable. During the late 1990s industry consolidation stimulated attrition as many smaller club manufacturers left the industry. Even though longtime industry participants like Wilson, MacGregor, and Spalding were still in business and had attempted to introduce technologically advanced lines of clubs, they had all largely failed in regaining lost market share.

Manufacturing.   Most club makers' manufacturing activities were restricted to club assembly, since clubhead production was contracted out to investment-casting houses and shafts and grips usually were purchased from third-party suppliers. Most golf club companies offered two to four general models of irons and woods built around proprietary heads that were internally developed. Each clubhead model line was equipped with shafts of varying flex that were either proprietary designs or standard models purchased from shaft manufacturers. Grip manufacturers such as Eaton/Golf Pride and Lamkin offered a number of models, but club manufacturers usually chose to purchase a limited variety of grips from a single source, since most golfers did not have strong preferences for one brand of grip over another. Some club manufacturers used custom grips bearing the company name and logo, while others used standard grips.

The brand and type of shaft had a relatively important influence on golfers' perceptions of club quality and performance. Most golfers had a strong preference for either steel or graphite and some preference for certain manufacturers. True Temper had one of the best reputations in steel shafts and had dominated that segment of the industry since it had introduced the steel shaft in 1924. Most club manufacturers purchased standard steel shafts from a sole supplier rather than developing proprietary steel shafts or using multiple sourcing.

---

[8] *Fortune,* June 12, 1995, p. 110.

As the 1990s progressed, a larger and larger percentage of golfers' preferences shifted to graphite shafts for both drivers and irons. Graphite shaft manufacturers could easily produce a broad line of shafts with varying degrees of flex at a number of flex points. Many golfers were persuaded that the unique characteristics of graphite contributed to game improvement. Companies such as Aldila, United Sports Technologies, HST, Unifiber, and Graman USA were competent manufacturers of high-quality graphite shafts and had made it difficult for True Temper to build a dominant market share in the graphite segment as it had done in steel.

Some companies, such as Callaway Golf, independently designed their shafts, while others collaborated with shaft manufacturers to develop proprietary graphite shafts. Taylor Made's innovative "bubble shaft" was codesigned and manufactured by the respected graphite shaft producer HST. Cobra Golf was the only golf manufacturer to vertically integrate into shaft production and produce 100 percent of its shafts in-house. Cobra Golf was acquired by American Brands (renamed Fortune Brands in 1998 when its cigarette business was divested), which also owned Foot-Joy (a leading maker of golf shoes) and Titleist (the maker of the most popular brand of golf balls and also a producer of golf clubs and other golf equipment). Cobra's golf club shaft facilities were used to produce a portion of the shafts needed for Fortune's Titleist golf clubs.

Marketing.   As television networks aired increasing numbers of professional golf tournaments, endorsements by professional golfers started to play a major role in the marketing of golf equipment. The dollar volume of player endorsements was estimated to be three times greater than the projected total Professional Golfers Association (PGA) year 2000 prize money payout of $132 million.

Professional golfer endorsements had been instrumental in the success of some fledgling companies. In 1990 Cobra Golf offered Greg Norman shares of stock and Australian distribution rights to the new company's products in return for the golfer's use and endorsement of Cobra equipment. Norman accepted the offer and, after the company went public, sold 450,000 Cobra shares for $12 million. Norman received an additional $30 million from the sale of his remaining Cobra Golf shares when American Brands acquired Cobra in 1996. Norman's endorsement of Cobra golf clubs helped make Cobra Golf an almost immediately identifiable brand in the golf equipment industry and an attractive acquisition target. Fortune Brand's belief in endorsements led the company to offer Tiger Woods a $20 million five-year contract upon his professional debut in 1996 to endorse Titleist drivers, irons, and balls. Woods's endorsement of the company's newly designed lines of clubs resurrected the brand's presence in clubs, particularly in woods, where its new 975D driver became one of the top-selling clubs of 1999. Before Woods's endorsement of Titleist clubs, the company was primarily thought of as a golf ball company.

Tiger Woods's entry into the PGA set a new standard for endorsement contracts—the $20 million Woods received in 1996 for endorsing Titleist golf clubs and balls was surpassed by the $40 million he received for endorsing Nike apparel and footwear for a five-year period. In 1999 Woods signed a five-year renewal with Nike for $90 million. Tiger Woods also signed a two-year, $10 million to $15 million deal with Buick to appear in Buick ads and carry the Buick logo on his golf bag. Woods's five-year renewal with Titleist provided a $2 million annual fee to use Titleist balls and clubs in PGA tournaments; this contract was primarily a defensive measure for Fortune Brands since Woods's Nike and Buick contracts prevented him from appearing in Titleist advertisements or displaying the Titleist logo on his golf bag. Woods's success in landing large endorsement contracts had spilled over to other professional golfers to some degree, but in 2000 no other golfer had been able to garner contracts in the same range as those signed by Woods.

Most pro-line or high-quality golf equipment manufacturers distributed their products through on-course pro shops and a select number of off-course pro shops, such as Edwin Watts and Nevada Bob's. The off-course pro shops were quickly accounting for the largest portion of retail golf club sales because they carried a wider variety of brands and marketed more aggressively than did on-course shops. Most on-course pro shops sold only to members and carried few clubs since their members purchased golf clubs less frequently than apparel and footwear. In 1997 on-course pro shops carried on average 4 brands of drivers, 4 brands of irons, and 6 brands of putters, while off-course pro shops carried on average 12 brands of drivers, 18 brands of irons, and 17 brands of putters.

Pro-line manufacturers chose to limit their channels of distribution to on-course and off-course pro shops because they believed that PGA professionals had the training necessary to properly match equipment to the customer. Manufacturers such as Taylor Made, Callaway, and Ping all provided the pro shops with inexpensive devices that gave an estimate of the golfer's swing characteristics. The pro could take the readings from these devices and then custom-fit the golfer with the proper clubs. Custom fitting could be done more precisely with more expensive, specialized computer equipment, but most pro shops had not invested in the new technology. The Sportech Swing Analyzer aided in custom fitting by recording 12 swing variables, such as clubhead speed and path, clubface angle at impact, ball position, the golfer's weight distribution, ball flight pattern, and ball flight distance. The pro could use the fit data provided by the Swing Analyzer to select the appropriate club for the customer. Golf equipment manufacturers expected a larger percentage of golfers to demand more precise custom fitting from retailers in the future.

Pro shops generally chose to stock only pro-line equipment and did not carry less expensive, less technologically advanced equipment. Low-end manufacturers such as Spalding, MacGregor, and Dunlop sold their products mainly through discounters, mass merchandisers, and large sporting goods stores. These retailers had no custom-fitting capabilities and rarely had sales personnel who were knowledgeable about the performance features of the different brands and models of golf equipment carried in the store. The appeal of such retail outlets was low price, and they mainly attracted beginning golfers and occasional golfers who were unwilling to invest in more expensive equipment.

Callaway Golf Company

Callaway Golf Company's competitive strategy was rooted in Ely Callaway's philosophy that true long-term success comes from innovative products that are "demonstrably superior to and pleasingly different from" the products offered by industry rivals. Ely Callaway believed that due to the difficulty of the game of golf (there was tremendous room for variation in *each* swing of the club and for off-center contact with the ball), serious golfers would be willing to invest in high-quality, premium-priced equipment, such as the Big Bertha driver and the titanium Great Big Bertha driver, if such clubs could improve their game by being more forgiving of a less than optimum swing. Since the introduction of Callaway's S2H2 line of irons in 1988, the company had sought to develop, manufacture, and market the most technologically advanced golf clubs available. In addition, Richard Helmstetter and his team of engineers sought quantum leaps in club performance rather than incremental improvements with each new line of clubs introduced by the company.

Callaway's "Demonstrably Superior and Pleasingly Different" Value Chain.
Callaway Golf Company's ability to develop "demonstrably superior and pleasingly different" golf clubs was a result of activities performed by the company throughout its value chain. Callaway's differentiation was achieved through both its unique value chain and its ability to outexecute its rivals where value chain similarities existed.

Product Development and the Helmstetter Test Center.   When Ely Callaway purchased Hickory Stick USA, he believed strongly that developing "demonstrably superior and pleasingly different" golf clubs would be more closely related to the company's physics-oriented R&D than would a focus on cosmetics. Richard Helmstetter and his engineering team were critical to the execution of Callaway's competitive strategy. As of 2000 Callaway Golf had consistently outspent its rivals on R&D. In 1999 alone the company spent $27 million on research and development related to its golf club business, more than most of its key rivals' combined R&D budgets. The company's R&D efforts allowed it to beat its competitors to the market with new innovation continually. Callaway's engineers developed the first oversize driver in 1990, were the first to make clubheads even larger by using titanium, and were the first to use a combination of materials (titanium and tungsten) in clubhead design.

Callaway Golf opened the Richard C. Helmstetter Test Center in 1994 to support its research and product development efforts. The test center was about a mile from Callaway's main campus and included a laboratory and a golfing area. The test center laboratory was home to Helmstetter's engineers, who worked both on teams and individually to develop new models of clubheads and shafts. Callaway's products were designed on powerful workstations running computer-aided design (CAD) software similar to that used in the aerospace industry. The CAD software allowed engineers not only to design new clubheads and shafts but also to conduct aerodynamic and strength testing in a simulated environment. Actual physical models could be created from the computer-generated images through the use of numerically controlled systems. The center's "destruction and durability" laboratory used robots and air cannons to establish minimum thresholds of strength and durability for prototypes of new models of clubheads and shafts.

The club-fitting and specifications area of the test center used the company's Callaway Performance Analysis System to match equipment to a golfer's swing characteristics. The internally developed proprietary video and computer system used stereo imaging techniques to capture a sequence of eight multiple exposures of the clubhead and ball at various time intervals immediately before and after a golfer hit the ball into a net approximately 10 feet from where it was struck. Callaway's proprietary computer software analyzed the video images of the clubhead's approach to the ball and the ball's rotational patterns over its first few feet of flight to make a variety of calculations needed to project the ball's ultimate path. The projected path was displayed on a six-foot video screen that showed the ball's flight along the 18th fairway at Pebble Beach. The computer system also recorded the clubhead speed, ball velocity, side spin, back spin, attack angle, and launch angle to calculate the efficiency rating, carry, roll, total distance, and dispersion (deviation from a straight path). All these statistics were projected on the screen, along with the image of the ball's flight down the fairway. The equipment allowed the company to build a set of clubs for the touring professional that had the perfect swing weight, frequency, loft, lie, and length to maximize distance and accuracy.

The Helmstetter Test Center's golfing area was an 8.1-acre outdoor testing facility that included three putting and chipping greens, a deep pot bunker, a shallow fairway bunker, and a 310-yard fairway that was 80 yards wide at its narrowest point. Sensors along the fairway recorded the distance and dispersion of any ball landing in the test area. Atmospheric conditions such as wind speed, direction, temperature, barometric pressure, humidity, and dew point were recorded by three weather stations located around the test site. The facility also included an artificial tee box and green that accurately simulated a real green. Ball reaction on the simulated green was almost identical to that on the other three greens and allowed the company to continue testing while the natural test site was being irrigated or mowed.

The Helmstetter Test Center had two primary uses: It provided an ideal place to custom-fit clubs for the touring pros who used Callaway equipment, and it allowed Callaway R&D staff to test new products during their developmental stage. Once a professional's new clubs were fitted using the video and computer capabilities of the Callaway Performance Analysis System, the touring pro could then use the golfing area to hit balls and fine-tune his or her clubs by requesting minor modifications to the clubhead or shaft. Callaway included nontouring professionals in addition to engineers among its R&D staff. The golfing staff was critical to the product development process since engineers were able to refine new prototypes based on the feedback and recommendations of Callaway's R&D staff golfers. Callaway's engineers also tested prototypes with robots to evaluate the distance and accuracy of the club, but only a human could evaluate the feel of a golf club striking a ball.

Callaway's Purchasing and Production Processes.   Once its clubheads were designed on a CAD system and tested in the Helmstetter Center, stainless-steel master plates were cut by Callaway to the exact specifications called for by the system. Each clubhead mold was made by pouring liquid wax between the stainless-steel master plates. The wax clubheads were removed from the master plates and sprayed with a mixture of highly heat-resistant material. The wax was melted out of these heat-resistant molds, leaving a hollow core. The hollow molds were then sent to an investment-casting house, where stainless steel or titanium was poured into the molds. The casting house then broke away the mold and welded, sanded, and painted the clubheads before sending them to Callaway for further assembly.

Callaway Golf used five investment-casting houses, all of which underwent extensive screening and were closely monitored during the casting process. Callaway management believed that it was particularly important to supervise the casting process since poor casting could produce clubhead inconsistencies that could lead to poor performance or product failure. Callaway had entered into a joint venture with Sturm, Ruger & Company in 1995 to produce its clubheads but had since recognized that quality clubheads could be obtained through outsourcing. Even though Callaway Golf was certain it would obtain high-quality clubheads through its sourcing agreements, it made daily inspections of incoming clubhead shipments, using the materials analysis and durability-testing capabilities of the Helmstetter Center.

Like Callaway's clubheads, all of its shafts were designed and tested at the Helmstetter Center. Callaway manufactured all prototype shafts by hand at the testing center but contracted shaft production out to independent shaft manufacturers once specifications were established for the various graphite shafts used in its product line. As with clubheads, shafts were drawn from incoming shipments and tested at the company's R&D facility. Steel shafts were contracted out and inspected in a similar fashion. Callaway had produced as much as 50 percent of its graphite shafts internally during the late 1990s but outsourced 100 percent of its shaft requirements in 2000.

Callaway Golf's cell manufacturing process allowed the company to include quality control inspections throughout each club's assembly. In addition, the assembly plant was highly automated, with all processes requiring very tight tolerances performed by computer-controlled machinery. For example, the drilling necessary to produce Callaway's tapered bore-thru hosels was done by a series of precision drill presses that ensured that each hosel was drilled at the correct angle. Once the hosel had been drilled through, the clubhead moved to a production station that checked the lie and loft angles of the club and made any necessary corrections by slightly bending the clubhead to the proper angle.

Each shaft was inspected for fractures before insertion into the clubhead, and then the entire assembled club was weighed to assess the swing weight. Callaway production workers could choose between medallions of four different weights to bring a finished iron to the exact specified swing weight. The chosen medallion was permanently affixed to the back of the clubhead with a press. Swing weights for assembled woods were brought to their specifications by inserting epoxy through a small hole in the rear of the clubhead.

After undergoing a baking process that dried the glue used to attach the shaft to the clubhead, each club was fitted with a grip using a laser alignment device, airbrushed with details such as the club number and Callaway trademarks, and then visually inspected for blemishes or other imperfections. Each finished club was wrapped by hand to protect its finish during shipping.

Sales and Customer Service.   New product development at Callaway Golf Company was a cross-functional effort that included not only the R&D staff but also the company's sales and advertising staffs. Callaway sales and advertising personnel would evaluate new designs created by the company's aerospace engineers and recommend design changes based on their knowledge of the market. Once a new design was settled on, Callaway's sales force and internal advertising staff would create a name for the new product line, an advertising campaign, and promotional materials that would accompany the product launch in parallel with the R&D staff's developmental and testing processes.

Callaway's customer service department was viewed as a critical component of the company's overall level of differentiation. The customer service staff was made up of experienced employees who were offered a generous compensation package that included commissions for superior performance in meeting the needs of Callaway's retailers and consumers. Many of Callaway's rivals viewed customer service as a low-value adding activity and typically made customer service a place for entry-level employees to become acquainted with the business. Each of Callaway Golf's customer service representatives received eight weeks of training before being allowed to handle a customer service inquiry. No other company in the industry provided more than three weeks of training to its customer service personnel. In addition to providing extensive training, Callaway promoted a team-oriented atmosphere that allowed the company's knowledge base to expand through the mentoring of newer employees by longtime customer service employees.

The entire customer service staff was empowered to make a final decision regarding a consumer or retailer complaint or warranty claim. Callaway customer service personnel were allowed to make decisions that might be pushed to the CEO at some other golf equipment companies. For example, if a golfer was vacationing and had a problem with a club, a customer service staff member could instruct the consumer to visit a local retailer to pick up a replacement club. If the consumer was out of the country and was not near a Callaway retailer, the Callaway employee was allowed to send a new club to the customer via Federal Express. Callaway customer service staff members also were known to send a gift to club owners who had experienced problems with Callaway equipment. Callaway's two-year warranty on all of its products entitled the owner to replace any defective product with a new product rather than return the product for a repair. In addition, Callaway generally chose to replace defective or broken clubs for the life of the club rather than stick to its two-year warranty period. A Callaway sales executive remarked, "A bad experience with a Callaway product usually winds up making someone a Callaway customer for life."

Callaway Golf's Product Line.   *Metal Woods.*   Callaway Golf's Big Bertha driver was the most innovative club in the industry when it was introduced in 1990. Its key features were a bigger clubhead, a bigger sweet spot, and a longer shaft, all of which helped improve the consistency with which a golfer could drive the ball off the tee. Callaway wasted no time in capitalizing on the explosive popularity of its new driver; company managers understood that once a driver developed a following among golfers, those golfers usually wanted other woods to match it. The company subsequently introduced a series of fairway woods—a 2 wood, a 3 wood, a 5 wood, two styles of 7 woods, a 9 wood, and an 11 wood—to complement the Big Bertha driver. Many golfers rushed to buy not only the Big Bertha driver but also the company's other Big Bertha metal woods; it was common for Big Bertha enthusiasts to have three or four of the Big Bertha fairway woods in their bag.

Four years later the company again moved to set itself apart from rival equipment makers (most of whom had by then come out with imitative versions of the Big Bertha line) by introducing the Great Big Bertha driver, made out of strong, lightweight titanium. The driver had a clubhead 30 percent larger than the original Big Bertha driver but was just as light because of the substitution of titanium for stainless steel in the clubhead and the use of a graphite shaft; the Great Big Bertha (GBB) was the industry's most technologically advanced golf club and retailed for $500 (a heretofore unheard-of price for a single golf club).

Callaway's introduction of its titanium Biggest Big Bertha in 1997 again caught industry rivals off guard as they moved to match the size of the GBB. The Biggest Big Bertha (BBB) was 15 percent larger than the titanium Great Big Bertha (and the titanium clubs produced by Callaway's rivals) and was equipped with a 46-inch lightweight shaft. The total weight of the BBB was less than the total weight of the titanium GBB and the stainless steel Big Bertha drivers, which had 45- and 44-inch shafts, respectively.

The size of Callaway woods began to decrease with the introduction of its Big Bertha (BB) Steelhead metal woods in 1998 and Hawk Eye titanium metal woods in 1999. The BB Steelhead line was created in response to the popularity of the shallow-faced woods introduced by Orlimar and Adams in 1998. BB Steelhead drivers and fairway woods had a lower center of gravity than did GBB and BBB woods but had a higher profile than did Adams and Orlimar woods. The BB Steelhead line incorporated the best features of both competing club designs by maintaining a very low center of gravity but having a larger clubface, which prevented the golfer from hitting below the ball, as was frequently done by amateur golfers using shallow-faced woods.

The BB Steelhead Plus was introduced in January 2000 as an improvement of the BB Steelhead line of drivers and fairway woods. Like the BB Steelhead line, the BB Steelhead Plus included a precision-cast steel chip to lower the club's center of gravity but featured variable clubface thickness that optimized energy transfer between the clubhead and the ball. Callaway's Variable Face Thickness Technology, developed through computer modeling and player testing, allowed the company to vary the clubface thickness to maximize perimeter weighting while keeping an elliptical area near the center of the clubface relatively thick. This thickness directly at the sweet spot of the clubface provided more energy transfer when a ball was well struck, while the perimeter weighting and thin walls near the outside edges of the clubface provided more forgiveness if a ball was mishit. Callaway's BB Steelhead Plus metal woods and Variable Face Thickness Technology are described in the Callaway print ad shown in Exhibit 7. Callaway's Great Big Bertha Hawk Eye titanium drivers and fairway woods featured a titanium body and crown plate and Callaway's exclusive tungsten gravity screw, which accounted for only 2 percent of the clubhead volume but 25 percent of its overall weight. The lightweight titanium clubhead body and crown plate allowed Callaway to increase the overall size of the driver and the sweet spot, while the tungsten screw performed a number of functions. First, the use of tungsten low in the club created a low center of gravity, which helped the golfer produce a high trajectory. The tungsten screw also was strategically positioned in the sole of the clubhead to create Callaway's Draw Bias Technology, which drew the clubhead square at impact and reduced the likelihood of a slice. The tungsten screw also increased backspin, which helped produce greater distance. Exhibit 8 shows a print ad for Callaway's line of GBB Hawk Eye metal woods.

Irons.   To capitalize on the initial popularity of the Big Bertha metal woods, Callaway Golf introduced lines of stainless-steel and graphite-shafted Big Bertha irons in 1994. In 1997 the company introduced Great Big Bertha tungsten-titanium irons, which included a tungsten insert in the sole of the club that lowered the clubhead's center of gravity. The use of titanium allowed Callaway to increase the overall size of the clubface, creating a larger sweet spot, while the tungsten insert allowed Callaway to keep the center of gravity low and add weight to the sweet spot. The low center of gravity and concentration of weight in the sweet spot allowed the irons to hit higher, straighter shots.

Callaway's Hawk Eye tungsten-injected titanium irons, introduced in 1999, included innovative design improvements over the original GBB tungsten-titanium irons. The Hawk Eye titanium irons included a hidden cavity that ran the length of the clubhead and extended upward behind the hitting area. Small, uniform tungsten spheres were added by a computer weigh station to the cavity through a port and then covered with a dense molten metal to lock them permanently into place. Each iron contained a different number of spheres depending on the optimal center of gravity for the loft of the club. Once the appropriate number of tungsten spheres and the molten metal were added to the clubhead, the weight port was hidden by a Hawk Eye medallion. The Tungsten Weight Matrix that resulted from the addition of the spheres occupied only 27 percent of the volume of a Callaway Hawk Eye 5-iron yet accounted for 45 percent of the clubhead's weight. The weight matrix created a low center of gravity that acted much like the gravity screw used in Hawk Eye metal woods and allowed golfers to create a high shot likely to maintain a straight path.

Callaway Golf replaced its stainless-steel Big Bertha irons in 1998 with its Big Bertha X-12 irons. The X-12 line of irons included a number of improvements over the Big Bertha irons and became the best-selling iron in the company's history. The X-12 line featured a narrower sole than Big Bertha irons, which made it easier to hit shots out of the rough. Big Bertha X-12 irons also had a multilayer design effect on the back of the clubface that allowed Callaway designers to locate the center of gravity at the ideal location for each length iron. The introduction of a variable 360-degree undercut channel also aided Callaway engineers in placing the center of gravity at the best possible location on the clubhead.

Callaway replaced the X-12 line of irons in 2000 with the Big Bertha X-14 Steelhead line. The X-14 featured Callaway's Variable Face Thickness Technology, which tapered the clubface from top to bottom and from heel to toe to create better perimeter weighting than previous generations of Callaway irons.The technology also allowed Callaway engineers to move the center of gravity to the ideal location on each iron. For example,

EXHIBIT 7   **Sample Ad for Callaway Golf's New Big Bertha Steelhead Plus Metal Woods**

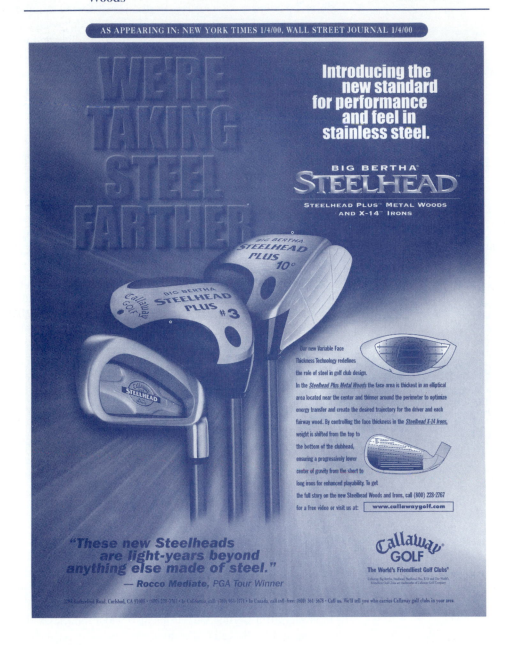

the X-14 short irons had a higher center of gravity to provide extra control on approach shots, while the midlength irons and long irons had a lower center of gravity to produce a higher ball flight. Exhibit 9 shows a sample ad for Callaway Golf's X-14 irons.

Putters.   Callaway Golf Company manufactured and marketed Bobby Jones, Carlsbad, and Tuttle lines of putters and the Odyssey brand of putters. Callaway had moderate success with its own Callaway putter lines, but its acquisition of Odyssey in 1997 made it the leading producer of putters in 2000. The 12 Bobby Jones putters and

EXHIBIT 8 Sample Ad for Callaway Golf's New Hawk Eye Metal Woods

four Carlsbad putters were all made from stainless steel and came in blade and mallet styles. The Tuttle putter came in one model, which was unique in that it actually resembled a Big Bertha driver but was the size of a putter. Odyssey became known as an innovator in putters when it became one of the first companies to introduce polymer clubface inserts. Many golfers preferred putters with an insert since the soft material created a softer noise and provided more feel when they were putting a ball. Callaway's

Exhibit 9 Sample Ad for Callaway Golf's New Big Bertha Steelhead X-14 Irons

AS APPEARING IN: GOLF WORLD 10/1/99, GOLFWEEK 10/2/99 AND GOLF MAGAZINE 11/99

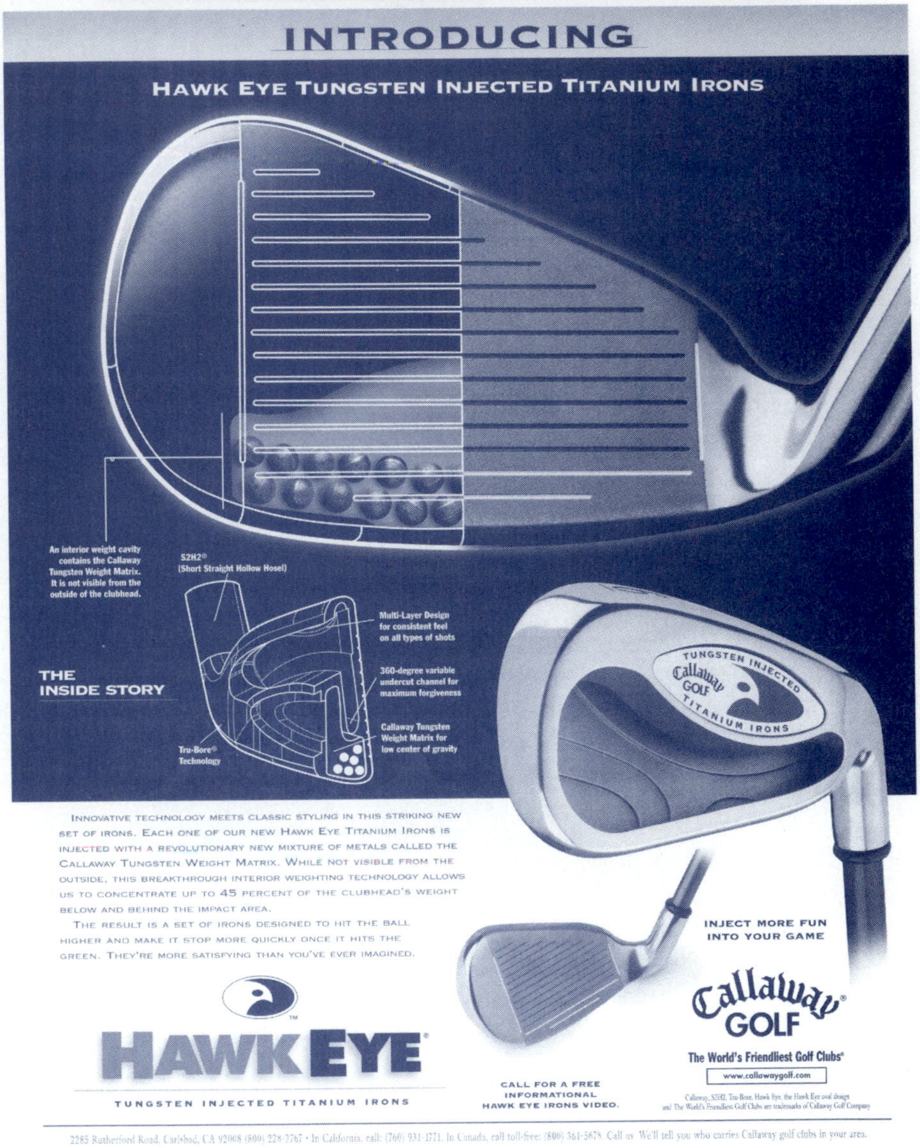

Odyssey putter was one of the two leading brands of putter in 2000 (Ping and Odyssey regularly exchanged the number one title) and was available in 26 different blade and mallet designs. Each of Odyssey's 26 models of putters featured its Stronomic polymer insert, which was available in three degrees of softness. In early 2000 Odyssey introduced its White Hot line of putters, which used Callaway's golf ball material as a clubface insert.

Callaway's Battle against Patent and Trademark Infringement. Ever since the Big Bertha driver had gained mass acceptance by professional and amateur golfers,

Callaway Golf had been attacked by small golf companies offering clubs that were so similar in design and appearance that they infringed on Callaway's patents and trademarks. Although they looked like the branded clubs, the knockoff clubs were of inferior quality and typically sold for as much as 75 percent less than name-brand clubs. Some knockoff brands outsold the brands offered by such well-known makers as Hogan, Cleveland, and MacGregor. Callaway Golf was extremely committed to battling the makers of knockoff and counterfeit clubs. The company hired a retired U.S. Army counterintelligence expert to investigate trademark infringement cases and also worked in this area with private investigators, U.S. Customs, and U.S. marshals. In early 2000, Callaway Golf carried out a four-state sweep against illegal club makers that netted $65,000 worth of Callaway golf clubs that had been stolen and were being sold over the Internet; officials seized 5,800 golf clubs, including Canterbury Big Bursar V-17 irons and Connection Golf Big Bernard Steelclad metal woods. However, even when patent infringers and counterfeiters were caught and convicted, it was difficult to collect damages because such companies usually had minimal assets to seize.

Callaway Golf also aggressively protected its legal rights when it believed that a branded rival infringed on its patents or made false claims about either its own products or Callaway's products. In 1998 Callaway brought a suit against Spalding Sports Worldwide for trademark violation after Spalding created a line of System C golf balls and claimed they were specifically designed for Callaway clubs. The two parties settled in 1999, with Spalding agreeing to pull the line of golf balls. In addition, after a legal challenge from Callaway, Orlimar Golf was ordered by the court to retract advertisements falsely claiming that it was the number one metal wood used on the PGA tour. In 1999 Callaway Golf saw that the vice president of Callaway Golf Ball Company could in no way be involved with Taylor Made's golf ball operations after the Callaway employee left with company trade secrets to become Taylor Made's president and CEO. Callaway Golf also forced an apology from the CEO of La Jolla Golf after Callaway found that La Jolla's chief executive had used a fictitious name to make untrue and disparaging remarks about Callaway golf clubs on the Internet.

Endorsements and Use of Callaway Products by Golf Professionals.   Callaway golf clubs were popular with both professionals and amateurs alike. Callaway drivers were endorsed by the professional golfers listed in Exhibit 10. However, many professional golfers used Callaway equipment even though they were not paid to endorse the company's products. In 1999 Callaway drivers were used in 61 wins, Callaway irons were used in 37 wins, and Odyssey putters produced 36 wins in a total of 186 PGA, LPGA, Senior PGA, Nike, and European PGA professional tournaments. A comparison of clubs used by professionals in all five tournaments is presented in Exhibit 11.

Callaway Golf's Major Competitors

Callaway management considered its strongest competitive rivals to be Ping and Taylor Made because of those companies' track records in product innovation and strong brand-name recognition: Ping irons had dominated the industry during much of the 1980s and 1990s (the perimeter-weighting feature pioneered by Karsten was a major technological breakthrough and had since become the industry standard in designing irons), while Taylor Made's distinctive bubble shaft was also considered a high-tech innovation. Other key rivals of Callaway Golf Company were Titleist, Adams Golf, and Orlimar Golf. Exhibit 12 presents a price comparison of golf equipment produced by Callaway Golf Company and its key rivals.

EXHIBIT 10   **Callaway Golf Company Staff Professionals, 2000**

Tour	*Staff Players*
Professional Golfers Association	Stephen Ames
	Paul Azinger
	Oline Browne
	Carlos Franco
	Brian Henninger
	Rocco Mediate
	Jesper Parnevik
	Paul Stankowski
Senior Professional Golfers Association	Bob Charles
	Jim Colbert
	Jim Dent
	Dave Eichelberger
	Bruce Fleisher
	David Graham
	Orville Moody
	Walter Morgan
	Bob Murphy
Ladies Professional Golfers Association	Jane Geddes
	Rachel Hetherington
	Rosie Jones
	Emilee Klein
	Leta Lindley
	Cindy McCurdy
	Liselotte Neumann
	Alison Nicholas
	Annika Sorenstam
European Professional Golfers Association	Mark McNulty
	Colin Montgomerie
	Eduardo Romero

Source: Callaway Golf 2000 catalog.

Ping.   Ping had not been well known for its drivers but had been one of the industry's premier manufacturers of irons since its Ping Eye 2-irons were introduced in the mid-1980s. The company's Ping Eye 3-irons that were introduced in 1999 were among the most popular irons with both professionals and amateurs. Ping Eye 3-irons were one of the two leading brands of irons sold in he United States and were frequently the most used iron in various professional tournaments. Ping Eye 3s were available with a compact blade-style clubhead designed for low-handicap golfers with an oversized clubhead that had greater perimeter weighting for more forgiveness. All Ping Eye 3-irons featured a custom tuning port that was very similar in appearance to Callaway's tungsten weight matrix port but functioned differently. Rather than acting as a port to add tungsten weights, Ping's custom tuning port allowed the company to make minor adjustments to the loft and lie of the club during custom fitting.

Ping had elected not to introduce a titanium driver until 1998 because the company's engineers believed that the material provided no advantage over stainless steel. However, in 2000 its 323-cc-displacement TiSI titanium driver was actually the largest custom-fit driver available. Ping also offered Ti3 titanium fairway woods that featured a zirconium soleplate and a tungsten bottom weight that were both intended to lower the

EXHIBIT 11   **Golf Club Use Comparison among Professional
Golfers, All Tours Combined, 1998–1999**

	1999	1998
Drivers		
Callaway	38.5%	55.2%
Titleist	24.2	16.9
Ping	13.4	n.a.
Taylor Made	5.3	8.0
Orlimar	3.0	0.1
All others	15.6	17.5
Total drivers	100.0%	100.0%
Fairway woods		
Callaway	52.1%	48.3%
Orlimar	17.9	10.5
Taylor Made	8.8	13.3
Titleist	4.5	5.1
Cleveland	3.1	n.a.
All others	13.6	20.3
Total fairway woods	100.0%	100.0%
Irons		
Callaway	18.3%	19.4%
Ping	15.0	15.3
Mizuno	15.0	14.1
Titleist	14.5	12.6
Taylor Made	4.4	4.7
All others	32.8	33.9
Total irons	100.0%	100.0%
Putters		
Odyssey	28.9%	31.0%
Ping	21.8	24.8
Titleist	19.8	18.7
Never Compromise	11.2	3.7
Tear Drop	4.0	n.a.
All others	14.3	16.0
Total putters	100.0%	100.0%

n.a. = not available.

Source: Callaway Golf Company annual reports and Darrell Survey.

club's center of gravity, Ping also offered an i3 line of stainless-steel fairway woods in
five different lofts.

Ping's greatest strength was in putters, where it alternated every quarter or so with
Odyssey as the number one brand in the U.S. and international markets. Depending on
the tournament, Ping putters often were used by professional golfers more than any
other brand. Ping had 46 models of putters that were made from antiqued manganese
bronze, stainless steel, or laminated maple. Certain Ping putters featured inserts made
from an elastomer compound, aluminum pixels, or copper pixels. Ping began offering
custom-fit clubs in the 1960s, and in 2000 all Ping metal woods, irons, and putters could
be custom-fitted to golfers who desired that service.

EXHIBIT 12   **Retail Price Comparison of Equipment Produced by Leading Golf Equipment Companies, March 2000**

Brand	Titanium Drivers	Graphite-Shafted Stainless-Steel Irons (Set of 8)	Putters (Price Range of Most Popular Models)	Golf Balls (Price per Ball—Based on Single Sleeve)
Callaway				
Golf/Odyssey	$400	$900	$90–$200	$3.60
Ping	$400	$850	$80–$140	n.a.
Taylor Made	$300	$750	$100	$3.33
Titleist	$400	$870	$270	$3.33
Adams Golf	$300	Not carried	n.a.	n.a.
Orlimar Golf	$300	$800	n.a.	n.a.

n.a. = not applicable

Source: Edwin Watts Golf Shops and International Golf Discount, March 11, 2000.

Taylor Made–Adidas Golf.   Taylor Made was founded in 1979 by Gary Adams, who mortgaged his home and began production of his metal woods in an abandoned car dealership building in McHenry, Illinois. Both touring pros and golf retailers were skeptical about the new club design until they found that the metal woods actually hit the ball higher and farther than persimmon woods. By 1984, Taylor Made metal woods were the number one wood on the PGA tour and the company had grown to be the third largest golf equipment company in the United States. In 1984 the company was acquired by France-based Salomon SA, which provided the capital necessary for the company to continue to develop innovative new lines of clubs. The company's sales had stalled during the late 1980s and early 1990s until it introduced its Burner Bubble drivers in 1994. The bubble shaft design allowed some of the shaft weight to be moved from underneath the grip to just below the grip. Taylor Made management claimed that his weight relocation decreased the club's inertia, which resulted in faster clubhead acceleration. The bubble shaft also featured a reinforced midsection that was said to minimize any twisting of the clubhead during the swing.

Many of the company's innovations in drivers and fairway woods mirrored those of Callaway Golf. In 1996, shortly after Callaway's introduction of the Great Big Bertha, Taylor Made had come out with an oversized titanium driver that had its differentiating bubble shaft and copper-colored clubhead. Taylor Made also produced and marketed a line of irons with its patented bubble shafts and introduced a line of bubble-shafted tungsten-titanium irons and a new titanium bubble-shafted T2 driver in 1997. The T2 and Taylor Made's tungsten-titanium irons appeared in retail locations at approximately the same time that the Biggest Big Bertha and the Big Bertha tungsten-titanium irons made their debut. Also in 1997, Taylor Made and its parent were acquired by the Germany-based sports conglomerate Adidas.

In 2000 Taylor Made offered titanium FireSole metal woods and irons that featured a tungsten sole plug and SuperSteel stainless-steel metal woods and irons. The FireSole was Taylor Made's answer to Callaway's Hawk Eye lines of metal woods and irons, while its promotion of its SuperSteel line touted many of the same benefits as Callaway's BB SteelHead Plus metal woods and X-14 irons. Taylor Made also offered FireSole Rescue clubs, which had a large tungsten sole attached to a reduced-size titanium clubhead that placed 75 percent of the clubhead's weight below the equator of the ball. The rescue woods had an ultralow center of gravity and could be used on either the fairway or the rough. In early 2000 Taylor Made's Rescue fairway woods were unique; no products of similar appearance were offered by other major club manufacturers. Taylor Made also had a line of putters that featured a polymer clubface. Taylor Made introduced its InterGel line of golf balls in 1999.

Fortune Brands/Acushnet (Titleist and Cobra Golf).   The Acushnet Company was a rubber deresinating company founded in 1910 in Acushnet, Massachusetts. The company opened a golf ball division in 1932 when founder Phil Young believed that a bad putt during a round of golf he was playing was a result of a faulty ball rather than his poor putting. Young took the ball to a dentist's office to have it x-rayed and found that the core of the ball was indeed off center. Young believed that Acushnet could develop and manufacture high-quality golf balls and teamed with a fellow MIT graduate, Fred Bommer, to create the Titleist line of balls. Young and Bommer introduced their first Titleist golf ball in 1935, and by 1949 Titleist had become the most frequently played ball on the PGA. In 2000, Titleist was still the number one golf ball on the PGA, being used by more than 75 percent of all professional golfers in tournament play. Acushnet also manufactured and marketed a Pinnacle line of golf balls, developed in 1980 as a lower-priced alternative to Titleist branded golf balls.

Acushnet's acquisition of John Reuter, Jr., Inc., in 1958 and Golfcraft, Inc., in 1969 put Titleist into the golf club business. Titleist's Reuter Bull's Eye putter became a favorite on the PGA tour during the 1960s, and its AC-108 heel-toe weighted irons were among the most popular brands of irons during the early 1970s. In 1996 the Acushnet Company was acquired by American Brands, which had increased its presence in the golf equipment industry in 1985 when it acquired Foot-Joy, the number one seller of golf gloves and shoes. Also in 1996 American Brands acquired Cobra Golf for $715 million. The company's golf and leisure products division had an operating profit of $147 million on sales of $965 million in 1999.

Acushnet's two golf club brands maintained separate sales forces, but every other value chain activity was combined for overall cost savings whenever possible. The Titleist brand of clubs had achieved only moderate success after Ping's perimeter-weighted clubs became popular in the 1980s, but Titleist had become much more successful during the late 1990s due to Tiger Woods's endorsement of the company's irons and metal woods. In 2000 Titleist's 975D driver, used by Tiger Woods, was among the more popular drivers with both professionals and amateurs. The 975D was an oversized titanium driver designed for a flatter ball flight to help a golfer achieve greater roll once the ball hit the ground. The Titleist titanium 975R was a variation of the 975D, which had a more shallow face and a slightly smaller clubhead. Titleist also offered a line of 975F stainless-steel fairway woods in 2000.

Titleist had two lines of stainless-steel irons: the DCI 990 and DCI 981. The DCI 990 was intended for low-handicap golfers and had a reduced clubface offset and more weight toward the lower portion of the heel, where better golfers were more prone to mishit a golf ball. The DCI 981 line, designed for higher-handicap golfers, had an offset clubface, a low center of gravity, and more weight toward the toe of the clubface of short irons. The overall design objectives of the 981 line were to produce higher trajectories and more forgiveness. The DCI 981 also was available in an SL series intended for seniors or other golfers with less clubhead speed. All Titleist irons and metal woods were available with either steel or graphite shafts. Titleist also marketed a line of 17 different Scotty Cameron putters in stainless-steel, teryllium, or platinum finishes. Some Scotty Cameron putters included an elastomer membrane covering the clubface.

In 1996, Cobra Golf held the industry's number two spot in irons and was number three in drivers and fairway woods (behind Callaway and Taylor Made). Cobra's popularity was a result of Greg Norman's endorsement of the clubs and the company's strategy of reducing the loft of its irons. The reduced loft added considerable distance to each club. For example, a golfer switching to King Cobra irons might pick up 20 yards or more on each club. Cobra Golf's King Cobra drivers were also considered a long-distance club.

After its acquisition by Acushnet, Cobra began to rapidly lose market share in both irons and metal woods. The company was forced to change its marketing approach since its high-profile, aggressive marketing practices clashed with the wishes of Acushnet's managers, who preferred a conservative approach to marketing. In addition, Acushnet management believed that Cobra should redesign its clubs to promote forgiveness at the expense of distance. Loyal Cobra customers were disappointed when they found that Cobra new models of clubs did not offer greater distance than other brands. The decline in demand forced Cobra into a practice of deep discounting, which encouraged golfers to wait for the company to cut prices before they purchased the latest Cobra products. Cobra Golf also lost a considerable number of retailers during the later 1990s. The combination of missteps by Acushnet and Cobra Golf managers had all but made Cobra an afterthought by 1999.

Cobra struggled to rebuild its image and market presence after its strategic gaffes of the late 1990s. In 1999 the company launched a Web site and print ads that promoted its products as hip, nonconformist alternatives to the more technology-based golf clubs on the market. In early 2000 Cobra abandoned this new image and recast itself as a more mainstream golf company.

Cobra's new products for 2000 included its Gravity Back drivers and fairway metal woods, which featured a titanium clubhead with a bronze alloy backweight placed at the rear of the clubhead. The bronze alloy backweight was designed to give the club a lower center of gravity. The Gravity Back fairway woods also featured a copper-tungsten sole weight to further lower the center of gravity. Cobra's CXI stainless-steel irons featured an X-like design on the backside of the clubface to more evenly disperse weight throughout the rear of the cavity back club. In 1999 Cobra Golf introduced Cobra Dista golf balls, which came in four models.

Adams Golf.   Barney Adams founded Adams Golf in 1987 in Plano, Texas, as a golf club components supplier and contract manufacturer. In 1995 the company introduced its Tight Lies line of fairway woods, which featured an innovative low-profile clubface with a very low center of gravity. The shallow clubface and low center of gravity enlarged the effective hitting area of the clubface and created shots with a higher trajectory than shots with traditional-sized metal woods of the same loft. Tight Lies fairway woods were named the "Breakthrough Product of the Year" in 1997 by the Golf Market Research Institute and were rated the "Best of the Best" fairway woods in an independent real-golfer comparison in 1998. Adams Golf went public in July 1998 at an initial offering price of $16. The company recorded 1998 sales and earnings of $85 million and $13 million, respectively. In 1997 Adams had revenues of $37 million and a net loss of $5 million.

Adams's success became more difficult to maintain after other leading golf club manufacturers offered new lines of fairway woods with a shallower face than their previous models. In 1999, Adams Golf's revenues had declined to $54 million and the company recorded a net loss of $11 million. The company's stock traded below $2 during the first three months of 2000. Adams Golf's product line for 2000 included its

Tight Lies 2 fairway woods, which had a deeper clubface than the original Tight Lies fairway woods. The new Tight Lies 2 retained the key features of the original Tight Lies line, but its deeper clubface made it easier to hit from the rough. In 1999 Adams introduced a line of SC series drivers, which were available in four different clubface curvatures designed to correct a slice, a fade, or a hook. One SC driver featured a neutral clubface curvature for golfers without swing path problems. Adams also offered Assault VMI (variable moment of inertia) irons, which were heavier than most other brands of irons and used a patented mathematical formula to determine the ideal weight of the club based on the overall club length, shaft length, grip weight, and shaft weight.

Orlimar Golf Company.   Orlimar Golf Company was founded in 1960 by Lou Ortiz in the basement of a converted stable in San Francisco. The company was a little-known maker of custom clubs primarily used by professionals and had annual sales of under $1 million in 1996. The company exploded onto the broad market for golf clubs in 1998 when it introduced its Tri-Metal fairway woods. Orlimar's Tri-Metal woods were made of stainless steel, copper, and tungsten and featured a low center of gravity and a shallower clubface than Callaway's GBB fairway woods. The combination of three metals and the low profile made the Tri-Metal instantly popular with professionals and amateurs alike. By year end 1998 the company's sales had grown to more than $50 million, and it was named the fastest-growing private company in the San Francisco Bay area.

The company added drivers and irons to its product line in 1999 as its sales of fairway woods began to decline after Callaway's fairway woods began to recapture market share lost in 1997 and 1998. Orlimar's 2000 lineup of new products included its Tri-Metal Plus fairway woods and drivers and Tri-Metal irons. Like Orlimar's original Tri-Metal woods, Tri-Metal Plus fairway woods and drivers were made from stainless steel and included a copper tungsten sole plate to lower their center of gravity, but the Plus line had a deeper clubface than the original Tri-Metals. The clubface of the Tri-Metal Plus metal woods was coated with an Alpha Maraging Face material that the company claimed was harder than titanium. Orlimar's Tri-Metal irons were made from the same materials as the company's metal woods and were designed to produce high trajectories and longer distance than competing clubs.

Callaway's Prospects for Growth and the February 2000 Launch of the Callaway Golf Ball.   Callaway's introduction of its new Rule 35 golf ball had been eagerly awaited since mid-1996, when Ely Callaway announced the formation of Callaway Golf Ball Company and the move of Charles Yash from Taylor Made to the new company. Whereas Nike had entered the golf ball industry in 1999 by outsourcing its production to Bridgestone and Taylor Made chose its mode of entry by purchasing an existing plant from a competitor, Ely Callaway had chosen a more time-consuming route to enter the market for golf balls by electing to construct a new golf ball facility and internally develop an all-new ball. He noted: "This is the first time in the modern history of the industry, to our knowledge, that anyone has built a major-production golf ball business from scratch. After analyzing all of our other options, which included buying an existing company, buying an existing plant or buying a golf ball from another manufacturer and merely stamping our name on it, we decided this was the best way to go in order to create a superior product now and for the future."[9]

---

[9] "Play Ball: Callaway Introduces the Rule 35," www.pgatour.com.

Callaway Golf spent three years developing in parallel its new golf ball and its state-of-the-art production facility. The company's entry into the market represented a $170 million investment in the research and development of the ball, the construction of the 225,000-square-foot production facility, and the development and purchase of special manufacturing equipment. Callaway's manufacturing facility and its equipment were designed specifically for the unique production requirements for the new ball.

Ely Callaway believed that the company's custom-designed manufacturing equipment and facility would contribute to the company's competitive strength and the ball's success: "No one else has the collection of late 90s equipment that we have, everything you need to make a better ball. No one has put it together and purchased it all the way we have. Some of the companies, because of the age of some of their equipment, just can't utilize the latest equipment without going outside."[10] Callaway's competitors were so interested in the company's new golf ball facility that they took aerial photographs of the plant's foundation as it was under construction.

Callaway Golf Ball Company engineers, recruited from Du Pont and Boeing, used aerodynamic computer programs (first used by Boeing and General Electric) to evaluate more than 300 dimple patterns and more than 1,000 variations of ball cores, boundary layers, and cover materials to create the new Rule 35 ball. Callaway engineers designed only two models of the Rule 35 ball, choosing to develop a "complete-performance" ball rather than separate balls developed for spin, control, distance, and durability. Ely Callaway explained the company's product development objectives as follows: "We have combined all of the performance benefits into one ball so players no longer need to sacrifice control for distance, or feel, or durability. Each Rule 35 ball contains a unique synergy of distance, control, spin, feel and durability characteristics. This eliminates confusion and guesswork in trying to identify the golf ball that is right for each individual golfer."[11]

Callaway's production process used computers to mill the rubber core, control the injection molding of a boundary layer, and deposit a proprietary urethane coating on golf balls as they were assembled. The golf balls then moved through a transparent tube to a battery of diagnostic machines that ensured that each ball was exactly the same. A laser was used to twice measure the depth of each of the ball's 382 dimples, and an electrical process was used to bond paint to the ball securely and evenly. Each ball was then x-rayed and machine-inspected before being packed or rejected. Callaway's production process included 16,000 quality assurance checkpoints, and Callaway employees were allowed to stop the flow of balls at the first sign of a defect.

Callaway's Rule 35 balls were differentiated from competing brands in a large number of ways. The name Rule 35 was a play on the 34 long-standing rules of golf published by the USGA and the Royal & Ancient Golf Club of St. Andrews. Ely Callaway suggested that there should be a 35th rule of golf—"Enjoy the game."[12] The complete-performance balls came in only two variations, whereas the golf balls offered by competitors came in as many as 10 models. The blue-logo Callaway ball was called the Softfeel and had all the same characteristics as its red-logo Firmfeel ball but had a slightly softer feel. Ely Callaway believed the availability of only two complete-performance balls and the avoidance of a discussion of the technical aspects of the balls' design and construction would make it easier for golfers to purchase golf balls: "We know there is a lot of complex science that goes into making a golf ball, but we

[10] "Long on Promises, Short on Explanation," *Golfweek,* February 5, 2000.

[11] "Callaway Enters the Ball Game," *Show News,* February 5, 2000.

[12] "Play Ball: Callaway Introduces the Rule 35."

don't think there should be a lot of complexity to buying one."[13] Callaway later commented, "We've come up with two balls. That's it. We're not gonna tell you much about them. We have only two, you make the choice. If you like a soft feel, you try this one (blue). If you like a firm feel, you try this one (red). We don't say a damn thing about how far they go. We don't say a word about compression or the construction or the details of the cover. We just say, 'Try them.' We believe that either one of them will give you more of what you've been looking for in one ball than anything else."[14]

Callaway Golf Ball Company's CEO, Chuck Yash, discussed the company's philosophy behind offering only two models of the Rule 35 and why the company refused to comment on the ball's technology: "Our basic aim in this process was to make a ball that reflects the parent company's philosophy and vision of creating a 'demonstrably superior and pleasingly different' product. We also set out to cut through the noise regarding the performance claims by most of the competitors' products, and all of the techno-babble about various polymers and compressions and dimple patterns and claims regarding the longest distance balls. What we have in Rule 35 is a very clear message. If you prefer a firm feel, our Firmfeel ball has everything you need in performance. If you prefer a softer feel, our Softfeel ball is the choice. It's that easy."[15]

Callaway golf balls were further differentiated by their logo and packaging. The Callaway name used a stylized script rather than the Old English script used on Callaway golf clubs, and the company's logo consisted of a letter C created from a rendering of the bottom of a golf cup. The balls were also packaged in sleeves of 5 and packs of 10 rather than sleeves of 3 or packs of 12 like other brands. Callaway Golf Ball Company's national sales manager explained why Callaway chose unique packaging for its golf balls: "When we were doing our research, we couldn't find a single person who could tell us why golf balls were packaged in sleeves of three or in dozens. When we discovered that the average golfer uses 4.5 balls per round, we decided the five-ball sleeve was the right way to go with packaging."[16] In addition, unlike the packaging of other brands of balls, Callaway's packaging included only the name and logo printed on a translucent plastic box rather than the name and product performance characteristics printed on a cardboard box. Callaway's use of a five-ball sleeve also allowed its golf balls to be placed away from other brands of balls since most retailers' display cases were designed for three-ball sleeves.

Even though the industry had long been dominated by Titleist and Spalding (see Exhibit 13), many analysts believed that Callaway's ability to develop technologically advanced products, its marketing expertise, and its established retailer network would allow the company to quickly gain a 2 to 3 percent share of the market and achieve $60 million to $70 million in sales during 2000. Analysts also speculated that Callaway Golf Ball Company could hit sales of over $200 million within two years of the ball's launch. It was expected that Callaway's golf ball operations would considerably affect the company's net profit since profit margins in the premium segment of the golf ball market ranged between 60 and 75 percent. In addition, golf ball sales were less seasonal since they were consumable items that were purchased throughout the year. Also, unlike a $500 driver, golfers could not delay the purchase of golf balls until they felt financially ready to make a large purchase. The company's objective was for the Rule 35 to capture a 10 percent share of the market within two years and ultimately become one of the

[13] "Callaway Enters the Ball Game."
[14] "Long on Promises, Short on Explanation."
[15] Callaway press release, February 4, 2000.
[16] "Callaway Enters the Ball Game."

Exhibit 13   **Estimated Manufacturing Shares of the Leading Producers of Golf Balls, 12 Months Ending September 30, 1999**

	Dollars	*Units*
Titleist	36%	29%
Top-Flite/Spalding	23	27
Pinnacle	11	14
Maxfli	8	7
Wilson	7	8
Slazenger	5	3
Precept	3	2
Dunlop	2	3
Taylor Made	1	1
All others	4	6
Total	100%	100%

Source: Callaway Golf Company

two top brands of golf balls. "We have 7 million people out there playing our products, and 80 percent of them think they're the best clubs in the world," said Ely Callaway. "We have almost a guaranteed 'try' on our new products."[17] Callaway further commented, "We're going to sell a lot of balls."[18] An advertisement for the Rule 35 golf ball is shown in Exhibit 14.

In February 2000 a survey of golf equipment company executives voted Callaway's Big Bertha driver the best golf product of the century by a margin of 2 to 1. The same group of executives called Ely Callaway the most influential golf trade person of the 1990s. As he approached his 81st birthday, Ely Callaway had vowed to retire by December 31, 2000, and make Chuck Yash the new CEO and president of Callaway Golf Company as well as Callaway Golf Ball Company. Just before the PGA Merchandise Show, Chuck Yash commented on his growing responsibility at Callaway Golf Company and the importance of its golf ball operations to the company's future growth: "The trust and faith Ely and the board of directors and the shareholders have shown in us is extraordinary. It has allowed me to use my 20 years of golf experience to build an organization and a team that, we believe, can have a significant impact. That is the way we are looking at things now, as a long-term commitment. It will take years before we feel we can compete with the leading companies in the golf ball market. But that is our objective. If we do that right, we have the potential to continue to grow."[19]

[17] "Rule 35 Tees Off," *San Deigo Union-Tribune,* February 4, 2000.
[18] "Play Ball: Callaway Introduces the Rule 35."
[19] "On the Spot: Chuck Yash," *Golf Product News,* January/February 2000.

EXHIBIT 14   **Sample Ad for Callaway Golf's Rule 35 Golf Ball**

Kevin Cage, general manager of Wind Technology, sat in his office on a Friday afternoon watching the snow fall outside his window. It was January 1991, and he knew that during the month ahead he would have to make some difficult decisions regarding the future of his firm, Wind Technology. The market for the wind-profiling radar systems that his company designed had been developing at a much slower rate than he had anticipated.

Wind Technology

During Wind Technology's 10-year history the company had produced a variety of weather-related radar and instrumentation. In 1986 the company condensed its product mix to include only wind-profiling radar systems. Commonly referred to as wind profilers, these products measure wind and atmospheric turbulence for weather forecasting, detection of wind direction at NASA launch sites, and other meteorological applications (i.e., at universities and other scientific monitoring stations). Kevin had felt that this consolidation would position the company as a leader in what he anticipated to be a high-growth market with little competition.

Wind Technology's advantages over Unisys, the only other key player in the wind-profiling market, included the following: (1) The company adhered stringently to specifications and quality production. (2) Wind Technology had the technical expertise to provide full system integration. This allowed customers to order either basic components or a full system, including software support. (3) Wind Technology's staff of meteorologists and atmospheric scientists provided the customer with sophisticated support, including operation and maintenance training and field assistance. (4) Finally, Wind Technology had devoted all of its resources to its wind-profiling business. Kevin believed that the market would perceive this as an advantage over a large conglomerate such as Unisys.

Wind Technology customized each product for individual customers as the need arose: the total system could cost a customer from $400,000 to $5 million. Various governmental entities, such as the Department of Defense, NASA, and state universities, had consistently accounted for about 90 percent of Wind Technology's sales. In lieu of a field sales force, Wind Technology relied on top management and a team of engineers to call on prospective and current customers. Approximately $105,000 of their annual salaries was charged to a direct selling expense.

The Problem

The consolidation strategy that the company had undertaken in 1986 was partly due to the company's being purchased by Vaitra, a high-technology European firm. Wind Technology's ability to focus on the wind-profiling business had been made possible by

This case was prepared by Ken Manning, Gonzaga University, and Jakki Mohr, University of Colorado at Boulder. This case is intended for use as a basis for class discussion rather than to illustrate either effective or ineffective administrative decision making. Some data are disguised. Copyright © by Jakki Mohr 1990. All rights reserved.

Vaitra's financial support. However, since 1986 Wind Technology had shown little commercial success, and due to low sales levels, the company was experiencing severe cash flow problems. Kevin knew that Wind Technology could not continue to meet payroll much longer. Also, he had been informed that Vaitra was not willing to pour more money into Wind Technology. Kevin estimated that he had from 9 to 12 months (until the end of 1991) in which to implement a new strategy with the potential to improve the company's cash flow. The new strategy was necessary to enable Wind Technology to survive until the wind-profiler market matured. Kevin and other industry experts anticipated that it would be two years until the wind-profiling market achieved the high growth levels the company initially had anticipated.

One survival strategy that Kevin had in mind was to spin off and market component parts used in making wind profilers. Initial research indicated that of all the wind-profiling system's component parts, the high-voltage power supply (HVPS) had the greatest potential for commercial success. Furthermore, Kevin's staff on the HVPS product had demonstrated knowledge of the market. Kevin felt that by marketing the HVPS, Wind Technology could reap incremental revenues, with very little addition to fixed costs. (Variable costs would include the costs of making and marketing the HVPS. The accounting department had estimated that production costs would run approximately 70 percent of the selling price and that 10 percent of other expenses—such as top management direct-selling expenses—should be charged to the HVPS.)

High-Voltage Power Supplies

For a vast number of consumer and industrial products that require electricity, the available voltage level must be transformed to different levels and types of output. The three primary types of power supplies are linears, switchers, and converters. Each type manipulates electrical current in terms of the type of current (AC or DC) and/or the level of output (voltage). Some HVPS manufacturers focus on producing a standardized line of power supplies, while others specialize in customizing power supplies to the user's specifications.

High-voltage power supplies vary significantly in size and level of output. Small power supplies with relatively low levels of output (under 3 kV)[1] are used in communications equipment. Medium-size power supplies that produce an output between 3 and 10 kV are used in a wide range of products, including radar and lasers. Power supplies that produce output greater than 10 kV are used in a variety of applications, such as high-powered x-rays and plasma-etching systems.

Background on Wind Technology's HVPS

One of Wind Technology's corporate strategies was to control the critical technology (major component parts) of its wind-profiling products. Management felt that this control was important since the company was part of a high-technology industry in which confidentiality and innovation were critical to each competitor's success. This strategy also gave Wind Technology a differential advantage over its major competitors, all of which depended on a variety of manufacturers for component parts. Wind Technology had successfully developed almost all the major component parts and the software for the wind profiler, yet the development of the power supply had been problematic.

---

[1] kV (kilovolt): 1,000 volts.

To adhere to the policy of controlling critical technology in product design (rather than purchasing an HVPS from an outside supplier), Wind Technology management had hired Anne Ladwig and her staff of HVPS technicians to develop a power supply for the company's wind-profiling systems. Within six months of joining Wind Technology, Anne and her staff had completed the development of a versatile power supply which could be adapted for use with a wide variety of equipment. Some of the company's wind-profiling systems required up to 10 power supplies, each modified slightly to carry out its role in the system.

Kevin Cage had delegated the responsibility of investigating the sales potential of the company's HVPS to Anne Ladwig since she was very familiar with the technical aspects of the product and had received formal business training while pursuing an MBA. Anne had determined that Wind Technology's HVPS could be modified to produce levels of output between 3 and 10 kV. Thus, it seemed natural that if the product was brought to market, Wind Technology should focus on applications in this range of output. Wind Technology also did not have the production capabilities to compete in the high-volume, low-voltage segment of the market or have the resources and technical expertise to compete in the high-output (+ 10 kV) segment.

The Potential Customer

Power supplies in the range of 3 to 10 kV could be used to conduct research, produce other products, or place as a component into other products, such as lasers. Thus, potential customers could include research labs, large end users, OEMs, and distributors. Research labs each used an average of three power supplies; other types of customers ordered a widely varying quantity.

HVPS users were demanding increasing levels of reliability, quality, customization, and system integration. *System integration* refers to the degree to which other parts of a system are dependent on the HVPS for proper functioning and the extent to which these parts are combined into a single unit or piece of machinery.

Anne had considered entering several HVPS market segments in which Wind Technology could reasonably compete. She had estimated the domestic market potential of these segments at $237 million. To evaluate these segments, Anne had compiled growth forecasts for the year ahead and had evaluated each segment in terms of the anticipated level of customization and system integration demanded by the market. Anne felt that the level of synergy between Wind Technology and the various segments was also an important consideration in selecting a target market. Exhibit 1 summarizes this information. Anne believed that if the product was produced, Wind Technology's interests would be best served by selecting only one target market on which to concentrate initially.

Competition

To gather competitive information, Anne contacted five HVPS manufacturers. She found that the manufacturers varied significantly in terms of size and marketing strategy (see Exhibit 2). Each listed a price in the range of $5,500 to $6,500 for power supplies with the same features and output levels as the HVPS that had been developed for Wind Technology. After she spoke with these firms, Anne had the feeling that Wind Technology could offer the HVPS market superior levels of quality, reliability, technical expertise, and customer support. She optimistically believed that a one-half percent market share objective could be achieved the first year.

EXHIBIT 1   HVPS Market Segments in the 3–10-kV Range

Application	Forecast Annual Growth (%)	Level of Customization/ Level of System Integration*	Synergy Rating†	Percentage of $237 Million Power Supply Market‡
General/univ. laboratory	5.40%	Medium/medium	3	8%
Lasers	11.00	Low/medium	4	10
Medical equipment	10.00	Medium/medium	3	5
Microwave	12.00	Medium/high	4	7
Power modulators	3.00	Low/low	4	25
Radar systems	11.70	Low/medium	5	12
Semiconductors	10.10	Low/low	3	23
X-ray systems	8.60	Medium/high	3	10

* The level of customization and system integration generally in demand within each of the applications is defined as low, medium, or high.

† Synergy ratings are based on a scale of 1 to 5; 1 is equivalent to a very low level of synergy, and 5 is equivalent to a very high level of synergy. These subjective ratings are based on the amount of similarities between the wind-profiling industry and each application.

‡ Percentages total 100 percent of the $237 million market in which Wind Technology anticipated it could compete.

Note: This list of applications is not all-inclusive.

Promotion

If Wind Technology entered the HVPS market, it would require a hard-hitting, thorough promotional campaign to reach the selected target market. Three factors made the selection of elements in the promotion mix especially important to Wind Technology: (1) Wind Technology's poor cash flow, (2) the lack of a well-developed marketing department, and (3) the need to generate incremental revenue from sales of the HVPS at a minimum cost. In fact, a rule of thumb used by Wind Technology was that all marketing

EXHIBIT 2   Competitor Profile (3–10-kV range)

Company	Gamma	Glassman	Kaiser	Maxwell*	Spellman
Approximate annual sales	$2 million	$7.5 million	$3 million		$7 million
Market share	1.00%	3.00%	1.50%		2.90%
Price†	$5,830	$5,590	$6,210	$5,000–$6,000	$6,360
Delivery	12 weeks	10 weeks	10 weeks	8 weeks	12 weeks
Product customization	No	Medium	Low	Medium	Low
System integration experience	Low	Low	Low	Medium	Low
Customer targets	Gen. lab.	Laser	Laser	Radar	Capacitors
	Space	Medical	Medical	Power mod.	Gen. lab.
	Univ. lab.	X-ray	Microwave	X-ray	Microwave
			Semiconductor	Medical equip.	X-ray

*Maxwell was in the final stages of product development and stated that the product would be available in the spring. Maxwell anticipated that the product would fall in the range of $5,000 to $6,000.

†Price quoted for an HVPS with the same specification as the "standard" model developed by Wind Technology.

expenditures should be about 9 to 10 percent of sales. Kevin and Anne were contemplating the use of the following elements:

1. Collateral Material.   Sales literature, brochures, and data sheets are necessary to communicate the product benefits and features to potential customers. These materials are designed to be (1) mailed to customers as part of direct mail campaigns or in response to customer requests, (2) given away at trade shows, and (3) left behind after sales presentations.

Because no one in Wind Technology was an experienced copywriter, Anne and Kevin considered hiring a marketing communications agency to write the copy and design the layout of the brochures. This agency would also complete the graphics (photographs and artwork) for the collateral material. The cost for 5,000 pieces (including the 10 percent markup for the agency) was estimated to be $5.50 each.

2. Public Relations.   Kevin and Anne realized that one very cost-efficient tool of promotion is publicity. They contemplated sending out new product announcements to a variety of trade journals whose readers were part of Wind Technology's new target market. By using this tool, interested readers could call or write to Wind Technology, and the company could then send the prospective customers collateral material. The drawback of relying too heavily on this element was very obvious to Kevin and Anne—the editors of the trade journals could choose not to print Wind Technology's product announcements if their new product was not deemed newsworthy.

The cost of using this tool would include the time necessary to write the press release and the expense of mailing the release to the editors. Direct costs were estimated by Wind Technology to be $500.

3. Direct Mail.   Kevin and Anne were also contemplating a direct mail campaign. The major expenditure for this option would be buying a list of prospects to whom the collateral material would be mailed. Such lists usually cost around $5,000, depending on the number of names and the list quality. Other costs would include postage and the materials mailed. These costs were estimated to be $7,500 for a mailing of 1,500.

4. Trade Shows.   The electronics industry had several annual trade shows. If it chose to exhibit at one of these trade shows, Wind Technology would incur the cost of a booth, the space at the show, and the travel and incidental costs of the people attending the show to staff the booth. Kevin and Anne estimated these costs at approximately $50,000 for the exhibit, space, and materials and $50,000 for a staff of five people to attend.

5. Trade Journal Advertising.   Kevin and Anne also contemplated running a series of ads in trade journals. Several journals they considered are listed in Exhibit 3, along with circulation, readership, and cost information.

6. Personal Selling.
   a. Telemarketing (inbound/inside sales).[2] Kevin and Anne also considered hiring a technical salesperson to respond to HVPS product inquiries generated by product announcements, direct mail, and advertising. This person's responsibilities would include answering phone calls, prospecting, sending out collateral material, and following up with potential customers. The salary and benefits for one individual would be about $50,000.

---

[2] *Inbound* refers to calls that potential customers make to Wind Technology, as opposed to *outbound*, in which Wind Technology calls potential customers (i.e., solicits sales).

EXHIBIT 3   **Trade Publications**

Trade Publication	Editorial	Cost per Color Insertion (1 page)	Circulation
Electrical Manufacturing	For purchasers and users of power supplies, transformers, and other electrical products.	$4,077	35,168 nonpaid
Electronic Component News	For electronics OEMs. Products addressed include work stations, power sources, chips, etc.	$6,395	110,151 nonpaid
Electronic Manufacturing News	For OEMs in the industry of providing manufacturing and contracting of components, circuits, and systems.	$5,075	25,000 nonpaid
Design News	For design OEMs covering components, systems, and materials.	$8,120	170,033 nonpaid
Weatherwise	For meteorologists covering imaging, radar, etc.	$1,040	10,186 paid

Note: This is a partial list of applicable trade publications. Standard Rate and Data Service lists other possible publications.

b. Field sales. The closing of sales for the HVPS might require some personal selling at the customer's location, especially if Wind Technology pursued the customized option. Kevin and Anne realized that potentially this would provide them with the most incremental revenue, but it also had the potential to be the most costly tool. Issues such as how many salespeople to hire and where to position them in the field (geographically) were major concerns. Salary plus expenses and benefits for an outside salesperson were estimated to be about $80,000.

Decisions

As Kevin sat in his office and perused the various facts and figures, he knew that he would have to make some quick decisions. He sensed that the decision about whether to proceed with the HVPS spin-off was risky, but he felt that not doing something to improve the firm's cash flow was equally risky. Kevin also knew that if he decided to proceed with the HVPS, there were a number of segments in that market in which Wind Technology could position its HVPS. He mulled over which segment appeared to be a good fit for Wind Technology's abilities (given Anne's recommendation that a choice of one segment would be best). Finally, Kevin was concerned that if they entered the HVPS market, promotion for their product would be costly, further exacerbating the cash flow situation. He knew that promotion would be necessary, but the exact mix of elements would have to be designed with financial constraints in mind.

Case 7–6
Slendertone (B)

BioMedical Research, Ltd., an Irish-owned company based in Galway, has successfully manufactured the Slendertone brand of body-shaping and cosmetic products since it acquired the brand in 1990 [Slendertone (A) provides in-depth information on the company and its product offering]. Available in mainland Europe, South America, Japan, and Australia, Slendertone was sold predominantly through distributors. With early 1996 calendar year sales indicating a banner year, the company had begun developing markets directly, recruiting new employees, and drawing up plans for factory expansion.

Slendertone in Turmoil

In late 1996 the size of the orders from the French distributor started to fall. Uncertainty about the reason for the sudden drop in French sales abounded, particularly as it was the buildup period to the normally busy Christmas season. The company quickly went from having a healthy cash surplus to being overdrawn. The banks were putting pressure on the company to address the situation. A decision was made to lay off all the temporary production workers. The situation continued to deteriorate. Over £1.5 million of raw material and stock, mostly for the French market, had accumulated in the factory. The staff was wondering whether the company could survive. McDonnell and his management team persevered with the plan to develop the UK market while addressing the serious situation developing in France.

After the slow start, sales in the United Kingdom were beginning to grow. Most sales were coming from direct response advertisements in magazines. Also, much public relations activity was being undertaken. Limited distribution had been secured in some nationwide retail chains, mostly on a trial basis in a few stores. Sales to Direct Shop (the television home-shopping company) were still disappointing, never rising above 4,000 Gymbody 8's a month. Sales in Ireland were up more than 30 percent over the previous year. Although sales to Ireland were now the highest per capita of any market, they still accounted for less than 10 percent of total sales. Sales to Colombia were about the same, while the sales of all the other distributors were down a little from the previous year.

The market in France deteriorated rapidly in early 1997. Subsequent analysis indicated that a number of factors were contributing to the dramatic loss of business there. The distributor had lost the television slot for the Gymbody 8 to a cheaper product. Other direct response channels seemed to have become "exhausted" or were being filled by cheaper products. To compound matters, a feature on EMS products in a consumer magazine gave poor ratings to many of the home-use products in the market. Although the Slendertone product range received the highest rating, this did not protect the company. A number of the low-quality competitors suddenly pulled out of the market, leaving a bad feeling in the "trade." The trade consisted of direct marketing companies that bought products from the distributors or manufacturers to sell to their existing customer base. It also included retailers: mostly pharmacies, sports shops, and a few department stores. The sudden fall in advertising for EMS products affected market demand and left many traders with unsold product. By the time BioMedical Research had received this information, it was too late to take any action. The company terminated its relationship with the French distributor later in the year, and all Slendertone sales in France soon came to an end.

At about the same time management ended its relationship with Direct Shop. The combination of lower than expected sales, low margins, and high return rates ensured that this was never going to be a profitable undertaking for the company. Furthermore, tension with existing distributors arose when Direct Shop began to broadcast across Europe, in many cases offering a price for the Gymbody 8 that was lower than what the distributors were charging for it locally. At least the company's own sales in the United Kingdom were growing. By selling direct to customers in the United Kingdom, BioMedical Research was earning a healthy margin (though the cost of the UK office and the increasing number of promotional campaigns had to be covered).

Restructuring

There had been a widespread belief throughout the company for many years that, in the words of one manager, "more marketing was needed." Efforts in 1995 and early 1996 to recruit a "marketing manager/marketing director designate," using advertisements in Irish and UK recruitment pages, were unsuccessful. It was suggested that the credibility issue concerning Slendertone might be having an effect on recruitment. With added urgency, the company succeeded in attracting O'Donohoe to the job of marketing director for Slendertone in April 1997. O'Donohoe had gained extensive marketing experience with Waterford Glass. He saw the opportunity to develop the Slendertone brand and welcomed the responsibility the job offered. But it was not easy at first: "When I joined in April, I had to go out to France, and everyone here in the office and factory would be waiting when I came back to see if I had gotten any new orders." Recognizing the opportunity presented by the trial placements for the Gymbody 8 in various UK stores, he immediately focused on developing the company's relationships in the retail channel.

While working on increasing retail sales, O'Donohoe initiated extensive research into the various markets for Slendertone. He started to build up a clearer picture of the markets for Slendertone and its brand positioning. His analysis of the French market identified the reasons for the drop in sales. It also revealed that Slendertone was not, or ever had been, the market leader in France. Based on the distributor's reports, the company had been under the impression that Slendertone had had some 70 percent of the home-use EMS market. O'Donohoe's findings revealed that Slendertone's market share had been only a fraction of that figure. His analysis also revealed that sales of replacement pads had always been extremely low, indicating low customer product usage; it previously had been assumed that the French distributor was using a different supplier for the replacement pads. Focus group research in a number of countries showed that Slendertone had a very confused positioning: It was variously associated with dieting, weight loss, health, fitness, exercise, toning, and body shaping. The focus groups also reinforced the credibility issue. Many people's first thought on seeing the product being advertised was, Does it work? Secondary data showed the size of the different markets for areas such as health, fitness, and cosmetics in different countries. O'Donohoe also gathered data on consumer behaviour and motivations relating to those different markets.

The Business Defined

The next stage for O'Donohoe was to decide exactly what business the company was in. "I've read about this business being described as everything from the 'EMS business,' whatever that is, to 'passive gymnastics.' Our consumer research showed that Slendertone had a very confused message. We're in the self-confidence business," he states emphatically. "Self-confidence through improved appearance." He now defines the Slendertone brand as "the most effective and convenient appearance solutions." The new slogan for Slendertone will be "living life and loving it." In terms of people's deeper motivations with regard to health and fitness activities, O'Donohoe stresses a core need to look good. He states that most people work out to look good rather than to be healthy. Likewise, "people diet not for the sake of losing weight but to improve their appearance through their weight loss." It is this core need to look good which O'Donohoe is targeting with Slendertone. In spite of the company's involvement in the health market with its NeuroTech range of products, O'Donohoe is clear that Slendertone is about appearance, not health. He sees it as misleading to talk in terms of health and beauty, a trade category into which many products are placed. He puts a value of $170 billion on the self-confidence market in Europe; this figure includes the combined markets for cosmetics and fashion.

Also included in this market are men. Originally recognized as only a niche segment, male users now represent an important and fast-growing market for EMS cosmetic products. In late 1997 BioMedical Research modified the Gymbody 8 by adding rubber pads and redesigning the packaging and launched the Gymbody for Men. This was very successful and opened up a new market segment for Slendertone.

The company has begun extensive consumer trials at a clinic in Galway to gain a better understanding of the exact physiological benefits of Slendertone and to identify new ways to measure those benefits. According to O'Donohoe, "We want to get away from the earlier measurements of effectiveness, such as 'inch loss.'" He is conscious of the added psychological benefits that these products might offer users. BioMedical's researchers also are using these trials to identify ways to improve product convenience and comfort.

Repositioning Slendertone

By early 1999 Slendertone products were being stocked in over 2,300 retail outlets, primarily in the United Kingdom. O'Donohoe states that the increasing emphasis on retail has to be seen in terms of a complete repositioning of the Slendertone brand. "Using Direct Shop [television home shopping] was the worst thing ever for this company. And look at these [French] magazine advertisements: lots of exclamation marks, sensational product claims, very cluttered, and the models used!" he remarks, reviewing the earlier marketing of Slendertone. O'Donohoe says it is these promotional tactics which have resulted in a "gadget" positioning for Slendertone, one he is working on changing. Furthermore, he says, by making excessive product claims the company was unlikely to meet customer expectations. This was jeopardizing the opportunity for repeat purchases of Slendertone products by existing customers. Gone, says O'Donohoe, are the promises of "effortless exercise": "We are telling customers they need to work with the products to get results. This is resulting in a different type of customer for Slendertone; we want to get away from the 'gadget-freaks.'" It is this different type of customer O'Donohoe hopes will also purchase other Slendertone-branded products in the future. The target market for Slendertone now is women and men age 20 to 60 years. The earlier niche segments, such as the "postnatals," no longer are being targeted separately. O'Donohoe believes it is important to keep the Slendertone message focused rather than having different messages for different segments of the market.

Central to O'Donohoe's strategy is the development of Slendertone into a brand in its own right. From now on O'Donohoe wants people to associate Slendertone with "effective and convenient appearance solutions" rather than EMS devices: "Slendertone will be a brand that just happens to have EMS products." The Slendertone range could in the future include many types of products. The company has just created the position of brand extensions manager to plan the development of the Slendertone range. O'Donohoe believes the company is now in a position to create an international brand: "People will tell you it takes hundreds of millions to create an international brand. We don't agree."

A priority for O'Donohoe in his goal to develop the Slendertone brand is an increased emphasis on the Slendertone name. In addition to a redesign of all the product packaging to reflect more "real" users in "real" situations (see Exhibits 1 and 2), all the product names have been changed. The original Gymbody 8 will now be marketed as the Slendertone Body, the Face Up is now the Slendertone Face, and the Celluforme has become the Slendertone Body Plus. The male products will be the Slendertone Body Profile and the Slendertone Body Profile Sports, which has been adapted from the Total Body unit. Along with the Slendertone Total Body, these products constitute the full Slendertone home-use range, reduced from some 25 products three years earlier. A new professional unit, utilizing innovative touch-screen technology and "space-age" design, is about to be launched. O'Donohoe sees the professional market playing an important role in the development of Slendertone. He does not believe that the home-use and professional markets are competing; the company's experience has been that promotions for the home-use products raise awareness (and sales) for the professional market. The company currently has four staff members dedicated to developing the professional market in the United Kingdom.

Accessing the Market

O'Donohoe continues to put greater emphasis on developing retail channels, which, he says, "still represent over 95 percent of sales for all products sold worldwide in spite of the current hype about direct marketing." He believes he is able to secure retail space from important multiples because he is offering them unique access to the body-shape section of the appearance market. For these retailers Slendertone represents a new category of good, with higher than average revenues. On a shop-shelf "mock-up" in a small room at the back of the office, there is a display of the new Slendertone range, alongside massagers and shavers and other personal care products. O'Donohoe is conscious of the attention Slendertone has been attracting from the big players in the personal care market. In some cases they have been losing vital shelf space to this relatively unknown company from Ireland. He believes that BioMedical Research's expertise in the marketing of EMS products, a strong brand, and greater company flexibility (because of smaller size) will enable the company to defend itself against the multinational companies now looking at the EMS market.

The focus on retail does not mean an end to the use of direct marketing. Direct sales still account for around half of all UK sales. O'Donohoe sees direct marketing continuing to play an important role in developing the UK market and newer markets. The new direct response advertisements have been changed to reflect the move toward a stronger Slendertone brand identity and away from the "oversell" of earlier years (see Exhibit 3).

EXHIBIT 1
The Cover of the Gymbody 8 Case (Used since 1994)

EXHIBIT 2
The Cover of the 'Slendertone Body' Case (Introduced in 1999)

The company will continue to use distributors for some markets. However O'Donohoe is determined to have greater company control over the brand than was the case in the past. By maintaining "control of the message" he believes the company can avoid a recurrence of what happened in the French market. Through a strong brand identity and a carefully controlled and differentiated image, he intends to protect the Slendertone name and market from the activities of other EMS companies. He does not plan to compete on price with the lower-quality producers; he believes that by investing in the Slendertone brand the company will be able to offer the customer greater total value at a higher price. The company will develop important markets such as Germany and France directly, as it has done successfully in the United Kingdom. Slendertone offices in Frankfurt and Paris have just been opened. O'Donohoe is conscious of the cost of establishing and maintaining international operations and the need to develop those markets successfully and promptly.

Slendertone: The Future

The company views the potential for Slendertone on two fronts: the existing potential for EMS-based products (including the existing Slendertone range and new, improved EMS products) and the potential for non-EMS Slendertone products. O'Donohoe believes he can restore Slendertone's fortunes in the French market: "The need is still there." He is conscious of bad feeling which may still exist within the trade, but other companies are operating again in this market (including BioMedical's former distributor, which now sells a lower-quality EMS product). There is still a lack of published secondary data for the EMS cosmetic market in any country. It is believed that the United Kingdom is now by far the largest EMS market. Company research indicates that the other markets with significant EMS sales are Spain and Italy. There is currently little EMS sales activity being observed by the company in Germany. In light of the level of sales being attained in Ireland (which has continued to grow every year since 1991) and the phenomenal recent growth in England, combined with a universal desire to look good, O'Donohoe envisages rapid growth for the existing Slendertone range in the short term. The potential for the extended Slendertone range in the longer term is much greater. Realizing this potential will depend on how effective the marketing strategy is in addressing all the issues and how well it is implemented.

For some the question might remain, Can Kevin McDonnell succeed in offering self-confidence to millions around the world from a factory in the wilds of Donegal? Certainly the locals in Bunbeg wouldn't doubt it.

CASE 7–7
LONGEVITY HEALTHCARE SYSTEMS, INC.

Kathryn Hamilton, president of Longevity Healthcare Systems, Inc., located in Grand Rapids, Michigan, was reviewing the 1993 annual statements. "We concluded another terrific year," she commented. "Our sales and earnings exceeded expectations, but I'm concerned about the next few years." Although Longevity was successful, it was beginning to experience competition and the uncertainty of health-care reform. In February 1994 a large hospital in Grand Rapids, Michigan, had converted an entire wing to a long-term care facility. The hospital also had initiated an aggressive sales and advertising campaign and was competing with Longevity for new nursing home residents.

Longevity's recent acquisition of seven nursing homes in Toledo, Ohio, was proving to be an unprofitable venture. Many of the residents were on Medicare and Medicaid, and those health insurance programs generally did not reimburse the full costs of care. Additionally, the families of the Toledo residents were becoming value-conscious and frequently commented about the quality and cost of nursing care. Kathryn realized that to improve the profitability, attention would have to be given to customer satisfaction and to attracting more profitable private-pay residents. Health-care reform was also a source of concern. It was her belief that reform of the health-care industry would be comprehensive, with increased emphasis on cost control, competitive pricing, and quality of care. She wondered what effect reform would have on Longevity and what the timetable for legislative action would be.

While increased competition and health-care reform seemed certain, the most profitable path for future growth was not clear because several marketing opportunities existed. An aging population had created a strong demand for long-term care in nursing homes. Alzheimer's disease was also becoming more common. Longevity recently had lost some nursing home residents to Alzheimer's treatment centers because the company did not offer a specialized facility. Kathryn had to decide whether offering Alzheimer's disease treatment would be desirable.

Opportunities to expand existing businesses were also an option. The Grand Rapids pharmacy acquired in 1992 had been successfully phased in Longevity, and Kathryn was wondering if a similar acquisition would work in Toledo. However, she was concerned about the impact of reform on the pricing of prescription drugs and medical supplies. To date, the pharmacy had been very profitable, but what would the future hold?

Geographic expansion of the firm's nursing and subacute care facilities also might be a profitable avenue for growth. Industry consolidation was making it possible to acquire nursing homes and unprofitable hospitals that could be converted to health-care facilities. However, Kathryn envisioned that a future industry trend might be toward vertical integration of health-care services. If so, it might make sense to further integrate Longevity's business in the Grand Rapids and Toledo markets before committing to additional geographic expansion.

This case was written by Professor Lawrence M. Lamont and Elizabeth W. Storey, Washington and Lee University. Case material is prepared as a basis for class discussion and not designed to present illustrations of either effective or ineffective handling of administrative problems. The names of the firms and individuals, locations, and/or financial information have been disguised to preserve anonymity. Copyright © 1994, Lawrence M. Lamont. Used with permission.

Beyond decisions on the future direction of Longevity, Kathryn wondered if it was time to begin thinking about a more formal approach to marketing. "I really need to get some ideas about marketing in our different businesses down on paper so I can see how they fit with my views on an overall corporate marketing strategy," she remarked.

History of Longevity Healthcare Systems, Inc.

In 1972 Kathryn Hamilton, R.N., was searching for a nursing home for her mother in Grand Rapids, Michigan. Discouraged by a six-month wait for admission, she decided to move her into the home she occupied with her husband, Richard. Dr. Hamilton, M.D., had a medical practice in Grand Rapids specializing in care for older adults.

A Nursing Home Business.   In 1974, Richard's mother and father joined the household and Kathryn and Richard continued to learn how to care for older adults. In 1976, the Hamiltons leased a small, outdated 40-bed hospital in a nearby suburb and converted it into a long-term care facility. After certification, the facility was opened in 1977 as the Longevity Nursing Home. In addition to their parents, 10 other adults over 65 entered the home during the year. All were "private-pay," meaning they paid directly for services with personal assets but without government assistance. By 1979 the nursing facility was fully occupied with private-pay residents. Longevity was incorporated, and Kathryn Hamilton became the president and director of nursing, while her husband provided medical services and continued his practice. The leased facility was purchased in 1979.

New Nursing Services.   By 1980 Longevity found it necessary to add additional nursing services for aging residents. Two levels of care were added, and professional nurses were hired to provide the services. The new services were favorably received, and the referrals from residents and physicians kept the facility filled.

Expansion by Acquisition, 1980–1985.   The demand for nursing care was strong in the early 1980s, and Longevity expanded. Eight unprofitable nursing homes with a total of 480 beds were acquired in Grand Rapids and nearby communities. All the homes were licensed, certified by Medicare and Medicaid, and occupied by residents requiring a variety of nursing services. Shortly after the acquisition, Dr. Hamilton left his medical practice to join Longevity full-time as its medical director. He added skilled nursing care for residents requiring 24-hour-a-day care, and rehabilitation services for those needing physical, speech, and occupational therapy.

Nursing Home Construction.   From 1986 to 1988 Longevity expanded by constructing three 70-bed nursing homes in nearby communities. Each provided the full range of nursing and rehabilitation services and was licensed for Medicare and Medicaid-patients.[1] The homes were quickly filled, and by the end of 1988 Longevity operated 12 nursing homes with a total of 730 beds. Employment had grown to 1,200 full-time and part-time employees.

---

[1] By 1988 all Longevity nursing homes were certified to receive Medicare and Medicaid patients. Medicare is a federally funded and administered health insurance program that reimburses health-care facilities for nursing and medical services. Medicaid is a state-administered reimbursement program that covers skilled and intermediate long-term care for the medically indigent. The benefits paid by Medicaid programs vary from state to state.

EXHIBIT 1 **Longevity Healthcare Systems, Inc., Historical Development, 1972–1993**

Date	Activity
1972–75	Nursing care for parents.
1976–77	Leased a 40-bed hospital and converted it to a nursing home.
1979	Business incorporated as Longevity Nursing Home.
1979	Corporation purchased leased nursing home.
1980–85	Acquired eight nursing homes in Grand Rapids area, 480 beds.
1986–88	Constructed three nursing homes in Grand Rapids area, 210 beds.
1990–91	Converted a 30-bed wing of Grand Rapids nursing home into subacute care.
1992–93	Constructed a 50-bed subacute care facility in Grand Rapids area.
1992	Acquired a retail pharmacy in Grand Rapids.
1992–93	Acquired seven nursing homes in Toledo area, 280 beds.
1993	Corporation name changed to Longevity Healthcare Systems, Inc.

New Business Opportunities. During a medical convention in 1990, Kathryn Hamilton noted a growing concern over the escalating costs of hospital care and the desire of insurance providers to shorten the hospitalization of patients requiring medical supervision but not the other services traditionally provided by hospitals. Sensing an opportunity, the Hamiltons converted a 30-bed wing of one of the Grand Rapids nursing homes to a subacute care facility for patients who did not need the full services of a licensed acute care hospital.[2] For patients moved from a hospital to the Longevity facility, the needed care was provided for about half the cost. The subacute care facility was licensed in 1991 and quickly filled with referrals from hospitals, physicians, and health-care insurers.

The growing recognition that treating patients requiring subacute care in low-overhead nursing facilities was a cost-effective alternative substantially increased the demand for Longevity's subacute care. In 1992, following marketing research, Longevity constructed a 50-bed subacute care facility near one of its nursing homes. It was completed in 1993 and within a few months operated at capacity with patients referred from insurance companies, physicians, and Longevity nursing homes.

As the demand for specialized nursing and medical care expanded, it became apparent that profitability could be improved by operating a pharmacy. In 1992 Longevity acquired a retail pharmacy in Grand Rapids from a retiring pharmacist. It was converted into an institutional pharmacy to provide prescriptions, medical equipment and supplies, and consulting services to Longevity facilities.

Geographic Expansion. Late in 1992 what appeared to be an exceptional business opportunity came to the attention of Kathryn and Richard Hamilton. A few hundred miles away, in Toledo, Ohio, a large health-care company was selling seven unprofitable nursing homes with a total of 280 beds for $12 million. The homes were occupied primarily

---

[2] Medical services fall along a continuum of intensive care, acute care, subacute care, nursing care, and home health care. Hospitals offer intensive and acute care for patients with complex medical conditions. They have fully equipped operating and recovery rooms, radiology services, intensive and coronary care units, pharmacies, clinical laboratories, therapy services, and emergency services. Subacute care facilities owned by nursing homes serve the needs of patients who require nursing and medical care but not many of the specialized services and equipment provided by an acute care hospital.

EXHIBIT 2   Longevity Healthcare Systems, Inc., Geographic Location of Facilities

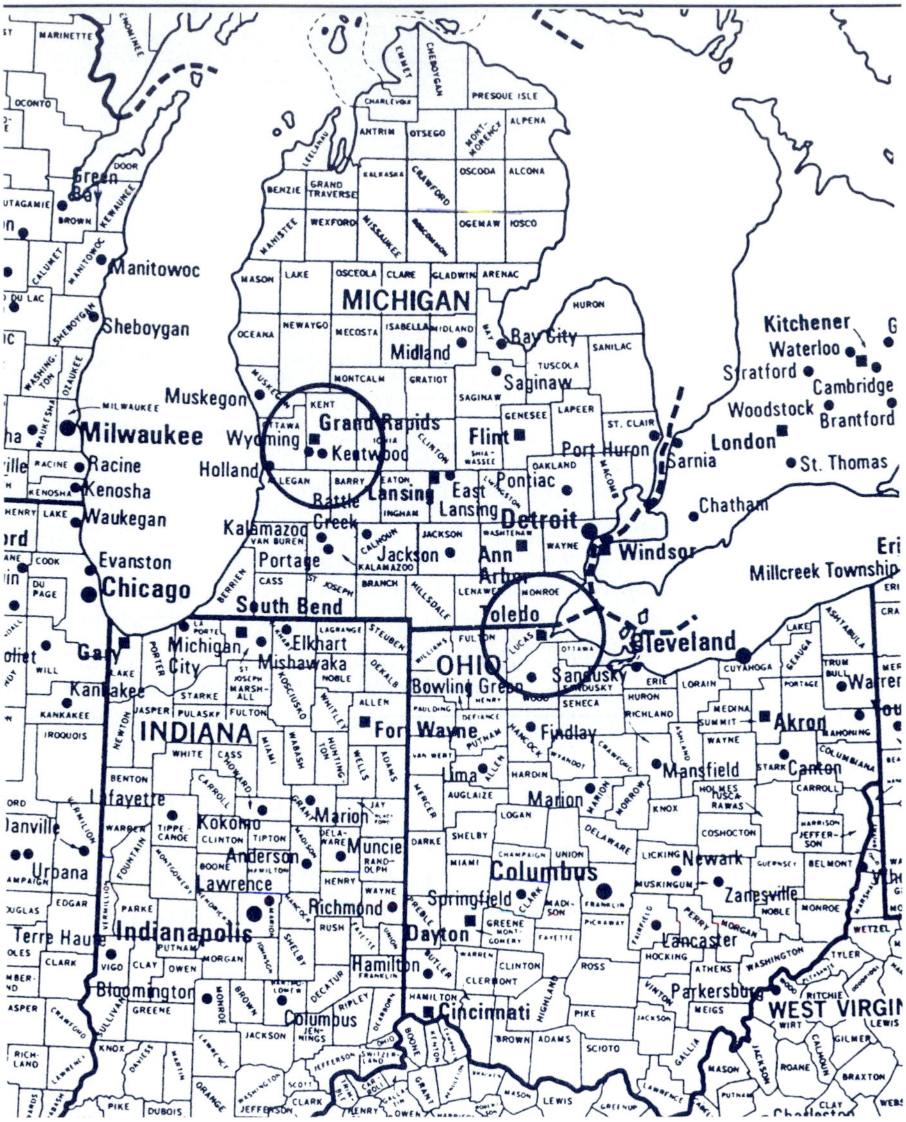

by Medicare and Medicaid patients and operated at 70 percent of capacity. The Hamiltons decided to take a one-year option on the facilities while they raised the money to complete the purchase. Eventually, 40 percent of Longevity's common stock was sold to a large insurance company, and some of the proceeds were used to exercise the purchase option. Kathryn Hamilton hired an experienced administrator and assigned him the task of returning the nursing homes to profitability. To reflect the company's broadening scope in the health-care industry, the Hamiltons decided to change the company name to Longevity Healthcare Systems, Inc. As shown in Exhibits 1 and 2, Longevity ended 1993 with 12 nursing homes, two subacute care facilities, and a pharmacy in Michigan and seven nursing homes in Ohio. Exhibits 3 and 4 contain the financial statements for the

EXHIBIT 3   **Longevity Healthcare Systems, Inc., Income Statement (Year Ending Dec. 31, 1993)**

Net revenues	
Basic LTC services	$45,500,000
Subacute medical services	9,000,000
Pharmacy services	3,000,000
Total revenues	$57,500,000
Operating expenses	
Salaries, wages, and benefits	$20,125,000
Patient services	21,275,000
Administrative and general	3,450,000
Depreciation and amortization	575,000
Total costs and expenses	$45,425,000
Income from operations	$12,075,000
Interest expense	1,726,111
Earnings before taxes	$10,348,889
Income taxes	4,139,555
Net income	$ 6,209,334
Net income per share	$ 0.78

EXHIBIT 4   **Longevity Healthcare Systems, Inc., Balance Sheet (Years Ending Dec. 31, 1993, and Dec. 31, 1992)**

Assets	1993	1992
Current assets		
Cash and equivalents	$ 841,770	$ 501,120
Accounts receivable	3,265,584	2,702,552
Inventory	2,262,816	1,624,399
Property, plant, and equipment		
Land	9,959,051	7,690,249
Buildings and improvements	27,002,416	13,622,079
Equipment	2,917,136	2,179,842
Accumulated depreciation	(4,028,149)	(2,464,535)
Other assets		
Goodwill	791,794	655,278
Other long-term assets	5,163,275	4,063,190
Total assets	$48,175,693	$30,574,174
Liabilities and Shareholders' Equity		
Current liabilities		
Accounts payable	$ 1,250,201	$ 1,043,648
Accrued expenses	708,447	586,301
Accrued compensation	416,734	344,883
Current portion of long-term debt	2,041,995	2,700,120
Accrued interest	196,694	203,954
Long-term debt (net)	10,506,622	12,871,452
Shareholders' equity		
Common stock, $.01 par value	50,000	50,000
Additional paid-in capital	17,870,666	3,848,816
Retained earnings	15,134,334	8,925,000
Total liabilities and shareholders' equity	$48,175,693	$30,574,174

EXHIBIT 5 **Longevity Healthcare Systems, Inc., Historical Revenues and Net Income**

Year	Revenues	Net Income
1993	$57,500,000	$6,209,334
1992	46,575,000	5,029,560
1991	37,260,000	3,017,736
1990	26,715,420	2,987,692
1989	21,799,783	1,334,147

EXHIBIT 6 **Longevity Healthcare Systems, Inc., Selected Pharmacy Information (Year Ending Dec. 31, 1993)**

Income Statement

Net revenue	$3,000,000
Operating expenses	2,430,000
Operating income	570,000
Net income	390,000

Financial Ratios

Current ratio	1.94
Inventory turnover	4.20
Profit margin (percent)	13.00%
Return on assets (percent)	9.29%

EXHIBIT 7 **Longevity Healthcare Systems, Inc., Operating Information for Facilities (Year Ending Dec. 31, 1993)**

	Grand Rapids	Toledo	Total
Payer mix			
Private and other	69.7%	18.7%	44.2%
Medicare	8.4	17.8	13.1
Medicaid	21.9	63.5	42.7
Occupancy	96.4%	81.2%	88.8%
No. of beds	780	280	1,060

year ending December 31, 1993. Exhibit 5 presents a five-year sales and earnings history, while Exhibit 6 provides some financial information for the pharmacy.

Longevity Marketing

Marketing was used to promote high occupancy in Longevity facilities, expand the percentage of private-pay residents, and increase the profits of its institutional pharmacy. Operating information for the health-care facilities is shown in Exhibit 7, and the products and services marketed by Longevity are summarized in Exhibit 8.

EXHIBIT 8   Longevity Healthcare Systems, Inc., Products and Services

Business	Products/Services
Nursing care	Custodial care
	Assisted living
	Intermediate nursing care
	Skilled nursing care
Subacute care for	Lung and heart disease
	Coma, pain, and wound care
	Spinal cord injuries
	Head injuries
	Intravenous therapy
	Joint replacements
Rehabilitation services	Occupational therapy
	Physical therapy
	Speech therapy
Institutional pharmacy	Prescription drugs
	Nonprescription drugs
	Medical supplies
	Medical equipment
	Consulting services

Nursing care was marketed locally. The administrator and admissions director of each facility designed a marketing strategy to increase awareness of the nursing home and its services in the market it served. Personal selling using telemarketing and direct contact was targeted to referral sources such as physicians, hospital administrators, home health agencies, community organizations and churches, senior citizens groups, retirement communities, and the families of prospective residents. Longevity also distributed promotional literature discussing its philosophy of care, services, and quality standards. Frequently the literature was provided to prospective residents and their families when they inquired about nursing or toured the facilities.

Marketing for subacute care was directed by Kathryn Hamilton, who contacted insurance companies, managed care organizations such as HMOs, hospital administrators, and other third-party payers to promote Longevity's services.[3] Kathryn also attended professional meetings where she maintained contact with the various referral sources.

The products and services of the institutional pharmacy were marketed by the pharmacy manager and his assistant through direct contact with Longevity facilities, other nursing homes, hospitals, clinics, and home health agencies. In addition to drugs and medical supplies, management also provided consulting services to help ensure quality patient care. These services were especially valuable because they enabled the nursing homes to admit patients who required more complex and profitable medical services.

---

[3] Managed care organizations provide health-care products that integrate financing and management with the delivery of health-care services through a network of providers (such as nursing homes and hospitals) that share financial risk or have incentives to deliver cost-effective services. An HMO (health maintenance organization) provides prepaid health-care services to its members through physicians employed by the HMO at facilities owned by the HMO or through a network of independent physicians and facilities. HMOs actively manage patient care to maximize quality and cost-effectiveness.

EXHIBIT 9 **Longevity Healthcare Systems, Inc., Example Resident Statement for Nursing Care (per Month)***

Semiprivate room, $105.00 per day	$3,150.00
Basic telephone service	15.00
Rehabilitation therapy, 7.0 hours per month	840.00
Pharmacy and other specialized services	360.00
Miscellaneous personal expenses	50.00
Total	$4,415.00
Per day	147.17

*Based on private pay. Includes room and board, 24-hour professional nursing care, meals, housekeeping, and linen services. Social and recreational activity programs also are included.

Nursing Home Services.   Longevity nursing homes provided room and board, dietary services, recreation and social activities, housekeeping and laundry services, four levels of nursing care, and numerous specialized services. Custodial care was provided to residents who needed minimal care. Assisted living was used by persons needing some assistance with personal care such as bathing and eating. Intermediate care was provided to residents needing more nursing and attention but not continuous access to nurses. Finally, skilled nursing care was available to residents requiring the professional services of a nurse on a 24-hour-a-day basis. Rehabilitation therapy was also available for residents who had disabilities or were returning from hospitalization for surgery or illness. Rehabilitation was an important part of Longevity's care because it helped residents improve their quality of life.

Most of the residents in Longevity nursing homes were female and over 65. Although rates depended on accommodations and the services used, a typical nursing home bed generated monthly revenues of $4,415. It was common for residents to initially enter the nursing home needing only custodial care or assisted living and to progress to higher levels of nursing care as they aged. Exhibit 9 provides a typical schedule of monthly charges for a resident in a semiprivate room with seven hours of therapy.

All the Longevity nursing homes were licensed in their respective states. Generally, the licenses had to be renewed annually. For renewal, state health-care agencies considered the physical condition of the facility, the qualifications of the administrative and medical staff, the quality of care, and the facility's compliance with the applicable laws and regulations.

Subacute Care.   Longevity marketed subacute care for patients with more complex medical needs that required constant medical supervision but not the expensive equipment and services of an acute care hospital. Subacute care generated higher profit margins than did nursing care, although patient stays in the facility were usually shorter.[4] Daily patient rates varied from $250 to $750, depending on the services and equipment required. Longevity's services included care for patients with lung and heart disease, spinal cord and head injuries, joint replacements, coma, pain and wound care, and intravenous therapy. Services at the subacute care facilities were not limited to the eld-

---

[4] Longevity profit margins for subacute care facilities were about 25 percent higher than those for nursing care facilities. The length of stay was usually 20 to 45 days versus eight months for private-pay nursing care and two years for Medicaid patients.

erly. Younger patients discharged from hospitals were attractive because of their longer life expectancy and eventual need for nursing and rehabilitation. Based on an average rate of $1,000 per day charged by acute care hospitals, Longevity knew that its prices were substantially lower for comparable services. Like the nursing homes, the subacute care facilities were subject to licensing by the state health-care agencies and certification by Medicare. All Longevity subacute care facilities were licensed and certified.

Pharmacy Products and Services. Longevity provided pharmacy products and services to nursing homes, retirement communities, and other health-care organizations. The pharmacy's products were frequently customized with special packaging and dispensing systems and delivered daily. The pharmacy also consulted on medications and long-term care regulations and provided computerized tracking of medications, medical records processing, and 24-hour emergency services.

The Market for Long-Term Health Care

Long-term health care includes basic health care (such as that provided in nursing homes), rehabilitation therapy and Alzheimer's care, institutional pharmacy services, subacute care, and home health care. In recent years spending for these and other health-care services has increased significantly. For example, in 1993, one out of every seven dollars that Americans spent went to purchase health care. Total expenditures are projected to increase from $585.3 billion in 1990 to $3,457.7 billion in 2010, an annual growth rate of over 9 percent.

Nursing homes are important providers of long-term health care. Expenditures for nursing home care are expected to increase at a comparable rate, from $53.1 billion in 1990 to $310.1 billion in 2010. This industry consists of about 16,000 licensed facilities with a total of 1,700,000 beds. It includes a large number of small, locally owned nursing homes and a growing number of regional and national companies. The industry is undergoing restructuring in response to stricter regulation, increasing complexity of medical services, and competitive pressures. Smaller, local operators that lack sophisticated management and financial resources are being acquired by larger, more established companies. At present, the 20 largest firms operate about 18 percent of the nursing facilities. Consolidation is expected to continue, but the long-term outlook is extremely positive for the businesses that survive. Nursing home revenues increased by about 12 percent in 1993 and are expected to experience similar gains in 1994. Several factors account for the optimistic outlook: favorable demographic trends, pressures to control costs, advances in medical technology, and a limited supply of nursing beds.

Favorable Demographic Trends. Demographic trends, namely, growth in the elderly segment of the population, are increasing the demand for health care and the services of nursing homes. Most of the market for nursing care consists of men and women 65 years of age and older. Their number was approximately 25 million in 1980 and is projected to increase to 35 million by 2000 and 40 million by 2010. The 65-and-over segment suffers from a greater incidence of chronic illnesses and disabilities and currently accounts for about two-thirds of the health-care expenditures in the United States.

Pressures to Control Costs. Government and private payers have adopted cost control measures to encourage reduced hospital stays. In addition, private insurers have begun to limit reimbursement to "reasonable" charges, while managed care organizations are limiting hospitalization costs by monitoring utilization and negotiating discounted rates. As a result, hospital stays have been shortened and many patients are discharged with a continuing need for care. Because nursing homes are able to provide services at lower prices, the cost pressures have increased the demand for nursing home services and subacute care after hospital discharge.

Advances in Medical Technology.   Advances in technology leading to improved medications and surgical procedures have increased life expectancies. Adults over age 85 are now the fastest-growing segment of the population, and their numbers are expected to double over the next 20 years. Many require skilled care and the medical equipment traditionally available only in hospitals. Nursing homes are acquiring some of the specialty medical equipment and providing skilled nursing care to older adults through subacute care facilities.

Limited Supply of Nursing Beds.   The supply of nursing home beds has been limited by the availability of financing and high construction and start-up expenses. Additionally, the supply has been constrained by legislation limiting licenses for new nursing beds in states that require a demonstration of need. The effect has been to create a barrier to market entry and conditions where the demand for nursing home services exceeds the available supply in many states.

National Health-Care Reform

The next decade will be a period of reform for the health-care system. Although it is not clear how comprehensive the reform will be and how it will be financed, the focus will be on controlling costs and providing universal access to quality health care. The most likely plan probably will reform the health insurance industry, build on the current employer-financed approach, and call for market incentives to control costs. To ensure universal access, insurance and managed care companies will be prohibited from dropping, rejecting, or pricing out of the market anyone with an expensive medical condition.

Reform will affect providers of long-term care such as nursing homes in several ways. It will regulate the insurance companies to make health insurance more price-competitive and affordable. This change will favorably affect long-term health-care providers by increasing the number of residents paying with insurance benefits. Reform also may extend Medicare coverage for home health care. A change such as this would encourage more older adults to receive health care at home instead of at a nursing facility, resulting in an unfavorable impact.

Employers also will have incentives to control costs and deliver quality care. Increasingly they will rely on managed care organizations, such as HMOs, that are likely to contract lower-cost providers, such as nursing homes, for subacute care and other cost-effective services. Companies capable of providing a variety of health-care services at attractive prices should see opportunities to expand demand.

Institutional pharmacies also will be affected by health-care reform. President Clinton's Health Security Act called for the addition of prescription drug coverage to the Medicare program. If adopted, this provision probably would decrease the prices of prescription drugs through regulation of pharmaceutical manufacturers. Price decreases, either legislated or achieved through managed care and the market system, may allow institutional pharmacies to earn higher profit margins while still providing medications at affordable prices to patients.

Regulation and Competition

Health-care providers are regulated at the state and federal levels. Regulation affects financial management and the quality and safety of care. Ensuring that health-care facilities are in compliance with regulatory standards is an important aspect of managing a health-care business. In addition, management increasingly is confronted with competition. Nursing homes and subacute care facilities compete for patients who are able to select from a variety of alternatives to meet their needs. Managed care and insurance organizations also negotiate aggressively with health-care providers to ensure quality care at attractive prices.

Financial Regulation.   The Health Care Financing Administration (HCFA) is the federal regulatory agency for Medicare and Medicaid. Both programs are cost-based and use a per diem payment schedule that reimburses the provider for a portion of the costs of care. Each facility must apply to participate in the Medicare and Medicaid programs and then have its beds certified to provide skilled nursing, intermediate, or other levels of care. A nursing home may have a mix of beds at any time, but it must match patient services to each bed. A facility cannot place a Medicare patient requiring skilled nursing care in a bed certified for intermediate care without recertifying the bed for skilled care. Recertification often requires a month or more.

Quality and Safety of Care.   Much of the current regulation facing nursing homes was developed in the Omnibus Budget Reconciliation Act of 1987 (OBRA 87). Facilities that participate in Medicare and Medicaid must be inspected regularly by state survey teams under contract with HCFA to ensure safety and quality of care. OBRA 87 also established a resident "bill of rights" that essentially converted nursing homes from merely custodial facilities into centers for rehabilitation. Nursing homes are now required to establish a care plan for patients and conduct assessments to ensure that the facility achieves the highest practical level of well-being for each resident.

Competition.   Longevity competes with acute care and rehabilitation hospitals, other nursing and subacute care facilities, home health-care agencies, and institutional pharmacies. Some offer services and prices that are comparable to those offered by Longevity.

Nursing homes compete on the basis of their reputation in the community, the ability to meet particular needs, the location and appearance of the facility, and the price of services. When a nursing facility is being selected, members of a prospective resident's family usually participate by visiting and evaluating nursing homes over a period of several weeks.

Some of the competing nursing homes in Grand Rapids and Toledo are operated by nonprofit organizations (churches and fraternal organizations) that can finance capital expenditures on a tax-exempt basis or receive charitable contributions to subsidize their operations. They compete with Longevity on the basis of price for private-pay residents.

Longevity competes for subacute care patients with acute care and rehabilitation hospitals, nursing homes, and home health agencies. The competition is generally local or regional, and the competitive factors are similar to those for nursing care, although more emphasis is placed on support services such as third-party reimbursement, information management, and patient record keeping. Insurance and managed care organizations exert considerable influence on the decision and increase the competition by negotiating with several health-care providers.

The institutional pharmacy market has no dominant competitor in the markets served by Longevity. Twenty percent of the market is accounted for by the institutional pharmacies owned by nursing homes. Independent institutional pharmacies control about 35 percent of the market, and retail pharmacies supply the remainder. Retail pharmacies are steadily being acquired by nursing homes and independents to gain market share and achieve economies of scale in purchasing prescriptions and medical supplies. Institutional pharmacies compete on the basis of fast customer-oriented service, price, and the ability to provide consulting and information management services to customers.

Marketing Issues and Opportunities

Kathryn Hamilton believed that Longevity could improve its marketing. She was concerned about the efforts of individual nursing homes and the need to improve the marketing of subacute care to managed care providers. Finally, she believed that customer satisfaction would become an important competitive factor and that Longevity would need to assess the reactions of nursing home residents and their families to the quality of its services.

Continued growth was also on Kathryn's mind. Population demographics and health-care reform would create outstanding opportunities for businesses that could design and implement successful marketing strategies. For some time she had been thinking about expanding into Alzheimer's treatment because of the demographics and the growing need for facilities in the Grand Rapids area. Additionally, she saw an opportunity to further integrate Longevity by establishing a pharmacy in Toledo or acquiring nursing homes in a new market such as South Bend, Indiana. Each marketing opportunity seemed to make sense, and so the final choices would be difficult.

Local Marketing of Health-Care Services.   Although local marketing had worked well, duplication of effort and overlapping market areas were becoming problems as the number of nursing homes in a market increased. Kathryn wondered what the marketing strategy for nursing home services should be and whether the marketing efforts of the Grand Rapids and Toledo nursing homes could be coordinated in each area to eliminate duplication and preserve local identity. One approach she was considering was to hire a marketing specialist to work with the nursing homes to attract more private-pay customers. Advertising was a related issue because it had not been used, and Kathryn questioned whether it should be part of the marketing strategy. Should an advertising campaign be created for all the nursing homes in a market, or should it be left to nursing home administrators to decide if advertising was appropriate in their strategy? If advertising was to be used, a decision would have to be made on the type of advertising, the creative strategy, and the appropriate media.

Marketing Subacute Care.   Subacute care was viewed as an attractive marketing opportunity because of the profit margins. However, to further penetrate the market, a marketing strategy would have to be developed. Kathryn noted that managed care organizations and other referral sources were like organizational buyers as they made decisions on subacute care for the cases they managed. Instead of marketing the service to physicians and patient families, Longevity would negotiate directly with HMOs and insurance companies to determine services and a rate structure based on the patient's medical needs. Personal selling would be used to build a relationship with the case managers for both the insurance company and the hospital. The marketing objective was to convince the insurance companies that the subacute unit could achieve the same patient outcomes at a lower cost than a hospital. If a marketing strategy could be developed along with appropriate staffing, it might be desirable to expand this part of Longevity's business. Economics favored the conversion of a wing of an existing nursing home into a subacute care facility at a cost of $25,000 per bed. One possibility existed in Toledo, where an unprofitable 80-bed facility was operating at 60 percent of capacity. If part of the facility were upgraded to subacute care, she expected that within a short time, it would operate at capacity.

Customer Satisfaction.   Occasional complaints from nursing home residents about the price and quality of care were of concern to management. Since Longevity depended on referrals, customer satisfaction was an important element of a successful marketing strategy. In thinking about the issue, Kathryn noted that the license renewal process generally assured the maintenance of high standards in each facility, but it focused heavily on the inputs necessary to provide quality nursing care, not on customer satisfaction. Kathryn needed to decide what should be done to monitor individual nursing homes to assure customer satisfaction with Longevity's services.

Acquisition of a Toledo Pharmacy.   One marketing opportunity being considered was the acquisition of a Toledo pharmacy. From management's perspective, an acquisition was interesting because it further integrated the existing health-care operations and provided an incremental source of earnings from the Toledo market.

Management had identified an institutional pharmacy serving 15 nursing homes with 700 beds. It was offered at a cash price of $1,050,000 and generated annual revenues of approximately $1,450 per bed served. The pharmacy was quite profitable, with an average profit margin of 12.5 percent over the past five years. To consider the profitability of the acquisition, Kathryn believed it was reasonable to assume that the pharmacy would be able to serve the Longevity facilities in Toledo and retain 60 percent of the nursing home beds it currently served if it was staffed with appropriate marketing support.

One concern was the impact of health-care reform. Most of the nursing homes served by the pharmacy had a high percentage of Medicare and Medicaid patients. If the reimbursement rates for prescription drugs and medical supplies declined, what seemed to be an attractive opportunity could quickly change.

Alzheimer's Treatment.   Alzheimer's treatment was being considered because the demand for care was not being met and the development of a cure or drug therapy for the disease was progressing slowly. Kathryn believed that the demand for Alzheimer's treatment would grow at least as fast as would the over-65 population. Projections from the U.S. Department of Health and Human Services indicated that by the year 2000, the Alzheimer's care market would increase by 50 percent from the base of 4,000,000 currently suffering from the disease.

Longevity was considering establishing an Alzheimer's wing in two of the Grand Rapids nursing homes that served areas near older community residents. Each unit would serve 30 patients and would be self-contained and secured to protect residents against their wandering habits. The furniture and fixtures would be renovated to meet the needs of the Alzheimer's patient, including softer colors, more subdued lighting, a separate nurses station, and a secured entrance. If an existing facility was converted, about six nursing rooms would have to be taken out of service to provide a separate activity and dining space. However, management reasoned that the revenue loss would be offset by average monthly revenues of $3,400 per patient and costs 15 percent lower than those for the average nursing home resident. Alzheimer's patients frequently required less costly care because of their younger age, better health, and a tendency to use fewer services. Longevity management had secured cost estimates that indicated that the conversion costs would be $2,000 to $3,000 per bed.

In thinking about the opportunity, Kathryn also recalled that Alzheimer's units typically had occupancy levels above 95 percent. Patients averaged a three-year length of stay and were almost always private-pay. The marketing for Alzheimer's units focused on Alzheimer's associations, Alzheimer support groups, and church groups. Kathryn would have to decide how to position and market the Alzheimer's units so that they would not appear to conflict with or be confused with the nursing home services. This would be a difficult but important marketing challenge because nursing homes that were known to operate Alzheimer's units tended to have better relationships with referral sources. Apparently they were perceived as providing an important community service.

Toward a Comprehensive Marketing Strategy

As Kathryn Hamilton completed her review of the financial statements, she was reminded of the need to make improvements in Longevity's marketing strategies. "I wish I could just write a one-paragraph statement of the corporate marketing strategy for this company. Then I could address each of the marketing issues and opportunities using my corporate strategy as a guide," she remarked.

Certainly one issue was improving existing marketing efforts. Marketing of nursing care, subacute care, and the institutional pharmacy had been reasonably successful, but Kathryn felt uneasy about going another year without making needed changes. Since

---

EXHIBIT 10   **Longevity Healthcare Systems, Inc., Selected Demographic Information**

Category	Grand Rapids* Number	Grand Rapids* Percent of Adult Population by Category	Toledo Number	Toledo Percent of Adult Population by Category	South Bend† Number	South Bend† Percent of Adult Population by Category
Retired	235,513	18.9%	161,630	19.9%	119,401	20.0%
Age, household head						
55–64	77,383	12.4	54,421	13.2	40,661	13.4
65–74	71,142	11.4	52,772	12.8	39,448	13.0
75 and older	56,165	9.0	40,816	9.9	30,951	10.2
Median age	44.5		46.1		46.7	
Life cycle stage						
Married, 45–64	87,992	14.1	58,544	14.2	44,910	14.8
Married, 65+	61,157	9.8	42,053	10.2	34,289	11.3
Single, 45–64	44,932	7.2	31,746	7.7	23,365	7.7
Single, 65+	56,789	9.1	43,702	10.6	30,951	10.2
Median income	$32,928		$32,194		$31,264	
Adult population	1,246,101		812,212		597,003	
Nursing facilities‡	439		988		590	
Total nursing beds	49,927		92,518		64,263	

Source: *The Lifestyle Market Analyst,* 1993. Health Care Financing Administration, 1991.

*Includes Kalamazoo and Battle Creek, Michigan.

†Includes Elkhart, Indiana.

‡Statewide statistics for certified Medicare and Medicaid facilities and beds.

most of Kathryn's time was now used to manage the business, additional marketing personnel would be necessary to develop and implement the marketing strategies for the various services. How many people would be needed and how the marketing effort would be organized also had to be decided.

Because Longevity was still evolving as a company with an uncertain marketing strategy, the most profitable direction for future growth was also important. Selecting attractive marketing opportunities was complicated because the choice depended on financial resources. Should Longevity expand the institutional pharmacy business or the subacute care business, or would resources be better utilized by offering Alzheimer's care? Each would bring Longevity closer to becoming an integrated health-care provider.

Just as Kathryn moved to turn her personal computer off for the day, she noticed an electronic mail message from the administrator of the Toledo nursing homes. It said that for the first quarter of 1994, the seven nursing homes were breaking even at 81 percent occupancy and 25 percent private-pay residents. When she arrived home that evening, she was greeted by her husband, who mentioned that she had received a telephone call from a commercial real estate broker in South Bend, Indiana. The broker had located five nursing homes with a total of 450 beds that were being sold in a bankruptcy proceeding for $5 million. During dinner that evening, Richard mentioned that they needed to discuss the South Bend opportunity because the homes were attractively priced in a desirable market. It was his belief that in the future, the most profitable health-care businesses would be vertically integrated and geographically diversified. Kathryn nodded in agreement as he handed her the summary information provided in Exhibit 10 and mentioned that a decision would have to be made in five days. She thought to herself, I wonder if it's financially possible?

Case 7–8
Can Amazon Make It?

Since the beginning of the year, it has been evident that Wall Street has become disenchanted with its former Internet darling, Amazon.com Inc. Sure, Amazon still had its impressive customer base, over $1 billion in cash, and expanding sales. But as with the smaller dot-coms, Amazon seemed a long way from profitability and was boasting an increasingly unjustifiable valuation. Top tech-fund managers began to reduce and even eliminate Amazon from their portfolios. It was the end of Amazon's fairy-tale existence as the one e-tailer with seemingly unlimited prospects. After hitting a peak of $106^{11}\!/_{16}$ on Dec. 10 and trending downward until mid-June, Amazon's stock price appeared to settle into a trading range between the mid-40s and mid-50s.

Holy War

Nonetheless, Amazon still had plenty of true believers among investors and the equity analysts. For them, it was the world according to Amazon CEO Jeffrey P. Bezos: The dot-com's balance-sheet negatives could be easily overlooked. Why? Because the company went into the red to build up a dominant position in e-commerce, and as triple-digit growth rates and expansion into new product lines led to far heftier sales, Amazon would eventually cross over into profitability.

Then, on June 22, Lehman Brothers Inc. debt analyst Ravi Suria released a scathing report about Amazon's deteriorating credit situation. And the Holy War began in earnest.

Suria painted the picture of a company hemorrhaging money. The only triple-digit growth that mattered, he argued, was in Amazon's cash-flow losses. The report shook many remaining stalwarts, and the stock dropped 19% in one day. Suria addressed Wall Street's darkest fears: that the business model on which Amazon—and for that matter, most e-tailers—is based may be flawed. Arguing that excessive debt and poor inventory management will make Amazon's operating cash-flow situation worse the more it sells, Suria suggested that cash was being devoured at such a rate that the company might eventually find it difficult to meet its obligations by the end of the first quarter next year.

This is scary stuff. After all, if Amazon can't make money in e-retailing, who can? Amazon was quick to scoff at the notion that its model is flawed, although it concedes execution could be improved as it ramps up from selling books and CDs to offering up everything from lawn chairs to power saws. Dismissing Suria's concerns as "baloney," Bezos claims the company will have positive operating cash flow over the next three quarters. And even though the company acknowledges that it may be forced to dip into its cash stash again in the first quarter of 2001, Bezos insists that Amazon is on the road to profitability (Exhibit 1).

Ticking Clock

On the surface, the debate appears to focus on arcane accounting issues. But underlying them is a fundamental question: Can Amazon deliver profits—and how soon?

Source: "Can Amazon Make It?" *Business Week*, July 10, 2000, 38–43.

EXHIBIT 1

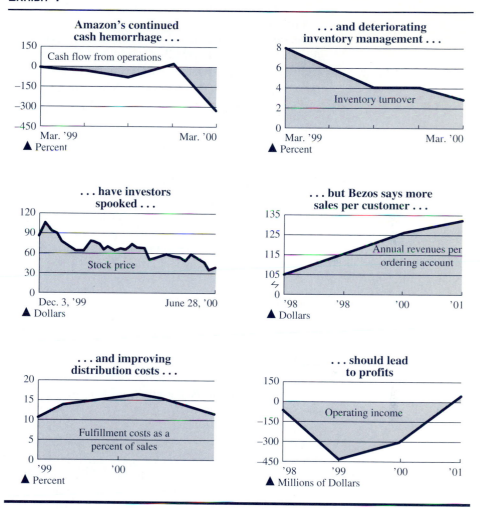

Source: Lehman Brothers Inc.; Goldman, Sachs & Co.; Bloomberg Financial Markets.

The timing is crucial, because until now, Amazon hasn't had to generate cash or profits. Its growth, critics contend, has been almost entirely funded by investors and the debt market.

But the dot-com implosion means that Amazon's access to new capital will likely be cut off now, so the clock is ticking. It must begin to replenish its cash through its operations rather than constantly depleting it. Although many analysts think Suria is overly pessimistic and give Amazon closer to six quarters before its bankroll runs out, that is still not far off.

Suria's report got Wall Street's attention because it had the audacity to evaluate this icon of the New Economy as a traditional retailer. Up until Suria, Amazon was usually viewed under a rose-colored microscope that overlooked divergence by dot-coms from standard business measures. Suria's reasoning was simple: Because Amazon has built up a vast infrastructure of warehouse and distribution centers to house burgeoning inventories of product lines, relies on brand-name identification, and needs to spend relentlessly to attract each dollar of sales, it faces many of the same difficulties managing its business as old-line retailers do.

So Suria used the standard yardstick of retail success—the ability to generate a positive cash flow. And for retailers, traditional or otherwise, this often boils down to an ability to properly estimate the right amount of inventories needed to meet demand, at the right price, without overstocking. Simply put, stock up too much, and the costs of holding that inventory far outweigh the thin margins you make on whatever you sell.

This is hardly the most becoming angle from which to view Amazon—and that classic retail error, Suria argued, is exactly the mistake Amazon made in last year's Christmas season. That's why he focused on the results of the first quarter of this year, when gross operating cash flow nose-dived from a positive $31.5 million to a negative $320.5 million. This performance was far worse than any in the previous nine quarters, only four of which were in the black. "As has been said before, cash is a fact, profit is an accounting opinion. And the company's inability to make hard cash per unit sold is clearly manifested in its weak balance sheet, poor working-capital management, and massive negative operating cash flow—the financial characteristics that have driven innumerable retailers to disaster throughout history," Suria wrote in the report.

Debt Trouble

Ironically, a key contributor to this first-quarter debacle was Amazon's efforts to implement its strategy for growth. By adding product lines such as electronics and toys, and building distribution centers all over the country, the job of policing its inventories became much more difficult, particularly for a retailer that concedes it is lacking in retail experience. On $676 million in sales in the fourth quarter, Amazon was forced to take a $39 million writedown on inventory. The question now is whether Amazon will manage the process any better this year, with far higher sales and an evermore complex product mix. "They may have to settle for a little lower growth," says Bob Grandhi, manager of Monument Fund Group's Internet Fund, who sold all its e-tailing stocks including Amazon when he joined in April. "We can't ask them to be profitable and also grow as fast as they have."

Suria and other critics also point out that Amazon's ability to turn over its inventory rapidly enough has declined since the end of 1998; that, too, is a classic measure of poor retail management. Amazon's rate of inventory turnover plummeted from 8.5 times in the first quarter of 1998 to 2.9 times for the first quarter of this year. In 1999, when Amazon's sales grew 170% from the previous year, its inventories ballooned by 650%, Suria pointed out. "When a company manages inventory properly, it should grow along with its sales-growth rate," he noted. When inventory grows faster than sales, "it means simply that they're not selling as much as they're buying."

Amazon's fast-growing debt load, which has risen to a staggering $2.1 billion, is also a source of concern. From 1997 through the latest quarter, the company may have reported as much as $2.9 billion in revenues, but it raised $2.8 billion to meet its cash needs—amounting to 95¢ for every $1 of merchandise sold, Suria noted. In the future, Amazon will be under far greater pressure to meet its obligations by generating its own cash. "Bondholders are in effect being paid cash from money they lent the company," says Marie Menendez, Moody's senior corporate finance analyst of the interest payments of about $150 million a year.

Not surprisingly, Amazon vehemently disagrees with Suria's portrayal. Bezos insists that the company is getting a handle on its costs and generating new sources of revenue

EXHIBIT 2 Big Jobs for Bezos

> *Will Amazon ever be in the black? To get there, it needs to bolster revenues and improve operations—fast. Here's what it must do:*
>
> Increase efficiencies in distribution and customer-service centers by reducing headcount and installing new computer systems and automation gear
>
> Open more new stores on its site to provide greater selection and draw more customers
>
> Persuade customers to turn to Amazon to buy more than books and music
>
> Demonstrate savvier merchandising, from anticipating product demand to personalizing offers to individual customers
>
> Sign up more e-merchant partners to bring in high-profit revenue

to take the place of market support. Bezos promises that Amazon will show positive operating cash flow for the last three quarters of this year, an assessment that equity analysts accept. He's not predicting what will happen in 2001's first quarter, however, when Amazon will have to pay suppliers for an expected $1 billion in holiday sales. But until then, he expects rising sales and greater efficiencies handling the company's vast, relatively new network of distribution centers to not only end the cash drain but also to produce cash flow (Exhibit 2).

Indeed, many analysts believe the Amazon of year 2000 is actually in better position than ever. Operating losses fell from 26% of sales in the fourth quarter to 17% in the first quarter. As a result, analysts expect operating losses to drop to a single-digit percentage of sales by yearend—when books, music, and video are expected to be profitable on their own—and they predict a companywide operating profit by the end of 2001. Says Merrill Lynch & Co. Internet analyst Henry Blodget: "I'm not at all concerned about the cash side."

Where Bezos and his band of Wall Street believers think Lehman's report went astray was in focusing on the one year of Amazon's greatest expansion and projecting those costs forward into the future. The costs came up front, but now, they argue, Amazon will exploit its ability to handle far higher volumes. "For a company that's changing at this velocity, looking only back at finances can lead to misleading conclusions," says Amazon.com Treasurer Russ Grandinetti.

One controversy seems to be over the vast network of distribution centers that Amazon built over the past couple of years. While largely empty and unused, the centers gave Amazon a leg up on online and traditional rivals last Christmas: It could ship on time over the holidays, creating an intensely loyal customer base. In the first quarter, repeat orders constituted 76% of sales.

Suria's critics claim he was looking at these one-time capital costs and assuming that Amazon would have to keep spending at those levels. Now that the centers are built, Bezos says Amazon can work on making them more efficient. In fact, the costs of the construction are not in the operating cash-flow calculations upon which Suria bases his criticism.

There is early evidence that Amazon is beginning to manage its unwieldy portfolio of products better, moving customers more quickly to new products. For instance, it became the largest CD seller after only four months. And sales of children's products, mostly toys, hit $95 million in the fourth quarter, less than five months after Amazon's "toy store" opened. Customers are also ordering more every quarter: Annual sales per customer rose to $121 in March from $107 a year before.

Amazon is also developing new sources of revenues other than direct sales. It is trying to line up partners, particularly ones that can handle highly regulated or difficult-to-ship products such as sofas and drugs. In return for cash payments of up to $150 million apiece over three to five years, Amazon allows other e-merchants, such as Living.com and Drugstore.com, to host stores on its site. While this on the whole is a strategic plus, the plan also leaves Amazon's revenue base vulnerable to the travails of its dot-com partners—some of which are already facing layoffs and difficulties raising capital.

Bezos and supporters also object to Amazon being lumped in with Old Economy giants like Wal-Mart, claiming that there are more differences than similarities. The argument: Amazon will not be forced to build new stores, stock shelves, or hire new people to generate sales. As Amazon's sales grow, analysts say it will require no more than a third of the investment of a brick-and-mortar retailer for the same amount of sales. Goldman, Sachs & Co., the company's original underwriter, estimates for the next year, Amazon's operating expenses will rise only 8% and marketing only 7% while driving a 59% jump in sales, to $4.5 billion. The ultimate result, says J. P. Morgan & Co. analyst Tom Wyman: "Their operating margin will be twice that of brick-and-mortar retailers."

Brand Power

Ultimately, Bezos contends, Amazon should be more profitable than conventional retailers, though he won't hazard by how much. Indeed, he implies that Amazon aims to produce not necessarily higher profit margins but higher profits overall—which he contends is more important to investors. His take: a company with $10 billion in sales and a 5% profit margin—that is, $500 million in profits—is much more valuable than a $1 billion company with 10% margins, which has $100 million in profits.

But whether Amazon is more or less like retailers, it certainly must contend with many of the same forces. Just like retailers, Amazon is highly dependent on brand recognition and identity to bring customers back to its site. And just like retailers that overextend themselves, some critics believe that Amazon's one-stop shopping mentality is a threat. Expanding beyond its signature items—books, CDs, and videos—could muddy the Amazon brand at a time in consumer history when success demands a clear image. "The most powerful brands in the world stand for something simple," says Al Ries, brand management consultant and author of *The 11 Immutable Laws of Internet Branding.* "Volvo stands for safety. Dell is a personal computer. Even Microsoft is software. Now Amazon is going to stand for books and charcoal grills. This makes no sense to me."

Bezos argues Amazon stands for high-quality customer service over the Web—and that customers looking for that will return again and again. But the debate is far from academic. The power of the retail brand has been demonstrated repeatedly over the past decade. The most successful retail chains, from Gap to Target Stores to the mighty Wal-Mart, have unadulterated images that stick with consumers and keep them coming back. Retailers that have stumbled, from Tandy Corp. to Kmart Corp., shared a common misstep: They failed to build a coherent theme for consumers by selling unrelated merchandise or not providing a consistent level of service.

Amazon and other e-tailers were fortunate in having been launched in a boom economy (Exhibit 3). But a consumer spending slowdown would endanger revenues at Amazon as much as at any other retailer.

Worse, Bezos is finding it necessary to cut prices on one of its newest lines: consumer electronics. True, low prices are what drew customers to the Web in the first

EXHIBIT 3   Commentary
By Heather Green and Norm Alster

Guess What—Venture Capitalists Aren't Geniuses

Wasn't it only a matter of months ago that venture capitalists were the smartest people on Wall Street? Investors were beating down their doors to throw billions of dollars at every high-tech prodigy they could bring public.

But as the Nasdaq has continued to stumble, and even the prospects of erstwhile high-tech superstars such as Amazon.com Inc. are being widely questioned, VCs are no longer undoubted financial gurus. Today, they are increasingly finding themselves forced back into the market to prop up flagging startups.

On Apr. 25, Benchmark Capital Partners LP, one of Silicon Valley's hottest venture-capital firms, bought 1.3 million shares in a private placement for its once celebrated E-LOAN, an online provider of consumer loans whose stock has fallen to less than 5 from a high of 74⅜ last July. Around the same time, Benchmark was also buying shares of luxury-goods Web site Ashford.com, which has seen its shares tumble to less than 10% of its November high of $35. Nor is Benchmark alone in lending a financial helping hand. On June 20, Internet holding company CMGI teamed up with Compaq Computer Corp. to provide $75 million to Engage Inc., the Web ad-delivery outfit whose stock has slid from a high of 94½ in March to 13⅜.

Resource Shift. Propping up failing stocks isn't exactly normal VC behavior. Typically, they don't look back after the entrepreneurial offspring leave the fold. But some VCs are eager to prop up the valuations of their lagging investments. So instead of putting money into new consumer startups, they're supporting old ones. "It's a defensive strategy," says C. Kevin Landry, CEO of venture firm TA Associates in Boston. "They're conserving capital to protect existing investments."

But don't shed too many tears: By and large, venture capitalists are responsible for their current predicament. The industry threw too much money at too many companies that were following the same business model. Last year, some $5.5 billion was invested in consumer e-commerce companies, up from $607 million in 1998, according to Venture Economics, a researcher that tracks venture funding. Nobody, but nobody, really believed the world needed that many new Net stores.

Then, in many cases, VCs took these clones to market way too soon. Instead of the four to five years it used to take before a company could get public investors to pony up, companies are now being pushed out after less than two years on average, estimates PricewaterhouseCoopers.Snowball. com Inc. beat even that: The teen-information and e-commerce site filed for its IPO a mere 10 months after its online debut. The problem with that kind of strategy is that neither the company nor its management has enough experience to prove consistent performance.

Indiscriminate Investing. Every VC was, instead, eager to have the next America Online Inc. or Amazon.com Inc. So they tossed huge amounts of money at redundant companies in an attempt to outspend and underprice rivals. As a result, heavily funded startups became locked into price-cutting strategies that turned into death struggles. Last Christmas, eToys duked it out with venture-funded companies KBkids.com, Toysmart.com, ToyTime, and Toysrus.com. Now, ToyTime and Toysmart.com are out of business, and KBkids pulled its initial public offering. And when the consumer market seemed to be played out, VCs engaged in some of the same type of indiscriminate investing in business-to-business Web sites, infrastructure, wireless, and optical networking. The same trends could eventually play out in those sectors. VCs could have handled this differently. Instead of pushing everything out the door, everyone would have been better served if the VCs had used their considerable business acumen to decide which companies were worth investing in for the long haul. And they could have done so with later rounds of private financing, not IPOs. Now, investors are disillusioned with the very model that promising e-tailers depend on for growth. And without further capital, many green e-tailers are getting a savage business lesson that may well spell their demise.

Green, in New York, and Alster, in Boston, track venture capital. Timothy J. Mullaney contributed reporting.

place. But from the start, Amazon has tried to depend on a wide selection to be its strongest drawing card.

Ultimately, Amazon and those on Wall Street who still back it have made a giant bet that none of these factors will be enough to keep it from boosting sales enough to get to profitability. At base, it is a bet on Amazon's ability to outrace the financial squeeze that all money-losing e-businesses now face. But as the difficulties of beating the debt clock increase—and the questions multiply about how the numbers will ever add up— a growing number of investors and analysts are bailing out, no longer liking the odds. Who is right? Coming down on either side ultimately requires something of a leap of faith. The only certainty: In its short life as a public company, Amazon's experience has often set the rules under which e-commerce companies operate. Survive or stumble, that will continue to be the case.

APPENDIX A
MARKETING FINANCIAL ANALYSIS

Several kinds of financial analyses are needed for marketing analysis, planning, and control activities. Such analyses represent an important part of case preparation activities. In some instances it will be necessary to review and interpret financial information provided in the cases. In other instances, analyses may be prepared to support specific recommendations. The methods covered in this appendix represent a group of tools and techniques for use in marketing financial analysis. Throughout the discussion, it is assumed that accounting and finance fundamentals are understood.

Unit of Financial Analysis

Various units of analysis that can be used in marketing financial analysis are shown in Exhibit A–1. Two factors often influence the choice of a unit of analysis: (1) the purpose of the analysis and (2) the costs and availability of the information needed to perform the analysis.

Financial Situation Analysis

Financial measures can be used to help assess the present situation. One of the most common and best ways to quantify the financial situation of a firm is through ratio analysis. These ratios should be analyzed over a period of at least three years to discern trends.

Key Financial Ratios.
Financial information will be more useful to management if it is prepared so that comparisons can be made. James Van Horne comments on this need:

> To evaluate a firm's financial condition and performance, the financial analyst needs certain yardsticks. The yardstick frequently used is a ratio or index, relating two pieces of financial data to each other. Analysis and interpretation of various ratios should give an experienced and skilled analyst a better understanding of the financial condition and performance of the firm than he would obtain from analysis of the financial data alone.[1]

As we examine the financial analysis model in the next section, note how the ratio or index provides a useful frame of reference. Typically, ratios are used to compare historical and/or future trends within the firm, or to compare a firm or business unit with an industry or other firms.

Several financial ratios often used to measure business performance are shown in Exhibit A–2. Note that these ratios are primarily useful as a means of comparing

1. Ratio values for several time periods for a particular business.
2. A firm to its key competitors.
3. A firm to an industry or business standard.

There are several sources of ratio data.[2] These include data services such as Dun & Bradstreet, Robert Morris Associates' *Annual Statement Studies,* industry and trade associations, government agencies, and investment advisory services.

Other ways to gauge productivity of marketing activities include sales per square foot of retail floor space, occupancy rates of hotels and office buildings, and sales per salesperson.

Contribution Analysis.
When the performance of products, market segments, and other marketing units is being analyzed, management should examine the unit's profit contribution. Contribution margin is equal to sales (revenue) less variable costs. Thus, contribution margin represents the amount of money available to cover fixed costs, and contribution margin less fixed costs is net income. An illustration of contribution margin analysis is given in Exhibit A–3. In this example, product X is generating positive contribution margin. If product X were eliminated, $50,000 of product net income would be lost, and the remaining products would have to cover fixed costs not directly traceable to them. If the product is retained, the $50,000 can be used to contribute to other fixed costs and/or net income.

Financial Analysis Model

The model shown in Exhibit A–4 provides a useful guide for examining financial performance and identifying possible problem areas. The model combines several important financial ratios into one equation. Let's examine the model, moving from left to right. Profit margin multiplied by asset turnover yields return on assets. Moreover, assuming that the performance target is return on net worth (or return on equity), the

---

[1] James C. Van Horne, *Fundamentals of Financial Management,* 4th ed. (Englewood Cliffs, NJ: Prentice Hall, 1980), pp. 103–4.

[2] A useful guide to ratio analysis is provided in Richard Sanzo, *Ratio Analysis for Small Business* (Washington, DC: Small Business Administration, 1977).

EXHIBIT A–1   Alternative Units for Financial Analysis

Market	Product/Service	Organization
Market	Industry	Company
Total market	Product mix	Segment/division/unit
Market niche(s)	Product line	Marketing department
Geographic area(s)	Specific product	Sales unit
Customer groups	Brand	Region
Individual customers	Model	District branch
		Office/store
		Salesperson

product of return on assets and financial leverage determines performance. Increasing either ratio will increase net worth. The values of these ratios will vary considerably from one industry to another. In grocery wholesaling, for example, profit margins are typically very low, whereas asset turnover is very high. Through efficient management and high turnover, a wholesaler can stack up impressive returns on net worth. Furthermore, space productivity measures are obtained for individual departments in retail stores that offer more than one line, such as department stores. The measures selected depend on the particular characteristics of the business.

Evaluating Alternatives

As we move through the discussion of financial analysis, it is important to recognize the type of costs being used in the analysis. Using accounting terminology, costs can be designated as fixed or variable. A cost is *fixed* if it remains constant over the observation period, even though the volume of activity varies. In contrast, a *variable* cost is an expense that varies with sales over the observation period. Costs are designated as mixed or semivariable in instances when they contain both fixed and variable components.

Break-Even Analysis.[3]   This technique is used to examine the relationship between sales and costs. An illustration is given in Exhibit A–5. Using sales and cost information, it is easy to determine from a break-even analysis how many units of a product must be sold in order to break even, or cover total costs. In this example 65,000 units at sales of $120,000 are equal to total costs of $120,000. Any additional units sold will produce a profit. The break-even point can be calculated in this manner:

$$\text{Break-even units} = \frac{\text{Fixed costs}}{\text{Price per unit} - \text{Variable cost per unit}}$$

[3] This illustration is drawn from David W. Cravens, Gerald E. Hills, and Robert B. Woodruff, *Marketing Decision Making: Concepts and Strategy,* rev. ed. (Homewood, IL: Richard D. Irwin, 1980), pp. 335–36.

Price in the illustration shown in Exhibit A–5 is $1.846 per unit, and variable cost is $0.769 per unit. With fixed costs of $70,000, this results in the break-even calculation:

$$\text{BE units} = \frac{\$70,000}{\$1.846 - \$0.769} = 65,000 \text{ units}$$

This analysis is not a forecast. Rather, it indicates how many units of a product at a given price and cost must be sold in order to break even. Some important assumptions that underlie the above break-even analysis include the use of constant fixed costs and one price.

In addition to break-even analysis, several other financial tools are used to evaluate alternatives. Net present value of cash flow analysis and return on investment are among the most useful. For example, assume there are two projects with the cash flows shown in Exhibit A–6.

Though return on investment is widely used, it is limited in its inability to consider the time value of money. This is pointed out in Exhibit A–7. Return on investment for *both* projects X and Y is 10 percent. However, a dollar today is worth more than a dollar given in three years. Therefore, when assessing cash flows of a project or investment, future cash flows must be discounted back to the present at a rate comparable to the risk of the project.

Discounting cash flows is a simple process. Assume that the firm is considering projects X and Y and that its cost of capital is 12 percent. Additionally, assume that both projects carry risk comparable to the normal business risk. Under these circumstances, the analyst should discount the cash flows back to the present at the cost of capital: 12 percent. Present value factors can be looked up or computed using the formula $1/(1 + i)n,$ where i equals our discounting rate per time period and n equals the number of compounding periods. In this example, the present value of cash flows is as shown in Exhibit A–7.

Because both projects have a positive net present value, both are good. However, if they are mutually exclusive, the project with the highest net present value should be selected.

EXHIBIT A–2   Summary of Key Financial Ratios

Ratio	How Calculated	What It Shows
Profitability Ratios		
1. Gross profit margin	$\dfrac{\text{Sales} - \text{Cost of good sold}}{\text{Sales}}$	An indication of the total margin available to cover operating expenses and yield a profit.
2. Operating profit margin	$\dfrac{\text{Profits before taxes and before interest}}{\text{Sales}}$	An indication of the firm's profitability from current operations without regard to the interest charges accruing from the capital structure.
3. Net profit margin (or return on sales)	$\dfrac{\text{Profits after taxes}}{\text{Sales}}$	Shows after-tax profits per dollar of sales. Subpar profit margins indicate that the firm's sales prices are relatively low or that its costs are relatively high or both.
4. Return on total assets	$\dfrac{\text{Profits after taxes}}{\text{Total assets}}$ or $\dfrac{\text{Profits after taxes} + \text{Interest}}{\text{Total assets}}$	A measure of the return on total investment in the enterprise. It is sometimes desirable to add interest to after-tax profits to form the numerator of the ratio, since total assets are financed by creditors as well as by stockholders; hence, it is accurate to measure the productivity of assets by the returns provided to both classes of investors.
5. Return on stockholders' equity (or return on net worth)	$\dfrac{\text{Profits after taxes}}{\text{Total stockholders' equity}}$	A measure of the rate of return on stockholders' investment in the enterprise.
6. Return on common equity	$\dfrac{\text{Profits after taxes} - \text{Preferred stock dividends}}{\text{Total stockholders' equity} - \text{Par value of preferred stock}}$	A measure of the rate of return on the investment that the owners of common stock have made in the enterprise.
7. Earnings per share	$\dfrac{\text{Profits after taxes} - \text{Preferred stock dividends}}{\text{Number of shares of common stock outstanding}}$	Shows the earnings available to the owners of common stock.
Liquidity Ratios		
1. Current ratio	$\dfrac{\text{Current assets}}{\text{Current liabilities}}$	Indicates the extent to which the claims of short-term creditors are covered by assets that are expected to be converted to cash in a period roughly corresponding to the maturity of the liabilities.
2. Quick ratio (or acid-test ratio)	$\dfrac{\text{Current assets} - \text{Inventory}}{\text{Current liabilities}}$	A measure of the firm's ability to pay off short-term obligations without relying on the sale of its inventories.
3. Cash ratio	$\dfrac{\text{Cash \& Marketable securities}}{\text{Current liabilities}}$	An indicator of how long the company can go without further inflow of funds.
4. Inventory to net working capital	$\dfrac{\text{Inventory}}{\text{Current assets} - \text{Current liabilities}}$	A measure of the extent to which the firm's working capital is tied up in inventory.
Leverage Ratios		
1. Debt to assets ratio	$\dfrac{\text{Total debt}}{\text{Total assets}}$	Measures the extent to which borrowed funds have been used to finance the firm's operations.
2. Debt to equity ratio	$\dfrac{\text{Total debt}}{\text{Total stockholders' equity}}$	Provides another measure of the funds provided the creditors versus the funds provided by owners.
3. Long-term debt to equity ratio	$\dfrac{\text{Long-term debt}}{\text{Total stockholders' equity}}$	A widely used measure of the balance between debt and equity in the firm's overall capital structure.
4. Times-interest-earned (or coverage ratios)	$\dfrac{\text{Profits before interest and taxes}}{\text{Total interest charges}}$	Measures the extent to which earnings can decline without the firm's becoming unable to meet its annual interest costs.
5. Fixed-charge coverage	$\dfrac{\text{Profits before taxes and interest} + \text{Lease obligations}}{\text{Total interest charges} + \text{Lease obligations}}$	A more inclusive indication of the firm's ability to meet all of its fixed-charge obligations.

Exhibit A–2   (concluded)

Ratio	How Calculated	What It Shows
Activity Ratios		
1. Inventory turnover	$\dfrac{\text{Cost of goods sold}}{\text{Inventory}}$	When compared to industry averages, it provides an indication of whether a company has excessive inventory or perhaps inadequate inventory.
2. Fixed-assets turnover*	$\dfrac{\text{Sales}}{\text{Fixed assets}}$	A measure of the sales productivity and utilization of plant and equipment.
3. Total-assets turnover	$\dfrac{\text{Sales}}{\text{Total assets}}$	A measure of the utilization of all the firm's assets; a ratio below the industry average indicates that the company is not generating a sufficient volume of business given the size of its asset investment.
4. Accounts receivable turnover	$\dfrac{\text{Annual credit sales}}{\text{Accounts receivable}}$	A measure of the average length of time it takes the firm to collect the sales made on credit.
5. Average collection period	$\dfrac{\text{Accounts receivable}}{\text{Total sales} \div 365}$ or $\dfrac{\text{Accounts receivable}}{\text{Average daily sales}}$	Indicates the average length of time the firm must wait after making a sale before it receives payment.

*The manager should also keep in mind the fixed charges associated with noncapitalized lease obligations.

Source: Adapted from Arthur A. Thompson, Jr., and A. J. Strickland III, *Strategy and Policy,* 4th ed. (Homewood, IL: Richard D. Irwin, 1987), pp. 270–71.

Exhibit A–3   **Illustrative Contribution Margin Analysis for Product X ($000)**

Sales	$ 300
Less: Variable manufacturing costs	100
Other variable costs traceable to product X	50
Equals: Contribution margin	150
Less: Fixed costs directly traceable to product X	100
Equals: Product net income	$ 50

Exhibit A–4   **Financial Analysis Model**

Profit margin		Asset turnover		Return on assets		Financial leverage		Return on net worth
↓		↓		↓		↓		↓
$\dfrac{\text{Net profits (after taxes)}}{\text{Net sales}}$	$\times$	$\dfrac{\text{Net sales}}{\text{Total assets}}$	$\rightarrow$	$\dfrac{\text{Net profits (after taxes)}}{\text{Total assets}}$	$\times$	$\dfrac{\text{Total assets}}{\text{Net worth}}$	$=$	$\dfrac{\text{Net profits (after taxes)}}{\text{Net worth}}$

EXHIBIT A–5
Illustrative Break-Even Analysis

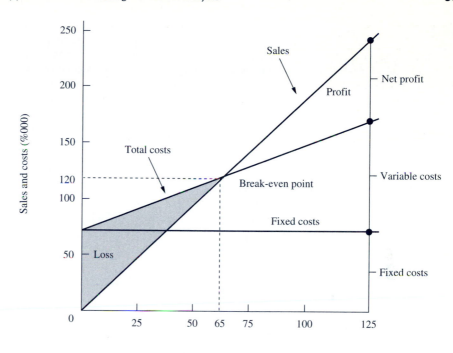

Number of units (000s)

EXHIBIT A–6   Cash Flow Comparison ($000s)

	Project X	Project Y
Start-up costs	$ ⟨1,000⟩	⟨1,000⟩
Year 1	500	300
Year 2	500	400
Year 3	200	600

EXHIBIT A–7   Present Value of Cash Flows

Time	Cash Flow	PV Factor	NPV of Cash Flow
Project X			
0	⟨1,000⟩	$1/(1 + 0.12)^0 = 1$	⟨1,000⟩
1	500	$1/(1 + 0.12)^1 = 0.8929$	= 446.45
2	500	$1/(1 + 0.12)^2 = 0.7972$	= 398.60
3	300	$1/(1 + 0.12)^3 = 0.7118$	= 213.54
		Present value	+ 58.59
Project Y			
0	⟨1,000⟩	$1/(1 + 0.12)^0 = 1$	⟨1,000⟩
1	300	$1/(1 + 0.12)^1 = 0.8929$	= 267.87
2	400	$1/(1 + 0.12)^2 = 0.7972$	= 318.88
3	600	$1/(1 + 0.12)^3 = 0.7118$	= 427.08
		Net present value	+ 13.83

Financial Planning

Financial planning involves two major activities: (1) forecasting revenues and (2) budgeting (estimating future expenses). The actual financial analyses and forecasts included in the strategic marketing plan vary considerably from firm to firm. In addition, internal financial reporting and budgeting procedures vary widely among companies. Therefore, consider this approach as one example rather than the norm.

The choice of the financial information to be used for marketing planning and control will depend on its relationship with the corporate or business unit strategic plan. Another important consideration is the selection of performance measures to be used in gauging marketing performance. Our objective is to indicate the range of possibilities and suggest some of the more frequently used financial analyses.

Pro forma income statements can be very useful when projecting performance and budgeting. Usually, this is done on a spreadsheet so that assumptions can be altered rapidly. Usually, only a few assumptions need be made. For example, sales growth rates can be projected from past trends and adjusted for new information. From this starting point, cost of goods can be determined as a percent of sales. Operating expenses also can be determined as a percent of sales based on past relationships, and the effective tax rate as a percent of earnings before taxes. However, past relationships may not hold in the future. It may be necessary to analyze possible divergence from past relationships.

APPENDIX B
GUIDE TO CASE ANALYSIS

A case presents a situation involving a managerial problem or issue that requires a decision. Typically, cases describe a variety of conditions and circumstances facing an organization at a particular time. This description often includes information regarding the organization's goals and objectives, its financial condition, the attitudes and beliefs of managers and employees, market conditions, competitors' activities, and various environmental forces that may affect the organization's present or proposed marketing strategy. Your responsibility is to sift carefully through the information provided in order to identify the opportunity, problem, or decision facing the organization; carefully identify and evaluate alternative courses of action; and propose a solution or decision based on your analysis.

This appendix provides an overview of the case method. It begins with a discussion of the role that cases play in the teaching/learning process. This is followed by a series of guidelines for case analysis. After carefully reading this material, you should be prepared to tackle your first case analysis. Even if you have had previous experience with cases, the discussion will provide a useful review.

Why Cases?

The case method differs substantially from other teaching/ learning approaches, such as lecture and discussion. Lecture- and discussion-oriented classes provide students with information about concepts, practices, and theories. In contrast, cases provide an opportunity to use concepts, practices, and theories. The primary objective of the case method is to give you a hands-on opportunity to apply what you have learned in your course work.

Consider this analogy: Suppose you want to learn to play a musical instrument. Your instruction might begin with several classes and reading assignments about your particular instrument. This could include information about the history of the instrument and descriptions of the various parts of the instrument and their functions. Sooner or later, however, you would actually have to play the instrument. Eventually you might become an accomplished musician.

Now suppose you want to become a marketing professional instead of a musician. You started with classes or courses that introduced you to the foundations of marketing management. Your prior studies also may have included courses in areas of specialization such as marketing research, buyer behavior, and promotion, as well as other business dis-

ciplines such as management, finance, accounting, economics, and statistics. You need practice and experience to become a professional. This is precisely the purpose of the case method of instruction. The cases in this book will give you opportunities to apply your knowledge of marketing and other business subjects to actual marketing situations.

Case studies help bridge the gap between classroom learnings and the practice of marketing management. They provide us with an opportunity to develop, sharpen, and test our analytic skills at

- Assessing situations.
- Sorting out and organizing key information.
- Asking the right questions.
- Defining opportunities and problems.
- Identifying and evaluating alternative courses of action.
- Interpreting data.
- Evaluating the results of past strategies.
- Developing and defending new strategies.
- Interacting with other managers.
- Making decisions under conditions of uncertainty.
- Critically evaluating the work of others.
- Responding to criticism.

In addition, cases provide exposure to a broad range of situations facing different types and sizes of organizations in a variety of industries. The decisions that you encounter in this book will range from fairly simple to quite complex. If you were the managers making these decisions, you would be risking anywhere from a few thousand to several million dollars of your firm's resources. And you could be risking your job and your career. Obviously the risk, or the cost of making mistakes, is much lower in the classroom environment.

A principal difference between our earlier example of learning to play a musical instrument and the practice of marketing lies in what might be called consequences. A musician's expertise is based on his or her ability to perform precisely the same series of actions time after time. The outcome of perfect execution of a predetermined series of actions is the sought consequence: a beautiful melody. Marketing, on the other hand, often is described as a skillful combination of art and science. No two situations ever require exactly the same actions. Although the same skills and knowledge may be required in different situations, marketing executives must analyze and diagnose each situation separately and conceive and initiate unique strategies to produce sought consequences. Judgment, as opposed to rote memory and repetition, is one key to marketing success. When judgment and a basic understanding of the variables and interrelationships in marketing situations are coupled, they form the core of an analysis and problem-solving approach that can be used in any marketing decision-making situation.

The Case Method of Instruction

The case method of instruction differs from the lecture/discussion method you have grown accustomed to since you began your formal education 14 or more years ago. It is only natural that you are a bit anxious and apprehensive about it. The methods of study and class preparation are different, your roles and responsibilities are different, and the "right" answers are much less certain. The case method is neither better nor worse than alternative methods; it is just different.

The case method is participative. You will be expected to take a more active role in learning than you have taken in the past. The case method is based on a philosophy of learning by doing as opposed to learning by listening and absorbing information. Case analysis is an applied skill. Thus, it is something you learn through application, as opposed to something someone teaches you. The more you practice, the more proficient you will become. The benefit you receive from case analysis is directly proportional to the effort you put into it.

Your Responsibilities.   Your responsibilities as a case analyst include active participation, interaction, critical evaluation, and effective communication.

Active Participation.   We have already noted that the case method is participative. It requires a great deal of individual participation in class discussion. Effective participation requires thorough preparation. This entails more than casually reading each case before class. The guidelines in the next section of this appendix will assist you in preparing case analyses. Also, keep in mind that there is a difference between contributing to a class discussion and just talking.

Interaction.   Interaction among students plays an important role in the case method of instruction. Effective learning results from individual preparation and thinking combined with group discussion. Whether you are assigned to work independently or in groups or teams, most instructors encourage students to discuss cases with other students. This, of course, is common practice among managers facing important business decisions. Case discussions, in and out of class, are beneficial because they provide immediate feedback regarding individual perspectives and possible solutions. Other important benefits of case discussions are the synergism and new insights produced by group brainstorming and discussion.

Critical Evaluation.   One of the most difficult responsibilities of student case analysts is learning to critique their peers and accept criticism from them. Typically, students are reluctant to question or challenge their classmates or suggest alternatives to the perspectives proposed by others in the class. Students find this difficult because they are generally inexperienced at performing these functions and also are unaccustomed to being challenged by their peers in the classroom. However, the case method of instruction is most effective when all parties engage in an open exchange of ideas. Good cases do not have one clear-cut superior solution. Don't be shy about expressing and defending your views. Moreover, the reasoning process you use and the questions you raise are often more important than the specific solution you recommend.

Effective Communication.   Each of the three responsibilities discussed above requires effective communication. It is important that you organize your thoughts before speaking. You will develop and refine your communication skills by making class presentations, participating in case discussions, and writing case analyses. Furthermore, the focus of the case method is the development and sharpening of quantitative and qualitative analytic skills. Your analytic skills will improve as you organize information, diagnose problems, identify and evaluate alternatives, and develop solutions and action plans.

Case analysis plays an important role in your overall education. What you learn in a course that uses the case method may be your best preparation for securing your first job and launching your career. If you ask a sample of recruiters to assess the students who are completing undergraduate and graduate programs in business administration today, you will probably hear that these students are extremely well-trained in concepts and quantitative skills but lack verbal and written communication skills and decision-making skills. The case method offers students an excellent opportunity to enhance and refine those skills.

A Guide to Case Analysis

There is no one best way to analyze a case. Most people develop their own method after gaining some experience. As with studying, everybody does it a little bit differently. The following suggestions are intended to give you some ideas of how others approach cases. Try these suggestions and make your own adjustments.

Begin by reading each case quickly. The purpose of the first reading should be to familiarize yourself with the organization, the problem, or the decision to be made and the types and amount of data provided and in general to get a feel for the case. Your second reading of the case should be more careful and thorough. Many students find it helpful to underline, highlight, and make notes about symptoms, potential problems and issues, key facts, and other important information.

Now you should be in a position to investigate the tabular and numerical data included in the case. Ask yourself what each figure, table, or chart means, how it was derived, whether it is relevant, and whether further computations would be helpful. If calculations, comparisons, or consolidations of numerical data appear useful, take the necessary action at this time.

A large part of what you will learn from case analysis is how to define, structure, and analyze opportunities and problems. The following information is intended to provide you with a general framework for problem solving. In essence, it is the scientific method with some embellishment. If your instructor does not assign a preferred analytic framework, use the approach shown in Exhibit B–1. A discussion of each step follows, and a detailed outline of analytic issues and questions is provided in this appendix.

Step 1: Situation Audit. The situation audit phase of the problem-solving process is basically a synopsis and evaluation of an organization's current situation, opportunities, and problems. This phase of case analysis is typically handled in a worksheet form rather than as a formal part of the written case. The primary purpose of the audit is to help you prepare for problem definition and subsequent steps in the problem-solving process. The situation audit interprets and shows the relevance of important case information. Thus, it is important that your situation audit be diagnostic rather than descriptive.

It is descriptive to recognize that "Company A's current and quick ratios are 1.03 and 0.64, respectively." A diagnostic look at these figures indicates that Company A may not be able to meet maturing obligations. The poor quick ratio shows that without inventory, the company's least liquid asset, short-term obligations could not be met. In other words, Company A is insolvent. If you have information about a number of different problems or challenges facing Company A, knowing that the company is insolvent helps you focus your attention on those that affect the firm's short-term survival needs.

The breadth and depth of an appropriate situation audit are determined by the nature and scope of the case situation, and your instructor's specific instructions. Each case will require a situation audit that is a little different from any of the others because of the information available and the decision to be made.

EXHIBIT B–1
An Approach to Case Analysis

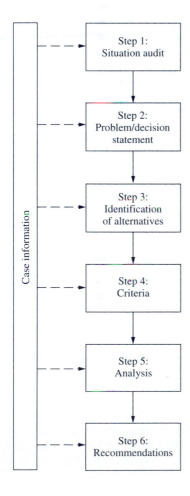

There are at least two philosophies regarding the appropriate depth and scope of a situation audit. One philosophy holds that the situation audit should include a thorough and comprehensive assessment of the organization's mission and objectives; each business unit of interest; present and potential customers and competitors; the organization's market-target objectives and strategies; its marketing program positioning strategy; its product, distribution, pricing, and promotion strategies; current planning, implementation, and management activities; its financial condition; and an overall summary of the organization's situation. If your instructor favors a thorough and comprehensive situation audit, you will find the outline for case analysis in this appendix quite helpful in organizing your work.

Some instructors, however, feel that the situation audit need not be a thorough and comprehensive study but rather a short, concise analysis of the organization's major strengths, weaknesses, opportunities, and threats—reserving the comprehensive effort for the analysis step. Some call this a SWOT analysis and recommend including only information that is crucial in preparing to analyze the case. The emphasis here is on *analysis, diagnosis, synthesis, and interpretation* of the situation. In a written assignment you should be able to present this in less than two pages.

A Note on Gathering More Data and Making Assumptions. Students often feel that they need more information in order to make an intelligent decision. Decision makers rarely, if ever, have all the information they would like to have before making important decisions. The cost and time involved in collecting more data are often prohibitive. Decision makers, like you, therefore have to make some assumptions. There is nothing wrong with making assumptions as long as they are explicitly stated and reasonable. Be prepared to defend your assumptions as logical. Don't use lack of information as a crutch.

For example, an assumption that Company A, mentioned previously, cannot borrow large sums of money is both reasonable and defendable. To assume that it could borrow large sums of money would require a clear explanation of why some lender or investor would be willing to lend money to, or invest money in, a firm with a quick ratio of 0.64.

Step 2: Problem/Decision Statement. Identification of the main problem, opportunity, or issue in a case is crucial. To paraphrase from *Alice in Wonderland,* if you don't know where you are going, any solution will take you there. If you don't properly identify the central problem or decision in a case, the remainder of your analysis is not likely to produce recommendations necessary to solve the organization's main problem.

You may become frustrated with your early attempts at problem/decision identification. Don't feel alone. Most students and many experienced managers have difficulty with this task. Your skill will improve with practice.

A major pitfall in defining problems/decisions occurs in confusing symptoms with problems. Such things as declining sales, low morale, high turnover, and increasing costs are symptoms that often are incorrectly identified as problems. You frequently can avoid incorrectly defining a symptom as a problem by thinking in terms of causes and effects. Problems are causes, and symptoms are effects. The examples cited above are the effects or manifestations of something wrong in the organization. Why are sales declining? Why is morale low? Why is turnover high? Why are costs increasing? The key question is why. What is the cause? Sales may be declining because morale is low and turnover is high. Why is morale low, and why is turnover high? These effects may be caused by an inadequate compensation plan, which in turn may be caused by inadequate profit margins. Profit margins may be low because products have been incorrectly priced or because the distribution system is outdated. As you can see, symptoms may appear in one part of the overall marketing program, and the true problem may lie elsewhere in the program. Keep asking why until you are satisfied that you have identified the problem (cause) and not just another symptom (effect).

Think about this analogy. You are not feeling well, and so you make an appointment to see a physician. The physician will ask you to describe what is bothering you. Suppose you say you have a headache, a sore throat, chills, and a fever. The physician probably will take your temperature, look in your throat, and perhaps examine you in other ways. The goal, of course, is to diagnose your problem so that a remedy can be prescribed.

How does this relate to case analysis? Your headache, sore throat, chills, and fever are symptoms of something wrong. They are signals to you to seek help. This information also assists your physician in making his or her diagnosis. These symptoms are similar to the declining sales, poor morale, high turnover, and increasing costs we discussed earlier. They are the effects of some underlying cause. Your role in case study, like the role of the physician, is to analyze the combination of symptoms that can be identified and then to determine the underlying problem.

Let's carry the analogy a bit further. Suppose the physician's diagnosis is that you have a common cold. Since there is no cure for a cold, all he or she can do is prescribe medication to treat the symptoms. The cold will cure itself in a matter of days.

Now suppose the diagnosis of the cause is incorrect. Instead of just a common cold, you contracted malaria during a recent vacation in Southeast Asia. If the physician treats the symptoms or effects, they will be temporarily reduced or eliminated, but they will soon reappear. Each time they reappear, they will be more severe, until the ailment is properly diagnosed or you die. This is precisely what will happen in an organization if a symptom is incorrectly identified as a problem. Treating the symptom will temporarily reduce its dysfunctional impact on the organization, but sooner or later it will reappear. When it reappears, it will probably be more severe than it was previously. This is why carefully identifying the root problem, decision, or issue in your case analysis is so important.

When you identify more than one major problem or decision in a case, ask yourself whether the problems or decisions are related enough to be consolidated into one problem/decision statement. You may not yet have reached the central problem. If, however, you have identified two or more problems that are not directly associated with one another, we recommend that you rank them in the order of their importance and address them in that order. You may find that although the problems do not appear to be closely linked, the solutions are related. One solution may solve multiple problems.

A final suggestion regarding defining problems or decisions is to state them concisely and, if possible, in the form of a question. Try to write a one-sentence question that is specific enough to communicate the main concern. For example,

- Should Brand A be deleted from the product line?
- Should General Mills implement a cents-off campaign, or should it use coupons to stimulate trial of its new cereal Gold Rush?
- Which two of the five sales candidates should be hired?
- How should L.A. Gear define its marketing planning units?
- What is the best marketing program positioning strategy for Rollerblade?

In addition to your problem/decision statement, you may find it useful to provide a brief narrative describing the main parameters of the problem/decision. This is helpful when you have a compound problem/decision that can be subdivided into components or subproblems.

Step 3: Identification of Alternatives.
Alternatives are the strategic options or actions that appear to be viable solutions to the problem or decision situation you have determined. Often, more than two seemingly appropriate actions will be available. Sometimes they will be explicitly identified in the case, and sometimes they will not.

Prepare your list of alternatives in two stages. First, prepare an initial list of alternatives that includes all the actions that you feel might be appropriate. Group brainstorming is a useful technique for generating alternatives. Be creative, keep an open mind, and build on the ideas of others. What may initially sound absurd could become an outstanding possibility.

After you have generated your initial list of alternatives, begin refining the list and combining similar actions. Use the information you organized in your situation audit regarding goals, objectives, and constraints to help you identify which alternatives to keep and which to eliminate. Ask yourself whether an alternative is feasible given the existing financial, productive, managerial, marketing, and other constraints and whether it could produce the results sought.

That is, does the alternative directly address the problem or decision you identified in Step 2? If your problem/decision statement and your alternatives are inconsistent, you have erred in one step or the other. To help avoid this mistake, be explicit in showing the connections between the situation audit, the problem/decision statement, and the final set of alternatives.

Doing nothing and collecting more data are two alternatives often suggested by students with limited case experience. These are rarely the best actions to take. If you have identified a problem or a decision that must be made, ignoring the situation probably will not help. Likewise, recommending a survey, hiring a consultant, or employing some other options associated with gathering more data is rarely a viable solution to the central problem or issue. In some cases, a solution may include further study, but this normally will be part of the implementation plan rather than part of the solution. Most cases, at least those included in this book, are based on real business situations. You have the same information that was available to the decision maker when the decision was made. The major difference is that your data are already compiled and organized. If complete information were available, decisions would be easy. This is not the case in business situations, and so it may help you to become familiar with making decisions under conditions of uncertainty. Executives, like case analysts, must rely on assumptions and on less than perfect information.

Step 4: Criteria.
Next you should develop a list of the main criteria that you will use to evaluate your strategic options. By expressly stating the criteria you intend to use in evaluating alternatives, you make clear the measures you plan to use in assessing and comparing the viability of your alternative courses of action.

Perhaps the best place to start in identifying criteria is to ask yourself what factors, in general, should be considered in making a strategic decision regarding this particular problem. For example, assume that your task is to identify the most attractive product-market niche. Your alternatives are niches X, Y, and Z. Your question then would be, What criteria should be employed in assessing the choices of product-market niches? An appropriate set of criteria might include (for each niche) potential sales volume, variable costs, contribution margins, market share, total niche sales, business strength, and niche attractiveness. This will provide an evaluation relative to the market and to competition.

The single most important factor in many decisions is profitability. Since profits are a principal goal in all commercial organizations, nearly every marketing decision is influenced by monetary considerations that ultimately affect profits (or expected profits). Sometimes several profit-oriented criteria are involved. These may include future costs and revenues, break-even points, opportunity costs, contribution margins, taxes, turnover, sales, and market share, for example.

Many criteria are only indirectly linked to profits. Such things as the impact of a decision on employees, the local economy, the environment, suppliers, or even customer attitudes may not directly affect profits. Because profits are almost always the overriding criterion, all factors bearing on them, directly or indirectly, must be considered.

Step 5: Analysis. Analysis is the process of evaluating each alternative action against the issues that were identified in Step 4. Often, analysis includes assessment of advantages and limitations associated with each issue. A tendency exists when first starting a case analysis to identify important issues carefully and then analyze each issue superficially. The consequence is a weak analysis. Your analysis will be much more penetrating and comprehensive if you use the same criteria in assessing each alternative.

One way of assuring that you assess each alternative in terms of each critical issue is to organize your analysis in outline form as follows.

Step 5 Analysis
    Alternative A: (Specify the alternative.)
      1. Identify the criterion and thoroughly discuss Alternative A in terms of criterion number 1.
      2. For the remaining criteria, follow the same procedure.
    Alternative B: (Specify the alternative.)
      1. Criterion 1. Thoroughly discuss Alternative B in terms of critical issue number 1.
      2. Criterion 2-n. Follow the same procedure.

Following is a brief, unedited example from a student paper. The problem/decision was whether Wyler Foods, a powdered soft-drink subsidiary of Borden, should introduce a new line of unsweetened powdered drink mixes to compete with the market leader, Kool-Aid. One alternative was to introduce the product and attempt to compete head to head with Kool-Aid. Criteria identified by the student were

    1. Projected profit impact.
    2. Long-term growth implications.
    3. Competitor reactions.
    4. Resource requirements.
    5. Competitive advantages and/or disadvantages.

Analysis of the alternative in terms of each criterion follows. (*Note that the exhibits identified in the analysis are not included.*)

Step 5 Analysis
    Alternative A. Head-to-head competition with Kool-Aid
    1.1 *Projected profit impact.* The profit potential for head-to-head competition with Kool-Aid does not seem promising. Assuming that the product will perform nationally as it did during test marketing, it should achieve a 4 percent share of the $143.51

million unsweetened powdered drink mix (UPDM) market (see Exhibit 1).

This represents sales of $5.74 million. Long-term share could be as low as 2.5 percent of the overall market. A retail price of 12 cents per packet and cost of goods sold of 9.4 cents per packet will produce a contribution margin of approximately $1.24 million (see Exhibit 2). This level of contribution margin will not be sufficient to cover advertising and sales promotion expenditures, which will exceed $4 million and could rise to $8–10 million.

Quantity allowances to stimulate grocer acceptance will have to be in the $800,000 area. Adopting this alternative would lead to substantial first-year losses, minimally in the $4–5 million range and possibly much higher (see Exhibit 3).

    1.2 *Long-term growth implications.* Long-term corporate growth factors are dependent on how deeply the new product can penetrate the Kool-Aid-dominated UPDM market. If the product performs no better than the test market results indicate, this strategy would be a long-term money loser. The product will have to capture roughly 15.4 percent of the UPDM market to break even (see Exhibit 4).

    1.3 *Competitor reactions.* Kool-Aid can be expected to spend $10–12 million more on advertising and sales promotion than is proposed for the new product in its first year. Kool-Aid also can be expected to emphasize its traditional position as the favored UPDM. The leading brand is able to exercise considerable influence in established distribution channels to keep the new product line off the grocers' shelves, necessitating huge quantity allowances to achieve penetration. Through 50 years of acclimation, the consumer is now at the point of utilizing the Kool-Aid product as the taste benchmark; this imperils the new product line even before the contest starts. Perhaps of greatest importance, Kool-Aid may opt for price competition. Because of sales volume considerations, Kool-Aid can cut prices and maintain profitability. Wyler simply could not afford to match Kool-Aid's potential price cuts. To do so would further darken its bleak profit outlook (see Exhibit 5).

    1.4 *Resource requirements.* Wyler seems to be short on the financial resources necessary to implement this alternative (see Exhibit 5). Substantial cash infusions would be needed for some time before any cash outflows would be generated. Wyler's personnel seem to be capable of executing the strategy.

    1.5 *Competitive advantages and/or disadvantages.* Implementation of this alternative involves doing battle with Kool-Aid on Kool-Aid's home ground.

Rather than exploiting a key Wyler strength, this alternative seems to favor Kool-Aid's strengths and Wyler's weaknesses. Wyler will be playing by Kool-Aid's rules, which isn't likely to produce a successful outcome.

Although this is a fairly simple example without any financial comparisons, it illustrates a useful approach for evaluating alternative actions. Note that each alternative should be evaluated in terms of each criterion. After the alternatives are analyzed against each criterion, you should complete your analysis with a summary assessment of each alternative. This summary will provide the basis for preparing your recommendations.

One approach that students sometimes find useful in preparing their summary analyses is illustrated in Exhibit B–2. Its preparation involves the following five steps:

Step 1:   List criteria on one axis and alternative actions on the other axis.

Step 2:   Assign a weight to each criterion reflecting its relative importance on the final decision. For convenience, assign weights that add up to one.

Step 3:   Review your analysis and rate each alternative on each criterion using a scale of one to five, with one representing very poor and five representing very good.

Step 4:   Multiply the weight assigned to each criterion by the rating given to each alternative on each issue.

Step 5:   Add the results from Step 4 for each alternative.

It is important to understand that this type of analytic aid is *not* a substitute for thorough, rigorous analysis, clear thinking, and enlightened decision making. Its value lies in encouraging you to assess the relative importance of alternatives and criteria and helping you organize your analysis.

Step 6: Recommendations.   If your analysis has been thorough, the actions you recommend should flow directly from it. The first part of your recommendations section addresses what specific actions should be taken and why. State the main reasons you believe your chosen course of action is best but avoid rehashing the analysis section. It is important that your recommendations be specific and operational. The following example of a recommendation deals with whether a manufacturer of oil field equipment (OFE) should introduce a new product line.

> The key decision that management must make is whether viscosity-measurement instrumentation represents a business venture that fits into the overall mission of the firm. The preceding analysis clearly indicates that this would be a profitable endeavor. If OFE concentrates on the high-accuracy and top end of the intermediate-accuracy ranges of the market, sales of $500,000 appear feasible within two to four years, with an estimated contribution to overhead and profits in the $145,000 range. This is assuming that manufacturing costs can be reduced by 20 to 25 percent, that effective marketing approaches are developed, that further product development is not extensive, and that price reductions per unit do not exceed 10 percent.

The second part of your recommendations section addresses implementation. State clearly who should do what, when, and where. An implementation plan shows that your recommendations are both possible and practical. For example,

> OFE should initially offer two instruments. One should provide an accuracy of 0.25 percent or better; the second should be in the accuracy range of 0.1 to 0.5 percent. Top priority should be assigned to inland and offshore drilling companies. Next in priority should be R&D laboratories in industry, government, and universities, where accuracy needs exist in the range offered by OFE. Based on experience with these markets, other promising targets should be identified and evaluated.
>
> OFE needs to move into the market rapidly, using the most cost-effective means of reaching end user markets. By developing an original-equipment-manufacturer (OEM) arrangement with General Supply to reach drilling companies and a tie-in arrangement with Newtec to reach R&D markets, immediate access to end user markets can be achieved. If successful, these actions will buy some time for OFE to develop marketing capabilities, and they should begin generating contributions from sales to cover the expenses of developing a marketing program. An essential element in the OFE

EXHIBIT B–2   ABC Company Summary Assessment

Criteria	Relative Weights	Alternatives (ratings) (1)	(2)	(3)
Corporate mission and objectives	(.2)	(5)	(2)	(3)
Market opportunity	(.3)	(2)	(3)	(5)
Competitive strengths/weaknesses	(.2)	(2)	(3)	(2)
Financial considerations	(.3)	(1)	(1)	(4)
Index: Relative weight × Rating		2.3	2.2	3.7

marketing strategy is locating and hiring a person to manage the marketing effort. This person must have direct sales capabilities in addition to being able to perform market analysis and marketing program development, implementation, and management tasks.

The last part of your recommendations section should be a tentative budget. This is important because it illustrates that the solution is worth the cost and is within the financial capabilities of the organization. Too often, students develop grandiose plans that organizations couldn't possibly afford even if they were worth the money. Budgeting and forecasting are discussed in Appendix A.

Your instructor realizes that the numbers used in your tentative budget may not be as accurate as they would be if you had complete access to the records of the company. Make your best estimates and try to get as close to the actual figures as possible. The exercise is good experience, and it shows that you have considered the cost implications.

Students often ask how long the recommendations section should be and how much detail they should go into. This question is difficult to answer because each case is different and should be treated that way. In general it is advisable to go into as much detail as possible. You may be criticized for not being specific enough in your recommendations, but you are not likely to be criticized for being too specific.

An Outline for Case Analysis

The outline shown here is an expanded version of the approach to case analysis discussed in this appendix. Although reasonably comprehensive, the guide can be shortened, expanded, and/or adapted to meet your needs in various situations. For example, if you are analyzing a business unit that does not utilize channels of distribution, section VIIIB of the outline will require adjustment. Likewise, if the salesforce represents the major part of the marketing program, then section VIIIE should probably be expanded to include other aspects of salesforce strategy.

This guide is not intended to be a comprehensive checklist that can be applied in every case. Instead, it is illustrative of the broad range of issues and questions you will encounter in analyzing the strategic decisions presented in this book and elsewhere. The key is to *adapt the outline to the case,* not the case to the outline.

Step 1. Situation Audit

I. Corporate mission and objectives.
   A. Does the mission statement offer a clear guide to the product markets of interest to the firm?
   B. Have objectives been established for the corporation?
   C. Is information available for the review of corporate progress toward objectives, and are the reviews conducted on a regular (quarterly, monthly, etc.) basis?
   D. Has corporate strategy been successful in meeting objectives?
   E. Are opportunities or problems pending that may require altering the marketing strategy?
   F. What are the responsibilities of the chief marketing executive in corporate strategic planning?

II. Business unit analysis.
   A. What is the composition of the business (business segments, strategic planning units, and specific product markets)?
   B. Have business strength and product-market attractiveness analyses been conducted for each planning unit? What are the results of the analyses?
   C. What is the corporate strategy for each planning unit (e.g., growth, manage for cash)?
   D. Does each unit have a strategic plan?
   E. For each unit, what objectives and responsibilities have been assigned to marketing?

III. Buyer analysis.
   A. Are there niches within the product market? For each specific product market and niche of interest to the firm, answer items B through I.
   B. What are estimated annual purchases (units and dollars)?
   C. What is the projected annual growth rate (five years)?
   D. How many people/organizations are in the product market?
   E. What are the demographic and socioeconomic characteristics of customers?
   F. What is the extent of geographic concentration?
   G. How do people decide what to buy?
      1. Reason(s) for buying (What is the need/want?).
      2. What information is needed (e.g., how to use the product)?
      3. What are other important sources of information?
      4. What criteria are used to evaluate the product?
      5. What are purchasing practices (quantity, frequency, location, time, etc.)?
   H. What environmental factors should be monitored because of their influence on product purchases (e.g., interest rates)?
   I. What key competitors serve each end user group?

IV. Key competitor analysis. For each specific product market and each niche of interest to the firm, determine
   A. Estimated overall business strength.
   B. Market share (percent, rank).
   C. Market share trend (five years).
   D. Financial strengths.
   E. Profitability.

F. Management.

G. Technology position.

H. Other key nonmarketing strengths/limitations (e.g., production cost advantages).

I. Marketing strategy (description, assessment of key strengths and limitations).
   1. Market-target strategy.
   2. Program positioning strategy.
   3. Product strategy.
   4. Distribution strategy.
   5. Price strategy.
   6. Promotion strategy.

V. Market-target strategy.

A. Has each market target been clearly defined and its importance to the firm established?

B. Have demand and competition in each market target been analyzed, and key trends, opportunities, and threats identified?

C. Has the proper market-target strategy (mass, niche) been adopted?

D. Should repositioning or exit from any product market be considered?

VI. Market-target objectives.

A. Have objectives been established for each market target, and are they consistent with planning-unit objectives and the available resources? Are the objectives realistic?

B. Are sales, cost, and other performance information available for monitoring the progress of planned performance against actual results?

C. Are regular appraisals made of marketing performance?

D. Where do gaps exist between planned and actual results? What are the probable causes of the performance gaps?

VII. Marketing program positioning strategy.

A. Does the firm have an integrated positioning strategy made up of product, channel, price, advertising, and sales force strategies? Is the role selected for each mix element consistent with the overall program objectives, and does it properly complement other mix elements?

B. Are adequate resources available to carry out the marketing program? Are resources committed to market targets according to the importance of each?

C. Are allocations to the various marketing mix components too low, too high, or about right in terms of what each is expected to accomplish?

D. Is the effectiveness of the marketing program appraised on a regular basis?

VIII. Marketing program activities.

A. Product strategy.
   1. Is the product mix geared to the needs that the firm wants to meet in each product market?

2. What branding strategy is being used?

3. Are products properly positioned against competing brands?

4. Does the firm have a sound approach to product planning and management, and is marketing involved in product decisions?

5. Are additions to, modifications of, or deletions from the product mix needed to make the firm more competitive in the marketplace?

6. Is the performance of each product evaluated on a regular basis?

B. Channels of distribution strategy.

1. Has the firm selected the type (conventional or vertically coordinated) and intensity of distribution appropriate for each of its product markets?

2. How well does each channel access its market target? Is an effective channel configuration used?

3. Are channel organizations carrying out their assigned functions properly?

4. How is the channel of distribution managed? What improvements are needed?

5. Are desired customer service levels reached, and are the costs of doing this acceptable?

C. Price strategy.

1. How responsive is each market target to price variation?

2. What roles and objectives does price have in the marketing mix?

3. Does price play an active or passive role in program positioning strategy?

4. How do the firm's price strategy and tactics compare to those of the competition?

5. Is a logical approach used to establish prices?

6. Are there indications that changes may be needed in price strategy or tactics?

D. Advertising and sales promotion strategies.

1. Are roles and objectives established for advertising and sales promotion in the marketing mix?

2. Is the creative strategy consistent with the positioning strategy that is used?

3. Is the budget adequate to carry out the objectives assigned to advertising and sales promotion?

4. Do the media and programming strategies represent the most cost-effective means of communicating with market targets?

5. Do advertising copy and content effectively communicate the intended messages?

6. How well does the advertising program meet its objectives?

E. Sales force strategy.
1. Are the roles and objectives of personal selling in the marketing program positioning strategy clearly specified and understood by the sales organization?
2. Do the qualifications of salespeople correspond to their assigned roles?
3. Is the sales force the proper size to carry out its function, and is it efficiently deployed?
4. Are sales force results in line with management's expectations?
5. Is each salesperson assigned performance targets, and are incentives offered to reward performance?
6. Are compensation levels and ranges comparable to those of competitors?

IX. Marketing planning.
A. Strategic planning and marketing.
1. Is marketing's role and responsibility in corporate strategic planning clearly specified?
2. Are responsibility and authority for marketing strategy assigned to one executive?
3. How well is the firm's marketing strategy working?
4. Are changes likely to occur in the corporate/marketing environment that may affect the firm's marketing strategy?
5. Do major contingencies exist that should be included in the strategic marketing plan?
B. Marketing planning and organization structure.
1. Are annual and longer-range strategic marketing plans developed and used?
2. Are the responsibilities of the various units in the marketing organization clearly specified?
3. What are the strengths and limitations of the key members of the marketing organization? What is being done to develop employee skills? What gaps in experience and capability exist on the marketing staff?
4. Is the organizational structure for marketing appropriate for implementing marketing plans?

X. Financial analysis.
A. Sales and cost analyses and forecasts.
B. Profit contribution and net profit analyses and projections.
C. Liquidity analyses.
D. Break-even analyses.
E. Return on investment.
F. Budget analyses.
G. Pro forma statements.

XI. Implementation and management.
A. Have the causes of all performance gaps been identified?

B. Is implementation of planned actions taking place as intended? Is implementation being hampered by marketing or other functional areas of the firm (e.g., operations, finance)?
C. Has the strategic audit revealed areas requiring additional study before action is taken?

XII. Summary of the situation.
Has the situation audit revealed opportunities that would enable the organization to gain a competitive advantage based on its distinctive competencies?
A. What are the major opportunities available to the organization?
B. What are the major threats facing the organization?
C. What are the requirements for achieving success in selected product markets?
D. What are the organization's and the principal competitors' distinctive competencies regarding these requirements? Do these areas of strength complement a given opportunity, or do strategic gaps exist that serve as barriers to pursuing the opportunity?
E. What strategic gaps, problems, and/or constraints relative to competitors appear?
F. What time and resources are required to pursue an opportunity or close a strategic gap?
G. Does the organization's mission (or objectives) need to be redefined?

XIII. Opinions and assumptions.
A. Are opinions or assumptions provided by others? Are they reasonable, given the source?
B. Is it necessary to make assumptions about the organization's objectives, competition, the environment, or something else?

Step 2. Problem/Decision Statement

A. What are the symptoms that suggest a problem exists?
B. What is the major problem or decision that must be addressed?
C. Are there secondary problems or decisions?

Step 3. Identification of Alternatives

A. What actions might provide viable solutions to the problem or decision?
B. Can actions be combined?
C. Can actions be eliminated without further consideration?

Step 4. Criteria

What criteria should be used to evaluate the strategic options? Any of the items listed in the situation audit may be relevant issues in analyzing the alternatives.

Step 5.   Analysis

   A. Examine each alternative in terms of each criterion.

   B. What are the relative advantages and disadvantages of each choice in terms of each of the criteria?

Step 6.   Recommendations

   A. What specific actions, including the development of marketing or other plans, should be taken and why?

   B. Who should do what, when, and where?

   C. What are the expected costs and returns associated with your recommendations?

   D. What contingencies may alter the attractiveness of your recommendations?

INDEX OF CASES

682

SUBJECT INDEX